E

Geoffrey Parker is Andreas Dor........................ ....ory and associate of the Mershon Center at the Ohio State University, and Profesor Afiliado, División de Historia, Centro de Investigación y Docencia Económicas, Mexico City. Among his many awards is the 2012 Heineken Prize for History. He has published forty books, including *Global Crisis: War, Climate Change and Catastrophe in the Seventeenth Century*, *Imprudent King: A New Life of Philip II* and *The Grand Strategy of Philip II* for Yale University Press.

Further praise for *Emperor*:

'A remarkable book, a panorama full of astounding and memorable details, and a gripping read. No other living scholar could have organised and analysed the vast and dizzying array of source materials. Parker is both psychologically astute and sets Charles in the huge canvas against which he operated, always presenting the diplomatic, religious, structural and systemic contexts of the decisions he had to make. A monumental achievement.' Lyndal Roper, author of *Martin Luther*

'A meticulous and comprehensive account by a master of traditional biography, the powerful narrative of a military and political career like no other . . . Parker yields remarkable insights into the everyday life of the emperor.' R.J.W. Evans, *New York Review of Books*

'I cannot remember reading anything that offered so much depth of perspective on both the emperor as a ruler and the age as a whole . . . A masterpiece of historical reconstruction.' C. Scott Dixon, author of *The Church in the Early Modern Age*

'It is brave for a historian to attempt a biography [of Charles V]. While many have tried, Parker has succeeded triumphantly.' John Edwards, *BBC History Magazine*

'Parker is one of the most innovative and multifaceted historians of the last half century.' John Adamson, author of *The Noble Revolt*

EMPEROR

A NEW LIFE OF
CHARLES V

GEOFFREY
PARKER

YALE UNIVERSITY PRESS
NEW HAVEN AND LONDON

Published with assistance from the foundation established in memory of Oliver Baty
Cunningham of the Class of 1917, Yale College.

For information about this and other Yale University Press publications, please contact:
U.S. Office: sales.press@yale.edu   yalebooks.com
Europe Office: sales@yaleup.co.uk   yalebooks.co.uk

Set in Minion Pro Regular by IDSUK (DataConnection) Ltd
Printed in Great Britain by CPI Group (UK) Ltd, Croydon, CR0 4YY

Library of Congress Control Number: 2019935200

ISBN 978-0-300-19652-8 (hbk)
ISBN 978-0-300-25486-0 (pbk)

A catalogue record for this book is available from the British Library.

10 9 8 7 6 5 4 3 2 1

To my grandchildren, Cameron, Sienna and Cordelia

CONTENTS

CONTENTS

PART IV DOWNFALL

PREFACE

Does the world really need another book about Charles V, ruler of Spain, Germany, the Netherlands, half of Italy, and much of central and south America? The emperor himself composed his memoirs; hundreds of biographies of him have appeared in dozens of languages; WorldCat lists over 500 books published so far this century with 'Charles V' in the title. Nevertheless, no work is ever perfect. The emperor composed his triumphalist autobiography in 1550, while at the height of his powers, and several of the 'lives' are partisan (even some nineteenth- and twentieth-century biographers used his achievements for ideological ends).

Charles's modern biographers belong to one of two tribes: those who complain that their subject left too few records to allow the reconstruction of an accurate portrait, and those who protest that he left too many. In 2003, Scott Dixon, a member of the first tribe, declared that 'Charles left us little trace in the records of what he was really like . . . Of the many thousands of letters dispatched from his desk, very few make any mention of personal details.' The following year, Harald Kleinschmidt made a similar claim: 'There is an abundance of texts bearing Charles's name. But he never saw most of these and among the minority of letters that he did write with his own hand are some which do not reflect his own thoughts but those of his advisers.'[1]

Karl Brandi, author of a two-volume biography of Charles, belonged to the second tribe. 'Not for many centuries,' he wrote in 1937, 'could any prince compare with him in the number of revealing documents which he left behind.' A few years later, Federico Chabod went even further and claimed that 'Charles V left us more holograph documents than any other ruler in History.' In 1966, Fernand Braudel argued that previous historians failed to reconstruct Charles's 'thoughts, his temperament and his character' mainly because the surviving sources are too abundant. 'Looking for the emperor's personality amid the mass of papers,' he concluded, 'is like looking for a needle in a haystack.' In 2002, Wim Blockmans concurred: 'The body of source material' concerning the emperor 'is so massive, it is impossible to survey the whole of it'.[2]

Impossible? Certainly, the surviving sources are 'massive'. Charles signed his first letter at age four (Pl. 2), and by the time he died he had signed more than 100,000 documents in Dutch, French, German, Italian, Latin and Spanish, adding a holograph postscript to several of them. His holograph letters (those written entirely with his own hand in French, Spanish and occasionally German) cover thousands of folios. Charles's epistolary output survives in archives and libraries all over Europe, in part because he spent so much of his reign on the move. He spent almost half his life (over 10,000 days) in the Low Countries and almost one-third (over 6,500 days) in Spain; he spent more than 3,000 days in Germany and almost 1,000 in Italy. He visited France four times (195 days), and north Africa and England twice each (99 and 44 days respectively). He created a documentary trail in almost every place he went. He eludes historians only on the 260 days he spent at sea, travelling between his dominions.[3]

Although he never crossed the Atlantic, Charles also left a documentary mark on his American dominions. The viceroy of Mexico issued almost 1,500 orders in the emperor's name in 1542 and 1543 alone, many of them in response to a direct imperial order. Some of his warrants (*cédulas reales*) gained iconic status because they legalized new Mexica settlements (*altepetl*) and became coveted foundational documents of which copies were still made in the 1990s. Moreover, since 'in Pre-Hispanic Mexico, the founding of the various *altepetl* took place under the will and protection of the gods', Charles acquired an honoured place among the panoply of deities in several of the communities he founded.[4]

The emperor strove to achieve immortality in more conventional ways. He sat for portraits, sponsored histories, commissioned works of art, built palaces, and appeared in propaganda spectacles (notably urban 'entries': Pl. 7). Mass-produced images of him appeared on coins, medals, ceramics and even draughts counters (Pl. 30), as well as in books and broadsheets. Musicians composed works to celebrate his successes (the battle of Pavia; the imperial coronation) and sometimes his setbacks (the death of his wife). An international corps of poets, painters, sculptors, glaziers, printers, weavers, jewellers, historians, armourers and scribes strove to project an approved image. The emperor followed the advice of Baldassare Castiglione's study of etiquette, *The Courtier* (one of Charles's favourite books, published while the author was ambassador at the imperial court and translated into Spanish at Charles's command): he did everything – walking, riding, fighting, dancing, speaking – with one eye on his audience.[5] He would have been appalled that in the nineteenth century the Spanish government opened his tomb and exposed his naked mummified corpse as a tourist attraction, and that some visitors made drawings while others took photographs (Pl. 39). One bribed a guard to detach the tip of one of his fingers as a souvenir – although this vandalism belatedly proved a boon because forensic examination of the detached digit, now kept in a special receptacle, provided two pieces of important medical evidence: the emperor had suffered from chronic gout, just as he always complained, and he was killed relatively swiftly by a double dose of malaria (Appendix II).

Arma virumque cano ('I sing of arms and a man'): in an important article about the perils associated with writing the life of the emperor, Heinrich Lutz used the opening words of Virgil's *Aeneid* (a text familiar to Charles) to underline the need for his biographers to focus on those matters that absorbed his time, energy and resources – above all on war and preparing for war, both because hostilities took up so much of Charles's reign and because contemporaries noted that he was 'happiest on campaign and with his army'. Lutz argued that other developments, even the Renaissance and the Reformation, should appear only as and when they mattered to Charles, and that they must always be viewed through his eyes.[6]

Bearing in mind Lutz's strictures, this biography deploys the available sources, from documents to digits, to illuminate three key issues:

- *How* Charles took the crucial decisions that created, preserved and expanded the world's first and most enduring transatlantic empire.
- *Whether* Charles's policy failures arose from structural faults or from personal shortcomings: could a monarch with superior political skills have done better, or had circumstances created a polity too big for its own good and impossible to defend? In modern parlance, does agent or structure explain the failure to pass on his empire intact?
- *What* was it like to be Charles? While writing about one of Charles's role models, Alexander the Great, Plutarch (one of Charles's favourite authors) noted that 'The most glorious exploits do not always furnish us with the clearest discoveries of virtue or vice in men: sometimes a matter of less moment, an expression or a jest, informs us better of their characters and inclinations.' This biography draws on many such unscripted but revealing episodes.[7]

Inevitably, the available sources are uneven. Like every other human being, Charles slept, ate, drank and performed other bodily functions every day, but they left a documentary trace only when they caused a problem (he could not sleep; he vomited; he excreted 'hot piss'; the pain from his haemorrhoids 'made him cry like a baby'). He also spent part of every day at prayer, he regularly attended church services, and each Holy Week he secluded himself in a monastery where he refused to transact any public business – but historians have no idea what else he did at these quiet times unless something unusual happened (he fainted during a church service and lay unconscious for over an hour; he retired to pray or confess at an unusual time, such as just before or just after making an important decision).

Moreover, as Charles lamented in the confidential instructions he composed for his son and heir in 1543, some political decisions 'are so impenetrable and uncertain that I do not know how to describe them to you' because 'they are full of confusions and contradictions'.[8] He made at least one effort to clarify everything. In November 1552 his valet Guillaume van Male confided to a colleague that the emperor had just ordered him to:

> . . . close the doors to his chambers and made me promise to maintain the utmost secrecy about the things he was about to tell me . . . He held back nothing. I was stunned to learn what he told me. Even now I shudder when I think of it and would rather die than tell anybody but you. Now I can write freely because the emperor sleeps, it is the dead of night, and everyone else has left.

'It will take a long time to share all the details with you,' van Male continued tantalizingly, because the emperor had just 'told me everything that ever happened in his life', and 'even provided me with a handwritten paper that listed all his past misdeeds', including 'many things he should have handled differently, either because he forgot something or because he later made changes'. Unfortunately for historians, at this point sleep overcame van Male too, and he laid down his quill. If he committed 'all the details' to paper at some later date, then his letter (like the emperor's handwritten list of misdeeds) has perished.[9]

Nevertheless, enough sources have survived to resolve many of the 'confusions and contradictions' in Charles's life. Apart from the mountain of his own surviving correspondence, the emperor attracted the attention of a large number of people: friends and foes alike wrote more about him than about any of his contemporaries, even Martin Luther. From his birth until his abdication numerous foreign diplomats observed and reported his every action, word and gesture; and a dozen or more eyewitnesses described major public events (such as his coronation in Bologna in 1530 and his abdication in Brussels in 1555). Records multiplied whenever the emperor travelled by land – and over the course of his reign he stayed in over 1,000 different places, from Wittenberg to Seville and from London to Algiers (Map 1) – so that it is sometimes possible to reconstruct his movements hour by hour.[10] Charles was never alone. Courtiers and diplomats accompanied him on even his loneliest journeys, including his first weeks in Spain in 1517 when he hiked across the Picos de Europa to claim his inheritance, sleeping in hovels surrounded by livestock and beset by bears; and again during his flight across the Alps in 1552 to escape capture by his German subjects, when his staff had to commandeer emergency bed linen for him in remote villages. He was closely observed even after he retired to the small palace attached to the monastery at Yuste, in Spain's Gredos mountains. At least two monks kept a journal in which their august guest played a starring role; virtually every day his courtiers recorded what their master had said and done; and twenty eyewitnesses provided sworn testimony about what they had seen and heard as the emperor lay dying. Bizarrely, Charles's last days are the best-known period of his entire life.

'My God, how does one write a Biography? Tell me,' Virginia Woolf asked a friend (and fellow biographer) in 1938. 'How can one deal with facts – so many and so many and so many?'[11] Four centuries earlier the Spanish Humanist Juan Páez de Castro, whom Charles had commissioned to write 'the life of Your Majesty', wrestled with the same dilemma. Before he started work, Páez de Castro drew up an outline that explained to Charles how he planned to deal with 'so many facts'. First, he set out his own credentials: he claimed fluency in six languages (including Chaldean) and knowledge of law, natural history and mathematics. Next, 'since writing is not just the product of ingenuity or invention but also of work and effort to assemble the materials that will be written about, it is necessary to seek them out'; and so Páez de Castro planned to visit every place 'that has seen the banners of Your Majesty, in order to provide the lustre that I desire for this work'. At each location he would 'consult venerable and diligent people; read the inscriptions on public monuments and graves; dig into the old registers kept by notaries, where many things that make up history are found; and copy all previous histories, old and new, by good and bad authors'. Finally, 'it will be necessary to consult Your Majesty about many things, to find out the rationale' for controversial decisions. It was an excellent outline, but Charles died before Páez de Castro could interview him, and its author died before he had completed any part of his biography.[12]

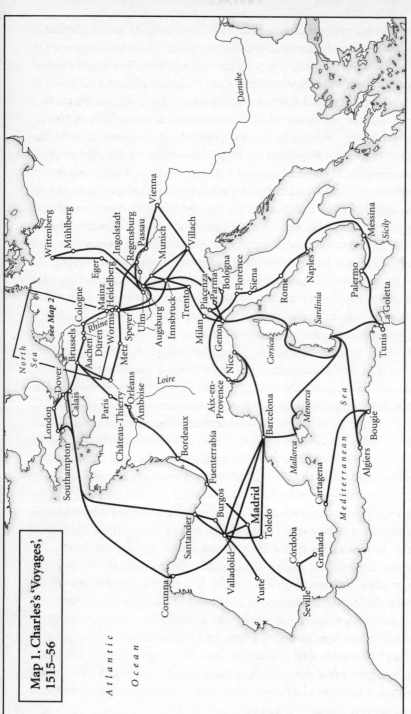

Map 1. Charles's 'Voyages', 1515–56

In his abdication speech in Brussels in 1555, Charles reminded his listeners that he had undertaken forty 'voyages' on their behalf. He would make one more, his last, to the convent of Yuste in Spain, making him the most-travelled monarch of early modern Europe.
Source: de Boom, 'Voyagé, pull-out

This volume presents Charles's life in four chronological sections separated by 'portraits' of how he appeared to his contemporaries at critical moments: in 1517, when he left the Netherlands for the first time; in 1532, when he reached full maturity; and in 1548, when he attained the height of his power. The only exception is a thematic chapter on 'The Taming of America'. Charles, the first European to rule significant parts of the Americas, developed a keen interest in the continent: although he focused primarily on how best to make the resources of the New World pay for his endeavours in the Old, the emperor also displayed lasting interest in its flora, its fauna and its people, both natives and newcomers. In particular, he sought to provide his native subjects with spiritual guidance and material security. He saw this as an issue that affected his 'royal conscience' because 'when he found out how all the native inhabitants of Hispaniola and Cuba, and the other [Caribbean] islands had died through being sent to the mines, he became convinced that he would go to Hell if he permitted the practice to continue'.[13] Few Netherlanders of his day cared about America – even Erasmus 'hardly let an allusion to the New World pass his pen' – and Charles was the only sixteenth-century ruler to make a principled stand for the rights of native Americans. His legislation 'long continued to be a powerful brake on the oppression of native Americans'. Charles's New World initiatives therefore merit detailed attention.[14]

Páez de Castro, too, intended to include Charles's New World achievements in his biography, but he planned to omit some other matters. Although he believed that historians should 'condemn and denigrate the bad, so that nothing similar should take place in future', as well as 'exalt and praise the good to encourage repetition', he distinguished between 'the details that are proper to history and those that, without compromising the truth, should remain in the author's inkwell'.[15] For better or worse, few details about the emperor remain in my own inkwell. On the personal level, I have exalted and praised his facility with languages (he eventually mastered Italian and Spanish as well as his native French, and could speak some Dutch and German); his prowess in marksmanship and horsemanship; and his personal courage when commanding troops under fire. He also knew how to foster loyalty and affection. According to a diplomat in 1531, Charles addressed a crowd 'in such a moving and gentle way that it almost made the audience weep' and by the time he had finished, his hearers 'were of one mind, as if they had become his slaves'; when he died, the sorrowing members of his entourage 'gave great cries, hit their faces and butted their heads on the walls'; and a few years later, Ferdinand told a confidant that 'I loved and revered the emperor as if he had been my father'.[16]

As for 'condemning and denigrating the bad', I have documented how Charles falsely denied that he had approved in advance the attack on Rome and capture of Pope Clement in 1527; how he lied about the murder of two French diplomats, Fregoso and Rincón, in 1541; and how he reneged on a solemn promise to marry his son Philip to a Portuguese princess in 1553. In some cases, Charles vehemently, publicly and repeatedly denied that he had lied (as in 1527 and 1541); in other cases, he simply refused to discuss his reprehensible conduct (when a Portuguese envoy came to protest the repudiation of the princess in 1554, 'we told him what was necessary, without wishing to justify or discuss the matter further, because when these matters are past it is best to dissimulate').[17] Charles could also behave badly in private. When he discovered in 1517 that his older sister Eleanor was in love with a courtier he forced her to appear before a notary and make a formal deposition renouncing her lover and promising to obey her brother in all things; the following year he forced her to marry an uncle more than twice her age. In 1530 he ordered that Tadea, one of his three illegitimate daughters, should receive a permanent 'mark on her right leg below the knee' (at best a tattoo, at worst a brand mark); and three years later he negotiated a marriage contract between his 11-year-old niece Christina of Denmark and a man four times her age, with the right to consummate the union immediately. Most shameful of all, Charles abused his mother Queen Joanna. He kept her confined and under guard until her death in 1555, and for some years he surrounded her with a fictional world, full of fake facts (such as insisting long after the death of her father, King Ferdinand, that he still lived). Moreover, on his visits to Joanna, Charles plundered her tapestries, jewels, books, silver goods and even liturgical vestments, which he recycled as wedding gifts for his sister and his wife, filling the empty chests with bricks of equivalent weight, hoping that his mother would not notice that he had robbed her until after he left.

These are perplexing paradoxes, and I have tried to understand them by establishing *how* Charles came to act as he did, before studying *why*. This methodological decision has some important consequences. As Christopher Clark observed in the preface to *The sleepwalkers*, his breathtaking study of the origins of the First World War:

> Questions of why and how are logically inseparable, but they lead us in different directions. The question of *how* invites us to look closely at the sequences of interactions that produced certain outcomes. By contrast the question of *why* invites us to go in search of remote and categorical

causes . . . The why approach brings a certain analytical clarity, but it also has a distorting effect, because it creates the illusion of a steadily building causal pressure; the factors pile up on top of each other pushing down on the events; political actors become mere executors of forces long established and beyond their control.

Like Clark, I have therefore tried 'to let the *why* answers grow, as it were, out of the *how* answers, rather than the other way round', even though asking 'how' inevitably privileges agency and contingency whereas asking 'why' foregrounds structures and continuities.[18]

To understand and explain how Charles behaved, like Páez de Castro I have learned several languages (though not Chaldean) and studied other disciplines (though not law, natural history or mathematics); I have visited the places 'that saw his banners' (and especially those that received his archives); I have read most 'previous histories, old and new, by good and bad authors'; and I have ransacked written records. Although I was unable to consult His Majesty in person 'about many things, to find out the rationale', more than enough material survives to allow readers to choose whether to believe those who revered the emperor or those who reviled him.

Should we side with Luis Quijada, who had known the emperor for over twenty years and after he watched him die declared him 'the greatest man that has ever lived'; and with Francisco de Borja, who asserted that when he spoke with Charles he spoke with God? Or should we believe Pope Paul III who claimed 'Your Majesty is an ingrate who only remembers his friends when he needs them'; and the French ambassador who echoed that 'If you examine the matter closely, you will find that the emperor has never cared for anyone, except insofar as he can make use of them'?[19] Do we join Gustave Bergenroth, who spent a decade in the archives of western Europe transcribing some 18,000 pages of documents by and about Charles, and rejoice as we watch the emperor 'break down, piece by piece . . . politically, morally, bodily, until he finishes his miserable life in his miserable retirement at Yuste', and deem his life 'one of the greatest tragedies ever enacted'? Or do we endorse the verdict of Karl Brandi, one of the few scholars to have read more documents than Bergenroth by and about the emperor, that he 'was a man, with the daily weaknesses and caprices of his kind, yet in the permanent motives of his desire, in the courage of his convictions, something more than a man, a great figure in the history of the world'?[20] Is there more to exalt than to denigrate about Charles V? Does the world really need another book about him? Gentle reader: the decision is yours.

NOTE ON CONVENTIONS

Where an established English version of a foreign place-name exists (Antwerp, Corunna, The Hague, Venice, Vienna) I have used it, otherwise I have preferred the style used in the place itself today (Mechelen, not Malines; Aachen, not Aix-la-Chapelle; Regensburg, not Ratisbon). The exception is the capital of the Ottoman empire: all references to it taken from original sources preserve the contemporary usage 'Constantinople'; all others refer to 'Istanbul'. Likewise, where an established English version of a protagonist's name exists (Francis I, Clement VII, Don John of Austria) I have used it, otherwise I have preferred the version used by the protagonist. Different people with the same name form an exception. Although the context usually clarifies their identity, 'Catalina' refers to Charles's youngest sister and 'Katherine' to their aunt, Katherine of Aragon; 'Margaret' means Charles's aunt Margaret, archduchess of Austria and dowager duchess of Savoy, and 'Margarita' means his illegitimate daughter, duchess of Florence and later of Parma (known in contemporary sources as 'Madama'); 'María' normally means Charles's older daughter; 'Marie' means his sister the queen of Hungary (after 1526 dowager queen); and 'Mary' means either Henry VIII's sister or older daughter, both of whom were at one stage betrothed to Charles.

Protagonists who changed their style or title present a special challenge. Antoine Perrenot de Granvelle (1517–86) used the style 'bishop of Arras' between 1540 and 1562 and thereafter 'Cardinal Granvelle', but he appears throughout this book as 'Perrenot' to distinguish him from his father, Nicholas Perrenot de Granvelle (1486–1550), who appears throughout this book as 'Granvelle'.[1] Charles's grandfather Maximilian (1459–1519) also changed his style. He started life as archduke of Austria, adding duke of Burgundy after 1477 when he married Duchess Mary; in 1486 he began to style himself 'king of the Romans' and after 1508 changed it to 'emperor elect'. After the death of his father Emperor Frederick III in 1493, however, his contemporaries normally referred to Maximilian as 'the emperor' and that is how he appears throughout this biography. Charles, too, was 'emperor elect' after he became king of the Romans, until the pope placed the imperial crown on his head ten years later; but after 1520 almost all his contemporaries referred to him as 'the emperor'. Charles himself followed the style used by the ruler in each of his dominions. In Spain, he used the title *Rey Católico* ('the Catholic king'), granted to his grandparents Ferdinand and Isabella, and signed all documents *Yo el Rey* ('I the king') even when writing to his wife or his children. He signed documents in Latin, German and Italian, 'Carol' or 'Carolus'; and those written in French, 'Charles'. In this book, Charles is referred to as 'emperor' from his coronation as king of the Romans in 1520 until he transferred the title to his brother in 1558; and 'the Empire' (with an initial capital) refers to the 'Holy Roman Empire of the German Nation' over which he ruled.

Finally, some terms changed their meaning over time, which can cause confusion. Thus 'Protestant' first appeared in 1529 as a political term for those who protested at the abrogation of the toleration granted to German Lutherans three years before. It acquired a doctrinal meaning the following year, when the followers of Martin Luther presented their Confession of Faith to the Diet of Augsburg; but, as Bob Scribner observed, throughout Charles's reign it remained 'something of a politico-religious centaur, a theological statement worked out under diplomatic and political pressure to meet the demands of a political situation'. The emperor used interchangeably the terms 'those who have deviated from the true church', 'Protestant' and 'Lutherans' (even for those who rejected aspects of Luther's teaching, such as Heinrich Bullinger in Zurich and Martin Bucer in Strasbourg); but in this book 'Lutherans' refer exclusively to followers of Martin Luther and 'Protestants' to all who rejected papal authority.[2]

PART I

YOUNG CHARLES

'We are delighted that our grandson Charles takes so much pleasure in hunting, because otherwise one might think he was a bastard.'

Emperor Maximilian to Margaret of Austria,
28 February 1510

ONE

FROM DUKE OF LUXEMBURG
TO PRINCE OF CASTILE, 1500–8

THE DUKE OF LUXEMBURG

'We will begin with his lineage': with these words Pedro Mexía commenced his biography of Charles V, written in 1548, and his first chapter – entitled 'Of the exalted, excellent and undoubted genealogy and lineage of this great prince' – listed his subject's ancestors over the previous thousand years.[1] Mexía had correctly identified Charles's greatest initial asset – his exalted family – but hindsight led to some exaggeration. At the time of Charles's birth in 1500, his father Archduke Philip of Austria ruled only a few provinces in the Netherlands inherited from Philip's mother, Duchess Mary of Burgundy, albeit he was also heir to the distant lands in central Europe ruled by his father Maximilian, head of the House of Habsburg. Charles's mother Joanna initially had no parallel expectations, since she was the third child of Isabella of Castile and Ferdinand of Aragon, both from the Spanish House of Trastámara and normally known as the Catholic Monarchs, a title bestowed upon them by a benevolent Spanish pope.

The three dynasties shared a number of common denominators. Above all, they all practised a policy of matrimonial imperialism. Several generations of the Aragonese and Castilian branches of the Trastámara intermarried with the express intention of uniting the kingdoms; and they also intermarried with the House of Avis, which ruled Portugal, in the hope of uniting the peninsula. The dukes of Burgundy embraced matrimonial imperialism from the first (in 1369 the first duke married the heiress of the county of Flanders), and they acquired most of their other Netherlands territories through inheritance. Habsburg rulers contracted marriages both to add territories and to strengthen bonds between different branches of their dynasty, giving rise to a slogan that first became popular just after the union of Maximilian of Austria with Mary of Burgundy in 1477:

Bella gerant alii; tu, felix Austria, nube
Nam quae Mars aliis, dat tibi regna Venus.
Others make war; you, happy Habsburgs, marry,
For the kingdoms Mars gives to others, Venus gives to you.[2]

Matrimonial imperialism nevertheless came at a cost. Polities created in this way were the antithesis of the modern state: dynastic loyalty was often their only common denominator, encouraging a ruler to see his dominions, however far-flung, as a personal possession, a patrimony, to be handed on to the next generation intact. In 1543, Charles assured his son, the future Philip II, that his principal goal would be 'to avoid leaving you less of an inheritance than the one I inherited'.[3]

Fear of France formed another common denominator between the three dynasties. Burgundy had signed anti-French treaties with Aragon in the 1470s, and a decade later Maximilian suggested the marriage of his only son with a Spanish princess; but negotiations languished until Charles VIII of France invaded Italy in 1494 and marched triumphantly to Naples to press his dynastic claims to the kingdom. The following year, Maximilian warned the Catholic Monarchs 'that once the king of France has gained Naples, he will want to occupy the other states of Italy'; and to persuade them 'that they should resist and attack the king of France' he proposed a double marriage: between his daughter Margaret and their heir, Prince John, and between his heir Philip and their younger daughter Joanna. The marriage contracts were signed in January 1495 and the Spanish princess reached Lier, near Antwerp, in October 1496, where the couple consummated their marriage. No one foresaw that their son would rule the greatest empire seen in a millennium (Fig. 1).[4]

The future Charles V first made his presence felt from the womb. In September 1499, Philip summoned 'a midwife from the city of Lille' to 'see and visit' Joanna; and four months later he sent a courier 'at the utmost speed, day and night, without sparing men or horses', to ask the abbot of a convent near Lille to lend its most precious relic, the 'ring of the Virgin' reputedly placed on Mary's finger by Joseph when they married, and said to 'bring solace to women in labour'. According to some accounts, the ring proved extremely effective: Joanna's labour began while she attended a ball in the palace of the counts of Flanders in Ghent, and she only got as far as the nearest latrine before giving birth to the future emperor. It was 24 February 1500, St Matthew's Day.[5]

Figure 1: The genealogy of Charles V and his siblings

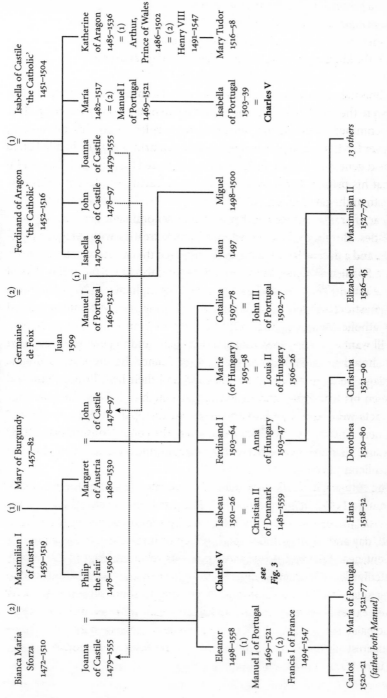

Most contemporary histories of Charles included his genealogy, and for good reason: a remarkable series of births, marriages and deaths united the possessions of four European dynasties under a single sceptre. None of Charles's grandparents desired this outcome, however, and it would have been undone had the unions between Princess Isabella and Manuel of Portugal, between Prince John of Spain and Margaret of Austria, or between Ferdinand of Aragon and Germaine de Foix, produced an heir that survived infancy.

As soon as the citizens of Ghent heard news of the birth, according to the city's leading poet, an eyewitness:

Great and small shouted 'Austria' and 'Burgundy'
Throughout the whole city for three hours.
Everyone ran about while shouting the good news
Of [the birth of] a prince of peace.

Meanwhile Philip signed letters instructing the major towns of the Netherlands to arrange 'processions, fireworks and public games' to celebrate the birth of his heir, and summoned the leading clerics of his dominions to attend the child's baptism.[6] He also sent an express messenger to his sister Margaret, then returning from Spain, 'begging her to hasten back so that she could hold the child in her hands at the font during the baptism' and serve as godmother. As soon as Margaret arrived she pressured her brother to call the child Maximilian, after their father, but Philip chose the name of their grandfather, Duke Charles the Bold of Burgundy – although he also conferred on his son the title 'duke of Luxemburg', a dignity held by several of Maximilian's ancestors.[7]

Charles's grandparents reacted in different ways. In Spain, 'when his grandmother Queen Isabella learned of his birth' on St Matthew's Day, 'remembering that Holy Scripture records that Jesus chose the Apostle Saint Matthew by chance, and understanding how much hope surrounded the birth of her grandson, who would inherit so many and such great kingdoms and lordships, she said: "Chance has fallen upon Matthew"'. In Germany, Maximilian declared himself 'entirely satisfied with the name' of the child 'on account of the affection I hold towards my dear lord and father-in-law, Duke Charles'.[8] Meanwhile, in Ghent, the magistrates prepared a series of triumphal arches representing the individual dominions that the infant would inherit from his father and grandfather, if he survived, while others represented the virtues of wisdom, justice and peace. On the evening of 7 March 1500 a long procession accompanied the infant over a special elevated walkway from the palace to the local parish church where his baptism would take place. Thousands of torches along the way 'turned night into day' (in the words of an awed chronicler) and allowed the vast crowd to watch as the officials and courtiers slowly passed by, culminating in Charles and his four godparents, each one destined to play a significant role in his early life: his great-grandmother Margaret of York, widow of Charles the Bold; his aunt Margaret of Austria; Charles de Croÿ, prince of Chimay, and Jean de Glymes, lord of Bergen, two of the foremost

Netherlands nobles. No one could have overlooked the symbolism of this arrangement: Philip, who would normally have occupied pride of place in the procession, ceded it to his son, who thus entered his secular inheritance by receiving the homage of his future subjects at the same time that he became a member of the Christian Church through baptism.

Philip had good reasons for this innovation. Although he boasted many titles, his ancestors had acquired them piecemeal over the course of a century, mostly by marriage. As Rolf Strøm-Olsen has pointed out: 'Charles's baptism presented a rare opportunity for the Habsburg court to make supra-regional claims about its legitimacy, power and authority', giving the ceremony in Ghent 'in ritual terms, some of the significance of coronation ceremonies found elsewhere in Europe, ceremonies not available to the rulers of the Low Countries.'[9]

Nevertheless, Philip did not entirely trust the people of Ghent. Three weeks before the birth he ordered that thirty archers and twenty-five halberdiers should henceforth 'stand on duty from the time when the archduke arises, and then accompany him on his way to Mass'. They 'must not leave the palace' without express permission but instead 'secure and protect the person of the archduke' day and night.[10] These were not idle precautions. After the death of Mary of Burgundy in 1482, Ghent had refused to accept her husband Maximilian as regent of the Burgundian Netherlands and guardian of their infant children. Instead, its magistrates seized young Philip, holding him as a hostage, and created a council of regency 'to maintain the right of our lord, your son, whom we hold to be our prince and natural lord, and none other'.[11] In 1485, at the head of troops from his German and Austrian territories, Maximilian crushed the dissidents and liberated his son, whom he moved to the loyal city of Mechelen; but three years later his autocratic behaviour provoked first his own capture and imprisonment in Ghent, and then his expulsion from the Netherlands.

Revolt, factional strife, and war thus characterized Philip's minority, which lasted until his fifteenth birthday in 1493, prompting the new ruler to adopt a very different style of government from his father. As Philip declared in 1497: 'Ever since we came of age and received the allegiance of our lands, we have always had the earnest desire, wish and inclination to end the great disorders that have prevailed here because of past wars and divisions, both in our own household and elsewhere in our said lands, and instead to introduce order.'[12] A decade later the Venetian ambassador at the court of Burgundy, Vincenzo Quirino, deemed this policy a success. Philip, he wrote, was 'by nature good, generous, open, affable, kind and almost intimate with everyone', and 'he sought to uphold justice with all his might. He was pious and he kept his promises.' Nevertheless, Quirino added, 'although he quickly understood complex issues, he was slow to deal with them and irresolute in action. He referred everything to his council.' Quirino also noted that 'I have learned from experience that decision-making at this court is very variable and mutable', because 'often they decide one thing in the council, and then do something totally different'. Gutierre Gómez de Fuensalida, the Spanish ambassador, agreed: the archduke, he wrote, 'is very fickle, and everyone has the power to change his mind'. Maximilian once reproached his son for listening to 'traitors and disloyal advisers who put [false] ideas in your head in order to create divisions between you and me' and suggested that 'it is better for you that I should know about your plans before your ministers instead of being treated like a stranger'. Yet Maximilian's repeated demands that his son should follow his lead, above all in waging war on France, left Philip (in Quirino's words) 'torn between paternal affection and the esteem and trust he places in his ministers'. In short, 'He finds himself in a labyrinth.'[13]

Olivier de la Marche, a veteran courtier of the dukes of Burgundy who became Philip's preceptor, appeared to agree with these unfavourable analyses, because at the end of his *Memoirs*, completed just before his death in 1502, he called the archduke 'Philip-believe-what-you're-told [*Philippe-croy-conseil*]'.[14] Nevertheless La Marche's 'Introduction', written a decade earlier, had expressly warned his pupil not to follow the example of his headstrong father Maximilian. 'Let me tell you the truth,' he urged Philip: 'Never give your subjects power over you, but always ask for their advice and assistance in forming and sustaining your grand designs.' La Marche praised the archduke because, after a quarter-century of war and rebellion, 'by listening to advice, you put the country back on its feet': he had united and pacified his disparate holdings; he had ensured universal acceptance of Habsburg rule; and he had established a cohort of over thirty trusted councillors, many of whom would also advise his son, creating a crucial element of political stability and continuity that helped to prevent a recurrence of the domestic unrest that had followed the death of his predecessors.[15]

The young duke of Luxemburg knew nothing of this. The daily accounts of his household show that a few weeks after giving birth, 'the archduchess and her noble children' (Charles and his sister Eleanor, fifteen months his senior) left Ghent for Bruges and then Brussels. There Joanna fell seriously ill and 'for forty-nine days continuously' Liberal Trevisan, Philip's personal physician and a member of his council, joined the 'other doctors and surgeons tending our very dear and much loved wife, to cure her of an illness'.[16] Charles would not have noticed. A Spanish diplomat reported that the duke of Luxemburg and his sister 'were being raised together in their apartments and no one has been added to their list of servants', with one exception: Barbe Servels, who, as Charles recalled four decades later, 'served as my principal wet-nurse for nine months'. A native of Ghent, Barbe began to nurse her august charge from the outset and Charles remained devoted to her: he stood godfather to her son, in whose career he took a keen interest, and when she died in 1554 he ordered her to be buried in the cathedral of St Gudule in Brussels and commissioned a prominent epitaph in her honour.[17]

The reports of Ambassador Fuensalida to Ferdinand and Isabella provide the earliest descriptions of Charles and his sister. In August 1500, after his first visit, Fuensalida wrote what grandparents everywhere want to hear: at five months 'the duke of Luxemburg is so tall and strong that he seems like a boy one year old', while his sister Eleanor, aged almost two, 'is so lively and clever that she seems as developed as a child of five'. Naturally, 'they are the most beautiful children in the world'. By the time of his first birthday, Charles was 'already taking steps in a baby walker (*carretonçillo*)' and 'walks with as much confidence and strength as a three-year-old'; and by August 1501 he was 'the strongest child for his age that I have ever seen'.[18]

The interest of the Catholic Monarchs reflected, in part, acute anxiety about the future of their dynasty. In 1497 their heir and only son John had died, leaving his wife Margaret of Austria pregnant, but their child died almost immediately. This made Joanna's older sister Isabel heir to all the territories ruled by the Catholic Monarchs, but she too died in 1498, immediately after giving birth to a son – who followed her to the grave two years later. On 8 August 1500 a letter from the Catholic Monarchs reached Philip, 'announcing the death of the child, so that my lord was now prince'. Three days later, for the first time, Philip signed a letter *Yo el príncipe* ('I, the prince'), the official style used in Spain by the heir apparent.[19]

These events profoundly affected the infant duke of Luxemburg. In the long term, as the oldest son of Joanna and Philip he would eventually succeed his father in Spain as well as in the Netherlands and in Austria. In the short term, his parents abandoned him because although Spain had no coronation ceremony, each new heir to the throne needed to appear in person before the representative assembly (*Cortes*) of each constituent state (Castile, León and Granada together; Aragon, Valencia and Catalonia individually) in order to receive their allegiance. Initially, Philip exhibited little enthusiasm for his good fortune. He did not inform his subjects of his impending departure for Spain until December 1500, when he asked his

Netherlands subjects to fund the costs of the voyage; and even then he suggested that he might travel alone. The archduke's ambiguity probably reflected both the fact that Joanna was pregnant with their third child, Isabeau (born in July 1501 and named after her grandmother, Isabella the Catholic), and also the hostility of his courtiers who, according to Fuensalida, 'would rather go to Hell than to Spain'. The new prince and princess did not begin their journey until October 1501, leaving their children under the care of Margaret of York in Mechelen (where Philip himself had grown up), assisted by a household of almost one hundred 'essential personnel'.[20] The children would not see their father again for two years, and their mother remained in Spain to give birth in March 1503 to another son, whom she named Ferdinand after her father. She did not return to the Netherlands until 1504.

As María José Rodríguez-Salgado has pointed out:

It was not unusual in this period for princes to be separated from their parents, to whom they were bound as much by political as by personal ties. We should not therefore expect aristocratic and princely dynasties of the time to be equipped with the emotional make-up of the contemporary bourgeois family. But even by the standards of the day, Charles had been born into an extraordinary and dysfunctional family.[21]

Fuensalida's letters to the Catholic Monarchs documented that dysfunction. He reported that during Joanna's absence in Spain, Philip 'had lots of fun' with his children 'and saw them many times', whereas after Joanna's return to the Netherlands she ignored them. In addition, Philip's infidelities caused such serious tensions between Charles's parents that in July 1504 Fuensalida (unfortunately for historians) dared not entrust details to paper but instead sent a special messenger to describe the discord to his sovereigns in person. The following month Philip visited Holland without his wife, and the ambassador noted with regret that 'Her Highness [Joanna] does not write to her husband and he does not write to her.' The archduke made an effort at reconciliation after he returned, bringing Charles and his sisters from Mechelen to Brussels to see their mother, 'thinking that if he brought them she would talk to them', but (according to Fuensalida) she 'did not seem to enjoy their company much'. Philip then tried another tactic: 'that night the prince slept in his wife's bedroom' (presumably the night that Joanna conceived another child, their daughter Marie). Relations between the couple soon deteriorated again. They regularly screamed at each other, and Joanna periodically retreated to her rooms and went on hunger strike; but after she grabbed a metal rod to beat the attendants appointed by her husband, Philip confined her to an apartment under guard. Obviously she could not be trusted with her children.[22]

In October 1504 another unexpected letter arrived from Spain: Ferdinand of Aragon announced that his wife Isabella seemed near to death. Therefore:

> The prince, my son, must immediately and secretly put his affairs there in order, so that everything is as it should be (although no one must know or understand why this is being done). He and the princess, my daughter, must also secretly prepare themselves so that if I should send a messenger they could leave at once and come here by sea with no delay.

Once again, Philip showed extreme reluctance to travel to Castile, complaining to Fuensalida that news of the queen's illness had 'come at a bad time', because he had just begun a war against Duke Charles of Guelders, a resolute and resourceful enemy of the dukes of Burgundy, 'and this is a major obstacle if I have to go to Spain: although Spain is of great importance, this is my real homeland and I must not lose it.' Even news of Isabella's death, which arrived in December 1504, failed to change Philip's mind: although he immediately styled himself 'king of Castile', he continued the war with Guelders until he had occupied most of the duchy – only to hand it back in return for a promise from Duke Charles that he would remain at peace while he went to Spain. The new king and queen of Castile finally set sail from Zealand in January 1506.[23]

THE UNIVERSAL HEIR

Although Charles never met his Spanish grandmother, her lavish obsequies in Brussels in January 1505 were probably the first public event he could remember. He, his sisters and their courtiers all wore special black coats and hoods lined with fur 'as mourning for the late queen of Spain', while they watched their parents kneel before the altar in the cathedral of St Gudule and listened to the magnificent 'Mass for Philip the Fair' by Josquin des Prés, the most famous composer of his day, composed for this occasion. After the service they heard the heralds proclaim the new 'king and queen of Castile, León and Granada, and prince and princess of Aragon and Sicily', and watched their parents solemnly process through the streets of Brussels, preceded by shields and banners 'on which all the king's titles were written, so that no one could plead ignorance'. Shortly afterwards, Charles and his siblings met their grandfather Maximilian for the first time, when he spent more than a month in the Netherlands, and they no doubt watched the numerous tournaments over which he presided 'in the great hall of the palace and in the park of Brussels', in one of which their father entered the lists with three of his courtiers, all dressed in yellow and red 'in the Spanish fashion'.[24]

The children likewise enjoyed the exotic animals imported by Philip from Spain – four camels, two pelicans, an ostrich and some guinea fowl, which joined the lions and bears kept in the palace gardens of Ghent and Brussels. Surviving sources record that Charles baited the lions with a stick, and fenced with the figures portrayed in the tapestries that decorated his apartments. He also pranced around on the hobby-horses given to him by Maximilian and by Count Palatine Frederick of Bavaria (both of whom would play an important role in his life); he drove his sisters around in a small cart drawn by ponies; and he organized his pages into armies of Christians and Turks, in which the duke of Luxemburg invariably commanded the former and invariably won.[25]

The children also learned to read and write. At first, Charles, Eleanor and Isabeau studied together under the direction of Juan de Anchieta, who served Joanna as both priest and composer – a common combination at the time, because musicians needed to write their own scores, and so were deft with a quill, while children normally learned elementary literacy by reciting and reading prayers. Indeed in April 1503 (when Eleanor was four and a half, Charles just over three, and Isabeau not yet two), Philip paid one of his chaplains who was also a copyist of musical manuscripts just over £2 'for a parchment book which he had illuminated, containing the gospels and prayers that were read' to the duke of Luxemburg and his sisters 'every day after they had heard Mass'. Seven months later, probably as a present for her fifth birthday, Philip gave Eleanor a 'book called "ABC", composed of large letters, with lots of pictures and some gold letters', which cost £12 – rather a lot for a child's primer, but a good investment because one year later she was able to send a letter written in her own hand to her grandfather Ferdinand.[26] Charles made slower progress. In January 1504, when a letter in Spanish went out in his name to his grandfather, asking 'Your Highness to excuse my discourtesy in not writing with my own hand' (reasonable enough for a boy not yet four), the prince could not even write his own name himself, instead copying the letters written on a separate sheet by Anchieta (Pl. 2).[27]

Anchieta returned to Spain and Luis Cabeza de Vaca, 'a Spaniard of noble blood who excelled in letters and good conduct', became preceptor to the royal children. He took immediate steps to create an environment more favourable to learning – a local carpenter supplied a special desk, with a cupboard for school supplies and seats, 'so that the prince and his sisters could go to school' – and for the next three years his three illustrious charges studied together (Pl. 1).[28] Still, Charles made slow progress. When, in September 1506, Maximilian expressed the desire that his grandson should learn some Dutch, his governor replied frostily: 'I will deal with your request once he can speak properly and has learned to read.' Perhaps illness delayed education, because in the course of 1505, a substantial quantity of 'drugs, medicine and spices' were 'delivered by order of the doctors to the prince and his sisters during their illnesses'. Isabeau suffered the worst, because she 'had an infection in her eyes' that obliged her parents to pay a master surgeon, who 'visited her every day for the nine months that she was ill'.[29]

In September 1505, just after the master surgeon had cured Isabeau, Joanna gave birth to Marie (named after her paternal grandmother), bringing the number of children in Mechelen to four; but this addition to Charles's family circle was balanced by losses. Margaret of Austria, his aunt and godmother, left to marry the duke of Savoy in 1501, while his great-grandmother and first governess, Margaret of York, died two years later. Although Charles was too young to be affected, he certainly noticed the departure of his parents. They visited Mechelen in November 1505, just before leaving for Zealand where Philip had assembled a fleet to take them back to Spain. Because unfavourable winds confined his fleet to port, Philip paid one last flying visit to his children in Mechelen in December, but it was the last time: he died in Spain less than a year later. Isabeau and Marie would never see him or their mother again, nor would they ever meet their youngest sister Catalina (born in spring 1507), because although Joanna survived until April 1555 she never left Spain, while Catalina, who outlived all of them (she died in 1578), never left the Iberian peninsula.

Although of course the new king and queen of Castile did not realize that they would never return to the Netherlands, the normal risks and perils of travel in early modern Europe led them to take appropriate precautions. In June 1505, Philip met both his father and his sister in the expectation (according to Ambassador Quirino) that Margaret, once again a widow, would 'govern the Netherlands while [Philip] was in Spain; but they could not reach an agreement, and so she returned to Savoy.' Instead Philip named Guillaume of Croÿ, Baron Chièvres and head of his treasury, as regent and commander-in-chief during his absence with full powers to take military, judicial and administrative decisions, as well as 'to make treaties, alliances and agreements' with foreign powers, 'and in general to do or cause to be done each and all the things that we ourselves would and could do'. Philip also named the prince of Chimay, Chièvres's cousin (and Charles's godfather), to be guardian of his children, assisted by Henri de Witthem, lord of Beersel, with instructions that the prince and his sisters 'must be carefully protected and also taught good behaviour and all manner of knowledge'.[30]

Finally, Philip made a will that revealed profound uncertainty concerning the future of his dominions. He decreed that if he died in Spain, he must be buried in Granada beside his mother-in-law Isabella, whereas if death overtook him in or near the Netherlands, he wanted to be interred in Bruges beside his mother Mary; 'but if the duchy of Burgundy should be in our hands' at the time of his death, 'I wish to be buried in the Charterhouse of Dijon, alongside the dukes of Burgundy, my predecessors'. Philip's will also directed that each of his young daughters must be well and honourably maintained, in keeping with their status, 'at the expense of my oldest son', and that when they married each should 'receive a dowry of 200,000 gold crowns' – a wholly unrealistic provision, since each dowry far exceeded his annual revenues from the Netherlands. Most perplexing of all, he named his male children jointly as 'universal heirs to all my kingdoms, duchies, counties, lands, lordships and other possessions', directing that 'I wish each of them to inherit and succeed to the various parts and portions according to the customs and usages of the places where my said possessions are and may be situated'.[31]

Evidently, Philip envisaged a partition of the immense but awkward inheritance created by the marriages and deaths of his Trastámara relatives (a prudent move contemplated by his successors on several occasions), but few at the time considered this a likely outcome. Henry VII of England predicted that Charles 'will be the sovereign of all and will be able to rule the world'; while Ambassador Quirino declared that since Charles was now the universal heir to 'all the Netherlands, and will succeed his mother [Joanna] as ruler of Castile when she dies, and his grandfather as Archduke of Austria, he will be a great lord'. However, the ambassador added ominously, although Charles was 'a handsome and happy child, in all his deeds he showed himself wilful and cruel, like old Duke Charles [the Bold] of Burgundy'.[32]

'A HANDSOME AND HAPPY CHILD'

For some time, the future of the 'handsome and happy child' hung in the balance. Philip took more than 400 courtiers, over 100 guards and some

2,000 German troops with him to Spain, and his sudden death there in September 1506 left them all destitute. 'There was not a man among us who had a penny,' one of them later complained, adding that 'by the time the king died, he had spent all his own money'. Since no one in Spain would help them, and 'fearing that an order would be issued preventing them from returning to our own country', the desperate courtiers immediately seized as much of the late king's goods as they could, starting with his jewels, gold and silver, 'selling everything for far less than it was worth'. Later, they 'sold their own clothes, their horses, and their other precious possessions in return for bread' and a passage home. The Burgundian survivors henceforth harboured a deep resentment towards Spain.[33]

News of Philip's death arrived in the Netherlands while Chièvres was absent from Mechelen, directing operations against the duke of Guelders who, encouraged by Louis XII of France, had resumed hostilities. The rest of the regency council panicked because (as one of them put it) 'we do not yet know how the news will be received by either the subjects or by the neighbouring friends and enemies'. They feared domestic disorders similar to those that followed the death of Philip's grandfather Charles the Bold in 1477 and his mother Mary in 1482; while although the king of France sent letters 'full of fine words as usual, it would be very dangerous to place much trust in them'. In addition, the regents observed ominously, Philip had died so suddenly that 'we did not even know he was ill', leaving Joanna in Spain and Charles too young to rule.[34] With some trepidation, they therefore summoned delegates from the representative assembly of each of his Netherlands provinces to convene as the States-General.

Philip had convened the States-General twenty-five times during his decade of personal rule, to discuss matters of peace and war as well as his demands for new taxes. Delegations from the four largest and richest provinces (Brabant, Flanders, Hainaut and Holland) almost always attended the States-General, normally joined by those from Artois, French-Flanders, Mechelen, Namur and Zealand, and occasionally by those from Limburg and Luxemburg. On each occasion the various delegations discussed the matters referred to them in three separate 'estates': prelates, nobles and towns. The same was true of the assembly that gathered in Mechelen on 15 October 1506 'to meet our revered lord, the archduke, prince of Castile, and to see if they will (as we hope) agree to offer advice on affairs here'.[35]

Philip's consensual style of government at home and abroad now paid dividends. Every community in the Netherlands gave vent to 'the greatest sorrow and lamentation you ever saw' on learning of his death, while both

Henry VII and Louis XII offered their protection to the young prince. Indeed, for the rest of his reign Louis respected the neutrality of all Charles's possessions (though he continued to provide clandestine aid to the duke of Guelders). Some of the regents (notably those with lands in the southern provinces, like Chièvres) favoured placing the Netherlands under French protection; but others, mostly those with estates in the maritime provinces (like Bergen), favoured an alliance with England. The States-General, however, deemed that Maximilian could best guarantee their future, and sent a delegation that included both Chièvres and Bergen to invite him to serve as guardian of his grandchildren and as regent.[36]

Maximilian had anticipated this decision: as soon as he heard of his son's death, he commanded the council of regency 'to continue to govern our Netherlands, as our late said son ordered you to do, in the name of ourselves and our very dear son Archduke Charles' until he could return to take charge, 'which will be in two to three weeks'. No doubt realizing that this timetable was totally unrealistic, he also summoned his daughter Margaret to join him.[37]

The archduchess, now aged twenty-seven, had led an eventful life. In 1483, aged three, she went to France as the fiancée of Charles VIII and spent the next eight years at the French court, until the king brutally repudiated her and married another. After living for two years with her grandmother in Mechelen, Margaret went to Spain to marry Prince John, but he died after only six months, and in 1500 she returned to Mechelen. Eighteen months later she left for Savoy to marry Duke Philibert, with whom she lived happily until he too died young in 1504. Margaret now concentrated on constructing the magnificent mausoleum for Philibert that still stands at Brou, in south-east France, and apart from a brief journey in 1505 to discuss with her father and brother the possibility of serving as regent of the Netherlands, she remained in Savoy until Maximilian summoned her the following year. The two spent several months together, apparently discussing how best to cope with the emergency caused by Philip's unexpected death, until in March 1507 Maximilian signed letters patent formally accepting:

The tutorship, guardianship, government and administration of our most dear and beloved [grand]children, Charles, prince of Castile, Ferdinand, archduke of Austria, and their sisters Eleanor, Isabeau, Marie and Catalina, all minors, as well as all their possessions, lands and lordships, as we are competent and entitled to do by right and by reason as their grandparent and their closest relative.

Since he could not yet exercise these powers in person, he appointed Margaret as his 'procurator' to receive an oath of obedience 'from our territories and lordships in the Netherlands', and he sent commissioners to swear an oath before the States-General by which he agreed to act 'irrevocably' as sole tutor and regent for Charles 'until the end of his minority'.[38]

This constituted a power grab of breathtaking proportions. Chièvres and his colleagues had governed the Netherlands successfully for eighteen months with minimal supervision: now Maximilian unilaterally dismissed them and claimed complete authority over the Low Countries and his grandchildren at Mechelen. He also claimed authority over the other territories left by his son and over his other grandchildren, Ferdinand and Catalina, both of whom lived in Spain. Since the emperor had no authority in Spain, Charles's inheritance in effect remained partitioned, much as his father had envisaged in his will: Joanna's father King Ferdinand did his best to control Castile (as well as Aragon and Sicily, of which he was sovereign, and Naples, which his troops had recently wrested from the French), and he raised his younger grandson and namesake as a Spanish prince, while Maximilian struggled to control the Netherlands and to make sure that Charles grew up as a Burgundian prince.

The children at Mechelen learned of their bereavement in October 1506 when their governor informed them that their father was dead. 'They showed the grief appropriate to their age, and perhaps even more so', Maximilian learned, and 'they said that they were lucky to have a loyal parent like you'. Charles now referred to the emperor as 'my grandfather and father'.[39] Although Maximilian did not visit them again for another two years, Margaret arrived in Mechelen in April 1507 and started to take care of her nephew and nieces. The children warmed to her immediately: when she left shortly afterwards to carry out her political duties, they burst into tears (according to an eyewitness) because 'they would no longer see their aunt and godmother – or more accurately their new mother'.[40]

ARCHDUCHESS MARGARET OF AUSTRIA, DOWAGER DUCHESS OF SAVOY

When Margaret returned to Mechelen two months later, she arranged solemn obsequies for her late brother in the cathedral of St Rombout, in which Charles appeared for the first time as a ruler. First she withdrew from the library of the dukes of Burgundy a magnificent illuminated manuscript prayer book, bound in black velvet and displaying the arms of Charles the

Bold, and presented it to his young namesake, no doubt so that he could use it during the service. Next she arranged for Charles to lead a solemn procession 'mounted on a small horse' and 'flanked on both sides by the archers of his bodyguard'. After Mass the principal herald shouted 'Long live Charles, by the grace of God archduke of Austria and prince of Spain'. The other heralds present then called out in turn his numerous other titles – duke of Brabant, count of Flanders and so on – after which Charles received the sword of justice 'in his tiny hands, and holding it with the point upright he went to the altar', where he briefly prayed before leading the procession back to the palace. There 'the noble young prince dubbed a new knight for the first time', thus demonstrating to everyone his new status. This detailed account of Charles's first public appearance as a ruler, written by Margaret's official chronicler Jean Lemaire des Belges, ended with the pious wish: 'May God grant that he may henceforth do as much as Charlemagne to defend public affairs and Christendom!'[41]

The events of the following day cruelly revealed the hollowness of such grandiose visions. Margaret had ordered the States-General to reassemble 'in the great chamber of the prince's residence, still draped in black', and there they listened as the chancellor requested new taxes to fund an effective defence against Guelders, to discharge the debts of the late king, and to 'pay for the household of My Lord and his sisters'. Margaret made a brief speech of support before turning to Charles to ask: ' "Isn't that true, nephew?" And then my lord Archduke, aware of his princely responsibilities despite his young age, begged the deputies for their consent by making a short speech that was better understood by watching his facial expressions than by listening to the sound of his boyish voice'. He spoke and gestured in vain: the assembly refused to vote any new taxes. Charles learned for the first time that paying for his enterprises required careful preparation.[42]

A few weeks later, Margaret introduced her nephew to the warriors who would absorb almost all the taxes provided by his subjects over the next half-century. She summoned her leading army officers to the great hall of the palace and pointed to Charles, saying: 'My lords: here is the person for whom you fight. He will never waver. Serve him!' The following day she and her nephew stood at the window while 500 cavalry troopers rode by the palace 'with banners unfurled and trumpets sounding' to defend the Netherlands against Guelders.[43]

When Maximilian named Margaret as his 'procurator' in 1507, he purchased for her a complex of buildings in Mechelen just across the street from the 'Keizershof' where his grandchildren lived. Soon refurbished, and known as the 'Hof van Savoy', it became Margaret's headquarters until her death in 1530. According to the account books of her household, more than 150 people sat down there to eat lunch every day, including visitors from all over Europe whom the archduchess wanted her nephew and nieces to meet. Some came from ruling families, like Count Palatine Frederick of Bavaria; others were related to Charles's ministers, like young Guillaume of Croÿ, Chièvres's nephew; but most came from less exalted families. One of them was Anne Boleyn, daughter of an English diplomat who desired her to become fluent in French. When she arrived in Mechelen in 1513, Margaret told Anne's father that 'I find her so refined and pleasant, despite her young age, that I am more indebted to you for having sent her than you are to me'. Anne stayed for over a year, learning the French that would later captivate Henry VIII and make her queen of England.[44]

Margaret's court soon became the foremost cultural centre in northern Europe. Her library contained almost 400 bound volumes, many of them exquisite illustrated manuscripts; she employed Bernard van Orley and Jan Vermeyen as her resident painters, and Peter de Pannemaker as her personal tapestry-maker; she also entertained the famous artists of her day, including Albrecht Dürer who in 1521 praised her paintings 'and many other costly things and a precious library'.[45] By the time of her death, the archduchess owned over 100 tapestries, over 50 sculptures and almost 200 paintings (including works by the finest Netherlands artists: Rogier van der Weyden, Hieronymus Bosch, Hans Memling and Jan van Eyck); and she took a keen personal interest in her possessions. She ordered a new hinge for van Eyck's great 'Arnolfini wedding' triptych, so that the wings would close properly; she summoned the celebrated painter Jan Gossaert to carry out expert restoration on her most valuable canvases; and an inventory of her possessions contains corrections and annotations written in her own hand that reveal her personal involvement in creating the collection. In the words of Dagmar Eichberger, who has studied Margaret's collections extensively, the archduchess 'could pride herself on having a comprehensive portrait gallery in her dining hall, a collection of ethnographic artefacts from the New World in her library, a painting gallery in her stately bedroom, and a beautiful array of small objects, scientifica and exotica in her two collection cabinets'. Margaret's example would inspire her young charges, each of whom later displayed exquisite artistic taste.[46]

Charles and his sisters became the family that Margaret had never previously enjoyed – and for the rest of their lives they would address their letters to 'Madame my aunt and my dear mother'; declare that 'the affection

I bear you is not only that of a nephew towards his aunt but that of a good son to his true and loving mother'; and sign them 'your humble niece and daughter' (or 'your humble son and nephew').[47] Margaret's surviving correspondence makes it easy to understand why the children adored her. When in 1507 Maximilian appointed a replacement for Friar Jean de Witte as confessor to his grandchildren, Margaret requested an exemption for Eleanor. Charles and his younger sisters, she reported, 'do not yet have great need' of spiritual direction, 'except to lead and encourage them to obey the commandments of God and his Holy Church', but Eleanor (then nine years old) 'already has a good understanding of good and bad conduct' and, since she liked Friar Jean, Margaret asked her father to leave him in post. Four years later, on hearing that their governor 'had forbidden the young ladies to dance', she informed him that 'this causes them much tedium and sorrow. Therefore, taking pity on them, I think that they should be allowed to dance just as before.' She taught her nieces sewing, needlework and the art of making preserves; and in 1514, when it seemed that Mary Tudor (sister of Henry VIII and also an orphan) would marry Charles and move to the Netherlands, Margaret sent her a pattern 'of the clothes that ladies here usually wear, so that it will be easier for you to dress in the local style when you get here'.[48] What mother could have done more? Long after her charges departed, Margaret served as a clearing house for family news. When in 1518 she received a letter from Charles in Spain, she immediately wrote to inform his sister Marie, then in Hungary, that 'every day he takes part in jousts and tournaments, and I bet he often wishes that you and I were there with him to enjoy ourselves'. Above all, as Annemarie Jordan Gschwend has noted, Margaret trained all members of the next generation 'to respect and serve the dynasty they were born into, instilling in her young protégés one principle they would honor their entire lives: a deep loyalty to the Habsburg house'.[49]

PROTECTING THE HEIR

The plethora of premature deaths among the Habsburg, Burgundian and Trastámara dynasties no doubt explains the obsessive anxiety concerning the health of Charles and his sisters. In 1508, when Maximilian returned to the Netherlands and suggested that 'for his recreation' his grandson should travel with him between Mechelen, Lier and Antwerp, a radius of no more than 18 kilometres, the prince of Chimay lodged a formal protest because of 'the young age of my lord, who is vulnerable and delicate'. If the emperor nevertheless insisted, Chimay continued, then after every day on the road the prince must 'stay put for a whole day, so that he will have two consecu-tive nights in which to rest and recover'. Six months later, it was Maximilian's turn to be over-protective. He learned that Liberal Trevisan, the Venetian physician who had attended Joanna 'for forty-nine days continuously' after her son's birth, planned to present Charles with a dog: 'Be on your guard against this,' he instructed Margaret, and keep both the dog and the doctor at bay 'during the current state of war that exists between us and the Venetians'. Shortly afterwards, he instructed her to expel Trevisan from the Netherlands 'because of our suspicions about him: since he is a Venetian we do not wish him to attend our grandson Charles any more.'[50] Margaret shared these fears. A few weeks later she insisted that her charges 'must reside [in Mechelen] permanently, without leaving the city until I get back there', because 'these days one does not know whom one can trust'. She also obsessed about their health because (as she once confided to Maximilian) 'even the slightest illness in people of such importance causes concern'. Thus when news arrived that the prince's sisters in Mechelen had contracted smallpox, she kept Charles in Brussels 'because the doctors say this illness is contagious, and that my nephew may catch it' (he caught it anyway, and was incapacitated by the agonizing and dangerous disease for over a month).[51]

Margaret's obsessions apparently did not extend to her nephew's education. The surviving evidence of Charles's early literacy suggests a very slow learner. 'At the age of seven', according to a courtier, Charles 'wanted to learn and understand Latin letters', but a surviving Spanish letter from 1508 contained only twelve words in his own hand and his signature as prince of Castile, while another in French ended with three words in his own hand and his signature as duke of Burgundy – and in both cases, although now eight, Charles still wrote each character separately and made no break between words (Pl. 3).[52]

His script would always remain poor. In 1532, on receiving a set of holo-graph instructions, his sister Marie complained that 'if I may say so, one or two words are so badly written that I was not able to read them, and I do not know if I managed to divine them correctly'. The description by a modern historian of the mature handwriting of their older sister Eleanor, taught by the same preceptors (Anchieta and Cabeza de Vaca), will sound depress-ingly familiar to all who have struggled with the emperor's calligraphy. Eleanor:

> Normally joined together as many characters of a single word, and even of several words, as possible, as if trying to commit as many letters as possible to paper without lifting her hand. She never hesitated to leave

erased words or to use every known abbreviation ... She never really used punctuation, although she sometimes indicated the end of a sentence with an oblique stroke ... She preferred efficiency to legibility.[53]

Charles and his siblings nevertheless came into contact at Mechelen with many cultivated men and women and their work. The accounts of the treasurer-general of the Netherlands recorded a payment of £10 in October 1504 'to Brother Erasmus of Rotterdam, a friar of the Augustinian Order, as a one-time gift from My Lord as charity to help support him at college in Leuven, where he is studying' (almost certainly a reward for the *Panegyric* on Philip's 'voyage to Spain and successful return home', delivered at court the previous January). Erasmus claimed that he also received an invitation to serve as Charles's tutor and although he turned it down, he dedicated two of his books to the prince and corresponded regularly with both ministers and courtiers.[54] The court also patronized musicians, artists and craftsmen. In 1504, Charles's father paid £15 to a bookbinder for 'making wooden covers for five large books, and for repairing and re-gilding several other works'; and £36 to 'Jeronymus van Aeken, called Bosch' for 'a very large painting measuring nine feet high and eleven feet wide which will show the Last Judgement, that is to say Heaven and Hell, which My Lord has ordered him to paint'. The following year, Philip paid £23 to 'a man who played a strange Spanish instrument, and to a young girl from Lombardy' who 'played several songs and performed acrobatics for him while he dined', as well as £25 to a painter who presented him with 'a picture of a naked woman' (payments that put the gift of £10 to Brother Erasmus of Rotterdam in perspective).[55]

COURTSHIP AND MARRIAGE

Just before his eighth birthday, Charles exchanged marriage vows – and not for the first time. In 1501 his father's diplomats had signed a treaty that betrothed him to Claude, daughter of Louis XII of France; but despite renewing that agreement on three separate occasions, Louis had no intention of honouring it, having already promised that his daughter would marry the heir presumptive to his crown: Francis, duke of Angoulême. As soon as the deception became public knowledge, Maximilian (in his capacity as tutor and guardian of his grandson) opened negotiations for Charles to marry Mary Tudor, daughter of Henry VII, and in December 1507, Bergen went to England as Charles's proxy and placed a wedding ring on the princess's finger, after which the couple exchanged their vows. A triumphalist English tract celebrated 'the most noble aliaunce and gretest mariage of all Christendome, considering the sundry and manyfolde regions and countrayes that the sayde yonge prynce . . . shal enherite', and Charles signed obsequious letters to 'the princess of Castile' (as she became known), whom he addressed as 'your devoted husband and companion' (see Pl. 3). The letters patent creating a separate household for Charles's sisters instructed their treasurer to include 'our very dear and beloved spouse, Mary of England'.[56]

Although Charles never consummated the 'gretest mariage of all Christendome', he gained one immediate advantage: Henry VII made his new son-in-law a member of the exclusive Order of the Garter. In February 1509, in the presence of Maximilian, 'the English ambassadors presented the archduke with the insignia of the Order, which he received solemnly, dressed in a purple coat made of velvet with a scarlet hood' and (tactfully) the cross of St George on his shoulder. A week of celebrations followed, including jousts in the marketplace of Brussels in which Maximilian took part, watched from the balcony of the city hall by his admiring grandchildren.[57]

Just before he left the Netherlands in spring 1509, Maximilian made two important innovations that affected Charles. First, he created a separate household for the prince, with up to twelve pages (who would later become squires and then knights) and between six and eight other young noble companions ('enfants d'honneur'), as well as a host of other attendants. Second, he conferred on Margaret the title 'regent and governor' of the Habsburg Netherlands and authorized her to preside over a Privy Council composed of twelve Knights of the Golden Fleece (Burgundy's exclusive chivalric order) who must accompany her at all times.[58]

According to the Belgian historian Henri Pirenne, these changes meant that 'never had a governess enjoyed such freedom of action'. Nevertheless, Margaret had hoped for far more: she urged her father to confer on her 'the same full authority that [he] exercises, without exception', and to grant that 'she alone can exercise [his] authority', but Maximilian insisted on retaining for himself control over finance, war, peace and patronage. 'Since I am guardian and grandfather of my [grand]children,' he chided her, 'it seems to me that I should retain some powers, both to supervise you and to maintain my reputation', and his correspondence with his daughter offers countless examples of decisions taken despite her opposition.[59] Above all, Margaret wanted to marginalize Chièvres, still in charge of the treasury. When the prince of Chimay wished to resign his position as First Chamberlain of the prince in favour of his cousin Chièvres, Margaret asked her father to appoint

Bergen instead. But Maximilian ignored her plea: Chièvres began to draw salary as First Chamberlain on 27 April 1509. He now became the prince's constant companion: the household accounts of that year record the purchase of matching fabrics 'for the coverlet of the bed of my lord [Charles] and the bed of my lord of Chièvres, his governor'; and when Charles later decreed changes for the household of his brother Ferdinand, he ordered that a confidant 'should always sleep in his bedroom as M. de Chièvres does in ours, so that when he wakes up he might have someone to talk with, if he wishes'.[60]

Although Maximilian prevailed on this important issue, he too had hoped for wider powers. In 1508 he announced to an assembly of the Knights of the Golden Fleece 'his intention of joining together his possessions, and unifying them into a single kingdom, to be called "Burgundy and Austria" for better defence against common enemies'. Although this initiative failed, two years later he announced his intention of taking Charles with him to Austria and 'immediately afterwards making him king of *Austrasia*' – a title virtually unknown since the days of Charlemagne – and in preparation, his advisers drew up 'Instructions for the household of the future king of Austrasia'. Once again, the initiative failed.[61] Meanwhile Chièvres strove to improve relations between the Burgundian Netherlands and France, while Margaret worked hard to strengthen links with England and Spain. In 1508 she informed King Ferdinand (her former father-in-law) that little Charles, 'despite his young age, on his own initiative asks about your health every single day and regards you (together with the emperor) as his true father who will, he knows, protect him from his enemies'. Henceforth these four powerful figures – Margaret, Maximilian, Ferdinand and Chièvres – competed ruthlessly for the heart and mind of the orphan prince.[62]

TWO

THE ORPHAN PRINCE, 1509–14

'MAXI'

In 1855 the French historian Jules Michelet hailed Archduchess Margaret of Austria as 'The real "strong man" of the family' whose efforts, above those of all others, 'made the House of Austria great'.[1] Rather like the eulogy of Henri Pirenne, this is an exaggeration: although the archduchess proved to be both a skilled administrator and a subtle diplomat, her father Maximilian achieved far more, for he not only prevented the French from annexing the Netherlands but also laid the foundation for four centuries of Habsburg domination in central Europe.

Even routine administrative documents revealed the archduchess's subordinate status: she signed ordinary missives 'by order of the emperor, Margaret', while proclamations went out 'By order of the emperor and of the archduke'. Her father also appointed all major officials, both clerical and secular, throughout the Netherlands. Although in 1510, 'weary of the petitioners who ceaselessly pester him', he promised to accept future recommendations forwarded by Margaret and her council, 'Maxi' (as he signed his letters) continued to bombard his daughter with orders – directly whenever he resided in the Netherlands and at other times by letter, many of them holograph.[2]

Periodically, the two clashed. In 1507, Margaret scribbled a note to one of her father's advisers begging that the emperor 'should tell me first what he has decided to do, and not do as he usually does – which is to write one thing to me and then do something else'. Two years later her father's decision to cede to one of his creditors a part of Franche-Comté, a province that he had given to her, provoked outrage. 'My Lord, I find myself speechless', Margaret protested 'because it seems to me that I, your only daughter, should be preferred to all others.' Nevertheless, she continued angrily, 'if you are determined to take these lands, then take them and do what you want with them – indeed don't take just them, but take the rest of the Franche-Comté and everything I own, because I do not wish to disobey you in anything.'³ Tirades like this sometimes provoked a counterblast. In 1508 the emperor claimed that his daughter's letters 'are so full of mysteries that it's impossible for me to understand them or even to identify the subject', and he provided her with a model of how to proceed in future (above all, 'write three lines instead of ten'). Two years later, he sent back those of her 'letters that we have not burned' because they seemed so 'unreasonable that I think you must take me for a Frenchman' (evidently the worst insult in the emperor's repertory). He then reminded her: 'I appointed you to your post as governess of our dominions and our subjects, always saying and proclaiming good things about you'; but, he concluded with a palpable threat, 'if you continue to write rude letters to me without cause, I think you will soon make me change my mind'.⁴

This was an empty threat, and Maximilian knew it: only his daughter could execute his policies effectively, and so he normally showed her both affection and consideration. Thus after telling her to drop everything she was doing and come to Luxemburg to receive his orders in person, he relented because, as he put it, 'that would interrupt your daily efforts to make sure the 12,000 troops in the Netherlands receive their pay, which is currently the most important of all our affairs; so we will make the effort to come and see you.' He also learned to accept her political advice. When Margaret discovered that her father intended to allow Ferdinand, Charles's younger brother, to become Grand Master of Spain's Military Orders she informed him crisply that it was a disastrous decision, 'which nothing on earth could justify', because 'it would suffice to deprive Prince Charles of the kingdoms of Spain'. Maximilian immediately relented.⁵

Margaret found it harder to disagree with her father in person. He made four visits to the Netherlands after Philip's death – between November 1508 and March 1509, in spring 1512, in summer 1513 and early in 1517 – and on each occasion, he spent much time with his daughter and his grandchildren. The first surviving letter written by Charles's older sister, Eleanor, informed Margaret that 'because you take pleasure in our pleasure, I wanted to tell you that our grandfather has come to visit us, which brought us all great joy'.⁶ The children's 'great joy' is easily explained: Maximilian was fun. He dined with them, danced with them, gave them money to play cards, and took them on trips in both boat and carriage to his various residences in and around Brussels and Antwerp. In 1509, just after Charles took the oath as count of Flanders, he and his grandfather made their way through the streets of Ghent 'shouting "Largesse" as they threw and scattered' coins among the crowd – something no nine-year-old boy would forget – and when Maximilian stayed in the ducal palace in Brussels he specified that 'our [grand]son should be in the room next to mine'.[7] He also gave the children thoughtful gifts. Once, after a day's hunting, he sent his granddaughters 'part of a deer that I killed today' so that it 'can be prepared for their dinner or supper'; and on another occasion he presented Charles with a pair of mounted knights made of brass with wooden lances, mounted on wheels and powered by a system of cords and pulleys so that he and his playmates could learn how to joust (Pl. 4).[8] In 1512 the emperor commissioned for the prince a suit of jousting armour decorated with gold and silver and displaying the insignia of the Golden Fleece. Maximilian also gave his daughter a 'large parchment book, full of sung masses' commissioned from a celebrated scrivener 'as a new year's gift' in 1511: the title page showed the emperor looking on benevolently while Margaret, Charles and his sisters sat at his feet – the epitome of a happy family (Pl. 5).[9]

Maximilian knew the value of such things. An only child, he had grown up in obscurity and relative poverty in east-central Europe until 1477 when, aged eighteen, he made a daring ride halfway across Europe to marry Mary of Burgundy. For the next fifteen years, he fought foreign and domestic opponents almost continuously in order to preserve her inheritance intact, and became so captivated by Burgundian culture that (according to his most eminent modern biographer, Hermann Wiesflecker) 'he became a Burgundian himself'.[10] Above all, Maximilian adopted the overarching Burgundian goal of 'rebuilding a Christian world empire'. This, he believed, required him to neutralize France as a prelude to leading a crusade that would regain Constantinople from the Turks. His dreams of grandeur knew no bounds. He styled himself Pontifex Maximus and aspired to be canonized as a saint after his death (like some of his imperial predecessors, including Charlemagne); he acted as pope as well as emperor, dispensing benefices, appropriating monastic revenues and the yield of crusade indulgences; and he treated popes as if they were his patriarchs, never understanding why (as he complained) 'throughout my whole life, no pope has ever kept his word to me' – a complaint that Charles would repeat, almost verbatim, to his own heir nearly thirty years later.[11] Likewise, although Maximilian had to abandon his 'great plan of war' conceived in 1496 to conquer and partition France, in 1513 he led the imperial contingent in person at the battle of Guinegate, where he routed 'the French, the eternal and natural enemies of our House of Burgundy'. He boasted to Charles that the outcome 'should cast down the pride of the French for at least ten years' and lead to 'the reconquest of the lands that rightly belong to our dynasty. Having thus shown you the way, I leave things to you, so you can valiantly defend what you have, as our predecessors have done for over a hundred years.'[12]

No doubt Maximilian imparted similar advice in person whenever he spent time with his grandson. Although their conversations have left no direct documentary trace, much can be gleaned from the quartet of semi-autobiographical works that Maximilian composed and presented to Charles. His *History of Frederick and Maximilian* chronicled the accomplishments of his early years; *The adventures and heroic life of Sir Theuerdank* related in verse his success in claiming the hand of Mary of Burgundy and in hunting and hawking; *Der Weisskunig* (meaning in German both *The wise king* and *The white king*) rehearsed in prose his education, princely upbringing and military accomplishments; and *Freydal* documented and illustrated each of the sixty-four tournaments in which he had taken part. The emperor closely supervised the composition of these works by ghost-writers (as we might call them today) with the express intention of producing a personal testament that would teach his heir by example how to govern himself, his subjects and the world.[13]

By the time Charles received his presentation copy of *Der Weisskunig* in 1517, Maximilian could point to four major successes. He had protected and reorganized the Burgundian Netherlands, whose political future had seemed bleak when he became their ruler forty years earlier. Likewise, he had overcome the obstacles posed by individual institutions, traditions and languages to forge the sub-Alpine lands he inherited from his father into a single state: 'Austria', ruled and taxed by a single administration that he created at Innsbruck. He had also reformed the chaotic central government of the Holy Roman Empire in ways that, though imperfect, would last almost until its demise three centuries later. Finally, by arranging strategic marriages for his grandchildren, he had established the House of Habsburg as the premier dynasty in central and eastern Europe, creating a polity that his successors would expand over the next four centuries. 'The truth is,' Maximilian observed to Margaret in 1516, 'that after serving God, I place the advancement of our dynasty above all things.' He repeated his boast a few weeks later (for the emperor rarely gave his opinion only once): 'My dear daughter: I think day and night of the affairs of my heirs'.[14]

Many of Charles's later actions closely reflected the goals and values of his grandfather, the only appropriate male role model available to him as an adolescent. He imitated Maximilian by marching at the head of his infantry 'with a pike over his shoulder'; he was crowned king of the Romans in a ceremony at Aachen 'designed according to archival research' done under his grandfather's supervision.[15] Charles challenged the king of France to meet him in a duel and invited the Ottoman sultan to participate in a tournament in order to settle their differences once and for all, just as Maximilian would have done; he schemed to regain the powers of Charlemagne, from whom the Habsburgs claimed descent; and he believed that he must neutralize France as a prelude to leading a crusade that would regain Constantinople from the Turks. When deciding how to punish Ghent after its rebellion against him in 1539–40, Charles studied the plans drawn up for his grandfather half a century before and then built a citadel in exactly the place proposed. Eventually he could echo Maximilian and claim that he had 'used up, lost and consumed the flower and manhood of our youth' in campaigning against his enemies and travelling around his dominions, despite 'deprivation of sleep, with other pains that our body has so often suffered, beyond measure, and more than our nature could bear and endure' (like his grandson, Maximilian left no heartstring unplucked).[16]

Charles also developed some of his grandfather's bad habits, such as pursuing policies that he could not afford. *Der Weisskunig* proclaimed that 'Every monarch fights his enemy with men and money, but a warlike regime and reputation count for far more than money': once again, words that Charles would pass on to his own heir. Both rulers, although punctilious about their honour, lacked all moral scruples where money was concerned so that, just like Maximilian, Charles left financial chaos when his reign ended.[17] Finally, Charles also imitated his grandfather by displaying (as Peter Burke has put it) an almost obsessional concern 'with his self-image and with the way in which he would be remembered by posterity'. Both rulers dictated their memoirs; commissioned over one thousand busts, portraits, medals and other images of themselves; compared themselves with the emperors of Classical Antiquity and the Middle Ages; asked to be buried under the altar of a church; made (or allowed others to make) explicit textual and visual comparisons with Biblical figures, including Christ; and regarded themselves 'not just as the leader of the Christian faith, but rather as a sanctified, even saintly, individual, eminently qualified to consider taking [religious] vows'.[18]

EDUCATION

Maximilian devoted almost half of *Der Weisskunig* to princely education. Some chapters stressed that a wise ruler should be prepared to learn from anybody, 'whether ordinary peasants and soldiers or nobles and generals'; other chapters explained why successful monarchs read all outgoing letters 'on great or small matters' before signing them, and learned how to give dictation to many secretaries at the same time in order to ensure efficient administration. Above all, *Der Weisskunig* insisted on the need to learn many languages, devoting a chapter each to how Maximilian had become proficient in 'Burgundian, which he learned from his wife', and in 'Flemish, which he learned from an elderly princess', as well as in English, Spanish, Italian and Latin besides his native German. This meant that 'since his soldiers spoke all of these seven languages, when the commanders of the various units came to him for consultation and orders, he was able to speak to each of them in their own language'.[19] Another five chapters explained how to excel in different types of jousts and tournaments, while six more described various methods of hunting, hawking and fishing. The emperor then paused to observe that:

> If someone who was not familiar with the subject read this, he might think that the young king [that is, Maximilian] did nothing else but hawk and hunt. That is not the case. The king did most of his hawking and hunting during great wars . . . Although he was the finest falconer, he was even better at making the mightiest kings, princes and lords do his will.[20]

Maximilian's distinctive pedagogic philosophy, which also suffused his letters, achieved considerable success. In 1506, and again seven years later, he expressed the wish 'that the Archduke Charles should soon learn Dutch'; and in 1515 Charles managed to take his oath as duke of Brabant in Dutch. He also eventually became fluent in both Spanish and Italian, and could carry on a limited conversation in German.[21] By contrast, Charles's command of Latin remained poor. At an audience in 1518 the English ambassador complained that Adrian of Utrecht, his former preceptor, constantly had to translate 'to the king in Frenche [what] I had spoken in Laten', while 'the said king catholyke answered forthwith his owne mowth in French'. Three years later another English ambassador complained that although Charles listened as letters in Latin were read out to him, because he knew 'not Latyn well' he 'commanded theyme [to be put] into Frenche, to the entente that he might better' understand them. 'La langue bourguignonne' would always remain his mother tongue: during his last years, secluded in a Spanish monastery, a member of his entourage reported that 'Here with His Majesty we speak only French.'[22]

Maximilian had more success in exposing his grandson to Humanism. Margaret extolled to her father 'the great and notable services rendered every day' by Luis Cabeza de Vaca, claiming that he had shown Charles 'how to behave, from which (given his age) he has profited greatly', as well as 'instructing him in letters' – a phrase that probably included the foundations of a Humanist education, rather than just 'reading and writing', since Cabeza de Vaca was a noted Humanist.[23] Two other members of Charles's entourage reinforced these efforts: Michel de Pavie, his first confessor and a former rector of Paris University (where he taught Erasmus, among others); and Adrian of Utrecht, from whom Charles would later declare that 'he had learned the little education and good manners that he knew'.[24]

Adrian was primarily a theologian. He first achieved fame in 1478 when, at the age of nineteen, he became top student of the year in the Faculty of Arts at Leuven University; and by 1491 he had attracted the attention of Margaret of York, dowager duchess of Burgundy, who paid for three days of celebration after he graduated as doctor of theology. By the time Adrian moved permanently to Mechelen to become the archduke's preceptor (and court preacher) in 1509, he was dean of the university faculty and 'the uncrowned king of the Leuven theologians of his day', an eminence reflected in his salary, for whereas Cabeza de Vaca received 12 shillings daily, Adrian received 24 shillings.[25]

No doubt Adrian imparted the problem-solving approach to knowledge practised at Leuven, where he lectured on philosophy as well as on theology; and he certainly made sure that his pupil's poor Latin did not deprive him entirely of Classical culture, providing French translations of the philosophical works of Aristotle and Seneca, the histories of Livy and Tacitus, and the military compendium of Vegetius. He also sponsored (and brought to his pupil's attention) the work of contemporary Humanists, including Juan Luis Vives from Spain (who made the Netherlands his base from 1512), Erasmus from Holland (who exchanged letters of considerable warmth with Charles as well as with many of his advisers), and Thomas More from England (who wrote the first part of his *Utopia* in Antwerp and published it with Leuven University Press in 1516).[26]

None of Charles's schoolbooks survive, but evidence of Adrian's pedagogy appears in the letters he sent to his former pupil while regent of Spain between 1520 and 1522. Sometimes he wrote those irritating 'I told you so' letters that many former teachers find irresistible. 'When we were in Santiago [in 1520] I told Your Highness that you had lost the love of all these subjects, but you did not believe me; but now I see it has come true,' he chided Charles in January 1521, after the outbreak of the Comunero rebellion. The following year he wrote: 'I'm glad that what you heard and learnt from me in school has not faded from your memory', adding pointedly that 'if others had absorbed the truth about this as diligently, I believe we would not have found ourselves in the troubles and dangers we face today'. Sometimes Adrian referred to texts that he and Charles had studied together ('Aristotle says in his *Politics* that people with lands adjacent to those of enemies with whom we have to fight must not be allowed to sit on the council of war . . .').[27] At other times, he delivered reproaches ('on this point [Your Majesty] always orders me to respond in a way that will prove ineffective'), and treated the emperor as if he were still at school ('For the sake of Your Highness's honour and conscience, you should keep the promises you made to the Cortes'; 'I beg Your Majesty to order that justice be done . . . *because that is why Your Highness is king*'). Charles must 'do your duty to God so that He will not abandon or ignore you in bad times'; and not be 'managed by others, as if Your Highness were a child and lacked reason, prudence and care. *Your Majesty must pay close attention to everything I have written*.' 'Believe me, Your Majesty, *if you are not more diligent* in understanding these matters, instead of letting others take care of things, Spain will never truly love you or obey your royal authority and person as it should.' This 'tough love' approach continued even after his former pupil acquired the upper hand:

> I beg Your Majesty not to let all this prosperity make you conceited or proud, but that you rather thank our sovereign God, from whom you have received such benefits, and that Your Majesty humbly recognize your obligation to give thanks for this, and do not display ingratitude so that God does not reject you *as he rejected Saul when he failed to obey His holy commandments*.[28]

Some contemporaries accused Adrian of indulging his pupil, but these powerful reprimands suggest otherwise.

CREATING AN ALTERNATIVE UNIVERSE

Nevertheless Charles's education included serious gaps. An early biographer, Willem Snouckaert van Schouwenburg, asserted that Adrian made his pupil 'read every day, as an adolescent, about the battles and victories of Caesar, Augustus, Charlemagne, Jason, Gideon, of ancient heroes, and of Dukes Philip and Charles of Burgundy'; and the books that Charles plucked from his palace library in Brussels to take with him to Spain in 1517 reflected this narrow focus. He selected only ten works, all written in French and most of them illuminated manuscript chronicles and books of chivalry, including 'The abridged chronicles of Jerusalem and of those who conquered the Holy Land with Godfrey of Bouillon', a magnificently illustrated account of the deeds of Netherlanders four centuries before, which no doubt served as a constant reminder of his Burgundian crusading heritage.[29] Such manuscripts were central to the culture in which Charles came of age. His father had taken some of the same works to Spain in 1501 and 1506; and among the almost 400 books owned by his aunt Margaret, only twelve were printed – the rest were manuscripts, many of them lavishly illuminated, more appropriate for a Cabinet of Curiosities than a modern library. Most works related to a specific time and place: the court of Burgundy in the fifteenth century, described by the eminent Dutch scholar Johan Huizinga as a 'dream world', dominated by 'a desire to return to the perfection of an imaginary past', recreated 'through conduct, customs, manners, costume and deportment, the illusion of heroic beings, full of dignity and honour, of wisdom, and, above all, of courtesy':

> Imitation of an ideal past made this possible: the dream of past perfection ennobled life in all its forms . . . The actions of princes, even daily and common actions, all assumed a quasi-symbolic form and tended to be elevated to the rank of mysteries. Births, marriages, deaths were set in a carapace of solemn and sublime formalities. The emotions that accompanied them were dramatized and amplified.[30]

In the words of Georges Chastellain, chronicler to Charles's great-grandfather Charles the Bold, a prince's household 'is the first thing that catches the eye: it is therefore vital to establish and run it well'; and he described in numbing details the complex rituals that accompanied every court ceremony, at which 'as prince and ruler of all, [Duke Charles] was always dressed more richly and magnificently than everyone else'. Olivier de la Marche, Chastellain's successor, provided even more numbing details in his 'Description of the Household of Duke Charles of Burgundy'. All his successors needed to do was follow this example.[31] La Marche, who served as preceptor to Archduke Philip, also promoted these values in his most famous work *Le chevalier délibéré* (*The resolute knight*), a melancholy verse epic delivered in the first person by a knight 'in the autumn of his life' as he prepared to fight his final tournament against Death, a female figure who had already killed Duke Philip the Good of Burgundy, his son Charles the Bold and his granddaughter Mary. The knight was determined to avenge these deaths before he retired to a monastery to die, but first he sought out those who could provide advice, both spiritual (the need for devotion and piety before the final combat) and practical (never act in anger; forget nothing).[32]

The resolute knight impressed Charles V immensely. He recycled much of the advice received by the knight in the holograph instructions he prepared for his son and heir Philip in 1543; seven years later he began to translate the entire work from French into Spanish 'with due regard not only for the language but also for the poetry and the exact meaning of the words'; and when in 1556 he retired to Spain, he took with him two manuscript copies (one in French and one of his Spanish translation, with nineteen illustrations) (Pl. 6).[33] It is thus no surprise to find in Charles's life so many reflections of the world of *The resolute knight*: his eagerness in 1528 and 1536 to resolve complex political disputes through duels; his statement to an ambassador in 1538 'that death is vncertaine, aswell the place as the time, and that God reserueth that to him selff alone. And so shall he remitt that to Him, knowing well that the suretie of his sonn, yea, and his lief also, must stand in His prouision'; his confessor's recollection in 1552 of 'something that I heard Your Majesty say: that the day a man loses his honour he should die, because he is now useless.'[34] His Burgundian heritage also explains Charles's veneration of the Order of the Golden Fleece (founded by Duke Philip the Good); his aspiration to recapture Constantinople (attempted by Philip's heir, Duke John); his desire to acquire glory and renown 'before it is too late'; and his periodic displays of fatalism. As Federico Chabod observed: 'The most profound motives of Charles's inner life, both mind and soul, arose from the culture of Burgundy.'[35]

HUNTIN', SHOOTIN' AND FISHIN'

Charles's limited scholarly prowess arose in part because he was a high-school dropout – his formal education ended when he was fifteen, and Adrian left for Spain as his special envoy – but long before then his preference for outdoor activities had become apparent. Juan de Zúñiga, a veteran courtier to whom Charles entrusted the education of his son, the future Philip II, once complained to him that his eight-year-old charge 'learns very well once he is out of school', adding mischievously, 'so that he somewhat resembles his father at the same age!'[36] A German chronicler supported his assertion that Charles had always 'loved arms more than books' by citing an exchange between Charles and the celebrated artist Lucas Cranach in 1547:

'In my apartment in Mechelen there is a portrait of me that you painted when I was a boy,' the emperor told the painter, 'and I would like you to tell me my age at that time.' Cranach answered: 'Your Majesty was then eight years old and Emperor Maximilian led you by the hand.' He continued: 'When I wanted to paint your portrait you had a preceptor who knew that, like other boys, you had a somewhat restless disposition, but loved to look at anything made of iron or steel. He therefore found a particularly fine iron crossbow bolt and placed it against the wall and turned the tip towards you. After that, you never took your eyes off it until I had finished my picture.'[37]

Important members of the prince's circle believed that too much book-learning was counter-productive. According to the Protestant historian Gregorio Leti, writing almost two centuries later, on one occasion when Adrian urged his illustrious pupil to spend more time trying to master Latin, the prince snapped back: 'Do you think that my grandfather wants to turn me into a schoolmaster?' Although Leti (as usual) cited no source, in *Der Weisskunig* Maximilian made exactly the same point, rejoicing that his own preceptor 'perceived that it would be neither good nor useful to burden him further with this instruction. If one wants to teach someone more than is necessary,' the emperor opined, 'it hinders other tasks.'[38] According to the historian Gonzalo Illescas, writing shortly after Charles's death, 'Emperor Maximilian often said that although it was very bad if a prince did not know his letters, it would be much worse if he lacked the ability to keep his kingdoms in peace and govern them with clemency, showing neither pride nor cruelty.' Indeed, Illescas suggested, the emperor chose Adrian as his grandson's preceptor precisely because 'he would not spend as much time teaching him letters as in instructing him in praiseworthy and honourable customs.'[39]

In *Theuerdank* and *Der Weisskunig*, as well as in his correspondence, Maximilian extolled the virtues of physical activities, especially hunting. In February 1510, in a characteristically flamboyant phrase, the emperor crowed to Margaret 'that we are delighted that our grandson Charles takes so much pleasure in hunting, because otherwise one might think he was a bastard'; and he suggested that 'after Easter, when the weather is mild', she should take him to the royal parks and 'make him ride, for the sake of his health and strength'. He reinforced this message whenever he visited, teaching his grandson both to shoot game with guns and crossbows and to snare them with nets.[40]

Charles de la Poupée, lord of La Chaux, another passionate proponent of the chivalric ideals of the Burgundian court, instructed young Charles on how to excel in both horsemanship and marksmanship – and the success of these lessons became manifest when he went to Spain and everyone admired 'his amazing dexterity with weapons, and his elegance in the saddle'. He was also able to hit targets more often than anyone else, becoming 'king of the musketeers' of Mechelen, and 'king of the crossbowmen' of Brussels. In 1512, Margaret summoned the English ambassadors at her court to 'see the prince shote at the buttes' with the longbow, England's national weapon, and they deemed that he 'handled his bowe right well'. Unfortunately, two years later when Charles 'went to the castle of Tervuren to practise with his crossbow on Whit Monday, he fired a bolt that fatally wounded a local artisan'. In her nephew's defence, Margaret protested that the victim was 'drunk and in bad shape', and reflected that 'there is no known way to avoid such misfortunes'; but there was clearly more to the homicide. Because 'many people may tell you things that are not true', she sent Chièvres, 'who was present, to give you a full account, so that you will know the truth'. He had, after all, just killed a man for the first time.[41]

By then, Charles played a prominent part in the annual cycle of court functions. Each New Year's Day he took £100 from his treasury 'to distribute and donate according to his noble pleasure'; he presided at the festivities on Mardi Gras and at Easter, pardoning some criminals on Good Friday; he lit a huge bonfire after sundown on St John's Day; he watched the jousts at All Souls; and he dined with the Knights of the Golden Fleece on St Andrew's Day.[42] Entries in his household accounts for 1512 indicate numerous other activities. A troupe of actors 'who in Lent staged several plays [*jeux de farches*] before my lord' received £13; 'some huntsmen and others who on several occasions furled and unfurled blinds made of cloth when my lord went hunting near Brussels' got £18 just for wine to sustain them as they worked; and 'a Dominican Friar who preached throughout Lent before my lord and his sisters in Mechelen' received £28 'in alms and charity'.[43] Charles and his sisters also played cards for money (especially when Maximilian was present to increase the stakes) and they enjoyed the company of jesters and Fools. In 1509 his treasurer purchased 'yellow, red and white cloth to make a fine costume for the little Fool, to make him look more respectable when in my lord's company', and Henry VIII thought it worthwhile to make a large payment to 'Master John, the prince of Castile's Fool'.[44]

Despite his lack of enthusiasm for reading and writing, young Charles enjoyed several other sedentary activities. In 1515, 'Jehannin the painter' received £100 'for teaching my lord the archduke how to paint', and Henry Bredeniers, 'organist of the archduke's chapel', received £200 a year in return for 'playing the flute, lute, clavichord, organ and other instruments for the leisure and entertainment' of the prince and his sisters 'each and every time they desired'. Three years earlier, Bredeniers had received payment (he claimed gracelessly) for teaching them *with great difficulty and effort* the principles of music and how to play several different melodious instruments'.[45] A surviving songbook created for Margaret gives an idea of the vocal music that Charles would have heard at Mechelen. Among other melancholy tunes, the song-book included two compositions by Josquin des Prés, the most famous musi-cian of his day: 'Plus nulz regrets', composed in honour of Charles's betrothal to Mary Tudor in 1507–8, and the better-known 'Mille regretz', later known as 'The emperor's song' because Charles liked it so much.[46]

The prince also loved to dance. In 1512 he danced with 'his susters and the yong folke' of his court for several hours during the celebration of St John's Day; and when his sister Isabeau got married two years later (aged thirteen), Margaret reported that once again Charles 'took part in all the dances to perfection, and perhaps a little more than his constitution could stand, because the next day he went down with a fever'. Four days later, Margaret reported with alarm, he 'cannot yet shake off the fever'; and only after another week was he 'free of his fever and doing well, so that his only concern now is to have fun'.[47]

Increasingly, the prince had fun outside Mechelen. Perhaps the trigger for this change was a strange protest in Brussels early in 1511, when an exceptional fall of snow and prolonged frost prompted the construction of numerous ice sculptures throughout the city. One of them, right outside the empty ducal palace, depicted the Virgin Mary holding a unicorn in her lap, which everyone understood as a plea that Brussels, not Mechelen, should henceforth protect Charles. Whatever the reason, he spent increasing amounts of time in the Coudenberg palace, whose spacious rooms, foun-tains, labyrinth and zoo left the German artist Albrecht Dürer (writing in 1520) breathless: 'Anything more beautiful and pleasing to me and more like a paradise, I have never seen.'[48]

THE THRESHOLD OF POWER

Charles also went hunting in two parks near his new capital: Tervuren and Heverlee. These two locations represented part of competing agendas, since Margaret of Austria provided access to the former, a royal park (then as now), whereas Chièvres owned the latter. The sharpest difference between the two agendas concerned foreign policy. Margaret favoured an alliance with England, the most important trading partner of the Netherlands, and war against Guelders, whose duke constantly challenged Burgundian power. Chièvres, by contrast, wanted an alliance with France and peace with Guelders. For most of Charles's minority, Margaret prevailed. Henry VIII, Charles's uncle by virtue of his marriage to Joanna's sister Katherine of Aragon, sent troops to assist Margaret against Guelders in 1511; the following year he sent a larger force to Spain to assist his father-in-law, Ferdinand of Aragon, against the French; and in 1513, Henry crossed the Channel in person at the head of a powerful army and joined forces with Maximilian to rout the French at Guinegate. The vanquished lost so many knights that the encounter came to be known (at least among the English) as 'the battle of the Spurs', and the French towns of Thérouanne and Tournai surrendered to Henry. Soon afterwards, Margaret took Charles on a visit to congratulate the victors. After attending Mass together, Henry led his nephew to Tournai, his new conquest, where together with Maximilian they watched the 'jousts royal' staged by the English to celebrate their victory. When Charles composed his autobiography four decades later, this, his first State Visit, was the earliest event he described.[49]

Henry professed himself 'much delighted with the conversation' of his nephew, and he persuaded Margaret and Maximilian that the marriage of the princess of Castile (as Mary Tudor had been known ever since the exchange of vows five years before) should take place within the next six months. The trio also agreed on a new regime for Charles's household that deprived Chièvres of his place as 'principal chamberlain': in future, the position would rotate between noblemen nominated by Maximilian, Henry and Ferdinand of Aragon. The emperor's nominee, Count Palatine Frederick, took precedence by virtue of his 'consanguinity' and his services to Charles's father (whom he had accompanied to Spain): he now became 'senior in all councils after Madame of Savoy [Margaret], and in her absence he would take her place in the said councils, for financial as well as for all other matters'.[50]

These changes seemed to mark the triumph of Margaret's agenda for Charles, but Thomas Spinelly, Henry's wily ambassador at her court, remained unconvinced. The archduchess, he noted, had only prevailed 'by cause of the minorite of my lord prynce' and he predicted that as soon as it ended (on Charles's fifteenth birthday, 24 February 1515) Chièvres and his Francophile allies would 'compelle' the prince to abandon both the English alliance and his marriage with Mary Tudor. His prophecy came true even earlier, thanks to a sequence of totally unexpected (and unrelated) events.[51]

In January 1514, Louis XII's wife Duchess Anne of Brittany died, leaving him a widower in his fiftieth year with only two daughters, neither of whom could succeed him on the throne because France's Salic Law allowed only male succession. Charles's relatives reacted to this development in totally – fatally – different ways. Ferdinand of Aragon proposed that Louis should marry Charles's sister Eleanor, now sixteen and thus capable of producing a son who would become king of France; Margaret declared herself willing to marry the French king herself; while Maximilian insisted that Charles must delay his marriage to Mary Tudor because (according to the English ambassador in the Netherlands) 'he was cownseld by phisicians that in case they folowyd *cum copula*, than of all likelihood yt shuld be the distruction of the lord prince, or [else] he shuld by that means lose *spem proles* [the ability to sire children]'.[52]

Margaret warned her father repeatedly that procrastination would alienate Henry VIII, who had become personally involved in arrangements for the wedding (deciding what the bride would wear, who would accompany her, and where they would lodge) as well as spending heavily on the festivities to follow (including the 'tents, houses and pavilions' from which the royal party would admire the 'jousts royal to be holden' after the wedding). On 6 July 1514, Margaret anxiously – and presciently – told her father that unless he immediately informed Henry that he approved the English match, 'I fear he will abandon you and our dynasty and make a deal with the French'.[53] It was too late: Louis had already exploited his rivals' disorganization and proposed to Henry a treaty of mutual defence, to be sealed by his own immediate marriage to Mary Tudor. On 30 July the princess of Castile, now eighteen, solemnly repudiated Charles; one week later Louis signed a promise to pay Henry one million crowns in return for his sister's hand; and on 13 August, while Mary lay naked in bed, Louis's proxy placed one leg 'naked from the middle of the thigh downward' against hers, thus officially consummating the marriage.[54]

How did Charles react to these dramatic events? As late as 20 May 1514 (scarcely two months before Mary repudiated him), when a courtier asserted that Charles was 'in love with a damoyselle of the court', the archduke 'answered that on hys faythe yt was not so, nor never wolld be of her or any other, onlye my ladye Marye [Tudor] reserved'.[55] Perhaps his younger sisters' tortuous path to matrimony contributed to this complacency. Maximilian had first arranged a wedding for Isabeau in 1510 when she was scarcely nine, but stipulated that she could only join her prospective husband, the duke of Guelders, when 'she reaches the age of sixteen, and then she can consummate the marriage'. After these negotiations fell through, in April 1514 the emperor signed a contract pledging Isabeau, now almost thirteen, to marry the king of Denmark – but refused to allow her to join him for another year.[56] That same month Charles's sister Marie, aged ten, left the Netherlands for the court of Maximilian, there to remain until he decided when she was physically capable of intercourse with her betrothed, King Louis of Bohemia and Hungary.

Maximilian was not alone in worrying that sex might kill or weaken his grandchildren: many of his contemporaries believed that excessive sexual activity had killed the heir of the Catholic Monarchs, Prince John, soon after his marriage – a falsehood that Charles himself would later use to regulate the sex life of his own teenage son after he got married (see chapter 14). Likewise, on hearing that Louis XII had married the eighteen-year-old Mary Tudor and, in a desperate effort to impregnate her, 'boasted of having ejaculated five times in their first encounter', a contemporary predicted that 'one must assume that he has just dug five graves with his hoe. If he manages to smell the flowers next spring, be assured that he will live to see fifty autumns' (and three months after her marriage, Mary Tudor was indeed a widow).[57]

Charles seems to have taken the collapse of the English match in his stride. A few months later he declared publicly that his new bride would be Louis XII's daughter Renée, who although only four years old was heiress to the duchy of Brittany. According to a courtier:

> One day his intimates [*mignons*] were joking with him and told him he was a cuckold [*coqu*] because he had lost his wife, and now needed a new one. They suggested to him either Madame Renée, or the daughter of the king of Portugal, or the daughter of the king of Hungary. I told these young gentlemen that he would prefer Madame Renée, and [Charles] replied at once: 'He is right, because the daughter of the king of France is the best prize – and if she should die first, I would be duke of Brittany.'

On 19 January 1515, Charles signed instructions authorizing a special embassy to discuss with the French king terms for his marriage.[58]

These documents reveal two things: that Charles had learned to subordinate his personal desires to political advantage, viewing his future wife primarily as a 'prize'; and that his minority had ended – indeed, signing the instructions was practically his first official act after his emancipation.

Although the minority of Archduke Philip had come to an end when he reached the age of fifteen, Margaret feared an earlier termination in the case of Charles. In November 1512 she begged her father to return to the Netherlands and assist her to face 'the extreme dangers' she perceived all around her, 'because I no longer know how to deal with them. The States are so hostile, and the common people so full of wicked words, that I greatly fear some evil will befall unless we find a remedy'. She begged Maximilian to 'take pity on me, because I no longer know which way to turn'. Many people, she continued, 'say that I am squandering everything just to please you', adding the colourful metaphor that she was 'so filled with regret about the situation' that 'I often wish I were back in my mother's womb'. Six months later, she repeated her appeal, reporting to Maximilian that posters had appeared on church doors 'deriding and condemning me', while some 'evil spirits' claimed that 'all I want to do is fight wars and ruin them', uttering 'other wicked words that might stir up the people'.[59]

She also found her nephew less malleable. By 1512 his court numbered more than 330 people (eighty guards, seventy-five nobles and knights, thirty-two members of his chapel, twenty-five 'valets, pages and young gentlemen-in-waiting' and so on), who between them drew salaries that totalled £180 a day (compared with only £37 a day a decade before). In September 1513 rumours that Charles 'was so masterful and headstrong that he can neither be controlled nor led' provoked a vigorous refutation from his chamberlain, the lord of Beersel. He began a long letter to Margaret, reasonably enough – 'If my lord, your nephew, were thus disposed I would know about it' – but then he counter-attacked:

> At all times and in all matters his lordship is entirely inclined, ready and prepared to comply with and carry out whatever he understands the emperor and you, Madam, might want and desire. As to other aspects of his actions, thus far I do not think I have seen or heard him do anything except comply and graciously acquiesce in all sound proposals and requests made to him. Indeed, Madam, all things considered, I do not think one could reasonably ask any more of him.[60]

Beersel was a controversial figure. A decade before, on his appointment as Charles's chamberlain, the Spanish ambassador in Brussels described him as 'a man who has the worst habits I have ever seen'; and perhaps now he protested too much, because a few months later Margaret and her nephew engaged in an unseemly public shouting match.[61] In January 1514, on the express orders of Maximilian, the regent arrested and imprisoned Don Juan Manuel, a Spanish supporter of Charles's father who had fled to the Netherlands because he feared the enmity of King Ferdinand; but Don Juan was a Knight of the Golden Fleece, and according to the statutes of the Order a knight could only be judged by his peers. Don Juan's relatives lodged a formal demand for due process with Charles, who would become Sovereign of the Order at his majority, and he led a deputation of seven knights into Margaret's presence to demand that she release the prisoner. Margaret angrily replied that since Maximilian (himself a knight) had ordered the arrest, she could not release Don Juan without his permission. Then, 'after expressing her annoyance that this assembly [of knights] had been convened without her permission', she rounded on Charles and 'told him that he should not be so ready to accept views opposed to the orders of the emperor, and to those who acted in his name' (meaning herself). Her scornful reply brought the meeting to an end, but four days later her nephew was back 'at the head of the knights' to protest once again that, according to their statutes, knights could only be judged by their peers. This provoked another blistering tirade. Margaret reminded Charles that he was still too young to be Sovereign of the Order, and then she told the knights that 'if she were a man instead of a woman, she would make them sing for their statutes'. Maximilian eventually defused the situation by transferring Don Juan Manuel to his court under guard, but Margaret's authority had been seriously compromised.[62]

Charles made no mention of all this in the *Memoirs* that he composed many years later, but he did state that during his time with Maximilian and Henry in October 1513 'the emancipation of the archduke [Charles] was discussed and agreed'. No written trace of this agreement has been found, but since the three principals spent almost a week together they no doubt took such a sensitive decision orally. Whatever the trio decided, six months later Margaret reported to her father that the States-General had refused to vote the taxes she requested, 'on the grounds that the minority of my lord [Charles] will soon end'. The following month she added that 'some people say that my lord's minority will end once he is married. If that is the case, you should advise me to arrange everything, so that you do not find that this causes matters to turn out otherwise than you expect'. She also warned her father that many members of the Netherlands elite 'are grumbling about us, and planting ideas in my lord's mind that are not good either for you or for me'. Worse, they were using the 'complaints and arguments' as a smoke-screen 'to end my lord's minority before you know it ... If you want to prevent it', her father must return to the Netherlands immediately, 'otherwise you will never get here in time'.[63]

In the event, Maximilian himself triggered the emancipation by demanding that his grandson should 'leave the Netherlands to come and join us' in Innsbruck, 'so that we can arrange for him to receive the oath of allegiance in all the lands and dominions of our House of Austria, to better assure his succession, and that of his brother, after my death' (evidence that he still dreamed of creating a unified 'Austrasia': see chapter 1). He therefore instructed his daughter to convene the States-General in December 1514 and ask them for the funds required for Charles's journey.[64] Instead, the States of Brabant demanded as a precondition of any further grant that Maximilian should emancipate his grandson 'and end his minority, so that the government of all the lands and dominions of the House of Burgundy should be placed in his hands', to which Charles (who was present) replied graciously: 'Gentlemen, I thank you for the honour and strong affection that you show towards me. Be good and loyal subjects, and I will be a good ruler.' Meanwhile, Chièvres and his allies promised to pay Maximilian 100,000 gold florins for his agreement. The emperor, always short of cash, immediately signed letters patent ordering a special session of the States-General to convene and authorize his grandson's emancipation.[65]

On 5 January 1515, in the presence of the elite of the Burgundian Netherlands assembled in the Great Hall of the ducal palace in Brussels, Count Palatine Frederick read out in Maximilian's name a formal declaration that Charles had come of age, and then 'they brought out the charters' on which Margaret's authority rested and 'in the presence of everyone tore them up. At the same time with sharp hammers they broke their seals into pieces' – a particularly brutal way of marking the transition of power. After that, everyone 'raised their hands, according to the custom of those lands, and swore to accept Charles as their lord'.[66]

THREE

THE DIFFICULT INHERITANCE, 1515–17

EMANCIPATION

On 8 January 1515, three days after 'it pleased the emperor, my lord and grandfather, to emancipate me and free me from his ward and guardianship, placing in our hands the governance of our lands and lordships in the Netherlands', Charles instructed all officials that 'our affairs shall in future be transacted in our name', and he helpfully appended a list of 'the titles that we intend to use from now on':

> By the grace of God prince of Spain, of Sicily and Naples, of Jerusalem, etc; archduke of Austria; duke of Burgundy, Lorraine, Brabant, Styria, Carinthia, Carniola, Limburg, Luxemburg and Gelderland; count of Flanders, Habsburg, Tyrol, Artois, Burgundy and Hainaut; landgrave of Alsace; prince of Swabia; marquis of Burgau, Holland, Zealand, Ferrette, Kyburg, Namur and Zutphen; lord of Friesland, Sclavonia, Portenau, Salins and Mechelen.[1]

Some of these titles were premature – notably Alsace and the Austrian lands, still ruled by Maximilian; Franche-Comté, the personal fief of his aunt Margaret; and Friesland, administered by Duke George of Saxony – but in May 1515, George sold Friesland to Charles. It was the first expansion of his inheritance.

According to a chronicler, after his emancipation 'my lord set off to take possession of his dominions, travelling from one town to the next' as he swore to respect local privileges and received oaths of allegiance (Map 2). His new subjects did their best to make him feel welcome. When Charles made his ceremonial entry into Bruges as count of Flanders, the first pageant that he encountered showed three angels presenting their new prince with a crown, a coat of arms and the keys of the city, just as the Three Wise Men

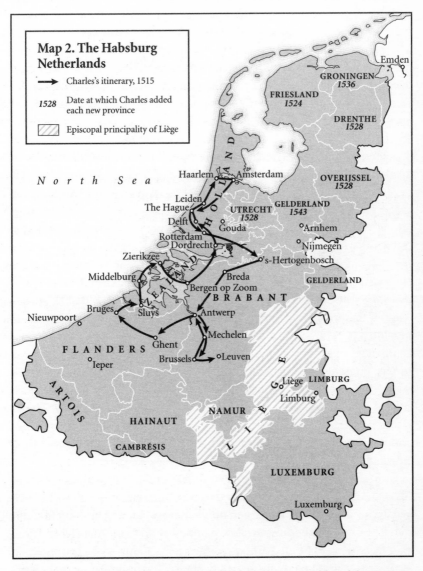

Map 2. The Habsburg Netherlands

→ Charles's itinerary, 1515

1528 Date at which Charles added each new province

▨ Episcopal principality of Liège

North Sea

Emden

GRONINGEN *1536*

FRIESLAND *1524*

DRENTHE *1528*

Haarlem — Amsterdam

OVERIJSSEL *1528*

Leiden
The Hague
Delft
Gouda

HOLLAND

UTRECHT *1528*

GELDERLAND *1543*

Arnhem

Rotterdam
Dordrecht

Nijmegen

Zierikzee

's-Hertogenbosch

Middelburg

ZEELAND

Breda
Bergen op Zoom

GELDERLAND

Bruges
Nieuwpoort

Sluys

BRABANT

Antwerp

Mechelen

FLANDERS
Ieper

Ghent

Brussels — Leuven

LIÈGE

Liège LIMBURG

Limburg

ARTOIS

NAMUR

HAINAUT

CAMBRÉSIS

LUXEMBURG

Luxemburg

After his emancipation in January 1515, Charles set off on a five-month tour of the Habsburg provinces in the western Netherlands, making a ceremonial entry into the principal cities to be acclaimed as ruler. He would later visit all the other hereditary provinces, and also Utrecht (acquired 1528) and Gelderland (conquered 1543); but he never managed to visit Friesland (acquired 1524), Drenthe and Overijssel (acquired 1528) or Groningen (acquired 1536).

had brought gifts to the Christ Child. Subsequent tableaux equated Bruges with Jerusalem, displayed the prince's descent from King David, and alluded to the various lands in Spain, Italy and Germany that he would soon inherit. It was heady stuff for someone scarcely fifteen, and Charles asked to see the whole show again the next day. He also commissioned a lavish manuscript record with thirty-two full-page coloured illustrations (Pl. 7), while the magistrates of Bruges prepared for publication a shorter illustrated version with woodcuts, printed in Paris, and a rhyming text in Dutch. This constituted the first systematic use of the media to glorify Charles.[2]

The new ruler and his principal advisers now took several important decisions. In January 1515, 'because we cannot by ourselves give sufficient thanks to God, our creator, for the grace, honour, health and success that He has granted us thus far, nor amass sufficient merit to secure the continuation of His grace in the future', Charles ordered processions and public prayers throughout the Netherlands to beseech God to continue 'to raise us in virtue and good customs, to govern our dominions and subjects in peace, union and concord, and to guide our affairs to His honour, our well-being, and the prosperity, utility and tranquillity of our said dominions and subjects'. He also started to issue legislation in both French and Dutch that began 'By order of the prince' and ended 'because such is our pleasure'. One of them appointed Jean Le Sauvage, a prominent lawyer and minister, as 'our *Grand Chancellor*', a new office, and charged him to 'administer justice to all', and 'to keep our seals and use them to seal and send all sorts of letters and provisions'.[3] Because the document did not limit Le Sauvage's jurisdiction, it implied that his authority would extend to all dominions ruled by Charles – which is exactly what happened: the Grand Chancellor accompanied Charles everywhere, and intervened in the affairs of each new territory from the moment of its acquisition.

In March 1515, Charles signed an order revoking all pensions granted before his emancipation 'in view of the great and weighty affairs with which we have to deal, which increase in number every day and crop up in many and various ways, and in view also of our great and excessive debts'. Seven months later he published a new regimen for his household, modelled on the instrument issued by his father in similar circumstances twenty years before (an event that many of his ministers could remember, since they had also served Philip):

Ever since our emancipation and entry into the lordship and governance of our Netherlands provinces, we have constantly tried and strongly desired and wanted to create good order and sound policies in all our affairs, and end the disorder that has existed in the past, because of the wars and divisions that prevailed as well as for other reasons, and even in the organization of our own Household, on which the well-being, honour and tranquillity of ourselves and of our ministers, dominions and subjects largely depends.

The document detailed the duties of almost 700 officials and guards. The prince also began to attend meetings of the Privy Council where (as Margaret noted with disapproval) he made each minister give his opinion and then 'required them to submit it in writing, signed' – the beginning of the *consultas* that would become central to his style of decision-making.[4]

Who determined these policy initiatives? Certainly not Margaret. Scarcely three weeks after her nephew's emancipation she informed Maximilian that she no longer gave orders, but instead obeyed those issued by 'my lord and his council'. Therefore, she huffed, 'I do not involve myself in any affairs of state now' and so if the emperor wanted something, 'it will be necessary for you to write to the lord of Chièvres and the chancellor'. Margaret particularly resented the secrecy that had preceded her demotion. She told an English envoy, 'almost wepying', how Maximilian 'without her knowledge, with the lord Chevers [Chièvres], hath handled the puttyng oute of tutela of the prynce, to a gret preiudice to her honor and reputacion'.[5] Worse soon followed. In March 1515, Margaret informed her father that Charles had just 'told me that he had heard that Louis Maroton [her confidential envoy] has become involved at your court in all sorts of plots and dealings that cause him harm, regret and displeasure, and he therefore requires me to recall him'. Finally, in August, she confronted Charles in person because, 'having patiently put up with the situation for a long while, I am well aware that people have tried by various means and methods to make you distrust me'. She asked that criticisms of her 'be voiced in your presence, and I will reply, for I prefer that people speak to my face than behind my back'. Then, after offering a detailed justification of her policies, foreign and domestic, and noting that she had often used her own resources to fund them, she concluded defiantly:

You can rest assured, my lord, that whenever it pleases you to make use of me, and to treat me and respect me as reason demands, I will serve you well and loyally, and risk my life and my goods (as I have done thus far); but if you are pleased to believe without verification what people tell you about me, and allow me to be treated as I now perceive, I would rather take care of my humble affairs and leave – something I have already asked the emperor to approve . . . So, my lord, I ask you to state your intentions about all this.

According to a note on the dorse of this document, Charles and his council responded lamely that 'Madame had done her duty well, with other fair words and promises'. Margaret thereupon commissioned an inventory of all her possessions, apparently as a prelude to leaving the Netherlands.[6]

Charles's emancipation also undermined Maximilian's authority. The emperor still expected his grandson to join him and tour his Austrian lands, where he would take the oath as heir apparent (chapter 2); but after that, he confided to Margaret, 'when I have him in my hands, it will be easy to make everything right'. Specifically, 'once he has left the Netherlands, you will govern them just as you used to do'. When Charles procrastinated, the emperor announced that 'he would travel soon to Worms and have the prince join him there . . . and should the prince not wish to come', he would 'go to the Netherlands myself and make trouble'.[7] As usual, Maximilian's other policy initiatives, combined with his perennial lack of money, thwarted these plans. Although the emperor optimistically empowered his personal bankers to receive the money promised for consenting to the emancipation, Charles did not authorize payment until May 1515 and did not start paying his grandfather's pension for another eighteen months.[8] Instead of travelling west, the emperor therefore stayed in Vienna, where he met with neighbouring rulers and concluded the double wedding of his grandchildren Marie and Ferdinand with the king of Hungary and Bohemia and his sister, thus laying the foundations of a new superstate on the middle Danube that would endure for four centuries.

Maximilian next attempted to regain his authority in the Netherlands by restoring Margaret's influence over his grandson. He informed her that he had written to Charles 'desiring him to keep you close to him and to treat you as a good nephew is obliged to treat such a virtuous and good aunt', and he ordered her 'to stay with our said grandson, and do not leave the Netherlands, because your presence there is essential *and will be of great benefit to me*'. The emperor also wrote to Charles that 'we have no doubt' that he would consult Margaret 'on all your greatest and most difficult affairs, and take and follow her advice' because it would always be better 'than that of anyone else'. He concluded that 'by nature and nurture she cares for our interests and honour, and also yours: indeed we consider the three of us to be one and the same, united by a single desire and affection'.[9]

Maximilian was wasting his time. Foreign ambassadors began to refer to Chièvres and Le Sauvage as Charles's 'governors' or as 'the regents', and for a while the Habsburgs virtually lost control over the affairs of the Netherlands. The ascendancy of the governors became immediately apparent in the deferential policy adopted towards France. The sudden death of Louis XII on 1 January 1515 created a delicate situation. As he had no male heir, he was succeeded by his cousin Francis, aged twenty, from the Angoulême branch of the House of Valois. At an audience two days after his accession Francis I informed Charles's representative that 'he would be a good relative, friend and lord [to the prince], because he is my vassal'; but, he added 'he did not wish to be led by him as the emperor and the king of Aragon [Ferdinand] had led the late king'. Stung by this gratuitous insult, the envoy shot back that although Charles would live peaceably with France 'as the king his father had done, I want you to know, sire, that you could never have a friend and vassal who could do you more harm'.[10] Charles's governors hastened to disavow this defiant stance and instructed the envoys sent to represent Charles at Francis's coronation to grovel. They must apologize that their master could not attend in person 'on account of our busy schedule and our recent accession as lord of our Netherlands provinces', and also convey his delight at the accession to the throne of France of 'such a valorous and virtuous prince, in the flower and full strength of his age'. Charles instructed his envoys to beg forgiveness 'in view of my young age' if 'anything had occurred during my minority that may have displeased' the new king, and then express the hope that the two rulers 'might do great things together for their own good, the public good, and the exaltation of our Holy Catholic Faith'. Finally, they must confirm Charles's eagerness to conclude a treaty of alliance to be sealed by his marriage to Princess Renée, then aged eight, who was not only the daughter of the late king but also the sister-in-law of Francis. When Maximilian wrote to urge the envoys to increase their demands regarding Renée's dowry, Charles and the governors quickly contradicted him:

> Although we want to please my lord and [grand]father, so that he will not have cause to complain and tell us that we have not followed his orders . . . you must do all you can to avoid giving the king [of France] and his people any cause or occasion to suspect or imagine that we have any wish to renege or risk breaking our alliance.[11]

The governors had good reasons for placating France. As an English diplomat observed, the emperor was now 'sikly, and the kynge of Arragon is of greet aage', and when they died Charles would inherit their lands and titles only if he could enforce his claims – and for that, it was imperative to guarantee the Netherlands against all risk of war. The treaty signed in Paris in March 1515 achieved this goal: Francis promised that he would not attack Charles's possessions, or assist any other aggressor (three weeks later he forbade the duke of Guelders 'to do any harm to the lands of the prince of Castile'). He also promised to support Charles's dynastic claims against all who challenged them. Concerning Renée, however, Francis stipulated that she would join her betrothed only in her twelfth year (which meant that Charles could sire no legitimate successor for at least four more years), and that she would renounce all claims to the strategic duchy of Brittany (which had first attracted Charles to her). Instead her dowry would consist of lands that would revert to France at her death. Moreover, if Charles reneged on his promise to marry her, he would have to forfeit all the territories he held as French fiefs. 'My lord,' Charles explained meekly to his grandfather Ferdinand of Aragon, 'I really wish that this treaty had been more to my honour and advantage than it is, but I accepted what I could get, recognizing that at present a good peace is worth more to me than a war, however just. I beg you, my lord, to remember my situation and take all this in good part'.[12]

Francis scored other notable successes during his first year on the French throne. In February 1515 he facilitated the clandestine marriage of Louis XII's widow Mary Tudor, the former 'princess of Castile' now aged nineteen, to the duke of Suffolk, whom Henry VIII had sent to escort her back to England. Thanks to Francis's complicity, Suffolk promptly boasted that he 'had lyen with' his new bride and that 'sche by wyet chylde' – which precluded her marriage to Charles (or anyone else).[13] Then, since the treaty of Paris obliged Charles not to attack him or to assist an attack by anyone else, Francis seized the opportunity to lead a large army across the Alps into Italy, and in alliance with the Venetian Republic he won a crushing victory on 13–14 September 1515 at Marignano over the forces assembled by the duke of Milan, assisted by his allies Emperor Maximilian, Ferdinand of Aragon and Pope Leo X.

French troops soon occupied both Milan and the adjacent republic of Genoa, and shortly afterwards Pope Leo surrendered to his former enemy the duchies of Parma and Piacenza (territories claimed by both the papacy and the dukes of Milan) and suggested, in his capacity as suzerain of the kingdom of Naples, that Francis might in due course succeed its present ruler, Ferdinand of Aragon. Almost immediately, the death of the Catholic King on 23 January 1516 offered an opportunity.

THE SPANISH SUCCESSION

Ferdinand of Aragon's demise was not unexpected. At age sixty-three he was the oldest monarch in Europe, and yet (as the English envoy John Stile observed) he had 'wylfully schorteyd the days of hys lyfe, always in fayre wether or fowle laboryng in hawkeyng or hwnteyng, foloyng more the cownsayl of hys fawkoners than of hys fesecyans [physicians]'. Stile went on to relate how unpopular Ferdinand had become in Castile, strikingly reflected in the fact that only one nobleman accompanied his corpse to Granada for burial, with 'no grete obsqwyys don for sayd Kyng, nor murneyng made, never less seyn for any prynce'. He concluded that although everyone in Spain 'wyth oon voyse' supported Charles, 'and no maner of person spekeyth to the contrary', still 'there ys lytyl love or stedfastnys' among the late king's subjects, and he predicted 'alterracyions and moveyngys' unless the new ruler arrived swiftly to claim his inheritance.[14]

Stile's analysis and prediction could hardly be bettered, because Ferdinand left a complicated inheritance. To begin with, 'Spain' did not exist. Although his marriage to Isabella had created a dynastic union between the crowns of Aragon and Castile, and their dependencies, it left intact the institutions, laws, currency and judicial structure of each component. The powers and policies of the crown differed in each area (Castile, Aragon, Catalonia and Valencia), and each state maintained its own tariff barriers and customs posts. They also retained different foreign-policy goals. Isabella and her advisers had shown great enthusiasm for attacks on Muslim north Africa, whereas Ferdinand, although also supportive of a crusade against Islam, favoured targets further afield (including the recovery of Constantinople and Jerusalem), and to this end he devoted far more attention to consolidating his hold over Italy.[15] He even spent the year 1506–7 in Naples.

Ferdinand's absence from Spain was not voluntary. His title of king consort of Castile had lapsed when Isabella died in 1504, and although under the terms of her will he became governor of the kingdom until Joanna and Philip returned to claim their inheritance, disagreements over policies and patronage multiplied. In 1505, Louis XII of France arranged for his niece Germaine de Foix to marry Ferdinand, and ceded to their offspring all of France's claims to Naples – offspring who would also inherit Sicily, Sardinia, Aragon and all of Ferdinand's other dominions. This development alarmed and infuriated Philip, who returned to Spain the following year with an escort of German soldiers as well as a large amount of cash to distribute as bribes. This combination of stick and carrot led most of

Ferdinand's supporters in Castile to defect to his rival, and when the two monarchs met on 27 June 1506 the new king appeared with a huge armed entourage whereas his father-in-law came virtually alone. Ferdinand thereupon signed an undertaking to leave Castile (in return for a guaranteed income) as well as an agreement with Philip that deprived Joanna of all her rights, claiming that to do otherwise 'would mean the total destruction and loss of these kingdoms on account of her illness and temperament which out of discretion are omitted here'.[16] Later that same day, however, the wily Ferdinand employed a technique that would haunt his grandson: he swore before notaries that he had signed both agreements with Philip under duress, because 'trusting his word and oaths, I went in good faith' to the meeting, only to find that 'his armed might put my royal person in notorious and manifest danger'. He claimed he had only agreed to deprive Joanna of her rights, and relinquished 'the administration of Castile, which is mine by right', because 'I was compelled by the said dangers and by fear'. He therefore did not consider these commitments binding.[17] Unaware of this development, one month later Philip met for over an hour alone with his father-in-law, during which Ferdinand claimed he had 'instructed and advised him in detail about what it seemed to me he needed to do for the sound government of these kingdoms, and to keep them in peace, and about other matters concerning our possessions and our friends . . . in all of which we remained in great harmony'.[18] Immediately afterwards he departed for Aragon, and on 4 September 1506, Ferdinand set sail for Naples. Three weeks later, Philip died.

Devastated by her husband's sudden death, and pregnant again, Joanna seemed unable to handle the everyday business of government and so Cardinal Francisco Jiménez de Cisneros, archbishop of Toledo and Primate of Spain, convened a meeting of the leading supporters of both Philip and Ferdinand and persuaded them to sign a formal commitment to refer any disagreements between them to an independent tribunal, instead of resorting to arms, until the Cortes of the kingdom could assemble and decide what to do next. Cisneros also created a council of regency, with which he governed the kingdom until Ferdinand returned in 1507.

Ferdinand remained in Castile for most of the rest of his life, taking numerous decisions that would have important consequences for Charles. Abroad, Ferdinand sent an expeditionary force to north Africa in 1509–10, which conquered several Muslim-held port cities, and another to Navarre in 1512, which wrested the southern part of the kingdom from its rulers. Although both successes proved popular in Spain, they would provoke the lasting ire of the Ottoman sultans and the French kings respectively. Charles would devote immense resources of men, material and money to retain his grandfather's territorial gains. At home, Ferdinand's presence helped to preserve public order after the death of Philip, ensuring that his grandson would inherit Castile intact; but two of his domestic initiatives directly affected the young prince of Spain. First, after his return to Castile he persecuted those 'anxious to see a new regime who wanted the prince or his grandfather the emperor to come to Spain', or who 'declared themselves to be exclusively servants of King Philip and sought to make King Ferdinand leave Castile'. Before long, most of those affected 'decided to leave the kingdom and go to the Netherlands'.[19] Second, Ferdinand mistreated his daughter, called by many historians 'Joanna the Mad', now queen of Castile in her own right and his heiress in Aragon, Naples, Sardinia and Sicily.

Not all her contemporaries considered Joanna 'mad'. In 1505 a Venetian ambassador to Spain, Vincenzo Quirini, noted that Maximilian spent several weeks in the Netherlands 'mostly with the queen [Joanna], keeping her entertained almost constantly with fetes' and trying to reconcile her with her husband before they left for Spain. He 'has tried everything he can to make her happy, because he knows that all her problems have arisen because she is depressed [*tuto el mal suo procedava da melanchonia*]'. In Quirini's opinion, Maximilian succeeded. Henry VII, who met Joanna a few weeks later when storms diverted her ship to England on her way to Spain, agreed: 'When I saw her,' he later told the Spanish ambassador, 'she seemed fine and she spoke in a restrained and gracious manner, never compromising her authority.' Moreover, 'although her husband [Philip] and those with him made her out to be mad, to me she seemed sane; and that is what I believe now.' Ferdinand, too, apparently harboured some doubts. At their meeting one month after declaring Joanna incapable of governing, the king urged Philip to tolerate Joanna's behaviour 'just as he had tolerated the behaviour of Queen Isabella, her mother, who in her youth was driven by jealousy to far worse extremes than those of his daughter right now; and with his support she regained her senses and became the queen that everyone knew.'[20]

Bethany Aram, who has made an exhaustive study of the contemporary sources, endorsed these verdicts, arguing that Joanna's principal goal was to preserve her late husband's extensive domains intact for her son Charles. To this end the queen steadfastly refused to consider remarriage and instead retreated to a convent, first near Burgos and later at Tordesillas, taking the corpse of her late husband with her. She gave her father a free hand to govern Castile and to use its resources as he wished, which allowed him to control

Joanna, and even to have her beaten: shortly after Ferdinand's death, Joanna's jailer at Tordesillas recalled wistfully that when she refused to eat as a protest, her father 'had given orders for her to be whipped in order to save her life, so that she would not die'.[21]

Ferdinand secured consent both from Maximilian (who had threatened to bring Charles to Spain and claim the regency for himself) and from the Cortes for his dual role as governor of Castile and as guardian of Joanna until she died, or until Charles turned twenty. So although Ferdinand did not solve the dilemma posed by Joanna's status as the sworn sovereign of the kingdom who refused to exercise her powers, he provided his grandson with a blueprint of how to control the queen in Tordesillas. But what of Aragon? In 1509, Queen Germaine bore Ferdinand's son, who immediately displaced Joanna as heir to all her father's kingdoms, including Aragon – but the infant soon died. The couple tried to produce more children, and (according to some) Ferdinand resorted to a 'potion' that would 'improve his potency', but (luckily for Charles) their marriage remained childless and the threat of disuniting the crowns of Castile and Aragon therefore abated.[22] Nevertheless, in 1512, Ferdinand signed a will that decreed that, in the event of his death, 'during the absence of Prince Charles, his brother Ferdinand should sign and enact all matters concerning the government' of Castile, while his own illegitimate son, Archbishop Alfonso of Zaragoza, would exercise similar powers in Aragon (as he had done during Ferdinand's prolonged absences). The following year the king went even further, proposing a partition of the territories that he and Maximilian would leave at their deaths, with young Ferdinand inheriting Milan and half of Austria.[23]

These developments alarmed Charles's governors in the Netherlands. In July 1515, Chièvres reassured King Ferdinand that Charles would do everything 'that a good and obedient son is obliged to do'; but, he continued (with more than a hint of menace), 'I humbly beg you, sire, that you will be pleased to reciprocate and not to give him [Charles] occasion to behave otherwise, which would make him deeply unhappy'. Three months later, another development alarmed the governors: they heard that the king's health was 'failing, so that it was feared that he could not last long'. Chièvres decided to send Adrian of Utrecht, Charles's preceptor and councillor, to discuss 'with the king of Aragon some important secret affairs that do not need to be explained here': namely that should Ferdinand die, Adrian must convoke the Cortes in Charles's name 'to declare our right to succeed in the two kingdoms'.[24]

Adrian eventually concluded a deal with Ferdinand. The king agreed to recognize Charles as his universal heir, and to persuade the Cortes of each kingdom to swear allegiance to him; he promised to send his grandson Ferdinand to the Netherlands as soon as Charles left them; and he undertook to restore part of the lands and income confiscated from the Spanish supporters of King Philip who had fled to Brussels. In return, Adrian affirmed that Charles would come to Spain promptly; that he would not bring with him foreign troops (as his father had done); that until then Charles 'would allow the king to hold the reins of government in Castile'; and that he would expel from his court those whom Ferdinand deemed to be his enemies.[25] In December 1515, Adrian boasted to a friend that he had served Charles 'better than most persons of my condition and state could manage', and promptly retired to the monastery of Guadalupe to celebrate Christmas, taking young Ferdinand with him. The king set out for Seville to raise an amphibious force that he planned to lead to north Africa on a new crusade.[26]

Suddenly, Ferdinand's health deteriorated, and 'having just and urgent cause to provide for the good government' of his kingdoms, on 22 January 1516 he dictated and signed a new will. Although he recognized Joanna as his universal heiress, with Charles as her successor, he stated that 'according to everything we have been able to ascertain, she is quite unable to understand the government of kingdoms, and lacks the necessary disposition for it'. Therefore, he continued, 'we name the most illustrious Prince Charles, our very dear grandson, as governor-general of all our kingdoms and lordships to rule, preserve, guide and administer them in the name of the most serene queen, his mother'. In addition, until Charles arrived, Ferdinand appointed his son Archbishop Alfonso of Zaragoza to govern Aragon and Cardinal Cisneros to govern Castile, both empowered 'to do the things that we did, and could have and should have done, during the time of our government'. The king died the next day.[27]

Ferdinand thus reneged on the deal concluded with Adrian the previous month. Instead of declaring Charles to be his successor as king, he merely named him governor-general in Joanna's name; moreover, until he came to Spain, agents whom Charles did not know would wield executive authority. To complicate this situation, as soon as he heard of his grandfather's death and 'not knowing the change that had been made in the Catholic King's testament [of 1512], believing that he had become governor', young Ferdinand summoned the royal council to join him at Guadalupe and started to issue orders in his own name. Adrian immediately enlightened Ferdinand about his grandfather's change of mind, and announced that Charles had empowered him, not Cisneros, to govern Castile should

Ferdinand die; but the arrival of Cisneros at Guadalupe complicated the situation yet further. The cardinal immediately objected that the laws of Castile (like those of Aragon) stipulated that no prince could govern until he reached the age of twenty and that, in any case, Charles was as yet unaware of the restrictive terms of his grandfather's will. 'Many discussions took place concerning this discrepancy' until 'it was eventually agreed to consult the prince, so that he could order what he wanted', and that meanwhile Cisneros and Adrian 'should govern and sign documents jointly, which is what they did for the time being'. As José Martínez Millán has noted, the cardinal's actions at Guadalupe amounted to 'a genuine coup d'état'. Afterwards, accompanied by Adrian, young Ferdinand and the council of Castile, Cisneros set off for Madrid, which for the next twenty months would serve as the kingdom's administrative capital.[28]

THE INTERREGNUM

News of King Ferdinand's death, and a copy of his last will, arrived in Brussels on 8 February 1516. Charles immediately called for 'six weeks of continual mourning' in every church in the Netherlands, 'just as was done after the death of the late king my father'. He also wrote to the brother he had never met, Ferdinand, commiserating on the 'solitude and sadness' that he must feel and assuring him that not only 'in us you have gained your only brother, but also (as you will see) a true father'.[29] These were the easy parts: the real challenge was how to respond to Cisneros's coup. At least his grand-father's bad faith allowed Charles to disregard the promise to expel from his court any of the Spanish refugees, known as *Felipistas* because they had supported Charles's father, Philip. At this point they numbered scarcely fifty, almost all of them junior members of urban patrician or aristocratic fami-lies (such as Juan de Zúñiga, to whose care Charles would later entrust the upbringing of his son and heir, Philip). None held a noble title, and only one held a see: Alonso Manrique, bishop of Badajoz, an outspoken supporter of King Philip whom Ferdinand of Aragon had imprisoned for three years, until he escaped to the Netherlands and joined Charles as his chaplain. Sensing that the time for revenge had come, the Felipistas now pressured Charles to take the title 'king of Castile' – a suggestion at which (Manrique reported) 'the prince, although he signs as "prince", laughs and smiles when they call him "king"'.[30]

On 14 March 1516, Manrique officiated at a funeral Mass for King Ferdinand held in the cathedral of St Gudule, Brussels, which closely resembled the exequies for Queen Isabella twelve years before (chapter 1). A procession of Knights of the Golden Fleece bearing Ferdinand's insignia preceded Charles into the cathedral and stood around the catafalque, on which lay 'a golden crown and a sword'. Thrice the chief herald listed the late king's titles and summoned him, but a mournful voice from the nave of the church answered 'He is dead'. After the third iteration, the herald proclaimed that Charles and Joanna had 'inherited these realms'. Then Manrique 'took the crown from the catafalque and went to Charles . . . and said: "Sire, this belongs to you as king". He then took the sword, and gave it to him saying: "Because you are king, here is the sword you will use to administer justice."' As the new king turned to face the crowd in the cathedral, trumpets rang out and choirs sang his praises. A week later, Charles signed a series of letters claiming that the pope and emperor, as well as many 'prudent and wise noblemen' and 'some provinces and lordships', had urged that 'together with the Catholic Queen, my mother, I should take the name and title of king. And so I did'. Then, apparently for the first time, he affixed the traditional royal signature that he would use for all his Spanish correspondence for the next forty years: *Yo el Rey* – 'I, the king'.[31]

These developments appalled Cisneros and the regency council in Madrid. A few days earlier, they had signed a letter to Charles stating that 'we understand that some people, out of zeal for the service of Your Highness, have urged you to take the title "King" now', but they disagreed: 'It seems to us that Your Highness should not do this, nor is it in the interest of God or the world to do so, because as Your Highness's kingdoms are peaceful . . . during the lifetime of the Queen our Lady, your mother, there is no need to call yourself king.' They also reminded him that 'wicked people in these kingdoms have always complained about whoever is ruling, and tried to make friends with whoever is about to succeed, so as to create discord and more easily tyrannize the kingdom'. Therefore:

> If Your Highness calls himself king now, it might cause difficulties and greatly damage Your Highness's interests, challenging (as it would) the title of the queen our lady . . . Those who are discontented in these kingdoms and those who are enemies of peace and unity would exploit this, using the language of loyalty as a disguise, with some claiming to serve Your Highness and others your mother.[32]

They wrote in vain, and after receiving news of the events in Brussels, Cisneros and his council had little choice but to acquiesce. On 3 April 1516 they authorized the ceremony of 'raising the royal standard', the traditional manner of marking the accession of a new monarch in Castile. Several cities immediately proclaimed 'Castile, Castile, Castile for Queen Joanna and King Charles, our sovereign rulers'; but others dragged their feet. Zamora did not raise the royal standard until 18 May, Plasencia not until 25 July. As the English ambassador John Stile noted, many Castilians 'do take grete dysplesure and dysdayne that the Flemyngys have proclaymeyd thayr prynce Kyng of Castyl wyth oute the[ir] asent'.[33]

Such uncertainty, coupled with the desire to win favour with their new ruler and his advisers, prompted several of Charles's new subjects to migrate from Spain to Brussels. In April 1516, according to the English ambassador in the Netherlands, there 'dayly cometh soo meny Spaniards that the court is full of theym', and three months later, according to Cisneros's agent in Brussels, 'they celebrated the festival of Santiago in the Spanish fashion: 24 knights attended Vespers and Mass.'[34] This marked an important development, because these knights came from the elite of Spanish society and therefore outranked the Felipistas. Other newcomers, later known as the 'Fernandinos', had served the late king but lost their posts when Cisneros took over. One of them was Francisco de Los Cobos, who had worked in Queen Isabella's secretariat since the 1490s and received rewards from Ferdinand since 1503. He thus boasted familiarity with the intricacies of the fiscal as well as the secretarial system of Castile and its American colonies: on 31 October 1516, Charles ordered Cisneros to pay Los Cobos's salary from the treasury of Castile, 'because he came here to serve us, and has been and is now in our service'. Six weeks later, Los Cobos took the oath as royal secretary and until his death thirty-one years later he would open, read and summarize thousands of letters addressed to Charles on almost every aspect of the government of Spain and its overseas possessions, and prepare responses for his master's approval and signature. In 1543, in the confidential holograph Instruction written for his son, Charles would devote more space to evaluating Los Cobos than to any other minister – noting, among other things, the enduring antagonism between Fernandinos like Los Cobos, who had entered his service relatively late, and Felipistas like Juan de Zúñiga who had fled from Spain a decade earlier.[35]

One of the few matters on which both factions agreed was the urgent need for Charles to return to Spain. As early as March 1516, Bishop Manrique reported that 'in a meeting of the council where everyone spoke and voted, it was decided that the prince our lord should leave for Spain' that summer. Manrique nevertheless harboured the same misgivings as those entertained about Charles's father a decade before (p. 10) – and for the same reason: although 'the prince spoke fine words about his determination to go,' he observed, 'people here are very fickle, and what they decide today is forgotten tomorrow'. He feared that 'if they do not set sail this summer, since winter is a dangerous time for navigation, the voyage will be postponed until next summer'. Manrique proved an excellent prophet. Six weeks later, Charles informed his brother Ferdinand that 'you cannot imagine the desire and enthusiasm I have' to come to Spain, and promised that 'you will be the first to know the place or port where we will disembark'. But for now, he added, 'we cannot yet be certain: God and the weather will decide.' In October 1516 he apologized again to his brother that 'certain matters of great importance have come up, so that for the security of all the other kingdoms and lordships ruled by the Catholic Queen, our mother, and by me, I must delay my voyage until the spring'. He therefore ordered a fleet to assemble in March 1517 in Middelburg, the same port from which his parents had set sail for Spain eleven years before.[36]

Manrique surmised that the main cause of delay was the need to protect Charles's patrimony against invasion while he was absent in Spain, and he identified three potential enemies: England, France and Guelders. The first proved easiest to placate. In April 1516, Henry VIII's diplomats in Brussels signed a treaty that settled outstanding trade disputes and promised English assistance in case anyone attacked the Netherlands during Charles's absence. Henry also promised to welcome Charles, should his fleet seek a friendly port as it carried him to Spain. Concluding a similar arrangement with France proved more difficult. Negotiations at the town of Noyon in May broke down over the parties' competing claims to Naples, but they resumed in August. Francis (who now styled himself 'king of France, duke of Milan and lord of Genoa') released Charles from his obligation to marry Renée but replaced it with a commitment to marry his own infant daughter, Claude, who would bring as her dowry the French claim to Naples. Until the wedding, Charles would pay 100,000 crowns annually as tribute for that kingdom – thus explicitly recognizing France's claim to it. The treaty of Noyon, signed in August, also obliged Charles to 'satisfy' Francis's ally, the king of Navarre expelled by Ferdinand, 'to the extent that he considers just, after studying his claims' within eight months of arriving in Spain. In return, Francis swore not to provide assistance to any enemy of Charles. No doubt Chièvres and Le Sauvage (who conducted the negotiations in person) considered concessions regarding distant Naples and Navarre a small price to pay for a guarantee that the Netherlands would be safe while Charles consolidated his authority over Spain and its overseas possessions. On paper, the obligation to marry Claude de France seemed more of a risk, since the princess was scarcely one year old, which meant that Charles might be unable to sire a legitimate heir until the 1530s – but perhaps the governors assumed that they could later renege on this part of the deal, just as Louis XII had reneged on his commitment to marry his daughter to Charles.[37]

The treaty of Noyon astonished and appalled Charles's English allies. 'The king of Castell, whiche is the gretyst prince by inheritaunce that hath ben thes five hundredth yeres,' Henry's diplomats observed, 'is like to be at the comandement of the Ffrench king.' Moreover, 'the said Ffrenche king is of that ambicion that he will suffer noo man to be in Italy of equalle or superior degree', so that both Naples and the papacy seemed likely to fall under his sway. Worse, Francis had 'affirmed' that 'the corone of th'empyre ought of right to be in the house of Ffraunce, which thinge he wolde attayne if he coulde' – and the new treaty made this outcome more likely. The English ascribed this adverse scenario to the fact that Charles had 'suche men about hym' (namely Chièvres and Le Sauvage) as 'had lever lose part of his right then displease others', and they saw little prospect of any change: instead, they predicted, the dominance of his governors would 'contynue until the king of Castell [see] the faulte hymself, which ys not like to be unto he come into Spain – and whether it shalbe then or noo, God knoweth'.[38]

Charles still needed to placate one more enemy before he could leave the Netherlands: Guelders. Philip I had faced an identical problem in 1506 (chapter 1), and although he had defeated Guelders and imposed a harsh peace, Duke Charles later used diplomatic and occasionally military means, sometimes with covert French assistance, to regain the influence he had lost. According to Bishop Manrique in March 1516, 'there is much to fear from the duke of Guelders' because 'the French tend to favour him in such times . . . It would be shameful, given how powerful the prince is, if [Charles] does not provide for this.' The bishop even urged Cisneros and the council in Spain 'to provide [aid] for the conquest of Guelders'.[39] Although that would prove the ultimate solution – in 1543, Charles used Spanish troops and treasure to conquer and annex Guelders – for the time being the urgent need to depart for Spain led the governors to prefer a peaceful settlement. At Noyon, they persuaded Francis to induce the duke of Guelders to guarantee a ceasefire while diplomats discussed the reconciliation of all competing claims, and they also dangled the possibility that the duke might marry Charles's youngest sister, Catalina. Although this came to nothing, for the time being it sufficed to neutralize Guelders.[40]

Still, Charles procrastinated. Perhaps the reassuring messages sent by Cisneros lulled him into thinking that Spain could wait. In August 1516 the cardinal had written:

All these kingdoms enjoy the greatest peace they have ever known ... and without doubt one must give thanks to God that in all these kingdoms, large as they are, there is not the slightest movement or suspicion of disturbances: not only the cities and towns but also the grandees, without exception, are so obedient and so peaceful that one could not ask for more.

A month later Cisneros repeated that 'all things in these kingdoms are peaceful and calm, as they always have been'.[41] Charles's leading Netherlands subjects also offered reassurance. In November 1516 he presided over an assembly of the Knights of the Golden Fleece for the first time. Having taken the oath as Sovereign of the Order, Charles proposed that the number of knights should increase from thirty-one to fifty-one, in view of the expansion of the territories ruled by the House of Burgundy since the foundation of the Order; and he proposed to reserve ten places for his most illustrious new Spanish and Italian subjects. The assembly agreed, and then exercised their unique privilege: a public review of each other's failings. After censuring a few knights for avarice, drunkenness and gambling, the assembly turned to Charles. Recognizing that his youth exempted him from most criticisms, they complained that he rarely consulted them about policy. The new sovereign promised to do better in future.[42]

Everything now depended on finding the necessary funds for the voyage to Spain. Charles explained to Cisneros that 'to leave everything here in a suitable state, so that I can come safely', he would need at least 100,000 ducats from Spain, while he asked the States-General to authorize taxes worth £400,000. Although this was the same amount that his father had requested for the same purpose a decade earlier, the delegates demurred. 'A vast sum of money is being demanded from the people, and, what is more, immediately', Erasmus noted, and then added waspishly: 'The request has been accepted by the nobility and the prelates – that is, by those who will pay nothing. The cities are considering the question now'. He also reported that Maximilian, 'who is normally unarmed, is now here with a body of troops splendidly equipped, and the country round is full of bands of soldiery'; and he wondered why.[43]

The answer was simple: the emperor had returned to the Netherlands in January 1517 in a final attempt to regain control of the provinces and of his grandson. The previous month, Margaret's agent at the imperial court had assured her that the emperor aimed 'to drive Chièvres and his colleagues from power' and 'would not leave until [Charles] had embarked, taking the government of the Netherlands in his own hands in order to place them in yours'.[44] It was uphill work. In April 1517, having exacted a promise from his grandson that he would make 'all hast and departe within iij or iiij wekes' from Zealand, Maximilian made enquiries 'to see what preparacons wer made, and repport was brought hym that ther had ben non, nor no mony laide out therfor'. Furious at the deception, Maximilian wrote 'a sherpe letter to the king his grandson puttyng hym in remembrance of his promyse', and he spent the first week of May in Zealand, assessing the 'preparacons' for himself. He then met Charles again in Lier, the city where Philip and Joanna had married two decades before, and although some detected coolness between the two men, Charles commissioned two huge stained-glass windows to commemorate their encounter. He would never see his grandfather again.[45]

Maximilian's nagging seems to have worked, because in June 1517 Charles announced his imminent departure to the States-General. According to an eyewitness, as Chancellor Jean Le Sauvage assured his audience how much their sovereign loved them, and how reluctant he was to leave them, many of the delegates started to weep, 'and even though the chancellor was a strong man, not easily reduced to tears, seeing the people all around cry' he first 'pretended to cough, and then wiped his nose with his handkerchief, to disguise the fact that his eyes were full of tears'. When he had regained his self-control, Le Sauvage made several promises in Charles's name: that he would return within four years; that he would arrange an effective government in his absence; and that he would send his brother Ferdinand to the Netherlands, so that a prince of the blood royal would live among them. Charles also repeated his request for money – but anticipating that it would not arrive in time, he persuaded Henry VIII to lend him 100,000 gold florins specifically to pay for the ships and crews assembled in Zealand to take him to Spain.[46]

Now, at last, Charles and his court travelled to Middelburg, and there he finalized his plans for the 'effective government' of the Netherlands in his absence. First, he appointed his closest confidant, Count Henry of Nassau, as commander-in-chief of all troops, with considerable latitude to decide how to deploy them. Then he declared that 'we have resolved that this time we will not appoint a regent' but instead 'we are establishing a Privy Council' of fourteen prominent nobles and ministers to handle civil affairs, specifying the numerous issues of policy, justice and patronage that they must refer to him. According to Charles, Maximilian (now back in Germany) had promised to return 'if any extraordinary situation should occur in the Netherlands ... and then he will become superintendent of the council'. Although Margaret's name headed the list of council members, she received no special powers except for custody 'of the stamp [*cachet*] we have made to print our name on all letters issued in our name with the consent of the council'. Although Chièvres and Le Sauvage would both accompany Charles to Spain, they clearly had no intention of losing control of the Netherlands.[47]

THE LETTER

Charles now issued an Ordinance for the Household he planned to take with him to Spain, which numbered over 600 members – almost twice the size of his father's entourage a decade before. They included a strong Iberian contingent, with eighteen senior officials, many of them already prominent figures (Alonso Manrique, now bishop of Córdoba, and Pedro Ruiz de la Mota, bishop of Badajoz; Juan de Zúñiga, Luis Cabeza de Vaca and Juan Manuel). Several German princes also appeared on the list, including Count Palatine Frederick, who continued to receive his annual pension of £5,000 as first chamberlain.[48]

Charles's older sister Eleanor also accompanied him. Initially, the complaints of his Netherlands subjects that her departure would remove from their midst the last child of Philip the Fair (Isabeau was now in Denmark, Marie en route to Hungary) led Charles to decree that she would remain in Brussels; but Eleanor sang songs of protest in the palace gardens 'and her ladies-in-waiting responded, until the king her brother took notice. His Highness came to console her, because he loved her very much, and promised to take her with him to Spain.'[49] There was more to the 'songs of protest' than met the eye. Charles's emancipation had also liberated his sister Eleanor, now nineteen, from the seclusion of Mechelen and both now made the Coudenberg palace in Brussels their base, living in adjacent suites of rooms. When Charles travelled around his dominions, Eleanor accompanied him and his courtiers – including the 'first prince of the blood', Count Palatine Frederick.

Born in 1482, and thus sixteen years older than Eleanor, Frederick had accompanied her father on his first journey to Spain, after which he fought alongside Maximilian in Italy. He also kept in touch with Charles: in 1505 he sent him a hobby horse, and no doubt other toys followed, while in 1513 he became one of the three chamberlains appointed to keep the prince constant company (chapter 2). Many credited him with curing Charles of a tendency towards anorexia.[50] Two years later, Maximilian appointed Frederick one of the commissioners empowered to emancipate his grandson, and over the next two years the Count Palatine accompanied the royal party on all its travels. Late in 1515, according to his biographer, Frederick became Eleanor's 'lover while they danced at balls, while they walked in the park that surrounded the royal palace, and while they went hunting; and when they could not exchange words, they communicated with signs and gestures.' By these means, he 'solicited and told the noble lady Madame Eleanor of Austria that he wanted to marry her'. Small wonder, then, that she sang 'songs of protest' when she feared that Frederick would leave for Spain without her.[51]

Charles also had a hidden agenda: he did not change his mind about leaving his sister behind because of her laments. In March 1517 their aunt María died, leaving King Manuel of Portugal a widower; and, now aged forty-eight, he sought a new bride. Charles offered him Eleanor's hand. This threatened her secret romance, and while waiting in Zealand for a favourable wind she promised Frederick that the next time 'she was alone with the king in our oratory', she would ask his consent to marry. Unfortunately for their plans, Frederick doubted her determination and wrote a passionate love letter that began: 'My darling, you can be the cause of my happiness or my misery . . . I am ready, and ask nothing more than that I should be yours and you be mine . . . Sweetheart, don't be angry if I burden your mind with so many irritating letters.'[52]

Eleanor never read his declaration of love. One of her ladies had observed the delivery of Frederick's 'irritating letters', which the princess hid in her bodice until she could read them in secret. Chièvres somehow found out, and informed Charles. Eleanor had just received Frederick's last desperate letter, and hidden it in the usual place, when her brother entered her apartments, as he did every morning, to exchange greetings:

'How are you,' he asked, to which she replied 'Well' . . . 'But I see,' the king responded, 'that your breasts seem bigger than usual today'; and on saying this he plunged his hand in and brought out the compromising letter. Eleanor, blushing, tried to regain this evidence of her secret love, but Charles prevailed and said as he left: 'Now I will find out what you have been doing.'

The king stormed back to his apartments, where he read the love letter before giving it to Chièvres, who forced each party to provide full details of their affair under oath before a notary. After reading the transcript, Charles immediately banished Frederick from his court and confined Eleanor to her quarters: there would be no chance to claim that 'sche by wyet chylde', as the duke of Suffolk had done to gain Mary Tudor, Charles's prospective wife.[53]

These dramatic events stunned the diplomats in Zealand waiting to sail with Charles for Spain. Cuthbert Tunstal marvelled at 'the soden departure hens off the Counte Palatine, which had al his stuff shypped to have gone with the kinge, and was off al the noble men next to the kinge at al tymes'. He also remarked with surprise that 'the kinge was inflexible' – but, he added, 'whedyr al that came off his own mynd or not I know not'. Tunstal, like many others, detected the hand of Chièvres, who bitterly resented the fact that Frederick was now 'depe in the king's favor' and may therefore have engineered his rival's downfall. By contrast Thomas Spinelly considered that the abrupt disgrace and dismissal of a close adviser revealed for the first time that Charles had a 'good stomak and cowrraggy, and that he shall not lyghtly forget the offences'. He predicted that the young king 'wyll be fast in his determynacions'.[54]

Nevertheless, unfavourable winds continued to prevent the royal party from leaving Zealand, and on 11 September, in Spain, an associate of Cisneros admitted that he, like many others, was 'hopeful that His Highness will not desert us in the year 1517, because we have bet more than 1,000 ducats on his arrival. I pray that God brings His Majesty safely to these kingdoms.'[55] He was already well on the way to winning his bet: four days earlier, the wind in Zealand suddenly changed and Charles, Eleanor and their entourage hurriedly confessed before boarding the ships waiting to convey them to Spain. The episode of the letter had demonstrated that Charles would trample over even those he loved if it suited his plans. It remained to be seen whether he also possessed the 'stomak and cowrraggy' to make difficult political choices and then 'be fast in his determynacions'.

PORTRAIT OF THE EMPEROR
AS A YOUNG MAN

Sancho Cota, a poet who fled from Spain to the Netherlands after the death of Philip the Fair and became secretary to his daughter Eleanor, provided an intimate portrait of Charles on the eve of his departure for Spain:

> Now let us speak about what King Charles was like when he was sixteen. He was of medium height, with a long face, blond hair, beautiful light-blue eyes, a narrow but well-proportioned nose, his mouth and chin not as beautiful as his other features . . . He was a graceful man in very good shape; an upright man in his life, eating and drinking in a measured fashion; very clever for his years; liberal and magnificent and very virtuous.[1]

Almost all accounts of Charles noted that distinctive 'mouth and chin'. The Italian diplomat Antonio di Beatis, who visited Charles just before he left for Spain, noted that although 'he is tall and splendidly built, with a neat, straight leg, the finest you ever saw in one of his rank . . . he has a long, cadaverous face and a lopsided mouth (which drops open when he is not on his guard) with a drooping lower lip'. Another Italian envoy at this time reported that Charles 'is fair and tall, does not talk much, always has his mouth open, and instructs others to speak for him'. Francesco Corner, the first permanent Venetian ambassador at Charles's court, provided more detail: 'Although he is not deformed, his mouth is always open, which makes him look very unbecoming . . . He is very prone to catarrh, and since his nostrils are constantly blocked he is forced to breathe through his mouth. His tongue is short and thick, which means that he speaks with great difficulty.'[2] Almost all contemporary sculptures and paintings show him with his mouth open and a prominent lower jaw.

Everyone agreed on another characteristic: the young man's piety. According to di Beatis, 'each day he usually attends two masses, said and then sung', and he usually went on a Retreat in Holy Week. Thus at Easter 1518, his first in Spain, Charles retired to a monastery accompanied by 'a very small entourage, to escape from all temporal affairs and to be almost alone, the better to examine his conscience and make a meaningful confession'. Afterwards he 'went to visit all the holy sites in the vicinity to gain pardons'. Two years later, the king again 'went to a monastery for Holy Week to perform his devotions', and refused to transact any official business.[3]

Some observers expressed concern about his health. One of the few matters on which his grandfathers agreed was that Charles's marriage to Mary Tudor, scheduled for May 1514, 'must be delayed because Nature did not endow him with much physical strength'. Three years later his physicians warned that he seemed 'soo feble that he cannot lyffe past two yere', which led his Netherlands ministers to request a postponement of his departure for Spain because he would have better 'helth in his natyfe contre'.[4] Such concerns contradict reports of Charles's prowess and endurance when hunting and jousting, and may simply betray the same prejudices displayed by the ministers of his father Philip, who 'would rather go to Hell than to Spain' (chapter 1), or of Erasmus, who turned down the offer of a Spanish bishopric because 'I do not care for Spain'.[5] Nevertheless, a dramatic event in January 1519 suggested that young Charles did indeed lack physical strength. According to the French ambassador, an eyewitness, 'while on his knees during High Mass, [Charles] fell to the floor and lay there for more than two hours, without moving and with his face contorted, as if he were dead. He was carried to his bedroom' and stayed there for several days. 'Everyone here is talking about this,' the ambassador stated, not least because Charles 'fell ill in the same way less than two months ago', while playing tennis.[6]

Yet although 'everyone' may have been 'talking about' this alarming episode (perhaps an epileptic attack) only one other eyewitness, the historian and royal councillor Peter Mártir de Anglería, seems to have recorded it – and even he played down its significance: 'While the king heard Mass he fainted and fell down, although he immediately recovered.' Mártir continued: 'Some say it was brought on in part by eating a huge meal the previous day; and a few attribute it to an excess of sex.'[7] The 'huge meal' explanation seems implausible: most of those who observed young Charles commented (like Sancho Cota) on his abstemiousness in food and drink. As for 'an excess of sex', after spending four years at Charles's court Francesco Corner stated categorically that Charles 'is not much of a womaniser'.[8] In this, however, he was mistaken.

In February 1517 an English diplomat in Brussels reported (without giving a source) that 'the Lord Chevers hath begun to satisfy the king's pleasure, and suffered him to play in the garden of Venus'. This suggestion might simply reflect the expectation that Charles would follow the example of his grandfathers, both of whom had sired illegitimate children (Maximilian left so many that 'he could not remember all of them'); or it might stem from the eternal interest of diplomats in sexual exploits at the courts where they resided.[9] But Charles himself provided some details in his earliest surviving holograph letter, written in January 1518 to Henry of Nassau, commander-in-chief of his troops in the Netherlands (Pl. 8). The opening greeting ('Henry') revealed an easy familiarity between the correspondents, as did the protest that he had received 'so many letters from you' that he had not been able to reply to all of them 'with my own fair hand' despite Nassau's threat that 'if I do not do so, I will be handed over to the devil'. Charles therefore declared that he would 'reply first to your silly letter [*fole lettre*], because everyone likes to talk about what they like best', and he joked about the amorous adventures of some of his courtiers. Next he unleashed a barrage of complaints about Spain: how much he missed the fish delicacies of the Netherlands; how he yearned for decent wine; and how 'I am very annoyed that I no longer see my Henry [*je suis bien mary de ne plus voir mon Henry*]'. Above all he missed 'pretty ladies [*belles dames*] because you scarcely find them here – although I believe I have found one who pleases me ... She does not amount to much, since she wears about a finger's width of makeup,' he continued unchivalrously, but 'if the lady is willing, I will get her more easily and more cheaply than over there'. Evidently he succeeded, because according to Laurent Vital, who had served as his valet for over a decade, at this time Charles 'conquered and possessed a lady through love [*avoit conquis et fait une dame par amour*]'. Who could the lady be? Only Ambassador Thomas Spinelly provided even a partial answer, informing Charles's uncle Henry that 'the king was amoreux of a goodly gentlewoman of the queen of Aragon', Germaine de Foix (Charles's step-grandmother).[10]

No other diplomat, minister or chronicler seems to have mentioned the lady, and their silence may seem surprising – but few of them found much of note to report about young Charles. Sancho Cota's *Memoirs* included only one example of Charles taking the initiative before he left for Spain: one day, almost certainly during the winter of 1515–16, he 'decided that he wanted a motto like other princes, and he used his dagger to write one on a window in his chambers in Brussels. The motto was "Plus oultre"': *Still further*.[11] The device, almost immediately linked with the twin columns of Hercules, had the double meaning that Charles would surpass not only the geographical limits of previous empires but also the valour, fame and glory of the heroes of Antiquity. It soon spread: in October 1516, Charles's doctor and adviser Luigi Marliano featured the device in his speech to a chapter of the Knights of the Golden Fleece, calling on the young king to be 'a new Hercules, a new Atlas', and a year later both motto and columns featured prominently on the mainsail of the ship that carried Charles to Spain.[12] A Latin version, *Plus Ultra*, appeared on the back of the stall where the emperor sat at the next chapter of the Fleece, in Barcelona, and later in a thousand other locations. Although Cota did not reveal where Charles got the idea for his motto – at once personal, heroic and chivalric – it probably came from the epic romance *The histories of Troy*, commissioned by Duke Philip the Good of Burgundy. Charles the Bold owned a magnificent illustrated manuscript copy, which entered the ducal library, and his wife Margaret of York, Charles's first governess, liked the work so much that she commissioned an English translation. By 1516, Charles would have heard the text read out several times, including the French inscription allegedly found on one of the columns of Hercules: 'Go no further if you want to acquire new lands', which included both the words 'plus' and 'oultre'.[13]

Like Cota, Laurent Vital found little memorable to write about the young Charles. He devoted a whole chapter of his chronicle of his 'First voyage to Spain' to 'The good customs that God has conferred on the Catholic King Our Lord', but offered few specific examples except that he 'could not abide swearing', that 'he was truthful in speech and just in deeds' and that 'he hated flatterers and tell-tales'. Moreover, Vital offered only one example in support of even these 'good customs': how at age twelve Charles rebuked 'one of his old servants', who had spoken ill of another in an attempt to get him dismissed.[14]

This absence of evidence no doubt reflects the fact that young Charles rarely did or said anything memorable. Vital included only one extended conversation in his detailed account of the long journey from Ghent to Zaragoza, which took nine months: an inconsequential exchange about sharing food and drink among the various ships of the royal fleet as they lay becalmed on their way to Spain. Di Beatis, writing just before the sea voyage, recorded that 'immediately after lunch or dinner His Majesty graciously gave audience to anyone where he sat, at the head of the table', although 'His Majesty did not speak'. Corner, too, noted that Charles 'speaks little in audiences and meetings'. Instead 'he gets the Grand Chancellor or some other minister present at the audience to respond, and when he does speak it is to say that he will refer the matter to the Grand Chancellor, to M. de Chièvres, or to someone else, according to the importance of the matter'.[15]

Corner and other ambassadors repeatedly referred to Chièvres as '*alter rex* [an alternative king]', while Erasmus noted that Chièvres's 'lightest word is law'. Vital justified Charles's willingness to 'favour and esteem the advice of older people' by invoking an Old Testament parallel: the example of 'Jeroboam, who was expelled from his kingdom because he ignored the old and wise and listened to the young and ignorant'.[16] Others were less charitable. A Spanish envoy in 1516 reported that Charles was 'being bossed around and does not know how to be any other way, or to say anything except what he is advised and told to say. He follows his councillors and is very bound by them'. The following year a Venetian diplomat asserted that 'he spoke little and was not a man of much intelligence'; two others stated that 'having been thrice in his presence they never heard him utter one single word, all matters being regulated by his councillors'; and an English diplomat opined with cruel simplicity that 'The king of Castell is but an idiote and hys counsail is corruptyde'.[17]

This was manifestly unfair. Laurent Vital knew exactly why Charles and his governors behaved as they did: they had to 'make a virtue out of necessity' and approve unpalatable concessions in order to avoid war and thus 'preserve the assets of this orphan prince' until he reached an age when he could successfully 'defend his rights' for himself. Chièvres carefully and consciously prepared the prince for that day. Martin du Bellay, a French diplomat with no reason to praise his master's principal rival, observed that during his visit to Charles's court in 1515: 'All the dossiers that came in from all the provinces were presented to the prince, even at night, and after he had seen them he reported their contents himself to his council, where everything was discussed in his presence'. When one of Du Bellay's colleagues expressed surprise that Chièvres 'should burden the spirit of the young prince, when he had the means to spare him', Chièvres replied: 'My cousin, I am his tutor and guardian while he is young ... If he cannot handle his affairs by the time I die, he is going to need another tutor because he has not been properly trained in the work of government'.[18]

Nevertheless, the micro-management by Chièvres, and before him by Margaret and Maximilian, seems to have stifled Charles's self-reliance and independence; and this probably explains his dependence on much older men – not only on Chièvres and Adrian of Utrecht, Maximilian's exact contemporaries, but also on Count Palatine Frederick and Henry of Nassau, both of them twice Charles's age. To be sure these men, together with the other surviving councillors of Philip the Fair, formed an important link with the world of his father, which explains some often overlooked continuities in policy; but Charles later came to realize the perils of placing too much trust in individual ministers. The secret instructions that he wrote in 1543 for his son Philip, then almost the same age as he had been when he first arrived in Spain, contained a strong warning against precisely the kind of dependence that characterized his relations with Chièvres:

> Always discuss your affairs with many, and do not become tied or obliged to any one of them, because while it will save you time it is not in your interest, especially at first, because they will immediately say that you are being governed – and that may be true. Anyone who receives such favour from you will become excessively proud and will elevate himself in such a way that he then causes a thousand problems; and in the end all the others will complain.[19]

Wise words indeed, yet the emperor only added them as an afterthought on a page that contains more emendations than any other in his instructions – a curiosity that may reflect his sense of shame and embarrassment that his own failure to follow this advice had provoked rebellions which almost deprived him of his Spanish inheritance (Pl. 9).

PART II

GAME OF THRONES

*'When you play the game of thrones, you win or you die. There
is no middle ground.'*

Cersei Lannister to Eddard Stark, *Game of Thrones*, series 1,
episode 7 (2011)

FOUR

FROM KING OF SPAIN TO KING OF THE ROMANS, 1517–19

SPAIN AT LAST

A few weeks after the death of Ferdinand of Aragon in January 1516, Ambassador John Stile wrote from Madrid that unless Charles came to Spain 'thys somer, wythoute fayle here wyl encreas many enconvenyentys and trobyllys'. For a time, it seemed that Stile exaggerated. Not only did Cardinal Cisneros send the new king a stream of reassuring messages about the state of Castile but in Aragon the *Justicia Mayor*, the kingdom's senior law officer, recognized Charles as both heir apparent and as legal guardian of Joanna for the duration of her 'illness, mental alienation and dementia'. Meanwhile the viceroy of Naples reported that 'the entire kingdom is as peaceful and lawful in obedience to the prince-king, my lord, as it was in the time of His Late Majesty'; and although some Sicilian barons rebelled when they heard of Ferdinand's death, the viceroy soon restored order. The stream of optimistic reports encouraged Charles to revive his grandfather's plan for a new campaign in north Africa: in May 1517, from Brussels, he ordered Cisneros to launch an amphibious assault on Algiers.[1]

By then Castile was spinning out of control. Despite the ambiguity of his position, at first Cisneros held his own with relative ease. When a delegation of grandees came to enquire 'by what powers do you govern', the cardinal 'pointed to a patio where, as in other commanding locations, he had placed and prepared many pieces of artillery, and said to them: "These are the powers that the king left me, and with them, and with the permission of the prince, I shall govern Castile until His Highness comes here or until he orders something else."' Such crude tactics could not work indefinitely. Looking back, the chronicler Bartolomé Leonardo de Argensola grumbled that 'the cardinal settled matters imperiously'. In particular, 'he deprived many people who had served him well of their offices, he took salaries from others, and rents and tax receipts from important people'. Many of those affected travelled 'to the Netherlands, to take refuge with the prince', which undermined the authority of Cisneros because 'one heard nothing in that court but complaints about the situation in Castile'.[2]

Many of those who remained in Spain also complained. Some nobles and cities openly opposed Cisneros's policies, and although the cardinal continued to accentuate the positive in his letters to Charles – 'everything is in peace and quiet' he claimed again in March 1517 – the leading cities of Castile threatened to convene the Cortes of the kingdom in October if Charles had not arrived by then. He just made their deadline, setting foot on Spanish soil for the first time on 20 September 1517.[3]

The new ruler came well prepared. Charles had sponsored books that promoted his legitimacy (including a new edition of *Decades of the New World* by Peter Mártir and the *Chronicle of John II*, Charles's great-grandfather); and he had secured copies of the daily accounts of his mother's household during her journeys to Spain a decade before, presumably to estimate how much he himself would need to spend.[4] Thanks to a loan from his uncle Henry VIII, Charles brought with him 40,000 ducats in Spanish coins newly minted in Antwerp with which to pay his way – but at first he found little to buy. The pilots aboard his fleet failed to identify their landfall correctly, and Charles, Eleanor and a few courtiers came ashore at the tiny Asturian port of Villaviciosa, which lacked the facilities to handle baggage and supplies. According to a member of the royal entourage: 'In 200 personnes – lordys, gentylmen and gentylwomen – was not 40 horses, and for to purvey any there was no way, ffyrst by cause that comonly for the great montaynes and manerre of the contray the princypaulles goyth afoute, and secondly that the chief places warre infected of the sicynes.'[5] 'The sickness' – bubonic plague – persisted throughout Charles's first visit to Spain, affecting his decisions and disaffecting his subjects.

Laurent Vital, who landed with his master, tried to put a positive spin on events: 'The king and his lords made a virtue of necessity,' he claimed, 'lending a hand' to whatever needed to be done 'pretending they were in some bucolic fantasy, feasting on omelettes and pancakes made with local eggs and flour'; but the pretence wore thin after 'a great part of them had to sleep on straw', and it vanished after they had eaten up all the local food. This compelled the royal party to move on, but because they found only a few oxcarts, in which the ladies travelled, and some packhorses and mules on which Charles and some others rode, the rest had to follow on foot.[6]

After struggling along the 'terrible and tiring coast road', braving torrential rain and 'a cold black fog', the bedraggled travellers eventually reached the port of San Vicente de la Barquera, where somewhat better accommodation and fresh food restored their spirits. Charles boasted to his aunt Margaret that 'along our route all the princes and grandees of the area have greeted us, triumphantly bringing many people with them, full of good will and obedience'. Indeed, he added pompously, 'We believe that never was a king here so universally welcomed and adored by everybody, as we are'; but almost immediately, he fell ill and took to his bed, scarcely eating while his doctors plied him with various drugs, 'often adding powdered unicorn horn'. He became so ill that 'even his jesters failed to make him laugh'.[7]

The doctors concluded that 'the sea air was the culprit' and so instead of pressing on to Santander, where his fleet had landed the rest of its supplies, the king and his small entourage set out directly for Castile over mountains that towered almost 2,000 metres above sea level – a foolish decision in any situation, but especially given Charles's fragile health. Villages where even 'in the king's lodgings bearskins replaced tapestries' gave way first to hovels with 'nothing but bare walls', and then to a place 'where we could not find a house that did not stink and was not full of diseases from the livestock that normally slept inside'. The royal party therefore pitched tents and prepared to sleep outside, but almost immediately another 'cold black fog' descended, followed by high winds, torrential rains and snow, forcing them indoors to spend the night surrounded by malodorous and flea-ridden livestock. Even the normally irrepressible Vital felt discouraged: 'Twenty-six days have passed since the king disembarked and arrived in Spain,' he wrote sadly, and yet they had travelled only 80 kilometres.[8]

Conditions improved somewhat once the royal party rejoined their supply train near Palencia, but their ordeal was by no means over. On 31 October they passed 'several villages where one saw only the church, because the houses and dwellings of the inhabitants were buried in the earth, in hidden and shadowy places, rather like rabbit warrens'; and after Charles made his solemn entry into the tiny town of Becerril de Campos, late on Halloween, 'he ordered Vespers to be solemnly sung in his lodgings but did not eat that night' – because there was nothing to eat.

The four months between Charles's departure from Ghent in June 1517 and his arrival at Becerril on Halloween were probably the most miserable of his life, and also the least productive: he transacted virtually no business during this period, despite dramatic developments elsewhere. In Africa, the Muslim defenders of Algiers destroyed most of the expeditionary force sent against them, causing dismay and anger throughout Spain. Further east, Sultan Selim supervised the conquest of Egypt and the Arabian peninsula, and claimed the title of Caliph. According to the Ottoman historian Andrew Hess, this 'not only catapulted the Ottomans into a position of leadership within the vast Muslim community, but it also gave the Istanbul regime resources sufficient to project its power north to the gates of Vienna and west to the Strait of Gibraltar'. In both places they encountered Habsburg defenders. So began 'the sixteenth-century world war' that would demand Charles's attention and consume his resources for the rest of his reign.[9] No less important for the future, Martin Luther, an obscure professor of theology at the university of Wittenberg in Saxony, prepared a list of objections to the theory and practice of indulgences, issued by the Church to those who made donations to pious causes. On 31 October, as Charles began his involuntary fast in Becerril de Campos, Luther published his *Ninety-five theses on the power and efficacy of indulgences* in Wittenberg. By year's end hundreds of printed copies had become available in German and Latin. Another 'sixteenth-century world war' had begun.

A MOTHER AND HER CHILDREN

Charles had arranged for the Cortes of Castile to assemble and acclaim him as king in Valladolid, and his courtiers now made their way there; but he and Eleanor went to Tordesillas instead. As he explained to his brother Ferdinand: 'My main reason for coming to these kingdoms was to see, serve and console Her Highness [Joanna] as much as I possibly could. To this end, I have decided that before doing anything else concerning the kingdom, I shall go straight to Her Majesty and kiss her hands'. On 4 November 1517, Charles and Eleanor rode into Tordesillas to visit the mother they had not seen for twelve years. After retiring briefly to the apartments prepared for them, each splendidly furnished with the tapestries that Joanna had brought with her from the Netherlands, Charles and Eleanor, accompanied by Baron Chièvres, entered the queen's presence to pay their respects. As he knelt before her, Joanna 'asked the king three times if he was really her son', adding 'How big you have grown in such a short time'. She then 'kissed him on the cheek, and likewise Madam Eleanor. Then she said "Go and rest now: you must be tired."'[10] Her children obediently retired to their apartments, but Chièvres stayed on and talked to the queen 'for a good half hour'. Joanna claimed to remember the baron well from her time in the Netherlands, and he exploited this advantage to suggest that 'you would be well-advised to grant [Charles] sovereign power now, so that during your lifetime he can learn to rule and govern your people'.[11] She agreed (or so his ministers would later claim). This critically strengthened Charles's authority in Castile, since the Cortes had recognized his mother (and only her) as their lawful sovereign. Henceforth, although she remained 'queen proprietress' of Castile until her death in 1555, and although her name appeared together with that of her son on all coins and official documents, Joanna never challenged Charles's right to rule in both their names.

In addition, Joanna did not claim the title 'queen of Aragon' – initially because those around her acted as if Ferdinand of Aragon still lived. The deception began when Cisneros and the council of regency decided, just after Ferdinand's death, that the news would upset the late king's daughter and therefore resolved not to tell her. The situation worsened after March 1518, when Charles appointed Bernardo de Sandoval y Rojas, marquis of Denia, as governor of both his mother's household and of the town of Tordesillas because, in the words of Bethany Aram, 'with the king's approval, Denia invented a fictional world' for Joanna.[12]

This fictional world depended on creating a double wall of silence around the queen. Denia forbade her to enter any room with a window, to prevent her from seeing or speaking with anyone outside: instead he 'locked her up in her chamber where no other light entered except candlelight'. He also allowed only hand-picked female attendants, supervised by Denia's wife, to attend the queen, while hand-picked guards excluded everyone else. They too were prisoners, forbidden to leave the palace or to communicate with anyone outside, not even with Charles's other ministers, because (as Denia put it) 'everything that happens here ought to be secret from everyone, especially from members of the council'. Denia also insisted that only he and his wife should converse with Joanna, and whenever it became unavoidable for an outsider (for example a doctor) to visit her, he made each one promise to say nothing that contradicted the fictional world that he had created.[13] When one day Joanna summoned Denia and 'complained much of me because I denied the death of the King, her lord [Ferdinand], and insisted that I tell her whether he was alive because it was very important to her to know. I answered that I had told and would always tell her the truth. If it were otherwise, I said, Your Majesty [Charles] would tell her so.' When news of Maximilian's death arrived, Denia immediately added another level of lies:

> I told her on this occasion that Your Majesty is emperor owing to the renunciation of the emperor, and a new election of the princes electors, and that her Highness ought to give thanks to our Lord. She answered, 'Is

it so, is the Emperor alive? for I believed that he was dead.' I assured her that he was alive.[14]

Why tell such lies? Why confuse and humiliate the queen, Charles's mother? Gustave Bergenroth, who published for the first time part of the heartless correspondence between Charles and Denia, surmised that they hoped to perpetuate the myth that Joanna was mad, and thus incapable of ruling; but this ignores the fact that no one outside the fictional world knew of its existence. It seems more likely that they fostered Joanna's belief that her father was still in charge because, as Denia explained, deception made her easier to control:

> I have told the queen our lady that the king my lord, her father, is alive, because whenever anything that is done displeases Her Highness, I say that the king orders and commands it so; for the love she bears him makes it easier for her to endure it than it would be if she knew that he is dead.

In addition, the deception allowed Denia to assure Joanna that her son 'had come to Spain principally with the intention to see that satisfaction be given to Her Highness', but so far 'you have not succeeded' because 'King Ferdinand' refused.[15]

These advantages no doubt explain why Charles did not merely tolerate the multiple deceptions but expanded them. In October 1518, when plague threatened Tordesillas, and prudence suggested evacuation to a safer place, Charles instructed Denia that if his mother refused to leave her palace, since 'Her Highness fears death, especially from the plague, you must tell her that the plague is so intense that those afflicted die in two days or even less; . . . and to this end it would be good if you could arrange for the clergy to pass in front of the palace carrying their cross several times a day, pretending that they are taking someone for burial.' Charles also reaffirmed his full support for the fictional world: 'As you say, no doubt it would be best if no one spoke to Her Highness about anything beyond what you judge appropriate. It seems best to me that whenever Her Highness asks about anyone, she should be told that they got the plague and were moved outside the town.' He also commanded all those in attendance on Joanna to obey the marquis 'as if I myself in person gave the order'. Charles never seems to have considered the harm that the lies and the prolonged confinement might do to his mother.[16]

Charles also treated his brother badly. Shortly before leaving the Netherlands, Charles received a report that some members of young Ferdinand's household were plotting to appoint their master 'governor of those kingdoms in the name of my lady, the queen'. He therefore sent an express courier to Cisneros and Adrian with instructions to dismiss and exile over thirty of his brother's officials. According to an eyewitness, 'The plan was executed in a single day, a daring move that surprised everyone because at present His Highness [Charles] has no heir or successor except' Ferdinand.[17]

Subsequent investigations allegedly revealed a conspiracy to spirit Ferdinand away to Aragon, and other plots too 'diabolical' to be mentioned; and, with the benefit of hindsight, Prudencio de Sandoval observed that 'all or at least most of those who served' Ferdinand in Castile 'joined the Comuneros when they rebelled two years later'. But that lay in the future: at the time, Charles concentrated on making sure of his brother's loyalty, writing a personal letter assuring him that 'everything is being done for your own good, and you should always keep in mind the love I have for you'. He promised that 'I will send a letter and make sure that orders are given concerning where you can join me. In the meantime, enjoy yourself and have fun.' Charles also urged Cisneros to make Ferdinand understand 'that the measures we have ordered are for his good and well-being, because the great love I have for him is always paramount. He must see me as a brother and a true father.'[18]

The cardinal was not convinced. Knowing that Charles planned to send his brother to the Netherlands, Cisneros begged that 'it is done in a way that leaves the kingdom content, that is: do not send him away poor and hopeless.' Perhaps, the cardinal suggested, 'he might be promised Your Highness's share of the lands that will be vacated when the emperor [Maximilian] dies'.[19] Cisneros died before he could meet Charles in person, which made it easy to ignore his advice – advice that was irreplaceable, since the cardinal had worked closely with both Isabella and Ferdinand as well as governing Castile on four separate occasions (1506-7, 1510, 1512 and 1516-17). He therefore knew from personal experience the strengths and weaknesses of every component of the kingdom, but these insights died with him. The cardinal's death also provided Charles with a poisoned chalice, for it left vacant the see of Toledo, worth 80,000 ducats a year. He decided to nominate as Cisneros's successor Guillaume de Croÿ, Chièvres's nephew and Charles's former page, and now at age nineteen a priest studying at Leuven university. It was the new king of Spain's first major error.

LOSING GROUND

Perhaps because he had no children Chièvres always strove to advance the career of his nephew, persuading Charles to nominate him abbot of two of the richest convents in the Netherlands as well as archbishop of Cambrai, bishop of Coria (in Castile) and finally cardinal. Chièvres now begged Charles to name his nephew archbishop of Toledo.[20] According to Vital, 'at first the king did not grant it or withhold it, saying that he would think about it', because others had also expressed an interest. He therefore 'asked his council to consider on whom he should confer this post, because he wanted first to hear their opinions'; but, Vital continued, 'the diversity of applicants left the king and his council really perplexed'. This reflected bitter divisions within the royal council. Erasmus later claimed that he had declined Charles's invitation to accompany him to Spain primarily because 'I saw the Court divided into so many factions, with sects of Spaniards, Jews and Frenchmen, supporters of Chièvres and the emperor [Maximilian], Neapolitans, Sicilians and who knows what'. In choosing a new archbishop of Toledo, perhaps predictably, the 'supporters of Chièvres' prevailed.[21]

Charles had already nominated foreigners to Castilian sees – Luigi Marliano as bishop of Tuy, and Croÿ himself as bishop of Coria – in clear breach of Queen Isabella's will, which declared that only natives of the kingdom were eligible for secular and ecclesiastical positions. Since this provoked some hostile comments, before nominating Croÿ archbishop of Toledo Charles took the precaution of signing papers that declared him to be a naturalized Castilian, but the appointment still proved controversial. Sancho Cota, Eleanor's secretary, reported that when news arrived that Alfonso de Aragón – King Ferdinand's illegitimate son, archbishop of Zaragoza and regent of the crown of Aragon since his father's death – was on his way to Tordesillas to ask for the see of Toledo, 'the king sent a message that he should not come, because he had named someone else as archbishop'. This insensitive response naturally alienated Alfonso: Charles would later plead in vain for his assistance in winning over the Aragonese. In Valladolid, according to Peter Mártir, 'everyone is saying that the king had behaved discourteously and rudely' towards his uncle Alfonso. Mártir also realized that the appointment of Croÿ 'contravened the laws and customs of the kingdom more blatantly, so that one day it may stir things up'. He predicted that 'time will tell what fruit will grow from these seeds'.[22]

While the seeds grew, Charles took care of some family business. At Tordesillas he and Eleanor spent time with their sister Catalina, now aged ten, and also arranged a belated funeral for their father, whose corpse Joanna kept in Tordesillas. The tomb itself was modest, since Charles intended to move Philip's body to Granada to lie beside the Catholic Monarchs, but performing the funeral rites for the late king before meeting the Cortes highlighted Charles's legitimacy as sovereign. Charles and Eleanor now left Tordesillas to meet another sibling: their brother Ferdinand, now aged fourteen. The king embraced him, dubbed him a Knight of the Golden Fleece, and 'explained several fine, worthy and chivalrous things concerning the Order'. Then, accompanied by an entourage that numbered 6,000, the three grandchildren of Queen Isabella made their ceremonial entry into Valladolid. According to Vital, even 'elderly burghers and merchants' of the city claimed that no one in Castile 'had seen the entry of such a noble and triumphant king as this one'.[23]

The Cortes of Castile almost immediately voted a subsidy of 600,000 ducats – substantially larger than any previous grant – and recognized Charles as king, jointly with his mother, but they also presented almost one hundred grievances for redress. Some were traditional and non-controversial ('that Your Highness prohibit games of dice'; 'that you order the minting of copper coins and other small change, because this kingdom does not have enough'). Others, though more critical, posed no threat ('they beg Your Highness to do us the honour of speaking Castilian' and 'grant a public audience at least twice a week'). Only a few displayed concern about recent developments: 'We beg Your Highness . . . to grant that Infante Ferdinand should not leave these kingdoms until you are married and have heirs'; that no office in Castile, whether secular or religious, 'should be conferred on foreigners'; 'that letters of naturalization should never be granted to a foreigner, and that any already granted should be revoked'; and that 'the archbishop of Toledo should come and reside in these kingdoms'.[24]

Charles addressed some of these complaints immediately, including his inability to speak Spanish. By spring 1518, according to a Burgundian minister, the king 'speaks with his nobles in Castilian, and has now mastered the language and the customs of the country'. Mártir concurred, informing some correspondents: 'The king has suddenly started to speak Spanish, and expresses himself as if he had been born and raised among you. It seems his apprenticeship was very short.' Charles also began to speak for himself at audiences – albeit in brief and often formulaic sentences – instead of relying on his governors to speak in his name.[25]

On Ferdinand's fifteenth birthday, Charles created a separate court for him and then, accompanied by Eleanor, the three siblings set off for Zaragoza to meet the Cortes of the kingdom of Aragon. En route, however, and apparently without warning, Charles defied the express wishes of the Cortes of Castile and ordered his brother to leave the land of his birth and travel by sea to the Netherlands and reside with their aunt Margaret. This, of course, fulfilled the promise Charles had made to his Netherlands subjects before his departure (chapter 3); but its abrupt execution reflected fear. According to Charles's chronicler Alonso de Santa Cruz:

> While talking to members of the Cortes in Valladolid, Chièvres and the Grand Chancellor [Le Sauvage] learned ... that King Charles was hated by many and that his brother Ferdinand was loved by everyone ... They therefore recommended that Ferdinand should be sent away from the kingdom, so that if one day some Spanish vassals should rise up they could not choose Ferdinand as their leader. His Highness considered this a good idea.

Sancho Cota, still travelling with the royal party, recorded that the infante's sudden departure 'greatly affected every Spaniard, lords and commoners alike, because they all like Ferdinand very much'; while the French ambassador echoed that 'people here are not very happy about it'.[26]

Even the normally obsequious Laurent Vital noted the growing hostility. While in Valladolid, several clerics refused to lodge the king's entourage and excommunicated the royal officials charged with finding accommodation. Posters appeared on church doors expressing frustration that foreigners now ruled the kingdom, and just after the king left the city a friar delivered sermons that contained 'scandalous words' against the Netherlanders who had 'imprisoned' the new ruler and had overturned the laws of Castile by appointing foreigners to office. The king instructed the magistrates to arrest the offending friar 'and make his punishment exemplary, so that in future others would preach only the truth'. The dislike was mutual. According to Mártir, Charles's Netherlands advisers – many of whom had been forced to flee from Spain so ignominiously a decade before (chapter 1) – 'held the Spaniards in contempt, as if they had been born in the sewers'.[27]

Perhaps these observers exaggerated? According to Lord Berners, an English diplomat at Charles's court, writing in September 1518, 'all the matteres in Spaine be in good trayne' except for 'a lytle jelosy and mistruste betweene the Spanyards and Burgunyanes'; and he expected the king's dexterity in 'dayly tryumphes, fightynge at the barres, justes and juga de kanes [the cane game]' to win the hearts of all who watched him.[28]

Nevertheless, Berners grumbled, the Aragonese are 'the moste prowde obstinat people of the world' and although 'they have swoorne him their kinge, and they swoorne his subiects, they nether give him obedience nor money'. Two months later, another frustrated diplomat predicted that the Cortes of Aragon would be 'infynyte and, as I suppose, without ende (for all that the king in his owne person is thayre twyse or thryce a weke)'.[29]

These delays had deep roots. As Manuel Rivero Rodríguez has pointed out, after King Ferdinand's death:

> Aragon regarded Charles only as prince, and the authorities did not open his orders, edicts and warrants, but instead saved them until he had been accepted as king. His orders issued as king rather than as prince were returned ... Since the law of succession did not accept inheritance through a female line, they treated both the oath to Joanna and to Charles as provisional.[30]

As Charles travelled slowly towards the Aragonese frontier in March 1518, he ordered his uncle Alfonso to meet him and swear allegiance; but, bruised by his treatment over the see of Toledo, Alfonso failed to appear. The royal party waited impatiently for a week, until a letter arrived from the magistrates of Zaragoza stating that before they could take the oath to Charles, they must first swear one to Joanna – in person. Although the Cortes eventually accepted that this was impossible, and reluctantly agreed to accept Charles's oath to respect all the laws of the kingdom, they refused to call him 'king' during his mother's lifetime; and even when he overcame that objection, the Cortes demanded permission to recognize Infante Ferdinand as 'crown prince'. Fighting broke out in the streets of Zaragoza between Castilian and Aragonese courtiers, and although Charles managed to reconcile them, negotiations with the Cortes dragged on for the rest of the year.

The prolonged power struggle in Zaragoza allowed the diplomats accredited to Charles's court to evaluate for the first time how decisions were taken in the new Habsburg state. The Venetian ambassador Francesco Corner repeatedly asserted that Chièvres was 'another king' at Charles's court, while Mártir began to call him 'the Goat' (a pun on the French word *chèvre*: goat), and (shamelessly mixing metaphors) asserted that Chièvres was 'the chain that imprisons' Charles. The French ambassador echoed that 'few people are involved in directing the affairs of this young prince', adding that Chièvres's influence remained undiminished. He was right: late in 1518, Charles named Chièvres marquis of Aarschot, count of Beaumont and baron of Heverlee – an unmistakable sign of continuing favour.[31]

Many considered Grand Chancellor Le Sauvage to be as powerful as Chièvres, but he died in June 1518. Some expected Mercurino Arborio de Gattinara, who took over as Grand Chancellor four months later, to challenge Chièvres but instead he became the marquis's biggest booster. Born in Italy and a lawyer by training, Gattinara had served Maximilian as a diplomat, and Margaret of Austria as a confidential councillor. According to the English ambassador, when 'Maister Mercurius' arrived at Charles's court, he was 'a man of 60 yeres, of muche gravite, of good lernyng and good Laten'. A Venetian envoy went further: the new chancellor was 'prudent, very learned (they say), just, and he understands Latin, Spanish, French and German', as well as his native Italian, 'and everyone welcomes him because of his languages' – a veiled criticism of Charles's other largely monoglot advisers.[32] Gattinara had attracted some attention at court in December 1516 through a curious manuscript addressed 'To the divine Charles the Great, Catholic King' and entitled: 'A supplicatory oration, including a dream of the last world monarchy and the triumph of Christianity, broadly stated, with the means of accomplishing it'. Although written in Latin, and therefore beyond the recipient's comfort zone, Gattinara took the precaution of giving the treatise to his countryman Luigi Marliano, Charles's physician as well as his councillor, in the hope that it would reach 'the ears of a certain adolescent'. After many pages narrating a dream in which Charles appeared as the Messiah who would pacify Italy, reform the Church, unite Christendom and bring universal peace, Gattinara noted the superior resources available to Charles in both Europe and America, and compared them with those available to other Christian states, to suggest how the dream might become reality. Gattinara would devote the rest of his life to making it come true.[33]

A few Spaniards also joined the team advising Charles. Francisco de Los Cobos now drafted most letters of state about Castile (including those to the marquis of Denia about perpetuating the fictional world that surrounded Queen Joanna). Early in 1519, in preparation for a proposed face-to-face meeting with Francis I to discuss outstanding issues, Charles 'convened four or five of the foremost clerics of Castile and Aragon to debate his right to the kingdom of Naples' (they advised him to surrender nothing – advice that he would follow).[34] But almost all those in charge of making policy decisions shared the Burgundian values of Charles, Chièvres and Gattinara.

Eventually, Charles left Zaragoza and led his entourage towards Barcelona, where he hoped to persuade yet another assembly of restless subjects, the Catalans, to recognize his succession and to provide funds. By the time he arrived, he had lost two more members of his family: his sister Eleanor and his only surviving grandparent. In October 1518 he sent Eleanor, his constant companion since birth, to join her future husband King Manuel of Portugal. (As with the exile of young Ferdinand, her departure 'was badly received by the whole court and the whole kingdom'.)[35] Four months later, while approaching Barcelona, Charles learned of the death of Maximilian, an event that transformed both his personal situation and the balance of power in Europe.

'BUY YOURSELF AN EMPEROR'[36]

Maximilian had first contemplated securing the imperial crown for Charles in 1513. His relative and confidant, Count Palatine Frederick, later recalled the emperor's exact words:

> You see that I have expended my blood, my money and my youth for the Empire, and got nothing for it. If we turn our hand to it, I would like this young lord, my grandson Charles, to be elected emperor, because as you can see there is no one with the capacity or the power to uphold the reputation of the Empire except him. If the Electors are willing, I would like to lay down this office.

According to the constitution of the Empire, such a change required the positive votes of at least four of the seven princes known as Electors (*Kurfürsten*) – the archbishops of Mainz, Trier and Cologne; the Elector Palatine; the margrave of Brandenburg; the duke of Saxony; and the king of Bohemia – at a special meeting convened to choose a 'king of the Romans' on whom the pope would later confer the title 'Holy Roman Emperor'. Shortly after his conversation with Frederick, Maximilian met with four Electors (including the Elector Palatine, Frederick's older brother) to test the waters, but they flatly refused his offer: 'None of us want you to lay down your office'.[37]

The subject seems to have remained dormant for the next three years, but then it became a 'fierce and prolonged poker game', with immensely high stakes, whose outcome remained uncertain until the final vote. Serious play began in November 1516, when the Elector of Trier sent an envoy offering to vote for Francis I as the next king of the Romans, as soon as Maximilian abdicated or died. In June 1517 the Elector of Brandenburg followed suit, pledging his vote in return for a promise that his son would marry Princess Renée (formerly promised to Charles), plus 150,000 crowns in cash and a pension for himself. As Robert Knecht has noted, 'Francis failed to see that the German Electors were interested less in his success than in promoting a contested election' that would allow them to sell their votes to the highest bidder. 'That he should have allowed himself to be thus exploited says little for his political judgment.'[38]

Nevertheless, the threat of a French candidacy terrified the Habsburgs. Charles heard rumours while waiting in Zealand for a favourable wind for Spain, and claimed that 'ever since we took leave of the emperor our grand-father, and received his blessing':

> We have given much thought to the imperial succession, and several times we have discussed the matter with our principal and most trusted advisers who are informed on the subject. We have increasingly realized how important this is to us, and wondered how best we could place the kingdoms, dominions, lordships and subjects of the emperor and ourselves in Germany, Spain and Italy as well as here in the Netherlands in permanent safety, peace and repose, so that no one could harm them; and that if any ruler, however powerful, should try to oppress, attack or invade, we would be strong enough to resist.

By contrast, Charles opined, if another ruler became emperor it would cause 'trouble and division, and risk total ruin' for him. He therefore informed his grandfather that he stood ready to distribute up to 100,000 florins in cash to the Electors who voted for him, with annual pensions to follow, as well as elevation to the Order of the Golden Fleece and other material rewards. Three months later, Charles reminded Maximilian of the need to ensure 'that after your death the Empire should not fall into the hands of the king of France', because it would 'greatly harm the House of Habsburg'. He there-fore exhorted his grandfather 'to spare neither gifts nor promises of pensions, benefices, or anything else'.[39]

It was almost too late. In October 1517, while Charles shivered in the mountains of Asturias, the Elector of Mainz (brother of the Elector of Brandenburg) also sold his vote to France, and six months later the Elector Palatine followed suit, giving Francis the majority he needed to secure elec-tion. Now it was Maximilian's turn to highlight the urgent need to match this outlay, but his grandson protested petulantly that 'it should not be necessary to buy the Empire', because thanks to his Austrian roots 'the entire

German nation will be more favourable towards us than towards the king of France'. In April 1518, Chièvres, who now controlled the public finances of Spain as well as the Netherlands, grudgingly sent letters of credit to Germany equal to the 100,000 florins already promised, but warned that 'this is as much as His Majesty can reasonably manage at present', adding loftily: 'Sometimes one must be content with what is possible, and find ways of filling the gaps by other means.' Maximilian was impervious to such arguments. 'If you aspire to gain this crown,' he informed his grandson, 'you must not hold back any resource', and he supplied a long list of the 'resources' required, including not only money but also the marriage of Charles's sister Catalina to the young margrave of Brandenburg with a substantial dowry (to prevent him from marrying Renée of France). Above all, Charles must 'leave all the decisions to me' because 'you are too far away for us to be able to tell you everything and ask for what we need: by the time we get your answer, everything may have changed'.[40]

In case the seriousness of the situation still escaped his grandson, a week later Maximilian wrote a passive-aggressive letter (an epistolary technique that Charles would later perfect): unless his grandson paid everything demanded, and unless he delegated full powers, Maximilian warned that:

> We see no way of conducting this matter as the desire and honour of both of us requires; and if there is any fault or negligence, we will feel greatly displeased that we have gone to so much trouble and effort throughout our life to aggrandize and exalt our dynasty and our posterity, and yet by your negligence everything should collapse and jeopardize all our kingdoms, dominions and lordship, and thus our succession.

'Take this matter to heart for the good of our dynasty, as we are doing,' he chided Charles in a holograph postscript.[41] A few days later Jakob Villinger, Maximilian's treasurer, sent a similarly reproachful message to Chièvres. If Charles 'really wants the empire', Villinger insisted, then he must send another 100,000 florins to Germany immediately, with no restrictions on how Maximilian chose to spend them. 'You already know the importance of this business,' he continued relentlessly, 'but let me refresh your memory'. The election of Charles would allow the House of Habsburg:

> To subjugate our enemies and those who wish us ill, while the reverse would plunge us into total misery and confusion, which we would always bitterly regret. We need to remember that just a small confrontation or

conflict, wherever it may occur, will soon make us spend and dissipate just as much – if not more – than this business will cost us. In addition, as you know, winning the Empire will solve many of the problems that might otherwise befall us.

'Pay attention to what I have just said,' Villinger concluded rudely, 'otherwise we will be lost. Don't fall asleep on this! . . . Don't even think of delaying matters!'[42]

After this unaccustomed verbal spanking, Chièvres meekly endorsed the letter 'Received at Zaragoza the 10th of June' and started to raise more money for Germany. He also overcame his rivalry with Archduchess Margaret, recommending to Charles that she should be granted at least some of the powers removed at his emancipation. She now became 'superintendent of all our finances in the Netherlands'; received sole authority to sign all official documents in her nephew's name (which must be obeyed 'as if we had signed the said documents with our own hand'); and acquired extensive powers of patronage.[43]

Charles now affirmed that 'he wanted to become king of the Romans, whatever it cost, without sparing any expense'; and Maximilian, confident that his grandson would underwrite all the promises he might make, convened a full meeting of the imperial Diet in Augsburg in July 1518.[44] For the next three months the city became the centre of international attention. Albrecht Dürer, the most famous artist in Europe, came to paint members of the German elite; Martin Luther arrived to explain to a papal legate his criticisms of church practices; and five Electors eventually promised that they would vote for Charles as the new king of the Romans. In return, Maximilian promised the Electors (in Charles's name) 500,000 florins on election day, as well as more than 70,000 florins a year in pensions and sundry tapestries, gold, silver and other bribes. Yet Maximilian's scheme had a fatal flaw: although he was universally styled 'emperor', he had never secured a papal coronation and was therefore still king of the Romans. As a French ambassador noted with glee, 'there could be no election until he himself has been crowned' emperor. Although he and Charles now tried to persuade the pope to rectify this oversight by authorizing a coronation at Trent, on the border between Germany and Italy, it was too late. Maximilian died on 12 January 1519.[45]

'Matters over here are very different now', one of Charles's envoys in Germany observed gloomily just after Maximilian's death: the late monarch 'knew how to take decisions, and was both loved and feared', whereas

Charles 'is far away and is little known in Germany'. In addition, 'the French have said many malicious things about him'. They did not just spread rumours. As soon as he heard of Maximilian's death, King Francis instructed a special envoy to remind the Elector Palatine of the need to choose an emperor capable of protecting Germany against a possible Turkish attack, and to contrast 'the immaturity and poor health' of Charles with his own 'strength, wealth, love of arms, expertise and experience in war'. The envoy must also exploit 'the insult done to Frederick [the Elector's brother] by the Catholic King, who expelled and exiled him from his household and would not let him wed his sister [Eleanor], even though she very much wanted to marry him'. Francis also began to make military preparations because, as he reminded his agents in Germany, 'In times like these, if you really want something – be it the papacy, the empire or anything else – you can only get it by using bribes or force.' Shortly afterwards, the pope promised Francis his support in the forthcoming election.[46]

In mid-February 1519, Margaret and her council in the Netherlands reluctantly concluded that Francis would prevail and therefore proposed to Charles a radically different strategy: he should abandon his own attempt to become king of the Romans and instead secure the election of his brother Ferdinand, who was now in the Netherlands and could easily travel to Germany, where he could secure Habsburg control over the dynasty's hereditary lands as well as negotiating directly with the Electors. Moreover, Charles should nominate an acceptable German prince, such as Count Palatine Frederick, as a compromise candidate if the Electors refused to elect another Habsburg. Margaret and her advisers informed Charles that unless they heard from him on or before 13 March – a mere three weeks away – they would implement their plan.[47]

Dividing the unwieldy Austrian-Burgundian-Trastámara inheritance between Maximilian's two grandsons made good sense, and Charles would eventually acquiesce; but in 1519 the suggestion provoked a furious rebuttal and rebuke from the young ruler, conveyed to the Netherlands both by letters and by a special envoy. After reaffirming that 'we are absolutely committed to spare nothing and to do our all to secure our election, which is the thing we desire most in this world', Charles stressed that he was not only Maximilian's 'eldest grandson but also the one whom [Maximilian] had chosen' to succeed him. Withdrawing his candidacy now 'would forfeit not only the Empire but also our honour and the money we have already spent'. He further claimed that splitting the inheritance with his brother 'would make it easier to break apart our common strength and entirely destroy our dynasty', because without direct access to the resources of Spain and the Netherlands, Ferdinand would not be able to defend himself. Charles even speculated that those who had suggested the partition 'are the same people who tried in the past to create difficulties between the king of Aragon and my father [Philip], and later with me, and now feed continual disagreements and divisions between me and our brother'. Finally, since couriers seldom covered the distance between Spain and the Netherlands in less than two weeks, he found Margaret's threat to implement her initiative within three weeks utterly outrageous.[48] Charles also conveyed his discontent in other ways. Margaret informed one of those involved in the discussions that 'God knows, he is angry about what we advised him, judging by the private letters he has written to me' (apparently now lost); and Charles's holograph post-script to another letter to her included the threat: 'Do what I have just told you, because otherwise you will displease me.'[49] The king nevertheless recognized that he needed to reassure and placate his brother, and so he made two important concessions: once elected king of the Romans, he promised to cede at least some of the Austrian lands to Ferdinand; and 'once we are crowned emperor, we can easily and without danger get [Ferdinand] elected king of the Romans, so that the empire can stay for ever in our dynasty'.[50]

Margaret responded coolly to her nephew's angry reproaches: 'We see only two ways for you to succeed in this election. One is through money', because each Elector now demanded far more in return for his vote than Maximilian had offered at Augsburg. 'The second way, sire, is to use force', which meant mobilizing troops in the Netherlands and Spain to deter armed French intervention, as well as in Germany to overawe the Electors – which of course would also cost money. Either way, she continued, since in order to win 'you intend to spare nothing [did that formula contain a hint of sarcasm?] you must give discretion to your ambassadors to offer and to pay more than the sums already promised, depending on how they find the situation ... without the need to refer everything to Your Majesty, because the long wait for your response may cause harm'. Specifically, Margaret insisted that Charles must authorize Jakob Fugger of Augsburg, the richest banker in Europe, to guarantee all his commitments, since that alone would surpass 'the prodigality of the French in this matter, which is unbelievable'. When her nephew vainly protested 'that the horse he seeks to ride is very expensive', Margaret replied crushingly: 'We are well aware that the horse is expensive, but it is of such a sort that if you do not want it, another buyer stands ready'.[51]

His aunt's logic left Charles no alternative, and so in May 1519 he reluctantly authorized his confidant Henry of Nassau to make all the payments that Margaret deemed necessary to improve his chance of election, and he asked Fugger to guarantee them. In addition, he forbade all bankers in the Netherlands to provide credit or transfer money outside the country without Margaret's express consent for the next six months, and he began a charm offensive – laboriously copying friendly messages to each Elector in German, character by character, in his own hand (Pl. 10).[52] He also recognized the need to make peace with the Elector Palatine's brother. According to Louis Maroton, the agent in charge of the charm offensive, Frederick 'has heard that [Charles] is not happy with him because of the queen of Portugal [Eleanor] and he told me this: "If I thought the king was still angry with me, Monsieur Louis, I would take steps that are not to his advantage."' A month later, Frederick repeated the threat: although he assured Maroton that he would work to procure Charles's election, 'it was conditional on keeping the promises made to him; and he wanted a firm assurance of this, reminding me of the rough treatment [*rude traictement*] that he had received once before'. Frederick also wrote directly to Margaret, assuring her that he would do his best to secure Charles's election 'unless someone gives me occasion to reconsider', and he closed his holograph letter, surely not by accident, by asking her 'to take in good part *my irritating letter*' – the exact phrase with which he had ended his last love letter to Eleanor two years before. Charles swallowed his pride: he wrote 'two nice and gracious letters with my own hand' to assure Frederick of his affection, he reinstated the count's hefty pension, and he promised further rewards after the election.[53]

Charles also courted other important German supporters, including Jakob Fugger who not only cashed letters of credit in Charles's favour issued by other bankers, and loaned him almost 550,000 florins from his own funds, but also refused to honour letters of credit received from France. Fugger made no secret of his position. In February 1519 he wrote a holograph note to the Elector of Brandenburg announcing that letters of credit had just arrived from Charles, 'of which I have orders to pay Your Grace 100,000 florins', and he attached copies of letters from Spain describing the arrangements being made for the marriage of Charles's sister Catalina to the Elector's son.[54]

No doubt the substantial unpaid loans made by Fugger to Maximilian, which only the king of Spain could repay, contributed to the decision to throw his full weight behind his candidacy, but he also supported Charles because he feared what Francis I might do if elected. He was not alone. In March 1519 the Elector of Mainz begged his brother the Elector of Brandenburg 'to consider in this matter the honour of the Empire, of yourself, of our dynasty and of the entire German nation', because if the French won, 'they would try to put everything beneath their feet and make themselves lords and masters for ever'. A few days later a spokesman for the nobles of the Rhineland declared that 'we will give everything, up to the last drop of our blood, to prevent a French success'. Margaret did her best to fan these flames, telling her agent in Germany: 'I rejoice that you find the people there disaffected towards the French, and beg you to find all possible ways of turning them even more against them, whether through preachers, town magistrates, or otherwise.' And indeed many sermons and illustrated broadsheets demonized King Francis and portrayed the 'servitude' of his subjects in damning colours, while exalting the liberty enjoyed under the House of Austria.[55]

Nevertheless, greed had become the principal if not the only factor for many. As a French diplomat in Germany observed: 'Matters have reached the point where whichever of the two kings gives and promises more will carry the day.' The Elector of Mainz switched sides six times in the two years leading up to the election, each time in return for a promise of greater rewards.[56]

Such venal behaviour made Charles more philosophical. In May 1519 he advised Margaret that 'since the election date will soon be upon us, we need to resign ourselves to God and wait and see what he will decide, while nonetheless always persevering to do my best' – a reflection of the stoic values he had learned at her court in Mechelen. He also became more belligerent, hiring an army of mercenaries and directing them to camp close to Frankfurt, the city where the Electors would meet. The combination of stick and carrot eventually triumphed: on 28 June 1519 the seven Electors unanimously chose Charles as the next king of the Romans.[57]

PLANNING FOR EMPIRE

Was it worth it? Henry VIII's envoy in Germany calculated that Charles had paid, in all, 1.5 million florins in cash, including 500,000 to the Electors and their advisers in return for their votes (the Elector Palatine did best, receiving 147,000 florins, with an additional 37,108 to his brother Frederick), plus lavish pensions and gifts to follow; the imperial troops raised and deployed near Frankfurt cost more than 250,000 florins; and so on.[58] These were huge sums, and they formed just a beginning: his election forced Charles to spend heavily in Germany against both foreign invaders (the Turks and the French) and domestic enemies (the Lutheran states). Nevertheless, the election

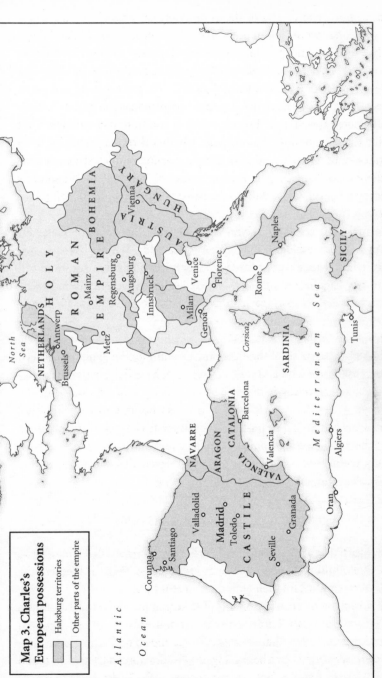

Map 3. Charles's European possessions

Habsburg territories

Other parts of the empire

Charles inherited the Habsburg lands in east-central Europe from his paternal grandfather, Maximilian, and the Netherlands and Franche-Comté from his paternal grandmother, Mary of Burgundy. He inherited Castile and its American possessions from his maternal grandmother, Isabella; and Navarre, Aragon and its Mediterranean outposts from his maternal grandfather, Ferdinand (although until her death in 1555 he nominally shared sovereignty in Castile and Aragon with his mother Joanna, confined in Tordesillas). He added the Holy Roman Empire in 1519 and Milan in 1535. In 1522 he ceded most of his eastern inheritance to his brother Ferdinand, who acquired Bohemia and much of Hungary in 1526. Between them, the brothers ruled almost one-half of Europe.

victory in 1519 proved an excellent investment. In the long term, it secured the imperial title for the House of Habsburg without interruption for four centuries; and even in the short term, Charles and many of his contemporaries felt that whatever the cost of winning, the cost of losing the election would be far higher. Just after Maximilian's death, the English ambassador Thomas Spinelly spelled out the escalation of potential disasters that would follow the election of another candidate: if Charles lost to Francis, he predicted, 'grete adversitie and domage shal unto hym ensue'. Specifically, the dukes of Bavaria would become hostile, given 'the ancient and late querrels they have with Austriche'; and the Swiss, the Venetians and 'al other his neighbors and borderers, by them selfs and by like instigacion, wil folowe sembable way, so that *oon losse shal lead [to] many others.*' Moreover, as emperor, Francis would not only retain his recent Italian conquests but might also in time acquire Naples, Austria and even the Netherlands, whereas Charles would never regain the Burgundian territories lost to France forty years before. In short, 'in this elecion consisteth his prosperitie and, for the defaulte of that, his [downfall]'.[59] The Grand Chancellor Mercurino Arborio de Gattinara agreed. According to his *Autobiography*, some ministers called on Charles to renounce the chance of gaining the imperial title. 'They complained that the election would bring more harm than good to Charles's kingdoms and lands in the future'; but the chancellor swiftly enlightened them:

> Under the shadow of the imperial title, not only could [Charles] serve his own hereditary lands and kingdoms, but he could also gain greater ones, enlarging the empire until it encompassed the monarchy of the whole world. However, if he rejected it, the empire might go to the French . . . [and then] Charles would not be able to maintain his hereditary lands in Austria and Burgundy, nor even the kingdoms of Spain itself.

'Charles heard this willingly', Gattinara continued, 'and the opinion of all his council having been changed, he settled the matter' by sending the funds required to secure his election (Map 3).[60]

The need to avoid such escalations of potential disasters would become a staple of Habsburg Grand Strategy. A second staple, also advanced in 1518–19 in favour of the imperial election, involved the issue of prestige – 'reputation' to use the contemporary term. Enforcement of claims and titles, however remote, formed the cornerstone of early modern international relations, and any ruler who did not press a claim, however tenuous, earned the contempt of contemporaries. The House of Habsburg had already held the imperial title for three generations: if Charles failed to retain it, he would imperil not only his own reputation but also that of his entire family. 'Take this matter to heart for the good of our dynasty, as we are doing,' Maximilian had once chided him, and Margaret agreed: the election of the king of France 'would be a permanent disgrace and reproach' to the entire Habsburg dynasty.[61]

The dramatic expansion of Charles's dominions affected the practice as well as the theory of his government. On the ceremonial level, when in March 1519 he presided over another chapter of the Order of the Golden Fleece, he conferred knighthoods on one Neapolitan, two Aragonese and eight Castilian nobles at a splendid ceremony in Barcelona cathedral. The Order had thus expanded its geographical reach in step with the dynasty. On the ministerial level, the 'fierce and prolonged poker game' to secure Germany forced officials and supporters in Charles's various dominions to work together as a single team. Foreign ambassadors in Spain noted (with a combination of envy and anxiety) the ease with which bankers anticipated the yield of Spanish taxes and transferred it to Augsburg, where an efficient team of ministers headed by Henry of Nassau and Jakob Villinger worked in unison to handle the distribution of funds and favours. Meanwhile the governors of the hereditary Austrian lands, although only just inherited by Charles, obeyed the orders of the absentee master they had never met 'to put everything to pledge' in order 'to accomplish his desire'; and in the Netherlands, Margaret of Austria sent letters of credit drawn on local revenues to Charles's agents in Germany, reminding them: 'Gentlemen, we know this is a large and substantial sum, but one must remember the quality and importance of the matter for which it will be used, and that if we fail for lack of money, we will suffer worse and much more harm.'[62]

Such integration transformed the transaction of business at Charles's court. Before the election, foreign ambassadors already complained about the delays in getting an audience and (even more) a decision. 'For the moste parte, what they saye shalbe done this daye is not done in 6 dayes following', an English envoy lamented from Zaragoza in 1518, while his French colleague added maliciously that 'if Barcelona and Valencia detain him as long as this town, he will be there for three years'. By February 1519, however, the same French ambassador noted that 'Not a day goes by without the arrival of a courier from Germany', and no doubt the volume of mail increased in the following months, because the historian Marino Sanuto recorded in his diary the arrival in his native Venice of almost 200 documents about the imperial election between February and July, more than one a day – and the letters received from Spain (he commented) 'speak of nothing but the Empire'.[63]

His election forced Charles to recognize that 'the great and continual tasks that face us and increase, as we try to bring order and transact the business of our kingdoms, dominions and subjects', required him to introduce major administrative changes. In particular, because 'for some time we will not be able to return to our Netherlands to deal with their affairs in person . . . by virtue of our personal knowledge, our own will, authority and power', he expanded Margaret's authority once again, naming her 'regent and governess' empowered to do everything 'as we ourselves do and cause to be done as long as we remain in Spain' with only a few restrictions, 'giving our word as a king to approve and maintain for ever whatever our noble aunt shall have done'. This would become the standard pattern of devolution for his empire.[64]

Six days after news of Charles's election arrived in Barcelona, Gattinara presented him with a blueprint for reforming the central government. After enjoining his master to give thanks to God, and to respect his mother, the pope and his confessor (in that order), Gattinara turned to the exiled Infante Ferdinand: 'you must honour whatever rights of succession, partition or appanages belong to him,' Gattinara stated, and also 'take him with you on your travels, and instruct him and employ him in major undertakings', because then 'you will be able to place more trust in him concerning major enterprises than in anyone else'. In addition, the chancellor warned, with 'so many and diverse kingdoms and provinces, and now the Empire, you may find a greater shortage of men than money'. Moreover, 'given the number of great matters with which you will have to deal, from the Empire as well as from your kingdoms and lordships in Spain, Austria, Flanders and Burgundy, it will not be possible for you to sign all dispatches with your own hand'; and so Charles should create a small council to travel with him at all times to give advice on issues that affected the entire monarchy, while delegating routine matters to the established local institutions in each dominion. The key was to distinguish 'matters that need speedy resolution' from those 'that can be considered and decided at leisure' – a permanent dilemma that would face both Charles and his successors. Gattinara offered a wealth of practical suggestions on how to separate them (for example: 'To speed up business and avoid keeping those who need a decision waiting, Your Majesty must listen to three or four items of business every morning as you arise and get dressed, because by doing so business will not build up as it does now').[65]

Such measures were doomed to fail because, as Karl Brandi observed, 'The unification of so many different states and people under one ruler inevitably produced almost insoluble problems.'[66] These manifested themselves almost at once in elementary administrative errors and oversights. For example, soon after Maximilian's death Charles signed a commission to the ministers trying to persuade the Electors to vote for him that omitted one name, that of the lord of Zevenbergen. The forgotten minister felt both frustrated and hurt, since he now lacked authority to act, and Margaret sought to comfort him by asserting that 'this does not stem from the king's displeasure, but from the fault, ignorance and stupidity of the secretary who drew up the documents.'[67] It nevertheless took Charles several weeks to rectify the error. Zevenbergen had already expressed resentment at the delays of 'the people in Spain' charged with executing policy decisions, asserting that 'if the king really cared about the affairs of the Empire, he would show greater diligence'; and another of Margaret's experienced advisers, Jean Marnix, complained that 'I find His Majesty's letters somewhat strange and ill-conceived'. Henry of Nassau was even more outspoken. When in March 1519 he received orders to raise troops in Germany to serve for only one month, he informed Margaret that this was a pointless exercise, since the election would not take place until June. He continued: 'I believe that their contracts should be made out for three months' – and coolly informed her that he had already begun to act accordingly. Perhaps anticipating a critical reply, Nassau added: 'Madame, you will issue the necessary orders as seems best to you, but if I were the king' – an unsubtle reminder that Charles called him 'my Henry' – 'I would not look at such matters too closely. The only things that might annoy His Majesty are negligence and deception.'[68] A successful outcome would excuse all deviations from the sovereign's commands.

Nassau was right. Charles managed to mobilize troops within Germany whereas Francis did not, and the Habsburg credit network delivered regular instalments of cash to the Electors whereas France's did not, thus fulfilling the sycophantic prophecy made by Erasmus in 1516:

You, noble prince Charles, are more blessed than Alexander [the Great], and will, we hope, surpass him equally in wisdom too. He for his part had seized an immense empire, but not without bloodshed, nor was it destined to endure. You were born to a splendid empire and destined to inherit one still greater, so that, while he had to expend great efforts on invasion, you will have perhaps to work to ensure that you can voluntarily hand over part of your dominions rather than seize more. You owe it to Heaven that your empire came to you without the shedding of blood, and no one suffered for it; your wisdom must now ensure that you preserve it without bloodshed and at peace.[69]

Charles had indeed succeeded spectacularly at the game of thrones, becoming king of Castile, Aragon, Naples and Sicily, and now king of the Romans – and all 'without bloodshed'. In late July 1519 letters arrived from Francis offering his congratulations, and the two monarchs renewed their promises to keep the peace. This meant, wrote Francesco Corner the Venetian ambassador, 'that all Christian princes have now sent their congratulations either to the king directly, or via their ambassador'.[70]

What next? As soon as certain news of the imperial election reached Barcelona, Corner realized that Charles needed to assemble a fleet large enough to transport him from Spain; yet although he 'has mortgaged all the revenues and the taxes voted by the Cortes of Castile' as well as 'spending the subsidies granted by these kingdoms' of Aragon, 'for six months the members of his court have not been paid'. To claim his new throne, Charles urgently needed to raise more money, and Corner wondered presciently how, where and when he would do so without provoking (as his English colleague John Stile had put it three years earlier) 'many enconvenyentys and trobyllys'.[71]

FIVE

FROM PEACE THROUGH REBELLION
TO WAR, 1519–21

THE RACE TO REACH ENGLAND

Charles's election as king of the Romans changed the European balance of power. Francis's victory at Marignano in 1515, followed by the occupation of Milan and Genoa, had made him the most powerful prince in Christendom – and also the most feared. One English diplomat claimed that 'The Frenche exaltacion is not to any cristen prince beneficial, because of their excessive ambicion and insaciable wil', while another asserted that the 'chief, principall and almost only cause' of all the troubles in Europe was 'the arrogant and supreme pryde and the insaciable appetite of the governaunce of the kingis of Ffraunce', who aspired to be 'the monarche of Christendom'. Now, in the words of a French diplomat, as 'emperor, [Charles] will think little of the other kings of Christendom because he considers himself the greatest'.[1]

Such fears were not unfounded. Some weeks before the election, one of Margaret's ministers in Germany predicted that although the Empire 'will prove an expensive commodity [*une chière merchandise*] for His Majesty', afterwards he 'can lay down the law to all of Christendom'. Grand Chancellor Gattinara agreed. As soon as news of the election arrived, he informed Charles and his council 'that the title of "empire" legitimizes the acquisition of the whole globe'. These sentiments duly appeared in Charles's acceptance speech to the German delegates who brought news of his election. He told them that after his initial delight, he worried that 'the distance that separated Germany from his kingdoms of Spain would prevent him from visiting Germany with the frequency that the Empire and his responsibilities might require'. Then, 'after thinking over and over again if he should accept or reject his election', he realized how the resources of 'the Empire were most valuable for the conservation of Austria' in case of a Turkish attack, and also of 'the Netherlands, which are adjacent to the Empire, and as a base from which to recover his duchy of Burgundy' – a clear challenge to Francis.

Finally, if he declined the honour, 'the king of France, would surely gain it' and would become intolerable.[2]

Such reasoning reflected the new political geography of Europe. A generation earlier, five major powers – England, France, Spain, Burgundy, and the Empire – had competed for the upper hand: now the same ruler controlled the last three. An English diplomat pointed out the consequences to his master with exemplary clarity: either Henry and Charles, 'which nature haath joynyd togedyr by blood, and alsoo the aunciente amyte that hath long contynuyd betwyne boothe youre howses', could become firm allies, and then 'withought fayle ye twayne shall sett all Crystendome in good ordyr and peace to the augmenttation of boothe your honours'; or else the 'thre yonge pwyssante prynces' – namely Henry (born 1491), Francis (born 1494) and Charles (born 1500) – would bicker, and then 'Crystendom shalbe drawin in pecis and maryed to warre infynyte, which weere to greett harme . . . and also greett blame to such as might have sett remedy in tyme.'[3]

For a while the 'thre yonge pwyssante prynces' recognized the dangers of 'warre infynyte' and upheld the peace treaties they had already signed. When, in September 1518, Charles heard of the death of the daughter of Francis to whom he was betrothed, he immediately sent condolences to his 'good father' and promised to marry her sister instead, as agreed in the treaty of Noyon (chapter 3). The following month, Henry's chief minister Cardinal Thomas Wolsey persuaded the representatives of Francis, Charles and many other Christian rulers to sign the treaty of London, which bound the signatories both to refrain from aggression against the others and to attack any state that broke the agreement. Nevertheless, distrust lurked close to the surface. When Francis suggested a personal meeting with Charles to settle all outstanding matters, Chièvres opposed the idea in 'remembrance howe the duk John of Burgoyne was handled' (a striking example of institutional memory, because Chièvres referred to the murder of Duke John the Fearless of Burgundy while conferring with a French prince one century before).[4] Instead, Chièvres, Gattinara and other senior ministers set out for the city of Montpellier to debate and resolve all differences with a French delegation led by Arthus Gouffier, Grand Master of France, preceptor and principal adviser of Francis. Since Gouffier had also led the French delegation that negotiated the treaty of Noyon, hopes were high; but his sudden death on 13 May 1519 halted all discussions.

Looking back, the perceptive French diplomat Guillaume du Bellay saw this as a fatal turning point: 'The death [of Gouffier] caused great wars, as you will learn, because if [he and Chièvres] had completed their talks, it is certain that Christendom would have remained at peace for the time being. Those who conducted public affairs afterwards did not care for the peace of Christendom as Chièvres and the Grand Master had done.' At least one of Francis's generals agreed. Since Chièvres and the Grand Master 'held all the affairs of their masters in their hands', wrote the lord of Florange, some 'two hundred thousand men, whom I am sure would have survived had he lived, perished after his death'.[5]

For some time Charles continued to appease Francis – in June 1519 he paid an instalment of the annual tribute required by the treaty of Noyon in respect of French claims to Naples; he and Francis exchanged holograph letters promising to keep the peace whichever of them gained the imperial crown – but Charles's election reduced his need to appease the French, even as it increased his need to appease the Germans.[6] The Electors, no doubt mindful of Charles's premature use of the title 'king of Spain', stipulated that he could not use the title 'king of the Romans' until he had been crowned, and that his coronation would take place only after he had sworn to honour the agreement (*Wahlcapitulation*) accepted in his name just after the election by the imperial commissioners in Frankfurt.

Did Charles realize the significance of the agreement? Admittedly, when he notified his Spanish subjects that a delegation from the Electors had arrived in Barcelona 'to request our departure, and to accompany us until we are in Germany', he acknowledged that they had also presented to him 'the decree of election in our favour, *together with the concessions required in return*' – but he provided no details on these concessions, perhaps because they were couched in ornate German, a language that 'he does not yet readily speak'.[7] Many of the agreement's clauses were routine (to respect the rights and privileges of the German princes, prelates and cities; to maintain justice; not to alienate any part of the Empire), while some reflected concerns about the potential consequences of electing a foreign ruler (Charles must employ only Germans in the imperial administration and issue all official documents in either German or Latin; he must not convene the Diet outside the borders of the Empire or arrive with foreign troops). By contrast, a few other clauses seemed likely to cause problems. Charles must swear never to involve the Empire in any alliance or conflict without the consent of the Electors, and never to allow any German ruler or subject to be summoned before a foreign jurisdiction. In addition, he must make Germany his habitual residence, and in his absence create a council of regency that included only Germans (some of whom must be Electors and princes); and he must swear to abolish everything the papacy had done contrary to the established practices of the German Church.[8]

The requirement that he travel immediately to Germany for his coronation presented Charles with a dilemma: he had promised to travel from Catalonia to Valencia to meet the Cortes of the kingdom and receive their oath of allegiance (and another subsidy). Chièvres argued that he should honour this promise, then sail from Spain to Italy and travel from there to Aachen to be crowned, even though it meant petitioning Francis for permission to pass through his new possessions, Genoa and Milan. Gattinara vigorously opposed this itinerary, largely because of a recent rapprochement between France and England. In October 1518, Francis had made three commitments to Henry: that his son and heir would marry Princess Mary Tudor when he turned fourteen; that Henry would immediately restore Tournai to French control; and that the two sovereigns would meet in person to resolve all outstanding issues. Initially, these agreements did not cause alarm among Charles's ministers – although Tournai soon changed hands, the betrothed children were both infants, and neither monarch announced plans to meet – but this changed early in 1520, when Francis suggested to Cardinal Wolsey that the two royal families should take part in a spectacular 'feat of arms' near Calais the following May.[9]

Gattinara now urged Charles to retrace his steps through Aragon and Castile to the port of Corunna in Galicia, where he would board a fleet and 'intercept the English king before he met with the French king . . . and if possible, prevent their meeting'. He would then travel through the Netherlands for his coronation in Aachen. Gattinara's plan required asking the Cortes of Castile to vote new taxes to pay for the fleet – a high-risk option given the existing tensions in the kingdom – but on 22 January 1520, Charles announced that instead of going to Valencia he would travel to Galicia, and thence by sea to the Netherlands and Germany. He left Barcelona the following day.[10]

Peter Mártir de Anglería, awaiting his master in Valladolid, warned Gattinara (to whom, as his compatriot, he wrote candidly):

It is said that upon the advice of the Goat [Chièvres] and the Spaniards who are with His Majesty, Castile will be asked for two things: first, that the Cortes assemble in Santiago de Compostela with the requirement that procurators for the cities with voting rights in the Cortes come with instructions to obey all the king's orders. It is whispered that these conditions will destroy liberty, and that such laws are imposed only on slaves bought in a public market. I see many who are inclined to refuse. The second request consists of a demand for a new tax, which Spaniards call a *servicio*, even though the previous one has not yet been collected. I see that the two requests have not been well received.

On 4 March 1520, as Charles attempted to leave Valladolid after a brief stay, alarm bells rang out and crowds ran to the gate through which they expected Charles to leave, planning to remonstrate with him. Although he got out first, the angry citizens 'began to rail against those who had voted the taxes' in the last Cortes.[11]

Charles ignored these dangerous developments, instead spending four days at Tordesillas with his mother and his sister Catalina on his way to Santiago, where (as usual) he 'spent Holy Week at his devotions in a local monastery'. He opened the Cortes on 31 March with a demand for another large *servicio* to pay for his journey to Germany.[12] According to Gattinara, Charles's council divided over this: 'Chièvres wanted to require a new *servicio* from them. Mercurino opposed it. He pointed out that the *servicio* from two years ago had not yet been collected, thus it did not make sense to require a new one. He predicted that doing so would provoke a popular rebellion.' Adrian of Utrecht shared the chancellor's fears, later reminding Charles that 'When we were in Santiago, I told Your Highness that you had lost the love of all these subjects, but you did not believe me.'[13] Instead Pedro Ruiz de la Mota, once a *Felipista* exile at Charles's court, gave an eloquent address 'by royal command' to the Cortes, announcing that:

> The glory of Spain, dormant for many years, has now returned. Those who have sung its praises say that whereas other nations sent tribute to Rome, Spain sent emperors [Trajan, Hadrian, Theodosius]. And now the Empire has come to Spain in search of an emperor, and our king of Spain, by the grace of God, has been made king of the Romans and emperor of the world.

The bishop reminded the procurators that 'Just as retaining what you have won is no less worthy than winning it in the first place, so failing to follow up a victory is no less unworthy than being defeated'; and he reassured them in Charles's name that 'with God's help he will return within three years – at most – of his departure'. He also promised that in future 'no office in these kingdoms will be given to a person who is not a native'. 'Immediately after the said address', the official record of the assembly continued, 'His Majesty himself gave to the procurators assembled in the Cortes' solemn confirmation of the promises Mota had just made.[14]

The speech soon achieved wider circulation in published form. Gattinara oversaw its metamorphosis into a Latin tract entitled *The Address of Charles, king of the Romans, in the Spanish Cortes, immediately before his departure*, in which Charles boasted that:

Anyone who believes that the empire of the entire world falls to anyone by [virtue of] men or riches, or through unlawful solicitation or stratagem, is wrong. Empire comes from God alone. I have not sought this responsibility of such extent for myself, because I would indeed have been content with the Spanish empire [*Hispano imperio*], with the Balearics and Sardinia, with the Sicilian kingdom, with great parts of Italy, Germany and France, and with another, as I might say, gold-bearing world [*pene alio aurifero orbe:* America].

But, Charles added, a 'fatal necessity' compelled him to accept:

[The] decision must also be taken out of proper respect for religion, whose enemy [the Turks] has expanded so much that neither the repose of Christendom, nor the dignity of Spain, nor finally the welfare of my kingdoms are able to withstand such a threat. All these are hardly able to exist or be maintained unless I link Spain with Germany and add the title of emperor to king of Spain.

To achieve all this, he needed just 500,000 ducats.[15]

It was fine rhetoric but, as Juan Manuel Carretero Zamora has noted, to many in the audience it seemed that 'the new crown that had descended on the head of Castile was actually a crown of thorns'. Unlike the representative assemblies of the Netherlands, Germany, and even Aragon, the Cortes of Castile – now by far Charles's richest possession – 'scarcely possessed any "constitutional" means of defence (whether institutional, democratic or fiscal) against a young monarch who viewed his new kingdom as the goose that lays golden eggs'. Several urban delegations refused to cooperate. Toledo sent no procurators at all: instead, two prominent citizens presented 'a petition that the laws of the kingdom should not be broken in such a blatant way' – but (according to Mártir) Charles 'listened to them in a very disagreeable way'.[16] Then, desperate to see Henry before he met Francis, he ordered the vexed procurators to follow him from Santiago to Corunna, where his fleet awaited. He also announced that he had chosen Adrian of Utrecht to serve as 'administrator and governor' of Castile, the Canary Islands and the Americas in his absence. He justified this decision by invoking 'our own initiative, reasoned consideration and absolute royal power, which we wish to use and do use as a king and lord who recognizes no earthly superior' – no doubt because the appointment broke the solemn oath he had recently given to the Cortes that 'no office in these kingdoms will be given to a person who is not a native'.[17] Almost immediately, a group of Castilian noblemen angrily 'reminded him that, according to the laws of Castile, when the king was a minor [*pupilo*], it was necessary to entrust the government to someone from Spain, not a foreigner', but the king snapped back that 'he was not a minor, and this is what he wanted to do' (the first recorded example of Charles speaking out for himself).[18] Although a combination of bribes and concessions persuaded the procurators isolated in Corunna to vote the *servicio*, some cities refused to contribute, on the grounds that 'it is not just that his imperial majesty should spend the revenues of this kingdom in his other dominions'. They also complained that Charles had accepted his imperial election 'without asking the advice or consent of these kingdoms'.[19] In April and May 1520, rioting in several cities of Castile forced royal officials to flee, giving way to communal governments (hence the name *Comunero*); but even though he spent six weeks waiting for a favourable wind in Galicia (almost as long as he had waited in Zealand three years before), Charles paid little attention to these developments. Instead, he and his ministers concentrated on the affairs of northern Europe.

The fleet finally set sail on 20 May, and after a voyage of only seven days it dropped anchor in Dover where Wolsey welcomed Charles ashore, and after supper led the way to the bedchamber prepared for him in the castle. When Henry heard the news, he impetuously mounted his horse, rode to the castle and entered 'the chamber where his imperial majesty was sleeping, and there they embraced and exchanged other demonstrations of mutual affection'. The next morning Charles met for the first time his aunt Katherine of Aragon, as well as Henry's sister Mary, the former 'princess of Castile'. The royal party dined and danced, interspersing the festivities with serious policy discussions that laid the basis for a closer alliance, and after three days, Charles re-embarked and sailed to the Netherlands.[20]

Henry, by contrast, left for Calais to meet Francis at the Field of the Cloth of Gold, a lavish event that lasted for almost three weeks, with many jousts and banquets. But it was not a success – in part because during an impromptu wrestling match, Francis humiliated Henry by hurling him to the floor; in part because Chièvres and Wolsey had secretly arranged for their masters to meet again immediately afterwards to continue their political 'conversation' (the word used by a Venetian diplomat: *abochamento*). On 14 July 1520, near Calais, Henry and Charles rode off alone and for a long time 'talked face-to-face, with the king of England speaking almost in the ear of the emperor'. Then 'they embraced very affectionately, their hats in their hands', and parted.[21]

The two monarchs had every reason to be both secretive and affectionate: they had just agreed to maintain a resident ambassador at the other's court; to hold another conference within two years to discuss their foreign policies, and until then to conclude no further alliance with France; and above all 'to succour the other if his dominions are invaded by an enemy'. Henry had become the arbiter of international affairs; Charles had gained the advantage over his principal adversary in northern Europe.[22]

SPAIN IN FLAMES

Charles's position in southern Europe, by contrast, had become perilous. Although his visit to Spain had lasted only thirty months, two major revolts broke out before he left: one in Valencia, known as the *Germanías*, and the other in Castile, known as the *Comunidades* or *Comuneros*. Lesser rebellions also broke out in Mallorca and Sicily. How did a sovereign whose presence had been so eagerly awaited in 1517 manage to alienate so many of his subjects so fast?

Probably no ruler could have satisfied all the expectations and tensions that faced Charles in Spain in 1517. First, bitter rivalries divided his councillors. Many Burgundian servants of his father Philip, forced to flee Spain ignominiously and impoverished after his sudden death (chapter 1), longed to seek their revenge and recoup their losses. The *Felipistas*, Spaniards who had remained loyal to King Philip and his heir, such as Juan de Zúñiga and Pedro Ruiz de la Mota, also longed for revenge on those who had stayed on to serve Ferdinand of Aragon, and they bitterly resented the favour shown by Charles after 1516 to *Fernandinos* like Los Cobos, who arrived in Brussels flaunting their wealth and experience after ten years in office. Furthermore, within Castile, several groups possessed incompatible aspirations. The city of Burgos, for example, enjoyed close and cordial relations with the Netherlands, and its merchants grew rich from exporting the wool produced by Castilian sheep to the clothiers of Flanders. The merchants bitterly resented a law of 1462 that required one-third of all wool sheared to be retained in Castile and sold to local clothiers. By contrast the clothiers, with their headquarters in Segovia, also resented the law, protesting that retaining one-third was not enough to secure their livelihood. No ruler could have pleased both Burgos and Segovia. Many other irreconcilable rivalries divided Charles's Castilian subjects, exacerbated by scarce harvests and a severe plague epidemic between 1517 and 1519.

Further east, in the kingdom of Valencia, torrential rains and floods that reduced harvest yields, followed by a plague epidemic, also exacerbated existing domestic rivalries. Above all, the urban guilds complained about the 'tyranny' of their magistrates 'some of whom are so exalted that they treat us like their prisoners'. In addition, the kingdom suffered frequent raids by Muslim corsairs, which meant that the guildsmen of all major towns needed to bear arms. This menace came to Charles's attention in May 1519, soon after he reached Barcelona, when a galley squadron from north Africa 'crossed in plain sight of His Majesty and his court', heading south. It was the new ruler's first direct contact with the military and naval might of Islam, and he ordered the militia of Valencia to mobilize. When the orders arrived, however, 'there were no gentlemen left in the city [of Valencia]: they had all left because of the plague', and so 'the common people took control of the city' and started to prepare for war. According to the detailed chronicle of the Germanías compiled by Martí de Viciana, an eyewitness, the guild leaders immediately saw a chance to 'free the population of Valencia from their servitude' because 'right now we have a new boy king who is governed by his ministers; and because his administration is new he will hear everyone, in order to learn what injustices are being committed and who are the victims, so that he might remedy matters for his vassals'.[23] Although the guildsmen were correct that the 'boy king' was 'governed by his ministers', they did not yet realize that those ministers were foreigners who would ignore their advice. They discovered their error in May 1520, when Charles appointed as his viceroy a Castilian nobleman (not a Valencian as local custom required). Citizens now rampaged through the streets shouting 'Long live the king! Death to the viceroy!' but Charles reacted by issuing contradictory orders to various protagonists. The revolt therefore spread.[24]

The first historians of the Comuneros of Castile also saw Charles's reliance on foreign advisers as a critical precipitant. Juan de Maldonado, writing in 1545, blamed the revolt above all on the fact that 'most of the grandees were very offended that after the king arrived in Spain he had scarcely informed them of important matters, and had not asked for their advice; and when he was preparing to leave he had not entrusted any part of the administration to them'. Three years later, Pedro Mexía asserted that the elite 'complained that the king seemed distant and aloof and it was not as easy to communicate with him as they would have wished'; and according to Alonso de Santa Cruz, in 1552, Chièvres 'managed to keep the king so withdrawn that few people could speak with him, so the Spaniards hated him and thought he was distant and poorly educated . . . In short, everyone hated the king.'[25]

Although all three historians had lived through the trauma of the Comunero revolt, none of them had participated directly: their accounts of Charles's responsibility, and of his reactions, were therefore second-hand. Nevertheless, many protagonists felt the same, including Adrian of Utrecht, who while Governor of Castile filled over one hundred letters to his master with complaints.[26] 'They say here that the Netherlanders have not left anything that they could take with them,' he informed Charles in June 1520, adding a few months later that everyone in Spain believed that 'Your Highness pays no attention to the matters of these kingdoms and that everything is handled by others, as if Your Highness were a child without reason, prudence, or concern.' In January 1521, he warned: 'Believe me, Your Majesty, if you do not start being more attentive in understanding matters, and cease delegating to others, Spain will never truly love you or obey your royal person and authority as it should.'[27]

Adrian articulated two other major complaints. He repeatedly criticized his master's silence. 'I am amazed that Your Majesty has not replied regarding what I wrote about these uprisings, and the delay in your letters is very dangerous,' Adrian wrote in June 1520; six months later he claimed that 'the whole world is shocked and amazed' that Charles had not yet answered any of his nine previous letters; and in January 1521 he protested that he had received no communication from the king for ten weeks. It is surely significant that scarcely any of the 105 original letters sent by Adrian to Charles during the Comunero crisis contain annotations or comments by the recipient and his advisers.[28] Adrian also rebuked his former pupil for failing to keep his promises: 'They say here that "The king makes promises but does not deliver."' In future, he chided, 'although it might later have negative consequences, for the sake of Your Majesty's honour and conscience you should keep the promises that you made to your subjects in the Cortes.'[29]

Above all, Adrian urged the king to return to Spain immediately. In April 1521 he informed Charles presciently that 'the resources of Spain can always be used to sustain the Netherlands and Germany, but their resources cannot sustain Spain'. Three months later he issued an extraordinary ultimatum:

Everything has become greatly confused and is on the road to total and irreparable loss, and for that reason some of the leading noblemen find themselves very perplexed. I must therefore tell Your Highness that *if you have not come here by the month of May they are determined to join with the Comuneros and protect their estates, and will leave Your Majesty to fend for himself.*[30]

As it happened, on 23 April 1521, three weeks after Adrian sent this threat to his former pupil, troops raised by the leading noblemen of Castile cornered many of the Comunero leaders and their followers near the small town of Villalar, near Tordesillas. A few hundred rebel soldiers fell in the brief battle that followed and hundreds more fell prisoner, including several leaders whom the victors executed the following morning. In the lapidary phrase of Joseph Pérez, 'And that put an end to the Comunero rebellion': by May 1521, only Toledo continued its defiance.[31] Soon afterwards, in Valencia, troops raised and led by noblemen defeated the forces of the Germanías and regained control of the capital.

CHARLES AND THE COMUNEROS

What part had Charles played in this dramatic reversal of fortune? Not much. The first news that 'in Spayn hade begynned some conmocyon' reached the king and his entourage in Brussels on 19 June 1520, two months after the revolt began, but since it came from 'the relacyon of strangers' they 'gave not trust' until letters from royal ministers arrived one week later, describing disorders in no fewer than seventeen towns of Castile. Charles failed to grasp the seriousness of the situation because (in the words of the English ambassador, Thomas Spinelly) 'for all theyr insurrectyons', the rebels 'suffer the kyngs revennuys to be contynwed and payed to the accustomed receyweurs withoute any contradyctyon'. Moreover, 'tyll now, noe grett lord or noblemann appyre to be adherent to such besynesse by any oppen demonstracyon' – and Spinelly predicted that this was unlikely to change because of the 'anchyens devysions, emnityes and envys that ben betwixt the lords of Spayn, in so moche that onne may not trust to the other. The whyche reason makes me belyve th'emperors absence may cause some perturbacyon, but not materre of moment.' Finally, Spinelly noted that all of the rebels' demands seemed to him 'yuste and reasonable': that the cities should administer their own sales tax revenues directly; that no foreigners should be appointed to secular or ecclesiastical offices in Castile; that no more gold or silver should be exported; and that the royal law courts should hear and decide all cases expeditiously. Adrian, too, recommended compromise, because 'at this point it is necessary to treat the towns and their citizens almost as if they were raw eggs that might crack unless they are handled with care'. He also warned (deftly switching metaphors) that 'things are balanced on a knife's edge, so the slightest movement puts everything at risk'. Since at this early stage Charles could have redressed grievances 'with honour and without losing reputation abroad', both Adrian and Spinelly were stunned when 'th'emperor wold not consent' to any concessions.[32]

Such inflexibility had important consequences, because Charles had withheld some crucial powers when he appointed Adrian as governor of Castile. Above all, only the king could grant pardons – a fatal limitation when in June a leading Comunero in Toledo offered to abandon the rebel cause in return for a pardon: Adrian did not receive permission to grant amnesties until it was too late.[33] Moreover, although Adrian advocated leniency, the president of the royal council, Antonio de Rojas, did not.

In practically his last message, Cisneros had warned Charles that Rojas 'is a wicked and evil-intentioned man who favours creating divisions' – but the cardinal's death meant that no one paid attention. The Constable of Castile, the senior nobleman of the kingdom, now made much the same point in a letter: 'The president of the royal council is very angry with me because I maintain that the kingdom will calm down if there are pardons and mild punishments. But he favours scorched earth and cutting people's throats, so the problems we face now are greater than those in the past, and those that lie ahead will be even greater.'[34] Charles ignored the Constable, just as he had ignored Cisneros, perhaps because for a time the harsh methods pursued by Rojas and the council seemed to succeed. On 6 July 1520, Spinelly reported that 'from Spayn th'emperor hathe good neweys and heres the conmocyons were ceased', followed three weeks later by assurances that there was no 'oppen demonstration of no lord or principall persons'. Instead 'the commoners . . . saythe they wol be trwe and obbediant to th'emperor in all thyngs except in suffryng monney go oute of the royalme, and [appointing] strangers to offices'.[35] Although the Comunero leaders created a central committee (the *Junta*) to coordinate activities, initially only four cities sent a formal delegation.

Everything changed in August. Adrian had sent troops to collect the royal artillery stored in Medina del Campo, intending to use it against rebel strongholds, but when his soldiers met with resistance they started a fire that destroyed a good part of the city. The burning of Medina gave the

Comunero cause a powerful recruiting tool: ten more towns sent delegates to the Junta, which moved to Tordesillas in the hope of persuading Queen Joanna to assume power and authorize their defiance of her son. Their cause also gained the open support of a 'principall person': Antonio de Acuña, bishop of Zamora.

News of these developments stunned the court in Brussels. On 6 September, according to Spinelly, Charles and his council debated two 'opinions' for dealing with what he coyly termed 'the inconvenience' in Castile. One group of ministers argued that Charles must proceed to Aachen as planned for his coronation as king of the Romans, and afterwards continue 'his iourney into Almayne [Germany], and with all diligence and good advise appease the differences betwene the lordes and the cities emperialle', and then 'with as greate power as he may, passe into Italy'. Only after that should he sail back to pacify Spain. The rest of the council vehemently disagreed, arguing that:

> The longer he tarieth to retorne into Spayne, the worse, for because the subgetts ther takith daily more courage, and considered howe swete is the libertie, and to lyve uppon other men's costs, *et quod nervus belli est pecunia* [and because money is the sinews of war], whereof withoute Spayne he cannot conveniently have; concluding therefore the most wisest deliberation were to receive the corone at Acon [Aachen], make a vicary [regency] in the Empire, and come hither agayne for to prepare an armie against the beginning of Merche [1521].

The 'armie' should be of 'sufficient nombre to reforme the contrey [Spain] and putt it in a perpetuall suertie'. Only after that might Charles 'goo to Rome' to be crowned.[36]

The emperor chose the second 'opinion', and announced several concessions: he named two Castilian noblemen as co-governors with Adrian; he agreed to forego the *servicio* voted at Corunna; and he granted the cities the right to collect their own sales tax. It was too little and too late. Before long, the Junta of Tordesillas started to act as if it possessed executive authority and (as Charles petulantly complained) 'they wrote to some cities in our Netherlands encouraging them to rebel as they had done'. Meanwhile Margaret and Chièvres argued openly 'in the king's presence' who was to blame, 'the oone laying charge to the other for the negligens'.[37]

Still Charles seemed incapable of grasping the true grievances of the Comuneros. When Cardinal Croÿ died in January 1521, leaving vacant the see of Toledo, the emperor proposed to transfer it to another of Chièvres's nephews – despite a lecture from one of his Spanish subjects that 'shewed that the first grudge and miscon[tentment] of all the realme beganne of the said Archbishop . . . and what g[reat in]convenient shulde at this time ensue if his mag[estie] wole geve it againe to the lord Chievres, saing that not oonneli [his] subjects shal be ofended, but also God, for the unhabilite and young eage of his other neveu'. Only Bishop Acuña's seizure of the assets of the archdiocese of Toledo prevented Charles from repeating his catastrophic error.[38]

Neither the *Memoirs* of the emperor nor the *Autobiography* of Gattinara shed light on why Charles and his ministers took so long to react, but a letter written in October 1520 by Luigi Marliano, not only the emperor's personal physician but also his intimate councillor ('nearly half Caesar's soul' as a contemporary remarked) reflects the prevailing opinion at court.[39] 'I have received many letters from you regarding this disturbance,' Marliano wrote to his cousin and compatriot Peter Mártir, and some blamed Charles. Specifically, many complained that Charles had failed to consult his Spanish subjects about policy, but Marliano pointed out that 'kings have no obligation to explain their decisions to the people'. In any case, 'not only the reason but the necessity for these matters is so obvious': namely 'the importance of acquiring the empire of the world, which he could not allow to pass to others, or lose by doing nothing'. As for the Comuneros' protests about 'money leaving the kingdom', Marliano claimed that practically no money remained to export after liquidating the debts of the Catholic Monarchs, paying for one sibling (Ferdinand) to sail to Flanders and another (Eleanor) to go to Portugal, funding a campaign in Africa, and dispatching 'two fleets to the New World, about whose admirable discovery you have yourself written' (a clever barb). Above all, Marliano asserted, 'neither the emperor nor his officials behaved arrogantly in Spain'.[40]

Mártir composed a devastating response. First he dismissed all Marliano's specific pleading with the lapidary phrase 'None of this caused the rebellion'; and he ridiculed the claim that 'neither the emperor nor his officials behaved arrogantly in Spain'. On the contrary:

Your expression, 'arrogantly' is not accurate, because it was not 'arrogantly' but rather 'with the highest degree of arrogance' that you people treated the Spaniards. We can clear the emperor himself of responsibility, because he was still a boy; but what could be more arrogant than calmly to allow Spaniards to be treated with the greatest rigour for the slightest offence toward a Netherlander while no judge dared to arrest a single Netherlander at court even if he had committed an atrocious act of injustice toward a Spaniard?

Mártir knew exactly who to blame: 'The Goat [Chièvres] and his entourage planted these seeds in the mind of the unfortunate king', of which the most destructive seed was 'when the Goat, violating the laws of the land, took for himself the archbishopric of Toledo as soon as he entered Spain, provoking hatred throughout the kingdom'. Barely able to control his indignation, Mártir concluded that 'Because of his poor education, the emperor does not pay the slightest attention to these kingdoms and his courtiers have even convinced him – in order to deceive him further – to feel hatred towards the Spaniards. These, then, my dear Marliano, are the thorns that have been sown to ruin the imperial harvest.'[41]

By then, the tide had turned against the Comuneros – but for reasons totally unconnected with Charles and his courtiers. In September 1520 peasants in several parts of Castile began to attack their lords, destroying their property, and for a while they enjoyed the support of the Junta. This led many nobles to overcome their anger against Charles, and throw their support behind his governors. In addition, Manuel of Portugal (Charles's brother-in-law) sent 50,000 ducats to Adrian, which encouraged some bankers to do the same, allowing the regents to raise the troops who routed the Comuneros at Villalar.[42] Charles therefore decided to remain in northern Europe and deal with Germany, where he issued an edict (once again invoking 'our absolute royal power, which we wish to use and do use') that authorized his governors to arrest and try those who normally enjoyed protection under the laws of Castile – even bishops and nobles – if they were guilty of 'the crime of treason against their king and natural lord'. The governors duly condemned as traitors almost 250 persons, including Bishop Acuña and some noblemen.[43]

KING OF THE ROMANS AND EMPEROR-ELECT

On 22 October 1520, Charles made his ceremonial entry into Aachen. After venerating the golden reliquary that contained the skull of his namesake and role model, Charlemagne (retrospectively called 'Charles I'), he entered the cathedral and 'prostrated himself on the ground with his arms outstretched'. Then he retired to the sacristy to venerate some more relics and swear to observe the Election Agreement 'that our commissioners in

Frankfurt had accepted' the previous year. The following morning Charles returned to the cathedral wearing the insignia of an archduke of Austria (a deliberate decision, because 'although the insignia of the king of Spain might be more exalted', he preferred something that asserted 'that someone from here, not a foreigner, had been elected'). Watched by a huge crowd, he prostrated himself again and then swore to protect the Church, defend the empire 'and do many other things that would benefit the said empire', after which the crowd acclaimed him as their ruler. Charles was then anointed and invested with the imperial sword, sceptre, orb and crown and then, seated upon Charlemagne's throne, he dubbed some knights (starting with Chièvres) as a token of his new power. The spectacle left Germany's foremost artist, Albrecht Dürer, almost at a loss for words: 'I saw all manner of lordly splendour, more magnificent than anything that those who live in our parts have ever seen', he wrote in his diary.[44]

The ceremony ended with a proclamation that 'the pope, having approved the election of Charles the Fifth, orders that henceforth he must take the title of "emperor"'. In addition, at Gattinara's suggestion, Charles adopted the style that he would use for the rest of his reign: *Sacred, Imperial, Catholic, Royal Majesty*. Next, after consulting the Electors, Charles signed a summons for all members of the imperial Diet to meet him in the city of Worms the following January. 'This was the first time I entered Germany and travelled up the Rhine', he later recorded in his *Memoirs*, adding laconically: 'At this time the heresy of Luther began to spread in Germany.'[45]

In November 1519 the theology faculty of Leuven university issued a formal condemnation of the writings of 'a certain Martin Luther', an Augustinian friar who taught at the university of Wittenberg in Saxony, and they sent a copy of their decree, together with some of his publications to their former colleague Adrian of Utrecht, now inquisitor-general of Spain. Adrian perused the material and found it contained several 'palpable heresies': he therefore called for the works to be burnt and their author forced to answer for his heretical opinions.[46] Since Adrian and Charles both resided in Catalonia at this point, they may have discussed Luther and his works; but if so, no trace seems to have survived. Charles's first encounter with the reformer's name might therefore have been in a letter written on 12 May 1520 by his ambassador in Rome, Juan Manuel. He reported that Luther 'is said here to be a great scholar, and he has thoroughly alarmed the pope', so that 'if the pope refused to make an alliance, or if having made one he reneges on it', then Charles 'could secretly show some favour to this friar called Martin'.[47]

The following month Pope Leo condemned Luther's opinions and ordered his works to be burnt in a bull commonly known by its first two words, *Exsurge, domine* ('Rise up, O Lord'). The 'friar called Martin' had already published several polemics in Latin criticizing the doctrines and practices of the papacy, notably indulgences, but in August 1520 he published an influential tract in German entitled: *Address to the Christian nobility of the German Nation respecting the Reformation of the Christian Estate*, which rejoiced that 'God has given us a young leader of noble blood' – Charles – and called on him to take measures 'starting on the day after his coronation' to restore the purity of Christ's teaching, even if it meant criticizing the pope.[48] Two months later Luther published an even more combative work entitled *The Babylonian captivity of the Church*: an exegesis of the sacraments that incorporated an angry attack on the pope, accused of being the Antichrist. Shortly afterwards Pope Leo's special envoy, Girolamo Aleandro, presented Charles with a copy of *Exsurge, domine* and exhorted him to burn Luther's writings and either to make their author recant publicly or send him to Rome to explain himself.

At first Charles hesitated. He had, after all, approved in March 1518 an ordinance that banned throughout the Netherlands 'until we decree otherwise' all 'pardons and indulgences brought, or that may be brought, from outside our dominions' – precisely what Luther's Ninety-Five Theses had called for; and when Charles returned to his homeland in June 1520, according to an eyewitness 'His Majesty's court was full' of Luther's writings, because 'while Luther confined himself to the reform of the Church and made statements about moral corruption . . . no one took exception to what he wrote'.[49] Nevertheless, while Charles resided in the university town of Leuven on 8 October 1520, in accordance with *Exsurge, domine* the authorities threw works by Luther onto a public bonfire, and although no order by Charles for this action has yet come to light, it can only have taken place with his knowledge and approval.

Exsurge, domine was a flawed document. It detailed forty-one errors in Luther's published work, and yet (as Hans Hillerbrand, an eminent historian of the Reformation, observed) 'at one point it seemingly condemned all of Luther's writings, at another only those containing any of the condemned forty-one errors'. Moreover, 'twelve of the forty-one propositions did not accurately quote Luther'.[50] This combination of intolerance and ignorance alarmed many of Europe's Catholic intellectuals, including one of Charles's most prestigious councillors: Erasmus. Shortly after the book-burning at Leuven, Erasmus complained to the university rector that:

I have never approved, and I never shall, the suppression of a man in this way by public uproar, before his books have been read and discussed, before a man's errors have been pointed out to him, and before he has been refuted with arguments and with evidence from Holy Scripture . . . The burning of his books will perhaps banish Luther from our libraries; whether he can be plucked out of men's hearts, I am not so sure.[51]

Soon afterwards, Erasmus shared his reservations with a far more important protagonist: Elector Frederick of Saxony, founder and patron of the university where Luther taught. On 4 November 1520, Aleandro handed Frederick a copy of *Exsurge, domine* and the following day, after his morning devotions, the pious but confused Elector summoned Erasmus to come and advise him how he should respond. The humanist evidently reiterated his opinion that Luther and his books must not be condemned without a hearing, because soon afterwards Frederick announced that 'it was not yet established that Luther deserved such treatment, and that the question must therefore be postponed to the Diet of Worms'.[52]

Imperial policy towards Luther remained ambiguous. On 12 November the authorities of Cologne threw Luther's works on a bonfire while Charles resided in the city, but two weeks later the emperor ordered Frederick to bring Luther to the Diet of Worms, promising that he would receive both a safe-conduct and an opportunity to recant his views. Aleandro immediately saw the danger of this concession. 'If Luther does not recant, and cannot be punished because of the safe-conduct,' he predicted, 'it will cause confusion throughout the world.' He therefore sought to persuade Charles and his leading advisers to change their minds, but in vain: Chièvres, he reported, declined on the grounds that 'the emperor is a true Catholic prince', who could be trusted to do the right thing; Gattinara went further, arguing 'that it would be good to let Luther come to the Diet'.[53]

Events would vindicate Aleandro – providing Luther with both a safe-conduct and a public platform proved a public-relations disaster for the papacy – but the emperor had little choice: legally, the election agreement that he had just confirmed obliged him both to heed the views of the Electors and to protect their subjects from standing trial before a foreign court. He could hardly now ignore Frederick's formal demand that Luther should not be condemned and sent to Rome without a prior hearing in Germany.[54] In February 1521, perhaps encouraged by Erasmus, Charles went further. He sent his confessor, Jean Glapion, to persuade Frederick to make Luther retract at least some of his propositions and thus avoid a high-risk confrontation at the Diet. Since the Elector refused to talk to a friar, Glapion made his case to Dr Gregor Brück, Frederick's chancellor, stating that 'Until the publication of *The Babylonian captivity of the Church* I was persuaded that Brother Martin was pursuing the noble goal of the universal reform of the Church, removing from it the abuses that have disgraced it for too long. In addition, his courageous example inspired the zeal and support of many right-minded people.' Glapion promised in Charles's name that if Luther would just retract the views expressed in *The Babylonian captivity*, or denied his authorship, he would escape prosecution and could continue to promote 'useful reforms, proceeding discreetly and silently'. He also assured Brück that 'the emperor believes that it is essential to reconcile such an eminent man with the Christian church'. Early in April, Glapion made a second effort, meeting with a group of Luther's allies to arrange a private setting in which the Augustinian could retract some of his propositions and thus defuse the situation. The proposal failed because Luther refused to forego his chance to explain his views in public before the Diet.[55]

Political considerations lay behind these remarkable initiatives. On the domestic front, Charles could not ignore the widespread support for Luther's views expressed by some of the princes and towns represented in the Diet: arresting Luther and sending him unheard to Rome risked unleashing another major uprising that, with rebellions raging in Spain, he lacked the resources to suppress. Abroad, according to rumour, the pope favoured the Italian ambitions of Francis I, and had signed an alliance with him, so that a critic of the papacy like Luther might prove (as Ambassador Juan Manuel had foreseen) a political asset. When, in March 1521, Aleandro 'exhorted' Chièvres 'to turn his hand to the suppression and extinction of this abominable heresy', the marquis shot back: 'Just make sure the pope does his duty, and deals straightforwardly with us. Then we will do everything His Holiness wants.' When Aleandro persevered, Chièvres became more belligerent: 'If *your pope* ceases to meddle in our affairs, he will get everything he could ask of us; otherwise, we will create so much trouble for him that he will find it hard to extricate himself.' Aleandro now realized, perhaps for the first time, that 'ever since the emperor talked with the Elector of Saxony in Cologne', his ministers 'have constantly tried to make use of the Luther question [*servirsi dell cose di Martino*]'. When the legate challenged Chièvres a third time, the marquis 'smiled and said that he himself did not think it would be so difficult to silence Luther' – to which Aleandro retorted tartly that, without a swift reaction, 'you will soon see such a fire that all the water in *your North Sea* will not extinguish it'.[56]

Charles had another practical reason to avoid executing *Exsurge, domine*: the Luther question was only one of the many German issues that required resolution. The Diet of Worms would debate over one hundred separate matters, including usury, monopolies, luxuries and the spread of 'wordy and far-fetched laws' that ordinary people could no longer understand (the unpopularity in Germany of 'Roman Law', which was fast displacing customary law at this time, can scarcely be exaggerated). As Charles had already discovered in both the Netherlands and Spain, persuading any large legislature to resolve such thorny issues required tact, patience and forbearance. He therefore worked hard to keep everybody happy. On the first day of the Diet he joined all its members at Mass, after which he 'spake certain brief words in Almain' (German: the first recorded occasion on which he did so); and for the next four months he consulted the Electors on a regular basis, as well as worshipping, hunting and hawking with leading participants in an effort to find common ground.[57]

THE REFORMATION AS TOURNAMENT

Aleandro did his best to disrupt the harmony. In his anxiety to secure Luther's immediate condemnation the legate submitted a draft edict of outlawry, but instead the emperor summoned 'Our dear Reverend Dr Martin Luther of the Augustinian Order' to appear in Worms within three weeks. He also issued the promised safe-conduct and on 17 April, 'at the time of Vespers, which would be at 4 p.m.', Luther appeared before Charles and the Diet. Over a decade later, an eyewitness still remembered the sense of general excitement: 'when Luther appeared in person, the whole world came to see him'.[58] The Diet itself comprised over one hundred members, accompanied by foreign and German dignitaries as well as members of the imperial court (including the future Inquisitor-General Fernando de Valdés) and many ordinary citizens – a total audience of perhaps one thousand. Charles sat on a stage in the great room facing Luther, who 'wore the habit of an Augustinian monk, with its leather belt', and to at least one eyewitness he seemed 'very tall, taller than most people'. Everyone fell silent as Johann Eck, who acted as 'spokesman for the emperor and for the Diet', rose to read out a list of books allegedly written by Luther, and a summary of their contents. The friar cheekily interjected, 'You haven't mentioned *all* my books!', but Eck ignored him and asked two questions, devised by Aleandro and communicated in advance to Luther: had he written all the books whose titles and contents he had just heard? And, if so, 'would you like to reconsider that, or else distance yourself from them as something insane and heretical?' After 'swearing his loyalty to the emperor', Luther replied in Latin and then again in German, 'with his face and gestures revealing his anxiety and discomposure: "As to the first point, those books were his; but concerning the second point, he asked that he be given until the following day to answer."' Surprised, Charles 'withdrew with his Privy Council to another place' to discuss their next move; and after they returned, Eck spoke to Luther again:

'What he was asked concerned important things that he himself had done, and about which he could not be ignorant, and so he should respond immediately and not request another delay; nevertheless His Majesty, showing his customary clemency, was willing to extend the term to the following day at the same time.' And with that, the ceremony ended for the day and the emperor went upstairs to dine.[59]

Charles had just made a critical error: Luther had indeed received advance notice of the two simple questions, and so there was no reason to grant him more time to prepare his responses.

The scenario that Aleandro dreaded now became reality. On 18 April, after a night of reflection during which he evidently overcame his 'anxiety and discomposure', Luther appeared before the Diet again at the same time, only to find that 'the emperor and the princes were upstairs in another room' (no doubt discussing what to do next). Therefore, 'the said Martin waited for an hour and a half before his examination', surrounded by (and perhaps energized by) 'the huge throng of people who had come with him'.[60] Eventually, accompanied by his councillors, Charles 'came down to the great room' and took his seat upon the raised dais. 'There were so many people that, except for the emperor, scarcely anyone had room to sit down'; and, as before, everyone fell silent when Eck rose to repeat his questions. This time Luther not only acknowledged his authorship of the books on display ('and of some others that were omitted'), but started to explain that they fell into three distinct categories. The first, he said, 'were written against our Most Holy Father, Leo X, because he could see that the whole German Nation was vexed and oppressed in Rome' – but Charles now intervened for the first time, 'telling him to be silent on this matter and to proceed to the others'. Luther therefore moved on to the second category, which consisted of 'books that he said he had written out of irritation with his critics', while 'the third category of books were about the Gospels'. He declared that 'he would not retract a single word he had written . . . unless he could be shown in a public debate to have erred, on the authority of the Old and New Testaments alone'; and he concluded 'by begging and exhorting the emperor not to try and impede the spread of his ideas, because that might prove detrimental not only to the most famous German nation but also to his other kingdoms and dominions'.[61]

Since Charles remained silent, Eck reminded Luther 'that everything that he admitted writing in his books. . . . was heresy that had long since been condemned by councils', and 'for that reason there was no point in discussing something that had already been discussed, declared to be evil, reproved and condemned by the Church, which had issued holy decrees and very good decisions on the matter'. Therefore, Eck pointed out smugly, if Luther 'spoke the truth, we must believe that our predecessors for the past thousand years were heretics and were not saved; and it would be reckless and a great error to think that one man, with little authority, wanted to condemn so many good Christians.'

When Charles again said nothing, Luther seized the opportunity to make his boldest and most famous statement:

> Unless I can be convinced by evidence from Scripture or clear reason –
> because I do not believe the decrees of either popes or councils alone,
> because it is clear that they have erred and also contradicted each other
> . . . I neither can nor will retract anything, for it is both sinful and
> dangerous to act against conscience. I have no choice: here I stand.

Eck arose once more and 'began to deny this', but Charles interrupted him. Although he could not understand the exchange in German, and although he still needed Latin texts to be translated into French 'so that I can understand them better', the emperor evidently grasped the significance of Luther's challenge, because he 'stood up and said "That is enough: I do not wish to hear any more from someone who denied the authority of the councils!"' And with that 'he went up to his apartments and the princes and Electors went to their quarters'.[62]

Chaos now broke out in the great hall. 'The Spanish equerries who were awaiting their masters stood at the door shouting "Burn him! Burn him!"' But they were no match for the Germans, who formed a protective escort around Luther and carried him on their shoulders as if he had just won a tournament – a conceit that appealed to the hero of the hour, because he left the hall 'raising his arms and making the sign with his hands and fingers that German knights do as a sign of victory when they have just won a joust' (a gesture that might have won the grudging respect of Emperor Maximilian).[63] The victor did not underestimate his predicament, however. He made a hasty exit from Worms before his safe-conduct expired, and two days later he wrote a letter assuring Charles that he had been prepared to recant and burn his books had he been convinced that he had erred – but the missive never reached its destination because no one dared to deliver it.[64]

CHARLES TAKES HIS STAND

Luther's half-apology would have made no difference. The confrontation before the Diet left Charles profoundly unsettled, and he spent the following night crafting a response. Early the following morning:

> ... he joined the princes and Electors in the upper apartment where he eats and asked them: 'What do you think about Martin Luther?' Before anyone could speak he said: 'I want to give you my opinion in this matter, before I hear yours', and he took out a sheet of paper with his writing on it.

Many manuscript copies of this sheet of paper have survived – in German, Italian, Latin, Spanish and French – not only because Charles ordered copies to be made in those languages but also because (perhaps for the first time) he was clearly speaking his own mind on a major policy issue. His paper began by reminding everyone that his ancestors – Spanish, Austrian and Burgundian as well as German – 'were all loyal sons of the Church of Rome until they died, having always defended the Catholic Church, its sacred ceremonies, decrees and customs', and that 'we have by God's grace lived thus far according to their example'. Next, he repeated a point made by Johann Eck in the debate: 'Assuredly a single monk must be wrong if his opinion goes against what Christians have believed for the past thousand years and believe now'. Therefore, Charles continued, 'I am entirely determined to dedicate my kingdoms and lordships, my friends, my body, my blood, my life and my soul' to combat heresy, because to permit:

> ... heresy or a diminution of the Christian religion to rest in the hearts of men through our own negligence would bring permanent dishonour on us and our successors. Having heard the perverse reply that Luther

gave yesterday in the presence of all of us, I tell you now that I regret having delayed so long before proceeding against him and his false doctrine, and I have decided to hear no more from him.

Although Charles promised to honour the safe-conduct, he forbade Luther 'to preach or teach his evil doctrine' and proclaimed that 'I have decided to treat and deal with him as I would with a notorious heretic'. He enjoined his hearers to do the same.[65]

Charles had declared 'Here I stand', much like Luther the previous day, but the speech of the theologian would echo down the ages, whereas that of the emperor was soon forgotten. The reasons were relatively simple. As the Reformation historian Heiko Oberman pointed out, Luther saw himself as the forerunner of the Apocalypse, anxious to gather in the congregation of the faithful 'in these last days' because he believed 'that these last days have already started, and that therefore the "last things" have commenced in our historical time, so that the eschatological clock has started to tick'. This gave his message an immediacy that Charles could not match. Printing accentuated this difference by giving Luther a far greater audience. When he stood before the Diet, more than 600,000 copies of his works were already on the market, and at least ten editions of his defiant speech soon appeared, in High and Low German as well as in Latin, firing up his base.[66] The reception of Charles's declaration was very different. The Electors 'asked for time to consult and decide on this matter. They went back to the emperor on several occasions, appearing to assent to his decree, but in reality raising many objections, so that nothing has yet been decided'. Some argued that 'another effort should be made to speak with and reprimand Luther'. Others openly opposed Charles's stance: posters appeared around the city 'claiming that 400 cavalry and 10,000 infantry stood ready to defend the proposition that Luther's works were good'.[67]

'I do not know what will happen next', the Venetian ambassador in Worms wrote anxiously, and he predicted that 'as soon as the emperor leaves, and this Diet is dissolved, Luther will provoke great disorders [tumultos] throughout Germany'. Alfonso de Valdés, a Spanish secretary in Charles's entourage, expressed the same fear in almost the same words:

Some imagine that this marks the end of the tragedy, but I believe it is not the end but the beginning. I see that the minds of the Germans are very agitated against the pope; and I also see that they do not attach much weight to the emperor's edicts, because as soon as Luther's books see the light of day, they are sold constantly and with impunity in every street and square. You can easily conjecture what will happen as soon as the emperor departs.[68]

In Spain, Adrian of Utrecht shared this fear, writing a holograph letter urging his former pupil 'to send and transfer Martin Luther to his judge, Our Holy Father, who will justly chastise and punish him as he deserves'. Charles scarcely needed reminding: the previous month he had instructed his officials in the Netherlands to seize and burn all Lutheran writings; to forbid the printing, sale, purchase or possession of any books attacking the Holy See; and to reaffirm decrees against the doctrines propagated by earlier heretics as well as those of 'a certain Martin Luther'.[69] But the risk of provoking another rebellion, so soon after Villalar, made Charles hesitate to enact similar measures in Germany. Although he approved the text of an edict that outlawed Luther, condemned all his works (again equating them with those of condemned heretics) and forbade the printing (without episcopal licence) of any work 'however small, that mentions or quotes the Holy Scripture, or any interpretation of the same', Charles refused to publish it.[70]

Aleandro, exasperated, protested to the papal secretary of state that 'the delay is not our fault', but that of 'the emperor, who says he wants to consult the princes about everything'. The legate saw this as 'very dangerous', because he had already identified several 'Lutheran princes' in the Diet, whom he feared might exploit the opportunity to dilute the language of the edict. He became even more anxious when news arrived that the king of France had encouraged attacks by the king of Navarre and the lord of La Marck on Charles's territories, so that 'in effect, war has broken out, and the imperialists say they want to raise the largest possible number of German troops', which made further concessions inevitable. He was correct: Charles refused to alienate 'the Lutheran princes' until the Diet had agreed to pay for an army to defend Germany against a French attack. 'May God make peace between Christian princes,' Aleandro sighed, 'or at least not allow the cause of Luther to become mixed up with secular affairs of state.'[71]

Finally, the day after the Diet voted funds to support 20,000 infantry and 4,000 cavalry and approved the creation of a council of regency under Charles's brother Ferdinand, the emperor signed the Latin and German texts of the edict outlawing Luther. Aleandro immediately took them to the printers, adding optimistically that 'although they said it would take six days, I have ensured that they will work night and day'.[72] Two developments dashed his hopes. On 24 May 1521 the French ambassador at Charles's court came to request a safe-conduct to return home – then, as now, an unmistakable harbinger of war – while four days later death removed the adviser whose opinions Charles had followed ever since his emancipation six years before, and who had 'hiderto stayed th'emperor from entring in hostillitie or breche with Ffraunce': Guillaume de Croÿ, lord of Chièvres and marquis of Aarschot.[73]

A SECOND EMANCIPATION

The Belgian historian Ernest Gossart was surely correct to claim that 'Charles V's political minority came to an end in 1521, at Worms, with the death of Chièvres.' Just the previous year, one of Charles's diplomats had suggested to Thomas Wolsey that the marquis might relinquish his position by the king's side once they returned from Spain to the Netherlands, 'and stay there to take his rest, and put someone else in [his] place' – but Wolsey scoffed that 'you do not yet understand the nature of men who hold such responsibilities': no one holding pre-eminent power would ever relinquish it.[74] Wolsey was correct: the marquis accompanied Charles all the way to Worms, where he continued to dominate both domestic and foreign-policy discussions at the Diet and to negotiate with foreign ambassadors and German princes 'in the name of his imperial majesty'. In February 1521, Erasmus opined that Chièvres 'stood so high with our Prince Charles that the whole empire almost seemed to be in one man's grasp'; and a few weeks later, in his Final Relation to the Venetian Senate, Ambassador Corner stated that the marquis 'holds the government of everything in his hands' because 'His Majesty not only loves him, but has great respect for him'.[75]

No amount of imperial love could protect the marquis, now aged sixty-three, against disease. The influx of some 10,000 visitors during the Diet soon created insanitary conditions in Worms. In March 1521, Charles 'spent a night and a day violently vomiting, and his courtiers say he is in great danger'; and no sooner had he recovered than both Marliano and Chièvres fell ill. The former died on 10 May, and on 20 May 'the doctors gave up hope' on the latter. Four days later Chièvres received extreme unction, and early on 28 May he died.[76] His power and influence died with him. According to Aleandro, 'no one in this court now mentions him in public, as if he had never existed', and Gasparo Contarini, the new Venetian ambassador, noted that instead of travelling to Austria as planned, Charles had decided to travel from Worms back to the Netherlands 'because he needs to return to Spain' – and 'my lord Chièvres, who dissuaded him from the journey, is dead'.[77]

The marquis left many positive legacies. In 1515 he had told a French envoy that he forced Charles to study all incoming dossiers 'even at night', and then 'report their contents himself to his council, where everything was discussed in his presence, because if he cannot handle his affairs by the time I die, he is going to need another tutor'. Chièvres was uniquely placed to monitor the young ruler's conduct because, as Charles himself noted, 'he always sleeps in my bedroom' so that 'when I awake I have someone to talk to'.[78] Charles evidently learned the lessons imparted by the marquis: after Chièvres left the stage, Aleandro reported that Charles 'displays every day an almost superhuman desire to do the right thing – something that is clear just now, when he is without a tutor [*pedagogo*]. We have seen many times that the rapid resolutions he takes are both appropriate and sensible'. Two veteran English diplomats at Charles's court provided even more explicit testimony:

> Th'Emperor usythe marvelous [diligence] in providynge to hys affaires, for he is daylye in hys council [chamber at] six or seven of the clock, and ther remaignythe unto he go to masse; and within one howre affter he hathe dynyd, he retournyth thydder agayne, and ther contenueth unto supper tyme. *And thys lyff hathe he ledde ever synthe the decesse of the lord Chevers.*

In 1538, Charles explained to another English envoy that he worked hard at the business of government because 'God hath not called him to such rule for his oune ease and pleasures.' 'Lord Chevers' would have felt proud.[79]

Charles's diligence seems to have increased his self-confidence. In August 1521 he invited Wolsey to join him in person to settle all outstanding issues, 'because you and I together will achieve more in one day than my ambassadors in one month', adding (with perhaps a hint of menace) 'I will also show you my army, from which you will see that I do not mean to sleep'. Wolsey expressed his astonishment at Charles's refusal to make concessions, but (Gattinara observed) that was because the cardinal had 'expected to find a boy in leading strings, as he was at the time when Lord Chièvres governed him, but instead he found someone very different' – someone 'who now holds the French king in contempt'. A few days later Wolsey opined that:

> For his age [Charles] is very wyse and wel understanding hys afferys rygth; colde and temperat in spech, with assuryd maner towchyng hys words rygth wel and to good purpose when he doth speke. And

undowgttydly by all appearance he shall prove a very wyse man, gretly inclyned to trewgth and observance of his promyse.[80]

This testimony speaks well for Chièvres's role as tutor; so do his numerous policy successes. He kept the Netherlands at peace with neighbouring powers, which (among other things) permitted his pupil to depart securely for Spain in 1517. Once there, the marquis persuaded Queen Joanna to recognize her son as sole ruler in both their names, and mobilized the funds required to secure Charles's election as king of the Romans. Later, he persuaded the Diet of Worms to enact measures that settled most outstanding matters: creating a viable council of regency; passing measures that restored the rule of law; voting the funds required to mobilize troops against France; and declaring Luther a heretic and an outlaw with a price on his head. Above all, Chièvres prevented a breach with France. Prudencio de Sandoval was not the only one to speculate that 'if he had lived, the enmity and war between the emperor and the king of France would not have started so soon, because he was ever the friend of peace'.[81]In other respects, however, Chièvres deserved censure. To quote Sandoval again:

> Chièvres would say that he had been responsible for every success, and demanded sole credit for it; but he blamed the king for all failures . . . I have seen a memorial on the subject prepared by a gentleman of the royal household, an eyewitness of the things he described, saying that since the king was young and knew little of public affairs, Chièvres would not allow anyone to speak with him without knowing first what he wanted to say, so that he could tell the king how he must respond. And if they refused to tell Chièvres first, they did not receive an audience.[82]

In addition, Chièvres did his best to exclude advisers whom he regarded as rivals, even those who had much to offer young Charles – most notably Margaret of Austria, whom he marginalized through the emancipation in 1515; Adrian of Utrecht, whom he sent to Spain later that year; Count Palatine Frederick, whom he managed to disgrace in 1517 (chapter 3); and young Ferdinand, whom he banished to the Netherlands the following year (chapter 4).

Worst of all, Chièvres showed insatiable greed in accumulating public offices and revenues for himself and his family, culminating in the appointment of his nephew as archbishop of Toledo, which did more than any other single act to precipitate the Comunero revolt. His entire handling of the most dangerous insurgency of Charles's reign ranks as one of his worst errors – rivalled only by his failure to appreciate the danger of the Lutheran movement in Germany, seeking instead to use it as a weapon to persuade Pope Leo X to abandon France and ally with his master. Yet despite the high domestic cost, in the short term both gambles paid off, with the result that when Francis finally declared war Castile was at peace again, while both Henry VIII and the pope sided with Charles, enabling him to end the year 1521 as the undisputed victor.

SIX

SNATCHING VICTORY FROM THE JAWS OF DEFEAT, 1521–5

CHARLES'S FIRST CAMPAIGN

The rivalry between Charles and Francis for influence in Germany led an English diplomat to predict in 1518 that 'There can be no peace between the two'. His Venetian colleague agreed: the two monarchs might 'adapt themselves to circumstances, but each one in reality harbours great hatred for the other'. For his part, a French minister had 'no doubt that the principal reason' for the war that lasted from 1521 until 1529 'was Charles's election as emperor', because Francis feared that it would inevitably cause the loss of his recent conquests, Milan and Genoa, both imperial fiefs.[1]

Not all contemporaries considered war inevitable. Looking back in the 1530s, the Italian soldier, diplomat and historian Francesco Guicciardini acknowledged that four major issues had led to war: Charles sought to recover Burgundy, lost by his ancestor Duke Charles the Bold, and resented French control of Milan and Genoa; Francis sought to recover Navarre, seized from its native dynasty by Charles's maternal grandfather Ferdinand of Aragon, and resented Spanish control of Naples. Nevertheless, Guicciardini continued, 'since each of them was so powerful, the risks of attacking one another kept them from taking the offensive' for some time. By way of example, he cited the jocular response of Francis to a Spanish delegation that had come to announce Charles's intention to seek the imperial crown: 'We must follow the example that one sometimes sees with two men who are in love with the same woman. Each exerts himself using all possible means to obtain her, but they do not for that reason fall out between themselves.'[2]

Initially, Francis accepted the election of his rival graciously. An ambassador at the Spanish court reported in June 1519 that 'the king of France recently wrote to His Imperial Majesty with effusive congratulations, saying that – apart from himself – there was no one in this world whom he would support for this position except for His Majesty'; while some French court-iers claimed that it was 'a good torne for the king here, and a great weale for his reaulme, that he is not emperor, for they say yf he had been, it shuld have putt hym to an infanite busyness, and impoverychyd and undoone his subjects'.[3] As late as January 1521, Francis resisted pressure from Pope Leo X to challenge Charles. The French king admitted that although 'with the empire, the kingdom of Naples and Spain all in the same hands, it would be much better to deal with future difficulties in advance than to seek remedies afterwards', and although the pope thought 'that I hold a greater advantage over the Catholic King now than after he enters Germany', it seemed to Francis 'that he will then have no fewer problems than he has now, and he may well have more'. Moreover, the king continued:

> Because his dominions are scattered in various places far from one another, and are as disobedient and difficult as we all know, [Charles] will be forced to hold and keep them without trying to acquire anything more. And because he owns so much, his care and concern must be to have peace, whatever the cost to him, to avoid the great and unsustain-able expense that he would have to maintain if he goes to war.[4]

A warrant signed on 14 February 1521 revealed that Francis had changed his mind. The king authorized Robert de la Marck, lord of Sedan, 'to serve with his person and property against everyone without exception, even the emperor', and in return he granted substantial sums to La Marck and three of his sons, who almost immediately raised an army and attacked towns in the Habsburg Netherlands. This, a French minister affirmed, 'was the first blow, the origin and the instigation of the war between the king [of France] and the emperor-elect that would later become so great and cruel', and he marvelled that 'this small spark started such a great fire'. In fact, La Marck's attack was just one of several sparks: Francis also clandestinely pledged his support for the king of Navarre's efforts to recover his kingdom; he encour-aged the duke of Guelders to invade Friesland and Overijssel; and he concluded a secret treaty with Leo X by which the pope promised that he would deprive Charles of the kingdom of Naples and refuse to crown him emperor. In addition, Francis announced that if any German troops chose to serve him, 'they shall have gode interteynment' – a clear sign that he would fight if necessary. In the words of Karl Brandi: 'A life and death struggle' between 'the Valois princes, Francis of France and Charles of Burgundy, was now about to begin in earnest'.[5]

News of these various acts alarmed Charles, still at Worms trying to settle the affairs of the Empire. Some of his advisers 'dyd counsail to prevent the French king, rather then to suffyr that stroke'; but Charles 'answereyd *of his owne mynd*' – still considered a novelty – 'that he wolde suffyr the French king furst to invade, if he were so disposyd, making a vowe that if he so dyd he wold venter al that God has callyd him unto, but he would destroy him or elles be destroyed himselfe'.[6] Illness prevented Charles from acting at once on his resolve – he 'spent a night and day vomiting' and for a few days 'did not leave his room, taking his medicine and transacting no business' – but on 1 April 1521 his personal envoy announced to Francis that 'the emperor took these actions as a declaration of war and a breach of the treaties; and since he had been attacked and provoked, he has decided to defend himself'. Meanwhile in Rome Ambassador Juan Manuel 'virtually assaulted His Holiness', insisting 'aggressively and with a very angry face' (according to his French colleague) on 'a yes or a no' answer to his demand that Leo immediately sign an offensive alliance against France. The pope soon succumbed: he nullified his treaty with Francis and promised to raise an army to help Charles to expel the French from Italy; to crown Charles emperor in Rome; and to bless two dynastic links devised by Maximilian and designed to protect central Europe in case of a Turkish attack – the marriage of Charles's brother Ferdinand to Anna, the sister (and heiress) of King Louis of Hungary and Bohemia, and of Louis to Charles's sister Marie. Charles for his part promised to restore to the Papal States the duchies of Parma and Piacenza (surrendered to France by Leo after the battle of Marignano), and to place all his Medici relatives under imperial protection.[7]

Charles was now eager to fight. On hearing that Francis had openly sent La Marck some of the troops recruited in Germany:

> ... he raised his hands to Heaven and said: 'Praise to You, Lord God, for granting that I did not begin this war, and because the king of France is likely to make me greater than I am! Thanks always to You, who have given me the means to defend myself. I hope that soon either I shall be an impoverished emperor, or he an impoverished king.'

When his aunt Margaret urged him to preserve the peace the emperor replied: 'No, Madame: if I were to negotiate with him now, in two months he would start to give me trouble again.' In the summer of 1521 imperial armies repulsed their enemies in the Netherlands, in Navarre and in Italy; and an English diplomat noted that the French 'have turned the leaf. For about half a year past, they would by their words have overrun the whole world . . . but now they would have peace with all their hearts.[8] Both rulers sent envoys to Henry VIII, protesting that the other had struck first and thus breached the terms of the treaty of London (p. 102), triggering an English declaration of war against the aggressor; but instead Cardinal Wolsey offered to preside over a peace conference at Calais.

In July 1521, just before the talks began, Gattinara presented Charles with a position paper that listed reasons for and against continuing the war. First he evaluated seven arguments in favour of a truce, most of them broad (the uncertain outcome of all wars; the inevitable cost; the difficulty of starting a war so late in the campaigning season), but some specific (La Marck and Navarre had already been defeated). Then followed ten reasons for continuing the war, most of them also broad (Charles's cause was just, and so would receive divine favour; he enjoyed widespread international support), but some specific (a truce would mean that the money already spent on mobilization would be wasted; the troops raised were ready and eager to fight). Gattinara devoted special attention to his final reason in favour of fighting:

> Above all things, Your Majesty must seek to acquire reputation, because up to now you have not engaged in any affair of state for which one can draw positive or negative conclusions, and the whole world has been waiting in the hope that you will do something worthy of such a powerful emperor, now you have such a fine opportunity . . . In addition, Sire, this is the first army you have raised, and these beginnings, on which you have spent so much, and mobilized so many resources, have got the whole world talking. Our job is to ensure that these beginnings result in an outcome that does not remove or reduce the reputation of Your Majesty, but rather maintains and increases it.

The Grand Chancellor therefore urged Charles to deploy his forces in the Netherlands against an easy target, such as Tournai, while making his main effort in Italy to wrest Milan and Genoa from French hands. In this way, he concluded, 'you will acquire reputation and astonish your enemies'.[9]

Gattinara's rationale came straight out of the chivalric traditions of Burgundy – which of course increased its appeal to his master, just as the wily chancellor had anticipated – but Charles nevertheless circulated the position paper among his leading advisers and asked them to discuss 'What the emperor should do this winter'. According to the detailed minutes of the debate, some ministers wanted an offensive treaty with England, to improve the chances of victory in the Netherlands, while others favoured a truce or peace with France that would permit Charles to return to Spain and restore order; but in the event, Charles took the decision himself after negotiating with Wolsey one-on-one.[10] A secret treaty on 25 August 1521 declared that Charles and Henry would 'remain friends and allies for ever, and act in unison' both in defending their existing possessions and 'in vindicating the rights withheld from them by others, without any exception'. The treaty would be sealed by Charles's marriage to his cousin Mary, Henry's daughter and heiress (and niece of the Mary Tudor to whom he had previously been engaged), as soon as she turned twelve. The emperor would also visit England, where the two monarchs would make public their alliance and finalize a grand strategy to dismember France.[11]

Gattinara now spent three months in Calais while Wolsey engaged in pageant politics, ostentatiously discussing truce terms with the French as a screen to conceal his secret treaty with the emperor; but Gattinara's prolonged absence from his master seriously undermined his influence. Initially, Charles assured his chancellor that 'you understand better than anyone else what we could and should do' and begged him 'to write to us often, once every day without fail, because we have set up a chain of postal stations at our expense that is at your disposal' – but letters like this, combining affection and dependence, soon ceased.[12] The change apparently began when, according to a Netherlands chronicler, on 2 September 1521, 'Emperor Charles put on his suit of armour and for the first time led all his troops against France'. Shortly afterwards he became extremely angry when his chancellor refused to countersign one of his warrants, 'which you could see was our express command', and he wrote imperiously that 'notwithstanding the objections you have put forward, we command you once and for all to countersign the said warrant and send it back to us without fail, because that is our pleasure'. The following month, when Wolsey tampered with the terms agreed for Charles's marriage with Princess Mary, the emperor declared – without consulting his chancellor – that he would scrap the whole treaty, exclaiming 'with an angry face':

> I can see clearly enough how the cardinal [Wolsey] wants to treat me: to make such unreasonable demands of me that my honour and advantage will not allow me to agree ... But he has mistaken his man [*Il l'a mal trouvé son homme*], because if one party rejects me, another will accept me. There is no shortage of brides; I don't need to pay so much.[13]

Charles's tantrum paid handsome dividends: Wolsey hastened to sign a treaty that obliged England, the emperor and the pope to make war on France. Moreover, the imperial armies in Italy and the Netherlands scored some notable successes, so that by the end of 1521 the emperor could boast that 'God has granted us His favour, because we are victorious on all sides, reducing Milan and several other [Italian] cities to our obedience, capturing Tournai, and recovering all that had been taken in Navarre.' In December 1521, Pope Leo died and a month later the cardinals chose as his successor Charles's former tutor, Adrian of Utrecht.[14]

EMPEROR, POPE AND KING UNITED

The emperor made haste to exploit this unexpected advantage. 'It has pleased Our Lord not only to raise us to this imperial dignity,' he reminded the new pontiff, 'but also to ordain that we should receive the imperial Crown from the hand of a person we know so well, from our own nation, and who has raised and taught us since childhood, and has a great and true love for us: namely Your Holiness.' More pointedly, he urged Adrian VI 'to remember what you once told me when I was your student, which I have since found to be true – and to make sure that you remember, I will remind you: that [the French] speak kind and sweet words, but in the end they seek only to deceive and fool you'. Nevertheless, he concluded: 'Your Holiness is so smart that you will know how to avoid doing anything that might be harmful or damaging to me.'[15]

Adrian's election created an urgent problem for his former pupil: the new pope could not continue to serve as governor of Castile, putting pressure on Charles to return to Spain. This, in turn, required him to appoint strong regents in both the Netherlands and Germany during his absence: for the former he chose Margaret, who was both able and willing to serve again; and he entrusted the latter to Ferdinand. At the Diet of Worms, he had ceded to his brother most of the Habsburg lands in Austria; now, anxious to return to Spain, he transferred the rest of his Austrian lands to Ferdinand and his descendants, and renewed his promise to arrange for his brother's election as king of the Romans as soon as he had himself been crowned emperor.[16] Charles also made his first will. He named Ferdinand his universal heir and successor; and, like his father, he specified that if he died in Spain his body should be interred in Granada beside the Catholic Monarchs, and if in the Netherlands in Bruges beside his grandmother Mary of Burgundy; but 'if at the time of our death our duchy of Burgundy should be restored to our obedience then we wish our body to be buried in the church of the Charterhouse of Dijon, beside the bodies of our predecessors Dukes Philip the Bold, John his son, and Philip the Good'. Charles still saw himself primarily as duke of Burgundy.[17]

The emperor and his entourage sailed from Calais to Dover, the first leg of their journey back to Spain, on 27 May 1522. Erasmus generously attributed their late departure to the weather – 'winds are the only creatures that do not know an emperor when they see one' – but that formed only part of the explanation. Some delays arose because the emperor was often absent from his desk. He sired at least three illegitimate children in twelve months (chapter 14), and he remained addicted to tournaments, hawking, hunting – and tennis. An English envoy who arrived at his court in February 1522 could not present his credentials because Charles was 'playinge at the paume [ball and court game]', forcing the ambassador to remain 'beholdynge the playe tyll it was almost nyght, at which tyme his majestie resortyd to his chambyr'.[18] A month later, Charles and his brother each led a team in a great tournament:

> Whanne they had salutyd the laadyes, and maade theyre towre about the fyelde and tylte, th'emperor began the playe, and brak his spere right freshly uppon oon of his brodyr's company, and the next course the Infant dyd in lyke wyse uppon one of th'emperor's company, insomuch that the rynniynge lastyd uppon twayne howrys, for the hundryrd speerys which weere brought in to be brookkyn constantly.

Thanks, no doubt, to all the hours Charles had spent practising:

> His maieste handyld his besynesse in moost gaallyande forme, and brak moo speerys thanne oony oothir, and in the ende, whanne alle the sayde speerys were brookkyn, th'emperor mountyd uppon a steaynge horsse, beinge dysarmyd of his armett and targett, uppon which horsse, afftyr that he had saluted the laadyes, he sportyd hymsylfe in the place lyke the prynce that maye well be callyd the patron of horsmen.

According to the Venetian ambassador, 'everyone present' judged that Charles 'excelled all others in this joust' and performed equestrian feats 'that no-one else could do'.[19]

Charles did not always place pleasure before business. Thus on 13 April 1522, when 'erly in the morning the post cam' from England, 'evyr sith, th'emperor and his Councell have ocupyid the tyme in councellynge boothe erly and laate, so that theey dyne late, suppe laate, and goe to bedde laate'. Two days later Charles wrote a holograph letter informing Cardinal Wolsey that henceforth, whenever 'something affects me personally', he would 'write this symbol ξ'; and for over a year his holograph letters to Wolsey often contained 'the symbol ξ that you and I know, meaning that the matter is very important to me'.[20] The emperor also spent much time attending in person to lesser public affairs. According to the amazed English ambassadors at his court, he himself supervised the embarkation of his entourage for his voyage to England – and when the diplomats expressed some doubt, an official showed them a register in which they saw many entries 'by th'emperor's owne hand'.[21] But the main reason for postponing the departure was lack of money.

According to a document drafted by Gattinara, the combined cost of the recent campaign and the imminent journey to Spain left the emperor with so little money that 'we are in danger not only of losing what we have conquered but also of placing at risk all our inherited dominions, leaving our affairs in ruins and at the mercy of Providence. In addition, we do not know how we shall be received by our Spanish subjects.' Charles turned first to Manuel of Portugal and requested a loan, but then Henry VIII offered both 150,000 ducats to prepare the imperial fleet and a naval escort to protect it against a possible French attack. Charles accepted, even though (in his own words) the arrangement involved 'some fairly harsh terms', including a promise 'not to conclude a peace or truce with France except with the knowledge and consent' of Henry and a diversion to England on his way to Spain.[22]

Nevertheless, 1522 started well for Charles. In April, victory over the French and their allies at Bicocca delivered not only Lombardy but also Genoa into Habsburg hands. The following month he crossed to England and on 6 June he and Henry entered London 'not merely like brothers of one mind, but both dressed in the same attire and with all the normal ceremonies, as if the emperor was about to be recognized as king in England'. Ten days later Henry published a declaration of war on France, and confirmed that Mary would marry Charles as soon as she turned twelve. The princess started to wear a brooch with jewels arranged to read 'the emp[er]our' (Pl. 11). Henry also provided his prospective son-in-law with a powerful train of English artillery 'to assist him in the pacification of his states', and sent an expeditionary force to attack Brittany. In addition, the two monarchs agreed that in 1524 they would launch a 'Great Enterprise': a simultaneous invasion of France, with Henry advancing on Paris from Calais and Charles from Vizcaya.[23]

After six weeks of feasting, jousting and negotiating in England, Charles took communion and then boarded a fleet carrying 3,000 German troops – far more than those brought to Spain by his father eighteen years before. He disembarked at Santander on 16 July 1522 and moved inland, 'hunting and enjoying himself', until he reached Palencia three weeks later. He reported to Henry that many 'grandees, nobles, prelates and important people have come to our court, displaying as much humility and devotion as we could desire, and all, great and small, have shown themselves our loyal subjects and servants'; and he felt secure enough to send his German troops to defend Spain's frontier with France, while he 'began to bring order into these kingdoms'.[24]

THE PACIFICATION OF SPAIN

But whose order would it be? As soon as he learned of Adrian's election, which meant that the new pope would have to leave Spain for Rome, Charles drew up a patent for his sister Eleanor (recently widowed) to act as his regent in Castile; and until she arrived he authorized the Admiral and the Constable of Castile to continue as joint governors. The Admiral urged his master to offer concessions and clemency to the Comuneros, since otherwise 'no one will sleep soundly in their beds because the slightest breeze will make them think that a magistrate has come to arrest them'. He reminded Charles boldly: 'You are not God who can be everywhere at once, but an emperor who must walk upon this earth. Love is a better way than fear to keep what you have.' Few ministers agreed with him. Even Adrian favoured repression, advising Charles to mobilize all his resources 'so that you may punish those who brought about sedition and rebellion in your kingdoms'; and the regency council, which had been humiliated and threatened by the Comuneros, began to imprison all the former rebels they could find.[25]

Jean Glapion, the emperor's confessor, had told him: 'You are endowed with every virtue, except for this one – you find it difficult to forgive insults'; and just like the knights of Burgundy in his books of chivalry, Charles regularly spoke and wrote about wreaking 'vengeance' on those whom he considered had offended him.[26] Now, as soon as he returned to Spanish soil, he ordered the execution of some German soldiers captured while fighting for the French in Guipúzcoa, 'to serve as an example to the rest, so that anyone who defies me will know the fate that awaits them for going against their emperor'. He also lost no time in punishing the Comuneros: he informed his aunt Margaret in August that he had 'started criminal proceedings against

10 or 12 of the principal delinquents from the Junta of Tordesillas, captured last year', adding that 'I plan to punish them in an exemplary fashion that will be remembered for ever'. Over the next two months, Charles approved almost one hundred condemnations of former Comuneros, including some granted a provisional pardon, until he is said to have remarked, 'That's enough for now: do not shed any more blood'. On 1 November 1522 a General Pardon – solemnly proclaimed in the city square of Valladolid in the presence of Charles, the foreign ambassadors accredited to his court, and his leading nobles and courtiers – granted amnesty to all but 293 named former rebels. Those denied amnesty (the *exceptuados*) included sixty-three nobles and gentlemen, and twenty-one clerics.[27]

The emperor took a close personal interest in the process of retribution. As Ferdinand's envoy, Martín de Salinas, noted: 'His Majesty is so well-informed about the nature of each person's offence that you would think he himself had taken down their confession'.[28] He rejected all suggestions of collective sanctions (such as removing the royal chancery from Valladolid or the commercial fairs from Medina del Campo), so that the defeat of the Comuneros did not transform the traditional structure of Castile; but the fines imposed on the leading cities involved in the uprising, and the taxes raised to pay reparations to loyalists who had suffered material losses, seriously weakened the industries and artisans of the kingdom.[29]

Charles acted with far greater severity against those involved in the Germanías of Valencia, starting after the death of their popular leader known as *El Encubierto* (The Hidden One), who claimed to be the posthumous son of Prince John, heir of the Catholic Monarchs (which would have made him, not Charles, the rightful king). The emperor appointed his stepgrandmother, Germaine de Foix, as vicereine with orders to regain control 'without granting or allowing any pardon whatsoever'. According to the Valencian chronicler Martí de Viciana, the arrest of rebel leaders (including, as in Castile, some of those already granted a provisional pardon) began in secret on the night of 10 January 1524, and over the next four years the queen approved the execution of some 800 former rebels, many of them after torture. Viciana estimated that the Germanías caused material damage worth 2 million ducats and the deaths of 12,000 people 'in battles, fights and skirmishes, and through judicial sentences'. Only the need to fund the war with France compelled Charles to call a halt, and sell pardons to most of the remaining rebels.[30]

The emperor refused to pardon Antonio de Acuña, bishop of Zamora, who had once styled himself Captain General of the Comuneros. In 1520 the Spanish ambassador in Rome persuaded Pope Leo to deprive Acuña of the normal legal protection enjoyed by clerics by telling him (without a shred of evidence) 'that he was another Martin Luther'. Two years later, in Valladolid, crowds watched as Rodrigo Ronquillo, a royal magistrate, 'led the bishop of Zamora through the middle of this city, with a guard of Spanish cavalry, to take him to the fortress of Simancas'. Charles now demanded that Pope Adrian permit the torture of Acuña (using the threat that 'if His Holiness does not grant this, we will be forced to resort to other means, as we see fit').[31] In desperation, Acuña offered Charles 60,000 ducats in return for his freedom; and when he learned that 'His Majesty does not want to accept, even though he really needs the money', he stabbed the castellan of Simancas to death and tried to escape. His attempt failed and Charles now ordered 'the bishop of Zamora to be taken to the torture chamber', where he would have 'his hands tied behind him with a rope linked to a pulley' and 'be hoisted slightly above the floor'. The bishop eventually incriminated three accomplices, one of them a priest who underwent torture so severe that he could not sign his own confession 'because his hand was badly damaged by the torture'. Ronquillo then 'garrotted the bishop without any further formality'.[32]

Charles exacted vengeance in other, lesser ways – in Zamora, a leading Comunero city, he ordered the houses of some rebels to be razed while those of others suffered the ignominy of having their coats of arms erased (as modern visitors to the city can still see) – and his resentment never entirely abated. He continued to nag both the king of Portugal and the pope to hand over fugitive Comunero leaders until the last of them died in exile; in 1532, on hearing that the regency government had reversed a sentence of exile imposed on one of the *exceptuados*, Charles ordered that 'in future no Comunero is to be pardoned unless I have been consulted first'; and four years later he ordered the arrest of a courier in Portuguese service as he travelled through Spain 'because he was once a Comunero'. Even in 1552, so desperate for money that he reluctantly agreed to sell knighthoods in Castile for cash, Charles specified 'that they should not be conferred on the son or grandson of any Comunero'.[33]

Such vindictiveness proved counter-productive. When 'some of the priests who supported the Comuneros' appeared before Adrian in June 1522 to 'demand justice', the new pope hesitated, fearing that if he refused 'they will go to France and help our enemies'; but Charles remained adamant and thus (as Adrian had predicted) created a cadre of implacable foes abroad.[34] They included 'a certain Cárdenas', who led the rebellious settlers of Chile in

1542 and had previously 'opposed Your Majesty during the Comuneros, and afterwards with Rincón' – the same Antonio Rincón who was 'one of the Comuneros from Medina del Campo' and entered French service, becoming a trusted intermediary between Francis and his anti-Habsburg allies. Cárdenas, Rincón and the rest joined the numerous Italian exiles who fled when the imperialists and their allies wrested control of each town from the French and their allies. As King Francis once observed, the Ottoman sultan made good use of 'the large number of exiles from the kingdom of Naples whom the war has forced to abandon their homes and goods'. Charles was fortunate that Francis also proved adept at turning his leading subjects into implacable enemies.[35]

THE GREAT ENTERPRISE

In summer 1522 intelligence reached the Spanish court that Duke Charles III de Bourbon, Constable of France, was preparing to rebel against his master. At first the news seemed too good to be true. Bourbon was a 'prince of the blood', nephew of Louis XII as well as cousin of Francis I, for whom he had commanded the vanguard at Marignano and jousted at the Field of the Cloth of Gold. Late in 1521 the duke captured Hesdin – one of the few French successes of the year – but everything changed a few months later with the death of his wife Suzanne, scion of a senior branch of the Bourbon line. Louise of Savoy, the king's mother, at once lodged a claim in the *Parlement* of Paris, the highest jurisdiction in France, that she now held the best title to the Bourbon estates. Francis, for his part, claimed that the entire Bourbon domain had escheated to the Crown.

Perhaps the king and his mother took these desperate steps because both were practically bankrupt. Francis had spent lavishly on the ceremonies connected with his accession, the Marignano campaign, and the Field of the Cloth of Gold, followed by a year of war on several fronts, causing him to run up debts greater than his annual income. Nevertheless, trying to seize the lands of his most powerful vassal and principal general was a rash move to make, especially in wartime, and almost immediately Duke Charles appealed for help to the emperor, who in August 1522 sent a special envoy 'to speak to the duke of Bourbon and bring to fruition the enterprise that he had begun'.[36] The duke suggested sealing the 'aliance with th'emperour by mariage of one of his susters'; and he made direct contact with Henry VIII to propose joining 'the king and the emperor with his strength and power at such tyme as they shall make actuall war in ffraunce'. The parties eventually agreed to execute the Great Enterprise – the invasion of France – in 1523, one year earlier than planned, and with an extra participant: while Henry invaded France from Calais and Charles attacked in the south, Bourbon would raise 500 cavalry and 10,000 infantry from his own estates in the centre of the kingdom and march on Paris.[37]

To pay for this initiative, Charles convened the Cortes of Castile, which opened in July 1523 with a triumphalist account by Gattinara of all Charles had achieved since the last assembly because 'God's hand is with Your Majesty' (his speech invoked God nineteen times). Charles apparently vetoed a passage in the chancellor's draft that admitted mistakes had been made during the last visit, and blamed 'ministers who were not born here' and were therefore 'uninformed about the laws, ordinances and customs' of Castile for causing the late unpleasantness. Without the apology, the deputies remained unenthusiastic: although they accepted that Charles enjoyed a special relationship with God – 'what comes from the mouth of Your Majesty comes from the mouth of God, who placed you here in His place' – they reminded him that at the last Cortes 'the deputies were not heard as they desired' and they demanded that this time the sovereign should hear and address their grievances before they voted another subsidy. According to the official record of the assembly, Charles replied immediately in fluent Castilian:

> What seems better to you: that you immediately grant me the subsidy (since I promised yesterday and promise again today that I will not dissolve the Cortes until I have responded to and acted on all things you ask of me) . . . so that it will seem that the concessions I make and the rewards I provide are done through my goodwill? Or would you have me first address the grievances that you bring, and have it said that I did it only so you would provide me with the subsidy?

He reminded the deputies that 'it has always been the case that the subsidy is granted first' and wondered 'why you are imposing such a major innovation on me?' 'Nothing remains a secret for ever,' he continued, 'and when this news reaches other rulers, both Ottoman and Christian, the fact that you are not treating me like other kings, my predecessors, will be very bad for my reputation, and the wicked will rejoice.'[38]

After a month of argument, Charles prevailed: the Cortes approved a substantial subsidy, in return for which the emperor addressed over one hundred separate grievances, starting with the demand that he fill his household with Castilians; that he hold public audiences at regular times each week; that he revoke all certificates of naturalization issued to foreigners (and grant no more); and that he appoint only 'those born in this kingdom' to all secular, ecclesiastical and diplomatic posts. He also promised to improve the defence of the realm and the administration of justice; to prohibit both carrying weapons in public and 'wearing masks' (a habit 'newly invented in this kingdom'); and to appoint qualified scholars to codify the laws and complete the chronicles of the kingdom. Only a few grievances dealt with policy. The deputies demanded that Charles marry his cousin, Isabella of Portugal, and make Spain his permanent headquarters; that he 'make no agreement with Portugal on the spice trade, so that we will not lose advantage and reputation (considering the cost in men and money of discovering [the Moluccas])'; and that he pursue 'peace with Christian rulers and war with infidels' (Ferdinand of Aragon's mantra). Finally, they demanded 'that Your Majesty give orders that the subsidy that we authorize, at a time when the kingdom is so exhausted and ruined, should be spent on the recovery of Fuenterrabía.'[39]

Given that scarcely a year had elapsed since the defeat of the Comuneros, the restrained nature of the grievances suggested that Castile and its ruler had reconciled; but some subjects remained disgruntled. In March 1523 the English ambassadors 'perceyve not very much love betwix the noblemen of Spayne and Flaunders'; while four months later Salinas reported that over a thousand soldiers had roamed the streets of Valladolid shouting 'Long live the king and death to the Flemings', and leaving several dead in the streets. In August, perhaps remembering the inflammatory sermons during Charles's last visit to the city, Salinas also expressed concern about 'what they say in the streets and the pulpits'.[40] Despite these warning signs, Charles left Castile again in October, naming his sister Eleanor regent of the kingdom, and moved to Navarre to direct the recapture of Fuenterrabía from the French, just as the Cortes had demanded.

Although the emperor eventually achieved this limited goal, doing so fatally compromised the 'Great Enterprise'. Charles remained on Spanish soil whereas Henry raised (according to Wolsey) 'a puissant armye of as tal, active and elect persones, with as expert and good captains, as hathe passed oute of this realme at any tyme this hundred yeres'. The 'puissant armye' advanced rapidly, forcing numerous towns in its path to surrender and swear allegiance to 'Henry, king of France', until in October 1523 it captured Montdidier, a mere 80 kilometres from Paris.[41] As panic gripped the French capital, the victorious invaders turned east to join forces with those of

Bourbon, but they were too late: Francis had already discovered Duke Charles's treason and he fled to Habsburg territory.

'MEN FIGHT BATTLES BUT GOD GRANTS VICTORIES'[42]

In November 1523, Charles suggested to Henry that they should 'abandon our plans for the Great Enterprise' and instead use 'my army of Italy to invade France as a substitute', to be funded jointly by the two monarchs.[43] This dramatic change of plan reflected not only the failure of Bourbon's conspiracy but also Gattinara's conviction that Milan and Genoa formed the fulcrum of his master's empire. Retaining them, he informed Charles:

> . . . must not be undervalued or left to chance, because they are the key to retaining and maintaining Naples and Sicily. They are also the true means of keeping the Venetians and all the rest of Italy under your control and entirely obedient to you, and through them to keep all of Germany and Switzerland in fear, and to do with them what you want. From that foundation you will be powerful enough on your own to make war on the Turks and other infidels in all parts and reduce them to reason.[44]

The following month, on hearing of the death of Pope Adrian, Gattinara submitted to Charles another comprehensive analysis of his strategic goals and how to achieve them. Two of them, entitled 'Reputation' and 'Securing Italy', concerned foreign policy. Under the first rubric, the chancellor stressed once again the need 'to maintain your reputation, which it is most necessary for you to uphold . . . whether in order to secure a favourable peace or truce, or (if that is impossible) to continue and end the war'. To this end, Charles must 'maintain the friendship of the king of England', and in view of the failure to support Henry's campaign adequately, 'we must not only apologize but also make good the damage . . . making clear that our past fault was not deliberate'. Gattinara turned next to 'Securing Italy'. To this end, the emperor must persuade the new pope (whose identity was not yet known in Spain) to sign a defensive and offensive alliance similar to that agreed with Adrian; betroth Duke Francisco Sforza of Milan to Eleanor's daughter Maria (which would postpone the duke's chances of siring an heir, since Maria was only two); and appoint Bourbon his lieutenant-general and personal representative in northern Italy. Charles ordered each of the six senior councillors who accompanied him to write down their opinion (*parecer*) in order of seniority.[45] Since everyone concurred, in December

1523 messengers left court armed with instructions to win over the new pope, Clement VII, from the same Medici family as Pope Leo, and for Bourbon as 'lieutenant-general in Italy' and thus (in the judgement of Ambassador Contarini) Charles's *alter rex*. Charles believed that 'The French have good reason to regret the presence of Monsieur de Bourbon because, with God's help, he will hold a dagger to their throats.'[46]

The initiative now passed to the imperial generals in Italy. Having spent the winter of 1523–4 driving the remaining French garrisons out of Lombardy, they resolved that Charles de Lannoy, viceroy of Naples, would stay behind to protect these gains while Bourbon invaded Provence, hoping that another English invasion in the northwest would distract Francis. They hoped in vain: his previous campaigns against France had cost Henry nearly 2 million ducats but brought no gains, and he saw no reason to spend more. This left Francis free to concentrate his forces against Bourbon, and although the imperial army captured Aix-en-Provence and laid siege to Marseilles, the approach of superior French forces led to an ignominious retreat into Italy – only to find that Francis had crossed the Alps by another route and arrived in Lombardy first, forcing the imperialists to take refuge in Pavia. Francis followed and tried to take the city by storm. When it failed he prepared for a full siege. Although besieging any fortress over the winter was rash, the king's confidence seemed justified because first the pope and then the Venetian Republic abandoned Charles and concluded an alliance with him.[47] Early in 1525, Henry followed their example, confiscating the correspondence of the imperial ambassador in London (a gross breach of diplomatic protocol) and proclaiming that he had better things to do than spend money on a liar (Charles), a harlot (Margaret), a child (Ferdinand) and a traitor (Bourbon).[48]

The pope, the Venetians and Henry would all soon regret this shift in allegiance because the emperor held two critical advantages. First, the success of the conquistadors in America resulted in the arrival of increasing quantities of treasure in Spain. In March 1524 the Venetian ambassador recorded the arrival of '60,000 pieces of gold, each one worth a ducat and a half', followed in January 1525 by a further '20,000 pieces of gold and 400 marks of pearls'. Charles used each consignment as collateral for the transfer of money to Italy – or, as the Polish ambassador put it, 'The emperor sends all the money that comes to hand to the armies, and puts up with extreme penury at home.' Furthermore, as Gattinara noted, Charles's greatest asset in Italy, 'after God, was the aid sent by the Archduke Ferdinand to reinforce the army of Caesar at precisely the right time'.[49] Moreover, Charles recognized his own military inexperience and empowered his generals to use their initiative and exploit any advantage without further direction. Thus his instructions to Bourbon in August 1524 contained some general advice on how to conduct the coming campaign, but concluded: 'Since you are on the spot, and you know that I have placed my complete confidence in you, it is not necessary to provide you with a detailed plan concerning the success of our common cause and the maintenance of our reputation'. A few months later, when Charles exhorted his brother 'to devote all your strength and do all you can for my cause', he added: 'Since you are so far away from me, I will not tell you what to do or how to do this, but rather leave that for you to decide for the best, according to your resources and the opportunities that arise.'[50]

Nevertheless, Charles wrestled with some grave doubts. According to the English ambassador, Richard Sampson, late in 1524 he became 'very feoble and nothing apt for the warre; his remedy is in Godis hande', and he began to feel deeply insecure about his overall position. Early in 1525 he composed a lugubrious memorandum to clarify his thoughts. If he could not get an honourable peace, he wrote, 'The solution seems to be war'; but 'how could we wage it? I lack the means to maintain my army right now' and 'my friends have abandoned me and left me in the lurch because they do not want to see me more powerful'. He continued: 'There are disadvantages to all courses of action, and some are impossible; but I wanted to write down my opinion in confidence.' Specifically:

Since time is passing, and we are all going to die, I do not want to disappear from the world without leaving something memorable behind. Time lost today cannot be made up tomorrow, and until now I have done nothing that brings me honour. If I delay any more, it will take that much longer to recover . . . I do not want anything to prevent me from doing something important.[51]

Charles concluded this remarkable self-analysis by affirming that 'in no way do I plan to take any risks, unless there is a very good reason' – but, almost immediately, Francis provided that 'very good reason'. The king haughtily declared that he intended to wrest not only Milan but also Naples from the emperor, and sent a powerful expeditionary force to conquer the southern kingdom. The division of his army decisively tilted the military balance in Lombardy. In late January 1525 it seemed to an English envoy with Bourbon that the imperial army was now 'well disposed to do some notable acte against thair enemyes' and so 'bataile is hourely loked fore'.[52] On 19 February, in Rome, the pope's chief adviser confided that 'His Holiness worries day and night' about the 'dangers that war involves' and fretted that 'since the armies are close', Francis 'might risk everything on a battle'; and a week later, Charles's ambassador warned his master that 'everything here is in an uncertain and dangerous state' so that 'Your Majesty must resolve to accept a defeat as you would a victory'. Little did he know that a battle fought 500 kilometres to the north had just transformed the entire military and strategic situation.[53]

Despite Charles's efforts to channel all available resources to Lombardy, his troops there had run dangerously short of funds – 'The defenders of Pavia did not wish to suffer any more, and the whole army was dying of hunger. The Spaniards were becoming insolent; the Germans were beginning to desert' – and his commanders therefore took the fateful decision to launch an all-out attack on the French besiegers, despite being outnumbered. 'We were forced to choose the lesser evil,' Lannoy explained to his sovereign, and 'therefore decided to confide in God, in our good luck, and in the valour of the army', even though it would 'incur some risk. In three or four days either the army will be united with the garrison of Pavia, or I will be dead. I hope to live and be victorious.'[54] On 24 February, the emperor's birthday, the imperial generals used the cover of night to deploy Spanish marksmen inside the French siege-works, ready to support a surprise attack at dawn.

Francis heard rumours that his enemies were on the move, and assumed that they were retreating. Perhaps spurred on by the prospect of capturing the hated Bourbon, the king unwisely ordered his forces to leave their fortifications as he led the heavy cavalry in several charges. At first the knights prevailed, only to be cut down by the concealed Spanish marksmen. Then the garrison of Pavia made a sortie that separated Francis from his men. For a while the king gallantly held his own, slaying several of his assailants, but when his horse was killed under him 'he fell on the ground. Some Germans wanted to kill him but he, fearing death, shouted out that they should not kill him because he was the king of France.' Two followers of Bourbon – men whom the king had recently declared traitors – found the king 'stripped down to his shirt' and persuaded him to surrender. 'All that is left to me,' Francis wrote sorrowfully that evening, 'is my honour and my life'[55] (Pl. 14).

An English diplomat on the scene rated Pavia 'as greate a victory as hath ben sene this many yeres', but he understated: the battle saw the greatest cull of French nobles since Agincourt in 1415, and the captives included not only Francis but also the king of Navarre, who four years earlier had helped to precipitate the war, and many other notables. The Venetian ambassador in Rome reported that 'the pope trembles with fear, saying that he and the Signory must come to terms with the emperor'.[56] Lope de Soria, a veteran diplomat based in Genoa, agreed:

> Let us give infinite praise and thanks to God, and to the glorious St Matthew, since on his day God blessed us with the birth of Your Imperial Majesty, and on that same day He granted us this wonderful victory, which has given Your Majesty more absolute power to settle the affairs of Christendom and lay down the law [*poner ley*] throughout the world.[57]

The balance of power in Europe had shifted decisively: Charles had replaced Francis as the most powerful prince in Christendom – and also as the most feared.

SEVEN

SNATCHING DEFEAT FROM THE JAWS OF VICTORY, 1525–8

WOE TO THE CONQUERED

'At about noon' on 10 March 1525, 'a courier from Italy who had travelled through France' arrived breathless at the Madrid Alcázar where Charles, 'sick and discontented, weighed down by his duties', resided. The courier:

> Was taken to His Majesty, who was talking with two or three advisers about Italy, and said: 'Sire, battle was joined before Pavia; the king of France is a prisoner in Your Majesty's power, and his entire army is destroyed.' Hearing just these words, [Charles] stood as if frozen, and repeated: 'The king of France is a prisoner in my power, and we won the battle?' Then, without saying any more, and without trying to ascertain anything else for the time being, he retired into another room alone and fell to his knees before an image of Our Lady that he kept at the head of his bed.

Charles 'spent a good half-hour secluded, praising God' before emerging to receive from the courier a letter sent by Charles de Lannoy, the victorious commander.[1] Lannoy took advantage of his long service with Maximilian as well as Charles to include in his letter a stern warning: 'Sire, I'm sure you will remember what Monsieur de Beersel [Charles's childhood chamberlain] used to say: that God gives each man one good harvest in their lifetime [*en leur vie ung bon aoust*], and that if they fail to bring it home there is a risk they will never see another one. I do not tell you this,' Lannoy continued, 'because I think Your Majesty will let this opportunity slip', but 'because whatever you decide to do should be done quickly'.[2]

As news of the victory spread, courtiers and ambassadors flocked to the Alcázar, where the emperor received them graciously, one after another, until nightfall (the exception was Ambassador Contarini of Venice, now

France's ally, whom Charles punished for the republic's defection by refusing to let him kiss his hand). Those present noted with admiration that 'one could not perceive in His Majesty any change in either expression or gesture beyond what is normal, even though this was such a notable occasion for rejoicing'. Charles also 'forbade any public celebration, except for a procession to praise God and pray for the dead, since the victory had been won against other Christians'; and the following day, 'having confessed and taken communion, he went to the church of Our Lady of Atocha where he proclaimed that the victory came from God, not him, so that everyone would be more inclined to give thanks for it'. The emperor told Richard Sampson, the English envoy, that:

> He considered the mercy that God had granted so much greater because it came from direct divine goodness, and not from any merit of his own. He therefore held it in high esteem for three reasons: first, because he thus knew that he enjoyed God's grace; second because he now held in his hands the means to prove his constant desire to bring peace to Christendom; and, third, because he could now pardon his enemies, grant another chance to those who had injured him, and reward the friends and dependants who had served him well.

Sampson relayed this message of modesty and moderation in a long letter to Cardinal Wolsey (no doubt eager for reassurance given his master's recent decision to abandon the emperor and ally with France), adding that Charles had shared his hope that:

> This victorie might be to the profette off his frends rather then his own ... And with humble words thanking God, he seyd that his dayly preyre is to have grace gevyn hym well to governe and ordre such possessions as he hath. And as towchinge his enemies, they schall well perceyve that ... his mynde is to use such moderation that in hym ther schalbe fownde no intent off crueltie or revengeance.[3]

His humility was a mask. Charles never forgot or forgave an injury, as Jean Glapion had perceived, and he had made detailed plans for 'revengeance'. After his initial military successes in 1521 he had instructed his diplomats 'to include in your opening communication' with their French counterparts 'details of the claims of all our ancient quarrels concerning the Empire, as well as concerning Castile, Aragon, Navarre, Sicily and Burgundy' – in other words, he sought to recover all the territories once ruled by his ancestors.[4] His goals remained unchanged. In February 1525, just after hearing that the pope and the Venetians had allied with France against him, he told his courtiers:

> I expect to receive bad news from both Milan and Naples, but I could not care less about it. I will go to Italy, and there I will have a better opportunity to get what is mine and to revenge myself on those who have opposed me – especially on that villain [*villaco*] the pope. Perhaps at some point it will turn out that Martin Luther is the one doing the right thing.

'These were remarkable words,' one ambassador noted, 'because they were spoken by the emperor, who is very reserved in his speech.'[5] Charles made a similarly intemperate statement to his ambassador in Rome, the duke of Sessa. He declared that despite the decision of Venice and the pope to ally with France:

> We are not neglecting, nor will we neglect, the support needed to maintain our army and, with God's help, to end this enterprise, dedicating to it the resources of all our kingdoms and states and even hazarding our own person, so that although the French may distract us with their accustomed wiles, our friends and allies will not find our strength abated. Instead, we will be a tough adversary, just as before.

He again asserted (no doubt to intimidate the pope) that 'given the way His Holiness treats us, now is not the time to discuss the Luther question.'[6]

The news from Pavia greatly increased Charles's self-confidence. His initial letters announcing the victory to his officials attributed everything to divine providence, but before long he also noted the coincidence that it had occurred on his birthday, as if that too was divine providence. An official account, composed by Gattinara's secretary Alfonso de Valdés and published by order of Charles's council, argued that the outcome of the battle – won at a time when 'all the friends and allies on whom he usually relied did nothing, and some were opposed' – showed that God 'had given him this victory, as he did with Gideon against the Midianites'. Specifically, Valdés gushed, 'God miraculously gave this victory to the emperor so that he could not only defend Christianity and resist the power of the Turk' but also:

> ... so that after the end of these civil wars (for that is what they should be called, since they are among Christians), he could seek out the Turks

and Muslims in their own lands and, exalting our Holy Catholic faith as his ancestors had done, win the empire of Constantinople and the Holy City of Jerusalem, which are occupied because of our sins, so that (as many have prophesied) under this most Christian prince everyone may accept our Holy Catholic faith, and the words of our Redeemer may come true: let there be one flock and one shepherd.[7]

To end the 'civil wars', seen as the vital prelude to achieving these lofty goals, Charles's ministers proposed two options: either the emperor could coordinate with Henry VIII the conquest and partition of France envisaged in the Great Enterprise, or he could force Francis to make substantial territorial concessions in return for his liberty. The duke of Bourbon favoured the first option, promising Henry that he could 'sett the crowne of Fraunce on your hed, and that shortly; and that there may be more doon now with 100,000 crownes for th'optaining of that than before might have been doon with 500,000, by cause the king with the most part of all the nobles and captaynes of Fraunce be taken and slayne'.[8] Others favoured the second option. Upon hearing of the victory, Charles's ambassador in Rome admonished his master (much as Lannoy had done): 'There is no time to waste: let the necessary efforts be made' to extract major concessions from the French. Ferdinand agreed: his brother must 'exploit your good fortune and ensure that neither the king of France nor his successors will ever have the power to threaten you or your successors'. In particular, Charles must 'avoid the fate of Hannibal after he won the battle of Cannae against the Romans', and the best way to do this (he continued) was 'to pluck some feathers from the wings' of the French king, 'so that he cannot fly, even if he wants to, and thus the emperor and his successors will be sure to enjoy perpetual peace'.[9]

Gattinara agreed, even citing the same Classical precedent as Ferdinand: 'they will say what they said of Hannibal: you know how to win battles but you don't know how to exploit them.'[10] The chancellor then presented to Charles and his council twenty concrete proposals showing exactly how one could pluck feathers from the French rooster, and stressing the need to detain Francis 'until we have a firm peace agreed and executed, with the advice and consent of all the Estates, law courts and other institutions of France'. Moreover, he continued, because 'it is much better, more honourable, and also more secure to deal with persons who are free than with prisoners', Charles should not negotiate with Francis but with his mother, the regent Louise of Savoy. She must immediately renounce, in her son's name, all claims to Artois, Burgundy, Flanders, Milan and Naples, and surrender

to Charles 'everything that the late Duke Charles [the Bold] held by the treaties of Arras, Conflans and Péronne' (signed in 1435, 1465 and 1468 respectively), later annexed by France. She must 'abandon all efforts to protect' the
duke of Guelders, Robert de la Marck and the others who had attacked
Charles; and she must 'restore and pardon Monsieur de Bourbon, giving
him Provence since it is an imperial fief', as well as all the duke's exiled
followers. In addition, Gattinara suggested that the pope 'must be induced
to convene a general council' to reform the Church, and that he and the
others who had recently turned against Charles (notably Venice) must
contribute to the upkeep of Charles's army in Italy.[11]

The emperor endorsed these comprehensive demands and in late March
his envoys left to present them to Louise. 'You must inform us promptly of
her response to all these points,' he insisted, 'so that we may know if there
will be peace, or whether we need to take another path to get what is justly
ours.' He laid out that 'other path' in a letter to Lannoy, reassuring the viceroy
that 'we do not intend to demobilize in any theatre of operations, so that if
we cannot have peace through mildness [*doulceur*] we will be all the more
ready to seek and obtain it by force'. If the French rejected his terms, 'or try
to make us waste time by procrastinating and using fine words', he would
himself lead an army into Languedoc while Lannoy and Bourbon invaded
either Dauphiné or Provence. They would join forces in Avignon. Meanwhile,
although Italian rulers who had 'shown their ill will towards us and our
affairs' deserved punishment, Charles felt that 'now is not the time to
proceed with rigour, to avoid alienating the pope and the Venetians, and in
consequence most of the rest of Italy'. The viceroy must therefore 'act as
seems best to you, either by acting graciously or by dissimulating until time
reveals what will be for the best'.[12] Beyond this, the emperor could 'not see
anything else to do except attack the infidels, something I have always
wanted to do, and especially now', and he begged Lannoy to 'help me to
arrange matters satisfactorily so that I can do something of service to God
before I become much older'.[13]

LOSING THE INITIATIVE

Charles had made the first of a series of catastrophic miscalculations. The
holograph letter that he sent to Louise of Savoy as a covering note for his
peace terms was not only unreasonable but rude. Instead of addressing her
as 'Madam, my good mother', as he had done in the past, his letter began
'Madam Regent' and ended coldly with the hope that 'you will not refuse

such just and reasonable' demands. Louise replied in kind. She told the emperor's envoys that she found his demands 'excessive and exorbitant', and 'with highe words' declared that she was 'redy to defende the realm thow the king be prisonier'. Moreover, although she might discuss a ransom for her son, she refused to surrender even 'oon fote of lande in Fraunce'.[14] Charles also miscalculated when he decided, despite Gattinara's advice, to negotiate directly with Francis as well as with Louise, sending him a copy of his peace demands as well as ordering Lannoy to transport his prisoner from Lombardy to Naples. Francis seized his chance. After reading 'the demands that it pleased you to make', he articulated some counter-proposals in 'the hope of satisfying you' (and also to avoid deportation to Naples). He declared himself ready to concede everything Charles claimed in Italy and the Netherlands, provided he could marry the emperor's sister Eleanor (now betrothed to the duke of Bourbon), with both Burgundy and Milan as an appanage to be ruled by their son. In addition, Francis offered Bourbon not only full restitution but also marriage to his cousin Renée (once Charles's betrothed). These proposals impressed Lannoy and he charged one of his lieutenants, Hugo de Moncada, to convey them orally to the emperor, urging his master 'for the good of your affairs, conclude nothing that concerns Italy until you have heard Don Hugo' – but Moncada did not arrive until 6 June.[15]

Some English diplomats rejoiced when they first heard about Francis's proposals. 'The Frenche king's high herte begynnyth somwhat to com lower', they chuckled, and 'for a begynnyng he offerith to th'emperor right well' – but they too miscalculated. The delay in waiting for Moncada meant that it was now too late (precisely as Francis intended) for Charles to coordinate the immediate invasion and partition of France. Meanwhile in Lombardy, trusting 'muche in his owne eloquens and in his owne wyt, and think[ing] with his rethorik to convert the emperor', Francis convinced Lannoy that if he could meet Charles in person they 'could settle everything with two words'.[16] So although the viceroy and his august captive travelled to Genoa and boarded the fleet assembled there to take them to Naples, as the emperor had ordered, once at sea they abruptly changed course for Spain. Francis entered Madrid in August 1525.

News of this development had dramatic consequences. Antonio de Leyva, now the senior imperial commander in Lombardy, warned Charles that Lannoy's 'departure with the king has upset all Italy. Everyone thinks that Your Majesty will reach an agreement with the king, which would mean their ultimate destruction; and they are therefore undertaking all the nego-tiations and initiatives they can to ally with France and unify all Italy, in order to oppose the grandeur of Your Majesty.' Ambassador Sessa reported much the same concerns in Rome: a 'great fear' concerning 'what Your Majesty may agree with the king of France, because they think and have convinced themselves that such an agreement would be to gain control of the whole of Italy and take power away from those who now hold it, leaving them so reduced that they will never be able to rise again'. According to Sessa, the republic of Venice had already begun to create a hostile alliance of Italian states, and he warned that without immediate reassurance Clement would join them and thus open a second front in the war.[17]

Charles now recognized his dilemma: the French would only surrender Burgundy 'if we apply more force', but 'we lack the money to achieve this'. Therefore, he declared, 'I do not plan to wage war this year, but instead I will concentrate on getting married and then sailing to Italy' both to restore order there and to be crowned emperor. Afterwards he would travel to Germany, 'where I will devote all my resources to exterminating the Lutheran sect', and then he would confront the Turks.[18] Since achieving these lofty goals required peace with France, Charles now belatedly followed the advice of his chancellor: he refused to deal with or even visit the French king, whom he kept confined in the Madrid Alcázar under humiliatingly close surveillance (guards checked throughout the night to make sure that Francis was in his bed). Meanwhile his councillors debated what concessions to demand. Lannoy, although steeped in the traditions of the Burgundian court, prioritized the strategic needs of the empire: Charles must secure Milan and Genoa because they would provide a vital link between his scattered dominions. By contrast Gattinara, although born and bred in Italy, saw Burgundy as the greatest prize, and he ransacked chronicles and archives for precedents and parallels to justify its restoration. The emperor eventually chose the past over the present because, as he explained to the English ambassadors at his court, in asking for Burgundy 'he askith nothing but his owne patrymonye, whereof his ancestors were possessyd to the dethe of duc Charles [the Bold in 1477], whiche is litle paste 40 yeres, and many of his subiectz be yet alyve'. The Englishmen remained unconvinced, reasoning that whereas Francis would find it relatively easy to renounce Italy because it was only a recent gain (and one already lost), he would not willingly 'delyvre oon fote of lande in Fraunce' to his arch-enemy.[19]

Initially, Francis tried to avoid making any concessions. First he attempted to seduce Eleanor. No doubt recalling Count Palatine Frederick's strategy eight years earlier, he wrote her a love letter; but Eleanor replied politely that in matrimonial matters, as in everything else, she did whatever her brother told her. Francis also used bribery until 'there are few men in the emperor's household, great and small, down to the pages in his chamber, whom the French king has not suborned'. He also attempted to escape (once, improbably, using black-face to impersonate the African slave who lit the fires in his room).[20] When all these ploys failed, he summoned a notary and signed a secret protestation that if 'by reason of his detention and prolonged imprisonment he was forced to cede and surrender to the emperor possession of the said duchy of Burgundy, or any other rights of the French Crown, it was and would remain of null effect, because made by force and constraint'.[21] And then the king fell dangerously ill.

The emperor was hunting near Segovia when he received an urgent letter from Francis's doctors, warning that 'if His Majesty wanted to see him alive, he must come at top speed'. He immediately rode to Madrid, covering 50 kilometres in two and a half hours (a remarkable equestrian feat), and strode into the bedchamber where Francis lay semi-conscious. The king 'embraced him with open arms and they remained there for a long time without speaking', after which Charles told Francis, ' "Sir, what I most desire is your health, and we will attend to that; everything else must be taken care of just as you wish." And the king replied "No: I am at your command." And, he added, "Sir, what I ask and beg of you is that there be no third parties between us." ' The two sovereigns spent an hour talking alone, holding each other by the hand, and afterwards 'the king said, "Death to those who have caused these disagreements between us! Is this the deformed, ugly, untalented stutterer [I have been told about]?" And he praised the emperor's prudence and his eloquence.'[22]

Francis expected these courtesies to lead to direct talks with Charles, but as soon as he recovered his health negotiations via 'third parties' resumed. The emperor demanded, as preconditions of Francis's release, not only the 'restitution' of Burgundy and the foundation of four convents 'to pray for the soul of Duke John of Burgundy, murdered by the French while under safe-conduct', but also a promise that Francis:

> ... would abandon all his friends and allies, and would only make alliances with those approved by the emperor. Apart from these terms, many say that the king must pay 4 million in gold and accompany the emperor to his coronation in person; must grant the State of Milan to the duke of Bourbon, who would no longer owe allegiance to the crown of France, but only to the emperor; and must surrender the Dauphin into

the emperor's hands as a hostage until he has performed all that he has promised.[23]

Charles's panicked reaction to news of his rival's illness nevertheless revealed an important weakness, which the French king proceeded to exploit in order to reduce these demands. In November 1525 the doctors attending Francis sent one of their colleagues post-haste to tell Charles 'that they did not believe he could live long' – but the wily Venetian ambassador, Andrea Navagero, who reported this news, suspected (correctly) that this time 'the king had persuaded the doctors to exaggerate his illness to persuade the emperor to reach an agreement sooner, stressing that if the king should die he would lose everything'.[24] Eventually, Francis agreed to the harsh terms asked of him, including the surrender of Burgundy, but on two conditions: first, he must be allowed to return to France at once because (he claimed) only his personal intervention could persuade his subjects to approve the alienation of French territory; second, he insisted on marrying Eleanor.

Initially, the emperor rejected both conditions, declaring that his agents must take possession of Burgundy before he released Francis, and that he had already promised Eleanor's hand to the duke of Bourbon. In a barrage of holograph letters to the emperor, Francis restated his objections, some-times with sarcasm ('some of the terms are the sort of things clerks and bankers handle, not gentlemen'), and sometimes with reproaches ('the kind things that it pleased you to say during my illness have led nowhere'), but he also presented Charles with an ultimatum. 'If you wish to keep me a pris-oner for ever, demanding impossible things,' he warned, 'I will take prison in my stride in the certainty that God (who knows I have not deserved this because I was captured fairly in war) will give me the strength to endure it patiently.' He therefore signed letters patent authorizing the proclamation of his eldest son as king, and he submitted to Charles the names of sixty servants whom he wished to constitute his permanent entourage in prison.[25] Such determination convinced the emperor that he must release Francis, provided he surrendered his two older sons as hostages until Burgundy was in Habsburg hands. He also ascertained that (despite the fact that 'everyone knows that the king of France has contracted venereal disease') his sister preferred to be queen of France than duchess of Bourbon and then, in the course of an awkward personal meeting, he persuaded the duke to relin-quish his claim to Eleanor's hand.[26]

Gattinara vehemently opposed these concessions, reminding his master that in the past 'the kings of France have never kept the promises they made to the House of Burgundy' and predicting that Francis, too, 'would keep none of his promises, claiming that he had been forced as a prisoner to do what he had done'. The chancellor also pointed out that since neither Charles nor Ferdinand had legitimate children, Eleanor was their heiress, so that 'by reason of such a wife' Francis could acquire the entire Habsburg Empire (much as Charles's father Philip had become king of Castile by right of his wife Joanna). He failed to convince Charles, who instead authorized Lannoy to receive the French king's solemn oath that he would honour the concessions demanded by the emperor as soon as he returned to France. The chancellor, for his part, refused his master's demand that he prepare, execute and seal the necessary papers on the grounds that the proposed agreement 'would be the emperor's ruin'.[27]

Gattinara defied his master without knowing that on 13 January 1526 Francis had summoned a notary to record a new secret Protestation that he would not honour any concessions made under duress compromising the integrity of France.[28] A few hours after doing so he affixed his signature to the treaty of Madrid, which conceded everything that Charles demanded: the king would surrender all claims in Italy and all disputed territories in the Netherlands; pardon the duke of Bourbon and his followers and restore all their possessions (or provide compensation); evacuate Burgundy within six weeks of his return to France; conclude a defensive and offensive alliance with Charles; and then join him in fighting both the Turks and the Lutherans. After signing the treaty 'as a prince and as Most Christian King', Francis 'promised and gave his royal word and undertaking that if he should fail to comply with the treaty he would return to Spain within six weeks and make himself a prisoner again'. He also made a personal pledge to Lannoy, 'on his honour as a knight', that he 'would rather die' than default on any of the promises he had just made. A few days later, Lannoy entered the king's bedroom as proxy for Eleanor, and declared that she and Francis were man and wife.[29]

Charles now visited his new brother-in-law again and introduced him to Eleanor. He also sent officials to take possession of Burgundy, and charged Lannoy with ensuring that Francis left Spain at the exact time his two sons entered it as hostages, and not before. Until then, the king must remain under constant guard and surveillance. Gattinara scored only one victory: Charles decided that Eleanor would not join Francis until after the king had publicly 'ratified and sworn to uphold the treaties and other matters agreed between him and me'.[30] Convinced that he had achieved all his goals, on 21 February 1526 the emperor headed south to conclude and consummate his own marriage.

MARRIAGE

Charles had been betrothed many times before – most recently to his cousin Mary Tudor, whom he had promised to marry when she turned twelve. The English diplomats sent to Spain to congratulate Charles on the victory of Pavia took with them an emerald ring from the princess as a 'token for a better knowlaidge to be had, whan God shal sende theym grace to be togedre, whither his Majesty do kepe himself as contynent and chast as with Godd's grace she woll' (perhaps an unsubtle reference to the illegitimate progeny already sired by the emperor). Charles accepted the ring 'verey thankfully, putting it on his litle fyngre, and saing he wolde were it for hir sake'; but he now demanded that Mary, although only nine years old, come to Spain at once. His subjects, he explained, did not want him 'to departe his realm until he had his spouse, my lady Princes, here in Spayn to the intente that a counsail aboute her mought stay the affaires of this realm from suche revolucion as was in his laste absence' (namely the Comuneros). The ambassadors replied that Mary was 'soe tender of age' that 'transporting by see were like to bee to her greate damage, besides the bringing of her into this hote countrie' – something 'we thought th'emperor shulde regard if he intended to have frute of her body'. Charles's brother Ferdinand agreed with this analysis, but drew a different conclusion. 'Considering Your Majesty's age and all your responsibilities, the age of the English princess, and the fact that there are only the two of us,' he wrote, the emperor must marry their cousin Infanta Isabella of Portugal 'so that, with God's grace, you can produce offspring that are the fruit of your marriage' (another unsubtle reference to Charles's illegitimate progeny). Charles agreed. 'Were this marriage to take place,' he mused, 'I could leave the government here in the person of the said Infanta', pocketing not only her magnificent dowry but also the additional taxes promised by the Cortes of Castile in return for a Portuguese match. He therefore issued an ultimatum: unless Mary Tudor came to Spain at once, accompanied by at least the first instalment of the agreed English dowry, he would cancel his engagement.[31]

Charles did not even wait for Henry's response: instead, in October 1525, his agents finalized the terms for the Portuguese marriage – but the pope delayed granting a dispensation to marry his cousin, for fear of offending Henry. As the emperor complained to his ambassador in Rome: 'Although we hold a general dispensation from the pope to marry any woman of any degree of consanguinity or relationship (except first-degree), which we obtained both with regard to the English marriage and this one, they claim that the general dispensation is not sufficient given the multiple degrees of consanguinity we share with the Illustrious Infanta.' The necessary documents did not arrive in Spain until February 1526, forcing Charles to use unseemly ruses in order to delay the wedding.[32] First he postponed choosing the courtiers who would receive his bride-to-be at the Portuguese frontier; then he ordered them to take her to Seville, far from Madrid, and to do so as slowly as possible. Isabella, who had taken to wearing a medallion inscribed *Aut Caesar aut nulla* ('The emperor or no one'), did not enter Seville until 3 March 1526, and even then she had to wait a week for her future husband to arrive.[33]

The emperor eventually rode into the bustling southern metropolis for the first time, watched 'by an infinite number of people who had come from all the surrounding communities to see His Majesty: some said more than 100,000 people lined his route that day.' Still in his travelling clothes and covered in dust, he dismounted in the courtyard of the Seville Alcázar and strode into the room where Isabella awaited him. After fifteen minutes of polite conversation with his fiancée, Charles changed into his finery, attended a nuptial mass and danced. Finally, as an Italian observer put it bluntly, 'the spouses went off to sleep together'.[34]

Two shadows tempered their nuptial bliss. News that the Comunero bishop of Zamora had been tortured and garrotted reached the emperor on the day after his wedding, and he immediately cancelled his plan to spend Holy Week in a local convent. He also petitioned the pope for absolution, citing the outrages that the bishop had 'committed and caused to be committed by others during the recent revolution and sedition in this kingdom', and until absolution arrived 'he did not attend any church services because he considered himself excommunicated'.[35] Charles nevertheless had no regrets. Francisco de Los Cobos, who had drawn up the warrant ordering torture and execution, reassured Alcalde Ronquillo (who had carried out the deeds) that 'His Majesty is very happy with what you did, as you will see from his letter', adding 'we are doing fine this Holy Week', even though 'His Majesty and I do not attend Mass or any service'.[36] The second shadow was the death of Charles's sister Isabeau, queen of Denmark. He had not seen her since dancing immoderately at her wedding a decade before, but according to Baldassare Castiglione, the nuncio (in whom Charles seems to have confided), 'the emperor grieved deeply for the death of his sister' and after 'the celebrations and jousts already planned for his wedding', the whole court went into mourning.[37]

The imperial couple nevertheless still had fun. A week after the marriage, the Portuguese diplomats who had accompanied the empress noted with satisfaction that she 'sleeps every night in her husband's arms, and they are much in love and very happy', and that 'they stay in bed until 10 or 11 o'clock'. When they emerged 'even though everyone is watching, they are always talking and laughing together'. Charles coarsely confided to a courtier that 'I cannot write with my own hand' because 'I am still a new bridegroom'. A month later, the Florentine ambassador complained that 'ever since His Majesty met his lady, he does not attend to business as promptly as he used to do; indeed nothing gets done in the morning'. In September, when Charles suffered some health problems even the refined Castiglione imputed them 'to trying too hard to be a good husband'.[38] When the temperature in Seville became oppressive, the newlyweds made a slow journey through Carmona and Córdoba to Granada to pay their respects to their common grandparents, the Catholic Monarchs, buried in the newly completed royal chapel of the cathedral, and then took up residence in the palace of the Muslim kings in the Alhambra. Charles did not intend to stay there for long – he promised his brother that he would sail from Barcelona to Italy at the end of June and suggested that they should meet in Milan – but irrefutable proof that Francis had reneged on his promises thwarted his plans.

The release of the king in return for the surrender of his two older sons took place under elaborate safeguards on the Franco-Spanish border on 17 March 1526. Just before he departed Francis repeated his promise to Lannoy that he would keep his word and ratify the treaty in the first French town that he reached; but at Bayonne later that same day, when the emperor's ambassador requested ratification, the chancellor of France replied that 'the king will perform whatever reason and honesty requires him to do' – a very different promise. When the ambassador tried again three days later, he was told that transferring Burgundy to Habsburg hands would take more time. Charles found this response 'very strange, making me suspicious about other things'. Worse, it 'leaves us and our affairs in suspense'.[39]

While in suspense, the emperor kept himself busy in Granada. When not in bed with his bride, he attended diligently to the avalanche of correspondence generated by his growing empire (for example, promising to defend Erasmus against his critics: 'the emperor stands by you, as a man strong in every branch of learning and in true piety, and he will defend your honour and reputation as he does his own').[40] He also took several steps to accelerate the Christianization of Granada, begun by the Catholic Monarchs: he founded one college to train priests for the royal chapel and another (offering instruction in logic, philosophy, theology and law) to train preachers – an institution that would become the university of Granada. Charles also presided over a commission convened to formulate orders (*Mandatos*) aimed at Christianizing the Moriscos (the subjects of the Muslim kings, and their descendants). Some orders prohibited Islamic practices, such as the circumcision of boys and the ritual slaughter of animals, while others forbade the use of spoken or written Arabic and the wearing of traditional Muslim dress – although none of these measures came into effect, because almost immediately the emperor agreed to suspend the *Mandatos* for forty years in return for a substantial payment from the Morisco community to help fund his wars.

While living in the Alhambra, the empress conceived the future Philip II. The English ambassador was the first to report the news, in September 1526: 'We can nowe speake openlie and assuredlie that the emperatris is with childe, whereof all this corte and this people takethe no litle ioye.' His Polish colleague confirmed the news two weeks later. 'They say it is now almost a month since the empress conceived and became pregnant (happy and fortunate event!). For that reason she spends most of her time in bed.'[41] He also predicted that the emperor would abandon his plan to go to Italy, leaving his pregnant wife to govern Spain in his absence, because renewed French hostilities made the journey too hazardous.

'FULL OF DUMPS AND SOLITARY MUSING'

Before leaving Seville, the English ambassador reported that 'Th'emperor is marvellously altered sithens his marriage. He is full of dompes and solitarye musing, sometimes alone 3 or 4 hours togider. There is no myrthe ne comfort with hym.' The trigger for his deep depression was confirmation that Francis had reneged not only on the treaty of Madrid, but also on his promise to return to captivity. When Charles's ambassador at the French court repeated his demand that the king ratify the concessions 'you have promysed to performe ... as soon as yow cam into your r[ealm]', Francis answered with a mordant jest: he would follow the procedure that 'he hadd lerned in S[pain] of th'emperor':

> For ther was never an article in the treatye of p[eace but the emperor] hadd with his counsel wel examened, discussyd and determened to his most profete, where he [Francis] hadd [neither] counsel, nor was in liberty to dispute hyt; wherefore now he wold as well use hys [own] cou[nsel] in the confyrmacion of the same as th'emperor dydd in the makyng.[42]

Meanwhile Francis refused to surrender anything.

Why had Charles missed his chance to bring home the 'good harvest' that usually comes only once in a lifetime? Francesco Guicciardini, a protagonist in the struggle between pope and emperor, began the relevant chapter of his *History of Italy* by asking that very question. 'Perhaps the desire of the Netherlanders to recover Burgundy, their ancient patrimony and the title of their rulers, was so strong that it did not allow them to see the truth', Guicciardini speculated, adding that 'it was said that some were influenced by the gifts and promises to them by the French'. In the end, however, Charles himself made the fateful decision. Although 'the great influence exercised' by Lannoy and the other Netherlanders with whom he had grown up had no doubt swayed the emperor, Guicciardini thought that Burgundy 'was what he really wanted'. The Venetian ambassador agreed: "The emperor believed himself more than he believed anyone else.'[43] On the surface, self-deception seems the most plausible explanation – after all, Charles hoped to be buried in Dijon, beside his Burgundian ancestors, and he dreamed of recovering the lands lost to France after the death of Duke Charles the Bold – but this ignores the numerous explicit promises of compliance made by both Francis and his mother. As soon as Louise of Savoy heard about the treaty of Madrid, she informed Charles that 'I shall set out for Bayonne tomorrow, determined to execute everything that you have been promised'; while from San Sebastián, Francis assured 'my good brother' of his eagerness to return to France 'so that I can put into effect what we resolved as soon as possible'.[44] We now know that these and several other similar letters, all holographs, were lies from beginning to end; but Charles could be forgiven for assuming at the time that his fellow monarchs, now united to him by marriage, would never engage in such shameless, sustained and blatant deception.

Nevertheless, few other contemporaries were deceived. 'All Christendom marvelled greatly at the treaty' of Madrid, wrote Guicciardini, 'because the liberation of the French king must precede the execution of its terms, and it was the opinion of everyone that once liberated he would refuse to surrender Burgundy.' More than a month before Francis signed the treaty, Nuncio Castiglione reported from Charles's court that 'Many people who are reputed wise say that before he has been out of prison for six months, the French king will wage war on the emperor more savagely than ever'; while in April 1526 he noted that 'almost everyone thinks that the French king will claim *Non stant foedera facta metu* [Treaties made through fear have no force]'.[45] In Rome the pope likewise assumed that:

Of all the matters King Francis has agreed with the emperor, he will only execute those that must take effect before his release, such as the surrender of his sons, and postpone all the other things he has been asked to do, such as his marriage with Queen Eleanor and the transfer of certain parts of Burgundy, until after his liberation – and then he will not do them. So the only effects of this treaty will be that the emperor will have custody of the sons instead of their father.

In London, Cardinal Wolsey came to an identical conclusion. Some of the articles of the treaty of Madrid, he noted:

Concernyng alienacion of the rightes of his crown, be not in [Francis's] power to performe, and the others whiche be in his power, be swo grete, that, being ons at liberte, it is not like that he intendeth to performe them; and specially in actual delyvere of the duchie of Burgoyne . . . [Therefore] I cannot persuade to myself that the Frenche king is deter-myned, after his restitucion unto libertie, to performe the same.[46]

Wolsey welcomed this outcome because he worried that if Francis surren-dered to Charles all he wanted, England would no longer hold the balance of power in western Europe. He therefore wrote to Louise of Savoy rejoicing at 'the deliverance of the king your son from the dangers and the cruel treat-ment he has suffered in Spain' and expressing the hope that 'no part of the dishonourable and unreasonable treaty violently extorted from your son will be observed'. He also pointed out that since Charles already ruled 'Germany, being the grettest part of Cristendome', as well as the Netherlands, southern Italy and Spain, 'the realme of Fraunce shal be envyronned on 3 parts, and scituated, as it wer, in the mydde of th'emperors countryes'; so whenever Charles or his successors decided to attack, the French would 'be inforced to stond at their defence on the said 3 parts'. Fear of Habsburg encirclement would dominate French foreign policy for over a century. To avoid this fate, Wolsey suggested that Francis should refuse to cede any of his territories and instead offer to ransom his sons 'for conuenient sommes of money', and he promised that in this England would act as 'a loving mediator'.[47]

For some time Francis maintained his deception. He continued to shower Charles with personal messages that reiterated his intention to honour all his promises in due course, but he also sought foreign support – moral as well as material. Pope Clement was one of the first to oblige, declaring that the king was 'not only free from his obligation to comply in his conscience, because he had acted under duress', and 'it is well known to all that obligations incurred through force are not valid'.[48] When Lannoy and Moncada, two men to whom Francis was personally indebted, arrived to urge the king to keep his promises, he received them graciously but insisted that 'he was not obliged to keep any promises that he was alleged to have made, because they were extorted from him through fear of permanent imprisonment'. Even Lannoy now realized that he had been deceived, and lamented to Charles that 'I wish to God that I had never become involved in this business', adding that he suspected that Francis 'wants to proceed by dissimulation and gain an advantage elsewhere as best he can'. This time, Lannoy was right: even as Francis feted his former captors at his court, he finalized an alliance with Venice, the pope, Florence and Francesco Sforza, whom Charles had recently deposed as duke of Milan. Henry VIII agreed to act as 'protector'.[49]

The Holy League of Cognac (as its signatories termed their agreement) called upon Charles to release the French princes for a reasonable ransom; to allow all Italian states to return to their pre-war boundaries; to reinstate Sforza as duke of Milan; to travel to his imperial coronation with a modest escort (the size to be determined by Venice and the pope); and to repay all his debts to England (which now totalled 800,000 ducats). Should the emperor fail to comply, the allies agreed to share the cost of mobilizing troops and galleys to seize Milan, Genoa and Naples.[50] On 23 June 1526, Clement sent an acerbic Brief to Charles that deplored his recent conduct towards the various members of the League: invading France unjustly; humiliating its king while in captivity; deposing Sforza; seizing goods and destroying property in the Papal States. Taken together, he stated, they 'have led me to form an alliance with those who care for the peace of Italy and Christendom', and he ended with a bold threat: 'Now if you wish to live in peace, it is good; but if not, be aware that I have both soldiers and weapons, and I shall use them to defend Italy and Rome.' As ambassador Navagero mused, all this marked 'a stunning reversal of fortunes. After being taken prisoner, losing so many men and suffering so much damage, the king of France is free and can now do more than ever before. It is in his power to make himself great and the emperor small.'[51]

FIGHTING ON TWO FRONTS

Hugo de Moncada, who travelled from the court of France to Rome once it became clear that his mission to Francis had failed, noted with alarm widespread anti-imperial sentiment throughout northern Italy. 'I have had to pass between pikes and guns, with cries of "Death to the Spaniards"', he told Charles, and on reaching Rome he found ambassador Sessa 'and his household standing to arms because the pope has declared Your Majesty to be his enemy, and begins to mobilize his troops'. Together, Sessa and Moncada sought to convince Clement that since neither Francis nor Henry could send the promised assistance in time, the Italian signatories of the League would have to face the emperor's wrath alone. This, they warned him, risked the 'destruction of the Apostolic See and confusion of Christendom', because the imperialists 'would declare war on His Holiness not only with weapons but also by using all other means that could produce a reformation in the Church'. They also played shamelessly upon Clement's greatest fear: 'We reminded him of the Lutheran heresy and the demands from Germany for a council.' As for the idea that threats might force Charles to reduce his demands, the envoys asserted that the emperor would rather 'lose all his states and kingdoms, one by one, spilling the blood of all his subjects and allies, than give in'. In their last stormy audience, the two Spanish envoys 'bade farewell to His Holiness, begging his forgiveness if we waged war on him in defence of Your Majesty's estates, because we are forced and compelled to do so'. They also advised Charles that 'after all these conversations, it appears to us that Your Majesty must consider the pope as your enemy, along with the kings of England and France, and the Venetians, who together are committed to ruining and undermining Your Majesty's glory'.[52]

Several of Charles's ministers elsewhere felt similarly belligerent. In June 1526 his ambassador in Savoy advised that 'Since the pope wants to set Christendom in flames, Your Majesty should set fires everywhere, punishing those who have taken up arms against your army'; and according to ambassador Lope de Soria in Genoa, 'All the damage Your Majesty might commit against His Holiness would appear legitimate, considering his ingratitude and the scarce interest he displays to serve God and good Christians. Moreover, only Your Majesty can punish the pontiff for not doing what he should.'[53]

Charles took these calls to 'punish the pontiff' very seriously. He asked his confessor, García de Loaysa, 'if with a just cause he could cease to obey the pope', and he also resorted (perhaps for the first time) to a technique that would become standard whenever the Habsburg rulers of Spain faced a moral dilemma: he 'summoned some theologians to his council' to determine whether 'in order to preserve and protect our lands', he could and should 'raise an army to fight everyone in the world, even the pope'.[54]

Apparently the theologians approved, because in June 1526 the emperor instructed Moncada that if the pope 'should ask you impossible things, or string you along with dissimulation and delays in order to gain time and make alliances with others, not with us, you should remember that it is better to prevent than to be prevented'. He also revealed that Cardinal Pompeo Colonna, a long-time supporter of Spain who had led the opposition to the election of Clement, had recently indicated 'that he was in a good position to expel the pope from Rome'. The emperor therefore ordered Moncada 'to negotiate with the said Cardinal Colonna so that he puts his plans into action *as if he were acting alone*, and *in secret* provide him with all the assistance you can'.[55] He also sent a small fleet to Lombardy carrying the duke of Bourbon and a few hundred soldiers.

These modest moves were a far cry from the emperor's proud boast earlier in the year that he would sail to Italy at the head of a large army, and Clement openly belittled his efforts. According to Charles's ambassador in Rome, 'They think little of M. de Bourbon's arrival, because he came without troops. I have heard it said that the pope laughed about it, saying that Your Majesty sent him here simply to get rid of him.' Clement would not laugh for long.[56]

Charles now made an important change in his plans. 'There is nothing in this world that I would rather do than go to Italy,' he explained to his brother in a long letter, 'not through any desire to make myself great, but solely to discharge the responsibilities God has given me and to secure the fruit that my journey might achieve for the benefit of Christendom, bringing it universal peace so that you and I can direct our united forces against the Infidel and extirpate the errors and heresies of Luther', perhaps by 'arranging a general council for the reformation of the church'. He also wanted to go in order to reorganize his troops in Lombardy, 'because if my army is lost, or forced to demobilize, I will soon lose Naples and Sicily, which would afterwards be hard to recover'. Conversely, 'if I can gain the upper hand in Italy, and be crowned emperor, I would be able to lay down the law to everyone and be the sovereign of everyone without resistance' (so much for lacking 'any desire to make myself great'!). But 'that is what the pope and other rulers fear most,' he continued, and 'I believe this is the cause of their present alliances against me.' The emperor again regretted that he would lack the troops, ships and money 'sufficient for my safety, honour and profit' if he sailed to Italy at once, let alone 'to support and assist as I desire' the king of Hungary. 'If we could have peace, you can be sure that I would deploy everything I have to Hungary; but if the wars concerning my own possessions are going to continue – and I see for sure that they will – I leave you to judge whether I should not look to my own defence and deploy all my resources for that.' The emperor therefore suggested a radically different strategy for Germany: he sent Ferdinand the draft of an edict that suspended the legal penalties he had imposed on Lutherans at the Diet of Worms, because 'some of my advisers think that through this suspension we could raise a substantial body of infantry and cavalry that could join with you wherever you wish to use them, for example to assist in Hungary'. In addition, as Gattinara shrewdly pointed out, the offer to tolerate Lutheranism, even for a short time, 'could serve as a vice to reduce the pope to reason'.[57]

The previously unthinkable idea of selling toleration to the Lutherans in return for funding troops to defend Hungary reflected the arrival at court of some alarming news. In April 1526, Sultan Suleiman had left Istanbul at the head of a huge army and siege train, and in July he entered Hungary for the first time. Ferdinand begged for urgent assistance, but Charles replied that 'I already have a tiresome Turk to deal with: the king of France.'[58] Then in August the sultan won a stunning victory at Mohács that left most Hungarian nobles and also King Louis dead on the battlefield. According to Ottoman tradition, the victory made Suleiman lord of Hungary: two weeks later he entered Buda and conferred the kingdom upon one of his vassals.

Thanks to his marriage to Louis's sister, Ferdinand almost immediately secured his own election as king of Bohemia (which Louis had also ruled) and then, ably backed by his sister Marie, Louis's widow, he defied Suleiman and claimed the crown of Hungary for himself. But his appeals for other Western rulers to fight the 'common enemy of Christendom' largely failed: despite copious information on the scale and immediacy of the Turkish threat, the struggle for northern Italy continued to absorb most of their attention and resources. Even Pope Clement, who paid the wages of 5,000 soldiers in Hungary, spent far more on the war in Lombardy. He was taken at a disadvantage when the combined forces of Moncada and the Colonna family entered Rome and took him hostage in September 1526. Charles later protested that 'We were greatly displeased by what the troops of Don Hugo tried to do', but he lied: by joining forces with the Colonna and invading Rome, Moncada had executed the emperor's express orders.[59]

Shortly before the news from Rome arrived at Charles's court, the ambassadors of the four major parties to the League of Cognac – England, France, the papacy and Venice – requested an opportunity to provide the emperor with formal notification of its demands. The audience went reasonably well until the French envoy 'summoned' Charles to release the French princes –

now aged seven and eight – in return for a ransom. At this, Nuncio Castiglione reported, 'everyone could see that His Majesty was very angry' and 'the reason for his anger, as His Majesty himself explained to me, was that word "summon"', which is 'normally used when addressing those under siege and ordering them to surrender, with overtones of menace and destruction'. The English envoy reported that Charles angrily:

> . . . turned to the ambassador of France, saying, 'I will not delyver them [the French princes] for monaye. I refused monaye for the father: I will muche lesse take monaye for his sons. I am content to render them upon raysonable treatie, but not for monaye. [Neither will I] trust any more the French king's promises, for he hathe deceived me, and that like no noble prince. And where he excuseth that he cannot fulfil some things without grutche of his subgettz, lett him fulfil that wiche is in his power, wiche he promised by the honor of a prince to fulfil; that is to say, that if he coulde not bringe all his promises to passe he wold return againe hider into prison.

The emperor concluded the audience by charging the French ambassador to relay a chivalric challenge to his master: if Francis refused to return to prison, 'may it please God that we can settle our differences in a duel, man to man, to avoid causing the death of so many Christians'.[60]

A few days later Charles sent Clement a bitter letter of reproach that did not even use the customary subservient conventions. He addressed the pontiff as 'tu', and commenced: 'You cannot be unaware that you became pope through my intercession and with my help' and yet 'you began hostilities against me before I could receive the Brief containing your declaration of war, and you intend not only to expel me from Italy but also to deprive me of the imperial title'. He expressed regret that he had not previously taken up the complaints about the papacy voiced by his German subjects, and threatened that unless Clement ceased to attack him he would convene a council himself to end the corruption and reform the abuses of the papal court. Castiglione considered the emperor's reply 'more acerbic than the Brief'.[61] Gattinara ordered the emperor's Latin Secretary Alfonso de Valdés to publish the texts of this exchange, together with a pointed commentary: immodestly entitled *A defence of Charles the Divine*, the volume soon appeared in Spain, Germany and the Netherlands.[62] In addition, Lannoy received funds to raise 9,000 troops in Spain to reinforce the duke of Bourbon. Although the galleys of the League of Cognac, commanded by the

Genoese patrician Andrea Doria, intercepted Lannoy and forced him to sail to Naples instead of Lombardy, Ferdinand sent another German contingent across the Alps to assist Bourbon, so that imperial forces now threatened Rome from both north and south.

It was at this point, 'when I had already raised and sent to Italy the last ducat in cash that I could find', that news of the loss of Hungary and the death of its king arrived in Spain, together with an urgent appeal from Ferdinand that his brother must 'make terms with the king of France and gain as many allies as [you] can', so that all Christian princes could unite and deploy their combined forces to halt the Turkish advance. Charles, still in Granada, immediately asked his council for advice and his ministers, like Ferdinand, 'begged Your Majesty to reach an agreement with the king of France, and if you cannot get the terms you deserve then you should accept whatever the current situation permits'. In addition, 'Your Majesty, God willing, should leave here as early as possible' and summon the Cortes of Castile to meet in Valladolid early in 1527. In light of the 'sad news' from Hungary, the council also recommended that all 'prelates, regular clergy and town councils should be admonished and instructed to arrange prayers and other devout interventions' and that 'all preachers should deliver sermons stressing the danger that faces Christendom in order to fire them up'. Charles himself must send as much money and as many troops as possible to his brother; he must moderate 'the expenses of his household and court, especially spending on food and dress, because we will order the whole kingdom to follow their example'; and he must make sure to pay and arm the kingdom's defenders.[63]

Charles needed no persuasion: the 'destruction of Hungary' shook him to the core. He told the nuncio in November 1526 that he was now willing to submit his dispute with Francis to the mediation of either Henry or Clement, and that to obtain 'a general peace he would consent to release the king's sons without payment, provided the king gave security for remaining at peace', so that he could travel to Austria and lead the defence of Christendom against the Turks in person. In a rare moment of self-analysis, Charles admitted to Castiglione that:

He was a mortal man and had defects, and amongst the rest he was tardy in making decisions, and had allowed many things to be delayed through neglect; but now he meant to conquer his nature and be very diligent, and would lose no opportunity whatsoever for arriving at this end. The whole world might wage war on him as much as they pleased, and the king of France could take Spain if he should think fit, but in order to defeat the Turks he would abandon everything.[64]

The loss of Hungary also affected Clement, freed from prison but acutely conscious of his inability to defend Rome alone against either Bourbon or Lannoy. He abandoned the League of Cognac, concluded an eight-month truce with Lannoy (apparently without realizing that it did not apply to Bourbon), and began to demobilize his forces.

TO ROME!

Francis's decision to renege on the treaty of Madrid seriously weakened the duke of Bourbon. His former master had confiscated his properties and revenues and transferred them to loyal ministers and nobles, leaving the duke not only penniless but also without hope of restitution. Admittedly, Charles had named him duke of Milan but the imperial army had exhausted all the resources available there, forcing Bourbon to lead his semi-mutinous army south in search of new areas to plunder. At first they threatened Florence, but finding it well defended they marched towards Rome and declared that they would only stop when Clement paid their arrears. The pope rashly rejoined the League of Cognac and declared Charles deposed as king of Naples. The imperial ambassador in Rome reported despondently that 'some are betting 5 to 1 that the pope will be master of Naples within 4 months'.[65]

The gamblers lost their bets: Clement's position was untenable. He had disbanded most of his own forces, and those of his principal allies – France, England and Venice – lay far away, whereas Bourbon now abandoned his siege artillery and used Roman roads to lead his army southwards at the astonishing speed of 30 kilometres a day.[66] At dawn on 6 May, boosted by volunteers who sensed the chance of plunder, the imperialists launched a surprise attack on Rome. Unfortunately for the city's defenders, Bourbon died in the first assault and no one else possessed sufficient authority to restrain his victorious troops. The sack of the city therefore lasted ten days, during which perhaps 8,000 Romans perished and the atrocities carried out by Charles's troops (an eyewitness reported) 'were so numerous that there would not be enough paper and ink – or memory – to record them all'. Indeed 'the extent of the destruction means that Rome will not be Rome again in our lifetimes, or in 200 years'.[67] Clement and a few cardinals found refuge in the Castel Sant'Angelo but, with no hope of relief, after a month they surrendered to the imperialists. Meanwhile the pope's Medici relatives fled Florence and their enemies proclaimed the city-state to be a republic once more.

For the second time Bourbon and his troops had 'made the emperor the absolute master of Italy', and Lope de Soria rejoiced that 'God clearly holds Your Majesty's affairs in his hands, because He guides and furthers them in such a miraculous way', so that all 'Christian princes may know that He desires their punishment by means of Your Majesty'. Ferdinand also offered his congratulations on the 'good news of the capture of Rome', and expressed the hope that since 'the pope is currently in your hands, or at least in a condition where you can do what you like with him', Charles would not release him 'until the general affairs of Christendom have been put in order'.[68]

The emperor had to decide what to do next without the assistance of Gattinara. Alienated by the rejection of his advice on how to negotiate with the French, the chancellor had abandoned the court and sailed to Italy to attend to his own affairs and so, in his absence, Charles convened all foreign ambassadors to explain in person what had happened in Rome. In the sarcastic words of an English diplomat, he made 'his excuse, avowing with his hands often layed opon his brest that these things were doone not oonlie without anye commission geven by hym but also against his will, and that to his utter displeasure and sorrow'.[69] The ambassadors did not believe him – and they were right. On 31 May 1527, when the first rumours of the sack of the city and the flight of the pope arrived at the imperial court, the Florentine ambassador reported that 'instead of inducing piety and sympathy in the emperor, they excited an excess of joy and such immoderate happiness here that, departing from his normal habit, he laughed and joked so much while talking to his entourage that he scarcely found time to eat'. The ambassador suspected that 'His Imperial Majesty has already begun to imagine himself as an absolute monarch, with everyone forced to accept his decisions'.[70] Charles himself confirmed these fears one week later, on 7 June. Not yet aware that Bourbon was dead, he sent him a letter that revealed that the capture of Rome and of the pope formed part of a broader strategy already communicated to the duke. Since 'a good peace is the thing I want most', the emperor claimed:

> I hope you will take care not to be deceived, and will secure firm guarantees that the said peace will be observed; and that you will also see to it that, if it can be done safely, *the pope comes here* to make the arrangements for a universal peace ... [because] as you well know, this

could have many favourable consequences for God's service, the good of all Christendom, and the advancement of my interests – and also your own.

In other words, Charles had already instructed his lieutenant not only to capture the pope, but to send him to Spain as a prisoner where he would be made to sign favourable terms under duress, just as he had made Francis do two years earlier. Charles continued, 'I do not know for sure *what you will have done with the pope after you entered Rome*' – further evidence of his earlier instructions to Bourbon – 'but in my last letters to you I wrote that the principal point is that if you can make a good peace, or some other arrangement, with the pope, you will then endeavour to lead my army into Venetian territory, to force them to pay its wages and compel them to come to terms too'.[71]

After hearing that Bourbon had died and Clement had surrendered to his troops, Charles granted Lannoy full powers to make war and peace 'as seems best for our reputation, given the complete confidence that we have in you'; and he informed one of his trusted diplomats, Baron Veyré, that since 'it has pleased God to grant this victory in Rome', and since 'the pope's capture seems to have been the handiwork of God, and by His permission, in order to permit and open the way to a good peace in Christendom, for its well-being and repose', the time was now ripe to convene 'a council for the reformation of the Church, so desired and so necessary as everyone knows, and also for the extirpation of the misguided sect of Luther'. Veyré must therefore travel to Rome and, while Lannoy applied diplomatic and military pressure, persuade the captive pope to make major concessions.[72]

CHARLES AT BAY

'Things over here are now in a very different state from what Your Majesty thought when I left,' Veyré ruefully observed once he reached Italy in September 1527. Indeed 'they are in such a bad state that they could not be worse': the mutinous troops in Rome (many of them German Lutherans) threatened to kill or abduct the pope; a new French expeditionary force had entered Lombardy under an experienced commander, Odet de Foix, lord of Lautrec; and the sudden death of Lannoy created a new power vacuum. 'For the love of God, Sire, think about making peace with the French, on whatever terms you can,' Veyré pleaded. After apologizing 'if I make Your Majesty despair', he repeated his urgent advice: 'I beg you to make peace with France, because it will be less dishonourable, and also you will gain the freedom to avenge yourself [*vous vengier*] on those who strive to harm you' in Italy.[73]

It was too late: Clement's humiliation had won him international sympathy and support. In August 1527, Henry VIII signed an alliance with Francis that offered his daughter Mary's hand to Francis's second son and repeated his promise to pressure Charles to release the French princes in return for a reasonable ransom. In addition, in the hope of persuading Clement to approve his plan to divorce Queen Katherine, Henry promised to resist all calls for a general council as long as the pope remained a prisoner, and to send troops and a subsidy to assist the French army in Italy.[74]

At first the allies' campaign prospered. After joining forces with the Venetians, Lautrec swiftly overran almost all of Lombardy while a naval force helped to regain for France the critical port of Genoa. A letter written by Antonio de Leyva, isolated in Milan, highlighted the perilous imperial position in northern Italy: 'More than two months ago' he had written 'to all Your Majesty's captains, informing them of the need in which I find myself', but although 'I have written two hundred letters to different places, I have received replies to none.' Leyva concluded with a bleak warning: 'Your Majesty places confidence in your good fortune, and with good reason; but it would be wise to reinforce it with deeds, and to remember that God does not perform miracles each and every day.'[75]

The situation of Charles's troops quartered in and around Rome was no better: although they remained a formidable fighting force, without a leader they continued to ravage the city as a way of maintaining pressure on Clement to pay their arrears (some 400,000 ducats). One of their commanders begged Charles:

> . . . to keep in mind what is owed to God, and not to acquire such an evil reputation in the world through the disorders, thefts and murders that your army carries out and has carried out in Italy, which will only increase unless they are paid . . . Your glory must not rest upon so many and such enormous evils, because neither God nor the world will permit it.

Like Leyva, he concluded that 'an agreement with France would be better' and suggested that 'if Your Majesty stops insisting on recovering Burgundy, perhaps the king might once again be your friend', but he pleaded in vain. In November 1527 diplomats representing France, England, Milan, Venice, Ferrara and the College of Cardinals signed a solemn league dedicated to 'the liberation of the pope'.[76]

According to ambassador Navagero, the emperor is now 'very doubtful about what he ought to do. On the one hand, he thinks it would be honourable to release the pope; on the other hand, he cannot be sure that if he does so the pope will be his friend'. At least Charles had the good sense to delegate critical foreign-policy decisions to his proconsuls: he instructed Ferdinand, Margaret and his generals in Italy 'to do the best you can, without having to consult me, or await orders from me, because such is my confidence in you that I have given you the power to make all decisions'.[77]

The emperor's spirits revived with the birth on 21 May 1527 of the future Philip II, the first prince to be born in Spain for fifty years. Charles signed jubilant letters to his leading subjects that same day, presenting his role in the process in Messianic terms: 'I trust in God that this will prove beneficial to His service and to these realms; and I hope it will please Him to allow me to serve Him even better in the future'. According to Ambassador Martín de Salinas, 'the Emperor is so happy and joyful and delighted with his new son that he does nothing but order celebrations for the gift God has sent us; and day and night there are jousts and cane games and all sorts of fun'. The celebratory plays performed at his son's baptism on 5 June featured prophets who predicted a glittering future for the infant, just as they had done for the Christ child.[78]

The rejoicing ceased when news of the sack of Rome arrived, but resumed as soon as the empress was fit enough to watch a new round of jousts and other spectacles staged by her husband. In August, Salinas reported that Charles and Isabella 'are the happiest spouses in the world', and three months later the empress was pregnant again.[79] But other observers noted that Charles had become impatient and even intemperate in audiences. In July 1527 he listened 'all lowering and [with] hevie countenuance' as the French ambassador yet again offered money and the partial surrender of France's claim to Naples in return for the repatriation of the two princes and the restitution of Francesco Sforza as duke of Milan. A few days later the emperor predicted to the English ambassadors that 'the Frenche king wold never sitt still untill his fedres be pulled' – by which he meant depriving him of Burgundy; and in October, Navagero reported that Charles had again 'used very rude words, and (contrary to his normal behaviour) shown extreme anger' during an audience, and raged that 'the king of France had decided to use force to make him do his bidding, but he deceived himself' because 'he would never be compelled to do anything under duress'. The ambassador reflected that Charles 'was young and accustomed to having good luck', which made it easy for him to be gracious, but 'now that his affairs do not go so well' he predicted that 'those who deal with him will need to proceed with great dexterity'.[80]

Luckily for imperial affairs, Gattinara returned to court in October 1527. According to the chancellor's autobiography, 'Caesar had agreed to and conceded more than was fitting in order to obtain peace. He [had] consented to conditions that were highly prejudicial to himself, his dignity and his situation.'[81] Gattinara resolved to put a stop to this, and matters came to a head in January 1528 when, at a joint audience, the ambassadors of France, England, Milan, Venice and Florence – the surviving members of the League of Cognac – demanded in the name of their masters that Charles restore Milan to Sforza and accept a ransom for the French princes, in return for which Francis would surrender Genoa and withdraw his army from Italy. The emperor flatly rejected this ultimatum, because (according to the Polish ambassador, Jan Dantiszek) 'he remembered what Cicero said, "Allowing oneself to be deceived once is unpleasant, the second time shameful, and the third time stupidity", a maxim that he followed, since he had been deceived before.' The members of the League had anticipated this negative response, and now 'the French and English heralds arrived and sent a message to His Majesty saying that they wished to give him a certain document, which His Majesty had been expecting for six months (because that is how long the heralds had been at his court). His Majesty graciously listened in the great hall of the palace in the presence of all the grandees, prelates and ministers' while the French herald 'declared war on him by land and sea', and the ambassadors of England, Florence, Milan and Venice then 'pronounced their "challenge" (as they call it)'.[82]

Thanks to his familiarity with the code of chivalry, Charles knew exactly what to do next. He 'responded in a strong voice so that everyone could hear him' as follows: 'For the past seven years the king of France has waged war on me without a formal declaration, and it is amazing that he should declare it only now, when according to the Law of War he is absolutely forbidden to do so because he is the emperor's prisoner and has betrayed the confidence placed in his hands ... And now you tell me', Charles continued, that your masters 'will compel me to return the princes. I shall therefore reply in a very different manner than I have done so far: I intend to keep them and will never return them under threat of force, because I have never been accustomed to do things under duress.' He then took the French herald aside, and charged him to deliver a special message to his master: 'Since he has neither abided by nor honoured the oaths he gave me, he should prepare to fight a duel with me. And tell him on my behalf, using the following words: He should look to his honour – that is, if he has any left.'[83]

Chivalric protocol obliged Charles to release the heralds unscathed, but he arrested all the diplomats sent by members of the League. They scarcely had time to pack before they were ignominiously marched out of town and into confinement 'accompanied by 50 horsemen and 100 soldiers of His Majesty's guards, as if we were criminals, watched by all the citizens who hung out of their windows and doors'. They remained in detention for four months ('which seemed like four years'), until Charles received confirmation that his own ambassadors were safe. He also punished the young French princes, moving them from one austere and uncomfortable castle to another until they reached the isolated fortress at Pedraza de la Sierra (Segovia), and separating them from their French servants (over one hundred of whom he marched to Barcelona and forced to serve on his galleys). Moreover, 'since we have been challenged, we cannot but uphold our honour and reputation, and preserve and protect our subjects and states as we are obliged to do': he therefore ordered all trade with England and France to cease, and he commanded all subjects of Henry and Francis to leave Spain within forty days.[84]

Charles also reminded his brother that this development 'affects you as much as me', and he therefore expected Ferdinand to 'send a herald to the kings of England and France to issue a challenge', and also to persuade 'the Electors and princes of the Empire to do the same because since we, their chief, have received a challenge it also applies to them, the principal members of the Empire'. These actions, Charles concluded optimistically, 'will raise our reputation among our friends, and spread terror and surprise among our enemies'.[85]

Such optimism was not misplaced. As Maurizio Arfaioli has pointed out, Francis's decision to launch another invasion of Italy was 'just a means and not an end'. Until his 'two sons returned home there could be no real French Italian policy' and so Lautrec's campaign aimed to 'allow his master to resume negotiations with the emperor from a less unfavourable position'. The king and his allies had divined – correctly – that Charles was more vulnerable to pressure on Naples, which he had inherited, than on Milan, which he had acquired only recently. They therefore resolved to 'fight for Lombardy in Naples'.[86] In January 1528, Lautrec left Lombardy and led southwards 'more than fifty thousand troops – an almost incredible figure – with the whole army spread over almost sixty square miles'. Heavily outnumbered, the imperialists retreated until they held only a handful of fortified towns in the kingdom of Naples, whereupon Lautrec placed the capital under siege by land while Doria's galleys cruised offshore to intercept all supplies and reinforcements. In April, Hugo de Moncada, who became viceroy of Naples upon the death of Lannoy, led all his available ships out in a desperate attempt to break the French blockade, but in 'the most cruel and bloody sea battle of our time' he and 1,400 of his men perished.[87] In just three years the emperor had lost all the advantages he had won at Pavia.

THE DUEL THAT NEVER WAS

Although Monsieur de Beersel would have reproved his former pupil for failing to 'bring home the harvest', he would doubtless have applauded Charles's efforts to recover his losses through a single duel. In March 1528 the emperor repeated for the third time his personal challenge to Francis, this time via a letter to the French ambassador (still in detention, but free to communicate with the outside world): 'Your master, the King of France, has behaved in an unworthy and wicked way by failing to honour the promises he made to me in the treaty of Madrid, and if he wishes to contradict me I will uphold my opinion in personal combat.'[88] This time Francis could not ignore the message, and he composed a blistering counter-challenge of his own. 'If you wanted to charge us,' he warned Charles, 'with having done something that a gentleman conscious of his honour must not do, then we say that you are lying through your teeth. Therefore,' Francis continued, 'henceforth do not write to us about anything: in future just name the place and we shall bring the weapons.' Until then, the taunting must cease. 'I trust' the challenge concluded, 'that you will reply like a gentleman instead of like a lawyer, in a duelling field instead of on paper.'[89]

Charles had no intention of forgoing paper as a weapon – on the contrary, he published the entire exchange with Francis as a small book – especially since for the first time he found himself popular among his Spanish subjects. Gattinara noted that 'the challenge of the duel, so rashly offered, provided a great incentive for the Aragonese, Valencians and Catalans to help Caesar and also get their revenge' on the French. Salinas reported that Charles's initial response to the heralds 'pleased all those present' and that 'everyone is so happy with the challenge that it seems as if it were directed towards them'.[90] The emperor capitalized on such sentiments to persuade the Cortes of Castile, meeting in Valladolid, to vote substantial new taxes to mount another campaign in Italy as well as swearing allegiance to Philip as prince of Asturias (the title held by the heir to the throne of Castile); and he now made the ceremonial visit to Valencia that he had avoided nine years before, leaving (for the first time) 'the empress as regent in all Castile'. As he returned, he met the Cortes of Aragon at Monzón and persuaded them, too, to vote new taxes.[91]

Before responding to Francis's challenge, Charles took the unusual step of consulting his leading subjects and ministers on etiquette: those of Aragon in person, since they were all at Monzón, and those of Castile by letter. The council of Castile stressed that 'such challenges are prohibited by Divine and Natural Law' and that the emperor, as the foremost ruler of Christendom, should set a good example and avoid duels; it also predicted that 'even if you accept this challenge, the wars and dissension will not cease but will rather (we believe) increase'. The empress, who had recently given birth to a daughter, María, also tried to dissuade her husband because 'she is afraid that Your Majesty will follow through with it' and leave her a widow.[92] The nobles, prelates and town magistrates of Castile each thanked Charles 'for the honour you do me in asking my advice on what you should do next', but then some expressed concern about hazarding his life with only an infant to succeed him, while others pointed out (in the words of the duke of Infantado) that 'the Code of Chivalry extends to princes, however powerful they may be, as well as to knights like us' – and that meant that an oath-breaker like Francis was not entitled to issue a challenge. The emperor should therefore ignore it.[93]

The rapid deterioration of the imperial position in Italy led Charles to reject this advice and instead accept Francis's challenge. He proposed that the duel should take place in a secured area 'by the river [Bidassoa] that separates Fuenterrabía and Hendaye', leaving Francis to choose 'how and with what we shall fight'. He added that unless Francis accepted within forty days, non-compliance 'will be imputed to you and added to the disgrace of not performing what you promised in Madrid'. On 24 June he entrusted this provocative message to his principal herald, named 'Burgundy', together with detailed instructions on how to deliver it to his rival. Soon afterwards he summoned Kolman Helmschmid, the celebrated Augsburg armourer who had recently made him a magnificent suit of armour monogrammed 'KD' – for 'Karolus Divus', 'Charles the Divine' – to come to Spain with 'materials and smiths in case I might need to fight'.[94] (Pl. 12)

The same rationale that led Charles to favour single combat led his rival to reject it. Francis refused to issue the safe-conduct that would allow 'Burgundy' to deliver the challenge because his troops seemed likely to gain mastery over all Italy, obviating the need to hazard everything on a duel. In a letter dated 28 July 1528 the king boasted that 'I feel so well that I could not possibly feel better', and reported that recently 'I have been hunting two or three times, and each day I stroll through my gardens and view the construction works' at his new palace of Fontainebleau, before rejoicing that his troops had forced the imperialists in Lombardy to retreat. This was 'such excellent news that things could not be better', because it:

> . . . removed from the enemy forces currently in Naples all hope that they will ever be relieved. This will make it very simple and easy for M. de Lautrec to execute the rest of his mission, and so I hope that in a very few days we will have more good news from that quarter . . . I leave you to guess how astonished my enemies will be as they see their forces daily weaken and diminish and see mine strengthen and increase as my cause prospers.[95]

'Good news from that quarter' never came. As Francis signed his triumphant message in Fontainebleau, 1,500 kilometres away in Naples, Andrea Doria defected to the emperor, breaking the naval blockade; dysentery and malaria decimated the besieging army; and Lautrec lay on his deathbed. God hates gloaters.

EIGHT

CHAMPION OF THE WESTERN WORLD, 1528–31

CAESARS'S LUCK

On 1 June 1528, confident that his siege of Naples was about to succeed, Odet de Foix, lord of Lautrec, reassured an Italian ally that the imperialists 'had not won victories in the past through valour', but through good luck. Now, he boasted, 'Fortune has turned against them and the heavens want to punish them'.[1] He erred: Andrea Doria, whose ships sealed Naples off from the sea, had just decided to abandon France. Charles acted swiftly on hearing rumours that the admiral might defect, declaring that he would 'do anything to persuade the said Andrea Doria to enter my service, whatever it may cost me' – an extreme position that he rarely adopted – and he approved a generous treaty that appointed the Genoese patrician his Captain-General of the Sea; granted him a full amnesty for past deeds; provided him with the munitions, manpower and money required to maintain twelve galleys in imperial service; and recognized him as 'perpetual magistrate' over Genoa and its former territories once they returned to the imperial orbit.[2]

Doria's withdrawal from the bay of Naples allowed the imperialists to send supplies and reinforcements into the city just as disease killed off the besiegers, including Lautrec. In August the surviving French forces retreated to the city of Aversa, twenty kilometres inland, but finding it indefensible they not only surrendered but also promised that 'all cities, lands, castles, places and fortresses' in French hands would surrender, so that everything 'would be as it was before my lord of Lautrec invaded'.[3] Doria led his galleys north to his native Genoa, which he entered in triumph in September 1528, driving out the French garrison and their Genoese allies (notably the Fregoso family). As Maurizio Arfaioli has noted, the impact of this double defeat exceeded that of Pavia because 'In less than two weeks, first Naples and its kingdom and then Genoa, "the gate and key to Italy", were lost to France' permanently.[4]

What made Doria change sides, and thus permanently tip the balance of power in Italy in Charles's favour? The emperor claimed that the primary motive was the French king's 'shameful treatment' of both Doria and Genoa, and this no doubt played a part in his decision; so did Charles's many concessions (including the right of 'all the Genoese living in the states of the emperor to be treated as if they were his natural born subjects': a licence to trade in the lucrative American market). But Doria himself told a different story. One day, in the emperor's apartment, a courtier indiscreetly asked why he had suddenly changed his allegiance and the admiral 'replied that for three nights, almost at dawn, a man appeared in his dreams who said "Go and serve the emperor", and that is why he acted'.[5] Although recorded by an eyewitness this could of course have been a rhetorical trope, but it fits well with the contemporary belief in Caesar's luck (*Fortuna Caesaris*): the idea, common since Antiquity, that a true emperor possessed the virtues of Clemency, Patience, Genius, Victory and *Fortuna*.

The idea that fortune (or misfortune) ruled all human lives was widespread in Renaissance Europe, but it seems to have become particularly intense in the sixteenth century. Charles himself often stressed his debt to fortune, and many of his contemporaries agreed. The birth of Prince Philip in 1527 prompted the Venetian ambassador Andrea Navagero to observe that:

> Throughout his life, from the beginning right up to now, we can say that Charles has always been very lucky and that his ventures have always prospered, and now in this too it seems that Fortune has favoured him as much as is possible, because the only thing that he lacked to bring stability to his affairs, and to make him adored throughout his realms, has now also been granted to him.

Thirty years later, when another Venetian ambassador reviewed the successes and failures of Charles's reign, he stated that 'Everyone agrees that the immense ship of state, kingdoms and empire of His Majesty has been guided by good fortune [*favorevole Fortuna*]'. His Florentine colleague agreed: 'Such is Caesar's luck that there is no point in trying to measure and discuss his ventures' according to rational calculation. After the recovery of Genoa in 1528, even the normally pragmatic Antonio de Leyva assured Charles that 'I put my trust in God and in Your Majesty's good fortune that you will become lord of everything, and that all the world will be convinced that God created you for this'.[6]

Clerics concurred. When a diplomat asked Pope Clement in 1529 why he had finally thrown in his lot with the emperor, the pontiff replied 'the world has seen that His Majesty's affairs always prosper, thanks to his good government and *good fortune*'. Three years later, Nuncio Girolamo Aleandro speculated that Charles's successes 'must stem from divine providence, because we see that despite all sorts of difficulties, God always gives him a happy outcome'. In 1552, when Charles rashly determined to besiege Metz despite the approach of winter, the nuncio travelling with him predicted that 'if he achieves anything with his army this year, it will be thanks to his customary *good fortune*'. Paolo Giovio, a bishop, included 50 references to the role of 'Fortuna' in the second part of his *History of his own time*, covering Charles's reign.[7]

THE PACIFICATION OF ITALY

In 1528 some imperial ministers nevertheless remained pessimistic. On hearing the good news from both Naples and Genoa, 'which exceeded all hope', Grand Chancellor Gattinara warned Charles 'not to let the fruits of these victories slip away as he had done with earlier ones'; and a Spanish ambassador echoed that 'it is necessary now to exploit this victory, and not lose the opportunity as has happened in the past'.[8] Charles paid heed and started by mending his fences with Clement.

The pope was vulnerable to imperial overtures because he craved both the restoration of Medici rule in Florence and the return of papal territory occupied by Ferrara and Venice – goals that he could only achieve with imperial support – and in April 1529, Charles made a crucial concession to win him over. Realizing how 'the matter of the council that the Germans say must be held in order to resolve the situation there distresses His Holiness, and given that it will be hard for the pope to swallow this', the imperial ambassadors in Rome suggested at an audience that it might be possible 'to resolve the insurgency and stupidity of the Lutherans' by convening a 'colloquy' rather than a full council. 'On hearing this the pope leapt out of his chair and said, "By my faith you are right, and what you say makes sense! In that case we could concede some of the less contentious demands!" From then on we found him to be more open and more cheerful.' Charles now promised Clement that 'if you are displeased with me, I am ready to beg your forgiveness, so that we can do what we need to do'; whereupon Clement sent an envoy to Spain with full powers to make peace, declaring that 'he was determined to live and die a supporter of the emperor'.[9]

Charles promised to compel Venice and Ferrara to return all their conquests in the Papal States; to make the Florentine republic accept the pope's nephew, Alessandro de' Medici, as their ruler; to betroth his illegitimate daughter Margarita, now seven years old, to Alessandro; and to confirm papal rule over Parma and Piacenza. Clement for his part issued a Brief, 'pardoning those who took part in, and those who condoned, the sack of Rome', and promised to transfer to Rome Henry VIII's suit to divorce Charles's Aunt Katherine. He also agreed to reinvest Charles with the kingdom of Naples (together with the right to nominate twenty-four senior clerics there) and to crown him emperor; to make Gattinara a cardinal; to grant both Charles and Ferdinand one-quarter of the income from all benefices in their dominions to support their struggle against the Turks; and to join them in a league to extirpate Lutheranism. Only the fate of Milan remained in limbo: Charles agreed to restore Duke Francesco Sforza provided he begged for forgiveness for his treason in joining the League of Cognac, failing which he would partition the duchy among its neighbours. The emperor ratified the treaty on 29 June 1529 in Barcelona.[10]

Charles's presence in Barcelona was no accident. On hearing of the relief of Naples, he announced his intention of 'getting myself to a place where I can win and increase honour and reputation'; and (he continued) 'some tell me that there is presently no better and swifter way to do this than by going to Italy'. He promised his brother that he would arrive before the end of 1528, and assemble an army with which he would first 'pacify Italy from one end to the other' and then reconquer Burgundy before returning to Germany. Although obstructionism by his Spanish ministers caused Charles to miss this deadline, popular sentiment now supported his imperial ambitions: 'All Spain is now in harmony with the will of their king, and everyone shouts "Caesar, Caesar is coming! The lord of the world is coming!"' [11] In March 1529, Charles signalled his impending departure by signing a series of important documents: a new Will; a declaration naming Prince Philip his heir should he die; and instructions for the various councils that he had either created or reformed during his time in Spain (Castile and Aragon; War and State; Indies, Inquisition and Orders). All would remain in Spain to advise the empress, who would act as regent during his absence. She too received an instruction detailing what she could and could not do without his express permission, after which Charles took his leave. He would not see his wife again for more than four years.[12]

In April, Charles authorized his ministers to sign a treaty with the Portuguese that provided him with 350,000 ducats in return for renouncing

Castile's claim to the Spice Islands (now the Moluccas); many Spanish noblemen, as yet unaware of this sell-out, arrived to accompany their sovereign to Italy. Only their exact destination remained uncertain. Charles received persuasive letters from Leyva, urging him to disembark in Genoa, and from the prince of Orange, insisting that he come first to Naples; and for a time he could not choose between them. 'Considering that the passage of time often changes the situation and causes options to change,' he told Leyva, 'we feel that we should postpone this decision about where we should disembark until the time when we wish to embark.'[13] Not until mid-May did he announce his decision in favour of Genoa.

Charles now made known both his optimal expectations for the pacification of Italy, and the concessions he was prepared to make (if required) to secure a settlement. In the case of Milan, 'which is the most important matter', he preferred to partition the duchy, with each neighbour buying a parcel from him as suzerain; but if the pope insisted on the restitution of Francesco Sforza, then 'saving our honour' he would comply in return for a hefty fine. Ferrara and Venice must restore all the places they had occupied in Naples and Lombardy as well as the Papal States, and also pay a heavy indemnity but 'without letting anything prevent reaching an agreement': his ministers could reduce the size of the indemnity in order to secure peace. Charles also declared that he would recognize the Florentine Republic, provided it allowed him to maintain a garrison in the city and paid an indemnity, although once again he authorized his ministers to waive the latter 'if you see it is impossible to reach an agreement with them in any other way'. The emperor knew that this outcome would infuriate the pope, but he also knew that much could change before his instructions reached their destinations, so here too he delegated full discretion to his lieutenants. 'We would not want something as important as this to be interrupted and not be carried out, or that it be delayed, and its effects delayed, by communicating back and forth,' he told them; therefore 'we declare to you our wish, but you may proceed as you think best without further consultation, and we promise to ratify whatever you conclude and agree, even if it is not covered by your other instructions and even if it directly contradicts them'.[14]

In June, Leyva routed another French army in Italy, inflicting heavy losses and capturing its commanders. On top of the losses at Pavia and Naples, France now lacked the generals as well as the troops and treasure to continue fighting, whereas ships, troops, supplies and money all flowed into Barcelona, prompting Gattinara to compose a Providentialist rhapsody that verged on incoherence:

The fact that everything happened at the same time, as though interwoven, from so many different parts of the world, all directed towards the same end, beyond the possibility of human hope, sent according to divine will, as it was said, brought a great deal of admiration into the hearts of men. It seemed almost as if Caesar's affairs had been directed miraculously by God himself. Everyone appointed to make the journey with Caesar would come together. One by one they would enter their assigned ships and galleys with their horses, arms and all of their supplies.

At last, on 27 July 1529 Charles boarded the royal galley commanded by Andrea Doria, and that same day they left for Italy. As the fleet headed for the open sea, those aboard shouted 'Emperor, emperor! Plus ultra, plus ultra! Ruler of the world!'[15]

HUMBLING FRANCE

Italian diplomats had filled their dispatches for months with speculation on where, when and indeed whether the emperor would arrive, so that his arrival at Genoa 'astonished some people so much that they almost could not believe it'. Nevertheless, news spread fast that the imperial fleet numbered over 100 ships and carried 12,000 infantry and 2,000 cavalry, and an entourage 'that with the servants and the various officials who always followed the Court must have numbered 5,000'. Moreover, 'word among the experts is that His Majesty has brought with him 2 million ducats in gold'. A steady stream of ambassadors, princes and cardinals therefore flocked to the city to pay their respects and (in several cases) to beg forgiveness for choosing the wrong side in the war – but the war itself continued.[16]

In October 1528, Charles wrote to 'several kings and princes' to publicize the refusal of Francis to accept his challenge to single combat and to announce his decision to revoke his offer to settle their differences in a duel, 'since I have adequately maintained my honour'. Instead he instructed his generals to 'keep everything on a war footing, so that our enemies will have more inclination to accept reasonable terms than they have done until now'.[17] Archduchess Margaret did the same: her agents concluded a truce with England and France to last for eight months, which allowed her to turn on Duke Charles of Guelders. By the treaty of Gorcum in October 1528 he recognized the emperor's suzerainty over Utrecht and Overijssel (two territories he had hoped to acquire himself); agreed that if he died without legitimate offspring the emperor would succeed him; and swore 'to forsake totally the king of France and to join the side of the emperor, and to serve him against all without exception' – striking successes that had eluded both Maximilian and his son Philip.[18]

Defeated and now isolated, Francis indicated to Margaret his willingness to conclude a 'universal peace'. She asked her nephew what terms he would accept. 'The king of France,' Charles replied loftily, 'knows very well what he must do to get peace, and to satisfy my honour as he should': he must fulfil all the terms of the treaty of Madrid except for the surrender of Burgundy, which the emperor consented to leave in French hands in return for a substantial cash indemnity. On that basis, in April 1529 he authorized Margaret to do 'everything that we ourselves would do and would cause to be done if we were present in person' and promised in advance to 'ratify, observe and execute inviolably' any peace terms she might conclude.[19] After a month's haggling behind closed doors with Louise of Savoy, with no ministers in attendance, the 'Ladies' Peace' (*Paix des dames*) obliged Francis to renounce all his conquests, claims and allies in both Italy and the Netherlands, and to withdraw all his troops from both. In addition, he promised to respect the rights of Bourbon's heirs; to marry Charles's sister Eleanor; and to pay over one million crowns in cash to ransom his two sons, still held in Spain as sureties for the execution of the treaty of Madrid. He also agreed to pay the emperor's debts to Henry VIII; to submit to arbitration some of Charles's residual claims concerning Burgundy; to persuade the Venetians to hand over to the emperor all their gains in the kingdom of Naples (and, should they decline, to assist the emperor to secure them by force); and to compel the Florentine republic to surrender. Margaret's agents also formalized terms for peace with England and both treaties were proclaimed at Cambrai on 5 August 1529.[20]

The terms delighted Charles, who told his wife smugly that 'they are just as good as I wanted, and in some cases even better. I am therefore very happy. It seems, my lady, that I have concluded matters as my honour and the good and peace of Christendom require.' One of the imperial diplomats whom Francis had humiliated over the treaty of Madrid felt less confident: 'The peace terms are so advantageous,' he mused, 'that some fear they may be meant to deceive us.'[21] How well he knew his man! Francis did indeed resort to the same tactic as before, registering a solemn protestation that Charles had used custody of the princes to extort concessions in Italy, especially the surrender of Milan and Genoa 'which as the whole world knows belong to us', and that consequently he was not obliged to comply; but this time, lacking allies, the king reluctantly withdrew his forces from beyond the Alps, surrendered his conquests in the Netherlands, and started to assemble the huge sum of money required to ransom his sons.[22]

The emperor, for his part, continued to treat the princes badly. After uncovering a plot to free them from captivity, Charles instructed their guardians at Pedraza de la Sierra that 'There is no need for them to go into the countryside, since they have good apartments inside the fortress. Also, you must keep out anyone sent to talk to or see them', in effect severing all contact with those who could speak to the boys – still only eleven and ten – in their native tongue. This mean-spirited behaviour produced a reprimand from Margaret of Austria (who had negotiated the peace of Cambrai with the princes' grandmother): 'Young princes like them, who have done nothing wrong, must not be made to pay for the enmities of their father; and it would be wise to treat them well, since the emperor's honour is at stake.' Charles complied, providing 1,000 ducats 'to make the princes some nice clothes, so that those who come to see them do not find them shabbily dressed' – but characteristically he insisted that this must be done 'without revealing the real reason'.[23] After receiving confirmation that Francis had fulfilled all his other promises, in June 1530 Spanish officials at the frontier examined and weighed the gold coins brought by their French counterparts one by one, and having exacted an additional 22,797 crowns to compensate for the light weight of some coins, the French princes accompanied Eleanor across the frontier. Thus ended four years of discomfort and humiliation that the younger of the two boys, later King Henry II, would never forget or forgive.[24]

Charles deliberately excluded Francis's Italian allies from the peace of Cambrai, forcing them to sue for terms individually. As the prince of Orange marched from Naples towards Florence at the head of a large army the emperor led another from Genoa, confident that overwhelming military superiority 'will uphold my reputation in all things, and serve to bring those still in arms' – namely Ferrara, Florence, Francesco Sforza and Venice – to make a hasty peace. If not, he threatened, 'I will use force wherever it seems most appropriate and necessary'. Scarcely had the ink dried on this letter than an express messenger arrived from Ferdinand with the alarming news that a huge Turkish army, led by the sultan in person, was advancing on Vienna. 'This affects His Majesty as much as me,' Ferdinand wrote frantically, and he must cross the Alps immediately.[25]

ITALY OR GERMANY?

The dilemma that now faced the Habsburgs was not unexpected. In October 1520, the same month that Charles had become king of the Romans, Prince Suleiman succeeded his father as Ottoman sultan. This coincidence led some observers to see the two rulers as 'twins' whose fates were inextricably entwined: Erasmus, for example, considered that they were locked in a deadly competition 'to decide the final outcome, whether Charles will be the sole ruler of the whole world, or the Turks. The world can no longer support two suns.'[26] The new sultan flexed his muscles almost immediately by leading a massive army up the Danube: in 1521 he captured Belgrade, bringing the frontier of his empire to the border of Hungary. The following year he laid siege to Rhodes, a Christian outpost in the eastern Mediterranean. Charles responded by announcing that he would organize a massive counter-attack, 'because that is what I have wanted to do since I was a child, and also to fulfil the responsibilities of my imperial title as chief protector and defender of our Christian religion'. Therefore, 'despite the vast costs and distractions that I face at present, on account of the war against the French, I have resolved to assemble a fleet as soon as I can to relieve Rhodes'. Charles also declared himself ready to 'spare nothing to preserve, defend and deliver Rhodes from these tyrannical infidel enemies, devoting all our kingdoms and dominions, and our person if necessary', and he urged his fellow monarchs to make peace and join him.[27] These boasts, made in August 1522 in Palencia, came far too late: 3,000 kilometres away, the island fell to the Turks the following December.

The situation in 1529 was different. When the Turks laid siege to Vienna, Charles was at Piacenza, less than 1,000 kilometres away, at the head of a powerful army. Two contradictory letters signed on 23 September reveal his dilemma. One assured his aunt Margaret that 'I am wholly decided and resolved to go in person to help my brother, because his need is so great and the peril so extreme that it does not merely threaten him but places all Christendom at risk. I cannot and must not abandon him, because of the office I hold and the obligations of fraternal friendship; and also because he is such a good brother to me.' Charles's letter to his 'good brother' struck a very different note. Although he recognized that the fall of Vienna would have catastrophic consequences for Christendom in general and for the Habsburg patrimonial lands in particular, he feared that 'without the prior pacification of Italy, it could happen that as soon as I leave to succour you, Venice, Florence, Ferrara and Francesco Sforza will ally together, pool all their resources, and invite the French to support them'. In addition, the treaty of Barcelona obligated him to see to the restitution of all territory taken from the pope and his relatives before he did anything else.[28] Charles therefore rated the loss of Austria as 'the lesser evil', compared with jeopardizing all his gains in Italy through a premature departure, and he instructed his generals to blockade Florence until it agreed to restore Medici rule, to attack Sforza so that 'the duke will be forced to do what he refused when we asked him nicely', and 'to do all the damage they can in the territories of Venice' to make 'their rulers come and negotiate as they should'. The one concession Charles made to Ferdinand was to abandon his plan to go to Rome: instead he asked the pope to meet him in Bologna – adding the veiled threat that, since 'I will need to take with me' to Germany the army besieging Florence, 'we need a swift decision by His Holiness in this matter'.[29]

The courage and skill of the Habsburg defenders of Vienna solved Charles's dilemma. They used their arquebuses to shoot down the Ottoman assaults, just as they had done with the French at Pavia four years before, and in October the besiegers retreated. The good news reached the emperor just before Francis's personal representative brought his solemn ratification of the treaty of Cambrai. Now, the emperor explained to Margaret, although his overall goal remained 'the peace and repose of Christendom, the expulsion of the Turks and the extinction of the current heresies', he would 'spend all his time' on 'the pacification of Italy'.[30]

Charles entered Bologna on 5 November 1529, preceded by his artillery train and thousands of troops, some 'arrayed in the manner of a phalanx of Alexander the Great's soldiers', others 'marching two-by-two, carrying leafy branches in their hands as a sign of victory'. The emperor rode beneath a canopy on a white horse wearing a complete suit of armour until he reached the city gate, where he replaced his helmet with a cap, which he 'doffed whenever he saw a beautiful woman at a window'. Two officials preceded him scattering coins among the crowd and 'shouting with a loud voice "Charles the emperor"'; and when he entered the main square 'the crowd suddenly cried "Charles, Charles, Empire, Empire, victory, victory!"' Thus far the ceremony resembled the 'triumphs' staged for victorious Roman emperors, but Charles now dismounted and fell to his knees before Pope Clement. Although the Venetian ambassador Gasparo Contarini could not hear 'the words uttered by the emperor, because he usually speaks in a very low tone', he did not miss the symbolism that 'Charles remained on his knees while speaking', and that the two leaders of Christendom occupied adjoining chambers in the same palace so that, 'as the pope showed me this morning, by opening a door one passes from the chamber of the emperor to that of the pope' without being observed.[31]

The pope also revealed to Contarini not only where the two rulers met but also how they transacted business: 'When [Charles] came to negotiate, he brought with him a holograph memorandum of all the points he had to discuss, in order not to forget any of them.' By chance, one of these memoranda has survived: a list of nineteen points, some annotated by Charles, which ranged from Henry VIII's divorce plans, through forgiveness for the sack of Rome, to proposals for extracting wealth from, and extending royal jurisdiction over, the Church in Spain (Pl. 13).[32] Topics discussed at other secret meetings can be surmised from the results – such as Clement's concession that Charles might nominate candidates to all ecclesiastical positions in the Netherlands – but the most important outcome became clear just before Christmas, when all the leading diplomats in Bologna gathered in Gattinara's lodgings to finalize three landmark treaties negotiated by the grand chancellor. One restored Francesco Sforza as duke of Milan, provided he paid Charles 400,000 ducats for his investiture and a further 500,000 as a penalty for his disloyalty. Until he handed over the money, Habsburg garrisons would remain in the duchy. Another treaty obliged Venice to restore to both pope and emperor all the places that they had captured, and to pay Charles another substantial indemnity. The third treaty created a defensive league among almost all the independent rulers of Italy, promising to declare war on any foreign power that threatened the peace of the peninsula.[33] Pope and emperor now attended Christmas Mass together, and after the leading cardinals had read some of the prescribed lessons, Charles 'arose from his seat and took off his robes, putting on others with a church vestment on the outside, and buckled on a sword that the pope gave him'. He then read a lesson himself. According to a member of the papal staff, it was 'a Mass of such solemnity that I do not believe there has been anything like it in our lifetime, nor do I think the like will happen in the future'. Charles's courtiers had 'never seen His Majesty so happy'.[34]

THE EMPEROR'S GRAND STRATEGY

Charles had every right to rejoice: he had resolved in his favour all the problems that faced him, and had forced his former enemies to make peace on his terms. Nevertheless, he felt uneasy, and on 11 January 1530 he composed a long 'state of the empire' message for Ferdinand's benefit. He wrote 'in secret, because I do not trust anyone to know these matters except you', and began by emphasizing his total commitment to support his brother against the Turks, adding that other princes had probably refrained from sending him help 'principally because we are brothers, and they think that the greatest part of your welfare is the same as mine, which no doubt it is, because we two are the same'. He urged Ferdinand not to seek a truce (however short) with the sultan, because 'if he sees himself free and secure in your area he will find another' in which to attack the empire. Charles noted with favour the pope's desire to unite all the princes of Christendom in a league against the Turks, which should provide more help in future; and he reiterated his intention to return to Germany and solve the religious problem.[35]

Charles next reviewed the peace treaties he had just concluded. The terms, he conceded, might not be perfect, but lack of money ruled out continuing hostilities. Eight years of war had left Italy depopulated and impoverished, and (Charles added sadly) 'You must realize, brother, that in Spain they abhor all the resources that I have spent for the sake of Italy' (between 1522 and 1529 he had sent over two million ducats from Spain to Italy). In addition, Henry VIII clearly intended to divorce Katherine, 'against all justice and reason, and without the desire or consent of the pope. If he does this, he will place us under a great obligation' to intervene. The principal imponderable was whether Francis would honour his promise to keep the peace. Charles predicted that if the war resumed, it would start in Italy and he therefore proposed to maintain 21,000 German and Spanish troops as a standing army in the peninsula.

Beyond that, the future seemed less clear, and so Charles sought his brother's advice. If possible, he still wanted to be crowned emperor by the pope in Rome and thence move to the kingdom of Naples to restore order before travelling through Germany to the Netherlands and so back to Spain; but should Ferdinand deem his immediate presence vital, Charles promised to accept a coronation in Bologna and come directly to Germany. Either way, he wrote, 'I assure you, brother, and you can assure the [imperial Diet] on my behalf, that I shall not cross the sea [to Spain] until I have visited Germany and laboured to make you king of the Romans' (a title Charles would automatically vacate upon his imperial coronation). The emperor concluded with an apology that although his multi-page 'letter is long, and contains many repetitions and errors, I still have other things I want to tell you at greater length, but they can only be discussed in person'.

As with his long analysis of the situation five years before, on the eve of the battle of Pavia, Charles may have committed his innermost thoughts to paper primarily for his own benefit; certainly he resolved several critical matters long before Ferdinand could reply – notably the decision to stay in Bologna and be crowned there. Choreographing this event had already begun. Pope Clement tried to make Bologna look like Rome (or rather, like Rome before Charles's troops sacked it): thus the cathedral of St Petronius, where the imperial coronation took place, was adapted both inside and out to resemble St Peter's basilica in Rome. Charles, for his part, asked Gattinara whether he should send for the Iron Crown of Lombardy. Although the chancellor advised against it, because during the last imperial coronation (a century before) 'Emperor Frederick [III] did not take it', in the end Bologna witnessed a double ceremony.[36] After forgiving Charles for any offences (including the sack of Rome), Clement placed the Iron Crown on his head on 22 February 1530, followed by the imperial crown two days later, the new emperor's thirtieth birthday and the fifth anniversary of the victory of Pavia. The pope took care to stress the sacral aspects of these ceremonies. During the imperial coronation Charles was invested as a canon of the Church, and Clement handed him a ceremonial sword as a sign that he now possessed the right to make war as the Church's champion, and a golden orb as a symbol that he now possessed dominion of the earth. Pope and emperor then processed around the city together under a single canopy.[37]

These ceremonies overwhelmed contemporaries. In Venice, Marin Sanuto filled twenty-five folios of his *Diaries* with transcripts of various descriptions, inserting two of the many engravings that circulated throughout Europe. Those who sought to ingratiate themselves with Charles commissioned commemorative images: frescoes in Florence, Rome, Verona and Pesaro as well as in Bologna; a handsome frieze erected by the magistrates of Tarazona; a massive sculpture in Florence; and so on.[38] Charles remained aloof. He refused to pay for a commemorative chapel and a frieze at St Petronius that featured his visit. He even offended Titian, whom the marquis of Mantua had brought to Bologna 'to paint the emperor'. According to an outraged Mantuan ambassador, Charles offered the painter 'just one ducat' for his portrait, even though 'he gives up to two ducats a night to any woman who sleeps with him'. The emperor left Bologna (he said) 'as happy as a man who has just escaped from prison'.[39]

Charles rode north to Mantua, where he hunted and hawked with the marquis (whom he elevated to the rank of duke and married to one of his cousins) and admired a replica of Trajan's column decorated with images of his own triumphs as 'master of the world'. He stayed in Mantua for almost a month, hoping that his troops would force Florence to surrender and thus end all hostilities in Italy before he left the peninsula; but since the city continued to resist, in April he reluctantly resumed his journey northwards. After a final delay at Trent, where Charles (once again putting pleasure before business) 'spent some time hunting bears', on 2 May he met his brother at the Brenner Pass. Ferdinand later erected a monument to commemorate the reunion: after all the procrastination, broken promises and delays, the appearance of the brother he had not seen for almost a decade as crowned and consecrated emperor must have seemed little short of miraculous.[40]

FROM THE BRENNER TO BRUSSELS

Much had happened in Germany since Charles's departure after the Diet of Worms in 1521. Besides the relentless Turkish advance up the Danube to the walls of Vienna, the Peasants' War, the greatest popular uprising seen in Europe for centuries, broke out in September 1524 and lasted almost a year. Although Ferdinand bombarded his brother with predictions that the rebels would consume all Germany, Charles largely neglected them (like the Turks) in the hope that the problem would simply go away. In both cases luck, combined with Ferdinand's skilful deployment of available resources, eventually prevailed. A third problem proved less tractable: the spread of heresy.

As Luther provocatively pointed out to the emperor just after his defiant stand at Worms: 'It did not suit anyone to refute, on the basis of God's Word, any erroneous articles [of faith] that my little books [*libelli*] are supposed to contain.' The refusal of the Catholics to engage him in debate certainly handed Luther a major moral and intellectual victory, and Charles did not intend to repeat this mistake. In the Netherlands he condemned to be burned all those who followed the teaching of thirteen named heretics (including Luther), along with all their writings, and in Germany he ordered both Lutherans and Catholics to present their arguments to him at a new Diet, summoned to meet at Augsburg.[41]

On the surface, the emperor's position seemed strong – France, Guelders and the Italian states had all made an ignominious peace; the Turks had retreated; the pope had pardoned and crowned him – and his solemn entry into Augsburg on 15 June 1530 reflected these successes. After greeting the German elite, 'shaking hands with each of them and uttering some gracious words', Charles progressed through the city's streets dressed all in gold astride a white horse beneath a canopy, flanked by Ferdinand and Aleandro, once again the pope's representative at the imperial court. The Electors preceded them and about 150 members of the Diet and the diplomatic corps followed, but this image of power and harmony was shattered the following day. When the emperor processed through the streets again as part of the Corpus Christi celebration, Germany's Lutheran rulers, who had already made a formal protest against the condemnation of their faith (hence their name 'Protestants'), refused to take part.[42]

Charles faced this major challenge to his authority without a senior statesman to advise him. On 5 June 1530, just as the imperial party prepared to leave Innsbruck for Augsburg, the Grand Chancellor died. As Rebecca Ard Boone has observed:

> Whether through talent or training, Gattinara's greatest asset as an advisor was his ability to see situations from the perspective of his opponents, subjects and patrons. Whether they were Aztec peasants in New Spain, Lutheran foot soldiers in Germany, duchesses in Brabant, kings in England or popes in Italy, they all had interests and motivations, and Gattinara made it his business to understand them.[43]

At Bologna, the chancellor had achieved not only his greatest diplomatic coup (persuading all Italian rulers save Florence to make peace on Charles's terms) but also a personal triumph: he persuaded his master to exile to Rome a hated rival, the imperial confessor García de Loaysa y Mendoza – but here his success proved transient. Loaysa had already prepared Charles for life without Gattinara, warning that 'if the chancellor should die, or leave your court, you should not appoint a successor'. Instead, 'I recommend that Your Majesty becomes his own Grand Chancellor, and that all business should pass through the hands of two other ministers': Francisco de Los Cobos and Nicholas Perrenot de Granvelle. Upon hearing of his rival's death, Loaysa restated his rationale: 'I always thought Secretary Los Cobos was a suitable repository for your honour and your secrets, because he knew how to make up for your negligence ... He loves you with great loyalty and is marvellously prudent. He does not tax his brains by saying clever or witty things as others do and he never gossips about his master.' The confessor also praised Granvelle, 'who is courteous, learned and a good Latinist, well-spoken and authoritative, a good Christian, faithful, trustworthy and he understands business well. He is a friend to the good and abhors the bad. He is not as charming in conversation as the secretary [Los Cobos] but he is extremely patient and I think he will resist temptation.'[44] Both ministers were with Charles when Gattinara died, and he accepted Loaysa's advice:

Granvelle became 'keeper of the seals', with general oversight over the affairs of northern Europe, and Los Cobos henceforth handled the affairs of Spain and its overseas dependencies in the Mediterranean and the Americas. Since the two men worked well together, they formed an enduring diarchy at the heart of the empire.

Charles would not regret his decision to accept Loaysa's advice – in 1543 he extolled the merits and services of both ministers in the confidential instruction that he drew up to guide his son (chapter 11) – but in June 1530 neither Granvelle nor Los Cobos possessed the experience or the cunning required to reconcile, as Gattinara might have done, the discordant religious groups that had sprung up in Germany. Neither did Loaysa, who initially advised Charles that 'if you decide to reduce Germany to order, I see no better way than to win over the leading men with gifts and smooth talk'. As for 'the common people, after you have issued your imperial edicts and Christian warnings, if they do not want to obey then the best medicine is force'. Loaysa concluded with a dangerous parallel: 'Force alone is what cured the [Comunero] rebellion in Spain, and that same medicine is what will cure Germany's betrayal of God.'[45]

Initially, Charles agreed. Shortly before the emperor entered Augsburg, Aleandro urged him 'to use the naked sword' against the heretics, 'to which His Majesty replied that the gallows, not the sword, was the best way to punish them'; but the ongoing siege of Florence tied up the resources required to intimidate the Lutherans, and Francis might yet declare war once his sons returned home, and so instead Charles decided to placate the Lutherans. When a Lutheran prince attending the Diet declared 'that he would rather lose his head than be either deprived of or denied the Word of God' the emperor replied anxiously, in his broken German, 'No chop heads! No chop heads!'[46]

The Lutherans knew exactly what they wanted. In April, in anticipation of the Diet, a group of Saxon officials met with Luther and some other theologians to finalize a Confession of Faith – twenty-one articles summarizing the essential elements of Luther's theology, and seven defending their religious innovations – and on 25 June they presented 'a document in both German and Latin, signed by themselves and their adherents', known henceforth as the Augsburg Confession. For two hours Charles and the Diet listened as the Saxon chancellor slowly read out the entire document in German. Who would have thought, Luther crowed, that his 'writings and preaching would be set before His Imperial Majesty and the entire Diet, right under their noses, so that they were forced to hear it and could not raise any objection?' A Saxon official considered it 'one of the greatest achievements that had ever happened on earth'.[47]

Loaysa now urged his master to take a more moderate course:

> Your Majesty should come to terms with all of Germany: just pretend that its heresies do not exist, and allow the Germans to live however they wish. You should work with them to abandon some past errors, and everyone should accept those that are easy. In this they should serve you as their lord, obey you as is only right, and join together to defend Germany and Hungary from the Turk. To that end they should provide you with paid troops for a time.

Charles did his best. According to a Lutheran wit, he even displayed neutrality 'in his public conduct, because having slept while our Confession was read out, he also fell asleep in the middle of the reading of the Response of our adversaries'.[48] More positively, the emperor created a succession of committees, each with different members, with orders to reach a theological consensus; and he spent much time feasting and hunting with the leading princes in an attempt to promote reconciliation. In August he gave a 'long speech' to the Diet in which he exhorted the Lutherans to return to the Catholic faith 'and follow the same practices as their predecessors had done for hundreds of years', otherwise 'he would be constrained to treat them as enemies and proceed against them by force, as the oath he had taken obliged him to do'. But after these inflammatory words, he repeated his desire to 'find some formula of reconciliation on the major issues' and declared his readiness to allow the practices in dispute to continue until a general council could meet.[49]

In part, Charles acted through fear. According to a Venetian observer in Augsburg: 'Take it for granted that unless these Lutheran matters are cleared up, and unless these German lords are reconciled with the emperor, if the Turks come again it will mean the destruction of Germany'; and yet, after ten weeks of talks, speeches, banquets and bonhomie, the Diet broke up 'without reaching any agreement'. Loaysa tried to console his master – 'The wilfulness and shamelessness of these heretics in defending their errors weighs deeply on my heart' – but Charles was inconsolable. 'These heretics have been so obstinate that no policy has worked or sufficed to get them to recognize their errors', he told Loaysa on 20 October. He continued: 'I can see that if there were a way of forcing them, we could justly move against them; but that is not the case now, nor do I currently have the means, because I am tired, alone and without help, and there are so many of them that great force would be needed to overcome them. The true remedy is to convene a general council.' Charles then changed his mind again. On 19 November 1530 he and the Catholic members of the Diet issued a decree condemning the major tenets of 'the doctrine previously outlawed' at Worms, 'which has kindled many errors among the common people'. All who failed to accept within five months the doctrine of the Catholic Church (which the decree helpfully spelled out) would be declared outlaws.[50]

Lyndal Roper has argued that both sides missed a golden opportunity at Augsburg – one that would never recur:

> Both sides had shown willingness to compromise and in the end the differences between them scarcely seemed big enough to justify the schism that resulted from the failure. But what kept the two sides apart was the absence of trust – on marriage, the sacraments and other issues, the evangelicals simply did not believe that the Catholics meant what they said, or that they would keep their word. They feared that concessions would lead to their being crushed at a church council that would be held outside Germany and set up to defeat them. The result was not inevitable, but rather a narrowly missed opportunity to prevent the splitting of the Catholic church.

Instead, the Elector of Saxony invited his fellow Lutheran rulers to meet in the town of Schmalkalden to form an alliance 'as a defence and protection for us, our subjects, and our relations against unjust coercion'. The Schmalkaldic League, led by the Elector and Landgrave Philip of Hesse, was signed on 27 February 1531.[51]

Not only did Charles fail to bring religious peace to Germany: he also failed to persuade the pope to reform abuses. He had discussed the matter with Clement during their meetings in Bologna, and on 20 October 1530 (the same day he vented his anger to Loaysa) he wrote a long holograph letter 'begging Your Holiness as earnestly as I can that you convene a general council with the urgency that the situation demands; and that, for optimal effect, Your Holiness should write to other princes and potentates, explaining why' – namely the need to create a united front against the expected Turkish attack, and to prevent 'the heresies that have recently appeared' from spreading further. He proposed convening the assembly at either Mantua or Milan, 'which are closest to Germany, which is where we find most of the errors with which the council must deal' (a reminder that at this stage

Charles saw Protestantism as essentially a German problem). Clement showed no interest. The messenger who delivered the imperial missive reported that 'He read it and in the middle gave a great sigh and another one at the end.' Clement's sighs, and his invincible opposition to convening a council, constituted another 'narrowly missed opportunity to prevent the splitting of the Catholic church'.[52]

Charles could nevertheless boast two victories elsewhere. In Italy, although the Republic of Florence resisted his forces for ten months, it surrendered in August 1530. Two months later the emperor imposed a constitution that restored to the Medici family the full powers lost three years earlier, and named as head of state Clement's nephew Alessandro, betrothed to Charles's daughter Margarita. The other victory involved his brother. While feasting and hunting in and around Augsburg, Charles persuaded the imperial Electors to accept Ferdinand as king of the Romans. Only the Lutheran Elector of Saxony refused: the rest agreed to deliver their votes in return for the rewards promised in 1519 (but still not paid in full), redress of individual grievances, and a share of 200,000 ducats taken from 'the ransom of the sons of the king of France'.[53] In January 1531, Charles hosted a lavish feast (albeit boycotted by most Lutherans) to celebrate the coronation of his brother in Aachen as king of the Romans. For the first time in half a century, Germany had both an emperor and an heir apparent, and according to an ambassador, 'His Imperial Majesty has shown so much jocularity and mirth, a sign of extreme happiness, that no one has ever seen a success have such an effect on him.'[54] Charles now returned, after an absence of almost nine years, to the land of his birth.

REORDERING THE NETHERLANDS

Margaret of Austria was no longer there to greet him. In November 1530, aged fifty, she dictated her last letter to Charles, claiming her only regret was that 'I will not be able to see and speak with you one more time before I die' – a final proof of her devotion to the nephew she had raised and served. She named him her universal heir, so that he gained the Franche-Comté of Burgundy ('which I beg you to retain in your own hands, so that the name of "Burgundy" may not perish'), her magnificent library and art collection, and also 'your Netherlands, which I have not only maintained just the way you left them, but also greatly increased' – a proud reference to the acquisition of Friesland (1515), Tournai (1521), Utrecht and Overijssel (1528).[55] Upon Margaret's death her two senior ministers immediately took charge, promising Charles that they would consult the rest of the council twice each day and 'transact as little important business as possible, until we hear from Your Majesty'. After expressing his sorrow, 'because I viewed her and treated her as my mother', Charles approved this interim arrangement – without revealing that he had already identified Margaret's successor: his sister Marie, dowager queen of Hungary.[56]

Marie had left Mechelen in 1513 to marry King Louis of Bohemia and Hungary, and after his death at the battle of Mohács in 1526 she stayed on to promote the election of Ferdinand as his successor. Charles did not see his sister again until the summer of 1530, and he asked her then whether she would be willing to govern the Netherlands should their aunt Margaret die or retire. She agreed in principle and early in 1531 Charles sent her a formal invitation, but he refused to discuss the details of her position 'until we are together, because when you and I are at leisure we can better discuss the best choices, and I will take the time to give you good advice so that you will be better able to put into effect your laudable desire to do everything well, and I can show you your responsibilities myself'.[57] This verbosity disguised an important innovation: henceforth Charles would groom in person and at length those to whom he planned to entrust the posts of greatest responsibility in his empire.

The Netherlands rejoiced at their ruler's return. The States-General presented him with a magnificent series of tapestries depicting the victory of Pavia over the hereditary enemy of the house of Burgundy (see Pl. 14); individual towns commissioned poems to celebrate his successes and his safe return, or else erected a commemorative pillar; Bruges completed a spectacular chimney breast with life-size statues of Charles and his four grandparents (Pl. 15).

The warm welcome seems to have raised the emperor's spirits. In a bulletin on 'the health of His Majesty' in late January, Fernan López de Escoriaza (Charles's personal physician) asserted that 'I have never seen him healthier and stronger' and he ascribed this to 'the joy he felt upon seeing the land and breathing the air of the country where His Majesty was born, and in conversing with the people with whom he grew up'. Dr Escoriaza's only concern was Charles's irregular eating habits – 'he eats nothing' at night 'because he eats during the day and at night he does not want to dine' – a problem that would continue to vex his physicians. Nevertheless, Charles soon provided a stunning example of his physical fitness. At a tournament in Ghent, he 'used and adapted to different weapons in such a way that the most accomplished warrior in the world could not have done better'.[58]

Domestic problems proved less tractable. As his sister Marie later recalled, on his return to Brussels in 1531 'His Majesty found many rivalries among his principal ministers, justice neglected, and the States very grudging'. The States of Holland proved particularly recalcitrant, demanding that their ruler redress grievances before they would vote any more taxes, to which Charles replied testily: 'I want to be trusted, and will not bargain with my subjects.'[59] Another of the problems listed by Marie worried him far more. He confided to Ferdinand that 'I found great enmities, personal passions, leagues and alliances' among his officials, 'constantly turning everyone against the rest'. Therefore, 'to see and ascertain the truth, I followed up the accusations against my fiscal officers made by their adversaries, and I examined their accounts from 1520 to 1530 – that is, for ten years – to see if they had robbed me as some claimed'. But 'although some matters were not as satisfactory as they should have been, I found no fault'. The spectacle of the most powerful ruler in the Western world checking ten years of public accounts in person would have delighted Chièvres, and Charles's diligence led him to an important conclusion: 'If there is a fault here, the principal cause is that everyone desires so many privileges in order to limit my sovereignty [*hauteur*] so that we would almost become colleagues and I would no longer be in charge [*casy nous demouryons compagnons et moy non seigneur*].'[60]

Charles therefore decided to overhaul the central government of the Netherlands. He established three 'collateral councils' to advise Marie: the Council of State for diplomacy, defence and religion; the Privy Council to prepare legislation and to hear both civil and criminal appeals from inferior courts; and the Council of Finance to supervise the collection and expenditure of revenues, the raising and repayment of loans, and the oversight of all state assets. His instructions to each body, and also to Marie, reserved a wide range of issues that only he could decide – no doubt to prevent Marie from following Margaret's example and creating her own agenda. In this he failed: after scarcely a year Charles allowed Marie to open any letters addressed to him that passed through her hands, just as their aunt had done, and her letters to him often included comments and advice about what he should do next. Charles also created a 'hotline': 'When something crops up that I want to remain secret, I will always write to you about it in my own hand,' he told his sister, 'and you should do the same.'[61]

Charles had little choice. Scarcely had he and his brother parted after the coronation feast in Aachen than Ferdinand begged him to return and deal with the threat of another Turkish invasion and the recalcitrance of the

Lutherans. Charles protested that the affairs of the Netherlands 'in truth require much more time and much more of my personal attention' than he had anticipated, while 'as you can imagine the affairs and needs of my kingdoms of Spain suffer greatly the longer I am away, causing my subjects to suffer and complain, so that I cannot postpone returning there for long'. The following month, with a fine display of passive-aggressive rhetoric, Charles informed his brother that he would return to Germany even though it meant 'postponing all other matters and the absolute necessity and importance of all other business which, as you can imagine, are very important to my kingdoms, dominions and subjects', and he warned that he would only stay 'for one month, maximum, because my other affairs cannot endure any more delay'. He nevertheless found a series of excuses for postponing his departure, such as pressing business in the Netherlands and 'a long and debilitating cold', but foreign ambassadors noted that they did not prevent his participation in frequent jousts and 'almost every day he goes hunting', so that 'he avoids transacting all business and spends his time at play'. Only the return of the papal nuncio Aleandro in November 1531 put an end to the procrastination.[62]

At his first audience, Charles later recalled, the nuncio began 'by reminding me of the past proceedings of the other Diet [of Worms] better than I remembered them myself, which astonished me' (perhaps the emperor recognized that he had then been wrong, whereas the nuncio had been right?). Aleandro exploited this advantage by stating boldly that 'Histories show that great heresies cannot be extinguished without bloodshed', and to this end he urged Charles to raise troops in Germany, Spain, Italy and the Swiss cantons. Almost immediately the emperor complied. On 3 January 1532 he informed his brother that 'I have put off and delayed writing to you until now, when I am certain of my departure, because I have written to you about it so many times and then defaulted, and I did not want to lie to you any more – nor will I.'[63] He promised to leave Brussels within two weeks, to meet the imperial Diet again in Regensburg and to campaign against the Turks in person. This time he kept his word.

PORTRAIT OF THE EMPEROR AS A RENAISSANCE PRINCE

In December 1531, Charles presided over a chapter of the Knights of the Golden Fleece in the city of Tournai, captured from France ten years before – an unsubtle way of stressing his success in defending and expanding his Burgundian heritage. According to custom, the chancellor of the Order collected information on the vices and virtues of each knight, which he then presented for discussion by the chapter. Since 'the conduct of the head and sovereign was not exempt' from this process, after recording 'the praise he had heard for [Charles's] virtue and his glorious exploits', the chancellor noted five complaints about him received from the knights:

> They considered that he was slow in dispatching business; that he spent a lot of his time on minor matters, neglecting the most important ones; that he seldom consulted his council, which lacked a sufficient number of members; that he did not take sufficient trouble to appoint suitable people to the judicial tribunals, which dealt with business very slowly; and finally that he paid both his ministers and his troops very poorly.

Charles listened to 'these complaints attentively and with good will' before offering a vigorous rebuttal:

> He blamed the alleged defects in the administration of justice on those whom he had charged with its execution during his absence, and on the major tasks that he faces constantly, which have prevented him thus far from devoting his full attention to putting his own affairs in order and to dealing with those of his subjects. Concerning his councillors, he stated that since he had failed to find men who were sufficiently experienced and loyal to him, in whom he could trust, he had been forced to take charge himself of many matters that he could have delegated to others.

For the rest, he promised to do everything he could to remedy promptly the various abuses that the knights had just stated.[1]

Although subjects everywhere complained about their rulers, few received a licence to do so in person, and fewer still had the right to expect a reasoned answer.

For a time, Mercurino Arborio de Gattinara also possessed a licence to reprimand his master. In a long memorandum of 1523 the Grand Chancellor told Charles that:

> You need to find qualified people who have your confidence, so that you can relax and rely on them; and to this end you need to follow the advice that God gave to Moses, through the mouth of Jethro, when He entrusted him with the task of ruling and leading the people of Israel, advising him that he should choose virtuous, wise and God-fearing people ... as ministers to render justice to the people constantly, and to refer to him the major matters while dealing with the lesser ones [themselves].

Indeed, Gattinara gushed, 'it is even more necessary for Your Majesty to do this because you have even more responsibilities than Moses himself, since God has entrusted to you this sovereign imperial title, which involves the administration of the whole world'. Charles passed the memorandum on to his council for discussion and all, both Burgundian and Spanish, enthusiastically endorsed the chancellor's call for delegation. 'It seems to me that you must do this', opined Henry of Nassau, 'because it is impossible for Your Majesty to do everything all alone'. Since Charles took no notice Gattinara soon returned to the attack. He reminded 'the young prince' that although God had raised him 'higher than any man anywhere in the world', this 'was not so that he might abuse all of the gifts and favours granted to him by God, but for the augmentation and exaltation of the Christian religion'. Therefore, 'when the emperor did not correct and castigate the abominations and evil deeds of his soldiers and ministers, when he did not administer justice, when he did not pay his debts, when he did not provide for those suffering damages, and when he did not remedy so many evils, he was reputed unjust by the just'. Once again Charles took no notice and early in 1527 Gattinara left court and sailed to Italy. Contrary to the chancellor's expectations he did not receive an immediate plea to return, because (as ambassador Navagero realized) 'the emperor never refuses anyone permission to leave his service, because he does not think he needs anyone so much that he cannot manage without them'.[2]

A NEW STYLE OF DECISION-MAKING

Charles's transition to political independence did not happen overnight. Some still considered him indecisive even after Chièvres's death. In 1521, Archduchess Margaret tried to soothe the wounded pride of a minister whose advice had been ignored: 'Our emperor has a head like everyone else, with ears into which one can whisper day or night,' she crooned, 'and sometimes change his mind.' Three years later, when an ambassador urged Charles to marry Isabella of Portugal, he added: ' "Your Majesty will consult with your council and form such resolve as shall seem fit to you"; to which the emperor snapped back: "Don't imagine that I now communicate everything with the council" ' (although he conceded 'that was true when M. Chièvres lived, because he controlled me').[3] The emperor even countermanded some decisions made in his name by others. In 1524 he revoked several appointments made by Margaret, but a minister warned her that protests would be futile because:

> The emperor did it himself, seeking advice from no one – as he normally does with matters that concern his will and authority. There is no one in his dominions great or wise enough to make him change his mind, unless he believes that common sense requires him to do so. I have observed many princes of various ages but I have known none who takes more trouble to understand his own affairs, and takes decisions more inflexibly on what affects him. He is his own treasurer in peace and war, and he confers offices, bishoprics and titles according to God's inspiration, without regard to any pleas he may receive.

The death of several veteran councillors over the next few years, including Margaret and Gattinara in 1530, removed almost everyone capable of restraining the emperor – and he had no intention of replacing them with a new cadre of strong-willed servants. In 1532 he flatly rejected a minister recommended to him to handle Netherlands business 'because I believe he will immediately want to involve himself in decision-making. I prefer someone else who is easier to handle [*manyable*] and will involve himself only in paperwork.'[4]

As the emperor gained in self-confidence, many praised both his intelligence and his diligence. Erasmus, who claimed that he had been 'often at court' while Charles resided in the Netherlands, informed a correspondent in March 1523 that the emperor 'is a young man with plenty of brains'; and that same month some English ambassadors reported that 'withowght fayle ther is no day but his majestie is very long with his counseyll, som tyms 5 or 6 [hours] contynually', and that 'he undyrstondith his affayres not lesse then ony othir off his counseyll'.[5] Many observers also noted that he refused to act in a hurry. In 1526, while discussing Italian politics, the nuncio Baldassare Castiglione told Charles that he 'should make up his mind, and fast, because delay is very dangerous', but the emperor calmly replied that 'his policy had always been to deal first with matters that were easier to resolve, and leave the most difficult ones till last'. Naturally, this infuriated those affected by the difficult decisions – including Castiglione, who complained shortly afterwards: 'Really, the norm here seems to be put things off indefinitely' – but others welcomed Charles's prudence. Three years later when some courtiers levelled an accusation of heresy against Alfonso de Valdés, Charles's Latin secretary and a devoted follower of Erasmus, 'the emperor, who is not in the habit of placing his confidence in anyone quickly, said he did not wish to make a decision until it could first be shown to him what errors [Valdés] had made'.[6]

Gradually, the emperor devised a system of decision-making that combined widespread consultation with deep reflection. Sometimes he would laboriously write out alternative rationales, starting with an analysis of the problems he faced in February 1525, composed 'even though there is no one who knows them better than me', because 'I want to put my opinions in the form of a confidential letter' (p. 146). During the winter of 1528–9, Charles added another weapon to his administrative arsenal. The efforts of his Spanish ministers to sabotage his plans to leave for Italy infuriated him so much that he created an alternative network of trusted Burgundian officials to circumvent them. He composed a long holograph letter informing the prince of Orange, viceroy of Naples, of his 'desire to get myself to a place where I can acquire and win honour and reputation' and demanded his urgent advice on how best to proceed. He then charged Baron Balançon, a member of his household, to deliver the letter in complete secrecy ('in an emergency you must not hesitate to throw this document into the sea; and whatever happens, make sure that it is seen only by the prince'). He even started to open letters addressed to his ministers. He ordered Antoine Perrenin (then a lowly clerk) to decipher an incoming missive 'without his master knowing'; and he sent a copy of one intercepted letter to Baron Montfort (another long-serving member of his household) along with his reply, together with orders to burn the former after reading it, and to 'reseal with a cord and a little wax the letter that I wrote' to make it seem unopened. Before he sealed his cover letter, he warned Montfort that 'I'm sending this to you via Perrenin. Please let me know if it has been opened'. Evidently, at this stage the emperor trusted none of his ministers except Balançon, Montfort, Orange and Perrenin, all of them from Burgundy: a truly extraordinary situation.[7]

The inability (or unwillingness) of his Spanish officials to raise the 300,000 ducats needed for his voyage to Italy particularly infuriated Charles. 'I constantly try to find the funds,' he raged to Montfort, and 'each evening it seems as if I have succeeded' but 'the next day I find myself further behind than ever'. He concluded that the paralysis arose because 'everyone here is so opposed to my departure, and knows (or thinks) that I am seeking money for this purpose', and he threatened that if necessary he would 'sell this town' of Toledo in order to raise the funds.[8] In the event he stopped short of such a drastic measure and instead circumvented his Spanish officials by renouncing his claim to the Moluccas to the king of Portugal in return for cash. The proceeds financed not only his journey to Italy but also victory over his Italian enemies and coronation by the pope. His alternative system of decision-making had allowed Charles to get his way.

When Gasparo Contarini, Venetian ambassador in Spain between 1521 and 1525, met Charles again at Bologna over the winter of 1529–30, he noted several changes. Although still 'prudent, reserved and extremely attentive to everything that concerns him', as well as 'more devout than ever', Contarini found that the emperor now 'speaks more – and more consistently – than he used to do in Spain. On some occasions I discussed business with His Majesty for two hours on end, something that never happened in Spain. He is also less obstinate in his opinions'. By way of example, Contarini reported that:

> One day, in a lively discussion with me, His Majesty said that by nature he tended to stick to his decisions; and I, wishing to reassure him, said 'Sire, sticking to good decisions is to be constant, not obstinate'. He replied immediately: 'Sometimes I stick to bad ones'. From this I deduce that prudence and good intentions have allowed His Majesty to over-come the defects of his natural inclinations.

Two years later, the Venetian ambassador Niccolò Tiepolo noted that 'His Majesty delegates only routine matters to his ministers. He himself wants to know about everything else, and to think about it, allowing nothing to happen without his intervention or at least his knowledge'. Cardinal Juan de Tavera, president of the council of Castile, once told his master (with a touch of irony) that 'although Your Majesty may have decided not to follow anyone's advice except your own, things may still turn out well *even if you trust the opinion of others*', but Charles remained adamant. In Tiepolo's words: 'He listens to the advice and opinions of all his ministers, but the decisions are his alone.'[9]

THE EMPEROR AT PLAY AND AT PRAYER

The emperor's increased workload scarcely affected his propensity to put pleasure before business. A register of household expenditure between 1530 and 1532 reveals some of his pastimes. He frequently gambled (sometimes with stakes as high as 300 ducats); he watched plays; and he sat to have his portrait painted with surprising frequency.[10] Hawking and above all hunting could keep Charles away from his desk for days on end. He once apologized to his sister Marie 'for taking so long to reply to your letter, because when it arrived I was so caught up in hunting [*tant enpesché en la chase*] that I put it off'; and when his brother begged him for a decision on a critical issue, Charles replied disarmingly that he was hunting and 'cannot decide what I ought to do while I am here at this country retreat'. Ferdinand and his problems would just have to wait.[11]

Until his forties, Charles seems to have spent little time reading – virtually no portrait shows him even holding a book – but the register of his household expenditure reveals that in 1530 and 1531 he bought some 'books written against Martin Luther'; and a few years later an inventory of his library in Brussels (653 items) showed that he owned several polemics against Lutherans as well as a few travel books, some items that might today qualify as soft porn (*Livre d'amours*), and handbooks on hawking and hunting. But how often did he read his books? According to the Venetian man of letters, Lodovico Dolce, Charles 'only enjoyed reading three authors, whose works he had translated into Spanish', namely Castiglione's *Courtier*, 'for the foundations of civilized life'; *The Prince* and *The Discourses* of Niccolò Machiavelli, 'for affairs of state'; and 'the *Histories* and all the other works of Polybius for military matters'.[12] Dolce overlooked two other categories of the emperor's favourite reading, however: books of chivalry and devotional works (his library contained fourteen Books of Hours, some of them exquisitely illuminated).[13]

Charles always took his devotions seriously. Just after his abdication an ambassador testified that 'Throughout his life His Majesty has heard Mass every day ... and sermons on holy days and throughout the forty days of Lent. Sometimes he attends vespers and other divine offices, and every day he has the Bible read to him. He has always confessed and taken communion four times a year.' Before he got into bed Charles normally knelt before a religious image and recited a simple version of the creed, and he practised mental prayer, perhaps aided by one of his Books of Hours.[14]

Charles periodically engaged in more ostentatious devotions. He owned two scourges, and (according to his son many years later) one 'was much used' and still bore traces of the emperor's blood.[15] In addition, the emperor went on retreat for a week every Easter. In 1529, just before departure for Italy, 'he left his wife and children on Palm Sunday' and remained in a monastery 'through the holy days, taking a break from official business, as was appropriate'; in 1535, just before his campaign in Africa, he again refused to transact any public business during Holy Week, which he spent in a monastery; and so on. The only exception occurred in 1526, when his decision just before Easter to torture and execute Bishop Acuña of Zamora led to Charles's excommunication – but as soon as he received the pope's pardon he went to a monastery, 'where he will spend a week in lieu of Holy Week, and will confess and take communion'.[16] Impatient ministers might pester their master at such times, but they got nowhere. During Holy Week 1531, Los Cobos prepared a *consulta* that summarized nine matters that (he believed) urgently required a decision and sent it, together with the relevant papers, to the monastery where Charles was on retreat. The emperor ignored it until after Easter, and then returned it with the lapidary reminder: 'It's hard to confess and write a lot at the same time.'[17]

Charles's exemplary piety allowed his confessors to influence his political choices. Jean Glapion, a Franciscan friendly with Erasmus, became imperial confessor in 1520 and the following year accompanied the emperor to the Diet of Worms and on campaign. Some thought he carried 'no less weight at Court than Christ himself'. His fiery Lenten sermons in 1520, delivered in Charles's presence, excoriated the shortcomings of both Church and churchmen and insisted that if clerical abuses continued, princes had a duty to intervene: 'It is your job to place your hand on your sword and ensure that such evils do not occur through the faults of the clergy' – a message that Luther himself might have delivered. A year later, Charles tasked Glapion with persuading Elector Frederick of Saxony to make Luther retract at least some of his propositions and thus avoid a high-risk confrontation at the Diet of Worms (chapter 5). It is therefore no surprise that a book by Glapion, 'His Imperial Majesty's confessor', later appeared on the Index of Prohibited Books.[18]

Glapion accompanied Charles to Spain in 1522, but almost immediately resigned in order to travel with other Franciscans from the Netherlands who wished to convert the indigenous population of America (he died first).

After almost a year, the emperor chose as his confessor the Dominican García de Loaysa y Mendoza. Like Glapion, Loaysa joined the council of state and in 1526 became president of the council of the Indies. Foreign ambassadors courted him because 'he is very much in His Majesty's favour, more than anyone else I know'.[19] Although few of Loaysa's exchanges with Charles from this period survive, their extensive correspondence from 1530 to 1533, when the Dominican served as the emperor's special representative in Rome, reveals much about their past interactions. Loaysa told Charles that 'since I have kept the title of confessor, as long as I live I have the duty to assist your salvation', and he felt this empowered him 'to speak to Your Majesty as if I were still in your apartments, as I used to be', so that 'my words reflect my long experience of telling you things in person, with the doors closed'.[20] 'Sloth and the desire for glory are in constant battle in your royal person,' Loaysa thundered, adding that 'crowns and triumphs have never rewarded laziness, self-indulgence, vice and recreation'. He even used the emperor's earlier confessions against him: 'Your Majesty once said that he wished to dedicate his life to defending the faith, because you did not feel that anything else would repay the infinite mercies that you have received from God. Now is the time for Your Majesty to show whether those words were hypocritical and false, or whether they were heartfelt and true.'[21]

Loaysa singled out Charles's self-indulgence for special criticism. In 1530 he marvelled that the emperor continued to eat fish when 'the whole world knows that your stomach cannot deal with fish'. Indeed, 'I hear from people there that sometimes your stomach is louder than your voice'. The following year he raged that 'God did not create you so that you could kill stags when the church stands in such need', and he reproached Charles for risking his health and perhaps his life:

> For the pleasure of drinking too much, of eating things that don't agree with you, and not acting prudently with your sleep and in other things. For the love of God, do not ignore my supplications, but rather leave aside such pernicious pleasures. God did not create Your Majesty so that you could have fun in this world but so that you would work ceaselessly to save the Christian Commonwealth![22]

In 1532 rumours of another Turkish invasion of Hungary led Loaysa to launch a new barrage of commands: 'Your Majesty must not think about leaving Germany but instead complete your tasks well and conclude the enterprise that you so gloriously took upon yourself.' In short, 'There must be no Castile, no wife, and no children until you have satisfactorily dealt with matters of state.' Most outspoken of all:

> I venture to say that now is the time, more than at any other time of your life, when Your Majesty has the greatest obligation not to waste a single hour. Each day you must consult your councillors and carry out their resolutions without delay ... I have always known that Your Majesty loved honour a thousand times more than life and wealth, and now that your honour is at stake you should not even eat or sleep without thinking about how to make it grow and not diminish.[23]

Loaysa wisely interspersed his criticisms with positive feedback. He praised 'the perfection of your faith and your honesty, because there is no one in this world who is more pure, and a greater enemy of lies and deception, than Your Majesty' (1530); and claimed that 'Everyone knows that Your Majesty is an angel' (1531).[24]

Charles seemed willing to accept the reproaches in return for such uplifting messages. 'I am very pleased,' he assured Loaysa in one of his holograph replies, 'to be counselled and advised by you', and 'so I beg you never to tire of doing so'. Or, with slightly less enthusiasm: 'Many thanks for the good advice that you are giving me. I would be delighted if you would continue, and always send me your advice on everything: I take it, and will continue to take it, in the same spirit in which you offer it.'[25]

The only reverse that shook Charles's faith appears to have occurred after witnessing the death of his nephew Hans, the fourteen-year-old son of his late sister Isabeau and her unpleasant husband Christian of Denmark. 'It has brought me the greatest sorrow you can imagine,' he wrote in August 1532, 'because he was the most handsome little boy for his age that you could find. I feel his death even more than the loss of my own son [Fernando, who had died two years earlier], because he was older and I knew him better, and treated him as my own son. Nevertheless we must accept the will of God' – but then he added angrily: 'May God forgive me, but I wish He had taken [Christian] instead of his son.'[26]

UNHAPPY FAMILY

Charles always held, and often expressed, strong views about his relatives. As María José Rodríguez-Salgado observed, he 'had been born into an extraordinary and dysfunctional family' – and, she added, he managed to perpetuate it. 'When we examine his relations to other members of the family he showed little affection for any of them; the most salient characteristic is his desire to control them.' Indeed, he treated some of them 'with profound suspicion which at times bordered on paranoia'.[27]

On hearing of the death of his aunt Margaret he claimed, 'I viewed her and treated her as my mother', yet he had often behaved towards her with stunning insensitivity, notably at the time of his emancipation. He also treated his biological mother appallingly. At their first meeting in Spain, he assured Queen Joanna that he and his sister Eleanor had come 'as humble and obedient children' to 'offer you our respect, service and obedience', but he perpetuated the fictional world, full of fake facts, created by her father (chapter 4). Even after the Comunero rebellion exposed Joanna to reality, Charles kept her confined at Tordesillas where he periodically helped himself to her possessions. In 1524, just before the marriage of his sister Catalina (who had spent almost all her life confined with her mother), Charles spent a month in Tordesillas removing tapestries, jewels, books, silver goods and even liturgical vestments from Joanna's collection to serve as part of his sister's dowry (thus saving Charles from paying it himself). He also removed items weighing 25 kilos of silver and 15 kilos of gold from his mother's apartments, and used them to fund Catalina's journey to Lisbon (thoughtfully filling the empty chests with bricks of equivalent weight so that his mother would not notice until after his departure that he had robbed her).[28] Charles also kept the wedding plans secret from Joanna for as long as possible, and 'when the time came for the bride to leave and join her husband, he left for Madrid to avoid being present, fearing that his mother would make a great demonstration of grief'. Despite his undoubted physical courage, the emperor was thus sometimes a moral coward.[29]

Charles also showed insensitivity towards his wife, whom he sometimes apparently regarded as primarily a regent and a breeder. In January 1522, though betrothed to Henry VIII's daughter Mary, he assured King John of Portugal unromantically that 'we are more inclined to marry his sister the Infanta [Isabella] than anyone else, because there is no daughter of a king as ready as her [*si preste comme elle*]'. Three years later he boasted to his brother that marrying Isabella would mean that almost immediately thereafter 'I could entrust the government to her' and leave Spain; and just before his marriage, he promised Ferdinand that he would abandon his bride-to-be and sail for Italy just as soon as he had impregnated her.[30] As his aunt Margaret reminded the empress, 'children are the only thing that [Charles] lacks to secure the great kingdoms and lands that God has given him', and she promised that 'when I see His Majesty I will ask him to return so that you may create another child' – but although the empress conceived at least nine times, except for their firstborn, after the pregnancy began Charles lost interest. When their second son died while he was absent in Germany, Charles belittled his wife's grief: 'Since our Lord, who gave [Fernando] to us, wished to have him back, we must bend to His will and thank Him and beg Him to protect what is left. With great affection, my lady, I beg you to do this, and to forget and leave behind all pain and grief.' A few years later, when Cardinal Tavera announced the birth of Infanta Joanna to his master, then in Africa, he felt it necessary to add: 'It seems to me that in your letter to the empress, Your Majesty must show great happiness about your new daughter because it will please her greatly.'[31] Most callous of all, Charles failed to inform his wife that he had promised Margaret of Austria that she would raise their second son in the Netherlands. The empress only learned about this commitment in an ecstatic letter from Margaret, congratulating her on the birth of Fernando: 'No news could have been as welcome to me. *Given what His Majesty promised me*, I hope that [Fernando] will be my son, a support to me in my old age, a consolation for the sadness I feel every day. I therefore beg you, madam: do not tell me I am mistaken.'[32]

Despite these occasional acts of selfishness, Charles clearly loved his wife. One day in 1532, in a letter to his sister Marie from Germany, he promised to include a portrait of Isabella, 'the most beautiful one I possess, which will be the one that resembles her most'; but then he changed his mind. 'I was writing to my wife when your letter arrived,' he explained, and now 'I want to look at her portrait myself, seeing the great beauty it contains' – adding self-righteously: 'I am such a devoted husband that other beautiful women now do nothing for me.' A few months later he apologized to Marie for the brevity of his letter, 'because otherwise it would be very badly written, since all I have done for the last two hours is write a letter to my wife.'[33] Charles and Isabella not only exchanged letters: periodically they also sent trusted messengers 'to bring news of your health and of how things are there, and also so that Your Majesty will learn about my health, and that of our children, and about things here'. The night after Charles left for Italy in 1529, apparently spontaneously, each of them dispatched a messenger to the other; and when they were apart, they also exchanged gifts – in 1537 the empress 'sent a post to th'emperor at Barcelona with a letle flower of silke of her owne making, enclosed in a box'.[34] Nevertheless, as Rodríguez-Salgado has shrewdly noted, only Isabella's death seems to have made the emperor fully 'appreciate what he had possessed, and he would show her memory a depth of sentiment not seen while she was alive. Now there was no pressure, no bitter reproaches, nothing that could counter the many admirable virtues she had embodied; no illness to distort the beautiful features'. In short, after her death she became 'more an icon than a real woman'.[35] In 1547, Charles summoned Titian to come and 'repair his portrait of the empress, which arrived two years ago somewhat damaged'. He took the painting with him to Yuste, and gazed on it for a long time the day he realized that his illness might be terminal. In his final agony, as he had always planned, he held and kissed the crucifix that Isabella had held when she died.[36]

The same combination of love, duty and abuse characterized Charles's relations with three of his siblings. He always addressed his elder sister Eleanor as '*ma meilleure sœur*'. She had been his constant companion until 1518, when he compelled her to marry King Manuel of Portugal, and after she returned to Spain following his death, Charles visited her every evening. As for duty, when he left to campaign in Navarre in 1523, Eleanor served as regent in Castile; and as queen of France between 1530 and 1547 she did her best to promote harmony between her husband and her brother, attending summits between them and on at least one occasion sending him a secret letter that revealed France's negotiating position (chapter 10). After Francis died in 1547 she joined Charles in Brussels and a decade later she accompanied him to Spain. On paper, the emperor always professed profound affection. In 1522, after Manuel's death, he instructed one of his trusted ministers to bring Eleanor back to Spain because 'she is the person whom we love most and cherish most in this world', and after her death he told his son about 'the great and special love we have always had for each other'; but the reality had been somewhat different.[37] In 1517, Charles brutally cut short the love affair of his 'meilleure sœur' with Count Palatine Frederick and forced her to marry Manuel, and when Frederick renewed his suit after Manuel's death Charles again thwarted it. Shortly afterwards, when trying to persuade Eleanor to return from Portugal to Castile, the emperor wrote ingratiatingly: 'If by chance you have been told that once you are here I will force you marry someone against your will, you must not give them any credence' because 'I have no intention of making you marry, unless it is someone you want. And you can be quite sure of that.' Almost immediately, he reneged on this undertaking and promised her hand to the duke of Bourbon. He later reneged on that too, offering her to King Francis instead. Although he later claimed that Eleanor preferred this 'to the marriage with the duke of Bourbon *which I had arranged for her*', he nevertheless prevented her from joining her new husband for four years.[38]

Charles's relations with Ferdinand and Marie were similarly volatile. He granted both of them immense latitude as his lieutenants (the former in Germany; the latter in the Netherlands), but when in 1531 he asked Marie to govern the Netherlands, he insisted that she first dismiss all the household officials who had served her since she left Brussels in 1514, and to appoint in their place only Netherlanders approved by him. He also asked her to accept the new post without knowing what powers she would receive because 'until we are together I cannot decide what they should be'. In the event Charles gave his sister exceptional powers – far broader than he granted to the empress – and he made her the ultimate executor of his will, empowered to decide the order of succession if both he and Prince Philip should die.[39] Normally, he ratified her decisions, even when she had acted before consulting him, but occasionally they disagreed. One outrageous example occurred after the death of their nephew Hans of Denmark in 1532. Charles decided that 'There is no other remedy but to find husbands' for both of the late prince's sisters, Dorothea aged twelve and Christina aged ten, whom Marie was raising at her court (their mother was dead, their father in prison). The following year he arranged for Duke Francesco Sforza of Milan to marry one of them, but in doing so he 'made a mistake, saying that the duke could marry the older one, when he meant to say the younger, because he is trying to marry the older one to the king of Scotland'. When the emperor realized his error, 'he told the duke that he could marry whichever one he wanted'. Francesco chose Christina, although he was almost four times her age, because he had learned that she was better-looking.[40] The contract stipulated that the marriage should be consummated immediately, to which Marie strongly objected; but Charles overruled her, in part because he continued to confuse which of his underage nieces he was giving away. He began his reply: 'As for the marriage of my niece Dorothea' (instead of 'Christina'), before explaining that 'She will find the duke satisfactory, because as for wealth, he is in good shape; and as for his person, although the limbs one can see and his manner may seem odd, his head and torso are perfectly formed. It is said he cannot live without a woman, but that is something we can take care of for him'. His callous attitude infuriated Marie even more: 'Our niece regards you as her lord and father, in whom she places her entire trust', but 'she is only 11½, and it is against both God and good sense to marry so young'. In addition 'as yet she shows no sign of being a woman' (that is, she had not begun to menstruate), and 'if she becomes pregnant before she is fully developed you will put both her and the child at risk'. Once again Charles ignored his sister's sensible arguments. 'The difference in age will present more of a problem for the duke than for our niece,' he smirked. Marie deployed a succession of excuses to keep Christina at her court but in 1534, aged thirteen, she made her ceremonial entry into Milan.[41] A year later, since talks of a Scottish marriage had fallen through, Charles arranged for 'my niece Dorothea' to marry Queen Eleanor's former admirer, Frederick, although he was thirty-eight years her senior. Neither union ended well. Francesco Sforza died eighteen months after Christina joined him in Milan; both Dorothea and Frederick became Lutherans; neither couple produced children.

Charles's most egregious bullying of Marie occurred near the end of his life. In 1555, having governed the Netherlands for a quarter-century, she retired and then travelled with her brother and Eleanor to Spain, where she took a 'solemn vow to God not to become involved in government again, either directly or indirectly'. Nevertheless, Charles's son Philip, in Brussels, determined that Spain alone could provide the funds he needed to defeat France, that only his presence there could secure them, and that he could not leave the Netherlands safely unless Marie returned to govern them. Since he knew she would refuse, he begged the emperor to persuade her. Charles toyed with the idea of summoning her to a personal meeting, but (according to an eyewitness) he recalled that the last time he had mentioned this, 'I found her so angry that I doubted she would agree to it; and so, fearing a repeat, it seemed better not to place myself in a situation where I would just get angry with her'. In August 1558 he therefore sent his sister a letter that declared flatteringly that Philip 'is as much your son as he is mine' before ordering that 'You must not permit the loss in our lifetimes of the honour and patrimony that we inherited from our parents and our ancestors, and which we have preserved at the cost of so many and such great trials.' He was confident that 'when you consider the risk of such a great loss, to avoid it you will drop everything' and return to the Netherlands, 'because it would be the greatest service you could perform for God and our dynasty'. Lest she should waver, he added a holograph postscript repeating that 'the salvation – or the loss, dishonour and ruin – of my son the king and of our dynasty depend on you'.[42]

It was vintage Charles: a shameless appeal to Marie's loyalty to him, to their dynasty, and to the country she had worked so hard to govern, followed by the threat that her intransigence imperilled all of them. It showed that, even three weeks before his death, he was still prepared to blackmail his closest relatives – and, as usual, he succeeded. Although Marie protested vehemently, she started to pack her things ready to return and help her nephew and 'our dynasty' in the Netherlands. She continued even after she learned of Charles's death, but the effort seems to have exhausted her: she died four weeks after her brother.

Charles subjected Ferdinand to a similar blend of flattery and bullying, starting in 1517 (before they first met) when Charles feared that some members of his brother's entourage planned to make him regent of Castile. He ordered their dismissal, while at the same time reassuring Ferdinand that 'the great love I have for him is always paramount. He must see me as a brother and a true father' (p. 81). At the same time, he promised the States-General of the Netherlands that as soon as he arrived in Spain his brother would come to live in the Low Countries – but without informing Ferdinand until the moment when he abruptly told him to leave. The Infante, aged only fourteen, 'who was very wise and obedient to his brother, replied that His Majesty should arrange matters as he wished', and he immediately left his homeland for the court of his aunt Margaret. Two years later, when Charles furiously opposed Margaret's attempt to put his brother forward as a compromise candidate for election as king of the Romans, once again, Ferdinand complied, assuring his brother that 'I place my entire fate in your hands, as in the hands of my lord and father, because that is how I see you and will see you for my whole life.'[43]

Ferdinand's eagerness to accommodate paid off. In 1521, Charles ceded to his brother the Austrian lands he had inherited and made a will that recognized Ferdinand as his universal heir; the following year he named his brother as vicar-general in the Empire; and in 1526 he granted Ferdinand full powers to act in Italy, too, 'able to give, sell, promise and do all the things that I could do, and cause to be done, if I were there myself, because I feel so much love and confidence towards you.'[44] Ferdinand's flexible temperament – so different from that of the emperor – also paid off in central Europe: he possessed the tact and patience required to cajole the political elite of Austria and Germany, as well as Bohemia and Hungary after he became their king in 1526. Charles learned to value his brother's advice. 'There is no one in the world whom I love and trust as much as you, holding you to be just the same as me [ung autre moy mesmes],' he wrote in 1524, repeating the phrase a few months later, and adding that 'I regard you not only as my brother but also as my oldest son.'[45]

Nevertheless, praise could swiftly turn to blame. In 1535 rumours about 'the poor administration' of his brother's household led Charles to humiliate Ferdinand's personal representative, Martín de Salinas, at a public audience. The emperor began roughly:

'Tell me, is my brother as poor as they say' — 'Yes sire.' — 'Does he pay his household officials?' — 'No, sire, not for a long time.' . . . 'Does he owe them much?' — 'He owes some people a year's salary, sire, and others more.' . . . — 'They say that my brother maintains a large household.' — 'True, sire: indeed I think it may be larger . . .'

Luckily for Salinas, the arrival of an urgent message interrupted this tongue-lashing, and when the audience resumed Charles had calmed down, saying 'My brother is smart: I do not want him to think that I wish to intervene in how he governs. Let him do what he wants.'[46] Charles also broke his promises to Ferdinand whenever it suited him. 'I will take care that you shall have everything possible,' the emperor wrote soothingly in July 1525, 'because you deserve so much more, since you are responsible for the victory' at Pavia, 'and besides, you know that my affairs are yours, and yours are mine'. Yet the very same letter revealed the limitations of his gratitude: 'I have been advised to do three things to safeguard my position in Italy' and 'I have done them' – two of them at Ferdinand's expense. Charles announced that he had made a separate peace with Venice 'on condition that they pay me 120,000 ducats', despite an earlier undertaking to extract concessions from the Republic in favour of Ferdinand; and that he had agreed to install Francesco Sforza as duke of Milan in exchange for 600,000 ducats, despite an understanding that he would confer the duchy on Ferdinand. In short, he had sold his brother's dreams to pay his own debts.[47] He did the same thing two decades later, after Ferdinand's military assistance proved equally critical in crushing the Schmalkaldic League. His brother had every right to expect Charles to grant him the duchy of Württemberg, since League forces had expelled Ferdinand's garrisons in 1534, but instead the emperor installed Spanish garrisons and administered the territory himself. Worst of all, during the winter of 1550–1, Charles forced Ferdinand to accept Prince Philip as the next king of the Romans (instead of his own son Maximilian), creating a disastrous breach between the brothers that almost proved fatal to the dynasty (chapter 14).

CHARLES THE CHARMER

Such callous behaviour did not pass unnoticed. 'The emperor's nature,' wrote Gasparo Contarini in 1525, 'means that he cares for nobody [*non sa accarezzare alcuno*]'; and, he asserted, such relentless selfishness explained 'why few people like him'.[48] But here Contarini erred. Even those whom

Charles slighted and bullied often remained devoted to him. In her last letter, dictated when she knew she was dying, his aunt Margaret claimed that her only regret was that 'I will not be able to see and speak with you one more time before I die'. One of Eleanor's last letters to him likewise asserted that 'As for myself, I have never wanted to take a decision without knowing the pleasure of Your Majesty, whom I regard as my sovereign and my father'. Marie likewise asserted that 'after God, Your Majesty means everything to me'; and even after Charles's death, Ferdinand remained completely loyal, telling a confidant that 'I loved and revered my brother the emperor as if he had been my father'.[49]

Their youngest sister Catalina was perhaps Charles's greatest fan. Her letters referred to him as her 'my true father and lord', and she welcomed any advice he cared to share with his 'daughter and sister'. Although they only met twice, Charles always remained her hero. In 1528 she claimed that reading his letter about the challenge issued by the king of France 'gave me the worst pain I have ever experienced, because I never want to hear or know about something that might involve the slightest risk to Your Majesty'. Four years later, when the Turks invaded Hungary, she had no doubt that 'Your Majesty, as the common father of us all, will save and remedy' everything.[50] Wherever he might be, Catalina sent Charles care packages from Lisbon containing delicacies and other gifts that she hoped would please him: scented gloves and embroidered handkerchiefs, ginger and cinnamon, marmalade and conserves that she made herself. In 1553 she sent a personal representative to Brussels to take care of him, and when he moved to Yuste after his abdication she sent a talking parrot and two cats from India to entertain him as well as a weekly consignment of Atlantic fish. She also did her best to promote Charles's political ends by acting as his advocate with her husband King John.[51]

Although his relatives were thus the emperor's leading boosters, they were not alone: many diplomats praised his ability to win the hearts of those around him. In 1530, just after he crossed the Alps for the first time, an old woman came to the bridle of his horse and begged for money: Charles 'placed his hand on her head, and spoke kindly to her' before ordering his almoner to see to her needs. A few weeks later, as he approached Augsburg, 140 German dignitaries came out to meet him and 'the emperor at once dismounted and spoke and shook hands with every one of them'. The following year, in the Netherlands, an ambassador expressed astonishment at 'the universal devotion of the entire population. Leaving aside those who venerate and adore him as if he were God, there is no one here who does not speak with some affection in praise of His Majesty'. Shortly afterwards, during the investiture of his sister Marie as regent of the Netherlands, 'the emperor spoke for more than an hour in such a moving and gentle way that it almost made the audience weep'. By the time he had finished, 'everyone was of one mind, as if they had become his slaves'.[52]

Charles repeatedly demonstrated his ability to work a crowd during his victory lap of Sicily and Italy in 1535–6, winning over subjects who had once opposed him, and even former enemies. When a group of French prisoners wanted to kiss his hands as a sign of submission, Charles refused and 'instead, with loving words, he placed his hands on their shoulders and chatted with them'. A decade later, a German observer noted the same graciousness: 'Whenever I saw the emperor come out of his apartments and into the court-yard', if any noblemen awaited him Charles 'was the first to remove his hat, and with a friendly gesture or look, he gave his hand to everybody'. Then when he returned, 'at the foot of the staircase he turned, removed his hat, gave everyone his hand and graciously bade them farewell'.[53]

At audiences, Charles would 'listen courteously, attentively and with great patience, not only to ambassadors, envoys and nobles but also to any inconsequential or poor person who wanted to explain or request some-thing, hearing whatever they wanted to say without ever interrupting'. He normally made himself available in this way twice each day: 'Whenever he came out of his apartments he stopped and either listened or held out his own hand to receive a petition, so that everyone has the freedom boldly to share concerns with him, and openly air their grievances without fear.' Likewise, after eating dinner 'he got up from the table and stood humbly while he listened and spoke to everyone equally'.[54]

Many observers also praised the emperor's self-control. In March 1525, Charles's impassive reaction upon hearing about the victory at Pavia and the capture of Francis impressed the Mantuan ambassador, who reflected that as a rule he 'does not gloat over successes or get depressed by adversity'. Five years later, on learning of the death of his young son Fernando, 'the emperor showed no sign of the sorrow that fathers, however stoic they are, normally show at such setbacks', and when his brother offered consolation, 'the emperor told him that one should not take offence at what Our Lord God was pleased to ordain', and he 'ended the conversation by saying that he and his wife were of a suitable age and condition to produce more children'.[55] Finally, foreign diplomats noted with approval Charles's restraint in food and drink. 'He always ate alone and in total silence', according to a Venetian account in 1530. Servers brought between twenty-five and thirty 'covered dishes to his table, and uncovered them so that he could indicate which ones he liked'; after which he chose '10 or 12 of them, taking 2 or 3 mouthfuls from each, eating with his hands from a silver platter', and drinking 'wine from a pitcher 3 or 4 times'. He ate 'very little bread and no salad'.[56]

At much the same time, the imperial preacher and chronicler Fray Antonio de Guevara composed an essay 'On the physiognomy and qualities of the emperor', which provided an intimate pen portrait that matched that of Sancho Cota a decade before (p. 66 above). 'He was of medium height, with large and beautiful eyes, aquiline nose and red hair . . . A small beard, a strong neck; large and powerful arms; small, rough hands; well-proportioned legs.' Like others, Guevara noted only one defect: 'His mouth, because his upper jaw was so badly aligned with the lower that his teeth never met. This had two unfortunate consequences: it made his speech hard to follow because he ate his words; and it made eating hard work for him, because his teeth could not chew what he ate, which meant poor digestion and often illness'.[57] After he had returned safely from his embassy to Spain in 1525, Contarini made the same point: the emperor's 'lower jaw is so large and so long that it seemed not to be natural but false' – he used the word '*posticcio*': a prosthetic artificially added to the body – but shortly afterwards the emperor took steps to conceal this defect.[58] Someone who watched him disembark in Italy in 1529 began his report by exclaiming that although 'his mouth is always open' he did not look at all like recent portraits because 'His Majesty has had his hair trimmed in the Italian style' and 'he has a pointed beard'. Exactly when this transition occurred remains unclear. A gold coin struck in Aragon in 1528 showed the emperor already sporting a beard, but still with long, straight hair in the Burgundian style (Pl. 16). He cut it short just before he left Barcelona for Italy, and his courtiers followed suit, albeit 'some of them wept' as they did so.[59] In normal times, ambassadors would have reported such dramatic changes, but Charles imprisoned most of the diplomatic corps in January 1528 and thus deprived them of the opportunity to observe him; so when he arrived in Italy, surprise added to the impact of his metamorphosis. As he entered Bologna for his coronation, 'what gave him added gravity was his blond beard and his golden hair, which he wore like the Roman emperors, cut at mid-ear length'. Instead of a duke of Burgundy, Charles had become Marcus Aurelius (Pl. 18).[60]

Thanks to Guevara, Marcus Aurelius provided Charles with more than a new coiffure. The friar claimed (almost certainly falsely) that he had found the Greek text of the late emperor's memoirs and some of his letters in an Italian library and had turned them first into Latin and then into Castilian while serving as preacher at Charles's court, starting in 1518. Ten years later, the first printed edition of *The Golden Book of the Emperor Marcus Aurelius* appeared in Seville, and by 1550 there were seventeen Spanish, nine Italian and nine French editions. It became (some claimed) the most widely read book in Renaissance Europe after the Bible.

In his lengthy dedication to Charles, Guevara remarked: 'I can see, sire, that you are one but have to deal with many; you are alone and cannot always be accompanied. I also see you engulfed by many matters.' Guevara offered his help in navigating this sea of solitude by 'persuading you to imitate and follow the example of Marcus Aurelius', because he had expanded the empire he had inherited through a combination of patience and justice, not through wars and conquests. In an expanded version of his book, also dedicated to Charles and first published in 1529, Guevara devoted five chapters to the evils of war, and three more to the particular evils of wars of conquest and of forcible colonization.[61]

Was the dedicatee one of Guevara's readers? The author claimed in 1525 that 'while His Majesty was ill with a fever, he asked me to spend time with him and do something to reduce his temperature. I therefore presented His Majesty with *Marcus Aurelius*, although it was not yet finished and revised'. The prologue to another of Guevara's works, *Alarm clock for princes*, expressed the wish that 'From time to time Your Majesty should make it a habit to dip into this book, and perhaps you will find some helpful advice that will be of benefit'. Charles certainly owned an illustrated manuscript copy, no doubt presented by the author; and both works formed part of the emperor's travelling library until 1542, when he deposited them in Simancas castle together with other books that he valued, to form the nucleus of an imperial library.[62] But if Charles actually read Guevara's works, he read them selectively, focusing on another passage in the prologue to *The Golden Book* that quoted with approval the example of Julius Caesar and expressed the hope that 'those of us who write about your century to enlighten future ages will testify that in order to live up to the words PLUS ULTRA, which form part of your emblem, you attempted the conquest of the whole world'. The decision to take Julius Caesar rather than Marcus Aurelius as a role model would involve high costs for Charles and his subjects, as well as for his enemies.[63]

PART III

'RULER FROM THE RISING TO THE SETTING OF THE SUN'

'Now [Charles] may as well wryte to his frendis, as [Julius] Caesar wrote to his frendis: I came, I saw, I conquered.'

Nicholas Wotton, English ambassador at the imperial court, September 1543

NINE

THE LAST CRUSADER, 1532–6

THE IMPERIAL INVALID

On 18 January 1532, the day after he reluctantly left Brussels for Germany, the emperor composed a letter of rare passion to his sister Marie: 'Although it's only a short time since I left you,' he wrote, 'I feel bored and irritated, mainly because I left you behind. You can be sure that after such a good time together I shall not forget it, or you, or my homeland, however far away I may be.' Ten days later he told Marie that he still felt 'displeased to be going further away from what I always have so many reasons to love and to hold: namely you, and the country where I was born and raised.'[1]

Charles tried to overcome his boredom and loneliness through hunting, overjoyed to encounter herds of up to 500 deer in the Rhineland, but his pleasure ended abruptly when 'the leash of his dog became wrapped around his horse's legs, as he was galloping to try and catch up with some deer. His horse threw him, and His Majesty's feet hit a large rock.' This, Charles reported, 'really damaged my leg: although it is not broken or dislocated, it is very painful.' He did not exaggerate: when his coffin was opened in the 1870s, observers noted 'the imperfect healing of a fracture in his leg, because the bones had knitted together laterally'.[2]

Thus began five months of health problems. Charles refused to be bled or purged – the remedies prescribed by most physicians at the time for most ailments – and initially he made a good recovery; but once he started to hunt again his leg became swollen and ulcerous, and the pain kept him awake at night. Some feared he might lose the leg and his doctors confined him to his room and put him on a diet to lose weight. 'The cure irritates me as much as the injury,' Charles raged, but the doctors had the measure of their illustrious patient: 'He could certainly go outside,' Dr Escoriaza confided to the empress, 'but if we doctors give His Majesty an inch we fear he will take a yard.' Therefore, 'we agreed to stand up to him as best we may'.[3]

The possibility of amputation led Charles to 'think about a wooden leg'. 'I can't deny that I have become afraid,' he told Marie, and yet 'I can't stop scratching the ulcers'. He paid a high price for his indiscipline. Escoriaza reported that 'He has an itch all over his body and he scratches a lot, especially his legs, and the scratching has caused a rash in many parts of his body, right up to his face', and his 'left eye became red and swollen'. When Charles appeared in public 'he wore a piece of green fabric over his left eye', and in private he complained that 'they cover me with an ointment that makes me look as if I had offended the carnival king because my face is more black than white. To tell you the truth, I am really angry that so many illnesses have come at the same time.' His only consolation was that (according to frustrated foreign ambassadors) 'on the orders of his doctors, His Imperial Majesty transacts business with no one'.[4]

In May, Charles thought he had recovered. 'Now I get up in the morning and go to bed early. I eat my main meal at 10 and afterwards have only a light supper.' He also started hunting again, but with predictable results: after spending 'three hours in the saddle, chasing a stag', he developed a fever. Nevertheless, a week later he spent 'two days hunting', covering 'half a league on foot', which he considered 'quite miraculous'; but the miracle did not last. After taking part in a procession through the streets of Regensburg, while 'talking with one of his courtiers' Charles 'suddenly felt a sharp pain in his leg' and, as a precaution, his doctors moved him to thermal springs nearby. Bathing there 'brings me two benefits', he joked to his sister: 'The first is that I can scratch myself as I recover; the other is that, with the doctor's consent, I can recommence my normal regimen' – that is, he could once more eat and drink as much and as often as he liked. In addition, 'I now have more leisure because I do not allow individuals to come and see me here'. Even Nicholas Perrenot de Granvelle, Charles's principal councillor on foreign affairs, only received permission to visit every other day to deliver important letters, discuss business and (when possible) get his master's signature. Charles even gave up hunting until mid-July, when he 'spent three days tracking a bear'. His health crisis abated just in time for him to oppose another Ottoman assault led by Sultan Suleiman in person.[5]

THE HEIR OF CHARLEMAGNE CONFRONTS
THE HEIR OF ALEXANDER

Charles and his brother had done much to provoke the attack. Soon after the deliverance of Vienna in 1529, Ferdinand had recaptured several towns in

Hungary and sought to make an anti-Ottoman alliance with the shah of Persia: both moves infuriated the sultan. So did Charles's imperial coronation. A spy in Istanbul reported that Suleiman 'always says "To Rome! To Rome!" and he detests the emperor, and his title of *Caesar*'. Instead, Suleiman 'caused himself to be called *Caesar*'. His agents commissioned Western emblems of sovereignty from Venetian jewellers, including a four-crown tiara (one crown more than the pope), and began a propaganda campaign that projected their master as heir to Alexander the Great. The Venetians, suitably impressed, began to refer to him as Suleiman 'the Magnificent'.[6] In April 1532 the new Alexander left Istanbul for his third campaign up the Danube, while his battle fleet headed for the western Mediterranean.

These developments placed Charles on the horns of a dilemma. Although he needed to support Ferdinand against the sultan as best he could, he dared not denude Italy of troops for fear of an Ottoman naval attack, perhaps with French support. As it happened, paying his huge ransom had deprived Francis of the means to attack Charles again, but the king used diplomacy to undermine his rival, above all by entrusting Antonio Rincón (a former Comunero now in French service) with a secret mission to divert the Ottoman army from Hungary to Italy. Suleiman received Rincón with every mark of favour, but refused to change his strategy. Instead, on 12 July 1532 he issued a personal challenge. 'The king of Spain [the sultan refused to recognize Charles's imperial title] has proclaimed for a long time that he wants to act against the Turks; and now, by the grace of God, I am advancing with my army against him. If he is a man who has balls and courage, let him come and draw up his army in the field ready to fight with my imperial host.' 'The issue,' he concluded, 'will be whatever God wills.'[7]

Charles welcomed the challenge. Having recovered his health, he informed his sister Marie that 'I have resolved to devote myself to the defence of Germany'; and 'because in all my affairs I place my hope and strength in God, my sovereign creator, who through his infinite goodness has always helped me', he asked her to arrange throughout the Netherlands 'pious processions and prayers' to mobilize divine assistance. He also mobilized earthly resources, raising troops in all his dominions (12,000 Germans, 10,000 Spaniards, 10,000 Italians, 4,000 Netherlanders); and he opened talks to persuade the German Lutherans to help him defend 'our Homeland'. Eventually, Lutheran and Catholic leaders alike converged on Regensburg to join the emperor at a new Diet: all seven Electors, over seventy secular and ecclesiastical rulers and delegations from fifty-five towns attended, each one accompanied by a host of advisers and officials – some 3,000 people in all.[8]

The Diet faced three major problems: the religious divisions of Germany; the need to mobilize resources against the Turks; and the risk that France might declare war. Girolamo Aleandro feared that the emperor's resolve might waver because, 'although he has good intentions . . . he is by nature very attached to advancing his own interests'. In particular Aleandro fretted that Charles might 'negotiate a deal with the Lutherans without the pope's permission', and at an audience he rashly reminded the emperor that:

> When Your Majesty was younger and less certain of your power, when you were buffeted by so many enemies of the church in the Diet of Worms, you alone held steady, paying attention only to God and your own conscience, which gave birth to that beautiful and sacred edict by which Your Majesty won both perpetual glory in this world and the prospect of eternal rewards in the next. All this may be lost if Your Majesty, now so much more prudent and sure of your power because God has granted you so many glorious successes, were to allow – I won't say make – unreasonable concessions in these talks with the Lutherans that would harm the universal Church.

This enraged Charles. 'The Edict of Worms was indeed good and sacred and reasonable,' he shot back, and 'it would have taken effect if the pope had chosen to do his duty, as we asked him at the time! Likewise if, after the Diet of Augsburg, His Holiness had done what he had discussed with me' – namely, convened a general council – 'we should not now be obliged to seek a deal with the Lutherans.' Surprised by this vigorous counter-attack, the nuncio wisely left the imperial presence, observing that, 'as Solomon said, "The hearts of kings are inscrutable"'.[9]

Aleandro did not realize that Charles had already negotiated 'a deal with the Lutherans', once again encouraged by his former confessor. 'Since you cannot use force, which is the true remedy,' García de Loaysa y Mendoza advised, the emperor should let the Lutheran princes 'live as heretics provided they do not spread their errors to other Christians' and 'make the best deal possible with them so that they will help you against the Turks . . . You should not scruple to make use of them, even though they are heretics because since your own heart is without sin, their errors will not prevent your success.'[10] Charles followed Loaysa's advice: in July 1532, by the peace of Nuremberg, he promised the German Lutherans that he would suspend the Edict of Worms until the pope convened a general council, and in return they agreed to provide and pay 40,000 foot and 8,000 horse to serve against the Turks. Even Luther said nice things. 'Caesar is an honest man [*probus*],' he told his guests at table one day. 'He is pious and quiet' – although he could not resist adding: 'I think he says as much in one year as I do in one day.'[11]

Marco Antonio Contarini, ambassador of the Venetian Republic at the imperial court, immediately saw the significance of this policy change. 'The Turks had counted on the Lutherans,' he observed, 'but they will be disappointed because they will soon bring to the imperial camp twice the number of men that they agreed to provide.' In Regensburg, 'almost every day you see companies of infantry passing through' as well as 'about 80 pieces of artillery purchased by His Majesty'.[12] In mid-August, Contarini reported that 'everyone is now united, so that without doubt there are more than 120,000 infantry and 20,000 cavalry' – and, he enthused, 'I am confident that no one has seen two larger armies in more than 800 years, or two such powerful emperors taking such a great risk.' Administrative records concur: a contemporary estimate of the rations required by the Christian host listed 114,000 soldiers, over 74,000 other personnel, and over 73,000 horses. Charles entered Vienna on 23 September, 'showing the world that he does not flee from conflict', and one month later Suleiman and his troops began their long retreat to Istanbul. Meanwhile the imperial navy under Andrea Doria, 'better equipped and organized than any other fleet for many years', wrested from the Turks the fortresses of Coron and Patras in Greece.[13]

Charles recognized his debt to Fortune. The rains that swelled the rivers of Hungary in June and July 1532, he wrote, seriously delayed the Ottoman advance and 'proved very beneficial because it allowed us time to repair and strengthen the fortifications of Vienna, and other more exposed fortresses, and provide them with supplies, artillery and munitions'.[14] Charles was also fortunate that, although the cost of his huge army and navy obliged him to raise some taxes and loans, the largest contribution came from France. In April 1532 he ordered his wife to transfer to Italy over 400,000 ducats from the French ransom 'with all possible secrecy and dissimulation'; and 'if you have to admit that you are withdrawing some money, you must not say that it is so much, so that both inside and outside Spain everyone will think that it is all still there'. Two months later, amid similar 'secrecy and dissimulation', he ordered her to transfer almost 500,000 ducats more.[15]

Despite this expenditure, and the concessions to the German Lutherans, Charles failed to bring the Ottoman army to battle, let alone defeat them, but he displayed excellent leadership, entrusting field command to Count

Palatine Frederick, who had been fighting wars for three decades, and solic-
iting and following advice of experienced military advisers such as Antonio
de Leyva and Fernando Álvarez de Toledo, duke of Alba.[16] Moreover, the
ability to assemble armed forces of unprecedented size against 'infidels'
vindicated the crusading tradition of the House of Burgundy exemplified in
the chronicles of chivalry on which Charles had been raised. When on 21
September 1532 the emperor boarded a boat at Linz that would transport
him down the Danube to take personal command of his vast army, dressed
in a gold jacket with a jaunty feather in his cap, he was indeed – and was
seen to be – the most powerful and successful ruler the Western world had
seen since Charlemagne (Pl. 17).

BACK TO SPAIN

Such success alarmed the pope. Although Clement recognized the need to
exploit the retreat of Suleiman, and 'break his head open so that he will
never think again of threatening Christendom as he has just done', he feared
that if the emperor should again 'campaign against the sultan in person . . .
France will immediately invade Italy, and encountering no resistance he
may do what he wants, and place His Holiness in jeopardy'. He therefore
pleaded with the emperor to meet him in Rome for more policy discussions.
Loaysa strongly opposed this. Writing as confessor as well as councillor, he
explained at length to Charles 'what is most suitable for your conscience and
your honour'. He warned that 'even if Your Majesty only sleeps 4 hours a
night while you are in Italy, and spends the rest of the 24 every day on the
business that must be concluded if Italy is to be at peace . . . you will not be
able to embark [for Spain] before the month of May' 1533. He therefore
urged him to go only as far as Bologna to discuss with the pope 'whatever is
relevant to your affairs and to the peace of Italy'.[17]

The emperor had reached the same conclusion. An outbreak of plague
led him to abandon Vienna in mid-October and he did not stop until he
reached Villach, the small town in the Austrian Alps to which he would flee
in ignominy twenty years later. From there, the only feasible route to Bologna
lay across the Brenner Pass and through Venetian lands, which created a
delicate situation because Charles now travelled at the head of 10,000
veteran infantry, 3,000 cavalry and an artillery train, as well as his court and
'6,000 or more women and boys'. Aware that only three years earlier he had
threatened to invade the republic, the emperor now made clear his pacific
intentions to the Venetian diplomats who came to pay their respects (and

keep their august visitor under surveillance). At an audience, 'dressed in his riding habit and standing the whole time', he explained that 'he was on his way to Spain', but 'first he wanted to talk with the pope' and create 'a union for the defence of Italy and its states that would maintain each of them within their present boundaries; and he said this not as emperor or king of Spain, but as king of Naples and an Italian ruler.' He predicted that he would be back in Spain by Christmas.[18]

His plan unravelled almost immediately because Clement delayed his departure from Rome, compelling Charles to postpone his departure for Spain. He therefore spent another month in Mantua where (the Venetian diplomats at his court noted disapprovingly) 'as soon as the sun has shone for an hour, His Imperial Majesty goes hunting with the nobles' until he 'injured the index finger of his right hand while hunting some very large boars', so that his signature became unrecognizable (Los Cobos attached certification that the emperor had indeed signed orders sent out in his name).[19] As occupational therapy, Charles attended balls, banquets and plays in the great Gonzaga castle, and when it snowed he had 'sledges in the German style' prepared, 'which gave great pleasure to the ladies, because they were new and unusual'. Everyone commented that Charles seemed 'very much at home' in Mantua, making do 'without any servants from his own household' and going out 'without any guards, and walking alone through the town and countryside'.[20] These walks took him to the house of Andrea Mantegna, with its distinctive design of a cube containing a circular courtyard. Suitably impressed, in November 1532, Charles 'gave orders to spend 12,000 ducats a year for four years in renovating the royal castle and palace in Granada, thinking to live there in tranquillity since they are the most beautiful places in the world'. His architects duly prepared a model of an Italian-style 'Palace of Charles V' at the heart of the Alhambra, and construction began the following spring.[21]

The month in Mantua left another notable artistic trace. Artists had done portraits of Charles since he was a child, but on the day he entered the city the duke summoned Titian. The result was a celebrated likeness of the emperor standing full length, his beard largely concealing his prognathism, while a hunting dog sniffs at his enormous codpiece. Titian did not work alone. Ferdinand's court painter, Jakob Seisenegger, had accompanied Charles to Mantua and produced an almost identical portrait, leading Diane Bodart to make the plausible suggestion that the emperor sat for both artists at the same time, perhaps in a competition similar to the one Alexander the Great had arranged between Lysippus and Apelles.[22] For almost a decade, their works became in effect an 'official portrait', imitated by all who wanted to display a likeness of the emperor (Pl. 19).

Clement eventually entered Bologna on 10 December 1532, and Charles joined him there three days later. As before, 'the pope and th'emprour be lodgid here both within wone house' so that they could talk together without being observed. When they first met 'the emperor with gret humyllite and reverence kyssed the pope's foot', and Clement took Charles 'up in his armys, and kyssed hym on hys cheike'. Afterwards Charles spent two hours 'describing everything that had happened since they parted', but then (the Venetian ambassador complained) 'although the emperor continues to meet with the pope alone, it is impossible to know what they discuss'. In their public appearances, pope and emperor showed complete amity – during a Christmas service Clement 'blessed the imperial sword' while Charles read one of the lessons – but 'after the Mass ended, they returned to their palace together' to resume their secret discussions.[23]

Clement announced a sensational consequence of these meetings just after New Year: he would summon a general council to settle outstanding religious problems and invite all the rulers of Christendom to attend in person. He then appointed a committee of cardinals to hold 'interviews almost daily' with imperial ministers (including Los Cobos and Granvelle) to finalize the details and thus 'save the two principals the trouble of confer-ring personally'. At least one observer in Bologna realized that this was just a device to 'waste the time of the Emperor's stay here without concluding anything' of importance concerning the general council:

> The pope professes to wish for it, but puts off the emperor with words, and deceives everyone. The two will never agree about the time and place. If Charles were wise, and saw the imminent danger to himself and all Italy, he would set about it in earnest, and not continue hoping . . . that time will bring a remedy; for the contrary is more likely.

Instead, Charles was foolish: just after taking his leave of Clement, he confi-dently assured Ferdinand that the council would meet in Bologna, Mantua or Piacenza and would prepare measures 'for the extirpation of the Lutheran heresy and the punishment of those who subscribe to it'.[24]

In his *Memoirs*, the emperor ruefully acknowledged that Clement had deceived him: their second (and last) meeting, he wrote, 'did not have the full effects that His Majesty had expected'. Why had he allowed himself to be duped by the pope, just as seven years earlier he had allowed himself to be duped by Francis? One common denominator is easily identified. The emperor brought to Bologna almost 10,000 troops 'beside his howsehold, and his counsel', and every night 500 men stood guard outside the palace where he and the pope resided, with another 200 inside. Faced with such overwhelming force Clement would claim (like Francis before him) that his concessions had been made under duress and so were not binding.[25] The concessions exceeded Charles's wildest dreams. On 24 February 1533, the emperor's birthday, and now also the anniversary of both the battle of Pavia and his coronation, Clement signed a secret agreement – 'so secret that only four people know about it' – by which he promised to persuade Francis to send assistance in case of another Turkish assault, to deny Henry VIII's petition to divorce Katherine of Aragon, and to make no treaties without Charles's consent. Three days later he also signed a 'league for the defence of Italy' that obliged him, as well as most other Italian states, to avoid providing any foreign power with either a pretext or an invitation to interfere in Italian affairs, and to create a war chest for mutual defence in case of invasion.[26]

While he distracted the emperor with these diplomatic ploys, Clement negotiated with the special envoys from both France and England who arrived in Bologna to press Francis's proposal that his second son Henry, duke of Orléans, should marry the pope's niece, Catherine de' Medici, and that Clement should meet Francis in person 'after the emperor leaves Italy'. The envoys also delivered a secret proposal: within eighteen months Francis would invade Italy and reconquer the duchy of Milan, which Clement would bestow on Henry of Orléans and Catherine.[27]

FAMILY LIFE AGAIN

Unaware of the pope's duplicity, Charles left Bologna in March 1533 to visit the battlefield of Pavia, where his generals showed him the exact spot where they had forced Francis to surrender, and the fortress of Pizzighettone, where the king had languished in prison. Then the emperor returned to Genoa where the galleys of Andrea Doria waited to convey him back to Spain – but the crossing took more than double the normal time. According to the Venetian ambassador, 'it was impossible to rest either by night or by day' because 'every galley, including that of the emperor, carried seventy or eighty men more than usual so that it was bad on deck and worse below'. In short, 'it seemed like hell'. The last stretch was the worst, because the wind became adverse as the galleys neared the Spanish coast, 'and the rowers, all of them naked, rowed two nights and almost two days until they were almost dead'. As soon as the imperial galley came within sight of the Catalan coast, 'without saying a word, except to forbid anyone to follow him', the emperor and a handful of courtiers went ashore in a small boat and commandeered 'such horses as they could find in a nearby village'. Riding throughout the night incognito towards Barcelona, the emperor covered 150 kilometres in just twenty-four hours and 'found the empress still in bed, because she had not yet got up. The emperor threw himself into bed too, and stayed there until 2 p.m. when they both got up and ate.'[28]

Charles had instructed his wife to bring their two surviving children to meet him when he disembarked. More than sixty years later Philip II still recalled the thrill of that reunion: 'In 1533 I went to Barcelona with the empress, my lady, there to await the emperor' and 'I turned six while in Barcelona'.[29] The prince had greatly changed since his father left him, four years earlier, and so had the empress. In her early months as regent, she had felt the need to solicit 'the general opinion of your subjects and ministers familiar with the matter' before referring it to Charles for final decision; but gradually she gained in self-confidence. When in September 1530 her husband instructed her to prepare to fight a campaign in the Mediterranean the following year, she objected forcefully. 'Each day we discover another shortage. We need to start preparing the equipment that the fleet will need immediately, because otherwise it will not be ready in time for next summer's campaigning season.' She also reproached her husband for keeping her in the dark: 'I beg Your Majesty to order that in future less time elapses without sending me a letter, so that every 20 days or so I would have news of you' – and she continually badgered him to come home because 'I have more reason to desire that than anyone'.[30]

Charles spent almost two months with his wife in Barcelona before leaving to celebrate Corpus Christi in Montserrat and then meet the Cortes of the Crown of Aragon at Monzón; but no sooner had he given the opening address than news arrived that the empress was 'very sick and at death's door', almost certainly because of a miscarriage. He now made the fastest journey of his life, covering in two days the 230 kilometres that separate Monzón from Barcelona to be by his wife's side. He did not leave until she had recovered.[31]

Charles would spend the rest of the year wrapped 'in the mortal coils of the Cortes' at Monzón, rejoining the empress in Zaragoza to celebrate New Year. Then the couple moved to Toledo, which became their capital until May when the summer heat led them to move northwards. The empress and most of the court went to Valladolid, but Charles travelled through the towns of Old Castile that had been prominent in the Comunero rebellion: Segovia, Ávila, Salamanca, Zamora and Toro.[32] He even visited Villalar, site of the decisive battle, and spent time at the university of Salamanca, 'saying that it was the treasure-chest that provided the judges and magistrates required' by the kingdom. Charles began by greeting the bishop, Luis Cabeza de Vaca, his first preceptor, and then 'he attended mass in the university chapel, and afterwards listened to a debate' on a very relevant subject: 'Whether a Christian prince may wage war to avenge injuries to an ally.' After this, the emperor attended lectures by the foremost university luminaries: Francisco de Vitoria on theology, Juan Martínez de Silíceo (soon to become preceptor to Prince Philip) on philosophy, and the rest on medicine and law. In each lecture hall the emperor 'sat down on a bench as soon as he entered' and listened (although since all instruction took place in Latin he probably understood little) before visiting the university library. In all, he spent four hours living like a student.[33]

Then a family tragedy occurred. While Charles visited his mother in Tordesillas, 'the empress miscarried a son in the eighth month of her pregnancy'. The chronicler Pedro Girón devoted a heavily corrected paragraph to this tragic event. Some doctors, he reported, asserted that it happened 'because she had become pregnant while convalescing from her serious illness in Barcelona, and the ligatures were not strong enough'; others said that 'while going to see her son the prince' the empress 'fell, and the fall killed the foetus. God alone knows the truth.' As with the death of his son Fernando, the emperor 'treated the empress's miscarriage as a Christian prince should', and urged her to accept the loss as God's will. He himself showed the way by indulging in hunting and sports until 'playing tennis too hard' left him 'somewhat lame in one foot'. He also resumed conjugal relations: by Christmas the empress was pregnant again.[34]

By then, important developments had transformed the international scene. Henry VIII not only officially repudiated his wife Katherine and declared their daughter Mary to be a bastard, but also married Anne Boleyn and had her crowned queen of England. Pope Clement proceeded to excommunicate Henry, who retaliated by threatening to renounce his obedience to Rome. The pope then travelled to Marseilles, where he officiated at the marriage of his niece to the duke of Orléans. He also coordinated an anti-Habsburg policy with Francis: the two rulers agreed to oppose both a general council (because it would strengthen Charles's position in Germany) and the new Italian League (because it would thwart French plans to conquer Milan).

Charles could not ignore Henry VIII's humiliation of his aunt and he urged his siblings – Ferdinand in Germany, Marie in the Netherlands, Eleanor in France, Catalina in Portugal – to join him in declaring their support for Katherine, 'because it is not only a matter that involves conscience but also, given the current state of public affairs in Christendom, we must support the judgement and declaration of the church'.[35] Significantly, his letter twice included the caveat that action should be delayed 'for the time being [*pour maintenant*]' because Clement and Henry had both left the door open to a negotiated settlement – the pope deferred publication of his sentence of excommunication, and the king delayed final consent to legislation severing England's ties with Rome – but in March 1534 the pope ended the impasse by declaring Henry's marriage to Katherine valid and their daughter Mary legitimate. In a letter from Rome announcing this decision, an imperial diplomat crowed that this constituted the greatest of the emperor's successes because it opened the path to the conquest of England; but Charles's Spanish councillors felt less enthusiasm. Upon receiving the news three weeks later, they urged the emperor to send envoys to Rome, Paris and London to explore the likely reactions to a Habsburg invasion of England, because 'doing it suddenly and alone will make them suspect that Your Majesty wants to settle the matter without them'. Therefore, Charles should announce that he would continue to do nothing 'for the time being' so that 'he could plan more effectively according to what time and events might bring'.[36]

Charles followed this advice. Despite general loathing in Spain for Henry's new queen, reflected in the insulting term *anabolena* (meaning troublemaker and sometimes prostitute), which remains in use in parts of Castile even today, the emperor did nothing to help his aunt.[37] In letters to his brother he blamed his inaction on the 'unrest and trouble in both Germany and Italy, which have heated up and caught fire ever since the summit at Marseilles'. In particular, Lutheran troops led by Philip of Hesse and funded by France invaded the duchy of Württemberg, restored the ruler exiled by Charles and Ferdinand, and drove out the Habsburg garrisons. Once again Charles failed to act, and he advised his brother to 'gain time by temporizing and dissimulating'. In September he repeated his message to Ferdinand: 'you would do well to forget or dissimulate the past' in order to preserve the peace of Germany.[38] It proved to be prudent advice: an Ottoman fleet of 160 galleys had just entered the western Mediterranean and seized Tunis, a Spanish tributary state in north Africa only 250 kilometres from Sicily.

CAROLUS AFRICANUS

Stung by the defeats of 1532, Sultan Suleiman now adopted a different Western strategy. He summoned to Istanbul Khaireddin Barbarossa, who had long used Algiers as a base from which to terrorize Christians throughout the western Mediterranean with his galleys, and named him commander of the imperial fleet. Two years later Barbarossa sailed west and took Tunis, forcing its pro-Habsburg ruler to flee, and the sultan marched east to campaign against the shah of Persia. Charles could not ignore this combination of challenge and opportunity. An English diplomat noted that because 'Tunis is a city as large as Rome, where Barbarossa can easily maintain his fleet and constantly menace Spain and Italy', the emperor 'will need either to become strong enough to be able to meet Barbarossa's fleet in combat, or else mobilize constantly to defend himself'. Charles agreed, informing his ministers in Italy that he had ordered 'the provisions and other necessary items to be prepared so that next spring we will have a great fleet capable of resisting and attacking that of our enemies, and we will expel them from Christian seas'.[39]

Then in September 1534 the pope died. Although Clement had been a fickle ally, often plotting to use France to check Habsburg dominance in Italy, he had steadfastly supported the emperor's efforts against the Turks. Charles worried that the next pope would renege on the defensive treaties signed by his predecessor and encourage Francis to enforce his claims to Milan and Genoa; but in the event Cardinal Alessandro Farnese, who became Pope Paul III, immediately declared that he would maintain all existing alliances and take tough measures to reform the Church. In his first conclave he also announced support for Charles's projected African campaign and proclaimed it a crusade; and in March 1535, on hearing that Suleiman had remained in Baghdad and begun a new campaign in Persia, Paul declared that 'this is a great opportunity for the emperor to attend not only to everything required for Africa but also for a greater and more honourable enterprise' – namely the conquest of Istanbul – and urged him 'not to waste this wonderful opportunity given by God'.[40]

Once again, Charles's councillors did not feel the same enthusiasm. Granvelle predicted an alarming escalation of potential disasters if Charles left to campaign in north Africa, because the French would then invade Italy to support the claim of the duke of Orléans to Milan, and afterwards 'find some excuse or pretext to occupy Naples' and perhaps some other independent states of the peninsula. Cardinal Tavera, president of the royal council and principal adviser to the empress when she served as regent, stressed the danger of 'tempting Fortune as many times as Your Majesty has done, leaving these realms [Spain] and putting yourself at risk on the sea and in lands that you do not rule . . . Starting a war is a dangerous, prolonged and uncertain business, as we have recently found,' he continued, adding unkindly: 'Your Majesty should remember that Emperor Maximilian, although such a valiant prince and so experienced in war, saw his great enterprises miscarry because he failed to match his ends to his means.' Tavera closed by repeating the arguments he had used to discourage a duel with King Francis: Charles must not 'take the same risks as a young knight, with nothing to lose and no one to whom he must explain himself . . . If Your Majesty should be captured, or if some other disaster should befall you', how could 'a child of tender age' like Prince Philip take over?[41]

At first, it appeared that the emperor would heed these warnings because in February 1535, from Madrid, he assured his brother that although he intended to travel to Barcelona, it was only 'so that from there I can observe and react to what Barbarossa might do, and improve the state of my own navy'. Charles promised that he would then return to Germany. Some believed him. Even though the naval and military preparations 'to make war in Africa against Barbarossa' impressed Pedro Girón, 'nobody thought at that time that His Majesty would go there in person'. Ferdinand's agent in Spain likewise reported complacently that the emperor travelled to Barcelona merely 'to get the fleet to sea and to prepare for any trouble from France'.[42] Their error first emerged through carelessness. On 28 February, Charles made a new will, stating explicitly 'that he had decided *to travel in person with his fleet*', and his secretary sent a copy to the emperor's sister Marie, who promptly shared the sensational news with Ferdinand – adding that their brother's 'reputation will not be maintained as it should be, because when all is said and done', he is 'going to war against a mere pirate'.[43] Three days after signing his will, the emperor set out for Barcelona, once more leaving his wife pregnant and depressed: according to one of the empress's ladies-in-waiting, 'she is as lonely as can be, God have pity on her'.[44] Three months later, the empress gave birth to another child, Joanna. As usual, she did so alone.

Rumours that Charles would lead the expedition in person galvanized his subjects, who now flocked to join him in Barcelona. According to an eyewitness, 'The excitement and the desire to attack the infidels was so great that the roadways were full of people. Fathers encouraged their sons to serve in such a just war . . . and wives went along with their husbands'. The participants included the empress's brother, Luis de Portugal, as well as the duke of Alba and a score of other prominent nobles from Spain. Contemporaries commented favourably on the quantity as well as the quality of the ships and soldiers converging on Barcelona. A Portuguese squadron of over twenty ships, including a galleon reputed to be the largest in the world that carried some 2,000 men, arrived in late April, joining contingents from Vizcaya, Andalusia and Málaga. A galley fleet also arrived from Genoa, led by Andrea Doria. 'When they passed before the emperor, they lowered their flags three times with a great shout of "The empire! The empire!"', after which Doria came ashore to salute the emperor and then 'they spent time alone together and made their plans in secret'.[45]

The emperor took important steps to ensure that Europe would remain at peace during his absence. Having won over the new pope, whom he expected to restrain France from attacking any of his own possessions, he instructed his lieutenants to refrain from attacking others – including Henry VIII. Henry of Nassau, commander of imperial forces in the Netherlands, received orders to 'avoid raising troops this year', because 'it would be difficult if not impossible to undertake two major campaigns at the same time'. When Nassau protested, Charles replied firmly: 'I fully understand that the matter of England is not something to be cast into oblivion, but we must adapt ourselves to the current situation and concentrate on the most pressing matters.' He likewise reminded Ferdinand that 'our intention and resolve is not to make war anywhere, unless we are forced to do so'.[46] Meanwhile, in Barcelona, 'the emperor did not rest by night or by day, going to see one thing and provide for another'. He presided while the mints of Barcelona coined crowns from gold received from America, and oversaw the manufacture of pikes, arquebuses and other munitions (Pl. 20). When he heard that a fleet carrying men and provisions from Málaga was approaching Barcelona, he 'rode to the top of Montjuïc hill because you could see the sails from there'.[47] Next, Charles held a general muster of his forces 'fully armed, seated among his officials'. When some courtiers inquired where they were going and who would command the expedition, the emperor replied:

'Do not seek to know your monarch's secrets, but I will show you your commander.' At that moment he gave orders to unfurl his standard, on which he had included a devout and splendid crucifixion scene, and said 'You will see here your general, and you will obey me as his lieutenant.'[48]

On 28 May, Charles 'left before dawn to visit the monastery of Montserrat' where 'he confessed and received the sacraments, returning the same evening to Barcelona'. Two days later, 'the royal trumpets sounded through the city', summoning the army to board, and after attending Mass again Charles entered Doria's galley. After 'making the sign of the cross and lifting his eyes to heaven as he said his private prayers, he called for divine aid', and his fleet of almost 250 vessels carrying 27,000 men set sail (Map 4).[49]

Meticulous logistical preparations ensured that Charles arrived at Cagliari in Sardinia just six days after the arrival of another imperial fleet of over 125 vessels, bearing troops and munitions from Germany, the Netherlands and Italy. It also brought many noblemen, including Ferrante Gonzaga, brother of the duke of Mantua, and Alfonso d'Avalos, marquis del Vasto. These men and their Iberian colleagues would bond together in the course of the campaign, creating at the heart of the monarchy a powerful international cadre on whose loyalty Charles could always rely. A hand-picked cultural entourage also accompanied the emperor (including the chronicler Jean Vandenesse, the poet Garcilaso de la Vega, and the war artist Jan Cornelisz Vermeyen), ready to exalt and disseminate his achievements. Thanks to them, and to the numerous foreign ambassadors embedded with the expeditionary force, it is possible to follow the Tunis campaign, and Charles's role in it, almost hour by hour.

While his fleet took on provisions in Sardinia, the emperor discussed strategy with his principal ministers and prayed in several churches until on 15 June the grand fleet, now comprising over 400 vessels carrying some 50,000 men, sailed for north Africa. They arrived the following day. 'The emperor very much wanted to be the first to jump ashore', the foot soldier Martín García Cerezada noted with approval in his journal, 'but he was prevented by his council of war'. Instead the fleet travelled to the site of ancient Carthage, where Charles and his troops disembarked and marched on La Goletta, the port of Tunis.[50]

They did not catch Barbarossa unawares – a diplomat sent by Francis to Istanbul had stopped at Tunis to update him on the emperor's preparations – but the pirate king relied on the heat and the improvised defences he had thrown up around La Goletta to decimate the invading force. He therefore failed to oppose the landing, allowing Charles time to pitch his camp about a mile from the town. The emperor spent almost a month 'making off trenches, fossys and bastions for the saveguard of hys host', acting as 'general, sergeant and soldier, calling some "my brothers" and others "my children"' and also taking part in the constant skirmishes. One day, 'grabbing his lance and shouting *Santiago*, he rode out against the Moors'; another day he entered the trenches, asked for an arquebus, and fired three rounds at the enemy. Then, 'as

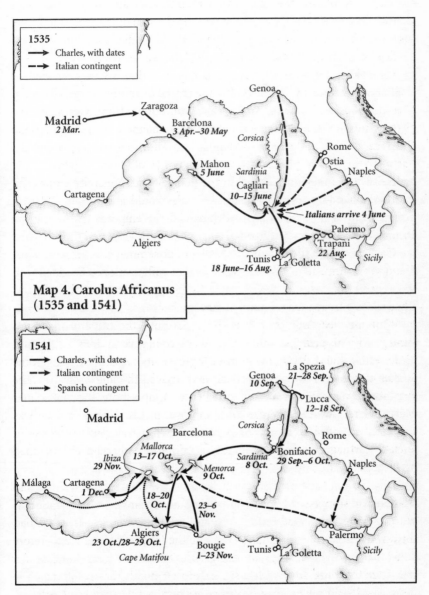

Map 4. Carolus Africanus (1535 and 1541)

1535

→ Charles, with dates
⇢ Italian contingent

Madrid
2 Mar.

Zaragoza

Barcelona
3 Apr.–30 May

Corsica

Genoa

Rome
Ostia

Naples

Mahon
5 June

Sardinia

Cagliari
10–15 June

Cartagena

Italians arrive 4 June

Palermo

Algiers

Trapani
22 Aug.

Sicily

Tunis
18 June–16 Aug.

La Goletta

1541

→ Charles, with dates
⇢ Italian contingent
⋯▸ Spanish contingent

Madrid

Barcelona

Corsica

Genoa
10 Sep.

La Spezia
21–28 Sep.

Lucca
12–18 Sep.

Rome

Mallorca
13–17 Oct.

Ibiza
29 Nov.

Sardinia
8 Oct.

Bonifacio
29 Sep.–6 Oct.

Naples

Málaga

Cartagena
1 Dec.

Menorca
9 Oct.

18–20
Oct.

23–6
Nov.

Algiers
23 Oct./28–29 Oct.

Bougie
1–23 Nov.

Tunis

La Goletta

Sicily

Palermo

Cape Matifou

In his African campaigns in 1535 and 1541, Charles laid meticulous plans for a combined operation by large forces that started from both Spain and Italy. Given the delays and obstacles inherent in such a plan, especially in the age of sail, the successful junction of the different forces off the African coast represents a remarkable logistical feat.

the time to open the battery approached, the emperor increased his efforts and took even greater care to provide whatever was necessary'. He offered a reward to 'whoever was the first to enter La Goletta' and:

> He visited the quarters of the German and Italian troops, and spoke with them; and when he came to the Spaniards he said 'I know that my words are not necessary to strengthen your spirits, because I know how determined you are, nor do they reflect any doubt about who you are. In the other battles you have won you fought for me, but you are fighting this one for God. In this campaign, I am just his lieutenant.'

On 14 July, after the emperor and his entourage heard Mass, the artillery in the trenches and on the galleys began the simultaneous bombardment of La Goletta. After eight hours they made a breach through which the infantry launched a successful assault and promptly sacked the town.[51]

At this point, Charles claimed, 'my entire council decided that we should abandon the campaign. I should embark, they said, because I had achieved what I came for'. Initially, 'as a new captain I accepted their advice', just as he had done in Hungary three years before; but now he overruled his generals and took the initiative. 'After discussing the matter further, I changed my mind, and so on Wednesday the 20th of this month [July] I set off for Tunis.'[52]

It was a rash decision because Tunis lay 10 kilometres away across barren sand. Since his 'army lacked carts to carry its baggage', Charles ordered every man 'to carry food and drink for two days'. Predictably, water soon ran short. Even Charles suffered. When he circulated among the troops, García Cerezada 'looked at his mouth, and noticed that his teeth were covered with black dust and grime – very surprising, given whose teeth they were'.[53] Barbarossa had deployed his troops outside the city and when his artillery opened fire on the approaching Christian army, Charles calmly took his place among his troops, speaking to each group in their own language. When a senior officer protested about the risk, 'the emperor laughed and reassured him that "There was no reason to fear, because no emperor has yet been killed by artillery"'. The imperial army then advanced and despite the heat drove off their adversaries, but afterwards the victors 'collapsed with thirst'. Some just sat or lay exhausted on the ground. Then the Christian slaves within the citadel rose up against their captors, 'shouting "Liberty!" and "Long live the emperor"', and the imperial army entered, freed all the Christian slaves (20,000 according to Charles), and started to plunder. Mosques, madrasas and homes were ransacked; and according to an English eyewitness, all Muslims 'ther found were sold lyke bestys, and many women and children, a pytyouse sight to behold'.[54]

'The continual anxiety, vigilance, and efforts appropriate to a regular captain rather than to an emperor' left Charles exhausted. When the Ferrarese ambassador arrived to present his congratulations, he found the victor sprawled 'on his bed, half dressed', because 'while taking care of business hither and yon' during the encounter with Barbarossa he had fallen under a horse' and injured his right leg. The next day, 'having entered the city, and wishing to intervene in person to prevent the disorders of some soldiers, he slipped on some wet paving stones and again fell under a horse, injuring his left leg'. The enforced rest made the emperor realize how fortunate he had been. He confessed that 'he had never thought Barbarossa could assemble so many troops', and that 'the citadel was so strong, and stocked with so much powder, shot, saltpetre and food' that it could have withstood a long siege. He also complained bitterly that his local allies had failed to provide the assistance they had promised. The emperor soon put these perennial perils of campaigning in north Africa behind him, and instead thanked God for granting him victory 'over an enemy who was not as weak or mean as we thought, but over one powerful on land and sea, in an operation that involved difficulty and determination'. He then restored the ruler deposed by Barbarossa, and imposed on him a treaty that permitted Catholic worship in the town, before moving back to La Goletta where his engineers repaired and improved the fortifications.[55]

Since it was only mid-August, and since Sultan Suleiman remained on campaign against the shah of Persia, some took up the pope's appeal that Charles should now attempt even greater things. According to Lope de Soria, now imperial ambassador in Venice, 'Everyone is convinced that you should go straight to Constantinople', because both Barbarossa and Suleiman were far away. Such a favourable conjunction, he warned, 'will not recur for many years'. The emperor remained unmoved: 'taking account of the season and what is possible', he stated that he preferred to quit while he remained ahead. 'Having discussed, weighed and considered everything, seeing that the sailing season is ending, and that a large number of our troops have fallen ill or been injured . . . in conformity with the season and the limits of the possible we have decided to embark together with our army and to visit our kingdoms of Naples and Sicily.' Having put a price on Barbarossa's head – '50,000 ducats to anyone who brought him in alive and 10,000 ducats to anyone who delivered him dead' – he re-embarked on his flagship and on 21 August set sail for Sicily.[56]

THE VICTORY LAP

According to an English diplomat, all Europe 'awaits the result of the emperor's enterprise because if it fails, the whole world' would abandon his cause. Moreover, 'if the emperor were to lose his life, or a great part of his army, or if he retreated', the French would 'enter Italy on the pretext of defending it' from Barbarossa, 'who, directly the emperor retreats, will be able to use his fleet to harass Genoa, Tuscany, Rome, Naples, and Sicily, which will be unprotected'. The commander of the papal squadron at La Goletta agreed: 'Since Barbarossa does not lack galleys, slaves and Ottoman troops,' he predicted, 'he will easily recover' from the loss of Tunis.[57] His prophecy came true the following month, when the pirate king sacked the town of Mahon on Menorca, killing or enslaving almost all its population, some 5,000 people. In spite of his relentless efforts and prodigious expenditure, Charles had thus failed to achieve his goal – 'to expel' Barbarossa 'from the Christian seas' – as the empress soon reminded him. 'The victories that Our Lord has given Your Majesty in Tunis have brought benefit to Italy,' she wrote pointedly, but in Spain it merely made the sack of Mahon 'hurt more than it would at some other time. They talk here of nothing else.'[58]

The emperor endeavoured to disguise this inconvenient truth by undertaking a victory lap. For the next eight months he travelled through Sicily and Calabria to Naples and thence to Rome, constantly presenting his African campaign as a game-changing success while propagating his vision of a united Italy under his protection and projecting a heroic image of himself as both Roman Imperator and Christian crusader. In this he once more defied his Spanish advisers. Before he left Spain, Cardinal Tavera had warned that 'if you go to Italy, Your Majesty would not be as strong or as well-provided as in Spain', because he would be 'among people who neither love nor obey you like your subjects here, and you would depend on people who place their own interests above your service – men who will try to bleed Your Majesty dry ... They would not worry if you were in danger because they would be thinking how to exploit it for their own ends.'[59]

Tavera's warning was well founded. Many members of the Neapolitan elite had supported the French during the siege of 1527–8; the nobles of Sicily had staged a rebellion during the transition from Trastámara to Habsburg rule in 1516–17, and in the 1520s several of them had tried to betray the island to the French. Nevertheless, as the first monarch to visit Sicily in a century, from the moment he landed at Trapani on the west coast in August 1535, Charles received a hero's welcome. In each town along his route the leading dignitaries received him outside the walls, often accompanied by local boys and girls (perhaps to demonstrate that the next generation would be more loyal than the last). After receiving from them the keys and some expensive gifts, the emperor confirmed local privileges and distributed some campaign booty before making his formal entry at the head of a procession composed of liberated Christian slaves, Muslim captives, soldiers and courtiers. He also visited the leading religious sites, which made his progress seem like a pilgrimage, and he rode on a horse beneath a canopy, dressed in gold and white, as he admired the triumphal arches that celebrated his recent victory in images and inscriptions, comparing him with Classical and Biblical heroes: Jason, Scipio, Augustus, Gideon, David. One memorable inscription, which greeted him first in Palermo and then in Messina, would later become an imperial motto: 'A SOLIS ORTU AD OCCASUM' (a phrase from Psalm 112, 'From the rising to the setting of the sun').[60] In addition, the emperor watched jousts, tournaments, plays and re-enactments (often Scipio's defeat of Hannibal and the destruction of Carthage) and he regularly went hunting; but he also worked hard. According to one chronicler, he 'immediately started to grant an audience to everyone, listening to quarrels and grievances'; while 'wishing to learn about the civil government, he studied the way in which magistrates administered justice and he even visited the royal archives'. The normally indefatigable Granvelle complained about 'being much occupied at present' in the domestic affairs of the island 'with which his Majesty is so engrossed, that, on my faith, I have scarce leisure to breathe'.[61]

Thanks to his careful combination of prayer, work and play, Charles's visit proved a resounding success. He presided in person over the Parliament of the kingdom, which voted him 250,000 ducats in taxes, and every town he visited seems to have commissioned a statue or at least a bust of its victorious sovereign, many of them still standing (Pl. 21). Other traces of his visit have survived: the city walls at Messina, designed in the 'modern' style at the emperor's direction, remain the essential skeleton of the city; the new town of Carlentini, near Syracuse, founded and named in his honour, now boasts 18,000 inhabitants; the city of Nicosia, where the emperor spent just one day, has preserved the special seat in which he sat and every year stages a re-enactment of his visit.

In November, Charles crossed to the mainland and progressed via the domains of important supporters, and places linked with the defeat of Hannibal, until he reached Naples. The city served as his capital over the winter, and his court staged jousts, banquets, hunts, plays, sightseeing and poetic competitions. On one occasion Charles 'showed great dexterity and elegance during a bullfight' and on another he took part in a cane game 'dressed in Moorish costume, in honour of his victory at Tunis'. Later, 'disguising himself with a mask he danced with the noblewomen, forfeiting some of his normal gravity'. In February 1536, although in mourning for Katherine of Aragon, who had died the previous month, the papal nuncio noted sourly that Charles attended a feast after which he 'danced and celebrated until dawn, showing how little the queen's death affected His Majesty'.[62]

In Naples, as in Sicily, the emperor combined business with pleasure. As he explained in a speech to the Parliament of the kingdom, he had not come 'just to visit, but to put things in order and to provide in this kingdom everything that will be of general and particular benefit to you, not only in matters that chiefly concern the proper administration of justice, and the peaceful existence of the people, but also in all your other concerns'. Charles had appointed as viceroy Pedro de Toledo, uncle of the duke of Alba, whose policy of executing and imposing exemplary punishments on those who had sided with the French during their failed invasion quickly made him unpopular. Some hoped that Charles would remove him from power, but they were disappointed: instead, Toledo remained at the helm until 1553, disciplining both the nobles and the cities and raising huge taxes to finance the emperor's various projects – starting with a parliamentary grant of 500,000 ducats 'towards past and present expenses, and a million ducats spread over certain future years'. Charles hoped to apply the proceeds to achieving the goal of capturing the Ottoman capital set by Paul III, because (in the words of the emperor's secretary of state) 'Everything is fine in La Goletta, Tunis, Bone and Bizerta, and the sultan does not have the power to capture La Goletta; but the emperor certainly has the power to capture Constantinople, and I pray that God will grant him favour so that we will see him triumph.'[63]

In March 1536, Charles resumed his triumphal progress towards Rome. The pope had made extensive preparations to welcome him, despite the fact that imperial troops had sacked the city only nine years before. According to the author François Rabelais, who served in the French embassy as a physician, Paul 'put half of his palace and 3,000 beds' at the emperor's disposal and 'demolished and razed over 200 houses and three or four churches' along the old *sacra via* so that the new Caesar could lead 5,000 Spanish veterans, 400 cavalry and his courtiers (which now included nobles from Sicily and Naples as well as from Spain) beneath the triumphal arches of Constantine, Titus and Septimius Severus, through the Campo dei Fiori and across the Tiber to St Peter's, to meet the pope.[64]

Since he arrived in Holy Week, Charles 'visited classical and curious sites privately, with only a few members of his household' (a marked contrast with his ostentatious behaviour in Naples and Sicily), and as usual he spent much time in devotions. He took part in the Palm Sunday procession, carrying a palm frond, and 'with great devotion heareth daily services in St Peter's chapel, in the presence of the pope and the cardinals'. On Maundy Thursday he washed the feet of thirteen poor men, and on Easter Saturday 'he visited the seven churches, accompanied by twenty courtiers but without any guards'. The following day he attended High Mass in St Peter's Basilica 'in pontifical robes' and wearing gloves 'like a bishop' before a crowd of 30,000. Throughout the service, pope and emperor presented a notable display of harmony: they rose and sat down in unison, and whenever the pope removed and replaced his tiara Charles did the same with his imperial crown, 'as the emperors of old used to do'.[65]

As Karl Brandi pointed out, entering Rome 'was like a homecoming' for Charles, because 'It was the culmination of all his desires':

> He had made a personal contact with each one of the states over which he ruled . . . He had summoned and attended the Estates General of the Netherlands; the Cortes of Castile and Aragon; the Electors, princes and estates of the German empire both in local sessions, and at the general Diet; and last of all the Estates of Sicily and Naples. He had included some of the leading men of each of these lands in his Order of the Golden Fleece.

To illustrate the cumulative impact of so many triumphs, the Humanist Christopher Scheurl of Nuremberg published a pamphlet that drew upon 'various letters in Italian and German' to describe *The emperor Charles's entry into the ancient imperial capital*. On the title page, under the emperor's portrait, appeared Abner's prediction to King David: 'Thou mayest reign over all that thine heart desireth' (Pl. 22).[66] Scheurl should have known better: the prediction had not turned out well for Abner, who was murdered soon afterwards by David's followers. It would not turn out well for Charles either.

TEN

YEARS OF DEFEAT, 1536–41

TO WAR WITH FRANCE AGAIN

'Charles, Charles, Caesar, Caesar, Empire, Empire!' The enthusiastic chant of Charles's subjects in Messina on 1 November 1535 encouraged him to start planning a return to north Africa the following year with the goal of capturing Algiers, but an event that same day, 1,300 kilometres to the north, changed everything: the death of the childless Duke Francesco Sforza of Milan. On hearing the news the French ambassadors in Rome predicted that 'either by gentle or violent means his death will resolve, once and for all, not only the affairs of Italy but of the whole of Christendom'. They were almost correct.[1]

Since Sforza's failing health had long given cause for concern, and since Milan was a fief of the Holy Roman Empire, Charles had taken some precautionary measures. Although in 1530 he had pardoned and restored Francesco, imperial troops continued to garrison some strongpoints in the duchy; and three years later he arranged the marriage of his niece Christina of Denmark to Francesco, with the expectation that she would bear children loyal to the House of Habsburg. If not, the duchy would eventually escheat to the emperor. Now, since Christina remained childless when her husband died, the Senators of Milan immediately 'took an oath of fidelity to His Majesty' and recognized 'Antonio de Leyva as their governor until new orders arrive from His Majesty'.[2]

Charles rejoiced that 'the duchy of Milan has devolved to us, because it is an imperial fief', and declared that it 'should be kept in peace and quiet in our name until we can take the further action that seems best for its benefit and for the good of Christendom and Italy'. Initially, he envisaged three options: cede the duchy to a member of the French royal family; keep it under direct imperial control; or bestow it on a deserving Italian.[3] For a moment the last option – the only one that could preserve the status quo –

seemed the likely outcome. Leyva reported that 'we have found in the archives of the duchy a privilege granted by Emperor Maximilian that if the legitimate line of the Sforza should die out, an illegitimate line may succeed', and he recommended to Charles the investiture of an illegitimate cousin of the last duke. The candidate set off for Naples to present his case, but died in mysterious circumstances on the way.[4] This left only two options: keep Milan, or bestow it on a French prince. Leyva, who had spent much of his career fighting to acquire the duchy for Charles, strongly favoured the former:

> It has pleased Our Lord to revert Milan to Your Majesty in peace, quiet and calm; and I am sure that God has done so for a reason – even though at present we cannot discern it. Your Majesty knows better than I what this duchy means to you; and please remember that it is linked to Genoa, which I think is of no less importance, given its naval power – and, again, Your Majesty knows better than anyone the importance of this.

Leyva nevertheless recognized that retaining Milan would 'cause a great war to start', in which the fighting would be 'more harsh and bitter than ever before'.[5]

Charles pondered his options while holding court in Naples, on his way from Messina to Rome. According to the diary of a Neapolitan official, 'throughout the time the emperor was here, overtly [nell'estrinseco] he attended entertainments and festivals but secretly [nell'intrinseco] he made serious preparations for war in case France attacked'.[6] The most obvious manifestation of the secret agenda was a flurry of diplomatic activity. The new duke of Florence, Alessandro de' Medici, arrived to marry the emperor's illegitimate daughter Margarita (as agreed in Charles's treaty with Pope Clement: p. 184 above), joining the dukes of Mantua, Urbino and Ferrara as well as envoys from Pope Paul, Venice and several other states. Their dilemma was clear. In the words of Lope de Soria, who boasted more than thirty years' experience as a Spanish diplomat in Italy, 'even if they now think of Your Majesty as a friend, in time they will think what they might do should Your Majesty wish to conquer Italy'. Charles's task, according to Soria, was to present himself as the best guarantor of peace in Italy, and Francis as the principal threat, and above all to play for time.[7]

Charles felt the same. Both Marie in the Netherlands and the empress in Spain protested that they lacked the resources to mount another campaign, and in January 1536 the emperor instructed his diplomats 'not to break off talks' with Francis and instead 'to buy time until we get to Rome, and then we can see what we should do, according to the king's behaviour'.[8] He did not have to wait that long: the following month Francis invaded the lands of the duke of Savoy, married to the empress's sister, using as his pretext a struggle over the city of Geneva, which had attempted to assert its independence from Savoy. Late in 1535 the duke attempted to subdue Geneva and he asked the emperor to send him military support. Leonard de Gruyères, Charles's special envoy to the Swiss Confederation, supported this request, reminding the emperor that 'it is necessary to choose the lesser of two evils; and therefore in my opinion it would be better to make war abroad than to have one at home'. Charles and his council disagreed. 'Given the season, and given that the Swiss are not accustomed to campaign for long at their own expense', they discounted the risk of an attack.[9] They miscalculated. Geneva had concluded a defensive league with the Swiss canton of Bern, France's ally, and in January 1536 Bern sent a herald to declare war on Savoy. The following month Francis followed suit, claiming that his alliance with Bern obliged him to do so, and in March French troops occupied Savoy and almost all Piedmont, bringing his forces to the border of Milan.[10]

This represented a major failure of intelligence. As Charles's principal councillor, Granvelle, ruefully admitted: 'We did not foresee the sudden invasion by Bern, or imagine that the king of France would take such an unfortunate, damnable and outrageous excuse to attack' Savoy.[11] Now Charles had to react. For a time he entertained the hope that the French had mobilized 'merely to improve their bargaining position', but 'in case they want to start something they must not find us unprepared', and so he started to raise troops in Lombardy, Germany, the Netherlands and Spain. He also ordered that 400,000 ducats 'coined from the gold and silver of Peru' now in Seville should be sent to Genoa immediately, together with 3,000 Spanish troops, albeit 'with the hope that matters will not come to rupture' – in which case, Charles concluded hopefully, 'we could undertake the enterprise of Algiers this summer, just as planned'.[12]

For a moment it seemed that a proposal from the pope might avert war: Charles's niece, the widowed Duchess Christina of Milan, would marry Francis's youngest son, Duke Charles of Angoulême, and they and their descendants would rule the duchy. The emperor accepted the suggestion, on condition that Angoulême renounce all claim to the French throne for ever and that if he and Christina died without children the duchy would revert to the empire 'as is the custom in imperial fiefs'.[13] Francis rejected this offer, insisting that Orléans, his second son, become the next duke of Milan; but a letter from Queen Eleanor, 'written in secret in her own hand', revealed that despite her husband's public statements he would in fact accept the investiture of Angoulême. Foolishly, the emperor ignored her, instead instructing his envoy at the French court to announce that he was prepared to discuss investing Orléans with Milan, but making clear in a cyphered addendum that he lied: 'We want to make it absolutely clear to you that we have always refused, and still refuse, to invest Orléans.'[14] He therefore directed the empress to 'prepare to suffer whatever God sends, which I hope will be favourable to us, and prepare everything in Spain with extreme diligence; so that in the end, with God's help, we will smash the heads of the French.' He assured his ambassador at the French court that he was making 'such excellent preparations for war that either the king of France will be forced to accept the terms that we dictate to him or we will make him regret renewing the war'.[15]

Outwardly, Charles continued to pretend that all was well. He met regularly with the pope, assuring him that 'we are happy to discuss giving the duchy of Milan to the third son of the King of France, with suitable guarantees', in return for which Paul would 'convene a general council and hold it in Mantua within a year'; but when a new ambassador arrived from France empowered only to discuss the transfer of Milan to the duke of Orléans, Charles pounced.[16] On 17 April 1536, Easter Monday, the pope, the College of Cardinals, and the diplomatic corps in Rome assembled at the emperor's request in the pope's apartments, expecting to hear him report on the Tunis campaign and request support for an attack on Algiers. Instead, for well over an hour Charles denounced the duplicity of Francis 'very calmly, without showing any anger; and he spoke in Spanish'.[17]

According to Salinas, 'The speech lasted a very long time, because it included a narrative of the Italian wars from their beginning until the present, justifying our conduct and detailing the excesses of the King of France.' Charles began by quoting 'the wise words of the emperor Maximilian on the last occasion the king of France made peace with him, saying: "This is the eleventh time I have made peace with the king, and now as on previous occasions I do so because of my desire to bring peace to Christendom and not because I think the king will not break it – as he has done on all previous occasions."' Charles went on to list the broken treaties before denouncing the links Francis had forged with both Barbarossa and the sultan. He then asserted that he had 'always wished to deploy with pride all the power and grandeur that God has given us against pagans and infidels, enemies of our Holy Catholic Faith', but 'the king of France prevented both the peace of

Christendom and the war we might have waged against the enemies of God'. He denied 'that I might want to be ruler of the world' and instead pointed to Francis's unprovoked invasion of Savoy and his insistence 'right or wrong' on acquiring Milan. To redress these injustices, Charles announced that he would leave the following day to join the army he had assembled in Lombardy and then invade France unless 'The king of France wishes to meet me in person on a field of honour, either fully armed or in our shirts with only a sword and dagger, on land or sea, on a bridge or an island, in a designated space or in front of our armies, or wherever and however he wants. I will say no more, except that I give him 20 days to make up his mind.' The two monarchs would wager Milan and Burgundy, with the winner taking both.[18]

In making this challenge, the emperor defied not only his rival but also his ministers. According to Salinas, 'Neither Los Cobos nor Granvelle knew about the speech in advance: His Majesty did it on his own initiative. I think it would have been more restrained if they had known about it – at least he would have omitted the part about the challenge.' When the French diplomats present asked Los Cobos and Granvelle for clarification, they replied that 'only the first part should be taken seriously' – that is, Francis should ignore the invitation to a duel.[19] Charles, by contrast, took his challenge very seriously: on 4 May he asked his ambassador in Rome if a reply had arrived because 'the twenty days that I gave the King of France to respond to the speech that I gave before His Holiness will expire next Sunday'. Francis eventually declined, joking that their swords were 'too short to fight each other at such a distance', but Charles immediately turned this careless response to his advantage, drawing a parallel with the abortive challenge of 1528: '[The king of France] is right to say that our swords are too short to strike at such a distance. I wonder if that is why in the past he only offered – in very insulting terms – to meet me in personal combat when I was in Spain and he was in Paris?'[20]

CHARLES ON CAMPAIGN

The emperor now left Rome to join the army assembling in Lombardy, passing beneath triumphal arches and receiving accolades in Siena, Florence and Lucca (each the capital of an independent state). Salinas reported that 'His Majesty has been very joyfully received in these cities, some through love and others through fear', because 'besides the court, he brings with him 5,000 Spanish infantry veterans and 300 mounted knights. Light cavalry fill the other roads, so that troops are now on the move all over Italy.' Salinas also reported that Charles 'shows great enthusiasm for this war, and I do not think he will welcome any diversion that prevents him from invading France'. Instead 'while he moves towards his army he spends time practising skirmishes . . . He is in good form – better than I have ever seen him.'[21]

Charles also ordered the empress, Marie and Ferdinand to mobilize the resources required to launch simultaneous attacks on Francis: 'I do not know if the king wants peace or war,' he told Marie, 'but I will first prepare my weapons, and then negotiate.' Marie agreed, confiding to Ferdinand that 'even though I have always hated war it would be better to fight now, because I am not sure that everything would favour His Majesty as much as at some other time.'[22] On 9 June, Charles announced to his brother that 'the moment I am ready to march, I will send a herald to declare war on the king of France', adding that 'I shall do what I can to get my revenge on him' – as usual, revenge featured prominently in his political repertoire – 'and I hope, with God's assistance, to attack him so vigorously by land and sea that he will regret having started the war'. Richard Morison, a well-informed Englishman in Italy, foresaw a rapid imperial triumph, because although the French had started well 'it's not much of a victory when no one opposes you'. It would be different after they met Leyva's soldiers, 'who are now used to drinking blood instead of wine'.[23]

The emperor knew exactly how to deploy these bloodthirsty troops. He had already asked both Leyva and Doria to prepare plans should Francis declare war again, and both favoured another invasion of Provence, but they recommended one change: 'When the duke of Bourbon attacked Marseilles' in 1524, 'France had to unite all its forces to relieve the city, and if we had brought a navy it would have fallen'; and so this time, Doria must use his fleet to blockade the city. The only outstanding question was whether Charles himself should direct operations, as he had done in Africa. Although Leyva 'advanced many reasons why His Majesty should not enter France in person', the emperor 'could not make up his mind and so he asked his council of war to discuss the matter. Eventually, after a thorough discussion of the rationale, His Majesty decided he would take charge' and on 17 July 1536 he set out for France, taking 'the most challenging but shortest route at the head of the Spanish and German infantry'.[24]

At first all went well. Charles, just like his grandfather Maximilian, 'dressed like a soldier' as he started up the mountain pass, 'wearing hose, a tunic and armour, with a sash of scarlet cloth, which is the distinguishing mark we all wear'. One of the Spanish veterans reported that 'we marched at top speed [*a toda furia*], loaded down like ants because we each carried biscuit and rations for 6 days'. The emperor suffered along with his men when 'we started to cross the mountain ... starting each day at midnight and travelling with torches'. On 25 July they crossed the French frontier, but since Charles 'was extremely tired, having visited his whole army to get it in order', everyone rested for three days. The emperor showed no mercy to stragglers and deserters. One day:

> He spotted a man abandon the ranks and followed him. He cornered him in some woodland and ordered him to be hanged. The man asked the emperor to pardon him this time, but His Majesty refused, and so he was hanged from one of the trees there. The emperor did this so that in future everyone in his army would obey orders.[25]

Meanwhile, Henry of Nassau led another army from the Netherlands towards the River Somme. Initially, this threat worried Francis far more because Paris lay only 150 kilometres beyond the Somme: he transferred some troops to Picardy from Provence, which he abandoned 'giving orders to remove as much as possible of the food in the region, and to destroy the rest, so that it will prove impossible for an army to subsist there'. Francis thus created a vast trap, from which the only exit was retreat.[26]

Charles pressed on regardless. He reached Aix-en-Provence on 5 August and declared himself count of Provence and king of Arles, two titles claimed by his imperial predecessors, perhaps hoping to annex the region; but developments elsewhere made this outcome unlikely. In Istanbul, Francis's agents concluded a formal treaty of military and economic cooperation with Suleiman, to last for the lives of both sovereigns, and the sultan immediately honoured it by launching an invasion of Hungary that prevented Ferdinand from sending an expeditionary force into France as he had promised.[27] In the Netherlands, Marie worried about the growing coordination 'between England, France and Guelders, and the way everyone is raising troops'. She begged her brother to authorize her to conclude a treaty of neutrality with France, but he refused, instead ordering her to support an attempt by their deposed brother-in-law Christian of Denmark to regain his throne. Although her troops seized the city of Groningen and the surrounding area (the Ommelanden), which she promptly annexed, they made little headway against the Danes. Worse, Ghent and other cities in the province of Flanders refused to pay any more taxes, which sabotaged Nassau's efforts to reach the Somme.[28]

In Provence, a French herald arrived to ask Charles to explain why he had invaded the kingdom. The emperor responded by reminding him of something 'that your king said: that our swords were too far apart for a duel. I have come here to reduce the distance as much as he wants, ready to meet him man to man or army to army. To that end I will await him here in arms, just as I promised the pope.'[29] Once again, the king ignored the challenge. The sudden death on 10 August of his eldest son, the dauphin, offered a possible resolution of the struggle, because the rulers of Italy were unlikely to accept Henry of Orléans, who now became dauphin, as duke of Milan; but Francis refused to negotiate as long as Charles 'remained in his kingdom with such a large and powerful army'. Instead he waited until starvation forced the invaders to withdraw. That point came on 4 September 1536: having lost 'between seven and eight thousand soldiers through disease and hunger since we arrived', and 'after consulting in great secrecy what I should do next', the emperor warned Nassau that he would have to retreat.[30] He promised not to execute this decision until after attempting to capture Marseilles one more time; but his efforts failed when Cesare Fregoso, whom Francis named his 'governor of Genoa', led a band of exiles in a surprise attack on the city, forcing Doria and his galleys to abandon their station off the coast of Provence and hurry back to defend their base. On 12 September, Charles and his army began their long retreat.[31]

As they advanced, the French found the abandoned imperial camp full of 'dead horses and men, some buried still wearing their armour, with pikes and other weapons scattered through the fields'; and as they pursued the imperialists, 'You could see men and horses all piled in heaps, the dying mixed up with the dead, presenting a spectacle so horrible and pitiful that even the most determined and pertinacious enemy felt sorrow. Whoever saw the desolation could not consider it less than what Josephus described during the destruction of Jerusalem.'[32]

This signal failure affected Charles deeply. Salinas described him as 'very discontented and not very well. I think his past exertions are responsible, and he may also have a touch of the same illness he had in Regensburg [in 1532], because he has an itch in his scrotum'. Perhaps pain explains the emperor's extreme reaction when a garrison of twelve French sharpshooters and two boys, concealed in a tower, fatally wounded his friend, the soldier-poet Garcilaso de la Vega. The garrison eventually surrendered in return for a promise that they would not be sent to the galleys: the emperor kept his word – and instead 'hanged the twelve men and cut the boys' ears off'.[33] After this, Charles pressed on until he reached Genoa. He had certainly inflicted harm on his enemy – one eyewitness estimated the damage done at three million ducats; another predicted that it would take Provence a half-century to recover – but his ignominious retreat, and the loss of half his army (including Leyva and many of the veterans 'used to drinking blood instead of wine'), meant that he had lost the campaign. His surviving soldiers had to winter in and around Genoa 'in great poverty, eating mushrooms for lack of bread'.[34]

Many rejoiced at the emperor's defeat. In Provence, citizens composed verse epics in denigration and a French diplomat ridiculed him for conducting a campaign on the basis of 'a map of the Alps and the plain of Provence in his hand or before his eyes. He studied it so often and so intently, using it to further his designs and his desires, that he began to think he had the country in his grasp instead of just the map.' In Italy, Michelangelo, still smarting over the fate of his native Florence, likewise jested that:

> If only the emperor had ordered a drawing to be made of the course of the River Rhône before he entered Provence, he would not have met with losses so severe, nor retired with his army so disarrayed; nor would he have been portrayed in Rome as a crab who moved backwards when he wanted to move forward, with the columns of Hercules and the motto Plus Ultra.

Another placard in Rome showed a river instead of the columns of Hercules, together with the legend 'NON PLVS VLTRA RHODANVS' ('No further than the Rhone'). Most cruel of all, a picture depicted the emperor on horseback with the motto 'PLVS RETRO' ('Retreat further!').[35] These jests contained an element of truth: for more than a year Charles had heard nothing but extravagant praise and lavish encomia that compared him favourably with both Classical and Biblical heroes. Perhaps it had convinced him that he was indeed invincible and invulnerable, guaranteed endless triumphs by 'favourable Fortune', and made him willing to take high-risk gambles.

THE STRANGE ROAD BACK TO PEACE

On 15 November 1536, although 'ill with a head-cold, and so overwhelmed with business that he cannot deal with matters as rapidly as some wish', Charles took another high-risk gamble: he ordered Doria's galleys to take him from Genoa back to Barcelona. This time Fortune smiled and he arrived safely three weeks later. Since he had ordered his family to meet him in Tordesillas, Charles now rode across Spain to join them. 'He experienced no problems,' Salinas reported, 'although he had some falls from his horse, as is usual with those who ride post-haste' – an interesting reminder of the everyday perils of riding on early modern roads – and afterwards 'he stayed to relax in Tordesillas for 7 days'.[36]

His relaxation soon ended because 1537 brought a stream of further setbacks. In January the emperor learned that Francis had declared forfeit the counties of Flanders, Artois and Charolais, which he held as fiefs of the French Crown; and that conspirators who hoped to restore a pro-French republic in Florence had murdered his son-in-law, Duke Alessandro. Then in April, when Charles asked the Cortes of Castile to provide him with funds, a group of city representatives, led by Juan de Mendoza of Seville, vociferously objected. 'When His Majesty learned what Don Juan had said he was furious and spoke opprobriously about him'; and when the Cortes ended and Mendoza requested the same reward as other representatives, 'His Majesty replied that to make an example, Don Juan should not get what he asked for.'[37]

The emperor did his best to relax with his family over Easter, with jousts and bullfights in which he occasionally took part – when a bull gored Luis de Ávila, Charles himself came to the rescue, 'hurling his lance right into the bull' – but as soon as 'he learned for certain that the empress was pregnant', he prepared to leave court again. The empress protested, telling her husband that 'she would come too, even if her womb came up to her throat', but she wasted her breath: Charles left for Aragon without her in July and Isabella again gave birth alone, this time to another son who received the Trastámara name Juan. He died six months later, leaving Prince Philip once more as the couple's only male child.[38]

Concern that his wife was approaching the end of her fertility led Charles to hurry back to 'create another child', but Pedro Girón (who as chief magistrate of the royal household had a privileged viewpoint) noted with surprise that, despite her husband's presence, this time 'the empress was very sad and made this plain to see in her face and her clothes. She never dressed as she used to do when the emperor was present, but instead dressed in black as she did when he was away.' If this was an attempt to make her husband feel guilty, it failed: after less than a month Charles once again abandoned his newly pregnant wife.[39]

Anxious to resume his north African crusade, the emperor went to Barcelona to oversee peace talks with France. In October he had authorized his sister Marie to conclude a local ceasefire – albeit with some misgivings because the terms she proposed:

> . . . may well cause resentment among my subjects in other kingdoms and dominions, as you can imagine. Nevertheless given the complete confidence that I have in you, and since you understand better than me how much this will mean to my subjects in the Netherlands, since you are on the spot and I am so far away, I authorize you to do whatever seems best to you, and you can promise that I will ratify it.[40]

Now the emperor authorized Los Cobos and Granvelle to travel to Salces on the Catalan frontier and begin formal talks for a general ceasefire with their French counterparts. Although he remained in Barcelona, Charles took a close personal interest in the outcome. When a messenger arrived from Salces in the middle of the night with draft terms 'His Majesty heard me at once', and 'having discussed his response at great length' with Loaysa (still the voice of Charles's conscience), 'His Majesty said that he had been thinking of other approaches, but it was not yet time to make them public, nor would he do so until it was the right time – not even to his ministers or his wife.' When Loaysa urged him to consult at least Los Cobos, Charles 'replied that he wanted to find a solution by himself' and refused to allow any other ministers or diplomats to visit Salces.[41]

The reason for such stealth became clear when Charles met a French envoy in secret. 'As you can see,' the emperor told him astutely, 'all the difficulties come down in the end to a lack of trust.' Although the two monarchs could continue 'to declare their wishes and intentions to each other by means of their ministers', he believed that a face-to-face meeting between him and Francis 'was the true and best means to conclude peace'. He joked that the monarchs 'were not yet so old that they could not catch a stag, or currently so far apart that they could not get together for a good cause'. Nevertheless, he recognized, 'since there is so much distrust between the two monarchs it seemed necessary to have a third party not only to mediate between them but also to guarantee their safety'. He proposed Paul III for this role.[42] The pope accepted and suggested the port of Nice, one of the few parts of the duchy of Savoy not in French hands, as a neutral venue. Charles arrived by galley from Barcelona on 9 May 1538, and he and Francis spent many hours in separate sessions talking with the pope. After three weeks of bargaining, the emperor promised to transfer Milan to Francis's younger son, Duke Charles of Angoulême, now promoted to duke of Orléans, who would marry one of Ferdinand's daughters; and Francis agreed to withdraw his support from Duke Charles of Guelders.

The two sovereigns left Nice on 20 June, having agreed to a ten-year truce. Although they never met face to face, they resolved to continue discussions in a less formal setting at Aigues Mortes, a port-city that lay midway between Nice and Barcelona (and thus implied equality and reciprocity between the principals). On 14 July, as soon as he spotted Charles's galleys approaching, Francis impulsively set forth without an escort to welcome his guest. Equally impulsively, Charles 'descended two steps of the ladder to receive the king, so they could come aboard together'. Standing on the poop deck, in full sight of their courtiers, 'with smiling faces they embraced five or six times'; and then (Charles reported) they spent about two hours alone together 'exchanging gracious words and affirming our desire to be and to remain good and true friends. We also resolved that we would not discuss details, but delegate them to our ministers.' When the monarchs emerged to dine, they strove to outdo each other in humility: they debated who should sit down first – ' "You are older," joked the emperor; "I admit it," replied the king, "Older and more foolish" ' – and throughout the meal 'the emperor usually tried to eat each dish only after the king had started'. It must have been a long evening.[43]

The trust shown by the French king in boarding his former enemy's galley alone impressed Charles, and although memories of the murder of Duke John of Burgundy a century before had not faded, the following day he reciprocated by accepting an invitation to come ashore. He nevertheless took everyone by surprise when the Dauphin and his younger brother came to receive him: he fell to his knees as he embraced them, an act of self-abasement that some saw as a request for pardon for the harsh treatment inflicted while the dauphin was his prisoner in Spain. After another enormous feast the two monarchs continued their amicable discussion and agreed 'not to believe, do or cause anything detrimental to the other'; 'to arrange some marriage alliances' to further unite their families; and to coordinate efforts against both the Lutherans and the Turks. They then exchanged rings, and Francis declared: 'I promise you, on my oath as a gentleman, that I will declare myself the enemy of all those who wish to act against your territories, pledging all my goods and placing at risk my person.' The emperor 'took a reciprocal oath'.[44]

No one seemed more surprised by this diplomatic breakthrough than the two monarchs. On the evening of 18 July, back aboard his galley, Charles informed Marie that 'God has inspired us to this reconciliation and restoration of our friendship', and instructed her to avoid any action that might jeopardize his 'true and perfect friendship' with Francis – who that same evening informed his ambassadors that 'no princes have ever felt as affectionate towards each other as we do' and ordered that 'henceforth the affairs of the emperor must be deemed and esteemed as if they were my own'.[45]

THE EMPEROR AND HIS CRITICS

Charles returned to Spain from Aigues Mortes 'determined to go in person' on the crusade against Algiers that he had planned for so long. He realized that he would need 'to keep his intention secret from our subjects here', because they would not want him to leave again so soon, but (he assured Ferdinand): 'I feel not only inclined but obliged to undertake this enterprise, which is more important than anything else, as much for you as for me and for our dominions'.[46] Developments in the central Mediterranean soon increased his determination. In September 1538, at Preveza at the entrance to the Adriatic, an Ottoman fleet under Barbarossa faced a combined Christian fleet, commanded by Andrea Doria. Eventually Doria withdrew, pursued by Barbarossa, but the following month storms destroyed many Turkish galleys and Doria seized the opportunity to capture the fortress of Castelnuovo (now Herceg Novi in Montenegro) after a short siege, leaving 4,000 Spanish troops as its isolated garrison.[47]

Charles now convened the Cortes of Castile, and the long opening speech made in his name detailed both the achievements of his recent wars (all fought outside the peninsula) and their cost (over six million ducats raised in loans to be repaid in Spain), concluding with a demand for yet more taxes 'to cover the cost of the campaign he wishes to launch' in the Mediterranean. These included a temporary excise tax (*sisa*) to be paid by everyone. The seventy-five noblemen present in the assembly debated the issue for three months before resolving that 'His Majesty should not mention this excise tax again, nor should he leave the kingdom for a while'.[48] Initially, the emperor 'did not display either irritation or anger, but rather a wise detachment', recognizing that the opposition 'did not come from pride or hatred towards him but rather from concern for the kingdom's exhaustion'. Some years later, however, when the historian Juan Ginés de Sepúlveda 'casually mentioned the Cortes of Toledo to him', the emperor replied: 'I think of that assembly as little as possible.' He would never again summon the nobles to attend the Cortes of Castile: henceforth each assembly consisted of only thirty-six members (two representatives from eighteen towns).[49]

'Everywhere I see darkening skies,' Salinas observed mournfully. 'I do not know when this eclipse will end, nor what will become of us'; but Charles seemed unaffected. He left 'to enjoy myself hunting for twelve days or two weeks' and on his return arranged a spectacular cane game, watched by his whole family as well as by a large crowd.[50] He also evidently spent time alone with the empress, because she conceived for the ninth time; but on 21 April 1539 she gave birth to another stillborn child. 'Ever since her pregnancy began,' according to Charles, his wife 'was always somewhat unwell'; and although she seemed better after the birth, ten days later she died.[51]

This unexpected tragedy left Charles devastated. 'I feel the anxiety and sadness that you can imagine at such a great and terrible loss,' he wrote to Ferdinand, just before retiring to the Jeronimite convent of La Sisla, outside Toledo, where he spent the next seven weeks grieving. The dynastic consequences of the empress's death did not escape Salinas. First, as he slyly reminded Ferdinand (who had been Charles's heir until 1527): 'Since the emperor has no spouse, and no intention of getting married again, the succession to these kingdoms consists of one boy and two girls. We cannot tell what God will do with us all, but we humans must think of all possible contingencies', and he predicted that 'recent events will lead to some changes' in what the emperor had planned. He referred to the emergence of open resistance in the Netherlands.[52]

Charles's sister Marie had drawn up a budget for 1538 that showed income of £233,628, expenditure of £441,184 and a debt of £1,356,381 (almost 700,000 ducats). For this critical situation she blamed the cost of the wars against France and Denmark, and she warned that she dared not raise more taxes – especially since the city of Ghent refused to pay another penny, despite an imperial letter reminding the city's magistrates that 'we have always maintained the belief and hope that in our absence you would strive to aid, assist and serve us more than any others, because we also come from Ghent'.[53] The emperor warned that if they did not pay voluntarily he would force them to do so, but Ghent took no notice. Its elite refused to accept tax demands or troops from the central government and even declined to join the delegation sent by Marie to offer condolences on the death of the empress. In August 1539 the city's guilds seized control of the council and soon afterwards orchestrated the trial and execution of one of the magistrates for allegedly tampering with the city's privileges. The following month they sent a secret embassy to Paris to request military assistance.[54] At much the same time, news reached Spain that after a six-week siege Barbarossa had forced the isolated garrison of Castelnuovo to surrender, and afterwards he executed the Spanish commandant and almost all the defendants in cold blood.

Luckily for Charles, in this time of adversity Francis remained faithful to the accord reached at Aigues Mortes, and he welcomed the emperor's suggestion that he should travel from Spain to the Netherlands 'through France so that he could see the king again, enjoy hunting with him and also spend lots of time relaxing with him and his sister the queen [Eleanor]'. For a time the emperor's 'great grief over the death of the empress keeps him in seclusion', but he could not ignore the worsening crisis in the Netherlands, with much of Flanders in open opposition.[55] As Marie told her brother bluntly, 'What is at stake here is whether Your Majesty will be master or servant': only his immediate personal intervention, she claimed, could now restore order and obedience. Other developments in northern Europe also caused concern. After the death of the childless Duke Charles, the Estates of Guelders recognized Duke William of Cleves as their new ruler; and Henry VIII chose as his fourth wife Anne of Cleves, the duke's sister who was also the sister-in-law of Elector John Frederick of Saxony, leader of the League of Schmalkalden. An alliance between England and disaffected German rulers posed a clear threat to imperial interests.[56]

Charles had intended Doria's galleys to come to Barcelona and take him to Genoa, where he would oversee arrangements for a new naval campaign against the Turks before crossing the Alps to reach the Netherlands; but in October 1539 the worsening situation in the north forced a change in his plans. Now he would travel through the heart of France, even though his decision required a double deception. On the one hand, he needed to explain this dramatic development to the pope and the Venetians, his allies in the Holy League, as well as to his own ministers in Italy; but, he explained to Luis de Ávila y Zúñiga, his special envoy to Italy, 'although they all need to know about this decision, at present it is better that they should not know more' – that is to say, that his decision reflected the weakness of his overall position.[57] The second deception involved his Spanish subjects. Charles feared a general outcry when they learned that he planned to throw himself on the mercy of their traditional enemy, and he therefore begged Francis and his courtiers to write 'affectionate letters to persuade me to make this journey, without mentioning that you already know exactly what I want'. He also asked for an assurance that no matters of state would be discussed while he was on French soil.[58]

As soon as the letters required to conceal his deception arrived from France, mindful of the rebellions that had almost cost him his throne the first time he left Spain, Charles took steps to create an acceptable regency government. He named his son Philip, now eleven, as his regent but invested executive power in Cardinal Tavera, who would serve as governor of the kingdom as well as president of the royal council and inquisitor-general. Charles also prepared two sets of instructions: one, addressed to his ministers, detailed their administrative duties and responsibilities (both towards the emperor and towards each other); the other was 'a warning, opinion and advice' to Philip so that, in case 'God is pleased to take me to Him' before he had achieved his policy goals, 'the said prince should know our plans' and would thus be prepared to follow the correct religious, dynastic and political strategies 'so that he may live and reign in peace and prosperity'. It was the first of many papers of advice that revealed to his son the emperor's innermost thoughts, and thus began the prince's long political apprenticeship.[59]

After enjoining Philip to love God and defend His Church, the emperor urged him to rely on his relatives:

> He should make and maintain a good, true, sincere and perfect friendship and understanding with our brother, the king of the Romans [Ferdinand], and with his children, our nephews and nieces; with the queens of France [Eleanor] and Hungary [Marie]; with the king and queen of Portugal [Catalina], and with their children ... to continue the friendship and understanding that exists, and has always existed, between us.

Charles then addressed three contentious issues: France, the Netherlands and Milan. He saw them as linked, because the current amity with King Francis would only continue if the parties agreed 'to remove and extinguish all quarrels and rivalries' concerning the Netherlands and Milan, sealing the deal with marriage alliances. Although he had just agreed that the duke of Orléans (the former duke of Angoulême) might marry his daughter María, with Milan as her dowry, Charles revealed that both he and the empress in their testaments had stipulated that 'should we have no other son than the said prince, as is now the case', María would marry one of Ferdinand's sons, and that the couple would rule the Netherlands. The issue had become of critical importance with the unrest in the Low Countries, caused by 'the multitude of sects opposed to our holy faith, created with the pretence of gaining liberty and a new form of consensual government, which could lead to their complete loss not only to our dynasty but also to our Holy Faith'. The emperor therefore stated his intention of reneging on all previous undertakings, so that María could marry Orléans and the Netherlands 'may pass to the said prince, our son, and that he may succeed us there if it can be arranged'. Nevertheless, he assured Philip, if in the end 'we should confer the said dominions on our said daughter and her future husband, it will be to avoid these aforesaid hazards, for the great benefit of Christendom and of our said son, and for the benefit, peace and wellbeing of the kingdoms and other dominions that he is going to inherit'. This convoluted provision contained two remarkable insights: Charles was willing to renege on solemn promises made to his brother, as he would do again at Augsburg in 1551 (see chapter 14); and he foresaw the risk of a Dutch revolt if Philip inherited both Spain and the Netherlands (as indeed occurred a decade after Charles's abdication).

The emperor's instruction next laid out the policy Philip must follow towards three other states: Portugal, Savoy and England. The emperor's daughter Joanna must marry the heir to the Portuguese throne, Prince John, and the French must evacuate Savoy and restore it to the duke. Regarding England, Philip must 'take great care not to agree carelessly to something that might prejudice our [Catholic] faith' and allow Protestantism to triumph. Moreover, family ties obliged Philip to promote the interests of Mary, the daughter of Henry and Katherine of Aragon, and 'to assist and favour her as much as you conveniently can do'. A codicil to Charles's will, signed the same day, repeated the arrangements set out in his instructions, with one addition: in the event of the emperor's death, his ministers 'must place the duchy of Milan in the hands of our brother ... the king of the Romans, and our presumed successor as emperor', whom he charged with executing the rest of his wishes.[60]

Although neither codicil nor instructions came into effect, because Charles survived, they identified several issues that would dominate Spanish foreign policy for the rest of the century: the need to maintain good relations with the Austrian branch of the family; to intermarry with the Portuguese royal family; to detach either Milan or the Netherlands (or both) from Spain; to restore the duke of Savoy to his dominions; and to uphold the Catholic faith and protect the Catholic claimant to the throne in England. The documents also revealed two practices that would undermine Spanish foreign policy for a century: the willingness to renege on solemn promises, and the reluctance to surrender any territory. Charles's instructions of 1539 thus highlighted in striking fashion both the strengths and the weaknesses of the monarchy his son would inherit.

THROUGH FRANCE TO THE NETHERLANDS

Charles took leave of his children and set out for France with a small entourage on 11 November 1539. His departure caused almost universal astonishment. The veteran diplomat and historian Francesco Guicciardini told a confidant that 'Even the emperor himself would not have believed this news, because it was unbelievable'; the French ambassador in London reported that 'the whole world is astonished, especially the king's ministers'.[61] Such incredulity is easily explained. Scarcely thirteen years had passed since the vanquished Francis had travelled to Spain, confident that he could settle his differences with Charles in one-on-one meetings, only to end up in prison under constant surveillance; and he had only secured his release by sending two of his sons into captivity, where Charles treated them badly. Nevertheless, now the dauphin, formerly one of Charles's hostages, re-entered Spain to meet and greet the imperial party and led them to Paris, which Charles entered on 1 January 1540, watched by perhaps 200,000 cheering spectators. The ruler who barely two years before had been execrated as head of an evil empire now encountered everywhere triumphal arches, fanfares and speeches of welcome. There was another reason for incredulity: undertaking such a long overland journey in December and January might seem the height of folly, but once again, Caesar's luck saved him: the winter of 1539–40 proved to be one of the warmest and driest on record in western Europe, with no precipitation recorded in some areas between October and March. As usual, Charles took it all for granted. 'We have been so well-treated and feted, with great affection and enthusiasm, that we could not have wished for more,' he reported, and 'we spend all our days hunting and hawking, and the nights whirling and dancing until it is time for bed'.[62]

Two considerations explain his effusive reception. After many years of war and numerous reverses, most French men and women rejoiced to see irrefutable evidence that peace had returned at last; and Francis was anxious to dazzle his guest with the extent and wealth of his kingdom, culminating in the gift of a luxurious suit of clothes worth 40,000 ducats when the two monarchs met. Although Charles declined the clothes, continuing to wear 'black garments with a black felt hat, without any insignia, because he mourned the empress', the overwhelming impression of wealth cannot have escaped him.[63]

From Paris the emperor continued his progress to the Netherlands, accompanied by Francis as far as the frontier. As agreed, the king refrained from raising the question of Milan, loudly proclaiming that a gentleman did not take advantage of his guests (as he had accused Charles of doing during his Spanish captivity), but Charles gave his promise that 'after our brother the king of the Romans arrives at Brussels, and we have consulted him, we can do what needs to be done' – which implied the transfer of Milan to the duke of Orléans.[64] First, however, he had to deal with his Flemish rebels.

The emperor took no chances. Before he entered Ghent in February 1540 he deployed over 3,000 German troops 'all around the palace so that they could easily come together if necessary', and 'they were all together in the market square until I had passed through' at the head of 'my entourage and my guards: five companies of men-at-arms'.[65] Charles sifted through the evidence of treason by citizens of Ghent and other parts of Flanders, and eventually had over a hundred men and women executed, mutilated or banished, often after torture. He also confiscated their property and imposed a heavy fine, as well as collecting all the back taxes the province had refused to pay; he revoked the city's privileges and abolished or weakened local institutions; and he confiscated all artillery and other heavy weapons. Then, as he had done in Valladolid after the Comuneros revolt, Charles presided over a final theatrical performance. On 1 May he retired to a monastery to commemorate the first anniversary of his wife's death, and two days later, having again deployed 'all the soldiers stationed in the city, fully armed, in the streets and crossroads', Charles watched from a stage as the entire urban elite filed in front of him, bare-headed, with nooses round their necks and wearing only their shirts. They knelt and begged his forgiveness, but for a time the emperor 'looked into the distance, saying nothing in reply, appearing to reflect on what the people of Ghent had done and whether or not he should pardon them', until Marie begged him to forgive them 'in honour and memory of his birth there'. This he graciously granted. He also laid the first stone of a citadel to be erected on the spot chosen by his grandfather Maximilian after an earlier revolt.[66]

Ferdinand joined his brother and sister in Ghent, and the three evidently discussed the partition of Charles's possessions after his death because the emperor now proposed to Francis a dramatically different way of settling their disagreements. He offered to bestow the Netherlands on his daughter María, who would marry Orléans, and in return Francis would renounce all claim to Milan and Savoy. Charles would do the same for Burgundy. However, the emperor insisted that his daughter and future son-in-law would only be his 'lieutenants' in the Netherlands – Charles would remain their sovereign until his death – and if María died without heirs, the provinces would revert to Habsburg rule. He also demanded that Francis promise to help Charles to extirpate Lutheranism in Germany; to assist Ferdinand to drive the Turks out of Hungary; to allow Prince Philip to marry Jeanne d'Albret, heiress to Navarre; and to endow Orléans with extensive lands in France.[67]

This proposal, which differed dramatically from the earlier one, was totally unacceptable to the French – yet Charles seemed oblivious. Even a decade later, he wrote in his *Memoirs* that he had 'sent letters to the king of France offering such great concessions that it was remarkable that he did not accept them, and that the desired peace did not follow'. The emperor apparently could not appreciate how evacuating Savoy would weaken France, how the marriage of Philip and Jeanne would strengthen Spain's northern border, and how his demand that Orléans should receive control of a large power-base inside France resembled the creation of an appanage for the dukes of Burgundy that had almost destroyed the kingdom a century before. The French ambassadors at the imperial court warned that 'it is public knowledge here that the king [Francis] dislikes the offers made by the emperor, and the common people here believe talks have broken down and some already fear the outbreak of war'. Their English colleague Thomas Wyatt agreed. 'The thinges of Fraunce,' he wrote, 'ar as cold as tho the thinges passid had bene but dremis', and he predicted that 'the donation of Millan shall not conclud, not now, not ever'. He also opined that Charles had so offended 'the Frenche kyng that men think he rather tymithe the matter till he be in redyness, then hopithe eni forder treting'. In short, he saw a new French declaration of war as inevitable. He was right.[68]

Although in May 1540, Francis proposed 'leaving things as they are for now', a suggestion that Charles accepted, both parties took secret measures to change the status quo. In July the emperor informed his brother that 'after thinking about public affairs, both yours and mine, I absolutely must return to Spain', both 'because of the state of my relations with France' and because in case of war 'I cannot be sustained except by my kingdoms of Spain'. Three months later he engaged in another major deception. Fearing 'a major war prejudicial to Christendom in general, as well as to our son, our kingdoms, dominions and subjects, and our brother' if Milan 'should fall into hostile hands, or those of someone unable to defend it', the emperor invested Prince Philip with the duchy as an imperial fief, and drew up a new codicil to his will revoking his previous orders that it should pass directly to Ferdinand 'whom we are sure will understand our reasons' – a phrase that proves that Charles had not informed his brother of this unilateral decision to reduce his inheritance.[69] For his part, Francis signed warrants worth 5,500 ducats in favour of Antonio Rincón, 'his chamberlain and ambassador in the Levant', and Suleiman granted Rincón an audience that lasted several hours – 'a thing which he had never done to any man in the world' – before sending him back to coordinate how he and his 'good friend and brother' Francis would attack the Habsburgs.[70]

Charles, meanwhile, took advantage of an unusually dry summer to tour his Netherlands provinces and reassert his authority in the wake of the troubles in Flanders. He also persuaded the States-General to approve a number of important economic, legal and religious proposals: they passed laws to regulate bankruptcies, monopolies, usury and the currency; to monitor the conduct of secular and ecclesiastical judges; to standardize regional legal codes; and to punish with death all those convicted of heresy. Charles also issued revised instructions to the three collateral councils that would advise Marie after he departed, adjusting their membership and protocols; and as usual he monitored developments in his other dominions, including approval of a suggestion from Los Cobos that he create a new archive in the fortress of Simancas, to which all surviving documents generated by the central government of Castile would be transferred.[71]

THE DIET OF REGENSBURG

By then, Charles had decided that he would return to Spain via Germany, where he hoped to resolve all religious divisions as a prelude to a second campaign in Africa. He recognized the difficulties inherent in this task. Since leaving Germany nine years before, in return for Lutheran support against the Turks he had suspended the Edict of Worms, with its penalties for non-conformity, and agreed to refer all differences between Lutherans and Catholics to a future church council. Since the former saw little chance that the council would endorse toleration, in 1535 the members of the League of Schmalkalden had voted to prolong its existence for another twelve years and also solicited expressions of support from foreign rulers (notably the kings of Denmark, England and France), provoking some Catholic rulers to form their own defensive league. In 1539, alarmed by Charles's rapprochement with France, both leagues declared that they would not use force against the other, or expand their membership. They also promised to send theologians to a series of 'colloquies' (or friendly conversations) arranged by the emperor in the hope of resolving their differences; while Charles sought 'the advice of my confessor and learned theologians' on the issues to be debated at the next Diet.[72]

The pope tried to derail the talks by summoning a general council to meet in Vicenza, in the Venetian Republic, and he asked Charles to forbid further discussion of religious issues at the Diet; Charles replied that the Lutherans would not attend any council held outside the Empire. He also pointed out that, unlike a Diet, a general council would not produce funds for the defence of Hungary against the Turks. Luther likewise dismissed the idea that a general council offered any hope of reform in another intemperate polemic entitled *On councils and churches*. He, too, favoured finding a solution just for Germany. The colloquies therefore continued.[73]

By January 1541 the German theologians had made considerable progress, and Charles gave orders for a draft text to be debated in his presence at the next imperial Diet, scheduled to open at Regensburg. He also tried to create a united Catholic front. Gasparo Contarini, formerly Venetian ambassador at his court and now the pope's special envoy to the Diet, reported that at his first audience the emperor asserted that everyone in the Catholic camp 'must speak with one voice, and not diverge from one another, if we want to bring this matter to a successful conclusion'.[74] To this end, Charles chose six theologians – three from each creed – and tasked them with finding common ground, and he appointed Granvelle and Count Palatine Frederick to preside over their discussions. On 6 April the Diet listened to 'a long statement recapitulating all that the Emperor had done' since they last met, namely his success in driving the sultan from Hungary; his attempt to make the pope convene a general council 'according to his promise at previous Diets'; his campaigns in north Africa (to defend Christendom) and Provence (to restore the duke of Savoy, a prince of the Empire); and his successful efforts to make peace with France and restore order in the Netherlands. Next the assembly heard a statement 'in his Majesty's name, in German (the Emperor not speaking that language fluently)', setting out his twin goals for the Diet: to find a formula of religious concord within the Empire and to prepare its defence against the Turks.[75]

In May, to general surprise, the theologians agreed upon the subject of Justification and turned to the crucial issue of the Eucharist, but Contarini denounced this as misguided on the grounds that the subject had been decided by previous general councils. Charles vehemently disagreed, not least because Sultan Suleiman once more approached Hungary at the head of a large army, which (as in 1532) made it imperative to make concessions that would secure Lutheran troops and taxes. He repeatedly expressed his frustration at the papacy's failure to understand his dilemma. When Contarini requested an imperial audience on 14 May and 'explained the errors of the

Lutherans on the sacraments of the Eucharist and confession' and 'how it was impossible to reach an accord unless they changed their mind', Charles 'listened attentively' and then told the cardinal that 'I had done my duty well, because he himself was not a theologian' (perhaps a sarcastic comment since Contarini, the former diplomat, had only been a priest for four years). His lack of theological training did not prevent the emperor from arguing that 'the difference between the two sides concerning the Eucharist consisted of just one word: "transubstantiation"'. How difficult could it be, he asked, to find a definition acceptable to all? Two weeks later, Granvelle repeated the emperor's message. 'The word "transubstantiation"' was 'a subtle concept [*una cosa sottile*] of significance only to the learned. It was irrelevant to ordinary people, who needed to know only that the body of Christ was in the Sacrament and must be revered.' Granvelle predicted that 'once we resolved this difficulty, it would be easy to reach agreement on the other articles'; but unless the two sides reached an accommodation 'within three months of the emperor's departure all Germany will be Lutheran'.[76]

At dawn the following day, 21 June 1541, Ferdinand arrived in Regensburg. On hearing the news, his brother arose and 'waited for him in his shirt at the window and after they had embraced and remained a short while together, they both retired to rest'. The brothers then pleaded with the Diet for funds to save Buda, now under Ottoman siege, but the Lutheran members of the Diet refused without guarantees that religious toleration would continue. As usual, they got their way: at the closing ceremony of the Diet, both groups agreed to refer all religious differences to the next general council, to be held on German soil, failing which a national council, or (if neither had taken place after eighteen months) at another meeting of the Diet. Until then, the toleration granted by the peace of Nuremberg remained in force and the Diet agreed to fund 24,000 troops to defend Hungary – but the compromise came too late to save Buda, which surrendered less than a month later.[77]

STORM OVER ALGIERS

Some contemporaries were astonished that Charles left Regensburg for Italy, instead of for Hungary, but this reflected a major change in his grand strategy. During his summit with the pope at Nice three years before, he had explained to a Venetian envoy that 'when the sultan advanced against Vienna, we saw that it is not always possible to force him to battle when one wishes, yet he commands so many horsemen that he can advance and retire, and devastate the countryside, at will'. This, Charles explained, led him to favour a defensive posture in Hungary, 'improving the fortifications and installing garrisons in the frontier strongholds, but otherwise not committing troops to any campaigns'. In future, he would make war on the Turks by sea; and, he told the ambassadors, 'having learned on my African campaign' that success required a far larger expeditionary force, he planned to raise and command 60,000 men, 200 galleys and 'as many ships as necessary' for an attack on 'Constantinople, which is surrounded by sea on three sides, via the Dardanelles, which I am told can be captured easily'.[78]

When Marie heard of this, she composed a blistering memorandum warning Charles of the risks involved:

> Although Your Majesty is the foremost Christian prince in honour and in the number of your dominions and subjects, you are not obliged to defend Christendom alone, or with only a little assistance, and even less to attack our common enemy, especially one as powerful as the Turks. Moreover, even if Your Majesty might want to do this you need to consider if you have the power to do it successfully ... However good and Christian the venture might be in itself, it should not be undertaken unless it will succeed.

Conceding that warfare 'is not my trade', Marie reminded her brother that 'I have listened to many people who are familiar with the Turks' (a reference to her years as queen of Hungary). She also reminded him of how much had gone wrong during his expedition to Tunis: 'In what state would you and your army have been if Barbarossa had not come out to do battle?' Yet Tunis 'is just at the doorway to your possessions': how would he overcome similar problems in the eastern Mediterranean? Next Marie condemned Charles's decision to campaign in person (the fact that her husband had perished in battle against the Turks gave her opinion added force). 'If some misfortune should befall you,' she asked rhetorically, 'what would become of your family and of us, your subjects and your lands, and of the entire Christian faith which, as everyone knows, depends wholly upon your life and your reputation? How would you answer to God if such a misfortune arose through your own fault?' She continued cruelly: 'Your Majesty's task is to vanquish, not to be vanquished':

> Even if the campaign starts so well that Your Majesty wins some town and begins to advance, if you lack the means to press on, think what a

disgrace and cause for regret it would be. And if Your Majesty wants to keep your gains, please consider what it would cost and how hard it would be to supply and defend them against such a powerful enemy, given the distances involved.[79]

Perhaps chastened by Marie's arguments, Charles scaled back his ambitions and set his sights on capturing Algiers, Barbarossa's base of operations and therefore the preferred target of his Spanish subjects. As with the Tunis campaign, his strategy required the junction of two amphibious forces, one from Spain and the other from Italy, both of which he would command in person, but with two major differences: this time he would sail with the Italian contingent and the operation would take place in the autumn.

Several reasons explain the fateful delay. Above all, the Diet of Regensburg dragged on far longer than Charles had expected, yet he felt unable to leave until he had exhausted all possibilities of finding a formula for religious concord, and secured funds to defend Hungary. At last, on 28 July, the emperor ordered his household to pack and the following day 'he appeared before the Diet in his riding clothes' to give his consent to the final resolution (the *Reichsabschied*).[80] He then travelled at top speed, sometimes covering sixty kilometres a day, over the Brenner Pass and on to Cremona in Lombardy; but instead of hastening to join his fleet he diverted to Milan, where he spent a week before proceeding to Genoa.[81] There he halted again while he and his advisers discussed what to do next. According to Francisco López de Gómara, who travelled with the imperial party:

> While the emperor was in Genoa, he learned from letters sent by his brother how Suleiman had captured Buda and all of Hungary. This led to different opinions among his councillors about going to Algiers. The marquis del Vasto [governor of Lombardy] said that it would be better to stay in Italy, so he could send aid to Ferdinand or return to Hungary if necessary, and also to safeguard Milan, since the king of France threatened it.

'Andrea Doria felt the same,' Gómara added, 'because it seemed too late to campaign on the African coast'; but the emperor argued that the departure of Barbarossa and his galleys to sail up the Danube with the sultan offered a unique opportunity, because Algiers would be too weak to resist him.[82]

Charles embarked at Genoa on 10 September but almost immediately stopped for another week while he met the pope at Lucca. Paul sought to dissuade him from attacking Algiers, 'because the season is far advanced and these troops should be in Hungary'; Charles countered by urging the pope to convene a general council on German soil and to uphold the truce with France, 'so that he could continue to defend Christendom against the Turks'.[83] After three days of fruitless discussion, and two months after leaving Regensburg, Charles and his fleet finally set out on 28 September to join the expeditionary force from Spain off Mallorca (Map 4).

Bad weather now delayed Charles and his fleet, and they did not reach Mallorca until 13 October. There they halted yet again because Charles 'felt great pain in his chest'. He used the enforced leisure to plan his agenda for the coming year, starting with a meeting of the Cortes of Castile in Seville as soon as he returned, after which he would visit Granada and inspect progress on his new palace in the Alhambra before travelling to Aragon, 'so that the prince could receive the oath of loyalty'. When his chest infection persisted, he summoned his principal secretaries, Alonso de Idiáquez and Juan Vázquez de Molina, and told them that:

> Since he might die of this illness, either at sea or having disembarked at Algiers before concluding the campaign, he wanted to leave instructions on how to proceed so that everyone would know his intentions. He therefore created two set of instructions, one signed 'Carlos' [for the contingent from Italy], which he gave to Idiáquez to keep, and the other signed 'Yo el Rey', which he delivered to me [Vázquez de Molina, for the contingent from Spain].

This impressive example of forward planning could not compensate for the late arrival of the expeditionary force from Spain, commanded by the duke of Alba. It left the peninsula only on 30 September and took two weeks to reach Ibiza, 130 kilometres from Mallorca. Given the lateness of the season, Charles now decided that the two fleets should set sail straight for north Africa and join forces there. It was a high-risk gamble: 'God grant that his decision succeeds,' Vázquez de Molina sighed.[84]

At first, the Creator seemed to favour Charles. The imperial fleet sighted Algiers on 19 October 1541, the day after leaving Mallorca, and although rough seas prevented an immediate landing the ships from Spain arrived four days later. Disembarkation began immediately. The emperor swiftly deployed his siege artillery around Algiers and planned to use it, as at La Goletta, in combination with the heavy centreline guns aboard the galleys (which could operate beyond the range of the artillery in the town and still bring down its walls); but on the night of 24 October a furious storm began.

Over the next three days, raging seas destroyed many of Charles's vessels and forced the rest to flee for shelter, while the high winds, freezing rain and hail demoralized his troops, 'who had disembarked without tents and without any coats or capes to protect them against the fury of the rains'. 'There was not a soldier who did not become in a moment as wet as if he had been thrown into the sea.' The storm also deprived the invaders of their tactical edge: 'Our firearms did not work because the rain ruined the powder and match', one of the participants complained, yet 'we were unfamiliar with making war with bows, crossbows, stones and other missiles', all of which their adversaries used to great effect. Unable to land provisions, 'without bread, wine, meat, salt or anything else', the troops only survived because the emperor ordered them to kill and eat the horses with his army: perhaps 2,000 animals perished. Once the storm abated, on 26 October, the invaders fled towards the surviving ships but no sooner had they re-embarked than another tempest arose 'so that each ship went wherever it could and many went in the opposite direction to the way that they should have gone'. Charles found safety in the fortified outpost of Bougie where he organized a fast and prayers for better weather until 23 November, when the winds abated and he led his fleet back to Mallorca. From there, most of the surviving troops and ships returned to Italy, while the emperor and the rest of the expedition made for Cartagena, where they staggered ashore 'half-dead' on 1 December.[85]

THE SEARCH FOR SCAPEGOATS

Sympathetic participants stressed Charles's personal involvement with all aspects of the campaign. According to a Genoese squadron commander, 'in spite of everything, this has been the best-organized war he has seen since he joined the imperial cause'; and once ashore, according to Gómara, 'the emperor was everywhere' and he showed no fear. When speaking to his men beneath the walls of Algiers, 'some of those whom he addressed were suddenly felled by enemy artillery, but the emperor showed no surprise on that account, neither interrupting his speech nor changing his expression. He continued with the same serenity and authority that he normally showed.' Likewise, when the storm began, 'although he was wet, because rain soaked his shirt, and although tired from all his efforts since he disembarked', nevertheless 'he would not go to his tent, asking his gentlemen not to rest until all the wounded were safe'. When his men started to slaughter and eat their horses, 'the emperor wanted to taste it, and to encourage the rest, as he ate he declared it delicious'. He behaved throughout as 'a most excellent captain, in the opinion of everyone, both in efforts and prudence' – but it was not enough.[86] The Venetian ambassador with the expedition, angry and scared as storms battered his ship off Bougie, blamed his predicament entirely on Charles's foolish over-confidence: 'Just as His Imperial Majesty conceived this venture in his own head, and against the advice of all his councillors and principal allies, so he worked out in his own head how to command it. In this he made a major error', resulting in the 'cowardly and disorderly retreat of this army from Algiers'. He added: 'His Majesty cannot escape the blame for this error ... All the Spaniards and Italians here complain about him.' So did the Burgundians: when Fery de Guyon compiled his memoirs twenty-five years later, he protested that 'it was the end of the campaigning season, but *nevertheless*, since His Majesty had made up his mind, we had to go' to north Africa.[87]

Charles himself gave two reasons for the failure: his detour to meet the pope ('this conference with His Holiness somewhat delayed His Majesty's embarkation'); and the judgement of God ('because God controls the weather, we embarked'). In others words, given the sacred nature of the cause, no doubt encouraged by his success against all odds at Tunis, Charles expected God to provide good weather. Muslim observers expressed remarkably similar sentiments: 'God the most high sent a violent storm' that 'drove many ships onto the rocks', wrote one; an imam whose prayers were said to have unleashed the storm became the subject of veneration.[88]

Certainly, the storm had decided the outcome. As Charles expected, the absence of Barbarossa and his galleys gave him an important advantage and he made the most of it, partly by using surprise, partly by pretending that he still intended to attack Istanbul. Even though the defenders of Algiers feared that they might be the emperor's real target, leading them to 'employ 400 Christian slaves to repair the walls, rebuild what had fallen down, and furnish it with towers and cannon', as well as 'cutting down the trees in the gardens around the town, so that the enemy could not use them for concealment in combat', they did not know when the blow would fall. According to an Algerian eyewitness, the city's greatest weakness was that 'in the case of an amphibious expedition, the target remains unknown until three days after it departs', and since the imperial fleet travelled from Mallorca to Algiers in just two days it inevitably took the defenders by surprise. They therefore failed to prevent the orderly disembarkation of the invasion force comprising 40,000 infantry and 4,000 cavalry who, by the evening of 24 October, had taken up their positions and installed their batteries and their galleys close to the town walls. In the opinion of Guyon, who boasted almost twenty years of military experience, 'If God had not sent the storm, I think the city would have been captured within two days.' The author of an anonymous German account agreed: 'Later information revealed that there were only 2,000 horse and 800 Janissaries in the city of Algiers and that the city was not so secure. If our forces had had provisions, without doubt, they would have won it without any difficulty.'[89]

Should Charles have foreseen the potential for disaster? After all, the ecology of the Maghreb did not favour major military operations, since the semi-constant skirmishing between Christians and Muslims dramatically limited food production, leaving most port cities permanently dependent on imports. Landing 44,000 men and their horses would inevitably strain local resources, and although Charles had anticipated this by loading copious stores onto his ships, the storms prevented disembarkation and created an acute food shortage ashore. Nevertheless, that was not the critical problem. As one survivor put it: 'We received some protection against the famine because the emperor allowed the slaughter of his horses', but 'we never found a defence against the rain'.[90]

Here, too, the risk should have been obvious. The months of October, November and December normally see the highest precipitation in and around Algiers, and much of it falls in torrential downpours. For example, 285 millimetres of rain fell in forty-eight hours in November 2001, and 227 millimetres of rain fell on Algiers in fifty hours in September 2012. Although those who endured the storm that began on 24 October 1541 had no means of measuring the downpour accurately (Andrea Doria, then aged seventy-four, merely stated that 'such a furious and terrible storm had never been seen'), they noted that rain and hail continued for fifty hours – very similar to the storms in 2001 and 2012. No army camped in the open could have withstood that unscathed.[91]

Invading an area with scarce resources in late autumn thus greatly multiplied the risks inherent in any complex amphibious operation undertaken in the age of sail. As Paolo Giovio observed, after meeting Charles at Lucca, 'I would never have believed that Caesar's brain, which is supremely cold-blooded, has turned into that of a lackey, because in spite of Doria and Vasto, to say nothing of Neptune and Aeolus [the gods of the sea and the winds], he wants to sail at top speed to Algiers' in early October.'[92] His decision cost the lives of almost half his army. Some died in action; others were overcome by hunger and cold; others still were drowned or cut down as they staggered ashore after their ships sank in the storm. The expedition also lost much equipment (including 200 artillery pieces), almost all its horses and over 100 ships (seventeen of them war galleys); and many survivors lost all their possessions (the English ambassador, saved from shipwreck wearing only his shirt, reported that he had lost over 7,000 ducats in goods and cash as well as the expensive silverware loaned by his sovereign; Hernán Cortés lost his jewels). Charles himself lost part of his archive and for a time his guards had to travel around Spain by mule 'because we lost so many horses at Algiers'. According to a French observer, 'The total material losses exceed 4 million in gold', to say nothing of the immense damage done to imperial prestige, and he predicted that 'the emperor will remember for the rest of his life the enormous loss he has just suffered'. Indeed, he 'has lost so much in this venture that he will not be able to put together another army for a long time'. There would therefore never be a better opportunity to break the truce of Nice and force Charles to make peace on disadvantageous terms. All Francis needed was a plausible excuse.[93]

ELEVEN

SETTLING SCORES, PART I:
GUELDERS AND FRANCE, 1541–4

MURDER MOST FOUL

On 2 July 1541, while Charles was still in Regensburg preparing for the Algiers campaign, Cesare Fregoso and Antonio Rincón embarked with a small entourage on two river boats near Turin, in French-controlled Piedmont, planning to sail down the Po to Venice. Both travelled as diplomats in the service of Francis I, who had ordered Fregoso to represent him in Venice while Rincón would proceed to Istanbul and communicate the king's acceptance of Sultan Suleiman's offer of alliance (chapter 10). Warned by friends that they might be ambushed, 'to deceive the spies they embarked all their goods and servants on another river boat', which departed a few days before, 'and also sent between 10 and 12 men in disguise on horseback, so that any observer would think it was them'. The attempted deception failed: just after the two ambassadors entered the duchy of Lombardy, Spanish soldiers intercepted, abducted and murdered them. They then buried the bodies and disappeared.[1]

Charles had tried to eliminate Rincón before. Three Spaniards had come to Venice to murder him as he returned from Istanbul to France in 1532; and when they failed, Charles placed a price on Rincón's head.[2] But although imperial spies kept the French diplomats under continuous surveillance, so that 'they could not take a step without it being known', on 23 June 1541 Charles instructed the marquis del Vasto, governor of Lombardy, to leave Rincón alone because 'even if you could detain him, it would be contrary to the truce of Nice, which must be preserved at all costs; and if you have already done so you must release him and set him free immediately, making it clear that he was detained without any order from me (which is the truth) and that as soon as we heard about it we gave orders to release him'.[3]

Although Vasto received this command before the assassination, he deliberately disobeyed. His grovelling subsequent apology stated that 'I would rather die a thousand deaths than allow this business to cause Your Majesty anger or disservice', but added 'the only thing that led me to do it [the murder] was knowledge that it would be to your advantage'. To make sure Charles understood his rationale he sent further details with a courier, begging Charles to hear the messenger 'in a place where only Your Majesty can hear what he says'.[4]

The emperor's response to Vasto's flagrant disobedience was of critical importance because murdering the ambassadors would bring about war with France. Charles's ministers had no illusion on this score. 'Given past disagreements, and with affairs in their current state, and since Your Majesty wants to avoid giving any grounds for a rupture', they opined that 'Your Majesty cannot approve what has been done. Nevertheless', they continued fatefully, 'we cannot deny that the deed has been well done, and is very appropriate to avoid something worse.' Therefore *the dexterity he [Vasto] has shown should be praised* – although to avoid any risks, this must be done in the utmost secrecy'. Although the emperor rejected the final suggestion, he neither reproached nor disavowed Vasto. His failure to do so would unleash war not only with France but also with the Turks.[5]

Charles's approval of the cover-up is surprising because (as in modern politics) lying about an action often caused more damage than the action itself. He was certainly capable of overruling the marquis because the following year, when Vasto threatened to disobey another direct order and withdraw his forces from Piedmont, claiming that he lacked the funds to sustain them, Charles delivered a blistering rebuke:

> We refuse to believe that you thought or think of doing what you wrote, unless you wrote it to stress how much you need money; but be that as it may, we do not wish to hear or read about it because it is unworthy that someone of your calibre, holding the position that we granted you, should even think such a thing let alone express it.[6]

Why did Charles fail to issue a similar reproach to Vasto for arranging the murder of the French ambassadors? The surviving evidence suggests that the emperor thought he could lie his way out of trouble – and lie he did. Three weeks after the deed, he signed a letter to his ambassador in France asserting that 'whatever had happened to those two people, we had nothing to do with it'; he assured the nuncio that although Vasto had informed him of the chance to arrest the envoys, 'I told him that he must do nothing to imperil the truce'; and 'at the request of the king of France' he appointed a special investigator to go to Milan to 'locate and liberate' Rincón and Fregoso.[7] A few weeks later Vasto requested permission for the assassins to escape from the prison where he had placed them, and for one of them to send him a written confession that they had acted alone. He helpfully sent a draft of what the document might contain. The emperor not only approved this further deception but recommended a change to the draft: 'If you decide to let the assassins escape, and one of them writes you the confession as we have discussed,' he told Vasto, it would be good if he added that they burned everything '*except for certain documents found on them, which detail the wicked and perverse plots that they were hatching*' – namely alleged plots to wrest control of Genoa from the hands of Andrea Doria. Charles further suggested 'that the person who writes the document should be of a rank appropriate to a leader in such a matter, one whom the others would obey'.[8]

RINCÓN'S POSTHUMOUS REVENGE

Charles's decision to lie proved both a logistical and a political disaster. Anxious to join the expeditionary force he had assembled to take Algiers, he interrupted his journey from Regensburg to make a solemn entry into Milan, where he and Vasto showed their mutual regard. The marquis had engaged Giulio Romano, one of the foremost artists and architects of his day, to prepare triumphal arches (one of them crowned by a statue of Charles, mounted and dressed as a Roman emperor, trampling down a Moor, a Turk and a Native American); and he accompanied his master everywhere until, flanked by two cardinals 'and all the dukes, princes and lords of his court, His Majesty went to the cathedral to carry the son of the marquis to his baptism', becoming the child's godfather. Shortly afterwards torrential rains and high winds destroyed most of the triumphal arches, which some saw as a harbinger of disaster. The emperor's ten-day sojourn in Milan, whether or not intended to demonstrate his confidence in Vasto, doomed the coming campaign: many believed that if Charles had arrived in north Africa ten days earlier, he would have captured Algiers before the catastrophic storms decimated his fleet.[9]

Charles's cover-up also proved a political disaster. As the French ambassador in Venice observed, once news arrived that the two diplomats had been abducted 'no one speaks of anything else', and he predicted (correctly) that it 'will be like the plague: as it spreads, no one discusses other illnesses'. King Francis – who had paid Rincón some 10,000 ducats just before his ill-fated departure – asked Henry VIII for 'council and advice on what I should do in this matter', and also sent a special messenger 'to tell the sultan the truth about what had happened to the envoys'. His chancellor angrily exclaimed that 'it was an act that not only violated treaties and promises but also international law, which guarantees the safety of ambassadors'.[10]

Although both Vasto and Charles continued to protest their ignorance of the murders, they chose their words with great care. The marquis insisted that he would never act contrary to 'the order issued by His Majesty when Rincón went to France, namely that neither he nor anyone with him should be troubled' (irrelevant, since Rincón had been coming *from* France). The emperor assured foreign diplomats that 'he had never given orders for his ministers to capture Fregoso and Rincón', and gave 'his solemn word that his officials would not have dared to undertake a thing of such importance and consequence without his knowledge and permission'.[11] Although these statements were technically true, they were also deliberately misleading – and Francis soon realized it. He therefore pressured Charles to release his diplomats, or at least to reveal where they were, by arresting and imprisoning George of Austria (one of Emperor Maximilian's numerous illegitimate progeny and thus Charles's uncle) as he made his way across France, and by seizing some Spanish merchants. He also sent a special representative to raise the matter at the imperial summit with the pope at Lucca, and although Charles 'refused to give the envoy an audience, or allow the matter to be discussed in his presence', Paul showed no such scruples and 'claimed for himself cognizance, trial and verdict in the case', on the grounds that 'he has jurisdiction over treaties of peace and truce between Christian princes, and particularly the one at Nice', which he had brokered. The emperor reported that the pope insisted 'I immediately deal with the restitution of Fregoso and Rincón, as if they were in my power and I could produce them!' Before he left Lucca, having further perjured himself with the claim 'on the soul of the empress that he knew nothing about the whereabouts of Rincón and Fregoso', Charles reluctantly agreed to submit the diplomatic incident to papal arbitration.[12]

The discovery in October 1541 of the mangled bodies of the ambassadors on Milanese territory outraged Francis even more. He told a special envoy from the pope that 'although he would take no action against the emperor until after [the latter] returned from his expedition to Algiers, he then expected His Imperial Majesty to give satisfaction'. According to an English envoy who overheard the conversation, the king defined 'satisfaction' very clearly: 'If th'empereur woold deliver him Milan, with th'appurtenaunces, "Then we have peace already"; but if th'empereur would not, "There is no point in talking about peace"'. When reminded that Charles had offered to cede the Netherlands to the duke of Orléans instead, Francis replied that he 'would not give his younger son the means to make war on the kingdom of France'. He wanted 'Milan and nothing els' for himself. Nevertheless, even after learning that Charles had survived his north African venture and returned to Spain, Francis remained cautious: when pressed by the nuncio, he admitted that although it would be easy for him to start a war immediately, 'there are now so many irons in the fire that the time is not right'.[13]

King James V of Scotland was one of the irons. In 1537 he had married one of Francis's daughters in Paris, amid lavish festivities, and after her death he married Mary of Guise, a prominent member of the royal court – an alliance guaranteed to keep Scotland in the French orbit. Francis used a similar strategy to win over the duke of Cleves. When Duke Charles of Guelders died childless in 1538, Charles V had a good claim to succeed, founded in the treaty of Gorcum (p. 186), but the representatives of the duchy instead recognized their neighbour William of Cleves as their new ruler. Marie urged her brother to hurry back to the Netherlands, warning him that 'to abandon them now would greatly undermine his reputation'. Charles replied that 'the campaigning season was too advanced to wage war on Guelders, and that next year he would be fighting the Turks'; but Marie countered boldly that a decision to 'fight the Turks and leave affairs over here in their current state' would lead 'a large number of your loyal subjects here to lose their affection towards Your Majesty'. The revolt of Ghent forced Charles to change his mind, and not long after he returned to the Netherlands, Duke William came to secure imperial recognition of his new title as duke of Guelders, hoping that the marriage of his sister Anne to Henry VIII would strengthen his hand; but the emperor turned him down flat.[14]

Perhaps his successful progress through France and the Netherlands made Charles over-confident. Sir Thomas Wyatt, the English ambassador at his court, reported that during an audience in December 1539 Charles had boasted that the duke of Cleves ' "shall do me reason" . . . laying his hand on his breast, "And he hath of one a sovereign, a neighbour, and a cousin; and otherways he shall lose all three"'. The following month, when discussing Guelders, Wyatt observed in Charles a 'vehemence that I have not bene acustomid to se. I notyd his lowder voice, his earnester looke and specially his imperius fashon in his words'. At another audience in February 1540, when Wyatt spoke up in favour of the duke of Cleves, the emperor merely 'smild and wagid his hed, with making a "Tushe" at the matter'.[15] Perhaps over-confidence explains why Charles apparently overlooked both the reports that 'all the triumphes' erected in his honour as he traversed France and 'left stonding after his departure in his memorie, ar now taken downe and broken in peaces', and the welcome extended by Francis to the duke of Cleves: the two signed a treaty that guaranteed mutual assistance in case of attack and allowed France to raise troops in Cleves in case of need, and promised Duke William the hand of Jeanne d'Albret, heiress to the kingdom of Navarre, whom the emperor had hoped would marry his son Philip.[16]

The winter of 1541–2 saw more diplomatic activity at the court of France. The king welcomed refugees from Ghent and elsewhere who had defied Charles; signed a 'lege defensive and offensive, freendes to freendes and enemye to enemyes' with Denmark; sent envoys to conclude alliances with Elector John Frederick of Saxony and with the king of Sweden; signed contracts by which several German mercenary leaders agreed to keep troops on standby for French service; and authorized his ambassador in England to propose a marriage between the duke of Orléans and Mary Tudor.[17] Most ominous of all, Francis finalized plans with the sultan for a coordinated campaign. Suleiman would lead an army of 60,000 men back to Hungary, and send Barbarossa with 150 galleys into the western Mediterranean; Francis promised to send a galley squadron to join the Turkish vessels, to allow their combined fleet to winter in a French port, and to attack the Habsburgs in Spain and the Netherlands.

In July 1542, since all his irons in the fire seemed hot, Francis unleashed attacks on multiple fronts and authorized his subjects to arm themselves and attack the emperor and his 'subjects and allies' wherever they could be found. The principal justification in his War Cry was that:

> The emperor has committed an injury so great, so execrable and so strange towards humankind, and especially towards those who boast the titles and qualities of princes, that it cannot ever be forgotten, suffered or tolerated: namely that by means of some of his ministers our ambassadors, Cesare Fregoso, a knight of our Order, and Antonio Rincón, were treacherously and inhumanly assassinated and killed as they were on their way to Venice on our business . . . In this, the emperor acted against the truce negotiated between him and me – something repugnant to all divine and human law, and contrary to the ancient and settled custom established and observed between kings and princes, states and republics, from the creation of the world until now.[18]

Suleiman used a similar rationale. In August 1541 he warned Ferdinand that he must 'secure the release of the ambassador [Rincón] who was coming to our Sublime Port on behalf of the emperor of France, whom your brother Charles has seized and arrested . . . unless you wish to cause the ruin of your own land'. The sultan also arrested the Habsburg ambassador at his court and threatened to inflict on him whatever 'outrage Charles had inflicted on Ambassador Antonio Rincón, who was on his way to see me'; and he later characterized his campaign against the Habsburgs as revenge for the 'great offence and indignity' of Rincón's murder. Thanks to the emperor's duplicity, from beyond the grave the former Comunero got his full measure of revenge.[19]

A NEW WAR BETWEEN CHARLES AND FRANCIS

The French declaration of war did not surprise Charles. In November 1541, Nicholas Perrenot de Granvelle, who had stayed in Italy after the Lucca summit, composed a perceptive position paper about the international situation based on the assumption that hostilities were virtually inevitable with either the French or the Turks, and possibly with both. He predicted that the principal blows would fall on either Navarre or Milan, perhaps preceded by an attack on the Netherlands 'under the aegis of the duke of Cleves'. The main obstacle to mounting an effective response, Granvelle thought, was that 'with so many things happening at the same time in different places', everyone would demand Charles's presence; the emperor must therefore 'make his decisions in the light of all these problems, and not deal with just one while abandoning the others'. For example, although the imperial presence in Germany would 'encourage the Germans to oppose the Turks, stimulate his affairs in Italy and the Netherlands, and restrain both the king of France and the Lutherans', leaving Spain would irritate his subjects there, since he had only just arrived; and 'it would cause desperation in Naples and Sicily if Your Majesty goes to Germany instead of going to their aid'. Moving to practicalities, Granvelle recommended extending the toleration enjoyed by the Lutherans of Germany, if necessary by twenty years, in return for a commitment to fight not only the Turks but also the French. He also advocated an alliance with England. Henry VIII might be a heretic, but that did not prevent Francis and other Catholic rulers from dealing with him; moreover (Granvelle added slyly) 'Your Majesty often negotiates with the German Lutherans, who not only deny papal authority but also reject important issues of Catholic doctrine'. Finally, he reviewed whether it would be better to wait for Francis to take the initiative or to launch a pre-emptive strike, concluding that 'since Your Majesty is so far from the Netherlands and Milan' prudence was preferable, but he urged the dispatch of funds to the emperor's lieutenants in both areas to create a strategic reserve.[20]

Charles submitted Granvelle's paper of advice to his Spanish ministers, and having received positive comments he implemented its principal recommendations. In December 1541 he informed Ferdinand that 'given the current state of affairs between France and me', should 'the Lutherans demand guarantees of continued toleration in return for military assistance against his enemy', his brother could concede them (albeit for as short a time as possible). That same day the emperor promised Marie that he would 'raise a large sum of money and disburse it in Italy and Germany as well as in the Netherlands so that we can always be ready in case of an emergency, wherever it might arise'; and he presciently predicted that hostilities might begin with a coordinated attack on Luxemburg by French, Danish and Guelders troops.[21]

A few days later, while visiting his mother at Tordesillas, Charles started to plan his counter-moves. 'As you know', he confided to Marie in a long holograph letter, 'I want to avoid war'; but given the overwhelming evidence that Francis 'intends to attack wherever he can cause me the most damage', namely in the Netherlands and in Navarre, 'I need to defend myself by thwarting his designs'. The previous summer he had devised 'plans to do everything in my power over the next two years to recover Guelders and punish the duke of Cleves', and 'I chose that timeframe because I need to put my other affairs in order, and to raise the funds that I lack for the venture here in Spain. But if France makes war on me again now, these plans will all be vain.' So, Charles wondered, might 'offence be the best defence', perhaps by marching through Italy and Germany to make a surprise attack on Guelders? He sought Marie's urgent advice on the matter because 'I cannot make up my mind what would be best for me do, since with Monsieur de Granvelle absent there is no one here whom I can consult' – a revealing admission – 'and if I raise the matter with the council here you can be sure that they will never agree that I should leave these kingdoms, but rather will do all they can to prevent me.'[22] By May 1542 he had made up his mind. He informed Ferdinand that he planned to travel to Barcelona 'with the intention of embarking there' for Italy, but 'all things considered, I cannot see how I can get to Germany until the end of the campaigning season ... My plan is to arrive next winter and hold a Diet at Speyer', he continued, 'and afterwards take steps to recover Guelders, if necessary by force.'[23]

The emperor would adhere closely to this plan, but another bout of ill-health delayed its implementation. He suffered 'so much pain in my body, my side and my neck, that I can't believe it is all happening to the same person. I often have to use a cane. So you can judge,' he jested to Marie, 'whether I can serve as your fearless champion' in the coming war. 'Time will show me what I need to do,' he concluded philosophically, 'and I hope God will guide me and reveal where I can do the most good.'[24] For some time, the Lord's guidance seemed ambiguous. Hostilities began in June 1542, when the Danes seized all ships and goods belonging to subjects of the emperor and sent troops and subsidies to the duke of Cleves, who mobilized 14,000 foot, 2,000 horse and eighteen artillery pieces. The following month, reinforced by vengeful exiles from Ghent and elsewhere, this army made a bold dash for Antwerp and summoned the city to surrender in the names of the kings of Denmark and France. By then, a Danish fleet cruised off the coast of Holland, a French army led by the duke of Orléans had conquered most of Luxemburg, another army under the dauphin stood ready to invade Artois, Francis himself prepared to besiege Perpignan, and the king of Navarre mobilized to regain his lost lands. This remarkable coordination caught Charles and his ministers unprepared. Marie warned him that:

> I do not believe that these Netherlands have been in the same peril as I see them now since the wars of our grandfather, the late emperor [Maximilian], because we are under attack on so many fronts that I do not know which one I should deal with first. The worst of it is that our enemies are prepared and we are not: they have taken us entirely by surprise.

She made haste to arrest, torture and execute all Netherlanders suspected of sympathy for the invaders, thus eliminating a potential fifth column, but she argued that only Charles's presence could save his ancestral lands. She argued in vain: as long as French forces remained on Spanish soil he dared not leave the peninsula.[25]

In the event, Charles survived the crisis of 1542 relatively unscathed. The duke of Alba organized an effective defence of the Catalan frontier and forced the invaders to retreat, but it had been a close call. As the English ambassador in Spain noted: 'Albeyt th'emperour, lyke a wise prince and a man of great experience, castyng upon the worste, made everye where great provision, yet the numbre and the diversitie' of the attacks almost overwhelmed him. Charles agreed, confessing to his brother:

The king of France thought he could not fail to surprise me here, attacking Roussillon as well as Navarre. He assumed that everything would be his, that I could not resist, and that having taken Perpignan by surprise he could press on as far as Valladolid. Well, to tell you the truth, if his army had set off at the time he intended, he would have placed me at a grave disadvantage because I never thought such an enterprise likely ... But God gave me time to fortify, repair and provision Perpignan.

French incompetence also saved the Netherlands. Orléans led his army south as soon as he heard rumours that his father planned to fight a major battle with Charles, which allowed Marie to recover most of her losses. Nevertheless, as in Spain, 'The attacks that the king of France and his adherents had planned against these Netherlands were so great, and so carefully and secretly prepared, that we must deem it a great miracle that their execution did not cause more damage here.'[26]

Once the crisis passed, Charles visited Catalonia and Valencia to persuade the Cortes there to vote taxes and recognize Prince Philip as his heir apparent, returning to Castile to celebrate Christmas with all three of his legitimate children (for the last time, as it transpired). Then on 15 January 1543 he ordered his household to prepare to accompany him to Italy, and six weeks later he set out for Barcelona. 'I cannot do everything and be everywhere,' he reminded Ferdinand, and so 'you must not count on my help, because I have enough problems – indeed, I fear, too many – of my own'. Nevertheless, he added with heavy sarcasm, 'I hope soon to reduce to reason our dear brother and friend, the most Christian King' (the etiquette used by Charles in happier times to address Francis).[27]

The process involved some important diplomatic initiatives. After intense negotiations, Charles's envoys in Portugal reached agreement on the terms for another double marriage: Infanta Joanna was betrothed to the heir to the Portuguese throne, Prince John, and his sister María Manuela would wed Prince Philip. The need to secure papal dispensation for the numerous relationships between the fiancés caused delay (see Pl. 28), but King John III (the husband of Charles's sister Catalina) agreed to pay half of his daughter's dowry in advance. Charles immediately used the money to fund his journey to Italy.[28]

He also turned to Henry VIII, once the pariah of Christendom but now courted by both Charles and Francis. The emperor enjoyed several advantages. Although in public Francis professed enthusiasm about a marriage between his younger son and Henry's daughter, Mary Tudor, in private he harboured serious misgivings; his close alliance with James V of Scotland profoundly irritated Henry; and the imperial ambassador in England, Eustache Chapuys, had persuaded a French embassy official to copy and share prodigious amounts of his master's correspondence, which he used to sabotage every move made by the French.[29] In January 1543, Charles authorized Chapuys to liaise directly with Marie and Granvelle in order to work out together 'the best means of carrying out our intentions', and the following month he signed a treaty that settled all outstanding grievances and committed both sovereigns to invade France to secure Burgundy and Picardy for Charles, and Normandy and Guyenne for Henry.[30]

The emperor remained uncertain about the most effective strategy for the allies to follow. The same letter that empowered Chapuys to make terms with Henry also informed him unhelpfully that although Andrea Doria's galleys would 'convey us personally to wherever the danger may be greatest, so as to resist the enemy with all our power, we cannot at this time tell you to which of those points we shall personally go, not knowing for certain what the enemy's designs may be'.[31] Nevertheless, in preparation for his voyage, the emperor gathered troops, treasure, ships and munitions at Barcelona, and welcomed nobles and other volunteers who wished to take part in his next campaign. He also signed instructions for all those who would govern Spain in his absence. He spent Holy Week secluded in a nearby monastery and then on 1 May 1543, 'after the exequies and masse doon there for th'Emperatrice' (the fourth anniversary of her death), Charles boarded Doria's galleys and left for Genoa.[32]

HOW TO BE KING

Almost at once contrary winds forced the imperial fleet to spend ten days in the small Catalan port of Palamós, 130 kilometres north of Barcelona. Some thought Charles waited there to allow latecomers to join his fleet, but the English ambassador Edmund Bonner knew better: 'It was bothe to be ridde of the infinite nombre of suters that combered hym at Barcelone, and also, beyng there in quyetnes, to settle and ordre all thinges fullye here in Spayne at this his departing'. Charles used the 'quyetnes' to compose some of the longest documents he would ever write: two holograph papers of advice for Philip, who at age sixteen would serve as his regent of Spain. In the first document, 'although I do not consider myself qualified to give you appropriate rules, nevertheless I trust that God will guide my pen as I tell you what is necessary'. Charles then provided a checklist of how a responsible ruler should behave: honour God and rule justly; avoid making promises that would prove hard to keep; and so on.[33] The second document was perhaps the most remarkable political analysis ever committed to paper by an early modern ruler. Although many monarchs provided written advice to their heirs, Charles himself had received none; and in any case, given the size and complexity of his transatlantic empire, the past provided no model for the lessons he now wanted to impart.

The emperor stressed that 'I am writing and sending you this secret document which will be for you alone: you must therefore keep it secret, under lock and key where neither your wife nor any other living person can see it' – and then he launched into a pessimistic assessment of the risks inherent in his voyage to northern Europe, 'which is the most dangerous imaginable for my honour and reputation, for my life, and for my finances'. He apologized that he had 'placed the kingdoms and dominions that I will bequeath to you in such extreme need' so that, if he died, 'my finances will be in such a state that you will encounter many problems, because you will see how small and encumbered my revenues are just now'. Nevertheless, he asserted grandiloquently, if he should lose his life in their defence, 'I will have the satisfaction of having lost it while doing my duty and helping you'.

He then laid out his grand strategy, so that 'if I should either be taken prisoner or detained on this journey', his son would know 'what I am planning to do':

> Should the King of France anticipate my actions and mobilize against me during my sea voyage and journey, I intend to defend myself from him; and, since I cannot sustain the cost, I may be forced to engage him in battle, risking everything. But if I find that he has not attacked me, I will attack him via Flanders or Germany, and this attack will be made with the intention of fighting him, if he so desires or finds himself compelled to do so. In order to reduce his strength, I intend the duke of Alba to invade Languedoc with the German and Spanish troops that are in Perpignan, together with the soldiers that the grandees and prelates and cities will raise; and to ravage Provence with the galleys by sea, and Dauphiné and Piedmont with the troops I have in Italy.

It was an excellent plan but, Charles noted regretfully, 'right now this cannot be done, partly because the necessary victuals are lacking, partly through the shortage of money and supplies, and partly because there will be great reluctance to allow these troops to fight outside the kingdom; and also because my galleys will not be free until I know what the Turks are going to do.' In any case, 'the risk that this journey involves for my honour and reputation is that I am going to undertake something so uncertain that I do not know what benefit or effect it will bring: time is running out, money is short, and the enemy is forewarned and prepared.' Nevertheless, he pointed to a possible solution for the financial crisis. Although after the Cortes of Castile in 1538 'I swore never to request' an excise tax (*sisa*), he did not consider that his oath bound Philip. Therefore in an emergency:

> I will write to you at once in broad terms about what needs to be done, with a note in my own hand to tell you that it is time for you to prove your worth, in doing what you should, both to aid your father and because it behoves you to relieve our poverty. At that point you can stand firm and speak to everyone, both in particular and in general, urging them to contribute [to an excise tax].

'With that, with what comes in from the Indies (if it comes), and with what my subjects elsewhere will provide', the emperor hoped that his daring strategy would 'push our enemies down so far that they would then leave us room to recover and end the expenses they impose on us every day'.[34]

After repeating his injunction that his advice 'must be for you alone and you must keep it very secret', Charles reviewed the strengths and weaknesses of each of the ministers whom he had groomed to help him govern Spain, and on whose opinions the prince would have to rely 'during my absence, especially if God should call me to Him during this journey'. The emperor had already warned his son orally of 'the animosities and alliances and practically cabals that were forming or that have already been formed among my ministers, generating much unease among them and much disservice to us'; but now, despite the risk that his misgivings might one day become public knowledge (as indeed proved to be the case), he repeated them in writing, because 'in public they will exchange a thousand compliments and sweet nothings, but in private they will do the opposite, and so you must be very aware of what they are doing'. Charles warned that every senior minister 'will attempt to come to you under the cover of darkness in order to convince you to rely on him alone'.[35] He started with Tavera, who 'will approach you with humility and holiness. Honour him and believe him in matters of morality, because he will give you good advice in them. Require him to advise you well and impartially in the matters he discusses with you, and in choosing good, impartial people for positions of responsibility. But in other matters do not place yourself in his hands alone, now or ever.' Next came the duke of Alba: although in military matters 'he is the best we currently have in these kingdoms', Charles had excluded him from the prince's innermost circle of advisers both because 'it is best not to involve grandees in the government of the kingdom', and because 'ever since I have known him, I have found that he has great aspirations and seeks to become as powerful as possible, even though he came on the scene genuflecting, all humble and modest; so just think how he will behave around you, my son, because you are younger!'

The emperor then turned to Los Cobos. 'He does not work as hard as he used to do,' Charles lamented; moreover, although 'until now, he has shown little partiality, now it seems to me that he shows some signs of it'. Nevertheless, 'he has experience of all my affairs and is very knowledgeable about them. I am sure you will find no one else who can serve you better in those matters, and I believe he will do so well and honestly.' Therefore, 'you would do well to deal with him as I do, never alone and not giving him more authority than is contained in his instructions'. He concluded: 'Favour him, because he has served me well. I believe that many wish him harm: he does not deserve this.'[36]

Charles felt the same about critics of Juan de Zúñiga:

You must realize that since all the people who have surrounded you in the past and who currently surround you are indulgent and want to please you, this may make Don Juan seem harsh; but if he had been like the others, everything would always have been the way you wanted, and that is not good for anyone, not even older people, let alone youths without the knowledge or self-control that come with age and experience.

Nevertheless, the emperor continued, Zúñiga 'is somewhat biased, mainly against Los Cobos but also against the duke of Alba . . . I think this partiality comes mainly from not having received as many rewards from me as he wanted, and thinking that Los Cobos has not helped him (and has even reduced)' the rewards. 'In addition, he measures the disparity of [their] lineages and the length of time in my service' – a reference to the fact that Zúñiga belonged to a prominent noble lineage and had served Charles since 1506, whereas Los Cobos came from a humble background and only joined Charles in 1516. 'Notwithstanding these partialities,' the emperor concluded, 'you will not find anyone who can advise you better, and more to my liking, than these two men.'

As for information about the foreign affairs of these kingdoms, and about Italy, the Netherlands, Germany, France and England, and other kings and potentates and their governments, I am certain that no one understands them better, and has dealt with them more both in general and in particular, than Granvelle. I have been, and still am, very well served by him in these matters. He is faithful (I do not think I am mistaken about this) and you would do well to employ him.

Charles also praised Granvelle's son Antoine Perrenot, who had been consecrated bishop of Arras in Philip's presence the previous year. 'He is young but has begun well. I believe he will serve you well.'[37]

Charles was far more critical of three other senior ministers. He had little good to say about the prince's former preceptor, Silíceo. 'You know him – and we all know him – to be a good man; but he was certainly not, nor is he now, the most suitable person for your education. He has been too anxious to please you.' Currently 'he is your senior chaplain and your confessor. It would not be good if he wanted to indulge you in matters of conscience as he has done in your education.' The emperor therefore recommended that 'you should appoint a good friar to be your confessor'. He then turned to Loaysa, his former confessor, now archbishop of Seville and the minister charged with oversight of American affairs. 'He used to be excellent in matters of state and he still is in the main, although less so due to his ailments. I used to seek his advice, particularly in my choice of ministers and other personal matters, where he indeed offered very good counsel.' Philip could 'try him out as you see fit, but be aware that it seems to me that now he simply follows the lead of others. Whenever he wishes to leave for his diocese, you would do well to encourage him to do so, but tactfully and without disrespecting him.' Finally, the emperor evaluated Fernando de Valdés, president of the council of Castile.[38] Although 'he is a good man, he is not, as far as I can see, the sort of man that such a council needs, but I cannot find, nor do I know, anyone who would do the job much better'. The prince must make the best use possible of Valdés's limited talents.

The emperor thus provided Philip not only with a candid assessment of each minister, but also with advice on how to deal with those who proved self-serving or ineffective, as well as on how to get rid of an unsatisfactory senior official 'tactfully and without disrespecting him'. The difficulty of composing these critical evaluations is reflected in the numerous additions and subtractions on these pages – more than in any other part of his instructions (see Pl. 9).

After almost three decades in power the emperor recognized more clearly than most statesmen the limits of the possible. 'I am well aware, my son, that I could and should tell you many other things', but:

> Of those I *could* say, some are not relevant right now, as I have already told you the most substantial ones; and each day, as need be, they will be repeated. The things that I *should* say are so impenetrable and uncertain that I do not know how to describe them, nor whether I should even offer you advice about them, because they are full of confusion and contradictions, either because of the state of affairs, or because of conscience.

So, if Charles died on campaign, Philip must:

> Take good advice so that you can make your peace with God, because I am so undecided and confused about what I must do that someone in my situation can scarcely tell anyone in the same situation what to do. Also the necessity in which I find myself is what causes my confusion. As I struggle to do what I must, I find no better solution than to place myself in God's hands so that He can order everything to serve Him best. I will be satisfied with whatever He does and orders.

Having filled forty-eight folios, Charles read and revised both documents before signing each one *Yo el rey* and sending them secretly to his son.

The eminent Belgian archivist and historian Luis Prosper Gachard hailed the instructions as 'monuments of wisdom and foresight, born of a mature experience in the art of government, and a profound knowledge of men and affairs. They alone suffice to place Charles V in the first rank of the statesmen of his day.' He had given a masterclass in 'how to be king'. As Ambassador Bonner observed, although the emperor 'is not like of longe tyme' to return to Spain, because he would need 'to tarie in other places, especiallye in Flaunders and Germanie', he had 'taken good ordre for all thies his realmes' while absent on his high-risk mission.[39]

THE DESTRUCTION OF GUELDERS

Charles and his fleet of 140 vessels reached Genoa on 25 May 1543. Although impatient to begin his journey to Germany, the emperor detoured to meet Paul III again to try and resolve their differences. As Loaysa reminded him, 'experience has taught us that little advantage or reputation comes from these meetings, but I still recommend that Your Majesty should endure it and dissimulate in order to get everything possible out of the Holy See'; and during the four-day summit, Charles fruitlessly urged the pope to declare war on Francis, in view of his open alliance with the Turks. The pope declined on the grounds that if he did so, the king would follow the example of Henry VIII and renounce his obedience to Rome. The emperor had more success in convincing Paul to convene a general council of the Church in the city of Trent on the southern border of the Empire, and therefore a location acceptable to his German subjects, and to raise and pay 4,000 soldiers to fight the Turks in Hungary. Then, much to Charles's surprise, Paul offered to pay one million ducats if the emperor would invest his son Pier Luigi Farnese with Parma and Piacenza, formerly part of the duchy of Milan, which he argued would bring peace to Italy. Charles promised to think about it.[40]

As he prepared to leave, the emperor met Paolo Giovio, the most celebrated historian of his day. 'With a smile on his face he [Charles] said to me casually: "You need to take up your pen again, Giovio, and make haste to write down in your *History* everything that has happened thus far, because the war that is about to start will provide you with a major new assignment."' Slightly more modestly, the emperor also assured his Netherlands subjects that 'we have decided to come to your rescue in person' so that 'with your assistance and that of our Creator we will ensure that our enemies, whether they want to or not, will in future leave you in peace'.[41]

Initially, Charles found himself surrounded by enemies, just as he had predicted. Sultan Suleiman led another huge army into Hungary, capturing Esztergom (Gran) and Székesfehérvár (Stuhlweissenburg); Barbarossa led the Turkish fleet into the western Mediterranean, joining forces with the French to lay siege to Nice; and French forces invaded Hainaut. The emperor decided to ignore all these threats, and instead led his Spanish and Italian troops to Speyer, where he joined several regiments of German veterans, a siege train of 120 artillery pieces and a flotilla of boats and barges 'to conveye his hole armye downe [the Rhine] by water'. This gave Charles the initiative, because he could now choose whether to 'begynne with the Duke of Cleves first'; or enter 'the Moselle, and so by Luxenbourgh to entre ynto France; or to comme streight' to the Netherlands. Giovanni Battista Ricasoli, the Florentine ambassador travelling with Charles, ruled out the first option because 'making war on one of his own vassals would bring little glory, while the uncertain outcome of wars meant he could easily lose it' – but Ricasoli erred.[42]

Charles and his army left Speyer on 3 August and sailed rapidly downstream until they reached Bonn, where they disembarked. The emperor then reviewed his whole army in person before advancing on Düren, one of the best-defended cities ruled by William of Cleves, and when it refused his summons to surrender Charles gave the order to 'punish its disobedience and rebellion, as an example to others'. His Spanish and Italian troops were happy to oblige: after executing a daring assault, they slaughtered some 700 defenders. All the rest were captured, and the emperor decreed that 'those who are most guilty – especially those who are our vassals in the Netherlands – will be punished'. According to a participant, in his presence 'they hanged prisoners found to be his vassals and severed two fingers from any German who had used them to swear an oath of obedience to the emperor'.[43]

As in his previous campaigns, Charles led from the front. Just before the final assault he mingled with his troops 'wearing full armour with a tunic made of cloth-of-gold, to make himself look good and to encourage his soldiers, as well as to communicate the hatred he bore the place and the revenge he wished to wreak on it'; and when someone, observing him 'armed and mounted', suggested that he should retire in case a cannonball hit him, 'His Majesty replied that this was no time to abandon his men, even if a cannonball took out his eyes'. Ambassador Ricasoli scoffed that 'He serves as general, colonel, sergeant-major, everything. The effort that he puts into going everywhere in full armour, constantly at work and wanting to see and do every little thing is truly astonishing. He is so diligent in this regard that he will soon be blamed because his desire to know everything will delay the campaign.'[44] Once again, the ambassador erred. Anxious to avoid the fate of Düren, one town after another surrendered and on 7 September 1543 William of Cleves, protected by a safe-conduct, came to the imperial camp, 'threw himself on his knees, and with his hands clasped begged forgiveness'. As he had done at Ghent three years before, the emperor looked severe as he 'reminded the duke of his past offences' and pretended for some time that he would take harsher measures. Even after William received permission to kiss the imperial hand, he had to sign an ignominious settlement that ceded all of Guelders to Charles. Soon afterwards the Estates of his new duchy swore allegiance to the emperor, and in return he promised to respect their traditional privileges.[45]

To Nicholas Wotton, an English diplomat travelling with Charles, this seemed:

> One of the straungest thinges that chawnsidde [chanced] these menye yeres, for I cowde never have beleevidde that for one towne cowardelye loste by assaulte, suche a great and stronge cowntrey shulde have ben

holelye lossed, withowte yn a maner stroke strickinge, so that now Cesar [Charles] may as well wryte to his frendis, as [Julius] Cesar wrote to his frendis, *I came, I saw, I conquered.*

Although the new Caesar did not use this presumptuous phrase himself, he told the duke of Alba that 'I rejoiced not a little with the victory that God granted me in Guelders, thanks be to Him for the great reward He has given me in removing such a thorn in my side'.[46] He had every reason to rejoice: the campaign had made safe the eastern border of the Netherlands (an achievement that had eluded both his father and his grandfather), and 'he had gained reputation everywhere, especially among the princes of Germany, all of whom are already trembling because he had obtained in a few days what they had thought and hoped would take him many months'. The king of France, by contrast, had 'lost all credit in Germany, where he is belittled, blamed and reproached by everyone' for abandoning his ally. To Wotton, 'It appeerithe that God hathe blyndidde, and entendithe to punisshe, the French Kinge, that hathe none otherwyse assistidde the duke of Cleves, for he moughte by hym have wroughte more displeasur to th'Emperour withe a smalle powre, then by hym selfe he shall be able to do withe fowre tymes as muche.' Now, Francis 'is lyke to have the warre holelye at home, and to have his owne cowntrey destroyed'.[47]

Campaigning nevertheless took its toll on Charles. He lost so much weight that when he tried on his armour he found it 'a greate deale to wyde for hym, notwithstandyng that he made hym a greate doublet' filled with cotton to wear as an undergarment. When he declared that he would join his army besieging Landrecies, on the French frontier, and force Francis to risk a pitched battle, a horrified Granvelle did his best to dissuade him. It was, he told his master, 'the most dangerous thing I have ever seen you undertake, and I would rather die a hundred deaths than approve this decision'. It was rash to campaign 'in a place so full of marshes that even the healthy often die': therefore Charles's decision to risk his life on campaign 'was to tempt God, and no confessor or theologian would approve. You are no longer a prince who can undertake the ventures appropriate to young men,' Granvelle concluded, and 'you should not venture your person more than your health will allow. If some misfortune should occur (which God forfend), it will jeopardize and efface all the good things that you could have achieved – without any adequate excuse to offer to God or the world.' After listening impassively to his principal adviser, Charles confessed, took communion, and left to join his army in the camp before Landrecies.[48]

At first, the emperor concentrated on his siege guns, which included some mortars that lobbed explosive bullets into the town (evidently an innovation). At least one of his senior commanders condemned this as 'a waste of time' because 'the fortress cannot be taken by force; but the emperor obsessed about opening the battery'; but Charles, who commanded 36,000 infantry and 6,000 cavalry, now sought battle – perhaps encouraged by Loaysa, who urged him to lure the French into 'another engagement, which will be worse for them than Pavia'.[49] When news arrived that Francis and his field army approached, Charles consulted his council of war and on 3 November 1543 drew up his forces 'in battle order. They then began to advance across fields so flat that no one could avoid seeing them', hoping that his 'enemies would remember all the boasts that they had made of wanting to come and find him and give battle'. As he directed operations, Charles lost his temper: 'A great lord kept asking him questions, until the emperor rudely told him to stop. The lord said "Is Your Majesty annoyed?" To which the emperor replied: "Yes, I'm annoyed because you are old and yet you keep asking me questions!"' No doubt this rebuke reflected the high stakes. If the two armies fought, wrote Bernardo Navagero, the Venetian ambassador, 'it will be the greatest thing ever seen in our time' – but in the end nothing happened. Perhaps remembering Pavia, Francis lost his nerve and withdrew his army 'at full speed' under cover of darkness. The imperial host 'gave chase as soon as we found out, th'emperour himself being on horsseback with theym', but they only captured a few enemy soldiers, 'of whome th'emperour commaunded to kill all such as were subjectes of th'empire'.[50]

Charles reconvened his council of war and pointed out 'that the tyme of the yere is farre past, and fowle wether now cumme at hand'. In addition 'the cuntre rownde abowte [was] sore wastyd, and vitayles hard to cumme by, so as this yere no good exploit cowld be don'. Francis had demobilized his army, with 'a gret part of the same bestowed in garrisons', and Charles proposed that he should 'do the same, asking all our oppynions, if we thought [it] not good so to do'. Everyone agreed, but before his troops dispersed the emperor entered the city of Cambrai, technically an imperial fief whose ruler had favoured France during the last campaign, and ordered the construction of a citadel. 'Without this,' he informed Ferdinand, 'Cambrai and the surrounding area would be lost to the Holy Roman Empire', whereas 'the citadel being built will safeguard its authority'. The king of France might have captured Landrecies, Charles told Navagero smugly, 'but I forced him to flee', adding 'The more the king tries to be a

Turk and a Lutheran, the more I rejoice, hoping that God will defend His cause.'[51]

PREPARATION

Both rulers now prepared for the next campaign, starting with a desperate search for allies. Francis had already compelled his subjects to evacuate the port of Toulon in order to accommodate the crews aboard Barbarossa's fleet of 115 galleys and 43 ships, which spent the winter there at French expense, ready to join in a French assault on Genoa, Naples or Sardinia in the spring; but in March 1544, Barbarossa realized that his host lacked the resources to mount a Mediterranean campaign and two months later he led his fleet back to Istanbul. Francis's ostentatious alliance with the Ottoman had alienated all other Christian rulers, Lutheran as well as Catholic, for no gain.[52] Charles, by contrast, finalized an impressive strategy for the coming campaign with Henry VIII. In January 1544 the parties:

> ... agreed that th'emperor shall with his armye make invasion into the realm of Ffraunce by the country of Champaign, and so marche towards Parys; and the kings majestie make the sayd invasion by suche passaige over the ryver of Somme as in the tyme of passaige shalbe thought most facible and easie, and from thens marche as commoditie maye serve towards Parys.

Both monarchs would invade in person no later than 20 June 1544, each at the head of an army of 32,000 men and 100 guns.[53]

Knowing nothing of this, Francis diverted his elite troops to make another effort to recapture Milan, and on 14 April 1544 at Ceresole d'Alba they won a dramatic victory over Vasto. According to Martin du Bellay, who as military governor of Piedmont saw his dreams about to come true: 'If the emperor had seen the duchy of Milan laid waste and in danger of being lost, especially given the powerful [Francophile] factions in the kingdom of Naples, he would have been compelled to re-deploy his forces to defend what he held rather than to conquer the territories of others, at the risk of gaining nothing.' But du Bellay's vision of war was out of date. On hearing of the defeat, the English ambassador at the imperial court observed that 'It seemith that the Frenche menne have had more glorye than profyt' from Ceresole, 'for I cannot perceive that sithe that tyme they have gotten anye one towne or castel, or that there is anye lykelihode of anye maner of innovation yn Lombardye for it.' Charles agreed, telling the Venetian ambassador that 'I grieve only for the poor soldiers who died in my service', because 'I have left the region strongly defended and well provided'.[54]

The emperor referred to a development in western warfare later known as the military revolution: transforming positional warfare so that defence became superior to offence, rendering battles largely superfluous. The architect Gian Maria Olgiati had already constructed a chain of bastions with interlocking fields of fire around Genoa before he moved to Milan to redesign existing works and add a constellation of star-shaped artillery fortresses to defend the duchy: in all, he would design or build new-style defences in almost seventy places. His circuit around Milan, anchored on the huge Sforza castle, successfully defended the city down to the 1790s, and even today dominates the traffic flow of the inner city. The Habsburgs also commissioned artillery fortresses north of the Alps. In Hungary, Italian engineers added bastions to the principal border fortresses, and in the Netherlands they provided numerous new-style defences along the French frontier, with powerful strongpoints in reserve. The citadel of Ghent, built after the revolt of 1540, boasted walls 385 metres long and over seven metres thick; the enceinte around Antwerp, begun after the attack by Guelders forces in 1542, extended for almost five kilometres and included nine bastions.

Across the frontier, by 1544 over a hundred Italian engineers worked under the general direction of Girolamo Marini to upgrade the defences of selected French strongholds, but they concentrated on fortresses along the northern frontier and a few outposts in Italy, largely neglecting the eastern border of the kingdom. Therefore, just as the Maginot Line in the 1930s did not continue into Belgium, so the new-style defences of Francis did not continue into Champagne. In both cases, it proved a fatal flaw.

Charles spotted his rival's weakness and sought to exploit it. First, he convened the imperial Diet at Speyer and sought its military support for an attack on France. Initially, he seems to have considered this mission impossible, informing the nuncio that 'when he considered the misfortunes and burdens that beat down on my head almost hourly, I want to die' – a remarkable admission for such a staunch Catholic – but he persisted. On 23 May 1544, in return for a promise to abandon for ever the cause of his brother-in-law Christian II, he signed a peace treaty with Danish diplomats; and on 10 June, in return for a promise that religious toleration in the Empire would continue unchanged until 'a general, free Christian council of the German nation' met to resolve all differences, the Diet declared that 'one must deem the king of France as much of an enemy to Christendom as the sultan, and use force against him as well as against the Turks'. It authorized Charles to raise 24,000 infantry and 4,000 cavalry 'to be employed partelye against the Turke, and partelye against the Frenche kinge as it shulde seeme beste' to him.[55]

Following this triumph, Charles spent three weeks in Metz awaiting the arrival of his siege artillery and reinforcements, including cavalry raised by Duke Maurice of Saxony and Albert Alcibiades of Brandenburg-Külmbach, two prominent German Lutheran leaders. Given the risks inherent in war, he also made another codicil to his will that explicitly revoked the various marriage commitments made after he met Francis at Aigues Mortes. Since, he claimed, 'experience has constantly shown us' that the same person could not govern both Spain and the Netherlands, because of the need to 'go from one to the other to take the measures that each requires, as we have often been forced to do at great risk, effort and expense', if he and Philip both died he stipulated that his daughter María would marry his nephew Maximilian and together they would rule Spain and its dependencies. His younger daughter Joanna would marry Maximilian's younger brother 'regardless of what we have solemnly agreed with the king of Portugal concerning her marriage to his son the prince', and together they would rule the Netherlands. Perhaps because of this breathtaking breach of previous promises, Charles sent a sealed copy of his codicil to Los Cobos, with orders to place it unopened with his will; and although he also sent 'a summary of the main points, which you can show' to the prince, Los Cobos must 'read it out to him, so that only you and he know about it'.[56]

Charles now concentrated on abasing France. Although his reliance on maps when he invaded Provence eight years before had provoked ridicule (p. 256), he now commissioned a huge panoramic map that showed Dijon, the capital of Burgundy on the far left and Paris on the far right, as well as all the major rivers – Marne, Seine and Yonne – and the bridges across them (Pl. 23). In the event, Charles never crossed any of the rivers, but he and his army still came within seventy kilometres of the French capital.[57]

'TO PUSH OUR ENEMIES DOWN'

The imperial campaign began in May 1544 with a surprise attack that recaptured all the places in Luxemburg taken by the French the previous year. The victors then turned south to Champagne, and invaded France – following not only the strategic plan recently agreed with Henry but also the route towards Paris followed by Charles the Bold of Burgundy two generations before (as recorded in one of the emperor's favourite books: the *Mémoires* of Philippe de Commynes, an eyewitness). Charles's forces, like those of his ancestor, initially made rapid progress. Commercy, which Francis had expected to resist for three weeks, surrendered after a furious three-day bombardment, allowing the imperial army to cross the River Meuse, and on 4 July it reached the Marne at St Dizier – but there it encountered for the first time an artillery fortress, designed and defended by Marini himself (Map 5).

The emperor was in high spirits – some thought they 'had not seen him as healthy, handsome and happy in the past ten years' – but others worried about the risks involved. 'Counting all the troops that he has in all his dominions,' the ambassador from Ferrara observed, 'the cost of this war to His Majesty cannot be much less than 500,000 ducats'; and, no doubt recalling the recent Algiers fiasco, he added: 'A delay of twelve or twenty days, or an unforeseen event, can have immense consequences.' His Venetian colleague agreed: each day's delay 'is seen as disadvantageous for the emperor and a boon to the king of France ... It is rare for things to turn out as planned, and even the best-laid plans always encounter some unforeseen obstacle.'[58] The first obstacle emerged just after Charles reached St Dizier. Worried that food and munitions alike were running short, he launched his Spanish and Italian troops in a surprise assault, just as he had done at Düren, but this time the defenders repelled them with heavy losses. Four hundred kilometres away, however, Henry VIII disembarked at Calais and joined the English and Netherlands troops besieging Montreuil and Boulogne, forcing Francis to withdraw troops from Italy and preventing him from relieving St Dizier. Once again, the emperor held the initiative.

After discussing with his council of war 'what to do for the rest of the year', on 20 July Charles explained his strategy to Marie. First, he would use artillery and mines to reduce St Dizier, because 'otherwise the enemy could harass my army and interrupt its supply of victuals'; then, 'as we had always planned, we will march on Châlons', further down the Marne. Henry's participation had led him to 'put on one side my personal interest in this enterprise, which is to enter the duchy of Burgundy, where I might have conquered some places and carried out some notable exploit'; but now 'we could not find a better target than Châlons', because 'it will astonish and hurt the king of France and his subjects more than any attack elsewhere; and the aim of this army has always been to penetrate into the heart of this kingdom, to reduce our enemies to reason'. As usual, Charles also

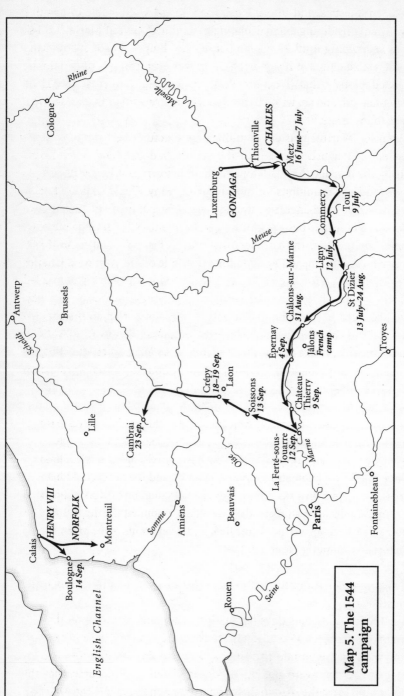

Map 5. The 1544 campaign

In August and September 1544, Charles led an army of 40,000 men and an artillery train through France virtually unopposed, travelling along the north bank of the River Marne from St Dizier to La Ferté-sous-Jouarre, seventy kilometres from Paris. He then turned north and marched towards an English invasion force led by Henry VIII – but at Crépy, Charles signed an advantageous separate peace with France.

considered logistics, and in particular 'how long I will be able to pay this army. After considering and calculating everything,' he told Marie, 'I think we can keep going until 25 September, but no longer.' While recognizing (like the ambassadors at his court) that 'in war everything is uncertain', he concluded piously that 'I cannot think of anything else that would be pleasing to God; and so, with His aid, we will do everything we can' to force Francis to his knees.[59]

Thanks to Marini's mastery of military architecture, St Dizier only capitulated on 17 August, after which the victors had to spend several days repairing the damage they had done so that the town could serve as a staple to store food and munitions for the advancing army. This unexpected delay forced Charles to change his strategy: he now planned 'to reconnoitre Châlons as if I mean to besiege it, although my intention, with God's blessing, is to press on to Paris'. The discovery that Francis had collected some 45,000 men in a fortified camp at Jâlons on the south side of the Marne led Charles to modify this plan too. He broke camp in the middle of the night, and led his army and artillery in a forced march by moonlight towards Épernay, where he hoped to cross the Marne and attack Jâlons from an unexpected direction; but he arrived just after the French secured the town and fortified the only suitable bridge across the river. Six years later, when dictating his *Memoirs*, the emperor indulged in a cautious counterfactual speculation about this outcome:

> If it is legitimate to pass judgement on the things that could have happened, one might well believe that if His Majesty had been able to reach Épernay that day (which he could not, even though it was less than three miles [five kilometres] away), so that he and the army could have crossed the river on a stone bridge in that town and on bridges of boats . . . they could have attacked the French encampment on the hill at a point that had not yet been fortified, and God would have given the victory to whomever He chose.[60]

The emperor therefore reverted to his original plan: to march down the Marne to Paris.

The foreign diplomats travelling with the emperor marvelled at the lack of French resistance: no skirmishers harassed the imperial host as it spread out to forage and to plunder; no troops protected the communities that lay in its path. As Navagero put it, 'Whoever would have thought that the French would leave the road to their own ruin open like this?' The Mantuan ambassador, Camillo Capilupo, who had considerable military experience, noted that 'between them, friends and enemies burned both sides of the river until the whole country seemed to be on fire. It was a terrible sight, and even the hardest heart was moved.'[61] As Nicholas Wotton observed, because 'th'emperor hathe deceyved the Frenche king's expectation, for he looked not for hym so nigh unto hym this yere', and because 'we have as fayre wether as we can wisshe and find plenty of al thinges by the waye', the imperial army advanced so fast that even larger towns failed to prepare adequate defences and instead surrendered without resistance. At one point Charles, who trav-elled with the vanguard, summoned a Burgundian cavalry unit 'and asked us what part of the country we were in'. In Rome, according to Giovio, 'Everyone here is in suspense, with sweat pouring from their foreheads, with supporters of both monarchs balanced between hope and fear' as they awaited news of the outcome.[62]

They did not have long to wait. On 12 September, with some of his troops at La Ferté-sous-Jouarre, only seventy kilometres from Paris, Charles suddenly turned north and forced Soissons to surrender, thereby gaining a bridgehead across the River Aisne, the only major obstacle between him and Henry – whose army forced the surrender of Boulogne two days later. The allies were free at last to join forces and advance on Paris.

This double blow placed Francis under intense pressure to make peace. He had tried to engage the emperor in negotiations almost since the start of the campaign, but (as Charles observed with satisfaction in his *Memoirs*) he tried 'much harder after he saw His Majesty bypass Châlons with his army'. The emperor played for time, reminding Francis that he could not make a separate peace without Henry but (he added smugly) 'since he had advanced so far into France, he had no news of what the king [of England] was doing nor had he the means of sending him his own news'. On 7 September, Charles secured a safe-conduct for Antoine Perrenot to travel to Boulogne and inform Henry of the peace terms under discussion, and to ascertain 'if he wishes to continue the war, and for how long? If he wishes to set his army on the march immediately? And if so, which route will he take?' Perrenot also carried a secret ultimatum: unless Henry 'was prepared to invade immediately, I will be compelled to withdraw my army and accept the terms offered by the French'.[63]

The bluster concealed a major dilemma. Should Charles conclude a separate peace with Francis that secured most of his goals, even though it meant abandoning his English ally, or should he coordinate with Henry a joint advance on Paris that would compel Francis to make even more concessions? Granvelle strongly endorsed the first alternative. Continuing the campaign, he argued, would mean ravaging more French territory, 'which would achieve nothing except to increase and perpetuate the enmity of the king of France and his subjects'. It would also oblige Charles to pay and supply the garrisons of the towns he had captured, but do nothing to unify Christendom as a prelude for a new crusade against the Turks. Granvelle concluded his advice with what a later age would call a dose of *Realpolitik*: 'There is, sire, a maxim in affairs of state, just as in other matters: that one must pay attention to the reality of the matters under discussion, to determine what is possible and what God and reason suggest is attainable, rather than take big risks because of personal considerations, as seems to be the case here.' Granvelle warned that Henry would never keep his promise to march on Paris: instead, once he had strengthened the defences of Boulogne he would go home. Charles must make a separate peace before that happened.[64]

Two practical considerations reinforced this rationale. Although the weather had been mostly favourable since the surrender of St Dizier, at any moment autumn rain could prevent further progress; and without money, the troops became restless – indeed on one occasion some German troops 'became so mutinous that the emperor had twenty of them drowned in the Marne and struck several more with his hand'.[65] Charles had originally calculated he could afford to campaign only until 25 September, and that date was fast approaching. Los Cobos warned that 'in all Spain there is nowhere to raise a ducat this year or next'; Loaysa urged him to settle as soon as possible 'even if it means forfeiting some of your rights'; and, after stressing that 'we have no way to raise money here', Prince Philip asserted that 'you would now gain as much honour in the world if everyone sees that when it is in your power to destroy your enemy, you granted him peace'. As for the Netherlands, the emperor complained that 'even though he had enough money there to pay his troops, he had no way of getting to it'.[66]

His situation appeared unsustainable until Francis received news of the fall of Boulogne, and in desperation agreed to concede virtually anything Charles asked in return for an immediate peace. Shortly afterwards, Perrenot arrived at the imperial headquarters bearing Henry's grudging consent to a separate settlement and on 18 September, at Crépy near Laon, ministers acting in the name not only of Francis but also of his two sons promised to surrender all claims to Naples and the Netherlands; to end the alliance with the Turks and instead contribute troops to a new crusade to be led by Charles; to return all conquests made since the truce of Nice (including

Landrecies); and to provide hostages to guarantee his compliance. In return, the emperor agreed to restore all his conquests within France and to renounce for ever his claim to the duchy of Burgundy. He also repeated his proposal that the duke of Orléans could marry either his elder daughter María, whose dowry would be the Netherlands (albeit Charles would remain sovereign until his death), or else Ferdinand's daughter Anna, whose dowry would be Milan (to take effect within one year of the treaty). The emperor promised to decide between the alternatives within four months, and Francis swore to evacuate Savoy-Piedmont as soon as the transaction took place, and to endow Orléans with a large appanage of territories in the heart of France.[67]

The next day, Francis signed a secret treaty that promised to provide both Charles and Ferdinand 'with our full assistance and favour in the reduction and pacification of religious discord in Germany whenever it is required'; to declare himself the 'enemy of those who seek to prevent the said pacification'; and to allow 'the assistance of infantry and cavalry that we have promised against the Turks to be used if necessary against the said heretics'. In addition, the king would send a full delegation to a general council, to be held at Trent 'or wherever the emperor wishes', to reform the abuses of the Church and end the religious schism; and he would persuade the Swiss cantons to return all territory that had once belonged to the duke of Savoy, including Geneva. Finally, if Henry VIII ever declared war on Charles, Francis promised that 'we will publicly proclaim ourselves to be the enemy of the said king of England'.[68]

Charles had won a stunning victory. For ten weeks he had marched through France at the head of some 40,000 men and a large artillery train, covering almost 300 kilometres, and he had either captured and garrisoned, or sacked and burned, the towns and villages along his route. His arch-rival had proved powerless to stop him, and in the end granted his every demand. The emperor had not only recovered the 'reputation' lost at Algiers, but also achieved the ambitious goal that he had outlined to his son eighteen months earlier: 'to push our enemies down so far that they would then leave us room to recover'.[69]

Paolo Giovio agreed. Upon learning the public terms of the peace of Crépy, he confessed to a friend, 'I don't know whether to laugh or cry over this peace', which would end hostilities and thus spare innocent civilians, and also create a united Christian front against the Turks, but left Charles supreme in Italy. He found it hard to believe that Francis 'had fought for the duchy of Milan for twenty-three years almost continuously to maintain his reputation, with so much money, effort and damage, only to sacrifice it with a stroke of his pen'. The king's promise to provide hostages while receiving none in return seemed particularly humiliating. 'The only trick' that Charles could still play on the French, Giovio chuckled, 'was to seduce their women'.[70] He was unaware of the secret clauses of the treaty: the emperor's next trick would be played not on the women of France but on the Lutherans of Germany.

TWELVE

SETTLING SCORES, PART II:
GERMANY AND ITALY, 1545–8

THE ALTERNATIVE

Having won another war against France, Charles now had to win the peace. This was not easy: after the imperial army demobilized, removing the immediate danger, many French men and women denounced the treaty of Crépy – led by the dauphin, who registered a legal protest against renouncing his claims to Naples, Flanders and the rest, as required by the peace. He also resented the provisions in favour of his brother the duke of Orléans, who would receive extensive lands in France as well as either the Netherlands or Milan, because they threatened to create a dangerous counterweight to royal authority.

Charles, for his part, regretted the need to alienate any part of his empire, but initially sublimated his sorrow in the normal way: in pastimes and prayers. On 2 November 1544, accompanied by his sister Eleanor and Orléans, he watched in the marketplace of Brussels as '60 men of armes, wel trymed after the Morisco, shewed the feate of the Jugo de Cannes'. Afterwards he retired to a monastery 'to be in quiet shryven and communicated', because he had not done so at All Saints. Then he went hunting and injured his knee, which forced him to transact business 'sitting in a very lowe chayre, with his legges wrapped in a blak cloth, and layde forth as high as his bodye'.[1]

The treaty of Crépy allowed Charles four months to decide between the Alternative (as it came to be known) of ceding either Milan or the Netherlands, and he spent the time consulting his close relatives, his ministers and his allies. Henry VIII, who was the first to provide advice '[out] of our freendly and amycable love and affection', strongly opposed giving away the Netherlands, 'considering the greate charges and defrayes th'empereur hath bene enforced to make by reason of these warres, and what dammage and trouble his subjectes have susteyned by the same', and also considering that the Infanta María would be 'heritier to th'emperour of all that he hath', should Prince Philip die. He therefore advised Charles to allow Orléans to marry one of Ferdinand's daughters. Moreover he noted that, as an imperial fief, Milan might 'after the deceasse of th'empereur, cume into sume controversie to whom it shalle descende, and yet canne not, when it is hadde, be kept without inestymable charges' – in other words, it was a poisoned chalice.[2] It was an excellent analysis, and many of Charles's ministers would concur.

On 1 November 1544, Alonso de Idiáquez, 'the chief manne abowte th'emperor that medelithe yn the affaires of Spayne', arrived in Valladolid where he explained to Philip and his advisers 'everything necessary to understand perfectly Your Majesty's intentions' concerning the Alternative. While the prince went to ascertain his sister María's preference, his senior ministers met 'four or five times' during his absence to discuss the options.[3] The prince ordered a secretary to record the opinion of each councillor at these meetings, and the record (punctuated with sighs that some 'gave a long speech', and others 'spoke at such length that it is not necessary to write it all down') clearly revealed the extent of 'the animosities and alliances and practically cabals' among his ministers that Charles had described to his son two years before (p. 290). Loaysa, who spoke first, noted that Charles had recently offered to cede the Netherlands to the French, but 'they did not want to accept', so there seemed little point in repeating the exercise. Moreover, since Francis 'had always preferred the duchy of Milan, he was convinced that even if we give him the Netherlands it would not bring an enduring peace because it is not what he wants'. Cardinal Tavera, who spoke next, took a similar position for different reasons. Not long after Charles left the peninsula in 1529, the cardinal had urged him to 'turn his thoughts to the conquest of Africa' which 'in the end . . . was what would last and could be bequeathed to his successors', whereas 'gains in Italy are a transitory glory'. He now repeated his view 'that no king of Spain should hold Milan, because of the great and continual expense that accompany it'. By contrast, 'what matters to His Majesty, and what will retain his pre-eminence in the Empire and Germany is possession of the Netherlands', because 'it played an essential role in keeping the king of France in check'. The duke of Alba, the only member of the council with practical experience of all parts of his master's empire in Europe, disagreed:

> [Milan] is the gateway through which we come and go to Germany and the Netherlands, and provide for the conservation of those states and maintain the authority and obedience of the Empire. Without Milan it

would seem that [the Empire] cannot be governed, and the kingdoms and states of Your Majesty will remain separated and divided from each other.

The duke supported his argument with a domino theory: 'Given the greed and ambition of the French, it goes without saying that if they gain a foothold in Milan they will try to gain Naples and Sicily, and Your Majesty will not be able to send them any help', because whoever held Milan would control Genoa, and 'no help can come from Spain because we will lack any port between Catalonia and Naples capable of sheltering a fleet'. Charles must therefore retain Milan and surrender the Netherlands.[4]

After presiding over a final meeting of senior ministers, Prince Philip summarized their divergent opinions in a letter to his father. Five councillors followed Loaysa and Tavera: Charles should retain the Netherlands and marry the duke of Orléans to Ferdinand's daughter, with Milan as her dowry. Five others agreed with Alba: Spain could not defend the Netherlands effectively from French aggression – indeed, they noted, previous attempts to do so had dangerously depleted the resources available to defend Spain and Spanish Italy – whereas Milan was the hub and heart of the entire empire. The prince himself sided with the second group: he advised his father to allow Orléans to marry María, with the Netherlands as her dowry.[5]

Charles's Netherlands ministers vehemently disagreed. Marie and her council prepared a dossier on 'Matters to consider concerning the declaration to be made on the Alternative contained in the treaty of Crépy'. It took the form of questions and answers, including:

- 'Which of the Netherlands nobles should the emperor consult on the matter, and should it be done individually or collectively?' (Answer: Do it individually, because it would then be easier to keep the consultation secret.)
- 'Would it be possible to find some expedient to gain time and defer the declaration?' (Answer: Not without raising French suspicions that the emperor might renege.)
- 'If His Majesty decides to allow the marriage of his daughter' to Orléans, with the Netherlands as her dowry, 'how will he secure the consent of his subjects here'? (Answer: 'Everyone here would prefer to remain the subjects of His Imperial Majesty and his descendants, failing whom the children of the king of the Romans [Ferdinand]. They would accept no one else.')

The council also reminded Charles that 'he is a native born in this country, who knows the great loyalty of his subjects here, the immense contributions, losses and damage they have sustained, their precarious location surrounded by enemies, and the danger of religious confusion'. They begged him 'not to abandon them or let them out of our hands as long as we live'.[6]

Charles's subjects in Milan made similar entreaties. A delegation arrived in November 1544 'to requyre th'emperour that He delyver not the state of Mylan to the Duke of Orléans', in part because the transition from Habsburg to Valois rule would force into exile those who had supported the emperor, and return their vengeful enemies to power. Charles had intended to travel to Germany to discuss his dilemma with Ferdinand in person, but 'my health has not allowed us to meet as we planned'. He therefore sounded out his brother 'by letter and via some of his trusted officials', ascertaining that Ferdinand, too, favoured the cession of Milan.[7]

According to the Venetian ambassador, Bernardo Navagero, the bitter debates on this dilemma at his court left 'the emperor greatly troubled in mind, because he does not want to renege on his faith and his word, yet every day he becomes more aware how fulfilling his promises might harm him and his descendants'. The ambassador thought the stress undermined the emperor's health, and he suffered another attack of gout which (Charles told his brother) 'started in my left shoulder, with pain throughout my arm and now my hand' – he started to put his left arm in a sling – and when it spread to his feet, he took to his bed. He also started a course of guayacán (*lignum vitae*), a remedy for gout recently imported from the Caribbean, but it produced jaundice, a urinary tract infection and a severe fever that kept the emperor 'weak and restless, constantly getting in and out of bed'. He could not procrastinate indefinitely, however, and in February 1545 he announced that 'we have resolved to give the duchy of Milan to the duke of Orléans', who would marry Ferdinand's daughter.[8]

PREPARING TO EXTIRPATE THE LUTHERANS

According to Charles's *Memoirs*, the swift collapse of Guelders in 1543 'had opened his eyes and alerted him to new possibilities, so that henceforth it seemed that the great pride of the Lutherans could be overcome by force, and that it could be done very easily if one chose the best time and strategy'.[9] An unrelated series of developments inside and outside Germany now permitted the emperor to turn those 'new possibilities' into reality.

The formation of the Schmalkaldic League in 1531 provided Lutheran princes and city-states with some protection. The League's lawyers blocked all attempts by the imperial courts to restrict freedom of spiritual and secular action (including the secularization of Church property), and their troops provided an effective defence – and sometimes offence. In addition, in 1534, at the head of an army funded by France, Landgrave Philip of Hesse forced the Habsburgs to evacuate Württemberg and restored its former ruler who soon imposed Lutheran worship. In 1541, however, Charles concluded a treaty with the landgrave: the emperor declared that since 'you have gained our affection and friendship, we have pardoned and forgiven everything that you may have planned or done against us or our brother'; and in return the landgrave promised not to ally with any enemy of the emperor (including France), and instead to support him both in the Diet and in international affairs.[10] The following year, together with Elector John Frederick of Saxony, the landgrave took advantage of his new alliance with the emperor to attack and occupy the lands of the Catholic Duke Henry of Brunswick, on the pretext that he had threatened two Lutheran towns. On this occasion, the princes failed to consult the other members of the League before acting; and when they belatedly demanded funds to maintain their troops, the Lutheran cities (which provided more than half the League's budget) refused, asserting that the occupation had 'until now brought us no benefits. Instead we have suffered damages and disadvantage because of this affair, and we have no reason to expect any advantage to come from it in the future.'[11] Charles offered to place the duchy of Brunswick 'in a third pair of hands' while the protagonists settled their differences but they refused. Instead in September 1545 hostilities resumed until Duke Henry surrendered against a promise 'that he would be treated as he deserved'. The landgrave promptly sent his rival to prison, prevented all contact with the outside world, and pressured him to convert to Lutheranism.[12]

The Brunswick war created a rift between the landgrave and his son-in-law, Duke Maurice of Saxony, who had personally assured Henry of Brunswick that he would receive generous terms if he surrendered. A rift already existed between Maurice and Elector John Frederick. The Saxon territories were the most extensive in the Empire after those of the Habsburgs, but a half-century earlier they had been partitioned: John Frederick held the Electoral title and ruled the larger segment, including Wittenberg where Luther lived and preached, leaving his cousin Maurice with a smaller segment. The rivalry between the two culminated in 1542 when John Frederick occupied some lands that had been administered jointly with Maurice, driving out the latter's officials. Unable to withstand his powerful cousin, Maurice decided to ingratiate himself with the Habsburgs: in 1542 he fought with Ferdinand against the Turks in Hungary; in 1543 and 1544 he fought with Charles against Cleves and France, and indicated that he might be willing to help the imperial cause yet more in return for support against John Frederick.[13]

Charles might not have dared to exploit these divisions among the German Lutherans without important international developments. In 1545, Francis launched an amphibious assault on England that occupied part of the Isle of Wight, and the following year Sultan Suleiman sent his army against Persia and his navy against the Portuguese in the Indian Ocean. The Schmalkaldic League thus lost simultaneously their most powerful foreign supporters. Charles nevertheless ordered the imperial Diet to convene at Worms in another effort to reconcile his Lutheran and Catholic subjects. He arrived in the city on 16 May, his tender left arm still in a sling, and two days later granted an audience to Cardinal Alessandro Farnese, the pope's secretary of state (and also his grandson). When the cleric began by apologizing for past disagreements, Charles graciously interrupted him – 'There was no need to talk about the past; we should open a new book' – and then Farnese revealed the purpose of his secret mission: to convey Pope Paul's offer to assist Charles with men and money if he agreed to wage war against the Lutherans.[14]

The emperor had already dispatched an envoy to Istanbul with instructions to liaise with the diplomats sent by Ferdinand and by France in order to seal a deal that would prevent 'those who have deviated from our Holy Faith, who call themselves Protestants, from taking advantage of the war in Hungary to reinforce their errors and make exorbitant demands', as they had done before. A few days later he informed Cardinal Farnese that although he welcomed the pope's offer of assistance, it needed to be improved before he could commit to a campaign. A month later a new papal offer arrived: if the emperor declared war on the Lutherans now, the pope would contribute 200,000 ducats in cash, with another 100,000 to follow, and also pay for an expeditionary force of 12,000 foot and 500 horse. In addition, Paul promised to authorize the sale of 500,000 ducats of monastic land in Spain to help finance the war.[15]

Charles ordered his ministers to draw up a detailed plan of attack, but they soon concluded that 'the season is too far advanced to prepare a campaign for this summer'. Specifically:

We cannot assemble an army before mid-September, and after that the rain and cold will make it difficult to wage war, especially in this country.

Starting the war without finishing it would be to exhaust our resources to no effect, and it would allow our enemies to prepare better, losing all fear and becoming more obstinate. It would then be difficult to recover our advantage.

Nevertheless, Charles added, 'although it is impossible to campaign now, I would be just as keen to do so next year'.[16] In August the emperor suspended the Diet – which had made virtually no progress towards resolving the religious issues facing Germany – and sailed down the Rhine to Cologne, where 'for the sake of his conscience' he berated the archbishop, Herman of Wied, for favouring Lutheranism. From there he went to Brussels, ready to invest Orléans as duke of Milan – but on 9 September 1545 the duke suddenly died.[17]

Five years later, Charles recorded in his *Memoirs* that news of the death reached him 'nine days before the deadline agreed in the peace of Crépy' for the investiture, and so 'it came at such a good time that it might seem as if God had arranged it for his secret purposes'. Naturally, he did not use this argument openly at the time, instead assuring Francis that he was 'determined to keep his word without deviating one iota', and suggested that Prince Philip (whose wife María Manuela of Portugal had just died) might marry a French princess, with Milan passing to their firstborn child. Although Francis seemed amenable to this, he refused Charles's demand to evacuate the lands of the duke of Savoy without prior agreement on the other issues. The emperor did not press the matter, because as long as the Anglo-French war continued Francis could do him little harm. Instead he encouraged the rumour that the money and men he was raising were destined for a third crusade in Africa.[18]

Paul III took advantage of these developments to take two critical initiatives. He invested his illegitimate son Pier Luigi Farnese, duke of Castro, with the imperial fiefs of Parma and Piacenza – something he would never have dared to do had Orléans become duke of Milan. Although the emperor refused to recognize the transfer, he did not disavow it for fear of jeopardizing Paul's support in Germany. The pope also summoned the long-delayed general council of the Church to meet in the town of Trent, on the border between Italy and Germany, in December 1545, and he charged it with redefining doctrine before turning to the reform of abuses – the exact opposite of what Charles wanted, but once again he accepted in order to avoid jeopardizing the pope's promise of support in Germany.

As the emperor prepared for war, his principal advisers urged caution. From Spain, Los Cobos expressed concern about 'the remedy to be applied to the German Protestants: since they are so numerous and obstinate, great trouble will be experienced'; and Prince Philip saw fit to 'remind Your Majesty that you should look carefully at what you plan to do, so that you have the protection and resources required for a favourable outcome', not least because although 'His Holiness now offers goodwill and aid, sometimes these things fail, and afterwards the burden and responsibility for everything will fall on Your Majesty alone'. From Brussels, Marie lamented that 'the accursed sect has expanded so much that it is hard to know who the good Catholics are', and she reminded her brother that a century before, Emperor Sigismund had 'attempted to reduce the Bohemians [Hussites] by force, and sent several armies against them to that end, assisted by all the princes of Germany, but they never succeeded. In the end they had to leave them as they were.' In addition, she observed, 'the Huns and Vandals came from just the same regions as the Lutherans today, and they ruined France, Spain and Italy before crossing to Africa'. It would therefore be better to leave them alone.[19]

Philip, Los Cobos and Marie all proved excellent prophets, but Charles ignored their advice – although he proceeded with great caution. In February 1546, after receiving confirmation that the sultan had signed a one-year truce, he re-entered Germany to preside over another imperial Diet in Regensburg with an escort of some 500 horsemen, inviting all whom he met on his route to 'see for themselves that he had brought with him only the entourage that always accompanied him, and that he preferred to solve the problems of Germany through peace and concord rather than by force and discord'.[20]

Although these assertions were totally false, they allowed Charles to travel through Germany unscathed, and to hold informal meetings with several Lutheran princes, including Philip of Hesse. The surviving accounts of their encounter shed interesting light on how far the emperor was prepared to lie about small things. His *Memoirs* claimed that 'in the landgrave's conversations with His Majesty in Speyer, he showed such great insolence that, with few words, His Majesty dismissed him'; but unknown to His Majesty, the landgrave kept a detailed record of their conversations. According to this source, Philip told Charles that although he doubted that a general council could bridge the religious divide, 'I have better hopes concerning a national gathering', just for Germany. The conversation then turned to the archbishop of Cologne's Lutheran leanings. According to Philip, the emperor asked jovially:

'How can that man introduce reforms? He knows no Latin and I hear he has celebrated Mass no more than three times in his life, and does not even know the *Confiteor* [one of the key prayers in the Mass].' To this I replied 'I want Your Majesty to know that he has read many books in German and has an excellent understanding of religion.' The emperor then said: 'Reformation does not mean introducing a new creed.'[21]

Another eyewitness account of the meeting confirms the cordial tone. When the emperor asked about the state of the League of Schmalkalden:

The landgrave replied enigmatically: 'My revered lord emperor, we lack only one person.' The emperor cautiously asked who it was, and the landgrave replied: 'I would like Your Imperial Majesty to join the godly, too.' This made them both laugh and Caesar said: 'No, no, I will not join those who are in error.'

This hardly amounts to 'great insolence', as Charles would later claim! Moreover, after conversing for 'more than three hours', the emperor, the landgrave and their courtiers went off hunting together. 'Judging by external evidence,' the Florentine ambassador reported, 'they all seem happy.'[22]

Despite the landgrave's apparent confidence, the League of Schmalkalden caused him grave concern. It now boasted thirty-six members but it 'suffered from its immense extent and inadequate density' from Strasbourg to Pomerania and from Constance to Hamburg. A common religion formed its sole common denominator, 'unsupported by common economic interests, common political traditions, or common problems of regional security'. The league 'was too large and too lacking in centralism to act like an effective state in the sixteenth-century manner'. As the landgrave lamented to some colleagues two months after meeting Charles:

We no longer have the spirit and feeling that we all used to have. When we were far fewer in number, we formed the League, took upon ourselves large tax burdens and with God's help achieved many great things, both individually and collectively. But now, when Fortune is on our side and our religion is in great need and faces a battle, we are so small-minded and so stingy with our money.[23]

By the time of the landgrave's lament, Charles had reached Regensburg where he remained for four months. He found time to hunt ('for my recreation I went to join the duke of Bavaria, where I spent 7 or 8 days hunting'), and to seduce Barbara Blomberg, the teenage daughter of a city artisan; but not everything went his way.[24] Despite Luther's death in February 1546, his creed continued to gain important converts, notably Frederick, erstwhile suitor of Charles's older sister and now Elector Palatine and husband of the emperor's niece Dorothea of Denmark. A few weeks before entertaining Charles at Heidelberg, Frederick and Dorothea expelled the Catholic clergy from their lands and brought in Lutherans. This increased the number of Lutheran Electors to three, none of whom attended the Diet. Ferdinand also stayed away from the Diet, claiming that he was too busy dealing with his own problems until Charles, furious, demanded that his brother join him within three weeks because 'the importance of the matter I want to discuss makes it more than necessary that we talk about it in person together . . . It cannot be handled by intermediaries or in writing.' He promised 'you can return to take care of your own affairs after we have talked together for four or five days' (an interesting insight on the importance the emperor attached to executive diplomacy); and he offered a clue about the matter he wanted to discuss by ordering Ferdinand to 'inspect and repair your artillery, to gather all the munitions you can', and to place on standby the Spanish infantry stationed in Hungary. The emperor concluded with a classic passive-aggressive flourish: 'You can see how much this matters to us, and that we are wasting time that cannot be recovered. I therefore beg you to make haste and be here as soon as possible, because this affects you more than anyone.'[25] Ferdinand dutifully dropped what he was doing and rode into Regensburg on 28 May 1546.

A few days later the brothers persuaded the duke of Bavaria to allow them to use his territories as a base for operations in case of war, and to contribute to their costs, in return for a promise that his son could marry a Habsburg princess; and they persuaded Maurice of Saxony to remain neutral should war break out with the Schmalkaldic League.[26] Charles also signed a formal agreement with the pope's representatives, triggering the dispatch of the promised troops and money from Italy, and ordered his German supporters to mobilize. On 9 June he also empowered the count of Buren to raise 10,000 infantry and 3,000 cavalry in the Netherlands for service in the Empire, because 'there is no way to deal with our problems here except by force of arms'; and he informed Marie that:

> I have decided to start the war against the Elector of Saxony and the landgrave of Hesse as disturbers of the common peace and the laws,

rejecting the authority of the Empire, citing their detention of the duke of Brunswick, his son and his lands. Although this covert pretext for war cannot prevent the Protestants from thinking that this is a war of religion, it may still provide a way of dividing them, or at least of delaying and complicating their mobilization ... As happened in the last war [over Brunswick], it may also deter [the Lutheran cities] from supplying Saxony and Hesse with money.

Charles also signed a series of letters to the leading princes and cities affirming that 'This warre is for the restitution of the Duke of Brunswike, and not for the cause of religion ... and repressinge of rebels'. A week later he signed patents and instructions to the staff officers of a new army to serve him in Germany.[27]

Had Charles planned to attack the Lutherans all along, despite his repeated assurances to them that he wanted peace? Sir John Mason, who had long served as a diplomat at the imperial court, could not believe that the emperor would lie like that, telling Frederick of the Palatinate:

I can hardelye be persuaded that he, who hath so often declared himself, both by speache and writing, to desyre nothing more then peax and the weale and quyet of Christendom, wolde now, all thinges being compownded and at a good poynte in the rest of the worlde, begynn a sturr, and that against himself. For I recken Germanye to be a parte of himself, and anything that he sholde move against that nation, to attempt it as it were against his owne entraylles.

Frederick knew better. When Mason asked him who the new imperial army would attack: '"The Protestantes", quod he, "against whome elles?"'[28]

Four centuries later, Karl Brandi reached the same conclusion. Brandi conceded that when Charles reassured his German subjects that 'he desired nothing more than peace and order, and would not appeal to arms unless he was driven to it, in a sense he was speaking the truth'; but, he added, 'it was not the whole truth'. Manuel Fernández Álvarez disagreed: 'We need to remember that Charles resorted to war because he thought that the Protestant princes would not be willing to negotiate, but prudence required that he should not make his thoughts public. That means that if he had found in Regensburg a greater deference among the Schmalkaldic League he might not have continued to think about war.'[29] Perhaps: but this overlooks both the extent and the cost of Charles's military preparations. We may discount as hindsight bias the emperor's claim in his *Memoirs* that he had decided to wage war on the German Lutherans as soon as he had defeated Guelders; but in February 1545, in the same letter that informed his son about his decision on the Alternative, intended to cement the peace with France, he announced that he would not be able to return to Spain on account of the 'pressing important affairs' in northern Europe, especially those of Germany. One year later he revealed to his son that he intended to crush his German Lutheran subjects using the same strategy that had worked so well in Guelders: if he could 'capture some territory and inflict on it an exemplary punishment, as it deserves, all the rest will surrender . . . Ending a matter of such importance will greatly advance God's service and our reputation, and secure our dominions, especially the Netherlands.'[30] One might argue, like Fernández Álvarez, that the intransigence of the Lutheran leaders at Regensburg meant that further negotiations would be futile, but Charles's complete failure both to exploit the favourable international situation, and to leverage his thinly disguised military preparations, strongly suggest that talks no longer interested him.[31]

THE WAR OF SCHMALKALDEN

Nevertheless, Charles had miscalculated. In June 1546 several prominent members of the League ordered their procurators to leave the Diet, and they sent agents to France and England to request financial assistance. Shortly afterwards they began to mobilize, and by mid-July the League had assembled 70,000 infantry, 9,000 cavalry and 100 artillery pieces at Donauwörth, only 130 kilometres from Regensburg. According to an English diplomat: 'By all men's voyces here, th'emperor hath begon a daungerous war, a war thretenyng greatly his estate, a warre of great moment.' His Venetian colleague agreed: 'Considering the time, the place, and the situation in which the emperor found himself, the decision to undertake this venture was the boldest – or more accurately, the most risky and most dangerous – that he has ever taken.'[32]

According to the semi-official campaign history by Luis de Ávila y Zúñiga, *Commentaries on the wars of Germany waged by Charles V, the greatest* [*el Máximo*], if at this point the Lutheran troops 'had arrived, they would have chased His Majesty from Regensburg, and in chasing him out of there, they would have chased him from Germany'.[33] The divided command structure of the League's army made it impossible to exploit this advantage. Alarmed by the unilateral action of the Elector and the landgrave in attacking

Brunswick, the League's other members insisted that in future all military decisions must be taken by a council of war, with ten members nominated by the cities as well as the princes. The decision proved a disaster: the council could not even agree on who should serve as commander-in-chief – John Frederick and Philip of Hesse competed for primacy with Sebastian Schertlin von Burtenbach, commander of the urban contingents and a veteran with extensive experience. Nor could they agree on the best campaign strategy: the Elector, fearing an attack on his home base, opposed Schertlin's proposal to occupy the Alpine passes and thus prevent the arrival of imperial reinforcements from Italy, and although Schertlin at first prevailed the council recalled his troops before they had achieved their goal.[34]

Charles's delicate military situation explains his intemperate reaction on learning that the pope had delayed sending the promised 200,000 ducats. He summoned the nuncio, who found him 'in a most evil disposition', because 'he had assumed that His Holiness would provide the entire sum immediately, and his failure to do so leaves us scandalized because the whole enterprise depends on it'. He complained bitterly that without these funds 'he would be forced to go and kiss the landgrave's feet'.[35] Although Charles stopped short of this, a few days later he fled Regensburg and rode south to Landshut, a fortified town in Bavaria, where he composed a letter of naked blackmail to his son, urging him to raise and send funds immediately because:

> If we are not able to keep our army in the field at least until the end of October it will imperil not only the Catholic faith but also our honour, our reputation and even the Netherlands and Italy. We cannot foretell how things will turn out, nor what will become of our person and those who are here with us, but we must not hazard everything for the sake of 300,000 or 400,000 ducats!

Charles also browbeat Los Cobos, using flattery rather than shame. He admitted that he had phrased his letter to Philip as if he feared that 'God might take me' and to show 'what he has lost' by recent developments. By contrast, he expressed complete faith that his loyal minister would know from experience what to do: although the scale of the new demands for money 'will cause you to shed some tears, do not be surprised because you have been with me in many similar situations, and since you got me out of them I trust that you will do the same this time'. After all, he was defending the cause of God, 'who has led me here for the sake of His faith and to serve Him'.[36]

No sooner had Charles signed these letters than the tide began to turn in his favour. Schertlin's troops reached Donauwörth on 5 August totally exhausted from their long and fruitless march to the Alps and back: they demanded four days' rest. The League's council of war used this hiatus to compose a formal renunciation of their allegiance to Charles on the grounds that he had broken his promise to tolerate those who subscribed to the Augsburg Confession. The Elector argued that they should not even address Charles as 'emperor', but as 'Charles of Ghent'; and although he was over-ruled, the document arrived 'in a forked stick, which is the way they declare war in Germany, when one ruler wishes to attack another'.[37]

The herald bearing the challenge arrived at the emperor's camp the day after papal and imperial reinforcements arrived from Italy (in flagrant viola-tion of Charles's Election Agreement never to bring foreign troops into Germany). The emperor refused to receive the challenge and instructed the duke of Alba, his principal field commander, to tell the herald and the page who accompanied him that 'the proper response to their mission was to hang them, but His Majesty would spare their lives because he wanted to punish only those who were to blame'. They returned with a copy of an imperial edict declaring the League's leaders to be traitors and rebels, and threatening all who supported them with loss of life and property.[38]

The emperor now commanded 10,000 Italians and 8,000 Spaniards, as well as 16,000 Germans, and he led them provocatively to Ingolstadt, a Bavarian city less than 60 kilometres from Donauwörth. Charles reconnoi-tred a suitable location for his camp in person, and also initiated a 'false alarm' to see how quickly his troops could reach their appointed station. Count Stroppiana, the Savoyard ambassador, reported this exercise 'was a splendid and inspiring sight. It was also good to see His Majesty, fully armed and wearing his helmet, moving through the camp, visiting each unit and surveying the trenches and the artillery and the places where the enemy might mount an attack'. Charles fortified his camp with bastions and ramparts made from 'barrels filled with earth', drafting not only soldiers but also 'women and children, of whom there are many in this camp'.[39]

These preparations were put to the test on 31 August 1546, when the Lutheran army took up position a few hundred metres away and began 'a battery with all their artillery, firing so fast and with such fury that it seemed as if were raining cannonballs'. Almost 1,500 rounds, some of them 'bigger than a man's head', landed in the imperial camp. Stroppiana reported that the bombardment 'made my heart beat triple-time, but the emperor displayed a fearless spirit. More than 27 balls passed between the feet of his horse or close to its head and cropper: they could not have come closer without hitting him'. Yet even when the emperor 'saw the bullets coming towards him, he did not move from his place but, immobile as a rock, he smiled'. Somewhat later, 'His Majesty was standing in the trenches to see when the enemy was about to fire his guns and although he shouted to those around him to duck, he himself remained standing'. Stroppiana speculated that 'without the special and all-powerful protection that God provides on special occasions, I believe that the emperor would no longer be among the living' (Pl. 24).[40]

The emperor made light of his courage. 'We are here, exchanging artillery fire with our neighbours and good friends,' he informed Ferdinand with heavy sarcasm, and 'the greatest pleasure they could give us would be to come and plant a kiss on our defences because, God willing, it would cost them dear.' Ferdinand was not impressed, rebuking his brother for risking his life, on which the success of the entire enterprise depended, and urging him to desist; but Charles replied: 'The truth is that while we were under attack we did not have enough men. That was not the time for me to set a bad example to others, and that was why I took those risks.'[41] Charles promised to take better care of himself in future, and on 4 September the League made this easier by retreating.

Some speculated that the besiegers withdrew because they lacked water, others that they 'wanted to tempt the emperor into following them'; but whatever the reason, the League's generals had lost their best chance of victory – and they knew it. Schertlin recorded in his autobiography that 'If my advice to launch an assault on the imperial camp had been followed, it would have meant the end of the House of Austria. In all his life, the emperor never experienced such anxiety and distress.' The landgrave agreed: 'If my advice had been followed,' he wrote in a confidential letter, 'we would have brought the emperor to battle – but too many councillors, too many heads and too many cooks spoiled the broth.' He continued:

The Lord God gave us a marvellous opportunity at Ingolstadt, if we had known how to exploit it, as I repeatedly told the Elector and the council of war. If it had been up to me, I would have ordered an assault, but they feared the walls and ramparts. I truly believe that we would have suffered fewer casualties from attacking the enemy than we did later from sickness.[42]

As the League army retreated and its casualties mounted, the landgrave became desperate. First he challenged his adversaries to a duel – 'If His

Imperial Majesty and the duke of Alba would bring 1,000 cavalry troopers into the field, the landgrave would also bring 1,000 to fight them' – and then he resorted to insults. When an Italian diplomat 'mentioned some proposal by "His Imperial Majesty" the landgrave objected and said "What Imperial Majesty? He is Charles of Ghent, just as I am Philip of Hesse, and if Germany could elect him emperor, it can also depose him." '[43] The emperor ignored the insult for the time being, even though he gained numerical parity with his adversaries when on 14 September Buren arrived at the head of 12,000 infantry, 5,000 cavalry and twelve field pieces from the Netherlands.

This remarkable logistical feat demonstrated the emperor's clear military advantage. He had ordered Buren to raise an army on 9 June, and the count began his march into Germany on 20 July although at that point neither he nor Charles knew where the rendez-vous would be (Buren even had to ask 'Your Majesty to tell me who are your friends and your enemies, so that I know which route to follow'). On 23 August the expeditionary force skil-fully crossed the Rhine near Mainz, where Buren received Charles's orders to march towards the Danube, through the heart of enemy territory, which required his troops to fortify their camp every night, in case of attack – and an attack seemed likely because the landgrave publicized his intention of intercepting Buren, so that either 'the emperour shal be forcidde to tempte the fortune of the batayle hymself', or Buren would march 'streighte to the boucherye'. But Charles sent constant intelligence on how best to avoid the Lutheran army, and Buren led his entire force safely into the imperial camp outside Ingolstadt, having covered over 800 kilometres in eight weeks.[44]

The emperor's expert directions reflected the 'paintings and maps that he took with him, some of all Germany and others of individual provinces, so that he knew the location of each place and the distances between them, and of the rivers and mountains'. He nevertheless accepted the risk-averse strategy proposed by Alba: to avoid a pitched battle and instead drive the army of the League northwards by constant skirmishes, capturing the hostile cities in his path until (in Charles's own words) 'one of the two armies is obliged to disband either through force, bad weather, hunger, or some other necessity'.[45]

The Lutheran army disintegrated first. When news reached the League's camp that Maurice and Ferdinand had signed an offensive and defensive alliance, and planned to invade Saxony, John Frederick led his forces back to defend their homeland, leaving his allies to fend for themselves, and on 16 November the League's council of war reluctantly decided that they must disperse into winter quarters.[46] Jacob Sturm, representing the city of

Strasbourg, protested to the landgrave that this would allow 'not only His Imperial Majesty but also the Antichrist in Rome' to subjugate the Protestant cities and states of southern Germany one by one, 'which will deprive us Germans of our reputation among the nations, and imperil the Protestant faith'. Surely, Sturm asked, either League members or their French and English allies could provide enough money to keep the Lutheran army in being for a little longer? In his reply from 'our camp', the landgrave berated Sturm for failing to understand the military situation. 'We now have 2,000 fewer cavalry and 8,000 fewer men than before,' he complained, 'and those that remain diminish daily through demoralization, sickness and desertion', whereas the emperor 'receives reinforcements and now outnumbers us'. As for money, 'one-third of the funds promised have not been paid ... and we have not yet seen a penny from England and France'. The landgrave concluded: 'We cannot and will not remain here any longer, having kept the army together thus far only through prayers and promises.' He seems to have signed his letter while in the saddle, because that same day he broke up 'our camp' and dispersed his army, abandoning Württemberg, all cities south of the Danube and even his wounded soldiers to their fate.[47]

The emperor did his best to exploit these advantages thanks to abnormally favourable weather. According to a diplomat travelling with the imperial army, 'This 100 yeres hathe not bene sene so good wether in this country this tyme of the yere, (as they say here). Yt rainithe sometyme; often tymes ther be fowle mistes, and colde nightes continually, but as yet neither suche accustomed snowe, nor suche frostes as was wont to kill bothe man and beste.'[48] Charles still suffered. On some days he travelled 'in a litter, because he suffered greatly from gout'; on others he managed to mount his horse, but 'because his right leg was badly afflicted by gout, he used a piece of fabric as a stirrup'. Nevertheless he 'reconnoitred enemy positions with his own eyes, to avoid making the wrong decision based on reports by others'; and whenever combat seemed possible he 'donned his armour and moved constantly from one contingent to another, talking to the soldiers of each nation and encouraging them to fight bravely'. His troops, 'seeing His Majesty come among them so unpretentiously, as if he were their equal and comrade, raised their arms and with a loud voice shouted "Emperor: to battle! Emperor: to battle!" '[49]

Although no battle took place in 1546, once the League's army disbanded the Lutheran rulers of southern Germany had little choice but to make their peace with Charles one by one, just as Sturm had predicted. Some surrendered when his army approached, others offered a submission at a humiliating public ceremony at which they 'fell to their knees' (*Fussfall*) before the emperor, who pardoned them in return for a large indemnity – thereby (in the words of a Spanish participant) 'reducing the strength of our enemies without losing anything ourselves'.[50] Frederick, Elector Palatine, who had rashly sent military support to the duke of Württemberg, was the first to submit. On 17 December he 'entered the chamber where his majesty sat on a seat, because of the pain in his legs,' and begged forgiveness. According to an eyewitness, after listening impassively Charles 'pulled out of his pocket a letter from the Elector that had been intercepted and said gruffly "Read this", adding "Go and discuss your business with Granvelle"'. Frederick now burst into tears and the emperor replied:

> Cousin: it hurts me to the core that you have recently taken sides against me. You are my relative and I raised you in my household, yet you sent troops to serve my enemies and against me, and you supported them for many days. Nevertheless, since we grew up together, and since you have expressed remorse . . . I have decided to pardon you and forget what you have done against me.

For Ávila, 'seeing a notable gentleman of such a venerable dynasty, the emperor's own cousin, with his white hair exposed and tears in his eyes', occasioned 'great compassion in those who witnessed it'. Charles remained suspicious, however: 'We need his actions to prove his good intentions,' he confided to Marie.[51]

Next, Duke Ulrich of Württemberg came to beg forgiveness. Charles pardoned him, too, in return for a fine of 300,000 florins ('in view of the great cost of this war to His Imperial Majesty'), the surrender of all artillery and munitions, and the admission of imperial troops to three of the duchy's fortified cities 'as a guarantee that the treaty will be honoured'. Ulrich hesitated before accepting these humiliating terms, but he eventually 'took up his pen and, turning his eyes to heaven, said: "If God has been pleased to grant the emperor two harvests in Germany in the same year, why should I not do what His Majesty wants?" And then he signed.' The Venetian ambassador, who described this scene, reported that even the normally imperturbable Granvelle showed elation at this further example of Caesar's luck: 'It is really something that when the affairs of His Majesty seem most adverse, at that very moment everything changes and he is successful again.'[52]

Charles assured Ferdinand, who had hoped to regain the duchy lost a decade before (chapter 9), that he had 'thought a lot about' whether or not to pardon Ulrich, but did so 'considering the present state of affairs', with both the Elector of Saxony and the landgrave still in arms, and also because of 'the insupportable cost that conquering Württemberg would involve' and the need to avoid the impression 'that we are putting our own interests first, given the widespread envy that exists towards our House of Austria'. Now, Charles mused, 'I cannot decide how best to exploit the advantage that it has pleased God to grant me'. His three long-term goals remained the same – 'to improve the religious situation in Germany'; to 'restore our authority in the Empire'; and to 'create peace and unity' so that Germany could better defend itself against foreign attack – but how best could he achieve them? He asked his brother for advice: should he convene the Diet at once and form a league with those who attended against those who remained in arms, or should he 'extirpate and defeat those who remained in arms, to gain the authority and reputation to convene the Diet, and then settle outstanding matters, notably the religious issue'?[53]

Charles favoured the second alternative: 'it is necessary to exterminate' both John Frederick and the landgrave, he told Ferdinand, 'otherwise it will not be possible to reduce and pacify Germany for the service of God, your authority, and mine'; and Ferdinand obliged by invading Electoral Saxony jointly with Maurice. Then news arrived that Francis I had at last offered support to the Lutheran leaders still in arms and was raising troops for their support. Publicly Charles made light of this development, reminding a French ambassador that 'I could be within your kingdom in two weeks, I know more than one way to enter it, and if necessary I also know how to remain there'; but privately he feared that Francis might mount a surprise attack, as he had done in 1542. 'I can't decide what to do,' he told Ferdinand, citing his usual dilemma: 'given the desire I have to come swiftly to your aid in person, and the need for me to be present elsewhere'.[54]

In the end, John Frederick forced a decision by laying siege to Leipzig, Maurice's chief stronghold, and by persuading some of Ferdinand's Bohemian subjects to rebel. Charles now led his troops eastwards to Bohemia, and although illness confined him to a litter or to a carriage heated by a travelling stove, the combined forces of Ferdinand, Maurice and Charles moved against the Elector. The allies sighted the Lutheran army across the Elbe on the evening of 23 April 1547, just as it encamped at the village of Mühlberg on the eastern bank. Imagining themselves safe, the Lutherans sent their artillery down the river towards Wittenberg and retired for the night, but Charles arose at midnight and prepared for immediate action. As his army crossed river under cover of a heavy morning mist, the emperor rode to battle in full armour mounted on 'a dark chestnut Spanish horse' with 'a caparison of red velvet edged with a golden fringe, wearing nothing over it except a broad crimson sash edged in gold. He wore a German morion and carried a gilded sword and a half-lance, almost a javelin, in his hands' – just as he appears in Titian's striking equestrian portrait (Pl. 25).[55]

The javelin conceit proved appropriate, because Mühlberg resembled a hunt rather than a battle. The Lutheran host lay spread out over several kilometres, and so offered little resistance. Nevertheless, the emperor 'spent 21 hours in the saddle, fully armed, without a break' and (according to a Venetian report) 'when he returned to his camp he dismounted from his horse and said cheerfully: "Get my dinner ready because I have spent the whole day hunting, and I have taken a boar – a very fat one"'.[56] He had indeed. John Frederick was easily identified because of his enormous girth, and Charles's soldiers surrounded him as he fled on horseback. To their surprise the Elector pulled out a pistol and killed one man, and struck down another with his sword; but then someone landed 'a heavy sword blow on the left side of his face', which meant that he could neither fight not flee. He therefore surrendered and was brought before the emperor, with blood pouring from his wound. 'He made three attempts to dismount, but lacking the usual and necessary assistance, on account of his huge size he remained on his horse', saying only: 'Most worthy emperor and lord, my fate has brought me here as Your Majesty's prisoner. I therefore ask that you treat me as my rank and name deserve.' The emperor replied coldly: ' "Now you call me emperor: that's a different title from the one you used to call me!" He said this because when the Elector and the landgrave were on campaign they referred to the emperor in their writings as "Charles of Ghent, who thinks he is emperor" '. Charles cut short the meeting with the same ominous phrase that the landgrave had used to Duke Henry of Brunswick: 'I will treat you as you deserve.'[57]

Despite the Brunswick precedent – and Duke Henry still languished in prison – John Frederick assumed that the emperor's statement meant that he would be well treated, but immediately after the victory Charles's Confessor Pedro de Soto argued at a meeting of the imperial council for the Elector's execution. Alba and Perrenot advised against it, however, because it risked making him a martyr and prolonging the war: better, they argued, for Charles to 'keep him alive and in his power, and take him round in triumph' to all the places that had supported his rebellion. On 10 May the emperor duly signed a warrant sentencing the Elector to death and confiscating all his lands, offices and goods, as punishment for his armed rebellion – but offering to spare his life provided the heavily fortified city of Wittenberg submitted to him. It did so nine days later.[58]

On 25 May 1547, Charles entered the city and visited (among other locations) the Castle Church where Luther lay buried. Bartholomew Sastrow, who resided in the imperial camp before Wittenberg, wrote in his *Memoirs* that when Charles and his entourage returned 'they claimed that the lamps and candles burned night and day before Luther's tomb and that prayers were recited constantly, just like with saints' relics in Catholic churches'; but he did not record an exchange that later became a legend. According to oral tradition, the duke of Alba called for the Reformer's bones to be exhumed and defiled, but Charles replied, 'Let them rest until Judgement Day'; and when Perrenot repeated the suggestion, Charles snapped back 'I don't make war on the dead, only on the living'. Some have doubted the veracity of this exchange, but an English diplomat who visited the imperial camp noted the intense hatred for Protestants in general, and for Luther in particular: 'The Spanish soldiers say nothing but the word: *Luther, Luther*.' It would have been strange if such hatred had not produced calls to desecrate his tomb when Charles entered the city and had the power to do so – calls that he resisted.[59]

After Wittenberg surrendered, Charles kept his promise to spare John Frederick's life, but insisted that he renounce his Electoral dignity, surrender most of his lands to Maurice, and solemnly swear 'that he would join the court of His Majesty, or of the prince his son in Spain, until further orders. His Majesty would choose the location and duration.' For the next five years, just as Alba and Perrenot had suggested, John Frederick accompanied the emperor as a prisoner, a constant reminder of the consequences of rebellion.[60] The harsh terms reflected a dramatic improvement in Charles's overall situation, both abroad and at home. The death of Henry VIII in January 1547, and of Francis I two months later, offered assurance that at least for a while he had nothing to fear from either England or France. The Bohemians who in March had opened talks with John Frederick made haste to reassure Ferdinand of their loyalty shortly after hearing about Mühlberg. News of the imperial victory also accelerated the conclusion of a five-year truce with Suleiman, signed on 19 June. The sultan now turned his resources against Persia, leaving Charles secure against Ottoman attack.[61]

These developments left the landgrave dangerously isolated. At first he made light of his plight. After hearing about Mühlberg, Philip of Hesse stated grimly that unless Charles granted reasonable terms, 'God willing we will defend ourselves in such a way that we can hold out for another year'; and a month later he ordered his subjects to prepare for a new campaign.[62] Early in June, however, he authorized Maurice and the Elector of Brandenburg (also his relative) to meet with Antoine Perrenot and the imperial vice-chancellor Georg Seld and negotiate his surrender. Their discussions secured far better terms than John Frederick had received: the landgrave would forfeit no territory; his life would be spared; and he would pay an indemnity of 150,000 florins, surrender all his artillery and munitions, and raze all fortifications in his dominions except for one (to be chosen by Charles). He would also abandon all his allies, both inside and outside Germany, and free all the prisoners he had taken during the war. In return the Electors promised in the emperor's name that the landgrave would not spend the rest of his life in prison. They also urged him to make his *Fussfall* before the emperor immediately, and to reassure him they issued their safe-conduct for his journey.[63]

ALWAYS READ THE SMALL PRINT

The landgrave reluctantly recognized that he was unlikely to secure better terms and on 19 June 1547, having ratified the terms agreed by Perrenot, Seld and the Electors, he entered the chamber where the emperor sat, surrounded by 'a crowd too large to count who had come to watch'. Before falling to his knees, however, the landgrave 'paused beside the Electors, talking and laughing with them. This greatly irritated the emperor', who refused to give his hand to the landgrave after his *Fussfall*, as he had done to other opponents. Instead (according to Bartholomew Sastrow, an eyewitness) Charles 'pointed his finger angrily and said, "Well, I will teach you to laugh"'.[64] The landgrave evidently did not take this threat seriously because after his submission he accepted an invitation to dine with the duke of Alba, who promptly arrested him and placed him under a Spanish guard.

This horrified the two Electors, who had not only persuaded Philip to accept the emperor's terms but also issued their personal safe-conduct, and late that night they engaged in an acrimonious debate with Alba and Perrenot that lasted until 2 a.m. the following morning, protesting vociferously that imprisoning Philip slighted their honour. The imperial ministers countered that the capitulation, which all parties had read and approved, only stated that he would be spared perpetual prison: it said nothing about incarceration for a specific period. When Charles heard about the debate the following day, he sided with his ministers. He also denied all knowledge of a safe-conduct. This outraged the Electors even more and they sent an embassy to Ferdinand (who had just campaigned with Maurice) complaining that they had issued their safe-conduct because they believed Charles had guaranteed that the landgrave 'would suffer neither pain of death nor any imprisonment'.[65]

It is important to establish Charles's personal involvement in this matter because, as with the assassination of Rincón and Fregoso five years before, his treatment of the landgrave would become a *casus belli*. Some contemporaries and many historians argued that the emperor deliberately chose the words '*einiger Gefencknus*' ('any imprisonment') in the draft agreement, so that with a single stroke of the pen it could later be changed without anyone noticing to '*ewiger Gefencknus*' ('permanent imprisonment'). The accusation is ingenious, but implausible. Although Charles could converse in German, he lacked the fluency to devise such a word-play. Seld later provided a more plausible explanation, during dinner with friends. He recalled that he and Perrenot (both eminent lawyers and both fluent in German) had first plied the two Electors with drink, and then negotiated with them while their legal advisers were absent. The Electors therefore failed to notice that a formula proposed by Perrenot, '*nit in ewiger Gefencknus halten* ['not to place him in permanent prison']', still allowed Charles to imprison the landgrave, subject only to the provision that the sentence not be permanent.[66]

Even if Charles did not devise the formula, however, he exploited its ambiguity. On 15 June, four days before the *Fussfall*, Charles pointed out to his brother that the landgrave 'expressly agreed to surrender unconditionally'. He continued:

> Admittedly the two Electors demanded a promise that I will not punish him in his person or in his possessions, except as specified in the treaty, or by perpetual imprisonment; and since they used the word 'perpetual' I accepted their proposal for the reason you already know: to keep him in my hands at least for a time. I therefore plan to detain him as my prisoner when he comes to make his submission. The Electors cannot object to this, because I will not be breaking the assurance that I gave them, which mentioned 'prison' with the added word 'perpetual'.

The emperor proceeded to ask his brother's advice on the nature and length of the detention after the landgrave had honoured all the other terms of the capitulation, given the risk that after his release 'if I am absent from Germany, he might do his worst'. Ferdinand recommended setting the captive free, once he had made all the agreed sacrifices and provided adequate securities for his good conduct, in order to avoid offending the Electors 'who have become involved, and also so that the landgrave does not become desperate'; but Charles disagreed.[67] In a letter to his brother written just after the *Fussfall* he argued that, unless the landgrave remained in prison, 'I have no other guarantee that he will execute what is in the treaty. Currently he is playing for time until I have demobilized my forces'. Furthermore, the emperor now felt that his honour was at stake. The Electors had 'impugned my honour by questioning whether or not I would keep my word'. This infuriated Charles, because (he claimed) 'I have always taken singular care to keep my word, even when I forfeited excellent opportunities for personal profit by doing so'. He therefore informed his brother that 'The matter has gone too far for me to withdraw: if I retreat from my position about imprisoning him, the world will think that I was wrong to do it, and that I have been forced to change my mind'. He would wait and 'see if the landgrave makes haste to proceed in good faith', and then decide on the duration of his incarceration.[68]

Once again, Ferdinand urged caution: although he agreed that the landgrave must remain in prison until he had fulfilled all his treaty obligations, thereafter, 'rather than alienate the two Electors, provided it can be done without great prejudice to your affairs, I think Your Majesty could agree to release him', perhaps taking the landgrave's sons as surety. But Charles rejected all calls for clemency and instead instructed his Spanish troops to keep Philip under close and constant guard. As Sastrow grimly observed, the landgrave found that 'the emperor's words "I will teach you to laugh" were not an idle threat'.[69]

Charles would later regret rejecting Ferdinand's advice, but initially his triumph seemed total. The landgrave's only consolation came a few days later. As he departed in a cart surrounded by Spanish soldiers Charles came out to gloat, 'wearing a velvet hat and a black cloak trimmed with velvet', but a sudden downpour of heavy rain forced the emperor 'to turn the cloak he wore inside out and to place his hat under it, letting the rain pour down on his bare head. Poor little man!', Sastrow jeered: 'He had spent so much gold on the war, but would rather stand bareheaded in the rain than let it spoil his velvet hat and cloak!'[70]

Sastrow was right about the immense cost of the German war. Charles took out loans payable in Spain worth almost three million ducats in 1546, and over 700,000 the following year, while Marie borrowed a further 750,000 in the Netherlands. Against this, the emperor could set only the papal subsidies (200,000 ducats), the fines imposed upon those who had defied him (perhaps 800,000 ducats in all) and the value of the heavy artillery confiscated from the various Lutheran towns and princes, which he ostenta-tiously redistributed around his dominions as a symbol of his victory.[71] It was not the only symbol. Although he demobilized much of his army before travelling to Augsburg, where he would meet a new Diet, Charles retained 3,000 of his troops 'to guard all the gates and squares of the city', with 20,000 infantry and 4,000 cavalry as garrisons in Ulm, Württemberg and elsewhere 'in the neighbourhood', leading the Protestants to dub the assembly 'the Armed Diet'. According to several sources, immediately after his victory at Mühlberg, Charles boasted: 'I came, I saw, and God conquered': he now aimed to exploit his overwhelming military advantage to solve once and for all the religious and political opposition he had encountered in Germany.[72]

THE ARMED DIET

Perrenot claimed that Charles approached the Diet 'hoping to complete his business there quickly', but added, 'in truth I believe that when it comes to hastening negotiations to get everything in proper order, we will encounter more difficulties than we expected'.[73] Perrenot was correct: the Diet would last ten full months, from 1 September 1547 to 30 June 1548, and generated documents that fill 2,760 printed pages. Imperial officials proposed a raft of initiatives designed to bolster the emperor's authority within Germany: measures to standardize law enforcement and the coinage; to strengthen and streamline the Imperial Chamber Court (*Reichskammergericht*); to recognize the emperor's various Netherlands territories as a distinct divi-sion (*Reichskreis*) of the Empire; to create a new League (*Reichsbund*) that would bind imperial subjects to the Habsburg dynasty (rather than to the Empire); to raise money for the defence of Hungary against a possible Turkish attack; and to create a reserve to fund the mobilization of an army of 27,000 men 'in case anyone in future wished to rebel against the edicts and commands of the emperor and the Empire'. Most controversial, they also proposed a new framework for religious unity in the Empire.[74]

Eventually the Diet would either approve all these measures, or allow the emperor to create special commissions to deal with the rest, but it is difficult to establish Charles's exact role in the debates and decisions. The detailed travel journal kept by his valet, Jean Vandenesse, recorded the emperor's presence at only a few major public events over the winter: on 30 November 1547 he attended a banquet of the Knights of the Golden Fleece; at Epiphany 1548 he attended Mass and 'offered three cups containing gold, frankin-cense and myrrh', just like the Three Kings; on 30 January he summoned the

Electors to his presence to discuss recognizing the Netherlands as a separate *Reichskreis*; and on 24 February, his birthday, 'in his imperial robes and on his imperial throne' he solemnly invested Maurice as the new Elector of Saxony. According to Vandenesse, the emperor missed other solemn occasions – even the opening ceremony, when Ferdinand's eldest son Maximilian deputized for him – but this concealed the fact that members of the Diet regularly came to the house of Anton Fugger (nephew of Jakob), where Charles resided, to discuss business with him face to face.[75]

Charles often failed to appear in public because he was ill. Sometimes he gave audiences 'seated, with one arm supporting his neck and his feet elevated on a stool with cushions'; and during the winter he sought relief from pain by climbing into a huge metal stove 'or, more accurately a furnace, in which most people would stay for a quarter of an hour, but he remains there the whole day'.[76] Pain no doubt helps to explain some of Charles's intemperate outbursts. In February 1547 he told a papal diplomat that Paul III had syphilis, adding 'we cannot help remembering what they say in Italy: you can forgive a young man for getting French Pox [syphilis], but not an old man'. When the diplomat protested that he knew nothing of this, so that it must be something 'new', the emperor 'continued on the same theme, saying that it must be a long-standing illness'; and when the envoy again tried to object 'we took our leave, saying it was now time to hear Mass'.[77]

Even without the pain, Charles had two reasons to be angry with the pope. Paul had withdrawn his expeditionary force from Germany (on the grounds that Charles had not made the vanquished rulers restore Catholic worship); and he had commanded the general council of the Church to move from Trent to Bologna, in the Papal States, a location totally unacceptable to German Protestants – and therefore to Charles. 'We will never accept this relocation,' he informed his commissioner at the council, and he ordered the prelates to remain in Trent 'for the sake of God's service and mine' (an arrogant equation that the emperor now used with increasing frequency).[78] He also resurrected the idea of finding a religious formula acceptable to all Germans – something Luther himself had advocated in his last major publication: 'Let our dear emperor make the pope hold a general, free, Christian council somewhere in Germany, or else hold a national council.' As usual, Granvelle took the lead in this initiative, issuing an ultimatum for the pope in August 1547: 'Either the council returns to Trent, or it must be suspended until we see the outcome of this Diet'.[79]

The situation changed dramatically the following month when Charles's troops seized the city of Piacenza, killing the pope's son Pier Luigi Farnese in the process (see below). Paul now declared that he would never allow the council to return to Trent unless the emperor restored Piacenza, and Charles responded by seeking an interim religious settlement just for Germany.[80] In February 1548 a commission comprising delegates chosen by him, by Ferdinand, by each Elector, and by the princes, the prelates and the towns represented in the Diet, convened to formulate a religious text acceptable to all parties. The Catholic rulers soon made clear that they did not recognize the ecclesiastical powers claimed by Charles, and since he lacked the means to coerce them, he authorized Catholic states to maintain their current religious practices. By contrast, he insisted that Lutheran rulers must follow the practices laid out in the new text, known as the *Interim* because it would last only until the general council made permanent decisions. This temporary status explains the document's many contradictions. For example, it declared clerical marriage and communion in both kinds, two of the most visible symbols of Lutheran liturgy, to be 'errors' temporarily tolerated in order to preserve the peace; and although it defined salvation as requiring faith and grace, but not necessarily good works, the document explicitly permitted Catholic ritual practices condemned by Lutherans (such as veneration of saints and memorial Masses for the dead, which implied a belief in purgatory).

Church historian Nathan Rein has suggested that the Interim contained so many 'similarities and echoes' of the Augsburg Confession of 1530 that they 'cannot be unintentional. In their phrasing and choice of metaphors, the Interim's authors were self-consciously making reference to the stock expressions of Lutheran thought, which no informed reader could have failed to notice.' Those same authors also skilfully separated the theology of salvation from the performance of ritual, which they left to secular rulers, who could now control the liturgical life of their subjects in the interests of preserving public order (at least until a general council decided otherwise).[81]

Charles decided to conceal the contents of the document from the pope and his representatives until the last moment. 'At lunch time' on 15 May 1548 he 'summoned all the princes to join him at 4 p.m. because he intended to publish the Interim'. Antoine Perrenot visited the nuncio 'just before 4 p.m.' and told him, 'by order of His Majesty, what the Interim would contain'. He also asserted that 'His Majesty had waited as long as possible, but now could delay no more.' At the appointed hour, in the presence of the emperor and the full Diet, Vice-Chancellor Seld read out the document, published almost immediately in both Latin and German.[82]

334

Now the hard part began: ensuring compliance. Paul III offered no help, instead sending a legate to reproach Charles 'for publishing the Interim without waiting for the authority of the Holy See'. At an audience that lasted two hours the legate protested that 'it does not conform to the doctrine and customs of the Holy Church, yet it regulates almost everything concerning the Christian life'. Charles immediately conceded that 'the Interim was not perfect, as he would wish, but people must be attracted back to the Catholic faith and our Holy Church little by little'. He was confident that 'a general council and the authority of the pope will do the rest and make it perfect'. Meanwhile, he continued, 'when Germany accepts this Interim, it will also accept the authority of the pope and of the Church – and it seemed to him that for this he deserved congratulations and not complaints'. The legate asked whether Charles would make any changes, for example on Mass and clerical marriage, but he replied that no alterations could be made because the Diet had ended.[83]

Some Lutheran rulers proved compliant. According to Sastrow, the Elector of Brandenburg accepted the Interim in return for payment of his debts; the duke of Württemberg and the landgrave endorsed the document in the hope of improving the terms of their surrender; Elector Maurice had already promised Charles that he would comply, and he pressured the theologians of Wittenberg (now his subjects) to cooperate. Almost all of them obliged, but some Lutherans elsewhere rejected the Interim, led by former Elector John Frederick who held fast to Luther's teaching even after Granvelle and his son put pressure upon him (first by hinting that compliance might secure his freedom and, when he refused, by confining him to his room, removing his books, and sequestering his chaplain). The Lutheran Church would remain divided for a generation.[84]

Once the weather warmed up, Charles appeared in person again. He presided at the solemn closing of the Diet on 30 June 1548, and five weeks later he deployed his soldiers to all strategic points in Augsburg, closed the city gates, and summoned all public officials to assemble in his presence. Seld ordered them to perform a *Fussfall* as a punishment for sending men and money to the League army, and then to swear a new oath of allegiance to the emperor. Next Seld announced the revocation of the city's charter, the dismissal of all its officials, and the abolition of all its guilds (which had previously chosen the council) before naming a new slate of office-holders to run the city, almost all of them members of its elite. Anton Fugger and Bartolomaus Welser, the emperor's bankers, took two of the seven seats on the new Secret Council. A few days later the emperor's

Spanish troops moved against Constance, another Protestant city that had sent troops and money to the League, leading its terrified magistrates to submit to Ferdinand, who suppressed its charter, restored Catholic worship, and then annexed the city to his own dominions. Charles briefly contemplated erecting a citadel in Constance (as he had done in Ghent, Utrecht and Cambrai) and desisted only because he feared it might provoke unrest in the Empire.[85]

The emperor next moved to Ulm, another city that had supported the League, and again presided over a ceremonial *Fussfall* after which Seld revoked the city's charter, dismissed its officials, abolished its guilds and imposed a new government run by patricians. He also ordered the city's Lutheran preachers to accept the Interim (something he had not done at Augsburg), arrested those who refused, and compelled clerics who conformed to abandon their wives and children. Lutheran preachers in Speyer, Worms and other Rhineland cities fled to avoid similar treatment; and in 1551–2 imperial officials revoked the charters, abolished the guilds and installed a new patrician governing council in twenty-five southern German cities.[86]

Some at the time, and many afterwards, claimed that Charles acted from confessional motives – 'The reform of the urban constitutions was a harbinger of the Counter-Reformation,' wrote Ludwig Fürstenwerth in 1893: 'The ultimate aim was the preservation or restoration of Catholic worship in the cities' – but this fails to explain why the emperor took steps to tighten his grip over Catholic as well as Lutheran cities, some of them staunchly loyal to him during the recent civil war. The eminent historian Wolfgang Reinhard searched the surviving papers of Charles and Ferdinand for 'some kind of manifest programme', but he failed to find one and concluded: 'This is not because so far it has escaped historians, but because none ever existed.' Rather, the emperor strove primarily to restrict urban independence in general, and the power of the guilds in particular, and only secondarily to combat Lutheranism. Therefore, the theatrical humiliation of Augsburg, Ulm and other German cities closely resembled Charles's treatment of Ghent in 1540.[87] Bartolomeo Cavalcanti, a Sienese exile, perceived a general pattern: 'The ministers of the emperor have always pursued the same policy,' he wrote in 1552. 'They have always tried to provoke civil discord, and then oppressed liberty and the common good by means of an oligarchic and tyrannical government.' He had in mind not only Charles's recent treatment of cities in the Netherlands and Germany, but also in Italy.[88]

SETTLING SCORES IN ITALY

The early successes of the Schmalkaldic League emboldened some of Charles's opponents in Italy to defy him. In Lucca, a small imperial fief in semi-constant rivalry with Florence, the patrician Francesco Burlamacchi and a group of exiles plotted to overthrow Medici rule and unite Lucca, Siena and Florence in a Tuscan republic. He was betrayed in August 1546, and condemned to life imprisonment in Milan.[89] Then, 'at midnight on January 3, 1547, the city of Genoa almost experienced a revolution'. Count Gian Luigi Fieschi, a prominent and popular figure who had studied 'the book of Niccolò Machiavelli called *The prince*', brought into the harbour of Genoa a war galley that concealed 200 followers. He invited Andrea Doria and his heir Giannettino to a banquet with the intention of murdering them both and then gaining control of the city.[90] Although Andrea accepted the invitation, he felt ill and did not attend; but Fieschi decided to go ahead with the plot anyway. Half his followers seized the city gates while the other half captured Doria's galleys in the Arsenal, freeing the oarsmen. Their jubilant shouts attracted the attention of Giannettino, who was fatally shot as he tried to regain control. Andrea Doria fled the city he had dominated since 1528 and crowds ran through the streets shouting 'Liberty! Liberty!' The coup failed only because Fieschi, wearing full armour, fell into the harbour and drowned. As Gómez Suárez de Figueroa, the veteran Spanish ambassador in Genoa, realized, his death 'was a gift from God, because had he lived everything would have been lost'.[91]

A few months later, Naples also almost experienced a revolution. Viceroy Pedro de Toledo caused a major upheaval when, at his request, the pope appointed a special inquisitor to root out heresy in the kingdom. The local elite immediately protested, but the viceroy ignored them. Then in May 1547 three local men tried to save a colleague arrested by the inquisitors and the viceroy had them executed, which provoked major demonstrations. Toledo used his Spanish troops to disperse the crowds and trained his artillery on the popular quarters of the city 'as if', a chronicler remarked, 'Naples was a French or Turkish city, instead of one belonging to the emperor'.[92] Those exiled after the imperial victory in 1528 began to return, and imperial authority hung in the balance until the arrival in August of a galley squadron sent by Doria from Genoa, carrying 3,000 Spanish soldiers. Once they had restored order, Charles deemed it prudent to pardon all but a handful of rebels.

This spate of challenges to Habsburg hegemony reflected both a powerful nostalgia for the return of an Italy 'where no prince could impose his will on another' and an astonishing complacency on the part of Charles and his ministers.[93] Fieschi had taken part in Fregoso's attempt to seize Genoa in 1536 (p. 255), but five years later, at Doria's request, Charles pardoned the count and granted him a pension. Rumours that one of Fieschi's relatives was in Paris trying to secure French support for a coup reached Genoa in May 1545, but neither Doria nor Figueroa took them seriously; and when news arrived that Fieschi had purchased four galleys from Pier Luigi Farnese, Figueroa assured his master that 'I believe it would be better for Your Majesty's service if the galleys were in the hands of [Fieschi] than of another.'[94] Such insouciance almost proved fatal, because Charles's relationship with Genoa depended on the personal bond (*condotta*) made with Andrea Doria two decades before. Ferrante Gonzaga, who became governor of Milan in 1546, warned Charles of the risk 'that a place like Genoa, so important to the affairs of Your Majesty in both Spain and Italy, should depend on the life of a man who is eighty years old, without any plan for what should happen after his death – something that could occur any day'. He requested instructions on 'what you would like us to do in the event of Doria's death'. One day later Fieschi and his supporters launched their revolution.[95]

Fieschi's failure (yet another example of Caesar's luck) produced a more aggressive imperial policy. Gonzaga immediately led 1,000 Spanish veterans to the frontier of the Genoese republic, ready to intervene if necessary; he advocated the confiscation of all Fieschi property in the duchy of Milan, to show what happened to those who opposed the emperor; and he sent a messenger 'to ascertain in complete secrecy [*con ogni dissimulatione*] what Your Majesty thinks'. Initially, the emperor felt helpless – 'Until we receive details concerning the origins of this event, and what else may have happened, we have no more to say' – but a few days later, having reflected on 'how beneficial it would be if we could secure and control that city and its forts' and 'not have to worry that anyone can do what they want when Doria dies', he instructed Figueroa to suggest how best to secure Genoa, for example by constructing a citadel.[96] At the same time he granted Gonzaga's request to seize all Fieschi fiefs.

Charles also authorized moves against Pier Luigi Farnese, the new duke of Parma and Piacenza, because in selling galleys to Fieschi 'he had failed to act in a way that advanced our affairs'. Therefore, 'with dissimulation and secrecy', Gonzaga must 'look into persuading some gentlemen from the area' to overthrow him. Charles even specified a timeframe: Gonzaga should 'win over supporters' in both cities so that 'should a good opportunity such as a *sede vacante* suddenly arise ... the plot would be ready for immediate execution.[97] The idea of waiting for a *sede vacante*, the period between the death of one pope and the election of his successor when the Papal States descended into chaos, made good sense – Paul III (like Andrea Doria) was almost eighty, and his death would remove his son's principal ally – but Charles soon changed his mind. The confessions of captured Fieschi plotters revealed that the pope and his son had provided support to the emperor's enemies: apart from the suspicious sale of the galleys, Pier Luigi had apparently promised to send 1,000 soldiers to Genoa from Piacenza 'before any other troops could come and dislodge them'. According to the Spanish ambassador in Rome, 'the suspicion grows by the day that what happened in Genoa was orchestrated by the pope'. Still Charles hesitated to grant Gonzaga a free hand to implement 'the plan to recover Parma and Piacenza, which seems excellent to us', because 'it is possible that when you decide to carry out the plot, the situation in Germany or France may make it inopportune to act against His Holiness and his interests, and it would be better to wait'. Therefore 'before you carry out the plot, since delay will not matter, you must consult us' so that 'according to the overall state of our affairs, we can inform you what would be best'.[98]

Charles finally abandoned his cautious stance when news arrived that Farnese had promised to support another plot to overthrow Doria's rule over Genoa, led by one of Fieschi's brothers and by Giulio Cibo Malaspina, marquis of Massa. Gonzaga promptly arrested Massa, and on 13 June 1547 he advanced two arguments why the emperor should give immediate approval for the conspirators he had recruited in Piacenza to act: the new citadel would soon be completed, making Piacenza impregnable; and, since the conspirators needed to act before then, if Charles did not promise aid and protection, they would call in the French. 'If we lose this opportunity to regain the city', Gonzaga added, 'another one may not arise for a long time', and he therefore sent 'an express courier to humbly' – humbly! – 'beg Your Majesty to make up your mind with the speed that the importance of the subject requires'. Two weeks later, with his principal enemies in Germany either reconciled or in custody, the emperor gave his consent – but on two conditions: 'under no circumstances must you lay hands on the person' of Pier Luigi, who must be exiled; and 'under no circumstances could it be said that it was done by our orders'.[99]

These restrictions placed Gonzaga in an awkward dilemma. He feared that if Farnese remained at liberty he would seek revenge both against him and against the conspirators; and he hesitated to take responsibility for 'the decision myself, to avoid repeating what happened in the case of Fregoso and Rincón'. He therefore devised an ingenious subterfuge to suggest that neither he nor his master had been involved: as soon as the plotters gained control of Piacenza, they would offer it to Charles provided he could take possession within twenty-four hours – a condition with which he obviously could not comply – after which they would feel free to offer it to the French. All Gonzaga needed to do was move close to Piacenza, with 400 horsemen, just before the conspirators struck. This ruse, he pointed out to the emperor, 'would require me to act without consulting Your Majesty, and would also justify my action as the result of necessity, not choice'. Charles approved the plan and on 10 September 1547 the conspirators seized control of Piacenza, murdering Pier Luigi Farnese in the process, and immediately offered the city to the emperor.[100] The following day the cavalry that Gonzaga had secretly stationed just across the frontier arrived, and on 12 September he took possession of the city in the name of the emperor. Although his plan to capture Parma by surprise failed, the following month imperial troops entered Siena and started work on a citadel.[101]

These successes sealed the fate of Charles's other enemies in Italy. On Gonzaga's orders, Francesco Burlamacchi of Lucca was beheaded in Milan in February 1548, and Giulio Cibo Malaspina of Massa followed him to the scaffold in May. Gonzaga also eliminated two of Charles's Florentine enemies. He captured Piero Strozzi, a prominent exile, and had him murdered at the Gonzaga residence now known as Villa Simonetta; and he sent two assassins to Venice where they stabbed to death Lorenzino de' Medici, the murderer of Duke Alessandro (Charles's former son-in-law) eleven years before.[102]

Everything now seemed to be going Charles's way, but appearances were deceptive. On 2 September 1548, at Speyer, Charles signed a letter to Philip that celebrated his success 'in making changes to the councils' of several German cities 'and replacing them with others who will be more amenable, and in expelling the Protestant preachers'; but then he made a startling admission. He now needed to demobilize his army because 'in no circumstances can we sustain the number of troops currently on foot, because of the excessive cost'; but this compelled him to return to the Netherlands because without those troops 'we do not want to risk remaining here [in Germany] on account of the lack of security for our person and also to avoid something happening in our presence that cannot be remedied, causing the loss of the reputation that (thanks be to God) we have recently gained'. To economize, he proposed to remove the German troops who currently garrisoned Württemberg and replace them with 2,000 Spaniards, who would be paid by the local population. A month later Ferdinand warned his brother of two other threats. Some Lutheran states in the north still 'refuse to submit to Your Majesty' and accept the Interim; moreover, despite his elevation as Elector, Maurice of Saxony remained resentful about the imprisonment of the landgrave. 'Because he has a hot head,' Ferdinand continued, 'he should not be driven to despair or be provoked to make an alliance or confederation with neighbouring cities and rulers.'[103]

By then, Charles faced another challenge to his authority: some 10,000 kilometres away, the conquistadors of Peru had rebelled. According to one courtier, 'although the emperor had faced other rebellions and uprisings by his Spanish vassals against his royal person, he resented none – not even those in Germany – as much as the revolt of Peru', led by someone else with 'a hot head': Gonzalo Pizarro.[104]

THIRTEEN

THE TAMING OF AMERICA[1]

THE FIRST AMERICA

In the dedication to his triumphalist *Hispania Victrix* (*Spain victorious*) of 1553, Francisco López de Gómara informed Charles that 'The greatest event since the creation of the world, apart from the birth and death of its creator, is the discovery of America'; and, he added, 'no nation has spread its customs, language and arms, or travelled as far by land and sea, as the Spaniards', especially in such a short time.[2] The truth of the second part of Gómara's claim is easily demonstrated. When Charles first set foot on Spanish soil, Castile's transatlantic possessions were confined to a few outposts on the isthmus of Panama and a few islands in the Caribbean, with a total area of some 250,000 square kilometres (about half the size of Spain) and a population of perhaps two million indigenous inhabitants, 5,000 Europeans and a few hundred African slaves. When the emperor abdicated forty years later, his possessions included not only the Caribbean islands but also two million square kilometres on the American mainland (four times the size of Spain), inhabited by perhaps ten million indigenous inhabitants and 50,000 Europeans, all of them incorporated into the Crown of Castile and treated (at least in theory) 'like vassals of our Crown of Castile, because that is what they are', as well as several thousand African slaves.[3]

Government activity also increased rapidly. In the 1540s the viceroy of Mexico issued over 500 orders (*mandamientos*) each year to officials and individuals, half of them Spaniards, and in the 1550s the annual total approached 800.[4] The church structure of the New World expanded in step: from four bishops at Charles's accession, all reporting to the archbishop of Seville, to two independent ecclesiastical provinces at his abdication, with three archbishops and twenty-one suffragans, all of them appointed directly by the Crown, and informal outposts of the Inquisition, reporting to the inquisitor-general in Spain.

As the Latin American historian Horst Pietschmann observed: 'The construction of a government structure in America proved perhaps the most successful venture that Charles ever undertook.' Admittedly, as Pietschmann also noted, 'The emperor's copious correspondence with members of his family and his closest councillors scarcely contain any detailed references to America'; but there were three major exceptions.[5] First came money. A few months after his proclamation as king in 1516, Charles ordered his regent in Castile to send 45,000 ducats 'from the money received from America' to Italy 'so that it can pay for our affairs of state there'; and throughout his reign he used gold and silver from America to pay for his imperial designs, especially expensive ventures such as the Tunis campaign in 1535 and the siege of Parma in 1551–2 (both of them funded in large part by treasure from Peru). A few weeks before his abdication in 1555, Charles's fiscal priorities remained undiminished: he ordered his regent in Castile to ensure that all the gold and silver available in Mexico should be embarked immediately and shipped to Spain to pay for his war against France.[6]

Charles also displayed a lifelong interest in exotic flora and fauna, perhaps stimulated by those he had seen while growing up in the Netherlands (chapter 1). Thus in 1518, from Valladolid, he thanked the officials of the House of Trade (the *Casa de la Contratación* in Seville: the body that supervised all commerce with America) for 'the dispatch of two American turkeys and a parrot that belonged to King Ferdinand, which we have enjoyed', and requested that 'you should send me the birds and similar things that may come from America which, because they are exotic, I will enjoy'. Almost forty years later, from his retirement home in Extremadura, Charles raved about 'two bedspreads lined with feathers' from America sent to keep him warm, and ordered 'dressing gowns and sheets for his bedroom made of the same material'.[7]

Charles's third abiding interest in America concerned its population. In 1518 he signed a warrant granting one of his Burgundian councillors an eight-year monopoly 'to ship to America 4,000 Black slaves, both male and female, from Guinea or any other part of Africa'.[8] A decade later he signed another contract, granting agents of the Welser company of Augsburg a similar monopoly to send another 4,000 African slaves to America over a period of four years in return for a payment of 20,000 ducats to the imperial treasury in lieu of import and customs duties. The contract specified that the slaves would work in gold mines – indeed it instructed the Welsers to 'bring fifty German master miners from Germany' – and the company vigorously prosecuted in the royal courts those who infringed their monopoly. Charles would grant many more licences to ship African slaves to America, in return for cash payments: the total number embarked rose from under 400 in the quinquennium 1511–15 to almost 4,000 in the quinquennium 1516–20, and the total shipped in the course of his reign exceeded 30,000.[9]

Ironically, this increase in the African slave trade reflected Charles's concern for America's indigenous inhabitants. Three months after arriving in Spain in 1517, he presided over a committee of leading advisers to consider (among other matters) an 'instruction for the well-being of the American Indians' written by Fray Bartolomé de Las Casas, who boasted extensive experience of the transatlantic colonies first as a settler and then as a missionary. The friar denounced in graphic terms the ruthless exploitation of the New World by those entrusted with its care, and called for major policy changes (including the decision to start shipping slaves from Africa, on the grounds that each one would save a native American from exploitation). He later claimed that his arguments had convinced Charles 'to see to the ordering of certain matters that redounded to the service of Our Lord and Ourselves, and the good of America and its inhabitants'.[10]

In other matters relating to the New World, as in so much else, Charles initially relied on the advice provided by his two 'governors': Le Sauvage and Chièvres. Ferdinand Magellan discovered this when he arrived in Valladolid early in 1518 eager to persuade the monarch to fund an expedition to the Moluccas, the fabled Spice Islands, following a 'route to them that the Portuguese did not use, by certain straits that he knew'. To make his point, 'Magellan brought a painted globe that showed the whole world' to a meeting with Le Sauvage, and 'showed him the route he would follow, except that he deliberately left the straits blank, so that no one else would use them'. The chancellor eventually 'spoke to the king and Baron Chièvres', but there is no indication that Charles made time to see the explorer (or his globe).[11] Nevertheless, in March 1518, Charles signed a contract that promised to provide Magellan with five vessels, together with stores and wages for their crews for two years, 'to discover the Spice Islands', adding 'I promise you and give my word as a king that I will keep and fulfil every promise made to you'. Interestingly, this promise did not satisfy Magellan, who (Charles noted) 'begged us to confirm and approve' his commitment, and the monarch obliged by invoking a formula that earlier kings of Castile had used when acting with dubious legal warrant:

By virtue of our own initiative, reasoned consideration and absolute royal authority, which in this matter we wish to use and do use as king and sovereign lord, not recognizing any temporal superior on this earth . . . we abrogate and nullify any laws, proclamations, sanctions and any customs and rights that are or might be contrary . . .

Charles also ordered Ferdinand, 'our most dear and well-beloved son and brother', and at that time also his heir, as well as all nobles and officials of the kingdom, to honour his promises 'for ever after'.[12] Reassured, Magellan travelled to Seville – only to find that the officials of the House of Trade lacked the 16,000 ducats required to honour Charles's promises. Magellan did not leave Spain for the Moluccas until August 1519.[13]

THE CONQUEST OF MEXICO

No sooner had Charles signed the contract with Magellan than Governor Diego Velázquez of Cuba asked the emperor to approve an expedition equipped at his own expense to 'place beneath our yoke and obedience' Yucatán (presumed to be another large island), recently discovered by agents of Velázquez in the western Caribbean. Charles agreed, providing from his own arsenal 'twenty arquebuses of eighteen kilograms each' for the expedition, and authorizing the governor to recruit up to 200 men from Spain's Caribbean colonies to carry out the 'discovery and pacification' of Yucatán. Even before he received these concessions, Velázquez had appointed his secretary, Hernán Cortés, to take command of a far larger force; and eleven ships carrying 600 soldiers and sailors, fourteen artillery pieces and sixteen horses sailed west from Cuba in February 1519.[14]

When Cortés reached the mainland he found a survivor of an earlier expedition, now fluent in the local language, who informed him of a rich and powerful state in the interior. After reconnoitring the Caribbean coast for some weeks in search of a suitable base, Cortés led some 600 men ashore and founded a settlement opportunistically called the 'Villa Rica de la Vera Cruz [Rich City of the True Cross]' on 'the island of Yucatán'. The fleet's officers became the new city's council and promptly chose Cortés as their chief magistrate. In June 1519 they sent Charles a long letter (approved if not dictated by Cortés) claiming that 'in our opinion, there is as much gold in this land as it is said Solomon accumulated for the temple' in Jerusalem. They also prepared and sent a 'sample' of almost 200 local objects, including gold, silver and jewels, escorted by six Totonac Indians in native dress, and a petition (*pedimiento*) to the emperor, signed by some 500 settlers, that asked him to invest Cortés 'with the offices of conquistador, captain-general and chief justice of these lands' until Yucatán 'has been entirely pacified and its indigenous inhabitants divided up among us. After he has conquered and pacified it, Your Majesty should appoint him governor for as long as you wish.' Cortés entrusted these items to agents who sailed for Spain on 26 July.[15]

Cortés was fortunate in his timing: the letter, the petition, the Totonacs and the 'sample' from Veracruz arrived in Spain soon after Mercurino Arborio de Gattinara succeeded Le Sauvage both as Grand Chancellor and as the minister with primary responsibility for New World affairs. Gattinara had placed 'a table in his apartment, with paper and writing-desk', where he ordered Las Casas to read all letters and papers that arrived for Charles about American affairs, and then condense 'the substance of each paragraph in one or two sentences, accompanied by: "To the first question that Your Majesty asked me about what it contained, I reply this and that etc."' Gattinara also presented to his master some proposals formulated by Las Casas for the peaceful colonization and evangelization of the mainland, after which 'the king ordered that Fray Bartolomé should handle the matter'.[16] The friar's vision was the exact opposite of the demand by the settlers of Veracruz that the new lands should be 'pacified and its indigenous inhabitants divided up'.

News of the arrival of messengers and goods from 'New Spain' (the term used by the royal clerks, perhaps for the first time) reached Charles in Catalonia, and his letters about them showed both immediate interest and clear signs of Las Casas's influence: 'I was delighted, and I give thanks to God that in my lifetime [*en mi tiempo*] a rich land has been discovered where the inhabitants show signs of ability and capacity to be baptized and receive instruction in Christian doctrine and our holy Catholic faith, which is my principal desire and wish.' The emperor also ordered that the Totonacs wear specially made European garments (silk and cloth of gold for the 'two leaders', fine textiles for the rest) and demanded that they and 'all the other things' from America be sent to him 'wherever I may be'.[17] In the event, they caught up with Charles in Valladolid in March 1520, just as he was desperately seeking money to fund his voyage to England and the Netherlands (chapter 5). He immediately put them on public display as evidence of his new-found source of wealth, and the effect proved electrifying. The nuncio speculated nervously that a powerful foreign prince had sent tribute and ambassadors to secure an alliance, which would greatly increase Charles's authority in Europe. His Venetian colleague reported how 'His Majesty summoned me for an audience, and showed me himself the presents sent to him by the ruler of the lands newly discovered', including 'a great moon made of gold, six feet in circumference' together with another one made of silver; statues of 'animals wrought and decorated in gold'; and items made of feathers from 'parrots and other birds unknown to us'. The Totonacs obligingly assured the ambassador 'that their country boasted lots of gold and silver'.[18]

As they waited at Corunna in May 1520 for a favourable wind for England, Charles's ministers debated the best way to advance his interests in the New World. Delegates sent by Governor Velázquez insisted that Cortés was a rebel who must be tried, condemned and executed for insubordination, but the royal council refused to kill a goose that laid such valuable golden eggs. Instead, they recommended to Charles a compromise likely to maximize receipts from America: they prepared documents that upheld Velázquez's authority over Cuba but made no mention of the mainland. Cortés was thus free to launch the conquest and partition of the American interior requested by the settlers of Veracruz.[19]

Charles left Corunna accompanied by many of the items sent by Cortés and he placed them on display as soon as he reached Brussels. Once again the effect proved electrifying. Albrecht Dürer confided to his *Diary* that in 'all the days of my life I have seen nothing that rejoiced my heart so much as these things, for I saw amongst them wonderful works of art, and I wondered at the subtle ingenuity of men in foreign lands'. Dürer (like Charles) did not realize that relatively few of the 'wonderful works of art' came from those who lived on the coastal plains around Veracruz: the rest were presents from envoys sent to Cortés by Montezuma, paramount ruler of the Triple Alliance of the city-states of Tenochtitlan, Texcoco and Tlacopan, often known as the Aztec Empire, which controlled the Valley of Mexico.[20]

Shortly after dispatching his letters and gifts to Spain, Cortés led some 500 Spaniards and hundreds of local inhabitants inland from Veracruz to the interior, encountering both allies and enemies along the way. Montezuma, who closely monitored the Spaniards' approach, welcomed them in November 1519 to Tenochtitlan, his capital, and quartered them in his palace complex. Perhaps he intended to arrest and later sacrifice them in a religious ritual, but Cortés struck first, arresting his host and sending out his companions to survey and appropriate the resources of the empire.[21] Despite mounting hostility from the Aztec leaders, and especially from the priests (whom the Spanish invaders prevented from carrying out their normal liturgical tasks, which included human sacrifice to placate the gods), Cortés's bold enterprise prospered until news reached him that an expeditionary force dispatched by Governor Velázquez had arrived at Veracruz with orders to arrest or kill him. Leaving a small Spanish garrison to guard Montezuma and his subjects, Cortés hastened to the coast where he won over almost all Velázquez's men; but in his absence the inhabitants of Tenochtitlan rebelled. Montezuma was killed and the Europeans and their allies fled to Tlaxcala, over 100 kilometres to the east.

Realizing the need to explain these traumatic events to Charles before others could discredit him, Cortés composed a lengthy letter to his master in October 1520 that cast everything in a rosy light. 'It seems to me,' he wrote obsequiously, 'that the best name for this country is "New Spain"'; and given its vast wealth Charles 'could call yourself emperor of it, with no less title than of Germany, which by the grace of God Your Sacred Majesty already rules'.[22] Despite the letter's imperial tone, Cortés could not disguise the fact that New Spain had now been lost. In normal times, he would have paid for such a catastrophic failure with his goods and perhaps also his life, but the Comuneros saved him.

As long as he remained in Spain, Gattinara took a keen personal interest in America: the records of the central government suggest that between his appointment in October 1518 and his departure from Corunna in May 1520, the chancellor read and approved every official communication sent to the New World. By contrast, the registers of orders issued by the royal council on American affairs contain no entries at all between August 1520 and April 1521 – a unique gap in the record – and when the council resumed its work, some warrants to its officials overseas complained that it had received no letters for 'many days'. For this it blamed the Comuneros: 'it is possible that the letters have been intercepted by the traitors who caused the cities here to rebel'. Not until September 1521 did the council inform its officials that 'it has pleased Our Lord that everything here is in peace and concord', and only then did it resume its customary vigilance over American affairs.[23]

During the hiatus in metropolitan control caused by the Comuneros, Cortés allied with anti-Aztec elements in the Valley of Mexico, notably Tlaxcala, and with their assistance he blockaded Tenochtitlan until August 1521, when the last native defenders surrendered amid the rubble of their capital. Cortés promptly rewarded the victors, who now numbered perhaps 2,000 Europeans, with *encomiendas*: the right to exact labour services and tribute from a specified group of indigenous inhabitants – precisely the outcome that Las Casas had hoped to forestall.[24] Cortés also sent a further selection of treasures to the emperor to back up his claims in another long letter. He dispatched not only 'pearls, jewels and other precious goods worth 100,000 ducats', but also one-fifth of all precious metals and stones discovered, as well as all 'regal' items (sceptres, any ornament decorated with eagles, and more giant gold and silver religious wheels). Cortés also boasted of the relative proximity to Mexico of the Pacific, where 'many islands rich in gold, pearls, jewels and spices are sure to be found' – provided (by implication) that he remained in charge.[25]

At much the same time, the survivors of Magellan's expedition returned to Spain, announcing that 'we have circumnavigated the world, sailing out to the west and returning from the east', and bringing with them 'samples of all the spices' and declarations of 'peace and friendship from all the kings and lords of all the islands' that produced spices. Charles reported excitedly to his aunt Margaret that the expedition 'went where neither Portugal nor any other nation has been . . . and I have decided to send to the Netherlands the spices that the said ship brought', to advertise to all Europe his newfound ability to procure them.[26]

TAMING NEW SPAIN

These spectacular developments led the emperor and his chancellor to take a closer look at the new 'gold-bearing world' across the Atlantic. Shortly after his return to Spain in 1522, Charles created a special committee, chaired by Gattinara, to consider once more the rival claims of Cortés and Velázquez. Their verdict (in the phrase of Luigi Avonto, an eminent expert on Gattinara) 'was based more on reason of state than on strict justice': the committee exonerated Cortés of the charge of rebellion, recommended that he be named 'governor and captain-general of New Spain', and urged that he be sent arms, horses and other provisions to consolidate and expand Spanish rule. The Crown would retain direct control only of the royal fisc, appointing a treasurer, inspector, accountant and other officials to maximize assets in New Spain.[27]

One year later, Gattinara submitted a wide-ranging memorandum to Charles on the problems that faced him, containing the recommendations of each member of a committee of trusted ministers. The first item concerned 'The Fear of God'. Although Gattinara recognized that the emperor 'is inclined by nature to fear and honour God', he proceeded to 'draw to your attention certain matters that, if you deal with them, may please God and make Him even more inclined to favour your cause'. One was the need to 'send enough qualified people to the New World that God has revealed to you' so that 'the Christian faith may be venerated and exalted there without oppressing and enslaving' the indigenous population. The committee unanimously endorsed this, and recommended the creation of a permanent council of the Indies, staffed by 'persons who boast both knowledge and experience, to meet at least twice a week'. It also accepted Gattinara's recommendation that Charles's confessor should preside over it. In August 1524 the emperor appointed García de Loaysa y Mendoza president of the *Consejo Real y Supremo de las Indias* to handle all official business concerning the New World, with Francisco de Los Cobos as secretary and the chancellor as a member.[28]

A few months later, in Mexico, Cortés penned another self-serving report to his master, dispatched with a further sample of the riches that were now (thanks to his efforts) at the emperor's disposal. The Venetian ambassador marvelled at 'a bird from those lands, the most beautiful thing in the world' as well as 'many things made with extremely beautiful feathers', concluding: 'Every day we see something new'. Charles and his ministers, who were more interested in gold than in parrots, particularly welcomed the 120,000 gold pesos that Cortés sent, because (as Gattinara informed an English embassy, with studied understatement) they 'shall help somewhat towardis his chargis' in fighting the French in Italy.[29]

The new council of the Indies nevertheless objected to the conduct of Cortés. Charles had given strict orders that no indigenous inhabitants should be forced to work for the conquistadors of New Spain: instead they 'must be allowed to live in liberty', paying only the same 'tribute and services that they rendered to Montezuma'; yet Cortés appeared to have disobeyed. Charles wrote reproachfully that 'I have received, in person and by letter, many statements against you and your administration'. He recognized that 'some of what people write and say will stem from jealousy and envy that you are serving us, but to comply with my obligation to uphold justice according to the laws and customs of that land', and also 'for the discharge of our royal conscience', he needed to take drastic action.[30]

Initially, Gattinara wanted Charles to announce that he 'planned to create and send a powerful fleet to reduce the lands discovered by Cortés to true obedience ... so that he could profit from all the riches that they contain', because he believed that the announcement alone, 'without actually sending a fleet', would make Cortés toe the line. The chancellor then thought of something more permanent – the transfer to the New World of an institution used by the Crown to control its officials in Spain: a government inspector (*juez de residencia*) who would report on 'how our officials in New Spain have used and exercised their offices'. In particular, after consulting with Cortés 'and with our officials, and with anyone else you choose, especially the friars', the inspector would determine 'the best method to convert the indigenous population of America to our Holy Catholic Faith, which is our principal desire and intention, and to ensure that they are well and justly treated' – instructions once again clearly derived from the views of Las Casas.[31] When news arrived that the inspector had died shortly after he arrived, followed by his designated successor, the council tried yet another approach. In a further lengthy report to Charles, sent from Mexico in 1526, Cortés had expressed the desire to return to Spain and explain his conduct; the following year Loaysa sent a letter 'requesting and advising him to come to Spain so that he could meet and get to know His Majesty'.[32]

Cortés found the offer irresistible. In May 1528 he arrived in Spain 'to address what had been said about him' by his critics, accompanied by an entourage that included a son and nephew of Montezuma and 'other prominent men from Mexico, Tlaxcala and other cities' as well as 'several of the principal conquistadors' and about forty indigenous people, including twelve of the athletes and jugglers who had entertained Montezuma. 'In short,' noted Gómara, Cortés 'came like a great lord.'[33] By chance, the German artist Christoph Weiditz arrived in Spain at the same time and his watercolours of the multicultural court reflected the tremendous impression made by Cortés and his entourage. Weiditz painted the conqueror, together with the caption 'This is the man who won almost all America for Emperor Charles V', as well as several of the Mexica athletes and jugglers who, he wrote, 'entertained His Imperial Majesty'.[34]

Cortés's tactics worked well. A royal letter in April 1529 informed him that Loaysa and Los Cobos 'have briefed me on what you request', and that he had instructed the council to draw up the necessary paperwork. The following month, Charles signed warrants that created Cortés marquis of the Valle de Oaxaca and granted him 'up to 23,000 vassals with their lands', some 500 kilometres south of Mexico City. The emperor insisted that this was an 'irrevocable grant for now and for ever' to reward the marquis's services to the Crown since leaving Cuba ten years earlier (a retrospective pardon for his previous insubordination), and he invoked the same formula as he had done with Magellan to guarantee the grant: he ordered Prince Philip (now his heir) and all his vassals to respect the donation inviolably, 'notwithstanding any laws that may contradict it', because the emperor abrogated them 'by virtue of our own initiative, reasoned consideration, and absolute royal authority'.[35] In addition, Charles took the first steps towards creating communities fully protected by law for his indigenous subjects. At the request of the new marquis, and of the delegates from Tlaxcala who accompanied him, he ordered his officials 'to investigate the role played by the inhabitants of Tlaxcala in the conquest of Mexico, and see if it would be right to protect them from being included in any encomienda, as they request, as a reward for their assistance'.[36]

TYING UP LOOSE ENDS

Issuing orders for America was easy; securing their execution was hard. In November 1527 the emperor decided to transfer to the New World another institution from Spain: he created an *Audiencia* in Mexico City, an appeals court with a president and five judges answering directly to the council of the Indies. Unfortunately for the plan, some judges took a year to reach Mexico, two died soon after they got there; and choosing a president took even longer. A special committee chaired by Cardinal Tavera, with members from the councils of Castile and Finance as well as the Indies, recommended the appointment of 'a sensible and prudent gentleman', but their first nominee claimed he was too ill to cross the Atlantic, and Tavera reported bitterly that although two others 'said that they would serve Your Majesty, they asked for such outrageous rewards that it seems they were not as willing to serve Your Majesty as they seemed at first. So we have begun to think of other people.'[37]

The emperor also had limited success in exploiting the lands beyond America to which he now laid claim. Soon after the return of Magellan's men in 1522, Charles signed a contract with a group of armourers to equip a second fleet to return to the Spice Islands because of 'the desire we have always had, and still have, to enlarge these kingdoms of Spain and enrich their inhabitants, our vassals' – but also, he confided to his aunt Margaret, 'because of the benefit that might arise for me'. He agreed to pay for a new House of Spice in Corunna, together with a new pier and three forts to defend the harbour.[38]

The emperor delayed the departure of this expedition because of protests from the Portuguese, who claimed that the Moluccas belonged to them according to the treaty of Tordesillas, which had created a notional demarcation line to divide the global claims of the two Iberian powers. It proved easy to establish the meridian – Africa, Asia and Brazil fell to Portugal, and the rest of America fell to Spain – but the ante-meridian proved almost impossible to locate, because no one knew the latitude of the lands that lay between Asia and America. Magellan had taken with him an impressive array of nautical instruments to establish the demarcation line, but he failed; so in 1524, Charles sent a team of diplomats, pilots and sailors (including some survivors of the circumnavigation) to debate the rival claims at a conference with their Portuguese counterparts. When the conference broke up after six weeks without reaching a resolution, the emperor ordered the fleet in Corunna to retrace Magellan's route to the Spice Islands, and he approved Cortés's request to send a flotilla down the Pacific seaboard of America to see whether 'there is some strait on that coast' that led to the Spice Islands.[39]

In March 1526, just before Charles married Isabella of Portugal, another special committee, this time including Gattinara and Loaysa, discussed how to reconcile the rival claims of the Iberian monarchs. Perhaps encouraged by the defeat and capture of Francis I, Charles refused to abandon his claims to 'our islands in the Moluccas' and instead repeated his order for Cortés to send a fleet from Mexico to locate and reinforce his subjects already there.[40] The resumption of war with France made Charles willing to sell his claim to the Moluccas to Portugal; but sensing his advantage, King John dragged out the negotiations in the hope of getting more for his money. 'I am thinking of breaking off the negotiations completely,' Charles fumed in a confidential letter to one of his Burgundian advisers in December 1528, 'and believe me, although we are brothers-in-law, [King John] will get no grain, anchors, weapons or any other commodity from my realms that he may need.' The emperor hoped that his threat of rupture would rekindle the talks, and thus produce instant cash, 'but if I could find any other source of funds, I would reject whatever offer he chooses to make'. He continued, in a rare example of unrestrained imperial wrath:

> [The deadlock] has hurt me more than anything else that could happen to me, because I based all my plans on this. Now that I see it slip away I believe the whole edifice has collapsed, with no hope of reconstructing it, and I despair of my voyage [to Italy]. You may wonder whether I feel positive and patient about this, but I can assure you that you will not find those qualities in me. I don't think I have ever felt so angry.[41]

Eventually, in April 1529, the need to fund his voyage to Italy and to assist Ferdinand in Hungary forced the emperor to give in: he surrendered his claim to the Moluccas, and agreed that any of his subjects subsequently found in the area would be 'chastised and punished as pirates and violators of the peace'. In return, Portugal agreed to pay Charles 250,000 gold ducats immediately and in cash, with 100,000 more to follow. The emperor now had enough money to fund his voyage, but the House of Spice closed its doors for ever. He had sacrificed the interests of Spain for dynastic advantage.[42]

New Spain presented the emperor with problems of a different sort. He complained that he had received many different opinions about what to do next, and because of that, and 'because those provinces are so far away, and their affairs so different from those of these kingdoms', he felt confused. Eventually, his desire to 'succeed in doing the right thing' for them, and for the 'discharge of our conscience', led him to take steps to create an enduring balance of power in New Spain. At the request of their representatives at his court, in March 1535 'we promise and give our royal word that now and for ever the city of Tlaxcala and its territory will never be alienated by us or by our heirs'. Instead the city would be permanently 'incorporated' into 'the royal Crown of Castile'. Charles even paid a court painter three ducats to create a coat of arms for the city.[43] The following month he appointed Antonio de Mendoza not only viceroy and governor of New Spain, but also president of the Audiencia.

Charles tasked his new viceroy with three major missions. Mendoza must ensure proper Christian instruction for the entire indigenous population because 'we are certain that this is the best way to make them love and fear us' and to make them 'live in peace and in continual and complete obedience'. At the same time, revenues must increase because 'at present, as everybody knows, we need great resources for the defence of our holy faith' in Europe. To this end, Mendoza must impose the same taxes in New Spain as those paid in Castile (notably the *alcabala*, a sales tax) and challenge all exemptions, especially those granted to the first generation of Spanish settlers (known in the documents as the *primeros conquistadores*: the first conquerors) and their families. Finally, the viceroy must keep Cortés in check, despite the broad powers he had received from the emperor's own hand. To that end, Charles authorized Mendoza 'to appoint someone other than the marquis [del Valle] to carry out orders, when occasions arise in which this seems desirable to you'.[44]

These and other measures so infuriated Cortés that in 1540 he returned to Spain 'to kiss Your Majesty's hands' and to 'plead for redress for the notorious provocations and injustices that I have received from Don Antonio de Mendoza'. Although he tried to gain a sympathetic hearing by participating with his sons in the ill-fated attack on Algiers, losing his jewels in the process, Cortés failed. In 1544, still in Spain, he filled three foolscap pages with his pent-up grievances:

> Sacred, Catholic, Caesarean Majesty: I thought that the labours of my youth would bring me rest in my old age, having spent forty years not sleeping, eating badly, or if not badly not well either, always with weapons ready, placing myself in danger, squandering my life and property – all in the service of God ... while spreading the name and patrimony of my king.

Nevertheless, Cortés asserted, 'defending myself against Your Majesty's attorneys is harder than winning the land of the enemy'. He wrote in vain: a secretary intercepted the letter and scribbled on the back 'No need to reply'. There is no evidence that Charles ever saw it.[45] Cortés never left Spain again – but at least he died peacefully in his bed, unlike the leaders who acquired a second American empire for Charles.

THE PROBLEM OF PERU

After securing Mexico, groups of Spaniards fanned out to find new riches elsewhere on the American continent. Two of them, Francisco Pizarro and Diego de Almagro, reconnoitred the coast of what is now Ecuador, on the edge of the Inca state, an empire that rivalled that of the Aztecs in size and resources; and when the governor of Panama refused them permission for a further expedition in greater strength, Pizarro returned to Spain to procure Charles's support. In May 1529 the emperor accepted the recommendation of his council of the Indies that Peru 'should be settled and that Captain Pizarro should be entrusted with populating and governing it for the rest of his life', but he insisted that the process must be peaceful:

> Because according to the available information about the area, its inhabitants possess the intelligence and capacity to understand our Holy Catholic Faith, so there is no need to conquer and subjugate them by force of arms. Instead they should be treated with love and generosity. We therefore give permission for [Pizarro] to take 250 men with him.

In December 1530, together with Almagro and other restless adventurers, Pizarro set sail from Panama for Peru.[46]

Like Cortés a decade before, Pizarro was fortunate in his timing. Although the Inca state covered almost a million square kilometres, unified by a sophisticated bureaucracy and a superb network of roads and bridges, it lacked a clear-cut succession policy: on the death of each ruler, his male relatives conducted a lethal struggle until one of them had subdued or killed all the others. Upon the death of the Supreme Inca in 1527 a bitter succession war broke out and lasted for five years until supporters of his son Atahualpa defeated and captured his rivals. In November 1532, Atahualpa marched in triumph at the head of 40,000 warriors towards the imperial capital, Cuzco, and had almost reached Cajamarca, where he encountered Pizarro, accompanied by 167 Europeans (one-third of them cavalry) and a few field guns, travelling to the same destination. Reassured by his huge numerical advantage, Atahualpa foolishly accepted an invitation to enter the city square where Pizarro had concealed artillery and soldiers in the surrounding buildings. Once the Supreme Inca had entered, Pizarro gave 'a signal to the gunner that he should fire his shots into the midst' of the packed square, and immediately afterwards his cavalry rode in to exploit the confusion. According to one of the victors:

> None of them fought back against the Spaniards because of the shock they felt at seeing [Pizarro] among them, and the unexpected firing of the artillery and the horses rushing upon them – things that they had never seen before; so in great confusion they tried to run for their lives rather than stay and fight.

Although the battle lasted scarcely half an hour, when it ended '2,000 native Americans lay dead in the square, not counting the wounded'. Each of the Europeans at Cajamarca must have killed more than ten adversaries in less than an hour.[47]

Atahualpa was one of the few survivors. Although after the massacre his captors stripped him of his golden robes and jewellery, and instead dressed him in 'ordinary native costume', Pizarro respected his role as Supreme Inca and (much as Cortés had done with Montezuma) allowed him to issue orders (including commands to execute most other members of the imperial family) and to collect all available precious metals to pay for his ransom, encouraging him to believe that his captors would then set him free to rule the empire he had won. Between March and July 1533 more than six tons of gold and twelve tons of silver arrived in Cajamarca and was melted down and forged into bars; but as soon as the operation was complete, Pizarro had Atahualpa summarily executed by garrotte.

Again like Cortés before him, Pizarro tried to secure Charles's approval of his initiative by sending a generous share of the loot back to Spain, earmarked for imperial ventures: intricate artefacts 'never previously seen in America, nor (I think) in the possession of any Christian prince' that would surely assist 'His Imperial Majesty in the war against the Turks, enemies of our Holy Faith'.[48] The treasures from Peru attracted as much attention when they went on display in 1534 as the treasures sent by Cortés from Mexico. Two decades later, the chronicler Pedro Cieza de León still recalled the excitement he felt at seeing 'those fabulous items displayed in Seville from the treasure that Atahualpa promised to give to the Spaniards in Cajamarca'. Charles felt less enthusiasm: 'I would love to see it all,' he told his officials in Seville, 'but given the time it would take to bring it here, I think it would be enough to send me some of the most unusual gold and silver work. You can coin all the rest.' In January 1535, given 'our need for money' to prepare his attack on Tunis, the emperor ordered that the remaining gold and silver be distributed among several royal mints so that it would all be available within two months as coins to pay his bills.[49]

Charles knew how to show his gratitude. Reversing his previous policy, 'on the advice of our council, and to show our desire to reward the conquistadors and settlers of that region, especially those who want to remain there', he informed Pizarro that 'we agree that there will be permanent allocations of the indigenous inhabitants' throughout Peru. Although the emperor scolded Pizarro for his conduct at Cajamarca – 'the death of Atahualpa displeased me, because he was a sovereign' – he added 'since it seemed to you necessary, we approve it for now'; and in 1537 he granted the perpetrator '20,000 vassals there, the title of marquis', and the right to name a successor 'from your own family, or whoever else you please'.[50]

Despite these massive rewards, Pizarro's position in Peru had become perilous. He distributed almost all of Atahualpa's ransom among those who had taken part in his capture – starting with himself (over 40,000 pesos of gold and silver) and his brothers (over 60,000 pesos) – whereas Almagro and his men, who had arrived after the Supreme Inca's capture, received only 20,000 pesos between them. This exacerbated the existing divisions among the conquistadors and led to a civil war that cost the lives of thousands, including both leaders. In 1538, Pizarro's brother defeated Almagro and executed him, but three years later a group of Almagro's followers cornered the governor, and although Pizarro managed to kill two of his assailants, his sword became stuck in a third, which allowed Almagro's son to stab him in the throat. After the governor fell, the rest inflicted on him over twenty wounds – an ostentatious killing typical of the feuds of early modern Europe and now transferred (like so much else) to the overseas colonies.[51]

THE NEW LAWS

These gruesome events soon became known in Europe because several conquistadors published best-selling accounts that described in detail the brutal nature of the conquest of Peru. The foremost professor of theology at the university of Salamanca, the Dominican Fray Francisco de Vitoria, lamented to a colleague that although few things that he read still shocked him, 'what is happening in Peru freezes the blood in my veins':

> I cannot see the justice of that war. I have gathered from those who were in the recent battle with Atahualpa that neither he nor his followers injured the Christians in any way, nor committed any act that required a declaration of war ... And I fear that the subsequent conquests over there have been even worse.[52]

Vitoria's fears were well founded. Some years later Viceroy Mendoza provided chilling detail on what hostilities in America involved. He boasted that he executed local inhabitants who opposed him in one of three ways: 'firing at them with artillery until they were cut to pieces; setting the dogs on them; or giving them to African slaves to be killed'. He justified such brutality not only because 'we need to set the dogs on them, or shoot at them, both to punish those who are most guilty and to make the rest more fearful', but also because he was following European precedent. As a young man he had taken part in the reconquest of Granada, during which (he reminded Charles) 'we used to beat and stone many Muslims who had reneged on our Holy Faith, and in such cases we did not involve the courts'. Any indigenous inhabitants who escaped such brutality, Mendoza added, 'were treated as slaves and divided up' among the Spanish settlers.[53]

Appalled by such reports, Pope Paul III issued a Bull in 1537 proclaiming that native Americans were not 'dumb brutes created for our service' but full members of the human race who 'should freely and legitimately enjoy their liberty and the possession of their property. They should not be in any way enslaved. Should the contrary happen it shall be null and of no effect.' He also ordered Cardinal Tavera to excommunicate any transgressors. The following year, when the Cortes of Castile debated Charles's demand for an excise tax, the senior nobleman present drew an ominous parallel between the exorbitant cost of imperial policies in Europe and America:

> I hold it a great disservice to His Majesty, who is still young enough to enjoy these kingdoms for many years, to place them under such a fiscal burden that in a few years its inhabitants will be ruined, just like the indigenous inhabitants of the New World. The resources of these kingdoms will be exhausted after a few years, if we act with such speed, just like the gold found in the early discoveries overseas.

Early in 1539, Vitoria delivered a series of public lectures in Salamanca that excoriated the behaviour of the conquistadors towards the indigenous inhabitants. It did not matter, he argued, whether or not the Spaniards had merely obeyed orders from the Crown: they had transgressed both natural and divine law. The lectures also questioned the basis for Spanish rule over America.[54]

Charles reacted vigorously to these criticisms. He prohibited the publication of the Bull in Spain and asked the pope to revoke it; and in November 1539, just before setting off for his overland journey through France, he ordered the prior of the Dominican convent in Salamanca where Vitoria and several of his colleagues resided to 'summon before you immediately' any academic who had discussed 'our rights to the Indies in sermons or in classrooms, publicly or secretly, and get them to declare under oath when, and in whose presence, they did so'. The prior must then deliver all declarations to a special commissar, who would bring them to court for examination. Furthermore, 'except with our express permission, neither now nor ever shall there be any sermon or discussion on the matter, nor should any writing on the subject be printed. I shall view anything to the contrary as a grave disservice to me'.[55]

The spectacular failure of his Algiers campaign in 1541 seems to have changed the emperor's mind, leading him to suspect that failure to protect his American subjects had cost him divine favour. Soon after he returned to Spain he initiated a thorough review of the policies executed in his name overseas.[56] The process began in April 1542 when the Cortes of Castile included among its petitions for redress: 'We beg Your Majesty to remedy the cruelties committed in America against the indigenous inhabitants, because God will be well served and America will be preserved – instead of being depopulated as happens now'. Charles responded by creating a special committee of thirteen experts, chaired by Loaysa and including Pedro de

Soto (his past and present confessors) as well as 'prelates, gentlemen, friars and some of our councillors' (Los Cobos and Zúñiga among them). In the emperor's presence they heard testimony from expert witnesses, including theologians like Vitoria and missionaries newly returned from America like Las Casas, who shared chilling evidence of Spanish brutality that a decade later would form the core of his *Very brief account of the destruction of America*. The friar claimed that Juan Martínez de Silíceo, Philip's preceptor, asked for a copy of his evidence and presented it to the prince. The committee then prepared *New laws and ordinances for the government of America, and for the better treatment and preservation of its indigenous inhabitants*. Convinced and chastened by what he had heard at the committee meetings, in November 1542, Charles affixed his signature.[57]

The document began, unusually, with an imperial apology:

> For many years I have been willing and eager to study the affairs of America thoroughly, given their great importance both for the service of God Our Lord and the increase of our Holy Catholic faith, and for the protection and sound government of those who live over there . . . [But] although I have tried to find time for this, it has not proved possible because of the many and continuing items of business that have cropped up, which I have not been able to neglect, and also because of my unavoidable absences from this kingdom.

Now, having convened the special committee on American affairs 'to discuss and deal with the most important matters that I have learned now require attention, and having heard debates about them on several occasions in my presence, and having secured the opinion of everyone, I have resolved to order the following things to be done . . .' Some of the forty clauses that followed aimed to 'preserve and augment the indigenous population, to educate them in the affairs of our Catholic faith, and to treat them as free people and our vassals, which they are'; others insisted that the tribute and labour services required of indigenous inhabitants must be 'moderated so that they are bearable'; others still reformed the procedures of the council of the Indies and created a viceroy and a royal Audiencia in Peru, as well as another Audiencia in Guatemala.[58]

Three other clauses provoked outrage among the Spanish settlers throughout America. One ordained that all indigenous inhabitants except those enslaved for an act of war or rebellion (and all enslaved Indian women and children) must be freed forthwith, and that in future no one could be enslaved 'even if involved in a rebellion'. Another forbade the grant of any new encomienda; mandated that 'when each encomendero dies, those who labour for him will be incorporated in Crown estates'; and ordered royal officials and ecclesiastical institutions holding encomiendas to surrender them at once. The third controversial clause decreed that 'those who played a leading role in the recent wars' between the followers of Almagro and Pizarro in Peru, 'will forfeit the labour of any indigenous inhabitants, who will be incorporated in Crown estates'. These clauses proved divisive not least because they contradicted a host of earlier royal directives. Several warrants in the 1530s had granted groups of conquerors 'permanent allocations of the indigenous inhabitants', so that on the death of each encomendero his legitimate children or his widow would inherit. Likewise, following Charles's express order in 1534, many colonists had enslaved indigenous inhabitants accused of resistance, captured in war, or judged guilty by a colonial court of an offence normally punishable by death, but commuted to penal servitude – 'all of which,' the Audiencia of Mexico tartly reminded Charles, 'Your Majesty told us enjoyed your approval'.[59]

To many Spanish settlers the New Laws seemed like a declaration of war, and their hostile reaction was swift and overwhelming. A letter sent to the council of the Indies in October 1543 by Jerónimo López, a magistrate in Mexico City and one of the 'first conquerors', was perhaps the most eloquent. After recognizing that 'some of Your Majesty's ordinances are very just and will help to protect and preserve this country as you desire', López protested that reneging on the promise that encomiendas could be inherited would mean that 'this land cannot endure, but will be lost and abandoned to its indigenous population'; while the order that 'no one should be enslaved, even if they rise up and rebel, is very dangerous because Your Majesty is giving them courage to rise up tomorrow because they can see that you have eliminated the punishment'. The emperor should remember that his new American possessions were 'so remote and separated from the presence and power of Your Majesty, where for every Spaniard there are at least a thousand natives', so that in case of trouble 'Your Majesty cannot send us help from Seville or Granada, because we would not have time to ask for it nor Your Majesty time to send it. Instead you must keep your reserves here.' Consequently, López continued:

If this land were like the Netherlands, Naples, Navarre or Granada, which Your Majesty can visit in person ... it would be good for you to come to see how to improve matters, but we are so far away here that Your

Majesty can neither see for yourself nor govern from there, because by the time you decide on a remedy for something the situation will have changed.

Herein lay a central problem of the first transatlantic empire: the obstacles posed by distance forced Charles to rely on the advice of others, but 'everyone gives you their opinion according to their point of view and the little they have seen and heard of this land'. López reserved special criticism for the political advice given to the emperor by friars, because 'few of them have experience of governing towns and villages, or even their own households' and therefore 'they speak as men who do not know how much labour and bloodshed or how many deaths are needed to keep such a vast enterprise working'. Instead 'they advise Your Majesty to take steps that will lose everything, and us with it'. The emperor should take advice only from those who knew whereof they spoke, and especially from conquistadors like López who 'had seen it all with my own eyes'.[60]

Like Cortés before him, López was wasting his time. Loaysa, president of the council of the Indies (which received the letter), was a Dominican friar like Las Casas, Soto and Vitoria: he was not likely to abandon the policies that he had just persuaded the emperor to adopt – but just to be sure, López's letter was endorsed: 'Seen: no reply needed.' Instead the council appointed one of its own members, Francisco Tello de Sandoval, a priest, as inspector-general of Mexico and ordered him to go and put the New Laws into effect there at once; and it appointed Blasco Nuñez Vela, a nobleman with extensive military and naval experience, as the first viceroy of Peru and issued him with parallel orders. The emperor's inner circle had scored a resounding victory – one that almost terminated Spanish rule in America.

THE REBELLION OF PERU

In Mexico and central America, Viceroy Mendoza immediately saw the dangers inherent in the New Laws and suspended promulgation until the emperor had heard and considered objections to them. In the words of a settler in Guatemala in 1545: 'The ordinances and New Laws from Spain are neither observed nor obeyed.'[61] Nuñez Vela was less prudent: immediately after his arrival in Peru in May 1544 he started to confiscate encomiendas from royal officials, ecclesiastics and those involved in the recent civil wars, as required by the ordinances. Naturally, his actions alienated the Spanish colonists, who now numbered at least 5,000, and many of them appealed for protection to Gonzalo Pizarro, brother and universal heir of the late Francisco and a charismatic leader in his own right.

Gonzalo began by composing a formal protest to the emperor in the name of the cities and encomenderos of Peru, asserting that specific clauses of the New Laws threatened the survival of Spanish rule, and he asked (like the viceroy of Mexico) that implementation be suspended until the emperor had heard the objections of those affected.[62] Unlike Mendoza, Nuñez Vela paid no heed to the colonists' complaints and instead behaved despotically, stabbing to death a senior treasury official who opposed him. The Audiencia of Lima therefore declared the viceroy deposed, imprisoned him and recognized Gonzalo as governor of Peru.

Charles was in the Netherlands when news of these alarming events arrived, and so Prince Philip's regency council was the first to debate how best to react. The duke of Alba advocated the immediate dispatch of an army to restore order because 'such great disrespect, boldness and violence as this could not be remedied or punished except by rigour and force'; but his colleagues pointed out that 5,000 kilometres separated Spain from the Caribbean, so that most troops would die on the transatlantic journey, and that Pizarro's fleet controlled the Pacific, through which the royal troops would have to sail.[63]

The situation in Peru continued to deteriorate. In 1545, Viceroy Nuñez Vela managed to escape from prison and regroup his forces, but Pizarro hunted him down and then, at the head of 800 men (some of them former Comuneros), defeated him and his few royalist supporters in battle, and killed him. The entire viceroyalty was now in open rebellion. According to one courtier, the 'boldness and rashness' of the rebels offended the emperor far more than the Comuneros, 'because when they rebelled in Spain, the authority and reputation of the emperor was less on account of his youth and lack of administrative experience'. Charles particularly resented the news that Gonzalo Pizarro, a commoner, planned to declare himself 'king of Peru'. 'Solving the problem of Peru,' Los Cobos opined in August 1545, 'has become the greatest challenge we have faced for a long time.'[64]

By then a deluge of letters, memoranda and personal testimony railing against the New Laws had arrived from Mexico: all urged the emperor to preserve hereditable encomiendas on the grounds that, although not perfect, the institution lay at the foundation of all trade, industry and evangelization. Even the Dominicans of New Spain claimed that if deprived of the Indians whose labour supported their missionary efforts, they would have to leave. Charles's councillors therefore recommended major concessions to avoid (in the words of Juan de Zúñiga) having to conquer America all over again – this time from its Spanish colonists. Prince Philip summarized the debate for the benefit of his father: 'All agreed that human efforts and forces will not suffice to pacify and recover Peru unless we also authorize negotiations by some person of great prudence, wisdom and experience.' In a separate message, Los Cobos suggested to the emperor that the ideal negotiator would be Pedro de La Gasca.[65]

Born into a family of modest means, La Gasca won a scholarship to read law and theology at both Alcalá and Salamanca universities, where he studied under Vitoria and Silíceo. Later he became a priest and in 1541 Tavera, inquisitor-general as well as president of the royal council, appointed him an inquisitor. Confident of support from the cardinal as well as from Los Cobos, La Gasca immediately accepted his appointment but refused to leave for Peru unless Charles granted him an unprecedented authority: the right to pardon all types of offence, civil as well as criminal, public and private; the power to wage war and make peace; and the authority to raid the royal treasury for funds to raise and support an army if necessary. This was outrageous, and for some time 'the council discussed and disagreed about La Gasca's demands'; but facing the unprecedented challenge of a major transatlantic rebellion they eventually advised Charles to accept.[66]

For a while the emperor hesitated, aware that 'the affairs of America are so weighty and so important that we need to examine and consider the measures that must be taken'; but in the autumn of 1545 he authorized some important concessions to the settlers. Although he refused to sanction the enslavement of Indians, he revoked 'the law that required indigenous inhabitants to become direct vassals of the Crown when each encomendero died': henceforth the widows and children of the first conquerors could inherit their encomiendas. 'Enforcement of the other ordinances that had caused rebellion is also suspended', and 'we order that everything should revert to its previous state'.[67] In addition, Charles recalled Nuñez Vela (not yet aware that he was dead), and authorized the dispatch of La Gasca with the power to suspend the viceroy and the judges of the Audiencia of Lima and send them back to Spain 'if they were at fault in anything', as well as 'to make war on any clerics' who defied him. La Gasca received all the powers he had demanded, as well as a copy of the king's own seal to affix to 'forty blank warrants that you can issue to individuals who have shown themselves loyal to His Majesty'. Finally, 'in view of the long journey, and the risks', Charles authorized La Gasca to 'name the person you consider best qualified' to succeed him; and the emperor instructed officials elsewhere in America

1. *Young Habsburgs study at school c. 1510.* Although we have no picture of Charles and his siblings at school, the autobiographical account dictated by their grandfather Maximilian of his own schooling contains a woodcut by Hans Burgkmair, prepared under the emperor's supervision, which may well reflect the schoolroom he observed when visiting his grandchildren in Mechelen.

2. *Charles's first signature, 1504.* In January 1504, not quite four years old, the prince allegedly dictated this letter begging his grandfather Ferdinand to allow his mother Joanna ('la princesa') to return to the Netherlands, but no child of his age could have composed such a complex document (let alone in a foreign language). He could not even sign it himself without help: the initial 'C' of 'Carlos' (at the bottom of the page) is reversed and he wrote the remaining five letters without lifting his quill from the page, probably copying a 'model' prepared by his tutor.

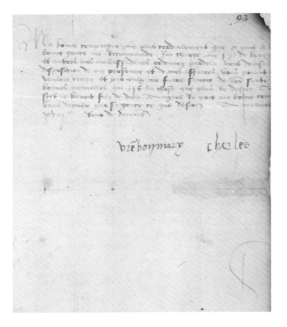

3. *Charles's first letter in French, 1508.* Although some erudite scholars have assigned the date 1513 to this letter, both the immature hand and the content show that Charles signed this love letter to Princess Mary Tudor 'Your good husband, Charles' five years earlier.

4. *Martial sports for boys, c. 1514*. Maximilian's autobiography, *Der Weiss Kunig* (meaning both 'The white king' and 'The wise king'), includes a woodcut that shows how the future emperor learned about war as a boy by playing with toy jousting knights and practising with a miniature cannon, a bow and a crossbow – precisely the toys that he gave to his grandson Charles. Two toy jousting knights from the imperial collection – perhaps the ones given by Maximilian – survive in a Vienna museum.

5. *Happy family, 1511.* This frontispiece of an illuminated hymnal presented by Maximilian to his daughter Margaret in 1511 shows the emperor sitting beneath the Habsburg double-headed eagle, with Margaret and Charles on chairs at his feet, and his granddaughters Eleanor (with an open book), Isabeau and Marie (with her back to the viewer) in the foreground.

6. *The resolute knight meets Death.* Charles V was so impressed by Olivier de la Marche's fantasy about knights at the court of Burgundy that in 1551 he began to translate the verse epic from French into Spanish, and took both the illustrated manuscript and a copy of the printed Spanish edition with him to his retirement home at Yuste.

7. *Charles makes his ceremonial 'entry' to Bruges as count of Flanders in 1515.* Remy du Puys created this handsome manuscript presentation copy for Charles, but also oversaw a printed version for the general public. The first pageant in the sequence shows three angels presenting the young prince with a crown, a coat of arms and the keys of the city, just as the three Wise Men had brought gifts to the Christ child.

8. *Charles unbuttons himself in a holograph note to his friend, Count Henry of Nassau, 1518.* The new king of Castile, miserable at Tordesillas with his mother, despite sledging in the snow and courting a possible paramour, missed his friends and his familiar lifestyle back in the Netherlands – and especially the addressee: 'mon Henri'.

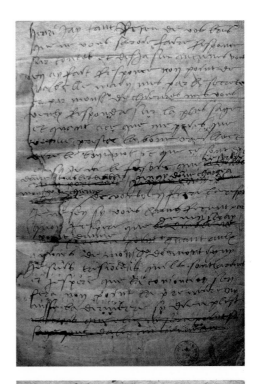

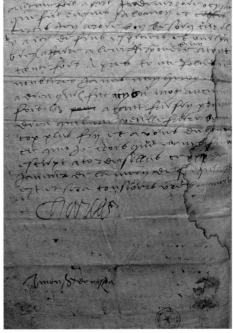

9. *Charles's secret instruction to Prince Philip, Palamos, 6 May 1543*. The emperor warned his son, 'always discuss your affairs with many, and do not become tied or obliged to any individual' – perhaps recalling the way in which Chièvres had once controlled him. The plethora of additions and corrections, between the lines as well as in both margins, shows how the emperor struggled to evaluate his principal ministers (in this case, 'the cardinal of Toledo' – Tavera – in the margin and the duke of Alba in the text).

10. *Charles almost writes in German, 1519.* Charles's desire to be elected king of the Romans led him to write letters in his own hand ('*manu propria*') to each Elector in German – but his ignorance of the language obliged him to copy each character from a 'model', just as he had done as a child when writing in Spanish.

11. *Mary Tudor wearing a brooch with jewels that reads 'the emp[er]our', 1522.* According to his diplomats in England, just before Charles's visit in 1522 the 'little princess' (aged eight) showed her charms by wearing 'on her bosom a golden brooch ornamented with jewels forming your majesty's name, which name she had taken on St Valentine's Day … which seems a happy augury'. In the event, Mary would remain a spinster until she married Charles's son Philip thirty-two years later.

12. *A suit of combat armour for Charles, 1525.* Kolman Helmschmid of Augsburg added the initials 'KD', standing for 'Karolus Divus' ('Charles the Divine') to this full suit of plate armour, made for the emperor around 1525. Three years later, if Francis had accepted Charles's challenge to a duel, this is what the emperor would have worn, perhaps after some refinements by Helmschmid, whom Charles summoned to join him in Spain.

13. *Discussion points drawn up for Charles before one of his meetings with Pope Clement VII in Bologna, 1529.* 'The matter of the queen of England' (Katherine of Aragon) was the first item for discussion, and the fifth was 'Changes to the brief of absolution for the matter [read: sack] of Rome', accompanied by several proposals for extracting wealth from, and extending royal jurisdiction over, the church in Spain. Charles made some annotations (in lighter coloured ink).

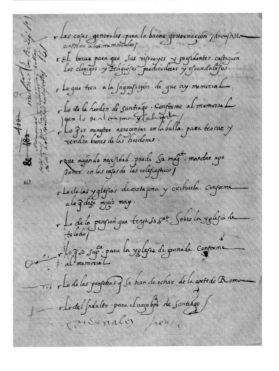

14. *Francis I captured at the battle of Pavia*. One of the seven tapestry panels commissioned to commemorate the victory of Charles's troops on his twenty-fifth birthday, 24 February 1525, and presented to him on his return to the Netherlands six years later. In the background the Spanish infantry emerge from the woods and advance towards the French cavalry, while in the foreground Francis I is pulled from his horse (with the fleur-de-lys clearly displayed).

15. *Charles and his grandparents in Bruges, 1531.* In 1528, the Brugse Vrije (a component of the county of Flanders) commissioned Lanceloot Blondeel to design a suitable monument in honour of Charles V for their Palace of Justice in the city of Bruges. It took three years to complete the magnificent chimneypiece in oak, marble and alabaster, with life-size statues of the emperor and his grandparents: Mary and Maximilian on the right, Ferdinand and Isabella on the left. The three males all boast supersized codpieces, no doubt as a reminder that marriage, not war, had united their four inheritances.

16. *Joanna and Charles, monarchs of Aragon, 1528.* This magnificent 100 escudos gold coin may be the first image of Charles with a beard – although he still wears his hair shoulder length in the Burgundian fashion. Joanna appears as a nun, albeit with a crown as a reminder that she and her son were joint rulers of Aragon as well as of Castile.

17. *Emperor Charles eclipses Sultan Suleiman, 1532.* Charles, supported by an angel, dominates the sultan in this striking bronze medal, almost certainly minted to commemorate his Hungarian triumph in 1532. The inscriptions reads: 'You are destined, o fortunate Caesar, to advance *plus ultra* / The imperial sword will remove the opposing head'.

18. *Charles with a book and gloves by Christoph Amberger, 1532.* One of the very few portraits that shows the emperor with a book, this painting displays the 'golden hair, worn short' described by eyewitnesses as well as the blond beard that scarcely disguised the emperor's prominent lower jaw. Note that the hand that marks the emperor's place in the book wears a glove, as if he is about to put the text down and go hunting.

19. *Portraits of Charles by Jakob Seisenegger and Titian, 1532–3.* During his prolonged residence in Mantua and Bologna over the winter 1532–3, Charles seems to have 'sat' for portraits by two celebrated artists: Titian, the duke of Mantua's favourite painter, and Jakob Seisenegger, court painter to his brother Ferdinand. The latter identified the dog that features so prominently in both portraits as '*ain grosser englischer wasserhundt*' ('a large English retriever').

20. *Charles reviews his army at Barcelona before embarking for Tunis, 1535.* The artist Jan Cornelisz Vermeyen accompanied Charles on his Tunis campaign and received a commission to design twelve commemorative tapestries. The second panel shows the emperor (holding a general's baton, and wearing armour and an early version of a baseball cap) riding by the scribes who note details of a general muster of the army at Barcelona. Charles appears as a logistician rather than as a warrior, while the monastery of Montserrat in the background (where the emperor went to pray before the campaign) reminds viewers of the religious nature of the venture.

21. *Statue of Charles in the Piazza Bologni, Palermo, 1535/1630.* The powerful bronze statue by Scipione Li Volsi, erected in 1630, shows the emperor in Roman dress with a laurel crown, holding his baton of command in his left hand while with his right he swears to uphold the laws and privileges of the kingdom of Sicily a century before.

Einrit Keyser Carlen 53.

in die alten Keyserlichen haubtstatt Rom / den 5 Aprilis. 1536.

Aus allerley Welschen vnd Teutschen Missiuen an Her
tzogen von Florentz/ vñ andere Herrn geschriben/
fleissig außzogen vnd verglichen.

CAROLVS.V.   ROM IMP. P. P.

Te assumam, & regnabis super omnia quæ desiderat
anima tua, erisq̷ Rex super Israel, iiȷ.Reg. xi.

22. *Charles enters Rome in triumph, 1536.* The frontispiece to a pamphlet celebrating
Charles's solemn entry into 'the ancient imperial capital, Rome' on 5 April 1536, published at
Nuremberg three weeks later by Christoph Scheurl. It included the Vulgate text of II Samuel
3:21, Abner's promise to David: 'Thou mayest reign over all that thine heart desireth.' Scheurl
evidently forgot that David's henchmen murdered Abner soon afterwards.

23. *Map of eastern France, 1544.* This enormous panorama (54 x 107 cm), shows France as Charles might have seen it from Metz, together with the route to three possible targets: from Troyes to Dijon on the left; from Troyes to Paris (beneath the hill of Montmartre) on the right; and from Dijon to Paris via Auxerre and Sens in the middle. The course of the Rivers Marne, Yonne and Seine, and the location of the principal bridges – essential knowledge for an army on the march – are clearly shown.

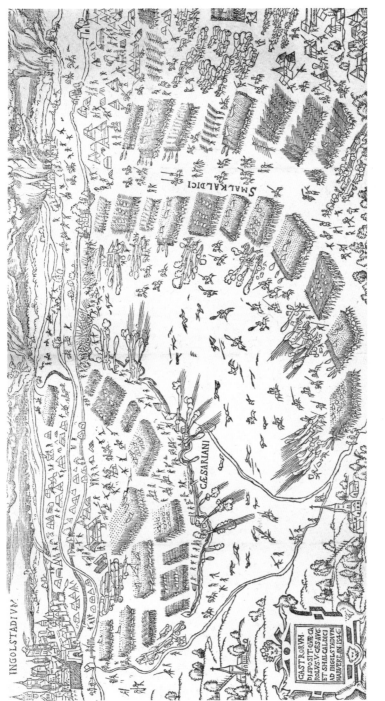

24. *Charles besieged in his camp outside Ingolstadt, September 1546.* According to Luis de Ávila, an eyewitness who later wrote a chronicle, the bombardment of the imperial camp before the Bavarian city of Ingolstadt lasted nine hours and made the ground shake like an earthquake, yet Charles stood resolutely beside the imperial standard. It made him both an obvious target to his enemies and an inspiration to his own troops.

25. *Charles at the battle of Mühlberg, 1547*. While residing at Augsburg, Charles commissioned a huge painting from Titian to commemorate his recent victory. The emperor – confident, tireless, resolute – appears as a light cavalry officer, with a short spear and a wheel-lock pistol, wearing the normal red insignia worn by Habsburg troops over a suit of Helmschmid armour that showed the Virgin and child: an image that combined Roman, German and Christian imagery. Unlike the Pavia tapestries (Pl. 14), no enemies are present, doubtless because Charles wanted to appear as a magnanimous ruler acceptable to German Lutherans, whose leaders had agreed to a religious settlement (the Interim).

26. *Charles and his war council, 1545.* The emperor gloried in war. In this contemporary woodcut he sits beneath a tree listening to his generals while dictating orders. One of the commanders is Count Reinhard of Solms, who had campaigned with Charles in France (directing the artillery and mines that forced St Dizier to surrender) as well as in Germany. The city of Lich (Hessen) shown in the background was his ancestral home.

27. *Charles in Augsburg by Titian, 1548.* Dressed in black, relieved only by his Golden Fleece, the emperor radiates calm, dignity and understated grandeur. Titian spent several months in Augsburg in 1548, accompanied by a team of assistants who helped him complete several commissions for Charles. Anton Fugger probably commissioned the portrait, which would explain why it portrays the subject as a bank customer, rather than as a victorious warrior, and also the prominence of the date (the emperor's residence in Fugger's palace marked the beginning of a new age).

Los parentescos q ay entre el principe de Castilla Don Phelippe hijo primo
genito del emperador y Rey de Castilla / y la 2.ª Infanta de Portugal
doña maria hija del s.or Rey don Ju.º de Portugal

- En primer lugar los dichos s.res principe y Infanta son primos hermanos y conjuntos
en segundo grado de consanguinidad por dos partes assi de parte de los
padres como de las madres / en esta manera /

- Porq el emperador padre del dicho principe es hermano de la s.ra reyna de portugal doña
Catalina madre de la dicha s.ra Infanta de portugal / y el dicho s.or Rey
de portugal padre de la dicha s.ra Infanta era hermano de la emperatriz
q aya gloria doña ysabel madre del dicho principe de Castilla / de manera q
los dichos s.res principe y Infanta son primos hermanos / dos vezes / hijos de
primos hermanos dos vezes / como dicho es /

De mas desto son conjuntos en tercero grado de consanguinidad dos vezes
por q el emperador y la emperatriz eran primos hijos de hermanas /
y el s.or Rey de portugal y la dicha s.ra reyna doña Catalyna y primas son
son primos hijos de dos hermas /

por otra parte son conjuntos en quarto grado por q el rey don manuel de
portugal padre de la emperatriz y la reyna doña ysabel abuela del empe.te
era y por su abuela del principe eran hijos de dos hermanos /

ay otro quarto grado de consanguinidad por q el rey don manuel padre de la
dicha emperatriz y el emperador maximiliano abuelo del emperador
eran primos hermanos por ser hijos de hermano y hermana /

En la dispensacion se ha de especificar señaladamente estos grados y parentescos /
y demas destos generales mas otros quales q sea parentescos assi de consanguinidad como de affinydad q entre los dichos s.res principe y Infanta
puede haver / q dependan de los q se declaron / y se pueda curar con la
dispension q se despacho por el casamiento del emperador y de la
emperatriz q aya gloria / como de otros quales q sea q queda q sener
dentro del segundo grado y de aquí abaxo / y tura bien de aquí mano
espiritual y de publica honestad y justicia / conforme a la mynistra
q con especifican /

29. *Charles vanquishes Fury by Leone and Pompeo Leoni, 1549–64.* The massive bronze statue of Charles, dressed as a Roman emperor, tramples on the figure of Fury, the Roman metaphor for war. Although defeated, Fury holds a lighted torch that might rekindle the fire of war – but Charles remains vigilant and composed, just the virtues projected two decades before by his chaplain and chronicler, Antonio de Guevara, in his books extolling Marcus Aurelius. Each piece of armour can be removed, revealing (for those interested) the emperor's naked body.

30. *Charles played at draughts.* The popularity of games of skill, such as chess and draughts with their military and chivalric associations, increased in the sixteenth century. This piece of pear wood, painted black and probably made in Augsburg in the 1540s, contains a gesso portrait of Charles with CAROLVS IMPERATOR carved around the border. No doubt it originally formed part of a set of thirty-two pieces.

31. *Charles and Philip by Leone Leoni.* Leone Leoni saw a combined image of Julius Caesar and his adopted son Augustus in 1550, inspiring him to carve an onyx cameo that portrayed Charles and his son on one side and the empress on the other. The artist's surviving correspondence shows that he completed his 'capriccio' in just three months, and that the emperor 'received it with the greatest admiration'.

32. *Charles abdicates, 1555*. Frans Hogenberg's engraving (done in 1569–70) shows several stages of the abdication ceremony in the great hall of the royal palace in Brussels on 25 October 1555: in the upper centre, surrounded by rich tapestries, Charles thanks his sister Marie for serving as his regent; slightly below, he renounces his possessions to his son Philip, and then leaves the hall ('Carolus'); in the centre one of his officials breaks up his seals and Dr Maes prepares to speak on behalf of the States-General.

33. *Charles after his abdication, 1556*. In this miniature, attributed to Simon Bening, the emperor wears the sort of 'tunic worn by citizens, made of Florence serge, a black German-style doublet' and a black hat – just as described by the French diplomats who visited Charles in Brussels in March 1556. This may be the last portrait done of the emperor from life, because he left for Spain three months later and commissioned no more likenesses.

34. *The Last Judgement by Titian, 1551–4.* The emperor's original commission referred to this enormous painting as 'The Trinity', but when he reached Yuste Charles called it 'The Last Judgement' because it showed him and his closest relatives – the empress and their son Philip, his sisters Eleanor and Marie – a few moments after his death, dressed in white linen as they prayed for God's mercy. The absence of his brother Ferdinand, present in Augsburg when Charles commissioned the work, is unlikely to be accidental.

35. *The imperial apartments at the monastery of Yuste.* Philip II commissioned the Dutch artist Antoon van den Wyngaerde to create a series of 'views' of Spain, and in 1567 he stopped at the Jeronimite monastery at Yuste. The artist's focus is the emperor's palace, abutting the convent church and reached by the ramp on the left (still standing), with the gardens and extensions that Charles built clearly visible.

36. *Funeral obsequies for Charles in Brussels, 1558.* On 29 December 1558, the emperor's funeral procession passed from the royal palace to the church of St Gudule, where four decades before he had been acclaimed king of Castile, Aragon, Naples and Sicily.

37. *Funeral obsequies for Charles in Valladolid, 1558.* Juan Cristóbal Calvete de Estrella had served Charles since 1533 and drew upon his knowledge of the emperor in designing his catafalque in Valladolid, then the administrative capital of Spain, for example by including scenes from Charles's favourite book, *The resolute knight* (Pl. 6). Calvete published a detailed description of his work, together with an illustration that clearly showed, in the second register, three scenes from the book.

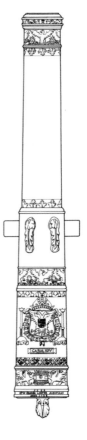

38. *A cannon confiscated from German Lutherans and embarked on the Spanish Armada.* After his victory in the Schmalkaldic war in 1547, Charles confiscated artillery from those who had defied him, including many pieces cast by Gregor Löffler for the city of Augsburg. Forty years later, his son Philip II distributed at least nine Löffler guns among the ships of the Armada, including this full cannon cast in 1538, weighing 5,230 lbs. Almost all the guns, including this one, were lost when the ships on which they sailed sank off the coasts of Scotland and Ireland.

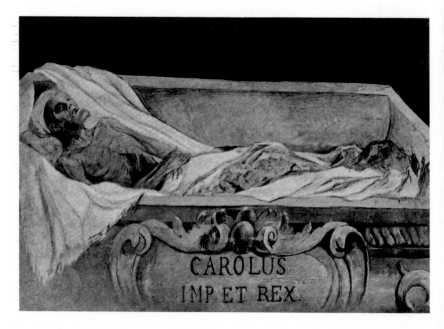

39. *Charles in his sarcophagus, 1870.* The emperor's body lay in a crypt at Yuste between his death in 1558 and 1574, when his son moved it to El Escorial. Each winter the temperature in the crypt fell below zero, which had the effect of 'curing' the corpse rather like the famous Jabugo hams cured, often for years, in high-altitude caves. A 'sketch in oils' by Vicente Palmaroli while the sarcophagus lay open to visitors, later photographed and published as a postcard, clearly shows Charles's mandibular prognathism and his powerful chest.

'to provide you with everything you may request, and to do everything you may ask'.[68]

Charles also sent his lieutenant a letter filled with good advice. 'Since small issues sometimes lead to problems that governments cannot solve', La Gasca must 'take care in everything, both in word and deed ... Because if you order one thing and do another, people will think you inconsistent and inconsequential.' 'Do not seek to judge every word and deed, but only those of men who stand accused. You must pretend that you do not know about the rest, because if every offence were to be investigated few people (or none) would remain unpunished.' Like his secret instructions to Prince Philip three years earlier, this document showed how much the emperor had learned about the art of government.[69]

In August 1546, as Charles faced his German rebels at Ingolstadt, La Gasca reached Panama and made it his headquarters while he undermined the Peruvian rebels. Only in December 1547, as he advanced towards Cuzco, did he feel strong enough to accuse Gonzalo Pizarro of rebellion and treason, contrasting his behaviour with that of the settlers in New Spain: they had submitted their objections to the New Laws 'without arms and disturbances', whereas Pizarro 'was not content to do likewise but behaved like one who had forgotten who is his king'. He rebuked Pizarro for executing the settlers who opposed him, for draining the royal treasury's resources 'to pay the costs of your rebellion against His Majesty', and for offering 20,000 pesos 'if I would be willing to go to Spain and recommend to His Majesty that he should appoint you governor . . . I laughed heartily at this bribe', La Gasca continued, 'and at Your Excellency for imagining that His Majesty would send a man likely to be corrupted with money'. He concluded with a grim counter-offer: if Pizarro refused to 'repent and return to the service of your Divine and secular rulers, you will lose both body and soul, as you will soon see'.[70]

La Gasca did not jest. In April 1548 he deployed his army of 1,500 men, supported by eleven artillery pieces, on a plateau just outside Cuzco, daring Pizarro to attack him. The ensuing battle involved fewer troops and caused fewer casualties than at Mühlberg, just one year before (only one royal soldier and forty-five rebels perished), but it proved just as decisive. After an artillery duel – the first on the American continent – many of the rebels fled, and since Pizarro 'and some of his captains neither fought nor fled' they all fell prisoner. La Gasca pondered 'whether we should take them in custody to Cuzco and deal with them there, or do so here', concluding that 'it would be better to act immediately, for fear they might escape and also because as long as Gonzalo Pizarro lived, it seemed that there could be no assurance of peace here'. Gonzalo and four of his lieutenants were beheaded on the battle-field, after which their severed heads were taken to Cuzco and exposed to public derision.[71]

If La Gasca had any qualms about this decision, they dissipated when he discovered that in Cuzco the rebels 'had removed the royal arms from the standard and burned them in a brazier' and 'planned to crown Gonzalo Pizarro king of this country as soon as they had defeated my army'. Local bishops exiled the numerous clerics who had supported Pizarro, including Juan Coronel, 'formerly a canon of Quito . . . who wrote a book entitled *De bello justo*, in favour and defence of the rebellion'; and secular judges executed at least fifty Pizarristas, some of them after torture and mutilation, and condemned perhaps 1,000 more to lesser penalties, usually including exile. These purges, combined with the '340 or so men that Gonzalo Pizarro and his followers executed during the rebellion', eliminated about a third of the first generation of conquistadors as well as most of the Inca royal family. As with the Castilian and Valencian rebels a quarter-century before, Charles also showed no mercy: he ordered his judges in Spain to treat the relatives of rebels who had repatriated money and goods with similar severity, confis-cating their lands, houses and other assets up to the value of what they had received from Peru. He even decreed the sequestration of dowries paid for their female relatives to enter a convent.[72]

The pacifier of Peru became an instant celebrity. In January 1550 the chronicler Gonzalo Fernández de Oviedo wrote to congratulate La Gasca on the success of his 'Caesarean venture' and begged obsequiously for a detailed account to include in his *History of the Indies*, commissioned by the emperor. Oviedo announced that his epic, which began with the voyage of Columbus, would end with the pacification of Peru since the news had providentially 'arrived in time to be immortalized in my third volume'. La Gasca duly starred in two chapters of the Great Work.[73] La Gasca's success also impressed Charles: 'We felt great satisfaction' after reading his account of the defeat of Pizarro, and the 'justice done to him and his followers'; and the emperor exulted that God and La Gasca had created the right conditions 'to resume the plan that we have always followed: the exaltation of the Holy Catholic Faith, and at the same time the restoration of peace and justice, avoiding the outrages, robberies and murders that have been cruelly inflicted on our subjects and vassals'. Charles then announced that he had appointed Antonio de Mendoza as the next viceroy of Peru, and that after La Gasca had briefed him, 'with God's blessing you may return to Spain, bringing with you the greatest quantity of gold and silver that you can – as we are sure you will do'.[74] Once again, La Gasca exceeded expectations: when he landed in Seville in September 1550 he brought over two million ducats in cash, a fabulous windfall that Charles compared (as he fantasized over how to spend it) with the ransom paid by King Francis two decades before. It 'has greatly enhanced my reputation and will allow me to execute all the plans I have devised'.[75]

Nevertheless, the 'Caesarean venture' had been a close-run thing. In the lapidary verdict of Viceroy Mendoza: 'The measures taken by His Majesty and the lords of the council were holy and just, but it cannot be denied that His Majesty's New Laws destroyed Peru.' He recalled (in an 'I-told-you-so' moment) that 'for many years before Peru rebelled I warned him what would happen'. Although 'I did not spell it out more clearly, because I would have suffered for it: I greatly regret that His Majesty, his councillors and the friars combined to destroy these poor people here.'[76] La Gasca found it necessary not only to preserve the encomienda system in Peru but to extend it, distributing grants worth over one million ducats a year to those who had supported him – and even that proved insufficient: some of those who had abandoned Gonzalo, but got little or no reward, rallied to the standard of revolt briefly raised by Francisco Hernández Girón in 1553.

On the positive side, the defeat of Pizarro revealed not only the strength of Charles's control over his American possessions but also his ability to coordinate their resources. From Panama in December 1546, soon after his arrival, La Gasca reminded other royal officials that 'we need all parts of America to obey His Majesty's orders and rally to his royal voice', adding that 'in a matter of such importance to his royal authority and interests' it was essential 'everyone should rally to him as if his royal person were present'. America, La Gasca argued, must show 'that good people here offer their persons and property to His Majesty no less than they did in Spain on similar campaigns in Hungary, Tunis and Algiers'. His rhetoric produced spectacular results, above all in New Spain where Viceroy Mendoza spent 192,000 pesos to raise an army of 600 soldiers for service in Peru, to be commanded by his son. In March 1547 he solemnly reviewed the expeditionary force. America had seen nothing like it.[77]

'ANOTHER GOLD-BEARING WORLD'

The speech given in Charles's name to the Cortes of Castile at Corunna in 1520 to justify accepting his election as Holy Roman Emperor promised that the acquisition of a 'New World of gold made just for him, because it did not exist before our own time', would shield his Spanish subjects from the full cost of his new commitments in central Europe. To some extent the promise was realized. In 1523, Martín de Salinas noted that 'ships have arrived from America carrying 800,000 gold pesos' and concluded 'it seems that God is taking charge of His Majesty's affairs because he is taking such good care of them'.[78] Ten years later, stunned by the size of Atahualpa's ransom as it passed through Panama en route for Spain, a treasury official exclaimed that:

> Since Your Majesty walks in the way of the Lord, serving Him and defending Christian society and the Church of our Holy Catholic faith, He provides this assistance and favour to raise your spirits and resources as you prosecute the holy enterprise, and wage war against the Turks, the Lutherans and other enemies of the faith.

In 1535, in Barcelona, Salinas noted with astonishment that Charles 'has ordered the mint masters of all his kingdoms to come to this city, and has brought here all the gold and silver from America so that it can be turned into coins'. He estimated their value at 500,000 ducats. In the words of James Tracy: 'The Tunis enterprise was possible only because Francisco Pizarro's conquest of Peru restocked the emperor's treasure chamber.'[79]

Most of this American largesse came from a tax imported from Castile: the 'royal fifth', which entitled monarchs to 20 per cent of all spoils taken in wars against enemies of the faith and of all minerals produced. In the course of the emperor's reign over half the receipts of his treasurers in Mexico, and four-fifths of the receipts of those in Peru, came from this source. Much of the rest represented the tribute paid to the Crown by indigenous inhabitants and from confiscations. On nine occasions Charles sequestered money remitted to individuals, using deceit to disguise his intentions. In 1523, to help fund an invasion of France, he ordered his officials at Seville to detain and inventory all gold, silver, pearls and merchandise on ships arriving from America, whether for the Crown or for 'merchants and individuals *in such a way that no one would know what I have ordered on this matter*'. In 1535 he decreed that if any ship should arrive 'from Peru or anywhere else with a large amount of gold, then *using dissimulation and whatever methods you think will best disguise your action*, send me a detailed list via a flying courier [*con correo volante*]'. Should the owners of the treasure protest and demand the release of their money, royal officials must lie to them: '*Lead everyone to believe that you cannot do it* because of the time it takes to turn all this gold and silver into money'. In 1543, as the emperor prepared his campaign against Guelders and France, he again commanded that 'from now on, if a ship or group of ships should arrive with up to 80,000 ducats or more of gold, you must sequester the gold, silver and pearls that they bring for any individuals, without exception, and *use whatever lies and deceit you like so that no one knows it is by my order*'.[80] In each case the individuals who lost their capital received compensation in the form of low-interest government bonds (*juros*).

Although Charles justified these lies by the need to safeguard 'our reputation and authority, and to defend our dominions', the repeated sequestrations involved major economic opportunity costs: the money exported, whether to pay the emperor's soldiers or his bankers, was money that could not be invested in domestic enterprise; and the annual cost of paying interest on the juros more than doubled in the course of his reign. Nevertheless, the temptation proved irresistible. As the Valencian chronicler Martí de Viciana later observed: 'His Majesty has derived such benefits from America that thanks to its treasure, and the soldiers of Spain, he could do more than all the other Christian rulers whenever he wanted.' At several critical junctures, as a later age might boast, America 'made Charles great again'.[81]

THE EMPIRICAL EMPIRE

To maximize his assets, Charles needed to overcome certain fundamental obstacles to effective transatlantic government. In Europe he deployed four strategies to control his scattered dominions: he visited each one as often as possible for as long as possible; he empowered his close relatives to represent him when he was absent; he cemented alliances through matrimony; and he created an institutional structure based upon a balance of power. Since he could not deploy the first three strategies in America, Charles relied more heavily on the fourth – but, as in his other dominions, faction and self-interest often got in the way. In 1551, Antonio de Mendoza, reflecting on his sixteen years' experience as viceroy, sent a Report to Charles complaining that 'men in New Spain prefer meddling in other people's business rather than attending to their own'; indeed 'their chief concern is public administration, especially in criticizing and judging every action'. Unfortunately, the viceroy continued, 'I have found many who counsel and criticize me, but few who help me when affairs do not go their way'.[82] This fundamental obstacle gave rise to another. To quote Mendoza's Report again: 'Your Majesty appointed me and others like me as viceroys and governors when we were new to our posts and had no experience; and you named judges there who would not be appointed magistrates back in Spain. You entrust them with a new world with no rationale or preparation.' He concluded bitterly: 'What does Your Majesty expect will happen, 2,000 leagues away? Everything will come crashing down when they attempt things of which they know nothing.'[83]

Charles was familiar with these structural problems. In 1526, frustrated by his inability to respond effectively to petitions from settlers in Cuba 'because we do not have information or complete data on the settlements and their population', Charles signed a warrant stating that 'I want to be informed of the houses, estates, yields and other things that we own on that island', and he ordered the governor 'that as soon as you receive this you must draw up a detailed account of everything'. A decade later, he charged Mendoza 'always to inform us of what you see and do . . . in those realms where we do not reside'. The new viceroy must commission 'a drawing or painting of the principal towns and ports . . . informing me of the situation and elevation of each settlement, and of the distances that separate them' and send the results to Spain.[84]

Charles also approved innovations in processing such information when it arrived. While he and the council of the Indies resided in Seville in 1526, they visited the House of Trade and charged it with reorganizing its haphazard collection of maps and documents, and with creating a systematic geographical database 'both in writing and in images, as you see fit, consulting each and every person who has knowledge and experience of navigation'. The officials must also ensure that all pilots sailing across the Atlantic 'compile a daily record of their voyage, starting in the port or place from which it begins and ending when they return to Seville . . . noting the distance they cover each day, the headings, and the latitude of all the lands they encounter'. According to Arndt Brendecke, 'It seems as if all the data were gathered in a single book which contained information supplied by more than 150 pilots.'[85]

The resulting flood of information provided the basis for a stream of legislation issued by Charles to regulate the economy, society and administration of the New World: 'In order to increase the prosperity of Hispaniola, we command that African slaves who marry, and their children, should not be set free' (1526); 'If necessary, brothels may be established in the city of Santo Domingo' (1526); coins struck in the new Mints in Mexico and San Domingo must all have 'on one side castles, lions and pomegranates' – the emblems of Castile, León and Granada – 'and on the other side two columns and a banner that says *Plus Ultra*, which is my royal emblem' (1544); and so on. By the time of his abdication in 1556, Charles had issued over 1,000 legislative acts for his possessions in the western hemisphere (compared with 700 for Spain). Some proved ephemeral, or were later rescinded, but 15 per cent of the acts recorded in the law code for Spanish America printed in 1680 were issued by Charles.[86]

The emperor also signed thousands of warrants that addressed individual issues. In 1536 he learned that a Spaniard in Nicaragua had raped a local woman and then set fire to her house, killing her, but although the provincial governor 'proceeded against him, you condemned him to a fine of just five pesos' – clearly inadequate, given the seriousness of the offence. Charles therefore ordered the governor to revisit the case 'and send an account of the punishment that you impose to our council of the Indies'.[87] Two years earlier, he authorized the payment of 1,000 ducats to create a prototype of the future Panama Canal, in response to a report forwarded by his officials in the isthmus concerning 'the utility of improving navigation on the River Chagre' and the need to improve the portage from Panama to Nombre de Dios.[88] This was a textbook example of 'sub-imperialism': a response to initiatives taken by officials on the periphery of the empire, and only afterwards referred to the Crown for endorsement. Another striking example occurred in 1550, when Charles received a *consulta* from the council of the Indies transmitting a report from Viceroy Mendoza (whose long service had clearly made him supremely confident) reminding everyone of his previous requests to found in New Spain 'a university where all forms of knowledge are taught, and where the indigenous population and the children of Spanish settlers may be educated'. Mendoza had now 'named people to start giving instruction in all faculties, in the hope that Your Majesty will be pleased to found and foster a university', with a constitution modelled on those of the universities of Salamanca and Alcalá. Noting that the local clergy strongly favoured the new institution, the council recommended that Charles provide an annual subsidy of 1,000 gold pesos. The imperial rescript read: 'It seems we should do what the council has advised', and in September 1551 a royal warrant authorized treasury officials in Mexico to pay 1,000 gold pesos a year to the new university. Teaching began in 1553 and continues to this day.[89]

Charles had already founded another American university, also in response to pressure from the periphery of his empire. In 1548 the Dominican friars of the Order's new province of Peru petitioned for a university attached to their monastery in Lima, and deputed their provincial to secure imperial approval. First he approached the city council of

Lima, which appointed him one of its procurators (La Gasca eventually served as the other) to persuade the emperor to create a 'college with the same privileges, exemptions and constitution as the university of Salamanca', because 'these regions are so far from Spain that if the local people send their sons to study in the universities of Spain, it would involve great expense; and so, for lack of opportunity, some will remain ignorant'. Later that year, after listening to the procurators in person, Charles allocated '3,000 gold pesos from the Royal Treasury for the maintenance' of the new college. The university of Lima (now Universidad Nacional Mayor de San Marcos) has taught students ever since.[90]

DID CHARLES REALLY CARE?

It would be easy to argue that Charles took little part in these and other initiatives for his American possessions, especially in the case of legislative acts that he did not himself sign. Thus the charters that created and funded the universities of Lima and Mexico in 1551 went out when the emperor was in Augsburg: the actual warrants were signed by his regent in Valladolid.[91] Yet they and other similar measures all required imperial approval, and some received considerable prior scrutiny. For example, the Report of Antonio de Mendoza that accused Charles of handling American affairs inconsistently and incompetently reached him in Innsbruck in March 1552: 'I listened intently as it was read out,' he told his son, because it contained 'important points that require careful consideration'. He therefore decreed that all the issues raised by Mendoza 'must be discussed and considered, so that I will be in full possession of the facts when I make my decision'.[92]

Some officials complained that the emperor intervened too often in American affairs, causing unnecessary disruption by changing his mind – and therefore his policies. 'His Majesty and his council and the friars,' Mendoza protested, 'waste so much time, and so much paper and ink, in doing and undoing, in giving grants that conflict with others, and in changing the system of government every day.'[93] Examples of such inconsistency abounded. For example, although the emperor solemnly decreed in 1535, and reiterated in 1541 and 1542, that 'neither we nor our heirs' would ever alienate 'the city of Tlaxcala and its territory from our royal Crown', he repeatedly broke his promise by making grants of land in the province to Spaniards; and although the viceroys supported the protests of the Tlaxcalans, such grants were seldom overturned.[94] It was much the same story with the New Laws, enacted in 1542 and partially revoked in 1546.

Charles's instructions to Luis de Velasco as viceroy in Mexico in 1550 commanded him to 'uphold everything mandated in the New Laws that we issued for the sound government of America' – and yet, like his predecessor, Velasco would issue many warrants allowing the sons of the first conquistadors to inherit encomiendas granted by Cortés, in clear contravention of the New Laws.[95]

Such measures nevertheless remained the exception: Charles resolutely resisted granting encomiendas 'in perpetuity'. Admittedly, in 1553 he asked Philip to consider 'what money might be raised from the encomiendas of America, something that has seemed to me complex and difficult because of the conflicting opinions that exist', and his son duly convened a committee of theologians to consider the matter; but when he reported that the members of the junta agreed that selling permanent titles to encomiendas constituted 'the only remedy for the conservation and pacification of those lands', Charles flatly refused: 'I have never liked this measure, as you know, and I have always tried to avoid it.' Philip must wait until he became ruler of Castile and its American colonies, and then 'you can do what you like and you can sign the relevant orders because it will all be yours; and I will not need to overcome my scruples.'[96]

'My scruples': what did Charles mean by that phrase? An exchange in 1549 between Las Casas and Domingo de Soto sheds some light. Las Casas wondered why the emperor had done so little to implement best colonial practices. Soto, Charles's confessor at the time, conceded that their master had failed to act, but in part because 'it is hard to find a remedy for the affairs of America since they are so far away, and especially because those who come from there have such different stories that it is difficult to know whom to believe'. Las Casas agreed, and added that not only was America 'so far away from the prince charged with its government, but the prince is also absorbed in many and various other matters much closer to him'. Finding a solution 'would require not only the mental and physical reserves of a single man, but of many'.[97] This suggestion apparently produced results: soon afterwards, Charles convened a committee 'to discuss the most appropriate methods of undertaking the conquest, discovery and settlement' of America 'and to examine the correct status of His Majesty's subjects there *without imperilling his royal conscience*'. The committee met in Valladolid (Spain's administrative capital) attended by nine ministers from the central councils together with two bishops and four theologians (including Domingo de Soto), and over the course of several weeks they heard and discussed presentations by Las Casas and the humanist Juan Ginés de Sepúlveda. Several members of the committee had experience of America, some direct (such as La Gasca and Tello de Sandoval) or indirect (the marquis of Mondéjar, who presided, was the brother of Viceroy Mendoza; Soto had helped to select missionaries). Eventually, they advised Charles that the acquisition of more territory and subjects in America by outright conquest would 'endanger the conscience of His Majesty' because of 'the damage and great sins committed in these conquests'. Las Casas now published the arguments he had presented to the committee in a slim volume entitled *A very brief account of the destruction of America*, dedicated to Prince Philip in the hope that he could 'with greater efficacy petition and persuade His Majesty [Charles] to refuse' future requests to continue abusive practices such as the grant of encomiendas.[98]

Charles was already programmed to receive. Jean Glapion resigned as his confessor in 1522 after requesting and receiving papal permission to become a missionary in America. Loaysa, who succeeded Glapion, became president of the council of the Indies, a position he held until his death in 1546. Soto also intended to go to America as a missionary before he became Charles's confessor, and afterwards played a leading role in the deliberations of the committee on American affairs in Valladolid in 1550–1.[99] Small wonder that several of Charles's decrees concerning America claimed that he acted 'for the discharge of our royal conscience'. To take two examples among many: the preamble to his Ordinances 'concerning the treatment of indigenous inhabitants' in 1528 argued that current practices constituted 'an offence against God' and also 'were a heavy charge on our royal conscience'; and the following year he ordered the council of the Indies to propose suitable legislation 'for the discharge of our royal conscience and for the preservation of New Spain'.[100]

Charles's ministers and subjects soon learned not only to respect his scruples but also to exploit them. In 1530 a procurator sent to Spain by Cortés couched his pleas to the emperor in the form of an appeal to 'Your Majesty's royal conscience'; the following year the judges of the Audiencia of Mexico claimed that sending more missionaries was essential 'for the good of your royal conscience'; and in 1533, Cortés asserted that a 'division of the entire state' among 'its conquerors and first settlers is essential not only for its conservation but also for Your Majesty's royal conscience'.[101] La Gasca made excellent use of this argument in a letter of 1549 to the magistrates of Arica, a Peruvian city that continued, despite the New Laws, to send indigenous inhabitants to labour in the silver mines of Potosí. He stressed that the clause prohibiting 'the dispatch of indigenous inhabitants to the mines' had not been revoked, and saw no prospect of change because 'when His Majesty found out how all the indigenous inhabitants of Hispaniola, Cuba and other [Caribbean] islands had died through being sent to the mines he became convinced that he would go to Hell if he permitted this practice to continue. He will therefore never agree to it.' 'Sending indigenous inhabitants to mines 170 leagues away,' La Gasca warned, 'is something that cannot be concealed without great offence to God and to His Majesty's delicate conscience, and it risks arousing his anger.'[102] The practice must therefore stop immediately.

La Gasca's rhetoric did not stand alone. The phrase 'the service of God and His Majesty' was often used to justify Charles's providential vision. His officials hailed the ransom of Atahualpa as a divine gift to enable the emperor 'to wage war against the Turks, the Lutherans and other enemies of the faith'. The first pamphlet published in Spain about the pacification of Peru described the outrages committed by 'this Lutheran, Gonzalo Pizarro, who had as little respect for religious affairs and beliefs as he did for the king's affairs': although there is no evidence that either Pizarro or any of his followers had Protestant sympathies, branding him a heretic fitted perfectly into Charles's vision. For the sake of his 'delicate conscience', as well as for material and ideological considerations, the emperor simply could not ignore the New World.[103]

PORTRAIT OF THE EMPEROR IN HIS PRIME

THE POLYGLOT EMPEROR

In 1557 a Venetian ambassador recalled that once upon a time 'Charles had been considered stupid and slothful by everyone, or almost everyone, but then suddenly and unexpectedly he awoke and became alert, committed and courageous'. A few years later a veteran minister observed that 'Habsburg men are slow developers, as we saw with the late emperor'.[1] The most spectacular 'late' improvement occurred in Charles's language skills. When he arrived in Spain in 1517 his new subjects were appalled that he spoke and understood only French; but within a year his spoken Castilian became fluent. In 1536, using only notes, he delivered in Spanish a speech that lasted well over an hour, and seven years later he filled forty-eight foolscap folios with detailed confidential advice in Spanish for his son: although he made a few grammatical errors, and used a number of French and Italian loan words and phrases, his meaning throughout remained clear.[2] The emperor's ability to communicate in Italian followed a similar trajectory. When he first arrived in the peninsula in 1529 and received welcome presents, 'he did not have the ability to thank the donors properly, so one of his Italian courtiers did it for him'; but eight years later an Italian ambassador reported that 'His Majesty always replied to me in Italian, and he made sure that I understood everything that he said.' His fluency did not desert him with age. At an audience in 1553 with an English ambassador 'His Majestie was horse at the begynnyng', and the ambassador 'could not well heare onles it wol please His Majestie to speak Italian; whereupon beyng willinger to speake Italian then able to speake lowder', Charles conducted the rest of the audience in Italian.[3] His command of German also improved. At his coronation in Aachen in 1520, an ambassador noted that Charles needed an interpreter 'because he still cannot speak German'; although when he opened the Diet of Worms a few weeks later, 'the emperor spake certain brief words in Almain'. By contrast, when the Polish envoy Jan Dantiszek addressed him in German at an audience in 1525, Charles 'with a smiling face, and blushing slightly' replied: 'I don't know how to reply to you: if I speak in Spanish, you might not understand everything, and I cannot speak German fluently.' Dantiszek replied obsequiously, ' "Your Majesty can communicate whatever you want in German." After that, he looked round to see if the Chancellor [Gattinara] was present, and since he was not he replied to me thus in German: I have recorded his exact words, as best I remember them . . .' Dantiszek then transcribed almost 100 words of German, idiosyncratic but intelligible.[4] By the time Charles presided over the Diet of Augsburg in 1530, he could hold his own in German; and in 1543, at the Diet of Speyer, Charles again 'replied in German' in all debates.[5] By then, if not before, the emperor also both spoke and understood Dutch – perhaps because he had acquired some competence as a boy, perhaps because 'he spoke a sort of German that was scarcely distinguishable from his "Flemish" '.[6]

Eventually, Charles even mastered Latin. In 1526 the English ambassador reported that unless Gattinara were 'present, the emperor gevethe me no audience bicause that although he will understand, yet he will not gladlie make answer in Laten'; and three years later, on arriving in Italy, Charles lamented that he could not understand 'the rhetoric and elegant phrases' in the Latin orations delivered by those he met, adding ruefully 'if I had listened to the words of my admirable teacher Adrian [of Utrecht], I would not need an interpreter here to know what you just said'. In 1540 he used the same excuse: 'I could not understand [an important document] properly because it was in Latin.' Three years later, he told his son that 'nothing could be more necessary or universal than the Latin language. That is why I strongly encourage you to work hard to learn it so that you will not be afraid, later, to speak it' – but he only followed his own advice during the siege of Metz in 1552, when his chamberlain, Guillaume van Male, used the Vulgate to teach his master Latin, with the result that 'the emperor sometimes brags about this'.[7]

Many contemporaries commented favourably on Charles's facility with languages. At Augsburg in 1530 a diplomat noted with approval that 'the emperor and his brother both speak very well, answering almost immediately and in many languages' – he specified Dutch, French, German, Italian and Spanish – 'so that it is a pleasure to watch them switch between various languages'. Two years later, other diplomats admired the emperor's ability to 'speak four languages – French, Spanish, Portuguese and German (although he finds the last one difficult) – besides Italian'.[8] Eventually, his linguistic prowess became the subject of a jest:

If I need to talk with God, the Emperor Charles V used to say, I would do so in Spanish, because the language of Spaniards suggests gravity and majesty; if with friends, in Italian, because the speech of Italians sounds friendly; and if to seduce someone, in French, because no language sounds more seductive; but if I want to threaten or scold someone I use German, because their entire language is threatening, harsh and emphatic.[9]

How did Charles acquire such polyglot proficiency? His formal education ceased when Adrian of Utrecht left for Spain in 1515, and he does not seem to have engaged other instructors; and yet in the sixteenth century, as today, acquiring fluency in a foreign language requires dedication, repetition and confidence.[10] Perhaps his insistence that his son must learn enough Latin to ensure that 'you will not be *afraid* to speak it' offers one clue: Dantiszek's testimony showed that the emperor was willing to practise, if necessary in public, in order to improve. A letter written by the humanist and diplomat Girolamo Aleandro in 1531 offered a second clue: the emperor found languages fascinating. Aleandro had just sat down one evening, 'beside a lamp at a table to read a memorial I had written [in Hebrew], when the emperor happened to pass by' and 'asked me what the script was'. When Aleandro told him, Charles 'recited the first two verses of the Bible in Latin, and asked if I could do the same in Hebrew. I did so, and His Majesty could not conceal his delight.' He asked Aleandro to do the same in Greek, which he did, and 'then asked if I could write in Greek, and when I showed him the dorse of the memorial, which was in Greek, he said "This is great: something beautiful and wonderful."' The nuncio rejoiced 'to see how much pleasure His Majesty took in the variety of languages', and speculated (plausibly enough) that 'he had inherited it from his grandfather Maximilian'.[11]

Charles also attempted to acquire as an adult another discipline absent from his formal education: mathematics. According to a biographer of Francisco de Borja, one of Charles's most trusted councillors, when the emperor returned to Spain in 1533 'he sought to escape the burden of affairs for a few hours by devoting them to the study of mathematics'; but 'feeling somewhat embarrassed to learn directly from the cosmographers', he asked Borja 'if he knew anything about the discipline'. The future saint confessed that he did not, and so Charles sent him to consult the experts, after which Borja:

Relayed for the emperor's better understanding what he had learned from the illustrious cosmographer Alonso de Santa Cruz, and from other mathematicians in the emperor's service; so that in little more than six months they managed to penetrate the most useful principles of the discipline, mastering the elements of Euclid, the speculations of Theodosius, of Apollonius etc . . .[12]

Knowledge of the emperor's proficiency soon spread. In 1543, 'because I know that Your Majesty loves mathematics', an agent of the Fugger company in Nuremberg urged the noted astronomer Peter Apian to perfect a special instrument to calculate latitude, commissioned by Charles two years before. He also forwarded a new book that advanced 'a marvellous theory, never before seen or heard or even thought of: that the sun is the centre of the universe, without an orbit, as all previous authors have asserted' – namely *On the revolutions of heavenly spheres* by Nicholas Copernicus.[13]

THE PERILS OF GOVERNING THE FIRST GLOBAL EMPIRE

Some contemporaries complained that the emperor's fascination with mathematics distracted him from dealing with pressing business. A few years after his brother's death, Ferdinand confided to his doctor that he considered Charles 'somewhat negligent' in this:

> I asked him more than once: 'Why does Your Majesty not read through the petitions and papers of your subjects instead of spending so much of your time and spare moments on mathematical books?' At this he laughed and said: 'At night I am fatigued and care-worn, and that makes it impossible for me to deal with business.'[14]

Nevertheless, Charles dealt with prodigious quantities of business in person, even when travelling. In 1541 a diplomat reported with surprise that 'I saw here today a wooden room constructed for His Majesty that contains a bed, a writing table and a small place to sit. It can be dismantled and placed in boxes to be transported by mules.' Charles also continued to handle the most sensitive issues in holograph letters – although he drew the line at writing them out twice: he once apologized to Los Cobos that 'I had written this letter in my own hand, and then spilled an ink-pot over it. Because I am too lazy to write it out again I have ordered [Francisco de] Eraso to cipher it.'[15] He also continued to make sure that he understood matters thoroughly before taking decisions. A Venetian ambassador observed that the emperor normally 'took advice from all sides, talking about each major item of business for four or five hours on end, sitting in a chair, and then he wrote out the reasons for and against to see which was better'.[16] In June 1546, when the pope expressed frustration at the emperor's procrastination in making war on the German Lutherans, an experienced diplomat explained that 'the reasons for His Majesty's delays are many and various [*molte e diverse*], but this is the main one: he does not want to begin such a major venture in Germany without sounding out several of the princes.' Three months later Charles showed the same prudence in practical matters. The Venetian ambassador in the imperial camp reported that 'yesterday evening His Majesty was with his council of war until after midnight, and again today until midday, discussing what to do'[17] (Pl. 26).

Charles realized that his ministers might try to deceive him, and he devised certain administrative procedures to counteract this. Ferrante Gonzaga, who had grown up at the imperial court and later became viceroy of Sicily, governor of Milan and commander of the imperial army, once told Charles that he spent too much time listening to those who criticized his ministers. 'His Majesty replied that he had not believed and still did not believe anything said against me, but that he wished to give a hearing to any man who wanted to speak to him' – which, Gonzaga noted bitterly, 'I took to mean "any man who wanted to speak ill of me"'. Gonzaga therefore instructed his agent at court, Natale Musi, to protest about the backbiting; but one of Charles's principal policy advisers reminded him that 'We have always listened to all sorts of grievances against all ministers. Refusing to do so would be tyranny on the part of His Majesty and an affront to human and divine law.' When Musi suggested that Charles should 'punish any person who accused a minister falsely', his interlocutor responded: 'That would never do, because such a punishment would frighten and discourage any other person who has a just grievance against the said minister.'[18] Titian's celebrated portrait of the emperor in Augsburg in 1548 captured this quality brilliantly: Charles's 'eagle eyes' (as contemporaries called them) coldly assess the viewer, searching for any sign of duplicity or deceit (Pl. 27).

The emperor continued to seek guidance from his confessor on public as well as private matters – although he did not always like or accept the guidance he received. Charles once complained to a confidant that Fray Pedro de Soto, his confessor from 1543 to 1547, had 'told him that he did not know how [the emperor] could be saved, and despaired of his salvation; and that His Majesty was very hurt by the friar's lack of confidence.' This exchange probably took place when Charles rejected Soto's advice about a tougher implementation of the Interim, which led to the confessor's resignation.

Although the emperor offered a bishopric or at least a pension if he would return, Soto refused and instead sent back a warning 'that His Majesty should remember the spiritual advice he had given him'.[19] Perhaps Charles acted belatedly on Soto's awkward advice when in 1550 he informed his regents in Spain that 'I have often been urged by my confessors to ban and abolish in all my kingdoms and lordships the practice of interest and loans, laying this as a charge on my conscience.' He continued: 'I more than anyone wish to address this issue, if it can be done, both to ease this scruple and to avoid the damage' to his treasury caused by high interest rates; but he worried that refusing to pay interest would destroy his credit. Nevertheless, 'since we know that all these things (and others that could be named) must cease when the safety and security of one's conscience is at stake', he ordered his ministers to assess the potential impact of unilateral action.[20]

By then, Charles had lost another confessor: Fray Domingo de Soto (no relation to his homonymous predecessor). According to a royal chronicler, 'when asked why' he had returned to Spain, Soto cited the emperor's neglect of 'poor petitioners' at his court and his practice of raising money by selling various privileges without regard for the calibre of the purchaser (such as public offices, knighthoods in the military orders, and exemptions to his own laws). Rumours of Soto's discontent evidently reached Charles, because six months later the former confessor protested that 'I have not told a living soul about my reasons for returning.' On the contrary, 'I have maintained complete secrecy concerning Your Majesty.' He thanked Charles for entrusting to him 'the part of royal conscience that Your Majesty was pleased to share with me' – an intriguing formulation — adding that since his return to Spain 'I have exonerated Your Majesty and taken the blame, saying that I gave advice on matters that, after much thought and counsel, you considered impossible.'[21] Although Soto did not identify these matters, his surviving correspondence suggests a few areas of activity. Inquisitor-General Fernando de Valdés wrote on several occasions to ask Soto to ensure that Charles dealt punctually with matters submitted by him on behalf of the council of the Inquisition; and other councils probably did the same. Bartolomé de Las Casas urged Soto to persuade the emperor to stop all conquests and perpetual grants of encomiendas in America (chapter 13), and other individuals probably took similar steps to get Charles's attention and favour.[22]

Nevertheless, as an English diplomat complained in 1546, the emperor often 'does things on his own, without consulting his friends' (meaning, in this case, Henry VIII); and six years later the papal nuncio echoed that 'the emperor is a man who likes to handle his affairs just as he pleases'. In particular, Charles liked to 'take his time to think things through, in the hope of gaining his ends without loss'.[23] Many found this style of decision-making frustrating. When the Knights of the Golden Fleece assembled for a formal chapter in 1546, they voiced many of the same complaints about their sovereign as at their last meeting fifteen years before (pp. 203–4): that Charles did not notify them in advance of his major decisions (notably his two African campaigns); that 'he exposed himself to danger too often in wartime'; that 'he was very slow in transacting business'; and that 'he had many debts, which caused his creditors to complain'. As usual, Charles 'replied graciously' but defended himself vigorously. He reminded the knights that both his African campaigns 'needed to be executed in the greatest secrecy, to avoid giving his enemies a chance to prevent them' (although he claimed that he had 'notified some of the knights who were then with him'). 'Concerning the slow transaction of affairs, he stated that this had always worked out well for him'; and the emperor affirmed that he had already ordered his treasurer to ascertain exactly how much he owed as a prelude to repaying his debts. He continued: 'As for the rest, if he had offended, he had done so through inadvertence rather than through some wicked design; and he concluded by assuring the assembly that in future he would be more attentive to carrying out his duties properly.'[24]

THE TYRANNY OF DISTANCE

Charles might have offered another explanation of why 'he was very slow in transacting business': the communications system on which his government relied. Fernand Braudel was the first historian to devote sustained attention to this problem, writing in 1949:

> Understanding the importance of distance in the sixteenth century – understanding the obstacles, the difficulties and the delays that it caused – leads one to view the administrative problems faced by sixteenth-century empires in a new light. Above all, the enormous Spanish empire . . . which involved (for its time) a massive infrastructure of land and sea transport, and required not only the ceaseless movement of troops but also the dispatch of hundreds of orders and reports every day – links that were silent but vital.

He suggested that 'a good half of the actions of Philip II can only be explained by the need to maintain these links', and the same might be said of his father. For both of them, in Braudel's memorable phrase, 'Distance was public enemy number one.'[25]

Many complaints by Charles and his contemporaries support this assertion. In 1525, from Basel, Erasmus grumbled that he had written to an
imperial secretary in Spain, but 'whether that letter ever reached you, I have
not yet been able to find out. So many mountains and plains and seas separate us that you seem to live in a different world!' Four years later another
imperial secretary warned Erasmus from Barcelona: 'Please send nothing to
me or the chancellor [Gattinara] without first checking where in the world
we are, for our destination is still uncertain.' Pedro de Toledo, Charles's long-
serving viceroy of Naples, jested that 'if he must wait for death, he hoped it
would come in a letter from Spain, because then it would never arrive'.[26]

Perhaps they exaggerated? Charles and his ministers had access to a
postal network of unprecedented extent and sophistication. In 1505 his
father named Francisco de Taxis his postmaster-general and paid him to
maintain thirty-five men in a network of postal stations linking Brussels and
the Spanish frontier. The following year Maximilian signed a contract with
the Taxis company to establish fifteen postal stations linking Augsburg and
Brussels; and a decade later Charles signed a contract with Taxis that established standard delivery times for letters travelling between the leading
cities in Germany, Italy and Spain (twelve days between Brussels and Toledo
in summer, fourteen in winter; and so on). By the 1530s, members of the
Taxis family served as postmasters in Augsburg, Brussels, Innsbruck, Rome
and Spain, while another often travelled with Charles to ensure an efficient
service wherever he might be.[27]

Charles once wished that his couriers 'could fly', in order to keep him in
touch better with developments – and sometimes they almost did. In 1519
news of his election as king of the Romans in Frankfurt reached Charles in
Barcelona, over 1,300 kilometres away, in seventeen days 'by means of fast
couriers who seemed to fly on very fast horses'. Three years later, a courier
covered the 1,500 kilometres that separated Rome from Brussels in twelve
days, bringing Charles the news that 'Master Adrian [of Utrecht] has been
elected pope'; and in 1545 a courier from Rome reached him in Worms,
1,300 kilometres away, in less than six days. These were truly remarkable
feats: an average speed of 76, 125 and 220 kilometres per day respectively. By
the end of Charles's reign, letters seem to have travelled faster than anything
else in the early modern world.[28]

The problem was that letters did not travel at uniform speeds. Although
we lack a systematic study of the rhythms of Charles's correspondence,
Pierre Sardella's analysis of 10,000 letters received by the government of
Venice from all over Europe between 1497 and 1532 provided a helpful

Figure 2: The time taken for official letters to arrive at Venice, 1497–1532

Place of origin	Number of letters	Shortest time (in days)	Longest time (in days)	Normal time (in days)	Received in 'normal time'
Rome	1,053	1½	9	4	38%
Naples	682	4	20	8	38%
Vienna	145	8	32	13	22%
Palermo	118	8	48	25	19%
Brussels	138	9	35	10	17%
Paris	473	7	34	12	13%
Valladolid	124	12	63	23	12%
London	672	9	52	24	12%
Innsbruck	163	4	16	6	10%
Augsburg	110	5	21	12	6%

Two Venetians, Mario Sanudo and Girolamo Priuli, recorded in their diaries the date on which more than 10,000 official letters arrived in Venice and also when and where they were written. From this raw data Pierre Sardella calculated the longest, the shortest, and the 'normal' time taken by letters from various destinations. His findings revealed 'normal' to be a meaningless category, especially for more distant locations: thus of the 124 letters received from Valladolid, the administrative capital of Spain, only fifteen arrived after the 'normal' time lapse of fifteen days – others took less than two weeks and one took over two months. Such unpredictable communications undermined government planning.
Source: Sardella, *Nouvelles*, 56–7

parallel (Fig. 2). Sardella set out to establish the 'normal time' – that is, the most common interval between dispatch and receipt – for letters travelling to Venice on various postal routes. Not surprisingly, the closer the location, the higher the proportion of letters that arrived at the normal time: only one in ten letters from Innsbruck, and one in eight from London, Paris and Valladolid, but one in five from Palermo and Vienna, and more than one in three from Naples and Rome. Even so, almost two-thirds of the 1,053 letters from Rome received in Venice did *not* arrive at the normal time: some took less than two days whereas others took over a week. Such unpredictability made it hard for the Venetian government to make and execute plans.

The same problem must have affected Charles's government even more, since his possessions eventually spanned one-quarter of the globe. The correspondence between Charles and Ferdinand in the 1520s shows that although on average their letters took forty days to arrive, some arrived in less than a month whereas others took more than two months. Such disparities directly impacted decision-making, because neither the sender nor the recipient could be sure when a letter would arrive. Even a critical communication, like Ferdinand's letter of 22 September 1526 containing news of the catastrophic defeat of Mohács almost a month before, did not reach Charles (in Granada) until fifty-one days later.[29] The same was true even on the most-travelled postal routes. In 1558 news of Charles's death at Yuste on 21 September did not reach his son in the Netherlands until 1 November; the previous year, a bishop in Spain complained that a letter written in Brussels had taken so long to arrive that 'it could have gone to America two or three times and still got here sooner'. Of course the bishop exaggerated: few letters written in Mexico arrived at court in less than three months, and those from Peru often took twice as long. On 20 August 1555 a courier arrived in Spain 'from Peru, with the news that the tyrant Francisco Hernández Girón had been executed' the previous December – a delay of almost nine months despite the importance of the news.[30]

Even if a letter arrived in record time, its contents might not be immediately actionable. Above all, the use of cypher could cause serious delays. In 1525 the English ambassadors in Spain received a letter from their master in code, 'wherupon we unciphred the letter, whiche is long and cost us welnigh the labor of 2 daies'; three years later, at a critical point during the French siege of Naples, it took the Spanish viceroy five days to break the code of a vital intercepted letter; in 1546 an agent of Count Fieschi (finalizing his conspiracy to capture Genoa) carelessly left part of a cyphered letter in Rome, but although it reached the Spanish ambassador he had to send it to Florence to be decoded.[31] The arrival of many letters at the same time could also cause delays. In 1543, Edmund Bonner, Henry VIII's ambassador in Spain, anxious to transact his master's business, despaired when a galley from Genoa arrived bearing letters 'in a great multitude to th'emperour out of Flaunders from the regent [Marie of Hungary], out of Germanie from Grandevele and others, and out of Italie from the Marques of Guaste [Vasto] and other th'emperours frendes there'. Despite 'all my diligent sollicitation and labour', it took Bonner several weeks to get from Charles the decisions he desired.[32]

James Tracy offered a felicitous simile for the dilemma posed by the combination of an information network of unprecedented sophistication with an empire of unprecedented size: 'Charles and his inner circle had regular reports on the affairs of dozens of kingdoms and principalities in Europe and overseas, and occasional reports on many others. Tracing the interconnections among these separate histories would require a gargantuan effort of the mind, a simulcast on thirty or forty different channels.'[33] The emperor adopted various strategies to process this simulcast. He continued to delegate decisions to trusted ministers, but insisted that they deluge him with news. In 1522, since his plan to return to Spain required the loan of both money and warships from Henry VIII, he instructed his ambassadors in England 'to write to me what you hear every day, so that we can better prepare our voyage'. Soon after reaching Spain he reminded his aunt Margaret, whom he had left in the Netherlands as his regent, that 'I greatly desire news so that I always know what is going on there. I therefore ask that you keep me informed as often as you can.' In 1525 he reminded his ambassadors in Rome to continue 'advising us continuously of what is happening'; and four years later, he instructed his new ambassador in Genoa 'always to take very special care to write to us many times by different routes, by sea as well as by land, everything that you think we need to know'. He asked no less of Juan de Vega, whom he sent to Rome as his ambassador in 1543, and made a reciprocal promise: 'We will write and tell you what items of business you need to monitor, because changes occur in them daily if not hourly, and we need to change our views accordingly.'[34]

The emperor also directed his officials to keep in close contact with one another. 'We are pleased when our ministers are in complete conformity and maintain good intelligence and correspondence among themselves,' he told the duke of Alba, 'because, as you know, it will help to advance our interests.'[35] When in 1529 he appointed Gómez Suárez de Figueroa as his ambassador in Genoa, Charles ordered him to consult his long-serving predecessor, Lope de Soria, who was moving to the Venetian embassy, 'before he leaves: find out from him with great secrecy and discretion the standing of the leading members of that republic, in general and in particular, which of them are more and less attached to our service, and from whom he usually gets information on what is happening there'. Ten years later, when Charles moved Soria from Venice, he insisted that 'you must wait there for twenty or thirty days after the arrival' of his successor, in order to brief him 'by word of mouth as well as in writing' and to hand over all relevant papers 'so he will be better informed and do his job better'. Soria must also share 'the general cipher that we use with our ministers' in Italy, and also spend time 'transacting business jointly with him, so that he will better understand it, and the way to handle affairs'.[36]

MASTER OF WAR

The perceptive Venetian ambassador Bernardo Navagero noted that Charles 'cannot conceal the pleasure he takes in war. He is happy then, he comes alive.' Whereas normally 'he always seems very solemn, in the midst of the army he wants to be everywhere, he wants to see and meddle in everything, and forgetting that he is such a great emperor he will even do the work of a simple captain. Many say,' Navagero continued:

> That the emperor's desire to take part in operations brings with it many drawbacks, because when he is present in person it is always necessary to be more cautious when on the move and more prudent in combat, and to undertake only those operations that have a chance of success. By contrast, when the emperor is not present, his generals would be more audacious in tempting Fortune, knowing that even if they lose an army they can easily raise another one.

According to Navagero, 'many people, especially the Spaniards, say that the emperor would do better not to go on campaign himself', citing the example of his grandfather Ferdinand who, 'without leaving Spain, gained the kingdom of Naples and many cities in Africa'. Indeed, he continued, 'the emperor, too, has always won striking and notable victories when he has left the conduct of war to his ministers. But,' the ambassador added, 'others say that given the type of armies he commands, things might have turned out worse in his absence than they did in his presence, and on certain occasions some ventures succeeded that might otherwise have failed'.[37]

The ambassador accurately summarized the passionate disagreements on this subject among Charles's ministers. When Archduchess Margaret discovered in 1529 that her nephew planned to go to Italy 'and hazard your person in war', she reminded him that 'my grandfather Duke Charles [the Bold] died defeated in battle', adding with heavy sarcasm, 'I'm sure you have heard about this several times'; and that 'the late King Charles [VIII] of France, who wanted to go to Naples, found everyone his ally' until he ran out of money, after which 'everyone abandoned him until he had only 5,000 or 6,000 men, with whom he was forced to fight at great risk and danger to his life in order to return to France'. She therefore begged her nephew to let his armies do the fighting until all his enemies had made peace. Six years later, when his sister Marie learned of Charles's plans for the Tunis campaign, she argued that 'His Majesty should not be present in person, because many things that could be risked in his absence cannot be attempted in his presence'.[38] Charles himself had periodic misgivings on this subject. When he heard that his wife's brother, Prince Luis of Portugal, had taken part in a night attack while campaigning against the Sharif of Morocco, he stated unequivocally:

We are vehemently opposed to him taking part in any action, even if he is well supported and supplied, because of the great risk involved, especially since the size of the army that the Sharif will have with him means that [the prince] can achieve little. It is better that he should be free to order and arrange any relief or other operation that may be required.

But Charles did not follow his own advice. In 1544, when he joined his troops besieging St Dizier, he took personal command, as he had done in both African campaigns, because 'almoost a dousen [dozen] diverse nations' served 'in myn armey', and since they did not always agree 'if I be not there myself, I am sure no man can rule them'.[39]

The emperor prided himself on his ability to organize a campaign. At the beginning of operations against John Frederick of Saxony, despite suffering from 'a hot piss that gives me no peace either by day or by night' (presumably a urinary tract infection), on 26 March 1547 he provided his brother with a detailed plan of campaign. He promised that he would lead his army out of Nuremberg the following day and 'with God's help' reach Ferdinand's camp at Cheb (Eger), 150 kilometres away, in nine days: 'I cannot come any faster, because it is not possible for troops to travel more than two leagues a day. You are eighteen leagues away, which means nine days.' He and his army marched into Cheb on 5 April, exactly nine days later – a remarkable feat.[40]

THE EMPEROR CLOSELY OBSERVED

Many observers took an obsessive interest in the emperor's physical health, noting anything unusual. Periodically he impressed everyone with a display of physical strength and endurance. After the battle of Mühlberg in 1547, according to an eyewitness, he 'returned to his quarters at 1 a.m., having spent twenty-two hours without dismounting'; four years later, an ambassador reported that Charles was still such an eager hunter that 'several nights he slept fully clothed, to be ready to ride out at dawn', adding 'when necessary, he is fit enough to do anything he wants'. An imperial physician, Dr Cornelis van Baersdorp, painted a very different picture. In a series of health bulletins written after Mühlberg he reported that Charles caught a severe cold (May); had a stomach ache until cured by a powerful laxative ('His Majesty himself said that he had three large bowel movements, and felt much better afterwards': June); was bitten in the foot by a rodent (July); and 'was kept awake by asthma' for several nights (August).[41] In 1550 the French ambassador Charles de Marillac provided a pessimistic overall health assessment. He asserted that the emperor 'suffered from three chronic illnesses, each of which sometimes becomes acute: the first is his haemorrhoids, which lead him to lose a lot of blood.' Second, 'he is asthmatic with a constant draining of catarrh into his lungs, and sometimes a racking cough so strong that it is a wonder he has endured it so long'. Third, 'he suffers from gout in his arms, shoulder and head so badly that in winter he climbed into some sort of sauna [*un poisle, ou pour mieux dire en une fournaise*] in which most people would stay for a quarter of an hour, but he remains there the whole day' to try and mitigate the pain. 'That he is still alive,' Marillac concluded (with evident regret), 'is a miracle and contrary to the laws of nature.'[42]

Charles himself agreed. He filled letters to his relatives with numbing detail on his various ailments, and when he composed his *Memoirs* in 1550 he obsessively recorded the time and place of seventeen attacks of gout.[43] It is easy to see why. According to Marillac, sometimes the intense pain of his gout made the emperor 'weep and say farewell to the world, taking the last rites in great haste'. When Charles left Ghent in January 1545, after a prolonged episode, Navagero claimed that 'everyone who saw the poor monarch felt compassion for him because he appeared so weak, pale and feeble. He left, swaddled and secured, in a litter that he could only reach with great difficulty'. After another attack three years later, a Florentine colleague asserted that a recent portrait (quite possibly the one by Titian in 1548) showed him 'looking very pale and lacking colour', adding 'and no wonder, since he has had so many purges and was on a diet'.[44]

'Diet' was a flexible term where Charles was concerned. The ruler praised for being abstemious when a young man (p. 66) periodically succumbed to gluttony as he got older. Dr Baersdorp complained in 1548 that the emperor sometimes overate, especially fruit ('five dozen cherries at one meal'; enormous quantities of melon). Two years later, Roger Ascham watched Charles gorge himself on 'roast mutton, baked hare' and a chicken, and drink prodigiously ('he had his head in the glass five times as long as any of us, and never drank less than a good quart at once of Rhenish wine'). Marillac considered the emperor 'the most self-indulgent man in the world when it comes to food'.[45] Yet Bartholomew Sastrow, normally a severe critic of Charles, told a different story: 'I often saw him eat dinner in public' in the 1540s and he 'drank only three times during each meal' from 'a crystal goblet' – albeit 'he drained it to the last drop, pausing for breath two or three times'. As for food, although 'there were always four courses, each with six dishes', Sastrow recalled that:

As the servers uncovered each one, the emperor shook his head when he rejected it and nodded and drew towards him the others. They took away enormous pastries, large pieces of game, and the most succulent dishes, while His Majesty ate a piece of roast, or a calf's head or something similar. No one carved for him, and he made little use of his knife except to cut his bread, and also his chosen dish, into pieces small enough to swallow whole. He then put down his knife, and instead used his fingers, holding his plate under his chin with the other hand.[46]

Although Sastrow thought that 'he ate so naturally, and at the same time so cleanly, that it was a pleasure to watch him', presumably Charles's delicate table manners reflected his prognathism, which made it impossible for him to chew food. A couple of accidents exacerbated this problem. In 1550 the Florentine ambassador, while marvelling at the emperor's marksmanship ('he is certainly a crack shot'), reported that he used 'an arquebus with such a long range that perhaps it was too much, because its recoil was so powerful that it affected those of his teeth that were not securely anchored in his jaw'. The following year, while travelling in and around Augsburg in a sort of gun-carriage 'of his own design', he fell out and 'loosened the few teeth that nature had left him'.[47]

The extreme oscillations in the emperor's health led some to suspect that he exaggerated his ailments either to buy time or to avoid unwelcome decisions. The English ambassador, William Paget, had no doubt. 'When I cam to him,' he wrote in March 1545:

I sawe no gret cause why he shuld not speke with any ambassadour; for as for his sicknes, howsoever it greveth him inwardly, I know not, but outwardly I sawe in his face, and of the quicknes and lowde and lyvely speking of him, a greater apparaunce of helth then he showed to have at my being with him in somer. And, to saye truely to you my fantazie, I think verily *he hath ben no more sick then I am, but useth it for a policye.*

Paget made a similar comment nine months later – 'Th' emperor's gowte *servith hym to purpose allway*' – and after an audience at which Charles lay 'in a low chair with his leg elevated', the nuncio likewise observed that '*some suspect that he is just pretending to be ill*'.[48]

The truth only emerged when Charles's naked body was exposed to public view in the 1870s (see Pl. 39). Although a spectator commented on both his 'corpulence' and 'his broad chest and broad shoulders', a modern laboratory analysis of a detached phalanx from one of his fingers confirmed that he had suffered from extreme gout. The investigators found that 'massive gouty tophi [had] completely destroyed the distal interphalanx joint and extended to the neighbouring soft tissue'. Presumably the emperor's other joints were similarly afflicted, so it is small wonder that he complained of chronic pain and sought relief by spending his days in a sauna.[49]

Contemporaries also monitored variations in the emperor's behaviour. Sastrow noted that in the 1540s Charles ate his meals in the presence of 'his jesters [*Schalksnarren*], who stood behind him', but 'paid little attention to them, with just a little chuckle [*mit einem halben Lachlin*] when they said something particularly amusing'.[50] Nevertheless, the emperor had a good sense of humour and sometimes made jokes at his own expense. Thus, when trying to arrange a private interview with Francis I in 1538, he stressed to a French envoy the importance of 'doing everything possible to create trust, because sometimes a single word can do a lot, provided that (and here he smiled) one does not bite; and *although His Majesty often has his mouth open*, you can be sure that he lacks the teeth to do that.' At an audience a decade later, after the Florentine ambassador had summarized a document, Charles asked him to read out the full text to make sure he had understood everything. The ambassador felt embarrassed, 'because I had never had to wear my spectacles when reading to His Majesty, and tried to get out of it. But he started to laugh and said "There are others here who depend on them", pointing to himself.'[51] Charles was similarly gracious to others. At Thomas Wyatt's first audience in 1537, the emperor 'gently entreteigned [him] not with pompe and setting furth of himself, but with sobre and discrete words, like a wise man'; and on hearing of the birth of Henry VIII's son and heir, Edward, the emperor indulged in 'good and long rejoicing and laughing which I never saw in him so heartily nor so pleasantly'.[52] In 1543, according to the Spanish exile Francisco de Enzinas, every day after dinner Charles 'got up and spent a long time leaning on a cane' to hear the assembled petitioners 'as if he had nothing else to do than listen to what we had to say to him'. When Enzinas's turn came, he presented the emperor with his translation of the New Testament 'into our Spanish language. "Into Castilian?" His Majesty asked'. After affirming this, Enzinas revealed that he had dedicated the book to Charles and asked for an exclusive licence to sell it. 'What you request will be done,' the emperor replied, adding prudently 'provided that it contains nothing forbidden'. He then 'went into an adjacent room', taking the book with him.[53]

Occasionally, Charles was not so gracious. In 1551 he 'used very pungent words' during an audience with the French ambassador, 'shaking his fist in a gesture of defiance as he said to him: "Make your king understand that we shall tolerate no hostile act"' towards himself or his allies. A few days earlier he also raged to an English envoy that 'I will not suffer' Mary Tudor 'to be evil handled ... Is it not enough that mine aunt, her mother, was evil entreated by the King that dead is, but my cousin must be worse ordered by councillors now?'[54] Some thought that such outbursts revealed the emperor's true feelings. According to Marillac that same year, 'If you examine the matter closely, you will find that he has never cared for anyone, except in as far as he needs them', citing Charles's cavalier treatment of his brother-in-law Christian of Denmark, his aunt Katherine of Aragon, and above all his brother Ferdinand.[55] In 1552 a nuncio at his court reached a similar conclusion. 'The emperor is by nature very good and a good Christian,' he wrote, 'but it seems to me nevertheless that he has become so miserly, and so short of money and of everything else that could be useful to him and his interests' that 'little reliance and little confidence should be placed in his friendship, unless it is something that brings him some direct benefit.'[56]

The Strasbourg Reformer Martin Bucer (no friend of the emperor) brilliantly captured the various paradoxes in Charles's nature after observing him at the Diet of Speyer in 1543. He informed a colleague that 'the emperor is a man with a sharp mind who pursues his plans with the greatest determination', and he 'is imperial in word, deed, look, gesture, gifts, everything. Even those who have been with him a long time are amazed to see in him such enthusiasm, willingness, determination and majesty.' He predicted that 'The emperor could achieve a great deal, if he would only act like a German emperor and a servant of Christ.' Bucer and his fellow Protestants would soon learn that Charles could also achieve a great deal while acting like a medieval emperor and persecuting heretics.[57]

PART IV

DOWNFALL

'You need to ask yourself...'

'I don't need to do anything: I'm the king!'

Joffrey Baratheon, first of his name; exchange between
Cersei Lannister and her son, *Game of Thrones*, series 3,
episode 2 (2013)

FOURTEEN

PATERFAMILIAS, 1548–51

SEX AND THE EMPEROR: I. THREE ILLEGITIMATE DAUGHTERS

In 1530 a Mantuan diplomat asserted that Charles 'gives up to two ducats a night to any woman who sleeps with him'; in 1548 a Venetian ambassador claimed that the emperor's 'doctors and those who know him well say that he was and still is by nature much inclined to sensual pleasures and has made love to many women'; his successor in 1557 stated that Charles 'has freely indulged in venereal pleasures in every place he has visited, with lower- as well as upper-class women'. Since none of these diplomats revealed their source, it would be easy to dismiss their claims as salacious gossip – except that Charles acknowledged four illegitimate children, two of them conceived with teenage servants (Fig. 3).[1]

Late in 1521, while residing in the castle of Oudenaarde in the Netherlands for six weeks, Charles seduced one of the servants, Jeanne van der Gheynst. By the time Jeanne gave birth the emperor had returned to Spain; but he left instructions that his daughter be named after his aunt Margaret and then taken away to Brussels to be raised by a courtier. In return for her agreement to sacrifice the child, Charles granted Jeanne a modest annual pension and arranged for her to marry someone far above her social station; and twenty years later, on learning of her death, he transferred her pension to her legitimate children.[2] Archduchess Margaret took a keen interest in her great-niece and namesake, buying her presents, teaching her to ride and to hunt, and occasionally inviting her to court functions; and Charles toyed with marrying 'my bastard daughter who lives in the Netherlands' to an Italian prince – first the son of the duke of Ferrara, then the heir to Mantua, and finally Alessandro de' Medici, the pope's nephew – as a means of winning them over. In 1529 he granted his daughter the right to use the family style 'of Austria', and issued a declaration of legitimacy; and when he returned to Brussels two years later he met her for the first time. Soon afterwards, at Pope Clement's request, he agreed that 'my very dear and much loved

Figure 3: The family tree of Charles V and Isabella

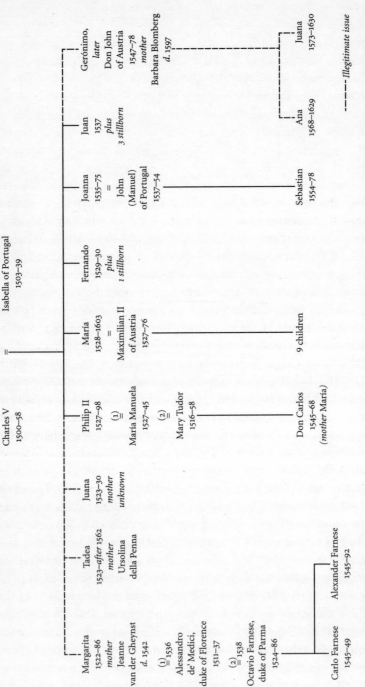

Empress Isabella had nine pregnancies, but only three of her children outlived her, and of those only two produced more than one heir: María, who gave birth to nine children, and Philip II, whose four wives produced only two children who outlived the king. Charles also sired four illegitimate children, of whom two entered a convent (Tadea and Juana); one never married but sired at least two illegitimate children (Gerónimo, later known as Don John); and the other (Margarita) gave birth to twins, of whom one died in infancy.

daughter' should reside in Rome, and he instructed her governess on what 'Margarita' (as she became known) should study and how she should behave. In 1536 he presided over her wedding, when she was aged thirteen, to Alessandro de' Medici, now duke of Florence, but their union did not fare well: a year later a discontented relative assassinated Alessandro.[3]

Although the young widow began to sign her letters 'sad Margarita', she made the most of her new freedom until Charles stepped in. In January 1538 the emperor informed her chamberlain (whom he had appointed) that 'I understand that the duchess [Margarita] sometimes goes out hunting and stays away two, three and even four days', and ordered him 'to stop her doing this by whatever means you can. If she wants to go hunting, she must return home each night.' The following month Charles accepted the suggestion of Pope Paul that his grandson, Octavio Farnese, should marry Margarita and soon afterwards the ceremony took place in the Sistine Chapel.[4] Once again, the union did not fare well. On their wedding night Octavio, aged fourteen, could not consummate the union and afterwards Margarita refused to sleep with him. She wrote a rude letter to her father complaining about this unsatisfactory situation, prompting Charles to compose 'the first letter that I have written to you with my own hand'. After criticizing her language, 'which you should not use to any Christian, especially not to me, since I am your father', he adopted the same passive-aggressive tone he used periodically with others close to him: 'So far I have not used force, nor would I wish to use it. I prefer to admonish you as a father concerning what you should and ought to do, and I hope and trust that my admonition, advice and pleas will prove more beneficial than all the force and threats that others might have used.' He concluded with the hope that God 'will guide, lead and induce you to do all that you should, and also what you owe to me and to yourself, like the good daughter you are; and I promise that you will always find me a good father'. Margarita evidently replied with further complaints about her husband because a few weeks later Charles wrote another holograph letter. This time he apologized that if he 'had known these things at the beginning' he would not have forced the marriage upon her; but now, he continued, 'I would not discharge my duties as a good father, or justify the confidence you have placed in me, if I did not advise and exhort you to do what you must to satisfy your honour and your conscience' – namely to 'live as a wife' with Octavio.[5] Nevertheless, the emperor did his best to address his daughter's complaints: he took her husband with him when he left for Algiers in 1541 and kept him in his entourage for two years. This temporarily solved the couple's conjugal difficulties. When they met again, according to a well-informed source, 'the first time Duke Octavio slept with his lady, he ejaculated four times'; and in August 1545 she gave birth to twin boys. Charles 'showed great pleasure in asking after [his grandsons], wanting to know how big and chubby they were, and if they differed from one another in any way'.[6] Two years later, the emperor changed his tune again on finding that Octavio had contracted syphilis: now he did 'everything he could to prevent the duchess from being infected'. Margarita would bear no more children, and she and Octavio reluctantly complied with Charles's demand that they send Alessandro, now the only surviving twin, to be brought up in Spain.[7]

Charles also seduced Ursolina della Penna of Perugia, the 'very beautiful' widow of a nobleman, while she resided at his court in the Netherlands in 1522. As soon as the emperor realized Ursolina was pregnant he sent her back to Italy, where she gave birth to their daughter, Tadea. The child was entrusted to the nuns of a neighbouring convent, but eight years later, shortly before his coronation, Charles summoned Tadea to meet him in Bologna. After publicly recognizing her as his daughter, he 'caused a mark to be made on her right leg below the knee, which was an $\overset{\wedge}{\text{IHS}}$' – that is, he caused someone to make a permanent mark (an abbreviation of the name of Jesus) on his daughter, presumably with a sharp instrument: an extraordinary act.[8] Tadea returned to her convent until 1532, when Charles summoned her for another brief visit and then sent her back with instructions that 'she must not be given to her mother or to anyone else until His Majesty authorizes it'. No doubt he intended to use her (like Margarita) as a dynastic pawn and he was therefore furious when Ursolina's half-brothers broke into the convent, seized Tadea, and forced her to marry a local nobleman. The emperor wrote Ursolina a reproachful letter, but soon calmed down: 'Although I was very angry with you, nevertheless Your Ladyship will feel gratitude towards me because I am sending with the bearer 3,000 gold crowns to be spent to the benefit and use of our daughter.' In 1550, after the death of her mother and husband, Tadea went to Rome and became a nun, but on hearing that Charles had abdicated and moved to Yuste she wrote to ask his permission to come to Spain. In 1562, having received no reply, she sent a messenger to Philip II bearing the same request, together with documents that proved her august paternity. With characteristic insensitivity Charles had failed to inform Philip that he had another half-sister, so this was probably the first the king knew about her existence. With similar insensitivity, Philip archived her plea and did nothing for Tadea.[9]

Charles's third illegitimate daughter was born in Valladolid in 1523, probably the fruit of a liaison with the daughter of an exiled Venetian nobleman.[10] The emperor immediately sent both mother and baby, named Juana, to a convent at Madrigal de las Altas Torres where Prioress María de Aragón (an illegitimate daughter of Ferdinand the Catholic and thus Charles's aunt) looked after them. The following year the prioress reported that the child 'has a marvellous body for her age, and about a month ago she started to walk when you hold her little arms', adding pointedly 'every day she looks more like the emperor'. She also stated that the child's mother 'is very sad because His Majesty has never thought of her, or sent to find out how she fares, since he sent Juana here'. She pleaded for a visit from Charles when next he went to see his mother at Tordesillas, which was not far away; but in 1530, Juana apparently drowned in the convent well and was buried at Madrigal without ever meeting her father.[11]

Charles appears to have abandoned his promiscuous ways while he was married, but temptation was seldom far away. While creating a household for his sister Marie as regent in the Netherlands in 1531, he named 'the young widow Egmont' as one of her attendants and defended his choice at suspicious length to his brother Ferdinand: 'To prove to you that I have not allowed myself to be carried away by affection for young women, I delayed making the appointment until now, when I am about to leave, so that no one can falsely say or think that I have done it with evil intent. I am not such a bad husband.'[12] Charles's confessor, García de Loaysa, was not so sure, chiding him 'never let your wicked sensuality govern you'; and several observers commented on the emperor's manifest 'affection for young women'. Thus in 1530, when 'sixty local women, young and old, beautiful and plain', came out to welcome Charles to Innsbruck, 'he shook the hands of all of them, and gave the younger ones a kiss'. Charles himself admitted flirtatious behaviour when he made his ceremonial entry into Naples five years later. 'Everyone knows the attractiveness of the city and the beauty and graciousness of the women who live there,' he told his courtiers, continuing:

I am a man just like other men, and I wanted to earn their favours. On the morning of my arrival, I summoned my barber to trim, shave and perfume me. He placed a mirror before me. I looked at myself and saw [some grey hairs] . . . Shocked and astonished I asked 'What are those?' My barber replied 'Two or three white hairs.' There were more than a dozen. 'Remove those hairs,' I told him, 'and don't leave a single one'.

'And do you know what happened next?' the emperor asked rhetorically: 'A short time afterwards, wanting to see myself in the mirror again, I found that for every white hair that had been removed, three more had appeared; and if I had wanted to have those removed, in no time at all I would have been as white as a swan.'[13]

Despite the white hairs, during his residence in Naples over the winter of 1535–6 (according to a member of his entourage) 'the emperor took advantage of the festivals to get to know all the ladies and gentlewomen of Naples'. In particular, he saw the duchess of Salerno daily and one evening at a masked ball he 'asked insistently, once, twice and a third time to kiss her hand'; and to win her favour he granted everything she asked him (including her request that he pardon a convicted murderer, an appalling lapse for which he later expressed regret).[14] Two years later, at a masked ball in Barcelona, 'the emperor talked and laughed no less than other gentlemen. It happened that he told a lady with whom he was talking that he was the emperor, and took off his mask so that she would recognize him, and then told the lady to pretend that she did not know him, and to treat him just like any other gentleman.' Rumours about the 'masquerading' soon reached the court and the empress's secretary Juan Vázquez de Molina reproached his uncle, Los Cobos, for taking part. He replied: 'What they say about my coming in at midnight is a lie', but then admitted that he had gone out masquerading on three occasions, one of them 'with the emperor. And since His Majesty enjoys it, the gossip does not have much weight.' The gossip certainly weighed on the empress, however. Charles had once more left her behind, pregnant, and according to one of her ladies-in-waiting 'she feels very bitter about his departure'.[15]

SEX AND THE EMPEROR: II. ONE ILLEGITIMATE SON

The death of his wife allowed Charles's flirtatious side to flourish once more. While he resided in Regensburg between April and August 1546, dealing with the Diet and preparing to attack the German Lutherans, he seduced Barbara Blomberg, a teenager exactly the same age as his son Philip. The daughter of a leatherworker, Barbara was also related to the landlord of the inn where Charles stayed, and so she could come and go without attracting much notice. On 24 February 1547, Charles's birthday, she gave birth to his son and named him Gerónimo. He would later be known as Don John of Austria.[16]

Charles's initial reaction resembled his behaviour after the birth of Margarita – he arranged for the child to be separated from his mother and taken to Brussels – but whereas he had crowed over 'my little bastard daughter', and used her as a dynastic pawn, he kept the existence of his son secret. In 1550 he forced François Massi, one of his musicians, to sign an affidavit stating that the emperor's principal usher, Adrian Dubois, had empowered him to take his illegitimate son to Spain 'because Adrian does not want his wife to know', and to raise him there until further notice. The affidavit is only known because Charles attached a copy to a secret codicil to his will, written and signed without witnesses in 1554, admitting that he – not Dubois – was the father: 'When I was in Germany after the death of the empress, I sired an illegitimate son with an unmarried woman. His name is Gerónimo.' He commanded that the affidavit and codicil remain sealed and secret until after his death – no doubt because he felt ashamed of his affair with a teenager when he was forty-six.[17] Meanwhile, the emperor arranged for Doña Magdalena de Ulloa, the wife of his comrade-in-arms Luis Méndez de Quijada, to supervise the upbringing of his secret son at their castle in Villagarcía de Campos, fifty kilometres from the court in Valladolid. There he remained until the summer of 1558, when the emperor ordered Quijada to bring Gerónimo to live near Yuste. Charles met his son only once before he died but declined to recognize him, leaving his legitimate children to discover for themselves that they had another sibling (chapter 15).

Charles treated Barbara Blomberg somewhat better. She later married Hieronymus Kegel, a minor imperial clerk to whom the emperor granted £100 'in consideration of certain good services he has rendered to the emperor, and to cover his expenses while he awaits some suitable position from His Majesty'. Shortly afterwards Kegel also received an annual pension of 100 florins 'with the obligation to reside in the Netherlands and, whenever required, to attend on the regent [Marie] and carry out her orders'. Barbara and her husband made Brussels their base, where they raised three children.[18] Although Barbara and Charles both lived in Brussels between 1553 and 1556, she probably saw him (if at all) only from afar; nevertheless, as he lay on his deathbed the emperor thought of her fondly, ordering a trusted aide to withdraw from his privy purse '600 crowns in gold' – a substantial gift – and deliver it to her. He then lost consciousness and died the next day.[19]

EDUCATING THE HEIR

Charles always paid close attention to his son and heir: Prince Philip. He stayed with the empress for his birth, a unique event, and he rejected suggestions that the boy should receive a traditional Trastámara name, such as Fernando or Juan, but instead called him after the father he had scarcely known, Philip. According to an ambassador, 'the emperor was so happy and takes so much pleasure in his new son that he does nothing except organize celebrations' (chapter 7). When Charles set sail for Italy in 1529 he left behind two legitimate children, Philip and María (born 1528). Shortly after his departure the empress gave birth to another son, Fernando, but he died a year later. Another daughter was born while the emperor was absent in Africa in 1535: Joanna.

While on his travels between 1529 and 1533, Charles invited three admirers of Erasmus whom he met to serve as the prince's preceptor – Francisco de Bobadilla y Mendoza, who taught at the university of Salamanca; Joachim Viglius van Aytta from Friesland, professor of law at the university of Padua; and Juan Luis Vives, one of the foremost humanists of his day, living in the Netherlands – but although all three would later serve him in other roles, none accepted the offer of preceptor. Charles therefore appointed a small committee to select a teacher. They soon reduced a list of fifteen candidates to three, one of whom was Juan Martínez del Guijo, normally known by the Latinized version of his surname, *Silíceo*, a forty-eight-year-old priest of humble origins who had studied at Paris and published books on both philosophy and mathematics before becoming a professor of philosophy at Salamanca, where the emperor heard him lecture in June 1534. Shortly afterwards he appointed him preceptor to his son.[20]

A year later Charles created a separate household for Philip, and he chose as its governor Juan de Zúñiga y Avellaneda, one of the *Felipistas* who had come to the Netherlands to serve him twenty-five years before. The emperor did not model his son's household on Burgundian lines, like his own, but instead sought to imitate that of his uncle Juan, the last native prince of Castile, and he instructed Zúñiga to obtain detailed descriptions of the late prince's household from its surviving members. One of them – the historian Gonzalo Fernández de Oviedo – came to court for an interview, and was later asked to write down everything he could remember because the emperor wished his son 'to be raised and served in the same way as the prince, his uncle'. Philip was to become 'a true prince of Castile'.[21] Henceforth, the prince's entourage comprised only male servants – the emperor appointed about forty of them – and Zúñiga (or his deputy) slept in Philip's chamber at night and kept him under constant surveillance by day. 'I am only absent,' Zúñiga stated, 'when I am writing to Your Majesty' or when the prince 'is in school, or with his mother somewhere that I may not enter'.[22]

Zúñiga's exclusion from school reflected the Castilian tradition that 'the prince should have two people to teach him different things: a master who will teach him letters and good behaviour, and a governor who would instruct him in military and knightly exercises'.[23] So it was Silíceo who taught the prince and six of his pages how to read, write and pray – albeit progress was slow because the preceptor was indulgent. In February 1536, Silíceo informed Charles that he had 'suspended for some days' the prince's Latin assignments 'because the first principles are difficult'; and four years later, when the prince was thirteen, he announced that 'we have just started Latin composition'.[24] Silíceo's relaxed regime, and his hostility to Humanism, did little to stimulate the prince's intellect: by the end of 1538 his library contained just sixteen books, all of them devotional except for an 'imperial genealogy' and three books of Spanish and Latin grammar. Moreover, as José Luis Gonzalo Sánchez-Molero noted, 'many of the books used to educate the future Philip II between 1535 and 1541 were manuscript volumes' so that, like his father two decades earlier, 'he apparently studied according to the aesthetic and cultural criteria of the previous century'.[25]

Silíceo had more success in stimulating Philip's religious devotion. Even the stern and godly Zúñiga was impressed, noting as he took over as governor in 1535 that 'the fear of God comes so naturally to the prince that I have not seen anything like it in someone of his age'; and the prince soon acquired several religious objects, including three small but richly bound liturgical works, apparently intended to be hung from his belt or placed on his bedside table; a Book of Hours; and a beautifully illuminated pocket *Rosario*.[26] After 1535, Philip devoted most of his mornings to prayer and worship followed (when he was healthy) by lessons in the company of the sons of Zúñiga, Los Cobos and Francisco de Borja. In August of that year, aged eight, he felt so happy on hearing of his father's victory at Tunis that he 'decided to write a letter to Your Majesty in his own hand'; but voluntary forays into literacy remained rare. Zúñiga grumbled that 'he learns very well once he is out of school!'[27]

The unexpected death of the empress in 1539 led Charles to decree important changes in the life of his children. He ordered his daughters to move first to the town of Arévalo in Old Castile and then to Ocaña south of Aranjuez, where they could grow up away from the bustle of the court. Henceforth Charles controlled their lives both directly (even when he claimed to be too busy to answer official letters, he found time to compose orders changing his daughters' residence) and indirectly (by instructing Philip to enforce his directives for them, such as his plan to marry María to Charles of Orléans in 1544 and to Maximilian four years later: chapter 11).[28] After María's marriage, Charles decreed that Joanna must live apart from her siblings in places so small and isolated that no nobleman could demand by right the honour of paying her a visit, eventually sending her to Aranda del Duero, an insalubrious town where he required her to look after his grandson Don Carlos, ten years her junior. The emperor denied María permission to visit her sister, and although in 1550 he moved Joanna (now fifteen) to Toro, he forbade her to stop and see her sister on the way. The following year he reluctantly allowed Joanna to visit María and Maximilian before they left for Germany, but they would never meet again.[29]

Charles also closely controlled his son. After the death of the empress he increased the size of Philip's household and promoted Zúñiga to be its chamberlain (*mayordomo mayor*) while still remaining the prince's governor. Two years later, frustrated by Silíceo's failure to teach his son Latin, Charles charged Zúñiga, Tavera and Los Cobos to meet as a committee and propose a suitable new preceptor. They recommended Juan Cristóbal Calvete de Estrella, raised in Catalonia, noting that he was not only 'a very learned man' but also 'of pure blood' (*limpio de sangre*: that is, he had no Jewish or Muslim ancestors). Charles duly appointed him 'to teach grammar to the prince and all his pages'. He soon added three other instructors: Honorato Juan, from Valencia, to teach him mathematics and architecture; Juan Ginés de Sepúlveda, from Córdoba, to teach him history and geography; and Francisco de Vargas Mexía, from Toledo, to teach him theology. Although all four preceptors were Spaniards (albeit from different regions), each had travelled extensively in Europe and boasted a cosmopolitan outlook that would broaden the horizons of the prince and his fellow students in the palace school.[30] Calvete, unlike Silíceo, was enthusiastic for Humanist learning and within a year he had purchased 140 books for the prince, more than doubling the size of his library.

In 1542 the emperor took his son to Navarre, Aragon, Catalonia and Valencia. The principal purpose was to ensure that each kingdom recognized Philip as heir apparent, but Calvete, Juan and Sepúlveda – all of whom accompanied Philip and his father – seized every opportunity to teach him about the different languages, cultures and histories of his future vassals. The prince admired ancient ruins, coins and inscriptions along the route; met an ambassador of the shah of Persia and a brother of the king of Congo; and received from Fray Bartolomé de Las Casas a dedicated manuscript copy of *A very brief account of the destruction of America* (chapter 13). When news arrived that the French had laid siege to Perpignan, the second city of Catalonia, Sepúlveda led a debate among courtiers on the best way to save it – Philip's first exposure to military strategy. In addition, throughout the tour and after their return to Madrid, Charles instructed his son in the art of government. He no doubt intended to make such lessons a regular fixture, but his departure in 1543 to direct military operations against France and Guelders put an end to them. It also prevented him from superintending Philip's marriage.

In September 1542, Charles had 'asked the king of Portugal for the hand of his oldest daughter', María Manuela, because 'the age of the prince my son makes it more than necessary to arrange his marriage, in order to continue the dynasty'. Since the princess was not only the daughter of his sister Catalina but also the niece of the late empress, Charles had to request multiple dispensations from the pope to cover 'each and every instance of consanguinity and affinity that exists between the prince and the princess' (Pl. 28).[31] This delayed the wedding, leading Charles to explain his son's marital responsibilities in writing: he devoted almost four pages of his May 1543 instructions to the subject of sex.

'My son, God willing, you will soon be married,' the emperor began, even though sexual intercourse at the age of sixteen 'can be dangerous both for the body's growth and for its strength: it can often lead to such weakness that it interferes with conceiving children and even causes death.' He had already interrogated his son to make sure he was still a virgin ('I am certain that you have told me the truth about the past, and that you have kept your word to me [to remain celibate] until you are married'); now he demanded that the prince show equal restraint after the wedding. 'I require and request that once you have consummated the marriage, you plead some illness and keep away from your wife and do not visit her again so quickly or so often. And when you do return, let it be for only a short time.'[32] Charles backed up this astounding request both with pathos (if too much sex killed the prince, 'your sisters and their husbands would inherit in your place: just imagine what cold comfort this would bring me in my old age!') and with measures to compel the young couple's compliance. He sent his instructions to Zúñiga, ordering the prince to 'read them in his presence so that he can remind you of what they contain whenever he deems it necessary'. Moreover, 'to make certain there are no shortcomings in this matter', he ordered that 'even though it may anger you, I order [Zúñiga] not to refrain from saying and doing all he can to see that you comply in this matter'. Most humiliating of all, he ordered Francisco de Borja and his wife 'to do the same' once María Manuela arrived in Spain, and to 'keep her away from you except for the times when your life and health can stand it'. A more effective way to create a complex about sex in a boy scarcely sixteen would be hard to imagine.[33]

PHILIP COMES OF AGE

In retrospect, Philip dated the beginning of his personal rule from the day his father left Spain. In 1574 he reminded a minister 'I began to govern in 1543', and two years later he rejected a suggested change to his administrative style because 'I have been dealing with public affairs for almost thirty-three years'.[34] He was correct. Although the emperor had originally intended his son to sign only 'the warrants and other documents concerning his household', and otherwise to do as he was told, he soon discovered that he had miscalculated. In October 1543, at the end of a letter instructing his son to send money to sustain his war with France, Charles added a holograph postscript that came close to blackmail: 'My son: I'm sure that when you read what I have written here, and see how much it affects me, you will do everything that a loyal son is obliged to do so as not to abandon your father in this situation . . . Do not fail to send me the soldiers and money that I have requested.' Barely two weeks later the emperor picked up his quill again to maintain the pressure: 'My son,' he crooned after another long plea for soldiers and money from Spain, 'once again I beg you to show me what a loyal son you are.' The prince remained unmoved. No doubt encouraged by his Spanish advisers, who worried that fiscal pressure might provoke unrest, the prince did not reply until February 1544 – four months later! – and then explained at some length why he intended to do nothing:

> I beg Your Majesty as earnestly as I can to take what I say in the same spirit as I write it. I do not seek to circumscribe Your Majesty's ambitious plans, which are the fruit of your imperial valour, but to remind you of the current state of affairs, the misery in which Christendom finds itself, the exhaustion of your kingdoms, the harm that follows from major wars (however justified they may be), and the danger in which we find ourselves, with enemy fleets at hand and few resources with which to resist them.

Ending all wars was the only realistic strategy, Philip emphasized, 'if Your Majesty wishes to avoid an irreparable disaster'.[35]

José Luis Gonzalo Sánchez-Molero has argued that in this letter 'Philip revealed his political opinions for the first time', and they no doubt irritated Charles profoundly.[36] So did some other developments. In February 1545 the emperor sent Zúñiga a long letter filled with complaints about his son, now almost eighteen, lamenting some 'little things that have started in my absence'. Charles recognized that many 'little things' could not be remedied. Thus although 'it would be better if he did not return so late when he goes hunting', or neglect his studies:

> Seeing that he is now married, and busy with affairs of state, and past the age where it might be worth urging him to do more than he wishes to do of his own free will, it seems to me that he should be allowed to do what he wants. We should not nag him so much that he becomes irritated with everything.

The emperor expressed more concern about some of the other 'little things' – 'the disorderly manner and the time wasted in getting up and going to bed, and in getting dressed and undressed'; 'the lack of attention he shows in devotions and confessions'; and above all 'what happened at the house' of the prince's jester – but once again he did nothing.[37]

Charles had reluctantly recognized that his dependence on support from Spain circumscribed his parental authority. On the very day that he wrote his complaint to Zúñiga, the emperor sent Philip yet another plea for money: 'Believe me: if this time the impossible does not become possible, I cannot maintain my various enterprises', because without the funds that only Philip could raise, 'I will be left in the dirt'. Charles simply could not afford to alienate his son. In addition, once María Manuela became pregnant, warnings about the risks of teenage sex gave way to jokes about the prince's prowess: 'Many congratulations on her pregnancy: you have done better than I expected, because I thought it would have taken you another year!' Henceforth the emperor meddled with his son's private life less often, telling Zúñiga that 'I will be writing to you less than before, because this poor old sinner can do no more. And I will do the same with my son.'[38]

Philip gained in independence as the 'older and mature men' whom his father had appointed to guide him disappeared. Zúñiga, his most 'faithful councillor' and moderator of his sex life, died in 1546 and Charles did not appoint another governor. That same year Cardinal Tavera, the senior minister, died; the duke of Alba left to join the emperor in Germany; and illness forced Francisco de Los Cobos to retire to his estates, where he soon died. In June 1546, Charles formally recognized the inevitable: as a prelude to investing Philip as duke of Milan, an imperial fief, he signed a declaration that henceforth his son 'would be emancipated and free from our paternal control'.[39]

Henceforth, Charles sought to control Philip's conduct primarily through correspondence; but, just as he had done with the empress, he dictated almost all of his letters to a secretary, only occasionally adding a short post-script in his own hand. Perhaps this explains why his letters to his son (as earlier to his wife) seem cold, in contrast to his letters to his siblings Marie and Ferdinand, many of which were holographs and often contained inti-mate details and even jokes at his own expense. It would be hard to find anything similar in the 500 or so surviving letters written by Charles to his son. In August 1545 he even dictated his consolation for the death of Philip's wife, expressing his personal grief in a letter to Los Cobos: 'Cobos: Since God has been pleased to afflict me and my son in this way, there is little to say and much to regret; but in all things we must accept His will, and that's what I am doing. Work with my son, so that he accepts it too, and console him.'[40]

SECURING THE SUCCESSION: I. A BLUEPRINT FOR EMPIRE

After crushing the last of his European enemies, Charles's thoughts turned to the future of his possessions and on Christmas Day 1547, from Augsburg, the emperor informed his son that 'we have decided that you should come here as soon as possible'; that María should accompany her brother; and that 'now that we have finalized the conditions' for her marriage to Maximilian, Philip must secure his sister's consent. A few weeks later, Charles learned that his daughter had expressed a desire to remain within the peninsula and he therefore sent more insistent orders. 'I am certain,' Charles told his son, that María 'will obey me, as is only right because, given my love for her, I must look out more than anyone else for her well-being and happiness'; but should there be resistance Philip must 'reduce her to reason, and explain to her in detail the reasons why she cannot do anything else'. As with the Alternative four years earlier, Charles expected his daughter to sacrifice herself for the greater good of the dynasty.[41]

On 18 January 1548 the emperor completed a long policy evaluation for his son's benefit, sometimes known as his *Political Testament* and composed (like his secret instructions five years before) because he feared that he might die before he could explain his vision to Philip in person. 'My past preoccu-pations have led to a recurrence of some infirmities, and recently my life has been in peril,' he admitted. Therefore, 'unsure of what might happen to me, depending on God's will, I decided to convey to you my current thinking in this letter, in case the worst happens'. Unlike the secret instructions of 1543, this document enjoyed wide circulation. At least twenty-eight manuscript copies survive – one of them among Granvelle's papers, which suggests that Charles may have involved his principal minister in their composition – and in 1606, Sandoval printed the full text in his semi-official *History of the life and deeds of the Emperor Charles V*.[42]

The emperor began, as he had done in his papers of advice in 1539 and 1543, by urging Philip to 'submit all your desires and actions to the will of God' and to make the defence of the Catholic faith his primary responsibility. He then regretted the cost of 'the wars that I have been forced to fight so many times and in so many places' to defend the Empire – even though, he noted with a trace of smugness, 'with God's help (for which let Him be thanked) I have preserved, defended and added other territories of great quality and importance'. The primary need, therefore, was to assure a period of peace during which his vassals could recover. However:

> Avoiding war and keeping it at bay is not always in the power of those who want it ... especially of those who rule realms as great and as numerous and as far-flung as God, in His goodness, has given me and which, if He pleases, I shall leave to you. Rather this depends on the good or ill will of neighbours and other states.

So Philip must always be ready to fight, if necessary, to preserve what was his.

Charles now surveyed the defensive capacity of each territory, focusing on the challenges that his son might encounter. 'Common sense and experience,' he began:

> Show that unless you watch and take the trouble to understand the actions of other states and rulers, and maintain friends and informants in all areas, it will be difficult if not impossible to live in peace, or to avoid, oppose, and remedy anything that is attempted against you and your possessions ... especially since (as I have already noted) they are separated one from another, and the object of envy.

Therefore, 'your first and most secure friendship and trust' must be with Ferdinand, Charles's brother and designated successor as Holy Roman Emperor. On the one hand, his uncle Ferdinand would be a valuable councillor; on the other hand, as emperor, his support would prove vital for Philip's control over northern Italy and the Low Countries as well as for secure and easy communications between them.

Next, Philip must always maintain good relations with the pope –
although, as in his earlier papers of advice, the emperor recognized that this
was easier said than done. 'You already know how the present pope, Paul III,
has treated me,' Charles complained; and although he expressed the hope
that a change of pontiff would improve matters, he identified two areas that
would continue to produce conflict: papal claims to suzerainty over Naples
and Sicily, and royal patronage over the Spanish Church. He therefore
advised his son to 'behave with the submission of a good son of the Church'
towards future pontiffs, 'and without giving them any just cause to be
offended with you. But do this without any prejudice to the pre-eminences,
prosperity and peace of the said kingdoms.' Philip must give nothing away,
not even to the head of the Catholic Church.

Charles now reviewed his relations with the major independent states of
the peninsula. The republic of Venice had previously opposed Spain, he
noted, but the treaty of 1529 had settled all earlier differences and his son
must uphold its terms and 'keep good friendship with [the Venetians],
favouring them as good allies as much as possible'. Charles also noted that
'ever since I entrusted' Duke Cosimo de' Medici with Florence in 1537 'he
has been very solicitous for me and my affairs; and I think he will befriend
you too, since he has received so many favours.' Moreover, the duke 'has a
good brain and good judgement, and keeps his territories well-ordered',
which made it all the more important that his son should 'favour him in all
things'. Likewise 'you can trust the duke of Mantua, as I do'; and he felt
confident that the republics of Lucca and Siena would retain their traditional pro-imperial stance, because their overriding political goal would
remain preserving the general peace of Italy. The Republic of Genoa constituted Spain's most important ally in Italy, both because of its economic ties
with various Habsburg dominions, and because it permitted access from
Naples, Sicily, Sardinia and Spain to Lombardy, Germany and the
Netherlands. Philip must therefore do his utmost to preserve and strengthen
the authority of Andrea Doria and his allies, and rush to their rescue whenever they encountered difficulties (just as Charles had done the previous
year: chapter 12).

The emperor expressed concern about only two Italian rulers. The duke
of Ferrara had married Renée of France, once Charles's fiancée, and although
he had recently shown exemplary loyalty (for example, sending a contingent
to join the imperial army against the Schmalkaldic League) because of the
French connection, Philip should 'treat him with care, and monitor his
actions carefully'. The emperor also advised his son to keep careful watch

over the new duke of Parma, Octavio Farnese. Although the duchess, his daughter Margarita, 'has been most obedient to me', Charles feared that his decision to retain Piacenza might create problems. He assured Philip that there were many reasons 'why you can and must retain Piacenza, which is yours by right and by reason'; but nevertheless his son should 'make an offer to the pope to review and examine the situation, with the intention of reaching an agreement'.[43]

Venice, Florence, Mantua, Lucca, Siena, Genoa, Ferrara and Parma were just the largest of almost 300 independent states in northern Italy. Most of the rest lay in the hands of local dynasties and Charles had created a sophisticated and complex 'system' – perhaps the first of early modern times – aimed to maintain Spanish preponderance there. On the positive side, the emperor sometimes ceded adjacent territory, arranged a marriage with a Habsburg princess, or appointed a member of the ruling dynasty to prestigious posts in the Monarchy (as he had done with Ferrante Gonzaga, brother of the duke of Mantua). He entertained members of other Italian princely families at his court, where they received both lavish entertainment and encouragement to see the world through Habsburg eyes. To them and others, Charles offered pensions, presents, offices and honours culminating in a knighthood of the Golden Fleece, with the right to be called 'my cousin'. He advised Philip to do the same.

The spate of recent rebellions in Italy showed that diplomacy must be backed up by force. Charles had constructed state-of-the-art fortifications in Sicily, Naples and above all Milan, and installed a well-trained tercio of Spanish infantry and some cavalry companies in each of them. He also maintained several squadrons of galleys to protect the western Mediterranean. 'Even though you will inherit large debts and exhausted countries, and will need to look for savings wherever you can, you must not for that reason avoid keeping at all times some Spanish garrisons in Italy,' the emperor warned, because they offered the best defence against 'outbreaks of war and attempts to seize territory'. For the same reason, Philip must also maintain the galley squadrons that defended each major port in the Spanish Mediterranean.

As usual, Charles saw the French as the greatest potential security threat because their kings had 'often made a peace or truce with me, none of which they kept – as is well-known – except during the periods when they could not renew the war or wanted to wait for an opportunity to harm me clandestinely'. No doubt, he mused, they would continue their efforts to regain the territories and rights he had compelled them to renounce by the treaties of Madrid, Cambrai and now Crépy; but Philip must stand fast:

You must insist that the said renunciations shall remain for ever in being and in force, and in no way depart from them, because I captured all of them, and you will inherit and possess them, with full rights and evident justification. And if you should show weakness in any part of this, it will open the door to bringing everything back into question ... It will be better to hold on to everything than to let yourself be forced later to defend the rest, and run the risk of losing it. If your predecessors with the grace of God held on to Naples and Sicily, and also the Low Countries, against the French, you should trust that He will assist you to keep what you have inherited.

Philip must also try to compel the French to evacuate all the territories that they had occupied, including those of his allies (notably the duke of Savoy), 'so that all will see and know that you take the requisite care of your own security and of [your allies] too'.

The emperor reviewed other international issues more rapidly, reiterating several points made in earlier instructions. His son must 'maintain good relations with Portugal'; 'remain a friend of England, making sure to uphold the treaties made by me with the late and the present kings [Henry VIII and Edward VI]'; reach a trade agreement with Scotland; and maintain the treaty made with the current King of Denmark 'without becoming involved in the arguments concerning King Christian [II]', the deposed husband of his late sister Isabeau – indeed, he continued callously, Philip should make sure that Christian 'never regains his liberty, so that he cannot start a war and harm the Netherlands, as he has done before'.

Finally, the emperor turned to how best to govern his own territories in the future. In Europe, even with Ferdinand succeeding him as emperor, Charles wondered whether he should partition the rest of his dominions. The idea was not new. In 1505 his father's will had made Charles and Ferdinand joint heirs, with the implication that each would rule part of the lands he had acquired; and a decade later, since the Austrian lands 'are partible', Cisneros's agent at Charles's court assumed that since 'God has granted him such a rich inheritance, with more to come, he will divide it with his brother'.[44] This partition took place in 1521–2, but since then Charles had acquired important new territories in both the Netherlands and northern Italy. The former 'have been fortified, and are still being fortified according to the designs that I have approved, and all the provinces are as willing and loyal as one could wish'; but would Philip be able to govern them effectively when he 'cannot reside there, or visit them frequently' because of his obligations in Spain and

Italy? Might it be better to entrust the Netherlands to the emperor's daughter María and her future husband Maximilian? Charles could not make up his mind 'given the great importance of the matter. I therefore do not wish to make a decision on this until you arrive here, and you have seen the country for yourself, and grasped its significance and its character ... God willing, everything will be decided after you get here.'

Charles closed with a consideration of Spanish America, urging Philip to 'take care and keep a constant watch on whether the French want to send a fleet there': if they tried, they must be stopped. Even without a French challenge, it was essential that his son should maintain a tight control over all colonial officials, 'because if you do not, it will allow the viceroys and governors to become more absolute and cause your vassals to despair'. In addition:

> It is essential that you take good care to know and understand what is happening in America, both to keep it constant in the service of God and to maintain their obedience to you, so that it will be governed in justice, and can be repopulated and remade, so that the oppression of the conquistadors will be forgotten.

In particular, Philip must investigate 'the encomienda system for the native population, about which information and opinions differ'. This was an understatement – even as the emperor wrote these instructions, as Philip well knew, Peru was in open revolt! – but Charles chose to deal with this challenge to his authority by concentrating instead on the stability of New Spain, which by implication clarified what he thought might work elsewhere.[45]

The emperor's Political Testament drew upon his experience of government during the previous thirty years, often by trial and error. It marked an improvement on his instructions to Philip in 1543, in which he deemed some issues to be 'so impenetrable and uncertain that I do not know how to describe them, nor whether I should even offer you advice about them'. Now, having vanquished all his European enemies, he exuded confidence. In the perceptive formulation of Horst Pietschmann:

> Charles was not concerned primarily with the character or details of the problems that faced him, but with how to solve them in a way that maintained the sovereign's pre-eminence intact. Given the enormous number of problems that he faced, the only sensible way to govern was to work through the established institutions and to make sure that those institutions were always in the hands of people whom he could trust.[46]

Charles's Political Testament thus offered both a frank overview of the current state of his empire and its problems, and a blueprint for dealing with future problems whose nature could not be foreseen. It is hard to think of a similar (let alone a superior) document prepared by any other ruler in Renaissance Europe.

SECURING THE SUCCESSION: II. THE NETHERLANDS

Charles made the first major departure from the plan laid out in his Political Testament only three months later, in response to fears that in the absence of both Philip and María from Spain, 'grandees might enter the government, which would be something that would cause resentment' among his subjects. He refused to appoint as regent either his daughter Joanna, because at thirteen he considered her too young, or her older sister María alone, 'because it is never a good thing for the transaction of business – nor can I ever accept – to allow women to be involved in government unless they are married'. Instead 'it would be better if Prince Maximilian, my nephew, goes to Spain and consummates the marriage that has been agreed upon', and afterwards stay on as regent jointly with María. Philip must remain in Spain until Maximilian arrived, and then 'instruct him in whatever you think he should know ... about the grandees and other gentlemen who come to court, and about the councils and ministers with whom he will have to deal' – in other words, his son must provide the same sort of intimate advice to Maximilian that he had himself received in the emperor's secret instructions five years before.[47] The emperor made a second notable departure soon after he returned to Brussels in September 1548. His subjects 'let off fireworks and staged several plays in their language in the Market Place, as a sign of rejoicing, after which all the clergy took part in an honourable and beautiful procession to thank God for His Majesty's victory in Germany and his good health'.[48] Touched and impressed by this display, Charles now ordered his son to meet him in the Netherlands instead of in Germany.

After persuading the Cortes of Castile to raise taxes to cover María's dowry and the costs of his own journey to the Netherlands, and after initiating Maximilian and María into the mysteries of government, the prince and a large entourage left for Barcelona, where a galley fleet waited to take them to Genoa. In Brussels, Charles feared 'that it would be thousands of hours before he could see and enjoy the company of his son again, and his affection prevented him from thinking of anything else – so much that he has become unusually generous, paying no attention to the expenses run up by his son'. Over the next few months, 'moved by his paternal affection, His Majesty sent four to six men to report step by step where his son was and when he was likely to arrive'.[49]

Given the numerous acts of aggression recently carried out by the emperor and his ministers in Italy (chapter 12), the prince's advent caused fear as well as excitement – and initially his conduct offered little reassurance. In Genoa, he supported those who favoured the construction of a citadel, and when the duke of Ferrara and others arrived with splendid gifts, 'the prince made small countenance to anie of them, wherupon he obtayned throughe all Italye a name of insolencye'.[50] The prince relaxed somewhat when he reached Trent and met a welcoming party of eminent Germans, both Lutheran and Catholic, led by Maurice of Saxony: unfazed by meeting Protestants for the first time, Philip joined them in prolonged eating and heavy drinking. From there, he rode through Germany to Brussels, where on 1 April 1549 he met the father he had not seen for six years.

Although in his Political Testament Charles had promised his son that everything concerning his successor in the Netherlands 'will be decided after you get here', he had already taken two important preliminary steps. He persuaded the Armed Diet to recognize the seventeen provinces of the Netherlands that he ruled, both those he had inherited and those he had acquired, as a single Circle of the Empire.[51] This measure enhanced the powers of the central government in Brussels in two important respects. It exempted the Netherlands from the laws of the Empire, including the religious compromises that had allowed Lutheranism to flourish in Germany; and it obliged the German members of the Diet to defend the Low Countries should they be attacked. Charles also took the momentous (and ultimately disastrous) decision that Philip would succeed him in the Netherlands as well as in Spain, persuading the representative assemblies (*Staten*) of each province to recognize his son as heir apparent and to agree that, notwithstanding their particular privileges, they would henceforth all follow the same succession protocols and choose the same sovereign in order to remain for ever united.

Soon after Philip arrived, Charles took him on a tour of the most prosperous southern provinces – Flanders, Artois, Hainaut and Brabant – where the local authorities solemnly swore to accept the prince as their next sovereign. Everywhere they went, father and son encountered allegories in both triumphal arches and plays that made extravagant claims. Some compared them with David and Solomon, or with Atlas and Hercules; others stressed that although powerful enemies surrounded them, divine and worldly weapons would allow them to prevail. For his part, Philip repeatedly showed his chivalric prowess, taking part in a cane game in Ghent, a joust at Antwerp, and extravagant celebrations in and around Marie's palace at Binche – one of the few events from Charles's life still commemorated, because every Shrove Tuesday local men (the 'Gilles') march through the streets of Binche wearing exotic costumes inspired by those worn in the celebrations of 1549.[52]

By the time they returned to Brussels, relations between father and son had soured. Some Netherlanders had objected to swearing the new oath of allegiance, in part 'because they did not wish to be governed by a foreigner', especially by a Spaniard, 'but much more because they are scared by the difficult personality of the prince, who makes no effort to cherish them'. According to an ambassador, 'Neither the persuasion of His Majesty, who mentions it to him every day, nor the more restrained reminders of Granvelle, have improved the prince's attitude.' Perhaps these tensions persuaded Charles to remain in Brussels while the prince and Marie visited the principal northern cities. In any case, by the time they returned relations had evidently improved: during the annual Mass attended by Knights of the Golden Fleece on St Andrew's Day, 30 November 1549, the same ambassador noted that 'the prince left his seat and moved next to His Majesty, and they spent the entire service talking to each other . . . so that it seems they have overcome the differences that left them discontented'.[53] Now, representatives of the territories acquired by the emperor joined those from his hereditary possessions in a States-General and collectively reaffirmed their oath to accept Philip as heir apparent. The prince spent the next seven months in Brussels, feasting, dancing, hunting and jousting, as well as receiving instruction from his father 'in matters of importance: the emperor made him come to his apartment to spend two or three hours every day, partly in council and partly to instruct him alone.'[54]

IN COMMAND OF HISTORY

In May 1550, after solemnly commemorating the eleventh anniversary of the empress's death, Charles and his son left Brussels to meet another Diet, and at Cologne the imperial party embarked on Rhine barges, 'with goodly glass windows, with seats of fir, as close as any house', so that they 'knew not whether it went or stood'.[55] As they made their way upriver over the next two weeks, 'during his free time the emperor set about writing down his travels and campaigns' in French. According to his chamberlain, Guillaume van Male, a Humanist from Bruges, 'the work is admirably polished and elegant, and the style attests to a strong spirit and eloquence'. Indeed, van Male added patronizingly, 'I would never have thought the emperor possessed such qualities, because he told me himself that he had learned little from his education and that he simply relied on his thoughts and his deeds.'[56] Charles continued the project after reaching Augsburg. 'Not a day passes,' an ambassador reported, 'that the emperor does not spend two or three hours writing with his own hand to immortalize his deeds, assisted by Guillaume van Male'. In the end, his *Memoirs* covered 150 manuscript pages.[57]

Why did Charles bother? The emperor asked Francisco de Borja during his visit to Yuste in 1557: 'Do you think there is any trace of vanity when a man writes about his own deeds?' Without waiting for an answer he then:

Intimated that he had chronicled all his campaigns . . . motivated neither by a desire for glory nor by vanity but so that the truth should be known – because the historians of our time whose work he had read had obscured it, either out of ignorance or out of partiality and bias.[58]

Perhaps this explains the emperor's decision to write his *Memoirs* in the third person, and to omit many personal details – including his entire childhood. Although he mentioned meeting Henry VIII with his grandfather Maximilian in 1513, 'where, among other things, the emancipation of the archduke [Charles] was discussed and agreed', the narrative began only after the provincial estates of the Netherlands 'received him as their lord' two years later. It ended with his return from Germany to Brussels in the summer of 1548.[59] Stylistically, the *Memoirs* fall into two parts. Until the conquest of Guelders, Charles provided a terse account of the events in which he felt he had invested personal energy and properly executed his duties as sovereign. He even listed the frequency of certain activities: how often he had met the kings of England and France (three times each); appointed his aunt and his sister regent in the Netherlands (three for Margaret, five for Marie); sailed the Atlantic (three times) and the Mediterranean (eight times); suffered attacks of gout (seventeen since 1528); and so on.[60] Both the tempo and content of the *Memoirs* changed significantly when Charles reached 1543: it metamorphosed from a travelogue into a campaign diary, and devoted twice as much space to the next five years as to the previous thirty. The emperor provided a detailed account of his role in the campaigns against France and the Schmalkaldic League, as well as a rationale for several of his own important decisions (what would have happened if he had captured the Marne bridge at Châlons in 1544) as well as those of his enemies (he noted six 'errors' committed by the German Lutheran leaders between March 1546 and April 1547 and explained how, 'thanks to God's support of the imperial cause', they brought about his enemies' 'total ruin').[61]

These stylistic changes formed part of a broader campaign by Charles and his entourage to rewrite history in his favour. In 1548 a copy of a flattering history of Emperor Maximilian written by the Seville historian Pedro Mexía reached Charles in Augsburg, and 'he, his confessor, Domingo de Soto, and other prominent courtiers read it with such satisfaction' that Charles commissioned Mexía to write a similar account of his own reign.[62] Two years later Paolo Giovio, perhaps the most celebrated European historian of his day, completed his 'universal history' and sent Charles a copy of the chapter concerning the Tunis campaign 'so that it may be perused and revised by Your Majesty before I send it to the press'. Giovio obsequiously promised 'to change, add and reduce it as seems best to Your Majesty's rich memory and flawless judgement'. No doubt to his surprise, the emperor took this invitation literally and gave the manuscript for evaluation to Luis de Ávila y Zúñiga (a veteran of the campaign, who subsequently served Charles as an intermediary with other historians). According to the Florentine ambassador at Charles's court, 'His Majesty covets glory so much that it appears to him that Giovio has detracted from his achievements' and 'continually seeks to belittle them', whereas Charles wanted his deeds 'to be celebrated more than they are'. Ávila therefore sent Giovio a list of changes that 'emphasized the emperor's selfless courage, and the manner in which he had exposed himself to danger', to ensure that his 'name and glory are not obfuscated by the mists of passion'. Since the book was to be published in Florence, Ávila also asked Duke Cosimo to 'make certain to correct [Giovio's] errors and not consent to publication' until the changes were made – but although Giovio rectified a handful of factual errors he refused to modify his treatment of Charles.[63]

Charles was more successful in censoring another history book that annoyed him: Francisco López de Gómara's *Spain victorious: The first and second part of the general history of America, with all the discoveries and notable events that have occurred down to the year 1551*, published at Medina del Campo in August 1553. It not only presented the conquest of Mexico as almost entirely the work of Hernán Cortés but also blamed Charles for neglecting America: 'Much more could have been discovered, conquered and converted if Your Majesty had not been so busy fighting wars elsewhere.' This time Ávila worked through his protégé van Male, who asked Pedro de La Gasca to provide a detailed account of the principal events in his pacification of Peru specifically to correct errors in Gómara. Three months later a royal warrant decreed that *Spain victorious* 'should not be sold or read, nor should more copies be printed; rather those already in circulation should be collected and brought to our council of the Indies.' Royal officials interrogated every bookseller about copies of the work they had handled: 'from whom they had acquired them, and to whom they had sold them and at what price, because His Majesty needs to know'.[64]

Ávila himself fared poorly in the emperor's *Memoirs*. Although Charles plucked details from Ávila's *Commentaries on the wars of Germany* without acknowledgement, he portrayed several events in a very different light – naturally, a light that shone primarily on himself. Perhaps the most egregious case involved the duke of Alba: Charles normally referred to him (when he referred to him at all) as 'his commander' and claimed credit for every major action – even discovering the crucial ford across the Elbe, just before Mühlberg, which both Ávila (an eyewitness) and Charles himself (in his first report of the victory) clearly stated was the work of Alba. Furthermore, although he named the allies whose support he had skilfully mobilized – the count of Buren and the Netherlands troops, Octavio Farnese and the papal contingent, Maurice of Saxony, and (albeit rather late in the narrative) 'the king his brother' – Charles himself was always the star.[65]

As Richard L. Kagan observed, 'Charles presided over what today would be called a publicity agency', and after the battle of Mühlberg, the emperor and his supporters commissioned numerous works of literature and art that portrayed him as the foremost champion of Christendom. Charles summoned Titian to Augsburg, where he began work on two of his most memorable portraits: an emperor victorious in war, and wise in peace (see Pls 25 and 27).[66] Shortly afterwards, Charles commissioned from Leone Leoni a series of heroic sculptures (statues, busts and reliefs in bronze and marble), including seven of himself, three each of Philip and the empress, and two of Marie. The largest item, a life-size statue of the emperor wearing armour that could be removed to reveal his nude body, showed him standing vigilantly above his vanquished enemies, poised to take up arms again if necessary (Pl. 29). Meanwhile Marie commissioned Willem de Pannemaker to weave a series of vast tapestries, based on cartoons by Vermeyen, to commemorate the victorious Tunis campaign (see Pl. 20); and Charles's ambassador in Venice oversaw the publication of both Ávila's *Commentaries* and a series of engravings commemorating each of the emperor's recent triumphs.[67] Not all images were commissioned by the emperor and his ministers. Some bookbinders in the Netherlands stamped their work with a portrait of their sovereign (often in armour) and his *Plus Oultre* device; town halls and even some churches displayed statues and portraits of him. In 1521, Anna Büschler, the 'mischievous, insolent and disobedient daughter' of the burgomaster of Hall, asked one of her clandestine lovers, then at the Diet of Worms, to 'please have a sketch of the emperor made for me, one that portrays him as neither more handsome nor any uglier than he really is, for such a sketch would be worth something'. Many of her compatriots collected (and no doubt used) game pieces that carried the imperial likeness to play chess and draughts (the popularity of both games increased markedly during Charles's reign; Pl. 30).[68] In 1550, Leoni happened to see a 'fantastic gem' that portrayed both Caesar and Augustus, which gave him the idea of creating a magnificent onyx cameo that showed the empress on the reverse and Philip and Charles on the obverse, the emperor wearing a laurel crown as well as his Mühlberg armour: once again, a reminder that he excelled in war as well as in peace, and that he had sired a worthy successor (Pl. 31).[69]

SECURING THE SUCCESSION: III. GERMANY

The emperor composed his *Memoirs*, at least in part, to impress his brother. He repeatedly stressed how he had supported Ferdinand and furthered his interests, both directly (by securing his election as king of the Romans; by sending troops and treasure to defend his possessions against the Turks) and indirectly (by compelling the pope to convene a general council primarily to bring religious peace to Germany; by smashing the Schmalkaldic League). He ordered van Male to translate the work from French into Latin, ready for publication, but it never materialized, perhaps because of the enmities generated by the family summit convened by Charles in Augsburg to discuss the succession to his various dominions: in Italy, where his investiture of Philip as duke of Milan dashed Ferdinand's hopes of acquiring the territory; in the Netherlands, where he had reneged on his promise to make Maximilian and María his successors; in Spain, where if Charles predeceased his mother, Ferdinand might challenge Philip for the role of co-sovereign of Castile; and, above all, in the Holy Roman Empire.[70]

Jacob Sturm from Strasbourg was apparently the first to divine Charles's grand design. In December 1547, from the Armed Diet, he reported rumours that the emperor had summoned his son to Germany with the express intention of arranging for his succession to the imperial throne. Four months later the Venetian ambassador picked up the story, and in June 1548 the nuncio in

Augsburg reported not only that 'many suspect that His Majesty wants to have his son elected king of the Romans, and thus perpetuate the imperial dignity in his family', but also that many opposed it. Nevertheless, he added sarcastically, 'His Majesty, proceeding with his accustomed authority and gravity, pays little attention' to contrary opinions. Indeed, he continued, 'whereas he used to receive the Electors with great solemnity, now they seldom get an audience – and if they do, they first have to wait for an hour or more in his antechamber'. The nuncio also reported an outburst by Archduke Maximilian one evening at dinner: 'That he was a good German, and he would never tolerate anyone other than a true German as emperor', and he railed against the idea that 'the Spaniards might think of governing Germany'.[71]

Ferdinand chose to disregard all this evidence until the spring of 1549, when he protested to Marie about 'something that seems to me totally unbelievable': namely rumours that 'in the court of Prince Philip my nephew, and in the Empire, people say openly that my lord the emperor has discussed with me the transfer of the office and title of king of the Romans to the prince'. He denied that any such discussion had taken place, and added 'I cannot believe that such a thing could have occurred, or would ever occur, to His Majesty in his thoughts or dreams, because I consider him such a good brother – and not only brother but also my true father'. Marie reassured Ferdinand that such stories were idle gossip – albeit adding ominously that 'I am absolutely certain that His Majesty would only decide such a matter with you in person'.[72]

There the matter rested for another year, with Charles, Philip and Marie in the Netherlands, Ferdinand in Austria, and Maximilian in Spain; but just before the emperor and his son set out for Augsburg in May 1550, Marie wrote a letter to Ferdinand 'in complete confidence, which is intended for you alone and should be burnt after you have read it'. She proceeded to communicate 'what I have learned of the intentions of our brother and nephew', adding that it was 'something that I would rather have told you in person, if it could have been arranged'. She confirmed all the rumours she had previously denied. Prince Philip, she began:

> Shows a strong inclination to take responsibility for the Empire after you, advancing a wide-ranging rationale because it seems an essential step to maintain our whole dynasty. The emperor sees reasons for and against, and therefore will not take a decision until he joins you, so that you can decide together what would be most advantageous for our dynasty and best for all Christendom.

She also stressed the need to secure Maximilian's concurrence, because his opposition to Philip 'would generate an eternal enmity and rivalry that would inevitably ruin both of them'; and she concluded by reminding Ferdinand of how much he owed to Charles, notably 'the favour he did you in supporting you ahead of his own son' as king of the Romans. Now it was time to return the favour, and support Philip ahead of Ferdinand's own son.[73]

It was a skilful argument, obviously constructed with the emperor's blessing, but it reneged on Charles's promise to his brother, often repeated, that Maximilian would succeed him. Deeply hurt by this brusque demand, yet reluctant to offend 'his true father', Ferdinand came to Augsburg and suggested that Philip and his successors could become permanent Imperial Vicar (deputy) in Italy instead – a sensible suggestion that offered Philip far more than he eventually received – but Charles rejected this and repeated his demand that Ferdinand must persuade the Electors to choose Philip as his immediate successor, perhaps as a second coadjutor. Ferdinand predicted disaster: 'If we try prematurely and by violent and inappropriate means to ensure that our dynasty retains the empire,' he warned Marie, 'we will lose it and create an opportunity for our enemies to secure it.' Changing the order of succession 'may give food for thought to others who are powerful, and closer to the Empire than Spain'. Therefore, he continued apprehensively, 'I hope we shall get by without discussing' the pre-election of Philip:

> In my view, that would be the best for many reasons – and among them, not the least is that I think it would be impossible to obtain it, and that proposing it would generate hostility and resistance, in many places and in many ways, which for my part I would willingly avoid. If it is proposed, I think you will find that I have told you the truth: that it would have been better if it had never been proposed.[74]

Charles disagreed, and instead ordered Marie to drop everything and come and help him convince Ferdinand, because 'the point to be settled at Augsburg outweighs all other considerations'. Just before she arrived, the sudden death of Granvelle on 27 August 1550 removed an important voice of moderation, and although Charles ordered Perrenot to take over his late father's work, he lacked the same authority.[75] Relations between the brothers rapidly deteriorated until, one evening in November, Ferdinand announced that in view of rumours of another Ottoman invasion of Hungary he would again demand help from the imperial Diet. Charles interrupted his brother more than once, arguing that since Hungary was not in imminent peril, its situation did not justify using money raised by the Diet, which he intended to use for his own purposes in Germany; but Ferdinand remained adamant. He stated that his conscience and his honour, as well as the need to protect his own possessions, all obliged him to mobilize German assistance for another campaign in Hungary. This infuriated Charles, who berated his brother for 'always justifying everything you want to do as a matter of conscience and honour'. He also asserted that Ferdinand had received the lion's share of all previous taxes voted by the Diet, 'while I got nothing; yet you still want everything for yourself. In the end,' Charles told Ferdinand, 'we need to establish who is emperor: you or me', and he threatened that if his brother persisted in requesting funds from the Diet, he would openly oppose him. Ferdinand stormed out of the room.[76]

After relating these bitter exchanges to Marie, Charles pouted that 'nothing that the late king of France [Francis] did to me' had affected him 'as much as the way that the king our brother treats me. What I resent the most' is that 'when we are together I see no sign of repentance or shame in him. I therefore have no choice but to put my trust in God, begging Him to grant sense and wisdom to my brother, and strength and patience to me.' He begged in vain. The brothers refused to speak to each other.[77] Charles now summoned Marie back to Augsburg where in March 1551, after weeks of heated discussion, she brokered a settlement between her brothers. The imperial succession would alternate between the two branches of the family: Ferdinand would succeed to the imperial title, but promised to delegate imperial powers over Italy to Philip and to arrange his nephew's election as king of the Romans; next, as emperor, Philip would secure Maximilian's election as his successor, and while absent from Germany would appoint Maximilian as his regent. The prince also promised to support Ferdinand and Maximilian in the Empire and in Hungary; to abstain from intervening in imperial affairs except when requested by Ferdinand; and to marry one of Ferdinand's daughters.[78]

Although Maximilian grudgingly gave his verbal consent to this Family Compact he refused to sign it, complaining that the 'standard operating procedure' of his uncle (and now father-in-law) 'was to be always superior to everyone and to always keep a tight rein on his associates so that he could control them'; and although Ferdinand signed the agreement, he remained resentful. Some years later he recalled that he had warned Charles of 'the difficulties, uprisings and disorders that this could provoke in the Empire, and that he would not prevail', but after the emperor insisted that we 'bow to his will, we had to do what we did [*hubimos de hacer lo que se hizo*]; and shortly afterwards we found that I had been a better prophet than we would have wished because when the princes of Germany discovered our plan, they took up arms against His Majesty.'[79]

The Family Compact jeopardized all of Charles's hard-won achievements since Mühlberg. As Roger Ascham observed, by the summer of 1551 there were 'few Princes in all the Empire' but 'some good big matter of unkindness hath bene offered unto them by the Emperor. Yea *Ferdinand* his brother, *Maximilian* his nephew . . . have bene shrewdly touched therewith'. But both Charles and his son seemed oblivious to all this. Convinced that they had triumphed, Philip left Augsburg in May 1551 to resume his regency in Spain and soon afterwards Charles departed too – perhaps, as Richard Morison (Ascham's successor as English ambassador) shrewdly suggested, he left the city because he felt as all 'fathers do, and wold be away from that howse a season where his son and he had been so long and now were sundered'. Philip would not see his father again for more than four years, and by then the Habsburg world had been transformed.[80]

FIFTEEN

THE EMPEROR'S LAST CAMPAIGNS, 1551–4

THE EMPEROR AND THE UNITY OF CHRISTENDOM

After leaving his father in Augsburg, Philip paused on his journey south in Trent, to observe one of Charles's most remarkable achievements: the second session of the general council of the Church. The murder of Pier Luigi Farnese in 1547 had poisoned relations between his father Pope Paul III and the emperor, and prevented further cooperation on the council; but Paul died two years later. Soon after his election in February 1550, Pope Julius III declared that the general council could reconvene either in Trent or, 'if that location seems inconvenient, somewhere deeper in Germany' acceptable to the emperor. Charles was overjoyed: Julius could not have done anything 'that we would appreciate more', he informed his ambassador in Rome, and he hastened to exploit the new opportunity to achieve his long-term religious goals – although he could not resist pointing out that deviant religious 'opinions in Germany are now many and various', complicating a reconciliation that 'could have been effected some years ago, when the differences were confined to a few issues, and each opinion had fewer followers'. Charles insisted that the German Lutherans 'must be given a hearing on any subject they choose to propose' so that later 'they cannot recuse themselves from the council on the grounds that they will not be heard'.[1] He was therefore furious to discover that the Bull convoking the council failed to mention Lutherans by name, and he signed a notarized protest witnessed by Prince Philip, Antoine Perrenot and the duke of Alba. For the time being he kept it secret, and instead sent letters to all prelates and selected theologians in his various dominions ordering them to attend the council. Thanks to these efforts, Charles's subjects made up more than half of its participants. Francisco de Toledo, the imperial ambassador, exploited this numerical advantage so well that (according to the pope) a joke circulated in Rome that 'the council of Trent was really the council of Toledo'.[2]

Initially, the emperor accepted Julius's demand that the council should first resolve outstanding issues of doctrine, because many Catholics yearned for clarification of what was orthodox and what was heresy, but he insisted that this time (unlike the first session) the council also devote some attention to reforming abuses, 'to eliminate and remedy the scandals that have grown up in the Church, because to do otherwise will mean that the errors will gain ground, and the heretics will continue their criticisms of them'. He continued: 'just as it is not our intention to reduce the authority of His Holiness . . . so His Holiness should not fail to do his best to remedy the abuses, because that is what has given rise to these problems in Germany'. In November 1551, shortly after writing this, Charles and a small entourage travelled to Innsbruck, less than 200 kilometres from Trent, in part to ensure that the assembly addressed at least some 'of the abuses that scandalize the faithful . . . because that is what we owe to God and to the world'.[3]

Early in 1552 some Lutheran theologians arrived at Trent. The emperor considered their participation 'the only remedy for the ills that afflict the Church', and he worked tirelessly to ensure that they would receive a hearing. He was therefore outraged when Julius threatened to suspend the council if the Lutherans spoke. 'I do not want to hear about a suspension,' he thundered to Diego Hurtado de Mendoza, his ambassador in Rome: 'Such a thing should not be proposed, let alone agreed, because it would obviously damage my reputation, which is the same as the service of God' – an amazing claim. The emperor insisted that his ambassador tell the pope personally that: 'If His Holiness and his ministers should do something else, and some disorder occurs, it needs to be clear . . . that it was not His Majesty's fault, so that he is free of blame before both God and the world'. Julius remained unimpressed by this passive-aggressive bluster: 'We are sure that His Majesty is admirably sound in all his opinions, and has good will towards us,' he informed his legate at Trent, but 'like everyone else he must respect the power given to us directly by God'.[4]

Charles remained optimistic. 'Since these matters depend on time and circumstances,' he reminded Mendoza at the end of February 1552, the ambassador must send constant updates so that he could make adjustments to his plans 'from time to time, according to how things seem elsewhere'. Little did Charles suspect that a few weeks later 'circumstances' – in the shape of a hostile German army – would not only lead those attending the council to flee Trent, thus ending the last meaningful attempt to reconcile Lutherans and Catholics, but also force the emperor to flee Innsbruck to escape capture by his own subjects.[5]

NEMESIS

In 1553, Roger Ascham, who had resided for some time at Charles's court, noted with surprise 'how the emperor, being at peace with all the world' three years earlier, 'had soon after so many enemies as he knew not which way to turn him'; and he attributed this remarkable deterioration to the 'great confusions of alliances, dissensions, plunderings, wars, various changes of fortune, and very serious disruptions; all these disasters compounded by ingratitude, treachery, perfidy, lust, avarice, ambition, tyranny and enmity toward God, as liberty was driven out, the law violated, religion besmirched, and God himself scorned'.[6] In international affairs the 'disasters' began in March 1550 when the regents for Edward VI of England, anxious to buy peace abroad, agreed to restore Boulogne to France, to withdraw all their troops from Scotland, and to allow Mary, queen of Scots, to marry the heir to the French throne. On hearing the news, the emperor displayed 'a notable pensiveness, and seemeth to be troubled', because 'this peace was concluded both without him and contrary to his expectation, whereby he is in fantasy that his reputation is much blemished – as indeed it is, both in Almain [Germany] and in Italy'. Peace with England also secured Henry II of France's western flank as he prepared to exact revenge for his four years of imprisonment in Spain in the 1520s, and for the humiliating terms of the peace of Crépy. According to a Venetian ambassador: 'The king cannot conceal his hatred of the emperor, desiring for him every evil that one can wish upon one's enemy. No medicine can cure this condition except the death or destruction of his enemy'.[7]

Unaware of these developments, Charles had already weakened his position by authorizing Andrea Doria and his fleet to capture Mahdia, a north African port-city that served as headquarters to Dragut, now the leading Barbary corsair, who made his living by preying on shipping from Habsburg Naples and Sicily. When news of Doria's success arrived in September 1550, the imperial court indulged in 'the greatest rejoicing' and staged a tournament in which Prince Philip took part; but the defeated Dragut sailed to Istanbul and requested the sultan's help against what he claimed to be naked Habsburg aggression. Charles wrote to the sultan asking – almost pleading – that these actions be regarded as actions against north African piracy, and not as contraventions of the truce concluded between them three years earlier; but since he refused to return his conquests, in 1551 Dragut led a huge Ottoman fleet against Mahdia and then against Malta. When both operations failed, Dragut launched a surprise attack on the important Christian outpost of Tripoli, which surrendered on terms negotiated by the French ambassador to the sultan (who travelled aboard the Turkish fleet).[8]

Ascham deemed Charles's aggression in the Mediterranean a catastrophic error because 'The Turk being once disclosed an open enemy to the emperor, many mean men began to be the bolder to put out their heads to seek some open remedy for their private injuries; France being at every man's elbow to hearten and to help whosoever had cause to be aggrieved with the emperor.'[9] These included Duke Octavio Farnese of Parma, Charles's son-in-law, who despaired of ever recovering Piacenza, seized by Ferrante Gonzaga, governor of Lombardy, after the murder of his father (chapter 12). In June 1551, on his way back to Spain, Prince Philip visited Piacenza, guided by Gonzaga, and then made his way to Parma, where he met for the first time his half-sister Margarita and her husband. Although the visit went smoothly, shortly afterwards Pope Julius declared Octavio a rebel and proclaimed that 'our cause is the same as that of His Imperial Majesty in all things'. The duke retaliated by signing a treaty that placed his possessions under French protection, and Henry's troops soon ravaged part of the Papal States and occupied several strongholds in Piedmont. Gonzaga begged the emperor to send him reinforcements from Germany to prosecute the siege of Parma.[10]

Charles was happy to oblige, given the importance of Parma to the security of the duchy of Milan (to which it had once belonged). In addition, as he explained to his brother, 'it is impossible for me to maintain any longer the Spanish troops that currently garrison the fortresses in Württemberg, since they have already added so much to the unbearable burden of my expenses'. Therefore, confident that the Interim and the Family Compact had secured his hold on Germany, in October 1551, Charles ordered the Spanish garrisons to cross the Alps, followed by many of his German veterans.[11]

Charles had made another catastrophic error because several Lutheran states in north Germany defied him. Early in 1550 the duke of Mecklenburg and some of his Protestant neighbours formed a league 'for the defence of princely liberty and the Lutheran faith'. The printers of Magdeburg published almost 150 books and pamphlets denouncing the Interim, earning their city the title (albeit only among Protestants) of 'the chancery of God'. Although Maurice of Saxony raised an army in Charles's name to besiege Magdeburg, his efforts remained half-hearted.[12]

Charles overlooked the significance of these developments, in part because he lingered in Brussels and only reached Augsburg, where he had convened another imperial Diet, in July 1550. Luckily for him, for a time Henry II also overlooked their significance. 'There are few people in

Germany in whom we can place much trust,' he lamented, 'and I see little chance of improving the situation because of the divisions that exist among them, and the fact that their hearts are so weakened that I see no prospect of them agreeing about anything.' The king detected only two glimmers of hope: the first was the discord between Charles and his brother 'on the imperial succession, which might ignite matters somewhat – although I see little chance of this, because I believe the emperor takes such good care of his affairs that he will not stir up trouble there'; the second was the arrival in France of a secret envoy from Maurice of Saxony.[13]

The new Elector harboured several grievances. Like other German Lutherans, Maurice felt threatened by the reconvened council of Trent; and although at the emperor's request he sent representatives, they insisted that all earlier decisions taken in their absence be regarded as invalid. Naturally Charles refused. The plan to have Philip elected king of the Romans also alienated Maurice, along with the other Electors, on the grounds that arranging the imperial succession in advance (as had happened in 1530–1) undermined its elective nature. Once again, Charles refused to listen. Finally, and most galling, was the continued imprisonment of Maurice's father-in-law, Philip of Hesse.

Initially, Maurice tried to win the landgrave's release by cultivating the friendship of Charles's relatives. In 1549 he visited Prague where, according to Ferdinand, 'the outstanding quarrels between this crown of Bohemia and the House of Saxony were resolved very advantageously for us and much to my satisfaction'. The new Elector also hunted and caroused with Prince Philip of Spain, and persuaded him to petition 'his father for the landgrave's delivery', but Charles refused. Ascham deemed this another serious error:

> Men may say it was not the wisest deed that ever the emperor did, to deny the prince this suit; for if the prince had been made the deliverer of the two princes [Hesse and Saxony] out of captivity, he had won thereby such favour in all Germany, as without all doubt he had been made coadjutor with the king of the Romans his uncle, and afterward the emperor.[14]

Instead, Charles's chancery drafted a secret declaration condemning the landgrave to 'ten years of continuous prison' – which Charles himself struck through and increased to 'fifteen years': in effect a life sentence, since the prisoner was by then forty-six years old.[15]

In December 1550 the landgrave orchestrated a plan to escape from his prison in Mechelen, with the aid of conspirators in France, Germany and the Netherlands, culminating in a shoot-out with his Spanish guards. The breakout failed, but this challenge to Charles's 'jurisdiction in our patrimonial provinces, and the attempt to kill the captain of his guards and those with him' so enraged the emperor that he instructed his officials to threaten that if Philip of Hesse 'does not tell you the truth voluntarily, we will make him do so by force'. The strategy worked: the landgrave burst into tears and named his associates (many of whom soon joined him in prison), whereupon Charles ordered his removal to a windowless cell and deprived him of cash, servants and all contact with the outside world. Maurice, concluding that Charles would never release his father-in-law, negotiated a secret agreement with the duke of Mecklenburg and his allies, pledging to secure the landgrave's release and also to 'defend the liberties of Germany', if necessary through an alliance with France.[16]

In October 1551, just as the Spanish garrisons left Württemberg for the siege of Parma, Maurice and his north German allies signed a secret 'treaty of confederation and alliance' with the king of France 'against the Emperor Charles V, to conserve the privileges and liberties of the Electors, princes and estates of the Empire', and to thwart Charles's efforts to reduce them 'to the bestial, insufferable and everlasting servitude that he has created in Spain and elsewhere'. Henry II promised to provide a monthly stipend to sustain a confederate army to fight for German liberty, Lutheran worship and the liberation of the landgrave; and he also promised to seize the French-speaking imperial cities of Metz, Toul and Verdun in Lorraine, and to 'light fires in the Netherlands so that the enemy will need to put them out, forcing him to divide his forces'. In return, the German confederates promised to help Henry recover all the territories France had lost to Charles, and to favour his election as the next emperor.[17]

GROUPTHINK

It proved impossible to keep such a widespread conspiracy secret and many of Charles's ministers relayed warnings to his court – but, amazingly, no one there listened. Part of the problem lay in a mindset that a later age would call 'groupthink': the creation of a false appearance of unanimity among decision-makers by discouraging any expression of dissent while guiding discussions in ways that minimize disagreement. The problem was not new. One of the ministers sent into Germany by Margaret of Austria to arrange Charles's election as king of the Romans in 1519 already detected the danger. 'To tell you the truth,' he confided to Margaret, 'the lords here dare not say or write what they think, for fear of displeasing the king' – just before begging her to keep his dissenting views to herself. Charles's reliance on summaries of incoming reports, rather than on the originals, exacerbated the problem, because it allowed ministers in his entourage to suppress items that they did not like. Thus in 1544 a letter from García de Loaysa offered congratulations on the imperial victory over Cleves and then begged 'Your Majesty to make some move towards peace, even if it means losing some of your undoubted rights'; but Charles never read the letter, relying instead on an abstract read out to him by a secretary – who omitted the advice to make a settlement.[18] By 1551, according to Ascham, the emperor 'hath many irons in the fire, and every one able alone to keep him in work enough; the Turk by land and sea; the French sitting on his skirts on all sides', besides Magdeburg and other centres of resistance in north Germany; and yet, he continued, 'blinded with the over-good opinion of his own wisdom, liking only what himself listed, and contemning easily all advice of others (which self-will condition doth commonly follow, and as commonly doth hurt all great wits)', Charles allowed himself to be deceived.[19]

The circle of ministers whom Charles consulted had dwindled. In 1545 a courtier opined that 'His Majesty has decided to discuss his affairs only with Monsieur de Granvelle, whom he has found faithful and extremely prudent'. Three years later, the nuncio reported that Antoine Perrenot, bishop of Arras, jointly with his father Granvelle, now monopolized the emperor's affairs: 'they do everything, and unless business passes through their hands, nothing gets done, *because His Majesty is only the third most important person in this court*' – a remarkable assertion. The nuncio also stated that 'this is a court where you have to make donations, or else no business is successfully transacted'. He held up the example of Duke Cosimo of Florence, who (he claimed) plied Granvelle and his son with presents and therefore 'obtains whatever he wants in this court'. His Venetian colleague was more specific. He claimed that Cosimo gave 15,000 crowns a year to Granvelle as a regular pension, with supplements for special requests, and that 'with all the donations from individuals in Germany, Spain and the Netherlands, Granvelle received 100,000 crowns every year'.[20]

It would be easy to dismiss these accusations as spiteful gossip, but Cosimo kept such excellent records that historians can document many bribes. For example, early in 1543 the duke sent Granvelle warm furnishings for his bed and his bedroom 'because I know you are going to the cold climes of Germany'. Two years later he sent several cases of sweet wine, an altarpiece painted by Agnolo Bronzino, and an engineer to drain the swamps on Granvelle's estates, with his salary paid by Cosimo for 'three or four months, or more if necessary'. In 1547 the duke sent some red satin bedcovers to Granvelle, linked with a request to sell him Pontremoli, an estate confiscated from the Genoese rebel Count Fieschi, at the bargain price of 25,000 crowns.[21]

Those who wanted or needed something from Charles seem to have tolerated the corrupt system run by Granvelle, but after his death in 1550 some complained bitterly about the rapacity of his son Antoine. According to Ferrante Gonzaga, whereas Granvelle had always 'understood the importance of never disrespecting the ministers of His Majesty', between 1551 and 1553 Perrenot levelled twenty-three specific criticisms regarding Gonzaga's conduct as governor of Milan, including his seizure of Piacenza ('which he sees as the cause of all setbacks') and his failure to capture Parma ('which has cost 1½ million gold ducats'), so that 'at present, even if I were Caesar or Hannibal, he would not be satisfied with me'.[22]

Those who disagreed with Granvelle and his son were soon either marginalized or dismissed – another essential aspect of groupthink. Not even the imperial confessor was immune. In August 1548, Granvelle arranged a compromise with the Lutheran preachers of Augsburg that allowed them to retain their livings provided they endorsed and observed the Interim. Fray Pedro de Soto, who had always urged Charles to use force towards the German Lutherans, vehemently objected to this measure and called instead for an imperial edict that would deprive the preachers of their livings unless they abjured their errors and followed Catholic teaching in all things. The emperor ordered Granvelle to convene a committee of ministers and theologians (including Soto) to discuss the matter, and all except the confessor agreed that 'His Majesty lacked the resources to enforce such an edict'. The next day Soto protested to Charles, and when the emperor upheld the majority decision, the confessor resigned and insisted on returning immediately to a monastery in Spain, saying (at least according to Granvelle) 'several impertinent things'. Charles thus lost an important source of independent advice.[23]

Some thought the emperor was losing touch with reality. His nephew and son-in-law Maximilian, who had seen him at close quarters on campaign in Saxony and later at the Augsburg Diet, as well as from afar when he served as regent in Spain, considered Charles's greatest fault to be 'the tenacity and inflexibility that he normally shows when dealing with his own affairs'. Perrenot voiced a different complaint. 'I find His Majesty more lethargic than is appropriate,' he complained to Marie:

In everything His Majesty despairs of finding a remedy, replying to whatever is proposed to him that 'One must find the least bad remedy for each problem . . .' When it is suggested to him that we should court the English, the Venetians, the German princes and others, and win the good will of people, he seems to set so little store by it, holding them all in such low esteem.[24]

THE NADIR OF THE REIGN

Groupthink, combined with the absorption of the emperor and those around him with other matters, led to the neglect of Germany, including the potential threat posed by Maurice of Saxony. 'Although I do not place much reliance on his goodwill,' Perrenot informed Marie (one of those who relayed warnings of a conspiracy building up against Charles):

I do not believe [Maurice] would dare move openly against His Majesty because . . . he is too fearful of undertaking a great enterprise, too poor to sustain great expenditure, and too unpopular in Saxony. He also fears that we might set free Duke John Frederick who, broken though he is, could still – thanks to his popularity in the area – easily chase out [Maurice].[25]

Marie responded by stressing that 'we have many enemies and ill-wishers, but few friends and well-wishers', and repeating that 'everyone agrees that Elector Maurice has contacts in France' as well as 'with all those in Germany who are hostile to His Majesty'. She therefore urged that her brother should move north from Augsburg into the German heartland, the better to monitor the situation there.[26] Yet again, Charles refused to listen: instead, he moved south to Innsbruck, thus isolating himself further from developments in the Empire.

Ascham's analysis resembled that of Marie: Charles had indeed offended many of his German friends and well-wishers. By way of example, Ascham cited Luis de Ávila's recently published *Commentaries* on the Schmalkaldic war (chapter 12), which belittled or criticized the conduct of several German princes, including Elector Frederick of the Palatinate (who complained to Charles in person about his portrayal in the book), Margrave Albert Alcibiades of Brandenburg (so enraged that he challenged Ávila to a duel), and the duke of Bavaria (who became 'more friendly to the princes confederate, than else peradventure he would have been'). Although a courtier may 'please his own prince' in the short term, Ascham reflected, 'yet he may perchance as much hurt him in the end, as Luis de Ávila did hurt the emperor his master in writing of this book', because the emperor would later lack 'both their hearts and their hands when he stood in most need of friends'.[27]

Perhaps Charles was distracted by the arrival in Innsbruck on Christmas Eve of his daughter María and her two children – the first of his grandchildren whom he had met. According to the Florentine ambassador, as soon as he saw María the emperor 'arose from his seat, removed his hat and walked towards her smiling'. He 'kissed her face most tenderly and then they started to laugh together'. Afterwards he kissed his grandchildren 'many times, which showed how much they pleased and delighted him'. Soon after the New Year, 'to increase the emperor's pleasure', Ferdinand's younger daughters 'joined him and so they enjoy themselves in their solitude' – but at a cost: the nuncio noted with irritation that 'this means that [the emperor and his ministers] pay no attention to business, which is transacted in this court so slowly and with so many delays'.[28]

The nuncio also regretted that although 'His Majesty, as good gladiators do, will take advice' before making decisions, 'his affairs pass through so few hands': in short, groupthink continued to characterize the imperial court.[29] On New Year's Day 1552, Perrenot belittled a correspondent who reported that convoys of French gold had been observed heading into Germany, while 'as to the league between Saxony, Brandenburg, Hesse, Mecklenburg and Pomerania, I promise you that it's nothing [che non è niente]'. Three weeks later Perrenot again dismissed the rumours of plots and foreign alliances, and also the news that Maurice refused to demobilize his army after the capitulation of Magdeburg because, he declared loftily, the Elector had no reason to break with the emperor – and even if he did, neither Maurice nor his putative allies 'have the brains or the funds' to sustain a successful rebellion. As late as 26 February 1552, Charles detected 'nothing serious to reprove' in Maurice's behaviour and 'could see no grounds to proceed against him'; but that same day, in Brussels, Marie found irrefutable proof of the plot in some intercepted letters from Maurice to his German allies containing details of his conspiracy and some commissions to raise troops. She sent the compromising correspondence to her brother by express messenger.[30]

This finally broke the spell. Charles now signed letters to the towns and princes of Germany, urging them to reject the confederates' offers, and he asked Ferdinand to placate Maurice by promising that he would set the landgrave free and pay any outstanding debts to Lutheran rulers – but this was an empty promise, because his treasury was empty. 'The devil take this war of Parma!' Charles lamented to his sister. 'It has ruined me, because I have used all the money that has come from America to fund it, and now it has almost gone.'[31] Two Lutheran armies, one commanded by Maurice and the other by Albert Alcibiades, now marched southward and almost every town on their route opened its gates to them: in each of them the princes restored the magistrates and the Lutheran preachers whom Charles had removed. They entered Augsburg in triumph on 4 April 1552. A few days later Metz opened its gates to the French and its magistrates recognized Henry II, 'being in his lodgings in the city', as 'protector and defender of German liberty'.[32]

The emperor was now bankrupt and isolated. As he explained sadly to Marie, 'I cannot find a penny, or anyone who wants to lend me one, or a man in Germany who seems ready to declare support for me.' He even suspected his brother's loyalty: 'Seeing that this unrest is so universal, and considering that the news of current events provided to us by [Ferdinand] has been so vague, and since he has offered us neither help nor advice on what we should do' – a grossly unfair accusation – 'we begin to wonder whether he might have some secret understanding with the authors of this conspiracy', which makes him less solicitous for what affects us.'[33] Worst of all, Innsbruck lay far from Charles's principal power-bases, making it hard for reinforcements to reach him. He begged his son to send money and troops from Spain, but expressed confusion about where to send them: the French army's advance into Germany cut him off from the Netherlands, yet joining Ferdinand in Vienna would place him under obligation to his brother and thus perhaps jeopardize the gains promised by the Family Compact. So the emperor of half the world reluctantly concluded that he could only be safe if he stayed put in Innsbruck – although he felt so insecure even there that he sent his son the text of his *Memoirs* 'to avoid the risk of losing it. Make sure it is kept safe and unopened.'[34]

The fall of Augsburg dramatically worsened Charles's situation. On hearing the news, he analysed his predicament for the benefit of Ferdinand: 'If I stay here any longer I shall surely be captured one morning in my bed', yet if he fled across the Alps 'I hold it certain that all Italy would immediately rebel, and the Low Countries would be at the mercy of France.' 'This would be,' the emperor concluded bitterly, 'the greatest humiliation and disgrace that any prince ever received.' Therefore:

Trusting in God and placing myself in His hands, I have decided that I would rather be taken for an old fool than to lose everything in my old age without doing everything I can – and perhaps more than my infirmities and ailments suggest that I should do. Seeing the situation in which I find myself at this moment, and the obstacles already mentioned, and seeing that I must either undergo a great humiliation or else place myself in great danger, I have chosen the path of danger because the remedy will then lie in God's hand. I will not wait here to be humiliated.

He declared his intention to leave Innsbruck secretly in a bid to reach the Netherlands, where he would be safe. 'If God is pleased to grant me a favourable outcome, I hope it will be for the best; and if He disposes otherwise, I will feel better about ending my days either in death or in captivity, in doing what I can, than to live longer in greater comfort. May God arrange what is best for His service.'[35]

Charles's reliance on Providence proved misplaced. Although he managed to leave his palace undetected, he had not even travelled eighty kilometres towards the Netherlands when he learned that Maurice's forces blocked his route. He therefore returned apprehensively to Innsbruck and redoubled his pleas for assistance from Spain. Realizing that Maurice's intention 'will be to come towards me, with the aim of driving me out of Germany', he begged Philip to send him 'without losing a minute' as many Spanish troops as possible, 'and above all pay attention to sending money, because you can see how it affects our honour and reputation, as well as the preservation of the lands that God has given us' – the use of 'us' once more serving as an unsubtle reminder that whatever Charles lost, Philip would lose too.[36] The emperor now resolved to swallow his pride and seek refuge in Vienna but (he complained) Ferdinand 'repeats in many letters that I should under no circumstances come to him, because it would ruin both him and his affairs, and that he cannot provide from there any help for mine.' The Family Compact forced upon him the previous year gave Ferdinand little incentive to fight for his nephew's inheritance.[37]

Ferdinand instead tried to remain neutral. First he travelled to Maurice's headquarters to find out what he wanted, and then to Innsbruck to ascertain what concessions Charles was prepared to make; but the emperor's best offer was to free the landgrave of Hesse two weeks after the rebel army demobilized, and to refer a permanent religious settlement to the imperial Diet, where the Catholics predominated. Maurice and his army therefore continued to advance, fighting their way over the Alpine pass that stood between them and Innsbruck. Sandoval's *History* imagined the scene when Charles heard the startling news of this on 19 May: 'There was not even time to grab the emperor's furnishings and clothes. He left at midnight, and some say that it was such a close call that as he left by one door, Maurice's troops entered by another.'[38]

Sandoval may have exaggerated slightly, but Charles's humiliation could hardly have been greater: he had to flee south across the Brenner pass, fifty kilometres away, to find safety. 'We rode almost all that night in wind and rain, and in the deepest darkness the world has seen,' an ambassador complained; and when the imperial party at last reached 'a small and uncomfortable village', they needed to commandeer 'a couple of sheets in which His Majesty could sleep, because his baggage had not arrived'. Five days and 300 kilometres later, 'in a litter and crippled by gout', Charles and his entourage reached the comparative safety of Villach, a remote town in the Austrian province of Carinthia, where they would spend the next two months.[39]

Count Stroppiana, the ambassador of Savoy, summarized the strategic dilemma that Charles now faced. He needed not only to avenge 'the disgrace of his flight from Innsbruck' by restoring his authority in Germany, but also to 'counter the audacity and gains made by the French', otherwise 'he stands in great danger of being chased out of both Germany and his hereditary lands'. Worse, if Henry II 'should mobilize against the emperor all the resources of France, and a good portion of those of Germany, Poland and the Turks, and makes trouble in Italy, he may lose both Italy and the Netherlands. His only remedy,' Stroppiana concluded briskly, 'is to castrate the French rooster and turn him into a capon.'[40]

Charles agreed with this bold analysis, but he needed to buy time. He therefore sent his brother back to negotiate with Maurice, now in Passau, with instructions to procrastinate until troops and money arrived from Spain, but the threat of French intervention led Ferdinand to disobey. Instead he offered major concessions: permanent freedom of worship for all Lutheran rulers and their subjects; the immediate liberation of the landgrave of Hesse; no further obligation for German princes to serve against France; and an undertaking that all political grievances against the emperor would be settled by an assembly of confederate rulers. Ferdinand even promised that if Charles did not observe these terms, he and his son Maximilian would declare war on him. In a holograph note that accompanied these concessions, 'your most humble and most obedient brother' warned Charles that unless he was prepared to wage all-out war, he must accept these terms as they stood.[41]

Charles could hardly believe his eyes as he read these documents and he composed a blistering reply. Although 'I do not intend to make war on the Lutherans, nor have I presently the means to do so', he found their terms – especially the demand that he grant permanent toleration – 'exorbitant':

> I cannot accept the bridle that they want to place on me . . . I would have to promise not to act against heresy for ever afterwards, although there could come a time and an occasion when my conscience would oblige me to do this. . . . As I have written and told you so often, I will never consent, for anything in this world, to something that goes against my duty and my conscience.

He pointed out that the religious concessions demanded of him would 'undo the decisions taken by the last two Diets without the participation of those who have a stake in them. This I cannot and must not do, especially in something of such importance to them.' Above all, Charles continued, the concessions would invalidate 'the Interim, and everything that has been achieved in religious matters, with such effort and cost'. He asserted that he was not motivated by pride, 'because if it only involved humiliation, I would easily suffer that in order to have peace . . . The problem is that, along with the humiliation that can be overcome, there is a burden of conscience that I cannot endure. And so I cannot accept the treaty.'[42]

Instead Charles agreed to 'bind myself with all the sureties they desire that in matters of religion I will accept whatever may be determined in the next Diet' – that is, his conscience allowed him to make another temporary concession, but not a permanent one. As he had done many times before, he granted full powers to Ferdinand 'since you are close to events', to negotiate in his name, but this time he included:

> A proviso, which I share with you now for future reference: that I do not wish or understand myself to be obliged to observe any concession beyond those indicated above. And in this sense, the more exorbitant it is the better, because my intention is to refer to the next Diet the wickedness [of the confederates], and the reasons why I do not wish to consider myself obliged [by consenting now], given the duress applied.

This was precisely the ruse that had so outraged Charles when Francis I employed it before signing the treaty of Madrid in 1526. In addition, in a holograph postscript, the emperor urged his brother to prolong deliberations as much as possible, since 'time is the greatest advantage for our side:

time to weaken our enemies and to allow my forces to assemble – all I need is fifteen to twenty days.'

Two other letters at this time shed light on the emperor's resilience under extreme threat. Having learned of the death of María and Maximilian's first child, on whom he had doted at Innsbruck the previous winter, despite 'a finger on my right hand that torments me' he wrote a holograph note of condolence to remind Ferdinand that 'in the end we must accept what God grants', followed by a prayer that 'God will help you to deal with current problems as His Holy Service and the prosperity of our own affairs require'. He then wrote a similar holograph letter of consolation to Maximilian (whom he addressed as 'my son', signing off 'Your good father, Carolus'): 'God be praised for all He does. We must accept His will and at the same time beg Him to watch over those of us who remain, and bless us.' Despite the personal and political setbacks, Charles remained convinced that God would advance his interests and those of his family.[43]

A few days later, Charles informed Marie that he was prepared 'to leave Germany and transfer the imperial crown' to Ferdinand and authorize him to make the concessions demanded by the Lutheran princes, because 'he says that his conscience will let him do it, while my conscience tells me the opposite'; but before a courier could leave with the letter, Charles was able to retrace his steps to Innsbruck – a move that (he told Marie) would 'encourage some and amaze others'. The balance of power had shifted dramatically in his favour: the duke of Alba approached at the head of 5,000 Spanish infantry, accompanied by 'many gentlemen who had decided to spend their personal wealth serving His Majesty' together with 'two million ducats minted into coins, or ready to be minted', brought from Peru; and everywhere his lieutenants raised troops to serve him. As the nuncio travelling with him realized, Charles could now 'not only defend himself but also attack his enemies and *get revenge*'.[44]

THE EMPEROR STRIKES BACK

'The arrival of the duke of Alba, with his Spaniards and the money has greatly raised our spirits,' wrote a member of Charles's entourage. 'Now the council of war meets in the duke's apartment for long and detailed discussions.' The arrival of these reinforcements also strengthened Ferdinand's bargaining position, and a week later at Passau he and Maurice reached a tentative agreement: on his brother's behalf, Ferdinand promised an unconditional pardon for all who had taken up arms, the immediate release of

Philip of Hesse and John Frederick of Saxony, and the summoning of an imperial Diet to find a permanent solution to the religious issue and to address all alleged abuses of power by the emperor and his agents since Mühlberg. In return, the confederates agreed either to disband their troops within ten days or to send them to defend Hungary. Almost immediately Maurice led his men to fight the Turks, while Charles entered Innsbruck 'on horseback, showing himself more robust than usual, with his arquebus upon his saddle'. The emperor who only a month before had seemed 'old and weighed down by his many infirmities' now commanded over 68,000 troops in Germany with a further 41,000 in the Netherlands and 24,000 in northern Italy. What would he do with them?[45]

One possibility was a campaign in Italy, where the successful defiance of Parma had called into question Charles's ability to impose his will; but in July 1552, Venice rejected France's offer of alliance, which led almost all other Italian rulers to maintain their neutrality too. Only the republic of Siena threw caution to the winds – the citizens of its capital chased out the Spanish garrison amid cries of 'France, liberty and victory' – and Charles decided that his ministers in Italy possessed sufficient strength to prevent the 'contagion' spreading to other parts of the peninsula. Instead he announced that 'We have resolved to deal, for the present, principally with finding a remedy for the affairs of Germany, on whose pacification the success of our affairs mostly depends'.[46]

This decision led to the worst strategic catastrophe of Charles's reign: the siege of Metz. Luckily for historians, a profusion of surviving sources – above all, the correspondence of the emperor himself and of the ambassadors attached to his court – make it possible to reconstruct in detail his path to disaster.

Although the treaty of Passau restored peace to most of Germany, Charles still faced two important enemies. Albert Alcibiades of Brandenburg seized Trier at the head of some 12,000 men, ravaged adjacent Catholic lands, and threatened the Habsburg duchy of Luxemburg; and the French left a powerful garrison in Metz. The imperial army now marched towards the Rhine in two divisions: Charles, once again wearing full armour, rode at the head of the main contingent, which lodged each evening in the quarters vacated that morning by the vanguard under the duke of Alba. Nuncio Camaiani reported (with a mixture of admiration and irritation) that he could not divine their objective; and although in September he realized that Charles aimed to cross the Rhine at Strasbourg, he remained unsure whether the ultimate target would be Trier or Metz. Although 'almost all the courtiers here believe that

His Majesty intends to do his best to recover Metz from the hands of the French', the nuncio fretted about the high risks involved in campaigning so late in the year, when prolonged periods of rain and cold were inevitable. Nevertheless, he recognized that either retaking Metz or neutralizing Albert Alcibiades 'will boost His Majesty's reputation', especially if he participated in person.[47] Charles had already reached the same conclusion. When his physicians warned him that 'he must not take part in the campaign, both because he lacked the health for it and because he would create more problems than if he were absent', the emperor 'responded that, come what may, he was resolved to press on'. He also informed his son that:

> Although there are obstacles, because the season is well advanced and because of the other problems that usually occur in such great enterprises, let us hope that God will hold everything in His hand, and guide me and bring about a successful outcome. At least I will do everything possible on my part, risking (whenever it is appropriate and necessary) my own person.[48]

Despite his apparent confidence, Charles harboured some misgivings. Already in June he predicted that a French army would lurk 'near to the frontier of Luxemburg to keep our troops at bay while they finish the fortification of Metz'; and three months later, perhaps recalling his own experience at Ingolstadt, he worried that once Metz acquired modern defences, 'we can abandon hope of finding a way to recapture it'. Moreover, 'if the city remains in French hands, it will provide them with a highway into Germany as far as the Rhine', and also 'sever a secure passage between the Netherlands and Burgundy'. Time, therefore, was of the essence. Charles conceded that the lack of victuals, the lateness of the season, the size and resources of the French garrison, and his own lack of money meant that 'we cannot mount a blockade that will starve them out and thus force them to surrender'; he therefore asked Marie to consult anyone who 'knows the place, and has seen it recently' to declare 'whether or not Metz can be taken by storm'. If not, her experts must 'tell me what they think the army I command should undertake, in order to inflict the maximum damage on our enemies in what remains of the campaign season'. In any case she must send sappers (together with surplus entrenching tools, 'since several break when they are used, and sometimes it is necessary to make the soldiers dig'); all the gunners she could spare ('since one always needs experts where artillery is concerned'); and engineers ('since if I need to build siege-works, I will need good engineers both to explain to others what they must do, and to design the siege-works and oversee their construction').[49]

Given the numerous disadvantages listed by her brother, Marie predictably advised him to leave Metz alone and instead attack somewhere closer to the Netherlands and to safe winter quarters. Equally predictably, Charles countered with providential arguments – indeed he used almost the same rhetoric he had used to justify his perseverance with the Algiers campaign a decade before. 'As far as I can see, we have no other course of action, because if we abandon this enterprise I will have to disband my army, having spent so much money without achieving anything. I have therefore decided to spend even more, and await what God pleases to give us, rather than to quit without seeing what Fortune brings.'[50]

This decision seems particularly rash in view of the military evaluation by Camaiani. 'In terms of numbers, the emperor's army is equal to any enterprise,' the nuncio conceded:

> But as to the state and quality of the soldiers, the majority of the German infantry is very poor: badly armed and lacking military experience. The Spanish infantry includes the excellent veterans who served at the siege of Parma, but the majority of those just arrived from Spain are also very poor and there are many who are sick ... The cavalry is inferior in numbers to that of our enemy.

Camaiani agreed with Charles that 'if this army achieves anything this year, it will owe more to the emperor's customary good Fortune than to anything else'.[51]

For a time, Fortune once again favoured Charles. In the Netherlands, his troops captured Hesdin, forcing Henry II to relocate soldiers and resources from the eastern to the northern frontier of his kingdom. In Germany, Alba persuaded Albert Alcibiades to accept the treaty of Passau and join him in the siege of Metz. Charles lamented the need to ally with the odious self-proclaimed 'priest-eater [*Pfaffenfresser*]' – 'We would be glad not to do this, so that we could punish him as he deserves' – but he reluctantly overrode his conscience because, without Albert Alcibiades's troops, 'we would not be able to complete the siege of this city, given its size, so that relief could enter it whenever they want'. Secretary of State Francisco de Eraso, travelling with Charles, also felt pessimistic: besieging Metz, he opined, 'was better than doing nothing', because then critics would jest that 'this huge army was assembled merely to escort His Majesty to the Netherlands'.[52]

'THE BEST SIEGE THAT EVER WAS'

The imperialists started digging trenches around Metz on 23 October 1552, but the emperor did not stay to watch. According to Eraso, the previous month Dr Baersdorp 'insisted that His Majesty must not go to the trenches under any circumstances, because his health would not allow it, and that his presence would create greater difficulties', but the emperor 'told him that, come what may, he was determined to take his chances'. He only changed his mind when, as he approached Metz, 'I felt so much pain from my gout that I had to stay in bed today' and decided to go to Thionville, thirty kilometres to the north, 'where I can live with less discomfort than in the camp, and can make a swifter recovery'.[53]

His troops before Metz suffered far more than 'discomfort'. Over the summer the French garrison had erected thick ramparts punctuated by bastions, and demolished all buildings outside the walls, creating an artillery fortress. This worried the commander of the Netherlands contingent in the imperial army because 'I have never met a man who has seen or heard tell of towns thus defended being taken by assault'. He soon complained about 'the attacks launched every day by the defenders, gallant fighters who know their business'.[54] After a month of stalemate, Charles worried that 'since things were not going well my reputation has become involved, as if I were personally present since I was so close. Moreover, if I were there I might be able to attend to some things'. He therefore arose from his sickbed at Thionville and travelled south, arriving at the camp before Metz with a 'happy and cheerful countenance'. On 22 November, accompanied by Alba and Albert Alcibiades, he 'rode around the trenches and the batteries, looking good on his horse', and the following day he entered the trenches to direct a bombardment so ferocious 'that you could hear the thunder of the guns beyond Strasbourg', 200 kilometres away.[55]

Nevertheless, a week's bombardment brought down only twenty-five metres of the curtain wall and his troops refused to launch an assault because the defenders' guns on the bastions overlooking the breach remained intact. Next, 'to avoid permanent regret for failing to try everything imaginable to prevail in this enterprise', Charles exploded gunpowder mines placed under the walls; but like the artillery barrage, they achieved nothing. Some considered this wasted effort, 'because Metz cannot be captured by mines', and they blamed the emperor 'for an unwillingness to change his mind, which might be called obstinacy'. A week later Charles returned to Thionville, and according to the Venetian ambassador, 'Now both the court and the army openly begin to lose whatever hope they may have had of capturing Metz.'[56]

A decade later, the French soldier and writer Pierre de Bourdeille, lord of Brantôme, deemed the emperor's attempt to take Metz 'the best siege that ever was', but it did not seem that way to the men in the trenches. 'The soldiers cannot resist the cold, which kills them like flies; and the rest flee as far as they can, because they cannot find food or fodder', wrote the Savoyard ambassador, while his English colleague claimed that 'I never since I was born felte such cold as hath ben herre thys Christmas'. Even twenty years later, Perrenot could still 'feel in my legs the cold that I experienced before Metz.'[57] Charles also suffered. From his sickbed in Thionville he complained bitterly to Marie that 'I eat so little that I'm beginning to think starvation cannot kill a man. You should know that I have lost all the spare flesh that I had before and that I lack the strength required for the trade [*mestier*] that I currently practise' – namely to wage war. 'I hear Mass in bed and get up only for lunch, and the cold and my weakness compel me to retire again after 4 or 5 o'clock.' While there, Guillaume van Male read aloud to him passages from Classical works, notably *The Jewish War* by Josephus (a history full of successful sieges), and from the Old Testament, especially the book of Daniel and the Psalms (full of courage and eventual triumph in the face of adversity). Charles even compiled 'a book composed of fine texts from the Psalms that he has chosen', which La Gasca, the pacifier of Peru and now a bishop in Spain, considered 'very devout and a testament to His Majesty's sacred and devout intention.'[58]

Evidently it did not suffice to placate the Creator: while the emperor's main army lay impotently before Metz, the French blockaded Hesdin. That tipped the balance for Charles: 'Madame my good sister', he wrote to Marie, 'the French actions against Hesdin may have important consequences, and having attempted everything possible against this city [Metz] without any sign that we may be able to take it, in order not to lose more men through illness without purpose, and to be able to relieve Hesdin ... I have finally decided to raise this siege'. Alba skilfully concealed the withdrawal and at 11 p.m. on New Year's Day, 1553, the imperial army silently abandoned the trenches.[59]

The unvanquished defenders unfurled banners and issued medals that parodied Charles's motto: an eagle chained to the columns of Hercules and the slogan NON ULTRA METAS, with the double meaning 'Not beyond Metz' and 'Not beyond these limits'.[60] According to the Venetian ambassador, the siege had 'cost the lives of 25,000 soldiers, not counting boys, women, sutlers and others, and 25,000 horses'; and Stroppiana reported that 'mortality on the imperial side was far greater than stated: there are no courtiers left, because all are dead or dying'. More soldiers were left to the mercy of the French because they were too ill or injured to be moved, and Alba abandoned 'armour, guns, pikes, swords and other weapons, an infinite amount of baggage and most of their tents', and threw a further thirty guns with their carriages into the river on the retreat.[61] It could have been worse. Just sixty kilometres away, and seventy-five years earlier, a foolish decision to besiege Nancy in winter had led to the catastrophic defeat and death of Duke Charles the Bold of Burgundy – a precedent well known to the emperor, because two years before he had ordered his ancestor's mortal remains to be exhumed from their humble tomb in Nancy and triumphantly transported to Habsburg territory.[62]

Although the emperor left the siege of Metz alive, he almost immediately provoked a major row among his ministers by ordering 'that, since he lacked the money to pay the German troops, the duke [of Alba] should pacify them with words, promising payment in Trier. The duke replied that he did not know how to perform miracles', and suggested that Charles should delegate the task 'to those ministers' – meaning Perrenot – 'who had advised him to persevere with the siege of Metz but had not provided, as they should have done, the necessary money and materials ... This caused great confusion among his ministers'; and while they argued, the French recaptured Hesdin.[63]

THE EMPEROR AT BAY

All of Charles's plans had miscarried. Parma, Siena and Metz had successfully defied him; he had lost Hesdin; and he had agreed to renew toleration for the Lutherans of Germany. Moreover, his unprecedented and prolonged mobilization had ruined his finances. James Tracy has calculated that the loan contracts signed by the treasury of Castile in the course of 1552 were 'by far the largest total for any year of Charles's reign' – 3.7 million ducats – while 'the next highest totals were for 1553': 2.2 million. In the Netherlands, treasury spending soared from £1.3 million in 1550 to almost £6 million in 1552 and even more in 1553 – likewise, the largest totals of the reign.[64]

The emperor had also ruined his health. On Christmas Eve 1552, van Male reported that his master constantly 'complained about intestinal problems and diarrhoea' but still insisted on drinking 'ice-cold beer that has been left out all night exposed to the cold. For some time he has been addicted to these excesses and will not give them up.' Van Male warned that 'no one, not even someone with strength and good health, could survive drinking iced beer before daybreak in winter, let alone someone of his age, with his health undermined by illness, travel and hard work'. He also complained that Charles constantly 'devoured oysters – which he consumes raw, boiled and fried – and almost all types of sea fish', despite the fact that 'every day before dawn, I hear his groans and sighs produced by the pain'. A week later, although 'his stomach and his haemorrhoids are better', Dr Baersdorp noted that Charles had lost his appetite 'and subsists on eggs and soups'. After an audience in January 1553, Ambassador Richard Morison wrote that he had never seen Charles 'so nigh gone, never so dede in his face, his hand never so leane, pale, and wan; his eyes that were wont to be full of life whan all the rest had yelded to sycknes, were now heavy and dull, and as nigh death in their look as ever I saw.'[65] It took the emperor over a month to get back to Brussels, a distance that he had previously covered in a week, and he entered the city cradled 'in an open litter, his eyes always raised to heaven'. According to Stroppiana, 'His Majesty is very weak, and takes no pleasure in either eating or drinking. He is in a lot of pain, without having any specific illness. His condition makes me very fearful.'[66]

Charles still dreamed of revenge. In February 1553, despite his infirmities, he appeared before the States-General of the Netherlands to ask them to vote new taxes worth 1.5 million ducats, but first he delivered a tirade against French treachery. King Henry had occupied parts of the Empire 'in order to take them over and reduce them to the same cruel servitude in which he held his own kingdom'; he had fomented rebellion in Germany; above all, he had encouraged the Turks to attack both in the Mediterranean and in Hungary. Exhausted by his efforts, Charles then withdrew to his apartments in the Coudenberg palace, where he spent the next four months (according to the Venetian ambassador) 'complaining about everything' and everyone.[67]

The emperor appears to have suffered a physical and psychological collapse. According to Nicholas Nicolay, a Netherlands councillor, arthritis 'has spread to all the limbs, joints and nerves of his body', and as usual cold weather increased the pain. In addition, catarrh so affected him that 'when he has it he cannot speak, and when he speaks he cannot be heard or scarcely understood by his attendants'. Finally, 'his haemorrhoids have swollen and hurt him so much, but they cannot be put back in without great pain and tears'. The combination of these ailments, Nicolay continued, had crushed the emperor's spirit, so that instead of being gracious and affable 'as he used to be', he had become sad and pensive, 'and often he cries violently, and sheds many tears, just as if he were a child . . . His Majesty does not want to hear about business, or to sign the few [papers] that are prepared.' He refused to give audiences or appear in public, and he banished from his presence one veteran minister, Louis de Praet, 'because he insisted on talking to him about business'. He even lashed out when Antoine Perrenot complained that he had received much public opprobrium but little recompense for his many services, and requested a lucrative office: 'As for what you say about others having received rewards for services when you have not, given the amount of business you handle, if I had to reward you for each one it would not be in my power to satisfy you.' Nicolay claimed that Charles now:

> Occupied himself day and night with adjusting and synchronizing his clocks ... At night, since he cannot sleep when he wants to, he often wakes up his valets and others and orders them to light candles and torches, to help him dismantle some clocks and then to reset them. He has spent and still spends many days reading the psalms of David and the Commentaries on them.

According to Nicolay, Marie had taken over the government of the Monarchy in order to forestall disaster, but everyone realized that this could only be a temporary measure.[68]

At Marie's insistence, probably unknown to the rest of the court, Charles signed a letter on 2 April 1553 commanding his son to return to the Netherlands in order 'to gain reputation and to make yourself known, so that the world, including your enemies, will see that you will not give them the chance – as perhaps they expect – to undertake anything'. The emperor believed that the best way to achieve this was for Philip in person to lead a successful campaign against the French, but since the Low Countries could pay no more, 'you must bring with you such a large sum of money that it will serve to sustain these provinces adequately. This is the only remedy for the present situation', and it would also avoid the need 'to ask the provinces for new taxes as soon as you arrive, which, since they are so exhausted, will not only cost you their affection but also cause them to resent twice as much (as subjects often do) the sacrifices you ask of them'. Therefore, 'since the situation is so desperate', Charles reviewed a series of dubious expedients for raising in Spain the funds he needed. He proposed the sale of knighthoods for 2,000 ducats each (except to descendants of Jews, Muslims and Comuneros); he petitioned the pope for permission to sell more church property; and he even authorized discussion of 'what we might raise from the encomiendas in America'. In the meantime, Charles declared, he planned 'to return to Germany to hold a Diet in late June', provided 'my health and my other commitments will allow it'; and from there he would travel 'in the autumn first to Italy, and from there to Spain'. He continued:

> I would like very much to have you here before I leave, so that I can talk to you about the things that seem important to me, and to hear from you in person the things that should not be written down about the state of [Spain]. I do not think that these provinces should be left at a time like this without the presence of one of us, and so while I am in Germany I want you to hold the fort here.[69]

Charles then turned to micro-managing the sex life of his son, now aged twenty-six, as he had done a decade before: 'So much time has passed since the death of the princess [María Manuela] that I think it is both opportune and necessary for you to marry again, given your age and given the need for the heirs that I hope God will give you.' As usual the perfect choice seemed to be a cousin, specifically María, daughter of Charles's sister Eleanor and the late King Manuel of Portugal, now aged thirty-two and one of the richest women in Europe. Nevertheless, 'it seems that a great obstacle lies in the way of this business': namely that, as part of the Family Compact at Augsburg, Philip had promised to marry another cousin, one of Ferdinand's daughters. Although Charles could and did break solemn promises whenever it suited him, this time he worried about the possibility that if his son 'defaults on the marriage [Ferdinand] will claim that everything is linked together' and renege on his promise to arrange Philip's succession as emperor. 'Nevertheless,' he continued, 'we agreed that the marriage is to take place after your election [as king of the Romans], of which there is little hope as long as Germany remains in such disorder. Until that changes, I cannot recommend that you accept the Empire, even if you were offered it.' Charles therefore instructed his son to give Ferdinand an ultimatum: 'You are now of marriageable age and for that reason, as well as to please our subjects, you should not be tied down or impeded from doing so; and since the agreement on your marriage to one of his daughters is linked to your election, you should ask him either to take steps to make this happen or else release you to marry whomever you want.' Since apart from Ferdinand's daughters 'we cannot see a suitable match for you anywhere else', the emperor urged his son to conclude his negotiations with Lisbon as soon as possible so that he could consummate the marriage before leaving his wife and coming to the Netherlands.[70] In June 1553, Philip obediently sent a confidant, Ruy Gómez de Silva, to finalize the marriage terms with his aunt (and former mother-in-law) Catalina and her husband, King John III.

Meanwhile French military pressure forced Charles to wage another campaign in the Netherlands instead of travelling to Germany as he had intended. This time, he triumphed. First he sent an experienced general, the count of Roeulx, to capture Thérouanne, a heavily fortified French enclave in the Netherlands. Realizing that 'unless we wage a cruel war, we will never gain our objective', during the three-week siege of Thérouanne Roeulx's artillery fired an average of 800 rounds a day (compared with 300 a day at Metz) and he exploded five gunpowder mines to force the dazed garrison to capitulate. Even before its surrender, the emperor had decreed that the city 'will be immediately sacked, and then razed to its foundations. Not only will secular buildings be destroyed, but also the churches, the monasteries and the hospitals. Not a vestige of its walls will remain.' He kept his word. According to François de Rabutin, a hostile French commentator, when the emperor heard that Thérouanne had fallen, 'he was as pleased as if it had been Constantinople' and over the next two months further gunpowder mines razed the city to the ground. Although today trees grow along the lines of the pre-1553 fortifications, only fields exist within: of the city and its cathedral, no trace remains. The victors then laid siege to Hesdin and, according to Rabutin, 'every hour, day and night, they maintained the most furious battery that anyone living could recall'. After the garrison surrendered, the imperialists once more used mines to destroy the city.[71]

Then news arrived that Henry II in person had laid siege to Cambrai. Yet again, the emperor rose to the occasion. On 28 May the nuncio found Charles 'so weak that he lacked the will to speak', and reported that even Marie and her ministers 'have had trouble in making him speak even one word in a week'; but a few days later Perrenot revealed that:

> We are trying to prepare His Majesty to appear in public, sometimes getting him dressed as if he were healthy and sometimes making him wear his sword and cloak. We also make him speak more loudly and vigorously than he normally does, on account of his weakness and debility. In short, we are doing everything to make him appear more comely and lively [più bella et vivace].

The makeover seems to have worked, because at his first audience since the retreat from Metz, on 9 June 1553, the nuncio reported that 'although his face shows some pallor, he has been like that for many years', but now his 'eyes were lively and sparkling' and 'he hears and speaks with the same attention and gravity as ever'. The imperial temperament also remained unchanged: when the nuncio relayed a French peace offer, Charles observed that Henry II was just like his father – always trying to revisit issues already decided, and allying with Turks 'despite his title of "Most Christian King", so that you could not trust any promise he might make'. Therefore, Charles continued, 'he believed it would be better to continue the war because he would lose nothing by doing so, and even if he should lose he would prefer it to being assassinated when he least expected it'.[72] In August, motivated by his 'deep hatred of the king of France and his fear that for lack of good leadership some misfortune might befall his army', Charles decided to take the field himself, 'even though it will be hard on his system, since he has not left his small apartment for seven whole months'. Accompanied by Marie, who looked after him, he travelled to Mons and from there joined his army in the field until King Henry withdrew. To celebrate, the emperor then spent a whole 'daye in hunting of the bore', and 'liked that daye his passetyme so well' that he did 'the same again on the morrow'.[73]

Delight at developments across the English Channel no doubt contributed to the emperor's remarkable recovery. Edward VI, king of England and Ireland, died on 6 July 1553, and although (at the direction of his councillors) he had signed a 'Device' naming as his successor his Protestant cousin Lady Jane Grey, she found few supporters. After a few days of uncertainty Edward's Catholic half-sister Mary Tudor defeated Jane's adherents and ascended the throne. Almost immediately the new, unmarried queen of thirty-seven turned for advice to Charles, her cousin and former fiancé, and indicated that she would look favourably on a renewed offer of matrimony. The emperor, assisted by Marie and Perrenot, skilfully exploited this windfall. Charles claimed that he lacked the energy to wed Queen Mary himself, and offered his son instead. He carefully explained to her the advantages: it would provide a 'husband who could take charge in wartime and perform other duties that are inappropriate for women', such as organizing an invasion of Scotland that would 'make it subject to the kingdom of England' and a campaign to 'recover Guyenne, unjustly possessed by those who now hold it, and perhaps even the kingdom of France'. In addition, gaining the crown of England would allow Philip to rule both Spain and the Netherlands effectively, even without becoming king of the Romans, while creating a new Anglo-Netherlands state to be ruled by the heir of Philip and Mary would permanently secure Habsburg domination of the Channel and North Sea, and thus 'keep the French in check and reduce them to reason'.[74]

Nevertheless, Mary Tudor felt limited enthusiasm for marriage. A few days after her accession she told Charles's ambassador, Simon Renard, that she had always been single and had never experienced love. As a woman, Mary continued, she had no wish to change her status, but as a queen she recognized that for the good of her realm both a marriage and a child were now essential. She 'laughed not once but several times' with embarrassment as she discussed these unfamiliar topics with Renard, and expressed the hope that whoever Charles 'proposed and put forward for her [husband] would be a Catholic; that she would have a chance to meet him first; and that he should not be too young.' When the conversation turned to Philip as a possible suitor, the queen responded that she understood he was already promised to María of Portugal, that he was twelve years her junior, and that 'in addition, His Highness would want to stay in Spain and govern his other dominions'. Renard forwarded her concerns to Charles, who hastened to address them. Mary's 'desire to see her future husband' in advance, he pointed out, 'would be hard to arrange' because 'no prince equal to her in rank would wish to take the risk of going there and being rejected'. Instead he sent her a flattering portrait of her suitor by Titian, done at Augsburg three years before; and assured her that after their marriage Philip would reside frequently in England.[75]

It was almost too late. A courier had already left Philip's court bearing his final approval of the terms of his marriage contract with María of Portugal when an express messenger arrived from Charles ordering him to marry Mary Tudor instead. The prince recalled his courier, so that the letter of approval never reached its destination, and he ceded full powers for his father to negotiate an English Match on his behalf.[76] Hard bargaining took place between Mary's councillors and Charles's envoys, led by Renard, who only prevailed by 'explaining to her the benefits that would come to England if, through her children, the kingdom were united with the Netherlands'. In October 1553, Renard triumphantly advised Philip that Mary Tudor had made up her mind to marry him, so that 'it would be advisable for Your Highness to practise speaking French or Latin'.[77]

The emperor favoured cementing the union by proxies, which would take immediate effect, but the English preferred that 'the wedding should be concluded and solemnized in the presence of both spouses'. Charles therefore demanded that his son send 'two powers of attorney, drawn up like the attached drafts, so that we can use whichever one is needed without wasting any time'. Once again, the prince complied – but with serious reservations. On 4 January 1554 he executed before a notary a deed stating that he will 'approve, authorize and swear to the said articles so that his marriage to the most serene queen of England may take place, but this does not bind or oblige him and his possessions, or his heirs and successors, to execute or approve any of them, especially those that involve his conscience'.[78]

The prince had little choice but to accept whatever marriage terms the English offered, because he had now burned his bridges with both Ferdinand and María of Portugal – but the emperor treated both broken promises with his usual insouciance. When a Portuguese envoy arrived in Brussels and 'gave vent to his discontent . . . we told him what was necessary, without wishing to justify or discuss the matter further'. Charles advised his son to do the same, 'because when these matters are past it is best to dissimulate'.[79]

After his success in arranging the English Match, Charles's interest in public affairs seems to have waned again. According to an ambassador in December 1553, he rarely signed letters of state, 'and although he has held a few audiences, they are mere formalities, because those who come are ordered not to discuss business . . . Some ministers have used stratagems to get him to hear and sign many matters, but nothing really works'. Eraso (whose constant attendance on the emperor gave him considerable insight into his master's state of mind) warned Philip of the precarious situation he faced. Charles now seemed determined 'to abandon all business, and his aim really does seem to be to go to Spain'; but 'there are signs that if God chose to remove His Majesty, dangers would soon arise here if Your Highness were not present'. Charles himself alerted his son to his failing health: 'I have recently had a setback, and the pain from my gout is beginning to spread so that I now have more pain than I would wish on all my left side and some, although less intense, in my right arm.' Shortly afterwards he apologized again that 'I have spent five weeks in bed beset by gout and other ailments, and so have not been able to transact business', and he told his son:

> I am well aware that it would be better if I returned to Spain before you left, and it is something that I really want to do; but my health will not let me travel and even if I could do so, it would be impossible to get a fleet together in time . . . It therefore seems best to me that I should leave after you arrive, and after I have discussed with you the affairs of [the Netherlands] and arranged what needs to be done here. So I will do everything I can to be able to leave, if God wills, next August or September.[80]

Charles now lived in a cottage in the park surrounding the royal palace in Brussels: a suite of apartments 'approached by a stairway of ten or twelve steps', with an antechamber that 'opens onto his receiving room and bedroom, none of them larger than twenty-four square feet', while a corridor linked his bedroom to a small chapel where he worshipped. The only decorations in the public space were his coat of arms and his motto, *Plus Ultra*, prominently displayed both on the walls and in special roundels in each window. It was, a nuncio asserted (somewhat implausibly), 'a little house no larger and no better than the quarters of a Carthusian'.[81] Another papal diplomat reported that 'inside the cottage, His Majesty spends part of his time beside a clock that includes all the planetary movements': he referred to the eight-sided spring-driven planetary clock known as the 'Microcosm' constructed and maintained by Janello Torriani from Cremona, whom Charles hailed as 'the prince of clockmakers'. It was 'circular, almost two foot in width and a little more in height', powered by perhaps 1,800 gears, 'showing all the motions of the planets and everything we know about astrology'.[82] A provincial lawyer who visited the imperial court in April 1554 recorded the general excitement when the clock and its inventor arrived from Italy: 'Its novelty led the emperor to make such a fuss of it that would astonish you, and he took pleasure in the clock above all things.' Charles's obsession with time pieces became the butt of a joke at this time. One day he complained to his major-domo, Baron Monfalconetto, that the food served to him was always bland and unappetizing, 'to which the baron replied: "I just don't know any other way to please Your Majesty, unless I try to create a new dish for you: *clock soup*." At this, the emperor laughed louder and longer than anyone had ever witnessed before.'[83]

The emperor's prolonged absence from Spain, combined with his preoccupation with his clocks, his health and his responsibilities elsewhere, allowed Prince Philip to take many decisions on his own initiative. As one nobleman put it crudely: 'I beg your Highness to authorize a response to the memorial that I gave you in Madrid, because we all know that you can transact all affairs of state without awaiting permission from Germany' – that is, without consulting Charles.[84] Philip proved the truth of this assertion in spectacular fashion as he prepared to leave for England in the spring of 1554. The emperor strongly opposed the appointment of his daughter Joanna as regent – 'you know that the princess is very haughty, and I have heard that her household is badly run,' he warned Philip – yet the prince persuaded her to return to Castile after the death of her husband, heir to the Portuguese throne, and then spent several days with her (as he coolly informed his father) 'to inform her of matters that she needs to know' before she took over as regent. Having got his way on this key issue Philip hand-picked Joanna's advisory council, once again studiously ignoring the nominations and suggestions made by his father. Finally, he issued instructions to his sister that explicitly overlooked or overrode Charles's directives. Joanna 'must not sign any document except those prepared by the secretaries indicated by me'; she must send him copies of all her correspondence with Charles; and she must consult him before taking any major decisions concerning Spain, Spanish Italy or Spanish America.[85]

At last on 13 July 1554, with his treasure chests full of cash to fund another campaign in the Netherlands and in command of a fleet large enough to deter any hostile attempt to intercept him, Philip left Spain to marry Mary Tudor and then take over from Charles in the Netherlands. After all the delays, the fleet took just seven days to sail from Corunna to Southampton, where both English and Netherlands envoys awaited him. The English brought him greetings and presents from his bride-to-be; the Netherlanders brought Charles's renunciation of his title to Naples in favour of his son, who thus became a king in his own right on the eve of his wedding. In addition, a special messenger brought Mary the tapestry series woven to commemorate the conquest of Tunis in 1535, 'which is one of the fayrest peces of worke that hathe bene made in our tyme'.[86]

These were gracious gestures by the emperor, who also sent his son a copy of the new will he had made. This document, written in Spanish although signed in Brussels, offers a fascinating overview of the emperor's preoccupations as his reign neared its end.[87] First came the conventional pious injunctions: 30,000 Masses must be said within a year for the repose of his soul, and his body must be conveyed to Granada and buried in the royal chapel beside his wife, his father and the Catholic Monarchs – he made no mention now of Bruges or Dijon, as in his earlier testaments: a reflection of how Spain had displaced the Netherlands and Burgundy in his imperial vision. He urged Philip always to uphold justice, protect widows and orphans, and revere the Catholic Church; and 'I particularly charge you to favour the Holy Office of the Inquisition.' Then came a series of more specific obligations. The sum of 30,000 ducats must be placed in the fortress of Simancas, in a locked chest to which only Charles had the key, to fund three charitable causes dear to his heart: to ransom 'Christians held captive in the lands of infidels . . . with preference for those who were captured during campaigns when I myself was present'; to create dowries for poor virgins; and to succour the deserving poor. Charles commanded his son to pay the dowries promised to his daughters María and Joanna (but never paid); to distribute the money and jewels left to each of them by their mother's will (also never paid); and, so that 'our conscience will be discharged', his heir must pay not only all of Charles's outstanding debts but also those of his father Philip, his aunt Margaret, and all four of his grandparents (more obligations that Charles himself had failed to discharge), as well as finding 10,000 ducats 'to be distributed in good works for the soul of Her Highness', Queen Joanna, still living in seclusion at Tordesillas, with whom Philip must rule jointly 'in the same form and order as I have done and do'. Furthermore, the young king must respect an important clause in the marriage treaty just concluded with England: his son by María Manuela, Don Carlos, 'must be removed and excluded from the succession to our Netherlands possessions'. Philip must also retain and defend Milan, both because 'whenever it has been ruled by someone who did not possess other states' war had broken out in Italy, and because of 'the immense sums that retaining the duchy has cost our kingdoms of Castile and Aragon, and the large number of our vassals and subjects, from all parts, who have died or shed their blood' in its defence. By contrast, Philip must 'take immediate steps to determine openly and sincerely whether justice and reason requires the return' of the kingdom of Navarre, conquered and annexed by Ferdinand of Aragon in 1512, 'or an offer of satisfaction or compensation to a third party'.

The emperor ordered Philip 'to honour and favour' his illegitimate daughter Margarita (although 'he is not obliged to do more for her, unless he wants to'), but although it covered forty-nine pages, his new will did not mention two other surviving illegitimate children: Tadea, then a nun living in Rome, and Gerónimo (later Don John of Austria). Instead, that same day the emperor wrote and signed a separate codicil about the latter – with the proviso that 'No one is to open this document except the prince' (or, should Philip predecease him, Don Carlos). Charles did not even reveal the boy's whereabouts, telling his son (or grandson) that 'if you do not know where this Gerónimo is', one of his aides would tell all. Charles preferred that the boy 'should become a member of one of the strict religious Orders', but 'if he prefers a secular life and lifestyle, I desire and require that he should receive a regular income of 20,000 or 30,000 ducats a year', equivalent to the income of a count or a marquis.[88] This generous settlement saddled Philip with yet another financial obligation – to say nothing of a half-brother who would serve as a permanent reminder of his father's incontinence at age forty-six with a teenage domestic servant. The emperor's failure to impart this information to Philip in person showed great moral cowardice. Charles also sent his son 'a document in Latin, together with my last will, by which I bequeath him all my property and lordships so that he can administer and treat them as his own from the date thereon'.[89]

THE EMPEROR'S LAST CAMPAIGN

As with his previous testaments and codicils, Charles acted through fear of imminent death – this time on campaign. According to the English ambassador at the imperial court, writing on 4 June (two days before Charles signed his testament): 'Th'emperor is in very good estate of body, and is able to walke two or three howres in the daye', while a week later 'he was not more lustye these foure years then he is at this present' – so 'lusty' that when he 'tried on his armour [he] found that the corselet and a jerkin of buckskin which he wears under it were tighter for him than usual, by three fingers breadth, so he is stouter than he was'. Of course, Charles still complained about his health. He began an audience with the Florentine ambassador on 9 June 'by telling me about his indispositions, and in particular about the pain that his haemorrhoids have given and still give him. Then, suddenly remembering that the same ailment had given me a lot of trouble in the past, and since it seemed to him that I now looked well he wanted me to share some details.' Charles overcame this obstacle, too: now 'he is hable to arme himself, and ys on horssebacke in his parke some tyme three howres togither'.[90]

Charles had not planned to fight another campaign, but Henry II invaded the Netherlands in person and captured the newly constructed fortress of Mariembourg, 'which is extremely dangerous at the present time, because it is a place from which he can easily invade the duchy of Brabant. There is no fortress here that could stop him,' Charles informed his son. Nevertheless, although his field army was inferior to the French, the emperor decided to take personal command – and he expected Philip to join him. 'Make plans to come here,' he wrote, adding coldly: 'Once you have celebrated and (with God's blessing) consummated your marriage with the queen [Mary Tudor], leave her after six or eight days.'[91]

On 7 July 1554 the emperor left Brussels in his open litter, accompanied by his leading nobles and cheered on by the citizens. 'As he left, he said that if the French wanted to fight, he was willing to finish the war' in a single stroke. In this, and in assuming personal command of his army, the emperor defied 'his Counsell and all other men', who had tried to dissuade him by stressing 'the puissance of his ennemye, the unhablenes as yet of his army to encounter with them, the daunger of their chopping of ties between him and this towne [Brussels], the hazards of himself, his estate, and of all these countries' should he meet with defeat. 'Yett was ther no remedy, butt forth [Charles] wolde, and commanded them they shulde march *sans plus replique*.' The English ambassador, Sir John Mason, feared the worst, recalling that Charles's 'headynes hath often putt him to greate hinderance, specially once by land att Metz, and another tyme by sea att Argell [Algiers]'. He warned that 'this enterprise is more daungerous than them both'.[92]

Initially, the ambassador's pessimism seemed justified. Charles could not prevent the French from capturing several places 'buylded altogether *à l'antiqua*, without any kynde of such defenses as are requisyte for the wars of nowe a dayes' – including Binche, where they burned Marie's sumptuous palace to the ground.[93] Shortly afterwards some of his troops mutinied, but Charles turned the tide by boldly riding towards them. 'According to his custom, he shook hands with all the German colonels and captains, and saluted all the rest by bowing his head.' Then he approached the mutineers, listening attentively to their complaints, after which he told them:

> My soldiers, approaching me in such a disorderly fashion is not appro-
> priate, because it dishonours you, your captains, and your nation, and it
> does me little credit. I am displeased that you have been wronged, but
> whenever something similar happens in future let me know through
> your colonel or your captains. I will never fail to render justice. I will be
> a good emperor and a good king to you. As for the wrong that you claim
> has been done to you, I will take steps to find out what happened and I
> shall not fail to punish those who erred.

'At this, the mutineers returned to their duties', and Charles 'slept in the camp' among his troops 'and rode around taking care of everything'. At a general muster of his army 'he appeared on horseback in full armour, raising everyone's spirits'; and according to one of the cavalry troopers 'the shouts of "Long live the emperor" lasted for an hour and were so loud that the king of France must have heard them in his camp'. When rumours of a French surprise attack circulated, 'His Majesty drew his army up in battle order and rode up and down the ranks, preceded by a large red banner with the kettle-drums beating.'[94]

Thanks to the money brought by his son's fleet to provision and reinforce his army, Charles gained the advantage and forced the French to retreat from Binche, and he pursued them with 'soch celerytie' that he 'marched in one day xxj myles; yet coulde he never overtake them'. On 4 August the frus-trated emperor held a council of war to decide 'what can be done with our army in the present state of affairs; and we decided to invade France and wreak the same destruction that they have done here'. But where? After discussing several alternative targets, Charles admitted weakly to his son, 'we cannot make a decision because everything depends on what our enemies will do'. The only point on which he and his councillors agreed was that now 'under no circumstances' should Philip leave England and join his father, because 'you are more likely to lose reputation than to gain it . . . and it is so important to gain it in your first campaign, when you want to impress the world'. He therefore granted his son permission to remain more than 'six or eight days' to enjoy the company of his new bride.[95]

A week later the French laid siege to Renty, another town that lacked 'such defenses as are requisyte for the wars of nowe a dayes', in the hope that Charles would risk a battle to relieve it. Instead he skilfully advanced without exposing his troops to attack, while Renty continued to resist, and on 14 August, Henry reluctantly withdrew 'under cover of night, and of a thick mist the following morning' with 'great loss of reputation because they had to abandon their attack [on Renty] and dared not await something that they have so often boasted that they sought', namely a battle. The retreat ended only after they had re-entered France.[96]

Mason had no doubt about the significance of this victory, and of Charles's personal role in achieving it. 'Th'emperor, in thies 9 or 10 daies followinge of his ennemye, hath shewed a greate courage and no lesse skillfulness in the warr; but muche more notablye', in seeking out and challenging the main French army 'against th'advice and perswasion of the substance of all his captains, which, yf he had not done', the Netherlands would have been ravaged on a scale 'as woulde longe after have been remembred. By his onlye wysdome and unconquered courage' he had decisively repulsed his enemies. By contrast, the French campaign had achieved nothing beyond 'the burninge and spoylinge of [all] sorts of poure people, which was easye to be done and as easy to be revenged'.[97]

Charles, as usual, attributed the favourable outcome to divine intervention. On 15 August, the day after the French withdrew, he wrote to his son (still in England): 'Son, God has guided this as He has been accustomed to do with my affairs. If there has been error it is mine, but still He has remedied it better than we had hoped.' His letter that same day to the duke of Alba (also in England, advising Philip) was less optimistic: 'Duke: You can imagine how I feel . . . Although some said yesterday that we should retreat, which would have involved great risks, instead He caused the enemy to retreat. Moreover Renty, which we feared was lost, has been saved.' But now, Charles declared, his fighting days were over: 'Although at the moment I enjoy better health than I expected, I am not strong enough to withstand the sort of health setbacks I suffered last year and this.' He likewise told Marie that 'I am in such a state that I fear falling to pieces', so that 'I need to avoid being in the field as much as possible'.[98] Two days later he left his army for the last time, and two weeks later he informed Philip that since 'it has pleased God to bring matters to a satisfactory conclusion, regaining some of the reputation that had been lost', and since Philip now 'is now so close' he wanted his son to take over from him. Charles hoped that the transfer of power could take place in January 1555, when 'we can spend some time together and enjoy ourselves', preferably with Mary, 'wherever you like. Then, after giving you my blessing, I will leave you and continue my journey' back to Spain.[99] It all sounded too good to be true. And it was.

SIXTEEN

RESTLESS RETIREMENT, 1555–8

THE DIARCHY

On 9 October 1554, Charles returned to Brussels, once again victorious. He passed 'through the Greate Streate in his lictier', according to Sir John Mason, 'to no small comfort of the beholders to see him after so greate travaile in so good a plight'. He was soon well enough to go hunting again, and at an audience a month later Mason 'found him sitting very cheerfully at a table. His face, that was wont to be somewhat more full than naturally it ought to be, is now come to the very natural; his colour much amended; his arms at commandment . . . He was so lively as I have not of long seen the like lustiness in him'. It did not last. At the end of November, a minister lamented that 'so many poor people are complaining in the streets that they await the emperor's signature, something that His Majesty could deal with in little more than an hour'; but at an audience on Christmas Eve, Mason again found the emperor 'in right good estate and in such disposition as, to be looked upon, he was not these ten years better'. Charles then 'entered into a great discourse of the difference between governing with rigour and governing in such sort as the prince and his subjects *can understand and appreciate each other*'.[1]

Charles did not feel that his son understood this difference. Shortly after Philip arrived in England, a courtier reported that the prince 'keeps the queen happy and knows how to overlook her defects . . . As for his dealings with the noblemen here, even they admit that no king of England has ever gained the goodwill of everyone so quickly.' In Brussels, Secretary of State Eraso received this news 'in praise of our boss' and immediately shared it with Charles, who listened 'with immense pleasure and gave many thanks to God for all His favours' – before adding spitefully 'The king has obviously changed a lot!'[2] Charles's confidence in his son's social and political skills sank so low that in September he sent Eraso to England with instructions to tell Philip that although 'I never cease to thank God that the queen is so happy and satisfied', he had heard complaints that his son seldom consulted his English subjects, and 'I hear they are dissatisfied because they see Spaniards coming and going so often [to see you].'[3]

Such criticisms only abated after Mary Tudor announced she was pregnant and insisted that her husband must stay to provide support as her confinement approached. Now Charles plied Ambassador Mason with blunt questions such as 'How goeth my daughter's belly forward?' – to which he replied that the queen would say nothing until she was sure, but volunteered that 'her garments wax very straight [tight]. "I never doubted," quoth [the emperor], "of the matter but that God, that for her had wrought so many miracles, would make the same perfect by assisting of nature to his good and most desired work. And I warrant it shall be," quoth he, "a man child". Mason affirmed that any healthy child would be a boon because 'by that shall we at the least come to some certainty to whom God shall appoint, by succession, the government of our estate'. By contrast, he warned Charles, if the queen should die 'without fruit, the realm were as good also to die. "Doubt not," quoth he: "God will provide both with fruit and otherwise." '[4]

Throughout the pregnancy, Philip sent a stream of orders to his ministers in Spain and Italy – and since Charles did the same (according to the Venetian ambassador in Brussels) 'all persons who have any business to transact complain that they can obtain no decisions from the ministers either of the emperor or of the king', because no one knew whom to obey.[5] Above all, Philip sought to outmanoeuvre his father on the most important policy issue: ending the war with France. In this he worked closely with Reginald Pole, the Cardinal of England, empowered by Julius III to promote peace throughout Christendom as well as to reconcile England with Rome. In November 1554, Philip informed his father that (thanks to Pole's efforts) a French envoy had just arrived in London with a request that England should serve as mediator in the conflict between Henry II and Charles. Claiming (implausibly) that 'the queen and I did not have time to consult Your Majesty', they accepted. Construction began at once on a special conference centre near Calais, 'with a separate tent containing rich tapestries for each nation in the middle of a field' where delegates of the two sides met with Pole, representing the pope, and with English ministers representing Philip and Mary.[6]

Charles reluctantly declared himself willing to join the talks – albeit insisting that he had not entered the war through 'anny desyre he had to enlarge his lymitts, which God had given him large enough, but for the defence of that was naturally his lymitts' – but they had made little progress when the death of Julius in March 1555 fatally compromised the peace initiative.[7] Two months later Gian Pietro Caraffa became pope and took the name Paul IV. The new pontiff – an open enemy not only of Charles, whose government of his native Naples he considered corrupt and tyrannical, but also of Pole, whom he considered soft on heresy – boasted that the Habsburgs' 'possessions are like an old house which, when a simple stone is removed, falls to pieces; when we here in Italy give him a slight blow, everything will be laid in ruins'. News of Paul's election arrived at the peace conference on 2 June, and four days later the French delegation departed. The pope now began to plan an attack on Charles by France and several other hostile Italian states, assisted by the Ottoman fleet.[8]

THE LONG GOODBYE

In Brussels, Charles gave few audiences and tried to avoid handling business. When in May 1555 the Florentine ambassador presented him with a letter from Duke Cosimo, the emperor told him that 'since it was almost dinner time, and since the letter contained vexing matters, he would take it away with him: tomorrow he would read a summary of it and then decide what to do.' Although, according to a French visitor, Charles still 'retained knowledge and authority in public affairs', he relied almost entirely on Perrenot, 'who conveys his advice to his son and his council'.[9]

Perrenot could not help his master withstand the cold. Despite the presence of several stoves, the emperor's gout intensified as temperatures fell, leaving him 'very yll trobled' throughout the winter. On 1 April 1555 he received Mason for an audience 'lying in bed', and halfway through 'he pawsed, being (as shoud seme) somewhat weary of speaking'. A few days later, while bidding farewell to Ferrante Gonzaga, who had served him for a quarter-century, he burst into tears and confided that his ailments made him 'weary of this world, showing his hands crippled with gout, saying this was the worst time of his life'. He had rallied somewhat by St George's Day (23 April), when 'very sollemply in his chambre of presence' he celebrated his membership of the Order of the Garter, reflecting on 'the ancientie of th'order, and the long tyme that he had enioyed the same; so as nowe he said he was the most ancyent thereof, having bene a knight thereof the space at the leaste of 44 yeres.' Mason predicted that 'with this seasonnable weather ... he is lyke dailie to growe to more perfeccion of health and more.'[10]

This proved too optimistic. A visitor from Portugal reported that the emperor's 'teeth look awful, because they are black'; while Fray Cipriano de

Huerga, a professor at the Universidad Complutense at Alcalá, asked rhetorically 'Who has changed our emperor so much that we scarcely recognize him?', adding: 'Who has turned his hair white before its time? Who caused all those premature wrinkles and made his lively eyes sad? Who removed the flesh from around his teeth and paralyzed his legs and hands with gout?' Fray Cipriano had no doubt: the emperor's exhaustion stemmed from 'the desire to free God's flock in Germany, using steel and fire as well as the balm of God's word'.[11]

While Charles anxiously awaited the birth of his English grandchild, after which Philip could cross the Channel and join him, he occasionally rode around the royal park on a mule (he could no longer manage a horse) and inspected the exotic animals in the adjacent zoo, as he had done as a boy. He rarely talked to anyone except for Perrenot, his sisters Marie and Eleanor, and his household servants. Nevertheless, two thorny problems were resolved that spring. In Spain his mother Queen Joanna died in April 1555 at the age of seventy-five. Although Charles vowed to wear mourning in her memory for the rest of his life, now at last he became sole ruler of Spain and Sicily, and Philip would not have to share his title as envisaged in the emperor's last will.[12] In Germany, the death of Maurice of Saxony from wounds reduced the political temperature and facilitated a settlement of outstanding religious divisions. Charles, however, wanted no part in this process. In 1552 he had reluctantly approved toleration for Lutherans until the next meeting of the imperial Diet; now he informed Ferdinand that although 'God knows that the zeal and affection I bear towards the Holy Roman Empire and the German Nation, as well as the care I take to support you and uphold our house of Austria . . . make me want to find the remedy for the troubles of Germany and get involved myself', nevertheless he had many 'scruples regarding the religious settlement'. He therefore empowered his brother to convene another imperial Diet in Augsburg 'as if I were in Spain, not invoking my name or my specific authority'; and on hearing that the Diet planned to make toleration for Lutherans permanent, Charles cited 'my ongoing reluctance to become more involved in this religious question' and delegated a final decision 'to you and your ministers who are on the spot'. On 25 September 1555, Ferdinand signed the Religious Peace of Augsburg, which recognized the right of individual German rulers to practise either Catholicism or Lutheranism legally, and to impose it on their vassals (the principle later known as 'cuius regio, eius religio'); to renounce the use of force to gain their goals in matters of faith; and to permit free transit to any subjects who wished to emigrate on religious grounds.[13]

By then it had become clear that, despite her protestations to the contrary, Mary Tudor was not pregnant. Philip now left England and returned to Brussels on 8 September, riding straight to the imperial cottage where his father 'embraced and kissed him so affectionately that the tears came to his eyes'. They had not seen each other for four years. Charles 'instructed all his ministers to inform [Philip] of all public affairs transacted since he left Augsburg [in 1551] down to the present'; and thereafter the two monarchs spent every 'morning and afternoon together, two hours at a time', sometimes sitting at a table 'with a tray of documents before them' as they took care of business. Two weeks later, Charles signed a proclamation announcing that he would cede all his territories in the Netherlands to Philip, and ordering the representative assemblies of each province to choose 'a good number of deputies' to gather in Brussels and witness the transfer of power.[14]

Ominously for the future, the emperor had to delay the ceremony because two provinces refused to send deputies, on the grounds that a valid transfer of sovereignty could only take place within their borders, while two more simply failed to send anyone; but eventually about 1,000 members of the Habsburg Netherlands elite gathered in Brussels to participate in the largest and most diverse gathering of the States-General to that date. Before addressing the assembly, Charles convened the Knights of the Golden Fleece for the last time, informing them of his intention to cede to his son not only his possessions but also his position as Chief and Sovereign of the Order. He invited the knights to transfer their obedience to Philip, and enjoined his son always to consult them and follow their counsel.[15]

On Friday 25 October 1555, at 2.30 p.m., Charles mounted his mule and rode from his cottage to the Brussels palace. An hour later he walked slowly into the great hall for the last time, supported by a cane on one side and by Prince William of Orange on the other, followed by Marie, Philip and the Knights of the Golden Fleece. He wore 'a doublet of simple black cloth, the biretta worn by lawyers, and the double insignia of the Golden Fleece'. As a sign of respect, 'the deputies all rose to their feet as the royal party entered' and then a councillor explained why the emperor had decided to abdicate and retire to Spain. After one of the delegates had made a gracious reply, Charles stood up unsteadily, 'and after collecting his thoughts', he 'put on his glasses and looked at a piece of paper that he held in his hand, on which he had written seven pages'.[16] He then addressed his subjects. With a fine sense of history, he began by observing that 'several of you will remember how, forty years ago on the eve of the Epiphany, it pleased the emperor [Maximilian] my grandfather to emancipate me, when I was only fifteen, and that it happened in the same place and almost at the same time as I am speaking to you now'. Next he provided a chronology of all his travels since then:

> Nine voyages to Germany, six to Spain, seven to Italy, ten to the Netherlands, four to France (in peace as well as in war), two to England and two to Africa, which make forty in all . . . To do this, I was compelled to cross the Mediterranean eight times and the Atlantic three times, not counting the journey that I plan to make next, with God's blessing, which would make four.

Next Charles listed his campaigns 'for the defence of these states and of my other realms', as well as 'for the preservation of the Empire and the benefit of religion'. But now, 'not feeling in himself the vigour which the government of so many states required, and knowing that his son was capable of supporting weighty duties, he wished to give the remainder of his own life to the service of God, and to cede these states, as he had done and would do with the rest, to his son'. At this point 'his heart seemed overwhelmed by grief, and his sobs prevented him from speaking, while tears poured down his cheeks' – perhaps, Mason thought, 'provoked by seing the hole company to doo the lyke before [him], being in myne opynion not one man in the hole assemblee' that during 'his oration poured not owte habondantly teares'. Eventually, 'having recovered his breath somewhat, he put on his glasses again and, looking at the notes in his hand he said: "My sight and my memory are no longer what they used to be, and increasingly I feel too weak and feeble to undertake the tasks required to protect you and this country. That is the main reason why I have decided to return to Spain – not so that I can live longer, because that is in God's hands."' Charles concluded by urging everyone present to uphold the Catholic faith as the sole religion – 'what inconvenience might rise by swarving [deviating] therin, he referred them to learne at their neighbours handes' (that is, from the religious strife in Germany) – and to obey his son 'as theire naturall seigneur'.[17]

Standing up to speak for over half an hour had left the emperor exhausted, and as he collapsed into his seat Philip rose and (in Spanish) begged his father to stay and govern a little longer so that he might 'learne of him by experience soch qualetyes as to soch a gouvernment are most necessary'. Then he too sat down, and turning to the assembly spoke the only words of French he is known to have uttered: 'Gentlemen, although I can understand French adequately, I am not yet fluent enough to speak it to you. You will hear from the bishop of Arras [Perrenot] what I want to say.'[18] Philip's failure to learn the languages of his subjects – and his decision to sit while addressing them, instead of standing as Burgundian protocol demanded – caused needless disappointment, which Perrenot did his best to dispel, stressing at length that the king had not wanted his father to abdicate and assuring the audience that Philip would remain in northern Europe as long as required to secure peace and prosperity. Thereafter, like his father, he would return whenever needed (a wise promise that the king would not keep). The ceremony ended with the reading of Charles's formal proclamation transferring all his authority in the Netherlands to his son, ending: 'We thus override, with our plenary and absolute power, all laws, constitutions, and customs that might contradict or impede it, because such is our pleasure.' The emperor then ordered that his personal seals be broken, just as those of Margaret and Maximilian had been broken during his emancipation in that same room forty years before; and with that, 'between six and seven o'clock this important ceremony ended, and the emperor went immediately through the park to his cottage' (Pl. 32).[19]

Despite all the pomp and emotion, this ceremony transferred only the emperor's territories and titles in the Low Countries. He intended to travel back to Spain before ceding his rights over Castile and Aragon and their overseas dependencies (the Americas, Sardinia and Sicily), but in November 'the emperor had such an increase of gout' that 'he was unable to feed himself with his own hands' and 'keeps his bed from fever'. The following month, although all the transfer documents had been prepared, Charles could not sign them, 'the emperor's hand being bandaged'.[20] At last, on New Year's Day 1556, Charles rallied. He confessed and took communion, and two weeks later he summoned his son and a small group of courtiers to his cottage, where he 'spoke for nearly an hour':

Saying first that he thanked God that he at last found himself in a condition to fulfil his obligations, to him and to his vassals, to make his renunciations ... [H]e knew there had been much murmuring in many quarters because there had been so long a delay in carrying his intentions into effect; but that still, in executing his determination, he would rather be blamed for slowness than for doing anything with inconsiderate haste ... Then, as when he abdicated the sovereignty of these provinces, he recounted in the same order and one by one all the expeditions and enterprises which he had undertaken in the course of his life, showing how all of them had been prompted rather by necessity than by inclination, and recommended to the king his faithful and valiant vassals, exhorting him to do them justice and to honour them according to their deserts.[21]

He also gave his son a box containing 'many testaments in both Latin and Castilian and many instructions' and then he signed deeds of abdication for Castile and its overseas possessions, next for the Crown of Aragon, and finally for Sicily. Charles also signed a renunciation of his imperial title, but at Ferdinand's request he did not make it public. Instead he appointed Philip imperial vicar-general in Italy.[22]

Charles's spirits continued to revive. Three days after this abdication ceremony, Ambassador Federico Badoer of Venice reported that he 'seemed more cheerful than for a long while, saying several times that he thanked God, who, after the renunciation of all his states, caused him to experience the mental repose which he had indeed hoped for' and 'he said several jocose things to his chamberlains, asking how they would address him for the future', concluding that once he had ceased to be emperor 'he was content to be called Don Carlos de Austria'. He likewise assured his nephew (and son-in-law) Maximilian that 'I feel much better and very happy now that I have now renounced' all his titles.[23] In March 1556, Badoer found the emperor 'in very good bodily health, and more cheerful in his eyes and movements than I had ever seen him before'. He was also more loquacious. Charles told him:

'As to my renunciation of power, I made that of my own free will, and in pursuance of a long-cherished desire, and I am well pleased with it; for I am enfeebled both by age and illness, and it was time that my son should no longer postpone the cares of government. I was never at any time solicitous to bear these burdens, and to this step I have been long looking forward. Men may now see how far that has been true which has been said by many, that I wished to make myself monarch of the world. Such a thought, I assure you, never came into my mind, nor would it, had the thing been attainable even by words instead of deeds.' He then held up his hands crippled by gout, and, after a pause, proceeded: 'Now I have no thought but how to pass my remnant of life as free from care and pain as I can; and I desire to retire to some place where I may finish it in the service of God.'[24]

A French delegation led by Admiral Gaspard de Coligny, sent to ratify the truce recently concluded between the belligerent monarchs, also left a vivid pen-portrait of Charles at this time. Initially, their mission did not go well because both sides deliberately insulted the other. Coligny's entourage tactlessly included the sons of the late Cesare Fregoso (chapter 11), while Philip decorated the great hall of the Brussels palace where he received them with Bernard van Orley's tapestries celebrating the defeat of the French at Pavia, 'the most monumental panoramic landscape conceived in the sixteenth century' (and thus impossible to ignore), which 'showed the story of the capture of the late, great King Francis' (see Pl. 14). The French delegates probably felt relief when they entered Charles's cottage, where the emperor received them seated, because of his gout, dressed simply 'in the short knee-length tunic worn by citizens, made of Florence serge, a black German-style doublet, wearing a hat' (Pl. 33). Admiral Coligny began by delivering a personal letter from Henry II, but since it was 'sealed more tightly than normal letters', Charles's arthritic fingers could not open it and he reluctantly handed it to Perrenot. He then looked up, and 'with a gracious smile' said to Coligny, 'What would you say about me, my Lord Admiral? Do I seem like a bold knight ready to joust and break a lance when I can scarcely open a letter?' But then the insults resumed. Charles commented that 'I have heard that your king has already begun to go grey', adding that 'it seems only a few days since he was in Spain as a young prince, a boy without a trace of a beard' – a tactless and unnecessary reference to Henry's incarceration in Pedraza de la Sierra. Next, catching sight of the famous French jester, Brusquet, Charles asked 'Do you remember the Battle of the Spurs?' (the rout of a French army at Guinegate in 1514) – but this time he miscalculated. 'Why yes, sire,' Brusquet shot back, 'I remember it well: that was the time you acquired those beautiful rubies and carbuncles that you have hidden in your fingers' – a reference to Charles's crippled hands. At this 'everyone else present burst out laughing, and then the emperor said: "I shall be sure to remember a lesson I have learned from you: never make fun of anyone who appears to be a Fool." '[25]

Perhaps this sparring match improved Charles's spirits, because just afterwards the Florentine ambassador reported that 'everyone who sees His Majesty says that he looks better than he has for the past four years, with very lively eyes and a great sense of humour'. In June 1556, Mason wrote that 'Th'emperour rydith upon a mulle so lustely as thies 7 yeres he shewid not so great a cheare'.[26] Charles nevertheless continued to postpone his travel plans: first, he claimed that he lacked the money to pay the salary arrears of the members of his household who would remain in the Netherlands; next he claimed that the weather in the Channel and North Sea would be too dangerous; then rumours arrived that Pope Paul planned to declare both Charles and his brother deposed because in the recent Diet the latter 'had agreed that Germany could live according to the [Lutheran] Augsburg Confession, and the emperor had approved'. On hearing this, Charles 'gave vent to the most violent rage' and 'every day, without awaiting the hour assigned for the meeting' summoned the council of state to assemble 'in his presence, his whole discourse being about papal matters, always in a very angry tone', telling his ministers that '"Such and such must be done" [*bisogna far così e così*], always adding an illustration derived from what has happened to himself with former popes and how he had conducted himself with them' – ominous comparisons, since his troops had sacked Rome.[27]

Ferdinand and Maximilian also managed to delay Charles's departure. In November 1555 he had written that it 'would be a great consolation for me' to see them both in Brussels 'and discuss business before I set out on my voyage to Spain'. Ferdinand declined outright – the brothers would never meet again – and although Maximilian and María accepted the invitation, lack of money delayed their journey and they did not reach Brussels until 18 July 1556.[28] Over the next few days they met with Charles several times to discuss his abdication as emperor, persuading him to permit Ferdinand to choose the best time and place to convene the Electors in order to recognize his succession. Until then, Charles would continue to reign, though not to rule, as emperor. The next day he left Brussels and 'was seen to weep, turning round several times as he went, to look back on the familiar walls which he was leaving behind for ever'.[29]

Charles did not travel alone. Although he had reduced his household from over 750 to only 150, paying off many and transferring others to the service of his son or his brother, his two sisters had decided to accompany him. Eleanor wanted above all things to meet her daughter, María, whom she had not seen since she left Portugal over thirty years before: she therefore wished to return to Spain ('which, according to her, she likes better than the Netherlands'). Marie of Hungary had grown close to her older sister during the decade they had spent together in the Netherlands, and she feared that when Eleanor and Charles left 'I would find myself alone in a land that I would have to get to know afresh, living in a very different style to the one to which I am accustomed'. Although she had never been to Spain, Marie therefore sought and received permission to accompany her brother and sister.[30] In August all three went to Ghent where Charles took his leave of Philip and his Netherlands ministers, and granted a final audience to selected foreign diplomats, starting with the Florentine envoy. Although the emperor 'spoke with great difficulty, so that he could scarcely articulate the words', he declared: 'Ambassador: my departure is unavoidable. You can be certain that if the king my son cannot solve the problems of the world, I would not be able to do so if I stayed here.' He attributed all these 'problems' to the 'hypocrisy and wickedness of the pope', adding smugly (but wrongly) that 'since the pope is old, he cannot live much longer'.[31]

The imperial entourage travelled from Ghent by litter and barge to Flushing in Zealand, where a fleet of over fifty vessels awaited them. The emperor emerged from his barge 'supported under both arms', and some spectators averred that 'you never saw a prince with a face so pale, so thin and weak, his hands crippled, his voice weak and broken: it seemed that only his spirit remained.' Just as on his first journey to Spain four decades earlier, Charles toured Walcheren (this time in a small cart) as he waited for a favourable wind. He boarded his flagship on 13 September, entering a special cabin seventeen feet square, followed by twenty courtiers each of whom had their own cabin (among them Guillaume van Male, 'who reads a variety of things to him', and Janello Torriani, 'with the clocks he made for him'); but another storm soon forced them back. This news led Philip to ride to Zealand, where he managed to 'talk for an hour and a half' with his father before 'a skiff took him back to Flushing'. On 17 September the imperial fleet made sail again, and this time the wind carried it into the North Sea. Charles would never see his son, or his homeland, again.[32]

THE LAST JOURNEY

According to the pope, Charles's decision to retire to the Jeronimite monastery of Yuste in Spain's Gredos mountains was 'the strangest thing that has ever been seen'; and the emperor himself provided three distinct narratives of when and how he made up his mind on the subject. During a visit to Yuste by his former courtier, Francisco de Borja, the emperor asked him:

'Do you remember what I told you at Monzón in 1542, that I would
   retire and do exactly what I have done?'
'I remember very well, Sire,' Father Francisco replied.
'Well you can be sure,' said the emperor, 'that I have told no one else
   except you and so-and-so', naming a prominent gentleman.

Fray José de Sigüenza, historian of the Jeronimite Order, repeated this story, adding that Charles not only took the decision to retire in 1542 but also determined the location, sending some 'learned and prudent men to survey the buildings, location, aspect and layout of the Jeronimite monastery at Yuste, and they brought him a detailed account of everything'.[33]

In September 1554, in a confidential message to his son, Charles offered some alternative facts. He confirmed that 'I decided to retire and withdraw several years ago, and was only waiting until you had increased in age and in experience of public affairs . . . and I thought I could do so this year, as soon as you had arrived [in northern Europe] and got married, and for that reason I ordered the construction of an apartment at the monastery of Yuste.' Then the outbreak of war with France caused a postponement, but now 'I recognize that I cannot do what my conscience tells me, and what my subjects and vassals require of me', and so had resolved to abdicate. Eighteen months later, just before leaving Brussels, 'placing his hand on his breast', Charles provided a few more details in an audience for the Venetian ambassador: 'Ever since my victories over the duke of Saxony and the landgrave of Hesse [in 1547] I have been thinking of making this renunciation.' He claimed that he had started to draw up the necessary documents, and always carried them round with him, but did nothing further until 1554, when 'I was in the field at Renty and had determined to give battle to the king of France'. He realized then that:

> If the battle had taken place, and I had by evil fortune lost it, as might well have happened seeing the inferiority of my forces to those of the king, I would have been either slain or made prisoner, there being no hope of escape from one or other of these chances. [T]hen, had I been slain, my son would have succeeded as heir to all my states; and, if I had remained in my enemies' hands, I was anxious that [Philip] should not be put to the expense of ransoming me as a sovereign, but merely as a private gentleman.[34]

Early in 1558, Charles gave a Portuguese ambassador who visited Yuste yet another account of his decision to retire to a monastery. He repeated that he gave it serious thought 'after the end of the German war' in 1547, 'admitting that he should have done it then because he would not have lost reputation thereby, unlike the present time because of subsequent events'; but he claimed that he had first considered abdicating after his victorious Tunis campaign in 1535, although he did nothing then because his son was too young.[35]

Each of these three narratives is plausible – indeed, given Charles's familiarity with *The resolute knight*, who also planned to retire to a monastery, and given his grandfather Maximilian's desire to abdicate, the emperor may have decided even earlier to lay down his burden: one contemporary document claimed that 'he had planned to do this since his childhood'.[36] Whatever his previous thoughts and intentions, however, he did nothing until June 1553, when he signed a warrant to pay the General of the Jeronimite Order 3,000 ducats 'to be distributed on certain things that we have commanded'. A holograph note to his son explained that this payment was specifically 'for the construction of a house next to the monastery of Yuste suitable for me to live there as a private person [persona particular] with only essential servants and officials'.[37] The emperor also ordered his son to inspect the monastery in person. Philip complied in May 1554 and gave his approval; and immediately afterwards 'materials began to arrive for the apartments that His Majesty ordered at Yuste'. The imperial architect Luis de Vega visited the site and drew up plans that showed how 'there is a large room inside the monastery that serves as a dormitory for the novices. If it is divided up in the manner shown, we could create a sitting room and bedroom, and from the bed one would see the principal altar' in the church. The emperor approved.[38]

Charles also assembled the items he planned to take with him. In 1551 he summoned Titian to join him in Augsburg, where he commissioned an enormous painting entitled *The Trinity* (later known as *The Last Judgement*), which, according to the painter, Charles 'always intended to hang behind the altar of a monastery where he would spend his last days'. In the inventory of the paintings selected for his last journey, *The Trinity* headed the list (Pl. 34).[39] Charles commissioned other paintings, and copies of paintings, from Netherlands artists: in 1555 he paid Jan Vermeyen to paint a '*Man of sorrows* just like the one done by Titian', duly delivered to his chamberlain, where it joined twenty-four other religious paintings, and portraits of his favourite relatives – the empress and Philip (painted by Titian), his daughter-in-law Mary Tudor (painted by Antonio Moro: or, as the imperial inventory improbably claimed '*By Thomas More*'), the children of María and Maximilian – and several portraits of himself at various ages.[40]

The inventory of 'silver and gilded items, and other goods' that would accompany Charles on his journey began with the contents of his private chapel: a chalice and other essentials for celebrating Mass, vestments for the priests, frontals for the altar, missals and service books, crosses and crucifixes (including 'a gilded cross with a crucifix, with Our Lady and St John on each side, and in the middle of the foot of the crucifix the arms of His Majesty'). Next came household items, ranging from 'two small silver vases for His Majesty's chamber, used for flowers' to 'a silver urinal [*ung pispot* d'argent]'; other gold and silverware used by his barbers, his apothecaries, his cooks, and those who served his meals; and a list of the clocks Charles wished to take with him, including the 'Microcosm' designed by Torriani, two other large clocks (one of them showing all twenty-four hours), and 'three small round portable clocks'.[41]

As in 1517, when he first travelled to Spain, Charles selected some volumes from his library to accompany him on the journey, but this time they were mostly printed, not manuscript: French and Spanish editions of *The resolute knight*; the *Commentaries* by both Julius Caesar and Luis de Ávila (perhaps to help him as he revised his *Memoirs*); Peter Apian's enormous *Astronomicum Caesareum*; various large maps and city views (often of places he had visited) to hang on the walls; and missals, psalters and Bibles (perhaps including one in French), and books of devotion and consolation, mostly about preparing for death. He took with him few illuminated manuscripts besides the 'Statutes of the Order of the Golden Fleece', illustrated by Simon Bening and others between 1531 and 1547, which showed the armorial bearings of 214 knights, past and present. In all he took with him fifty volumes, packed in a single box.[42]

Charles also spent many hours in spiritual preparation. In January 1556 he informed his nephew Maximilian that the renunciation of all his titles left him 'free to search and purge my conscience'; and according to a monk at Yuste, 'for about a year before he left the Netherlands and came to Spain, he gathered together five learned theologians and lawyers with whom he shared all his affairs, and all his remaining doubts and scruples'. Charles himself confirmed this. Not long after he arrived in Spain, Fray Juan Reglá, the Jeronimite whom he had chosen as his confessor, protested ' "Sire, I do not feel adequate, nor do I have the necessary gifts required to serve you" ... To this His Majesty replied: "Look, Friar Juan, you have nothing to fear. I spent a whole year with five learned men in the Netherlands so my conscience is clear: all that remains now is matters that arise each day." On hearing this, Fray Juan dropped his reservations.'[43]

In 1556, as in 1517, Charles's arrival took many in Spain by surprise. When the news reached Yuste, the General of the Jeronimites 'was delighted, because it refuted many doubters who considered Your Majesty's coming too good to be true'. The central government had apparently believed the doubters, because despite letters from Philip on 23 July and 11 August confirming that the emperor would embark 'with the first good weather', when he landed at Laredo on 28 September he found nothing ready and virtually no one to receive him. 'His Majesty is very annoyed by the oversight, since so many necessary items are not available,' wrote his secretary, Martín de Gaztelú: no 'cleric to say Mass for him', no doctors, and 'no official of the postal service'. Above all, 'no one has written him a letter, or sent to see how he is doing', all of which made Charles 'say some very opprobrious words'.[44] To make matters worse, it rained continually. When Luis Quijada, who would head the emperor's household, reached Laredo on 5 October he found everyone 'fed up and disillusioned, not knowing what would become of them'. Given the 'bad roads and worse quarters', and the difficulty of finding provisions through lands that seldom produced surpluses, Quijada divided the royal entourage so that 'I alone travelled beside His Majesty' in his litter, with only 'a magistrate and five guards'. They travelled one day's journey ahead of the rest, and (he grumbled) 'I am ashamed to see how few we are', adding that 'when I see how many law officers accompany us, it looks as if he and I are travelling while under arrest'.[45] Eventually on 21 October the emperor entered Valladolid, where he met for the first time his grandson and namesake Don Carlos, now aged eleven.

Charles's last voyage to Spain resembled his first in another way: critical events occurred elsewhere while he was on the move. In July 1556, before the emperor left Brussels, the pope arrested the imperial postmaster in Rome, tortured him and seized his mail. Two months later, as Charles sailed through the English Channel, Paul IV delivered a tirade about the perfidy of the House of Austria and its supporters, recalling how the military assistance provided by his predecessor Paul III had 'rendered the emperor master of Germany' and how, 'to reward the pope, he had his son assassinated, and robbed him of a city' (Piacenza). Going back further (because Paul IV had a very long memory for slights), he denounced 'the resolve formed by the imperial council when the Lutheran sect first sprang up, that it should be encouraged because it would render the emperor master of Rome'. A month later, just before Charles entered Valladolid, the pope denounced him publicly to the Venetian ambassadors as 'diabolical (*indiavolato*), soulless (*senza anima*), thirsting for the blood of Christians, a schismatic born to destroy the world'. Having thus warmed up, Paul described how Charles had ruined all the states he ruled – the Netherlands, Milan, Spain and especially Naples – before predicting that 'when we are devoured, you Venetians will be a side salad (*una insalata a costoro*) . . . Do not deceive yourselves: these imperialists seek . . . to make themselves masters of Italy', and ultimately the world. Shortly afterwards the pope opened legal proceedings against the emperor and his son for rebellion.[46]

Charles could not have cared less. When Quijada joined his master at Laredo he reported with astonishment that the emperor 'is so anxious to withdraw from public affairs that he will not speak, listen or act about any business item'; and although, in Valladolid, Charles discussed some affairs of state with his daughter Joanna, the regent, and with Juan Vázquez de Molina (nephew and successor of Los Cobos as secretary of state), on 4 November he took his leave of them, as well as of his sisters and his grandson, forbidding anyone except an entourage of about 100 to accompany him any further. After passing by Simancas and spending the night in Medina del Campo, he left the post road (which meant that government couriers would find it harder to locate him) and exclaimed: 'Thanks be to God that from now on we will not have any visitors, or formal receptions!' He flatly refused to discuss domestic affairs: 'Concerning the affairs that you say you would like to discuss with me,' he informed one minister brusquely, 'when we left our realms we also left them behind.' His letters now referred to things that had happened 'in my time' – meaning that he considered his rule at an end.[47]

RETIREMENT AT LAST

Charles could not ignore the cold, however. As winter approached 'he began to feel the cold at night, and since the places where we spent the night had no chimneys, we hand-carried a fine iron stove, sending the boy who looked after it ahead to our lodgings to heat up his bedroom.'[48] Charles also suffered in other ways. According to Quijada, the road into the Gredos mountains was 'the worst that I have ever travelled', so that 'the mules could not carry the imperial litter without the risk of it plunging down' precipitous slopes. For three leagues local men therefore 'carried His Majesty on their shoulders' until he reached the castle of the counts of Oropesa at Jarandilla, only fourteen kilometres from Yuste. There he had to stay because his apartments at the convent were not ready.[49]

After only one night at Jarandilla, Charles complained about his apartments and insisted on moving to others 'with a corridor adjacent to his bedroom where the sun shines all day, and there is a nice view of the orchards and greenery' – not that he saw much of the sun, because 'the mist never lifted' (indeed 'you could not see a man twenty paces away'). Quijada complained that 'it is really cold here and very humid' after which it rained continuously for twenty-seven days and, he opined, 'more rain falls here in an hour than in Valladolid in a day'. In addition, food was scarce and expensive so that 'His Majesty is fine but the rest of us really hate it here'.[50]

Throughout their four months at Jarandilla, Gaztelú and Quijada complained ceaselessly about the rain, the boredom and their master's demands for 'comfort foods' produced in other parts of Spain – partridges, oysters, sausages, olives, pomegranates and anchovies – and the deleterious consequences of his overindulgence. Sir William Stirling-Maxwell exaggerated only slightly in *The cloister life of the emperor Charles V* when he wrote that:

> [Quijada] never acknowledged the receipt of the good things from Valladolid without adding some dismal forebodings of consequent mischief; and along with an order he sometimes conveyed a hint that it would be much better if no means were found of executing it. If the emperor made a hearty meal without being the worse for it, the mayordomo noted the fact with exultation ... and he interposed between his master and an eel-pie as, in other days, he would have thrown himself between the imperial person and the point of a Moorish lance.[51]

At Christmas 1556 the emperor suffered a serious attack of gout and spent two weeks in bed – his right hand now 'is only good for cleaning his teeth' – but two months later, having paid off the rest of his servants and given them leave to return home, Charles travelled in his litter to Yuste accompanied by fifty-one servants and eight mules.[52] After attending a service in the chapel, he met the thirty-eight monks in residence and toured the monastery. Then he entered his own apartments built on the sunny south side of the convent, where he planned to spend the rest of his life.

The fact that the emperor died only nineteen months after his arrival in February 1557 has distorted our understanding of Yuste. Charles Clifford, an English traveller who spent 'two days and nights in that solitary and desolated spot' in 1858, and took the first photographs of the monastery, declared that it was 'the last resting-place of that great monarch, who here shut out from the distracting cares of active government, in strict monastic seclusion, sought to prepare himself for the end which his declining health but too plainly indicated must soon terminate his long and brilliant career'. This is a classic case of hindsight bias. As the art historian Antonio Perla noted: 'Charles wanted a palace where he could retire, not where he would die; a place of recreation surrounded by plants, artificial lakes and various animals.'[53]

Work to enlarge and improve the palace began soon after the emperor's arrival, and under his personal direction. Although no plans have survived, and although the site fell into ruin in the nineteenth century, the major changes can be reconstructed from the surviving accounts combined with a detailed sketch made in 1567, when the new edifice remained intact (Pl. 35). The builders added two entire wings: the lower floor of the east wing contained the imperial kitchens (a fire had seriously damaged the old ones), with new quarters for Quijada above; the lower floor of the south wing contained the emperor's pharmacy and pantry, with accommodation for his doctors and others above. Outside, Charles ordered the construction of a 'small hermitage named Bethlehem', where he occasionally went to relax, about 100 metres from his palace; and of a ramp so that he could be carried in a litter between his living quarters on the upper floor and his gardens and fishponds below. These too received a face-lift:

> There are two ponds to the south of the [imperial] apartments, with a fountain between them that flows into a pool with blue tiles, which His Majesty has stocked with tench. Windows surround the whole building, which is one of its most agreeable and beautiful features, and through them comes the fragrance of the lemon, apple and orange trees . . . To the east of his apartment there is a large patio with a fountain in the middle.

'His Majesty', wrote Quijada, 'spends much time overseeing the creation of a garden with working fountains.'[54]

Before the onset of his first winter at Yuste, Charles also oversaw the workmen who installed in the imperial apartments a large metal sauna specially brought from Germany. It was an impressive structure – the building accounts mention 'twelve iron crosses to hold the glass that goes in the windows of the sauna', 'a table made of walnut on which to place His Majesty's books inside the sauna', and 'a little desk' – and, as he had done in Augsburg a few years before, Charles spent most winter days within.[55]

Quijada ensured that the palace pharmacy always stocked the herbs, balsams, ointments and objects thought to have curative powers (such as a unicorn's horn and 'two bracelets containing bones that they say are good for haemorrhoids'); while the barber's shop boasted many perfumes (to counteract the smells from the kitchen and the toilets) as well as the instruments (mostly of gold and silver) required to clean the imperial teeth, ears and tongue, and to cut the imperial finger- and toenails. Charles surrounded himself with furniture and ornaments that were simple but elegant. He summoned Quijada with a little silver bell decorated with the device 'Plus Ultra'; he used a golden quill 'to write down in a small book the things he wanted to remember'; and his apartments boasted twenty-five tapestry panels and seven rugs. Unaware that his end was near, Charles continued to add items – on 4 July 1558 'three consignments of clothes, together with the books of His Majesty' arrived at Yuste – and when his personal goods were sold at auction after his death, their transport required more than sixty mules and their combined value approached 20,000 ducats.[56]

Fray Hernando del Corral, an eyewitness who composed a *Brief and summary history of how Emperor Charles V, our lord, decided to come to shelter in the monastery of San Jerónimo de Yuste*, devoted an entire chapter to 'How His Majesty divided his days and what he did in them'. Every morning, Corral wrote, 'as soon as his apartments were opened, Janello [Torriani] entered at once to see and wind up the planetary clock [the 'Microcosm'] that the emperor kept by him on top of a buffet'; and after he left 'Fray Juan Reglá, his confessor, entered to pray with him'. Fray José de Sigüenza provided a somewhat different account in his *History of the Jeronimite Order*, written two generations later. Now Reglá, not Torriani, 'entered each morning as soon as the imperial apartment opened' and after prayers together he 'explained the mysteries that were shown in the Book of Hours, so that the lofty thoughts that filled his soul in the morning might last the whole day'. If the Book of Hours was the magnificent French illuminated manuscript from Charles's collection, acquired with other booty when the tent of Francis I was captured at Pavia (now in Spain's National Library), its use might have triggered less lofty thoughts: the emperor would surely have taken special pleasure in contemplating images prepared for his defeated rival.[57]

After his daily prayers, according to Corral, the emperor's barbers and surgeons entered his apartments:

> Together with Dr Mathys, and they did whatever was necessary according to His Majesty's current ailments. Meanwhile his officials carried out their tasks so that everything was ready by 10 a.m., when everyone scheduled to attend His Majesty at table, including the gentleman who was in charge, ate their meal. His Majesty dressed at this time, and when that was done, the officials ended their meal and went with His Majesty to hear Mass, and then those who had dressed him went to eat. While His Majesty heard Mass, the officials on duty laid the table and got everything ready so that His Majesty could eat as soon as he had heard Mass.

Charles often had company while he ate. Instead of the jesters who had entertained him at mealtimes in Augsburg a decade earlier:

> While His Majesty was eating Dr Mathys and Guillaume van Male debated certain issues, because they were both wise and well read: sometimes history, at other times war ... And at other times His Majesty

478

summoned Friar Juan Reglá while he ate, and told him to bring a work by St Bernard [of Clairvaux] or some other edifying work, and after the meal the friar would read a little until His Majesty got sleepy, if it was time to sleep, or else until it was time for a sermon or a lesson.

Corral's next chapter described 'How the emperor spent each day'. At 3 p.m. on Sundays, Wednesdays and Fridays he heard sermons, and on the other days a 'reading from the Bible (normally from Paul's Epistle to the Romans)' surrounded by 'the monks wearing their robes, in great solemnity'. In addition 'every day, at His Majesty's command, four Masses were said in this monastery': one each for his mother and father; one 'at 8 a.m. for the empress'; and the other for him, 'which His Majesty heard every day, although sometimes rather late if His Majesty had not slept well'. Other Masses were said for his son Philip, as well as 'for Knights of the Golden Fleece who died while His Majesty lived at Yuste'; and every Thursday began with 'a sung Mass with much music' – although 'since His Majesty found it hard to get up so early' he normally sent a chamberlain to represent him and listened in his bedroom.[58]

The prior of Yuste later remembered that Charles loved to hear choral devotions so much that he sometimes interfered. One day 'a contralto from Plasencia who was very good' came to sing for him, but the emperor disapproved and sent a message telling 'the prior that the singer should be dismissed from the choir'. At other times, when listening to the choir, 'if anyone made a mistake he muttered to himself "Son of a bitch! That man erred."'[59] Sandoval repeated this story and (as in some other cases) added details from his own experience. A chorister from Seville Cathedral 'called Guerrero, *whom I knew*' – namely Francisco Guerrero, later a celebrated composer – came to Yuste and:

> Presented the emperor with a volume of motets that he had composed, and of Masses. His Majesty ordered the choir to sing one of the Masses for him, and after the Mass he summoned his confessor and said to him 'Son of a bitch [*hideputa*], that Guerrero is a crafty thief! This passage comes from so-and-so [*fulano*] and this passage from someone else.' At this, all the singers stood amazed, because they had not spotted any of this until they looked again.[60]

Charles also spent time at Yuste polishing his record for posterity. From time to time he and van Male worked on his *Memoirs*, and in April 1557 he granted Juan Ginés de Sepúlveda's request for an interview, so that the historian could clarify some details in his biography of the emperor. According to Sepúlveda, the emperor promised that 'if you want to know anything from me, just ask and I will not refuse you an answer'. During his visit, Luis de Ávila showed Sepúlveda a copy of the *Commentaries on the state of religion and public affairs under Emperor Charles V*, recently published in Strasbourg by Johannes Sleidan, official historian of the Schmalkaldic League, and afterwards sent Sepúlveda a copy 'assuring me that it would come in useful for revising what I had written on events in Germany'. Two months before his death, Charles insisted that should either Sepúlveda or the chronicler Florián de Ocampo 'die before their work is printed (because both of them are old) care should be taken that it should be published and not lost'.[61]

A GRUMPY OLD MAN

Charles also endeavoured to control the present as well as the past. Corral asserted that at Yuste 'His Majesty would always attend the sermons and lessons, except when he received important letters from his son King Philip or his daughter Princess Joanna: at these times he sent word that we should not wait for him because he was busy'. Gaztelú likewise told a colleague that 'His Majesty was delighted' on hearing the latest news on foreign affairs, 'and when couriers arrived he asks them what else they know, in order to get information by all possible means'. Almost 250 letters from Charles on state business signed at Yuste survive – more than one for every two days of his residence.[62]

All this might give the impression that, in the words of María José Rodríguez-Salgado, the emperor 'continued to influence, even to dictate his son's policies'; but she proceeded to demonstrate that this 'is simply not the case', listing numerous initiatives in which Charles tried to shape events but failed.[63] He attempted to resolve the rival claims to Navarre, as he had promised to do in the treaty of Noyon at the beginning of his reign and often since, but Joanna and her regency government in Valladolid thwarted him. He also endeavoured to attract his niece María of Portugal, Eleanor's daughter, to Castile but King John III refused; and when John died, leaving Joanna's infant son Sebastian as his successor, Charles strove to have Joanna named regent of Portugal, but his own sister Catalina (John's widow) outmanoeuvred him and became regent herself. Each of these (and several other) initiatives involved the exchange of numerous letters and the visit of envoys and ambassadors to Yuste – but they achieved nothing.

The emperor also lost his influence with Philip. Admittedly, soon after he moved to Yuste, his son asked him to take charge of Spain once more:

Begging Your Majesty with all humility and insistence to agree to act, helping and assisting me not only with your advice and council, which is the greatest asset I could have, but with your own presence and authority, leaving your monastery and going to whatever place would be best for your health and for dealing with public affairs ... because the fate of everything depends on your decisions.

In addition, he asked 'Your Majesty to send me your opinion concerning the war, and about where and how I can best undertake and participate in this campaign in order to achieve the greatest results.'[64] Charles duly bombarded his son with the requested advice, but Philip soon ceased to pay attention. In November 1557 a report that French troops were returning home from the Italian peninsula alarmed the emperor. 'If the enemy finds that you have demobilized,' he warned Philip, 'he may decide to concentrate his forces and make an attempt this winter to recapture some of the places he has lost – or to gain some new ones.' His son should maintain a large force in arms over the winter, so that 'you can use those troops to challenge the enemy with greater assurance and prevent him from achieving any of his goals'. But Philip never saw the letter: bored by his father's verbose and often self-centred missives, he read only the summaries prepared by Eraso. This time, the secretary of state endorsed the letter 'Nothing to respond to here' and omitted Charles's insight from 'the points and items that the emperor raises with Your Majesty in his letters of 8 August, 17 and 22 September, and 15 November.'[65] When in January 1558 the French troops withdrawn from Italy attacked the English enclave of Calais, Philip looked on helplessly as they conquered everything within three weeks.

Many of his former ministers also ignored Charles. In April and May 1557 he tried to squeeze a loan to pay his son's army in the Netherlands from Fernando de Valdés, the former president of the council of Castile whom he had secretly denigrated as 'not the sort of man that such a council needs' (chapter 11). Charles had subsequently nominated Valdés to the see of Seville, one of the wealthiest in Spain, yet the archbishop refused outright to provide the war loan, 'which astonished us not a little, since we promoted you, and you have enjoyed the profits of that diocese for so long'. Unless the archbishop paid up at once, the emperor huffed, 'the king will not hesitate to make an example of you, and I will support him' – but Valdés continued to stall.[66] On hearing that a senior minister had spent much time 'with the emperor in Yuste' in the autumn of 1557, one of his colleagues opined that 'to negotiate with him is to negotiate with a dead man'. A few months later, according to one of the regent's advisers, when orders arrived from Yuste 'we explain to the emperor our rationale for doing the things that he wants, but we do not actually do anything' – a classic example of the maxim followed by Habsburg officials everywhere: 'I obey but do not execute [*obedezco pero no cumplo*]'.[67]

As time passed, Charles became increasingly outspoken about public affairs. He did not disguise his disappointment that Philip had not been present at the spectacular defeat of the French at St Quentin ('He is upset that his son was not in the battle'), or his disapproval of the generous terms granted to Pope Paul IV ('the peace sent him into a rage, because he considers it a disgrace').[68] He told Joanna that if Oran were lost, 'I would not want to be in Spain or America, but in some place where I would not hear the news'; and he complained to Philip that the loss of Calais 'is something that has caused me more sorrow and anxiety than anything else could do'.[69] News that officials of the House of Trade in Seville had failed to follow his express orders to confiscate and send to the Netherlands all the specie landed by the latest fleet from America provoked a particularly ferocious outburst. Charles railed that 'if I had the health for it, I would go to Seville myself and find out whence this wickedness comes. I would sequester every official of the House of Trade and treat them in such a way that I would get to the bottom of this business.' Then, 'after arresting them, I would throw them in prison and take them in chains to [the fortress of] Simancas in daylight, to shame them, and I would not put them in a cell or a tower there, but in the dungeon'.[70]

No one paid heed. One of the regent's advisers coolly observed to a colleague that 'we are bombarded from Yuste with commandments', containing 'things to cry over and things to laugh about'. 'One of the things that made me laugh,' he continued, was the demand that 'the council should hang the officials of the House of Trade' because 'in this kingdom no man would take responsibility for doing that'. In this and other matters, because no one 'wants to have on his conscience the extreme measures demanded by Our Lord the emperor', his former ministers simply ignored him.[71]

The discovery of Lutheran cells in Valladolid, Seville and elsewhere in Spain unleashed another volley of furious commandments from Yuste. Charles urged Joanna to abandon the normal procedure by which heretics who admitted their error 'are forgiven their first offence provided they showed some remorse', and instead 'proceed against them as you would against traitors, rioters and disturbers of the peace, showing them no mercy'. Then, 'once you have ascertained the truth, burn the recalcitrants alive and cut off the heads of those who admit their fault'. He ended his letter: 'Believe me, daughter, if this is not punished and remedied at the outset, to put a stop to such a great evil without excepting anyone, I do not think the king or anyone else will be able to do it later'. He sent a copy of this outspoken message to Philip, adding a similarly dire warning in a holograph postscript: 'This evil business that has developed here leaves me as shocked as you can imagine. Take a look at what I have written to your sister on the subject. You need to write to her, and you must tackle the whole issue with rigour and with brutal punishments'.[72]

Such intemperate outbursts from a man who had allegedly entered a monastery to find tranquillity may seem puzzling. Rodríguez-Salgado has compared Charles at Yuste with Shakespeare's King Lear – a monarch who had relinquished his power and could no longer force his children to obey him – and she noted perceptively that each outburst tended to be triggered by the memory of something that had either thwarted him or made him look impotent.[73] Thus the failure to exploit St Quentin and the defiance of the pope recalled his own failure to exploit Pavia and the sack of Rome; the risk of losing Oran reminded him of the disastrous Algiers campaign; discovering that officials in Seville had ignored his order to sequester treasure angered him 'because *when I was in similar straits, with water up to my nose*, the officials there did what they liked; and when a large shipment of money arrived *they never told me about it*'. Finally, finding Lutheran cells in Spain infuriated him in part because '*it is happening in my presence*' and 'now that *I have come here* to retire and relax', but also because it reminded him that '*I have endured and suffered* so many setbacks and expenses in Germany, and *sacrificed part of my health*' in a vain attempt to extirpate Lutheranism.[74]

'My health': Charles made these outbursts while in almost constant pain. Almost every letter written by members of his entourage at Yuste mentioned some ailment that made the emperor's life miserable. Sometimes he became fatalistic, telling Quijada on one occasion: 'Do you know how I feel? I would regret *not* having an attack of gout, because if that does not cause me pain, something else surely will. Since I might get asthma or some other illness that would give me more trouble, I would not regret an attack of gout'. Four months later he told one of his doctors that 'of his many painful illnesses, he normally prefers the ones that he tolerates the best'.[75]

The visits of old friends could temporarily lift his spirits. His entourage noted the pleasure he took in conversing with Francisco de Borja (who came twice) and Luis de Ávila ('who, since he resided in Plasencia, often came to kiss His Majesty's hands'), as well as the company of his sisters Eleanor and Marie. Another pleasure was meeting for the first time his son by Barbara Blomberg, still known as Gerónimo. Charles had entrusted the boy to Quijada and his wife, Magdalena de Ulloa, who carefully supervised his education at their secluded castle near Valladolid until July 1558, when at Charles's request Quijada brought his wife 'and the rest [*y lo demás*]' (meaning Gerónimo) to reside close to Yuste. Later that month Magdalena 'brought the boy' to the palace, no doubt disguised as a page because the emperor continued to insist that his son's existence 'should remain secret until the arrival' of Philip.[76] Since Charles had expressly invited Magdalena 'and the rest' to live nearby, he no doubt anticipated more visits. He certainly gave orders that his younger son 'should be taught and learn the things that are appropriate to his age and condition' so that he would be ready to participate in court life once Philip returned to Spain; but death put paid to these plans. The next time the boy entered the convent, he would stand beside Quijada while the monks conducted a solemn funeral for his late father.[77]

LAST DAYS

'Three canopies of fine silk in three sacks, to be placed beneath the curtains against the mosquitoes.'[78] This entry in the inventory of the late emperor's possessions at Yuste, made one week after his death, is the only contemporary reference to the true cause of his demise: *Plasmodium falciparum*, the most severe strain of malaria that infects humans, transmitted through the bite of an infected *Anopheles* mosquito. Although the senior members of Charles's retinue – Quijada and Gaztelú, Mathys and Baersdorp – were all obsessed by his health, most of the time they concentrated on either his gout or 'his normal ailment', chronic haemorrhoids, and the possible remedies (over the winter of 1556–7 the search for a herbal cure for the latter involved experts from Italy and the Netherlands as well as from Spain). They also monitored his condition by recording exactly what he ate and drank each day, how much he slept and how long he stayed awake each night, and the quantity and appearance of the substances excreted by each imperial orifice.[79]

Charles already seemed weaker in February 1558, when Ávila reported that 'I found the emperor in bed and extremely feeble, with very poor complexion and no desire to eat'; and two months later one of his doctors lamented that 'he rarely takes more than fifteen or twenty steps in the course of the whole day', causing his feet to become 'somewhat numb, with sores'.[80]

The situation deteriorated further when the heat of August led the emperor to 'sleep with the windows and doors open'. Quijada complained that one of his servants had died, with 'thirteen or fourteen more ill, including me: I have had fever a couple of times' – presumably due to bites from the mosquitoes that evaded the canopies of fine silk and flew in through the open windows and doors.[81]

Corral thought Charles had a sudden premonition of his own death on 31 August 1558, because 'today His Majesty wanted to get out of the room in his apartment that faces west', but:

> While he was sitting there in a chair he ordered the portrait of the empress to be brought out. After gazing at it for a while, he also ordered *The prayer in the garden* to be brought out, and he spent a long time looking at it and thinking. Finally he asked for *The Last Judgement*, and while he was looking at it he turned to Dr Mathys with his whole body shaking and said: 'Doctor: I feel ill.'[82]

The following day, Charles 'felt a deep chill that spread from his back to his sides and his head', until after three hours 'he began to feel hot, with great pain in his head'. According to Dr Mathys, 'we could tell that His Majesty felt fearful with this new fever, because immediately he wanted to revise his will'; but before he could do so, Charles went 'out of his mind, so that he could not remember anything that happened that day'. When he recovered he developed a raging thirst and although his courtiers tried to limit his liquid intake, 'he constantly demands that we give him water'. Moreover, Quijada added, 'I have never seen him without some sort of doublet until today, when he wore just his shirt and was naked except for a sheet up to his chest.' He noted that 'His Majesty's whole body looks somewhat yellow.'[83]

On 9 September, Charles 'ordered the copy of his will that we have here to be read to him, to see if anything needed to be added or deleted. He then made a codicil.' It began with an injunction to his son to extirpate heresy, summarized in a sidebar that read: 'Lutherans to be punished harshly'. Charles then directed that his corpse should be buried in the church of the monastery (although he empowered Philip to decide his final resting place – provided his body lay beside that of the empress). If he remained at Yuste, he wanted his son to provide a 'retablo of alabaster or marble' with figures of him and his family 'as they appear in the painting by Titian called *The Last Judgement*'. He also instructed Philip to pay another schedule of 'grants and pensions', this time to those who had served him at Yuste. He then took up his pen for the last time and wrote 'Carlos' with almost as much difficulty as he had done with his first signature, fifty years before (see Pl. 2).[84]

The emperor's physical condition now worsened rapidly, leaving him 'weak and very tired'. Quijada cautiously suggested that 'it might be appropriate to see what we should do, in case God should wish that this illness progresses so far that his life could be in danger'. His prudence proved well-founded. Over the next two weeks the emperor suffered a debilitating sequence of chills, convulsions, fevers, headaches, vomiting and diarrhoea; he did not eat and he constantly complained about the pain. On 19 September 'we could not get His Majesty to speak for more than 22 hours', and he 'said later that he could not remember anything that happened yesterday'.[85]

Charles revived somewhat on 20 September, and his thoughts turned to Barbara Blomberg. Although they had apparently not met since their affair a decade before, Charles now summoned Quijada and ordered him to give a special messenger '600 gold crowns from his privy purse, and use them to buy an annuity worth 200 florins a year for the person whom he will name'. In explaining this mysterious gift to Philip, Quijada made clear that the emperor referred to 'the mother of the person known to Your Majesty', namely Gerónimo.[86] The gift was apparently the emperor's last act. Later that day Bartolomé Carranza, whom Philip had nominated as archbishop of Toledo and sent back to Spain to deliver some confidential papers to his father, arrived at Yuste.

DID THE EMPEROR DIE A LUTHERAN?

Despite the extreme rhetoric at the end of his life about unleashing the Spanish Inquisition against Lutherans, Charles had sometimes shown them favour. Until the publication of *The Babylonian captivity of the Church*, like some members of his entourage (including his confessor Jean Glapion), he seems to have felt some sympathy for Luther's critique; and even in 1525 he speculated that 'perhaps at some point it will turn out that Martin Luther is the one doing the right thing' (chapter 7). In 1530, Charles solemnly presided over the imperial Diet as a Lutheran spokesman read out the Augsburg confession, and he later approved temporary toleration for German Lutheran rulers. Although he attacked them in 1546, shortly afterwards he appointed as his chaplains and court preachers two men who would later be condemned for heresy (Constantino Ponce de la Fuente and Agustín Cazalla) and nominated another, Juan Gil (normally known as Dr Egidio), as bishop of Tortosa. The small imperial library at Yuste included works by several authors later condemned for heresy (not only tracts by Constantino but also by Fray Luis de Granada and Erasmus: after the emperor's death the book by Constantino was immediately delivered to the Inquisition and the one by Granada was burnt on the spot). In addition, Charles probably possessed a vernacular Bible, like his sisters Marie and Eleanor, and also like Dr Mathys. In May 1558, Mathys declared that 'with His Majesty's permission he had brought a French Bible with me from the Netherlands', and 'asked if I could keep and read it'. The Inquisitors refused, and so the following month 'in the presence of His Majesty's confessor, I burned it'. Since no French Bible appeared in the inventory post-mortem of Charles's goods, if Charles also possessed one, Mathys probably burned it along with his own. In any case, as José Luis Gonzalo Sánchez-Molero wryly observed: 'Heresy arrived at Yuste in the emperor's own baggage.'[87]

Charles may have had another close encounter with heresy on his deathbed. As part of his campaign to prove that Archbishop Carranza had Lutheran leanings, Inquisitor-General Fernando de Valdés collected sworn depositions by twenty individuals who had witnessed the emperor's final hours, making them the best documented of his entire life.

Some found Charles's reception of Carranza somewhat cool, perhaps because of rumours that some suspected him of heresy. Certainly, his first words were reproachful – 'You are late, archbishop' – but then he perked up and 'asked: "How is my son doing?"' The archbishop replied, 'Doing well, and at Your Majesty's service.' Next the emperor asked 'What is being done about the heretics in Valladolid?', to which Carranza answered: 'The only thing that matters at the moment is Your Majesty's health.' At this 'the emperor closed his eyes and lay back on his pillow'.[88]

Carranza now withdrew, but a few hours later Charles's entourage recalled him because their master seemed close to death. The emperor asked 'for the portrait of Christ crucified which he had kept in readiness for this moment, ever since his wife died, and as he gazed at Jesus – apparently as a means of resisting the temptations of Satan – he begged forgiveness for all his sins'.[89] Carranza now read Psalm 129, 'Out of the depths', and when Charles asked him to stop the archbishop assured him that 'Your Majesty must place all your hope in the passion of Christ, our Redeemer, because nothing else matters [todo lo demás es burla]'.[90] This statement seemed to several of those gathered around the emperor's bed like Lutheranism – they would testify to that effect when the Inquisition proceeded against Carranza for heresy – but if Charles noticed, he showed no sign. Instead, his pulse stabilized and he rested until the middle of the night, when he suffered new paroxysms.

Carranza hurried back and offered him the crucifix that the empress had held when she died. Their hands touched as the archbishop warned him: 'Do not let the devil disturb Your Majesty with the memory of your sins, which often happens at moments like these, but place your hope in Him who has already redeemed them. Since Your Majesty has done all that a Catholic Christian should do, receiving the sacraments of the Church, no harm will come to you.' 'Judging by his feeble gestures' at this point, 'some thought these words comforted His Majesty', but Carranza wanted more. When a nobleman sat next to him 'at the foot of His Majesty's bed' and said '"I am astonished by the serenity of a dying man who has done so many things", the archbishop replied "Such confidence does not please me at all"'. Nevertheless Carranza gave him final absolution (without securing a further confession: another irregularity duly noted by others and later used against him) and at 2 a.m. on 21 September, Charles whispered: 'Help me, I'm dying.' With Carranza's assistance he grasped a candle in one hand and his wife's crucifix in the other, 'holding it up until it reached his lips'. After five paroxysms 'he gave a deep breath and said "Now it's time"' and 'after two or three more breaths, he rendered his soul to God'.[91]

OF DEATH AND DIGITS

The rhythm and intensity of Charles's paroxysms had led his doctors to conclude – correctly – that he suffered from 'a very powerful double tertian fever' and they therefore intensified their regime of blood-letting and purges, further weakening their patient; but they could not identify the cause of his ailment, let alone devise an effective treatment. This is hardly surprising: the *Plasmodium* parasite that causes malaria was not discovered until 1880; and although the anti-malarial properties of cinchona bark were known in 1558, that knowledge remained confined to the emperor's Quechua subjects in faraway Peru. Certainty concerning the cause of his failing health and death only emerged in 2004, when a medical team conducted clinical tests on a detached phalanx from one of Charles's fingers that revealed 'malaria parasites in large quantities'. The team considered that their photographs taken via a microscope could serve as 'a textbook example of tropical medicine or the history of medicine: fossil parasites were clearly visible', revealing 'two generations of parasites'. This proved that the emperor had suffered a double dose of *Plasmodium falciparum* malaria.[92]

Almost certainly, Charles contracted the fatal disease only after he reached Yuste, a region that remained 'one of the most malarious areas of

Spain until recent times'. Dr Julián de Zulueta, the specialist on the disease who oversaw the clinical tests, thought that Charles might not have become infected until August 1558:

> In a study of the receptivity of malaria in the area, a high density of *Anopheles atroparvus*, the main vector of the disease in Spain, was found in the immediate vicinity of the monastery of Yuste . . . The time of year of the emperor's illness at Yuste, the end of the summer and the beginning of autumn, corresponds to the time when *P. falciparum* was most prevalent in Spain.[93]

Charles's decision to build fishponds and a fountain adjacent to his apartments created the perfect breeding ground for mosquitoes, and therefore the perfect incubator for the disease that killed him at the age of fifty-eight.

SEVENTEEN

THE EMPEROR IN LEGEND AND HISTORY

For a long time I went to bed early. Sometimes, when I had just put out my candle, my eyes closed so quickly that I did not even have time to say 'I'm going to sleep'. Half an hour later the thought that it was time to go to sleep would awaken me . . . While asleep I had been thinking constantly about what I had just been reading, but my thoughts had run into a channel of their own, until I myself seemed actually to have become the subject of my book: a church, a quartet, the rivalry between Francis I and Charles V.

Marcel Proust, *Du côté de chez Swann* (Paris, 1913), 1[1]

HIS LATE SACRED MAJESTY

A few hours after Charles died, Luis Quijada (who had served him for thirty-seven years) wrote that 'The greatest man who has ever lived, or will ever live, just died in Christ's arms.' He added: 'I cannot believe he is dead.' He was not alone in his denial. Like Quijada, Luis de Ávila and Martín de Gaztelú 'gave shouts and cries, hit themselves in the face and beat their heads against the walls; they seemed to have taken leave of their senses, as indeed they had, with the pain they felt at seeing their master dead.' Six months later, in the Netherlands, Charles's librarian Willem Snouckaert van Schouwenburg included 'saintliness' in the title of his sycophantic biography: *On the public affairs, life, customs, deeds, reputation, religion and saintliness of the emperor Charles V.*[2]

The idea was not new. The pageants celebrating Charles's entry into Bruges in 1515 compared him with Christ (chapter 3 and Pl. 7); he patronized sculptures that portrayed him as one of the Wise Men; he also became the subject of prophecies – a particularly striking one, also from 1515, foretold that the young prince would conquer the English and the Italians; that he would destroy Rome with fire; that he would capture Jerusalem. 'No one would be able to resist him', the prediction continued, 'because God's arm would be with him, and he would ... gain the universal dominion of the earth.'[3] In 1532, Charles confronted two people who claimed to be the Messiah. One of them, Sultan Suleiman, who now began to wear a special tiara with four crowns, symbolizing the rule of the last world emperor, used the title *Sahib-kiran* ('World Conqueror') and encouraged histories and prophecies that compared him with both his namesake Solomon and Alexander the Great, or hailed him as *mujaddid* ('renewer'), the eschatological figure who appears in each age to 'renew' the Islamic community. Meanwhile, as he prepared for battle against the sultan, Charles granted an audience to Solomon Molcho (a Portuguese convert to Christianity who had returned to Judaism and circumcised himself), who arrived with 'a Hebrew banner together with a shield and sword consecrated in the name of the Hebrew God' that he proposed to use when he led 'all the Jews to make war on the Turks'. According to Nuncio Aleandro (who also met Molcho and took an instant dislike to him), 'His Majesty listened to him most attentively for two hours and asked him about many things', apparently impressed by his visitor's charisma; but the following day Charles had second thoughts and had him arrested. Molcho was sent to Italy, where he was burnt at the stake.[4]

Soon afterwards, 'our great king Charles V' achieved semi-divine status in parts of Mexico because he 'was the first to grant lordship and patrimony' to many indigenous communities, and their municipal charters included thanks to him as well as to the Trinity for their foundation.[5] In Spain, when the monks of San Lorenzo de El Escorial opened Charles's coffin in 1654, just before moving it to the new Pantheon of the Kings, they noticed that the emperor's body 'was still intact, ninety-six years after his death' and concluded that 'such a prodigy must be the work of a higher power, and since it occurred naturally it was one of those rarities that transgress the limits of the natural world' – in other words, a minor miracle. A century later, a visitor to Charles's tomb in the Pantheon reported that 'the friars here consider him a saint'.[6]

COMMEMORATING THE EMPEROR

As news of Charles's death spread, lavish exequies celebrated his life and achievements. Gregorio Leti claimed that more than 2,400 churches organized a procession and erected a catafalque in honour of the late emperor – 527 in Spain, 382 in Naples, 292 in the Papal States, and so on – and in many places 'the crush of people was so great that it seemed as if the whole world had gathered together'.[7] Special pamphlets described commemorations in Valladolid (where his grandson Don Carlos was the principal mourner) and in Brussels (where his son Philip resided), both in December 1558, and in Augsburg (where his brother Ferdinand presided at a 'great commemoration of the dead' on 24 February 1559, Charles's birthday).[8] Partly because they drew on different funerary traditions, these events differed significantly. Juan Calvete de Estrella designed an elaborate catafalque for the funeral ceremony in Valladolid that depicted the humiliation of the German Lutherans in 1547; Charles's conquests in America and Africa; the capture of Thérouanne and Hesdin from France; scenes from *The resolute knight*; and, beneath the motto ANIMO INVICTO ('unvanquished spirit'), a picture of 'Ingolstadt with two encampments facing each other. In one of them, the emperor appeared at the entrance of his tent, fully armed, surrounded by the many cannonballs fired by the enemy's artillery that fell close to his feet and his tent. His face was strong and manly, showing no trace of fear but rather animating and encouraging his men.'[9] These were surely the achievements that Charles himself would have selected (Pl. 37).

By contrast the book published to commemorate the Brussels ceremony contained only a short text (which facilitated translations in five languages) to accompany thirty-four lavish spreads (hand-coloured in some copies) that showed Philip and the Knights of the Golden Fleece processing through the streets of Brussels from the Coudenberg palace to the cathedral of St Gudule, where four decades before Charles had been acclaimed king of Castile, Aragon, Naples and Sicily (Pl. 36). According to the vivid account of Richard Clough, an English eyewitness, the ritual followed precedent precisely:

> There went a nobellman unto the herse (so far as I coulde understand, it was the prince of Orange) who, standing before the herse, strucke with his hand uppon the chest and sayd, 'He is ded.' Then standing styll awhyle, he sayd 'He shall remayne ded.' And then, resting awhile, he strucke again and sayd, 'He is ded, and there is another rysen up in his place greater than ever he was.'

One of the knights then stepped forward and in a dramatic gesture his colleagues threw back his hood to reveal Philip, who led the procession back through the streets of Brussels to the palace. 'It was sure a sight worth to go 100 myles to see,' wrote Clough in awe: 'The lyke of thys I think hath not been sene.'[10]

Although Gregorio Leti probably exaggerated the number of exequies for Charles in Europe, he omitted those staged in America. In Lima, on hearing in July 1559 'that His Majesty is dead', the viceroy of Peru immediately started to make preparations based on the catafalques he had seen in Spain for deceased members of the royal family. On 11 and 12 November 1559 a procession of perhaps 250 people went to pay their respects at the simple catafalque made of wood, decorated with flags and shields representing the late emperor's possessions. Although the official record of the exequies remained in manuscript, because Lima still lacked a printing press, they provided a powerful symbol of the integration of the city and the viceroyalty into the Spanish Monarchy after a generation of conquest, chaos and civil war.[11]

Far grander exequies took place in Mexico on 30 November 1559 (the feast of St Andrew: the day on which Charles had normally hosted a banquet for Knights of the Golden Fleece). Before a crowd estimated at 40,000, the viceroy led a procession to a catafalque filled with tributes in Latin and Spanish to the late monarch's deeds, notably those in America. The choir sang the motet *Circumdederunt me* by Cristóbal de Morales, who had met Charles in 1536 – a striking example of the transatlantic culture that thrived under the emperor – and nine of the twenty-two painted scenes on the catafalque contained direct references to the conquest. One picture showed 'Ferdinand of Castile' (*sic*: for Ferdinand of Aragon) kneeling before the pope 'receiving a New World with both hands'; another revealed Montezuma and Atahualpa, 'emperors of this New World', kneeling before Charles 'with cheerful faces, showing that they were happy to have been vanquished'; a third celebrated the fact that 'the emperor had created a university in Mexico to instruct and educate the native population'. The structure was painted to look like *tezontle*, the native stone used to rebuild Mexico City, and other local references included a drawing of the catafalque that included a skeleton (in Mexica tradition a skeleton accompanied each dead ruler to the Underworld). The combination of elements from both colonial and precolonial traditions revealed that although Spaniards designed and described the catafalque, Mexica students from the College of Santa Cruz of Tlatelolco did the paintings.[12]

In Spain, the emperor's executors arranged the 30,000 Masses he had requested for his soul, and began to distribute the 30,000 ducats in gold that he had placed in a locked chest in the fortress of Simancas to pay legacies to prisoners of war, poor virgins and deserving paupers (chapter 15). It is possible to monitor the payments made in each category because many monasteries in Castile sent certificates detailing the number and frequency of the Masses they had arranged; the officials sent to north Africa to ransom prisoners kept full records; and several bishops sent lists of those they deemed deserving and poor enough to receive the imperial largesse.[13] Paying Charles's other bequests proved far harder. In July 1559, Philip made 80,000 ducats available to his father's executors, but it soon emerged that Charles owed far more – and not only to his own servants but also to the creditors of his parents and grandparents, 'because he had fought major wars and spent heavily ever since he was sworn king of Castile and Aragon' and therefore lacked the funds to honour their bequests. The executors reminded Philip that 'sixteen months have passed since His Imperial Majesty died, yet not a penny has been spent to discharge the obligations set out in his will'; but they wrote in vain. In 1579, when they again requested more money to pay off the emperor's creditors, the king replied dismissively: 'I would certainly like to be able to deal with this at once, but there are so many other commitments and so little money for them.' Instead, he suggested, 'it would be good to find out if any of His Majesty's assets remain from which his debts could be paid'.[14] The executors and their successors would continue their efforts to pay all the emperor's debts well into the seventeenth century.

THE EMPEROR'S LONG SHADOW

Philip's rescript epitomized his ambiguous feelings about his father. Publicly, he always showed deep respect. In 1572 he approved a plan for a funeral group of seven figures (his parents and their two sons who had died as infants, as well as his aunts Eleanor and Marie and his sister María), which resulted in the larger-than-life gilded bronze statues cast by Pompeo Leoni and his atelier that now kneel beside the main altar at El Escorial as if they had joined the monks in perpetual prayer. They constitute (as Rosemarie Mulcahy observed) 'the most impressive royal funerary sculptures in European art'.[15] Two years later, Philip spent 318 ducats on moving Charles's cadaver from Yuste to the Escorial, and he devoted several hours to deciding what should be inscribed on the emperor's coffin. When the king authorized a restoration programme at the royal Alcázar of Seville in 1577, he included a set of magnificent tiles (*azulejos*) to commemorate the wedding of his parents there fifty-one years before; and on 20 and 21 September 1584 a minister noted that Philip had neglected his paperwork 'because yesterday he attended vespers and today he participated in services for the anniversary of his father's death'.[16] In private, the king showed less enthusiasm. He never displayed the magnificent life-size bronze statue of Charles V as a Roman emperor, commissioned from Leone Leoni in 1549 (Pl. 29) – instead it remained in the Madrid workshop where it had been designed and cast – and he left Titian's great canvas *Charles V at the battle of Mühlberg* (Pl. 25) in the storeroom of the Madrid Alcázar.

Philip was less ambiguous when it came to the art of government. In 1574, when he thought he would have to leave Spain, he searched for Charles's instructions 'from when I started to govern, in 1543' because he expected to find useful guidance 'in the advice that the emperor wrote out for me then in his own hand'.[17] The king evidently learned other political habits from his father, including how to write passive-aggressive letters to the pope. When in 1569, Pius V seemed to ignore his wishes, Philip instructed the Spanish ambassador in Rome: 'When you are alone you will lodge a protest on my behalf that any damage caused by this, and by His Holiness's refusal to believe me and to act, *will be on his conscience and not on mine*' – a turn of phrase that would have doubtless pleased the emperor.[18] More dangerously, Philip also inherited his father's comprehensive messianic vision. Both rulers believed that God had charged them to achieve His purpose for the world and that He had granted them special protection expressly so that they could achieve these goals (although the process might not be swift, obvious or easy). Both rulers also believed that God would bridge with a miracle any gap between ways and means whenever necessary, a certitude that led them to take foolish risks. Thirty years after Charles's disastrous decision to persevere with his attack on Algiers, against the advice of his experts, Philip in 1571 authorized a complex amphibious attack on England, against the advice of his experts, because 'I am so attached to it in my heart, and I am so convinced that God our Saviour must embrace it as His own cause, that I cannot be dissuaded'; and thirty-five years after the emperor's equally disastrous decision to besiege Metz, Philip in 1587 ordered the Armada to sail against England even though 'We are fully aware of the risk that is incurred by sending a major fleet in winter through the Channel without a safe harbour.' He assured his commanders that 'since it is all for His cause, God will send good weather'.[19] Finally, father and son both found it hard to swallow their pride and admit defeat if doing so might imperil their 'reputation'. Charles decided to persist with the siege of Metz because 'if we abandon this enterprise I will have to disband my army, having spent so much money without achieving anything. I have therefore decided to spend even more, and await what God pleases to give us, rather than to quit without seeing what Fortune brings.' His son deployed the same logic in his struggle to suppress the Dutch Revolt: 'I have no doubt that, if the cost of the war [in the Netherlands] continues at its present level, we will not be able to sustain it; but it would be a great shame if, having spent so much, we lost any chance that spending a little more might recover everything.'[20]

Charles's vision continued to shape strategic thinking long afterwards. At least twenty-eight manuscript copies of the Political Testament of 1548 survive, and the Spanish ambassador in Savoy evidently had one in front of him in 1600 when he reminded his sovereign, Philip III, 'of what His Majesty the emperor said in the instructions that he gave the late king our lord [Philip II] about the schemes of the French and the distrust that one should have about any peace made with them'. He insisted that this advice, based on providential principles, still held good. Six years later Prudencio de Sandoval printed in full Charles's paper of advice in his best-selling *History of the life and deeds of the Emperor Charles V.* Henceforth everyone could read, admire and imitate it.[21]

The emperor cropped up posthumously in many different places. Lope de Aguirre, the 'cruel tyrant' who attracted much support in Peru when he rebelled in 1561, addressed a formal challenge to 'King Philip, Spaniard by birth, son of Charles the invincible'. A few years later, alarmed by the rapid spread of Protestantism in the Netherlands, the fire-eating Fray Lorenzo de Villavicencio warned Philip that 'The holy bones of the Emperor your father are complaining and his spirit will demand God's punishment against you if you allow the loss of those provinces, without which Spain cannot live in safety.' More positively, in the 1560s, Jerónimo Sempere and Luis Zapata de Chaves both extolled Charles's deeds in lengthy epic poems (*La Carolea*, 1560, and *Carlos famoso*, 1566); and Luis de Ávila y Zúñiga added to the marble bust of the emperor in the 'Charles V room' of his palace in Plasencia the triumphalist inscription:

Charles V
That's enough because
The whole world knows the rest.[22]

In 1568 the count of Olivares, who had accompanied Charles on the Tunis campaign and now wanted to build up his picture collection in Seville, asked Duke Octavio of Parma 'to procure for me a painting of when the emperor, wearing full armour, crossed the River Elbe because it is not fair that those who served him should lack a copy of such a fine portrait. I believe Titian has the master copy of this, and since he lives close to Your Excellency, please order him to make a copy for me.' His postscript asserted that 'The whole world has a duty to remember the deeds of such a valorous prince and fortunate emperor.' When in 1570, Philip composed a paper of advice to his brother, Don John, on how to crush the rebellious Moriscos of Granada, he concluded 'I tell you this as someone who loves you and wants you to succeed in everything because you are our father's son.' In 1588 several ships of the Spanish Armada sank off the coasts of Scotland and Ireland carrying heavy artillery pieces cast by Gregor Löffler of Augsburg and confiscated after the defeat of the Schmalkaldic League, each one resplendent with Charles's imperial insignia (Pl. 38). The following year, Alonso de Ercilla, who had spent time in the emperor's entourage as a boy, included fifteen references to 'Charles the Great' and 'the great emperor, Charles the Invincible' in his epic poem about the conquest of what is now Chile: La Araucana.[23]

Even after the death of those who had known him personally – Barbara Blomberg in 1597; Philip II in 1598; his daughter María in 1603 – the emperor continued to attract favourable comments. In 1604, in his history of the evangelization of Mexico, Gerónimo de Mendieta praised 'the most pious emperor Charles V, of immortal memory'. Two years later, when Prudencio de Sandoval narrated Charles's funeral at Yuste in his History, noting that those who knew him had 'shed many tears when they buried him', he added 'as well they might because I, who only know of his life by reading about him, shed tears too'. In 1611, Sebastián de Covarrubias's entry on 'Carlos' in his Spanish Dictionary read: 'We have had five emperors of this name, and the fifth was Charles, monarch of the world.' Shortly afterwards, the emperor made two appearances in Miguel de Cervantes's Don Quixote (as the 'most invincible Charles V' for his capture of the fortress of La Goletta outside Tunis in 1535, and as the 'great emperor Charles V' during his visit to Rome the following year). In 1638 the count-duke of Olivares, chief minister of Philip IV, drew to his master's attention the dilapidated state of the 'royal apartments' at Yuste and requested appointment as guardian of the 'Imperial palace' there in order to superintend a programme of restoration to create a worthy monument to its first and only occupant. Olivares would reproduce many of its features in the palace and monastery complex that he constructed on his estate at Loeches.[24] The emperor's popular reputation also remained high in the Low Countries, thanks to such works as The heroic and amusing deeds of Emperor Charles V, first published in both French and Dutch in 1675, which presented him as 'the worthiest hero you could ever imitate'. In 1999 a census of legends, anecdotes, fairy tales and riddles in Dutch included some 160 items about 'Good

Old Charles'.[25]

Public monuments in honour of the emperor continued to appear long after his death – such as the life-size statue erected in Palermo in 1631 (Pl. 21) – and in his treatise on the greatness of the Spanish Monarchy the Dominican Tommaso Campanella proposed that a statue of Charles be erected at the South Pole as a sign that his rule had encompassed the entire world: *Plus ultra*, indeed.[26] Equally striking, from the 1590s (if not earlier) manuscript copies circulated in Italian, German and English of a document entitled 'The last instructions which the Emperor Charles the Fifth gave to his son Philip before his death', until by 1750 at least fifty manuscript and two printed copies of the text existed. All of them were either forgeries or based on forgeries – the emperor composed no such document – but the combination of his achievements and the wide circulation of his genuine instructions evidently conferred an almost mythical authority that made it worth attaching his name to a document written by someone else.[27]

The same apparently remained true in the twentieth century. The Fascist regime of General Francisco Franco encouraged Spanish historians to see Charles as a great unifier and an epitome of Spanish values: in 1942 the university of Valladolid established a 'Seminar on the history of the empire' dedicated to publishing relevant documents from the archives of Simancas; and in 1958 a Centenary Committee arranged commemorative conferences, oversaw the repair of the palaces of Charles V at both Yuste and Granada, and staged exequies at the Escorial on 21 September attended by Franco himself. One eminent alumnus of the 'Seminar on the history of the empire', Manuel Fernández Álvarez, became an enthusiastic promoter of the 'European vision of Charles V', presenting the emperor as 'the great precursor of the political unity of Christian Europe'.[28] In this he was not alone. The French president Charles de Gaulle gave a speech in 1962 that included the emperor in the list of those who had 'dreamed of European unity'; and three years later Viscount Charles Terlinden published *Carolus Quintus: Charles V, emperor of two worlds*, lavishly illustrated. It would appear in nineteen editions and seven languages, claiming that the emperor had pioneered the idea of a united Europe. Such arguments evidently convinced the governments of Belgium and Spain, both of which issued écu coins in the 1980s (when it seemed likely that the écu, rather than the euro, would become the common currency of Europe) that depicted Charles as Titian had shown him: on horseback at Mühlberg as his Spanish troops routed the German Lutherans – a curiously divisive image to choose for the European Union. In 1994, Enrique Barón Crespo, past president of the European Parliament, delivered a lecture entitled 'The Europe of Charles V and the Europe of Maastricht', which argued that Charles 'created a Europe that in essence coincided with the European Community today, *except for France*' – an exception so substantial that it made nonsense of the parallel.[29]

THE EMPEROR AND HIS CRITICS

De Gaulle, Terlinden and Barón Crespo all ignored the warning of Peter Rassow in 1958: '*Who would want to turn such a failed personality into an ideal leader?* The historical Charles cannot serve as the figurehead of the ship of European unity.' They also ignored the contemporary critics of His Late Sacred Majesty. In Italy a 'farce' composed in Calabrian dialect lampooned the emperor's progress in 1536 through the town of Cava de' Tirreni (between Salerno and Naples). In 'The reception of the emperor in Cava', whose inhabitants were often portrayed on stage as ignorant and argumentative bumpkins, the emperor appeared as the *tedeschino* (the little German chap), with an inscription on his brow that read 'You can do anything with money' and a notable disregard for his subjects. He offended the citizens by refusing to stop either to eat the local delicacies (a sausage and a glass of wine) or to revere the numerous local relics (said to include half an ear from Balaam's ass and a sneeze from the nose of Christ himself, preserved in a vial).[30] Some French writers went further, portraying Charles as an existential threat. The chronicler Claude Haton, writing just after the emperor's death, claimed that 'France could rightly call him her Attila, in other words her great enemy and persecutor'. Most Protestants felt the same. John Knox recalled with pride in his *History of the Reformation in Scotland* that, while a refugee in Germany in 1554, he had called the emperor 'no less enemy unto Christ than ever was Nero' because he 'do maintain and advance idolatry'.[31]

The emperor also had critics in Spain. *The history of Charles V* by Juan Ginés de Sepúlveda, completed in the 1560s, claimed that Charles had fought too many wars ('some of them undertaken because they were necessary for defence but others, although for just cause, less necessary') and that their cost had impoverished his subjects. Sepúlveda also criticized the emperor for obstinacy ('once he had taken a decision, it was very difficult to make him abandon it'); for selling exemptions to his laws to raise money; for consulting too few ministers in his later years; and for refusing 'after he turned fifty' to transact affairs of state promptly 'because he was afflicted by melancholy'. Not surprisingly, Philip II refused to print Sepúlveda's text.[32] In 1611, Antonio Daza, a Franciscan based in Valladolid, published a history of his Order that included several dreams by his colleagues, including one by Friar Gonzalo Méndez while preaching in Guatemala, who reported a vision of the soul of the late emperor ascending into Paradise 'four years after his death', that is in 1562. In Daza's opinion, God had left Charles to languish in Purgatory 'because he did not punish Luther when he could have taken him' at the Diet of Worms – although apparently Caesar's luck prevailed even in the realm of imagination: some of those who dreamed about Charlemagne soon after his death had pictured him in Hell with 'an animal tearing at his genitals'.[33]

Predictably, most later Protestant writers showed hostility towards the emperor. When the Scottish philosopher and historian David Hume learned that his colleague William Robertson proposed to write a biography of Charles, he protested that 'your hero, who is the sole connexion, is not very interesting'. Furthermore, 'though some parts of the story may be entertaining, there would be many dry and barren; and the whole seems not to have any great charms.' Robertson nonetheless persevered and prospered: his three-volume *History of the reign of the Emperor Charles V*, published in 1769, soon became the standard work, with translations into German (1770–1), French (1771), Russian (1775–8), Italian (1836), Arabic (1842) and finally Spanish (1846). The author secured an advance of £3,500 for his book– an unprecedented sum – and its publication 'sealed his reputation as the leading historian in Europe'. Robertson praised the 'careful and deliberate attention' that Charles had devoted to 'every subject that demanded his consideration', but discerned numerous 'defects in his political character'. Specifically, his 'ambition was insatiable'; he engaged in 'continual wars, which not only exhausted and oppressed his subjects, but left him little leisure for giving attention to the interior police and the improvement of his kingdoms'; above all, he 'engaged in schemes so complicated as well as arduous, that, feeling his power to be unequal to the execution of them, he had often recourse to low artifices, unbecoming his superior talents, and sometimes engaged on such deviations from integrity as were dishonourable in a great prince'. Robertson's negative sentiments even peppered his index: the entry for 'Charles V' contained references to the emperor's 'cruel', 'unjust' and 'haughty' behaviour, his 'dissimulation' (three entries), the 'intoxicating influence of success on his mind', and of course 'his intolerant bigotry'.[34]

Public archives were closed to scholars when Robertson wrote, but access to manuscript collections at first did little to improve the emperor's image. The German pioneers of archive-based history, Leopold von Ranke and Hermann Baumgarten (both descended from Lutheran pastors), saw

Charles primarily as an anachronism whose efforts to build a supra-national state and halt the spread of Protestantism were doomed to failure. Their Scottish contemporary Sir William Stirling-Maxwell resorted to multiple mixed metaphors to condemn Charles as:

> One of the most tiresome writers who ever drove the quill of political or diplomatic correspondence . . . Even in argument, his vivacity is cramped and crippled by the fence of caution and reserve which ever hedges his path. Very rarely does it happen that any spark of human feeling or passion illumines his weary records of the daily toils of power . . . of selfish intrigues and ignoble rivalries; and of all the dusty plans of an ambition which never soared above the family tree of Hapsburg.[35]

French historians likewise found much to deprecate in the emperor: compared with Francis I, wrote Jules Michelet in his influential *History of France*, Charles 'was a pale bookworm, learned and eloquent but a bad writer and a self-serving graceless speaker'. Most Italian historians were equally critical, harping on the way the emperor had 'snuffed out the liberty of Florence and Siena, conquered Milan, marginalized Venice, yoked Genoa to his wagon, sacked Rome and lent a hand to the popes' efforts to extinguish every voice opposed to the established order'. As Giuseppe Galasso observed in 2001, this did not leave much to like.[36]

Many Spanish historians also saw their first Habsburg ruler as 'a foreign-born monarch, proud and implacable, the epitome of an absolute king'. They tended to focus (if they focused on the period at all) on his contemporaries – his mother Queen Joanna, Cardinal Cisneros, the conquistadors, the leading Comuneros – leaving Charles 'a second-rank figure'. Of the 265 articles dealing with the sixteenth century published in the *Bulletin* of Spain's Royal Academy of History between 1877 and 1901, not one dealt directly with Charles V. Most eloquent of all, when the photographer Charles Clifford visited Yuste in the 1850s, after travelling by mule from the village of Cuacos 'through large oak forests and scrambling mountain paths, only known to and visited by the peasants of the neighbourhood', he found 'grim decay and crumbling walls': 'All is damp, ruin and decay', with 'an utter disregard and neglect of all repairs'. Clifford declined 'the offer of having our bed littered down in the emperor's chamber, being unwilling to dispute the tenancy with the present occupants, the bats and night-birds that streamed . . . into the desolate, roofless church'.[37]

Little had changed one century later, when Manuel Fernández Álvarez retraced Clifford's route from Cuacos to Yuste, and the sight of 'the monastery and the imperial apartments all in ruins' produced in him 'a feeling of great sadness for a lost world – sometimes glorious, sometimes confused – that could scarcely be glimpsed amid the desolation'. But by then, the recovery of that lost world was well under way. Above all, after three decades of research on the emperor, between 1937 and 1941 Karl Brandi published a pioneering two-volume biography 'based almost exclusively on a new and thorough examination of the best and most immediate contemporary evidence'. Admittedly, Brandi harboured some reservations about his subject, opening with the lapidary verdict: 'There are in history certain men whose productive energy is more than human. They create out of their own elemental strength, and lay down the laws of thought and action for centuries to come. The Emperor Charles V was not one of these.' Nevertheless, Brandi continued:

Many as are the seeming contradictions in the life of Charles V, it had an inner unity. His career was dominated by the dynastic principle, which found more vital and effective expression in him than in any other ruler in the history of the world. Both as a man and as a sovereign, he was subjected to the moral pressure of this principle, which beset his path with perilous temptations.[38]

Brandi's 'agent versus structure' formulation has been applied to many statesmen, sometimes in the guise of the 'fox and the hedgehog' metaphor made famous by Desiderius Erasmus, Charles's sometime councillor, in the year of the future emperor's birth: 'The fox knows many things, but the hedgehog knows one big thing.' This adage implied that hedgehogs have a focused worldview and strong convictions, which they apply to all situations, whereas foxes are more pragmatic, adjusting their views in response to events – in short, hedgehogs are belief-driven whereas foxes are evidence-driven – and for Brandi, Charles was the quintessential hedgehog. But what about the more basic question: could anyone, whether fox or hedgehog, have ruled his inheritance with greater success than Charles? What was the balance of his reign?[39]

THE BALANCE OF THE REIGN

> History can never be reduced to a single entry in a ledger . . . The
> history of Charles V must be the sum of all possible explanations of
> his life, his achievements, and his times. It is essential that nothing
> be omitted from the book-keeping, whether money, actions, inten-
> tions, certainties, or luck.
>
> Fernand Braudel (1958)[1]

CAESAR'S LUCK RECONSIDERED

Late in 1550 the veteran French diplomat Charles de Marillac tried to
explain to his master 'the causes of the grandeur' of the emperor, then at its
apogee. He focused first on the negative: 'The first and principal cause' of
Charles's success, Marillac argued, 'was that those with whom he had to deal
committed errors'; and he started with his own compatriots. Although he
did not offer specifics – writing only that 'we withdrew when we should
have advanced, and acted too fast when we should have waited' – examples
are easy to find: had Francis not behaved so rashly during the siege of Pavia
in 1525, it is hard to see how the imperial army in Lombardy could have
long survived as a fighting force; had he offered military assistance to the
Schmalkaldic League in 1546, it is hard to see how Charles could have
defeated the German Lutherans; and so on. 'The second cause of his grandeur,' Marillac continued, was Charles's ability to 'create dissension among
allies by winning over those favourable to him' and 'sow doubts about loyalty
among his enemies, so they became less willing to attack him' (he cited the
duke of Bourbon, Andrea Doria, 'and a thousand others' in the case of
France). Third, Marillac asserted, Charles had also triumphed by 'making
the world believe that he was a pious, just and honourable prince, so that
one might more easily trust him', with the result that 'if it happens that one
of his actions is seen as wrong, the blame falls on his ministers without

suspecting that it could proceed from a pious prince like him'. But, the ambassador continued angrily, 'This is true hypocrisy', and he offered numerous examples: condoning the sack of Rome; retaining Navarre, Milan, Piacenza and Utrecht; suppressing the Florentine republic; erecting citadels in Siena and Cambrai; abandoning to their fate his own relatives, such as Christian of Denmark and Katherine of Aragon.[2]

The ambassador oversimplified: although these negative factors certainly contributed to imperial success, Charles also benefited from positive influences, notably luck. Marillac's Florentine colleague, writing an evaluation of the emperor at almost exactly the same time, highlighted this: 'Such is Caesar's luck that it allows him to defeat any difficulty and overcome the hostility and snares of his rivals, and also vanquish any feeling of depression when his affairs appear to be in a bad, even desperate, state.'[3] No doubt the ambassador had in mind the numerous political and military situations in which Fortune seemed to favour Charles, starting with Pavia and culminating in a series of errors by his enemies that brought him victory over the superior Lutheran forces ranged against him (chapter 12); but there was much more. Biologically, a sequence of marriages, births and deaths between 1488 and 1509 (culminating in the death of Ferdinand of Aragon's only child with Germaine de Foix) conspired to leave the young duke of Luxemburg as sole heir to four previously separate states: had any of the outcomes been different, Charles would have ruled far fewer territories. In 1545 the death of the duke of Orléans saved him from surrendering either Milan or the Netherlands, as the treaty of Crépy obliged him to do. In addition, good luck saved Charles's life on several occasions. During the summit at Nice in 1538 he led his courtiers across a bridge from the shore to the galley on which his sister Eleanor had just arrived 'and while they were embracing' the bridge gave way and they fell into the water: both monarchs 'got soaking wet but were soon rescued'; the following year, when visiting Amboise in France, the emperor rode his horse into a primitive elevator that linked the floors of the castle, illuminated by torches and candles: the machine burst into flames but Charles emerged unscathed.[4]

Charles's lifestyle choices regularly placed him in harm's way, but he survived almost unscathed. Just after the capture of Tunis in 1535 he twice fell under a horse that kicked him, injuring both his legs (chapter 9); and two years later, when he rode at top speed from Barcelona to join his family at Tordesillas, an ambassador reported that 'he had some falls from his horse, as is usual with those who ride post-haste'. He was less fortunate in 1532, when his horse threw him while hunting: he landed feet-first on a rock so hard that it damaged his leg and made him somewhat lame for the rest of his life – but, even so, he escaped the fate of his grandmother, Mary of Burgundy, and his son-in-law, Prince John of Portugal, both of whom died as a result of falling from their horse.[5] Charles was also lucky to survive repeated participation in war, despite exposing himself to enemy fire at Tunis, Algiers, Düren, Ingolstadt and elsewhere. Among monarchs, his great-grandfather Charles of Burgundy and his brother-in-law Louis of Hungary died in battle, and another brother-in-law (Christian of Denmark) became a prisoner of war and died in confinement. Among his generals, Bourbon died in action while both Philibert and René of Orange died of wounds – the latter struck by a cannonball 'while sitting in the seat where the emperor normally sat'.[6] Charles likewise survived his many tournaments and at least one assassination plot: in 1546 'three Italians promised the king of France that within four months they would kill the emperor'. The following year he confronted mutinous troops who, with their firearms loaded and primed, demanded from him 'either money or blood', and a drunken soldier fired his arquebus at Charles; but on both occasions he survived unscathed.[7] Others were less fortunate: a group of Protestants ambushed and murdered his Secretary of State Alonso de Idiáquez in 1547 as he rode through Saxony; and a jousting accident killed his arch-rival Henry II of France in 1559.

Of course, luck could have helped Charles even more. If King Francis had been killed at Pavia, as almost happened, leaving a successor who was only six; if Grand Chancellor Gattinara had lived a few months longer, to oversee mediation between Catholics and Lutherans at the Diet of Augsburg in 1530; if Popes Leo or Clement had convened a general council to reform Church abuses and clarify doctrine, as the council of Trent would later do; if Charles had disembarked his forces at Algiers a few days earlier and conquered the town before the storms decimated his troops and his fleet; if Mary Tudor had lived as long as her sister Elizabeth, and died in 1587 (or even as long as her mother Katherine and died in 1567), instead of in 1558, and thus allowed time to re-catholicize England thoroughly – all of these alternative outcomes would have enabled Charles to achieve even more.

HOW TO MAKE THINGS WORSE

Charles could also have achieved more by avoiding some self-inflicted wounds. In 1551, Count William of Nassau, brother and heir of Charles's Favourite ('mon Henry'), complained to a friend that 'those who wish to serve the emperor must now be Spanish: he only calls on people of our nation

[Germans] in case of need and to advance his agenda.'[8] It would be easy to dismiss this charge as biased – after all, the count had recently forfeited imperial favour by supporting the Schmalkaldic League – but Charles's own actions confirmed it. After Jean Glapion left his service in 1522, Charles chose only Spaniards as his confessors; whereas in 1522–3 he entrusted his three illegitimate daughters to Netherlanders, in 1550 he entrusted his illegitimate son, the future Don John, to a Spaniard; and he made sure that his heir, Philip, grew up as a 'true prince of Castile'.[9] The same turn towards Spain occurred in public affairs. In 1523 English diplomats noted that Charles now consulted 'the great lords off Spayne' every day, whereas 'before this tym they war nevyr callyd to no counseyll'. A decade later, the majority of Charles's inner circle of advisers came from the peninsula. So did the majority of his funds: in 1540 he confided to his brother that, having exhausted the resources of the Netherlands, 'I cannot raise any more money' there to fund his projects, now 'I cannot be sustained except by my kingdoms of Spain'. This imbalance increased over time: in the 1550s the emperor borrowed four times as much money in Castile as in the Netherlands to pay for his wars.[10]

William of Nassau was also correct about Charles's lack of German advisers. Although some of his relatives married prominent German princes – his nieces married the Elector Palatine and the dukes of Cleves and Bavaria – the emperor failed to build up a network of rulers committed to advancing his political and religious agenda in Germany. He also failed to build a cadre of competent ministers. Therefore, as he strove to resolve the religious divisions of Germany late in 1541, when his German Secretary Obernberger fell ill he found 'no one here to translate my instructions into German' and was therefore reduced to sending his chief negotiator 'a signed blank sheet, so that the said instructions can be entered later'. The cost of this neglect soon became apparent. In May 1542, Ferdinand complained that Charles had signed documents granting toleration to Lutherans even in the lands of Catholic rulers. When Charles demanded an explanation for this unprecedented concession, Obernberger protested that 'the documents had reached him ready to be signed, approved by those members of the council who were then dealing with them. Therefore,' Charles explained to his brother, 'trusting that they were as they should be, and because they were in German, I signed without reading them first.' Unfortunately, he continued, 'I cannot revoke these concessions because I do not have a copy of them' – and in any case he still lacked 'a secretary with me able to write in either Latin or German'. Small wonder that so many of Charles's policies in the Holy Roman Empire miscarried.[11]

Charles periodically encountered other shortcomings among his minis-ters. In 1520 his ambassadors in England, one a Spaniard and the other a Netherlander, apologized for writing confidential messages to him in clear text: 'Although we received your orders that all important matters should be cyphered, at present we do not know how to do this, and our secretary cannot read French.' Eight years later, Charles suspended Secretary of State Jean Lallemand from office on suspicion of treason and corruption, but dispatches continued to arrive from officials abroad in codes that only Lallemand knew, so that the emperor could 'only reply to the passages that we can understand'. He sent an urgent message to Lallemand 'asking him to send me a copy of the cypher key'; but even after it arrived, Charles managed to forget the names of his representatives in Rome and therefore dictated a message 'to Tweedledum and Tweedledee, my ambassadors'.[12]

These were all oversights and omissions, but Charles also made matters worse for himself by acts of commission. The refusal to forgive and forget wrongs, noted by his confessor Jean Glapion in 1521, created many prob-lems. The following year Gattinara informed a colleague that their master '*wants vengeance* for the harm and wrongs done to him' by the French; and thirty years later, as he travelled across Germany with a huge imperial army, the nuncio realized that Charles could now 'not only defend himself but also attack his enemies and *get revenge*'.[13] Horst Pietschmann has suggested that 'the confrontation with Luther and the rupture of religious unity, together with the Comunero revolt' underlay Charles's determination to make rebels pay, even if his severity created a host of implacable enemies: the double defiance by subjects in 1520–1 'had such an impact on the young emperor that they led him to react violently when confronted with the real or presumed liberties of towns, and with religious heterodoxy, not only in Germany but also in Spain and America'. Charles would have agreed with Pietschmann. In 1522 he declared his intention of punishing the Comunero leaders 'in an exemplary fashion that will be remembered for ever', and even thirty years later he still penalized the 'sons and grandsons' of former rebels. In 1531, on learning about riots and looting in Brussels, he ordered his sister Marie 'to punish the vile mutineers in such a way that others will take note'. When she protested against his severity, he replied: 'You may think that I am taking vengeance without due cause, but I make no apologies.' Suspects therefore continued to be arrested, tried and executed, often after torture, for another four years.[14] Charles could also impose severe punishments on those who were not his subjects, including the young French princes left by King Francis as hostages for the execution of the treaty of Madrid: in 1529 he ordered that they could not go hunting or receive any visitors from France, and he left them wearing shabby clothes, provoking his aunt Margaret to observe reproachfully that 'Young princes like them, who have done nothing wrong, must not be made to pay for the hostile behaviour of their father.' A few years later, Charles condoned the judicial murder of a rebel leader with the chilling phrase: 'Dead men don't wage war.'[15]

Charles also created problems for himself by selfishness – or what others perceived as selfishness. Just before he left the Netherlands for the last time, an ambassador observed that 'His Imperial Majesty preferred taking to giving', echoing similar comments by many others earlier in the reign. In 1539 the English ambassador at Charles's court considered the emperor both 'wise and wily', always prone to 'keep his shins whole for himself than break them for another man's pleasure, except he might have thereby right great assured honour and also very much profit'. Five years later a French minister asked rhetorically: 'If th'empereur might lyve alwayes, what is his freendeship? He careth not if freend, father and all togedre shuld sinke so [long as] as his insatiable desyre to reign might be satisfied ... He is a covetous man.' In 1547, more concisely, Paul III asserted at an audience that 'Your Majesty is an ingrate who only remembers his friends when he needs them.'[16]

Above all, Charles created serious problems for himself by telling lies – a charge he would doubtless have denied, since he once assured his brother Ferdinand that 'I have always taken singular care to keep my word, even when I forfeited excellent opportunities for personal profit by doing so.'[17] Nevertheless, evidence abounds that he lied repeatedly when it suited him, even to his closest relatives (for example, by creating a fictional world around his mother). In 1541 he solemnly swore, 'on the soul of the empress, that he knew nothing about the whereabouts of Rincón and Fregoso', even though he had taken steps to shield the officials who had murdered both diplomats from any legal consequences. A decade later, despite promising not to condemn Philip of Hesse to life imprisonment, Charles secretly extended his sentence by another fifteen years – which, since the landgrave was already forty-six, meant that he would probably die in prison. In 1547 he denied prior knowledge of the capture of Piacenza from Pope Paul III's son, Pier Luigi Farnese, orchestrated by his lieutenant Ferrante Gonzaga, but nevertheless refused to return it to Farnese's heir, Octavio. Such lies had consequences. Francis used the assassination of his ambassadors to justify a declaration of war against Charles; keeping the landgrave in prison helped to propel his son-in-law, Maurice of Saxony, into revolt; Paul refused to reconvene the council of Trent until Charles returned Piacenza to Octavio. Some of these lies also had a long afterlife. In his novel *Gargantua and Pantagruel*, first published in 1552, François Rabelais denounced Charles's imprisonment of Philip of Hesse as an act of treachery. In 1576, Jean Bodin flagged 'the base and filthy murder of Fregoso and Rincón' as an infamous breach of international law in his *Six books of the Republic*; and many writers on international law would repeat his criticisms. When two of its diplomats were murdered in Austria on their way to a peace conference in 1799, the French government portrayed the crime as a 'frightening extension of the series of atrocities with which the House of Habsburg has stunned Europe, ever since Charles V provided the precedent of placing himself above the laws by ordering the assassination of the ambassadors that the king of France had sent to Venice and Constantinople'.[18]

THE THREE REVOLUTIONS OF THE EARLIER
SIXTEENTH CENTURY

Although these self-inflicted wounds weakened Charles, their impact paled before the challenges presented by three revolutions in the earlier sixteenth century: military, religious and administrative.

The development of the artillery fortress, an interlocking system of star-shaped bastions and outposts beyond reinforced walls, known as *alla moderna* and *à la manière moderne*, revolutionized the art of land warfare in Europe because they normally only surrendered after a complete blockade by armies of unprecedented size. Steven Gunn has estimated that in the 1550s 'forces of 40,000 or more operated in a region which had in the 1520s supported armies only a quarter of the size'. Securing the surrender of an artillery fortress by blockade normally took weeks if not months, and sieges became the hinge on which campaigns turned.[19]

Charles first encountered this truth in 1529. A few years before, anticipating a siege, the republic of Florence had reconfigured existing towers and gateways into angular bastions, adding thick revetments of earth to reinforce the medieval walls, and creating forts beyond the walls to cover weak points. The military stalemate created by these initiatives infuriated Charles's commander at the siege of Florence, Prince Philibert of Orange, whose holograph letters complained repeatedly that the lack of artillery, men and money jeopardized the outcome of the siege. In October 1529, describing himself as 'the most desperate man in the world', the prince warned Charles that 'if you really want the town you can have it, but not with the few troops I have here because – please believe me – it would take me years to conclude the matter. If you want victory now, you must send immediately 10,000 or 12,000 men to complete the siege-works on the other side of the river, together with a good artillery crew.'[20] He did not exaggerate: Florence held out for eleven months. Artillery fortresses would again derail Charles's campaign in 1544 (St Dizier halted his invasion of France for over a month) and sabotage his strategy in 1551, with the unsuccessful siege of Parma, and in 1552, with the unsuccessful siege of Metz.

Supporting the large armies required to subdue an artillery fortress created another problem: organized indiscipline. As the prince of Orange complained during the siege of Florence: 'Your whole army is ready to mutiny through lack of money ... If God does not work a miracle, as He usually does, and you do not provide a remedy, I hold a general mutiny to be certain.' Others shared the prince's concerns. The insubordinate behaviour by the imperial troops in Italy led the duke of Ferrara to inform the emperor that 'we do not dare to accept just now the command of such a disobedient and unbridled [exfrenato] army'. Ferrara was wise: the Spanish troops in Lombardy had mutinied briefly before their victory at Pavia, and thousands of their successors would mutiny again in Italy in 1537–8 (after the failed Provence campaign), in Germany in 1547 (after defeating the Schmalkaldic League) and in the Netherlands in 1553 (after the siege of Metz).[21]

Artillery also transformed naval warfare during Charles's reign. In the Mediterranean, oared galleys now deployed huge centreline guns either against targets ashore (as at La Goletta in 1535) or against each other (as at Preveza in 1538). At the same time, the operational range of galley fleets increased dramatically. The viceroy of Sicily observed wistfully in 1557 that:

Things are different today from what they were thirty or forty years ago. Back then we talked about the Turks as if were talking about the Antipodes, but now they come so close and they are so familiar with the affairs of Christendom that what happens in Sicily is known as quickly in Constantinople as in Spain; and it is normal for their fleet to sail by this island every year.[22]

In the Atlantic, too, naval warfare became more complex as sailing warships began to deploy heavy artillery on their lower decks (thanks to the invention of the gun port). In 1545 the galleons of Francis and Henry VIII engaged in an artillery duel when a French expeditionary force attempted to land on the Isle of Wight; and in 1558 bombardment from Spanish galleons offshore helped to defeat the French troops trapped on the sands near Gravelines.

These developments greatly increased the cost of naval operations. Unlike infantry or cavalry regiments, warships – whether galleons or galleys – could not be mobilized at the beginning of a campaign and demobilized at its end. Rulers needed either to maintain a standing navy or else find and fund someone else to do so. In 1522 the emperor managed to sail through the Atlantic to Spain only because Henry VIII loaned him ships from the Royal Navy; and in 1529, 1535, 1541 and 1543 he managed to cross the Mediterranean only because the galley fleet maintained by Andrea Doria escorted him.

James Tracy has calculated that these innovations in land and sea warfare increased the cost of Charles's campaigns from an annual average of 430,000 ducats in the 1530s to 900,000 ducats in the 1540s – more than double – with further increases in the 1550s. Moreover, whereas windfalls (above all the French ransom and the spoils of the Aztec and Inca empires) covered almost half the emperor's military expenditure in the 1530s, they produced less than one-fifth in the 1540s and even less in the 1550s, leading him to secure loans from bankers and to sequester his subjects' private property, creating a sovereign debt that could not be repaid. A few months after his accession, Philip II's financial advisers calculated that he owed over ten million ducats in his various dominions, and that he had committed all his revenues for the next four years to their repayment; shortly afterwards, for the first time in Spanish history, the treasury defaulted on its obligations and forcibly converted outstanding high-interest loans into low-interest bonds.[23] Charles's wars also involved an important opportunity cost: when the emperor campaigned in person, as he did for at least 600 days between 1532 and 1554, he found time for little else. According to a disgruntled diplomat travelling with Charles during his last campaign, 'In wartime His Majesty does not attend to other business.'[24]

The religious revolution unleashed by Martin Luther also periodically absorbed Charles's attention. The published *Acta* of each imperial Diet give some idea of the hours taken up by religious debates: according to a simple page count, 'Discussions with and about Luther' at Worms constituted more than a quarter of the total business. The discussion of religious concessions at Regensburg in 1532 absorbed almost as much time, and crafting a religious formula acceptable to both the Lutherans and Catholics at the Diet of Augsburg in 1547–8 represented one-eighth of the total business.[25] Sometimes the emperor intervened in person (as he did at Worms in 1521);

at other times he sat through the debates (as he did at Augsburg in 1530 while the Lutheran Confession was slowly read out); and, behind the scenes, he spent many hours feasting and hunting with the leading German princes in an effort to win their support for his religious programme. He also devoted precious time at summits with the pope and at audiences with his envoys, as well as in writing holograph letters, in order to win Rome's support for his religious initiatives.

Charles's efforts to silence Luther and his supporters failed in large part because Ottoman advances up the Danube repeatedly obliged him to authorize religious concessions in return for military assistance from Lutheran rulers. The Lutheran leaders fully realized their advantage: as Philip of Hesse informed Luther in 1529, since he and his colleagues 'are the greatest and chief source of help' to the Habsburgs in resisting the Turks, 'we thought we should all agree not to provide or give any help unless His Majesty first promised to leave us in peace and not to disturb us on account of the Gospel'.[26] This policy produced a series of concessions from Charles that allowed Lutheranism not only to prosper in the states where it already existed but also to expand. Only the conclusion of a five-year truce with the sultan in 1547 allowed the emperor to attempt the forcible reconciliation of Germany's religious divisions.

Charles also faced unprecedented administrative challenges in ruling his empire. In his remarkable study of supreme power and its pitfalls in the United States, *The impossible presidency*, Jeremi Suri suggested that sometimes large states become too complex for any one individual to handle. Specifically, Suri argued that Franklin Roosevelt, who 'built the postwar presidency' in America, was also 'the last to master it':

> The problem for Roosevelt's successors was too much power, too much responsibility, and too much temptation. Roosevelt was the last great president because the office was still small enough for him to control it, just barely. After him, the continued increase in presidential power exceeded executive capacity ... [until] by the start of the 21st century, the inhuman demands of the office made it impossible to succeed as president ... The pressure to react quickly and globally left little space for thought and creativity about policy.

It had become, in short, 'the impossible presidency'.[27] The surviving sources suggest a parallel between Charles and Roosevelt: the primary architect of the Habsburg Empire was also 'the last to master it'. He ruled, in effect, an impossible empire.

Although Charles's ceremonial entry as count of Flanders at Bruges in 1515 included pageantry that alluded to the various lands that he might inherit, nothing prepared him or the rest of Europe for the spate of territories that fell under his sceptre during the next few years. In 1516, Erasmus noted that 'Prince Charles is being sent for to take over several kingdoms (nine or ten they say)' in Spain and Italy; and, he added presciently (though in vain), 'I pray it may turn out well for our country and not only for the prince.'[28] Charles soon added both the Holy Roman Empire and the Aztec lands, creating a transatlantic state of unprecedented size, to which his lieutenants would annex the duchy of Milan, several provinces in the Netherlands and many more lands in the Americas, including the Inca Empire. Moreover, the population of all his European dominions grew throughout his reign – that of the kingdom of Naples doubled. These developments prevented Charles from turning to the recent past for inspiration – not even Charlemagne seven centuries before had controlled such extensive territories – and the absence of precedents helps to explain the apparently haphazard nature of his decision-making. Charles had no choice but to learn by trial (and sometimes by error).

In this he was not alone. In his pioneering book of 1953, Geoffrey Elton called the explosion of central government activity in England during the reign of Henry VIII the 'Tudor revolution in government', centred on the administrative innovations of Thomas Wolsey and Thomas Cromwell, who served successively as Henry's chief minister. Four centuries earlier, the phenomenon had attracted the attention of Steven Vaughan, an English merchant and diplomat in the Netherlands. In 1534, Vaughan compared Cromwell's workload with that of Jean Carondolet, 'the emperor's chief counsillor in these parts' and predicted that 'the excellent mynds and wytts' of both ministers would be 'dulled with the contynued travayle' caused by the rising tide of public affairs. This would leave them 'lesse able and disposed to endure a long travayle in the prince's causes and other matters', and increase the risk that they would 'hasteth [their] dethe byfore [their] tyme'.[29]

Gattinara would have strongly agreed with Vaughan – though he would no doubt have grumbled that Charles's administrative habits unnecessarily increased the 'travayle' of his ministers. In a bitter memorandum in 1523 the Grand Chancellor complained that 'ever since I entered your service, I have toiled to introduce proper order into your affairs, submitting to you several papers of advice on the subject', but 'it was never possible to make you deal with them [ne fut jamays possible de vous reduisre a y entendre]'. Evidently, the emperor neglected this paper, too, because shortly afterwards Gattinara composed another one, even more outspoken. 'My heart is full of regret that it takes so long to decide most of the important matters that occur daily that either the situation has changed or the opportunity is lost,' he began. 'I cannot imagine where this failing originates, unless Your Majesty wants to follow the methods of the late Emperor Maximilian who also took too long to make up his mind, using the excuse that he lacked the money required. But Your Majesty cannot use the same excuse because of all the money at your disposal.' Charles's dangerous procrastination, Gattinara asserted, stemmed not from a lack of resources but from a failure to deploy effectively the ample resources at his disposal.[30]

MESSIANIC IMPERIALISM AND THE LIMITS OF THE POSSIBLE

Gattinara's memoranda linked his master's slothful decision-making with his Messianic Imperialism. According to the chancellor, the emperor chose to leave 'everything unresolved in the expectation that God will always perform miracles in your affairs, as He has done until now; but this is very dangerous, because by leaving everything up to God one may well anger Him.' Once again, Charles paid no attention. During the Tunis campaign of 1535 he claimed more than once that he served merely as God's lieutenant and relied on the Creator to arrange a successful outcome; in autumn 1541 he persevered with his attack on Algiers, against the advice of his experts, 'because weather lies in God's hands'; and in autumn 1552 he likewise decided to besiege Metz because 'God will hold everything in His hand and guide me, and bring about a successful outcome'. Charles periodically turned to his confessors (and occasionally to a special committee of theologians) for reassurance that his actions and aspirations enjoyed divine favour, and they rarely disappointed him. His confessor Loaysa once promised him that 'More than ever, I believe that Your Majesty will overcome all the present difficulties and that God will place all your enemies at your feet. Moreover, because it is God's will that your victories come only after surmounting obstacles, Your Majesty must be patient and proceed with a joyous heart.' On another occasion, after suggesting an alternative course of action, Loaysa backtracked and assured Charles that 'if Your Majesty persists in following contrary advice (which I would regret, because I cannot see any advantage), I would be consoled by my belief that Your Majesty is guided by God in what you want, and the rest of us do not know what we are talking about'. Such reinforcement helps to explain why miracles formed an integral part of the strategic culture of Habsburg Spain.[31]

Charles's Messianic vision had several consequences. At a basic level, the evidence of divine favour encouraged self-righteousness and inflexibility; it could also lead to imprudence and over-confidence. Antoine Perrenot once boasted that 'in desperate situations, just when one least expects it, something happens that rescues His Majesty'; but this created a dangerous feedback loop, in which the perceived miracles of the past strengthened the expectation that, despite the obstacles, more would follow.[32] In addition it discouraged making contingency plans: if God fought for the emperor, any attempt to plan for potential failure might be seen as evidence of a lack of faith. It also discouraged a willingness to abandon or even to adapt confession-based policies when they ran into difficulties, allowing his enemies time to coordinate their resources in order to thwart Charles's strategic goals.

Despite his confidence in miracles, and his reliance on those who reinforced it, for most of his reign Charles heeded the advice of Erasmus in 1517: 'A prince called on to reign over so many kingdoms ought to despise no man's counsel zealously offered, and should then choose out of it all what he judges most worthy to be followed.' Three decades later, Count William of Nassau acknowledged that the emperor had indeed chosen his ministers 'with no attention to family or wealth or estates, but only to experience and past achievements'; and he could have cited by way of illustration the careers of Adrian of Utrecht, Francisco de Los Cobos, Pedro de La Gasca, and many others whose merits lifted them from relative obscurity to prominence in imperial service.[33] Charles also wisely delegated many critical decisions to his lieutenants on the periphery of his empire, a practice that started early: in August 1516, puzzled by conflicting accounts of the situation in Castile, Charles sent two sets of instructions from Brussels to Cardinal Cisneros, his governor there, 'so that you can use them according to your discretion and prudence'. The decision, Charles repeated, 'rests with you'. In 1531 he likewise waived the restrictions on the powers delegated to his brother as his lieutenant in Germany: Ferdinand might disregard them 'in matters of great importance' whenever 'time and circumstance' did not allow him to consult the emperor first.[34]

Charles usually succeeded when he recognized the limits of the possible. In April 1532 he decided that 'our plan for the year is to see to the defence of Christendom and to resist the Turks, recognizing that it will be impossible to take the offensive so soon'. The following year, when his sister Marie protested that she could not cope with all the challenges that faced her, Charles responded soothingly that 'I have also had all these [negative] thoughts, as well as some others, but after chasing them away I have often found that I had the means to be able to do better, and cope with the tasks that faced me.' He added: 'Sometimes you just have to persevere and do what is possible, because no one is obliged to do the impossible. God does not want people to work themselves to death.' As was his wont, Charles made the same point again later in the same document: 'I can give you good advice on this, because I have experience. I don't want to say that I do everything that I should – and I believe that few do so, or can do so – but we should do the best that our natural strength can stand. God does not require us to do more than is possible.'[35] On the last day of his meeting with the French royal family at Aigues Mortes in 1538, Charles said to the dauphin: 'Sir: you and my son must not be as stupid as your father and I have been'; and the following year he reluctantly delayed the Mediterranean campaign he had planned with Venice and the papacy because 'Even though I am emperor, I can only do what is humanly possible, because I am only a man.' In 1542 he informed Ferdinand that 'the urgency of some public affairs means that I must do what is possible, not what I want.'[36]

The emperor meant what he said. In 1535 he abandoned other ventures in order to devote all his resources and his attention to the Tunis campaign because 'we must adapt ourselves to the current situation and concentrate on the most pressing matters'. In 1552, realizing that he lacked the funds to maintain a garrison at Mahdia in north Africa, captured amid great fanfare two years before, he ordered its fortifications to be razed and abandoned; and three years later, when the Florentine ambassador doubted his declaration that he planned to retire to Spain, 'His Majesty replied: "Yes, it's true: that is still my intention. But with great plans, things can arise from one hour to the next that force you to give up what you had resolved to do." '[37] Charles showed the same realism concerning words as he did towards deeds. When Marie complained that the Netherlands nobles levelled wounding criticisms at her, Charles replied that 'I am so familiar with reproaches like these that I pay no attention to them.' Likewise, when the English ambassador complained at an audience about the hostile sermons against his master delivered by Spanish clerics, Charles reminded him: 'Prechers woll speke agaynst my sellff, when ever there is cause. That can not be let [stopped].' When the ambassador persisted with his protest, Charles replied: 'Kynges be not kinges of tonges, and if men gyve cause to be spoken off, thei woll be spoken off: there is no remedy.'[38] Charles ignored unwelcome praise as well as criticisms. During the coronation festivities in Bologna in 1530, Paolo Giovio, historian and the pope's master of ceremonies, 'told him in a loud voice, "Today, invincible king, you are called to the crown of Constantinople" ' – but, Giovio reported with regret, 'At this His Majesty just smiled.' Five years later, after the conquest of Tunis, Charles again ignored calls to sail against Constantinople and declared that he would proceed 'in conformity with the season and the limits of the possible'.[39]

THE IMPERIAL REPERTOIRE

Henry Kissinger, the US National Security Advisor and Secretary of State in the 1970s, has claimed that 'In retrospect, all successful policies seem preordained. Leaders like to claim prescience for what has worked, ascribing to planning what usually starts as a series of improvisations.' Historians Jane Burbank and Frederick Cooper agreed. Their impressive study, *Empires in world history*, noted that 'empires were not all alike; they created, adopted, and transmitted various repertoires of rule'. Moreover, 'an imperial repertoire was neither a bag of tricks dipped into at random nor a pre-set formula for rule. Faced with challenges day by day, empires improvised.'[40]

The diffuse nature of Charles's empire increased the need to improvise because, as Helmut G. Koenigsberger observed in 1958 (the fourth centenary of the emperor's death), Charles 'was no Alexander or Napoleon who had conquered his empire, but the hereditary and legitimate ruler of each of his states whose laws and customs he had sworn to maintain'. This meant that the emperor was often reactive, not proactive – and above all reactive to the priorities of the dominion where he resided.[41] Between 1522 and 1529, while confined to Spain, the sub-imperial agenda of the peninsula normally prevailed, whereas between 1543 and 1556, when he shuttled between Germany and the Netherlands, Charles often privileged issues important to his proconsuls and subjects there. Competition between various sub-imperial agendas could place the emperor under intense pressure. The 'Alternative' in 1544–5 offered one example of this, with the governing elites of Milan, the Netherlands and Spain providing incompatible advice on which part of his empire Charles should surrender to France (chapter 12); and the oscillations in his policy on the enslavement of native Americans, in response to the distinct agenda of the friars and the colonists, offer another (chapter 13). Nevertheless, despite the need to improvise, innovate and compromise, Charles's imperial repertoire included a pre-set formula consisting of four core elements: dynasty, chivalry, reputation and faith.

The emperor's dynastic commitment is easily demonstrated: he constantly sought ways to recover lands that had once belonged to his ancestors, especially to the dukes of Burgundy. He had demanded restitution of the whole inheritance at the treaty of Madrid in 1526, and although he renounced most of his claims three years later in the treaty of Cambrai, in 1534 he assured his sister Eleanor, queen of France, that he 'would persevere in recovering the duchy of Burgundy, which is part of our ancient inheritance, and more important to us than Milan'. In 1539 an English diplomat deduced from Charles's conversations about grand strategy that 'he myndith more Geldre in his hert then he dothe Millan or all Italy'; and the following year, the emperor dangled before France 'the renunciation of all our rights and claims to the duchy of Burgundy, albeit they are well and justly founded in law', as if they were still worth something.[42]

Charles's fidelity to Burgundy included loyalty to its chivalric values. He believed that political problems could be solved by duels; that it was worth jousting to win a lady's smile; and that he might lead a crusade to recover Constantinople for Christendom. As Loaysa noted in 1532, 'you love honour a thousand times more than life and wealth'; and when eight years later Henry VIII demanded the immediate surrender of an Englishman in imperial service, whom the king regarded as a traitor, Charles angrily responded that even if he were himself a prisoner 'in the Towre of London, I wold not consent so to charge myn honour and my consciens' by sacrificing a faithful servant. Shortly afterwards, he told his confessor that 'the day that a man loses his honour, he should die – because he is now useless'.[43] Lastly, he always venerated the Burgundian Order of the Golden Fleece: his *Memoirs* included details on every Chapter over which he presided, and an illustrated manuscript of its statutes was one of the few works that he took with him to Yuste.[44]

Charles also loved reputation 'more than life and wealth'. His self-evaluation of 1525 obsessed about 'maintaining my reputation' and worried that 'since time is passing, and we are all going to die, I do not want to disappear from the world without leaving something memorable behind' (chapter 6). After he left Spain in 1529, although he paid lip service to the difficulties that faced his regent, the empress ('I am well aware of the problems that exist in those kingdoms . . .'), he always regarded the difficulties that he himself faced as superior because 'my honour and my life are at stake', so that failure to send him the troops and treasure that he demanded 'will place at great hazard and danger my person, my dominions, and my reputation' – an unsubtle attempt to make the empress (and her advisers) feel personally responsible for any harm that befell him.[45] In 1543 he assured his son and heir that everything 'I have done has been necessary to guard my honour' and revealed that he planned to attack his enemies 'for the sake of my honour and my reputation, which is why I leave on such an uncertain venture' (chapter 11). The following year, as he prepared to invade France, Charles warned his ministers in Spain that if they did not immediately send him money, 'it will hazard not only the great sums already spent thus far but also our reputation, which is what we would resent most'. In 1551 he declared that 'we are so involved' in the siege of Parma 'that we could not abandon it without great loss of reputation'. The following year he insisted that Lutheran theologians must be allowed to speak at the council of Trent because to do otherwise 'would obviously imperil my reputation, which is the same as the service of God'; and he entered the trenches around Metz in person because 'things were not going well there, so that my reputation has become involved'.[46]

Finally, it is easy to document the emperor's solid faith and its impact on his political choices. Throughout his life he performed daily devotions and he retired to a monastery each Easter and also after his abdication. He made good on the promise he made on the day after he confronted Luther at the Diet of Worms in 1521: 'I am entirely determined to dedicate my kingdoms and lordships, my friends, my body, my blood, my life and my soul' to combat heresy, because to permit 'heresy or a diminution of the Christian religion to rest in the hearts of men through our own negligence would bring permanent dishonour on us and our successors'. In 1540, when the English ambassador requested at an audience the release of some English merchants arrested by the Inquisitors of Toledo, Charles flatly refused because 'I cannot lett [prevent] the Inquisition. This is a thing that towchith our faythe', adding, 'I assure yow I woll not altre my inquisition.' ('*My* inquisition'!)[47] The emperor's fear 'that he would go to Hell if he permitted [a given] practice to continue' also led him to reject several policies that would have brought him important political advantages, notably granting permanent toleration to the Lutherans of Germany and granting encomiendas to the American colonists in perpetuity. In 1554, 'for the discharge of our conscience', he instructed his son to examine the justice of his occupation of both Piacenza and Navarre. The following year he claimed that he had decided to abdicate 'because I know that I cannot fulfil what I owe to my conscience'.[48]

DO IT YOURSELF

Charles's policies displayed one more core element throughout his life: confidence that he alone could solve the problems that faced his empire. Admittedly, he occasionally expressed misgivings – not only in his self-analysis of 1525 ('until now I have done nothing that brings me honour') and his instructions of 1543 ('I am going to undertake something so uncertain that I do not know what benefit or effect it will bring'), but also in 1552 as he fled from Innsbruck

('God may be angry with me' and might punish him for pride because he had composed his *Memoirs*) – but such doubts were relatively rare.[49] The emperor's self-confidence manifested itself most clearly in his resort to 'executive diplomacy': face-to-face meetings with other monarchs to resolve outstanding disputes. To this end he met Henry VIII four times; Clement VII twice and his successor Paul III three times; and Francis I also three times (although since the latter was his prisoner in Madrid in 1525–6, it hardly counted). Not everyone approved of executive diplomacy – in 1519, Chièvres vetoed an invitation from the French king to a meeting, on the grounds that Duke John of Burgundy had been murdered when responding to a similar invitation a century before; in 1525–6, Gattinara urged his master not to negotiate directly with Francis while in captivity; and in 1543, after a papal summit, Loaysa tutted: 'Experience has taught us that little advantage or reputation comes from these meetings' – but the emperor persisted. Although monarchs could continue 'to declare their wishes and intentions to each other by means of their ministers', he believed that a face-to-face meeting between them 'was the true and best means' to settle outstanding issues.[50]

Although Charles eventually abandoned summit diplomacy, he continued to travel: indeed between 1529 and 1550 he was almost constantly on the move, covering thousands of kilometres (see Map 1). María José Rodríguez-Salgado has speculated that Charles enjoyed his travels because they allowed him to appear:

> ... ever the knight in shining armour to his hard-pressed regents and governors. As one chronicler put it, his presence was looked for with as much desire as parched land longs for rain. Charles was sustained by the universal belief that his presence or his time alone would solve the most excruciating problems. The responsibility was great but so was the sense of achievement and worth. Fired with adrenalin he would rush from internal political crisis to war and back again.

This judgement seems too harsh. As Horst Rabe and Peter Marzahl have noted: 'Rule was as yet no abstract concept' in Charles's day. 'It was not a body of rights and duties that could be delegated easily.' Rather, 'Rule meant the concrete and personal demonstration of power and authority. Therefore a ruler's absence potentially enfeebled or even endangered his authority', whereas 'the actual presence of the ruler remained a political fact of the utmost importance. Substitute arrangements were far too often uncertain and remained insufficient.'[51]

Charles himself never doubted that his physical presence made the critical difference between success and failure in his ventures. In February 1529 he informed his Spanish subjects that he must leave Spain for Italy because 'my ministers there advise me that only my presence can remedy the situation' and ensure that 'Christendom and what God has given me will not be lost in my time'. In letters written shortly afterwards 'from the royal galley' in Barcelona harbour, he repeated that it would be impossible 'to end the wars in progress and the problems that face Christendom without our presence' in Italy. Two years later, he informed the empress that unless he remained in northern Europe (instead of returning to Spain as she asked), 'all the evil that happens would be my fault, and I would believe that it happened because I did not do enough'.[52]

Paradoxically, rushing 'from internal political crisis to war and back again' brought other benefits. Successful leaders must carve out time from their schedules for reflection and creativity, and travelling allowed Charles to fulfil this need. His secret instructions to his son in 1543 provide a rare insight into this process. The emperor embarked on his galley fleet in Barcelona on 1 May, but the following day bad weather forced him to take refuge in the small port of Palamos, and between then and 6 May, isolated from the normal press of business, he composed and revised 48 sheets of detailed advice for Philip, written entirely in his own hand and alone. Charles's frequent hunting expeditions brought similar benefits: apart from keeping him fit (at an audience in 1547, the nuncio told him that his two weeks of 'hunting and the country air have done us good, and helped us recover our colour and strength'), it gave him time to reflect on the problems he faced and how best to solve them. Although the administrative benefits derived from his leisure activities are hard to document, it cannot be coincidence that Charles often took a series of decisions just after he returned from hunting.[53] Moreover, since he never travelled or hunted alone, the emperor's outdoor activities provided opportunities to bond with members of his entourage and dazzle them.

CREATING CHARISMA

In his path-breaking study of the role of ideology in sustaining the Roman Empire – a subject that intrigued Charles and his ministers – Clifford Ando argued that the power wielded by Augustus and his successors rested to a remarkable degree on personal charisma: the emperors manipulated messages and media to achieve a consensus among members of the elite, encouraging the perception that they were participants in the imperial venture rather than mere subjects.[54] Charles, too, used his personal charisma to create consensus across his empire, and like Augustus he began with his extended family, favouring not only his siblings, nieces and nephews, but also members of his household. In the Netherlands, he granted pensions to his first wet-nurse, Barbe Servels, and to the mothers of two of his illegitimate children, Jeanne van der Gheynst and Barbara Blomberg, as well as providing jobs for members of their families. In Spain, he publicly honoured his first preceptors: in 1519 he granted Juan de Anchieta an annual salary for life, even though he was then 'too old' to serve at court, 'because of the many excellent services the said Juan has performed for us'; and in 1523, Charles appointed Luis Cabeza de Vaca bishop of the Canaries, promoting him in 1530 to Salamanca and making much of him on his visit to the city four years later.[55]

Such gracious acts could create lifelong devotion among recipients. The ingenious inventor from Cremona, Janello Torriani, 'told the emperor one day that he owed more to him than to his natural parents, because the latter had merely given him a short life whereas the emperor would make him immortal'. In 1548 the count of Buren, commander of the Netherlands contingent that had crossed the Rhine to reach Charles at Ingolstadt two years before, learned that he only had a few hours to live and immediately sent for his closest colleagues in the imperial entourage, as well as his finest clothes and his insignia of the Golden Fleece. He then called for a 'fine goblet' (perhaps the one presented to him by Charles that depicted the Rhine crossing), drank his master's health, made a speech thanking him for all his favours, and 'wrote with his own hand two entire sheets to the emperor' before he died. In 1550, Fray Domingo de Soto, back in Spain after serving eighteen months as Charles's confessor, assured Secretary of State Francisco de Eraso 'that I have never in my life felt such deep love [*tan entra-ñable amor*] as I do' for the emperor and that 'the modesty and sweetness of his conversation gives me an infinite desire to see him again and serve him'. Two years later, Soto assured Eraso that news of the emperor's flight from Germany 'has truly awakened a great desire in me to go and die with him, if only my journey would do some good'.[56] Some held up Charles's behaviour as an example for others. In January 1552, Perrenot rejected the request of a Spanish bishop to leave the council of Trent and go home on the grounds that he was semi-paralyzed with gout, because 'His Majesty himself suffers from several maladies, especially gout, and he believes that if someone is ill he can find a cure wherever he may be.' The following October, during the siege of Metz, Marie rejected a request from William of Orange to leave his unit on the French frontier 'because of the bad weather'; instead he should 'follow the example of His Majesty, and of so many excellent nobles with him, who remain in the field despite the contrary weather'.[57]

Charles's efforts to project an imperial charisma drew strength from the fact that many of his subjects shared both his values and his outlook. In the Americas, the chronicles written by the Spanish conquistadors invoked God, on average, three times in every thousand words: God gave them strength, courage, consolation, inspiration, aid, support, victory and health; He delivered, preserved, rewarded, foresaw and forgave; He led, saved, wished and directed. The only words used more frequently in the chronicles of conquest were 'war', 'gold' and, above all, 'the king' or its equivalents ('His Majesty', 'emperor' and 'royal'), which appeared eight times in every thousand words. In Europe, Gattinara constantly urged his master to place God first, and his own conduct provided a striking practical example: in August 1517, just before Charles left the Netherlands for Spain, his future chancellor entered the Carthusian convent of Scheut, a ducal foundation just outside the walls of Brussels, and spent seven months secluded there to fulfil a vow. Even hard-nosed merchant bankers began their business letters with 'Jesus' and the sign of the cross, peppered the contents with 'God willing', and ended 'Christ be with you'. The *Memoirs* of Fery de Guyon, a professional soldier from Burgundy, described the multinational armies in which he served as 'the emperor's men', never happier than when fighting 'the infidel'. Guyon devoted several pages to 'one of the best tournaments ever seen' (staged by the marquis del Vasto in Milan) and included details on the pilgrimage he undertook with three companions from the imperial court to Santiago de Compostela, 'witnessing many fine devout acts along the way'.[58]

Many contemporaries also lionized Charles. In Spain, the Cortes of Castile assured him in 1523 that 'what comes from the mouth of Your Majesty comes from the mouth of God, who placed you here in His place'; three years later, after hearing of the Ottoman victory at Mohács, some of his Castilian subjects affirmed that 'Your Imperial Majesty is not only lord of the Christian religion but of the whole world'; and in 1528 one of his Spanish vassals begged the Creator to protect and prosper Charles's cause 'for ever, making you lord of the world', while an obsequious diplomat in Rome claimed that some people 'no longer believe in God, but rather in Your Majesty'.[59] In Italy, Ludovico Ariosto included in his most famous poem, *Orlando furioso* (*Angry Roland*), set in the time of Charlemagne, a prophecy that Charles, 'the wisest and the most just emperor that there had been or ever would be since Augustus', would one day 'rule the world', because God 'wants there to be only one flock and one shepherd'. In the Netherlands, the chamber of Rhetoric at Leiden might have won the international sycophancy stakes with their entry for a competition to identify 'Who has won the most noble and powerful victories?' They answered 'Charles V' and their verse play included the figures of Jupiter with his eagle, Hercules with his columns and Jason with the Golden Fleece – but Charles surpassed them all.[60]

Many shared other core beliefs of their master, including the conviction that only Charles's presence could save them from catastrophe. In 1548 the Cortes of Castile declared that 'the presence here of our king and natural lord is of such importance that all other resources are of less weight'; six years later, a lawyer from Arras opined that the appearance of his sovereign, mounted and at the head of his army, 'encouraged everyone' who saw him and 'contributed to the retreat of the French'.[61] Some shared Charles's ability to recall ancient injustices and injuries and seek revenge: when the French garrison of Hesdin surrendered in 1553, the same lawyer from Arras noted with satisfaction that the prisoners included the grandson 'of Mr. Robert de la Marck, whose defiance of the emperor started the war in the year 1521'.[62] Others detected and denounced the menace of heresy everywhere. The Spanish bishop of Venezuela warned in 1535 that 'Your Majesty should not permit any Germans to come over here', especially not 'those of low degree, because we have found that some of those in this province have followed the opinions of the heretic Martin Luther': although he only provided one name, the bishop had identified a development likely to grab the emperor's attention.[63] Others still pleaded their conscience as a reason for making difficult policy choices: in 1537, Charles's lieutenant in Lombardy begged him to moderate his tax demands on the duchy 'to satisfy my conscience', and a decade later the last testament of his successor pleaded for repayment of the loans contracted in the emperor's name 'for the unburdening of the testator's soul'.[64] When Charles deployed similar rhetoric, therefore, many members of his audience were already programmed to receive.

A GAME OF GLOBAL CHESS

In an essay about Charles first published in 1966, Fernand Braudel called on modern historians to imagine the emperor engaged in 'a long and difficult game of global chess, so let us try to put ourselves in the player's seat'. It was, Braudel stressed, 'a chess game that did not follow the normal rules', because Charles's opponents, foreign and domestic, determined many of his moves and forced him to choose where he should go, what he should spend, and how he should attack. By the time of the emperor's abdication, Braudel deemed, he had largely failed in the Mediterranean; neither won nor lost against France; clearly won in Italy and the Americas, and apparently also in England and the Low Countries; and ensured, for better or worse, that his son would not inherit his German problems. Nevertheless, Braudel cautioned, 'Politics is like Penelope's weaving: it never ends': two months after Charles's death, Philip ceased to be king of England, but six months later France concluded a humiliating peace and soon lapsed into civil war.[65]

In 2000, Michèle Escamilla, one of the few historians since Braudel to draw up a balance sheet of the reign, also suggested that 'since a full global assessment apparently remains so difficult to establish, we should attempt a series of assessments by region'. Let us take up her invitation, starting in the Netherlands where Charles's reign began and ended. The emperor's constant fiscal demands, and the devastation caused by his wars, drained resources and sparked some rebellions; but his piecemeal acquisition of provinces to the east of those he had inherited brought political unity and improved defensive capacity. Without Habsburg resources to defend them, the Burgundian Netherlands would surely have succumbed to French aggression and lost their independence. Instead, all three modern Benelux countries can claim Charles as their founder.[66]

The state of Germany changed dramatically between Charles's election as king of the Romans and his abdication, largely (as Friedrich Edelmayer has observed) because of 'the religious problem. All the other problems that faced the Empire during these thirty-six years either stemmed from the Lutheran Reformation or were related to it' – with one exception: the emperor's decision in 1530–1 to support the election of his brother Ferdinand rather than his own son Philip as king of the Romans, and therefore his successor as emperor. This presaged the division of his dominions, and after acrimonious discussions about the succession in 1550–1, Ferdinand succeeded in turning Germany into a pluri-confessional state with a fragile balance between the rival blocks: the first of its kind anywhere in the world.[67]

Italy likewise changed dramatically in the course of Charles's reign. The peace treaties negotiated by Gattinara in 1529 ended the internecine wars that had racked the north of the peninsula for decades, and also effectively terminated French claims to Naples. Six years later the emperor annexed the contentious duchy of Milan, on the extinction of its native dynasty, and eventually decreed that it would pass, together with Spain and the rest of Spanish Italy, to his son Philip. Taken together, these successes guaranteed Spanish control of the Italian peninsula for a century, and of southern Italy for even longer.

Charles also transformed Spain, and especially Castile. He became the first monarch since Visigothic times to rule all of Spain, and thus played a crucial role in furthering the process of unification begun by his Trastámara predecessors; and he also declared uncompromisingly that Castile 'is the chief among our kingdoms'. In economic terms, the consequences proved disastrous. Juan Manuel Carretero Zamora has calculated that the taxes paid by Castile tripled during Charles's reign, producing in all eleven million ducats, almost all of which 'ended up with the bankers of Augsburg, Genoa and the Netherlands, who used it to raise the loans with which Charles funded policies that were often contrary to the interests of those who paid the bills'. Moreover, the emperor left huge debts that would force his son to declare a state bankruptcy just after his accession.[68]

The emperor's call for extreme measures against all those accused of heresy (chapter 16) also transformed Spain. Two weeks before his death, his regent signed a proclamation that forbade 'printing or owning any book prohibited by the Holy Office', as well as 'printing any book without a licence', and 'circulating any book in manuscript'. The following year, Inquisitor-General Valdés issued a Catalogue of prohibited books that listed almost 700 titles, almost half of them in vernacular languages, including works by Jean Glapion, Bartolomé Carranza and Francisco de Borja – all members of Charles's inner circle – as well as 'any and all sermons, letters, treatises, prayers and any manuscripts that quote or discuss the Holy Scripture or the sacraments'.[69] The climate of fear and uncertainty created in Castile by these and other measures caused the flight of several authors whose works appeared on the Index – including Borja, who had recently consoled Queen Joanna at Tordesillas as well as Charles at Yuste. The future saint fled to Portugal in 1559 and then, when summoned to Rome two years later, traversed Spain incognito, fearful that he might follow Carranza into prison.[70] The spate of arrests and accusations in 1558–9 meant that (in the words of one of Philip II's confidants): 'Before long we will no longer know who to call Christian and who to call heretic.' Henceforth, he opined, 'it is better to keep quiet'.[71] Although these harsh measures prevented the spread of Protestantism in Spain – there would be little circulation of heretical books; and although the Inquisition continued its vigorous persecution of Protestants in both Aragon and Castile, almost all were foreigners – they also prevented much intellectual innovation.

In Spanish America, finally, although Charles bears some responsibility for the dramatic decline of the native population in the decades after first contact, he ruthlessly disciplined the men who had carved out an empire for him, including Hernán Cortés and the Pizarro brothers: once they had triumphed, Charles either marginalized or eliminated them, gaining for himself permanent access to the resources of the continent to be used to fund his dynastic goals in Europe. He also enacted legislation that offered some protection to the indigenous inhabitants of the Americas against those seeking to colonize them, and funded schools to provide them with free education.

THE POISONED CHALICE

Charles's greatest failure lay elsewhere. According to Sir Thomas Wyatt in 1538, the emperor realized that his dominions 'lie farr off one from another', but nevertheless hoped that 'as he hath hitherto with labor and trauaile gouerned them, so to continew them and that his sonn (or thei that he shall leaue them to) shall if thei will kepe them, learne to be industrious and to think that thei haue them of God, that in such case will woorke His pleasour' – in other words he hoped that, with diligence and divine favour, his empire would survive intact after his death.[72]

Charles's ambitious goal overlooked two factors. First, as the emperors of Rome had discovered, 'charismatic authority possesses the inherent flaw that its holder cannot have a true heir precisely because of his own exceptional nature', and Charles's heir proved a disappointment. Prince Philip alienated many of his father's allies and subjects on his Grand Tour in 1548–9, and for some months he and Charles were not on speaking terms (chapter 14). The same thing happened again after Philip became king of England (chapter 15). The emperor himself was partly to blame for this disappointment, because his relentless micro-management fostered in the prince an obsessive (or, as Freud would have said, an 'anal') personality, ill-suited to ruling a global empire. In the 1560s, Philip's inflexibility would provoke major rebellions by important groups of his subjects in both Spain and the Netherlands, and for much of the 1570s he fought major wars on two fronts.[73]

A second endemic weakness stemmed from Charles's tenacious policy of matrimonial imperialism. The emperor acquired most of his European dominions as the result of endogamy: intermarriage over several generations among a very few dynasties. Although the practice enabled his son to unite Spain and Portugal, it also produced long-term disadvantages. Intermarriage had already reduced the dynastic gene pool before Charles's birth: Mary of Burgundy had only six great-grandparents instead of eight, and her son Philip married his third cousin Joanna, daughter of Ferdinand

and Isabella, themselves descended from numerous intermarriages among the branches of the House of Trastámara. Even taken together, however, this created an 'inbreeding coefficient' for Charles of only 0.037; but his marriage to his double-cousin, repeated by his son Philip, led to a dramatic increase. With only six great-grandparents, instead of the normal sixteen, Philip's son and heir Don Carlos boasted an inbreeding coefficient of 0.211, almost the same as the offspring of a brother and sister, or a parent and child (0.25).[74]

Historians like Pedro Mexía and Prudencio de Sandoval were justified in seeing the emperor's 'lineage' as his greatest asset, but neither they nor Charles apparently paused to question whether the failure of at least five of Isabella's pregnancies to produce a healthy child might reflect the impaired fertility that often accompanies the marriage of very close relatives. A crisis in the empress's own immediate family provided a chilling warning: four of King John III's children and four of his siblings (including the empress) died between 1537 and 1540, leaving as his heir Prince John who, even at three years old, 'although he hears and understands well enough, cannot talk yet. They say here that *if he survives* he will soon start to talk', but 'he is so weak' that María Manuela seemed likely to succeed. And how did the Habsburg and Avis dynasties address this crisis? By arranging the marriage of both María Manuela and Prince John to double cousins: Charles's children, Philip and Joanna. In the event each couple had only one child – Don Carlos and King Sebastian respectively – both of whom died without issue.[75]

The few contemporaries who pointed out the dangers of such inbreeding were ignored. In 1568, Pope Pius V refused to grant the necessary dispensation for Philip II to marry his niece Ana, daughter of his sister María and their cousin Maximilian, informing him pointedly that 'we have seen that bad results always follow from these marriages of the first degree' – an unsubtle reference to Philip's decision to imprison his son Don Carlos earlier that year because of his 'natural defects' – but the king went ahead and married Ana anyway. Only one of their children survived infancy: the future Philip III.[76] Two generations later, during discussion of a possible marriage between Louis XIV of France and his double cousin Maria Theresa of Spain, one diplomat reported that 'the talk turned to hunting dogs, and I said with a smile that our masters were already closely related and that hunters recognized that if you want strong dogs you must mix pedigrees'. Yet again such reservations made no difference: the marriage took place, and only one of the couple's six children survived infancy.[77]

In addition to these high biological costs, matrimonial imperialism created serious political problems. On the one hand, some of the territories acquired through incest lay far from the centre of government and possessed their own enduring strategic rivalries and political agendas; on the other hand, the configuration of Charles's empire posed a passive yet palpable threat to some of his neighbours. The Polish historian Władysław Pochieca has argued that the election of Charles as king of the Romans in 1519 marked 'the point after which maintaining the balance of power in Europe became the defining problem of western politics' because Habsburg hegemony was unacceptable to the international community. The political history of western Europe for the next two centuries therefore revolved around attempts to separate the various territories accumulated by Charles.[78]

Many contemporary observers agreed. Upon hearing about the imperial occupation of Lombardy after the victory at Pavia in 1525, Cardinal Wolsey pointed out that France was now 'envyronned on 3 parts, and scituated, as it wer, in the mydde of th'emperors countryes', so that whenever Charles or his successors decided to attack, the French would 'be inforced to stond at their defence on the said 3 parts'; and for the next two centuries, French foreign policy aimed to break what it perceived as a Habsburg stranglehold.[79] The papacy also felt encircled by Charles's territories: Sardinia to the west, Naples and Sicily to the south, Milan and other imperial fiefs to the north. Habsburg troops captured the papal capital in 1526 and 1527; Rome normally depended on grain exports from Sicily; and the commerce of the Papal States by sea and land lay at the mercy of the surrounding Habsburg bases. Papal support for Charles's crusades against infidels, whether in the Mediterranean or Hungary, or against heretics in Germany, therefore tended to remain muted because further imperial successes might tighten the dynasty's grip on central Italy.

But what was Charles supposed to do? He could scarcely decline the windfalls produced by the carefully crafted matrimonial policies of his forebears; and the only serious discussion about trading land for peace – the Alternative of 1544 – revealed that neither his subjects nor his advisers could agree on which territories should be traded. That is perhaps why, four years later, the emperor's Political Testament instructed his son never to surrender any of his possessions because 'if you should show weakness in any part, it will open the door to bringing everything back into question . . . It will be better to hold on to everything than to let yourself be forced later to defend the rest, and run the risk of losing it.'[80]

Royall Tyler, one of the emperor's modern biographers, postulated other deleterious consequences of the imperial election. Charles borrowed recklessly to become king of the Romans, and thereafter he deployed immense resources in Germany to fight both the Lutherans and the Turks, only to find that 'the means at his disposal to face the demands upon him always fell short of what he needed to exploit a victory or a diplomatic success'. Tyler then asked rhetorically: 'Debt and heresy, heresy and debt! How could he have avoided them?'[81] But once again, what was Charles supposed to do? Neither of the major problems he would face in Germany – the spread of Protestantism and the advance of the Turks – were evident at the time of his election. No previous ruler of Germany had faced simultaneously international threats from the Turks and the French as well as a domestic challenge from the Lutherans, as Charles did after 1521.

SUCCESS IS NEVER FINAL

Antoine Perrenot once reminded a foreign ambassador that although his master might 'occasionally be pinched for money', because 'he rules so many realms, including Peru', he could always overmatch the king of France, 'who has just one kingdom'.[82] This boast, though true, missed a crucial point: although Charles could indeed overmatch each of his enemies in isolation – the pope in 1526 and 1527; the sultan in 1532 and 1535; France in 1529 and 1544; and the German Protestants in 1547 – sooner or later the vanquished formed a hostile alliance that forced Charles to embark on yet another campaign. The emperor may have expected that victory at Pavia would lead to a favourable peace that would allow him to travel to Germany to extirpate the followers of Martin Luther, and then to Hungary to lead the forces of Christendom against the Turks; but instead, Francis concluded the anti-Habsburg League of Cognac with the pope, England, several Italian states and eventually allied with the Ottoman sultan. Sooner or later a balance of power nullified each of Charles's victories.

Many years later, the Lutheran magistrate Bartholomew Sastrow interrupted the narrative of his *Memoirs* to highlight 'Emperor Charles's good and bad fortune', a contrast that he attributed to the religious policy imposed at the Armed Diet of 1547–8:

> Let my children bear in mind the great success attained by the emperor, and how at the summit of that prosperity, when everything proceeded according to his desires, he thought he could break his promise to undertake nothing against the Augsburg confession. For love of the pope, His Majesty contemplated storming Luther's safe stronghold [𝕯. 𝕷ut𝔥ers 𝔙este 𝔅urg]. From that moment, the emperor's great good fortune turned into misfortune and all his enterprises failed.

One day at Yuste, Charles himself mused that he should have abdicated 'after the end of the German war' because then he 'would not have lost reputation thereby, unlike the present time because of subsequent events'.[83]

For once the Lutheran burgomaster and the Catholic emperor agreed: until 1548, Charles had scored one success after another in both Europe and the Americas. It is easy to overlook the magnitude of this achievement, and the odds against it. In May 1532, as Charles recovered after being thrown by his horse and prepared to do battle with both the German Lutherans and the Turkish army and navy, Loaysa wrote: 'I beg Your Majesty to be cheerful and not oppressed by the scale of the problems surrounding you. Because they are very difficult, and beyond the ability of human force, you may be sure that your good intentions and firm faith will triumph over them gloriously.'[84] Shortly afterwards, the emperor rose from his sickbed and overcame all the immediate challenges. So why did he fail to do the same after 1550?

Some contemporaries considered failure inevitable. In the spring of 1542, in the wake of the emperor's disastrous Algiers expedition, a French minister asked his English colleague a series of rhetorical questions that suggested that Charles ruled a doomed empire:

> England is a kingdom perpetuel, and so is Ffraunce. Our masters, their childern, their succession may royne foreuer; we be undir one clyme and of one complexion, we be at hande one to another. Th'empereur is but one, and whenne he is dead sum Almayn [some German] may be empereur, I wote [know] not who. Truth it is Spayne is a kingdome, but what is that alone? ... And as for Italy, when th'empereur is dead who shalbe master?[85]

None of these predictions came true. Spain alone sufficed to make Philip II the most powerful ruler of his generation; and although the emperor failed to pass all his dominions on to his son, as he had wished, they all remained under Habsburg rule. Moreover, although the creation of a restricted gene pool and the emergence of an adverse balance of power ultimately thwarted Charles's ambitions, better management could have delayed the fragmentation of his empire – above all had he continued the policy of devolution that underlay his earlier successes. Instead, after 1548 he ignored or rejected advice that he did not like, accepting only opinions and evidence that reinforced his own views. Groupthink eventually permeated all senior levels of the imperial government. In September 1551, Diego Hurtado de Mendoza, the imperial ambassador in Rome and normally a man of resolutely independent views, sent the emperor a review of potential threats to the general council at Trent, including the risk that the German Lutherans might use force against it. Mendoza did not rule this out totally – 'certainly it is possible, because everything is possible' – but 'we can assume it is impossible because the authority of Your Majesty is so great in Germany, more than ever before because the Lutherans lack leaders'. This is exactly the message that the emperor and his immediate entourage wanted to hear, and so they accepted it even though (unfortunately for them) it proved mistaken.[86] Groupthink, reinforced by the conviction that either Caesar's luck or a miracle would always make the impossible possible, deprived Charles of his advantage in Germany and fatally undermined the integrity of his empire.

In 1945, Johan Huizinga claimed that 'The entire political career of Charles V amounted to little more than an initial series of unexpected strokes of luck, followed by an almost uninterrupted series of errors, short-sighted acts and failures.' Fifty years later, John Robertson flatly rejected this judgment: 'The Monarchy of Charles V recast the mould of European politics. Modern historians may wish to emphasize the limits upon the effective exercise of his authority', but 'the sheer extent of his inheritance made possible monarchy on a scale not seen since the Roman Empire'.[87] Through a combination of good luck and superior resources, Charles managed to preserve and improve his international position. Of the three 'yonge pwyssante prynces' who in 1515 had seemed likely to wage 'warre infynyte' – Charles, Henry and Francis – Charles alone remained until in 1554, seven years after the death of both his rivals, he led his army on a final successful campaign against France, and his son became king of England. Failure, like success, is relative. Despite his frustrated ambitions, Charles wielded greater power for longer than any other European ruler before or since, and the extent of his dominions on both sides of the Atlantic far exceeded those of any predecessor. By those metrics, the ones by which he himself might have chosen to be judged, his successes far outweighed his failures.

But why should we accept the emperor's preferred metrics? In 1972 Fernand Braudel issued a mischievous warning about the risks that attend the biographers of eminent sixteenth-century figures:

In writing of him or her, will we not unconsciously write too much about ourselves, about our own times? Erasmus as portrayed by Marcel Bataillon resembles Marcel Bataillon. I myself have spent more than forty years in the company of Philip II. I have tried to be careful to keep my distance from a complex person, but increasingly I find myself attempting to excuse him, no doubt in the hope of understanding him and thus bringing him back to life.[88]

Have I likewise attempted to excuse Charles in the hope of understanding him better and thus bringing him back to life? Have I always kept a proper distance from my subject? Unlike his son Philip, who spent a large part of his life secluded in his study, Charles relished the spotlight. He generated a multitude of sources himself, and others produced even more: an abundance of material therefore exists by which to judge him. Although by twenty-first century standards his personal defects and shortcomings tarnish his image, the emperor's contemporaries were surely correct to deem him an extraordinary man who achieved extraordinary things.

APPENDICES

The validity of two sources on which this book relies has been questioned: the *Memoirs* written by the emperor, and a digit detached from one of his hands. Although both lack a clear chain of provenance that leads back to Charles, the available evidence supports their authenticity. By contrast, I reject as false a third source on the emperor that others have regarded as authentic: a set of 'Last Instructions' prepared for his son Philip in 1556. I also conclude that Charles did not sire an illegitimate child during his first visit to Spain in 1517–20, as claimed by Manuel Fernández Álvarez and other historians. My rationale for each choice appears in the following appendices.

APPENDIX I: THE EMPEROR'S *MEMOIRS*

At some point between 1620 and 1791 the French Royal Library in Paris acquired a manuscript entitled 'Historia do invictissimo emperador Carlos quinto, rey de Hespanha, composta por sua Mag. Cesarea ... Traduzida da lingoa francesa e do proprio original. Em Madrid. Anno 1620'. It contains sixty-eight folios written in a neat hand, with topic summaries in the margin in another hand, and it covers the years between 1515 and 1548. Written in the third person, like the *Commentaries* of Julius Caesar (and like the autobiography of Gattinara and other Renaissance figures), the manuscript was originally given the shelfmark BNF *Fonds français* 10,230, and is now BNF *Ms. Port.* 61. It has been digitized and can be consulted at: http://gallica.bnf.fr/ark:/12148/btv1b10036839z. But is it genuine?

In 1559, Willem Snouckaert van Schouwenburg, Charles's librarian and one of his first biographers, stated categorically that 'like Christ, Socrates and Alexander, our Emperor Charles never himself wrote Commentaries about his deeds'. In his edition of BNF *Ms. Port.* 61, published in 1989, Vicente Cadenas y Vicent opined that 'there are so many doubts that no historian should accept' as authentic 'this translation of a document whose veracity cannot be proved'. Specifically, 'The watermark of the paper does not correspond to anything from Spain or Portugal', and 'the arrival of the volume in Paris is shrouded in mystery, so that no one knows how it reached the Royal Library'.[1]

These objections are all easily refuted. The watermark of the paper used in *Ms. Port.* 61 resembles one from Perpignan, the second city of Catalonia, dated 1595; and the volume probably entered the Royal Library of France in 1668, along with other manuscripts from the collection of Cardinal Mazarin, leading adviser to Charles's great-granddaughter, the regent Anne of Austria. It had certainly entered the collection before 1791, when it became the property of the French Republic, because it bears royal stamps.[2] The eminent bibliographer, Benito Sánchez Alonso, suggested that the manuscript had been prepared in Madrid in 1620 for Manuel de Moura, marquis of Castel Rodrigo, and came to the Royal Library of France together with other items in the Castel Rodrigo collection acquired by Mazarin.[3]

The claim by Snouckaert van Schouwenburg that 'Charles never himself wrote Commentaries about his deeds' is conclusively refuted by a letter written by the emperor's chamberlain Guillaume van Male in July 1550: 'During his free time while sailing up the Rhine' the previous month, 'the emperor undertook to write his travels and campaigns from the year 1515 until now'. Van Male stated that although he had provided his master with some 'texts and suggestions', the emperor wrote largely from memory and that, still assisted by van Male, he revised his autobiography in Augsburg later that year.[4] José Luis Gonzalo Sánchez-Molero has suggested that this venture formed part of a 'great autobiographical enterprise', perhaps modelled on the projects of self-aggrandisement undertaken by his grandfather Maximilian (p. 28 above), or perhaps intended to guide the professional historians he hoped would write his life.[5]

A note in Spanish inserted at the beginning of BNF *Ms. Port.* 61 states that Charles took his *Memoirs* with him to Innsbruck in 1551 but sent them to his son in Spain the following spring when he feared that a Lutheran army might capture him and his possessions.[6] The emperor may have intended to resume work on his *Memoirs* at Yuste, because his small library there contained several historical works, and his few visitors included two historians, Juan Ginés de Sepúlveda and Luis de Ávila y Zúñiga; but if so, the sudden onset of his last illness frustrated his plans. The emperor was certainly reunited with his manuscript at Yuste, because van Male complained bitterly that when his master died, 'Luis Quijada took from him, almost by force, the *Memoirs* that he had composed with His Majesty'. The Inventory Post-Mortem of Charles's goods mentioned 'A black velvet folder of papers belonging to Guillaume van Male, containing some important sealed papers, taken by Luis Quijada to be delivered to His Majesty [Philip II]'. Perhaps the *Memoirs* were among them?[7]

The Spanish antiquary Ambrosio de Morales, who worked closely with Philip II, mentioned the *Memoirs* in a letter of 1564 that praised the emperor because 'despite the fury of his wars he himself managed to write a most admirable, diligent and continuous History of his deeds' – phrasing that implied that Morales had seen the work. At some point Philip entrusted the *Memoirs* to his secretary Francisco de Eraso, because in 1569 Juan Páez de Castro, a protégé of van Male and a royal chronicler, informed a colleague that 'I begged His Majesty to permit me to see what the emperor wrote about the justification for each of his wars, and especially for the German war [of 1546–7]. He replied that he consented, and told me to speak to Eraso.'[8] Perhaps after Eraso's death the *Memoirs* migrated to El Escorial, because a list of manuscripts related to Charles held by the monastery's library in the early seventeenth century included one entitled 'His history, written in French'; but after this, the original text of Charles's *Memoirs* disappeared from view.[9] It was evidently in Madrid in 1620, when someone commissioned a Portuguese translation; but both versions disappeared from view until 1860, when the Belgian scholar Kervijn de Lettenhove stumbled upon the Portuguese text while on a research visit to Paris, and prepared a French translation, published two years later. Although marred by numerous errors, Kervijn's text immediately appeared in English, Spanish and German translations.[10]

In 1913, Alfred Morel-Fatio printed in his *Historiographie de Charles-Quint* a transcription of the Portuguese original accompanied by a far better French translation, an erudite introduction, and numerous notes. In 1958, to mark the quatercentenary of Charles's death, Manuel Fernández Álvarez published a Spanish translation of the Portuguese text, together with a helpful introduction (reprinted in *CDCV*, IV, 459–567); and in 1989, Cadenas y Vicent published in *Las supuestas 'Memorias'* a photocopy of each folio of the Portuguese original with a Spanish translation on the facing page, together with an introduction that cast doubt on its authenticity.

Despite Cadenas y Vicent's assertion that BNF *Ms. Port.* 61 'lacks even the slightest guarantee of veracity', it seems that the manuscript is exactly what it claims to be: a translation into Portuguese, made in Madrid in 1620, of the *Memoirs* written in French by Charles, with some assistance from van

Male, in the summer and autumn of 1550. I have therefore made use of it extensively in this biography. In 1913, Alfred Morel-Fatio expressed the hope that the original of both the *Memoirs* and Charles's secret instructions to his son of 6 May 1543 would one day be found. His second wish came true a century later, when I identified HSA *Ms.* B 2955 as the original holograph instructions. Perhaps his first wish will also one day be realized, but until then historians of Charles V must rely on BNF *Ms. Port.* 61.[11]

APPENDIX II: THE AFTERLIFE OF CHARLES V'S BODY[12]

Charles V died in the Jeronimite convent at Yuste in Spain's Gredos mountains on 21 September 1558 and was buried in the convent there, as he had requested. Sixteen years later Philip II moved his father's body to a mausoleum for his dynasty created at the new royal monastery of San Lorenzo de El Escorial. In 1654, on the orders of Philip IV, the monks were about to transfer the imperial cadaver reverentially from the 'old coffin' to a 'new one made of seasoned wood' in the newly completed Pantheon of the Kings when they noticed a 'spectacle worthy of Caesar':

> ...a remarkable thing, worthy of eternal admiration: his body was intact, ninety-six years after his death; and so perfect that, even looking closely, the heroic composition of his body seemed flawless: his strong face, whose physiognomy reflected the great intelligence with which heaven had endowed him; a broad brow, capable of accommodating all those laurels; his eyes open; his full beard, which made the enemies of the Church tremble so many times; his chest strong and vigorous, denoting his invincible valour and his valiant heart; his inflexible strong arms, which defended the faith.

Indeed, 'all his parts were so free of corruption that even the nails on his feet and hands (which in life suffered so much from gout) were entirely intact'. The emperor's uncorrupted corpse 'led some to consider him a saint'.[13]

In the twenty-first century, Julián de Zulueta y Cebrián, a specialist in tropical diseases (especially malaria) with a strong interest in history, offered an alternative explanation for the uncorrupted state of the imperial cadaver. He noted that Charles died in late September, exactly the time when in places like 'Jabugo, the hams are shut away in caves' where, as in the small crypt at Yuste that contained the imperial sarcophagus, each winter the temperature fell below freezing, in effect 'curing' Charles's corpse like a ham.

By 1574, when his son supervised the move to El Escorial, it had turned into a mummy.[14]

In 1654 the coffin remained open for a while so that 'everyone could view it'; but thereafter (except when invading French troops briefly opened the tomb in 1809), the emperor's mummy lay in peace until it became a tourist attraction immediately after Spain's Glorious Revolution of 1868. On 9 December 1870 the Spanish government invited several members of the diplomatic corps, and their families, to travel from Madrid to the Escorial to view the imperial sarcophagus, which now lay open. The British ambassador, Sir Arthur Layard, described what he saw that day:

> The body is wrapped in white linen and red silk. On the head is a skull-cap of white linen embroidered with gold. One or two persons present pretended that they could recognise the features from Titian's portrait, but this appeared to me an exaggeration. The only feature which bears this resemblance is the chin, which is very characteristic (as you will perceive by the photograph), and is thoroughly Austrian. It is covered with a short red beard. The body is well preserved, for a mummy. The hands and feet are small and delicate.

Another observer noted 'the imperfect healing of a fracture in his leg, with the bones healing laterally' – almost certainly the consequence of the emperor's fall in 1532 (p. 225). Layard ordered the Madrid painter Vicente Palmaroli y Rodríguez to make a 'sketch in oils' on the occasion of his visit, which was later photographed and distributed as a postcard (Pl. 39).[15]

Eighteen months later the novelist Pedro Antonio de Alarcón y Ariza attended the twentieth 'public exhibition of the emperor's body, at the request of the fair ladies of Madrid who spent their summer there'. After descending into the Pantheon of the Kings, 'we saw for ourselves the open tomb of Charles V, and in front of it, on scaffolding constructed for the purpose, a coffin whose lid had been replaced by a piece of glass' through which they viewed the emperor's 'robust mummy from head to foot, completely naked but perfectly preserved, albeit somewhat wizened'. He noted in particular 'the high and very full thoracic cavity, his broad and prominent shoulders, his characteristic skull with facial features typical of the House of Austria, including his open mouth and prominent chin, caused by his mandibular prognathism'. He stressed that 'this was not a skeleton, but flesh covered by dark skin, on which you could still see a few eyelashes and eyebrows as well as his beard and a neat head of hair'.[16]

In the autumn of 1871, when no glass covered the coffin, the painter Martín Rico y Ortega spent several days sketching the imperial cadaver. He, too, left a detailed description of what he saw: 'I noticed that his full beard, neatly trimmed around his mouth, was still a dark chestnut colour and not grizzled, almost white, as shown in the portraits of him at that time.' He complained that 'I have never encountered such difficulties, nor worked with so many obstacles and nuisances as when making this sketch, because apart from the position in which I had to remain – a posture that turned my body into a perfect "C" – the distance between my position and my subject was only 30 centimetres.' An engraving based on his sketches appeared in the periodical *La ilustración de Madrid* in January 1872.[17]

Rico's uncomfortable efforts to capture an accurate image of the emperor, together with Palmaroli's painting, settled one question about his physiognomy. The art historian Diane Bodart has noted how, as Charles grew older, fewer people mentioned the mandibular prognathism that occasioned widespread comment in his early years, while artists like Titian disguised it, to the point where some doubted whether it was real. Palmaroli's painting settles the matter: the emperor's lower jaw was indeed extremely prominent.[18]

In 1936, Julián de Zulueta, then a Republican exile in Paris, 'saw a photograph taken during the [Spanish] Civil War and published in the international press in which a militiaman appeared to cuddle, half in jest, the mummified emperor. The mummy had its eyes open and seemed as if it were about to speak.'[19] Fifty years later, Zulueta read about a new technique for rehydrating mummies in order to conduct clinical tests on them, and recalled both the photo that showed the emperor's body as a mummy and rumours that Charles died of malaria. Zulueta therefore asked permission of King Juan Carlos to examine the imperial cadaver in the Pantheon of the Kings.

Permission was denied, but in 2005 a member of Spain's Patrimonio Nacional alerted Zulueta to the existence of 'a pinkie of the emperor kept outside the sarcophagus in a box in the sacristy of San Lorenzo de El Escorial', because a visitor to the emperor's sarcophagus after the revolution of 1868 had managed to secure it. This remarkable assertion is supported by an obituary of Martín Rico, which recalled that while he resided at El Escorial, visiting the Pantheon every day, the official who possessed the key tired of his requests to enter, and so 'entrusted it to Rico, who left it in his house when he did not need it. A guide who became aware of this custom came to Rico's house, and in the name of a foreigner' – a foreigner: of course! – 'anxious to view the emperor's mummy asked for and received the key'.

While Charles's body lay on a scaffold in front of his tomb in a coffin, unprotected by glass, it seems that the inquisitive visitor took advantage of the lax security to 'offer 20 reales to one of the guards in return for a part of the emperor. The guard put his hand into the coffin and removed the digit from a finger.'[20]

On 14 September 1870 – thus before the visits of Layard, Palmaroli, Alarcón and Rico – the digit somehow came into the possession of the marquis of Miraflores and his sister, the dowager marchioness of Martorell; and on 31 May 1912 they returned it to King Alfonso XIII together with a letter assuring him that the digit 'came into our hands involuntarily, because we never attempted to acquire or keep it'. Alfonso sent it back to the Escorial where, rather than reopen the tomb, the prior placed it in a locked red box in the sacristy.[21]

Inspired by this information, Zulueta asked King Juan Carlos for permission to examine the digit, and this time he received it. In 2005 he returned to El Escorial accompanied by Dr Pedro Alonso, whose laboratory sought a vaccine against malaria at the Hospital Clinic d'Investigacions Biomèdiques August Pi i Sunyer in Barcelona. Zulueta later recalled that the prior of San Lorenzo opened the locked red box 'with the digit wrapped in special paper – not the normal paper that we use for typing. The prior opened the paper and put on white gloves, to touch the object with greater respect.' The mummified digit, which was still in good condition, travelled 'in a hearse, escorted by the Guardia Civil', to Barcelona where tests revealed 'large quantities of malaria parasites – ones that had killed an emperor'. They also revealed severe gout.[22] Afterwards the detached pinkie returned to the locked red box in the sacristy of the Royal Monastery of San Lorenzo de El Escorial, where it is now Patrimonio Nacional, # 10044506.

But did the detached pinkie in the locked red box really come from an imperial hand? One piece of evidence counts against this attribution. In a letter to the painter Mariano Fortuny in 1871 describing Charles's cadaver, Rico asserted that: 'The three centuries that have elapsed since he was buried have left scarcely any trace on him; and *contrary to what you may have read or heard*, I can assure you that he remains intact and that *he lacks nothing, absolutely nothing*.'[23] Rico evidently sought to refute a story then circulating that some part of the imperial anatomy was missing; and since the marquis of Miraflores claimed that the digit was in his possession by September 1870, presumably Rico referred to rumours about this. Interestingly, although Rico sketched the emperor from many different angles, none of them showed his left hand in full: his portrayal of the left pinkie always stops precisely at the final joint. Could Rico perhaps have insisted that the cadaver remained intact lest someone suspect that he had connived in removing the digit?

DNA tests would settle the authenticity of the item, but the Hospital Clinic did not receive permission to perform them and so the detached pinkie in the locked red box cannot be definitively linked either with the cadaver in the sarcophagus or with someone who has certified Habsburg genes.[24] Nevertheless, three considerations support the presumption. Although the marquis of Miraflores did not reveal how he had acquired the digit, or how he knew it came from an imperial hand, he was an eminent courtier and his sister was a matron of honour of both the queen and the queen dowager: they would not have offered to return it to the king unless they believed that it belonged to Charles V. Likewise, the prior of San Lorenzo de El Escorial in 1912 evidently accepted this attribution, since he placed the digit in a locked red box wrapped in special paper and put it in the sacristy. Most convincing of all is the evidence collected by the Hospital Clinic in Barcelona from the rehydrated mummified digit: their tests demonstrated that the pinkie belonged to someone who suffered from extreme gout, who suffered a double dose of malaria that almost certainly proved fatal, and whose cadaver was mummified. All three descriptors fit Charles. The same combination may be true of other cadavers, of course, but the chances are slim. I therefore accept the argument of Julián de Zulueta and his colleagues that they examined a digit detached from an imperial hand.

APPENDIX III: THE EMPEROR'S LAST INSTRUCTIONS TO PHILIP II[25]

The advice of Charles the Fifth, Emperor of Germany, and King of Spain, to his son Philip the Second upon his resignation of the crown of Spain has been printed in both English (London, 1670) and French (Berlin, 1699). In addition, one German, at least twenty-five Italian, and at least twenty-three English manuscript versions survive. With two exceptions, the manuscripts belong to one of three groups: those that cover forty folios or less, those that cover between forty and eighty folios, and those (including both printed texts) that are far longer, arranged in two parts.[26]

One of the two exceptions is the *Ragionamento de l'imperatore fatto, quando rinontio tutti suoi regni et stati al re, suo figiuolo* in the Haus-, Hof- und Staatsarchiv in Vienna. The document describes a meeting held in the presence of leading nobles and ministers at 4 p.m. on 16 January 1556 in the emperor's cottage in the royal park in Brussels, at which Charles gave his son a box containing 'many testaments in both Latin and Castilian and many instructions' together with the seal he had used on a document declaring that, should the French take him prisoner while on campaign, Philip should refuse all demands for a ransom.[27] Most of the meeting was taken up by reading out the various formal documents ceding to Philip the kingdoms of Castile, Aragon and Sicily, after each of which Charles declared 'I consent and confirm', and then he and several of those present affixed their signatures. The anonymous author mentioned that Charles expressed his regret that he had not abdicated six years before when his affairs were in a better state, and opined '"Everyone can do three things: protest . . ." but then he paused for a while and said that he did not remember the other two things.' The document then referred tantalizingly to 'the many other most prudent things' that Charles said, 'which induced wonder and compassion, considering that the most powerful man in the world spoke with such humility' – but provided no details.[28]

Perhaps these 'most prudent things' are summarized in the other outlier: the only known Spanish text relating to final instructions, a single sheet entitled *Points that the Emperor Charles V, of glorious memory, gave to his son King Philip when he departed for Spain: concerning the best way to govern.*[29] The *Points* are so terse that they would make little sense on their own. They may therefore be either notes made by the emperor before he met his son (a technique he had used when meeting Pope Clement in 1529–30 – see Pl. 13 – and when delivering his abdication speech for his Netherlands possessions a few months earlier: p. 465), or minutes taken down by someone when the two monarchs met – perhaps on 16 January 1556.

Although undated, both these documents seem authentic. Those named in the *Ragionamento* are known from other sources to have attended the meeting on 16 January, at which the transfer of the testaments and the signing of the acts of renunciation really took place. Charles may well have given a speech to mark the solemn occasion, and the *Points* may well refer to what he said on that occasion. We find the 'vos' form that Charles normally used when addressing his son; and most of the *Points* repeated advice already given in earlier instructions. The only exceptions are the suggestion that 'it will be necessary to keep a register containing the names of good officials', to ensure that he rewarded only the deserving; and the command 'Expel the Moors from your kingdoms', something Gattinara had urged him to do more than three decades before.[30] So perhaps Charles did impart a final lesson to his son 'concerning the best way to govern' before they parted in September 1556, but if so he did so orally – and this is the only surviving record.[31]

The same confidence cannot be extended to the other manuscripts that purport to contain the emperor's last instructions. The lack of an original is not significant, because the same is true of other similar documents of undoubted authenticity, such as Charles's Political Testament of 1548, his *Memoirs* and (until 2009) his secret instructions of 1543. The major problem lies in the style, including the salutation 'Most dear son' (whereas Charles invariably used the austere form 'Son [*Hijo*]') and the abundance of Classical references (something seldom found in Charles's other writings). Furthermore, the plausible passages are mostly platitudes found in many early modern 'Letters of Advice from a Father to his Son'; none of the detailed political advice relates to events after 1553; and many of the dates and events are incorrect.[32]

The earliest dated text of the last instructions is 20 August 1592, a generation after the emperor's abdication, in an Italian manuscript presented to King James VI of Scotland by his Italian tutor, Giacomo Castelvetro. James certainly considered them genuine, because he used them as a model six years later when drafting *Basilicon Doron*, a political testament for his own son. So did John Pemberton, who prepared a Spanish edition of *Basilicon Doron* – indeed he specifically linked the two treatises: 'just as the instructions of Charles V to his son Philip were translated into most languages and quite well into English, so may these instructions of Your Majesty in English be turned into Spanish without diminution and I trust without losing their force'.[33] Pemberton's assumption that a Spanish original existed probably stemmed from Lord Henry Howard, courtier of Queen Elizabeth and minister of King James, who composed several versions of a purported English translation that he presented to the queen. One text claimed that it was 'A Copy of the last instructions which the Emperor Charles the Fifth gave to his son Philip before his death, *translated out of Spanish*'; another that it was 'The Emperor Charles Vth's political instructions to his son Philip II on his resignation of the crown of Spain. *Translated from the Spanish*.'[34]

The claim that the instructions were delivered when Charles abdicated as king of Spain suggests that Howard may have used a genuine original, since it matches the two authentic documents; and so, at first glance, does his claim that 'This briefe treatise first compiled in the Spanish tongue and cominge unto my hand by chance'; but Howard never claimed that he worked from a Spanish original.[35] It seems more likely that he translated an

Italian text. Since Howard probably presented his translation to the queen in December 1592, he may have plundered Castelvetro's text: after all, Castelvetro spent time in England on his way to Scotland, and he and Howard moved in the same circles.[36] So either Castelvetro created the original of the numerous short versions of the Italian text of Charles's last instructions, or else he copied a text already in existence (none of the similar surviving Italian texts are dated, so one or more of them might have been written earlier; but none link back to anything written by Charles himself).

Howard suggested that a longer version of the instructions existed: the dedicatory epistle to his English translation informed Queen Elizabeth that 'This treatise seemeth only to have bene an abridgement of a larger worke wherein the rulers of government were more at large delated by this thoroughly experienced emperor'; and he lamented that 'it is not possible by any labour to procure a sight theirof, either because tyme, the grave of worthy monuments, hath overwhelmed it, or the kinge of Spaine (as some affirme) hath reserved it as the Romans did Sybill's oracles to special use'.[37] Perhaps one of the longer surviving Italian texts already existed in 1592, when Howard presented his manuscript to Queen Elizabeth; certainly, some of them existed a century later when Antoine Teissier, councillor and historiographer of Elector Frederick of Brandenburg, published a French translation for the edification of the Elector's son. Teissier stated that he had used an Italian text that had come into the possession of Queen Christina of Sweden, later purchased at great cost by 'Monsieur *** [sic]', who 'made it available to the translator, who has turned it from Italian into French, because His Serene Highness understands the second language better than the first'.[38] Teissier divided the instructions into a section on how to govern in peacetime followed by a section on how to lead in wartime. Some other versions – such as the German and Italian texts prepared circa 1740 for the children of King Augustus of Saxony and Poland – introduced a formal division into two parts and covered over 100 pages.[39]

Although the rulers of Brandenburg and Saxony, like James VI of Scotland and 'Monsieur ***', believed that the texts they commissioned were genuine, it is hard to dissent from the verdict of E. W. Mayer in 1919: that all of the Italian versions of Charles's 'last instructions' are based on a forgery, which means that all the translations are also based on a forgery. It is also hard to dissent from the opinion of Karl Brandi that the combination of the emperor's status and the wide circulation of copies of his other (genuine) instructions, notably his Political Testament of 1548, gave him an almost mythical authority that made it worthwhile to attach his name to a document written by someone else, and (with the passage of time) worthwhile to add new material. But whoever composed the 'Last Instructions', it was not Charles V.[40]

APPENDIX IV: 'INFANTA ISABEL OF CASTILE, DAUGHTER OF HIS MAJESTY THE EMPEROR'[41]

In 1536 the will of Germaine de Foix, widow of Ferdinand the Catholic and wife of Fernando de Aragón, duke of Calabria, included a major legacy: 'Item, we bequeath and leave the string of 133 large pearls, which is the best that we possess, to the Most Serene Infanta Isabel of Castile, daughter of His Majesty the emperor, my son and my lord, on account of the great love that we feel for His Highness.' Germaine died a few days later and Calabria sent a copy of her will to Empress Isabella 'so that Your Majesty can see the bequest of the pearls that she left to the Most Serene Infanta'.[42]

In 1998, in an article entitled 'Sobre una posible hija', Jaime de Salazar drew attention to these two documents, and suggested that Infanta Isabel of Castile was the fruit of a liaison between the emperor and Germaine. Manuel Fernández Álvarez accepted this identification in both *Felipe II y su tiempo* (pp. 811–12) and *Carlos V: el César* (pp. 98–9), but neither he nor Salazar cited any evidence except Germaine's will and Calabria's covering letter. Admittedly, the night before he died, King Ferdinand wrote a letter begging his grandson 'always to take care to aid and succour Her Serene Majesty, my most dear and much loved wife', but incest with one's step-grandmother seems improbable, even for a Habsburg.

In an article entitled 'Una calumnia gratuita', Vicente de Cadenas y Vicent dismissed Don Manuel's claim as 'mental masturbation' (pp. 626–7) and denied that an Infanta Isabel of Castile had ever existed; but then he changed his mind. In another article shortly afterwards, entitled 'Aclarada la calumnia del académico y catedrático Manuel Fernández Álvarez', Cadenas y Vicent argued that Isabel was a descendant of the last Trastámara kings of Naples and that she died in 1550. He asserted that 'of Castile' was an error, and that 'daughter' was just a courtesy term applied to all female relatives of the emperor. In 2012, Pere María Orts i Bosch offered another identification in an article entitled 'Margarida o Isabel', which argued that Germaine left her pearls to Charles's illegitimate daughter Margarita of Parma, despite the fact that Margarita was never an 'Infanta of Castile' (indeed she never visited Spain). All these assertions are wrong.

In her biography *Germana de Foix*, Rosa Ríos Lloret correctly pointed out that the queen's will proved only that Charles had a daughter named

Isabel, who was alive in 1536 (although apparently unmentioned in any other source). It did not identify her mother.[43] Moreover, the fact that Calabria offered to send his late wife's legacy to the empress, rather than to Charles, suggested that the Infanta was not illegitimate – otherwise the duke would surely have written secretly to the emperor. So who was she?

An entry in a genealogy of Charles composed in French offers a clue. The author stated that Charles and his wife 'Isabeau of Portugal' had 'four children, namely Philip, Ferdinand (who died in infancy), Isabeau and Joanna'. Confirmation that the name 'Isabeau' was not an error comes from Francesc Joan, a Valencian chronicler, who recorded in his *Llibre de memòries* the births of all members of the royal family according to the name by which they were known in Valencia. In 1527 he recorded the name of Charles's heir as 'Felipe Juan' (and continued to refer to him thus until 1555), and the following year he noted the birth of a sister, 'Doña Isabel'.[44] Since Germaine was vicereine of Valencia in 1536, the notary who drew up her will no doubt adopted the Valencian name for the emperor's elder daughter. Therefore 'on account of the great love that we feel for His Highness', Germaine bequeathed her finest necklace to the Most Serene Infanta known as María in Castile and Isabel in Valencia.

This identification is confirmed by the inventory of the precious goods left by Empress Isabella at her death in 1539, and divided between her three surviving children in 1551. The lengthy dossier includes a letter sent by Charles to his daughter María, at the time queen of Bohemia and regent in Spain, with the clause: 'Item: it is our will that you, queen of Bohemia, should receive the 133 pearls of Queen Germaine.' This is obviously the item left to the 'Infanta Isabel of Castile' in Germaine's will. Since the inventory valued each pearl at forty-five ducats, the string of 133 large pearls was indeed a magnificent legacy – and it can still be admired today in a portrait of María from circa 1557 that hangs in Schloss Ambras.[45] The emperor did not sire a daughter named Isabel: neither with Queen Germaine nor with anyone else.

ACKNOWLEDGEMENTS

On 1 April 1841, William Hickling Prescott settled upon his next historical project: the conquest of Mexico. 'I propose to write about 1,000 pages of my own composition,' he confided to his journal, at the rate of 'four printed pages per diem, i.e. when composing. Allowing two days' reading for one of writing – it will give me a vol. of 450 printed pages per annum, or 1¼ printed pages per diem, thro' the year.' Prescott kept to his gruelling schedule and sent his *History of the conquest of Mexico* to the printer in August 1843. Writing a much shorter life of Charles V has taken me far longer, not only because I lack Prescott's iron discipline as a writer but also because I succumbed to a temptation that claims many biographers:

> I became utterly absorbed in the forensics of the project: the piecing together of clues in correspondence, for example, that brought to light previously unrecorded events and actions or newly illuminated character and motive. I experienced those transcendent moments, familiar to all historical biographers, when the author seems to touch the hand or face of their subject.[1]

I almost touched the hand or face of Charles as a boy. On meeting the emperor for the first time in 1550, the English Humanist Roger Ascham thought he 'looked somewhat like the parson of Epurstone [sic]. He had on a gown of black taffety, and a furred night-cap on his head, Dutch-like, having a seam over the crown, like a great cod-piece.'[2] The village of Epperstone lies only a few miles from Nottingham, where I grew up, and on Sunday afternoons my parents and I often walked through the village; but I did not encounter a codpiece, great or small, or any other trace of the emperor. Instead, I first came upon Charles in 1957 when I spent three weeks in Belgium on a school exchange. My host family came from Binche, and they took me to see the ruins of the great palace where four centuries before the emperor's sister Mary had staged magnificent festivities in his honour. Ten years later I spent three months in Belgium as a doctoral student researching the reasons why Spain failed to suppress the Dutch Revolt, but Charles (although often cited by both sides) remained a peripheral figure. In between those two visits I encountered Helmut G. Koenigsberger. I read his articles on Charles V while an undergraduate – a wise choice because (unknown to me) he would serve as external examiner for my final exams, and on the paper 'Europe since 1494' he set the question: 'Were the resources available to Charles V equal to the needs of his empire' (a puzzle I have been trying to solve ever since). We first met in 1966, and both then and after- wards I learned much in conversations with Helli about Charles V, one of them recorded on tape by Sussex Publications. Listening to it again reminds me of what a perceptive scholar we lost when he died in 2014. How I wish I could present him with a copy of this book.[3]

I did not actually 'touch the hand or face' of the emperor until December 2009: while working on another project in the reading room of the Hispanic Society of America, I realized that HSA Manuscript B 2955 contained Charles's long-lost holograph secret instructions for his son Philip in May 1543. I decided there and then to write his biography. I thank the expert cura- tors who welcomed me to the HSA both then and subsequently – Mitchell Codding, Patrick Lenaghan and John O'Neill – as well as Bethany Aram, Rachael Ball, Richard Kagan and David Lagomarsino, all of whom provided assistance in deciphering and interpreting the instructions. In 2014, Rachael and I published a critical edition of the manuscript, in Spanish and English.[4]

Like all other historians of the emperor, I owe a special debt to Karl Brandi (1868–1946). During a university career that spanned fifty years, he published over eighty books on topics from Charlemagne to World War I, directed or examined 122 doctoral theses, and formed the first research team ever to work on the emperor comprising ten scholars, most of them his former advisees at the university of Göttingen. Between 1930 and 1941 the 'Göttingen Project' had identified some 23,000 documents from Charles's reign, printed several of them, and provided detailed descriptions of the archival collections generated by the imperial government in a series of twenty fascicles entitled *Berichte und Studien zur Geschichte Karls V*. Brandi had served as an infantry officer in World War I (winning an Iron Cross both first and second class), and his mili- tary experience provided him with important insights into command, logis- tics and combat that enriched his account of the emperor at war.[5] Brandi and his subject had other things in common. Just as Charles offered to settle his disputes with other rulers through a duel, when publicly slighted by an academic colleague Brandi (then aged sixty-five) 'asked the speaker if he was prepared to meet me with weapons in hand, to give satisfaction'. Like Francis I, the colleague declined.[6] In 1937, Brandi published the first volume of his biography: *Kaiser Karl V. Werden und Schicksal einer Persönlichkeit und eines Weltreiches*, which went through seven editions and has been translated into five languages.[7] Four years later he published the second volume, *Kaiser Karl V: Quellen und Erörterungen*, which described, discussed and often transcribed the sources cited on each page of the German version of its predecessor. Although reprinted in 1967 it has never been translated.

Brandi's publications about the emperor were so numerous, and his judgements so sure, that they called to mind another passage from the Journal of W. H. Prescott, written as he composed his *History of the conquest of Peru*. 'Beware of Robertson', Prescott reminded himself, referring to William Robertson's *History of the reign of the Emperor Charles the Fifth*, published eighty years before. 'Never glance at him till after subject moulded in my mind and thrown into language.'[8] By the twenty-first century, Robertson (who conducted no archival research) seemed less of a threat, but while writing about Charles, I learned to 'Beware of Brandi': I tried not to consult his biography until after I had drafted each chapter – only to find, in many cases, either material that I had missed or a brilliant analysis that presented familiar documents in a novel way, leading me (with suitable acknowledgement) to amend my text.

After Brandi, I owe my greatest academic debt to Gustave Bergenroth (1813–69), who in the 1860s collected materials for a biography of Charles V based on what he called 'real State Papers: the despatches and instructions to the ambassadors, ministers and councillors, etc., and the letters and despatches received from them'.[9] This approach took Bergenroth to numerous European archives and libraries, where up to ten scribes copied the documents he deemed important to his project. He also decoded himself several hundred documents for which he could find no cipher key (which makes his copies superior to the originals). By the time Bergenroth died in 1869 his biography remained incomplete, but his transcripts filled over 20,000 folio pages, most of them arranged in a single chronological order that provides historians with a unique opportunity to measure the administrative pulse of Charles's empire.[10]

Archival research in the 1860s was not for the faint-hearted. An English visitor to Bergenroth reported that 'In Simancas all is as primitive, as native, and as shameless as the days of Adam. None of the decencies of life are to be found there ... Nothing but the strongest desire to do service to history could reconcile any man to so much hardship, and Mr. B., in speaking of his residence there, does not exaggerate when he calls it the life of a hermit.' It was while living in Simancas that Bergenroth contracted the typhus that killed him.[11] Everything had changed by the time I first worked there in 1966, and according to the archivists (who closely monitor every move made by *los señores investigadores*) since then I have consulted more than 2,000 bundles and volumes of their documents. Without the unique researcher-friendly methods of archive management practised at Simancas, this book could never have been written, and I thank in particular the archivists Ricardo Magdaleno Redondo, Asunción de la Plaza, José Luis and Julia T. Rodríguez de Diego, and Isabel Aguirre Landa; the *bedeles* who delivered those 2,000 bundles and volumes (usually within a few minutes of my request to read them); and the reprographic staff who made countless microfilm, Xerox and latterly digital copies for me.

I am also deeply grateful to the expert curators of other collections of documents concerning Charles V, especially Juan Manuel Calderón at the Alba Archive (Madrid); Leopold Auer and David Fliri at the Haus-, Hof-, und Staatsarchiv (Vienna); Ernest Persoons, Hugo de Schepper and Lucienne van Meerbeeck at the Algemeen Rijksarchief (Brussels); Hervé Passot at the Archives Départementales du Nord (Lille); Pierre-Emmanuel Guilleray and Henry Ferreira-Lopes at the Bibliothèque Municipale d'Étude et de Conservation (Besançon); Michael St. John-McAlister at the British Library (London); Clay Stalls and the late Bill Frank at the Huntington Library (San Marino); and Mitchell Codding, John O'Neill and Patrick Lenaghan at the Hispanic Society of America (New York).

Archival research is never cheap, and I thank the National Endowment for the Humanities (which awarded me a senior fellowship for this project in 2014–15) as well as the History Department and the Mershon Center of The Ohio State University for their generosity. I also thank Bethany Aram for vital support during my final bout of research in Spain, provided under the aegis of the exciting project that she directs: HAR2014-52260-P, 'Comercio, conflicto y cultura en el istmo de Panamá. Una artería del imperio y la crisis global, 1513–1671', financed by the Spanish Ministry of Economy and Competivity (MINECO), 2015–18.

I am very grateful to David Lincove, Brian Miller and Tonya Johnson of The Ohio State University Library: David, our History Librarian, purchased every book that I requested and approved an institutional subscription to both *ODNB* and *SPO*, two vital resources for my research; Brian and Tonya, of the Interlibrary Loan section, secured copies of every book, article and book chapter that I ordered (sometimes sending me an electronic copy within twenty-four hours).

ACKNOWLEDGEMENTS

I am grateful to other friends and colleagues who helped me acquire and interpret documents: Bethany Aram in Brussels, Lille and Seville; Fernando Bouza Álvarez, Alberto González Martínez, José Luis Gonzalo Sánchez-Molero, Santiago Martínez Hernández and Felipe Vidales del Castillo in Spain; Sheilagh Ogilvie and Hamish Scott in Britain; Lucien Bély, Indravati Félicité and Sanjay Subrahmanyam in France; Annemarie Jordan Gschwend in Austria; Arndt Brendecke and Franz Mauelshagen in Germany; Sebastiaan Derks, Raymond Fagel, Dries Raeymacker, Hugo Soly and Steven Thiry in the Low Countries; Maurizio Arfaioli, Michael Levin, Andrea Ottone and Michele Rabà in Italy; Clara García Ayluardo in Mexico; Richard Kagan in the United States; and Cameron Jones in Peru. I also thank Annemarie Jordan Gschwend, Hilary Macartney and Patrick Lenaghan for help with iconography; James Estes and Saskia Limbach for advice on German aspects of this project; and Christine Meyer, who provided vital assistance as I navigated the 'Political Correspondence of Charles V Collection' at the university of Konstanz.

In the countdown to publication, I was very fortunate that Bethany Aram, Maurizio Arfaioli, Ruth MacKay and James Tracy read and critiqued everything; that Byron Hamann and Robert Sargant read the proofs; that Kate Epstein gave me good advice; and that Robert Baldock, Percie Edgeler, Rachael Lonsdale, Marika Lysandrou, Clarissa Sutherland and my copyeditor Richard Mason of Yale University Press guided me through the final stages. This is the fourth book (so far) that Robert has commissioned from me, and I recall with pleasure his exemplary patience as well as his expert editorial skills. I also thank James Amelang, Maurizio Arfaioli, James Estes and Tom Nelson for pointing out some errors in the first edition.

Finally, I thank my family for their patience and support. James Atlas has eloquently described the miserable fate of the family of a biographer: a writer obsessed with 'someone who is not strictly speaking dead but not entirely present either', a figure who 'demanded vast amounts of my time, my energy, and my mental attention', and for this he offered his apologies.[12] The emperor and I therefore bow low and offer our apologies to my partner Alice Conklin, to my children Susie, Ed, Richard and Jamie (all Simancas veterans), and to my grandchildren Cameron, Sienna and Cordelia (as yet too young to decipher Habsburg handwriting but with plenty of time to learn) for any neglect, both perceived and actual, over the past nine years.

Geoffrey Parker
Columbus, 30 November 2018, St Andrew's Day
A day of special significance for Charles V and for me

CHRONOLOGY

	SPAIN, ITALY AND THE MEDITERRANEAN	THE NETHERLANDS, FRANCE AND THE EMPIRE	ENGLAND, SCOTLAND AND THE AMERICAS
1494			Treaty of Tordesillas (7 June): Portugal and Castile agree to partition newly discovered lands beyond Europe
1496		Archduke Philip of Austria and Infanta Joanna of Castile and Aragon marry (20 Oct.)	
1497	Juan, heir to the thrones of Aragon and Castile, marries Archduchess Margaret of Austria (3 Apr.), and dies (4 Oct.)		
1498	Infante Miguel, heir to the thrones of Aragon, Castile and Portugal, born (23 Aug.)	Charles's older sister Eleanor born (15 Nov.)	
1499			
1500	Infante Miguel dies (19 July), making Philip and Joanna heirs to the crowns of Castile and Aragon	Charles, duke of Luxembourg, born in Ghent (24 Feb.)	
1501		Charles's sister Isabeau born (18 July); Joanna and Philip sail for Spain (31 Oct.), leaving Charles and his sisters under the care of their great-grandmother Margaret of York.	Arthur Tudor, Prince of Wales, marries Charles's aunt Katherine of Aragon (14 Nov.)
1502			Prince Arthur dies (2 Apr.)
1503	Charles's brother Ferdinand born (10 Mar.)	Philip returns to the Netherlands (Oct.); Margaret of York dies (23 Nov.)	
1504	Queen Isabella of Castile dies (26 Nov.), succeeded by Joanna and Philip	Joanna returns to the Netherlands (May) and is confined in her apartments (Nov.); war between Philip and Duke Charles of Guelders begins	

	SPAIN, ITALY AND THE MEDITERRANEAN	THE NETHERLANDS, FRANCE AND THE EMPIRE	ENGLAND, SCOTLAND AND THE AMERICAS
1505	Ferdinand of Aragon marries Germaine de Foix (19 Oct.)	Charles meets his grandfather Maximilian for the first time; Luis Cabeza de Vaca replaces Juan de Anchieta as Charles's preceptor; Charles's sister Marie born (15 Sep.)	
1506	Philip returns to Castile (12 July), is acclaimed as king, then dies (25 Sep.); Queen Joanna confined in Tordesillas	Philip and Joanna leave for Spain (Jan.); States-General of the Netherlands acknowledge Charles as their lord (15 Oct.)	
1507	Catalina, Charles's youngest sister, born (14 Jan.)	Margaret of Austria becomes regent of the Netherlands for Emperor Maximilian, and guardian of Charles and his siblings (Apr.); Charles's first public appearance as ruler of the Netherlands at Philip's exequies (July)	Charles married by proxy to Princess Mary Tudor, daughter of Henry VII (July)
1508		Charles contracts smallpox (Oct.); Maximilian in the Netherlands (Nov.–Mar. 1509)	
1509	Birth and death of the only child of Ferdinand and Germaine de Foix (May)	Charles made Knight of the Garter (Feb.); Guillaume de Croÿ, lord of Chièvres, becomes Charles's chamberlain; Adrian of Utrecht becomes his tutor	Henry VIII succeeds as king of England (21 Apr.), and marries Katherine of Aragon (11 June)
1510			
1511			
1512		Maximilian in the Netherlands (spring)	
1513	Giovanni de' Medici elected pope (9 Mar. as Leo X); Niccolò Machiavelli completes *The prince*, which circulates in manuscript until published in 1532	Maximilian and Henry VIII defeat the French at Guinegate (16 Aug.); Charles makes his first state visit and attends Henry's victory jousts (Oct.)	English rout Scots at Flodden Field (9 Sep.)
1514		Marie leaves the Netherlands for Vienna (Apr.); Charles kills a man for the first time in a hunting accident (June)	Mary Tudor repudiates Charles (30 July), and marries Louis XII (13 Aug.)
1515	Francis I victorious at Marignano (13–14 Sep.), occupies Milan and Genoa	Louis XII dies (1 Jan.), succeeded by Francis of Angoulême (Francis I); Charles's emancipation (5 Jan.); Jean le Sauvage appointed Grand Chancellor (17 Jan.); Charles betrothed to Princess Renée of France; Isabeau leaves to marry Christian II of Denmark (June); Marie leaves to be betrothed to Louis II of Bohemia and Hungary (July); Charles sends Adrian to Spain as his ambassador to Ferdinand (Sep.)	

	SPAIN, ITALY AND THE MEDITERRANEAN	THE NETHERLANDS, FRANCE AND THE EMPIRE	ENGLAND, SCOTLAND AND THE AMERICAS
1516	Ferdinand of Aragon dies (23 Jan.); Cardinal Cisneros and the council of Regency acknowledge Charles as king of Castile (3 Apr.)	In Brussels, Charles devises his motto *Plus Ultra* and is proclaimed king of Castile and Aragon (14 Mar.); Erasmus publishes *Education of a Christian prince*, dedicated to Charles (May); Charles signs treaty of Noyon with France (13 Aug.), and presides over a chapter of the Order of the Golden Fleece for the first time (Oct.–Nov.); Francisco de Los Cobos becomes royal secretary	Katherine of Aragon gives birth to Princess Mary Tudor (18 Feb.)
1517	Charles's aunt Queen Maria of Portugal dies (7 Mar.); Charles and Eleanor reach Spain (20 Sep.) and visit their mother Joanna and sister Catalina (4 Nov.); Cisneros dies (8 Nov.); Charles and Eleanor meet their brother Ferdinand for the first time (19 Nov.)	Maximilian's last visit to the Netherlands (Jan.–May); Charles forces Eleanor to end her affair with Count Palatine Frederick (Aug.), and sails with her to Spain (7 Sep.); Martin Luther publishes his Ninety-five Theses (31 Oct.)	
1518	Charles meets Cortes of Castile (Mar.), sends Ferdinand to the Netherlands (Apr.), and meets Cortes of Aragon (May); Grand Chancellor Le Sauvage dies (7 June), Mercurino Arborio de Gattinara succeeds (8 Oct.); Eleanor sent to Portugal to marry King Manuel (Oct.)		Non-aggression Treaty of London (Oct.)
1519	Charles loses consciousness during Mass (Jan.); presides over chapter of the Order of the Golden Fleece in Barcelona (Mar.); receives news of his election as king of the Romans (6 July)	Emperor Maximilian dies (12 Jan.); Charles elected king of the Romans (28 June); Habsburg troops occupy Württemberg	Hernán Cortés sails from Cuba to Yucatán and sends Charles a first *muestra* of goods (July); Ferdinand Magellan's expedition leaves Seville for the Moluccas (10 Aug.); Cortés enters Tenochtitlan and meets Aztec Emperor Montezuma (8 Nov.)
1520	Charles receives in Valladolid the *muestra* sent by Hernán Cortés (Mar.), meets Cortes of Castile in Santiago and Corunna (Apr.–May), and sails for England from Corunna, leaving Adrian of Utrecht as regent (20 May); *Comuneros* revolt begins in Castile (May) and *Germanías* revolt in Valencia (July); Suleiman the Magnificent becomes sultan (1 Oct.)	Charles lands at Vlissingen (1 June); Francis I and Henry VIII meet at the Field of the Cloth of Gold (7–24 June); Charles and Henry meet (12–14 July); Luther's books, condemned by Leo X, burned at Leuven (8 Oct.); Charles crowned king of the Romans at Aachen (23 Oct.)	Charles reaches Dover (26 May), meets Henry VIII, and sails to the Low Countries (31 May); Montezuma killed (28/30 June); Cortés and supporters flee Tenochtitlan (*Noche triste*, 30 June/1 July)

	SPAIN, ITALY AND THE MEDITERRANEAN	THE NETHERLANDS, FRANCE AND THE EMPIRE	ENGLAND, SCOTLAND AND THE AMERICAS
1521	*Comuneros* defeated at Villalar (23 Apr.); Leo X, Henry VIII and Charles form an alliance against France (May); Leo X dies (1 Dec.); King Manuel of Portugal dies, leaving Eleanor of Austria a widow, and John III succeeds (13 Dec.)	Leo X excommunicates Luther (3 Jan.); Francis I promises support to enemies of Charles (Feb.); war between Charles and Francis (1 Apr.); Charles confronts Luther at Diet of Worms (17–18 Apr.) and outlaws him (26 May); Ferdinand marries Anne of Hungary (26 May); Chièvres dies (28 May); Suleiman captures Belgrade (29 Aug.); Charles dons a full suit of armour and leads his army on campaign for the first time (2 Sep.)	Magellan reconnoitres archipelago later known as the Philippines, where he is killed (27 Apr.); Cortés and allies besiege Tenochtitlan (10 May–13 Aug.), and after its fall the Spanish conquerors begin to take over Aztec Empire; secret treaty of Bruges between the emperor and England (25 Aug.)
1522	Adrian of Utrecht elected pope (9 Jan. as Adrian VI); French defeat at Bicocca (29 Apr.); Charles lands in Spain again (16 July); Charles's confessor Jean Glapion dies (22 Sep.); Charles issues General Pardon for most *Comuneros* (1 Nov.)	Charles makes his first will (22 May), sails from the Netherlands to England and Spain (26 May), leaving his aunt Margaret as regent; Jeanne van der Gheynst gives birth to Charles's daughter Margarita in or near Oudenaarde (July)	Charles in England (26 May–7 July), agrees with Henry to mount a 'Great Enterprise' against France, and to marry Henry's daughter Mary when she turns twelve; Duke Charles of Bourbon joins Great Enterprise (Aug.); survivors of Magellan's expedition reach Seville (8 Sep.); Charles agrees to fund a House of Spice in Corunna, and names Cortés governor and captain-general of New Spain
1523	Ottomans conquer Rhodes (1 Jan.); Ursulina della Penne gives birth to Charles's daughter Tadea in Bologna (23 Jan.); Fray Garcia de Loaysa becomes Charles's confessor (May); Charles's illegitimate daughter Juana born in Valladolid (June?); Adrian VI dies (14 Sep.); Giulio de' Medici elected pope (19 Nov. as Clement VII); Charles campaigns in Navarre (winter), and appoints Bourbon his lieutenant-general in Italy (Dec.)	Christian II of Denmark deposed (Jan.): he and Isabeau seek Charles's protection	English invasion of France (Aug.–Dec.)
1524	Charles establishes the council of the Indies and reorganizes State and Finance; Bourbon leads unsuccessful imperial invasion of Provence (June–Sep.); Francis invades Milan (Oct.); Clement concludes alliance with France and Venice (Dec.)	Peasant Revolt in Germany begins (summer); Francis names his mother, Louise of Savoy, regent of France, and leaves to campaign in Italy (Oct.)	Charles authorizes two expeditions to the Moluccas: one from Corunna and one from Mexico

	SPAIN, ITALY AND THE MEDITERRANEAN	THE NETHERLANDS, FRANCE AND THE EMPIRE	ENGLAND, SCOTLAND AND THE AMERICAS
1525	Catalina marries King John III of Portugal (10 Feb.); Imperial victory at Pavia, Francis captured (24 Feb.); Francis brought to Madrid a prisoner (Aug.)	Peasants' Revolt crushed (summer)	Charles breaks off his engagement to Henry's daughter Mary (June)
1526	Francis signs the treaty of Madrid (14 Jan.); Charles marries Isabella of Portugal (11 Mar.); Francis returns to France, leaving two sons as hostages in Spain (17 Mar.); Bishop Acuña of Zamora tortured and executed at Simancas (24 Mar.); Charles's troops and Colonna forces capture Rome (Sep.)	Isabeau of Denmark dies (19 Jan.); Francis I returns to France (17 Mar.), reneges on his promises to Charles, and forms the anti-Habsburg League of Cognac with the papacy, Florence and Venice (22 May); King Louis of Hungary defeated and killed at Mohács (26 Aug.); Ferdinand elected king of Bohemia (24 Oct.) and Hungary (17 Dec.)	
1527	Bourbon dies leading Imperial troops who storm Rome (6 May); Rome sacked (6–16 May); Gattinara on leave from Imperial court (May–Oct.); Prince Philip born (21 May); Republic of Florence proclaimed (June)		Anglo-French treaty of Amiens (18 Aug.); Charles creates an Audiencia in Mexico City (Nov.)
1528	On behalf of the League of Cognac, the heralds of France and England declare war on Charles, who arrests all ambassadors of the League (22 Jan.); League of Cognac blockades Naples by land and sea (Feb.–Aug.); Charles challenges Francis to a duel (18 Mar.); Infanta María born (21 June); Andrea Doria enters Charles's service (19 July); League of Cognac troops abandon siege of Naples and surrender at Aversa (27 Aug.); Doria seizes Genoa (12 Sep.); Margaret of Austria forces duke of Guelders to surrender Utrecht and Overijssel to Charles (3 Oct.)		Cortés returns to Spain (May) and meets Charles
1529	Charles signs his second will (3 Mar.); Antonio de Leyva defeats another French army in Lombardy (21 June); Charles signs the treaty of Barcelona with Clement (29 June), sets sail for Italy (27 July), arrives in	Peace of Cambrai between Charles, Francis and Henry (5 Aug.); Ottoman siege of Vienna (23 Sep.–14 Oct.)	Cortés created marquis of the Valle de Oaxaca (1 Apr.) and returns to Mexico; Charles cedes all claim to Moluccas to Portugal by treaty of Zaragoza (22 Apr.) and closes House of Spice; Francisco

	SPAIN, ITALY AND THE MEDITERRANEAN	THE NETHERLANDS, FRANCE AND THE EMPIRE	ENGLAND, SCOTLAND AND THE AMERICAS
1529 *cont.*	Genoa (12 Aug.), lays siege to Florence (Sep.), and enters Bologna to meet Clement (5 Nov.); Infante Fernando born (22 Nov.); Charles makes peace with Venice and Duke Francesco Sforza of Milan, and creates league for the defence of Italy (29 Dec.)		Pizarro authorized to conquer Peru (24 May); peace between Charles and Henry VIII (5 Aug.)
1530	Charles meets his daughter Tadea (Jan.–Feb); Clement crowns Charles king of Lombardy (22 Feb.) and Holy Roman Emperor in Bologna (24 Feb.); Charles crosses the Brenner into Austria (2 May); Infante Fernando dies (30 July); Charles's illegitimate daughter Juana dies at Madrigal; Imperial-papal siege forces Florentine republic to surrender (Aug.), and Charles restores Medici rule (Oct.)	Gattinara dies (5 June), and Los Cobos and Nicholas Perrenot de Granvelle become Charles's principal ministers; Charles opens the Diet of Augsburg (15 June) and hears the Augsburg Confession (25 June); French princes return to France upon payment in full of their ransom (1 July); Eleanor of Austria marries Francis (7 July); Charles condemns Lutherans in closing act of the Diet (19 Nov.); Margaret of Austria dies (30 Nov.)	Pizarro and Diego de Almagro lead an expedition from Panama to Peru (27 Dec.)
1531		Ferdinand elected king of the Romans (5 Jan.); Charles enters Brussels (25 Jan.); landgrave of Hesse and Elector of Saxony form the Schmalkaldic League of Lutheran states (27 Feb.); Charles appoints Marie, dowager queen of Hungary, his regent in the Netherlands, advised by three Collateral Councils (Sep.–Oct.), and holds chapter of the Order of the Golden Fleece in Tournai (Dec.)	Henry VIII claims the title of Supreme Head of the Church of England (11 Feb.)
1532	Charles crosses the Brenner into Italy with an army (Oct.) and enters Bologna (13 Dec.) for more talks with Clement; Machiavelli's *Prince* published posthumously	Charles leaves Brussels for Germany (17 Jan.); suffers a hunting accident and a series of health crises (25 Feb.–July); challenged by Suleiman to battle (12 July); agrees to the peace of Nuremberg (23 July) granting German Lutheran rulers toleration in exchange for military support; enters Vienna (23 Sep.); Ottoman army withdraws from Hungary (Oct.)	Francisco Pizarro captures the Inca Atahualpa at Cajamarca (16 Nov.) and sends *prendas* to Charles

	SPAIN, ITALY AND THE MEDITERRANEAN	THE NETHERLANDS, FRANCE AND THE EMPIRE	ENGLAND, SCOTLAND AND THE AMERICAS
1533	Charles signs pact for the defence of Italy (24 Feb.), leaves Bologna (28 Feb.) and sets sail for Spain from Genoa (10 Apr.); Charles rejoins his family in Barcelona (22 Apr.)		Henry VIII repudiates Katherine of Aragon, marries Anne Boleyn (25 Jan.), and is excommunicated by pope; Pizarro executes Atahualpa (26 July); Elizabeth Tudor born (7 Sep.); Pizarro captures Cuzco (15 Nov.)
1534	*Prendas* sent by Pizarro reach Spain (Jan.); Charles visits university of Salamanca (June); empress gives birth to stillborn son (29 June); Clement VII dies (25 Sep.); Alessandro Farnese elected pope (13 Oct. as Paul III)	Landgrave of Hesse leads Lutheran troops into Würt-temberg, drives out Habsburg garrisons, and restores Duke Ulrich (Apr.–June)	Clement reaffirms the validity of Henry VIII's marriage to Katherine of Aragon (Mar.); Henry ends England's obedience to Rome
1535	Charles makes his third will (28 Feb.), leaves Spain (28 May), and captures Tunis (16 June–20 Aug.); Infanta Joanna born (24 June); Charles establishes an independent household for Prince Philip (June); Charles undertakes victory lap through Sicily (21 Aug.–2 Nov.) and Naples; Barbarossa sacks Mahón in Menorca (Sep.); Duke Francesco Sforza of Milan dies (1 Nov.) and Leyva takes possession of duchy in Charles's name		Charles incorporates Tlaxcala into the Crown of Castile (13 Mar.) and appoints Antonio de Mendoza his first viceroy of New Spain (25 Apr.)
1536	Charles presides in Naples at the marriage of his daughter Margarita to Duke Alessandro de' Medici of Florence (18 Jan.), enters Rome (5 Apr.), and again challenges Francis to a duel (16 Apr.); Charles leads army into France (25 July); Germaine de Foix dies (15 Oct.); Charles retreats defeated to Genoa (28 Oct.) and sets sail for Barcelona (15 Nov.)	Francis occupies Savoy and Piedmont (Feb.–Mar.), and ne-gotiates alliance with Suleiman (Apr.); Charles invades Provence (July) but has to retreat to Italy (Sep.–Oct.)	Katherine of Aragon dies (7 Jan.); Henry VIII has Anne Boleyn executed (19 May), and marries Jane Seymour (30 May)
1537	Duke Alessandro de' Medici murdered (6 Jan.); Infante Juan born (19 Oct.)		Prince Edward Tudor born (12 Oct.); Queen Jane Seymour dies (24 Oct.)

	SPAIN, ITALY AND THE MEDITERRANEAN	THE NETHERLANDS, FRANCE AND THE EMPIRE	ENGLAND, SCOTLAND AND THE AMERICAS
1538	Charles sets out for Nice (12 Feb,); Infante Juan dies (29 Mar.); Ottoman fleet defeats Christian fleet at Prevesa (28 Sep.); Margarita of Austria marries Octavio Farnese, grandson of Pope Paul III and future duke of Parma (4 Nov.)	Charles and Francis meet the pope in Nice (9 May–20 June); Duke Charles of Guelders dies (30 June), and his subjects recognize Duke William of Cleves as his successor; Charles meets Francis at Aigues-Mortes (14–15 July)	Pizarro brothers defeat and execute Almagro (8 July)
1539	Empress gives birth to another stillborn son (21 Apr.) and dies (1 May); Charles names Philip regent (5 Nov.) and writes his first set of 'instructions' for his son before setting out for the Netherlands (11 Nov.)	Revolt of Ghent begins (17 Aug.); Charles enters France en route for the Netherlands (Nov.) and joins Francis (10 Dec.)	Francisco de Vitoria delivers his *Relectio de Indis* at the university of Salamanca (Jan.)
1540	Charles approves creation of a government secret archive in the fortress of Simancas (Sep.)	Charles enters Paris in triumph (1 Jan.), enters Ghent at the head of his troops (14 Feb.) and punishes rebel leaders (3 May)	Cortés returns to Spain (June); Henry VIII marries Anne of Cleves (6 Jan.), rejects her (9 July), and marries Catherine Howard (28 July)
1541	Marquis del Vasto, governor of Milan, arranges murder of French ambassadors Antonio Rincón and Cesare Fregoso (3 July), subsequently approved by Charles; Charles meets Paul III in Lucca (15–18 Sep.) before leading his forces in an unsuccessful attack on Algiers (23–28 Oct.); returns to Spain (1 Dec.)	Charles presides over the Diet of Regensburg (23 Feb.–29 July); sets out for Italy (29 July); Ottomans defeat Habsburg forces besieging Buda (21 Aug.) and occupy most of Hungary	Allies of Almagro murder Pizarro (26 June); Catherine Howard executed (23 Nov.)
1542	While at Monzón to meet the Cortes of Aragon (June–Sep.) Charles contemplates abdication and retirement to a monastery; French siege of Perpignan fails (Sep.)	Denmark and the duke of Cleves declare war on Charles (June), followed by France (10/12 July): the allies attack the Low Countries, Catalonia and Navarre	Charles allies with Henry VIII to attack France and Scotland (11 Feb.), and signs the New Laws, suppressing *encomiendas* in America (20 Nov.); English defeat Scots at Solway Moss (24 Nov.); James V of Scotland dies (14 Dec.) and his heiress, Mary Stuart, flees to France
1543	Charles sets sail for Genoa (1 May), and in Palamos he compiles secret holograph instructions for Prince Philip, left as regent (4 and 6 May); Charles meets Paul III at Busseto (20–23 June); Philip marries his cousin María Manuela of Portugal (14 Nov.); Barbarossa and Ottoman fleet winter in Toulon	Charles marches through Germany and attacks Cleves, taking Düren by storm (24 Aug.); Franco-Ottoman forces sack Nice (6 Sep.); Duke William of Cleves submits and surrenders Guelders to Charles (7 Sep.); Charles advances on Landrecies and offers battle to Francis, who retreats (3 Nov.)	Charles appoints Blasco Nuñez Vela his first viceroy of Peru (28 Feb.); Henry VIII marries Catherine Parr (12 July)

	SPAIN, ITALY AND THE MEDITERRANEAN	THE NETHERLANDS, FRANCE AND THE EMPIRE	ENGLAND, SCOTLAND AND THE AMERICAS
1544	French victory over imperial army under Vasto at Ceresole d'Alba (14 Apr.)	Charles presides at the Diet of Speyer (Feb.–June), which votes funds for war against France; Charles invades France, captures St Dizier (17 Aug.), and signs the Peace of Crépy which includes many French concessions (including a secret promise to provide aid against the German Lutherans) but obliges Charles to surrender either Milan or Netherlands to Francis's son, Duke Charles of Orléans (18–19 Sep.)	Nuñez Vela arrives in Peru (May); *encomenderos* in Peru rebel, led by Gonzalo Pizarro (Aug.)
1545	News of rebellion in Peru arrives in Spain (May); Don Carlos born (8 July); María Manuela of Portugal dies (12 July); Paul III offers to send Charles money and troops for war against Lutherans (June) and invests his son Pier Luigi as duke of Parma and Piacenza (Sep.); council of Trent opens (13 Dec.)	Charles announces his decision to surrender Milan to Charles of Orléans (1 Feb.); Charles of Orléans dies (9 Sep.), allowing Charles to retain both Milan and the Netherlands; landgrave of Hesse and the Elector of Saxony defeat and imprison Duke Henry of Brunswick and seize his lands (Oct.)	Los Cobos recommends appointing Pedro de La Gasca to pacify Peru (30 June); French forces invade Isle of Wight (21 July)
1546	Charles sends Philip his 'letter of emancipation' (30 June)	Charles holds chapter of the Order of the Golden Fleece in Utrecht (Jan.); Martin Luther dies (18 Feb.); Charles travels to Regensburg to meet Diet (Feb.–June), seduces Barbara Blomberg, and mobilizes troops in Germany, Italy and the Netherlands, ostensibly to restore the duke of Brunswick (June); landgrave of Hesse, Elector of Saxony and other leaders of the League of Schmalkalden mobilize and sign an Act of Diffidation, renouncing Charles's rule (11 Aug.); League's army bombards Charles and his army in their camp before Ingolstadt (31 Aug.–4 Sep.); League's army withdraws (4 Sep.) and demobilizes (22 Nov.); Frederick of the Palatinate and Ulrich of Württemberg submit to Charles (Nov.–Dec.)	Viceroy Nuñez Vela of Peru defeated and ex- ecuted by rebels (18 Jan.); Pedro de La Gasca leaves Spain for Peru (Mar.); France and England make peace (6 June); La Gasca reaches Panama (Aug.)
1547	Fieschi leads revolution in Genoa (2–3 January); Paul III relocates the general council from Trent to Bologna (Mar.); riots in Naples against the introduction of the Inquisition	Barbara Blomberg gives birth in Regensburg to Charles's son, called Gerónimo, later Don John of Austria (24 Feb.); Paul III withdraws his troops from Germany (Feb.); Francis I dies (31 Mar.), succeeded	Henry VIII dies (28 Jan.), succeeded by Edward VI; La Gasca lands in Peru and advances towards Cuzco (June); English

	SPAIN, ITALY AND THE MEDITERRANEAN	THE NETHERLANDS, FRANCE AND THE EMPIRE	ENGLAND, SCOTLAND AND THE AMERICAS
1547 *cont.*	(May–Aug.); Los Cobos dies (17 May); five-year truce between Charles and Suleiman (19 June); Duke Pier Luigi Farnese murdered in Piacenza (10 Sep.) and Imperial troops occupy the city; Cortés dies (2 Dec.)	by Henry II; at Mühlberg Charles defeats and captures the Elector of Saxony (24 Apr.), who surrenders his lands and titles; landgrave of Hesse surrenders to Charles (19 June) who imprisons him; Charles sends Spanish garrisons into Württemberg, presides at the 'Armed Diet' of Augsburg (opened 1 Sep.), and summons Philip and María to join him in Germany (25 Dec.)	defeat the Scots at Pinkie (10 Sep.)
1548	Imperial agents in Venice assassinate Lorenzino de' Medici, Duke Alessandro's murderer (26 Feb.); Charles's daughter María marries Ferdinand's son Maximilian and they become joint regents in Spain (Sep.); Philip leaves Spain for Genoa (Oct.) and travels through northern Italy into Germany	Charles sends his *Political Testament* to Philip (18 Jan); Charles orders Philip to join him in Brussels after Maximilian arrives and marries María in Spain (9 Apr.); Diet of Augsburg enacts the Interim (15 May); Diet declares the Netherlands a separate Circle of the Empire (30 June); Charles starts purging German city councils as he returns to Netherlands (Aug.)	La Gasca defeats rebellious *encomenderos* of Peru in battle outside Cuzco (8 Apr.), has Gonzalo Pizarro executed (10 Apr.), and starts purge of rebels and their relatives
1549	Council of Trent/Bologna prorogued indefinitely (17 Sep.); Paul III dies (10 Nov.)	Philip joins Charles in the Netherlands (1 Apr.), and both tour southern cities and attend festivals, notably at Binche (21–31 Aug.); Pragmatic Sanction unites the seventeen Habsburg provinces of the Netherlands (4 Nov.)	
1550	Giovanni del Monte elected pope (7 Feb.: Julius III); Charles makes his fourth will (19 May); Charles's illegitimate son Gerónimo sent to Spain (June); Junta de Indias meets in Valladolid to discuss royal policy in America (Aug.–Sep.); Habsburg forces conquer Mahdia and other ports in north Africa (Sep.)	Charles travels to Germany with Philip and starts writing his *Memoirs* (June); presides over the Diet of Augsburg; Nicolas Perrenot de Granvelle dies (27 Aug.); bitter arguments with Ferdinand over imperial succession	Treaty of Boulogne reconciles England with France and Scotland (24 Mar.); Charles appoints Antonio de Mendoza viceroy of Peru and Luis de Velasco viceroy of Mexico (Apr.); La Gasca reaches Spain with two million ducats from Peru (Sep.)
1551	Junta de Indias reconvenes in Valladolid (Apr.–May); Philip travels from Augsburg via Trent to Spain (May–July); Duke Octavio Farnese switches his allegiance to France and Imperial-papal forces lay siege to Parma	In Augsburg, Ferdinand and Philip sign a Family Compact concerning the imperial succession (9 March); council of Trent reconvenes, to which Charles insists that Lutherans must be invited (1 May); Charles's agents start to remodel	Charles creates institutions of higher education in Mexico and Peru (May)

	SPAIN, ITALY AND THE MEDITERRANEAN	THE NETHERLANDS, FRANCE AND THE EMPIRE	ENGLAND, SCOTLAND AND THE AMERICAS
1551 *cont.*	and La Mirandola (July); Ottomans capture Tripoli (15 Aug.)	the charters of twenty-five South German cities (Oct.); Henry II and German Lutheran princes led by Maurice of Saxony sign the Treaty of Lochau (5 Oct.); Charles orders the Spanish garrisons in Württemberg to join siege of Parma (Oct.), and moves to Innsbruck with his court (Nov.)	
1552	Infanta Joanna marries Prince John of Portugal (11 Jan.); end of the War of Parma (25 June); successful pro-French uprising in Siena (26 July); Charles orders garrison to raze fortifications of Mahdia and abandon it (Sep.)	Lutheran forces occupy Augsburg (4 Apr.); Metz recognizes Henry II as its suzerain (21 Apr.); council of Trent suspended (May); Charles flees from Innsbruck to Villach (19 May), agrees to free the imprisoned rulers of Hesse and Saxony, and ratifies the treaty of Passau, bringing the German war to an end (15 Aug.); Charles joins his army at Augsburg (20 Aug.), marches across Germany, and lays siege to Metz (23 Oct.)	Bartolomé de Las Casas publishes *Brevíssima relación de la destrucción de las Indias* in Seville
1553	Charles orders his son to break off negotiations to marry Maria of Portugal, the daughter of Eleanor (Aug.)	The Imperial army abandons the siege of Metz (1 Jan.); Charles reaches Brussels (6 Feb.), addresses the States-General (13 Feb.), and summons Philip to the Netherlands; Imperial troops besiege and destroy French-held Thérouanne and Hesdin (June)	Edward VI of England dies (6 July), and Mary Tudor succeeds; Charles urges Philip to marry Mary (30 July); Francisco Hernández Girón rebels in Peru (12 Nov.)
1554	Prince John of Portugal dies (2 Jan.); Infanta Joanna gives birth to Prince Sebastian (20 Jan.) and returns to Castile; Philip briefs Joanna on serving as regent of Spain, then leaves for England (13 July); Charles abdicates as king of Naples in favour of Philip (24 July)	Charles approves the terms of the marriage of Philip and Mary Tudor (4 Jan.); Charles drafts his fifth (last) will and secret codicils (6 June), leaves Brussels to join his troops (7 July), relieves Renty and forces French to withdraw (14 Aug.), and returns to Brussels in triumph (9 Oct.)	Mary crushes Wyatt's rebellion (3 Feb.) and imprisons her sister Elizabeth; Philip marries Mary Tudor (25 July), becomes king consort, and resides in England; England reconciled with Rome; Hernández Girón defeated in battle in Peru (8 Oct.) and is executed
1555	Julius III dies (23 Mar.); Queen Joanna, Charles's mother, dies (12 Apr.); Siena surrenders to Florentine-Imperial forces (17 Apr.); Marcello Cervini elected pope (9 Apr.: as Marcellus II) and dies (1 May); Gian Pietro Caraffa elected pope (23 May: as Paul IV); Ottoman forces capture Bougie (Aug.)	Philip returns to Brussels (8 Sep.); Ferdinand signs the peace of Augsburg (25 Sep.), which guarantees toleration for Lutherans in the Empire; Charles abdicates as ruler of the Netherlands (25 Oct.) and as Sovereign of the Order of the Golden Fleece (26 Oct.) in favour of Philip	Philip leaves England for the Netherlands (4 Sep.)

	SPAIN, ITALY AND THE MEDITERRANEAN	THE NETHERLANDS, FRANCE AND THE EMPIRE	ENGLAND, SCOTLAND AND THE AMERICAS
1556	Paul IV excommunicates and declares war on Charles and Philip (Sep.); Charles lands at Laredo (28 Sep.) and travels to Jarandilla	Charles abdicates as king of Sicily, Aragon and Castile, in favour of Philip (16 Jan.), whom he names imperial vicar-general in Italy; truce of Vaucelles with France (Feb.–July); Charles and his sisters Eleanor and Marie leave the Netherlands for Spain (17 Sep.)	
1557	Charles moves into his quarters at Yuste (3 Feb.); Philip begs his father to leave Yuste and govern Spain again, but he refuses (23–24 Mar.); Philip issues his first *Decreto* suspending all payments from the treasury of Castile (May); John III of Portugal dies (11 June), succeeded by infant grandson Sebastian, with Charles's sister Catalina as regent; Paul IV makes peace (14 Sep.)	Philip's army defeats French at the battle of St Quentin (10 Aug.), and invades France (Sep.–Oct.	Philip returns to England (18 Mar.–6 July); England declares war on France and Scotland (7 June)
1558	Eleanor of Austria dies (25 Feb.); Luis Quijada brings Gerónimo to Yuste and presents him to Charles (July); Ottoman fleet sacks Ciutadella on Menorca (July); Charles reviews his last testament and makes some changes (9 Sep.); Charles dies (21 Sep.); Marie of Hungary dies (18 Oct.); exequies for Charles in Spain and Italy (Dec.)	Charles's abdication as Holy Roman Emperor accepted by Electoral College (14 Mar.); Ferdinand succeeds him but denies Philip the title of imperial vicar-general in Italy; Philip's army defeats French at the battle of Gravelines (13 July); exequies for Charles in the Netherlands (Dec.)	England loses Calais (7 Jan.); Mary Tudor dies (17 Nov.), succeeded by her half-sister Elizabeth; exequies for Charles in London (Dec.)
1559	Paul IV dies (18 Aug.); Giovanni Angelo de' Medici elected pope (25 Dec. as Pius IV); Philip returns to Spain, meets his half-brother Gerónimo, whom he renames Don John of Austria, and welcomes him to his court (Sep.)	Exequies for Charles in Augsburg (24 Feb.); Peace of Cateau-Cambrésis ends Habsburg-Valois wars (3 Apr.); Philip appoints his half-sister Margarita his regent in the Netherlands and sails to Spain (Aug.)	Peace of Cateau-Cambrésis ends Anglo-Scottish and Anglo-French wars (3 Apr.); exequies for Charles in Lima (11–12 Nov.), Mexico City (30 Nov.), and elsewhere in Spanish America
1562		Charles's daughter Tadea, now a nun in Rome, begs permission to come to Spain (12 Oct.); Ferdinand secures the election of his son Maximilian as king of the Romans (24 Nov.)	Gonzalo Méndez, a Franciscan friar in Guatemala, observes Charles's soul ascend from Purgatory to Paradise

ABBREVIATIONS IN THE
NOTES AND SOURCES

AA	Biblioteca de Liria, Madrid, Archivo de la Casa de los Duques de Alba, with caja and folio
ADN	Archives départementales du Nord, Lille
B	*Archives civiles, Série B (Chambre des Comptes de Lille)*, with register or liasse and (where one exists) immatriculation
AGI	Archivo General de Indias, Seville, with legajo and ramo, or libro and folio
IG	*Indiferente General*
Justicia	*Papeles de Justicia*
Lima	*Audiencia de Lima*
México	*Audiencia de México*
Patronato	*Patronato Real*
AGNM	Archivo General de la Nación, Mexico D.F.
Mercedes	*Instituciones coloniales: Mercedes*
AGPM	Archivo General del Palacio Real, Madrid, Sección histórica
AGRB	Archives Générales du Royaume/Algemene Rijksarchief, Brussels
Audience	*Papiers d'État et d'Audience/Papieren van Staat en Audientië*
Gachard	*Collection Gachard/Collectie Gachard*
MD	*Manuscrits divers/Handschriftenverzameling*
AGS	Archivo General de Simancas, Simancas (Valladolid)
CC	*Cámara de Castilla*
CJH	*Consejos y Juntas de Hacienda*
CMC	*Contaduría Mayor de Cuentas* (with época and legajo)
CS	*Contaduría del Sueldo* (with época and legajo)
CSR	*Casas y Sitios Reales*
E	*Negociación de Estado*
GA	*Guerra Antigua*
PR	*Patronato Real*
AHN	Archivo Histórico Nacional, Madrid
Inquisición	*Sección de Inquisición*
AHN Nobleza	Sección Nobleza del Archivo Histórico Nacional, Toledo
Frías	*Archivo de los duques de Frías* (until 1987 housed in the castle of the dukes of Frías at Montemayor, Córdoba)
AHR	*American Historical Review*
AMAE	Archivo del Ministerio de Asuntos Exteriores, Madrid
ANF	Archives Nationales de France, Paris, Archives de l'Ancien Régime
Série J	*Trésor des Chartes*
Série K	*Monuments historiques*
ANTT	Arquivo Nacional da Torre do Tombo, Lisbon
CC	*Corpo cronológico*
AS	Archivio di Stato
ASF	Archivio di Stato, Florence
MdP	*Mediceo del Principato*
SDO	*Signori, Dieci di Balia e Otto di Pratica. Legazioni e commissarie, missive e response*
ASMa	Archivio di Stato, Mantua
AG CE	*Archivio Gonzaga: Corrispondenza estera*

ASMo	Archivio di Stato, Modena
CDA	*Cancellaria ducale: ambasciatori*
ASP	Archivio di Stato, Parma
CF	*Carteggio Farnesiano*
GG	*Archivi di Famiglie e di Persone: Gonzaga di Guastalla*
AST	Archivio di Stato, Turin
LM	*Lettere di ministri*
B&S	*Berichte und Studien zur Geschichte Karls V.*, with issue number (a series of 20 fascicles published in *Nachrichten von der Gesellschaft der Wissenschaften zu Göttingen, Philologisch-Historische Klasse* between 1930 and 1942 by Karl Brandi and his students. See bibliography for details.)
BAE	Biblioteca de Autores Españoles
BAV	Biblioteca Apostolica Vaticana, Vatican City, Manuscript collection
Vat. Lat.	*Codex Vaticanus Latinus*
BCRH	*Bulletin de la Commission Royale d'Histoire*
BH	*Bulletin Hispanique*
BHO	*British History Online*
BIHR	*Bulletin of the Institute of Historical Research*
BKK	Brandi, K., *Kaiser Karl V: Quellen und Erörterungen* (Munich, 1941)
BL	British Library (formerly British Museum Library), London, Department of Western Manuscripts
Addl. Ms.	*Additional Manuscripts*
Cott. Ms.	*Cotton Manuscripts*
Eg. Ms.	*Egerton Manuscripts*
Harl. Ms.	*Harleian Manuscripts*
BMECB	Bibliothèque Municipale d'Étude et de Conservation, Besançon
Ms. Granvelle	*Collection Manuscrite Granvelle*
BNE *Ms.*	Biblioteca Nacional de España, Madrid, *Colección de Manuscritos*
BNF	Bibliothèque Nationale de France, Paris, *Section des Manuscrits*
Dupuy	*Collection manuscrite Dupuy*
F. f.	*Fonds français*
Ms. Esp.	*Manuscrit espagnol*
Ms. Port.	*Manuscrit portugais*
BNMV	Biblioteca Nazionale Marciana, Venice, Manuscript collection
BNP	*La Bibliothèque Nationale à Paris. Notice et extraits des manuscrits qui concernent l'histoire de la Belgique*, ed. L. P. Gachard, 2 vols (Brussels, 1875–7)
BR *Ms.*	Biblioteca Real (formerly Biblioteca del Palacio Real), Madrid, *Colección de Manuscritos*
BRAH	*Boletín de la Real Academia de la Historia*
BRB *Ms.*	Bibliothèque Royale de Belgique/Koninklijke Bibliotheek, Brussels, *Cabinet des Manuscrits/Handschriftenkabinet*
BSLE *Ms.*	del Real Biblioteca Monasterio de San Lorenzo de El Escorial, *Colección de Manuscritos*
BZ	Biblioteca de Zabálburu, Madrid, Manuscript collection (with caja and folio)
CADMA	Centre des Archives Diplomatiques du Ministère des Affaires Étrangères, La Courneuve (previously Archives du Ministère des Affaires Étrangères)
MDE	*Mémoires et documents: Espagne*
CCG	*Correspondance du Cardinal de Granvelle*, ed. E. Poullet and C. Piot, 12 vols (Brussels, 1877–96)
CDCV	*Corpus Documental de Carlos V*, ed. M. Fernández Álvarez, 5 vols (Salamanca, 1973–81)
CLC	*Cortes de los antiguos reinos de León y de Castilla*, 7 vols (Madrid, 1861–1903)
CMH	*Correspondance de Marie de Hongrie avec Charles-Quint et Nicolas de Granvelle*, ed. L. Gorter-van Royen and J.-P. Hoyois, 2 vols (Leuven, 2009–18)
CODOIN	*Colección de Documentos Inéditos para la historia de España*, 112 vols (Madrid, 1842–95)
CODOIN … América	*Colección de Documentos Inéditos relativos al descubrimiento, conquista y organización de las antiguas posesiones de América y Oceania*, 42 vols (Madrid, 1864–84)
CODOIN … Ultramar	*Colección de Documentos Inéditos relativos al descubrimiento, conquista y organización de las antiguas posesiones españoles de Ultramar*, 25 vols (Madrid, 1885–1932)

CR	*Corpus Reformatorum*, ed. K. G. Bretschneider et al., 101 vols to date (Halle, 1834–)
CSPF	*Calendar of State Papers, Foreign Series, of the reign of Edward VI, 1547–1553*, ed. W. B. Turnbull (London, 1861)
CSP Milan	*Calendar of State Papers and Manuscripts in the Archives and Collections of Milan, 1385–1618*, ed. A. B. Hinds (London, 1912)
CSPSp	*Calendar of Letters, Despatches, and State Papers, relating to the negotiations between England and Spain, preserved in the archives at Vienna, Simancas, Besançon, Brussels, Madrid and Lille*, ed. G. A. Bergenroth, P. de Gayangos et al., 13 vols, (London, 1862–1954)
CSPSp Supplement	*Supplement to volume I and volume II of Letters, Despatches, and State Papers, relating to the negotiations between England and Spain, preserved in the archives of Simancas and elsewhere*, ed. G. A. Bergenroth (London, 1868)
CSPSp Further Supplement	*Further Supplement to Letters, Despatches, and State Papers, relating to the negotiations between England and Spain, preserved in the archives at Vienna and elsewhere, 1513–1542*, ed. G. Mattingly (London, 1947)
CSPV	*Calendar of State Papers and Manuscripts relating to English Affairs existing in the archives and collections of Venice*, ed. H. F. Brown et al., 38 vols (London, 1864–1947)
CWE	*The Collected Works of Erasmus: The Correspondence*, ed. W. K. Ferguson, J. Estes et al., 18 vols to date (Toronto, 1974–2018)
EHR	*English Historical Review*
FBD	G. Parker, *Felipe II. La biografía definitiva* (Barcelona, 2010)
GRM	*Retraite et mort de Charles-Quint au monastère de Yuste. Lettres inédites publiées d'après les originaux conservés dans les archives royales de Simancas*, by L. P. Gachard, *Introduction* and 2 vols (Brussels, 1854–6)
HHStA	Haus-, Hof- und Staatsarchiv, Vienna
	Länderabteilungen: Belgien-Niederländisches Departement
Belgien DD	*Belgien Repertorium DD*
Belgien PA	*Belgien Repertorium P Abteilung A*
Belgien PB	*Belgien Repertorium P Abteilung B*
Belgien PC	*Belgien Repertorium P Abteilung C*
	Handschriftensammlung
Hs. Blau	*Handschrift Blau*
HMC	*Historical Manuscripts Commission*
HR	*Historical Research* (formerly *Bulletin of the Institute of Historical Research*)
HSA	Hispanic Society of America, New York, Manuscript collection
Altamira	Manuscripts from the Society's Altamira collection, with box, folder and document
B	Manuscripts from the Society's main manuscript collection
HC	Documents purchased by the HSA from Karl Hiersemann, with catalogue and document
Hunt	Huntington Library, Art Collections and Botanical Gardens, San Marino (California)
HA	*Hastings Manuscripts*
PL	*Pizarro-La Gasca Collection*
IVdeDJ	Instituto de Valencia de Don Juan, Madrid, with envío and folio
KB	Koninklijke Bibliotheek, The Hague
KFF	*Die Korrespondenz Ferdinands I. Die Familienkorrespondenz*, ed. W. Bauer et al., 5 vols to date (Vienna, 1912–2015)
LCK	*Correspondenz des Kaisers Karls V., aus dem königlichen Archiv und der Bibliothèque de Bourgogne zu Brüssel*, ed. K. Lanz, 3 vols (Leipzig, 1844–6)
LGC	*Correspondance de l'empereur Maximilien Iᵉʳ et de Marguerite d'Autriche, sa fille, gouvernante des Pays-Bas, de 1507 à 1519*, ed. A. J. G. Le Glay, 2 vols (Paris, 1839)
L&P Henry VIII	*Letters and papers, foreign and domestic, of the reign of Henry VIII*, ed. J. S. Brewer, J. Gairdner, and R. H. Brodie, 21 vols, some in multiple parts (London, 1872–1920), plus revised and expanded editions of the first two volumes
LWB	*Dr Martin Luthers Werke, Kritische Gesamtausgabe. Abteilung 4: Briefwechsel*, 18 vols (Weimar, 1930–85)
LWS	*Dr Martin Luthers Werke, Kritische Gesamtausgabe. Abteilung 1: Schriften*, 56 vols (Weimar, 1883–1929)
LWT	*Dr Martin Luthers Werke, Kritische Gesamtausgabe. Abteilung 2: Tischreden*, 6 vols (Weimar, 1912–21)
MHE	*Memorial Histórico Español*

MÖStA	*Mitteilungen des Österreichischen Staatsarchivs*
NBD	*Nuntiaturberichte aus Deutschland. Nebst ergänzenden Aktenstücken, Erste Abteilung 1533–1559*, ed. W. Friedensburg, L. Cardauns et al., 17 vols, with two *Ergänzungsbände* covering 1530–2 (Gotha, 1892–1981)
ODNB	*Oxford Dictionary of National Biography* (Oxford, 2004; updated online resource: *www.oxforddnb.com*)
ÖNB	Österreichische Nationalbibliothek, Vienna, manuscript collection
PEG	*Papiers d'État du Cardinal de Granvelle*, ed. C. Weiss, 9 vols (Paris, 1841–52)
RAH *Ms.*	Real Academia de la Historia, Madrid, *Colección de Manuscritos*
Muñoz	*Colección manuscrita Muñoz*
Salazar	*Colección manuscrita Salazar y Castro*
RTA	*Deutsche Reichstagsakten, jüngere Reihe. Deutsche Reichstagsakten unter Kaiser Karl V.*, ed. A. Kluckhohn et al., 20 vols, some in multiple parts (Gotha and Munich, 1893–2009)
RVEC	Rodríguez Villa, A., *El Emperador Carlos V y su corte según las cartas de don Martín de Salinas, embajador del Infante don Fernando, 1522–1539* (Madrid, 1903)
SCJ	*Sixteenth Century Journal*
SLID	Sánchez Loro, Domingo, *La inquietud postrimera de Carlos V*, 3 vols (Cáceres, 1957–9)
SP	*State papers, published under the authority of His Majesty's Commission. King Henry the Eighth*, 5 parts in 11 vols (London, 1830–52)
SPO	*State Papers Online* (online resource: *https://www.gale.com/uk/primary-sources/state-papers-online*)
TNASP	The National Archives (formerly The Public Record Office), Kew, London, State Papers
TRHistS	*Transactions of the Royal Historical Society*

NOTE ON DATES AND QUOTES

Dates in the earlier sixteenth century present the historian with multiple challenges. According to the French Style used in most of northern Europe during Charles's lifetime, each year began with Easter (which, then as now, fell on different dates in successive years); but according to the Roman Style, widely used in Italy and Spain, each year began on 1 January, while in Venice it began on 1 March. Thus Charles was born on 24 February 1500 according to the Roman style; but since Easter that year fell on 19 April, most documents written in Venice, France, Germany, England and the Netherlands stated that he was born on 24 February 1499. This difference between calendars only affected the months between New Year and Easter, and some letter-writers would add 'before Easter' to make clear that they were using the French Style (Venetians sometimes add 'm.v.': *more veneto*), but several writers who provide critical information on Charles used more than one calendar. Margaret of Austria normally used French Style but adopted Roman Style when she wrote to correspondents in Spain, and her father Maximilian often dated letters according to the style used in the place where he happened to be writing – if indeed either of them bothered to include a date or place at all. These inconsistencies mean that some letters can only be dated from internal evidence. Unfortunately the French archivist André Le Glay, who expertly deciphered and published much of the correspondence between Maximilian and his daughter, assigned the wrong date to perhaps one-third of their letters. For example, one of Margaret's letters to her father stated that Charles had just killed a man while hunting with his crossbow earlier that day, which was 'Whit Monday'. Without revealing his rationale, Le Glay confidently dated this letter 'May 1513' and placed it alongside other letters written that month. Almost all subsequent historians have accepted Le Glay's date without question, even though Andreas Walther demonstrated long ago that Margaret wrote her letter on 5 June 1514. Unless otherwise stated, this volume uses the dates proposed by Walther and gives all dates in Roman Style: thus Charles was born on 24 February 1500 and he killed a man for the first time on 5 June 1514.[1]

The dispatches of Italian diplomats, which feature prominently in this book, present a further complication because they usually marked the passage of time according to a twenty-four-hour clock that began half an hour after sunset, which occurred at 'ore 2330' each day, whatever the season of the year. For example, in 1521 the Venetian ambassador in Brussels reported that Charles left his palace to welcome King Christian of Denmark 'at around 21 hours' on 4 July, returning 'at half-an-hour in the night'; and the following evening he recorded wearily that the two monarchs, having dined, had started to dance even though 'it is two o'clock at night, and they are still at it'. Since in July the sun sets in Brussels around 10 p.m., in this book the events recorded by the ambassador occurred at (respectively) 7.30 p.m. and 11 p.m. on 4 July, and he wrote about them at 12.30 a.m. on 6 July.[2]

Quoting sixteenth-century documents also presents challenges. First comes orthography: even familiar syntax and vocabulary can be obscured by frequent abbreviations and bizarre spelling. Jason Powell has calculated that the twenty-four surviving letters of Sir Thomas Wyatt, most of them written while he was English ambassador at the imperial court between 1537 and 1540, contain almost 30,000 words, 'among which are 3,380 abbreviations. That is to say that there is one abbreviation for every 8.43 words in Wyatt's holograph prose.'[3] A similar ratio probably characterized the correspondence of Charles and his other European contemporaries (curious readers should feel free to check). As for vocabulary, even the same document may contain several different spellings of the same word. And then there is repetition. Correspondents in the earlier sixteenth century seldom used one word when they could use two or more, creating a tedious parade of synonyms. Charles would 'order and command'; he 'travelled and journeyed'; an action must be carried out with 'dissimulation and secrecy'; and so on. In this book I have respected both the original orthography (for documents in English) and the repetition, but expanded the abbreviations. Readers interested in the original quotations from Spanish sources will find them in Geoffrey Parker, *Carlos V: una nueva vida del emperador* (Barcelona: Editorial Planeta, 2019).

NOTE ON SOURCES

The historiography of the reign of Charles V, wrote Benito Sánchez Alonso in his classic *Sources of Spanish and Latin American history* in 1952, is 'the most interesting of all periods' – but it is also 'extremely copious and confused'. He proceeded to list some 2,500 separate sources in ten languages on 'Spain in the period 1516–1556'. The literature has of course become yet more copious and confused since 1952 – for Spain, for Latin America and for other parts of Charles's empire. The historiographical essays in the excellent volume *The histories of Emperor Charles V*, published in 2005, covered almost 300 pages but included only works published in various European countries and the former Ottoman Empire, ignoring how Latin American writers had portrayed him.[1]

The principal primary sources on the emperor's life and reign can be divided into six broad categories: collections of data; ego-documents; administrative archives; diplomatic archives; chronicles and histories; and cultural records.

I. COLLECTIONS OF DATA

Seven collections of data – four printed and three manuscript – provide a wealth of information on Charles and his world.

1. CHARLES'S TRAVELS

Manuel de Foronda y Aguilera spent almost fifty years ransacking all sources available to him to establish where Charles spent every night and day of his life, and (where possible) what he did there. He published the definitive edition in 1914. Two compilations by Vicente de Cadenas y Vicent, *Diario del emperador Carlos V* and *Caminos y derroteros*, provide both more and less than Foronda: on the positive side, they include many events important for Charles, even though he was not personally present; on the negative side, they omit the copious archival references provided by Foronda. Currently, Alain Servantie and others are creating a website 'Itinera Carolus V imperator/The European routes of Emperor Charles V: Itinera Carolus V|Las Rutas del Emperador.'[2]

2. THE POLITICAL CORRESPONDENCE OF CHARLES V: THE UNIVERSITY OF KONSTANZ COLLECTION

In the 1960s, Horst Rabe and a team at the University of Konstanz started to collect photocopies of the political correspondence of Charles V from archives and libraries in Austria, Belgium and Spain. By 2000 they had catalogued over 120,000 missives sent to or by Charles, from almost 1,500 distinct bundles, written in Dutch, French, German, Italian, Latin and Spanish. They assigned each document a number and then published an index, arranged by date and correspondent (Rabe, *Karl V., politische Korrespondenz*), and an overview of the collection (Rabe, 'Die politische Korrespondenz'). The photocopies of the letters in the Konstanz University Library are arranged in *Schuber*, according to the archive, series and bundle (*legajo, liasse* or *Konvolut*) from which they came, usually with two lists of contents at the front: one organized by the letter number of each document in the box, the other by the folio in the original archive bundle. The essential details – sender and recipient; date and place of signature; archive call-number and Schuber number; status (original, minute, cyphered and so on) – have also been entered into the database POLKAweb: http://karl-v.bsz-bw.de/. The arrangement of all the letters in a single numbered sequence by date tracks the uneven flow of paperwork over time and measures the pulse of empire much as Charles did – a remarkable work of historical reconstruction in itself.[3]

3. THE BERGENROTH TRANSCRIPTS OF DOCUMENTS FOR A *HISTORY OF CHARLES V*

After a colourful life in Europe and California, Gustave Bergenroth spent a decade locating and reading manuscripts in European archives and libraries in preparation for his projected *History of Charles V*. Bergenroth employed up to ten copyists to make transcripts and by the time of his death in 1869 (from typhus contracted while living at Simancas) he had accumulated almost 20,000 pages of copies. Almost immediately, his 'intimate friend' Paul Friedmann offered Bergenroth's 'Charles V collection' to the British Museum for £1,500, and the Keeper of Manuscripts asked an eminent historian, Lord Acton, to assess their value. Although Acton regretted that Bergenroth's 'power of detecting what was important and new was superior by far to his manner of using what he had obtained', he deemed the collection 'eminently worthy of a place among the treasures of the Museum'. The Trustees approved the purchase in 1870. Bound in a single chronological order, regardless of the archive in which they were found, the twenty-six fat folio volumes of the Bergenroth collection (BL *Addl. Ms.* 28,572–28,597) afford a unique opportunity to see the world through Charles's eyes.[4]

Shortly after purchasing the collection, the British Museum librarians discovered that Friedmann had withheld eleven more volumes. Although he later offered them for sale, the Museum declined and in 1896 Friedmann donated them to the Preussische Staatsbibliothek, Berlin. After World War II, they were acquired by the Biblioteka Jagiellońska (Jagiellonian Library), Kraków, accessioned as *Ms. Hisp. Fol.* 27–37. The first six volumes contain more transcripts prepared for Bergenroth, arranged by themes (*Ms. Hisp. Fol.* 29 contains copies of documents from various collections concerning Charles and the Inquisition; *Ms. Hisp. Fol.* 30 includes copies of Charles's correspondence about the council of Trent; and so on). The rest contain Bergenroth's list of all the documents he had consulted and transcribed, those in London as well as those in Kraków, organized by archive and series.[5] All eleven volumes have been scanned and made available online: http://info.filg.uj.edu.pl/fibula/pl/manuscripts/5

4. THE COURT OF CHARLES V

In 2000, José Martínez Millán and a group of colleagues (mainly from the Universidad Autónoma of Madrid) published a five-volume study of Charles's court and government. The first two volumes contain essays; the rest include lists and biographies of many ministers and household officials.[6] The volumes are all available online at https://dialnet.unirioja.es/servlet/libro?codigo=4519

5. THE EMPEROR'S GOODS

In 2010, Fernando Checa Cremades and an international team of experts transcribed and published almost all the extant inventories left by Charles, his siblings, and other close relatives, each one listing and describing in detail what they owned at various stages of their lives. The inventory for each member of the family is preceded by a helpful essay in both English and Spanish.[7]

6. CHARLES'S RETIREMENT

The period of Charles's final sojourn in Spain (September 1556–September 1558) is the best-documented of his entire life. Immediately after the emperor's death, at the request of his daughter Joanna, Prior Martín de Angulo of Yuste composed a short *Vida y fin que ha tenido la cesárea, sacra y real majestad de nuestro señor Don Carlos, en este monasterio de San Jerónimo de Yuste*.[8] Some decades later, Fray Hernando del Corral wrote a far more detailed *Historia breve y sumaria de cómo el emperador Don Carlos V, nuestro señor, trató de venirse a recoger al monasterio de San Jerónimo de Yuste*, which began with the emperor's abdication and ended with the relocation of his body in 1574 to a new Jeronimite house, San Lorenzo el Real de El Escorial, but concentrated on his nineteen months in the imperial apartments attached to the convent.[9] Their more celebrated successor, Fray José de Sigüenza, shamelessly plagiarized both Angulo and Corral for the second part of his *Historia de la Orden de San Jerónimo*, published in 1600 – albeit with some subtle additions and omissions – and Prudencio de Sandoval did the same in a final segment of his *History*: 'Historia de la vida que el emperador Carlos V rey de España hizo retirado en el monasterio de Iuste'.

In addition to the emperor's correspondence, the correspondence of many in his entourage, the audited accounts of his household, and the inventory of his possessions while at Yuste all remain largely intact in Simancas. Many of these sources appeared in print for the first time in the 1850s, apparently in preparation for the third centenary of his death, some transcribed by the archivists of Simancas, Tomás and Manuel

González, others by their successor, Manuel García González, working for the Belgian archivist and historian Louis Prosper Gachard.[10] In 1957–8, Domingo Sánchez Loro published almost all of the surviving sources on the emperor's last two years in three volumes containing almost 2,000 pages. Volume III published a day-by-day reconstruction of the 'Retiro, estancia y muerte de Carlos V en Yuste' compiled from the Simancas documents transcribed by Tomás González, with the texts of the corresponding documents inserted in over 500 footnotes.[11]

Charles's final illness can be reconstructed almost minute-by-minute thanks to these sources, complemented by the sworn depositions from twenty of those gathered around his deathbed, collected by the Inquisition as part of its investigation of the archbishop of Toledo, Bartolomé Carranza, for heresy. José Ignacio Tellechea Idígoras, who worked tirelessly on Carranza, published the twenty depositions in three places: *BRAH*, CXLIII (1958), 155–227; along with other documents in *Fray Bartolomé Carranza. Documentos históricos* (1962–94); and in a special volume entitled *Así murió el emperador* (1995).

7. CHARLES'S DEBTS

AGS *CSR* legajos 128–180, known as *Descargos de Carlos V*, comprise fifty-two boxes filled with manuscript accounts and petitions to the executors of Charles's last will from those who claimed that he still owed them money: a total that exceeded 500,000 ducats. The claimants ranged from his ministers and household officials, or their heirs (including the widow of Francisco de Los Cobos, who had to produce his will before she received his salary arrears as Charles's principal secretary), to Barbara Blomberg, the mother of Don Juan de Austria (who was still begging for payment of her son's debts in 1597). Their stories shed a unique light on the emperor's world. An index of the names of all petitioners mentioned in the collection, compiled in 1898, is available in the Sala de los Investigadores at Simancas.[12]

Nevertheless, all seven collections of data remain incomplete. Although Foronda consulted manuscripts from collections all over Spain and at Lille, elsewhere he relied largely on published works. The University of Konstanz researchers deliberately excluded everything from Charles's early years (the first letters from Charles in their collection date from June 1517) and also overlooked many documents held in private archives. Bergenroth gathered copies of many but by no means all important manuscripts concerning Charles. Checa Cremades and his team omitted a partial inventory of the items that accompanied Charles on his first journey from the Netherlands to Spain in 1517.[13] The index entries for the *Descargos de Carlos V* do not mention the documents attached, and in any case the series covers only Charles's creditors in Castile.

II. EGO-DOCUMENTS

In 1958 the Dutch historian Jacob Presser coined the term 'ego-document' to cover 'those historical sources in which the user is confronted with an "I", or occasionally (Caesar, Henry Adams) a "he", continuously present in the text as the writing and describing subject.'[14] Historians, particularly early modern European historians, have subsequently developed important methodologies to deal with the problems surrounding ego-documents, such as memories so painful or embarrassing that writers either could not recount them or else (whether unconsciously or consciously) edited them. Although no contemporaries seem to have recorded Charles's mealtime conversations, as they did for his brother Ferdinand and for Martin Luther, the emperor wrote an autobiography, delivered policy speeches based on notes written in his own hand, and composed countless instructions, position papers and letters in which he revealed his inner thoughts. As Federico Chabod observed: 'Probably no other ruler in History left holograph documents comparable in quantity with those of Charles V.'[15]

1. AUTOBIOGRAPHIES

While sailing up the Rhine on his barge in 1550, assisted by his chamberlain Guillaume van Male, Charles composed *Memoirs* in the third person that covered his public life between 1515 and 1548 (see Appendix I). Two members of Charles's inner circle also wrote life stories that involved him. Emperor Maximilian supervised the composition of an illustrated autobiography in four parts: *Theuerdank* (1505–16); *Der Weisskunig* (1510–17); *Freydal* (1512–16); and *Historia Friderici III et Maximiliani I* (1515–16). He presented special copies of all four to his grandson Charles (chapter 2).[16] Charles's Grand Chancellor Mercurino Arborio de Gattinara wrote his autobiography, also in the third person, just before sailing for Italy from Barcelona with Charles in July 1529. In 1915, Carlos Bornate published the text of the document, which covered forty-seven large folios written in Latin in Gattinara's distinctive

NOTE ON SOURCES

neat script, heavily corrected, together with some memoranda and letters that clarified the chancellor's assertions (Bornate, 'Historia'). Almost a century later, Rebecca Ard Boone published an English translation as an appendix to her study of the chancellor, including most but not all of Bornate's erudite notes (Boone, *Mercurino*). As Bornate observed bitterly, Gattinara's 'style is verbose and prolix', and he sometimes 'weighed down his rationale by interminable sentences and overlong digressions', so that (in the words of Manuel Rivera Rodríguez) on reading the *Autobiography* 'We have the impression that we are subjected to a monologue.' Nevertheless, it contains much material not found elsewhere.[17]

2. INSTRUCTIONS

Like other rulers of his day, whenever Charles appointed someone to carry out an important task – diplomatic, military, administrative, personal – he composed detailed instructions, some public and others secret. For example, when he left Spain in May 1543 he drew up and signed dozens of instructions to those who would govern in his absence, including two written in his own hand for his son Philip, each one covering over twenty pages. The second document, intended only for the eyes of his son, included Charles's thoughts not only on how Philip should govern but on the strengths and weaknesses of those who would assist him.[18]

3. POSITION PAPERS

In 1551, the Venetian ambassador Mario Cavalli noted that when faced by a complex decision, Charles liked to 'write down the reasons pro and contra to see which one offered the better rationale'. Many of these introspective documents have survived, starting with a consideration of his dilemmas in February 1525, composed because 'I wanted to write down my opinion [the reasons pro and contra] in confidence, even though no one knows them better than me'.[19] Some of the emperor's holograph letters to his brother served the same purpose: see, for example, his holograph 'state of the empire' message in January 1530, which covered fourteen folios, some heavily corrected, composed expressly so that 'it will serve as a memorandum when we are together, and I will explain to you everything necessary concerning what I have written'.[20]

4. SPEECHES

Some considered Charles taciturn – in 1532, Luther jested that 'he says as much in one year as I do in a day' – but we know that the emperor, too, could be loquacious because ambassadors always recorded, often verbatim, what he said at audiences (see below). Moreover, some of his formal addresses appeared in print (e.g. his speeches when he opened a meeting of the representative assembly of a dominion; and his lengthy responses to criticisms of his conduct voiced by the Knights of the Golden Fleece at their formal chapters recorded by the Greffier of the Order).[21]

Contemporaries paid special attention to Charles's public speeches, such as his harangue to the pope and the College of Cardinals in Rome in April 1536, which lasted well over an hour, and his abdication address to the States-General of the Netherlands in Brussels in October 1555; and although on both occasions Charles spoke from notes, not from a text, many eyewitnesses later recorded what they thought he had said. The most detailed versions were those relayed to foreign governments by their ambassadors, and because they sat at the front of the audience they presumably heard and saw everything of importance.[22] Others were less fortunate – the report by a Spanish eyewitness of the abdication speech was probably typical: 'I can only narrate what happened according to what I saw myself, because there were so many people that you could not hear anything' – but some at the back of the hall took notes and later published them anyway.[23] Pontus Heuterus from Holland was one of them: in 1598 he printed in his *Affairs of the Netherlands and of Austria* (in Latin) a version of Charles's speech forty-three years before, but it differed significantly from the most detailed surviving text: 'Receuil [sic] de ce que l'empereur dit de bouche aux estatz generaulx de pardeça le xxvᵉ d'octobre 1555 . . . noté par quelque bon personnaige estant à ladicte assamblée', probably compiled by Antoine Perrenot from the notes used by Charles.[24] Unfortunately, the best-known text – that published by Prudencio de Sandoval in the last volume of his *History* (1606) – relied on Heuterus; and therefore those who have relied on Sandoval (like Fernández Álvarez, *Carlos V: el César*, 782–8) included the same errors as Heuterus. To take a single example, Heuterus, Sandoval and Fernández Álvarez all claimed that the emperor said that 'my much-loved mother, who died recently, was out of her mind after the death of my father, so she was never fit to govern' – an extraordinary admission – whereas according to the 'Receuil', the emperor stated (far more plausibly) that he had gone to Spain in 1517 'to attend to the indispositions of the queen his mother (who died recently)'.

NOTE ON SOURCES

5. LETTERS

In 1892, after working for a decade on his history of the emperor's reign, Hermann Baumgarten wrote that 'The most important source is Charles V's correspondence' – but not all letters are equal. Lyndal Roper's admirable study of the correspondence of Martin Luther (which fills eighteen printed volumes) pointed out that letters in the sixteenth century 'functioned rather like email, readily forwarded and semi-public'; and like Luther, Charles composed some of his letters with a view to publication, such as those challenging Francis I to a duel in 1528. Many of the emperor's other letters were cyphered, to prevent anyone except the intended recipient from reading them, and he wrote other letters entirely in his own hand, sometimes even addressing and sealing them himself, explicitly so that his ministers would not know what he had written.[25] Many letters survive in multiple copies, but (again) not all are equal. Secretaries often summarized incoming letters and papers, and read those summaries out to the emperor, making a note in the margin of how he wished to respond; they would then draft a letter, which the emperor might revise (often by commenting as they were read out to him). Therefore, the annotated summaries and drafts often provide more evidence than the original correspondence of the emperor's decision-making process.

Almost 100,000 letters exchanged between Charles and his siblings Ferdinand and Marie survive in half a dozen different archives and libraries. Marie's correspondence down to 1533 has appeared in a modern edition, with more volumes promised; the correspondence of Ferdinand with other family members, including Charles, has now reached 1,536 letters in five volumes, the most recent one accompanied by English summaries of the documents and an English translation of the introduction. More volumes are promised but Christopher Laferl, the general editor, has warned that although the series began publication in 1912 only a quarter of the surviving letters have so far been printed. 'At this rate,' he concluded with grim humour, 'publication of his family correspondence should be completed in the year 2558, just in time for the millennial commemoration of the death of Charles V.'[26]

Charles also exchanged intimate letters with his wife, but none appear to have survived: the 114 printed letters from the empress to her husband between 1528 and 1538 reveal little affection or intimacy, although they allude to other personal missives now apparently lost.[27] Two of Charles's surviving letters in 1536 to Ursolina de la Penna, who had borne his child fourteen years before, were certainly personal, but they concerned 'our daughter Tadea' and were written in French by a secretary, with a sentence in Italian enjoining her to take the letters to a local friar 'should you not understand what I have written'. Charles himself only signed his name.[28] We find nothing like the passionate love letter written to his sister Eleanor by Count Palatine Frederick in 1517, addressed to 'Ma Mignonne' (it survives only because Charles confiscated the letter and, having read it, took it with him to Spain and placed it in the archives of Simancas).[29] The same is true of Charles's correspondence with his son and heir: of the 500 surviving letters he wrote to Philip between 1543 and 1558, often with holograph postscripts, none exude genuine warmth. Charles was certainly capable of raising intimate issues with his children, as he did with his daughter Margarita of Parma, but his sixty letters to her perished when German soldiers destroyed much of AS Naples in 1943. Only a few had already appeared in print.[30]

By contrast, intimate letters exchanged by Charles with other members of his circle have survived. Both von Höfler and Gachard published correspondence between Adrian and his illustrious former pupil between 1516 and 1523. Aude Viaud published forty-five epistles written to Charles by his youngest sister Catalina between 1528 and 1532, with a brilliant introduction that stresses the importance of such correspondence in holding the imperial family together.[31] In 1530, Charles sent García de Loaysa y Mendoza, his confessor, to Rome as a special representative and for the next three years Loaysa bombarded the emperor with letters full of intimate advice which frequently referred to equally intimate matters discussed while they were together in the 1520s. Two editions of Loaysa's letters to Charles appeared almost simultaneously, but the minutes of some of Charles's replies, in AGS E 1558/56–96, remain unpublished (except for English summaries in CSPSp, IV/2).[32] Although Fray Pedro de Soto accompanied the emperor as his confessor between 1542 and 1548, we know only of his role in negotiating peace with France and in urging war against the German Lutherans.[33] Many more letters have survived from Pedro's successor as confessor (1548–50), Domingo de Soto, and they appeared in print with a commentary in Beltrán de Heredía's biography of the Dominican. These documents are revealing because (as Soto claimed in one of his letters to Charles) 'nobody knows the Christian soul of Your Majesty as well as I do'.[34]

Other surviving correspondence that reveals personal details about the emperor includes the letters exchanged between his aunt Margaret and grandfather Maximilian between 1506 and 1519 (see p. 580 below); medical reports on him by his doctors (Fernando de Escoriaza's letters in Spanish to the empress in 1530–2; Cornelis van Baersdorp's letters in French to Marie of Hungary in 1548–52; Henri Mathys's letters in Latin and halting Spanish to Juan Vázquez de Molina in 1556–8; and thirty-four 'intimate letters' in Latin from his chamberlain Guillaume van Male to a colleague between 1550 and 1553.[35] St

Francis Borja, one of the emperor's most trusted councillors who became a Jesuit, later described his conversations with Charles at Yuste to Pedro de Ribadeneyra, who included them in his *Life* of the future saint (reproduced with embellishments by Sandoval).[36]

III. CHARLES'S ADMINISTRATIVE ARCHIVES

By the time he abdicated each of Charles's dominions boasted a central archive. In addition certain libraries acquired segments of Charles's administrative archives, often filed with other items. The following are the most important collections, grouped by country:

1. AUSTRIA

(a) Haus-, Hof- und Staatsarchiv, Vienna (HHStA)

As its title suggests, HHStA contains documents concerning the dynasties that have ruled Austria, as well as their households and governments, and collections from other territories ruled by the Habsburgs. An e-guide is in progress at http://www.archivinformationssystem.at/detail.aspx?ID=1.

Four sections are of special interest to Charles's biographers:

* *Habsburgische-Lothringische Hausarchive: Hausarchiv, Familienkorrespondenz*, which contains four boxes of Charles's correspondence between 1534 and 1555.
* *Länderabteilungen: Belgien-Niederländisches Departement*, which contains the extensive administrative correspondence of both Charles and Marie (much of it removed from the archives of Brussels in the eighteenth century): see *Belgien PA, Belgien PC* and *Belgien DD-B*. Rabe, 'Stückverzeichnis' (with nine parts), provided basic data on 7,165 documents in the series *Belgien PA 1–PA 35/1* (letters from 1480 to 1542).
* *Diplomatie und Aussenpolitik vor 1848, Staatenabteilung Grossbritannien (England), Diplomatische Korrespondenz 1–17*, which contains Charles's correspondence with his regents in the Netherlands and his ambassadors in England between 1505 and 1555. Summaries of many of these items were published in English in *CSPSp*. Unfortunately, the call-numbers in the Calendars no longer correspond with those currently used in the archive. For example, Charles's letter to Ambassador Eustache Chapuys dated 14 March 1542, summarized in *CSPSp*, VI/1, 480–3, with the call-number *Länderabteilungen Belgien PC*, Faszikel 233, folios 9–18, is now *Staatenabteilung England, Diplomatische Korrespondenz*, Faszikel 9, folios 3–7.[37]
* *Handschriftensammlung: Handschriften Blau 595* and *596/1–2*, three registers containing copies of Charles's letters to his brother (1524–48, 1548–51 and 1551–8 respectively).

In the 1930s, Karl Brandi and his research team published a guide to relevant HHStA documents in *Berichte und Studien zur Geschichte Karls V. [B&S]*: 'Die Überlieferung der Akten Karls V. im Haus-, Hof- und Staatsarchiv, Wien', organized in four parts: I, 'Die Burgundische Kanzlei' (the emperor's correspondence with his aunt Margaret and his sister Marie: *B&S*, IV, 241–77); II and III, 'Die Kabinettskanzlei des Kaisers' (correspondence with his Austrian lands and with foreign powers: *B&S*, V, 18–51, and VII, 229–59); and IV, 'Die deutsche Reichskanzlei Karls V.' and 'Die österreichische Kanzlei' (*B&S*, XI, 513–78). HHStA has changed many call-numbers since then, which complicates the use of Brandi's lists, but they still indicate what is there. Voltes Bou, *Documentos*, provided brief descriptions of documents in HHStA relating to Spain, arranged in a single chronological list.

Karl Lanz, *Monumenta Habsburgica*, vol. I, promised a complete edition of Charles's letters and state papers in HHStA, but unfortunately his first volume (which printed 170 documents) proved to be the last: *Aktenstücke und Briefe zur Geschichte Kaiser Karls V. (1513–1521)*.[38] The Charles V collection at the University of Konstanz contains photocopies of most letters written to and from the emperor in HHStA (see above); and von Bucholtz, *Geschichte der Regierung Ferdinand des Ersten*, vol. IX, 'Urkunden Band', printed extracts from many documents (including many letters exchanged between Ferdinand and his brother) cited in earlier volumes. The volume is available online at http://reader.digitale-sammlungen.de/resolve/display/bsb10015425.html

(b) Österreichische Nationalbibliothek (ÖNB)

The collection contains numerous items owned by or related to Charles. Here are four examples, together with their provenance:

* Codex 1859: a Book of Hours in Latin and French presented to Charles by his aunt Margaret with seventy-six miniatures (from the Jesuit College at Wiener Neustadt, which acquired it from Archduke Leopold William, governor-general of the Netherlands):[39] http://archiv.onb.ac.at:1801/view/action/

nmets.do?DOCCHOICE=7174926.xml&dvs=1527614220163~484&locale=en_US&search_
terms=&adjacency=&VIEWER_URL=/view/action/nmets.do?&DELIVERY_RULE_ID=1&divType=
&usePid1=true&usePid2=true

* Codex 2591: the original illustrated manuscript of the 'Solemnelle entrée faicte sur l'advenement de Charles Archidux d'Autriche en Bruges, 1515' by Remy du Puys (bequeathed to the library by Emperor Mathias in 1619): http://data.onb.ac.at/rec/AC13947423

* *Codex Vindobonensis Palatinus* 9363: a collection of Latin documents from the imperial chancery about the imprisonment of John Frederick of Saxony and the landgrave of Hesse in 1547–52. A detailed analysis is available at http://www.vhmml.us/research2014/catalog/detail.asp?MSID=19262

* *Codex Vindobonensis* S. N. 1600: the *Cartas de relación* sent to Charles from Mexico by Hernán Cortés, and many other important documents about the Americas from the 1520s, forwarded to King Ferdinand. See the facsimile edition: *Cartas de Relación de la conquista de la Nueva España*, ed. C. Gibson (Graz, 1960).

2. BELGIUM

Charles spent almost half his life in Belgium, and he took several steps to streamline the central government (above all by creating three Collateral Councils in 1531, and a special German secretariat in 1548). Some archives perished in wars and fires (the archive of the Council of Brabant burnt during the bombardment of Brussels in 1695; a fire at the royal palace in 1731 destroyed almost the entire archive of the council of Finance). Others were housed in places now outside Belgium (notably ADN *Chambre des Comptes* at Lille, now in France), or migrated to Vienna when Habsburg rule ended abruptly in the eighteenth century. Once Belgium became an independent state in 1830, its government sought to recover migrant documents (notably those in Vienna) and sponsored the publication of surviving sources in its own archives. It also paid its archivists to travel abroad to locate and transcribe relevant sources in foreign archives, which it then published (for an example, see the works of L.P. Gachard in the bibliography to this volume).

(i) Brussels

(a) Archives Générales du Royaume/Algemene Rijksarchief, Brussels (AGRB)

* *Chambre des Comptes/Rekenkamer:* The Burgundian state decentralized the task of auditing its various officials and the Chambre des Comptes in Brussels handled the accounts of some officials of the central government (the rest are at ADN: see below) as well as all of those from the duchy of Brabant and some from the county of Flanders: see details in Janssens, 'Fuentes flamencas', 200.

* *Collection Gachard/Collectie Gachard:* Louis Prosper Gachard (1800–85) became an archivist in 1822, and served as head of the AGRB from 1831 until his death, undertaking numerous visits to foreign archives in search of documents relating to Belgian history and publishing the results. In 1842 another eminent Belgian historian called him, with only slight exaggeration (and perhaps a hint of envy), 'emperor of the archives'.[40] Although Gachard published thousands of pages of edited documents (see the bibliography of this volume), his papers contain notes, summaries and unpublished transcripts of many more manuscripts, some now lost (e.g. AGRB *Collectie Gachard* 565, 569 and 572 contain his notes on documents relating to Belgium in AS Naples, whose originals perished in 1943) as well as materials gathered for his publications (e.g. AGRB *Collectie Gachard* 628–637, material for his projected biography of Charles V).[41] Wellens, *Inventaire*, provided a guide to the collection: see items 467–840 for material related to Charles.[42]

* *Papiers d'État et d'Audience/Audientië:* This large series contains papers of both the Council of State and the Privy Council under Charles, including much of his correspondence with his aunt Margaret and his sister Marie, and with Granvelle, as well as the correspondence of Marie while regent of the Netherlands: see Janssens, 'Fuentes flamencas', 204–5.

* *Secrétairerie d'État allemande/Duitse Staatssecretarie:* Much of Charles's correspondence with German rulers, military personnel, and institutions (above all the Diet and the Reichskammergericht) is archived here. In the 1840s, Karl Lanz published 1,009 documents from Brussels in *LCK*, with 100 more in *Staatspapiere*: many came from the *Secrétairerie d'État allemande*.[43]

(b) Bibliothèque Royale de Belgique/Koninklijke Bibliotheek van België, Brussels (BRB)

The BRB manuscript collection contains items from Charles's library as duke of Burgundy as well as subsequent additions, such as the earliest surviving intimate letter written by Charles: a holograph missive to his confidant Count Henry of Nassau ('mon Henri') in 1518, one of very few in which he discussed his sex life (Pl. 8). BRB purchased the item at auction in 1892 as part of the collection of

575

autographs assembled by Johannes van Vollenhove, chaplain of the Stadholder-King William III (who inherited the archive of 'mon Henri').[44] Van den Gheyn, *Catalogue*, VII, 278–90 and 418–32, described manuscripts in the collection concerning Charles, but several items have migrated to AGRB since he published: for example, BRB *Ms.* 16068–72, 'Recueil de documents relatifs à Marguerite d'Autriche 1515–1530' (van den Gheyn, VII, 430–2) is now AGRB *Audience* 41bis.

(ii) Mons

Archives de l'État, Mons

Charles de Croÿ, prince of Chimay (1455–1527), was one of Charles V's godparents and his first chamberlain. In the mid-nineteenth century the archives of his descendants at Beaumont castle still contained several items relating to the emperor. In 1838, Émile Gachet published a brief inventory of the collection, and seven years later Louis Prosper Gachard published a more detailed description: both noted a 'Registre tenu par le seigneur de Boussu des sommes reçues et payées par lui, par le commandement de l'empereur', 1 Aug. 1530–31 Jan. 1532. Charles reviewed and signed Boussu's account at the end of each month.[45] Some of the papers formerly at Beaumont are now in the Archives de l'État, Mons, *Dossier famille de Caraman-Chimay*, with an inventory by P.-J. Niebes, *Inventaire des archives de Chimay. Château de Beaumont* (2013: available online), which correlates items listed by Gachet with the collection in Mons. Alas, the Registre is not among them. Beaumont castle was sold in 1931, and part of its archive was sold between then and 1986, when AGRB bought the remains: once again, the Registre was not among them. Presumably it now graces some private library, but I have been unable to locate it. But what of Charles's personal spending in other years? It seems unlikely that the 1530–2 register stood alone, but neither Gachet nor Gachard mentioned any similar registers before 1530 or after 1532, so they belong to the tantalizing category 'Unknown unknowns' (see below).[46]

3. GERMANY

http://www.manuscripta-mediaevalia.de provides listings for 90,000 manuscripts (many of them digitized) in German libraries. Typing 'Personenname' and 'Karl V. Kaiser' produces 187 links. Between 1873 and 1896 four volumes of *Briefe und Akten zur Geschichte des 16. Jahrhunderts ... Beiträge zur Reichsgeschichte 1546–1555*, edited by August von Druffel (the last volume completed by Karl Brandi), included extracts (often lengthy) from documents held by the principal archives of Germany, supplemented by some from HHStA and AGS, concerning Charles's relations with his German subjects during the last decade of his rule. See also the section on the *Deutsche Reichstagakten* below.

4. ITALY

(i) Milan and Naples

The relevant archives of two important areas ruled by Charles – Milan and Naples – largely perished in 1943: in August aerial bombardment destroyed much of AS Milan, and in September, German troops set fire to the most important series of AS Naples (including its large collection of Farnese papers, moved from Parma in the eighteenth century). Nevertheless, a few relevant documents remain (such as AS Milan *Autografi*, Folders 220–230, which contain many of the letters received by the governor of Milan); and copies of some items destroyed in 1943 have been preserved elsewhere, including the correspondence of Governor Vasto of Milan with Charles in 1540–2 (p. 578); and Gachard's notes from AS Naples (p. 575). Others had already appeared in print: for example, Chabod, *Lo stato*, quoted copiously from AS Milan; and *CSP Milan*, 381–588, published English abstracts of numerous documents from Charles's reign from the same repository.[47] Gachard printed two of Charles's holograph letters to his daughter Margarita about her marital problems from AS Naples, *Carte Farnesiane*; and *NBD* included excerpts from letters in the same series sent by nuncios at the imperial court to Cardinal Farnese, papal secretary of state from 1538 to 1549. Nevertheless, most of the documents from these two archives destroyed in 1943 are irreplaceable.

(ii) Parma

Allied bombardment in 1944 seriously damaged the Palazzo della Pilotta, which housed the Archivio di Stato at Parma (ASP). Its diligent archivists have reconstructed as much as possible of the surviving documents, including the official correspondence of Dukes Pier Luigi and Octavio Farnese, in the series *Carteggio Farnesiano interno* (arranged in a single chronological order) and *estero* (arranged in chronological order by place of provenance: 'Genova', 'Roma', 'Spagna' and so on); as well as that of their archenemy Ferrante Gonzaga, imperial courtier and commander, viceroy of Sicily and governor of Milan: ASP *Archivi di Famiglie: Gonzaga di Guastalla* and ASP *Racolta Ronchini*.

5. MEXICO

Archivo General de la Nación, Mexico D.F. (AGNM)

The first four registers of the series AGNM *Libros de Mercedes* (appropriately entitled *Libros de Gobierno*), supplemented by three volumes in other collections, contain in chronological order many of the warrants (*mandamientos*) issued by the two viceroys of New Spain appointed by Charles: Antonio de Mendoza (1535–50) and Luis de Velasco (1550–64). In the words of Peter Gerhard, who compiled an analysis and index of the four volumes that cover 1548–53: 'We have here a daily record of all business transacted at the viceregal court in Mexico during a period of transcendent importance, involving people from all social levels and all regions.'[48] Nothing like it has survived for any other part of Charles's empire, which enhances the importance of these volumes. The full sequence in chronological order is as follows:

* AGNM *Civil* 1271: copies of 92 warrants issued Dec. 1537–Sep. 1538 and Mar. 1550.[49]
* AGNM *Mercedes* I: copies of almost 500 warrants issued Mar.–Oct. 1542.
* AGNM *Mercedes* II: copies of over 750 orders warrants issued Jan. 1543–Apr. 1544.
* AGNM *Mercedes* III: copies of almost 800 warrants issued Mar. 1550–May 1551.
* Library of Congress, Washington (D.C.), *Kraus Ms.* 140: copies of some 800 warrants issued Nov. 1550–May 1552.
* Newberry Library, Chicago, *Ayer Ms.* 1121: copies of some 800 warrants issued May 1552–Dec. 1553.
* AGNM *Mercedes* IV: copies of over 200 warrants issued Mar. 1554–Sep. 1556.

Several warrants quote the text of a royal order demanding action, and more of these are copied into AGNM *Cédulas reales duplicadas* I, which runs from April 1548 to November 1566. AGNM *Hospital de Jesús* contains the archive of an institution founded by Hernán Cortés, which houses his corpse and many of his papers. AGI contains many more documents concerning the viceroyalty (see below).

    Semboloni Capitani, *La construcción*, Gráfica 3 and Mapa 10, used the warrants registered in the early 'Libros de Gobierno' to chart the steady geographical expansion of viceregal authority in New Spain. Martínez, *Documentos cortesianos*, printed virtually all the documents concerning Cortés between 1518 and 1547 currently in AGNM and AGI.

6. PERU

The Archivo Arzobispal, Lima, *Sección histórica*, *Papeles importantes*, contains copies of over thirty warrants issued by Charles to Peruvian institutions, but the majority of the surviving documents from his reign concerning the viceroyalty survive only in AGI or the Huntington Library (see below).

7. SPAIN

Starting in 1992, *Portal de Archivos Españoles* (PARES) has made available online thousands of documents from the reign of Charles V in various Spanish archives, so that someone in (say) Columbus, Ohio, can locate, read and print them, without a reader's card and without charge, even at times when the archives that hold the originals are closed.[50] The principal relevant archival series are as follows:

(i) Simancas (Valladolid)

Archivo General de Simancas (AGS)

After 1540, Charles sought to turn the royal fortress in the village into a repository for the documents generated by the government of Spain, then based eight kilometres away in Valladolid. Even after the seat of government moved to Madrid, the archives remained at Simancas. The major series with material from Charles's reign are:

* *Consejos y Juntas de Hacienda*: letters and papers addressed to the king 'en manos del secretario de Hacienda', and *consultas* sent to Charles by his council of Finance, sometimes bearing a royal rescript. For the audited accounts of those who disbursed government funds or provided government loans, see four other AGS series: *Contaduría Mayor de Cuentas*, *Contaduría del Sueldo*, *Contadurías Generales* and *Dirección General del Tesoro*.
* *Estado*: the papers of the council of State organized geographically, with one series for each European country ruled by the king (Aragon, Castile, 'Flandes', Milan, Naples, Sicily and so on) or governed by others (England, France, Germany, Portugal, Rome, Savoy and so on), plus 'Armadas y Galeras' (about the Mediterranean fleet) and 'Despachos diversos' (including registers of the secretary of state's outgoing correspondence).
* *Guerra Antigua*: papers handled by the council of War about the defence of Spain by land and sea, including garrisons in north Africa.

* *Junta de Obras y Bosques*, founded in 1545 to deal with public building and works: its papers are today divided between AGS *Casas y Sitios Reales* and AGPM *Sección histórica* (see below). AGS *CSR* also contains accounts for the households of members of the royal family, including the registers of Philip's household as prince of Asturias from 1535 (AGS *CSR* 36). AGS *CSR legajos* 128–180 contain the *Descargos de Carlos V*: see above.

* *Patronato Real*: a collection of ninety-two *legajos* containing documents to which the central government attached special importance, such as testaments, treaties and instructions. The entire series is available online via PARES.

Many AGS documents from Charles's reign have appeared in print. Manuel Danvila y Collado, *Historia crítica* (*MDE*, XXXV–XL), published some 4,000 documents from AGS related to the Comunero rebellion, albeit with many errors of transcription (perhaps because he worked from nineteenth-century copies rather than from the originals in AGS *PR*).[51] Von Höfler, 'Zur Kritik und Quellenkunde', published 755 documents (in whole or in part) from AGS dated 1521; Maurenbrecher, *Karl V*, printed almost 100 'Akten aus dem spanischen Staatsarchiv von Simancas' concerning the emperor's German policy between 1530 and 1555; and more appeared in von Döllinger, *Dokumente*, in *CODOIN*, and in *CDCV* (see below). *CSPSp* published lengthy summaries in English of many AGS documents, albeit often taken from the transcripts made by or for Gustave Bergenroth and not from the originals (see above: all volumes of *CSPSp* are available in digital form via *BHO*).

The majority of the relevant documents in AGS nevertheless remain unpublished. Laiglesia, *Estudios*, III, 75–82, provided a helpful guide to material on Charles in the series *Patronato Real* and the sections of *Estado* for which a published catalogue existed; but he omitted the series *Estado K* (papers of the council of State concerning France, housed in the French Archives Nationales between 1812 and 1941) and in *Estado* 8334–8343 (mostly documents stolen from Spanish archives in the nineteenth century, held until 1941 by CADMA: p. 581 below).[52] In the 1930s, Hasenclever, 'Die Überlieferung', listed all the documents in these collections from the reign of Charles V: *B&S*, X, 437–69. In addition, Looz-Corswarem, 'Die römische Korrespondenz Karls V', *B&S*, XIII, 109–90, listed all imperial correspondence with Rome in the archives of Simancas and Madrid (Biblioteca Nacional, Biblioteca Real, Real Academia de la Historia) arranged by year (first letters to and then letters from Charles). Looz-Corswarem, 'Die Korrespondenz Karls V. mit Philipp und mit der Regentschaft in Spanien (1539–1556)', *B&S*, XV, 227–68, listed Charles's correspondence with his regents in Spain in AGS by year (first letters to and then letters from Charles).

(ii) Madrid
(a) *Archivo de la Casa de los Duques de Alba (AA)*
Caja 4 contains Charles's letters to the III duke of Alba in the 1540s and 1550s, and his replies (the latter published in Berwick y Alba, *Epistolario*, I). Two other important items in AA have been published: the letters of Gutierre Gómez de Fuensalida, Spanish ambassador at the court of Burgundy 1500–9 (Berwick y Alba, *Correspondencia*); and the correspondence of the marquis del Vasto, governor of Milan, with the emperor in 1540–2 (Berwick y Alba, 'Correspondencia', but note that letters to Vasto written by Charles while in Regensburg and Innsbruck dated '1542' in the article were actually written in 1541).

(b) *Archivo General del Palacio Real, Madrid (AGPM)*
Sección histórica, *Cédulas reales*, 1–3, contain register copies of all warrants issued by the Junta de Obras y Bosques between 1545 and 1556 in chronological order.

(c) *Biblioteca Nacional de España (BNE)*
The *Sección de manuscritos* is a collection of collections, containing many important documents by or about Charles. For example:

* *Ms.* MR43/283 (formerly *Ms.* 283), 'Descripció de parte de Francia por donde entró el emperador', is the huge map apparently commissioned to help Charles prepare his invasion of France in 1544 (Pl. 23 in this volume).

* *Ms.* 917, 'Registrum epistolarum Caroli V imperatoris et hispaniae regis et aliorum', contains copies of 292 letters in Latin issued by the imperial chancery between 1518 and 1523.[53]

* *Ms.* 5578 and 5938 contain proposals by Juan Páez de Castro on how to write a history of the emperor.

* *Ms.* 18,634/58 is a *consulta* sent by Francisco de Los Cobos to Charles while he was on retreat in Holy Week 1531, returned with the memorable reproach: 'It is hard to confess and write a lot at the same time.'[54]

Laiglesia, *Estudios*, III, 87–99, described these and other BNE manuscripts concerning Charles by topic ('Alcabalas', 'Alianzas y tratados' and so on). Many have been digitized and can be read online via http://www.bne.es/es/Colecciones/Manuscritos/

NOTE ON SOURCES

In 1899 the BNE acquired the library of Pascual de Gayangos, which included many important manuscripts concerning Charles and his entourage, notably seven volumes of correspondence that once belonged to Cardinal Antoine Perrenot de Granvelle: now *Ms.* 20,209–20,217, many of them digitized and available online. Roca, *Catálogo*, described the BNE Gayangos collection, which has been little used by historians.

(d) Biblioteca Real (BR: formerly Biblioteca del Palacio Real)

Laiglesia, *Estudios*, III, 415–16, listed some manuscripts in BR concerning Charles, but provided little detail. He also omitted the most important collection: the papers of Antoine Perrenot, Cardinal Granvelle, chief minister of both Charles and Philip II, who died in Madrid in 1586 leaving an archive that contained the papers of his father Nicholas Perrenot as well as his own. Today perhaps 100,000 of their surviving letters are scattered through archives from Sweden to Sicily, and from Austria to America, written in hundreds of different scripts and in seven languages (Dutch, French, German, Greek, Italian, Latin and Spanish.) A large part of Perrenot's archive – some 14,000 letters – came to the BR manuscript collection in 1806, now bound into over 100 volumes: II/2188, II/2192–2194, II/2201, II/2203–2204, II/2206, II/2210, II/2248–2325 and II/2549, and parts of II/2229–2233 and II/2238. Documents from the 1550s are particularly numerous and important.[55] In addition, BR *Ms.* 1960 and 1960*bis* contain La Gasca's papers concerning the pacification of Peru (BR *Ms.* 409 contains copies of the same).

(e) Real Academia de la Historia (RAH)

Laiglesia, *Estudios*, III, 101–413, listed manuscripts concerning Charles in the RAH collection *Salazar y Castro*, in chronological order. The searchable catalogue of the collection, available online, includes a detailed description of each document, arranged by volume and folio. RAH *Salazar y Castro* A–17 to A–44, full of Charles's correspondence with his ministers in Italy between 1521 and 1529, arranged chronologically, are of particular importance.

RAH also acquired the archive of Lope de Soria, one of Charles's veteran diplomats in Italy. Ibarra y Rodríguez and Arsenio de Izaga, 'Catálogo', described the collection: RAH *Ms.* 9/1951–1954. The first two volumes contain almost 100 original letters from Charles to Soria between 1523 and 1538 (sometimes duplicating items in *Salazar y Castro*). In addition, RAH *Ms.* 9/4817 (formerly Muñoz A–83) contains minutes and drafts of Charles's letters to the duke of Sessa, his ambassador in Rome, 1522–6, often annotated by Chancellor Gattinara (to whom the volume apparently once belonged): see details in *Catálogo de la colección de Don Juan Bautista Muñoz*, I (Madrid, 1954), 205–16.

Looz-Corswarem, 'Die römische Korrespondenz', provided a useful guide to letters exchanged between the papacy and the Spanish court archived in Simancas and Madrid: see above.

(iii) El Escorial (Madrid)
Real Biblioteca del Monasterio de San Lorenzo de El Escorial (BSLE)

Laiglesia, *Estudios*, III, 83–5, noted that a catalogue of the Spanish manuscripts in the library described 303 codices concerning Charles, many of them compiled by the royal chroniclers Florián de Ocampo, Bernabé de Busto and Juan Páez de Castro. In addition, the Panteón de los Reyes contains Charles's mummified corpse: see Appendix II for details.

(iv) Seville
Archivo General de Indias (AGI)

AGI contains the majority of the papers handled by the council of the Indies. As at AGS, documents that the government considered especially important (treaties, concessions, papal bulls) are filed in *Patronato*. The disarmingly named series *Indiferente General* contains many of the *consultas* sent by the council to the king. The council's correspondence with royal officials and others in the Americas is organized geographically (AGI *México*, *Perú* and so on); and its papers on judicial matters (including those generated by the *Visita* that scrutinized the actions of Antonio de Mendoza, the first viceroy of New Spain) are in AGI *Justicia*.

(v) Sant Cugat del Vallès
Arxiu Nacional de Catalunya (ANC)

ANC Fons *Arxiu del Palau-Requesens*, lligalls/legajos 35–100, contain the papers of Juan de Zúñiga y Avellaneda, Prince Philip's governor, including his correspondence with Charles, mostly published by March, *Niñez* (March prudishly excised passages from some documents). Lligalls/legajos 118–157 of the collection contain papers left by Mencía de Mendoza, marchioness of Zenete, and her husbands, Count Henry of Nassau and Ferdinand of Aragon, duke of Calabria.[56] Bofarull y Sans, *Predilección*, printed in full 131 letters (some in Catalan) addressed by Charles and his regents to Catalan officials and institutions, preserved in Catalan archives.

(vi) Toledo

Archivo Histórico de la Nobleza (AHN Nobleza)
A separate centre for the archives of Spanish noble families was created in Toledo in 1993, and shortly afterwards the first collections migrated from the AHN. By 2018, AHN Nobleza contained the archives of almost 260 noble families. Many have been digitized and can be consulted through PARES. Many contain correspondence with Charles.

In addition, the archives and libraries of two other countries have acquired important collections of documents generated by Charles's government: France and the United States.

8. FRANCE

(i) Lille

Archives départementales du Nord (ADN)
ADN contains the majority of the surviving documents concerning Charles's first seventeen years, when he resided in the Netherlands, and much relevant material down to 1530. This reflects two circumstances.
a) The dukes of Burgundy created four *Chambres des Comptes* to audit the accounts of their various dominions (at Brussels, Dijon, Lille and The Hague). The auditors at Lille handled not only regional accounts but also those of the central government, including the huge registers in which the Receveur Général des Finances summarized his accounts for each year, always organized in the same categories, accompanied by files containing the original warrants and receipts. *Inventaire sommaire des Archives Départementales antérieures à 1790. Nord: Archives civiles, Série B: Chambre des Comptes de Lille*, vols 1–8, provides the best guide to this collection (many entries include lengthy quotations). In addition, each loose document in the series has a unique *numéro d'immatriculation*. In this volume, references appear in the following format: ADN *B* 2170 (72,193) – that is, ADN *Archives Anciennes Série B, liasse* 2170, *numéro d'immatriculation* 72,193. Citations from registers in the series retain their original foliation, except that I have rendered the Roman numerals into Arabic: thus 'folio vi^{xx}xij' (= six-vingts douze) becomes 'folio 132'.
b) ADN *Lettres missives* includes the letters received and sent by the chancery of Margaret of Austria, dowager duchess of Savoy and regent in the Netherlands, for most of the period between 1507 and 1530: a total of perhaps 20,000 letters (the majority concerning Margaret's own domains in Franche-Comté and Savoy). On her death they entered the archives of the Chambre des Comptes at Lille and in the 1840s they were reorganized and bound into twenty registers. So far, over 1,000 of Margaret's letters, many of them exchanged with her father Maximilian about Charles, have appeared in print in the following collections (in chronological order of publication): Godefroy, *Lettres du roi Louis XII*; Mone, 'Briefwechsel'; Le Glay, *Correspondance*; van den Bergh, *Gedenkstukken*; Chmel, *Urkunden*; Gachard, *Lettres* and *Correspondance de Marguerite*; Kreiten, *Der Briefwechsel*; Walther, *Die Anfänge* and 'Review of Kreiten'; and Bruchet and Lancien, *L'itinéraire*.[57]
The *Lettres missives* series presents historians with three problems. First, about half of the letters are either undated or at least lack a year, and their earliest editors proposed erroneous dates. Second, several correspondents wrote hastily (and, in Maximilian's case, sometimes while intoxicated) so that transcribing their prose can pose almost insurmountable problems. Finally, at least until 1517 many of the minutes of Margaret's letters lack an addressee (although the salutation usually offers a clue: 'Treschier et bien aimé' indicated a letter directed to ambassadors or officials; 'Mon cousin' meant that the addressee was a prince of the blood or a Knight of the Golden Fleece; and 'Mon très redoucté seigneur et père' can only refer to her father). When in doubt, I have accepted the dates, addressees and readings proposed for each published letter by Andreas Walther in his 1908 'Review of Kreiten', 268–84.[58]

(ii) Paris

Several Paris archives and libraries contain documents related to Charles: see the list in Hasenclever, 'Die Überlieferung der Akten Karls V. in Pariser Archiven und Bibliotheken'. The most important collections are as follows:

(a) Bibliothèque Nationale de France (BNF: formerly Bibliothèque Royale, Bibliothèque Impériale and then Bibliothèque Nationale de Paris)

The library's manuscript collection contains many documents generated by the French government concerning Charles (especially in the series *Fonds français* and *Collection Dupuy*) as well as many other items collected or confiscated by the French (notably in the series *Manuscrits Espagnols* and *Manuscrits Portugais*). Laiglesia, *Estudios*, III, 417–21, listed all relevant items in BNF *Ms. Esp.*

The online catalogue http://archivesetmanuscrits.bnf.fr/ark:/12148/cc7296x provides descriptions of items in the various BNF manuscript collections, organized by language, together with a link to individual manuscripts that have been digitized. Thus typing 'Charles-Quint' into the box 'Refine' produces details on hundreds of manuscripts about the emperor that can be consulted online. For an example, go to 'Portugais' in the list of languages, choose '61', and you can read online the only surviving text of the emperor's *Memoirs* (see Appendix I for more details on this document).

Gachard, *BNP*, provided descriptions and some extracts of documents in the library that concerned the history of Belgium, with a helpful list of entries in chronological order at the end of each volume (I, 530–4, and II, 580–6, list documents from Charles's reign). Vol. II, 36–114, summarized the surviving dispatches of French diplomats at the imperial court: fragments of the dispatches of La Roche-Beaucourt (1518–19: fifteen letters) and Vély (1535–6: seven letters); and three registers of correspondence kept by Marillac (1548–50).[59]

(b) Centre des Archives Diplomatiques du Ministère des Affaires Étrangères, La Courneuve (CADMA; formerly Archives du Ministère des Affaires Étrangères)
In the nineteenth century, Melchior Tirán, a French official sent to inspect Spanish archives, looted numerous documents and delivered them to CADMA (some were later transferred to the Archives Nationales). At a meeting in October 1940, General Francisco Franco asked Adolf Hitler to compel the defeated French to repatriate these documents, and the Führer followed through: CADMA made photocopies before sending them back and these, as well as a few originals and documents from non-Spanish repositories, remain in the series *MDE*. See the description of each volume currently in the series at https://www.diplomatie.gouv.fr/IMG/pdf/md-espagne-1-369.pdf.[60]

(iii) Besançon
Bibliothèque Municipale d'Étude et de Conservation, Besançon (BMECB)
In 1694 the Bibliothèque Municipale of Besançon acquired eighty-two volumes of papers from the heir of Nicholas and Antoine Perrenot de Granvelle, which became the *Collection manuscrite Granvelle*. The first six volumes, 'Mémoires de ce qui s'est passé sous le ministère du chancelier et du cardinal de Granvelle', cover the reign of Charles (*PEG* printed over 700 documents from this source, though not always in full). In 1992 the library acquired ten more volumes of Granvelle papers from the archive of the marquis of Downshire (Trumbull papers).[61] BMECB has now scanned virtually the whole Granvelle collection and made it accessible online, together with an index to each volume and hotlinks to each document: http://memorevive.besancon.fr.[62] Some items are sensational, such as the transcript of a secret codicil to Charles's will concerning his illegitimate son, the future Don John of Austria, signed in 1554 (BMECB *Ms. Granvelle* V/265–8: see chapter 15), and the various position papers composed by and for Nicholas Perrenot between 1530, when he became the emperor's principal adviser on foreign affairs, and his death in 1550.

Publication of the Granvelle papers began in the later sixteenth century, and the most recent collection – Grata, *Des lettres pour gouverner* – provides a helpful list of previous editions of Antoine's correspondence as well as the text of all his letters contained in two of the Trumbull volumes: 149 letters in Italian exchanged with fifty-three people between August 1551 and February 1552. Most of the correspondents were obscure men – soldiers, lawyers, printers, merchants, clerics – who held humble posts scattered through Burgundy, Germany, Lorraine, the Low Countries and Spain as well as Italy, and they wrote mostly about minor matters; but paradoxically their relative obscurity proved an unexpected strength, because the routine nature of the letters revealed the vast network that helped Perrenot and his father to influence Charles's decisions. For another major collection of Granvelle papers, see p. 579 above.

9. UNITED STATES OF AMERICA

Two cousins, Archer and Henry Huntington, shared a love of Spain and inherited enough money both to acquire most of what they wanted and to endow a suitable repository to preserve their acquisitions.

(i) New York City
The Hispanic Society of America (HSA)
Although the HSA contains relatively few documents by or to Charles, two of them are outstanding:

* *Ms.* B 2954: a collection of eleven autograph or holograph letters exchanged between Charles and other rulers 1525–31, purchased by the founder of the HSA, Archer M. Huntington, c. 1900.
* *Ms.* B 2955: the original holograph instructions sent by Charles to his son in May 1543, purchased by Huntington in 1906: see Ball and Parker, *Cómo ser rey*.

A typescript 'Reference List: Charles V', available in the HSA search room, describes these and other items in the collection and provides their call-numbers.

(ii) San Marino (California)

The Huntington Library, Art Collections and Botanical Gardens (Hunt)
The rebellion of the settlers of Peru in 1544–8 allegedly caused Charles more grief than any other revolt (chapter 13), and by a happy coincidence a unique collection of documents allows historians to reconstruct both its genesis and its suppression. Following the defeat and execution of Gonzalo Pizarro, Charles's lieutenant Pedro de La Gasca acquired his archive, and after his triumphant return to Spain he entrusted it, together with many of his own papers, to Juan Cristóbal Calvete de Estrella whom La Gasca charged with writing a chronicle of his achievements (Calvete de Estrella, *Rebelión*, written in 1565–7 but unpublished until the nineteenth century). In 1925, Henry E. Huntington acquired at auction a collection of almost 1,000 of La Gasca's documents, subsequently rearranged in ten boxes in a single chronological order: Hunt *PL* 1–946. The Library also possesses a microfilm copy of the collection, and a volume of nineteenth-century transcripts, for which a typescript index exists: 'Pizarro-La Gasca transcription volumes: Table of Contents'. English summaries, not always accurate, were published in the 1925 sale catalogue, entitled *From Panama to Peru*. In 1964, Juan Pérez de Tudela Bueso published *Documentos relativos*, transcribing another set of nineteenth-century copies of the originals now in the Huntington: RAH *Mss.* 9–9–5–1830 and 1831 (formerly in the Colección Muñoz).[63]
  Consultation of this important collection is complicated by two factors:

(a) The Huntington microfilms and transcripts, and the RAH copies, all follow the same idiosyncratic order, copied by Pérez de Tudela. By contrast the originals (Hunt *PL* 1–946) and the translated extracts in *From Panama to Peru* both follow a strict chronological order. The various texts can be collated through the folio numbers provided in both published works, although the task is further complicated because vol. I of the RAH texts, and therefore of *Documentos relativos*, corresponds to vol. II in the Huntington, and therefore in *From Panama to Peru*, and vice versa. Thus the English summary of Gonzalo Pizarro's initial letter to the emperor in August 1544 criticizing the New Laws is at *From Panama to Peru*, 17–20 (from Huntington vol. I, ff. 455–60, of the original pagination), and at *Documentos relativos*, II, 383–95 (from RAH *Ms.* 9–9–5–1831, ff. 455–60). The original document is now Hunt *PL* 623.
(b) Although Pérez de Tudela Bueso obtained a microfilm of the originals from the Huntington Library, and used it to improve his transcriptions, *Documentos relativos* omitted many of the originals, notably Huntington vol. I, ff. 784–920, which contain most of La Gasca's correspondence with Charles and the council of the Indies in the period 1545–51. An eight-page typed 'Preliminary inventory' of these omissions is available in the Huntington Library reading room.[64]

  In addition, Charles left a documentary trail wherever he travelled – and he visited over 1,000 different places in the course of his reign, many of them repeatedly. For the scale of the available documentation, see Vincenzo Saletta's careful reconstruction from local sources of the emperor's 'victory lap' from Trapani in Sicily to Savigliano near the French frontier between July 1535 and July 1536, which covers almost 200 printed pages.[65]

IV. DIPLOMATIC ARCHIVES

In the preface to the final volume of his *History of Charles V*, Hermann Baumgarten wrote that although a generation earlier Leopold von Ranke established admirable protocols for historical study based upon the newly accessible diplomatic archives of Venice, 'if he were sitting today in the archives of Vienna, he would concentrate above all on Charles and his entourage. Set beside the correspondence of the emperor, his siblings, his councils and his ambassadors, the Final Relations and dispatches of the Venetian ambassadors become a second-class source.'[66] This is unfair. Charles's unique importance attracted extensive international attention, starting with Gutierre Gómez de Fuensalida, a special ambassador sent in 1500 by Isabella of Castile and Ferdinand of Aragon in part to report on the health and temperament of the grandson who would eventually succeed them. Thanks to the register of his dispatches in the Alba archive, we have several detailed descriptions of Charles as an infant (see chapter 1).

Fuensalida was a member of an exclusive group, because resident ambassadors were still a rarity. In 1512 English diplomats urged Henry VIII to keep a permanent representative at the court of Maximilian because 'a letter is soon seen, and lightly cast [away and] forgotten, where the presence of one of your ambassadors' could 'force hym to declare his mynd'.[67] The number of resident ambassadors at the courts of Europe steadily increased, and so did the frequency of their dispatches. Already in 1476 the duke of Milan had warned his envoy to Duke Charles of Burgundy, the emperor's great-grandfather, that 'I demand and require you expressly, on pain of death, to write to me every day'; and half a century later, many ambassadors did just that.[68] By the time of Charles's abdication, over a hundred different diplomats sent by the pope, England, Ferrara, Florence, France, Mantua, Milan, Poland, Portugal, Venice, and also by his brother Ferdinand, had written tens of thousands of dispatches describing the emperor's words and deeds as well as events, people and places from the vantage-point of Charles's court. 'Ambassadors', according to an experienced minister of Henry VIII, should be 'chosen men of experience' who could observe the sovereign to whom they were accredited so closely that they could 'fishe out the bottom of his stomake', and 'feale the depenes of his harte'. Admittedly, as Elizabeth Gleason has pointed out, several ambassadors began very young. Gasparo Contarini of Venice, for example, at first 'wrote like a novice, loading his reports with peripheral detail', but in the course of writing almost 400 letters from Charles's court between 1521 and 1525 he became increasingly shrewd, judicious and well-informed.[69]

Ambassadors took special care to record what happened at their audiences, 'merking and noting in suche wise the dyscourses, procedinges and communicatyons to be had there; their continuance, fasshyon and vehemence, with the very woordes and aunswers'. Even when Charles 'used so many words to explain everything' that afterwards an ambassador could not recall all of them, he nevertheless 'wrote down all the conversation I could remember'.[70] Several hundred accounts survive of how Charles appeared at audiences (his dress, his gestures, his expressions, his complexion), and some are very vivid. The dispatches of Sir Thomas Wyatt, a leading poet who served as English ambassador to the emperor from 1537 to 1540, are (in the words of his first editor) 'some of the most lively and dramatic pieces of writing that I know. They place the emperor before our eyes; we see his every look, and every gesture; and trace in all he says and does, that refinement of political cunning for which he was so remarkable.' Nevertheless (in the words of his most recent editor), we should recall that Wyatt and other diplomats often told 'good stories, employed humor or drew fascinating portraits of places and characters' at least in part 'with the aim of overshadowing their failures'. Whatever the motive, however, the ambassadors who accompanied Charles provided uniquely vivid portraits of him laughing and frowning, interrupting their 'tale, with imperius and brave words', and 'wagging his head and making a "Tush"' when he heard something he did not like.[71]

Then as now, a shrewd ambassador might overmatch the emperor's 'political cunning' through skilful questioning. In December 1543, Henry VIII and Charles agreed to mount a joint invasion of France, and a few months later Nicholas Wotton, Wyatt's successor at the imperial court, received instructions to find out whether the emperor intended to honour his promise and, if so, when and where he would strike. Wotton therefore asked Granvelle a leading question:

'I trust we shall now shortelye departe owte of this rude cowntrey [Germany], and go downe to that merye and pleasant cowntrey of Brabant againe.' But Granvele had me streight, and perceyvid right well that it was neither the rudenesse of this cowntrey nor the playsantnes of Brabant, that cawsed me to move that questyon, and said, 'Ah! Yow maye not aske me that questyon, for I maye not answer yow'.

Granvelle would only assure Wotton that the emperor 'entendithe to folow his cownsell, and to entre into France, and to keepe that waye, that the king hathe advysed and cownseiled him to do'. Wotton transmitted this answer to Henry in the hope that 'though it be darke to me, [it] maye peradventure gyve summe lighte to Your Hieghnes'. It did indeed, because the two monarchs had agreed 'that th'emperor shall with his armye make invasion into the realm of Ffraunce *by the country of Champaign*, and so marche towards Parys'. Granvelle's affirmation that his master would adhere to the agreed plan may have been 'darke' to Wotton, but it shed all the light that Henry needed. Both monarchs invaded France as planned a few months later.[72]

Like all sources, diplomatic dispatches have their limitations. Many ambassadors expressed frustration at the lack of reliable information because Charles refused to see them when he was ill, or when 'during this military emergency he is not dealing with ordinary business', or when he sought to create a news blackout. Thus in September 1552, just before besieging Metz, Charles announced that 'no agent, secretary, or man of any ambassador shall be suffered to write or tell out what is done' in his camp, and banished all of them to Speyer, 200 kilometres away. The diplomats remained there, largely isolated from the sovereign to whom they were accredited, for almost five months.[73]

Sometimes ambassadors inadvertently reported fake news. One English envoy in the Netherlands 'repented the writing' of some recent letters because 'here flye suche swarmes of lyes that he who writes nothing does best'; and when the perceptive Polish ambassador Jan Dantiszek arrived at Charles's court in 1519, he compared himself to a freshman student entering university. He discerned four faculties: 'the first teaches one patience, the second offers instruction in distrust, the third in dissimulation, and the fourth and largest in how to lie'. The court, Dantiszek opined, 'is a magnificent school in which to perfect all these skills'.[74]

Luckily, the abundance of sources created by diplomatic alumni of the imperial court normally allows historians to separate truth from falsehood. For example, in September 1526, Charles granted a joint audience to the ambassadors of three signatories to the hostile League of Cognac – France, the pope and Venice – and the diplomats wrote full reports for their masters immediately afterwards. Since each provided much the same account of what Charles said, their reliability seems assured.[75] At the very least, ambassadors provided an accurate record of when and where certain events took place – something that can be surprisingly difficult to document from other sources. For example, controversy surrounds the date and place when Charles first saw the treasure and other gifts, including some native Americans, sent to him from Veracruz by Hernán Cortés; but the descriptions included in the dispatches of the nuncio and the Venetian ambassador prove that this happened in Valladolid in early March 1521 (chapter 13 above).

Ambassadors also made copies of important documents for their masters, and in some cases they provided the only surviving record. Thus we lack the original text of Charles's angry condemnation of Martin Luther in 1521 at the Diet of Worms, composed the night after their only meeting; but Henry VIII's envoy, Thomas Spinelly, who had resided at Charles's court for over a decade, travelling with him through Spain, the Netherlands and Germany, secured a transcript of the original written in French in Charles's own hand. It is preserved in The National Archives in England, and is as close to the holograph original as historians are ever likely to get.[76]

Ambassadors expressed frustration when heads of state met in person to resolve policy via direct negotiation. Early in 1538, after eighteen months of war, Charles told a French diplomat that although he and Francis could continue 'to declare their wishes and intentions to each other by means of their ministers', he believed that a face-to-face meeting between them 'was the true and best means to achieve the peace that they desired'. Two summits between them soon took place, first at Nice with the pope as a mediator and then at Aigues Mortes between the two monarchs alone. No diplomat attended their discussions.[77] Monarchs also exchanged numerous holograph letters, some containing matters that they wished to conceal from the eyes of diplomats. Charles wrote numerous letters in his own hand to Francis (whom he saw in 1525–6, 1538 and 1539–40), to Henry VIII (whom he met in 1513, 1520 and 1522), to Adrian VI (whom he already knew well), to Clement VII (holding summits in 1529–30 and 1532–3), and to Paul III (with summits in 1538, 1541 and 1543).[78] But at other times the thousands of surviving dispatches from diplomats at Charles's court in the archives and libraries of England, France, the Low Countries, Poland, Portugal, Scandinavia and the independent states of Germany and Italy provide an invaluable source on the emperor and the problems he faced. The main series are as follows:

1. ENGLAND

(i) The National Archives, Kew (TNA: formerly The Public Record Office)

The series *State Papers*, divided by reign, contains (among other things) correspondence between the central government and its diplomats abroad:

* *State Papers* 1 (246 vols). An artificial collection of public and private letters, memoranda and papers from the reign of Henry VIII (1509–47), arranged in the nineteenth century into a single chronological order irrespective of provenance and covering both foreign and domestic affairs.
* *State Papers* 2 (20 vols). An artificial collection of folio-sized public and private letters, memoranda and papers from 1516 to 1539, arranged in the nineteenth century into a single chronological order, irrespective of provenance.
* *State Papers* 68 (15 vols). Letters and papers relating to foreign countries and to Calais from the reign of Edward VI (1547–53), arranged in chronological order, first for foreign countries and then for Calais.
* *State Papers* 69 (13 vols). Letters and papers relating to foreign countries from the reign of Mary (1553–4) and Philip and Mary (1554–58), arranged in chronological order.
Many documents in TNA *SP* are also available via *CSP*, *L&P Henry VIII*, *SP* and *SPO*: see details below.

(ii) The British Library, London (BL: formerly British Museum Library)
a) Cotton Manuscripts
Sir Robert Cotton (1571–1631) started collecting manuscripts when he was eighteen and eventually owned perhaps the most important collection of manuscripts ever assembled in Britain by a private person. He

arranged them in a series of presses surmounted by busts of the twelve Caesars and two of their consorts. In 1702, Cotton's grandson donated the collection to 'the British Nation' and in 1753 it entered the library of the newly opened British Museum (now the British Library), which retained Cotton's unique classification system (Galba A.1–E. XIV; Vespasian A.1–F. XVII; and so on.). BL *Cotton Mss.* today contains more than 1,400 manuscripts, many of them from the earlier sixteenth century, many of them removed from the State Paper Office. In the 1990s a team from the University of Sheffield re-catalogued the entire collection and provided new descriptions of its contents: http://www.hrionline.ac.uk/cotton/cotframe.htm

b) Additional Manuscripts

Other BL manuscript collections contain numerous documents by or about Charles. They are best identified through the BL site 'Explore archives and manuscripts': http://searcharchives.bl.uk. Type 'Emperor Charles V' into the 'Advanced Search' option to bring up more than 600 items ranging from individual charters (e.g. *Addl. Charter* 74,946, Charles's appointment of Johann Obernberger as his German language secretary in 1538) to entire volumes (e.g. *Addl. Ms.* 28,706, a volume containing 114 folios about the marriages of Charles's children Philip and Joanna with their Portuguese cousins, collected by Charles's secretary Alonso de Idiáquez, who negotiated the match in 1542–3). BL *Addl. Mss.* 28,572–28,597 contain transcripts of thousands of documents concerning Charles made in European archives by or for Gustave Bergenroth: see above.

Several tools facilitate consultation of these series. Pride of place goes to *State Papers Online* (hereafter *SPO*), a commercial venture only accessible via institutional subscription (and in the words of Diarmaid MacCulloch, 'one of the great scholarly achievements of the modern age'). *SPO* provides online access, via its 'Browse manuscript' feature, to all volumes in TNA *SP* and to the volumes in BL *Cott. Ms.* that once belonged to that series. They are accessed through their archival signature (TNA *SP* 1/220, using the numbering stamped in print on the manuscripts; BL *Cotton Ms.* Galba B.VI, using the most recent sequence of numbering; and so on).[79] *SPO* also provides online access, via its 'Browse Calendar' feature, to the following relevant printed sources:

* *State Papers, published under the authority of His Majesty's Commission . . . King Henry the Eighth*, vols 6–11 ('Part V: foreign correspondence'): full transcripts of almost all the official correspondence of English diplomats abroad between 1473 and 1547 preserved in TNA *SP* 1 and *SP* 2.
* *Letters and papers, foreign and domestic, of the reign of Henry VIII*, 21 vols, some in multiple parts: summaries of all the documents generated by the government of Henry VIII now in TNA *SP* 1 and 2 and in BL *Cott. Mss.* and other collections, as well as in numerous printed sources. Each entry includes a précis, often with lengthy quotations. The original editor, J. S. Brewer, first catalogued all materials in TNA for the reign of Henry VIII by arranging them in a single chronological series – no mean feat, since the documents were divided between several locations and the majority bore no year so that 'the chronology could only be ascertained from internal evidence by an elaborate and comprehensive study of the whole correspondence, long before any attempt was made to summarise their contents in a calendar'.[80] Brewer published the first four volumes of the series and his assistant, James Gairdner of TNA, completed the project after Brewer's death, latterly assisted by another archivist, R. H. Brodie, who also published a 'second edition revised and greatly enlarged' of the first volume, in two parts, covering 1509–14. These erudite editors sometimes transcribed words now illegible, and located documents subsequently mislaid.
* *Calendars of State Papers, Foreign Series (CSPF)*, for the reigns of Edward and Mary. Once again, there is a close correlation between the calendars and TNA *SP* 68 and 69: both archival series are arranged according to the calendar entry numbers.

Only a few relevant manuscripts escaped the editors, such as 'A diary iournall of the actions in France done by Henry 8th in the 5 yeare of his raigne', in which John Taylor, clerk of Parliaments, kept a record in Latin of the 1513 campaign, including a description of Charles at his first summit meeting with other heads of state (BL *Cott. Ms.* Cleopatra C.1, # 4, f. 92).

Although *SPO* provides links between the Calendar summary and the original document, they do not always match because *L&P Henry VIII* and *SPO* both used the original foliation for BL *Cotton Mss.*, not the current one. It is therefore necessary to browse the scanned volume to locate the original document and its current call-number. Conversely, most entries in *State Papers* and *L&P* either provided outdated call-numbers or no call-number at all for documents in TNA *SP*; but *SPO* personnel used 'a key available at the National Archives' to identify the original documents. Therefore, the *SPO* scanned texts of *L&P Henry VIII* include a 'Browse Manuscript' link that leads directly to the item summarized, and provides its current call-number as well as another link to scans of each document, making *SPO* an outstanding online resource for Charles's reign.

NOTE ON SOURCES

2. FRANCE

In the late nineteenth century, French archivists adopted the Calendar technique pioneered by their British colleagues and published summaries of the dispatches of three ambassadors from Francis and Henry II to England preserved in CADMA: Castillon and Marillac in 1537–42 (Kaulek, *Correspondance*) and Selve in 1546–9 (Lefèvre-Pontarlis, *Correspondance*). Gachard, *BNP*, provided helpful summaries of the surviving dispatches from French ambassadors to Charles's court in BNF, together with call-numbers, but none have been published: see details above.

3. GERMANY

Only one German ruler maintained a permanent representative at Charles's court: his brother Ferdinand (also, until the birth of Prince Philip in 1527, Charles's heir). A register of 400 letters written by Martín de Salinas between 1522 and 1539 was published in *RVEC*, albeit with the omission of 'private matters and economic measures that lack any historical value'.[81] Salinas recognized at an early stage the importance of the new lands acquired for Charles by Hernán Cortés, and he not only encouraged Ferdinand to correspond directly with the conqueror of Mexico but also made copies of important documents about America and sent them back to his master. Gradually, Salinas's nephew Alonso Gamiz took over his functions: AGS *Estado* 641bis contains correspondence between Ferdinand and Gamiz, 1542–1556 (acquired at auction in 1983), with more in the *Archivo Familiar Gamiz* in the Archivo Histórico Provincial de Álava (acquired in 1998 and accessible through PARES, by typing 'Alonso de Gamiz' into 'Búsqueda Sencilla'; many letters are digitized).

4. ITALY

(i) Florence

Archivio di Stato (ASF)
Although the Florentine Republic and later Duke Alessandro de' Medici, Charles's son-in-law, maintained a resident ambassador at the imperial court, few of their dispatches have survived. By contrast, after Cosimo became duke of Florence in 1537 dispatches abound in the series ASF *Mediceo del Principato (MdP)*, with most documents concentrated in the volumes of the sub-section *Germania: Corte Imperiale*.[82] Many dispatches from Averardo Serristori in 1537–8 and 1541 were printed by his descendant: Serristori, *Legazioni*.

Many diplomatic dispatches from ASF *MdP* have been analysed and entered into the Medici Archive Project (MAP), available online. Users need to obtain a username and password to log in, and they may then type 'Habsburg Karl V' in the 'Simple Search' field on top of the Main Menu, and click 'go'. The right screen will show all people with those elements in their names: click on the emperor's name and his profile will appear on the left screen. Alternatively, log in and follow this link: http://bia.medici.org/DocSources/src/peoplebase/SharePerson.do?personId=253

This leads to the emperor's profile. At that point click on the 'More info' button, and at least 569 documents related to Charles V will appear (the number constantly increases as MAP expands). Each entry contains a transcription and at least a partial English translation. Although the project began as a database on material culture, and therefore does not focus on politics or military matters, it still contains fascinating details – such as a description of the portable wooden office constructed to accompany Charles on his travels in 1541, enabling him to deal with public affairs while on the move.[83] In addition, since MAP is currently digitizing the Medici archives, the full texts of many documents related to Charles V are available online.

Finally, although documents related to the emperor are scattered across ASF, there is one remarkable exception: *MdP: Carteggio Universale* filza 329 consists entirely of letters and diplomas sent by Charles to Duke Cosimo between 1530 and 1556. It has been fully digitized, and is available either via Basic Search or through the link: http://bia.medici.org/DocSources/src/volbase/ShareVolume.do?summaryId=890

(ii) Vatican City

Archivio Segreto Vaticano (ASV)
The correspondence of the papal diplomat Girolamo Aleandro in 1520–1 has been published twice: Balan, *Monumenta*, printed the original letters, and shortly afterwards Brieger, *Quellen*, provided the texts in the register of his correspondence. Brieger corrected most of the dates proposed by Balan for Aleandro's letters, printed many more of them, and provided a concordance between the two (*Quellen*, xiv–xv), but Balan sometimes provided superior readings. Serassi, *Delle lettere*, published many of the dispatches of Nuncio Baldassare Castiglione from Spain 1525–7. The dispatches of the papal nuncios in

Germany between 1533 and 1556, most of them in ASV, were printed in calendar form in the seventeen vols of *NBD: Erste Abteilung*. Charles appears prominently in vols VI and VII (1540–4), VIII–XI (1545–9), XII–XIV and XVI (1550–6), and in two important *Ergänzungsbände* covering the Legation of Lorenzo Campeggio and the Nuntiature of Girolamo Aleandro in 1530–2. In addition, Pastor, 'Correspondenz', Dittich, 'Nuntiaturberichte' and Schultze, 'Dreizehn Depeschen', all published dispatches from papal agents at the Diet of Regensburg in 1541. For direct communications between Charles and Popes Adrian and Clement, see Gachard, *Correspondance de Charles-Quint et d'Adrien*, and Vañes, 'Cartas', respectively.

(iii) Mantua

Archivio di Stato (ASMa)
Archivio Gonzaga: Corrispondenza estera contains dispatches from Mantuan diplomats at the imperial court. The duke evidently shared many of them with Venice, because Sanuto copied them – or parts of them – into his *Diarii*. But did the duke share the whole dispatch and nothing but the dispatch? Only a close comparison of the two texts will tell.

(iv) Modena

Archivio di Stato (ASMo)
Cancellaria ducale: ambasciatori, sub-series 'Alemagna', 'Italia' and 'Spagna', contain dispatches from the diplomats sent to Charles's court by the dukes of Ferrara.

(v) Turin

Archivio di Stato (AST)
French troops invaded the duchy of Savoy in 1536, forcing Duke Charles and his heir Prince Emanuel Philibert to flee until after the peace of Cateau-Cambrésis in 1559. Since support from the emperor offered the only realistic chance of expelling the French, the duke maintained a permanent ambassador at the imperial court: Jean-Thomas de Langosco, count of Stroppiana, provided much detail in his dispatches to both the duke and the prince – not least because, according to another (envious?) diplomat, Stroppiana 'sleeps in the emperor's bedchamber'.[84] The originals are in AST *Lettere di ministri: Vienna*, mazzi 2, 3 and 4. Greppi, 'Extraits', published French summaries of many of them for 1546–59 (with transcripts of many Italian originals in the notes).

(vi) Venice

Every Venetian ambassador composed a *Relazione* after returning from his embassy, and after 1524 each one had to read his text to the Senate and submit it in writing two weeks later. These were substantial documents: it took Gasparo Contarini over three hours to read out his *Relazione* in 1525, after fifty-two months at the court of Charles V, and his text covers over sixty printed pages.[85] Most of each *Relazione* dealt with the same issues: geography and resources; wealth of cities and nobles; recent history; and the character, appearance and health of the ruler, his immediate family and his principal advisers. Thanks to this custom, historians can find intimate portraits of the emperor at different ages by Vincenzo Quirini in 1506, Francesco Corner in 1521, Gasparo Contarini in 1525, Niccolò Tiepolo in 1532, Bernardo Navagero in 1546, Alvise Mocenigo in 1548, Marino Cavalli in 1551, and Federico Badoer in 1557.[86] In the nineteenth century, Eugenio Alberì published the *Relazioni* of most Venetian ambassadors (but in an apparently haphazard order); and a century later, Luigi Firpo started to republish many of them, together with a few more printed elsewhere, arranged by country and then by date. Vols II and III (*Germania 1506–1554* and *Germania 1557–1654*) and IX (*Spagna 1497–1598*) contain the *Relazioni* composed by ambassadors to Charles V. All except those of Quirini and Corner are available online at http://www.bibliotecaitaliana.it.[87]

In addition, like envoys sent by other rulers, each Venetian ambassador sent regular dispatches to his home government, and extracts from them appear in two printed sources: *CSPV* (available in digital form through *BHO*) and the *Diarii* of Marino Sanuto: see http://onlinebooks.library.upenn.edu/webbin/metabook?id=sanudodiary

Sanuto was already a historian with some works to his credit when in 1496 he decided to create a chronicle of his own times by collecting relevant materials every day, recording Venetian documents and debates that he considered important until September 1533, just before his death. The republic's political elite recognized the value of his enterprise, granting him special permission to scour archives in order to keep his *Diarii* up to date. Sanuto himself boasted that 'I have seen and understood the truth, not only about the city but about the entire world, and I can state that no writer will be able to undertake a good history of modern times without consulting my *Diarii*.'[88] His material would fill fifty-eight large printed volumes, arranged (according to Sanuto's design) according to the year, month and day on which each document arrived in Venice. This may confuse historians trying to follow a particular 'thread' of correspondence, because dispatches from diplomats in different places describing the same event arrived at an uneven pace; but Sanuto shows historians of Venice what the government knew and when they knew it, and allows historians of communication to measure the speed of couriers on official business (see Fig. 2). Nothing similar exists for any other government.

Rawdon Brown, who edited the early volumes of *CSPV*, often used Sanuto's transcriptions of incoming dispatches, rather than the originals, but he did so before the publication of the *Diarii* provided the volume and folio of the original, which differ from the references in the published text, making it difficult to calibrate the two. In addition, Brown made several errors of transcription.[89]

The dispatches of four Venetian ambassadors at Charles's court have been published in whole or in part: von Höfler, 'Depeschen' for Quirino; Cicogna, *Delle Inscrizioni*, VI, for Andrea Navagero; Gachard, *Trois années*, for Bernardo Navagero (from a register of his correspondence in ÖNB); Stirling-Maxwell, *Notices*, for Badoer. Two other registers of diplomatic dispatches have survived: BNMV *Ms. Italiani Clase VII*, cod. 1009, contains Contarini's letters from Charles's court, 1521–5; BAV *Vat. Lat.* 6753 contains those of his successor, Andrea Navagero, 1525–8. Turba, *Venetianische Depeschen*, provides summaries and extracts of the dispatches sent by ambassadors at the imperial court, now in the Archivio di Stato of Venice, from 1538 onwards.

5. POLAND

Johannes von Höfen, a humanist and poet from Danzig (hence his name Johannes Dantiscus in Latin, Dantisco in Spanish and Dantiszek in Polish), served as ambassador of King Sigismund of Poland-Lithuania at Charles's court in 1518–19, 1522–3 and 1525–32. Perhaps because of boredom (a recurring complaint in his correspondence) Dantiszek filled his dispatches with descriptions of the places and peoples he saw, as well as of events, and so provided more information than most diplomats. He also corresponded with Cortés and others about the Americas, and collected materials from the New World which he sent back to Poland.[90] Many of Dantiszek's official dispatches were published in Górski, *Acta Tomiciana*: the papers of the Polish statesman Piotr Tomicki, collected and preserved by his secretary. The first thirteen volumes are available online: http://www.wbc.poznan.pl/publication/32217. Many of the 6,000 surviving letters (mostly in Latin and German) written by and to Dantiszek are also available in full-text, searchable form: *Corpus of Joannes Dantiscus' texts and correspondence* (http://dantiscus. al.uw.edu.pl/?menu=clat&f=clat). In 1994, Fontán and Axer, *Españoles y polacos*, published a Spanish translation of over forty of Dantiszek's diplomatic dispatches from Charles's court (as well as many other fascinating items, including his correspondence about America).

6. PORTUGAL

The Houses of Austria and Avis maintained close family ties: King Manuel married two of Charles's aunts and then his sister Eleanor; Charles married the sister of John III, who married Catalina of Austria; their son Prince John married Charles's daughter Joanna, and Charles's son Philip married the prince's sister, María Manuela. These links meant that the Portuguese ambassadors to the imperial court took special care to describe Charles's behaviour – especially towards scions of the House of Avis. See, for example, the dispatches from 1526–7, when the imperial couple were still 'very much in love and very happy', printed by Braamcamp Freire, 'Ida'. These dispatches came from ANTT *CC*, a series created in the wake of the chaos caused by the Lisbon earthquake of 1755, with most surviving documents placed in a single chronological sequence by date of composition, irrespective of provenance, addressee or date received. ANTT *CC*, Part I, maço 21 (1517) to maço 103 (1558) contain (among many other documents) dispatches received from the emperor and from diplomats at his court. https://digitarq.arquivos.pt/ details?id=3767259 provides a brief description of each document in the series.

V. CHRONICLES AND HISTORIES

The final group of important documents on Charles are the chronicles compiled by protagonists. In the Netherlands, Jean Molinet (1475–1507), his nephew Jean Lemaire des Belges (1507–12), Remy du Puys (1515–16) and Heinrich Cornelius Agrippa of Nettesheim (1530–2) all served as chroniclers (*indiciaire*) at the court of Burgundy, but few published much history. Paradoxically, although never appointed official chronicler, in 1559, Charles's librarian Willem Snouckaert van Schouwenburg published a 300-page biography of the emperor: three other editions had appeared by 1563, with two more in the 1590s.[91] In

Castile, nine scholars served Charles as royal chroniclers: Antonio de Nebrija (1509–22), Peter Mártir de Anglería (1520–6), Bernardo Gentile (1523–6), Antonio de Guevara (1525–45), Juan Ginés de Sepúlveda (1536–73), Florián de Ocampo (1539–58), Bernabé de Busto (1546–57), Pedro Mexía (1548–51) and Juan Páez de Castro (1556–68). All of these men had a Humanist training and boasted a university degree, but only three (Mexía, Ocampo and Sepúlveda) had previous experience of writing history. All of them seem to have spent too much time researching (or working on other projects) and not enough time writing.[92]

Morel-Fatio, *Historiography of Charles V. Part I* (1913), provided an outstanding evaluation of the work of each of the Spanish chroniclers, although in several cases a subsequent edition has appeared. Thus a typescript of almost 4,000 pages was created from the manuscript of Santa Cruz's *Chronicle of Emperor Charles V*, and published in Madrid in five volumes between 1920 and 1925; a critical edition of Mexía's chronicle appeared in 1945; between 1953 and 1957, José López de Toro published a four-volume Spanish translation of the letters of Peter Mártir; a full edition of Girón's history came out in 1964; and a magnificent edition of Sepúlveda's *The deeds of Emperor Charles V*, with the original Latin and a Spanish translation on facing pages, appeared in six volumes between 1995 and 2010.[93]

Of the official chroniclers only Sepúlveda interviewed Charles and asked him to explain his motives and his feelings about certain episodes, and he included a highly critical evaluation of the emperor in his final years (book XXX); but his *History* did not appear in print until the 1780s.[94] Three other chroniclers did not need an interview because they already knew the emperor well: Guevara was his chaplain, Girón served as his Alcalde de Casa y Corte (the magistrate tasked with maintaining discipline in the court of Spain), and Santa Cruz taught Charles mathematics and accompanied him on journeys.[95] Other contemporary historians who left personal records of their time with the emperor included the following (in chronological order):

1. Jean Vandenesse kept a diary of Charles's movements from 1506 to 1551 that included detailed descriptions of several major events.
2. Sancho Cota did the same from 1510 until October 1518, when he left for Portugal with Eleanor.
3. Laurent Vital kept a day-by-day record of life at Charles's court between June 1517, when he left the Netherlands with Charles, and April 1518, when he returned with Ferdinand.
4. Francesillo de Zúñiga, 'Official gossip-monger of the Spanish court [*chismógrafo official de la corte Española*]', accompanied Charles between 1517 and 1529, holding the office of court jester from 1522. After he fell from favour, Zúñiga compiled a scurrilous account of life at court, full of barbed comments about its denizens, and it began to circulate widely in manuscript almost immediately. The sting of his barbs can be judged by the fact that one of his targets had him stabbed to death in 1532.[96]
5. Martín García Cerezada, *Treatise*, is an account of a foot-soldier's campaigns in Charles's service between 1522 and 1545, with great detail (often day-to-day) on those periods when, 'as an eyewitness', he watched the emperor in action at the head of his troops.
6. Fery de Guyon, from Franche-Comté, began to serve in Charles's armies as a page in 1523, rising in 1539 to become an 'archer of the guard', which gave him the opportunity to observe his sovereign at close quarters. Guyon was completely absent from some parts of his *Memoirs* (apparently composed for his family after 1566), but he appeared prominently as a protagonist in other parts and provided some unique details on the logistics of Charles's principal campaigns, including some criticisms of 'our emperor' from the perspective of a junior officer.[97]
7. Luis de Ávila y Zúñiga composed and in 1548 published flattering *Commentaries* on the Schmalkaldic war, based on his experience at Charles's side, and also acted as imperial *proto-cronista*, overseeing the work of other historians.[98]
8. Charles was the central figure in the second half of Paolo Giovio's *History of his own times*, ending in 1547 and first published in 1552. Apart from wide reading, Giovio conducted interviews (sometimes in person, more often by letter) with Charles and his leading lieutenants as well as with his enemies (Giovio interviewed some Muslims captured in Tunis and brought by the emperor to Rome in 1536; and he sent questionnaires to John Frederick of Saxony and the landgrave of Hesse in August 1547, when both languished in prison, asking for their views on why their rebellion had failed).[99] He also drew on his personal experience, based on his meetings with Charles in 1529, 1536, 1541 and 1543.[100]
9. In 1555, Johannes Sleidan brought out his *Commentaries on the state of religion and public affairs under Emperor Charles V*, initially in Latin but soon with translations into several vernacular languages. Sleidan boasted at the outset that 'This work of mine is based entirely on documents collected with the utmost diligence', but as official historian of the Schmalkaldic League he collected documents about religion and public affairs, rather than about Charles: he therefore allocated fifty pages to the recent war in Germany, but only six lines to the Tunis campaign. Sleidan wrote virtually nothing about

the emperor's appearance or inner thoughts. Although (not surprisingly) Charles disliked his work, Sleidan provided important insights on the emperor's German policies, and their opponents.[101]

10. Francisco López de Gómara composed his *Annals of Charles V* in 1557–8, although some passages remain in the form of notes rather than as a finished work. The author had accompanied Charles on his Algiers expedition and was perhaps an eyewitness to other events, which gives his account great vividness.[102]

11. Although Florián de Ocampo only published five of a projected eighty-four chapters of his *Chronicle*, he left some notebooks full of relevant material concerning conditions in Spain: BNE *Ms.* 9936 and 9937, covering the years 1521–43 and 1550–8, were both copied from BSLE *Ms* V-II-4, 'Relación de cosas sucedidas en la Cristiandad desde 1510 hasta 1558', annotated by Páez and perhaps by Busto.

12. The life of Fray Prudencio de Sandoval, born in circa 1551, scarcely overlapped with that of the star of his *History of the life and deeds of the Emperor Charles V*, first published in 1604–6, and he borrowed extensively – often literally – from the chronicles compiled by Gómara, Guevara, Mexía and Santa Cruz. Nevertheless, his claim to have read or held in his hand many of the documents quoted in his *History* reminds us that he had access to numerous state papers, including some now lost; and where the originals survive, they confirm that Sandoval cited his sources accurately.[103]

Charles appeared in many other contemporary accounts over which he had no control. He featured frequently in the *Memoirs* of Bartholomew Sastrow, from Stralsund, who observed the emperor on many occasions in the 1540s; in the *History of Italy* by Francesco Guicciardini, which ended in 1534; and in the biography of Frederick, first Count and then Elector Palatine, composed by Thomas Hubert (also known as 'Leodius'), who served as Frederick's secretary and special envoy from 1522 until his death in 1555. Hubert recorded many conversations with his master about members of the imperial family (including Charles's sister Eleanor, whom Frederick tried to marry in 1517 and again in 1522) as well as citing documents from the Palatine archives.[104] Charles also appeared in the legion of chronicles devoted to his various campaigns: Voigt, 'Die Geschichtschreibung', published carefully researched bibliographical articles on the Tunis and Schmalkalden operations, which are still valuable. Nordman, *Tempête*, edited an exemplary collection of texts, both Christian and Muslim, concerning the Algiers fiasco.

VI. CULTURAL RECORDS

I. BUILDINGS

All four palaces in the Low Countries where Charles resided have been destroyed. In Ghent, commemorative frescoes depicting his great deeds were installed in 1685 in the room where he was born in the Hof Ten Walle (subsequently renamed the Prinsenhof in his honour), but it burned down in 1835. The Keizershof in Mechelen, where Charles spent most of his adolescence, became a monastery and was demolished at the beginning of the eighteenth century (now restored). The enormous ducal palace in Brussels, in which Charles staged many key events, including his emancipation in 1515 and his abdication forty years later, was almost entirely destroyed by fire in 1731 – although recent excavations have uncovered traces of several additions made during the emperor's reign. Nothing remains of the cottage in the palace park where he lived between 1553 and 1556 because it was demolished in 1778.[105]

Only two of Charles's palaces survive more or less intact, both in Spain. Charles commissioned the Renaissance construction in the heart of the Alhambra of Granada during his visit to Mantua in 1532, and although he made plans to return on more than one occasion, he never actually saw it.[106] By contrast the emperor reviewed and approved architectural plans for another major construction: the apartments at Yuste where he would spend the last nineteen months of his life. They became part of the convent shortly after his death, but in 1809 French troops sacked, looted and burnt the site, and the entire complex fell into ruins soon after the monastery was abandoned in 1837. Serious restoration work began just before the 400th anniversary of Charles's death, in 1958, and was triumphantly completed between 1999 and 2002.[107]

II. REPRESENTATIONS

Charles and his entourage closely supervised visual representations of the empire by painters, sculptors, engravers and other artists. Wohlfeil, 'Retratos', Checa Cremades, *Carlos V*, and especially Burke, 'Presenting', provide excellent overviews. Surviving images range from the full-length life-size paintings known as 'state portraits' (see Pl. 19), through stained glass and statues in wood (Pl. 15) and bronze (Pls 21 and 29), to coins and medals (Pls 16 and 17), tapestries (Pl. 20), cameos (Pl. 31) and miniatures (Pl. 33). Pieces and tokens used to play games could also be used for propaganda by placing the likeness of the emperor and his family on the upper side (Pl. 30).[108] Many images could be mass-produced thanks to printing, and the same was true of the ceremonial entries of the monarch into each city in his realms, starting at Bruges in 1515 (Pl. 7 and chapter 3 above) and reaching its apogee in the triumphal arches as Charles and his son progressed around the Netherlands in 1549 reproduced in Calvete de Estrella, *El felicíssimo viaje*. Jacquot, *Fêtes et cérémonies*, included many examples, and new studies of individual commemorations continue to appear, such as Borrás Gualis, *La imagen triunfal*, about the impressive frieze created in Tarazona, Spain, to commemorate Charles's coronation as emperor at Bologna in 1530.

Many of Charles's ministers acquired portraits and other memorabilia to remind them of their late master (or they sought to acquire them: see the unrequited effort of the first count of Olivares to secure a copy of Titian's painting of Charles at Mühlberg in chapter 17). Luis de Ávila y Zúñiga, whom some regarded as the emperor's Favourite, almost certainly convinced Charles to retire to Yuste, near to his own palace in Plasencia where he created a veritable 'Caroline Museum' decorated with frescoes of the emperor's leading battles (when Ávila described the one of Renty, Charles objected that it was not accurate) and full of memorabilia given to him by the emperor, including a marble bust by Pompeo Leoni dated 1555. The Palacio de Mirabel in Plasencia still boasts a *Salón de Carlos V*, but its contents may not remain there for long: the Leoni bust from the collection was offered for sale at auction in 2017 for 400,000 euros before being withdrawn.[109]

III. MUSIC

Young Charles learned to play several musical instruments at Mechelen, and throughout his life he heard much fine music. He evidently listened attentively because he recognized that some of the motets by Francisco Guerrero performed for him at Yuste were based on compositions by others (chapter 16). In her fine study of music at Charles's court, Mary Tiffany Ferer acknowledged that 'any personal involvement in both the patronage of music and musicians has failed to emerge'; but strong evidence links certain compositions with specific events (the imperial coronation at Bologna, the opening of the imperial Diets, the death of the empress and so on).[110] The best introduction to the emperor's music remains the long and richly documented essay by Ignace Bossuyt, a professor of musicology at the university of Leuven, 'Charles V: a life story in music', which provides a chronological outline of Charles's political career through music.

In addition, fine recordings exist of many works by composers known to Charles (Josquin des Prés, Peter Alamire, Juan de Anchieta, Luis de Narváez, Jean Courtois, Francisco Guerrero, Nicholas Gombert, Cristóbal de Morales and so on). Dedicated Carlophiles are fortunate that ensembles sometimes recreate the music performed for the emperor: for example, in October 2018, at Trinity College, Hartford (Connecticut), the Ensemble Origo performed a partial reconstruction of the music sung at Charles's coronation in Bologna on 24 February 1530.

VII. PRINTED PRIMARY SOURCES

The Belgian historian and archivist Louis Prosper Gachard, who published more documents about the emperor than anyone before or since, discerned only one chronological gap in the record: 'History only took an interest in [Charles] after he began to sparkle,' he complained in 1842:

> It would be intriguing to know just how a prince who would fill the world with the sound of his fame and his power was raised. Above all, it would be interesting to follow, step by step, the development of the mind that would, for almost half a century, exercise such a striking influence on the fate of Europe ... But unfortunately it does not seem that the sources survive.

For once, Gachard erred: in 2011, Anna Margarete Schlegelmilch published a 650-page study on precisely this subject, based on a dazzling range of sources in seven languages, entitled *The adolescence of Charles V: The cultural environment and education of a Burgundian prince*. Her meticulous multi-lingual research proved that material on Charles 'before he began to sparkle' has survived in prodigious quantities.[111]

For the rest of Charles's life, printed sources that include material from only one archive (AGS, ASV), or only one source (the Venetian *Relazioni*), are described above in the entries on individual archives; but some important publications include documents from many sources, notably:

I. SPAIN

CODOIN, a series of 112 volumes, contained many documents by or about Charles from Spanish archives (Laiglesia, *Estudios*, III, 61–73, listed them in alphabetical order). *CLC*, vols IV and V, published documents generated by the Cortes of Castile of Charles's reign (now available online: https://biblioteca-digital.jcyl.es/es/consulta/registro.cmd?id=16930). Facsimile editions of the last wills of Ferdinand the Catholic and Charles were published in 2016 and 1983 by J. M. Calderón Ortega, and by M. Fernández Álvarez and J. L. de la Peña, respectively.

Pride of place among printed sources published in Spain goes to *CDCV*. In 1956, Manuel Fernández Álvarez received the instruction: "Álvarez: the centenary of Charles V approaches and we need to do something." Ever since then,' Don Manuel recalled, 'I have committed myself to accumulating material on the emperor.'[112] Thanks to major research grants for foreign research, and a publication subsidy of 500,000 pesetas, the 2,800 pages of *CDCV* appeared in five volumes between 1973 and 1981, containing 825 documents (almost all published in their entirety) and a Spanish translation of the emperor's *Memoirs*, together with cumulative indexes.[113]

II. GERMANY

In 1893 the first volume of *Deutsche Reichstagsakten, jüngere Reihe. Deutsche Reichstagsakten unter Kaiser Karl V.* (*RTA*) appeared, containing a documentary history of the process by which Charles became king of the Romans (1516–July 1519). Vol. II (1896) covered the period from his election to the end of the Diet of Worms (July 1519–May 1521). Both volumes printed the relevant dispatches of foreign ambassadors as well as internal documents and, as Henry Cohn has noted, they 'invalidated everything written beforehand' – yet they have been little used by historians outside Germany.[114] Of the other assemblies over which Charles presided in person, *RTA* vol. X (1992; 1,602 pages in three parts) printed documents from the Regensburg Reichstag of 1532; vol. XV (2001; 2,404 pages in four parts) those from Speyer in 1544; vol. XVI (2003; 1,740 pages in two parts) those from Worms in 1545; vol. XVII (2006; 596 pages) those from Regensburg in 1546; vol. XVIII (2006; 2,760 pages in three parts) those from Augsburg in 1547–8; and vol. XIX (2005; 1,681 pages in three parts) those from Augsburg in 1550–1. Two volumes currently in preparation will cover the other Reichstage over which Charles presided: Augsburg in 1530 (IX) and Regensburg in 1541 (XIV). The lack of the former can be partially replaced by the sources printed by Förstemann, *Urkundenbuch*. Von Druffel and Brandi, *Briefe und Akten*, vols II–IV, published many documents concerning the Reichstag of 1546–55.

Kohler, *Quellen*, printed 120 important documents about Charles, all translated into modern German. The majority came from printed primary and secondary sources (see the list at pp. XV–XXII). Few of the sources were originally in German, but # 10 is a fascinating exception: the accounts of Charles's 'Receiver-General in Germany' for 1520, recording the payments made on Charles's behalf to secure his election as king of the Romans.[115] Kohler quoted and discussed each document in his admirable biography, *Carlos V*.

In 2001 the Akademie der Wissenschaften und der Literatur in Mainz began to digitize its *Regesta Imperii* project, a chronological record of the activities of all popes and emperors down to 1558, in the form of abstracts ('Regesten': more than 130,000 are currently available). Since then it has added details on literature that cites or extends the Regesta, for example providing a detailed list of the contents of relevant edited volumes and collections of essays, with links to any contributions available online. Currently, over two million titles are available. See further details in http://www.regesta-imperii.de/en/research/ri-online.html#c958. For an example, see the description of Boone and Demoor, *Charles V in context*, with one chapter available online: http://opac.regesta-imperii.de/lang_en/anzeige.php?sammel werk=Charles+V+in+context.+The+making+of+a+European+identity&pk=973091

III. BELGIUM

Publications of sources from Charles's reign include six huge volumes that contain all the ordinances issued by his government (*Recueil des Ordinnances*) and a history based on (and often quoting) Belgium's local and central archives: Henne, *Histoire du règne de Charles-Quint en Belgique*, in ten volumes.

IV. ITALY

Shortly after Henne's history appeared, Giuseppe de Leva began to publish a similar study for Italy, reproducing material drawn from an impressive range of foreign as well as Italian archives and libraries down to 1552: *Storia documentata di Carlo V*, in five volumes.

VIII. SECONDARY LITERATURE

Thousands of biographies of Charles have appeared in at least a dozen languages, starting in the emperor's lifetime. Over 100 had appeared by 1600. In 1956, Royall Tyler opined that among all available studies 'pride of place' belonged to the biography published by Karl Brandi: *Kaiser Karl V. Werden und Schicksal einer Persönlichkeit und eines Weltreiches*, the first volume published in 1937 and soon translated into many languages. Brandi had started work on a biography of Charles in 1907, intending to complete the unfinished three-volume study by Hermann Baumgarten, but he later resolved to start from scratch and worked through primary and secondary sources for much of the next three decades. In 1941, Brandi published a companion volume, *Kaiser Karl V: Quellen und Erörterungen*, which described and often transcribed in part the sources cited on each page of the German version of his biography (supplemented by an article in *B&S*, XIX, 161–257, 'Aus den Kabinettsakten des Kaisers', which included some documents of outstanding importance that Brandi discovered after publishing his biography).[116] Some might criticize Brandi for devoting so much space to political and religious developments in Germany, and so little to economic and social issues, or for citing so few documents in the archives of Lille and those of Spain, but his biography – especially if one reads the two volumes together, as he intended – continues to occupy pride of place. It still sets the standard by which all other works about Charles should be judged.[117]

A spate of biographies appeared around 1958, the quatercentenary of Charles's death, together with sixty-seven papers delivered in various languages at four international conferences: Kohler, *Carlos V*, 403–4, provided full details. Another spate of studies of the emperor appeared around 2000, the quincentenary of his birth. Above all, the *Sociedad estatal para la conmemoración de los centenarios de Felipe II y Carlos V* sponsored five international conferences and six exhibitions in 2000, and published the corresponding proceedings (275 individual contributions) and catalogues, as well as numerous monographs and sources concerning Charles – a total of some 25,000 printed pages. Blockmans and Mout, *The world*, 1–11 and 337–47, provided full details. Belgium, too, celebrated the quincentenary: the 286-page report of the Flemish 'Charles V Commission' detailed the various activities concerning the emperor that it had supported in 2000, including a list of thirty-eight relevant publications.[118]

Chaunu and Escamilla, *Charles*, 1,133–60, provided an excellent survey of publications down to 2000, and subsequent publications can be tracked via three online resources: by typing 'Karl V' into the Online *Katalog der deutschen Nationalbibliothek*: https://portal.dnb.de/opac.htm?method=simpleSearch &query=118560093; by typing 'Carlos V', 'Karl V' and 'Charles-Quint' into Dialnet.unirioja.es; and by consulting the 'Carlos Quinto' portal on *Biblioteca Virtual Cervantes*.[119]

IX. THE ABSENTEES

In his excellent study of biographies and their obsessed authors, James Atlas observed: 'You could never get it all down. The story would always remain unfinished. It was a hazard of the trade . . . Biography, like [psychiatric] analysis, remains incomplete; the subject, like the patient, remains unknown.'[120] There are two types of unknown, however: those you are aware of, and the rest.

1. THE KNOWN UNKNOWNS

War has destroyed many of the documents written by, for or about Charles. The archives of the States of Brabant perished in 1695 when the French bombarded Brussels; advancing German troops destroyed those of Leuven and Ieper in 1914; retreating German troops burned those of Naples in 1943. Other documents perished in shipwrecks. In 1542, Charles apologized to an ambassador that he could not find some relevant papers because they were 'lost on the Algiers campaign' the previous year.[121] Worse, 'All the papers of the emperor and of the king our lord since the year 1540' until 1559, when Philip II sailed from the Netherlands back to Spain, perished when the ship carrying them foundered, and 'with them we lost an important source on past events'.[122] Another important loss – that of holograph messages from Charles to his brother – is known because shortly after his brother's death, Ferdinand ordered their entire correspondence since 1522 to be copied into special registers: HHStA *Hs. Blau* 595, 596/1–2 and 597/1–3. Although his archivists 'collated their copies with the original letters', they systematically omitted the emperor's holograph postscripts after the first few words, perhaps because Ferdinand considered them too sensitive. We know what Charles wrote with his own hand when the original of his letters also survives, but for the rest we know only that something – presumably something important – is missing.[123]

Many other surviving documents withhold their secrets from researchers, at least in part. Some made little sense even to contemporaries: Henry VIII's chief minister Thomas Cromwell once complained that the letters sent by an envoy at Charles's court were 'so obscure that hard itt was for any man to understand the same'. Even when the syntax is clear, the surviving documents are written in a bewildering variety of scripts, some of them all but impenetrable. One of the editors of *The family correspondence of Ferdinand I* observed wearily 'that in every generation of historians there should be someone who can edit the letters exchanged between Ferdinand I and his siblings, letters which are sometimes extremely difficult to decipher'. Charles himself was one of the worst offenders. His sister Marie sometimes reproached him for the illegibility of his letters: 'If I may say so, there were one or two words so badly written that I was not able to read them properly, and can't be sure I divined them correctly.'[124] (See Pls 8 and 9 for examples of Charles's challenging script in both Spanish and French documents.) But since the emperor expected all recipients to be able to read what he wrote, historians must persevere.

Many papers once legible have subsequently been damaged. Several volumes of the manuscripts collected by Sir Robert Cotton were burnt by fire before they reached the British Library, so that it is now impossible to read the outer parts of dispatches from many English diplomats at Charles's court; a volcanic eruption in Guatemala in 1541 unleashed flood waters that destroyed the colonial capital, including most documents, damaging the rest; and so on.

In addition, many documents were written in code for which no 'clear' text survives, either because the recipient was so familiar with it that they could cypher and decipher it in their head, or because the key has not survived. In 1516, Emperor Maximilian received at least one letter from his daughter 'which you cyphered with your own hand'; and a decade later Charles reassured his brother that 'I decoded myself what you wrote to me in your letter of 9 May' – two examples among many.[125] Gustave Bergenroth encountered some fifty different cyphers in Simancas alone, and carried out an 'immense labour, injurious to my health' trying to decode them until he stumbled on a box in the archive that contained numerous keys. Some were 'of use to me in deciphering page after page; others were useful only for reading a few lines'; but thanks to his labours, documents transcribed by or for Bergenroth can now be read in their entirety, whereas the originals in the archives contain extensive passages still in cypher. To tackle the rest, Stix, 'Die Geheimschriftenschlüssel', provided keys to twenty-four cyphers used by Charles's chancery (together with seven plates showing the cypher and decrypt).[126]

In some cases we know we lack some information only because a correspondent announced tantalizingly that a particular matter was too important or too sensitive to commit to paper. Thus Maximilian informed Margaret that he had 'explained our plans orally' to a special messenger who 'can advise you with greater secrecy and candour what we have decided to do'; Margaret told Cardinal Wolsey that her special envoy would explain her plans to him in person 'because these are matters better communicated orally than in writing'; and Charles's regent in Spain likewise communicated sensitive information via trusted messengers because 'affairs here are much worse than I can express in my letters'.[127] Charles likewise sometimes insisted on handling sensitive business orally. In 1528 he informed the count of Haro that 'it is necessary for you to come here so that I can tell you some important matters concerning my service' (almost certainly to appoint and instruct the count as guardian of the French princes held as hostages). Two decades later he told his brother that 'The importance of this matter makes it more than necessary that we discuss it together in person … It cannot be handled by third parties or in writing.' He envisaged 'talking together for four or five days'. (The 'matter' was making war on the German Lutherans.)[128]

Finally, although Charles himself committed an extraordinary amount to paper, he also sometimes took steps to conceal matters of state. In 1515 he sent his preceptor, Adrian of Utrecht, from Brussels 'to Spain to see the king of Aragon *about some important secret affairs that do not need to be explained*'. The same phrase appears frequently in the records of his Netherlands government throughout his reign: forty years later, his treasurer in Brussels paid a minister £500 'for some important matters concerning His Majesty's service *that need not be specified*', and another received £50 'to be distributed by him on some secret matters *that His Majesty does not wish to be specified*'.[129] Charles also sometimes ordered the destruction of sensitive papers. In 1536, when war with France seemed imminent, he instructed his ambassador at the French court to 'burn the minutes and other papers in your possession that should not be seen'. Seven years later, he prefaced the secret advice sent to his son Philip on the eve of another war with France: 'I am writing and sending you this secret document which will be for you alone. You must therefore keep it secret, under lock and key where neither your wife nor any other living person can see it.' The emperor repeated his stern admonition at the end: 'Because we are all mortal, if God were to call you to His side, be certain to put it in a place where it will be returned to me under seal, or have it burned in your presence.'[130]

2. THE UNKNOWN UNKNOWNS

Historians are fortunate that the instructions of 1543 were not burnt, because the emperor composed them alone and made no copies. Some other 'secret matters that His Majesty does not wish to be specified' can be recovered with a measure of luck and ingenuity, because normally secretaries kept a draft, copy or minute of outgoing letters, or else sent duplicates or even triplicates, of which at least one copy survives. Nevertheless, some gaps will inevitably remain unknown. The registers of Charles's private expenditure (p. 576 above) illuminate the problem: we know that the register covering 1530–2 once existed, because although now lost it was inventoried in the nineteenth century, but other volumes may have covered the period before 1530 and after 1532 and have since disappeared without trace. Historians do not know.

The problem of the 'unknown unknowns' is particularly serious for political and military history, as Robert Caro found when composing his monumental biography of the US President Lyndon B. Johnson. Caro began work in 1975, two years after his subject's death, when 'most of his contemporaries were still alive' and available for interview. This proved a vital asset. Although written sources about the thirty-sixth president have survived on a scale that awes biographers of Charles V (the Johnson Library and Museum in Austin, Texas, contains 34,000,000 documents), they still leave many things obscure; but Caro could and did consult those who had known Johnson personally, 'and when the meaning of documents in the Library was not clear, they often made it clear'. But this led to other frustrations, because Caro soon found that not all interviewees were equal. 'You don't really know how power is being used until years later,' he complained, when 'people are more willing to talk in interviews. Then you go back and you see what was really happening.'[131]

In the case of Charles V, this is not an option – although Vicente de Cadenas y Vicent made a gallant attempt in his *Interviews with Emperor Charles V*. Having published many sources concerning his subject, Cadenas y Vicent used his knowledge to ask more than a thousand searching questions, together with an answer (usually brief) from 'the emperor', followed by references and excerpts from actual documents as supporting evidence. Although Cadenas y Vicent emphasized that he offered only 'entertainment', his questions pinpointed many issues to which every biographer of the emperor longs for answers. Unfortunately for historians, since an impeccable source observed Charles's soul in transit between Purgatory and Paradise in 1562, some of the unknowns are likely to remain unknown.[132]

NOTES

PREFACE

1. Dixon, 'Charles V', 105–6 (Dixon also claimed – incorrectly – that the emperor 'left no personal reflections'); Kleinschmidt, *Charles*, xv.
2. Brandi, *The emperor*, 16; Chabod, *Carlos V*, 128 (from a lecture course originally delivered in 1938–9); Braudel, 'Charles-Quint', 205; Blockmans, *Emperor*, 1–2. Note the distinguished lineage: Brandi helped Chabod with his research (Chabod, *Lo stato*, Prefazione); Chabod aided Braudel; Braudel inspired Blockmans.
3. I thank Claudia Möller Recondo and Alain Servantie for help in calculating the emperor's movements. See also the table showing where Charles spent his days in Anatra, 'Itinerarios', and the diagram in Vilar Sánchez, *Carlos V*, 401.
4. AGNM *Mercedes* I and II (now *Signaturas servibles* 15792 and 15793), counting each 'expediente' as a *cédula*; Ruiz Medrano, *Mexico's indigenous communities*, 112 (reinforced by a conversation with Lidia Gómez García in Mexico in 2015 about Charles's 'divinity').
5. Dolce, *Le vite*, f. 525v, claimed that *El cortesano* was one of the few books that Charles read thoroughly; and in 1533 the emperor signed a privilege to print a Spanish translation. In 1516, Erasmus, *The education*, dedicated to Charles, had made the same point: 'Whenever [the prince] goes out, he should take care that his face, his bearing, above all his speech are such that they will set his people an example, bearing in mind that whatever he says or does will be seen by all and known to all' (99).
6. Lutz, 'Karl V', 181; ASF *MdP* 4301/179, Ricasoli to Duke Cosimo of Florence, from the imperial camp, 30 Aug. 1543. See also Firpo, *Relazioni*, II, 465–6, Relation of Bernardo Navagero, Venetian ambassador, July 1546: Charles 'cannot conceal the pleasure he takes in war. He is happy then, he comes alive.'
7. *Plutarch's Lives*, II, 139, translated by John Dryden.
8. Ball and Parker, *Cómo ser rey*, 130, Charles's secret instruction to Prince Philip, 6 May 1543.
9. De Reiffenberg, *Lettres*, 28–33, van Male to Louis de Praet, 11 Nov. 1552, Latin.
10. For the paper trail created by one imperial visit, consider the sources generated during the three days that Charles spent in Aigues Mortes in 1538 deployed by Le Person, 'A moment of "resverie"' – and multiply them by 1,000.
11. Nicolson and Trautmann, *The letters of Virginia Woolf*, VI, 225–6, Woolf to Vita Sackville-West, 3 May 1938 (Woolf had been commissioned to write a biography of the artist and art critic Roger Fry).
12. BNE *Ms.* 5578/77–99v, 'Méthodo para escribir la Historia por Dr Juan Páez de Castro, chronista de el emperador Carlos V, a quien le dirige', copy. The original, once in BSLE, seems to have disappeared. Esteban, 'De las cosas', printed a flawed transcription of this manuscript, then BNE *Ms.* Q-18. De Courcelles, *Escribir*, 316–28, claimed to provide a new transcription of the document, but still used the discontinued call-number 'Q-18' and included exactly the same errors as Esteban. Although the document is undated, a letter written by Páez de Castro in Brussels dated 12 July 1556 described 'what I need to write in my history': Domingo Malvadi, *Bibliofilia*, 430–1. Presumably by then Páez de Castro had submitted his outline to Charles, who was still in the Netherlands.
13. Pérez de Tudela Bueso, *Documentos*, II, 544–7, Pedro de La Gasca to a cabildo in Peru (Arica?), 28 Sep. 1549.
14. Smith, *Erasmus*, 34–5; Bataillon, 'Charles-Quint', 91.
15. BNE *Ms.* 5578/87v–88, 'Méthodo para escribir la Historia'. For two modern studies on Páez de Castro, see Domingo Malvadi, *Bibliofilia*, and von Ostenfeld-Suske, 'Juan Páez'.

16. Sanuto, *I diarii*, LV, cols 68–9, copy of a letter from Brussels, 7 Oct. 1531; *SLID*, II, 136 (Hernando del Corral); Neefe, *Tafel-Reden*, 2–3, relating Ferdinand's conversations with his doctor in 1563–4.
17. *CDCV*, III, 667, Charles to Philip, 13 Mar. 1554.
18. Clark, *The sleepwalkers*, xxix–xxx. I thank Mary Sarotte for bringing this passage to my attention.
19. GRM, I, 405–7, Luis Quijada to Juan Vázquez de Molina, 26 Sep. 1558 (five days after Charles's death); AGS *E* 874/17–18, Juan de Vega, imperial ambassador in Rome, to Charles, 19 Feb. 1547; von Ranke, *Deutsche Geschichte*, V, 366–70, Charles de Marillac's report on his embassy, 1550.
20. Cartwright, *Gustave Bergenroth*, 153–5, Bergenroth to David Douglas, 1 Aug. 1866; Brandi, *The emperor*, 644.

NOTE ON CONVENTIONS

1. In *CSPSp*, V/1, viii, Gayangos incorrectly asserted that Antoine Perrenin, Charles's secretary of state (1525–38), was in fact Antoine Perrenot de Granvelle, and throughout the *Calendars* that he edited he incorrectly attributed to the latter several letters written to or by the former.
2. Scribner, *The German Reformation*, 2–4, provided a helpful overview of the changing meaning of the terms 'Protestant' and 'Reformation'. He argued that Ranke was the first to use the latter term in its current broad sense, but this ignores John Knox, who between 1559 and 1571 composed a work entitled *The history of the Reformatioun of Religioun within the realme of Scotland* in defence of 'the Protestants of the Realm': Knox, *History*, Preface. For an example of Charles using the terms 'protestans', 'lutheriens' and 'les desuoyez de la foy' interchangeably in the same letter see *LCK*, II, 486–91, Charles to Marie, 9 June 1546.

CHAPTER 1: FROM DUKE OF LUXEMBURG TO PRINCE OF CASTILE, 1500–8

1. Mexía, *Historia*, 4–5 (stating that he was writing in 1548). Hieronymus Gelweiler, a Humanist from Alsace, and Pietro Mareno, a papal notary, both affirmed Charles's descent from Noah; Ludovico Ariosto, a best-selling Italian poet, traced it back to Hector of Troy; Fray Prudencio de Sandoval began his biography of Charles with a genealogy going back 119 generations to Adam: Burke, 'Presenting', 418.
2. A verse based on Ovid, *Heroides*, XII, 84 ('Bella gerant alii: Protesilaus amet'), attributed to Matthias Corvinus, king of Hungary, in the 1480s.
3. Ball and Parker, *Cómo ser rey*, 154, Charles's instructions to Philip, 6 May 1543. Weber, 'Zur Heiratspolitik Karls V', remains the best analysis of how the emperor pursued matrimonial imperialism particularly towards France.
4. AGS *E K* 1482/14, Maximilian to Catholic Monarchs, 23 June 1495. On the broader context, see Angermeier, 'Der Wormser Reichstag 1495'. Cauchies and van Eeckenrode, '"Recevoir madame l'archiduchesse"', 263–6, provided the best guide to the complex antecedents of the double Spanish marriage. Kohler, *Carlos V*, 28, noted that Maximilian had only two legitimate children, and so marrying both of them into the House of Trastámara exhausted his options.
5. ADN *B* 2165/205, payment to 'une saige femme de la ville de Lille nommée Ysabeau', Sep. 1499; ADN *B* 2169/58v and 136v, payments to George de Dôle, who left Ghent on 1 Feb. 1500 'à extrême diligence', and to 'deux religieux de l'abbaye d'Anchin' who brought the ring to 'la ville de Gand où ilz avoient séjourné par l'espace de quinze jours entiers, actendant la délivrance de madicte dame'. The 2001 movie *Juana la Loca* (*Mad Love*) – hailed by one critic as a 'bodice-ripper for intellectuals' – includes a spectacular recreation of Charles's birth in a privy, but Schlegelmilch, *Die Jugendjahre*, 22 n. 15, dismisses the story as baseless gossip. Pity.
6. Van Salenson, *Die warachtige geschiedenisse*, sig. B, poem by Lieven Bautkin, stanza 2 (Bautkin wrote 'een *paeyeselick* prince', which meant both peace, *paix*, and Easter, *paas*); AGRB *Gachard*, 611, unfol., Philip to the city of Ieper, 24 Feb. 1500. Tondat, 'De Geboorteplaats', claimed that Charles was born in the town of Eeklo, 20 km from Ghent, but the numerous orders signed by Philip in Ghent in the course of Feb. 1500, as well as sources like Bautkin, rule this out.
7. ADN *B* 2169/62v–63, payment to Gillart Michiel, *chevaucheur*, dispatched on 25 Feb. 1500; Gachard, *Lettres inédites de Maximilien*, I, 105 n., Maximilian's reply to Margaret, undated but March 1500 (dispute about the name); Rodríguez Villa, *Juana la Loca*, 43–5, Villaescusa to the Catholic Monarchs, 28 Mar. 1500 (arguments about the title).
8. Zurita, *Historia*, IV, iii, expanding on the anecdote recorded in the *Anales* of Isabella's councillor, Lorenzo Galíndez de Carvajal (*CODOIN*, XVIII, 297; the queen referred to Matthew: 9:9); Gachard, *Lettres inédites de Maximilien*, I, 105 n.
9. Strøm-Olsen, 'Dynastic ritual', 36.

10. AGRB *Audience* 22/133–5, warrant of Archduke Philip, 1 Feb. 1500, in Spanish (an unusual circumstance in the records of the Burgundian household).

11. Blockmans, 'Autocratie ou Polyarchie?', 282 n. 1, council of regency to Maximilian, 15 Oct. 1483. Ghent had also rebelled against Duke Philip the Bold in the 1450s and would do so against Charles V in 1539–40.

12. Finot, *Inventaire Sommaire*, VII, xcvii–xcviii, Philip's Household Ordinance, 2 Mar. 1497. No formal act of emancipation seems to exist for Philip, but Cauchies, *Philippe*, 84–6, argues plausibly that his minority ended in July 1493, just after his fifteenth birthday, when he started to sign documents in his own name, albeit remaining Maximilian's 'procurator' until 1495.

13. Firpo, *Relazioni*, VIII, 33, Quirino's closing Relation, 1506; Berwick y Alba, *Correspondencia*, 332, Fuensalida to Ferdinand of Aragon, 5 Mar. 1505; Cauchies, *Philippe*, 225, Maximilian to Philip, undated but Sep.–Dec. 1496; von Höfler, 'Depeschen', 147–8, 160–1 and 215–17, Quirino to the doge of Venice, 31 Aug. 1505, 21 Sep. 1505 and 15 May 1506.

14. La Marche, *Mémoires*, III, 315–17. (La Marche perpetrated a dreadful pun here, since 'Croÿ' ['Believe'] was the surname of two of Philip's leading councillors: Chimay and Chièvres.)

15. La Marche, *Mémoires*, I, 163, and III, 318. I follow Millar, 'Olivier', ch. 3, in dating the 'Introduction' to the *Mémoires* to 1488–91. Cauchies, '"Croit conseil" et ses "ministres"', named and discussed the cohort of councillors.

16. ADN *B* 2170 (72,017) and *B* 2171 (72,193), warrant of Philip dated 4 Aug. 1500 to pay Liberal Trevisan, 'conseiller et phisicien de monseigneur l'archiduc', and Trevisan's receipt dated 6 Aug. 1500.

17. *BKK*, II, 72, Charles to Marie of Hungary, 24 Dec. 1540 (support for Barbe's son); van der Elst, *Basilicae Bruxellensis*, II, 43 (Barbe's epitaph); Rodríguez Villa, *Juana la Loca*, 43–5, Villaescusa to the Catholic Monarchs, 28 Mar. 1500 (Barbe's origins).

18. Berwick y Alba, *Correspondencia*, 138, 182 and 190, Fuensalida to the Catholic Monarchs, 4 Aug. 1500, and 22 Mar. and 27 Aug. 1501.

19. ADN *B* 2169/149, payment by Philip of £123 to the special messenger from Spain; Cauchies, '"No tyenen"', 121, Philip to the Catholic Monarchs, 11 Aug. 1500.

20. Berwick y Alba, *Correspondencia*, 181, Fuensalida to the Catholic Monarchs, 22 Mar. 1501. Historians disagree about the date of the archduke's departure, but ADN *B* 2177/1v, the first account of Simon Longin as 'Maître de la chambre aux deniers' for Charles and his sisters, stated that on 31 Oct. 1501 their parents 'partirent au matin de la ville de Malines ou ilz laissèrent messeigneurs ses enffants'.

21. Rodríguez-Salgado, 'Charles V and the dynasty', 28.

22. Berwick y Alba, *Correspondencia*, 203, 259, 265 and 300, Fuensalida and colleagues to the Catholic Monarchs, 19 Jan., 15 July, 16 Aug. and 1 Nov. 1504. For an evaluation of Joanna's behaviour at this time, see Aram, *Juana*, ch. 3.

23. Berwick y Alba, *Correspondencia*, 286–7, Ferdinand to Fuensalida, 26 Sep. 1504 (the king repeated the warning on 15 Oct., promising to send news 'with a courier who can fly' should his wife die: ibid., 292); ibid., 314, Fuensalida to Ferdinand, 3 Dec. 1504; BRB *Mss.* 7386–94/17v, 'La nouvelle d'icelle mort vint à Monseigneur l'Archiduc en sa ville d'Anvers le 11 décembre [1504]'. On Philip's tempestuous relations with Charles of Guelders, including the duke's broken promise to accompany Philip to Spain, see Struick, *Gelre*, 58–76.

24. ADN *B* 2191/355, 359–60, 370v–371, 380–1 and 393–4, Account of Receiver-General Longin for 1505, payments for decorating St Gudule for the funeral service, 14–15 Jan.; for the jousts held on 4 and 11 Sep.; and for 'three great banquets hosted in Brussels on 4, 7 and 11 Sep. 1505'; ADN *B* 2193 (74,099), warrant to pay for 'le deul de feue la royne despaigne' worn by Joanna and her children, 6 Jan. 1505; BRB *Mss.* 7386–94/17–25 and *Mss.* 16381–90/45–51, accounts of the funeral ceremony (splendidly described by Aram, *Juana*, 79–81).

25. ADN *B* 2181/42v–43 and 136, account of Receiver-General Longin for 1503, payments to 'the guardian of the two ostriches' and 'the guard of the *papegay*' that 'My Lord had sent from Spain', and for constructing and heating 'a large cage for the *papegay*'; ADN *B* 2189 (73,620), payment for the 'guard and food for four camels and two pelicans that my lord had brought from Spain', 3 Jan. 1504; AGRB *Audience* 22/186–187v, payments to the guard for the 'papegay, de l'ostriche, et des gélines d'inde', 1504; ADN *B* 2193 (74,065), payment 'pour ramener les bestes et oiseaux d'Espagne à Bruxelles', 28 Aug. 1505; ADN *B* 3462 (121,649), warrant to pay for the ironwork required 'pour le cheval que le roy des Romains donna au prince, et aussi faire regarnir le cheval que le Comte Palatine donna au prince', 30 Sep. 1505. Other details from Vera y Figueroa, *Epítome*, 21–2. In 1521, Albrecht Dürer visited the royal lions in Ghent and sketched them: Dürer, *Diary*, 87 and plates 18–19. In 1549 an Italian visitor to Mechelen admired 'l'ucello già di Massimiliano imperatore ... col becco largo e lungo' (thus a pelican): Brizio, '"The country"', 77.

26. ADN B 2195 (74,346), receipt for £100 signed by Anchieta, 'Maistre d'escole de monseigneur le prince de Castille et de mesdames Lyénor et Isabeau', 26 Sep. 1505; ADN B 2181/124v–5 and 135, payments to Martin Bourgeois, Apr. 1503, and to Jehan Loupez, Dec. 1503; Berwick y Alba, *Correspondencia*, 309, Fuensalida to the Catholic Monarchs, 18 Nov. 1504. See also Schilling, 'L'education', 5–6, and Gonzalo Sánchez-Molero, *El César*, 41–2.

27. RAH *Salazar* A-10/35 (formerly f. 42), Charles to Ferdinand, Jan. 1504, discussed in Rassow, 'La primera firma'. Charles did not forget his first tutor: in 1519, at Barcelona, he granted a generous salary for life to Anchieta, who had become a prolific composer (see details of his life and compositions in Preciado, *Juan de Anchieta*).

28. Mártir de Anglería, *Epistolario*, III, 101–2 (# 515), letter to Luis Hurtado de Mendoza, 13 Jan. 1513 (on Vaca); ADN B 3462 (121,649), payment of £5 10s to 'un escraignier de Malines qui a fait bancq atout des armoyres et une table pour aller le prince et mesdames ses soeurs à l'escolle', 30 Sep. 1505.

29. Chmel, *Urkunden*, 253, Chimay to Maximilian, 9 Sep. 1506 (responding to the emperor's insistence 'qu'il apprendra le Brabanchon'); ADN B 3462 (121,621), payment to Evrard Sparcke for 'plusieurs drogheries, médecines et autres espiceries . . . pour mesdits seigneur et dames durant leur maladies', 31 July 1505; and ADN B 2195 (74,333), receipt signed by Jacques de Rubbe, 'maistre cururgien', 12 Sep. 1505. On Charles's subsequent ability to speak Dutch, see p. 377 below.

30. Von Höfler, 'Depeschen', 112, Quirino to the doge of Venice, Cleves, 8 June 1505; ADN B 2193 (74,137), appointment of Chimay as 'gouverneur et premier chambellan de nostredit filz le prince', 13 Oct. 1505; Gachard, *Voyages*, I, 461 ('Deuxième voyage', written by a member of Philip's entourage) and 491–3, Philip's commission to Chièvres as lieutenant-general, 26 Dec. 1505.

31. Cauchies, *Philippe*, 265–7, testament of Philip, Bruges, 26 Dec. 1505. At that time Philip had only two sons, Charles and Ferdinand, but the phrasing of his will left open the possibility of a multiple partition if he sired more.

32. Berwick y Alba, *Correspondencia*, 461, Fuensalida to Ferdinand of Aragon, London, 5 July 1508, reporting a long audience with the English king; Firpo, *Relazioni*, VIII, 34, Relation of Vicenzo Quirino, 1506.

33. Gachard, *Voyages*, I, 452–3, 'Deuxième voyage'; Fagel, 'Un heredero', 118.

34. Chmel, *Urkunden*, 257, Berghes to Maximilian, 5 Oct. 1506.

35. Ibid., 258–60, council to Maximilian, Mechelen, 7 Oct. 1506.

36. Gachard, *Voyages*, I, 455, 'Deuxième voyage'. Fagel, 'Un heredero', 121–2, analyses the pro-French and pro-English factions that had developed during Maximilian's regency.

37. Laurent, *Recueil*, I, 4, Maximilian to the council, 27 Oct. 1506, his first orders after receiving news of Philip's death.

38. Ibid., I, 8–9, Maximilian's letters patent, 18 Mar. 1507.

39. Chmel, *Urkunden*, 253 and 260–7, Chimay to Maximilian, Mechelen, 9 Sep. and 7 Oct. 1506; AHN Nobleza *Frías* 22/91, Charles to the count of Oropesa, 7 Feb. 1508.

40. Lemaire des Belges, *Chronique*, 49.

41. ADN B 3510 (123,922), warrant signed by Margaret, 10 July 1507 (discussed in Wijsman, 'Philippe le Beau', 62–5, who tentatively identified the volume as BSLE Vitrina 14); Lemaire des Belges, *Chronique*, 113, 127, 129.

42. Lemaire des Belges, *Chronique*, 129, 131.

43. Cauchies, *Jean Lemaire des Belges, Le carnet*, 55–6.

44. ADN B 18,862 (31,117), Margaret to Thomas Boleyn, undated but spring 1513. See also *HMC, 15th Report, Appendix, Part II*, 30, Boleyn to Margaret, 14 Aug. 1514, asking her to return 'ma fille, la petite Boulain'; and Paget, 'The youth'.

45. Dürer, *Diary*, 95–6 (entry for 6 June 1521).

46. Checa Cremades, *Inventarios*, III, 2391 ('Il a necessité d'y mettre une serrure pour le fermer, ce que madame a ordonné faire'); and Eichberger, 'Margaret of Austria', 2353. Eichberger, 'A noble residence', provided a vivid reconstruction of the Hotel de Savoy (or Hof van Savoy) opposite the Keizershof (or Hotel de Bourgogne). Strelka, *Der burgundische Renaissancehof*, described the cultural ambience of Margaret's court and its influence. When in 1535 and again in 1548, Charles organized the household of his son, he chose the solemn Burgundian style that Margaret had perfected at Mechelen.

47. Van den Bergh, *Correspondance*, II, 87–8, Charles to Margaret, 6 Oct. 1513; *BKK*, II, 75–6, Eleanor to Margaret, undated; Altmeyer, *Isabelle d'Autriche*, 43, Isabeau to Margaret, 7 Aug. 1515.

48. Bruchet and Lancien, *L'itinéraire*, 336, Margaret to Maximilian, 1507 (Witte would remain Eleanor's confessor until his death in 1540: Moeller, *Éléonore*, 182–3); ibid., 348, Margaret to Chièvres, Sep. 1511; and 365, Margaret to Mary Tudor, sister of Henry VIII, 23 Feb. 1514 (and not to Marie of

Hungary, as stated in van den Bergh, *Correspondance*, II, 88–9). See also Mary Tudor's reply to 'Ma bonne tante' in Sadlack, *The French queen's letters*, 163–4 (the date must therefore be 13 Apr. 1514).

49. Bruchet and Lancien, *L'itinéraire*, 375, Margaret to Marie of Hungary, Feb. 1518; Jordan Gschwend, 'Ma meilleure sœur', 2,569.

50. Gachard, 'Particularités', II, 129, Remonstrance of Chimay to Maximilian, 28 Sep. 1508, article 1 (date from Gachard, 'Notice des archives de M. le duc de Caraman', 202); *LGC*, I, 129–30 and 172, Maximilian to Margaret, 27 Apr. and 30 July 1509.

51. *LGC*, I, 202–3, 424–5, and II, 260, Margaret to Maximilian, 29 Oct. 1509, 16 June 1514, and late July 1510.

52. Gachard and Piot, *Collection*, I, 461, from the 'Relation' of Philip's second journey to Spain, probably written by Philippe Dale, master of the king's household, in 1507; BNF *Ms. Esp.* 318/24, Charles to Ferdinand of Aragon, 26 Oct. 1508; BL *Cott. Ms.* Galba B/III f.109, Charles to Mary Tudor, 18 Dec. 1508 (here plate 3). For another example of Charles's abysmal writing from the same year, see his holograph postscript to AHN Nobleza *Frías* 22/91, Charles to the count of Oropesa, 7 Feb. 1508. By contrast, BNE *Ms.* 20210/14/4, Charles to Ferdinand, 12 June 1510, with a holograph salutation and signature, showed some improvement in his calligraphy.

53. *CMH*, I, 384–9, Marie to Charles, 3 Aug. 1532, holograph minute; Pardanaud, 'Plaider', 197.

54. ADN *B* 2185/162, account of Receiver-General Longin for 1504, payment to 'Frère Erasme, Rotterdamensis, religieulx de l'ordre de Saint-Augustin', Oct. 1504; *CWE*, II, 77–9 (# 179), Erasmus to Nicholas Ruistre, Feb. 1504. Erasmus, *The education*, 111–45, printed extracts from the *Panegyric* in English translation. Mesnard, 'L'expérience politique', 47–8, noted that Erasmus revised and republished this work, showing that he valued it highly.

55. ADN *B* 2185/227v–8 and 230v, account of Receiver-General Longin for 1504 (payments to the bookbinder and Bosch); and ADN *B* 2191/294v and 297, account of Longin for 1505 (payments for the music, the acrobat and the nude painting).

56. Gairdner, *Letters*, I, 301–3, Maximilian to Henry VII, 14 Sep. 1506; Gairdner, 'The "Spouselles"', 15 and 31 (on pp. xi–xii, Gairdner convincingly proved that Charles's letter, dated 1513 in *L&P Henry VIII*, I. ii, 1108, and here plate 3, was in fact written in 1508); ADN *B* 3351, letters patent dated 27 Feb. 1509. Cauchies, *Philippe*, 144–51, provides an excellent overview of the early marriage negotiations concerning Charles; Sadlack, *The French queen's letters*, 28–30 and 44–8, presented Mary's side of the story.

57. Cauchies, *Jean Lemaire des Belges, Le carnet*, 63–4 ('l'empereur joua ledit jour les joustes') and 99 (Margaret, Charles and his sisters watched 'den steeckspele op den merct' on 18 Feb. 1509).

58. Laurent, *Recueil*, I, 79–81, letters patent of Maximilian, 18 Mar. 1509; Wiesflecker-Friedhuber, *Quellen*, 172–5, Zyprian von Sernstein to Paul von Liechtenstein, 3 Apr. 1509; Walther, *Die burgundischen Zentralbehörden*, 93, Jean Marnix to Margaret, 9 June 1508.

59. Pirenne, *Histoire*, III, 74; *LGC*, II, 431 n., undated draft (in the hand of Gattinara) of the powers sought by Margaret, and idem, I, 122–5, Maximilian to Margaret, undated holograph but Apr. 1508 and apparently a response to Gattinara's draft). The emperor's French (not his native language) is particularly challenging in this letter: 'i me semble, veu que je suis mainbour et grand-père de mes enfans, que je retieng quelque chose avecq vous, pour vous gouverner, et pour nostre reputation'.

60. Kreiten, *Der Briefwechsel*, 246–8, Margaret to Maximilian, undated holograph (but early 1508); ADN *B* 2211 (75,365), warrant to pay Chimay £8,000 because Chièvres now serves as 'premier chambellan', 27 Apr. 1509; ADN *B* 2210/398, matching bed accessories purchased in Nov. 1509; *PEG*, I, 92, Charles to Cisneros and Adrian, 7 Sep. 1517.

61. Walther, *Die burgundischen Zentralbehörden*, 93, Jean Marnix to Margaret, 9 June 1508; Reiffenberg, *Histoire de l'Ordre*, 279–80, minutes of a meeting of the knights, 22 Nov. 1508; Gossart, *Charles-Quint et Philippe*, VIII and 48–9, 'Règlement de la maison du future roi d'Austrasie' (undated but mid-Dec. 1510).

62. BNE *Ms.* 20212/67/1, Margaret to Ferdinand, 2 Aug. 1508.

CHAPTER 2: THE ORPHAN PRINCE, 1509–14

1. Michelet, *Histoire*, 146 ('Celle-ci est le vrai grand homme de la famille, et, selon moi, le fondateur de la maison d'Autriche').

2. Walther, *Die burgundischen Zentralbehörden*, 96, Maximilian to Margaret, Dec. 1510.

3. Bruchet and Lancien, *L'itinéraire*, 335 and 338, Margaret holograph memorandum, 1507, and Margaret to Maximilian, Apr. 1509.

4. *LGC*, I, 122–5 and II, 204–7, Maximilian to Margaret, Apr. 1508 and Aug. 1510, both holograph (dates from Walther, 'Review of Kreiten', 271).

5. Kreiten, *Der Briefwechsel*, 249–50, Maximilian to Margaret, 29 Apr. 1508, holograph (also published in van den Bergh, *Correspondance*, I, 98–9, with the wrong date and some misreadings of the text); *LGC*, I, 271–2 and 274–5, Margaret to Maximilian, 21 May 1510, and his reply 31 May 1510.

6. Boom, *Marguerite*, 100, Eleanor to Margaret, undated but during Maximilian's visit in 1508–9. Visits calculated from von Höfler, 'Depeschen', 137–8 and 142–4, Quirini to the doge of Venice, 11 and 24 Aug. 1505 (the first visit) and von Kraus, 'Itinerarium Maximilian I', and Foronda, *Viajes* (for the rest).

7. *LGC*, II, 12–14, 182–3, Maximilian to Margaret, 20 and 23 June 1512, and 23 July 1513; ADN *B* 2210/429, payment £86 'en comptant' to Maximilian and Charles, 24 Feb. 1509 ('largesse'); ADN *B* 3351/10–12v, account of Didier Boisot, treasurer of the household of Charles's sisters, payments for their trips with Maximilian in June 1512. Other details from Moeller, *Éléonore*, 64–5.

8. *LGC*, II, 13, Maximilian to Margaret, 22 June 1512, for the stag; Thomas, *Gesammelte Schriften*, I, 161–70 and II, 1602–7, for the martial toys, some of them on display in the Kunsthistorisches Museum, Vienna.

9. ADN *B* 2218/337, account of Receiver-General Micault for 1511, payment on Maximilian's order to Pierre Alamire (Pieter van den Hove), 'escripvain des livres de la chappelle domestique de monseigneur' and a noted composer, for 'deux gros livres de parchemin plains de messes de musique … donné à Madame de Savoye sa fille pour son nouvel an'.

10. Wiesflecker, *Kaiser Maximilian*, I, 389 ('völliger Burgunder'), and 228–47, 'Das burgundische Erlebnis'.

11. Ibid., III, 370, and IV, 414. See p. 410 below for Charles's complaint in 1548.

12. Wiesflecker, *Kaiser Maximilian*, II, 40–1 (the 'grosser Kriegsplan' of 1496); Walther, *Die Anfänge*, 218–19, Maximilian to Charles, Sep. 1513.

13. Silver, *Marketing Maximilian*, 3, reproduces a drawing of Joseph Grünpeck presenting a copy of the *Historia Friderici et Maximiliani* to his grandson, under the emperor's benevolent gaze. The beautifully illustrated manuscript prepared for Charles, with holograph notes by Maximilian, is today in HHStA *Hs. Blau* 9, Cod. 24; while the copy of *Theuerdank* that Maximilian gave him is at BSLE X-I-3.

14. *LGC*, II, 335–8 and 245, Maximilian to Margaret, 1 Jan. and 2 Mar. 1516 (dates from Walther, 'Review of Kreiten', 286).

15. Wiesflecker, *Kaiser Maximilian*, I, 176 notes 6–7, and V, 518 (trailing a pike in 1485, 1504 and 1505); Lhotsky, *Festschrift*, I, 77 (Aachen).

16. Gunn, *War*, 247, quoting a speech by Maximilian to the States-General of the Netherlands in 1499.

17. Boone, 'From cuckoo's egg', 90 (the citadel at Ghent); Wiesflecker, *Kaiser Maximilian I*, III, 229 (quoting *Der Weisskunig*) and V, 204 ('Finanzchaos').

18. Burke, 'Presenting', 411; Silver, *Marketing Maximilian*, 110. Charles never seems to have felt qualified to become pope like Maximilian: see *LGC*, II, 37–9, Maximilian to Margaret, 18 Sep. 1511 (date from Walther, 'Review of Kreiten'), a remarkable letter signed 'Maximilianus, futur pape'.

19. Maximilian, *Der Weisskunig*, 341 (ch. 47), 332 (ch. 26) and 348–9 (chs 62–9). All of Part II (chs 13 to 69) dealt with the appropriate education for a young ruler.

20. Maximilian, *Der Weisskunig*, 338–9 (ch. 40).

21. Chmel, *Urkunden*, 253, Chimay to Maximilian, 9 Sep. 1506; *LGC*, II, 176, Maximilian to Margaret, 7 July 1513. Maximilian practised what he preached: in 1498 he 'proposa fort élégamment, par l'espace de heure et demye, en lengaige thiois' to the States-General of the Netherlands (Molinet, *Chroniques*, V, 106). Schlegelmilch, *Die Jugendjahre*, 176–84, provided a good overview of young Charles's limited linguistic skills. For his later linguistic proficiency, see pp. 376–8 below.

22. BL *Cott. Ms.* Vespasian C.I/194, archbishop of Armagh and Lord Berners to Henry VIII, Zaragoza, 17 Sep. 1518; BL *Cott. Ms.* Vitellius B. XX/218, Tunstal to Henry VIII, decrypt, Feb. 1521; GRM, II, 414, Dr Mathys to Juan Vázquez, 30 May 1558.

23. *LGC*, I, 35–6 and II, 115–16, Margaret to Maximilian, Dec. 1507 and early 1514.

24. Gachard, *Correspondance de Charles*, p. XVII, Charles to his envoys in England, 21 Jan. 1522. See also Gonzalo Sánchez-Molero, *El César*, 39–40. Charles appointed his former tutor to a succession of lucrative dioceses, including Salamanca where in 1534 he paid Cabeza de Vaca a visit: see ch. 9 below.

25. Verweij, *De paus*, 5 (quotation); ADN *B* 3465 (# 121,766), list of all members of Charles's household, and their wages, on 4 Apr. 1512 ('Maistre Louis de Vacques' and 'Maistre Adrien Florency'). Other details from Stone, 'Adrian of Utrecht and the university'.

26. See Stone, 'Adrian of Utrecht as a moral theologian', and Schlegelmilch, *Die Jugendjahre*, 251–317, on Adrian; and Strelka, *Der burgundische Renaissancehof*, for other details on the Humanist network based on Mechelen.

27. Danvila, *Historia*, II, 624–9, Adrian to Charles, 4 Dec. 1520; ibid., III, 31–41, Adrian to Charles, 16 Jan. 1520; *LCK*, I, 60–2, Adrian to Charles, Zaragoza, 3 May 1522, holograph. Adrian's use of the word 'croy' while reproaching Charles's more gullible councillors was probably a pun aimed at the Francophile Guillaume de Croÿ, lord of Chièvres. Fagel, 'Adrian', 45, listed the surviving letters written by Adrian to Charles between June 1520 and June 1522; *LCK*, I, and Gachard, *Correspondance de Charles*, printed letters exchanged after Adrian became pope.

28. Danvila, *Historia*, I, 376–86, II, 515–16, and III, 31–41, and Gachard, *Correspondance de Charles*, 252–3, Adrian to Charles, 25 and 30 June 1520, 28 Nov. 1520, 16 Jan. 1521 and 17 Jan. 1522 (italics added): five examples among many. See also *LCK*, I, 58–62 Charles to Adrian, 7 Mar. 1522, holograph, a more cordial letter recalling the warnings about French perfidy that Adrian 'told me some time ago when I was your pupil [*estant vostre escolier*]'.

29. Snouckaert van Schouwenburg, *De republica*, 34; ADN B 2268 (# 79,071), 'Aucunes livres que le roy ordonne porter avec luy', part of an inventory of precious goods that Charles planned to take with him to Spain, 30 June 1517. *Inventaire Sommaire*, IV, 350–1, transcribed the titles (with some errors); Gonzalo Sánchez-Molero, *El César*, 74–7, and *Regia biblioteca*, I, 240–1, discussed the *Chroniques de Iherusalem abrégés*. Laurent Vital recorded that during the sea voyage 'aulcuns se mectoient à lire des chronicques' (Gachard, *Collection*, III, 69).

30. Huizinga, *Herfsttij*, 40–5. Wijsman, 'Philippe le Beau', 82–7, described the books taken to Spain by Philip; Debae, *La bibliothèque*, reconstructed Margaret's collection.

31. Chastellain, 'Chronique', 364–5 and 368–9 (written in 1468); *L'État de la Maison du duc Charles de Bourgogne, dit le hardi* (composed in 1474), in La Marche, *Mémoires*, IV, 1–94.

32. La Marche, *Le chevalier déliberé* – a bilingual edition.

33. Reiffenberg, *Lettres*, 15–16, Guillaume van Male to Louis de Praet, Augsburg, 13 Jan. 1551: 'Caesar maturat editionem libri, cui titulus erat gallicus, *Le chevalier déliberé*. Hunc per otium a se ipso traductum … ad numeros rithmi hispani … cum non solum linguam, sed et carmen et vocum significantiam mire expresserit'. The emperor charged Hernando de Acuña with completing and publishing his Spanish translation: *El cavallero determinado* (Antwerp, 1553), dedicated to Charles V. Speakman Sutch and Prescott, 'Translation as transformation', noted that the Spanish translation added the Catholic Monarchs, Philip I and Maximilian as rulers vanquished by Death. In the inventory post mortem of Charles at Yuste, the first entry in the books section was 'un libro de cavallero determinado en lengua françesa', and the fifth was the manuscript of the Spanish translation: Checa Cremades, *Inventarios*, I, 525. Checa Cremades, 'El caballero y la muerte' reproduced all 19 illustrations.

34. Powell, *The complete works*, I, 127, 'Note of remembraunce by Sir Thomas Wiat', Dec. 1538; Beltrán de Heredía, *Domingo de Soto*, 654–5, Soto to Charles, 25 Aug. 1552 (recalling something said while Soto served as imperial confessor, 1548–50).

35. Chabod, *Carlos V*, 12, with a plethora of telling examples at pp. 17–38.

36. March, *Niñez*, I, 227, Zúñiga to Charles V, 25 Aug. 1535.

37. Chytraeus, *Chronicon*, 561 (Latin) and 110 (German), paraphrasing the 'Aufzeichnungen' written down in 1556 by Matthias Gunderam, Cranach's cousin, printed in Lüdecke, *Lucas Cranach*, 84–8, used here. I thank Patrick Lenaghan for help in interpreting this passage. In 1609, Valentin Sternenboke included in his *Historia* a somewhat different account of the exchange, derived from Cranach's son (printed in Lüdecke, *Lucas Cranach*, 89–91). Alas the portrait once in Charles's apartment at Mechelen, done in Feb. or Mar. 1509, has disappeared.

38. Leti, *Vita del invitissimo imperadore*, I, 55; Maximilian, *Der Weisskunig*, 328 (ch. 20).

39. Illescas, *Segunda parte*, 196v–197.

40. *LGC*, I, 241–2, Maximilian to Margaret, 28 Feb. 1510 (date from Walther, 'Review of Kreiten', 271). ADN B 2224/342–3, records payments in June 1512 to the huntsmen who 'furled and unfurled' almost 100 metres of 'hunting nets when [Charles] went hunting with the emperor'.

41. Mártir de Anglería, *Epistolario*, III, 300–1, letter to the marquesses of Los Vélez and Mondéjar, 12 Feb. 1518; BL *Cott. Ms. Galba B III*, f. 36v, Wingfield, Young and Boleyn to Henry VIII, 29 June 1512; *LGC*, II, 155–6, Margaret to Maximilian, undated but 5 June 1514 (see Walther, 'Review of Kreiten', 282).

42. Moeller, *Éléonore*, 61–5, describes the annual calendar of court events; ADN B 2210/ 379 and 2224/430, accounts of Receiver-General Micault for 1509 and 1512 (New Year's largesse).

43. ADN B 2224/342–3, account of Receiver-General Micault for 1512.

44. ADN B 2210/398, payment in Nov. 1509 ('pour le petit narre fol'); Brodie, *L&P Henry VIII*, II/2, 1442 (from 'The king's book of payments', July 1509, signed by Henry VIII). In the 1540s, while Charles ate his Fools told jokes: see p. 391 below.

45. On 'Jehannin le paintre', see ADN B 2242/306, account of Receiver-General Micault for 1515. On Bredeniers, see ADN B 2218/107, B 2224/191v–2 and B 2227/169–70v, accounts of Micault for 1511,

1512 and 1513; ADN *B* 2250, quittances for 1515, italics added; and Burbure, 'Bredeniers', cols 922–3: ADN *B* 2222/126.

46. Bossuyt, 'Charles', 88–90 (on Margaret's songbook, now BRB *Ms.* 228, containing 58 compositions) and 132–3 (on *Mille regretz*, already known as 'La canción del emperador' by 1538). See also Ferer, *Music and ceremony*, 216–17. For performances of 'La canción del emperador' see https://www.youtube.com/watch?v=cWxDG-f8OQc (cornet) and https://www.youtube.com/watch?v=QYruB57dJ60 (vihuela).

47. BL *Cott. Ms.* Galba B III/33 and 35v, Wingfield and Young to Henry VIII, 19 and 27 June 1512 (summarized in Brodie, *L&P Henry VIII*, I/1, 572–5); *LGC*, II, 260–1 and 265, Margaret to Maximilian, 16, 20–21 and 25 June 1514 (dates from Walther, 'Review of Kreiten', 271).

48. Pleij, *De sneeuwpoppen van 1511*, described the remarkable ice sculptures; Dürer, *Diary*, 63 (entry for 27 Aug. 1520) and plate 75 (a sketch of 'der diergarten und dis lust hinden aws dem schloss' in Brussels.)

49. Brodie, *L&P Henry VIII*, I/2, 1046, payments for preparing pennants for Charles at the 'jousts royal' at Tournai; Ibid., 1053–4, Henry VIII's 'oblations' for 16 Oct. 1513 'with Lady Margaret and the prince of Castell'.

50. Brodie, *L&P Henry VIII*, I/2, 1047–8, Henry VIII to Pope Leo X, 12 Oct. 1513, and 1049–50, declaration of Henry, Lille, 15 Oct. 1513; Walther, *Die Anfänge*, 210–11, payment to the Count Palatine rehearsing the letters patent of Charles and Maximilian, 1 Feb. 1514. Walther, *Die Anfänge*, 117–19, and Fagel, 'Un heredero', 129–30, both discussed the new Household Ordinance, which came into effect on 19 Oct. 1513.

51. Brodie, *L&P Henry VIII*, I/2, 1080, Spinelly to Henry VIII, Ghent, 15 Nov. 1513.

52. BL *Cott. Ms.* Galba B.III/15, Dr William Knight to Cardinal Wolsey, Mechelen, 2 May 1514, holograph. Ferdinand of Aragon agreed, urging Maximilian to 'delay the marriage of the prince' and 'avoid uniting him with his wife prematurely': AGS *E* 635/11, Ferdinand to his ambassador at the imperial court, Apr. 1514, draft.

53. Walther, *Die Anfänge*, 233, Margaret's instructions to Louis Maroton, 6 July 1514. Details of Henry's preparations from Brodie, *L&P Henry VIII*, I/2, 1159–62 and 1194.

54. Details from Brodie, *L&P Henry VIII*, I/2, 1325, 1341 and 1351.

55. BL *Cott. Ms.* Galba B.III f. 218v, Wingfield to duke of Suffolk, Mechelen, 20 May 1514 (unfortunately, fire damage has rendered illegible several other passages of potential relevance).

56. *LGC*, I, 245–8 and 383, Maximilian to Margaret, 16 Mar. 1510 and 30 Apr. 1514.

57. Mártir de Anglería, *Epistolario*, III, 157–9 and 162–4 (# 539 and # 542), to Luis Hurtado de Mendoza, 2 June 1514 (early death of Prince John) and 13 Nov. 1514 (early death of Louis XII).

58. Le Glay, *Négociations*, I, 595, Philippe Dalles to Margaret, Paris, 3 Jan. 1515 (in the event, Charles would marry the princess of Portugal in 1526). Charles did not forget his humiliation: in 1530 he told a papal legate that 'he thought royal marriages rarely had the desired results' and cited 'my own case, since I was betrothed to the sister of the king of England when she was of marriageable age but I was not' (*NBD, 1. Ergänzungsband 1530–1531*, 132–9, Campeggio to Salviati, 23–24 Aug. 1530).

59. Walther, 'Review of Kreiten', 266, Margaret to Maximilian, [29] Nov. 1512, holograph (Margaret evidently had second thoughts about some of the protests, because she crossed them out); *LGC*, I, 504–7, same to same, [28] Mar. 1513 (date from Walther, 'Review of Kreiten').

60. Le Glay, *Négociations*, I, 550–2, Beersel to Margaret, 16 Sep. 1513.

61. Berwick y Alba, *Correspondencia*, 193–4, Fuensalida to the Catholic Monarchs, 27 Dec. 1503. For an important lesson imparted by Beersel to his illustrious pupil see p. 149 below.

62. Reiffenberg, *Histoire de l'Ordre*, 382–93, report of Laurent du Blioul, Greffier of the Order (using the Burgundian calendar, in which each year began at Easter, so the events he described took place between Jan. and Mar. 1514). Ibid., 300–2, the proceedings of the first chapter of the Order after Charles became its Sovereign, in Nov. 1516, show how he ensured the rehabilitation of Don Juan.

63. *CDCV*, IV, 486 (Charles's *Memoirs*); *LGC*, II, 234 and 247–50, Margaret to Maximilian, 14 Mar. and 28 Apr. 1514; Walther, *Die Anfänge*, 233, Margaret's instructions to Louis Maroton, 6 July 1514.

64. Laurent, *Recueil*, I, 307–8, letters patent of Maximilian, 23 Dec. 1514, referring to an earlier summons now lost.

65. GRM *Introduction*, 3 n. 1 (Charles's speech); BL *Cott. Ms.* Galba B.III/313–16v, Spinelly to Henry VIII, 29 Jan. 1515 (specifying that Chièvres promised Maximilian 100,000 florins 'for setting oute the prynce of tutela').

66. Keniston, *Memorias*, 50. Charles apparently kept the fragments of the seal, because an inventory of his goods in 1536 recorded 'Ung cachet de l'Empereur Maximilien, d'argent blancq, le quel est cassé et martellé' (Checa Cremades, *Inventarios*, I, 141). His own reign would end 40 years later with the same ritual in the same room.

CHAPTER 3: THE DIFFICULT INHERITANCE, 1515–17

1. Laurent, *Recueil*, I, 309, Charles to the Great Council of Mechelen, 8 Jan. 1515. Van den Bergh, *Correspondance*, II, 113–14, published an identical order to the council of Flanders: Charles must have signed similar orders to all other institutions in the Netherlands.

2. Gachard, *Voyages*, II, 55 (Vandenesse, 'Journal des voyages'); Du Puys, *La tryumphante entrée* (the 'encore' at p. 12). A lavish French manuscript of Du Puys's account, probably a presentation copy for Charles, is ÖNB Codex 2591. *De triumpe gedaen te Brugghe binner ter intreye van Caerle*, a copy of the Dutch text, published in Antwerp on 25 June 1515, is at KB, 225 G 11.

3. Laurent, *Recueil*, I, 378, Ordinance of Charles to the magistrates of Bruges, 13 Apr. 1515, beginning 'De par le prince' and ending 'Car tel est nostre plaisir'; Gachard, *Analectes*, V ('14ᵉ série'), 11, Charles to magistrates of Valenciennes, 13 Jan. 1515; and Gachard, *Analectes*, I ('2ᵉ série'), 50–2, appointment of Le Sauvage as 'Grand Chancelier', 17 Jan. 1515.

4. Laurent, *Recueil*, I, 337–8, order dated 28 Mar. 1515; Gachard, *Voyages*, II, 491–501, 'Ordonnance de Charles ... pour le gouvernement de sa maison', 25 Oct. 1515; Walther, *Die burgundischen Zentralbehörden*, 109 n. 1, Margaret to Maximilian, 1 Mar. 1515.

5. *LGC*, II, 284, Margaret to Maximilian, 28 Jan. 1515 (date from Walther, 'Review of Kreiten', 282); BL Cott. Ms. Galba B.III/ff. 319–26, Spinelly to Henry VIII, 6 Feb. 1515 (see also ff. 313–16v, Spinelly's letter of 29 Jan. 1515, reporting Margaret's lament that 'the besynes of the world hertofor hath so succedyd that she is compellyd to folow the opyneans of the Lord Chevers'.

6. *LGC*, II, 276–7, Margaret to Maximilian, 18 Mar. 1515; van den Bergh, *Correspondance*, II, 117–27, Mémoire of Margaret presented to Charles and his council, 20 Aug. 1515.

7. Walther, *Die Anfänge*, 238–9 and 135 n. 4, Maroton to Margaret, Innsbruck, 4 and 17 Feb. 1515, reporting conversations with the emperor.

8. Gachard, *Analectes*, I ('3ᵉ série'), 168–70, Charles's warrant to pay £150,000 to Maximilian for his expenses in defending the Netherlands during his minority and also 'pour consenter nostre émancipation', over and above the £50,000 'par an qu'il a et prend ordinairement de noz deniers de par deçà', Bruges, 7 May 1515; and Gachard, *Analectes*, V ('17ᵉ série'), 465–70, Charles warrant of 22 Nov. 1516.

9. Walther, *Die Anfänge*, 243, Maximilian to Margaret, holograph, May 1515 (italics added); van den Bergh, *Correspondance*, II, 133–6, same to same, 18 Jan. 1516.

10. Le Glay, *Négociations*, I, 593–6, Philippe Dalles to Margaret, Paris, 3 Jan. 1515.

11. Gachard, *Analectes*, I ('2ᵉ série'), 53–5, Charles's commission to Henry of Nassau and others, 19 Jan. 1515; Le Glay, *Négociations*, II, 2–8, instructions of the same date, 'ainsi conclu et ordonné par monseigneur en son conseil'; Verweij, *De paus*, 166–8, Charles to Nassau and others, 5 Mar. 1515.

12. TNA *SP* 1/10/49, Robert Wingfield to Henry VIII, Innsbruck, 7 Feb. 1515; *Ordonnances des rois de France. Règne de François Iᵉʳ*, I, 147–72, treaty of Paris, 24 Mar. 1515; Doussinague, *El testamento*, 432–3, Charles to Ferdinand, 15 May 1515.

13. *L&P Henry VIII*, II/1, 25–7, Suffolk to Henry VIII, early Feb. 1515, and 73–4, Suffolk to Wolsey, 5 Mar. 1515. Avoiding a resurrection of her engagement to Charles was apparently Mary's express intention: she claimed that 'she would rather to be torn in pieces' than 'married into Flanders': Sadlack, *The French queen's letters*, 102–3.

14. *L&P Henry VIII*, II/1, 447–51, Stile to Henry VIII, Madrid, 1 Mar. 1516. Zurita, *Los cinco libros*, f. 405, also noted that 'most of the grandees of Castile showed great satisfaction and joy' on hearing of Ferdinand's death.

15. Doussinague, *La política*, 483–511, stresses the strong crusading element in Ferdinand's foreign policy – an element that his grandson Charles would share.

16. AGS *PR* 56/27–2, 'Scriptura que otorgó el Rey don Felipe para no consentir que gobernase la reyna doña Juana', Benavente, 28 July 1506, original (AGS *PR* 56/27–1 is a copy of Ferdinand's version of the agreement, printed in Gachard, *Voyages*, I, 543–4). Gachard, *Voyages*, I, 438–43 (Deuxième voyage') stressed Philip's military superiority, and printed the terms of the public treaty.

17. AGS *PR* 56/30, Ferdinand's 'protesta', Villafáfila, 27 July 1506, original.

18. AGS *PR* 56/31, Ferdinand to an unknown correspondent, Aranda del Duero, 5 July 1506 (the day of the meeting), confirmed by von Höfler, 'Depeschen', 239, Quirini to the doge of Venice, 7 July 1506.

19. Zurita, *Los cinco libros*, f. 159. Martínez Millán, *La Corte*, I, 110–11, provides an astute analysis of the 'partido felipista'.

20. Von Höfler, 'Depeschen', 149–51 and 239–40, Quirini to the doge of Venice, 5 Sep. 1505 and 7 July 1506 (Quirini claimed that Cisneros, the only eyewitness, leaked to him what Ferdinand had told Philip at the secret 'raxonamenti'); Berwick y Alba, *Correspondencia*, 461–2, Fuensalida to Ferdinand, London, 5 July 1508, reporting on his audience with Henry VII.

21. *CSPSp Supplement I*, 143, Mosen Ferrer to Cisneros, 6 Mar. 1516. The phrase used was 'dar cuerda': Gustave Bergenroth, op. cit., xlii, argued that this meant putting Joanna on the rack, but thrashing her with a rope seems more plausible.

22. *CODOIN*, XVIII, 350, 'Anales' of Lorenzo Galíndez de Carvajal, reported that 'many believed' that the 'potion [*potaje*]' had killed Ferdinand.

23. Calderón Ortega, *Testamento*, published the different versions of Ferdinand's will; *CSPSp*, II, 118–21 and 185–8, Ferdinand's instructions to Pedro de Quintana, 21 May 1513, and to Juan de Lanuza, 20 Dec. 1513 (on partitioning the inheritance).

24. AGS *E* 1004/60, Chièvres to Ferdinand, 3 July 1515, French; RAH *Salazar* A-16/6, letters patent of Charles, 17 Sep. 1515, copy; ADN *B* 2249 (# 77,795) receipt signed by 'Adrien Florency, dit d'Utrecht' for his travel expenses, 1 Oct. 1515. Chièvres derived an additional advantage from sending Adrian to Spain: it separated pupil and teacher.

25. Mártir de Anglería, *Epistolario*, III, 211–13 (# 565), letter to the marquis of Mondéjar, Guadalupe, 22 Jan. 1515 (*recte* 1516), written just before Mártir de Anglería learned of Ferdinand's last testament and death. Leonardo de Argensola, *Primera parte*, 8–9, printed the terms.

26. Fagel, 'Adrian', 28, letter to Floris van Egmont, 13 Dec. 1515.

27. Calderón Ortega, *Testamento*, 36–8, last testament of Ferdinand of Aragon, 22 Jan. 1516. See *CODOIN*, XVIII, 342–51, 'Anales' of Lorenzo Galíndez de Carvajal, an eyewitness, on the animated discussions between Ferdinand and his advisers concerning his final dispositions. *L&P Henry VIII*, II/2, 447–51, John Stile to Henry VIII, Madrid, 1 Mar. 1516, accurately summarized these arrangements.

28. *CODOIN*, XVIII, 354–7, 'Anales' of Lorenzo Galíndez de Carvajal; Martínez Millán, *La Corte*, I, 100 and 158 on the coup d'état.

29. Gachard, *Analectes*, I, 177–8, Charles to the magistrates of Mechelen, 10 Feb. 1516; Spielman and Thomas, 'Quellen', 21–2, Charles to Ferdinand, 15 Feb. 1516.

30. Gachard, 'Mémoire', 30, Manrique to Cisneros, 8 Mar. 1516; Martínez Millán, *La Corte*, III, 256–7 (biography of Manrique); Keniston, *Memorias*, 42 (a list of over 50 exiles).

31. Keniston, *Memorias*, 78–9; *CODOIN*, XVIII, 368 n. 2, Charles to the Chancillería of Granada, Brussels, 21 Mar. 1516.

32. *CODOIN*, XVIII, 363–8, royal council to Charles, Madrid, 4 Mar. 1516.

33. Gayangos and La Fuente, *Cartas*, 109, Cisneros to López de Ayala, 12 Apr. 1516 (describing the standard-raising ceremony in Toledo and Madrid); *L&P Henry VIII*, II/1, 486–8, John Stile to Henry VIII, 3 Apr. 1516. Other details from Aram, *Juana*.

34. BL *Cott. Ms.* Galba B. VI/27–28v, Spinelly to Henry VIII, Brussels, 24 Apr. 1516; La Fuente, *Cartas*, 212, Diego López de Ayala to Cisneros, Brussels, 28 July 1516.

35. Cedillo, *El cardenal Cisneros*, II, 425–6, Charles to Cisneros, 31 Oct. 1516. Keniston, *Francisco de Los Cobos*, chs 1–2, provided an excellent account of the rise of Los Cobos. See ch. 11 below on Charles's evaluation in 1543. Giménez Fernández, *Bartolomé de Las Casas*, named the two rival Spanish factions at Charles's court the 'partido felipista' and 'partido fernandino'.

36. Gachard, 'Mémoire', 28, Manrique to Cisneros, 8 Mar. 1516; Spielman and Thomas, 'Quellen', 25–6 and 28–9, Charles to Ferdinand, Brussels, 22 Apr. and 10 Oct. 1516.

37. *Ordonnances des rois de France. Règne de François Ier*, I, 409–30, treaty of Noyon, 13 Aug. 1516. The verdict of Karl Brandi, *The emperor*, 76, that 'this treaty was nothing but an outward show', seems too harsh: the treaty allowed Charles to secure Spain and Francis to consolidate his hold on Italy without interference from the other.

38. BL *Cott. Ms.* Galba B.V/73–81, the earl of Worcester, Cuthbert Tunstal, and Robert Wingfield to Henry VIII, Mechelen, 12 Feb. 1517 (two letters).

39. Gachard, 'Mémoire', 28–9. Manrique to Cisneros, 8 Mar. 1516.

40. Struick, *Gelre*, 244–66, discusses the tortuous negotiations between Burgundy and Guelders, including the possibility of a marriage to seal the deal, in 1517–18.

41. Gayangos and La Fuente, *Cartas*, 138 and 159, Cisneros to Diego López de Ayala, his personal envoy to Charles, 12 Aug. and 27 Sep. 1516 (repeated word for word on 14 Oct., p. 171).

42. Reiffenberg, *Histoire*, 293–335, account of the 18th Chapter of the Order; Gachard, *Voyages*, III, 19–25 (account of Vital).

43. Cedillo, *El cardenal Cisneros*, III, 575–8, Charles to Cisneros, 21 Apr. 1517; *CWE*, IV, 270–3 (# 543), Erasmus to Thomas More, Antwerp, 1 Mar. 1517.

44. Walther, *Die Anfänge*, 246–7, Louis Maroton to Margaret, Hagenau, 12 Dec. 1516.

45. BL *Cott. Ms.* Galba B.V/209–11v, earl of Worcester to Henry VIII, Antwerp, 26 Apr. 1517 (narrating a conversation with Matthew Scheiner, Cardinal of Sion, a trusted minister of the emperor); ADN *B* 2267/297, warrant dated 26 Nov. 1517 to pay £125 for 'deux verrieres' at Lier: they may still be admired in the church of St Gummarus, where his parents had married. Wiesflecker, *Kaiser Maximilian*, IV, 381, notes the coolness at the meeting; Von Kraus, 'Itinerarium', 313–16, recorded Maximilian's movements around the Netherlands, including the trip to Zealand 1–7 May 1517.

46. Gachard, *Voyages*, III, 27–32 (account of Vital); *L&P Henry VIII*, II/2, 1109, obligation of Charles, king of Spain, for repayment of the loan, 18 July 1517; Keniston, *Memorias*, 145, reported Charles's promise 'de bolver y los visitar dentro de cuatro años'. Charles did not exaggerate his fiscal needs: ADN B 2267, the account of the Receveur-Générale des Finances for 1517, showed an expenditure triple the size of normal years.

47. Gachard, *Analectes*, I, 9 ('4ᵉ série'), 353–6, Commission to Henry of Nassau as 'chef et capitaine-général de l'armée', Middelburg, 12 July 1517; Laurent, *Recueil*, I, 578–81, Instructions to the Privy Council, 23 July 1517.

48. Fagel, 'Het Bourgondische hof', 79–135, 'Estat et ordonnance de l'ostel du roy', 21 June 1517; ADN B 2268 (# 79,089), warrant to pay Frederick's stipend, 19 Feb. 1517.

49. Keniston, *Memorias*, 144 (Sancho Cota composed the laments that Eleanor and her ladies sang).

50. ADN B 3462 (# 121,649) payment to Adrian de Beaumarais to 'faire regarnir le cheval que le Comte Palatin donna au prince', 30 Sep. 1505. See *LGC*, II, 240–1, Margaret to Maximilian, c. 28 June 1514 (date established by Walther), about Charles's improved appetite; and Thomas, *Annalium*, 50, claiming 'Caroli nutritor appelabatur Fredericus' at this time.

51. Thomas, *Annalium*, 53, briefly reported the love trysts of the couple, and Moeller, *Éléonore*, 205–14, speculated on when and where they may have taken place. Frederick himself stated in Aug. 1517 that 'it was now more than two years since he had suborned, solicited and told the noble lady Madame Eleanor of Austria that he wanted to marry her' (Moeller, *Éléonore*, 337–9).

52. Moeller, *Éléonore*, 327, printed Frederick's holograph letter to Eleanor, and 337–9, the Procès-verbal of the interrogation of the couple on 16 Aug. 1517.

53. Thomas, *Annalium*, 58, presumably based on what Frederick told him some years later, but confirmed by BL *Cott. Ms.* Galba B.V/338–9, Tunstal to Wolsey, Middelburg, 27 Aug. 1517, thus a week after the events, reporting that 'the king found [Frederick's letter] in my lady Elianor's bosome hym selff'. Other details from Moeller, *Éléonore*, 337–9, notarized Procès-verbal, 16 Aug. 1517.

54. BL *Cott. Ms.* Galba B.V/338–9, Tunstal to Wolsey, Middelburg, 27 Aug. 1517, holograph, and ff. 348–50v, Spinelly to Henry VIII, Middelburg, 28 Aug. 1517, holograph.

55. La Fuente, *Cartas*, 130–4, Varacaldo to López de Ayala, Aranda del Duero, 11 Sep. 1517.

PORTRAIT OF THE EMPEROR AS A YOUNG MAN

1. Keniston, *Memorias*, 142. See the similar portrait of young Charles in Mártir de Anglería, *Epistolario*, III, 101–2 (# 515), letter to Luis Hurtado de Mendoza, 13 Jan. 1513.

2. Di Beatis, *The travel journal*, 89–90; Sanuto, *I diarii*, XXIII, col. 11, letter from Giovanni Badoer, 23 Oct. 1516; idem, XXX, col. 324, Final Relation of Francesco Corner, 6 June 1521.

3. Di Beatis, *The travel journal*, 90; Gachard, *Collection*, III, 261–2 (Vital); Sanuto, *I diarii*, XXVIII, col. 488, Corner to the Signory, Santiago de Compostela, 12 Apr. 1520.

4. Mártir de Anglería, *Epistolario*, III, 157–9 (# 539), letter to Luis Hurtado de Mendoza, 2 June 1514 (see also the sources quoted on p. 39 above); BL *Cott. Ms.* Galba B.V/202–6, Worcester, Tunstal and Wingfield to Henry VIII, Antwerp, 19 Apr. 1517, reporting a conversation with Margaret of Austria.

5. *CWE*, V, 6–13, Erasmus to Thomas More, c. 10 July 1517: 'non placet Hispaniae'.

6. *BNP*, II, 66–7, La Roche-Beaucourt to the Grand Master of France, 8 Jan. 1519.

7. Mártir de Anglería, *Epistolario*, III, 347–8 (# 633), letter to the marquesses of Los Vélez and Mondéjar, 12 Jan. 1519; Crouzet, *Charles Quint*, 21–5, discussed this episode, noting that it occurred at Epiphany, and speculated that it had psychological roots. In Book XXX, ch. 35, of his *Historia de Carlos V*, Juan Ginés de Sepúlveda (who had known his subject personally) stated that until he married, the emperor suffered from 'morbus comitiali', or epilepsy.

8. Di Beatis, *The travel journal*, 90; Sanuto, *I diarii*, XXX, col. 325, Final Relation of Corner, 6 June 1521.

9. *L&P Henry VIII*, II/2, 94–5, Knight to Wolsey, 16 Feb. 1517; *KFF*, I, 70–1, Ferdinand to Charles, 25 June 1523, having discovered some documents written in their grandfather's hand, 'par lesquelz declaire ainsi qu'il ne peult souvenir les bastars qu'il a delaissé', but charging his two grandsons to look after them all.

10. BRB *Ms.* II-2270, Charles to Nassau, 22 Jan. 1518, holograph (printed in Gossart, *Charles-Quint: roi d'Espagne*, 217–20); Gachard, *Collection*, III, 159 (Vital); BL *Cott. Ms.* Vespasian C.I/121–4, Spinelly to Henry VIII, Valladolid, 7 Jan. 1518 (Spinelly inserted 'gentle' between 'goodly' and 'woman'); Morgan, *Ireland 1518*, 13–15, discussed Vital's career and his chronicle.

11. Keniston, *Memorias*, 73. Although Cota did not provide a date, he wrote of '*prince* Don Carlos', which means that the incident occurred before his proclamation as king of Castile in March 1516. This detail is important because it means that the incident pre-dates all other examples of the motto discussed in the two erudite and richly illustrated articles by Earl Rosenthal, 'Plus Ultra' and 'The invention'.

12. Many authors, including Rosenthal, have claimed that the device originated in Marliano's speech at the chapter of the Golden Fleece on 28 Oct. 1516 (printed in full by Freher, *Rerum*, III, 146–9). Bataillon, 'Plus oultre', 23–7, noted that this attribution is only found after 1830, and (although unaware of Cota's claim) he deployed dazzling erudition to suggest that historians should look elsewhere for the origins of the motto.

13. Raoul Le Fèvre, Philip the Good's chaplain, presented a manuscript of *Le recoeil des histoires de Troyes* to the duke in 1464. It soon became popular far beyond the court of Burgundy: twenty-five manuscripts and five incunabula are known, and the English translation was the first book ever printed in English. Le Fèvre asserted that one of the columns of Hercules bore the minatory inscription: 'Ne passe oultre pour quérir terre/ Ne pour loingz royaulmes conquerre./ Plus en Occident t'en yras/ Et moins de terre trouveras.'

14. Gachard, *Voyages*, III, 264–9.

15. Ibid, 67–87 (Vital); Di Beatis, *The travel journal*, 90; Sanuto, *I diarii*, XXIV, col. 272, Hironimo de la Vedoa to the Doge, Brussels, 4 May 1517; ibid., XXV, cols 306 and 326–7, and XXVII, cols 70–1, Corner to the Signory, 24 Feb. 1518, 8 Mar. 1518 and 25 Feb. 1519.

16. Sanuto, *I diarii*, XXX, col. 325, Final Relation of Corner, 6 June 1521; *CWE*, V, 6–13 (# 597), Erasmus to Thomas More, c. 10 July 1517, and 72–5 (# 628), Erasmus to Beatus Rhenanus, 23 Aug. 1517; Gachard, *Voyages*, III, 266 (Vital).

17. Gachard, 'Mémoire', 23, Manrique to Cisneros, 8 Mar. 1516; Sanuto, *I diarii*, XXIV, col. 89, Relation of Dr Marin Zorzi, 17 Mar, 1517; *CSPV*, II, 420, Ambassador Marco Minio to the Signory, 16 Sep. 1517, relaying the report of two diplomats just returned from Charles's court; BL *Cott. Ms.* Vitellius B.XX/55, Richard Pace to Wolsey, 17 May 1517.

18. Gachard, *Voyages*, III, 12–14; Du Bellay, *Mémoires*, I, 58.

19. Ball and Parker, *Cómo ser rey*, 155, Charles's instructions, 6 May 1543. Frederick was born in 1482, Henry in 1483.

CHAPTER 4: FROM KING OF SPAIN TO KING OF THE ROMANS, 1517–19

1. *L&P Henry VIII*, II/1, 486–8, John Stile to Henry VIII, 3 Apr. 1516; Walther, *Die Anfänge*, 160 n. 4, Viceroy Cardona to Margaret, 27 Mar. 1516; Aram, *Juana*, 109, 'Escritura otorgada por el lugar-teniente del Justicia de Aragón', 12 Mar. 1516; *CDCV*, I, 58, Viceroy Moncada to Charles, 12 Apr. 1516; Gayangos and La Fuente, *Cartas*, 264–9, Cisneros to Charles, 18 Mar. 1517, responding to 'a holograph letter from Your Highness in which you informed me of your royal wishes concerning the war in Africa'.

2. Leonardo de Argensola, *Primera parte*, 65–6.

3. Gayangos and La Fuente, *Cartas*, 264–9, Cisneros to Charles, 18 Mar. 1517. On the threatening letter dispatched in June 1517 by a group of cities led by Burgos, see Pérez, *La revolución*, 108–9.

4. Gonzalo Sánchez-Molero, *El César*, 113–15; ADN *B* 17,876, Chambre des Comptes at Lille to Charles, 14 July 1517, together with copies of Joanna's expenses in 1501 and 1505.

5. BL *Cott. Ms.* Vespasian C.I /111–13, Spinelly to Henry VIII, 29 Sep. 1517.

6. Gachard, *Collection*, III, 89–95.

7. BL *Cott. Ms.* Galba B.V/369, Charles to Margaret, 1 Oct. 1517, copy; Gachard, *Collection*, III, 97–120 (Vital).

8. All details in this and the following paragraph come from Vital's day-by-day account in Gachard, *Voyages*, III, 97–130. The satellite view available through Google Maps reveals the challenging itinerary from San Vicente to Reinosa chosen by the royal party. According to TripAdvisor, 'It is obviously unlikely that anyone is going to walk around Cantabria on foot.' TripAdvisor obviously needs to learn some Habsburg history.

9. Hess, 'The Ottoman conquest', 55.

10. Keniston, *Memorias*, 146 (account of Sancho Cota, Eleanor's secretary); and Gachard, *Collection*, III, 135 (account of Laurent Vital, with a line missing from the manuscript used by Gachard supplied from BNF *F. f.* 5627/65–6).

11. Gachard, *Collection*, III, 136.

12. Aram, *Juana*, 120.

13. *CSPSp Supplement*, 166–9, Denia to Charles, 30 July 1518, and 396–401, Infanta Catalina to Charles, 19 Aug. 1521.

14. Ibid., 202–4 and 197–200, Denia to Charles, undated but 1520 and 1519, respectively, both holograph. Joanna only discovered the truth in August 1520 when a group of Charles's ministers, fearful that she might throw in her lot with the Comuneros, and totally ignorant of the fictional world created with Charles's consent, came to Tordesillas to inform her 'of many things that had happened

in her kingdoms since the death of the Catholic King'. The secret was out (ibid., 204–5, notarized account of an audience with Joanna on 23 Aug. 1520).

15. Ibid., 154–6, Denia to Charles, undated but 1518. See ibid., 'Introduction', for Bergenroth's explanation. See further examples of Charles's callous treatment of his mother on p. 212 below.

16. Aram, *La reina Juana*, 340–3, Charles to Denia, 30 Oct. 1518; Aram, *Juana*, 221 n. 54, Charles to Beltrán de Fromont, deputy mayordomo, and Guillem Punçon, wardrobe master, 28 Apr. 1519; *CDCV*, I, 82–3, Charles to Denia, 14 Jan. 1520. See also *CSPSp Supplement*, 257–60, Charles to Adrian, 26 Sep. 1520 (approving all Denia's actions).

17. *CDCV*, I, 75–8, Charles to Cisneros and Adrian, 7 Sep. 1517 (also published in *PEG*, I, 89–100); La Fuente, *Cartas*, 135–41, 151 and 174–7, bishop of Ávila to López de Ayala, 23 Sep., 25 Sep. and 22 Oct. 1517.

18. Sandoval, *Historia*, I, 112; Spielman and Thomas, 'Quellen', 29–34, Charles to Ferdinand, 7 Sep. 1517 (also in *CDCV*, I, 71–4, from a copy) and 26 Oct. 1517; *CDCV*, I, 79–80, Charles to Cisneros, 27 Sep. 1517.

19. La Fuente, *Cartas*, 139, bishop of Ávila to López de Ayala, 23 Sep. 1517, conveying Cisneros's advice. *CDCV*, I, 64–9, included the text of a paper of advice apparently prepared by Cisneros for Charles around this time, but the many internal contradictions in the document (a later copy) cast doubt on its authenticity.

20. Bietenholz, *Contemporaries*, I, 367, s. v. Croÿ, provides details of Guillaume's promotions. *CWE*, V, 72–5 (# 657), Erasmus to Beatus Rhenanus, 23 Aug. 1517, noted that Croÿ was now 'so they tell me, coadjutor of the archbishop of Toledo'.

21. Gachard, *Collection*, III, 138–9; *CWE*, V, 164–71 (# 694), Erasmus to Willibald Pirckheimer, 2 Nov. 1517, slightly amended in light of the original text of Erasmus, *Opus*, III, 116.

22. Keniston, *Memorias*, 148 (see also p. 151, where Cota suggested that Alfonso poisoned the Cortes of Aragon against their new king); Mártir de Anglería, *Epistolario*, III, 285–7 (# 602), letter to marquesses of Los Vélez and Mondéjar, 10 Nov. 1517 (so just two days after the death of Cisneros). Martínez Millán, *La Corte*, I, 158–66, described the troublesome regency of Alfonso in Aragon, which may also have alienated Charles.

23. Gachard, *Voyages*, III, 141 (Catalina), 144 (funeral), 149 (Order), 151 (Entry). Sanuto, *I diarii*, XXV, cols 128–9, Ambassador Corner to the Signory, 19 Nov. 1517, also stressed the splendour of the event.

24. *CLC*, IV, 260–84, list of eighty-eight grievances from the Cortes of 1518, together with Charles's response to each.

25. Walter, *Die Anfänge*, 209 n. 5, Laurent Gorrevod to Margaret, 28 May 1518; Mártir de Anglería, *Epistolario*, III, 306–8 (# 613), letter to marquesses of Los Vélez and Mondéjar, 15 Mar. 1518. For examples of Charles speaking directly to ambassadors, see *BNP*, II, 45 and 59, La Roche-Beaucourt to Grand Master, 15 May and 25 Nov. 1518.

26. Santa Cruz, *Crónica*, I, 182–3; Keniston, *Memorias*, 151 (Cota explicitly stated that Charles gave his brother no advance warning of his decision); *BNP*, II, 42, La Roche-Beaucourt to Grand Master, Apr. 1518.

27. Gachard, *Collection*, III, 179–81 (clerical opposition) and 234–5 ('libelles diffamatoires'); Pérez, 'Moines', 98 n. 8, Charles to president of the Chancery of Valladolid, Zaragoza, 16 May 1518; Mártir de Anglería, *Epistolario*, III, 298–300 (# 608), letter to marquesses of Los Vélez and Mondéjar, 12 Feb. 1518.

28. BL *Cott. Ms.* Vespasian C.I /196 and 181, Berners to Wolsey, 18 Sep. and 26 July 1518. On the 'cane game [*juego de cañas*]', derived from the 'djerid' practised in Muslim Granada, see Fuchs, *Exotic nation*, 89–102.

29. BL *Cott. Ms.* Vespasian C.I /181, 203 and 232, Berners to Wolsey, 26 July, and to Henry VIII, 8 Oct. 1518, and the archbishop of Armagh to Wolsey, 17 Dec. 1518, all from Zaragoza.

30. Martínez Millán, *La Corte*, I, 177, a section written by Rivero.

31. Sanuto, *I diarii*, XXV, 242–3, 306, 326–7, Corner to the Signory, 11 and 14 Jan., 24 Feb. and 8 Mar. 1518; Mártir de Anglería, *Epistolario*, III, 306–8 (# 613), letter to marquesses of Los Vélez and Mondéjar, 15 Mar. 1518; *BNP*, II, 40 and 49, La Roche-Beaucourt to Grand Master, Apr. and 25 Oct. 1518.

32. BL *Cott. Ms.* Vespasian C.I/226, Armagh to Wolsey, 6 Dec. 1518; Sanuto, *I diarii*, XXVI, cols 223–4, Corner to the Signory, 6 Oct. 1518. For Gattinara's praise of Chièvres, see the concluding recommendations in his paper of advice in July 1519: Bornate, 'Historia', 413.

33. BL *Addl. Ms.* 18,008, 'Ad Divum Carolum Maximum, Regem Catholicum, Mercurini Arboriensis di Gattinaria . . . Oratio supplicatoria', discussed by Boone, *Mercurino*, ch. 2, from which I have taken all translations. Erasmus presented his *Institutio principis christiani* to Charles that same year, but it seems unlikely that the recipient read it.

34. *BNP*, II, 67, La Roche-Beaucourt to Grand Master, 22 Jan. 1519.
35. Keniston, *Memorias*, 152.
36. The catchy title of a popular German study: Günter Ogger, *Kauf dir einen Kaiser: Die Geschichte der Fugger*, first published in 1978.
37. Von Druffel, *Beiträge*, I, 673, Gerhard Veltwyk to Charles V, July 1551, reporting the account given by Frederick, now Elector Palatine, of what Maximilian said 'ung jour, après la guerre que luy et les Anglois firent ensemble contre roi Louis de France' in 1513. The idea of abdication was one more precedent that Charles would follow.
38. Cohn, 'Did bribery', 1; ANF *série J* 995A pièce 7, Letter of credence by the Elector of Trier, 18 Nov. 1516; ANF *série J* 952 pièce 1, 'Promesse de l'ambassadeur de Brandenbourg', 27 June 1517; Knecht, *Francis*, 72. Mignet, *Rivalité*, 120–3, discussed the deals struck with Trier and Brandenburg, but gave some incorrect dates for the key documents.
39. Chmel, 'Review of Lanz', 186–93, Instructions to Jakob Villinger, Maximilian's treasurer, [17] Aug. 1517; *RTA*, I, 71 n. 4, Charles to Maximilian, 12/13 Nov. 1517.
40. *RTA*, I, 73 n. 2, Charles to Villinger and other ministers at Maximilian's court, 8 Mar. 1518, and 75 n. 1, Chièvres to the same, 15 Apr. 1518; Le Glay, *Négociations*, II, 125–33, Maximilian to Charles, 18 May 1518. Mignet, *Rivalité*, 122–3, gave the terms of the deal struck by each Elector with Francis.
41. Mone, 'Briefwechsel', cols 13–14, Maximilian to Charles, 24 May 1518. For examples of how Charles later deployed the same passive-aggressive style, see chapters 8 and 15 below.
42. *RTA*, I, 81 n 2, Villinger to Chièvres, 28 May 1518.
43. Walther, *Die burgundischen Zentralbehörden*, 203–4, La Chaulx to Margaret, 24 July 1518 (specifying that the initiative for devolution came from Chièvres), and Margaret to Maximilian, 25 Oct. 1518 respectively; Laurent, *Recueil*, I, 656–7, Ordinance of Charles, 24 July 1518.
44. Gachard, *Rapport*, 149, Courtewille to Charles, 27 May 1518 (quoting Charles's letter of 1 May).
45. *BNP*, I, 57, La Roche-Beaucourt to Francis, Zaragoza, 20 Nov. 1518. Total commitments from Mone, 'Briefwechsel', cols 407–9, 'Estat de l'argent'; and Gachard, *Rapport*, 151–5, Maximilian's instructions for Courtewille, Augsburg, 27 Oct. 1518. Núñez Contreras, *Un registro*, pp. LXX–LXXI, recorded almost a dozen letters from Charles to Rome in Dec. 1518 and Jan. 1519, pleading for his grandfather's coronation.
46. Le Glay, *Négociations*, II, 189–93, Zevenbergen to Margaret, Augsburg, 1 Feb. 1519; Mone, 'Briefwechsel', cols 283–5, Henry of Nassau to Margaret, Bonn, 23 Mar. 1519; *RTA*, I, 169–75 and 198–200, Francis to his envoys, late Jan. and 7 Feb. 1519; ANF *série J* 952 pièce 10, Leo X to Francis, 12 Mar. 1519. See also Laubach, 'Wahlpropaganda', 210–25, on the arguments against electing Charles deployed by the French. On Frederick's ill-starred courtship of Eleanor, see chapter 3 above.
47. Le Glay, *Négociations*, II, 253–62, Margaret and her council to Charles, 20 Feb. 1519 (see p. 257 for the threat to send Ferdinand to Germany 'le premier dimanche de quaresme prochain' – which in 1519 fell on 13 Mar., three weeks ahead).
48. *RTA*, I, 352–8, Charles to Margaret, 5 Mar. 1519, cyphered; Le Glay, *Négociations*, II, 303–10, Charles's instructions to M. de Beaurain, 5 Mar. 1519.
49. Gachard, *Rapport*, 173, Margaret to Nassau, 13 Mar. 1519; *RTA*, I, 358 ('Ensieuvez ce que vous escrips cy-dessus, car autrement n'auroie cause me contenter').
50. *KFF*, I, 11, Charles to Ferdinand, 5 Mar. 1519, holograph; Le Glay, *Négociations*, II, 303–10, instructions to Beaurain (charged with explaining Charles's views to both Ferdinand and Margaret), 5 Mar. 1519.
51. Le Glay, *Négociations*, II, 316–27, Margaret and her council to Charles, 9 Mar. 1519; Gachard, *Rapport*, 155–6, Margaret to La Chaulx, 18 Jan. 1519.
52. *RTA*, I, 633, Charles to the Elector Palatine, 2 May 1519 (with another example at ibid., 747).
53. Mone, 'Briefwechsel', cols 17 and 118–19, Maroton to Margaret, 21 Jan. 1519, and Frederick to Margaret, 2 Mar. 1519 ('ma fasceuse lettre'); Le Glay, *Négociations*, II, 278, Paul Amerstorff to Margaret, 25 Feb. 1519. On Charles's grovelling, see Mone, 'Briefwechsel', cols 132–3, Jean Marnix to the count of Hoogstraeten, 16 Mar. 1519 (pension of £2,500), and 403, Le Sauch to Margaret, 26 Apr. 1519 (Charles's holograph letters delivered); and Le Glay, *Négociations*, II, 333–40, Charles's instructions to Le Sauch, 13 Mar. 1519 ('ayons desjà escript par deux fois *de nostre main* bonnes et gracieuses lettres' to Frederick).
54. *RTA*, I, 220–1, Jakob Fugger to Brandenburg, 12 Feb. 1519, holograph. Other details from von Pölnitz, *Jakob Fugger*, II, ch. 18, and Häberlein, *The Fuggers*, ch. 2.
55. Mignet, *Rivalité*, 174–5, Mainz to Brandenburg, 1 Mar. 1519 (from a copy sent to Margaret); Mone, 'Briefwechsel', col. 124, Nassau to Margaret, 11 Mar. 1519, quoting the count of Koenigstein; *RTA*, I, 317–19, Margaret to Zevenbergen, 28 Feb. 1519. Laubach, 'Wahlpropaganda', 225–38, also described Charles's charm offensive.

56. Mignet, *Rivalité*, 188, Joachim von Moltzan to Francis, 26 Feb. 1519 (he concluded his letter, which begged Francis to send him yet more money, *Cito, cito, cito*: 'haste, haste haste').

57. *RTA*, I, 734–5, Charles to Margaret, 31 May 1519. Cohn, 'Did bribery', 25–7, provided strong evidence that on 27 June 1519, the day before Charles's election, Frederick of Saxony was offered the position, but declined.

58. BL *Cott. Ms.* Vitellius B.XX/161–2v, Richard Pace to Wolsey, Frankfurt, 3 July 1518, holograph. This figure – 1.5 million florins – is roughly double the total normally quoted (852,189 florins), but the latter is based solely on the accounts of Charles's German treasurer, Johan Lucas, printed in part by Kohler, *Quellen*, 63–70, which included only expenditure *within* Germany to the Electors, to the troops and so on. It excluded expenditure elsewhere, such as the cost of mobilizing troops in the Netherlands.

59. BL *Cott. Ms.* Vespasian.C.I/257–60, Spinelly to Wolsey, 9 Mar. 1519, holograph (italics added).

60. Boone, *Mercurino*, 91–2, Gattinara's *Autobiography*. See also Crouzet, *Charles Quint*, 29, for a similar rationale attributed to Charles himself at this time 'en débat en soy mesme s'il debvoit accepter son élection ou s'en excuser'. For subsequent use at the court of Spain of the 'argument from the escalation of potential disasters', see Parker, *The Army of Flanders*, 109–11.

61. Le Glay, *Négociations*, II, 194–202, Margaret's instructions to Jean Marnix, Feb. 1519. On the significance of the term 'reputation' to Charles, see Hatzfeld, 'Staatsräson'.

62. BL *Cott. Ms.* Vespasian C.I /247–54, Spinelly to Wolsey, 20 Feb. 1519; Bruchet and Lancien, *L'itinéraire*, 380, Margaret to Charles's agents, Apr. 1519. Häberlein, 'Jakob Fugger', 73–8, identified and described the ministerial team that worked so well together in Germany; Reiffenberg, *Histoire*, 346–53, chronicled the chapter of the Order held in Barcelona.

63. BL *Cott. Ms.* Vespasian C.I/196, Berners to Wolsey, 18 Sep. 1518; *BNP*, II, 63 and 71, La Roche-Beaucourt to Grand Master, Nov. 1518 and 20 Feb. 1519; Sanuto, *I diarii*, XXVII, cols 1–543 (quotation at col. 71).

64. Laurent, *Recueil*, I, 682–4, Royal ordinance, 1 July 1519 (issued by virtue of 'nostre certaine science, propre mouvement, auctorité et pleine puissance', a formula previously used in Spain), and idem 687–9, Margaret's acceptance on 28 July both of her new powers and also of certain restrictions (mostly the requirement that she should consult her councillors on policy and Charles on important appointments). Lanz, *Aktenstücke*, I, 92–103, and Gachard *Analectes*, V ('16e série'), 306–11, also printed these crucial documents.

65. Bornate, 'Historia' 405–13, Paper of advice dated 12 July 1519 (on working while getting dressed, see p. 412). See also ibid., 414–20, a further paper of advice by Gattinara in Oct.–Nov. 1519, presented to Charles 'because it seems Your Majesty has done nothing about the measures and remedies I proposed' in Barcelona. Once again, Charles largely ignored it: Martínez Millán, *La Corte*, I, 184–6 (date taken from 186 n. 261).

66. Brandi, *The emperor*, 84.

67. Gachard, *Rapport*, 164–5, Margaret to Zevenbergen, 28 Feb. 1519. Margaret erred, however: Charles had omitted Zevenbergen's name in the belief that he had left Germany to take up a position in the Swiss cantons. Note that Margaret urged Zevenbergen to do and say nothing that 'might risk losing the king's esteem, or the honour and excellent reputation that your prudence, diligence and dexterity have won for you'.

68. Gachard, *Rapport*, 162, Zevenbergen to Margaret, 18 Feb. 1519; Le Glay, *Négociations*, II, 359–63, Jean Marnix to Margaret, 22 Mar. 1519; Mone, 'Briefwechsel', cols 127–8, Nassau to Margaret, 14 Mar. 1519.

69. *CWE*, III, 239, Erasmus to Charles, Mar. 1516, preface to *The education*.

70. Sanuto, *I diarii*, XXVII, col. 581, Corner to the Signory, 28 July 1519 (Corner noted one absentee: Venice itself).

71. Ibid., Corner to the Signory, 28 July 1519.

CHAPTER 5: FROM PEACE THROUGH REBELLION TO WAR, 1519–21

1. BL *Cott. Ms.* Vespasian C.I/257–60, Spinelly to Wolsey, 9 Mar. 1519, holograph cypher with decrypt; BL *Cott. Ms.* Vespasian C.III/158–75v, Tunstal, Wingfield and Sampson to Henry VIII, 2 June 1525; *BNP*, II, 70, La Roche-Beaucourt to Grand Master, 20 Feb. 1519.

2. *RTA*, I, 366–70, Marnix to Margaret, 7 Mar. 1519, holograph; Boone, *Mercurino*, 92 (*Autobiography*); Crouzet, *Charles Quint*, 29 (Charles's rationale).

3. TNA *SP* 1/10/49, Robert Wingfield to Henry VIII, Innsbruck, 7 Feb. 1515.

4. Le Glay, *Négociations*, II, 166–9, Philibert Naturelli to Margaret, 24 Oct. 1518; BL *Cott. Ms.* Vespasian C.I/261–2v, Spinelly to Wolsey, Barcelona, 20 Mar. 1519. Charles would have been familiar with the

prediction in La Marche, *Mémoires*, I, 197, written in the 1470s, that the passions generated by the murder of Duke John in 1419 would never die. See Crouzet, *Charles Quint*, 124–5, and Huizinga, *Herfsttij*, 18–20, on the persistence of fear and suspicion in Renaissance Europe.

5. Du Bellay, *Mémoires*, I, 95; Florange, *Mémoires*, I, 257.

6. Sanuto, *I diarii*, XXVII, cols 416–17 and 514–15, Corner to the Signory, 2 and 29 June 1519, on the payment and letters.

7. Lanz, *Aktenstücke*, 108–13, Charles's instructions to Bernardo de Mesa and Jean de le Sauch, 12 Dec. 1519 (italics added). Sanuto, *I diarii*, XXIX, col. 371, Corner to the Signory, Aachen, 23 Oct. 1520, reported that Charles 'non parla anchora molto promptamente lo idioma aleman'.

8. *RTA*, I, 864–76, printed the *Wahlkapitulation*, signed in Frankfurt by Charles's commissioners on 3 July 1519 (six days after the election). Kohler, *Quellen*, 53–8, reprinted most of it.

9. *Ordonnances des rois de France. Règne de François I*er, II, 299–341 and 351–6, agreements concluded in London between 1 and 8 Oct. 1518, and ibid., 565–75, arrangements for a personal meeting and an 'armatorum congressus' agreed on 10 Jan. 1520 and ratified 26 Mar. 1520.

10. Boone, *Mercurino*, 94; Sanuto, *I diarii*, XXVIII, cols 246–8, Corner to the Signory, 22 Jan. 1520; Santa Cruz, *Crónica*, I, 221.

11. Mártir de Anglería, *Epistolario*, IV, 14–15 (# 663), to Gattinara, 24 Feb. 1520, and 17–18 (# 665), to the marquesses of Los Vélez and Mondéjar, 'From the rebellious city of Valladolid', 14 Mar. 1520. See also Pérez, *La revolución*, 147–8, on the riots on 4 Mar. 1520.

12. Sanuto, *I diarii*, XXVIII, 488, Corner to the Signory, Santiago, 12 Apr. 1520. Charles's travels reconstructed from Foronda, *Viajes*.

13. Boone, *Mercurino*, 94 (Gattinara wrote his *Memoirs* in the third person); Danvila, *Historia crítica*, III, 31–41, Adrian to Charles, 16 Jan. 1521.

14. *CLC*, IV, 293–8, speeches of Mota and Charles, 31 Mar. 1520.

15. *Caroli Romanorum regis recessuri adlocutio in conventu Hispaniarum*, based on the translation in Headley, *The emperor*, 10–11. The pamphlet was published at Rome and Augsburg in Latin, and at Leipzig in German. Headley, 'The Habsburg world empire', 52–3 and 72 n. 28, made a convincing case that composing both the speech and the printed text represented 'a collective enterprise' by Charles's ministerial team.

16. Carretero Zamora, *Gobernar*, 397–8; Mártir de Anglería, *Epistolario*, IV, 19–20 (# 666), to the marquesses of Los Vélez and Mondéjar, 5 Apr. 1520.

17. Gachard, *Correspondance*, 237–42, Provision of Charles and Joanna (the formula always used in Castile until her death in 1555), 17 May 1520. On the antecedents for Charles's use of his 'absolute royal power', see Sánchez Agesta, 'El "poderío real absoluto"', and Owens, 'By my absolute royal authority', ch. 2. See also chapter 13 below.

18. Sanuto, *I diarii*, XXVIII, 488, Corner to the Signory, Corunna, 9 and 23 Apr. 1520.

19. Pérez, *La revolución*, 150, manifesto of the friars of Salamanca, and 232, letter to the king of Portugal.

20. Sanuto, *I diarii*, XXIX, cols 225–54, 'Ordine di lo abochamento del Serenissimo re d'Ingaltera, con la Cesarea et Catholica Maestà et con il Cristianissimo re', incorporating much material from ibid., XXVIII, cols 595–7, Corner and Surian to the Signory, 27 May 1520, and XXIX, cols 73–4, report of Lodovico Spinelli, 12 July 1520.

21. Sanuto, *I diarii*, XXIX, cols 225–54, 'Ordine'.

22. Bornate, 'Historia', 424–5, secret treaty between Henry and Charles, Canterbury, 29 May 1520, ratified at Calais, 14 July 1520 (Lanz, *Aktenstücke*, 179–81; English précis in *CSPSp*, II, 312). See also Gwyn, 'Wolsey's foreign policy', 762.

23. Viciana, *Libro quarto*, 11–17, quoting a speech by Joan Llorenç, a prominent guildsman of Valencia.

24. Ibid., 126–7, and *poderes* issued by Charles to Diego Hurtado de Mendoza, count of Mélito, 4 May 1520.

25. Maldonado, *La revolución comunera*, 76; Mexía, *Historia*, 89; Santa Cruz, *Crónica*, I, 165–6.

26. Both Danvila, *Historia*, and Martínez-Peñas, *Las Cartas*, published the cardinal's letters, in whole or in part (the latter with modernized spelling), but both made errors of transcription. Scans of 105 original letters, covering 546 folios, are now available via PARES in a collection entitled 'Correspondencia de Florencio Adriano de Utrecht', with the etiquette 'AGS Patronato Real, leg. 2'. I cite Danvila's transcripts except when they contain errors; in such cases I cite the original.

27. Danvila, *Historia*, I, 373–6, II, 515–16, and III, 31–41, Adrian to Charles, 25 June and 28 Nov. 1520, and 16 Jan. 1521. Pérez, *La revolución*, 121, affirmed that 'the court behaved in Spain as if it were a conquered country', and his section entitled 'La codicia de los flamencos' (pp. 121–6) provided numerous examples.

28. Danvila, *Historia*, I, 373–81, II, 660–2, and III, 11–17, Adrian to Charles, 25 June 1520 (two letters), 15 Dec. 1520, and 16 Jan. 1521 (royal silence since a letter dated 7 Nov. 1520). Although some

nineteenth-century historians scrawled summaries and comments on these letters, Charles and his ministers did not.

29. AGS *PR* 2-I-2 (images 5–9), Adrian to Charles, 25 June 1520.

30. Danvila, *Historia*, III, 31–41, Adrian to Charles, 16 Jan. 1521 (it would take Charles another two decades to recognize that 'I cannot be sustained except by my kingdoms of Spain': ch. 10 below); AGS *PR* 2/395–6 (images 347–9), Adrian to Charles, 3 Apr. 1521 (italics added). The nobles' threat resembled that of the towns of Castile in 1517 to assemble without royal warrant unless Charles came at once: chapter 4.

31. Pérez, *La revolución*, 314.

32. BL *Cott. Ms.* Galba B.VI/191–5, Spinelly to Wolsey, Brussels, 27 June 1520, 'at five of the clooke at afternoon'; AGS *PR* 2-I-2 (images 5–9), Adrian to Charles, 25 June 1520, incorporating the proposals made by the city of Toledo to the other cities with a vote in Cortes on 8 June (see Pérez, *La revolución*, 169–70).

33. Pérez, *La revolución*, 174 n. 56, documented this error, concerning Pero Laso de la Vega.

34. Gayangos and La Fuente, *Cartas*, 225–6, 'Quejas contra el consejo real', dictated by Cisneros, 28 Sep. 1517; Danvila, *Historia*, I, 386–8, the Constable's instructions to Pedro de Guevara, his envoy to Charles, 24 June 1520.

35. BL *Cott. Ms.* Galba B.VI/199–200 and 204–9, Spinelly to Wolsey, 6 and 27 July 1520.

36. BL *Cott. Ms.* Galba B.VI/227–8v, Spinelly to Wolsey, undated (but 6 Sep. 1520). Spinelly noted that Chièvres, whose advice Charles normally followed, was 'not in small perplexite' because of 'the general murmure that reigns against hym; and for my parte I thynke he cannot telle whether he would goo or tary, considering that Spayne for hym is loste for ever'.

37. *CDCV*, I, 83–4, Charles *poder* to his governors, Mechelen, 22 Sep. 1520; BL *Cott. Ms.* Galba B.VI/360–1v, Spinelly to Wolsey, 19 Sep. 1520, citing indiscretions by Audiencier Hanneton, who had attended the council where the accusations flew. Margaret had lived in Castile as princess and maintained many contacts there.

38. *L&P Henry VIII*, III/2, 1574–7, Spinelly to Wolsey, 24 Jan. 1521. Sanuto, *I diarii*, XXIX, 561 and 581, Corner to the Signory, 11 Jan 1521, made the same claim (Charles had already nominated Robert de Croÿ to succeed his brother as archbishop of Cambrai). See Pérez, *La revolución*, 316–49, on Acuña and the struggle for the see of Toledo in 1521.

39. Mártir de Anglería, *Epistolario*, IV, 161–5 (# 722) to Los Vélez, 7 June 1521.

40. Ibid., IV, 86–9 (# 696) to Los Vélez and Mondéjar, Valladolid, 13 Nov. 1520, enclosing a letter from Marliano to Mártir de Anglería, Aachen, 20 Oct. 1520.

41. Ibid., IV, 102–4 (# 703) to Marliano, Valladolid, 29 Nov. 1520. Marliano was another foreigner whom Charles had appointed to a Spanish see (Tuy). Espinosa, *The empire*, 61–5, noted that the clerics of Toledo, furious at the appointment of a foreigner as their archbishop, began the city's revolt.

42. *CDCV*, I, 106, 'Capitulaciones matrimoniales de Carlos V e Isabel', 24 Oct. 1526: '50,000 cruzados of gold which King Manuel loaned him during the time of the Comuneros of Castile'.

43. Danvila, *Historia*, II, 777–85, Edict of Charles V, Worms, 17 Dec. 1520, proclaimed in Burgos, 22 Feb. 1521.

44. Details from *RTA*, II, 95–100, including the text of Charles's oath to observe the *Wahlkapitulation*; Sanuto, *I diarii*, XXIX, cols 370–9, Corner to the Signory, Aachen, 23 Oct. 1520; and Dürer, *Diary*, 70. Immediately after his proclamation as duke of Burgundy in 1507, Charles had also dubbed some knights as a sign of his new authority: see p. 18 above.

45. Volpi, *Opere*, 282–5, Baldassare Castiglione to Cardinal Bibiena, Cologne, 2 Nov. 1520 (the conclusion of a fine eyewitness account of the coronation); Keniston, *Francisco de Los Cobos*, 57 (the new style); *CDCV*, IV, 489–90 (Charles's *Memoirs*).

46. *LWS*, VI, 174–8, condemnation of Luther's works by the Leuven theologians, 7 Nov. 1519, and Adrian's response, 4 Dec. 1519. The two documents were published together in Feb. 1520.

47. RAH *Salazar* A-45/7–9, Manuel to Charles, Rome, 12 May 1520 (copy made from the partly cyphered original: idem A-19/386–9). No doubt it reached Charles after he had left Spain. For the career of Manuel, a prominent *Felipista*, see Martínez Millán, *La Corte*, III, 264–9, and ch. 2 above.

48. Luther, *An den christlichen Adel deutscher Nation von des christlichen Standes Besserung*, began by addressing Charles ('Der allerdurchläuchtigsten grossmächtigstenen Kaiserlichen Majestät') and rejoiced that 'Gott hat uns ein junges, edles Blut zum Haupt gegeben'.

49. Laurent, *Recueil*, I, 620–1, Ordinance of 5 Mar. 1518; Redondo, 'Luther', 113 (other supporters) and 115–17 (testimony of Juan de Vergara to the inquisition of Toledo, summer 1533). Erasmus agreed with Vergara, asserting that at this stage 'even the emperor was sympathetic to Luther's teaching' (*CWE*, X, 452–60 (# 1526), Erasmus to Duke George of Saxony, 12 Dec. 1524). Many have taken two letters written from Charles's court by Alfonso de Valdés to Peter Mártir, dated 31 Aug. and 25 Oct.

1520, as reliable contemporary analyses of the imperial court's assessment of Luther, but internal evidence (notably references in both letters to things that happened afterwards) shows that both must have been written, or at least extensively revised, some months later: see Tubau, 'Alfonso de Valdés', 23 n. 19, and Egido, 'Carlos', 226–7.

50. Hillerbrand, 'Martin Luther'. The bull dealt only with works published by Luther in 1518 and 1519, above all his Ninety-Five Theses.

51. CWE, VIII, 68–74 (# 1153), Erasmus to Godschalk Rosemondt, Leuven, 18 Oct. 1520.

52. Ibid., 77–9 (# 1155) and 105–8 (# 1166), Erasmus to Johann Reuchlin, Cologne, 8 Nov. 1520, and to an unknown patron, Leuven, Dec. 1520. Mencke, Scriptores, II, col. 604, printed entries from the diary of George Spalatin, Frederick's councillor, about the events of 4 and 5 Nov. 1520; Erasmus, Erasmi opuscula, 329–37, published the Axiomata Erasmi pro causa Martini Lutheri, which contained his advice to Frederick.

53. RTA, II, 466–7, Charles to Frederick, 28 Nov. 1520; Brieger, Quellen, 16–22, Aleandro to Cardinal Medici (the future Clement VII), Worms, 14–15 Dec. 1520. Luttenberger, 'La política', 46–9, stresses how the imperial government deliberately chose 'a strategy based on ambiguity' towards Luther until he appeared in person at Worms. Egido, 'Carlos', 240, suggested that it did so 'because there was no other solution'.

54. According to Sandoval, Charles told the monks at Yuste that 'I erred in not killing Luther', and that 'I was not obliged to honour the safe-conduct I had given' because he was a heretic, and one did not keep faith with heretics; but the emperor evidently forgot that he had issued the safe-conduct to Elector Frederick, and that breaking it would have created a major uproar (Sandoval, Historia, 'Historia de la vida que el emperador . . . hizo . . . [en] Iuste', Book X).

55. RTA, II, 477–94, account of his meetings with Glapion by Chancellor Brück (characterized by Aleandro as 'Lutheranissimo') in Feb. 1521; and Brieger, Quellen, 63–5 and 131–42, Aleandro to Medici, 18 Feb. and 13 Apr. 1521, describing the visit by Glapion and Paul von Armersdorff, Charles's chamberlain, to discuss a settlement of the 'Luther problem' with Ulrich von Hutten and Martin Bucer. As Luttenberger, 'La política', 48–9, observed, it is 'hard to imagine' that Glapion acted without the knowledge and consent of Charles's inner circle.

56. Brieger, Quellen, 89–95, Aleandro to Cardinal Medici, Worms, 8 Mar. 1521, italics added (also printed in Balan, Monumenta, 130–4, with variant readings and under the date 19 Mar. 1521). On the secret treaty between France and the papacy, see Barillon, Journal, II, 176–7, and Mignet, Rivalité, I, 232–3. Redondo, 'Luther', 112, gave examples of how Juan Manuel, Charles's ambassador in Rome, used Leo's anxiety about the reformer to extort concessions for his master. Tubau, 'Alfonso de Valdés', 25–6, endorsed Aleandro's analysis that the principal councillors who accompanied Charles – Chièvres, Gattinara, Marliano, Valdés – all seriously underestimated Luther.

57. L&P Henry VIII, III/1, 428–30, Spinelly to Wolsey, Worms, 2 Feb. 1521; RTA, II, 156–68, details on Charles's interactions with other members of the Diet.

58. RTA, II, 526–7, Charles to 'dem ersamen unsern lieben andechtigen doctor Martin Luther, Augustiner Orden', Worms, 6 Mar. 1521; Redondo, 'Luther', 118, testimony of Vergara in 1533.

59. RTA, II, 632–8, 'Relación de lo que pasó a el emperador en Bormes [Worms] con Lutero, año de 1521' (anonymous, but written from the viewpoint of 'el emperador mi señor'); Brieger, Quellen, 144–9, Aleandro to Medici, 17 Apr. 1521.

60. RTA, II, 555, 'Doctoris Martini Lutheri Oratio coram Caesere Carolo'.

61. This and the succeeding paragraphs rely on RTA, II, 533–94, various accounts in Latin and German (especially 555, 'Doctoris Martini Lutheri Oratio coram Caesere Carolo'), and 632–8, 'Relación'; Brieger, Quellen, 149–55, Aleandro and Nuncio Caracciolo to Medici, 19 Apr. 1521; RTA, II, 879–82, Corner and Contarini to the Signory, 28 Apr. 1521; and CSPV, III, 116–17, Contarini to Mateo Dandolo, 26 Apr. 1521.

62. On Charles's limited understanding of both German and Latin at this stage, see Sanuto, I diarii, XXIX, cols 371–2 (Charles needed a German interpreter at Aachen), and Balan, Monumenta, 249, Aleandro to Cardinal Medici, 26 May 1521 (Charles's reluctance to read documents in Latin). I thank James Tracy for pointing out to me that many theologians, initially including Luther, regarded an ecumenical council as the highest Church authority: questioning the authority of popes was one thing, but rejecting the authority of councils was very different.

63. RTA, II, 632–8, 'Relación'. Brieger, Quellen, 153, Aleandro and Nuncio Caracciolo to Medici, 19 Apr. 1521, also reported this striking act of defiance: when 'Martino uscitò fuora della sala Cesarea, alzò la mano in alto more militum Germanorum, quando exultano di un bel colpo di giostra' (my italics).

64. LWB, II, 307–10, Luther to Charles, 28 Apr., 1521, endorsed by Spalatin, 'Hae literae Caesari non sunt redditae, quod in tanta vi procerum ne unus quidem esset, qui redderet'. Luther later became less apologetic and instead took to gloating over his appearance at Worms: see his 'Table Talk' on the

subject in Sep. 1533 and autumn 1536 (*LWT*, III, 284–9 # 3357b, and 343–4 # 3474); and summer 1540 (*LWT*, V, 65–8, # 5342a).

65. *RTA*, II, 594–6, printed the document from the French copy 'fait de ma main' on the night of 18–19 Apr. 1521 and sent to Henry VIII (TNA *SP* 1/22/9). Sanuto, *I diarii*, XXX, cols 214–16, provided an Italian translation; *RTA*, II, 636, 'Relación', contained a Spanish text (see also Sandoval, *Historia*, Book X, ch. 10).

66. Oberman, 'The impact', 21. Figures from Moeller, 'Luther', 240, who estimated that by the time of Luther's death, 682 of his works had appeared either singly or as collections, in 3,897 editions, with some items translated into ten vernacular languages. *LWS*, VII, 814–87, provided full bibliographic information on the publications of the speech.

67. *RTA*, II, 632–8, 'Relación'; Sanuto, *I diarii*, XXX, cols 210–14, Contarini to Mateo Dandolo, Worms, 26 Apr. 1521, Latin (English précis in *CSPV*, III, 116–17).

68. Sanuto, *I diarii*, XXX, cols 210–14, Contarini to Mateo Dandolo, Worms, 26 Apr., 1521; Mártir de Anglería, *Epistolario*, IV, 161–5 (# 722), to the marquis of Los Vélez, 7 June 1521, with a copy of Alfonso de Valdés's letter to him from Worms, 13 May 1521.

69. Gachard, *Correspondance*, 244–6, Adrian to Charles, 9 Apr. 1521, French, holograph; Laurent, *Recueil*, II, 71–2, Ordinance of 20 Mar. 1521. See also Danvila, *Historia*, III, 581–3, Adrian and the council to Charles, 12 Apr. 1521, warning him that Lutheran writings were circulating in Spanish, which risked provoking trouble 'since several cities of this kingdom are in rebellion'.

70. *RTA*, II, 640–9, German text of the Edict of Worms, 8 May 1521.

71. Balan, *Monumenta*, 232–4 and 240–7, Aleandro to Cardinal Medici, 22 [*recte* 18] and 24 May 1521.

72. Ibid., 248–55, Aleandro to Cardinal Medici, 26 May 1521. Laurent, *Recueil*, II, 73–83, edict of 8 May 1521, is a Dutch copy of the Edict of Worms – but Aleandro stated that it was not available for publication in the Netherlands until July: Balan, *Monumenta*, 271–3, Aleandro to Cardinal Medici, 16 July 1521.

73. BL *Cott. Ms.* Caligula D.VIII /46–7, Wingfield to Fitzwilliam and Jerningham (Henry's envoys in France), Worms, 29 May 1521 (decoded text of BL *Cott. Ms.* Caligula E. III/33–v, the original).

74. Gossart, *Notes*, 55; Lanz, *Aktenstücke*, 135–45, Le Sauch to Chièvres, London, 7 Apr. 1520.

75. *RTA*, II, 893–5, Corner and Contarini to the Signory, Worms, 4 May 1521; Sanuto, *I diarii*, XXX, 324–6, Relation of Corner, 6 June 1521; *CWE*, VIII, 153–4 (# 1184), Erasmus to Guillaume Budé, 16 Feb. 1521.

76. Sanuto, *I diarii*, XXX, 61–3, Corner to the Signory, 14 Mar. 1521; Brieger, *Quellen*, 214–18, Aleandro to Medici, 18 May 1521 (stating that this was 'the fourteenth day of Chièvres's fever').

77. Balan, *Monumenta*, 248–55, Aleandro to Cardinal Medici, 26 May 1521; BNMV *Ms. Italiani*, Classe VII, cod. 1009/22v–23, Contarini to the Signory, 28 May 1521.

78. Du Bellay, *Mémoires*, I, 58; *CDCV*, I, 75–8, Charles to Cisneros and Adrian, 7 Sep. 1517 (also printed in *PEG*, I, 89–100).

79. Balan, *Monumenta*, 248–55, Aleandro to Medici, 26 May 1521; BL *Cott. Ms.* Galba B.VII/29–31, Wingfield and Spinelly to Wolsey, 19 June 1521 (italics added); Powell, *The complete works*, I, 127, 'Note of remembraunce by Sir Thomas Wiat', Toledo, Dec. 1538.

80. BL *Cott. Ms.* Galba B.VII/102–3, Charles to Wolsey, 7 Aug. 1521; BNMV *Ms. Italiani*, Classe VII, cod. 1009/82, Contarini to the Signory, 22 Aug. 1521; TNA *SP* 1/23/28, Wolsey to Henry VIII, 28 Aug. 1521, holograph, 'To the king's grace, ys owne hands onely' (printed with some errors in Burnet, *History*, III.ii, 11–12).

81. *RTA*, II, 729–43, *Reichsabschied*, and 659–61, Edict of Worms against Luther, both dated 26 May 1521; Sandoval, *Historia*, Book X, ch. 14.

82. Sandoval, *Historia*, Book V, ch. 2.

CHAPTER 6: SNATCHING VICTORY FROM THE JAWS OF DEFEAT, 1521–5

1. *L&P Henry VIII*, II/2, 1293–4, Spinelly to Henry VIII, 20 May 1518; Sanuto, *I diarii*, XXIX, col. 166, Antonio Giustinian's report to the Senate after his French embassy, 7 Sep. 1520; Barrillon, *Journal*, II, 178, reporting the views of Barrillon's master, Chancellor Duprat of France.

2. Guicciardini, *Istoria d'Italia*, 193, 187 (entry for the year 1518, written between 1537 and 1540).

3. Górski, *Acta Tomiciana*, V, 68–70, Dantiszek to Sigismund, 29 June 1519 (Spanish translation in Fontán and Axer, *Españoles y polacos*, 142); Ellis, *Original letters*, 1st series I, 154–6, Thomas Boleyn, English ambassador in France, to Henry VIII, 4 July 1519.

4. Barrillon, *Journal*, II, 151–62, Francis to the count of Carpi, 31 Jan. 1520, French style (highlights printed in *RTA*, II, 114–18, but with the date 1 Jan. 1521).

5. ANF *série K* 82/1bis, warrant signed by Francis in favour of La Marck and his children, 14 Feb. 1521, granting over 10,000 crowns in cash and 16,000 more in annual pensions; Barrillon, *Journal*, II, 177; *RTA*, II, 829–31, Tunstal to Wolsey, 22 Mar. 1521; Brandi, *The emperor*, 153.

6. *RTA*, II, 812–15, Tunstal to Wolsey, 6 Mar. 1521 (italics added).

7. Sanuto, *I diarii*, XXX, cols 61–3, Corner to the Signory, 14 and 16 Mar. 1521; Barrillon, *Journal*, II, 181, statement of Philippe Naturel, 1 Apr. 1521, and letter of Carpi to Francis, Rome, 17 May 1521; Dumont, *Corps*, IV, *Supplément*, 96–9, 'Tabulae Foederis stabiliter inter Carolum V Romanorum Imperatorem & Leonem X Pontificem Maximum contra Gallos', 8 May 1521.

8. Ruscelli, *Delle lettere*, I, ff. 93–5, Lorenzo Aleandri de' Galeazzi to his father, Brussels, 3 July 1521 (English précis in *L&P Henry VIII*, III/2, 559–61); Sanuto, *I diarii*, XXXI, cols 504–6, 'Edictum imperiale contra regem Gallum', Antwerp, 12 July 1521; *L&P Henry VIII*, III/2, 1579–80, Fitzwilliam to Wolsey, 6 Aug. 1521.

9. Lanz, *Staatspapiere*, 1–9, 'Gutachten' of Gattinara, 30 July 1521 (also printed in Le Glay, *Négociations*, II, 473–82; German summary in Lanz, *Aktenstücke*, 231–3; English summary in *L&P Henry VIII*, III/2, 588–90).

10. Lanz, *Aktenstücke*, 236–42, 'Sur ce que fera l'empereur durant cest hyuer', giving the opinions of nine councillors, followed by Gattinara's recommendation and Charles's resolution.

11. Sanuto, *I diarii*, XXXI, cols 318–19, Contarini to the Signory, 16 Aug. 1521; BL *Cott. Ms.* Galba B.VII/109–19, secret treaty of Bruges, 25 Aug. 1521, original signed by Wolsey and Margaret (printed by Lanz, *Aktenstücke*, 244–67, from a copy; English précis in *CSPSp*, III, 365–71, and *L&P Henry VIII*, III/2, 620–1). Russell, 'The search', 174–5, documented the private meetings between Charles and Wolsey.

12. Lanz, *Aktenstücke*, 323 and 325, Charles to Gattinara, 15 and 'mid' Sep. 1521. Dunham, 'Henry VIII's whole council', 41, coined the phrase 'pageant politics' for this phase of Wolsey's diplomacy.

13. Weert, 'Cronycke', 88; Lanz, *Aktenstücke*, 399, Charles to Gattinara, mid-Oct. 1521; and ibid., 441–3, Margaret to Berghes, 14 or 15 Nov. 1521, holograph minute, relating 'what I heard [the emperor] say today'.

14. *L&P Henry VIII*, III/2, 760–1, treaty between England, the emperor and the Pope, 24 Nov. 1521; Lanz, *Aktenstücke*, 496–500, Charles to his envoys in England, 13 Dec. 1521.

15. Gachard, *Correspondance de Charles*, 24–5, Charles's instructions to Lope Hurtado de Mendoza, his envoy to Adrian, 25 Jan. 1522; *LCK*, I, 58–60, Charles to Adrian, 7 Mar. 1522.

16. Laurent, *Recueil*, II, 167–9, Charles's ordinance appointing Margaret his regent in the Netherlands, 15 Apr. 1522. Bauer, *Die Anfänge*, 239–64, the agreements between Charles and Ferdinand at Worms (Apr. 1521) and at Brussels (30 Jan. and 7 Feb. 1522).

17. *PEG*, I, 252–6, Testament of Charles V, Bruges, 22 May 1522 (a short document that lacked any provision for his succession beyond Ferdinand). For his father's will, see ch. 1 above.

18. *CWE*, IX, 64–8, Erasmus to Jean Glapion, Charles's confessor, 21 Apr. 1522; BL *Cott. Ms.* Galba B.VII/5–6, Wingfield and Spinelly to Wolsey, 11 Feb. 1522. For other similar complaints see BL *Cott. Ms.* Galba B.VI/188–90, Spinelly to Wolsey, 19 June 1520; Sanuto, *I diarii*, XXIX, cols 665–6, Corner to the Signory, 8 Feb. 1521; ibid., LIV, col. 501, Tiepolo to the Signory, 1 July 1531; and LV, col. 258, Tiepolo to the Signory, 30 Nov. 1531.

19. BL *Cott. Ms.* Galba B.VII/12–13, Wingfield and Spinelly to Wolsey, 3 Mar. 1522; BNMV *Ms. Italiani Classe VII* cod. 1009/195, Contarini to the Signory, 5 Mar. 1522.

20. BL *Cott. Ms.* Galba B.VII/305, Wingfield and Spinelly to Wolsey, 14 Apr. 1522 (the letter that caused consternation was sent by the imperial ambassadors in England on 6 Apr., containing the terms for a truce offered by the French: *CSPSp Further Supplement*, 113–16); BL *Cott. Ms.* Galba B.VIII/33–4, Charles to Wolsey, 15 Apr. 1522, holograph (copies at AGRB *Audience* 370/37 and HHStA *Belgien DD* Abt. B fasz. 4); BL *Cott. Ms.* Vespasian C.II/187, Charles to Wolsey, 18 Aug. 1523, holograph (the symbol also appears in *Cott. Ms.* Titus B.I/336). European rulers had used special signs to authenticate their letters since at least the 1450s: see Ilardi, 'Crosses and carets'.

21. BL *Cott. Ms.* Galba B.VII/321, Wingfield and Spinelly to Wolsey, 15 May 1522.

22. Piot, 'Correspondance politique', 80–3, Gattinara to Barroso, 13 Jan. 1522 (request for a Portuguese loan); HHStA *Belgien PA* 2/2/13–14, 'Ce que le sieur de La Chaulx debvra dire et declarer à nostre sainct père, sans le comuniquer en Angleterre', undated but presumably 15 Jan. 1522, minute by Gattinara (terms demanded by England).

23. Gachard, 'Charles-Quint', 540, Charles to La Chaux, 9 June 1522; *CSPSp*, II, 434–6 and 438–40, treaty and secret treaty of Windsor, 16 and 19 June 1522; *CSPSp Further Supplement*, 69–73, ambassadors in England to Charles, 5 Mar. 1522, Latin; *CSPSp*, II, 442, Charles warrant of 20 June 1522, promising to repay Henry's loan of 150,000 ducats. See also Robertson, 'L'entrée de Charles-Quint à Londres en 1522'.

24. *RVEC*, 55–9, Salinas to Salamanca, Palencia, 10 Aug. 1522; *CSPSp Further Supplement*, 142–3, Charles to Henry, Palencia, 11 Aug. 1522.

25. HHStA *Belgien PA* 2/2/15–16, Supplementary instructions to Lachaulx, 17 Jan. 1522, minute by Gattinara (about the government of Castile after Adrian departed); Danvila, *Historia*, V, 198–201, Admiral to Charles, Aug. 1522; Gachard, *Correspondance de Charles*, 104–7, Adrian to Charles, 5 Aug. 1522. See Pérez, *La revolución*, 567–85, on the early stages of the repression. In his *Autobiography*, Gattinara claimed that he was one of the few who 'advocated clemency': Boone, *Mercurino*, 98.

26. BNMV *Ms. Italiani Classe VII*, Cod. 1009/66v–67, Contarini to the Signory, Ghent, 30 July 1521, quoting a conversation with Glapion. The exchange evidently took place at least two months earlier, when Aleandro mentioned it in a letter to Cardinal de' Medici on 26 May 1521: Balan, *Monumenta*, 248–55.

27. *RVEC*, 55–9 and 62–6, Salinas to Salamanca, 10 Aug. and 1 Sep. 1522; HHStA *Belgien PA* 2/4/68, Charles to Margaret, 25 Aug. 1522; Pérez, *La revolución*, 588 (quoting Mexía, *Historia*, I, 320), 585 (total condemnations) and 628 (punishments).

28. *RVEC*, 73–83, Salinas to Salamanca, 4 Nov. 1522. Danvila, *Historia*, V, 239–51, printed the list of *exceptuados*; Pérez, *La revolución*, 474–92 and 585–95, analysed them and their assets (quotation from p. 477).

29. Pérez, *La revolución*, 592–4 (collective sanctions) and 650–65 (reparations).

30. Viciana, *Libro quarto*, 546–56, with additional data from García Cárcel, *Las Germanías*, 141–2, and Ríos Lloret and Vilaplana Sánchis, *Germana de Foix*, 40–9.

31. RAH *Salazar* A-45/25, Manuel to Charles, 31 Dec. 1520; *RVEC*, 66–71 and 221–6, Salinas to Salamanca, 7 Sep. 1522 and 2 Oct. 1524, and 155–7, Salinas to Ferdinand, 16 Dec. 1523; Gachard, *Correspondance de Charles*, 171–2, Charles to Sessa, 10 Jan. 1523, conveyed the threat.

32. *Causa formada*, 54–9; *RVEC*, 308–14, Salinas to Ferdinand, 27 Mar. and 8 Apr. 1526; *CSPSp*, III/1, 614, 'Bishop Acuña's confession'. See also Pérez, *La revolución*, 629–33: 'Apéndice: la ejecución de Acuña', and p. 160 below (on the spiritual consequences of the execution for Los Cobos, Ronquillo and others).

33. *CDCV*, I, 375–9 and 482, Charles to the empress, 9 Aug. 1532 and 5 Mar. 1536 (about Gonzalo de Ayora); *CDCV*, III, 472–3, Charles to Philip, 18 Sep. 1552. Pérez, *La revolución*, 565–680, analysed the fate of individual Comuneros.

34. Gachard, *Correspondance de Charles*, 94, Adrian to Charles, 19 June 1522.

35. Anon., *Cartas de Indias*, 482, Cristóbal Vaca de Castro de Charles, Cuzco, 24 Nov. 1542; Charrière, *Négociations*, I, Francis to Ambassador Dinteville, 25 Jan. 1532. Rincón's Genoese associates were Cesare Cantelmo and Cesare Fregoso. I deduce Rincón's presence as a French agent in Poland from *LCK*, I, 98–113, Jean Hannart to Charles, 13 Mar. 1524; in England from TNA *SP* 1/53/144, Rincón to Wolsey, undated but Apr. 1529; and in Hungary from Setton, *The papacy*, III, 312–22. Some historians have doubted that Rincón had a Comunero past, but in 1530 the Spanish ambassador in Venice stated unequivocally that 'Rincón is one of the Comuneros from Medina del Campo': AGS *E* 1308/58–9, Rodrigo Niño to Charles, 18 June 1530.

36. Gachard, *Voyages*, II, 66–7 (Vandenesse's 'Journal'). *CSPSp Further Supplement*, 148–9, Charles to his ambassadors in England, 5 Sep. 1522, also mentioned Bourbon and his 'Great Enterprise'. Crouzet, *Charles de Bourbon*, Part III, provides a good guide to the lawsuit and the conspiracy.

37. TNA *SP* 1/26/51–56, Instructions to Sir Thomas Boleyn and Dr Richard Sampson, signed by Henry VIII (undated but 25 Sep. 1522); *CSPSp Further Supplement*, 190–4, Charles to his ambassadors in England, 8 Feb. 1523.

38. *CLC*, IV, 334–51, prints Gattinara's opening speech, delivered 14 July 1523 (*BKK*, II, 153–4, printed the omitted parts of the draft); ibid., 354–8, petition of the Cortes and Charles's reply, 15 July 1523.

39. *CLC*, IV, 363–402, list of grievances together with Charles's responses, 24 Aug. 1523.

40. BL *Cott. Ms.* Vespasian C.II/106–20, Boleyn and Sampson to Wolsey, Valladolid, 8 and 18 Mar. 1523; *RVEC*, 122–30, Salinas to Salamanca, 2 July, and to Ferdinand, 14 Aug. 1523.

41. TNA *SP* 1/28/181–93, Wolsey to Sampson and Jerningham, 30 Aug. 1523. On the English campaign, see Gunn, 'The duke of Suffolk's march'.

42. Barrillon, *Journal*, II, 151–62, Francis to the count of Carpi, 31 Jan. 1521.

43. *CSPSp Further Supplement*, 286–9, Charles to Louis de Praet, Pamplona, 15 Nov. 1523.

44. Claretta, *Notice*, 84–92, 'Deuxième représentation de Mercurin de Gattinara à l'empereur', in Italian, with passages from the French original in Bornate, 'Historia', 311 n. 4. *BKK*, II, 152–3, convincingly argued that Gattinara prepared this document in April or May 1523.

45. Brandi, 'Aus den Kabinettsakten', 181–222, 'Denkschrift' published in full from the copy in HHStA *Belgien PC* 68/3–30. Brandi argued persuasively that it was composed in early Dec. 1523: p. 215 n. 1. Gossart, *Charles-Quint*, Appendix D, and 'Notes', 110–19, printed an abridged text from AGRB.

Martínez Millán, *La Corte*, I, 216–17, notes 422–4, published much of Gattinara's original text in AS Vercelli, albeit with some errors.

46. Sanuto, *I diarii*, XXXV, col. 365, Contarini to the Signory, 11 Nov. 1524; RAH *Ms.* 9/4817/171–84, Charles to Sessa, 14 Dec. 1523.

47. Clement signed the treaty on 12 Dec. 1524, and notified Charles on 5 Jan. 1525 (RAH *Salazar* A-34/3, Brief of Clement to Charles); Venice followed suit on 10 Jan. 1525, but tried to keep the treaty secret, although of course Charles soon discovered the truth (Setton, *The papacy*, III, 226 and 228).

48. BL *Cott. Ms.* Vespasian C.III/55–7, Tunstal, Wingfield and Sampson to Wolsey, Toledo, 2 June 1525 (the summary in *L&P Henry VIII*, IV/1, 616, does not do justice to the pungent words of the original – spoken at an audience by Charles himself, quoting Wolsey). Rodríguez-Salgado, 'Buenos hermanos', 450–3, provided an excellent overview of the unfortunate policies pursued by Henry and Wolsey in 1524–5.

49. Sanuto, *I diarii*, XXXVI, col. 419, and XXXVII, col. 661, Contarini to the Signory, 18–23 Mar. 1524 and 10 Jan. 1525; *CSPSp*, II, 691, Charles to his ambassadors in Rome, 10 Jan. 1525; Górski, *Acta Tomiciana*, VII, 172–9, Dantiszek to Sigismund, 7 Feb. 1525 (Spanish translation in Fontán and Axer, *Españoles y polacos*, 165–70); Boone, *Mercurino*, 100 (Gattinara's *Autobiography*).

50. AGS *E K* 1639 # 95, Charles to Bourbon, 14 Aug. 1524, copy; *KFF*, I, 250–3, Charles to Ferdinand, 4 Feb. 1525; RAH *Ms.* 9/4817/239–44, Charles to his ambassadors in Rome, 19 Dec. 1524 (draft partly in Gattinara's hand).

51. *L&P Henry VIII*, IV/1, 347–50, Sampson to Wolsey, 30 Oct. 1524; Brandi, 'Eigenhändige Aufzeichnungen', 256–60, original (undated but certainly written before news of the victory at Pavia reached Charles on 10 March 1525, and perhaps prompted by receiving Clement's Brief of 5 Jan. announcing that he had made an alliance with France, Florence, Ferrara and Venice). See similar statements in Charles's letters around this time in *PEG*, I, 427–41.

52. TNA *SP* 1/33/113–14, Pace to Henry VIII, 26 Jan. 1525.

53. Ruscelli *Delle lettere*, I, f. 147v, Giovanni Matteo Giberto to Girolamo Aleandro, Rome, 19 Feb. 1525; RAH *Salazar* A-34/150–63, Sessa to Charles, Rome, 24 and 25 Feb. 1525 (Sessa immediately added, 'I beg Your Majesty to pardon my boldness, which stems from the abundance of affection that I feel for Your Majesty, and the loyal service that I owe you').

54. *CODOIN*, IX, 481–5, marquis of Pescara to Charles, undated but 25 Feb. 1525; Brandi, 'Nach Pavia', 185–7, Lannoy to Charles, 25 Feb. 1525 (also printed in *LCK*, I, 150–1, from an imperfect copy); RAH *Salazar* A-34/133–4, Lannoy to Sessa, 21 Feb. 1525, copy.

55. Valdés, *Relación*, sig. A iii^v–A iv, quoting dispatches to Charles from the victors of Pavia; Champollion-Figeac, *Captivité*, 129, Francis to Louise of Savoy, undated but probably 25 Feb. 1525.

56. BL *Cott. Ms.* Vitellius B.VII/75–7, Russell to Henry, Milan, 11 Mar. 1525, copy; Sanuto, *I diarii*, XXXVIII, cols 47–8, Foscari to the Signory, 13 Mar. 1525. Champollion-Figeac, *Captivité*, 85–8, lists the French captives and casualties at Pavia. French sources referred to the captured Henry d'Albret as 'king of Navarre', but after 1512 the rulers of Spain claimed that title. Spanish sources therefore referred to Henry as 'son of the king' – viz. son of the last king of the Albret dynasty whose legitimacy they recognized.

57. Rodríguez Villa, *Italia*, 10, Lope de Soria to Charles, 26 Feb. 1525. Just in case his master missed the point, Soria repeated in a postscript: 'This has been a noble victory, which Your Majesty can now use to lay down the law [*poner ley*] and establish your pre-eminence throughout Christendom.'

CHAPTER 7: SNATCHING DEFEAT FROM THE JAWS OF VICTORY, 1525–8

1. Sanuto, *I diarii*, XXXVIII, cols 205–7, Giacomo Suardino to the marquis of Mantua, 15 Mar. 1525 (English précis in *CSPV*, III, 415–17). Fernández de Oviedo, 'Relación', 407, stated that the courier arrived on 3 Mar., but all other sources say 10 Mar.

2. Brandi, 'Nach Pavia', 185–7, Lannoy to Charles, 25 Feb. 1525 (also printed in *LCK*, I, 150–2, from an imperfect copy).

3. Valdés, *Relación*, sig. A vij^v; Sanuto, *I diarii*, XXXVIII, cols 205–7, Suardino to Mantua, 15 Mar. 1525 (quoting what Sampson had told him); Ellis, *Original letters*, 1st series I, 260–7, Sampson to Wolsey, 15 Mar. 1525. See the similar accounts of Charles's modesty on hearing news of Pavia by other diplomats: Sanuto, *I diarii*, XXXVIII, cols 203–5, Contarini to the Signory, 12 and 14 Mar. 1525 (English précis in *CSPV*, III, 413–15); Górski, *Acta Tomiciana*, VII, 188–200, Dantiszek to King Sigismund, 16 Mar. 1525 (Spanish translation in Fontán and Axer, *Españoles y polacos*, 171–2); Serassi, *Delle lettere*, I, 146–8, Castiglione to Piperario, 14 Mar. 1525.

4. Lanz, *Aktenstücke*, 322, Charles to his diplomats at the conference of Calais, 15 Sep. 1521.

5. BNMV *Ms. Italiani Classe VII*, cod. 1009/410, Contarini to the Signory, 6 Feb. 1525, reporting the emperor's indiscretions in an audience with Giovanni Corsi, who represented both Florence and the pope (which may explain Charles's provocative comment about Luther: he intended his 'remarkable words' to alarm Clement).

6. RAH *Ms.* 9–4817/249–52, Charles to Sessa, 9 Feb. 1525, minute (with the last phrase struck through; English summary in *CSPSp*, II, 699–701).

7. Redondo, 'La comunicación', 260, Charles to Germaine de Foix, 10 Mar. 1525; Villar García, 'Cartas', 69, Charles to Rodrigo Mexía, 12 Mar. 1525; Valdés, *Relación*, sig. A vij'–A viij.

8. BL *Cott. Ms.* Vitellius B.VII/75–7, Sir John Russell to Henry VIII, Milan, 11 Mar. 1525 (printed with errors in Ellis, *Original letters*, 2nd series I, 297–303).

9. BNE *Ms.* 20214/52/9, Sessa to Charles, 26 Feb. 1525, 'a iiij horas de noche', holograph; *KFF*, I, 273–6 and 277–81, Ferdinand to Charles, and Instructions to Salinas, Innsbruck, 14 Mar. and 2 Apr. 1525 (also in *LCK*, I, 154–6 and 683–90). Ferdinand quoted the rebuke to Hannibal by one of his generals after Cannae: 'Vincere scis, Hannibal; victoria uti nescis' (Livy, *History of Rome*, 22.51). At this point, Ferdinand was his brother's heir and successor.

10. Górski, *Acta Tomiciana*, VII, 188–200, Dantiszek to Sigismund, 16 Mar. 1525, quoting Gattinara (Spanish translation in Fontán and Axer, *Españoles y polacos*, 173).

11. Brandi, 'Nach Pavia', 195–211, Position paper prepared by Gattinara for Charles, undated but submitted between 10 Mar. (when news of the victory arrived) and 25 Mar. 1525 (when Charles signed orders implementing his chancellor's proposals).

12. Champollion-Figeac, *Captivité*, 149–59, Charles's instructions to his ambassadors to Louise of Savoy, 28 Mar. 1525; Halkin and Dansaert, *Charles de Lannoy*, 267–70, Charles to Lannoy, 27 Mar. 1525. The emperor sent a similar message to his brother: *KFF*, I, 277–81, Charles to Ferdinand, 25/26 Mar. 1525.

13. *PEG*, I, 265–6, Charles to Lannoy, undated but probably written on 26 Mar. 1525 (see the similar phrases in *LCK*, I, 157–9, Charles to M. de Praet, his ambassador in England, 26 Mar. 1525).

14. *PEG*, I, 263–5, Charles to Louise, undated but 25 Mar. 1525, followed by her response (date supplied by Champollion-Figeac, *Captivité*, 136 n. 2); TNA *SP* 1/34/153 Sampson to Wolsey, Toledo, 2 May 1525, holograph. Although the report from Beaurain (Charles's envoy) has apparently not survived, on 10 Apr. 1525 Beaurain informed Margaret of Austria that Louise 'shows no sign of wishing to surrender anything': Le Glay, *Négociations*, II, 598–9.

15. *LCK*, I, 161–2, Lannoy to Charles, 3 and 6 May 1525; TNA *SP* 1/35/17–18, 'Ce que don Hughe de Montcade ... a dit à l'empereur notre seigneur que le Roy de France luy avoit divisé pour la paix' (translated from Moncada's notes in Spanish into French; cf. the terms printed in Champollion-Figeac, *Captivité*, 170–3).

16. BL *Cott. Ms.* Vitellius B.VII/146–9, John Clerk to Wolsey, Rome, 14 June 1525 (quoting Clement on Francis's 'eloquens'); Rodríguez Villa, *Italia*, 52, Nájera to Charles, 7 May 1525. See also Halkin and Dansaert, *Charles de Lannoy*, 278–9, Lannoy to Charles, 27 Apr. 1525: 'the thing that [Francis] desires most is to talk to you'. Some suspected that it was Lannoy's idea to bring Francis to Spain, but one of the king's ministers later stated on oath that Francis 'procura envers le vis-roy de Naples d'estre mené en Espagne, et jusques à bailler ses propres gallères pour luy conduyre': Champollion-Figeac, *Captivité*, 432–3, Report of Philibert Babou, 18 Dec. 1525.

17. BNE *Ms.* 20212/43/9, Leyva to Charles, 7 July 1525; BNE *Ms.* 20214/52/10, Sessa to Charles, 12 July 1525.

18. Halkin and Dansaert, *Charles de Lannoy*, 284–7, Charles to Lannoy, 15 June 1525. Some have suggested that Charles knew in advance that Francis was coming to Spain but this letter, written five days before the news arrived at court, proves his ignorance of Lannoy's initiative. See also RAH *Ms.* 9/4817/261, Charles to Sessa, 8 June 1525, ordering the ambassador to consult Lannoy on how to negotiate with the pope – clearly assuming that the viceroy was still in Italy.

19. BL *Cott Ms.* Vespasian C.III/107–27, Tunstal and Sampson to Henry, 2 Dec. 1525, reporting on their audience with Charles on 19 Oct. See also BAV *Vat. Lat.* 6753/18, Venetian ambassadors to the Signory, 13 June 1525, reporting the statement of one of Charles's Netherlands ministers that 'Burgundy belongs to His Imperial Majesty just as the shirt on your back belongs to you, but King Louis XI of France fraudulently occupied it'. In 1544–5 Charles faced a similar choice of whether to sacrifice part of his heritage or a recent strategic acquisition: see ch. 12 below.

20. BAV *Vat. Lat.* 6753/29v–30 and 69v, Venetian ambassadors to the Signory, 10 July and 5 Oct. 1525 (Francis certainly knew all about the love letters, because in 1519 he cited them while attempting to win Frederick over: p. 91 above); Serassi, *Delle lettere*, II, 9, Castiglione to the archbishop of Capua, papal secretary of state, Madrid, 9 Dec. 1525, postscript (on bribery); BAV *Vat. Lat.* 6753/97, Navagero to the Signory, 11 Dec. 1525 (on the bungled escape in blackface: English summary in *CSPV*, III, 508).

21. *Ordonnances des rois de France. Règne de François Ier*, IV, 88–92, 'Première protestation' of Francis, 16 Aug. 1525, registered on 22 Aug.

22. Fernández de Oviedo, 'Relación', 418 (an eyewitness account); Górski, *Acta Tomiciana*, VII, 328, Dantiszek to Sigismund, 1 Nov. 1525 ('Pereant illi, qui inter nos dissidia ista fecerunt. Istene est juvenis tam deformis aut monstrum et sine ingenio balbutiens?'; Spanish translation in Fontán and Axer, *Españoles y polacos*, 180). Francis apparently suffered from an abscess that pressed upon his brain: as soon as it burst, he recovered (BAV *Vat. Lat.* 6753/62v–67, Navagero to the Signory, 24 Sep. 1525: 'una appostema in la testa').

23. BAV *Vat. Lat.* 6753/70v, Navagero to the Signory, 10 Oct. 1525.

24. BAV *Vat. Lat.* 6753/84v, Navagero to the Signory, 4 Nov. 1525. Francis later confirmed that he had used this ruse, explaining to some diplomats 'almost derisively [*quasi irridento*]', that while in Madrid 'the physicians told the emperor that I was consumptive and that it would be well to exchange me for my sons'. And, Francis added with a malevolent smile, 'I was content that he should entertain that opinion': *CSPV*, V, 613–15, Venetian ambassadors in France to the Signory, 17 Feb. 1531.

25. Champollion-Figeac, *Captivité*, 363–9, 'Les moyens de paix baillés par le conseil de l'empereur', 9 Oct. 1525, and Francis's rejection the following day; ibid., 384, Francis to Charles, undated but almost certainly the same day; and ibid., 416–25, letters patent, Nov. 1525 (the day left blank). See also Le Glay, *Négociations*, II, 650–2, de Praet to Margaret, Lyons, 22 Dec. 1525, passing on the news that Francis 'is absolutely determined to remain in prison rather than return Burgundy'.

26. BAV *Vat. Lat.* 6753/29v, Contarini, Navagero and Priuli to the Signory, 10 July 1525 ('che il re come si sapea da ognuno havea havuto et havea di molto mal francese').

27. Boone, *Mercurino*, 109–10 (*Autobiography*); Sanuto, *I diarii*, XLV, cols 616–18, Suardino to Mantua, 12 Dec. 1525; Bornate, 'Historia', 318 n. 1, 478–9 and 482–3, Navagero to the Signory, 11 Dec. 1525, 29 Jan. and 8 Feb. 1526; Halkin and Dansaert, *Charles de Lannoy*, 289–91, Charles's commission to Lannoy, 16 Dec. 1525, specifying the approval of five councillors but omitting the name of the chancellor. Castiglione, who noted that Gattinara 'either cannot or will not conceal his discontent', recorded the verbal duel between the emperor and his chancellor over preparing the treaty: Serassi, *Delle lettere*, II, 29–33, Castiglione to Capua, 24 Mar. 1526.

28. *Ordonnances des rois de France. Règne de François Ier*, IV, 165–78, Second Protestation, 13–14 Jan. 1526. Although Charles would denounce this as base behaviour unworthy of a gentleman, twenty years earlier Ferdinand the Catholic had used precisely the same legal device, making a 'protest' before notaries when Charles's father extorted concessions from him under threat (ch. 3), and Charles would do the same twenty-five years later when his German opponents forced him to make concessions (ch. 15).

29. Gachard, *Captivité*, 66–70, based on Sandoval, *Historia*, Fernández de Oviedo, 'Relación', and a procès-verbal of the various ceremonies kept by the emperor's secretary of state, Jean Lallemand (the king's oath as a knight printed pp. 66–8); *Ordonnances des rois de France. Règne de François Ier*, IV, 178–219, treaty of Madrid, 14 Jan. 1526.

30. Sanuto, *I diarii*, XLI, cols 36–8, Suardino to Mantua, 5 Feb. 1526; *LCK*, I, 192, Charles to Louise, 16 Feb. 1526 (also printed in Le Glay, *Négociations*, II, 654–5, and, with an English translation, in Bradford, *Correspondence*, 216–18).

31. TNA *SP* 1/34/118–19, Wolsey to Tunstal and Wingfield, 3 Apr. 1525; BL *Cott. Ms.* Vespasian C.III/158–75v, Tunstal, Wingfield and Sampson to Henry VIII, 2 June 1525; *KFF*, I, 305–11 and 322–6, Charles to Ferdinand, 25 June 1525, and reply, 1 Sep. 1525; *L&P Henry VIII*, IV/1, 621, Charles's ultimatum, delivered in London, 7 June 1525.

32. *CDCV*, I, 100–15, marriage treaty signed 17 Oct. 1525; RAH *Ms.* 9–4817/272–4, Charles to Sessa, 31 Oct. 1525, draft corrected by Gattinara (English summary in *CSPSp*, III/1, 419–23); RAH *Salazar* A-36/176–8, Sessa to Charles, 13 Nov. 1525 (asserting that Clement had delayed in part because of his prior dispensation for Charles to marry Mary Tudor and wanted to avoid offending Henry); *CSPSp*, III/1, 461–3, two versions of the dispensation, 13 Nov. 1525, not received by Charles until 8 Feb. 1526.

33. Fernández Álvarez, *Carlos V*, 329–38, notes Charles's procrastination; BAV *Vat. Lat.* 6753/80, Navagero to the Signory, 28 Oct. 1525; *CDCV*, I, 100–15, marriage treaty, 17 Oct. 1525, specified a dowry of 900,000 ducats, minus the unpaid dowry due for Charles's sister Catalina (who had married King John III of Portugal the previous year), and minus the 50,000 ducats loaned by Portugal during the Comunero uprising.

34. Sanuto, *I diarii*, XLI, cols 171 and 342–5, Suardino to Mantua and Zuan Negro to his father, both 15 Mar. 1526. Gómez-Salvago Sánchez, *Fastos*, documented the adorable couple's ceremonial progress through Seville – and its cost.

35. *RVEC*, 308–14, Salinas to Ferdinand, 27 Mar. 1526; Serassi, *Delle lettere*, II, 33–5, Castiglione to Capua, 30 Mar. and 9 Apr. 1526; RAH *Ms.* 9–4827/299–300, Charles to Sessa and to Clement, 30

Mar. 1526; BAV *Vat. Lat.* 6753/169, Navagero to the Signory, 8 Apr. 1526. See also BL *Cott. Ms.* Vespasian C.III/239–41v, Lee to Wolsey, Seville 15 Apr. 1526, noting with approval that the emperor 'euer sithe wedding and afore Ester hathe patiently absteyned his communion'.

36. *Causa formada*, 61, Los Cobos to Ronquillo, 28 Mar. 1526. Charles received his absolution on 30 Apr. 1526 (BAV *Vat. Lat.* 6753/182, Navagero to the Signory, 1 May 1526), but Clement delayed for more than a year before commuting the penitence imposed on Los Cobos ('because they say that he was the first to advise Your Majesty to proceed against the bishop as you did') and to absolve Ronquillo and his associates: Rodríguez Villa, *Memorias*, 226–8, Secretary Pérez to Charles, Rome, 26 June 1527; and Serassi, *Delle lettere*, II, 142–3, Castiglione to Capua, 13 Mar. 1527.

37. *KFF*, I, 376–80, Charles to Ferdinand, 30 Mar. 1526; *RVEC*, 308–14, Salinas to Ferdinand, 27 Mar. 1526; Sanuto, *I diarii*, XLI, cols 342–5, Zuan Negro to his father, Seville, 15 Mar. 1526; Serassi, *Delle lettere*, II, 29–33, Castiglione to Capua, 24 Mar. 1526.

38. Braamcamp Freire, 'Ida', 609–12, Antonio de Azevedo Coutinho to the count of Vimiosa, 16 Mar. 1526, and 616, marquis de Vila Real to Antonio Carneiro, 17 Mar. 1526; Halkin and Dansaert, *Charles de Lannoy*, 293–4, Charles to Lannoy, Mar. 1526 (explaining why his hand was too weak to write a holograph letter); ASF *SDO* 58/21, Domenico Canigiani to the Eight, 7 Apr. 1526; Serassi, *Delle lettere*, II, 64–71, Castiglione to Cardinal Salviati, 8 Sep. 1526 ('troppo diligenza circa l'essere buon marito').

39. Hauser, *Le traité*, 150–3 'Mémoires délibérés au conseil du Roy touchant le traité de Madril', Bayonne, 17 Mar. 1526; HHStA *Frankreich: Varia*, Konv. D/1, 1526, 14/1 ff. 84–90 and Konv. E, 1526 ff. 24–9, French royal council to Louis de Praet, Bayonne, 20 Mar. 1526; Halkin and Dansaert, *Charles de Lannoy*, 298–9, Charles to Lannoy, 27 Mar. 1526.

40. *CWE*, XII, 266–7 (# 1731), Charles to Erasmus, 4 Aug. 1526, Latin, minute.

41. BL *Cott. Ms.* Vespasian C.III/273–v, Lee to Henry, 30 Sep. 1526; Górski, *Acta Tomiciana*, VIII, 335–64, Dantiszek to Sigismund, 12 Oct. 1526 (Spanish translation in Fontán and Axer, *Españoles y polacos*, 186).

42. BL *Cott. Ms.* Vespasian C.III/239–41v, Lee to Wolsey, Seville, 15 Apr. 1526, decoded original; BL *Cott. Ms.* Caligula D.IX/183–5, Taylor to Wolsey, 4 Apr. 1526, narrating what Francis had told him at an audience the week before. See also Le Glay, *Négocations*, II, 656–8, 'Explications du roi', on why he had not ratified the treaty, 2 Apr. 1526.

43. Guicciardini, *Istoria*, III, 402 (from Book XVI, ch. 6, written between 1537 and 1540); BAV *Vat. Lat.* 6753/183–7, Navagero to the Signory, 14 May 1526. See also Castiglione's assertion that Francis had bribed most members of Charles's entourage: p. 156 above.

44. HSA *Ms.* B 2954/8, Louise to Charles, c. 31 Jan. 1526 (a promise repeated in HSA *Ms* B 2954/7, same to same, c. 15 Feb. 1526), and Champollion-Figeac, *Captivité*, 517–18, Francis to Charles, San Sebastián, Mar. 1526, all holograph.

45. Guicciardini, *Istoria*, III, 405; Serassi, *Delle lettere*, II, 9 and 35–9, Castiglione to Capua, 9 Dec. 1525, postscript, and 26 Apr. 1526.

46. *L&P Henry VIII*, IV/1, 881–2, Ghinucci and Casale to Wolsey, Rome, 7 Feb. 1526 (quoting Clement); BL *Cott. Ms.* Galba B.IX/3–4, Wingfield to Wolsey, Antwerp, 9 Feb. 1526, with marginal comments dictated by Wolsey.

47. TNA *SP* 1/37/212, Wolsey to Louise of Savoy, undated (but 20 Mar. 1526), French, copy; BL *Cott. Ms.* Caligula D.IX/172–8, Henry's instructions to Sir Thomas Cheyne, his envoy to France, undated (but 22 Mar. 1526).

48. HSA *Ms.* 2954/1–2, Charles to Francis and Louise, Mar–Apr. 1526, both holograph, replying to their recent letters promising compliance; Guicciardini, *Opere inediti*, IV, 6–8, Guicciardini to Gambara, the pope's special envoy to England, Rome, 21 Apr. 1526, conveying Clement's views.

49. Le Glay, *Négociations*, II, 660–4, Lannoy to Charles, 16 and 25 May, and to Margaret, 18 May 1526.

50. *Ordonnances des rois de France. Règne de François I*ʳ, IV, 238–52, text of the 'Sainte Ligue', Cognac, 22 May 1526. Sanuto, *I diarii*, XL, cols 613–14, Navagero to the Signory, 11 Dec. 1525, gives the total claimed by England.

51. *LCK*, I, 217, Clement to Charles, undated but 23 June 1526, probably incomplete; BAV *Vat. Lat.* 6753/183–7, Navagero to the Signory, 14 May 1526.

52. HHStA *Belgien PA* 65/4/122–31v, Moncada and Sessa to Charles, 20/24 June 1526.

53. Rodríguez Villa, *Memorias*, 16–18, Lope de Soria and Lope Hurtado de Mendoza to Charles, 20 and 28 June 1526.

54. Op. cit., 20–1, Pérez to Charles, 9 Sep. 1526; Sanuto, *I diarii*, XLII, cols 582–3, Suardino to Mantua, 9 Aug. 1526; Bornate, 'Historia', 489–96, Gattinara's 'Relación' to the royal council, and response.

55. *LCK*, I, 213–16, Charles's instructions to Moncada, Granada, 11 June 1526, italics added.

56. Rodríguez Villa, *Memorias*, 18–19, Pérez to Charles, 9 July 1526.
57. *KFF*, I, 407–21, Charles to Ferdinand, 27 July 1526, draft with extensive corrections; Bornate, 'Historia', 503, 'Discorso del gran Cancelliere' (undated, but composed just before 27 July 1526 because Charles repeated entire passages from this document in his letter to Ferdinand on that date: Brandi, 'Eigenhändige Aufzeichnungen', 248).
58. *RVEC*, 323–7, Salinas to Ferdinand, 4 Aug. 1526.
59. Rodríguez Villa, *Memorias*, 41–2, Charles to Secretary Pérez in Rome, 16 Nov. 1526. Compare with Charles's instructions to Moncada on 11 June 1526, above.
60. BL *Cott. Ms.* Vespasian C.III/257–66, Lee to Henry, 7 Sep 1526; Serassi, *Delle lettere*, II, 64–85, Castiglione to Cardinal Salviati and to Capua, both dated 8 Sep. 1526. BAV *Vat. Lat.* 6753/203v–15, Navagero to the Signory, 6 Sep. 1526, also summarized this exchange, although he confessed that 'I did not understand it then, since I understand little of the French language, but later some councillors explained it to me'. The audience took place on 17 Aug. In his *Memoirs* Charles recalled this as a formal challenge issued by France, England, Venice and the pope: *CDCV*, IV, 493.
61. *CSPSp*, III/I, 905–22, Charles to Clement, 17 Sep. 1526; *LCK*, I, 219–21, Charles to Clement, 18 Sep. 1526; Serassi, *Delle lettere*, II, 90–2, Castiglione to Capua, 20 Sep. 1526. *BKK*, II, 178–9, provided a concordance of the public exchanges between Charles and Clement and the drafts prepared by Gattinara, Valdés and others at this time.
62. Headley, *The emperor*, ch. 5, provided a detailed discussion of *Pro Divo Carolo eius nominis Quinto Romanorum Imperatore invictissimo, pro felice semper Augusto, Patrepatriae* and its dissemination.
63. *KFF*, I, 486–92, Charles to Ferdinand, 23 Nov. 1526 (also in *LCK*, I, 224–8); *CDCV*, I, 117–19, *consulta* of the council of state on what to do after news of Mohács, undated, but shortly after Ferdinand's letter arrived on 13 Nov. Charles told his brother that he had received reports of the disaster earlier, but had not believed them (cf. *L&P Henry VIII*, IV/2, 1153, Lee to Henry, 1 Nov. 1526, containing a full account).
64. BAV *Vat. Lat.* 6753/232, Navagero to the Signory, 2 Dec. 1526, reporting indiscretions from the nuncio about his recent audience (English summary in *CSPV*, III, 620–3). Serassi, *Delle lettere*, II, 125–7, Castiglione to Capua, 2 Dec. 1526, omitted these self-abasing comments.
65. RAH *Salazar* A-40/147–8, Pérez to Charles, 14 Feb. 1527.
66. *KFF*, II/1, 26–8 Charles to Ferdinand, 6 Mar. 1527. RAH *Salazar* A-40/212–20, Nájera to Charles, Rome, 3 Mar. 1527, noted Bourbon's use of the 'strada Romana andando hazia Bolonia'.
67. AGS *E* 847/180–1, Francisco de Salazar to Gattinara, 18 May 1527.
68. Rodríguez Villa, *Memorias*, 165–7, Soria to Charles, 25 May 1527; *KFF*, II/1, 81–3 and 85–8, Ferdinand to Charles, 30 and 31 May 1527.
69. BL *Cott. Ms.* Vespasian C.IV/166–8v, Lee to Wolsey, 27 June 1527 (describing an imperial audience two days before). See also Górski, *Acta Tomiciana*, IX, 216–17, Dantiszek to Sigismund, 17 Aug. 1527, describing Charles's claim at the same audience with similar disbelief (Spanish translation in Fontán and Axer, *Españoles y polacos*, 201–6).
70. ASF *SDO* 58/49, Domenico Canigiani to the Eight, Valladolid, 31 May 1527.
71. HHStA *Belgien PA* 66/3/281, Charles to Bourbon, 7 June 1527, minute, italics added. (Mignet, *Rivalité*, II, 330–1, followed by Rodríguez Villa, *Memorias*, 203, both quoted parts of this letter, but they linked together passages that are separate in the document, and gave an incorrect date.) Several other sources reveal that the emperor had planned for his army to capture – though not to sack – Rome, and to take the pope prisoner. (i) Charles himself repudiated the truce concluded by Lannoy with the pope (Halkin and Dansaert, *Charles de Lannoy*, 319–20, Charles to Lannoy, 12 May 1527); (ii) on the same day, Navagero claimed that Charles had ordered Bourbon to attack Rome (BAV *Vat. Lat.* 6753/260v–3v, to the Signory, 12 May 1527); (iii) HHStA *Belgien PA* 94/446, Gattinara to Charles, 28 May 1527, written at Palamos on the Catalan coast, stated that 'if before I embark [for Italy] certain news should arrive that the pope has come to Barcelona, I will remain here'; (iv) Charvet, *Lettres et documents*, 131–2, Agrippa von Nettesheim to Bourbon, Lyons, 30 Mar. 1527, revealed that the duke had already confided his plan to 'bring down those proud walls after a few days' siege', a revelation that came from Eustache Chapuys, who served as a courier between Bourbon and Charles (ibid., 132–4) – one more indication that Bourbon had been following Charles's orders; (v) Don Juan Manuel informed the Florentine ambassador that Charles's council had 'discussed many times what to do with His Holiness – whether to bring him here or leave him in Italy – and many were of the opinion that he should be brought here' (ASF *SDO* 58/52, Canigiani to the Eight, 12 July 1527). Rodríguez Villa, *Memorias*, 202–3, presented yet more evidence regarding Charles's complicity in the capture of Rome.
72. Halkin and Dansaert, *Charles de Lannoy*, 321–7, Charles's instructions to Lannoy, 30 June 1527, and to Veyré, 21 July 1527.
73. *LCK*, I, 248–56, Veyré to Charles, Naples, 30 Sep. 1527.

74. *Ordonnances des rois de France. Règne de François Ier,* V, 87–99, treaty of Amiens, 18 Aug. 1527 (confirming the terms of earlier treaties agreed at the More in August 1525 and at Westminster in Apr. 1527).

75. *LCK,* I, 235–48, Leyva to Charles, 20 July 1527, with postscripts down to 4 Aug.

76. RAH *Salazar* A-41/1–3, Instructions of Hernando de Alarcón to Alonso Gayoso, his envoy to Charles, Rome, 1 Dec. 1527 (printed in Rodríguez Villa, *Memorias,* 229–34, but incorrectly dated June 1527); Muratori, *Delle antichità,* II, 341–52, 'Capitoli della Lega . . . per la liberazione d'esso Papa Clemente', 15 Nov. 1527.

77. BAV *Vat. Lat.* 6753/283, Navagero to the Signory, 1 Aug. 1527 (English summary in *CSPV,* IV, 81); *KFF,* II/1, 119–23, Charles to Ferdinand, 8 Sep. 1527.

78. Fernández Álvarez, *Felipe II y su tiempo,* 621–2, Charles to the magistrates of Úbeda and Barcelona, 21 and 23 May 1527; *RVEC,* 359–60, Salinas to Ferdinand, 29 May 1527.

79. *RVEC,* 363–71 and 387–9, Salinas to Ferdinand, 19 Aug. and 23 Nov. 1527.

80. BL *Cott. Ms.* Vespasian C.IV/145–52, Ghinucci, Poyntz and Lee to Wolsey, 17 July 1527; and BAV *Vat. Lat.* 6753/295–7v and 300, Navagero to the Signory, 25 Oct. and 17 Nov. 1527 (English summary in *CSPV,* IV, 102–5). See also BL *Cott. Ms.* Vespasian C.IV/94–6v, Ghinucci to Wolsey, 16 Apr. 1527: Charles 'visus est ultra solitum tristis, turbatus et asper'.

81. Boone, *Mercurino,* 127 (*Autobiography:* see the original in Bornate, 'Historia', 355).

82. Górski, *Acta Tomiciana,* X, 61–5, Dantiszek to Sigismund, 29 Jan. 1528, quoting Cicero, *De inventione,* I, 71. The key word in the Latin original was '*diffidatio*'. (Spanish translation in Fontán and Axer, *Españoles y polacos,* 207–10.)

83. Loc. cit., Dantiszek to Sigismund, 29 Jan. 1528; *PEG,* I, 310–21, 'Declaration de Guerre', 22 Jan. 1528 (quotation from pp. 319–20).

84. Sanuto, *I diarii,* XLVIII, cols 149–50, Zuan Negro, secretary of the Venetian ambassador, to his father, 1 June 1528; RAH *Salazar* A-42/80, Charles warrant to the governor of Cerdeña and Rossellon, 22 Jan. 1528, minute. On the heartless treatment of the princes, see Pascual Barroso, *Dos niños príncipes.*

85. *KFF,* II/1, 176–85, Charles's instructions to William of Montfort, his envoy to Margaret and Ferdinand, 31 Jan. 1528.

86. Arfaioli, *The black bands,* 36 and 99–100 (quoting Giovio, *Delle historie*). Proof that his enemies had correctly discerned Charles's strategic priorities at this time comes from *KFF,* II/1, 148–52, Charles to Ferdinand, 21 Nov. 1527, copy of holograph: if both Milan and Naples are 'en eminent peril, j'aime mieulx secourir et remedier en Naples, qu'est du patrimoine de noz predecesseurs, que non pas ledit Millan que n'est de nostre heritage'.

87. Sanuto, *I diarii,* XLVII, cols 26–7, Ludovico Ceresara to the marquis of Mantua, 25 Feb. 1528; ibid., XLVII, col. 389, Pompeo Colonna to Lorenzo Campeggio, Gaeta, 1 May 1528. Arfaioli, *The black bands,* 198–203, provided the best account of the battle and its impact.

88. *PEG,* I, 349–50, Charles to Jehan de Calvymont, ambassador 'estant à présent à Poza en Castille', 18 Mar. 1528.

89. *PEG,* I, 350–9, 'Audience de congé' granted by Francis to Nicholas Perrenot de Granvelle, 28 Mar. 1528 (also printed in *LCK,* I, 265–70), and ibid., 372–4, Cartel of Francis, delivered in French and Spanish.

90. Bornate, 'Historia', 362 (Boone, *Mercurino,* 131, mistranslates 'Catellanis' as 'Castilians' instead of 'Catalans'); *RVEC,* 392–8, Salinas to Ferdinand, 4 Feb. 1528. García Martínez, 'Estudio', 130–1, noted that the Valencian chronicler Martí de Viciana allocated 'almost half the space devoted to imperial matters' for 1528 to the 'chivalric challenge to Francis, unequivocal proof that the affair fascinated contemporaries'.

91. *RVEC,* 404–10, Salinas to Ferdinand, 8 July 1528.

92. AGS *E* 8815/24–6, *consulta* of the royal council to Charles, 20 June 1528, and f. 29, Tavera, president of the council to Charles, 12 June 1528. This volume contains forty-two letters of advice sent to Charles by individual nobles, towns and prelates of Castile, as well as by its council, almost all holograph; *CODOIN,* I, 47–95, printed copies of most of them. Villar García, 'Cartas', 85, Charles to Rodrigo Mexía, 79–81, 10 Nov. 1528, revealed that the process of securing opinions concerning the cartel was far wider, involving councils, prelates, nobles 'and other gentlemen *[caballeros]* with whom we shared it'.

93. *PEG,* I, 384–7, duke of Infantado to Charles, 20 June 1528. The merchant community strongly disapproved, considering the resort to single combat to decide affairs of state, 'something almost unheard of, and truly unworthy of such princes': *CWE,* XIV, 258–61 (# 2024), Schets to Erasmus, Antwerp, 14 Aug. 1528.

94. *LCK,* I, 405–11, Cartel of Charles V, and instructions to his herald 'Bourgogne', 24 June 1528; BMECB *Ms. Granvelle* I/149, Charles to Baron Montfort, 19 July 1528, holograph postscript ('N'obliez

d'amener Colman avec estouffe et ouvriers, si d'auenture il me failloit combattre'. Presumably Helmschmid and his team would work on 'fitting' one of the garnitures they had already made for Charles, since they would not have time to create a new one). Bond, 'Costume albums', 72–87, documented Helmschmid's journey to the imperial court in 1529.
95. BNF *F. f.* 3001/15, Francis to Anne, duke of Montmorency, Fontainebleau, 28 July 1528.

CHAPTER 8: CHAMPION OF THE WESTERN WORLD, 1528–31

1. ASMa *AG CE* Napoli e Sicilia 810/125, Lautrec to the marquis of Mantua, 'From the camp before Naples', 1 June 1528. I thank Maurizio Arfaioli for this reference.
2. Robert, 'Philibert de Châlon', XXXIX, 174–81, Charles to the prince of Orange, 19 July 1528; Cadenas y Vicent, *El Protectorado*, 85–8, Articles agreed with Doria on 19 July, approved by the royal council on 10 Aug. and signed by Charles the following day (English summary in *CSPSp*, III/2, 765–8). Apparently, Charles had delegated full powers in this way only once before: to those handling his election as king of the Romans in 1519.
3. Sanuto, *I diarii*, XLVIII, cols 478–80, 'Capitoli et conventione afirmati' between the prince of Orange and the marquis of Saluzzo, Aversa, 30 Aug. 1528.
4. Arfaioli, *The black bands*, 165. Arfaioli's account of the siege ('See Naples, then die': ibid., 115–62) is the best available.
5. *CDCV*, IV, 495 (*Memoirs*); Salonia, *Genoa's freedom*, 141; Keniston, *Memorias*, 171 (Sancho Cota). For Doria's other motives, see Pacini, *La Genova*, 42–5.
6. *KFF*, I, 277–81, Charles to Ferdinand, 26 Mar. 1525; BAV *Vat. Lat.* 6753/264–5v, Navagero to the Signory, 23 May 1527; Firpo, *Relazioni*, III, 60, Relation of Federico Badoer, Feb. 1557; ASF *MdP* 4301/209–13, Ricasole to Duke Cosimo, 27 Sep. 1543; Bornate, 'Historia', 545–8, Leyva to Charles, 7 Jan. 1529.
7. AGS *E* 848/64–5, Praet and Mai to Charles, Rome, 12 Aug. 1529; *NBD, 2. Ergänzungsband 1532*, 102–7, Aleandro to Sanga, 25 Mar. 1532; *NBD*, XIII, 116–21, Nuncio Camaini to Cardinal del Monte, 16 Sep. 1552, coded postscript (italics added to all quotations). For a broader consideration of Fortune's role in human affairs during the Renaissance, see Buttay-Jutier, *Fortuna*, and Crouzet, *Charles de Bourbon*, 154–62 and 191–9. I thank Maurizio Arfaioli for reminding me of the importance of 'Fortuna Caesaris'.
8. Boone, *Mercurino*, 132 (Gattinara's *Autobiography*, apparently quoting his holograph instructions to the prince of Orange, 29 Dec. 1528: 'If God is pleased to give us victory ... let us not lose the fruit, as we have done with past victories': HHStA, *Belgien PA* 66/4/379–82v); RAH *Salazar* A-43/184–9, Alonso Sánchez to Charles, 21 Sep. 1528.
9. AGS *E* 848/36, Mai to Charles, Rome, 11 May 1529, reporting on his audience on 24 Apr. (partly printed, with some errors, by Heine, *Briefe*, 520–1); *LCK*, I, 296–8, Charles to Clement, Apr. 1529, copy of holograph original; AGS *E* 848/14, Mai to Charles, Rome, 8 June 1529 (reporting Clement's declaration).
10. Dumont, *Corps*, IV/2, 1–7, 'Tractatus confoederationis inter Carolum V ... & Clementem VII', Barcelona, 29 June 1529; AGS *E* 848/5–6, Brief of Clement VII, 6 Aug. 1529; *L&P Henry VIII*, IV/3, 2583–4, English ambassadors in Rome to Wolsey, 16 July 1529. Gattinara became a cardinal by Clement's declaration on 13 Aug. 1529.
11. *PEG*, I, 427–32, Charles's instructions to Baron Balançon, Sep. 1528, copy of holograph; *KFF*, II/1, 295–308 and 335–46, Charles's instructions to Baron Montfort, 8 and 28 Nov. 1528 (the latter superseded the former); Sanuto, *I diarii*, L, cols 279–81, ambassador Malatesta to the marquis of Mantua, 24 Feb. 1529; *RVCE*, 424–30, Salinas to Ferdinand, 3 Apr. 1529. On the efforts of his Spanish ministers to sabotage his trip to Italy, see pp. 206–7 below.
12. Sanuto, *I diarii*, L, cols 63–4, letter from Giovanni Battista Grimaldi to the Grimaldi company in Genoa, 10 Feb. 1529. *CDCV*, I, 137–54, printed various instruments and instructions signed by Charles on 8 Mar. 1529. No copy of the will he signed that day has survived: its existence is known only because his aunt Margaret acknowledged receiving a copy. It is impossible to provide a precise date for the creation and reform of most councils, since Charles often reorganized them several times: see, for example, Carlos Morales, *El consejo*, 25–34, for the gradual reorganization of the council of finance between mid-1522 and 16 Jan. 1525, the date when Los Cobos administered an oath to all council members. Espinosa, *The empire*, 281, provides a brilliant organogram of Charles's central government at this time.
13. RAH *Salazar* A-44/37–41, Charles to Leyva, 16 Feb. 1529, draft in Gattinara's hand, heavily corrected.
14. AGS *E* 267/161–3, 'Traslado de los capítulos que se enviaron a Don Ugo de Moncada, y después de su fallecimiento al príncipe de Oranges' in Naples, originally dated 19 Apr., but revised 16 May 1529, minute. Charles sent similar instructions to Leyva and other ministers in Lombardy.

15. Boone, *Mercurino*, 136, Gattinara's *Autobiography*, apparently written as he and Charles waited in Barcelona; Headley, 'The emperor', 35 note 20, quoting a German pamphlet: 'Keyser/Keyser/for uber/for uber/herre der weldt!'.

16. Sanuto, *I diarii*, LI, cols 399–403, 'Raporto', 20 Aug. 1529; Boom, 'Voyage', 62. A glance at 'Austria, Carlo di' in the index of Sanuto, *I diarii*, vol. 50, covering March–June 1529, reveals that the Venetian ambassadors were obsessed with when and whether Charles would come to Italy, and the possible consequences.

17. *KFF*, II/I, 315–17, Charles to Ferdinand, 4 Nov. 1528 (also printed in *LCK*, I, 291–2, and Le Glay, *Négociations*, II, 675–6); RAH *Salazar* A-44/37–41, Charles to Leyva, 16 Feb. 1529 (albeit with a postscript a week later stating that if he happened to encounter Francis in Italy, 'perhaps we can deal with his challenge'). HSA *B* 2854, Charles to Henry VIII, 31 Oct. 1528 (draft in AGS *E* 16/285), is one of the letters sent to other 'kings and princes'.

18. *L&P Henry VIII*, IV/2, 1918, treaty of Hampton Court, 15 June 1528 (summary); Dumont, *Corps*, IV/1, 514–15, Treaty of Gorcum, 3 Oct. 1528 (partial).

19. Gachard, 'Charles Quint', 567 note, Charles to Margaret, 15 Oct. 1528; BL *Cott. Ms.* Galba B.IX/220–1, Charles's appointment of Margaret as his 'procuratrix générale, spéciale et irrévocable' in the peace talks, 8 Apr. 1529, notarized copy (printed text in *Ordonnances des rois de France. Règne de François Ier*, V/2, 253–4, followed by the parallel power granted by Francis to Louise, 2 June 1529).

20. *Ordonnances des rois de France. Règne de François Ier*, V/2, 221–56, and Dumont, *Corps*, IV/2, 7–17, peace of Cambrai, 5 Aug. 1529, with the treaty of Madrid inserted (but not printed).

21. AGS *GA* 2/29–30, Charles to the empress, Genoa, 30 Aug. 1529; Le Glay, *Négociations*, II, 693–7, Praet to Granvelle, 31 Aug. 1529.

22. *Ordonnances des rois de France. Règne de François Ier*, V/2, 276–8, and Dumont, *Corps*, IV/2, 52–3, 'Protestation' of Francis against the peace of Cambrai before the Parlement of Paris, 16 Nov. 1529.

23. AHN Nobleza *Frías* C.457 D.43, 'Sentencia del Condestable' on Juan de Jalón, who tried to help the princes to escape, 28 May 1529 (Jalón was executed the next day); AHN Nobleza *Frías* C.23 D.26, Charles to the Constable of Castile and marquis of Berlanga, Palamos, 1 Aug. 1529; *CDCV*, I, 186, Margaret to the empress, 15 Dec. 1529; AGS *GA* 2/29–30, Charles to the empress, 30 Aug. 1529; and AHN Nobleza *Frías* C.23 D.27, empress to Berlanga, 27 Sep. 1529 (passing on verbatim her husband's orders).

24. AGS *CMC* 1a/590/1, 'Cuenta de Álvaro de Lugo' for the 'ransom received for the sons of the King of France', records the extra coins. Sanuto, *I diarii*, LIII, cols 344–5, Andrea Corsoni to Guido Rangon, Bayonne, 2 July 1530, recorded the 'endless assaying' of the coins before the hostages were released. A visit to Pedraza de la Sierra today reveals why Henry II never forgave or forgot his internment there.

25. *KFF*, II/2, 484–9, Charles to Ferdinand, Voghera, 5 Sep. 1529; and 473–6, Ferdinand's instructions to Count Noguerol, Linz, 18 Aug. 1529 (also printed in *CDCV*, I, 159–61).

26. *CWE*, XVIII, 19–22 (# 2481), Erasmus to Bernard Boerio, 11 Apr. 1531. Six decades later, the Portuguese chronicler Diogo do Couto added to this 'twins' conceit by claiming that Suleiman 'succeeded to the Ottoman empire on the same day that the invincible emperor Charles V was crowned' – but in fact Suleiman succeeded on 1 Oct. 1520, whereas Charles's coronation as king of the Romans took place on the 23rd: Lima Cruz, *Diogo do Couto*, I, 191–2 (década VIII, libro III ch. 1). My thanks to Sanjay Subrahmanyam and Jane Hathaway for these data.

27. *LCK*, I, 66–8, Charles to La Chaulx (his special envoy to Rome), and *BKK*, II, 151, Charles to Margaret, both from Palencia, 25 Aug. 1522.

28. Gachard, 'Charles Quint', 573, Charles to Margaret, 23 Sep. 1529; *KFF*, II/2, 499–509, Charles's instructions for Noguerol, returning to Ferdinand, 23 Sep. 1529.

29. AGS *E* 1555/130 and 131, Charles to de Praet and Mai, 16 and 20 Sep. 1529; AGS *E* 848/7, Charles's instructions to the archbishop of Bari, going to the pope, 9 Oct. 1529.

30. Gachard, 'Charles Quint', 575 n. 1, Charles to Margaret, 16 Nov. 1529. See also AGS *E* 1454/171, Gattinara to Charles, 1 Nov. 1529, written as soon as the good news arrived from Vienna: 'Since the Turks have now retreated, so that Your Majesty's journey to Germany is less urgent' the emperor should first 'arrange the affairs of Italy'.

31. Details from Giordano, *Della venuta*, 24–37 ('Carlo, Carlo, Imperio, Imperio, Vittoria, Vittoria!'), and Sanuto, *I diarii*, LII, cols 180–1, Gasparo Contarini to the Signory, Bologna, 5 and 6 Nov. 1529 (also in *CSPV*, IV, 234–5). Sanuto, op. cit., cols 182–99, contains other eyewitness accounts of the 'triumph'. Stirling-Maxwell, *Entry*, reprinted with commentary a set of sixteen images of Charles's entry published in 1530. In 1515, Francis and Leo X had also cohabited when they met in Bologna after Marignano.

32. Alberì, *Relazioni*, 2nd series III, 255–74, Relation of Gasparo Contarini, 4 Mar. 1530 (quotations from 264 and 269); AGS *PR* 16/96, 'Las cosas que Su Magestad ha de tener memoria para hablar y

suplicar a Su Santidad son las siguientes', undated but late 1529 (*BKK*, II, 248–9, printed this text with some errors, and without Charles's annotations; *CSPSp*, IV, 239, provided a summary that contains major inaccuracies and the wrong call number). Cadenas y Vicent, *Doble coronación*, 96, Clement to Charles, 29 Oct. 1529, revealed another discussion topic, promising that 'we will discuss further in person' plans to attack the Turks. Ibid., Part XI, listed the dates of the secret meetings between pope and emperor.

33. Laurent, *Recueil*, III, 3–4, papal grant, Bologna, 20 Feb. 1530; Dumont, *Corps*, IV/2, 53–8, treaty of alliance, and Sanuto, *I diarii*, LII, cols 422–32, Charles's treaties with Sforza and with Venice, both Bologna, 23 Dec. 1529. Florence remained unreconciled for the time being because its republican leaders refused to readmit Medici rule.

34. BL *Addl. Ms.* 28,579/288–91, Los Cobos to the empress, 28 Dec [1529]; Sanuto, *I diarii*, LII, cols 308–9, letter of Federico, secretary to the papal legate in Venice, to his master, 20 [*recte* 26] Dec. 1529.

35. *KFF*, II/2, 549–63, Charles to Ferdinand, Bologna, 11 Jan. 1530, minute with holograph corrections (also printed in *LCK*, I, 360–73). All the following quotes come from this document.

36. AGS *E* 1454/170, Gattinara to Charles, 29 Oct. 1529. (*CSPSp*, IV, 319–20, asserted that Gattinara referred to Emperor Frederick Barbarossa, but this is not correct: see Sanuto, *I diarii*, LII, cols 622–4, 'Copia de una lettera' about the coronation of Frederick III in 1452 – the Frederick to whom Gattinara referred.)

37. Details from Stirling-Maxwell, *The procession* (reproducing commemorative prints by Hogenberg). Other details from Boom, 'Voyage', 92; and the sources printed in Cadenas y Vicent, *Doble coronación*, part IX.

38. Sanuto, *I diarii*, LII, cols 603–79 (folios 423–48 of his annual compilation); and Borrás Gualis, *La imagen triunfal* (especially the 'Repertorio iconográfico' at 247–375).

39. Borrás Gualis, *La imagen triunfal*, 32–4 (projects proposed but never realized); Bodart, *Tiziano*, 209, ambassador Leonardi to the duke of Urbino, 18 Mar. 1530, reporting the complaint of his Mantuan colleague (at ibid., pp. 61–5, Bodart discussed this statement, which might merely reflect disappointment that Charles had not suitably honoured the marquis of Mantua, but concluded that other complaints about the emperor's 'extreme avarice' support the ambassador's claim); *RVEC*, 483–5, Salinas to Ferdinand, 28 Mar. 1530.

40. *RVEC*, 492–4, Salinas to Ferdinand, 24 Apr. 1530. Bodart, 'Algunos casos', 18, prints an engraving of the monument (which apparently no longer exists). Soly, *Charles*, 488, printed a replica in rock crystal of the imitation of Trajan's column erected at Mantua.

41. *LWB*, II, 306–10 (# 401), Luther to Charles, 28 Apr. 1521 (with a similar letter on the same day, in Latin and German, to the 'Electors, princes and Estates' at pp. 310–18, # 402); Laurent, *Recueil*, II, 578–83, Ordinance published 14 Oct. 1529 (the list of condemned Reformers included Wyclif and Hus, who had both been dead for more than a century: perhaps Charles felt that one can never be too cautious where heretics are concerned); Förstemann, *Urkundenbuch*, I, 1–9, Charles V's 'Reichstag Ausschreiben', Bologna, 21 Jan. 1530.

42. *LWB*, V, 366–70 (# 590), Justas Jonas to Luther, 18 June 1530, and Sanuto, *I diarii*, LIII, cols 318–19, Paxin Berecio to Thomas Tiepolo, 16 June 1530, describing the processions. The 'Protest' was lodged at a meeting of Lutheran rulers on 19 Apr. 1529.

43. Boone, *Mercurino*, 69.

44. Heine, *Briefe*, 355–7, Loaysa to Charles, 6 July 1530 (also printed in *CODOIN*, XIV, 36–9). Nieva Ocampo, 'El confesor', 661–2, documented the rivalry between Gattinara and Loaysa; Martínez Pérez, *El confesor*, 207–38, and Lehnhoff, *Die Beichtväter*, 34–59, chronicled the life and times of Loaysa. It seems noteworthy that ambassador Salinas had realized a year earlier that Granvelle would become a powerful minister, and advised his master to start courting him: *RVEC*, 435–7, Salinas to Ferdinand, 22 June 1529.

45. Heine, *Briefe*, 357–9, Loaysa to Charles, 18 July 1530 (also printed in *CODOIN*, XIV, 43–5).

46. *NBD, 1. Ergänzungsband 1530–1531*, 60–1 and 63–74, Campeggio to Salviati, 14 and 26 June 1530; *LWB*, V, 383–4 (# 1598), Andreas Osiander to Luther, 21 June 1530. (Osiander wrote in Latin but used German – and Black Letter – for Charles's reassuring words to Margrave George of Brandenburg-Ansbach: 'Cesarem respondisse, "𝕹𝖎𝖈𝖍𝖙 𝖐𝖔𝖕𝖋 𝖆𝖇𝖍𝖆𝖚𝖊𝖓! 𝕹𝖎𝖈𝖍𝖙 𝖐𝖔𝖕𝖋 𝖆𝖇𝖍𝖆𝖚𝖊𝖓!")

47. *CWE*, XVI, 343–5 (# 2333), Simon Pistoris to Erasmus, Augsburg, 27 June 1530; *LWB*, V, 453–9 (# 1633), Luther to Elector John of Saxony, 9 July 1530; Spalatin quoted by Roper, *Martin Luther*, 314.

48. Heine, *Briefe*, 359–62, Loaysa to Charles, 31 July 1530 (also printed in *CODOIN*, XIV, 52–5); *CR*, II, cols 245–6, Brenz to Isenmann, 4 Aug. 1530 – though see the dissenting view in *LWB*, V, 426–9 (# 1618), Jonas to Luther, c. 30 June 1530: 'Satis attentus erat Caesar', during the reading of the Augsburg Confession.

49. Sanuto, *I diarii*, LIII, cols 384 and 504–5, Marco Antonio Magno to Marco Contarini, 20 July 1530 (on the feasting) and 9 Aug. 1530 (on the threats); and ibid., cols 474–5, Paxin Berecio and Niccolò Tiepolo to Thomas Tiepolo, 7 and 10 Aug. 1530. According to Magno, Charles wrote his response in French, which was translated into German before being read out to the Diet.
50. Sanuto, *I diarii*, LIII, cols 428–9, Benedeto de Rani to Francesco di Contissi da Faenza, 2 Aug. 1530; Heine, *Briefe*, 377–8, Loaysa to Charles, 8 Oct. 1530 (also printed in *CODOIN*, XIV, 88–91); AGS *E* 1558/62, Charles to Loaysa, 20 Oct. 1530, minute (with the last pathetic phrase struck through, and replaced with 'in addition, the situation is very unfavourable'); Förstemann, *Urkundenbuch*, II, 715–25 and 839–41, *Reichsabschied*, Augsburg, 13 Oct. and 19 Nov. 1530.
51. Roper, *Martin Luther*, 339.
52. *CDCV*, I, 247–50, Charles to Clement, undated (but 20 Oct. 1530), copy of holograph sent with Pedro de la Cueva; AGS *E* 849/6, La Cueva to Charles, Rome, 17 Nov. 1530.
53. AGS *CMC* 1a/590, 'Cuenta de Álvaro de Luna', warrant dated Augsburg 4 Aug. 1530, authorizing payment of 200,000 ducats to Ferdinand's special agent (*CDCV*, I, 256–9, Charles to the empress, 6 Dec. 1530, explained the purpose); Lanz, *Staatspapiere*, 50–3, calculated the probable cost of the election, undated (but late 1530). Kohler, *Antihabsburgische Politik*, 132–59, listed the total payments, almost 500,000 florins, made to the electors.
54. Sanuto, *I diarii*, LIV, cols 268–72, Sigismondo de la Torre, Mantuan ambassador, to the duke, 11 Jan. 1531.
55. Gachard, *Analectes Belgiques*, I, 378–9, Margaret to Charles, 30 Nov. 1530; Dumont, *Corps*, IV/2, 73, Codicil to Margaret's Will, 28 Nov. 1530.
56. Gachard, *Collection de documents*, I, 293–4, Charles to Count Hoogstraeten, 3 Dec. 1530, and 296–9, Hoogstraeten and the archbishop of Palermo to Charles, 8 Dec. 1530.
57. *CMH*, I, 15–20, Charles to Marie, 3 Jan. 1531, holograph (also printed in Gachard, *Analectes Belgiques*, I, 381–6). Charles apologized for not asking her to serve while they were together at Augsburg, but he apparently erred: the queen's summary of the letter mentions '*les ofres que luy ay faites à Augsburg*' (ibid., 20), and she also told Ferdinand, on hearing of Margaret's death, 'J'ay en bonne memoire *l'ofre que ay fait* tant à l'empereur que à vous' at Augsburg 'que vous voroie servir et obéir' (*KFF*, II/2, Marie to Ferdinand, 26 Dec. 1530, italics added).
58. AGS *E* 496/94, Dr Escoriaza to the empress, Brussels, 29 Jan. (endorsed '1530', but evidently 1531); Sanuto, *I diarii*, LIV, cols 430–2, La Torre to the duke of Mantua, 26 Apr. 1531.
59. AGS *E* 8335/109, Marie of Hungary to Philip II, 4 Sep. 1558, copy, looking back on the situation in 1531; Tracy, *Emperor*, 90, quoting the Resolutions of the States of Holland, 29 Mar. 1531.
60. *KFF*, III/2, 280–95, Charles to Ferdinand, 1 Oct. 1531. I thank James Tracy for suggesting that 'hauteur' is best translated here as 'sovereignty'. Charles claimed that some of his officials '*cryent le murdre sur moy*' – a very strong statement – and concluded his letter: 'I did not wish these details to be written by any hand but mine, nor to anyone except you. I therefore beg you to keep this letter somewhere where it cannot be seen by anyone else.'
61. *CMH*, II, 28–33, Charles to Marie, 1 Feb. 1533. Laurent, *Recueil*, III, 236–54 and 260–79, contain the numerous commissions and instructions concerning the regency government of the Netherlands signed by Charles between 27 Sep. and 7 Oct. 1531. Henne, *Histoire*, V, ch. 18, reviews Charles's achievements in the Netherlands in 1531–2.
62. *KFF*, III/1, 89–100, 129–35 and 152–6, Charles to Ferdinand, 3 Apr., 16 and 21 May, and 14 June 1531, all holograph (also printed in *LCK*, I, 429–36, 456–7 and 479–84); Sanuto, *I diarii*, LIV, cols 501, Tiepolo to the Signory, 1 July 1531, and 566–8, La Torre to the duke of Mantua, 7 Aug. 1531.
63. *NBD*, 1. *Ergänzungsband 1530–1531*, 399–404, Aleandro to Salviati and Sanga, 14 Nov 1531 (two letters); *KFF*, III/1, 152–6 1 and 183–90, and III/3, Charles to Ferdinand, 14 June and 7 July 1531 (also printed in *LCK*, I, 479–84 and 490–4), and 3 Jan. 1532, all holograph.

PORTRAIT OF THE EMPEROR AS A RENAISSANCE PRINCE

1. Reiffenberg, *Histoire*, 375–6, a précis of the deliberations of the 20th Chapter of the Order held at Tournai in Dec. 1531, compiled by its Greffier.
2. Brandi, 'Aus den Kabinettsakten', 190–2, paper of advice submitted by Gattinara in late 1523, together with comments by the royal council and by Charles (Gossart, *Notes*, 100–19, also printed this important document, but from an imperfect copy); Boone, *Mercurino*, 112–13 (from Gattinara's *Autobiography* for 1526); BAV *Vat. Lat.* 6753/260–3v, Navagero to the Signory, 12 May 1527.
3. Lanz, *Aktenstücke*, 441–3, Margaret to Berghes, 14 or 15 Nov. 1521, holograph minute; BNMV *Ms. Italiani, Classe VII*, cod. 1009/399, Contarini to the council of Ten, 4 Dec. 1524, communicating the report of a spy concerning Charles's exchange with the nuncio.

4. AGRB *MD* 156/126, La Roche to Margaret, 17 Jan. 1524; *CMH*, I, 89–92, Charles to Marie, 18 Feb. 1532, holograph (the rejected minister, Jean de Le Sauch, did indeed have a mind of his own: see p. 126 above). Cauchies, '"No tyenen"', 128, noted the death in the 1520s of almost all those who might have restrained Charles: Chièvres and Marliano in 1521, La Roche in 1524, Lannoy in 1527, Gorrevod in 1529, and Lachaulx, Margaret and Gattinara in 1530.

5. *CWE*, IX, 441–52, Erasmus to Udalricus Zasius, [23 Mar.] 1523; BL *Cott. Ms.* Vespasian C.II/106–20, Boleyn and Sampson to Wolsey, 8 and 18 Mar. 1523.

6. Serassi, *Delle lettere*, II, 11–17, 29–33, Castiglione to the archbishop of Capua, papal secretary of state, 19 Jan. and 24 Mar. 1526 (also noting that Charles 'is tenacious in his opinions'); *CWE*, XV, 255–61, Valdés to Erasmus, 15 May 1529. Valdés was exonerated and Charles banished his principal accuser, Secretary of State Jean Lallemand.

7. BMECB *Ms. Granvelle* I/151–5, Charles to Montfort, 16 Nov. and 23 Dec. 1528, both holograph, and idem, ff. 172–7, Instructions to Balançon, Sep. 1528, copy of holograph (printed with some errors in *PEG*, I, 427–47). Stirling-Maxwell, *The chief victories*, 76–7, printed a facsimile of the first letter together with an imperfect transcription. Charles appointed Perrenin secretary of state in 1528.

8. BMECB *Ms. Granvelle* I/153–60, Charles to Montfort, 23 Dec. 1528 and 24 Jan. 1529, both holograph (printed with some errors in *PEG*, I, 441–7).

9. Alberì, *Relazioni*, 2nd series III, 255–74, Relation of Gasparo Contarini, 4 Mar. 1530 (quotations from pp. 269–70); Walser, 'Spanien und Karl V', 167–73, Tavera to Charles, Jan. 1535 (italics added); Firpo, *Relazioni*, II, 203–4, Relation of Niccolò Tiepolo, 23 Aug. 1533.

10. Gachard, 'Notice des archives de M. le duc de Caraman', 243–4, describing a Register kept by Baron Boussu, 1 Aug. 1530–31 Jan. 1532, signed by Charles in person at the end of each month (the volume is now apparently lost).

11. *CMH*, I, 12–13, Charles to Marie, Augsburg, 18 June 1530, holograph; *KFF*, IV, 240–6, Charles to Ferdinand, Galapagar, 28 May 1534.

12. Checa Cremades, *Inventarios*, I, 104–29 (a list of the 653 books owned by Charles in May 1536); Dolce, *Le vite* (1561), f. 525v. In 1533, Charles granted a privilege to print *Los quatro libros del Cortesano . . . traducidos en lengua castellana por Boscán* (Barcelona, 1534); and in 1550, 'knowing that for our relaxation we sometimes read from a book entitled *The discourses* of Nicolas Machiavelli', he granted a licence to print a Spanish translation (Howard, *Discursos*). Diego Gracián dedicated several of his translations of Plutarch to the emperor: Morales Ortiz, *Plutarco*, 199–200.

13. Reiffenberg, *Lettres*, 14–16, van Male to Praet, 13 Jan. 1551, stated that Charles had translated *Le chevalier délibéré* into Spanish the previous year; Gonzalo Sánchez-Molero, *Regia biblioteca*, I, 253–62, discussed the Books of Hours.

14. Firpo, *Relazioni*, III, 52–3. Relation of Federico Badoer, June–July 1557; Sandoval, *Historia*, III, 565–6 (prayers at bedtime).

15. In 1598, Philip asked to see the box containing his father's crucifix and a scourge. A monk at El Escorial noted traces of blood and asked the king whether they were his. He said no, they came from his father: Sigüenza, *Historia*, 184–5. A few years later, Sandoval began the section of his *Historia* entitled 'Virtud católica y cristiana del emperador' with the same story but cited as his source the king's valet, Juan Ruiz de Velasco.

16. Boone, *Mercurino*, 135 (*Autobiography*); Poumarède, 'Le voyage', 265, quoting a complaint by the ambassador of Ferrara, whom Charles refused to see; BAV *Vat. Lat.* 6753/181v–3, Navagero to the Signory, Seville, 1 June 1526.

17. BNE *Ms.* 18,634 no. 58 (formerly ff. 260–2), 'Lo que el Comendador Mayor scrivió a Su Magestad desde Gante con Ydiáquez, estando Su Magestad en Grumendala, [Groenendaal] y su respuesta.' Although undated, internal evidence showed that Los Cobos wrote during Holy Week, and the only year in which he and Charles were together in the Netherlands at Easter was 1531. Los Cobos wrote on 'Tuesday', which was 4 Apr. 1531; Charles stated in his reply that he was about to leave for Leuven, and Foronda, *Viajes*, showed that he got there on 13 Apr.; so he probably replied on 11 or 12 Apr. 1531. Sanuto, *I diarii*, LIV, cols 384–5, the Mantuan ambassador to the duke, Ghent, 4 Apr. 1531, reported that Charles had just entered Groenendaal and would remain there for a week. *CDCV*, I, 260–3, published this fascinating *consulta*, but with numerous errors of transcription and no firm date.

18. *CWE*, IX, 137–41, Erasmus to Pierre Barbier, [14 July] 1522, recorded Erasmus's contacts with Glapion (see also *CWE*, IX, 64–8, Erasmus to Glapion, [21 Apr.] 1521, the only one of several such letters to survive). Godin, 'La société', 344–59, and Lippens, 'Jean Glapion', XLV, 50–7 and 66–9, summarized his Lenten sermons in 1520 and 1522. Bujanda, *Index*, 186–7, noted the prohibition in 1546 of the Dutch translation of a book on pilgrimages 'gemaect by broeder Jan Glappion vander minrebroeder oorden, *der Keyserlijcker maiesteyt Biechtvader*' (my italics).

·19. *RVEC*, 347–55, Salinas to Ferdinand, 11 Mar. 1527.

20. Heine, *Briefe*, 381–2, 450–3 and 494–5, Loaysa to Charles, 16 Oct. 1530, 2 Oct. 1531 and 8 May 1532 (the second also published in *CODOIN*, XIV, 221–3).

21. Heine, *Briefe*, 350–2, Loaysa to Charles, 26 May 1530 (also in *CODOIN*, XIV, 25–8).

22. Heine, *Briefe*, 403–5, 462–5 and 444–5, Loaysa to Charles, 20 Dec. 1530, 1 Sep. 1531 (also in *CODOIN*, XIV, 203–5), and 9 Nov. 1531 (also in *CODOIN*, XIV, 242–7).

23. AGS *E* 25/211, Loaysa to Charles, 7 Mar. 1532; Heine, *Briefe*, 495–500, same to same, 17 May 1532.

24. Heine, *Briefe*, 390–5, Loaysa to Charles, 30 Nov. 1530 (also in *CODOIN*, XIV, 104–11); *CODOIN*, XIV, 134–6, same to same, 27 Mar. 1531; Heine, *Briefe*, 494–5, same to same, 8 May 1532.

25. AGS *E* 1558/60 and 66, Charles to Loaysa, 2 Aug. 1530 and 16 Feb. 1531. For more on Loaysa, see Nieva Ocampo, 'El confesor'.

26. *CMH*, I, 399–401, Charles to Marie, 13 Aug. 1532, holograph.

27. Rodríguez-Salgado, 'Charles V and the dynasty', 56.

28. Gachard, *Collection*, III, 136 (account of Vital). Checa Cremades, *Inventarios*, 890–3 (by Miguel Ángel Zalama) and 3,017–18 (by Annemarie Jordan Gschwend), documented Charles's disgraceful behaviour from contemporary testimony: in 1524, Charles 'mandó sacar muchas joyas de oro e joyas e piedras que estaban en la cámara de la reina nuestra señora . . . y de allí tomó lo que su majestad quiso, así para su majestad como para la reina de Portugal [Catalina]' (891–2). Gonzalo Sánchez-Molero, *Regia biblioteca*, I, 160–3, notes that after 1524 many of Joanna's books appeared in the inventories of Catalina's possessions. Two years later Charles repeated the exercise: he removed tapestries and other items from his mother's depleted collection and gave them to his wife as wedding presents.

29. Tamalio, *Ferrante*, 213–18, Pandolfo di Pico della Mirandola to Isabella d'Este, 7 Nov. 1524.

30. HHStA *Belgien PA* 2/2/1–12, Charles's instructions to M. de Lachaulx, 15 Jan. 1522; *KFF*, I, 322–6 and 366–8, Charles to Ferdinand, 1 Sep. 1525 and 2 Feb. 1526.

31. *CDCV*, I, 292–4, Charles to Isabella, 13 June 1531 (the emperor did not even write these words himself: they came in an official letter drafted by Los Cobos, amid a list of the political problems that would keep the emperor away from Spain for the foreseeable future); AGS *E* 30/113, Tavera to Charles, 24 June 1535. On how the death of her son Fernando devastated Isabella, see *RVEC*, 499–502, Salinas to Ferdinand, 14 Sep. 1530.

32. *CDCV*, I, 186, Margaret to Isabella, 15 Dec. 1529 (italics added).

33. *CMH*, I, 221–2 and 447–8, Charles to Marie, 7 May and 4 Sep. 1532, holograph. Mazarío Coleto, *Isabel*, published letters from the empress to her husband, and observed (pp. 102–3) that internal references to other correspondence suggests that 'there cannot be many letters missing from this series', but it did not include Charles's holograph epistles such as the one that took him two hours to write in Sep. 1532, which does not seem to have survived. By contrast, the archives of Simancas preserve a host of letters about patronage. Alvar Ezquerra, 'El gobierno', analysed 1,099 surviving warrants issued by the empress in 1531 and 1532, noting the abundant evidence of Charles's involvement in her decisions.

34. Mazarío Coleto, *Isabel*, 99–101 and 262, Isabella to Charles, 25 Jan. 1530; BL *Cott. Ms.* Vespasian C.XIII/258, John Brereton to Wriothesley, Valladolid, 23 June 1537. We only know of the empress's present because an English diplomat recorded that the authorities in Zaragoza 'insisted upon searching the bearer'. The diplomat also recorded that the gift, when examined, 'was not worth a cople of ducketts' – but, as always, it's the thought that counts.

35. Rodríguez-Salgado, 'Charles V and the dynasty', 74.

36. AGS *E* 644/107, Charles to Juan Hurtado de Mendoza, 21 Aug. 1547. Details on the emperor's last days in ch. 16 below.

37. Tamalio, *Ferrante*, 259–63, Pandolfo di Pico della Mirandola to Isabella d'Este, 9 Aug. 1526 (Charles went out riding every evening 'and when he returns His Majesty goes to visit his sister'); HHStA *Belgien PA* 2/2/1–12, Charles's instructions to M. de Lachaulx, 15 Jan. 1522; GRM, II, 365, Charles to Philip, 31 Mar. 1558. On Eleanor's secret letter to Charles in 1536, see ch. 10.

38. Piot, 'Correspondance', 109–10, Charles to Eleanor, 18 Dec. 1522; GRM, II, 334–5, Charles to Quixada, 19 Mar. 1558 (italics added). On Eleanor and Frederick see ch. 3 above, and Moeller, *Éléonore*; on the marriage negotiations with Bourbon and Francis, see ch. 8 above. Eleanor's feelings about the enforced four-year separation from Francis may be judged from indiscreet remarks by the king's sister four years later: Francis, she told an ambassador, complained that 'when he doth lie with [Eleanor], he cannot sleep; and when he lieth from her, no man sleepeth better. I said "Madam, what should be the cause?" She said, "She is very hot in bed, and desireth to be too much embraced"' (*L&P Henry VIII*, VI, 308–11, Lord Norfolk to Henry VIII, 19 June 1533).

39. Brandi, 'Die Testamente', 104–5, Charles's codicil signed on 21 June 1544, clause 9; *CMH*, I, 15–20, Charles to Marie, 3 Jan. 1531, holograph. Gorter-van Royen, 'María', 197–8, noted the contrast between the powers granted to Marie and Isabella.

40. *CMH*, I, 399–401, Charles to Marie, 13 Aug. 1532; Sanuto, *I diarii*, LVIII, cols 71–2, Giovanni Bassadonna (ambassador to Milan) to the Signory, 14 Apr. 1533 (reporting Granvelle's account of the emperor's mistake and his solution); Dumont, *Corps*, IV/2, 96–8, marriage contract between Christina and Sforza, Barcelona, 10 June 1533.

41. *CMH*, II, 244–61, 282–5, and 293–4, Charles to Marie, 31 July 1533; Marie to Charles, 25 Aug. 1533, and his reply 11 Sep. 1533 (the last two also in *LCK*, II, 87–9). Cartwright, *Christina*, published many holograph letters from Christina to her husband, suggesting cordial relations during their brief marriage. When she returned to the Netherlands in 1537, an ambassador reported that 'she is bothe widow and mayd' (*SP*, VIII, 6–7, John Hutton to Thomas Cromwell, 9 Dec. 1537). Four years later, Charles arranged her marriage to the duke of Lorraine, with whom she had three children. She died in 1590.

42. AGS *E* 8335/109, Marie to Philip, 4 Sep. 1558, copy sent to Charles (GRM, I, 341–52, printed the letter from an inferior copy, incorrectly dated 7 Sep.); GRM, II, 495–9, Garcilaso de la Vega to Philip, 7 Sep. 1558; GRM, I, xliv, Charles to Joanna, 27 Aug. 1558 (describing the letter he had sent to Marie, now apparently lost, to overcome her resistance. I have changed the third person to first person.)

43. *CDCV*, I, 79–80, Charles to Cisneros, 27 Sep. 1517; Keniston, *Memorias*, 151; Fagel, 'Don Fernando', 270, Ferdinand to Charles, Feb. 1519.

44. *KFF* I, 407–21, Charles to Ferdinand, 27 July 1526.

45. *KFF* I, 216–19 and 250–3, Charles to Ferdinand, 7 Sep. 1524 and 4 Feb. 1525.

46. *RVEC*, 667–84, Salinas to Ferdinand and Secretary Castillejo, 6 Dec. 1535. Laferl, 'Las relaciones', 112–14, provides further examples of Charles rebuking his brother.

47. *KFF*, I, 312–17, Charles to Ferdinand, 20 July 1525 (with postscript dated 31 July). When Sforza died a decade later Charles annexed the duchy of Milan, once again dashing Ferdinand's hopes.

48. Firpo, *Relazioni*, II, 120–1, Relation of Contarini, 16 Nov. 1525. See also the hostile evaluation of Contarini's predecessor, Vicenzo Quirino, in 1506: see p. 14 above.

49. Gachard, *Analectes Belgiques*, I, 378–9, Margaret to Charles, 30 Nov. 1530; GRM, II, 113, Eleanor to Charles, Nov. 1556; *PEG*, IV, 469, Marie to Charles, Aug. 1555; Neefe, *Tafel-Reden*, 2–3, relating conversations with Ferdinand in 1563–4. In 1536 the will of Germaine de Foix, Charles's stepgrandmother, likewise testified to 'el sobrado amor que tenemos' towards 'la Magestad del Emperador, mi señor e hijo': AGS *PR* 29/59, notarized copy.

50. Viaud, *Lettres*, 107 and 176, Catalina to Charles, 21 Aug. 1528 and 31 Jan. 1532.

51. Details from Checa Cremades, *Inventarios*, III, 3,018–19 (by Jordan Gschwend). Catalina seems to have defied the emperor only once: after her husband's death in 1557 she ensured that she, rather than Charles's daughter Joanna, became regent of Portugal (see ch. 16).

52. Sanuto, *I diarii*, LIII, cols 215–16 and 318–19, Paxin Berecio to Thomas Tiepolo, Innsbruck, 9 May 1530, and Augsburg, 16 June 1530; idem, LIV, cols 384–5, La Torre to the duke of Mantua, 4 Apr. 1531; idem, LV, cols 68–9, copy of a letter from Brussels, 7 Oct. 1531.

53. García Cerezada, *Tratado*, 133; Sastrow, *Herkommen*, II, 629 (for an alternative translation see *Social Germany*, 272).

54. Firpo, *Relazioni*, II, 212, Relation of Tiepolo, 23 Aug. 1533; Sanuto, *I diarii*, LII, cols 209–10, 'L'ordine del mangiar de l'imperatore' (undated but 1529–30).

55. Sanuto, *I diarii*, XXXVIII, cols 205–7, Suardino to Mantua, 15 Mar. 1525; idem, LIII, col. 505, Camillo Ghilini to the duke of Milan, 28 July 1530. Perhaps Ghilini exaggerated: Los Cobos reported that Charles 'felt the loss deeply' and 'carried with him a portrait of the late Infante': AGS *E* 635/89, Los Cobos to the empress, 1 Aug. 1530.

56. Sanuto, *I diarii*, LIII, cols 95–6, Antonio Zorzi to his brother, Vicenza, 30 Mar. 1530; ibid., LII, cols 209–10, 'L'ordine del mangiar de l'imperatore' (undated but 1529–30).

57. Santa Cruz, *Crónica*, II, 37–40. Redondo, *Antonio*, 330, demonstrated that Santa Cruz lifted the passage from the unpublished *Crónica* composed by Guevara between 1527 and 1536.

58. Firpo, *Relazioni*, II, 83–150, Final Relation of Contarini, 16 Nov. 1525. See also Bodart, 'Il mento "posticcio"', and the similar observations in Sanuto, *I diarii*, XXXVIII, cols 203–5, Contarini to the Signory, 26 Mar. 25; and LVII, cols 212–14, report of Marco Minio and other diplomats to the Signory, undated but Nov. 1532.

59. Sanuto, *I diarii*, LI, cols 369–72, letter from Genoa to the cardinal of Mantua, 17 Aug. 1529; López de Gómara, *Guerras de mar*, 127–8, reported the hair-cutting as an eye-witness ('yo vi algunos que lloraban').

60. Giordano, *Della venuta*, 35 (from a contemporary *Cronaca*). Giordano, op. cit., Tavolo XII, reproduced commemorative medals of the coronation, all showing Charles with a beard and short curly hair. Bodart, 'Algunos casos', reproduced and discussed images of Charles at this time; Civil, 'Enjeux et stratégies', 107–8, compared the written descriptions with the portraits of Charles c. 1530.

61. Guevara, *Libro áureo* (1528 edition), prologue. Fifty-two chapters of the *Libro áureo* appeared among the 144 chapters of the *Relox de príncipes*, so in effect they became a single work. Part III, chs 3–4 and 12–16, concerned war.

62. Guevara, *Libro áureo* (1528 edition), prologue (the presentation copy of the *Libro áureo* is today BSLE *Ms.* g-II-14, with a bizarre error in the dedication, which reads 'don Carlos *sexto*'); Guevara, *Relox de príncipes* (1529 edition), prologue; Gonzalo Sánchez-Molero, *El César*, 176–7, on the transfer to Simancas (part of a section dedicated to 'Guevara, Charles's favourite author').

63. Guevara, *Libro áureo* (1528 edition), prologue. Redondo, *Antonio*, 693–4, quoted passages from Charles's instructions to his son in 1543 and 1548 that resemble those in *Relox*, and claimed that they prove the emperor had read and digested Guevara; but all these passages are generalizations found in many other Renaissance books of advice for princes.

CHAPTER 9: THE LAST CRUSADER, 1532–6

1. *CMH*, I, 41–2 and 57–60, Charles to Marie, 18 and 28 Jan. 1532, both holograph.

2. Sanuto, *I diarii*, LV, col. 597, Tiepolo to the Signory, 25 Feb. 1532; *CMH*, I, 89–92, Charles to Marie, 18 Feb. 1532, holograph; Vilar Sánchez, *Carlos V*, 397–9 (description of the imperial cadaver).

3. *CMH*, I, 110–12 and 126–8, Charles to Marie, 8 and 12 Mar. 1532, holographs; *CDCV*, I, 334–5, Dr Escoriaza to the empress, undated (but 6 Apr. 1532); Sanuto, *I diarii*, LV, cols 658–9 and 671, Mantuan ambassador to the duke, and Venetian ambassadors to the Signory, Regensburg, 5 and 12 Mar. 1532.

4. *CMH*, I, 151–7 and 211–17, Charles to Marie, 24 Mar. and 3 May 1532, holograph; Sanuto, *I diarii*, LVI, cols 109–10, Tiepolo and Contarini to the Signory, 18 Apr. 1532, and 364–5, Contarini on 21 May 1532; Beltrán de Heredía, *Cartulario*, II, 450–1, Escoriaza to the empress, 22 Apr. 1532.

5. Pocock, *Records*, II, 259–62, Augustus Augustinus to Thomas Cromwell, Regensburg, 16 May 1532; Sanuto, *I diarii*, LVI, cols 250 and 261–3, Contarini to the Signory, 3 and 11 May 1532; *CMH*, I, 221–2, 295–9 and 347–50, Charles to Marie, 7 May, 19 June and 15 July 1532, all holographs.

6. *CSPV*, V, 619–21, Giovanni Antonio Venier to the Doge, 8 May 1531, relating an audience with King Francis. Necipoglu, 'Suleiman', described Suleiman's Venetian tiara and other insignia.

7. Von Gévay, *Urkunden*, I, part V, 87–9, Suleiman to Ferdinand, Esseg (Osijek), 12 July 1532, Latin with imperfect Italian translation – the latter also in Sanuto, *I diarii*, LVI, cols 784–5, from a copy brought to Venice by Rincón.

8. *CMH*, I, 281–2, Charles to Marie, 12 June 1532, minute. *RTA*, X, 149–55, discussed the inflated population of Regensburg during the Diet.

9. *NBD, 2. Ergänzungsband 1532*, 102–7 and 179–86, Aleandro to Sanga, 25 Mar. and 30 Mar./23 Apr. 1532 (narrating an audience with Charles on the 20th, changing the third to the first person).

10. *CODOIN*, XIV, 201–2, Loaysa to Charles, 31 July 1531 (also in Heine, *Briefe*, 369–70, but misdated 1530); AGS *E* 25/207, 'Relación de las cartas' of Loaysa to Charles, 15 Feb. 1532; Heine, *Briefe*, 500–1, Loaysa to Charles, 8 June 1532; *CDCV*, I, 375–9, Charles to the empress, 9 Aug. 1532 (with news of the peace of Nuremberg concluded with the German Lutherans on 27 July). More than a year earlier Charles had instructed his brother to 'offer concessions to the Lutherans and other deviants from the [Catholic] faith to make them more inclined and willing to repel the Turks': *KFF*, III/1, 49, Charles to Ferdinand, 4 Mar. 1531.

11. *LWT*, II, 182 (# 1687) and III, 233 (# 3245), two sources on the same dinner conversation in June–July 1532.

12. Sanuto, *I diarii*, LVI, cols 656–7, 717–18, 757–9, 812–13, Contarini to Doge, 18 July and 2, 4 and 10 Aug. 1532.

13. Ibid., cols 864–5 and 989–90, Contarini to Doge, 17 Aug. and 16 Sep. 1532, and cols 1,023–4, muster of the imperial fleet, 1 Sep. 1532; Turetschek, *Die Türkenpolitik*, 364–8, 'Überblick über das Kriegsvolk des Kaisers, König Ferdinands und des deutschen Reiches', 16 Aug. 1532.

14. *CDCV*, I, 375–9, Charles to the empress, 9 Aug. 1532.

15. *CDCV*, I, 345–8, Charles to Álvaro de Lugo and to the empress, 6 Apr. 1532; ibid., 361, Charles to the empress, 11 June 1532; AGS *CMC* 1a/590, 'Cuenta de Álvaro de Lugo'. Tracy, *Emperor*, 149–54, details how Charles funded the 1532 campaign.

16. Contarini recorded in some detail the advice given to (and accepted by) Charles both by Antonio de Leyva (skirmish, but avoid battle) and by the duke of Alba (break up the camp before supplies become exhausted): Sanuto, *I diarii*, LVI, cols 865–7 and 989–90, letters of 21 Aug. and 16 Sep. 1532.

17. *NBD, 2. Ergänzungsband 1532*, 559–80, Cardinal Ippolito de' Medici to Charles, Vienna, late Sep. 1532; Heine, *Briefe*, 512–15, Loaysa to Charles, Rome, 31 Oct. 1532. Earlier that month, Loaysa reproached Charles for his decision not to pursue the sultan as he retreated, because doing so would have redounded to 'God's glory and your perpetual honour' (Heine, ibid., 510, letter of 5 Oct. 1532); while Ferdinand declared that 'the loss of such a fine opportunity to serve God' caused 'me such regret that I don't know what future joy would be sufficient to make me forget it' (*KFF*, III/3, 628, Ferdinand to Marie, 21 Oct. 1532).

18. Sanuto, *I diarii*, LVII, cols 165-6, Venetian embassy with Charles to the Signory, 28 Oct. 1532, and 171-2, description of the imperial host by the podestà of Conegliano the following day.

19. Ibid., cols 284-6 and 309-10, Contarini and Basadonna to the council of Ten and the Signory, 24 Nov. and 1 Dec. 1532. Foronda, *Viajes*, 368, followed by many others (e.g. Keniston, *Francisco de Los Cobos*, 153), stated that Charles spent only the night of 7 Nov. 1532 in Mantua, entering Bologna on 13 Nov., but this is incorrect: he remained in Mantua for a month and did not enter Bologna until 13 Dec.

20. Sanuto, *I diarii*, LVII, cols 332-5, Contarini to the Signory, 7 and 18 [*recte* 8] Dec. 1532.

21. Ibid., cols 308-9, Contarini and Basadonna to the Signory, Mantua, 27 Nov. 1532. Rosenthal, *The palace*, 57 and 266-7, demonstrated that work on the new palace began in May 1533, with a budget of 50,000 ducats payable over six years. Brothers, 'The Renaissance reception', 91-2, and Tafuri, *Interpreting*, ch. 6, both noted the similarities between Charles's palace at Granada and the architecture of Mantua but seemed unaware that the emperor initiated construction while he resided in the city. Rosenthal, 'The house', 343, noted that 'the house of Andrea Mantegna' was 'the first Renaissance villa retonda actually constructed', and in 1532-3 it formed part of the Gonzaga 'Palazzo della Pusterla', so Charles would certainly have seen it.

22. Bodart, 'Frédéric Gonzague', 28. Other artists doing portraits of the emperor at this time included Parmigianino, Vermeyen, Amberger and Behaim.

23. TNA *SP* 1/71/154-5, Ambassador Nicholas Hawkins to Henry, 24 Dec. 1532, holograph; Sanuto, *I diarii*, LVII, cols 368-9, 383-5 and 388, Marco Antonio Venier (ambassador to the pope) to the Signory, 16, 18, 21 and 26 Dec. 1532; TNA *SP* 1/74/18-19v, John Hackett to the duke of Norfolk, 8 Jan. 1533. On the subjects discussed, see ch. 8 above.

24. Pocock, *Records*, II, 365-6, Clement to Henry, 2 Jan. 1533; *L&P Henry VIII*, VII, 7, Clement to Francis, 2 Jan. 1533, together with a rationale for the council (also sent to Henry); ibid., 70-2, Augustus Augustinus to Thomas Cromwell, 13 Feb. 1533; *KFF*, IV, 89-92, Charles to Ferdinand, 4 Mar. 1533.

25. *CDCV*, IV, 500, Charles's *Memoirs*; TNA *SP* 1/71/154-5, Hawkins to Henry, 24 Dec. 1532.

26. *PEG*, II, 1-19, secret treaty between Charles and Clement, 24 Feb. 1533, and defensive league, 27 Feb. 1533 (Sanuto made a copy of the latter, even though Venice did not join: *I diarii*, LVII, cols 600-10).

27. Hamy, *Entrevue*, CCLXXXV-CCXCVI, Francis's instructions to Cardinals Grammont and Tournon, 10 Nov. 1532, and CCLXXX-CCLXXXI, Francis's project for a secret treaty with Clement, holograph, Mar. 1533.

28. Sanuto, *I diarii*, LVIII, cols 196-9, Contarini to the Signory, 26 and 29 Apr. 1533, provided a detailed account of the galley journey from hell (noting bitterly that the sailing ships completed the same journey in four days); Girón, *Crónica*, 30, tallied Charles's hours in bed with his wife.

29. AHN *Inquisición* libro 101/695-7, Licenciado Hernando Arenillas de Reynoso to Philip II, 4 Dec. 1594, with rescript.

30. Mazarío Coleto, *Isabel*, 292-5, 262, 301-5 and 329-31, the empress to Charles, 16 Sep. 1530, 25 Jan. 1530, 12 Jan. and 16 Dec. 1531. For more examples of the empress's growing independence, see ibid., 119-38.

31. TNA *SP* 1/76/174-174v and 1/78/1, Hawkins to Henry VIII, 11 June and 16 July 1533; Sanuto, *I diarii*, LVIII, cols 472-4, Contarini to the Signory, 23-24 June 1533; Foronda, *Viajes*, 377 n. 1 (Charles's speed of travel).

32. *RVEC*, 545-7, Salinas to Castillejo, 12 Oct. 1533. Girón, *Crónica*, 41-4, and Foronda, *Viajes*, 388-90, provided the itinerary.

33. González de Ávila, *Historia*, 475-6; Girón, *Crónica*, 42-4, reported the debate; BL *Cott. Ms.* Vespasian C.XIII/327-8v, Mason to Starkey, 3 July 1534, recorded the topic.

34. *RVEC*, 604-7 and 614-17, Salinas to Ferdinand, 15 July and 4 Sep. 1534; BNE *Ms.* 3825/337 (showing the heavy editing: see also Girón, *Crónica*, 44). Since Princess Joanna was born 23 June 1535, I assume the pregnancy began in Oct. or Nov. 1534.

35. *KFF*, IV, 121-5, Charles to Ferdinand, 23/28 May 1533.

36. BL *Addl. Ms.* 28,586/191, Dr Ortiz to Charles, 24 Mar. 1534; and BL *Addl. Ms.* 28,586/223, 'Los puntos que se consultaron con su Magestad en Toledo a xij de Abril 1534 para responder a Roma sobre la sentencia de Inglaterra'.

37. According to a newsletter dated 14 Dec. 1536, 'all the grete men' of Spain had asked Charles's permission to 'assemble an armye at theyr cost and charges to sayle into England, there to revenge the injuryes don to Quene Kathryn, his aunt' (TNA *SP* 1/238/162). Salvador, 'El hablar', 80-1, recorded several insulting uses of 'anabolena' in twentieth-century Spain; and a wooden 'tarasquilla' representing the late queen still sits atop the fearsome dragon drawn through the streets of Toledo in the annual Corpus Christi procession. Did Charles perhaps remember that he had met Anne Boleyn when she spent a year at Mechelen (ch. 2)?

38. *KFF*, IV, 227–36 and 314–22, Charles to Ferdinand, 24 Apr. and 3 Sep. 1534. Nevertheless, Brandi, *The emperor*, 330–1, was surely right to marvel that 'the imperial dynasty, which was prepared to fight a whole generation for Milan, accepted the loss of Württemberg so philosophically'.

39. TNA *SP* 1/86/48–9, Sir Gregory Casale to Lord Rochford, Rome, 15 Oct. 1534; *CDCV*, I, 405–6, Charles to Soria, 4 Sep. 1534.

40. Poumarède, 'Le voyage', 267, papal secretary of state to Nuncio Poggio in Spain, 4 Mar. 1535.

41. *PEG*, II, 206–21, 'Arraisonnement sur ce à quoy le roy de France parsiste pour parvenir à establisse-ment de paix' by Granvelle, Oct. 1534 (see ch. 4 for earlier arguments based on the escalation of potential disasters); Walser, 'Spanien' 167–71, *consulta* by Tavera, undated but mid-Jan. 1535, holo-graph. The Cardinal had presided over the council of Castile since 1524.

42. *KFF*, V, 161–72, Charles to Ferdinand, 3 Feb. 1535; Girón, *Crónica*, 49; *RVEC*, 631–2, Salinas to Ferdinand, 21 Feb. 1535 – although he also noted that Los Cobos 'has not smiled since they announced the departure' and wondered why (ibid., 632–4, to Castillejo, that same day).

43. *KFF*, V, 211–12, Marie to Ferdinand, 12 Apr. 1535, italics added (see Ferdinand's reply, full of anger that Charles had deceived him: ibid., 223–7). The will has not survived. Charles also sent Marie a copy of his instructions to the empress as regent of Castile, dated 1 Mar. 1535, but they stated that he was going to Aragon, not to Africa: *CDCV*, I, 408–19.

44. March, *Niñez*, II, 224, Doña Estefanía de Requesens to her mother, Madrid, 3 Mar. 1535.

45. BNE *Ms.* 1937/102v and 104v, from Fray Alonso de Sanabria's *Comentarios y guerra de Túnez*. Girón, *Crónica*, 56, lists the nobles; so does BL *Cott. Ms.* Vespasian C.XIII/334 'The nobles as well Spanyards as Italiens that went with th'emperour to the conquest of the citie of Tunez in Africque.'

46. AGS *E* 1458/102–8, 'Lo que se consultó en Barcelona', Apr. 1535; *LCK*, II, 177–9, Charles to Nassau, 10 May 1535; *KFF*, V, 161–72, Instructions to Roeulx, Charles's special envoy to Ferdinand, 1 Feb. 1535, and letter to Ferdinand, 3 Feb. 1535.

47. BNE *Ms.* 1937/103v, Sanabria, *Comentarios*; BL *Cott. Ms.* Vespasian C.VII/43–4, 'Anno 1535. La Armada que o emperador leva de Barcelona'.

48. García Cerezada, *Tratado*, II, 7–8. Licenciado Arcos, another eyewitness, provided a very similar account of the same event in his *Conquista de Tunez por el emperador Carlos* (BNE *Ms.* 19,441/33).

49. BNE *Ms.* 1937/108, from Sanabria's *Comentarios* (the author, a Franciscan, paid special attention to Charles's devotions); total size from TNA *SP* 1/239/188, 'Minuta de l'armata e gente Cesariane'.

50. García Cerezada, *Tratado*, II, 21. The fleet first arrived off Ghar el Mehl (formerly known as Utica and Porto Farina) but sailed on.

51. Ibid., II, 24, 37, 43; BNE *Ms.* 1937/150v–1 (Sanabria); TNA *SP* 1/97/32–3, Peter Rede to Geoffrey Loveday, 27 Sep. 1535 (a particularly vivid account).

52. Gachet, 'Expédition' 37–40, Charles to Marie, 26 July 1535 (Sanabria also noted that the night after the sack of La Goletta 'en el consejo de guerra secreto ouo diversidad de opiniones': BNE *Ms.* 1937/160v.)

53. Foucard, *Ferrara*, 24–30, Alfonso Rossetti to the duke of Ferrara, 22 July 1535; Guyon, *Mémoires*, 61–2; García Cerezada, *Tratado*, II, 58.

54. Giovio, *Delle historie*, 377 (book XXXIV: an anecdote supplied by Vasto, which adds to its credibi-lity); Guyon, *Mémoires*, 63–4; TNA *SP* 1/97/32–3, Rede to Loveday, 27 Sep. 1535. See also the accounts of the sack cited in Nordman, *Tempête*, 253–6.

55. Foucard, *Ferrara*, 28–9, Rossetti to Ferrara, 22 July 1535; Gachet, 'Expédition', 37–40, Charles to Marie, 26 July 1535. *PEG*, II, 368–77, prints part of the treaty between Charles and Muley Hasan, 6 Aug. 1535.

56. AGS *E* 1311/20–3, Soria to Charles, 21 May 1535; *CDCV*, I, 441–4, Charles to Soria, 'data en nuestra galera, cerca de La Goleta de Túnez', 16 Aug. 1535; *LCK*, II, 200, Charles to Jean Hannart, 16 Aug. 1535; BL *Cott. Ms.* Nero B.VII/115, Bernardino Sandro to Thomas Starkey, Venice, 19 Aug. 1535.

57. TNA *SP* 1/94/173–8v, Sir Gregory da Casale to Thomas Cromwell, Ferrara, 27 July 1535, severely damaged Italian and Latin texts, augmented by the English translation in *L&P Henry VIII*, VIII, 439–40; Charrière, *Négociations*, I, 272–5, Virginio Orsini, count of Anguillara, to 'Monsenor Pietro', La Goletta, 28 July 1535.

58. Mazarío Coleto, *Isabel*, 410–11, the empress to Charles, 24 Sep. 1535. Vidal, 'La defensa', 562–80, describes the loss of Mahon and its consequences.

59. Walser, 'Spanien', 167–71, *consulta* by Tavera, undated but mid-Jan. 1535, holograph.

60. Morales Foguera, 'El viaje', 100, 106 (Psalm 112:3 in the Vulgate reads 'a solis ortu usque ad occasum laudabile nomen Domini').

61. Rosso, *Istoria*, 63 (about Charles in Naples); Di Blasi, *Storia*, 174 (about Charles in Palermo); *L&P Henry VIII*, IX, 146, Granvelle to Eustace Chapuys, Palermo, 26 Sep. 1535.

62. Rosso, *Istoria*, 66, 70; Poumarède, 'Le voyage', 282, Fabio Arcella to Secretary of State Ricalcati, 5 Feb. 1536 (Arcella wrote 'si stette in danze et festa fin alle X hore', which according to the Italian system of calculating time then in use, meant ten and a half hours after sunset). Charles received news of his aunt's death on 27 Jan.
63. Cernigliaro, *Sovranità*, 299, Charles's opening address to the parliament of Naples on 8 Jan. 1536; *CDCV*, I, 469–73, Charles to the empress, 18 Feb. 1536; Gilliard, 'La política', 229, Antoine Perrenin to Leonard de Gruyères, special envoy to the Swiss, 31 Dec. 1535.
64. Rabelais, *Lettres*, 33–64, to Geoffroy d'Estissac, 30 Dec. 1535 and 28 Jan. 1536; *KFF*, V, 452–8, Charles to Ferdinand, 18 Apr. 1536.
65. *L&P Henry VIII*, X, 265–74, Richard Pate to Henry VIII, Rome, 14 Apr. 1536; Cadenas y Vicent, *Discurso*, 35–7; *RVEC*, 714–19, Salinas to Castillejo, 22 Apr. 1536.
66. Brandi, *The emperor*, 371; Scheurl, *Einritt*, title page, quoting II Samuel 3:21.

CHAPTER 10: YEARS OF DEFEAT, 1536–41

1. Scheurer, *Correspondance*, II, 140–4, Jean du Bellay and Hémard de Denonville to Francis I, Rome, 12 Nov. 1535.
2. AGS *E* 1368/105, Gómez Suárez de Figueroa to the empress, Genoa, 13 Nov. 1535. *SP*, VIII, 6–7, John Hutton to Thomas Cromwell, Brussels, 9 Dec. 1537, reported that Christina of Milan, now aged sixteen, had returned to Brussels 'both wedowe [and] mayd'. Her aunt Marie's fears about the consequences of marrying young (p. 215 above) were thus not realized. Chabod, *Storia*, 6–9, described the steps taken by Charles and his ministers in 1534–5 to secure Milan in case Francesco died childless.
3. *CDCV*, I, 451, Charles to the empress, Naples, 18 Jan. 1536; AGS *E* 1180/86, Leyva to Charles, Milan, 27 Nov. 1535; *RVEC*, 667–71, Salinas to Ferdinand, 6 Dec. 1535, after a meeting in which Granvelle 'gave his opinion for and against three options' concerning the fate of Milan. The 'opinion' to which Salinas referred is surely Granvelle's 'Discours fait incontinent après le trespass du duc François-Marie Sforce sur la disposition de l'estat de Milan', printed in *PEG*, II, 395–410.
4. AGS *E* 1180/86, Leyva to Charles, 27 Nov. 1536. On the death of Giovan'Paolo Sforza on 12 Dec. 1535, perhaps by poison, see Leva, *Storia*, III, 153, and Scheurer, *Correspondance*, II, 141 note.
5. *BKK*, II, 254–5, Leyva to Charles, 3 Dec. 1535; BL *Cott. Ms.* Nero B.VII/113, Bernardino Sandro to Thomas Starkey, Venice, 14 Nov. 1535.
6. Rosso, *Istoria*, 65.
7. AGS *E* 1311/11 and 34–7, Soria to Charles 22 Aug. 1535 (see a similar verdict on Venice's ambiguous attitude towards Charles in Soria's letter of 9 Aug. 1535: AGS *E* 1311/40–2). RAH *Salazar* A-40/446–7, Soria to Charles, 25 May 1527, noted that 'I have been in Italy for 28 years'.
8. *PEG*, II, 427, Charles to Hannart, 23 Jan. 1536. See also Mazarío Coleto, *Isabel*, 430, the empress to Charles, 4 Dec. 1535, and *LCK* II, 657, Marie to Charles, 8 Feb. 1536, both complaining that they had no money.
9. Gilliard, 'La política', 233, Gruyères to Granvelle, 22 Dec. 1535; AGS *E* 1024/26, 'Lo que ha sido acordado, so el buen placer de Su Magestad, en lo que toca a los negocios de estado generalmente y a otros particulares deste reyno' of Naples, 31 Dec. 1535 (defective English translation in *CSPSp*, V, 304–8, incorrectly dated 26 Dec. 1536).
10. *L&P Henry VIII*, X, 40, 'Copie de la deffiance et lettres patentes mandées au duc de Savoye par ung herault d'armes, de la part de la seigneurie de Berne', 27 Jan. 1536; *Ordonnances des rois de France. Règne de François Iᵉʳ*, VIII, 18–22, mobilization of the ban and arrière-ban, and 'Pouvoir' to invade and 'recover' Bresse, Bugey and Valromey, both dated 11 Feb. 1536; ibid., p. 65, edict incorporating these areas into France, Mar. 1536.
11. *PEG*, II, 445–50, 'Mémoire remis à l'empereur sur la question de la guerre et de la paix', undated but Mar. 1536. The intelligence failure reflected in part Gruyères's absurdly over-optimistic reports from Switzerland, insisting that 'everything here continues uneventfully, with no word of any trouble' (Gilliard, 'La política', 231, Gruyères to the empress, 22 Dec. 1535); and in part explicit assurances from Francis that 'he would not attempt or do anything against the duke of Savoy' (*LCK*, II, 226, Charles to Hannart, 17 Apr. 1536).
12. *CDCV*, I, 455–64, Charles to the empress, 1 Feb. 1536.
13. Leva, *Storia*, III, 163–4, citing 'Minuta de las condiziones que se dieron al papa del parte de Su Magestad cerca de tratar del estado de Milan para el duque de Angouleme, en Roma, año de 1536'.
14. *PEG*, II, 414–18 and 431–6, Charles to Hannart, 14 Dec. 1535 (summarizing Eleanor's secret letter) and 21 Feb. 1536 (with 'ung billet apart ziffré').
15. *CDCV*, I, 473–6, Charles to the empress, 20 Feb. 1536, holograph; *PEG*, II, 443, Granvelle to Hannart, 30 Mar. 1536.

16. *CDCV*, I, 485–90, Charles to the empress, 18 Apr. 1536. Leva, *Storia*, III, 164–5, argued plausibly that the arrival of French ambassador Vély with powers only to negotiate the cession of Milan to Orléans triggered the emperor's speech.
17. Cadenas y Vicent, *Discurso*, 35–7, contemporary account.
18. *RVEC*, 712–14, Salinas to Ferdinand, 22 Apr. 1536, summarized the speech and forwarded 'a text that can be circulated, and if necessary printed', which was probably the version published by Morel-Fatio, 'L'espagnol', 212–14 (reprinted in Cadenas y Vicent, *Discurso*, 61–3). See also the text in *LCK*, II, 223–9, Charles to Hannart, his ambassador in France, 17 Apr. 1536; and the version reconstructed from memory by the French ambassadors in Rome: Charrière, *Négociations*, I, 304, Macon (who could not understand Spanish) and Vély to Francis, 19 Apr. 1536 (both of them reprinted in Cadenas y Vicent, *Discurso*, and in Rassow, *Die Kaiser-Idee*, Beilage 4 and 5). The ambassadors recorded that the emperor spoke from notes ('lisoit en ung billet qu'il avoit à la main'), just as he would do in his farewell address in 1555 (ch. 15).
19. *RVEC*, 712–14, Salinas to Ferdinand, 22 Apr. 1536; Charrière, *Négociations*, I, 304, Macon and Vély to Francis, 19 Apr. 1536.
20. AGS *E* 1564/40, Charles to the count of Cifuentes, 4 May 1536 (see also *PEG*, II, 459, Charles to French ambassador Vély, 7 May 1536, asking the same question); Du Bellay, *Mémoires*, II, 402–12, Francis to Paul III; *Recueil d'aucunes lectres*, unfol., Charles to Paul III, 19 May 1536.
21. *RVEC*, 707–9, Salinas to Castillejos, 21 May 1536 (and not 31 Mar. as the editor suggested); and ibid., 726–30, Salinas to Ferdinand, 30 May and 10 June 1536.
22. *LCK*, II, 658–9, Charles to Marie, 2 Mar. 1536; *KFF*, V, 495–9, Marie to Ferdinand, 25 May 1536.
23. *KFF*, V, 514–20, Charles to Ferdinand, 9 June 1536; TNA *SP* 1/103/120–1, Richard Morison (later English ambassador to Charles) to Thomas Starkey, 12 Apr. 1536.
24. AGS *E* 1367/46–7, Gómez Suárez de Figueroa to Charles, 8 July 1534, conveying the results of separate interviews with Doria and Leyva (copy at f. 48); *RVEC*, 751–5, Salinas to Ferdinand, 17 July 1536. For the debate about the merits of Charles's participation, see BL *Addl. Ms.* 28,589/3–5v, 'Las dificultades que ocurren que ay en la pasada de Su Majestad en Francia', 13 July 1536. Sherer, *Warriors*, 60, provides an excellent campaign map.
25. *RVEC*, 756–72, Salinas to Castillejo and to Ferdinand, 17 July 1536, 4 and 5 Aug. 1536; García Cerezada, *Tratado*, II, 151, 157–8.
26. Decrue, *Anne de Montmorency*, 271, Montmorency (who had superintended the defence of Provence) to Francis, 1 Aug. 1536.
27. *KFF*, I, 99, Charles to Ferdinand, 23 Jan. 1524 (proposing the recovery of Arles, Provence, Dauphiné); Leva, *Storia*, III, 169 (on whether or not Charles intended to annex Provence in 1536). *Ordonnances des rois de France. Règne de François Ier*, VIII, 29–37, printed the Protocol between Francis and Suleiman agreed in Feb. 1536; Setton, *The papacy*, IV, 401 nn. 20–1, demonstrated its authenticity.
28. *LCK*, II, 657–67, summary of letters exchanged between Marie and Charles in 1536.
29. García Cerezada, *Tratado*, II, 160.
30. *PEG*, II, 480–1, 'Substancial' of a report by the papal nuncio, c. 11 Aug. 1536; BNF *F. f.* 3008/144, Montmorency to M. de Humières, 2 Sep. 1536 (casualties); *LCK*, II, 248–52, Charles to Nassau, 4 Sep. 1536.
31. On Fregoso in 1536, see Pacini, *La Genova*, 588–90.
32. BNF *Ms. Dupuy* 265/297, Jean de Breton, royal secretary, to Jean du Bellay, Arles, 20 Sep. 1536; Du Bellay, *Mémoires*, II, 299, by Martin du Bellay, who emphasized that 'I write what I saw'.
33. *RVEC*, 772–86, Salinas to Castillejo, 14 Sep. 1536; García Cerezada, *Tratado*, II, 195–8; Cienfuegos, *La heroyca vida*, 64. For an example of the emperor's affectionate relationship with the poet see BNE *Ms.* 20212/7/2, Garcilaso de la Vega to Charles, Genoa, 20 May 1536, signed just 'Garcilasso' (one of the last letters he wrote).
34. Decrue, *Anne de Montmorency*, 286 (estimate of damage by the Venetian ambassador); Bourrilly, *Histoire*, I, 295 (prediction of Honoré de Valbelle of Marseilles); Guyon, *Mémoires*, 71.
35. Du Bellay, *Mémoires*, III, 118–19; Holanda, *De la pintvra*, 181–2 (reporting a conversation with Michelangelo); Bourrilly, 'Charles-Quint', 277–80 (rejoicing in Provence and Rome).
36. *RVEC*, 789–99, Salinas to Ferdinand, 14 Nov. 1536 and 18 Mar. 1537.
37. Girón, *Crónica*, 99–100. On the consequences of Duke Alessandro's murder see ch. 12 below.
38. March, *Niñez*, II, 337, Doña Estefanía de Requesens to her mother, 18 May 1537; *RVEC*, 794–9 and 820–2, Salinas to Ferdinand, 18 Mar. 1537, and to Castillejo, 18 Nov. 1537; Girón, *Crónica*, 110.
39. Girón, *Crónica*, 125.
40. HHStA *Belgien PA* 27/5/227, Charles to Marie, 6 Oct. 1537.
41. Rassow, *Die Kaiser-Idee*, 431–2, Idiáquez to Los Cobos and Granvelle, and to Los Cobos alone, 15 Jan. 1538. Ambassador Serristori of Florence, normally well informed, complained that Charles kept

the entire diplomatic corps 'in the dark [*al bujo*]' about his intentions: Serristori, *Legazioni*, 47–8, dispatch to Cosimo, 29 Dec. 1537.

42. Rassow, *Die Kaiser-Idee*, 433–7, 'Las pláticas que el emperador passó con el señor de Pressiu por la misma forma y palabras syn dejar nada', sent by Idiáquez to Los Cobos and Granvelle, Feb. 1538.

43. BNF *F. f.* 3015/123, 'Double des lettres' sent from Aigues Mortes, probably to Cardinal du Bellay, 15 July 1538; TNA *SP* 3/17/49–v, report sent by Sir Francis Bryan, English ambassador in France, 16 July 1538; *LCK*, II, 284–9, Charles to Marie, 18 July 1538.

44. Le Person, 'A moment', 20 (from an eyewitness account); *LCK*, II, 284–9, Charles to Marie, 18 July 1538; TNA *SP* 3/17/49–v (as in the preceding note). *RVEC*, 869–71, Licenciado Gamiz to Ferdinand, 18 July 1538, another eyewitness description, provided an almost identical account of the exchange of oaths and rings. Henry of Orléans became dauphin in 1536, after the death of his older brother: both had been Charles's prisoners in Spain from Mar. 1526 to June 1530. On the harsh treatment they received, see ch. 8 above.

45. *LCK*, II, 284–9, Charles to Marie, 18 July 1538; Kaulek, *Correspondance*, 69–70, Francis to Châtillon, 18 July 1538.

46. AGS *E* 867/64, Charles to the marquis of Aguilar, his ambassador in Rome, 7 Sep. 1538; *BKK*, II, 273, Charles to Ferdinand, 22 Sep. 1538.

47. Preveza and its significance is discussed by Guilmartin, *Gunpowder*, 42–56 (with a valuable map at p. 49); and in Colin Heywood's review of Guilmartin in *Bulletin of the School of Oriental and African Studies*, XXXVIII (1975), 643–6, which cites Ottoman sources on the battle.

48. *CLC*, V, 46–95, provides a transcript of the nobles' debates, after which only five peers followed the duke of Alba in approving the new tax.

49. Sepúlveda, *Historia*, XVIII, 18 (the chronicler said that the conversation took place 'in Madrid some years later', which can only mean the winter of 1542-3). See the admirable discussion of the Cortes of Toledo in Fortea Pérez, 'Las últimas Cortes', 245–60; but see also p. 290 below on Charles's injunction to Philip in 1543 to demand an excise in his own name if necessary.

50. *RVEC*, 879, Salinas to Ferdinand, 28 Oct. 1538; and 887–95, to Castillejo, 26 Nov. 1538 (two letters); idem, 897, Salinas to Ferdinand, 4 Feb. 1539 (two months later, once again, 'el emperador se va a holgar a la caza por algunos días': ibid., 903–6, same to same, 18 Apr. 1539).

51. *BKK*, II, 288, Charles to Ferdinand, 21 Apr. 1539. *RVEC*, 903–6, Salinas to Ferdinand, 18 Apr. 1539, stated that 'en este mes de Mayo que viene, entra [the empress] en el noveno mes de su preñado', so she had conceived the previous Sep.

52. *BKK*, II, 289, Charles to Ferdinand, 2 May 1539; *RVEC*, 913–15, Salinas to Ferdinand, 3 May 1539.

53. AGRB *Audience* 868/110–14v, 'Estat' of expenditure 'procédent des guerres de France, de Dennemarcke et d'Overyssel'; Gachard, 'Charles-Quint', col. 617, Charles to the magistrates of Ghent, 31 Jan. 1538.

54. Arnade, 'Privileges', provided an excellent short account of the revolt of Ghent, noting that the magistrates also allowed the city's Chambers of Rhetoric to stage plays with an openly Lutheran theme.

55. Ribier, *Lettres*, I, 368–70, Ambassador Tarbes to Montmorency, 6 Feb. 1539; *RVEC*, 920–4, Salinas to Ferdinand, 11 July and 7 Aug. 1539.

56. Gachard, 'Charles-Quint', col. 625n, Marie to Charles, 9 June 1538. *SP*, VIII, 203–5, Stephen Vaughan to Henry, Brussels, 19 Nov. 1539, brilliantly analysed the situation, discerning three reasons why Charles would risk travelling to the Netherlands through France: 'the mutyny of certeyn cities in these parties'; Henry's 'allyance ... with the howse of Cleve, whiche he greatly stomakithe'; and his 'confederacie (as they here call it) bytwene His Majeste and th'Almayns'. Vaughan then predicted (correctly) that after he had crushed his domestic opponents, Charles would 'sett upon Gelderlande' and afterwards the German Lutherans.

57. AGS *PR* 45/6–7, Charles's instructions to Luis de Ávila y Zúñiga, 24 and 26 Oct. 1539. (Both documents name Luis de Zúñiga, but subsequent correspondence proves that the envoy was Luis de Ávila y Zúñiga.)

58. Gachard, *Relation*, 249–51, Los Cobos and Granvelle to François Bonvalot, imperial ambassador in France, 27 Sep. 1539. Gachard, *Relation*, 258–62, printed the letters of invitation from Francis and several others, dated 7 Oct. 1539; Paillard, 'Voyage', 517–18, listed all the senders.

59. *CDCV*, II, 32–55, printed the instructions for Philip, and for Tavera and Los Cobos, both dated 5 Nov. 1539, with a French text of the former in *PEG*, II, 549–61. Manuel Fernández Álvarez plausibly argued that Charles composed his instructions for Philip in French, perhaps aided by Granvelle, and that the Spanish version is an imperfect translation.

60. *PEG*, II, 542–8, codicil dated 5 Nov. 1539, French copy of the Latin original, with two signed copies in Spanish – all of which, like the will made by Charles in 1535, have apparently perished.

61. Guicciardini, *Opere inedite*, X, 324–5, letter to Roberto Pucci, Florence, 29 Nov. 1539; Kaulek, *Correspondance*, 143–4, Marillac to Francis, London, 14 Nov. 1539. Charles's entourage included both the duke of Alba and Luis de Ávila.

62. Gachard, *Relation*, 653–8, Charles to Tavera, Paris, 6 Jan. 1540, and 'Relation du voyage'. Wetter, 'The year-long unprecedented European heat and drought of 1540', 357, and 'Supplementary Information', documents the warmth and the absence of snow and rain in the winter of 1539–40.

63. ASF *MdP* 4297/7, Alessandro Giovanni Bandini to Agnolo Niccolini, 7 Dec. 1539, from Loches, the day Charles and Francis met. Paillard, 'Voyage', and Knecht, 'Charles V's journey', provided useful overviews (p. 154 of the latter included a map of Charles's itinerary).

64. Gachard, *Relation*, 662–3, Charles to Tavera, 21 Jan. 1540. BL *Addl. Ms.* 28,592/1–2, Granvelle to Los Cobos, 6 Jan. 1540, confirmed that 'there has been no discussion of marriages or other business'.

65. Gachard, *Relation*, 668, Charles to Tavera, Ghent, 14 Feb. 1540.

66. Henne, *Histoire*, VII, 62–5 and 88–95 (lists of those punished in Ghent and elsewhere in Flanders); Gachard, *Relation*, 156–60, from a contemporary account of the 'amende honorable' on 3 May 1540. The submission is re-enacted in the streets of Ghent each July as part of the 'Gentse Feesten'. Boone, 'From cuckoo's egg', notes that Charles chose the site of the citadel after studying the plans drawn up for Charles the Bold in 1469 as well as for Maximilian in 1492. See *Recueil des ordonnances*, IV, 170–91, for the edicts condemning Ghent (30 Apr. 1540); 198 and 200, for those concerning the citadel (5–6 May 1540); and 206–7 and 211–16, for those condemning Oudenaarde (June 1540) and Kortrijk (17 July 1540) for rebellion. *SP*, VIII, 339–41, Dr Wotton to Thomas Cromwell, 30 Apr. 1540, noted the commemoration of the empress.

67. *PEG*, II, 562–72, Charles's instructions to Bonvalot, Ghent, 24 Mar. 1540.

68. *CDCV*, IV, 509 (*Memoirs*); Ribier, *Lettres*, I, 514–16, ambassadors de Selva and Hellin to Montmorency, Ghent, 11 Apr. 1540; Powell, *The complete works*, I, 246–59, Wyatt to Cromwell, Ghent, 5 and 12 Apr. 1540 ('not now, not ever' translated from Latin).

69. *PEG*, II, 597–9, Charles to Bonvalot, 9 June 1540, accepting Francis's proposal 'de laisser ainsi les choses pour maintenant'; and 599–604, codicil to Charles's will, 28 Oct. 1540; *NBD*, VI, 338–41, Charles to Ferdinand, 2 July 1540 (see p. 110 above for an identical view expressed by Adrian of Utrecht in 1521). Dumont, *Corps*, IV/2, 200–2, printed Charles's deed investing his son with Milan, 11 Oct. 1540.

70. *Catalogue des Actes*, IV, 106 (nos 11,485–6), warrants to Rincón, 1 May 1540; Setton, *The papacy*, III, 456 (Turkish original).

71. *Recueil des ordonnances*, IV, 229–30, 232–8 and 240–53, edicts enacted by Charles in Oct. 1540; AGS *E* 49/81–5, Los Cobos (alcaide of Simancas) to Juan Vázquez de Molina, 26 June 1540 (ordering his nephew to ensure that the emperor signed 'la orden para que se haga en Simancas' a new archive); AGS *CC*, 247/1, royal warrant, Brussels, 16 Sep. 1540.

72. *NBD*, VI, 319–23, Charles to Ferdinand, Brussels, 9 June 1540, sharing the advice of Pedro de Soto, his confessor.

73. Martin Luther, *Von den Conciliis und Kirchen* (Strasbourg, 1539).

74. Schultze, 'Dreizehn Depeschen', 150–6, Contarini to Cardinal Farnese, 13 Mar. 1541.

75. *CSPV*, V, 96–8, Francesco Contarini to the Signory, Regensburg, 6 Apr. 1541.

76. Schultze, 'Dreizehn Depeschen', 159–61, Gasparo Contarini to Cardinal Farnese, 18 Mar. 1541 (the nature of the Eucharist 'era già stato determinato' by the Fourth Lateran Council in 1215); Pastor, 'Correspondenz', 388–90, Contarini to Farnese, 15 May 1541; Dittich, 'Nuntiaturberichte', 465–72 and 620–3, Morone to Farnese, 29 May and 21 June 1541.

77. *CSPV*, V, 105–6 and 107–8, Francesco Contarini to the Signory, 22 June and 26 July 1541. In fact, by sleight of hand the Lutherans managed to gain more by the Regensburg Recess than they had enjoyed under the peace of Nuremburg: p. 228–9 above.

78. Turba, *Venetianische Depeschen*, I, 67–76, Tiepolo, Corner, Contarini, Venier and Mocenigo to the Doge, Nice, 24 May 1538.

79. Lanz, *Staatspapiere*, 263–8, memorandum by Marie, [10] Aug. 1538. See also Marie's letter to Charles on the same day on the same subject: *LCK*, II, 289–90.

80. ASF *MdP* 652/256, Agnolo Niccolini to Lorenzo Pagni, 1 Aug. 1541. He later found that the *Reichsabschied* that he signed differed from the one approved by his ministers, granting extensive concessions to the Lutherans: see p. 506 below.

81. Gachard, *Collection*, II, 189–90, Journal of Jean Vandenesse for Aug. 1541, shows that Charles reached Cremona, only 150 kilometres from Genoa, on 18 Aug. He then turned north for Milan, and away from Genoa.

82. Nordman, *Tempête*, 451. For evidence that Charles believed that attacking Algiers would reduce the pressure on Hungary, see ibid., 239–40. See also Guyon, *Mémoires*, 87, for another evaluation by an eyewitness of campaigning so late.

83. *CDCV*, IV, 511 (*Memoirs*); Friedensburg, 'Aktenstücke', 38–42, two documents about 'things to be discussed in Lucca', one by the papal nuncio travelling with Charles (which listed 'le cose private et particolari') and the other by Granvelle.
84. AGS *E* 53/67–8, Vázquez de Molina to Los Cobos, 15 Oct. 1541. The two instructions appear to have perished, but presumably they resembled the campaign plan that Charles provided for his son in May 1543: see p. 289 below.
85. Nordman, *Tempête*, 493 and 495 (Magnalotti); 356–7 and 381–3 (Nicholas Durand de Villegaignon); and 225–7 (Christian and Muslim sources on the number of horses eaten); Sandoval, *Historia*, 347; Guyon, *Mémoires*, 90; *CDCV*, IV, 512.
86. ASF *MdP* 4298, unfol., Alessandro Giovanni Bandini to Duke Cosimo, Bougie, 4 Nov. 1541 (quoting Giannettino Doria); Nordman, *Tempête*, 456 (Gómara), 493 (Antonio Magnalotti) and 358 (Villegaignon); Guyon, *Mémoires*, 92; and 'P. P.', 'L'expédition', 187.
87. Turba, *Venetianische Depeschen*, I, 434–6, Francesco Giustiniani to the council of Ten, Bougie, 10 Nov. 1541; Guyon, *Mémoires*, 87 ('néantmoins').
88. *CDCV*, IV, 511 n. 105, Charles to Cortes of Castile, 1542; and ibid., 511 (*Memoirs*); Nordman, *Tempête*, 564, quoting an Algerian eyewitness; and 212–13, the imam. Idem, 248–60, presents convincing evidence that success at Tunis 'tempted' Charles to behave rashly.
89. Nordman, *Tempête*, 178; Guyon, *Mémoires*, 91; Anon., *Warhafftige und gewise newe Zeytung*, unfol. (I thank Alison Anderson for this translation).
90. Nordman, *Tempête*, 381–3, Villegaignon to du Bellay, 25 Oct. 1541.
91. Op. cit., 497, Antonio Magnalotti, quoting Doria.
92. Giovio, *Opera*, I, 269–71, Giovio to Cardinal Pio di Carpi, 17 Sep. 1541.
93. *CSPSp*, VI/2, 105, Charles to Eustache Chapuys, his ambassador in England, 12 Aug. 1542 (apologizing that he could find few relevant documents 'ayant esté les aultres perdues au voyage d'Algey'); *CDCV*, II, 453–8, Charles to Prince Philip, 17 Mar. 1546 (mules instead of horses); Charrière, *Négociations*, I, 522–4, 'Rapport d'un agent à François Ier sur l'expédition d'Alger', Dec. 1541.

CHAPTER 11: SETTLING SCORES, PART I: GUELDERS AND FRANCE, 1541–4

1. Details from AGS *E* 638/106, Vasto to Charles, 7 July 1541, copy; AGS *E* 1374/167, Vasto to Los Cobos, 6 July 1541, and f. 238, Gómez Suárez de Figueroa to Charles, 8 July 1541; Ruble, *Le mariage*, 149–51, Charles de Boisot to Marie of Hungary, 12 Aug. 1541; and Tausserat-Radel, *Correspondance*, I, 361–3, Guillaume Pellicier, French ambassador in Venice, to Georges d'Armagnac, French ambassador in Rome, 23 July 1541; and ibid., 434–8, Pellicier to Francis, 6 Oct. 1541.
2. Sanuto, *I diarii*, LVI, col. 781, entry for 20 Aug. 1532, recording the presence in Venice of 'three Spaniards who sought to murder' Rincón. In 1541 both Vasto and Henry VIII attested that Charles had offered a 'grosse rescompense à ceulx qui le luy livreroient' Rincón: Tausserat-Radel, *Correspondance*, I, 349–53, Pellicier to Francis, 9 July 1541 (quoting Vasto), and Kaulek, *Correspondance*, 326–8, Marillac to Francis, 12 Aug. 1541 (quoting Henry).
3. Tausserat-Radel, *Correspondance*, I, 349–53, Pellicier to Francis, 9 July 1541; Alba, 'Correspondencia', 83–6, Charles to Vasto, Regensburg, 23 June 1541.
4. Alba, 'Correspondencia', 119–20, Vasto to Charles, 9 July 1541; AGS *E* 638/106, same to same, 7 July 1541, with postscript on 9 July (incomplete copy in Alba, 'Correspondencia', 117–19). The messenger was Pirro Colonna, sent to Regensburg by Vasto on 5 July.
5. AGS *E* 52/359, 'Lo que paresce que se deve screvir al marqués del Gasto', *consulta* prepared for Charles by Secretary Idiáquez, undated but mid-July 1541 (italics added); Alba, 'Correspondencia', 93, Charles to Vasto, Regensburg, 19 July 1541 (not 1542, as the text states).
6. Alba, 'Correspondencia', 93–4, Charles to Vasto, 20 July 1542 (see also the equally reproachful letter written one week earlier: ibid., 91–3).
7. *LCK*, II, 315–18, Charles to Bonvalot, 23 July 1541; *NBD*, VII, Contarini to Cardinal Farnese, 2 Aug. 1541; Alba, 'Correspondencia', 120–1, Charles's commission to Charles de Boisot, 23 July 1541. See also Ruble, *Le mariage*, 149–51, Boisot to Marie, 12 Aug. 1541, reporting on his mission.
8. Alba, 'Correspondencia', 94–6, Charles to Vasto, 8 Aug. 1541 (the printed version dates this letter 1542, but it refers to another letter sent 'yesterday from Innsbruck' and Charles was at Innsbruck on 6 and 7 Aug. 1541; he spent all of 1542 in Spain). This letter was (as a later age would say) a 'smoking gun', because it revealed that although the emperor may not have ordered the murder of the ambassadors himself, he certainly approved of the deed and did his best to protect the principal perpetrator. On Fregoso's role as leader of the anti-Doria exiles of Genoa, see Pacini, *La Genova*, 591–3.
9. Albicante, *Trattato del'intrar in Milano*, fourth and last engraving, shows the arch. See also Mitchell, *The majesty*, 175–6; and Venturelli, 'L'ingresso trionfale'. Chabod, *Storia*, 412, noted the destructive storms.

10. *Catalogue des Actes*, IV, 198 (no. 11,914) and 203 (no. 11,935), warrants to Rincón; Tausserat-Radel, *Correspondance*, I, 353–4 and 379–80, Pellicier to d'Armagnac, 9 and 30 July 1541; Kaulek, *Correspondance*, 322–3, Francis to ambassador Marillac, 26 July 1541; and *LCK*, II, 324–6, Bonvalot to Charles, 3 Aug. 1541 (the chancellor spoke of 'le droit de la société des hommes').

11. AGS *E* 1374/167, Vasto to Los Cobos, 6 July 1541; Tausserat-Radel, *Correspondance*, I, 398–403, Pellicier to Francis, 22 Aug. 1541.

12. Tausserat-Radel, *Correspondance*, I, 439–41, Pellicier to Captain Polin, 6 Oct. 1541; *LCK*, II, 326–7, Charles to Marie, 26 Sep. 1541; Giovio, *Opera*, I, 269–71, Giovio to Cardinal Pio di Carpi, 17 Sep. 1541.

13. Lestocquoy, *Correspondance*, 99–102, Niccolò Ardinghello to Cardinal Farnese, 1 and 3 Dec. 1541; *SP*, VIII (part V, vol. 3), 639–44, Ambassador William Paget to Henry, 7 Dec. 1541 (repeating what Francis had told Ardinghello in French, translated here); Lestocquoy, op. cit., 95–8, Nuncio Capodiferro to Farnese, 27 Dec. 1541.

14. *LCK*, II, 683–4, Marie to Charles and his reply, July 1538, and 289–90, Marie to Charles, 10 Aug. 1538. *SP*, VIII, 307–15, Wotton to Henry, 9 and 15 Apr. 1540, and to Cromwell, 27 Apr. 1540, are full of details on the duke of Cleves's efforts.

15. Powell, *The complete works*, I, 163–70, 182–201 and 201–12, Wyatt to Henry, 12 Dec. 1539, 7 Jan. 1540 and 3 Feb. 1540.

16. *SP*, VIII, 374–6, Pate to the duke of Norfolk, 4 July 1540; Dumont, *Corps*, IV/2, 196, treaty between France and Cleves, 17 July 1540.

17. Dumont, *Corps*, IV/2, 216–17 and 228–30, treaties between France and Denmark, 29 Nov. 1541, and France and Sweden, 1 July 1542; *SP*, VIII, 635–44, Paget to Henry, 21 Nov. and 7 Dec. 1541 (see 'Articles agreed upon by certain capitaines of Almayn, entreteined by the French king' at p. 640 n. 1); Kaulek, *Correspondance*, 327–31 and 347–51, Marillac to Francis, 12 Aug. and 12 Oct. 1541. Francis signed powers for Marillac to finalize terms for the marriage on 10 Feb. 1542: ibid., 388.

18. *PEG*, II, 628–31, 'Cry de la guerre ouverte', 12 July 1542 (English translation in *CSPSp*, VI/2, 62–3; Guiffrey, *Cronique*, 392–6, printed the same document from another copy, dated 10 July 1542); Kaulek, *Correspondance*, 431, Instructions to L'Aubespine, 8 July 1542, included the declaration of war. One year later, Francis still used the murder of his ambassadors to justify a demand for new taxes for his war against Charles: BL *Eg. Ms.* 38, Mandement to raise the *taille* in Quercy, 31 Aug. 1543.

19. Williams, 'Re-orienting', 21–2, Suleiman to Ferdinand, 12/21 Sep. 1541, and Jerome Laski to Ferdinand, Nov. 1541; Kaulek, *Correspondance*, 340–1, Rustem Pasha to Laski, forwarded to Francis by an agent in Belgrade, 18 Aug. 1541, and forwarded in turn to Ambassador Marillac in England. On the rich afterlife of the murder of Fregoso and Rincón, which remained a diplomatic *cause célèbre* until the 1790s, see p. 509 below.

20. Friedensburg, 'Aktenstücke', 45–57, Granvelle's position paper, beginning 'Affinque l'empereur se puisse mieulx determiner et mander son intencion', Siena, 28 Nov. 1541. The minister had obviously received copies of letters addressed to the emperor by his siblings (e.g. Árpad, 'Kiadatlan', 490–3, Ferdinand to Charles, 20 Oct. 1541; and *BKK*, II, 434, and plate 6, Granvelle's advice on how to reply to Marie's letters of 15 Oct. 1541).

21. Árpad, 'Kiadatlan', 497–9, Charles to Ferdinand, and *BKK*, II, 430–3, Charles to Marie, both dated 29 Dec. 1541

22. HHStA *Belgien PA* 32/1/7–10, Charles to Marie, Tordesillas, 26 Jan. 1542, a heavily corrected draft, mostly holograph (fair copy, perhaps a decrypt made for Marie, at *Belgien PA* 32/1/11–14). Charles mentioned the plan to recover Guelders 'that I prepared when I left Germany', that is in July 1541. As early as Nov. 1539, an English diplomat predicted that once Charles had travelled from Spain to the Netherlands he would first suppress 'the mutyny of certeyn cities in these partes', then attack Guelders and afterwards the German Lutherans: *SP*, VIII, 203–5, Stephen Vaughan to Thomas Cromwell, Brussels, 19 Nov. 1539.

23. Árpad, 'Kiadatlan', 514–18, Charles to Ferdinand, 10 [not 19] May 1542.

24. HHStA *Belgien PA* 32/4/332–4v, and *BKK*, II, 323, Charles to Marie, 13 May and 10 June 1542, both holograph.

25. HHStA *Belgien PA* 32/3/242–7v, Marie to Charles, 30 June 1542, minute, sent 'tout en cyffre forte'.

26. *SP*, IX, 157–63, Bonner to Henry, 9 Sep. 1542; HHStA *Hs. Blau* 596/1/38–40v, Charles to Ferdinand, 9 Oct. 1542, register copy; *LCK*, II, 364–7, M. de Praet to Charles, 24 Sep. 1542.

27. HHStA *Hs. Blau* 596/1/44–5, Charles to Ferdinand, 3 Nov. 1542, holograph, register copy (published with some errors in Árpad, 'Kiadatlan', 537).

28. BL *Addl. Ms.* 28,706 contains all the major documents concerning the Portuguese marriage treaty; HHStA *Belgien PA* 38/2/183–87v, Charles to Marie, 12 Apr. 1543, mentioned the advance payment

of 150,000 ducats of the dowry for his future daughter-in-law, which Charles planned to use 'to sustain me' in arranging 'my trip' out of Spain.

29. For examples of the intelligence provided by Jehan de Hons, see *CSPSp*, VI/1, 341–3, and VI/2, 8–9, Chapuys to Charles, 16 July 1541 and 7 May 1542. For his identity, idem VI/2, 427, Chapuys to Marie, 5 July 1543. As David Potter astutely noted: 'The mystery is how de Hons was able to find the time to copy out so many ciphered despatches of his master' (Potter, *Henry VIII*, 67–8).

30. *CSPSp* VI/2, 236–8, Charles to Chapuys, 23 Jan. 1543; Rymer, *Foedera*, XIV, 768–80, treaty between Charles and Henry 'contra Franciscum cum Turcha confoederatum, de guerra indicenda & Franciae invadenda', 11 Feb. 1543 (Roman style).

31. *CSPSp* VI/2, 236–8, Charles to Chapuys, 23 Jan. 1543.

32. *SP*, IX, 355–60 and 374–6, Bonner to Henry, 15 Apr. and 14 May 1543.

33. *SPs*, IX, 374–6, Bonner to Henry, 14 May 1543; Ball and Parker, *Cómo ser rey*, 149–59, from which this and all other quotations from the instructions of 4 and 6 May 1543 are taken.

34. The emperor's use of 'us' and 'our' is notable: perhaps for the first time, he saw himself and his son as a 'team'.

35. For vindication of this warning, see the evidence of factions among Charles's ministers revealed in Tellechea Idígoras, *Fray Bartolomé*, I, the testimony of over fifty courtiers during the recusal phase of Carranza's trial in 1559–62.

36. The emperor spent longer evaluating Los Cobos than anyone else. Regarding his faults, Charles informed his son 'I have warned him and I believe he will mend his ways'.

37. Antoine Perrenot (1517–86), Cardinal Granvelle after 1561, would serve the emperor and his son in Germany and the Netherlands until 1564 and in Italy from then until 1579, when he returned to Spain as chief minister. As Charles had predicted, 'he will serve you well'.

38. Fernando de Valdés Salas (1488–1568) served as president of the chancery of Valladolid (1535–9) and president of the council of Castile (1539–46); and as archbishop of Seville and Inquisitor-General from 1546 until his death. He had accompanied Charles to England, the Netherlands and Germany in 1520–2: see Colón de Carvajal, 'Don Fernando de Valdés'. See ch. 15 for his later interaction with the emperor.

39. *Bibliographie nationale de Belgique*, III (Brussels, 1872), col. 666, Gachard's entry on Charles; *SP*, IX, 355–60, Bonner to Henry, 15 Apr. 1543.

40. AGS *E* 60/193–4, Loaysa (a survivor of the 'summits' between pope and emperor in Bologna in 1530 and 1533) to Charles, 28 Sep. 1543, holograph; AGS *PR* 16/75, Charles's instructions to Juan de Vega, his new ambassador to the pope, 5 July 1543, with a full account of what he had discussed with Paul III at Busseto. Chabod, *Storia*, 84–7, discusses the pope's offer to buy Milan from Charles, pointing out the emperor had just accepted 150,000 ducats from Duke Cosimo of Florence in return for two fortresses occupied by imperial troops.

41. Giovio, *Delle Istorie*, 693 (book XLIII; at Busseto in June 1543); Gachard, 'Notice historique', 45–6, Charles to the Estates of Flanders, 13 June 1543 (HHStA *Belgien PA* 38/3 contains minutes of twelve similar letters).

42. *SP*, IX, 450–2, Nicholas Wotton to Henry, Brussels, 21 July 1543, holograph; ASF *MdP* 4301/104–10 and 141, Ricasoli to Duke Cosimo, Speyer, 2 Aug. 1543, and Mainz, 11 Aug. 1543.

43. *SP*, IX, 484–7, Bonner to Henry, Cologne, 24 Aug. 1543; Gachard, *Analectes historiques*, I, 246–57, Charles to Philip, 25 Sep. 1543; Gayangos, *Relaciones de Pedro de Gante*, 97. Arfaioli, 'A clash of dukes', notes that although Düren was not an artillery fortress, its fortifications had been partially modernized (like those of Florence in 1529–30 and Metz in 1552).

44. Brantôme, *Oeuvres*, II, 4; Gayangos, *Relaciones de Pedro de Gante*, 96; ASF *MdP* 4301/179, Ricasoli to Duke Cosimo, from the imperial camp, 30 Aug. 1543.

45. ASF *MdP* 4301/182, Ricasoli to Duke Cosimo, from the imperial camp, 12 Sep. 1543; *PEG*, II, 669.

46. *SP*, IX, 505–7, Wotton to Henry, 9 Sep. 1543 (quoting Caesar in Latin); AA 4/95, Charles to Alba, 27 Oct. 1543, holograph postscript (copy at f. 46).

47. ASF *MdP* 4301/182–5, Ricasoli to Duke Cosimo, 12 Sep. 1543; *SP*, IX, 505–7, Wotton to Henry, 9 Sep. 1543; *PEG*, II, 678–82, Charles's instructions to Baron Chantonnay, his special envoy to Henry to propose a joint Anglo-imperial invasion of France 'next year', 12 Sep. 1543.

48. *SP*, IX, 522–5, Sir John Wallop, commander of the English expeditionary force, to Henry, 21 Oct. 1543, after visiting Charles the previous day; Gachard, *Analectes historiques*, II, 216–19, Granvelle to Marie, 29 Oct. 1543 (placing the minister's reported speech into the first person).

49. ASF *MdP* 4301/280–1, Ricasoli to Duke Cosimo, 27 Oct. 1543, quoting the marquis of Marignano ('batterla era una *obstinatione* di Sua Maestà;'); *SP*, IX, 527–9 and TNA *SP* 1/182/39–41, Wallop to Paget, 22 and 26 Oct. 1543 (describing in great detail the 'artficiall boulets' fired by the mortars

'spowting fyer on every syde', which suggests that they were new); AGS *E* 60/193–4, Loaysa to Charles, 9 Sep. 1543, holograph.

50. Gayangos, *Relaciones de Pedro de Gante*, 105–6 (the advance) and 109 (the rebuke); Gachard, *Trois années*, 22, Navagero to the Signory, 2 Nov. 1543; *SP*, IX, 538–42, Wallop to Henry, 6 Nov. 1543.

51. *SP*, IX, 538–42, Wallop to Henry, 6 Nov. 1543; ibid., 543–5, Wallop to Paget, 7 Nov. 1543 with a postscript on 10 Nov.; HHStA *Hs. Blau* 596/1/57, Charles to Ferdinand, 19 Nov. 1543; Gachard, *Trois années*, 23, Navagero to the Signory, 28 Nov. 1543, with an addition overheard by his Florentine colleague: ASF *MdP* 4301/357, Ricasoli to Duke Cosimo, 10 Dec. 1543. See also Gachard, *Analectes historiques*, II, 34–8, Charles to Marie, 4 and 5 Nov. 1543.

52. Isom-Verhaaren, '"Barbarossa"', 419, quoting a letter from Barbarossa to Suleiman, 22 Mar. 1544.

53. TNA *SP* 1/182/157–64, 'Articles concluded between the viceroy [Gonzaga] and the king's highness commissioners for ye invasion of France', heavily corrected draft in several hands, but mainly Paget's (parts in French), undated but sent to Wallop on 4 Jan. 1544: *SP*, IX, 576–81. See also AGS *E*, 806/79, Chapuys to Prince Philip, 18 Jan. 1544, summarizing and updating the agreed terms.

54. Du Bellay, *Mémoires*, IV, 236; TNA *SP* 1/187/86–8, Wotton to Henry, 7 May 1544; Gachard, *Trois années*, 36–7, Navagero and Morosini to the Signory, 26 Apr. 1544, after an audience with Charles.

55. ASF *MdP* 4301/464, Ricasoli to Duke Cosimo, 1 Mar. 1544, decrypt, quoting the nuncio; *PEG*, III, 21–5, Response of the Diet to the emperor's proposition, Speyer, 10 June 1544. For the Danish dimension see Bregnsbo, 'Carlos V', 494–5.

56. Brandi, 'Die Testamente', 96–107, codicil witnessed and signed 21 June 1544, and sent sealed to Ferdinand; AGS *E* 500/73, Charles to Los Cobos, 7 July 1544.

57. BNE *MR*/43/283, 'Descripció de parte de Francia por donde entró el emperador', 56 x 107 centimetres, undated but from 1544.

58. ASF *MdP* 4301/503, Ricasoli to Duke Cosimo, 14 Mar. 1544; Rozet and Lembey, *L'invasion*, 545–6, Ambassador Hieronymo Feruffino to the duke of Ferrara, 7 July 1544; ibid., 539, same to same, 23 June 1544; ibid., 666–8, Navagero to the Signory, 22 June 1544. Rozet and Lembey, op. cit., 511–743, printed substantial extracts from almost 200 campaign dispatches written by envoys from Venice, Ferrara and Mantua to their home governments. *SP*, IX and X include those of the English ambassador.

59. HHStA *Belgien PA* 40/3/293–8, Charles to Marie, 20 July 1544. Charles concluded his campaign at Cambrai on 23 Sep. two days short of his target date.

60. HHStA *Belgien PA* 40/3/363–8, Charles to Marie, 31 Aug. 1544; *CDCV*, IV, 522 (*Memoirs*). Rozet and Lembey, *L'invasion*, 574–6, Feruffino to Ferrara, 4 Sep. 1544, and 638–48, Camillo Capilupo to the regents of Mantua, 19 Sep. 1544; both give excellent accounts of the moonlight march.

61. Rozet and Lembey, *L'invasion*, 713–15, Navagero to the Signory, '16 leagues from Paris', 6 Sep. 1544; ibid., 638–48, Capilupo to the regents of Mantua, 19 Sep. 1544.

62. TNA *SP* 1/192/36 Wotton to Paget, 6 Sep. 1544; Guyon, *Mémoires*, 109; Giovio, *Opera*, I, 348–50, Giovio to Cardinal Farnese, 23 Sep. 1544. France's military collapse in 1544 was thus almost as rapid and as complete as that in 1940, when another enemy mounted a surprise invasion from the east.

63. *CDCV*, IV, 523–4 (*Memoirs*); Rozet and Lembey, *L'invasion*, 574–6, Feruffino to Ferrara, 4 Sep. 1544; von Druffel, 'Kaiser Karl V', 266–70, Charles's instructions to Perrenot, 7 Sep. 1544.

64. AGS *E* 64/95, Los Cobos to Charles, 17 Sep. 1544; BMECB *Ms. Granvelle* III, 166–8, Granvelle's advice on making peace, undated but submitted to Charles on 14 or 15 Sep. 1544, a heavily edited draft (text in *PEG*, III, 26–9, without indicating the edits). Granvelle's analysis was correct: no sooner had his troops taken Boulogne than Henry started to plan his return to England.

65. Rozet and Lembey, *L'invasion*, 577–8, Feruffino to Ferrara, 11–14 Sep. 1544.

66. AGS *E* 64/95, Los Cobos to Granvelle, 17 Sep. 1544; AGS *E* 64/197, Loaysa to Charles, 5 Jan. 1545; *CDCV*, II, 282–4, Philip to Charles, 28 Sep. 1544 (an interesting articulation of the view of the theologians of the School of Salamanca, who argued that victors should not destroy the vanquished but instead offer them peace); *CDCV*, IV, 523–4 (*Memoirs*).

67. Dumont, *Corps*, IV/2, 279–87, treaty of Crépy, 18 Sep. 1544.

68. Hasenclever, 'Die Geheimartikel', 420–2, text signed 19 Sep. 1544.

69. HHStA *Hs. Blau* 596/1/69v–72, Charles to Marie, 19 Sep. 1544, register copy (parts printed in von Druffel, 'Kaiser Karl V', 270–1).

70. Giovio, *Opera*, I, 352–4, letter to 'a friend', Rome, 14 Oct. 1544; Zimmerman, *Paolo Giovio*, 197.

CHAPTER 12: SETTLING SCORES, PART II: GERMANY AND ITALY, 1545–8

1. *SP*, X, 178–87 and 202–7, Hertford, Gardiner and Wotton to Henry, 7, 9 and 17 Nov. 1544.

2. *SP*, X, 71–2, Henry to Wotton, [15] Sep. 1544 (thus written just before the peace treaty); Gachard, *Trois années*, 43, Chapuys and Corrières to Charles, 16 Sep. 1544, relaying the same message. The

only error in Henry's reasoning was that 'the Lowe Countrey, being the certaine inheritance of th'empereurs succession, out of all doubt and question', would be 'gardable without any greate charges' if it remained joined to Spain.

3. TNA SP 1/194/39–40, Wotton to the Privy Council, 21 Oct. 1544 (describing Idiáquez and his mission); CDCV, II, 300–1, Philip to Charles, 14 Dec. 1544 (not the 24th, as stated in ibid., p. 311).

4. Chabod, 'Milán o los Países Bajos?', 244–51, 'Los puntos que se apuntaron por los del consejo de Estado en las dos comunicaciones que se tuvo sobre la alternativa que ofreció Su Magestad', undated but Nov. 1544. Chabod also provided a brilliant analysis of the debate, situating it in the changing context of imperial grand strategy: ibid., 211–44.

5. CDCV, II, 299–311, Philip to Charles, 14 Dec. 1544 (misdated 24 Dec.). Just as Charles had predicted in May 1543, Los Cobos sided with Alba, and Zúñiga sided with Tavera: Ball and Parker, Cómo ser rey, 117.

6. PEG, III, 67–87, 'Ce que l'on doibt considérer sur la déclaration de l'alternative contenue au traité de Crespy', followed by 'Discours et arraisonnement des considérations que l'on peult prendre sur l'Alternative', undated but before 17 Feb. 1545, when Charles informed his son that 'las personas más principales y aceptas a Nos destos Stados' had 'dado por scripto' their preference concerning the Alternative: CDCV, III, 336–43, 17 Feb. 1545.

7. SP, X, 236–7, Wotton to Henry VIII, 27 Nov. 1544; AGS E 872/129, Charles to Juan de Vega, undated but 17 Feb. 1545 (with orders to inform the pope).

8. Dumont, Corps, IV/2, 288, printed Charles's declaration. Other details from Gachard, Trois années, 68–9 and 71, Navagero to the Doge, 22 Jan. and 27 Mar. 1545; ASF MdP 4302, unfol., Ricasoli to Duke Cosimo, 14 and 22 Feb., 1, 6 and 22 Mar. 1545; PEG, III, 55–8, Charles to Ferdinand, 1 Feb. 1545; CDCV, III, 336–43, Charles to Philip, 17 Feb. 1545. Gachard, Voyages, II, 306 (Vandenesse's journal), stated that the emperor also took 'palo de Indias' between 10 Feb. and 15 Mar. 1545; see also the vivid accounts of Charles's illness in ASF MdP 4302, unfol., Ricasoli to Duke Cosimo, 3 and 23 Jan. and 8 Feb. 1545 – just as the emperor wrestled with the Alternative.

9. CDCV, IV, 527 and 538. In summer 1543, Granvelle informed the nuncio that Charles would attack the German Lutherans as soon as he had defeated Guelders and France: NBD, VII, 441–4, Poggio to Farnese, 10 July 1543.

10. Lenz, Briefwechsel, III, 91–6, printed the treaty between Charles and the landgrave, 21 June 1541.

11. Close, 'City-states', 214–15, Ulm to other cities in the League, 18 June 1544.

12. Winckelmann, Politische Correspondenz, III, 504–7, Jacob Sturm to Strasbourg, Speyer, 18 Mar. 1544, noted the emperor's proposal to sequester Brunswick 'in eine dritte hand'. RTA XVI, 1474–94, documented the attempts by the imperial Diet to solve the Brunswick question; Brady, Protestant politics, 260–72, provided a clear and concise account of the Brunswick war.

13. Brandenburg, Politische Korrespondenz, I, 564–6, Christoph von Carlowitz's report to Maurice on his meeting with Granvelle, 28 Feb. 1543; HHStA Belgien PA 37/1/120–3, Granvelle to Charles, 1 May 1543, reporting on his talks with Carlowitz.

14. Maurenbrecher, Karl V, 37*–40*, Charles to Philip, 16 Feb. 1546; Gachard, Trois années, 83–4, Navagero to the Doge, 20 May 1545.

15. LCK, II, 435–45, Instructions to Gerhard Veltwyck, 22 May 1545; NBD, VIII, 170–7, Fabio Mignanello to Cardinal Santa Fiora, 28 May 1545, and 231–6, cardinal of Augsburg to Farnese, 6 July 1545.

16. AGS E 641/2, 'Relación de los negocios que embía el secretario Idiáquez' to Los Cobos, undated but c. 20 June 1545, with the request that the document 'be burned after it has been read' (luckily for historians, Los Cobos did not comply: English translation in CSPSp, VIII, 225–7). NBD, VIII, 221–6, Nuncio Verallo to Farnese, 1 July 1545, mentioned that Granvelle 'mi mostrò una carta con più di cinquanta capituli, tutti concernenti la impresa' against the Lutherans, that he was about to discuss with Charles; NBD, VII, 685–6, Granvelle to Marie, 8 July 1545, reported the decision to delay. RTA, XVII, 1201–1375, contained the religious debates at Worms, in which Ferdinand took a leading part until Charles arrived on 16 May, after which Granvelle acted as the principal imperial spokesman.

17. NBD, VIII, Mignanello and Verallo to Farnese, 9 July 1545 ('non per altro che per esser Sua Maestà quanto a Dio sicura in conscientia'). Gachard, Trois années, 98, provided more detail on Charles's testy interview with the archbishop.

18. CDCV, IV, 529–30 (Memoirs); TNA SP 1/208/38–40, Fray Gabriel de Guzmán to Charles, 20 Sep. 1545, reporting on his mission to reassure Francis; SP, XI, 19–20, Mont to Henry VIII, Frankfurt, 17 Jan. 1546, transmitting the African rumour (which he did not believe). See also PEG, III, 186–204, Granvelle's arguments for maintaining the peace despite the death of Orléans, using the parallel that the treaty would still stand even 'if God allowed an earthquake to destroy one of the towns specified for restitution'.

19. *CSPSp*, VIII, 229, Los Cobos to Charles, undated but 3 Sep. 1545; *CDCV*, II, 418–22, Philip to Charles, 3 Sep. 1545; *BKK*, II, 356–7, Marie to Granvelle, undated minute, late 1545. Marie's advice may of course have been coloured by the Lutherans at her court, and her contact with Luther himself, in the 1520s.

20. *CDCV*, II, 453–8, Charles to Philip, 17 Mar. 1546.

21. *CDCV*, IV, 532 (*Memoirs*); von Druffel, *Briefe*, III, 1–24, 'Protokoll der Verhandlung des Landgrafen Philipp mit Kaiser Karl zu Speier', 28 and 29 Mar. 1546 (parts also printed in *RTA*, XVII, 64–78).

22. Bernays, *Urkunden*, IV, 93 note 1, Sebastian Erb to Heinrich Bullinger, 1 May 1546 (in Latin, but with German for the reported speech); *NBD*, VIII, 623–4, Serristori to Duke Cosimo of Florence, 29 Mar. 1546.

23. Brady, *Protestant politics*, 273, 276; Lenz, *Briefwechsel*, II, 437–46, landgrave to Martin Bucer and Jacob Sturm, 15 May 1546.

24. *CDCV*, II, 471–4, Charles to Philip, 20 May 1546. For Barbara Blomberg, see chs 14 and 16.

25. HHStA *Hs. Blau* 596/1/103–4, Charles to Ferdinand, 18 Apr. 1546.

26. For details, see *LCK*, II, 648–52, secret treaty signed by Charles, Ferdinand and Bavaria, 7 June 1546; and Brandenburg, *Politische Korrespondenz*, II, 660–4, secret treaty signed by Charles, Ferdinand and Maurice, 19 June 1546.

27. Kannengiesser, *Karl V*, 199–201, Charles to Buren, 9 June 1546; *LCK*, II, 486–91, Charles to Marie, 9 June 1546; *SP*, XI, 219–21, Thirlby to Paget, Regensburg, 15 June 1546; AGS *CMC* 1a/1455, Accounts of García Portillo, patents signed at Regensburg, 21 June 1546.

28. *SP*, XI, 223–7, Mason to Paget, 25 June 1546, reporting on a meeting with Frederick at Heidelberg. On Mason's service at the imperial court, see *ODNB* s.v.

29. Brandi, *The emperor*, 541; *CDCV*, IV, 531, n. 144.

30. *CDCV*, II, 336–43, and Maurenbrecher, *Karl V*, 37*–40*, Charles to Philip, 17 Feb. 1545 and 16 Feb. 1546 (three letters). For an example of advance planning, see *CSPSp*, VIII, 183–4, Juan de Vega to Philip, Rome, 20 July 1545.

31. For the unsuccessful negotiations in the 1546 Reichstag at Regensburg, see the documents in *RTA*, XVII, 433–89. See also the uncompromising rationale in favour of war submitted to Charles by his confessor, Pedro de Soto, in Feb. 1546, printed in Maurenbrecher, *Karl V*, 29*–32*, with an English translation in *CSPSp*, VIII, 353–6.

32. TNA *SP* 1/123/100–3, Vaughan to the Privy Council, Antwerp, 12 Aug. 1546; Firpo, *Relazioni*, II, 605, Relation of Mocenigo, 1548. Mariotte, 'Charles Quint', 379, called the emperor's decision to open hostilities before concentrating his forces 'un coup de poker'. *RTA*, XVII, 484–9, printed the letters from the League members recalling their procurators from the Diet; Brady, *Protestant politics*, 299, lists the members of the League who mobilized in 1546 and their contributions to the war.

33. Ávila y Zúñiga, *Comentario*, f. 10v.

34. Firpo, *Relazioni*, II, 610, Relation of Mocenigo, detailed the flawed command structure of the League's army. A campaign plan prepared for Charles in May or early June 1546 deemed the league's fragmented command structure to be the emperor's greatest advantage in the approaching war: Friedensburg, 'Am Vorabend', 142–3.

35. *NBD*, IX, 158–66, Verallo to Cardinal Farnese, 30–31 July 1546; BL *Addl. Ms.* 28,595/42–4, Charles to Juan de Vega, 31 July 1546.

36. *CDCV*, II, 489–92, Charles to Philip, 10 Aug. 1546; AGS *E* 73/239, Charles to Los Cobos, 11 Aug. 1546, decoded holograph.

37. Núñez Alba, *Diálogos*, 48 (Ávila y Zúñiga, *Comentario*, f. 13, provided a similar account). *RTA*, XVII, 567–74, prints the 'Absagebrief', dated 11 Aug. 1547 and signed by eight princes and the representatives of five cities; Sleidan, *De statu*, 533 (book XVII), recorded the Elector's reluctance to address Charles as 'emperor'; HHStA *Hs. Blau* 596/1/104–6, Charles to Ferdinand, 17 Aug. 1546 (partially printed in von Druffel, *Briefe*, I, 14–15), reported that the declaration arrived 'sur ung baston fendu, qu'est la forme de défiance que l'on a accoustumé user en Allemaigne', known as a *Fehdebrief*. Spanish sources refer to it as a 'desafío'.

38. Ávila y Zúñiga, *Comentario*, f. 13 (similar account in Núñez Alba, *Diálogos*, 48). *RTA*, XVII, 552–62, printed the edict dated 20 July 1546 but not published until 14 Aug. Von Druffel, *Des Viglius van Zwichem Tagebuch*, 54, recorded 'Advenit Italicus exercitus' on 13 Aug., and 'Litterae ab lantgravio cum trompeta, quibus renunciabant jus vasallagii et fidelitatis' on 14 Aug.

39. Greppi, 'Extraits', 123–4, Stroppiana to the duke of Savoy, 6 Sep. 1546; Turba, *Venetianische Depeschen*, I, 662–3, Mocenigo to the Doge, 1 Sep. 1546. Núñez Alba, *Diálogos*, 72–8, also stressed the bastions and 'cavaliers' attached to the camps' defences; and the Lutheran commanders noted how 'by night and by day, the emperor fortified his camp': Schertlin von Burtenbach, *Leben*, 46. See the map of the siege in Schüz, *Der Donaufeldzug*, 39.

40. Greppi, 'Extraits', 125–31, Stroppiana to the duke of Savoy, 6 Sep. 1546; Mugnier, 'Les faictz', 279–80; Ávila y Zúñiga, *Comentario*, f. 21; Núñez Alba, *Diálogo*, 60.

41. HHStA *Hs. Blau* 596/1/106–7v and 108v–9v, Charles to Ferdinand, 2 and 19 Sep. 1546, holograph postscripts (partly published in von Druffel, *Beiträge*, I, 19 and 21). Others also reproached Charles for risking 'his person, on which alone the fate of Christianity depends': Greppi, 'Extraits', 127, Stroppiana to the duke, 6 Sep. 1546. Even Ávila y Zúñiga, *Comentario*, f. 31v, doubted whether it was wise that the emperor 'se ponga en estos peligros como vn capitan o soldado particular'.

42. *NBD*, IX, 226 n. 4, Serristori to Duke Cosimo, 4 Sep. 1546 (Lutherans' motives for retreat); Schertlin von Burtenbach, *Leben*, 46; Möllenberg, 'Die Verhandlung', 49–50, and Duller, *Neue Beiträge*, 60–1, Philip of Hesse to his wife Margareta, 11 and 21 Sep. 1546, both holograph.

43. Mogen, *Historia*, 291–2 § 89 (from the diary of the landgrave's secretary); Turba, *Venetianische Depeschen*, I, 673–7 and II, 66–7, Mocenigo to the Doge, 7/8 Sep. and 24 Oct. 1546 (Hesse's insults reported by a diplomat who had been detained in the Lutheran camp).

44. Kannengiesser, *Karl V*, 207–9, Buren to Charles, Roermond, 24 July 1546 (Kannengiesser provided an excellent account of this operation, including transcripts of Charles's correspondence with Buren). *SP*, XI, 256–9, Carne to Paget, 27 Aug. and 14 Sep. 1546, provided a vivid account of how Buren got his army across the Rhine; ibid., 299–300, Wotton to Paget, 17 Sep. 1546, assessed the risks.

45. Busto, *Geschichte*, 112; *CDCV*, IV, 550 (*Memoirs*). On the changing strength of the two armies, see the figures in Schüz, *Der Donaufeldzug*, 88–94.

46. Brandenburg, *Politische Korrespondenz*, II, 872–7, Defensive and offensive alliance between Ferdinand and Maurice, Prague, 14 Oct. 1546; Hortleder, *Der Römischen Keyser*, II, 506–8, 'Abschiedt zu Giengen gemacht, den 16 Novembris 1546' regarding the 'Abzug und Winterlager' of the League's army.

47. Bernays, *Urkunden*, IV/1, 494–7, Sturm to the landgrave, 21 Nov. 1546, and the landgrave's reply the following day, with holograph corrections. On the campaign, see Schüz, *Der Donaufeldzug*, based on personal reconnaissance of the terrain as well as printed sources, with seven maps; and Crouzet, *Charles Quint*, ch. 15.

48. *SP*, XI, 350–1, Thirlby to Paget, Dillingen, 21 Nov. 1546.

49. Ávila y Zúñiga, *Comentario*, ff. 35–6; Turba, *Venetianische Depeschen*, II, 10–14 and 19–22, Mocenigo to the Doge, 22 and 27 Sep. 1546 (quoting Charles's doctor, Cornelis van Baersdorp); Mugnier, 'Les faictz', 290–1 (entry for 4 Oct. 1546).

50. Núñez Alba, *Diálogos*, 173–4. Soly, *Charles*, 305, reproduces a painting done in 1551 by Matthias Gerung of Charles receiving the submission of the city of Lauingen five years before.

51. Ávila y Zúñiga, *Comentario*, ff. 61v–2v; Turba, *Venetianische Depeschen*, II, 125–6, Mocenigo to the Doge, 19 Dec. 1546; von Druffel, *Briefe*, I, 26–8, Charles to Marie, 23 Nov. 1546. On Charles's earlier dealings with Elector (formerly Count Palatine) Frederick, see chs 2, 3 and 4 above.

52. Dumont, *Corps*, IV/2, 326–7, treaty between Charles and Duke Ulrich, 3 Jan. 1547; Turba, *Venetianische Depeschen*, II, 151–2 and 156–60, Mocenigo to the Doge, 29 Jan. and 2 Feb. 1546.

53. *LCK*, II, 524–7, Charles to Ferdinand, 9 Jan. 1547 (copy at HHStA *Hs. Blau* 596/1/117–19v). Four years later, Maximilian indiscreetly revealed to a Venetian diplomat how much Ferdinand resented his brother's failure to give him Württemberg: Friedensburg, 'Karl V', 72–81, Giovanni Michele to the council of Ten, Dec. 1551.

54. *LCK*, II, 529–31 Charles to Ferdinand, 2 Feb. 1547 (copy at HHStA *Hs. Blau* 596/1/126–7v); von Druffel, *Briefe*, I, 39–46, Charles to St. Mauris, 19 Jan. 1547; *LCK*, II, 539–41, Charles to Ferdinand, 19 Feb. 1547 (copy at HHStA *Hs. Blau* 596/1/131–3v). See also *LCK*, II, 34–7, Marie to Charles, 10 Jan. 1547, warning that the French might mount a surprise attack 'as they did in 1542'. Glagau, 'Landgraf Philipp', 37–44, documented the negotiations between France and Hesse.

55. Ávila y Zúñiga, *Comentario*, f. 85. Crouzet, *Charles Quint*, ch. 16, provides the best modern account of the campaign.

56. Turba, *Venetianische Depeschen*, II, 234–42, Mocenigo and Lorenzo Contarini to the Doge, 25 and 26 Apr. 1548.

57. ASP *CF* 510/1, 'Avvisi mandati da Mr. Valerio Amano', 25 Apr. 1547; Mugnier, 'Les faictz', 341–2; Ávila y Zúñiga, *Comentario*, f. 90v; Núñez Alba, *Diálogos*, 210. See also the description of this incident in Turba, *Venetianische Depeschen*, II, 242–3, Mocenigo and Contarini to the Doge, 27 Apr. 1547. Sastrow, *Herkommen*, II, 16 (*Social Germany*, 196), attributed the ominous phrase to Ferdinand, but Sastrow had not yet arrived at the imperial camp; on the other hand, Sastrow alone recorded the Elector's salutation in German: 'Allergnedigster Keyser und Herr'. Crouzet, *Charles Quint*, ch. 18, provided a good modern account of Charles's triumph on the Elbe.

58. Kohler, *Quellen*, 373–5, published the debate at the imperial council; Dumont, *Corps*, IV/2, 332, printed the *Todesurteil* of Charles against John Frederick, 10 May 1547. See also von Druffel, *Briefe*,

I, 58, Perrenot to Marie, 'from the field of victory on the Elbe', 25 Apr. 1547: 'From what I can tell, His Majesty now wants to cut off John Frederick's head'.

59. TNA *SP* 1/226/152, Christopher Mont to Walter Bucler, 24 Nov. 1546; Sastrow, *Herkommen*, II, 22 (for an alternative translation see *Social Germany*, 200). Junghans, 'Kaiser Karl', 102, quoted the exchange first printed in 1707 by Johann Georg Neumann, a professor of theology at Wittenberg, along with other sources (though not the testimony of Mont and Sastrow), and concluded that we may accept oral traditions on the subject. A celebrated painting of the incident, done in 1845 by Adolf Friedrich Teichs, hangs in the Lutherhalle in Wittenberg. See pp. 34–5 above for another snapshot of a benign emperor as he awaited the surrender of Wittenberg.

60. Benavent Benavent and Bertomeu Masiá, *El secuestro*, 41–7, 'Artículos acordados con el prisionero Juan Federico de Saxonia debaxo de los quales el emperador a moderado la pena que avía meresçido por aver sido rebelde', Halle, 19 May 1547.

61. Petritsch, 'Der habsburgisch-osmanische Friedensvertrag', 68–70, printed the text of the truce, concluded in Istanbul on 19 June 1547 and ratified by Charles on 1 Aug. 1547; Pánek, 'Emperador', 143–8, covered the Bohemian dimension of the Schmalkaldic war.

62. Glagau, 'Landgraf Philipp', 42, Philip to Maurice of Saxony, 30 Apr. 1547; von Rommel, *Philipp*, III, 231–2, Philip to his regency council, 28 May 1547.

63. Von Rommel, *Philipp*, III, 248–53, printed the terms of the capitulation dated 19 June 1547, the day Philip signed but almost certainly drawn up on 3 or 4 June. See also a Spanish text in Benavent Benavent and Bertomeu Masiá, *El secuestro*, 50–2, 'Capitulación dada al Landgrave de Hessen sobre su libertad, sumisión y perdón'.

64. Preuschen, 'Ein gleichzeitiger Bericht', 148 (an anonymous account sent to the Elector of Mainz stating that Philip had 'mit den Churfürsten etwas geredt vnnd gelechelt'); Sastrow, *Herkommen* II, 29–30 (stating that the landgrave 'lachede gar schimpfflich', and that the emperor threatened him: 'Wel, ik zal u leeren lachgen'). See also the accounts in *NBD*, X, 24–7, Nuncio Verallo to Cardinal Farnese, 20 June 1547; and *LCK*, II, 585–95, Perrenot to Marie, 20 and 21 June 1547.

65. *LCK*, II, 585–95, Perrenot to Marie, 20 and 21 June 1547, and 'Touchant le prinse du landtgraue' (Spanish translation in Benavent Benavent and Bertomeu Masiá, *El secuestro*, 52ff); Brandenburg, *Politische Korrespondenz*, III, 443–5, Maurice's instructions to his envoys going to Ferdinand, 21 June 1547.

66. Stumpf, *Baierns politische Geschichte*, I, part 2, 287, note, Seld's account 'ubers Fursten von Baiern Tafel' of Perrenot's ruse at the meeting with the Electors in June 1548 (correct date from Mariotte, 'Charles-Quint', 401). Von Rommel, *Philipp*, III, 235–6, printed both words – 'einiger' and 'ewiger' – in his edition of the text of the landgrave's submission. The deception was mentioned in 1552 by Rabelais, *Les cinq livres*, book IV: at the end of ch. 17, Pantagruel sailed by 'les isles aussi de 𝕰niɡ et 𝕰uiɡ, des quelles par avant estoit advenue l'estafillade au Langrauff d'Esse' (Black Letter in the original; published while the landgrave languished in prison). Roger Ascham recorded the same story in July 1553: Giles, *The whole works*, III, 51–2. Issleib, *Aufsätze*, 258–64, provides an excellent analysis of whether or not Charles had intended to deceive.

67. HHStA *Hs. Blau* 596/1/144v–5, Charles to Ferdinand, Halle, 15 June 1547, register copy (partially printed in Issleib, *Aufsätze*, 458 n. 88, and von Bucholtz, *Geschichte*, IX, 427–8); HHStA *Hs. Blau* 597/2/251v–3, Ferdinand to Charles, 17 June 1547, with the interesting observation that since John Frederick was too dangerous to remain in Germany, he should be moved under Spanish guard to Tyrol and then sent to Spain (partially printed in Issleib, *Aufsätze*, 460 n. 89, and von Bucholtz, *Geschichte*, IX, 428–9).

68. HHStA *Hs. Blau* 596/1/148v–51, Charles to Ferdinand, 28 June 1547, register copy (see also the heavily corrected minute at HHStA *Belgien PA* 5/2/70–5, revealing the care that Charles took in drafting his account. Parts printed in von Druffel, *Briefe*, I, 63–8, and in von Bucholtz, *Geschichte*, IX, 429–33, but with several errors of transcription and the wrong date).

69. HHStA *Hs. Blau* 597/2/254v–5v, Ferdinand to Charles, 14 July 1547 (parts printed in von Bucholtz, *Geschichte*, IX, 433–4); Sastrow, *Herkommen*, II, 48 (for an alternative translation see *Social Germany*, 217).

70. Sastrow, *Herkommen*, II, 31 (for an alternative translation see *Social Germany*, 206).

71. Tracy, *Emperor*, 223–8; AGS *CMC* 1a/1189, accounts of Alonso de Baeza, and *CMC* 1a/1491, accounts of García Portillo. Several heavy guns cast before 1546 by Gregor Löffler of Augsburg sailed on the Spanish Armada in 1588: see ch. 17 below.

72. Busto, *Geschichte*, 185 (Ávila y Zúñiga, *Comentario*, f. 92, related the same anecdote). Military dispositions from *NBD*, X, 377–80, Santa Croce to Farnese, 15 June 1548.

73. *LCK*, II, 599–602, Perrenot to Marie, 11 July 1547.

74. Rabe, *Reichsbund*, remains the classic study of the 'Armed Diet' of 1547–8; but see also Press, 'Die Bundespläne', 71–85. *RTA*, XVIII, published the relevant documents, including the 108 articles of the

Reichsabschied (Recess) on 30 June 1548 (pp. 2,651–94). For more on the creation of the Burgundian Circle, see ch. 14 below.

75. Gachard, *Voyages*, II, 349–71, printed Vandenesse's Journal between 1 Sep. 1547 and 30 June 1548: see the relevant chronological entries. Rabe, *Reichsbund*, 197, noted that Maximilian presided at the solemn opening of the Diet in the Fugger residence on 1 Sep. 1547, even though Charles was present.

76. *NBD*, X, 76–9, Nuncio Verallo to Cardinal Farnese, 11–12 Aug. 1547; idem 185–9, Mignanelli to Farnese, 4 Nov. 1547; ASF *MdP* 3101a/1085, Francesco di Paolo Vinta to Duke Cosimo, 2 Apr. 1548; von Ranke, *Deutsche Geschichte*, V, 370–1, 'Sommaire de l'Ambassade de feu monsieur de Vienne vers l'empereur Charles V, en l'année 1550'. Charles took a German sauna with him to Yuste: see ch. 16 below.

77. AGS *E* 644/77, Charles to Diego de Mendoza, 11 Feb. 1547.

78. AGS *E* 643/32, Charles to Francisco de Toledo, 11 Apr. 1547. On Philip II's use of the same equation, see *FBD*, ch. 5.

79. *LWS*, LIV, 208, in *Wider das Babstum zu Rom vom Teuffel gestifft* (Wittenberg, 1545); AGS *E* 644/99, Granvelle to Mendoza, 29 Aug. 1547.

80. Beltrán de Heredía, *Domingo de Soto*, 212–17 and 221–30, demonstrated how Piacenza determined the fate of the general council as well as papal-imperial relations until the death of Paul III.

81. Rein, 'Faith and empire', 51, translated from the Interim, and 54. My summary of the Interim owes much to Rein's analysis. *RTA*, XVIII, 1910–48, printed the Latin text of the document, whose full title was revealing: *Der Römischen Keyserlichen Maiestat Erklärung, wie es der Religion halbe, imm heyligen Reich, biss zü Ausstrag dess gemeynen Concilii gehalten warden soll, auff dem Reichsstag zü Augspurg, den XV Maij im M.D.XLVIII Jar publiciert und eröffnet und von gemeynen Stenden angenommen*. Interestingly, until his death Philip II kept by his desk the copy of the Interim that he inherited from Marie. It is now San Lorenzo de El Escorial library 102-III-43.

82. *NBD*, X, 327–33, Nuncio Sfondrato to Cardinal Farnese, Augsburg, 16 May 1548. In a letter to Marie that same day, Perrenot was more candid: 'Since the pope had not done what he should have done, we persevered' (ibid., 329 n. 1).

83. *NBD*, XI, 15–18, Bertano to Farnese, Augsburg, 2 Aug. 1548 (the audience had taken place that morning).

84. Sastrow, *Herkommen*, II, 335–46, the view of an eyewitness (for an alternative translation see *Social Germany*, 247–52). *NBD*, XI, 29–32, Bertano to Farnese, 10 Aug. 1548, confirmed the harsher treatment of John Frederick.

85. Naujoks, *Kaiser Karl*, 57–8 (Augsburg); Dobras, 'Karl V', 215–21 (Konstanz).

86. Naujoks, *Kaiser Karl*, 61–4 (Ulm); Sastrow, *Herkommen*, II, 345–7 (the author travelled the same route as Charles a few days later; for an alternative translation see *Social Germany*, 249–50). See Naujoks, op. cit., xxiii and 169–99, on the twenty-five cities whose charters Charles remodelled.

87. Fürstenwerth, *Verfassungsänderungen*, 101, 34; Reinhard, '"Governi stretti"', 160; von Druffel, *Briefe*, I, 180–2, Charles to Ferdinand, 10 Dec. 1548. The treatment of Ghent alarmed some German cities: the magistrates of Strasbourg resolved in 1540 to 'reflect on the example of Ghent. In every way we should be more careful' (quoted by Brady, *Protestant politics*, 354).

88. Cavalcanti, *Trattati*, 231, from a treatise addressed to Henry II of France in 1552, but not printed until 1571 (the key phrase was '*governi stretti e tirannici*').

89. Details in Hewlett, 'Fortune's fool'. Burlamacchi would later be seen as a heroic herald of Italian unity: see Carlo Minutoli, *Il primo martire dell'unità italiana* (1844), and the statue in his honour erected in Lucca in 1863.

90. Levin, 'A failure of intelligence' (quotation from p. 20); Pacini, *La Genova*, 595 (Fieschi's study of *The prince*).

91. Ha-Kohen, *Sefer divre ha-yamin*, II, 421–32; Spinola, 'Documenti', 30–2, Figueroa to Prince Philip, 6 Jan. 1547. Like Burlamacchi, Fieschi would later be seen as a herald of Italian unity: see the introduction to a recent edition of an opera about him by cardinal de Retz, *La congiura* (1655/1990).

92. Castaldo, *Historia di Napoli*, 113. Hernando Sánchez, *Castilla*, 311–12, demonstrated that the inquisitorial initiative originated when the viceroy asked his brother, a senior inquisitor in Rome, to secure a brief from the pope. It did not originate, as Sandoval and other historians have claimed, with a request from Charles.

93. Vigo, *Uno stato nell' impero*, 14, quoting Guicciardini ('*dove non ci fusse principe che potesse dare le leggi agli altri*').

94. See Pacini, *La Genova*, 596–7, on Fieschi's opposition to Charles and Doria in 1536 and his pardon in 1541; and 603–4, Figueroa to Charles, 7 Dec. 1545 and 7 May 1546.

95. Spinola, 'Documenti', 11–13, Gonzaga to Charles, 2 Jan. 1547.

96. Spinola, 'Documenti', 40–4, Gonzaga to Charles, 9 Jan. 1547; idem, 47–8 and 55–7, Charles to Figueroa, 10 and 14 Jan. 1547; AGS *PR* 45/71, Gonzaga's instructions to Juan Gallego, his emissary to Prince Philip, about 'hazer una fortaleza en la ciudad' of Genoa, 1548.
97. Spinola, 'Documenti', 57–60, Charles to Gonzaga, 14 Jan. 1547.
98. Ibid., 64–5, Juan de Vega to Charles, 17 Jan. 1547; idem, 121–3, Charles to Gonzaga, 11 Feb. 1547.
99. Bertomeu Masiá, *La guerra secreta*, 458–9, Gonzaga to Charles, 13 June 1547; Podestà, *Dal delitto*, 90 n. 34, Charles to Gonzaga, 28 June 1547. Podestà, op. cit., 166–73, demonstrated that serious work on the citadel only began in Aug. 1547, when money for the project arrived from Rome, and argued that Gonzaga's concern was premature. However, the governor was in Milan, and had no access to the financial records used by Podestà: instead Gonzaga, like Charles, relied on hearsay – and what he heard alarmed him.
100. AGS *E* 1193/31, Gonzaga to Charles, 12 Oct. 1547; Bertomeu Masiá, *La guerra secreta*, 459–61, Gonzaga to Charles, 10 and 23 July 1547; Podestà, *Dal delitto*, 101, Charles to Gonzaga, 24 July 1547. The conspirators' concern about revenge was well grounded: Farnese agents soon assassinated two of them and the rest lived in constant fear of a similar fate.
101. AGS *E* 1465/248, Gonzaga to Charles, Piacenza, 12 Sep. 1547, describing the capture of the city as if Charles knew nothing about it; AGS *E* 1193/31, same to same, 12 Oct. 1547, announcing his plan to 'amazzare' Strozzi, 'valendome dei ministri del duca de Fiorenza'; Brizio, '"The country"', 55, on the citadel at Siena.
102. On the various judicial murders orchestrated by Gonzaga in 1548, see dall'Aglio, *The duke's assassin*.
103. *CDCV*, II, 659–62; Charles to Philip, 2 Sep. 1548; von Druffel, *Briefe*, I, 170–1, Ferdinand to Charles, 15 Oct. 1548 (Maurice 'a la teste chaulde'). Charles later boasted of 'dejando en tres fortalezas del Estado de Württemberg 2,000 españoles de presidio': *CDCV*, IV, 567 (*Memoirs*).
104. Calvete de Estrella, *Rebelión*, I, 101–2.

CHAPTER 13: THE TAMING OF AMERICA

1. When Charles and his contemporaries referred to the New World they normally employed the term used by Columbus: 'the Indies'. In this book I normally use 'America' but exceptions remain: notably 'the council of the Indies', the advisory body set up to handle the Crown's American business. I have translated *cédula* as 'warrant', and *provisión* as 'charter'. I have not found an adequate translation for *encomiendas* (grants of compulsory labour), *encomenderos* (the settlers who received them), or *repartimiento* (originally the process by which *encomiendas* were distributed, but later synonymous with *encomienda*), and therefore in each case I use the Spanish term.
2. Gómara, *Hispania Victrix*, dedication. Charles was not impressed, and ordered the book to be suppressed: see ch. 14. Brading, *The first America*, 44–50, offers an excellent analysis of the work and its reception.
3. Konetzke, *Colección*, I, 216–20, from the New Laws, 20 Nov. 1542. Many conflicting estimates exist of the population of America, both European and indigenous, during the earlier sixteenth century. I have followed those in Newson, 'The demographic impact', in Boyd-Bowman, 'Patterns', and in the sources they cite.
4. Figures from Semboloni Capitani, *La construcción*, 71, 185–6 and 314, calculated from entries in the surviving *Libros de gobierno* kept by the first viceroys (details on pp. 577 above).
5. Pietschmann, *Alemania*, 109; idem, 'Carlos V y la formación', 469; and idem, 'Carlos V y América', 265.
6. Cedillo, *El cardenal Cisneros*, II, 268, Charles to Cisneros, 28 June 1516; AGNM *Mercedes* IV/331v–332v, order of Viceroy Velasco, Mexico, 10 Apr. 1556, quoting a warrant from Princess Joanna, regent of Castile, 4 Sep. 1555.
7. Giménez Fernández, *Las Casas*, II, 77, Charles to the Casa de la Contratación, 25 Feb. 1518; *SLID*, III, 234–6 ('Retiro, estancia y muerte'). See also ibid., 235 n. 183, Quijada to Vázquez de Molina, 12 Nov. 1556, passing on Charles's praise for the bedspreads and his request for more.
8. AGI *IG* 419/7/78, warrant to Laurent de Gorrevod, Zaragoza, 18 Aug. 1518; AGI *IG* 420/8/37–8, warrant to Adam de Vivaldo, Tomás de Forne 'and company', 24 Jan. 1519. Charles also signed warrants for some others to import slaves: for example, AGI *IG* 419/7/110, licence for the marquis of Astorga, Zaragoza, 24 Sep. 1518, granting permission to transport 400 slaves, 100 during the period of Gorrevod's monopoly and the rest afterwards.
9. AGI *IG* 421/12/296–7, contract with Enrique Ehinger and Jerónimo Sayler, Burgos, 12 Feb. 1528; AGI *Justicia* 1169/4/2, a case brought by the procurator fiscal of the council of the Indies against those who infringed on the Welser monopoly, Feb. 1530–Aug. 1533. Numbers from http://www.slavevoyages.org/assessment/estimates.

10. Las Casas, *Historia*, IV, 368; Giménez Fernández, *Las Casas*, II, 90–1, royal warrant of 13 Jan. 1518. Idem, II, 57–60, discussed this document, considered in 'pleno Consilio Indiarum a XI de Diziembre de DXVII años' (a session over which, according to Giménez Fernández, Charles presided).

11. Las Casas, *Historia*, IV, 377 (Las Casas claimed that 'I was in the room' of the chancellor when Magellan arrived with his globe). Charles had evidently grasped the advantage of a globe by the time the surviving circumnavigators returned, because he sent to his brother 'una palla, dove è pinto tutto el ditto viaggio' (Morsolin, 'Francesco Chiericati', 231, Chiericati to Isabella d'Este, Nuremberg, 10 Jan. 1523); and the following year his negotiators at the Junta de Badajoz took with them two globes: Brendecke, *Imperio*, 164–9.

12. Fernández de Navarrete, *Colección*, IV, 116–21, 'Capitulación y asiento' between Charles and Magellan, 22 Mar. 1518, copy. For the precedents from Castile, see Owens, '*By my absolute royal authority*', ch. 2. For the first example involving America, see Nader, *The Book*, 265–7, the Catholic Monarchs to Columbus, 23 Apr. 1497.

13. AGI *Patronato* 34 ramo 2, Magellan to Charles, Seville, 24 Oct. 1518, holograph (printed by Fernández de Navarrete, *Colección*, IV, 124–7, but without the significant endorsement 'Recibida y proveydo en vj de noviembre'). Had Magellan arrived the following year, when the top priority for Charles and his ministers was funding his journey to Germany, his appeal for financial support would probably have failed.

14. *CODOIN . . . América*, XXII, 38–46, contract with Velázquez, 13 Nov. 1518. Martínez, *Hernán Cortés*, 131–41, evaluated the conflicting figures for the size of Cortés's expedition; but whether he commanded twelve ships or only eleven, its size differed significantly from the two previous expeditions sent by Velázquez, which consisted of only three or four ships.

15. Cortés, *Cartas*, 65, 'Carta de Relación' of the town council of Veracruz to Charles and Joanna, 10 July 1519; AGI *México* 95/1, 'Pedimiento que hiso Francisco Aluares Chico, procurador desta Villa Rica de la Vera Cruz', 20 June 1519 (transcribed with some differences by Schwaller and Nader, *The first letter*). The presence of the petition in AGI indicates that it was sent to Charles via the emissaries who brought him the 'Carta de Relación', to which the petition refers. Russo, 'Cortés's objects', described the *muestra* (sample) of 1519, noting that the great gold wheel represented the 'royal fifth' whereas the rest were gifts from the conquistadors 'over and above the fifth'.

16. Las Casas, *Historia*, V, 95, 98, discussed and dated by Giménez Fernández, *Las Casas*, II, 742–53.

17. AGI *IG* 420/8/173–5, Charles to the Casa de la Contratación and to the messengers from Veracruz, Molins del Rey, 5 Dec. 1519, register copies, endorsed by Los Cobos, 'Sobre la Nueva España'. See Ramos, *Hernán Cortés*, 175–6 and 199 notes 22 and 25 on the identity of the six young Totonacs (four males and two females); and Giménez Fernández, 'El alzamiento', on Charles's personal interest in them.

18. Cosenza, 'Copia litterarvm', Valladolid, 7 Mar. 1520; Sanuto, *I diarii*, XXVIII, cols 375–6, Cornaro to the Signory, 6 Mar. 1520. Cortés, *Cartas*, 71–6, stated that Charles received the sample 'en Valladolid en la Semana Santa en principio del mes de abril', but this is impossible because in 1520 Charles spent Holy Week in Galicia, not in Valladolid. The testimony of Cosenza, Corner and others proves that Charles received the gifts 'en principio del mes de *marzo*'. See Ramos, *Hernán Cortés*, 178–93, for an unsuccessful attempt to establish the date and place from government documents alone.

19. Giménez Fernández, *Las Casas*, II, 790–810, described the council debates on America between 12 and 19 May 1520, and at pp. 794–9 published the Corunna Declaration of 17 May 1520.

20. Dürer, *Diary*, 64, entry for 27 Aug. 1520. Although few items from this sample survive, two of them came from the area around Veracruz: the 'dos libros de los que acá tienen los yndios', now ÖNB *Codex Vindobonensis Mexicanus* I, and BL *Codex Zouche-Nutall*.

21. I accept the suggestion of Matthew Restall that Montezuma might have planned to arrest Cortés and his men (Restall, *When Montezuma*, 144–8). Apart from the reasons he provided, thirteen years later in Peru Atahualpa definitely had a similar plan: Pogo, 'The Anonymous', 246.

22. Cortés, *Cartas*, 80 and 181, Cortés to Charles, 30 Oct. 1520.

23. Giménez Fernández, *Las Casas*, II, 1182 and 1103 n. 3785, quoting warrants issued 11–14 Apr. 1521, and to Diego Colón and other Spanish officials, 6 Sep. 1521. Ibid., II, 1254–86, recorded the mark (*señal*) of Gattinara on each warrant concerning American affairs. I respectfully dissent from the assertion of Pérez, *La revolución*, 667, that 'It seems that the events in Castile had no repercussions in America'.

24. Cortés, *Cartas*, 182, coda to Cortés's second letter included in the first printed edition. Sanuto, *I diarii*, XXXIII, cols 501–3 and 557, Contarini to the Signory, 24 Sep. and 24 Nov. 1522, made clear that news of the loss of Tenochtitlan arrived in Spain at the same time as news of its recovery.

25. Cortés, *Cartas*, 275, Cortés to Charles, 15 May 1522; Haring, 'Ledgers', 175, recorded the funds taken to Spain by Treasurer Julián de Alderete. A French squadron intercepted and appropriated the

shipment, but not the relevant register, so that Charles knew what Cortés could deliver: see Johnson, *Cultural hierarchy*, 113 and 117–19.

26. AGI *Patronato* 48/20, Juan Sebastián El Cano to Charles, Seville, 6 Sep. 1522, copy; *LCK*, I, 73, Charles to Margaret, 31 Oct. 1522.

27. Avonto, *Mercurino*, 47–51, on the commission (quotation at p. 49); *CODOIN*, I, 97–100, and *CODOIN ... América*, XXVI, 59–70, Charles to Cortés, 15 Oct. 1522 (three warrants); AGI *IG* 415/2/451-63, register copies of instructions 'dispatched to New Spain in October 1522'.

28. Brandi, 'Aus den Kabinettsakten', 183–6, paper of advice from Gattinara, Nov.–Dec. 1523, with individual votes by Gattinara, Gorrevod, Lachaux, La Roche, Nassau and Hernando de Vega (the only Spaniard on the committee), and rescripts by Charles; AGS *Quitaciones de Corte* 20, *nómina* of Loaysa, 4 Aug. 1524.

29. *Libros de Antaño*, VIII, 368–76, Navagero to Giovanni Battista Ramusio, Toledo, 12 Sep. 1525; BL *Cott. Ms.* Vespasian C.III/158–75v, Tunstal, Wingfield and Sampson to Henry, 2 June 1525, reporting on their meeting with the Grand Chancellor.

30. *CODOIN ... Ultramar*, IX, 214–26, instructions to Luis Ponce de León, 4 Nov. 1525; *CODOIN*, I, 101–2, Charles to Cortés, 4 Nov. 1525 (in answer to his 'Carta de Relación' of 15 Oct. 1524).

31. Bornate, 'Historia', 458–76, 'Consigli del gran cancellier all'Imperatore', Sep. 1525, holograph minute (quotation at p. 460); *CODOIN ... Ultramar*, IX, 214–26, instructions to Luis Ponce de León, 4 Nov. 1525 (Avonto, *Mercurino*, 93–7, discussed this and a second instruction of the same date).

32. Gómara, *Hispania Victrix*, book 192, on 'Cómo vino Cortés a España', included the text of Loaysa's letter. On 5 Apr. 1528, Charles signed a warrant authorizing Cortés to come (Martínez, *Documentos*, III, 11–12), but since he left Veracruz in mid-April he clearly acted before it arrived.

33. Gómara, *Hispania Victrix*, book 192. Van Deusen, 'Coming to Castile', narrated the life histories of two humble native Americans who accompanied Cortés to Spain in 1528 and remained there.

34. Germanisches Nationalmuseum *Ms.* 22,474, pp. 1–14 (native Americans), 77 (Cortés) and 83 (Doria). Its beautiful paintings are available online at http://dlib.gnm.de/item/Hs22474/213/html; see also the discussion in Cline, 'Hernando Cortés'.

35. AGI *Patronato* 16/2/8, Charles to 'gouernador don Hernando Cortés marqués del Valle', 1 Apr. 1529 (incompletely and imperfectly printed in *CODOIN ... América*, XII, 379–80); AGI *IG* 737/1, Charles to the council of the Indies, 24 May 1529, ordering the preparation of the relevant documents; AGI *Patronato* 16/2/13, 14 and 15, royal warrants dated 6 July 1529, notarized copies (also at AGI *México* 1088/1 ff. 23–7, and printed in *CODOIN ... América*, XII, 291–7 and 380–6; and Martínez, *Documentos*, III, 49–61). Martínez, *Hernán Cortés*, 505–10, listed the villages granted to Cortés in 1529 and noted how they differed from those he had requested.

36. AGI *México* 1088/1/38–9, Charles to the Audiencia of Mexico, 10 Aug. 1528.

37. AGI *IG* 737/4, Tavera to Charles, 10 Dec. 1529. The future viceroy, Antonio de Mendoza, was one of those who demanded 'such outrageous rewards'.

38. Cadenas y Vicent, *Carlos I*, 261–71, 'Capitulación con los armadores sobre la dicha Specería', 13 Nov. 1522 (referring to the expedition under García Jofré de Loaysa to colonize the Spice Islands, which left Corunna in 1525); *LCK*, I, 73, Charles to Margaret, 31 Oct. 1522.

39. Brendecke, *Imperio*, 164–9; Cortés, *Cartas*, 325, 'Carta de Relación' to Charles, 15 Oct. 1524.

40. Fernández de Navarette, *Colección*, V, 440–1, Charles to Cortés, 20 June 1526. Cabrero Fernández, 'El empeño', 1,093, noted the abortive treaty of Seville.

41. BMECB *Ms. Granvelle*, I, 153–5, Charles to Baron Montfort, 23 Dec. 1528, holograph (printed with some errors in *PEG*, I, 441–4).

42. Cabrero Fernández, 'El empeño', chronicled the desperate bargaining over the terms of the treaty at Zaragoza, and printed the final text, signed by Gattinara and Loaysa on 22 Apr. 1529.

43. AGI *Patronato* 275/20, Charles to the Audiencia of Mexico, Madrid, 13 Mar. 1535 (Gibson, *Tlaxcala*, 229, argued on the basis of a copy in AGNM that the date was 13 May 1535, but the AGI copy clearly states 13 Mar.); AGI *IG* 422/16/201, royal warrant to pay Diego Rodríguez de Narváez, 12 May 1535.

44. AGI *IG* 415/2/352–364, draft instructions to Mendoza, 25 Apr. 1535 (endorsed 'dezima') and 14 July 1536 (endorsed 'duodezima', heavily annotated). *CODOIN ... América*, XXIII, 423–45 and 454–67, and Hanke, *Los virreyes*, I, 21–38, printed these documents, but without the annotations. Merluzzi, '"Con el cuidado"', 158–65, discussed Charles's various instructions to Mendoza in detail.

45. BNE *Ms. Res.* 261/70, Cortés to Charles, Madrid, 26 June 1540; AGI *Patronato* 16/1/19, same to same, 3 Feb. 1544 (endorsed 'no ay que responder' with the rubric of Francisco de Eraso).

46. AGI *IG* 737/1, Charles to council of the Indies, Barcelona, 24 May 1529 (the same letter announced the grant of a noble title and lands to Cortés); Porras Barrenechea, *Cedulario*, I, 18–30, royal warrants, 26 July 1529.

47. Details from Pogo, 'The anonymous' (Cristóbal de Mena), 242; and Xérez, *Verdadera relación*, 91-2 and 96.
48. *Libro primero de Cabildos*, III, 127, Hernando Pizarro to Charles, Seville, 14 Jan. 1534.
49. Cieza de León, *Primera parte* (1553), f. 234 (Part I, book 94); *Libro primero de Cabildos*, III, 127-8, Charles to the Casa de la Contratación, 21 Jan. 1534; Medina, *La imprenta*, I, 163-70, 'Relación del oro del Perú que recibimos', Feb. 1534, and Charles to the Casa, 30 Jan. 1535.
50. *CODOIN . . . Ultramar*, 2ª series X, 160-7, idem, XV, 113, and AGI *Patronato* 90A/1/10, royal warrants to Pizarro, 8 Mar. 1533, 21 May 1534 and 10 Oct. 1537.
51. Maples, 'The death', brilliantly matched the written accounts of Pizarro's murder in 1541 with the wounds on the skeleton that he examined in 1984.
52. Vitoria, *Relectio de Indis*, 137-9, Vitoria to Fray Miguel de Arcos, 8 Nov. 1534.
53. AGI *Justicia* 259/2/25-26v, 'Descargos del Virrey', Mexico, 30 Oct. 1546, descargo 38, answering charges that he had brutalized indigenous inhabitants in wartime. (I thank Bethany Aram for verifying this reference.) Martínez, *Hernán Cortés*, 135, discussed the practice of 'aperreamiento' accompanied by a disturbing image of the practice from an indigenous source.
54. Hanke, *The Spanish struggle*, 73 (papal bull); Sandoval, *Historia*, III, 70 (Book 24, ch. 8: the Constable of Castile); Vitoria, *Relectio de Indis*, 99. Vitoria wrote his *Relectio* in 1538 and delivered it in Jan. 1539. It was published for the first time in 1557, in France. Did Charles recall attending a lecture by Vitoria during his visit to Salamanca University in 1534 (p. 235 above)?
55. Pereña Vicente, 'El emperador Carlos V', 385-6; Vitoria, *Relectio de Indis*, 152-3, Charles to the prior of San Esteban, 10 Nov. 1539. He left for France the following day.
56. Pereña Vicente, 'El emperador Carlos V', 379, and Fernández Álvarez, *Carlos V: el César*, 641-3, both suggested a connection between Algiers and the New Laws. Although they cited no sources, the idea seems plausible.
57. Danvila y Collado, *El poder civil*, V, 313, petición 94 of the Cortes of Castile, Valladolid, Apr. 1542; Las Casas, *Brevíssima relación*, ff. 3-3v, claimed that Silíceo, Philip's former preceptor, 'siendo obispo de Cartagena, me las pidió e presentó a Vuestra Alteza'. Pereña Vicente, 'El emperador', 393, presented convincing evidence that both his friends and enemies were correct to see Las Casas as the 'godfather of the New Laws'.
58. *CODOIN*, LXXVI, 340-55, text of the New Laws, signed by the emperor in Barcelona on 20 Nov. 1542, but not published until July 1543 in Seville. Charles's apology came in the preamble: idem, 340-1.
59. *CODOIN . . . Ultramar*, 2ª series X, 86-93, charter of the empress to the governor of Santa Marta, 4 Apr. 1531; *CODOIN . . . América*, XLI, 198-204, royal warrant, 26 May 1536; Paso y Troncoso, *Epistolario*, IV, 60-1, the Audiencia of Mexico to Charles, 8 Oct. 1543.
60. Ibid., 60. Paso y Troncoso, *Epistolario*, IV, 64-75, López to the emperor 'en su consejo', Mexico, 25 Oct. 1543. See also the similar critique of Tomás López Medel, *Colonización*, 62-80, López Medel to Regents Maximilian and María, 25 Mar. 1551.
61. Cortijo Ocaña, *Cartas*, 60-5, Gómez Díaz de la Reguera to Alonso Díaz de la Reguera, San Salvador (previously Guatemala; now capital of El Salvador), 1 Aug. 1545.
62. Pérez de Tudela Bueso, *Documentos*, II, 383-95, Gonzalo Pizarro to Charles, undated (probably 2 or 3 Aug. 1544), and 193-7, 199-203, same to the Cabildo of Lima and to Blasco Nuñez Vela, 2 Aug. 1544, and to the Audiencia of Lima, 3 Aug. 1544. English summaries in *From Panama to Peru*, 17-25.
63. Calvete de Estrella, *Rebelión*, I, 97-9. Although Calvete wrote his study at La Gasca's request in 1565-7, he was the prince's preceptor at the time of the debate and so an important member of his court: there is no reason to doubt the veracity of his account. *CDCV*, II, 398, Philip to Charles, 30 June 1545, confirmed the gist of the council debates, which took place that month.
64. Calvete de Estrella, *Rebelión*, I, 101-2; Hampe Martínez, *Don Pedro*, 77, Los Cobos to La Gasca, 29 Aug. 1545. On the presence of former Comuneros among the rebels of America, see Calvete de Estrella, *Rebelión*, I, 280, and pp. 140-1 above. Pietschman, 'Carlos V y la formación', 446-54, compared the revolt of Pizarro with that of the Comuneros.
65. *CDCV*, II, 398-9, Philip to Charles, and Hampe Martínez, *Don Pedro*, 76, Los Cobos to Charles, both 30 June 1545.
66. Calvete de Estrella, *Rebelión*, I, 110, council debates on La Gasca's demands. Compare the council's refusal in 1529 to recommend for the new post of viceroy of Mexico candidates who demanded 'outrageous rewards': p. 352 above.
67. AGS, *E* 641/10, Charles to Los Cobos, Worms, 2 Aug. 1545; Konetzke, *Colección*, I, 236-7, Charles to the Audiencia of New Spain, Mechelen, 20 Oct. 1545; RAH *Ms.* 9/4846/66, Charles to the council of the Indies, undated but probably Feb. 1546.

68. *CODOIN . . . América*, XXIII, 507–19, Charles's instructions to La Gasca, Venlo, 14 Feb. 1546. See also BR *Ms.* II/1960 no. 12/85–93, La Gasca's copy of the draft instructions, with his holograph comments on each clause, revealing his non-negotiable demands. Merluzzi, 'Mediación', 96–7, summarized the powers eventually granted.

69. *CODOIN*, XXVI, 274–84, paper of advice on how La Gasca should behave, with neither date nor place (but probably Venlo, 14 Feb. 1546, like the instructions), and incorrectly attributed to Philip II. Hampe Martínez, *Don Pedro*, 84–8, ably discussed all these documents.

70. Pérez de Tudela Bueso, *Documentos*, I, 375–84, La Gasca to Gonzalo Pizarro, Jauja, 16 Dec. 1547 (also published in *CODOIN*, XLIX, 260–76; English summary in *From Panama to Peru*, 439–44).

71. Pérez de Tudela Bueso, *Documentos*, II, 401–21, La Gasca to Los Cobos, 3 May 1548.

72. Ibid., II, 401–21 and 258–77, La Gasca to Los Cobos, 3 May 1548, and to the council of the Indies, 26 Sep. 1548 (*CODOIN*, XLIX, 359–427, published the same letters, but some with different dates; English summaries in *From Panama to Peru*, 474–82 and 486–8). Other data on the punishment of those who had failed to oppose Gonzalo Pizarro come from Anthony, 'Intimate invasion', ch. 6, the best account currently available.

73. Pérez de Tudela Bueso, *Documentos*, II, 607–9, Fernández de Oviedo to La Gasca, 3 Jan. 1550 (also in *From Panama to Peru*, 517).

74. Hunt *PL* 122, Charles to La Gasca, 26 Feb. 1549 (a letter omitted by Pérez de Tudela Bueso, *Documentos*).

75. *CDCV*, III, 250–5, Charles to María, Augsburg, 30 Dec. 1550, and 243–6, Charles to Maximilian and María, 20 Oct. 1550.

76. AGI *Patronato* 180/7, 'Parecer del virrey don Antonio cerca de los seruicios personales', and *CDCV*, III, 255–7, 'Relación de don Antonio de Mendoça', both undated but 1550. For other examples of Caesar's luck, see ch. 8.

77. Saville, 'Some unpublished letters', facsimile of letter no. 2, La Gasca to the Audiencia of Guatemala, 15 Dec. 1546. Aiton, *Antonio de Mendoza*, 175–6, documented the Mexican expeditionary force prepared for Peru in response to La Gasca's appeal.

78. *CLC*, IV, 293–8, speech to the Cortes of Corunna, Apr. 1520; *RVEC*, 146–50, Salinas to Ferdinand, 4 Oct. 1523. In a letter dated 16 Dec. 1523, Salinas corrected his original figure from 800,000 to 180,000 *pesos de oro*.

79. Porras Barrenechea, *Las relaciones*, 38–40, Licenciado Espinosa to Charles, Panama, 21 July 1533; *RVEC*, 645–52, Salinas to Castillejo, 11 May 1535; Tracy, *Emperor*, 155.

80. García-Baquero González, 'Agobios carolinos', 313–14, royal warrants of 3 Sep. 1523, 22 and 30 Jan. 1535 and Jan. 1543 (italics added). Figures from Haring, 'Ledgers'. García-Baquero González, op. cit., claimed that Charles authorized eight sequestrations, but Carretero Zamora, *Gobernar*, 382, counted nine.

81. Viciana, *Libro tercero*, 324 (written c. 1564). Figures from Tracy, *Emperor*, 111.

82. Hanke, *Los virreyes*, I, 38–57, 'Relación, apuntamientos y avisos que por mandado de Su Majestad di a Luis de Velasco' by Mendoza, 1551–2.

83. *CDCV*, III, 255–7, 'Relación de don Antonio de Mendoça', undated but 1550 (also printed in Hanke, *Los virreyes*, I, 57–8). See the similar reproach of Jerónimo López in 1543, quoted on pp. 361–2 above.

84. *CODOIN . . . Ultramar*, I, 354–61, Royal warrant to the governor and officials of Cuba, 9 Nov. 1526; AGI *IG* 415/2/352–64, instructions to Mendoza, 25 Apr. 1535 and 14 July 1536.

85. Brendecke, *Imperio*, 184–5, with quotations from royal warrants dated 20 June and 6 Oct. 1526, and 16 Mar. 1527.

86. *CODOIN . . . Ultramar*, IX, 239–46, royal charters of 11 May and 21 Aug. 1526; Cadenas y Vicent, *Carlos I*, 258–9, royal warrant on coinage, 6 June 1544. Konetzke, *Colección*, I, 68–338 (nos 31–243), printed the social legislation relating to America issued by Charles; Cadenas y Vicent, *Carlos I*, 299–512, printed all the laws in the *Recopilación de Leyes de los Reynos de las Indias* issued between 1516 and 1556; Pérez Bustamente, 'Actividad legislativa', analysed the laws and calculated the totals. Bonal Zazo, 'Disposiciones Carolinas', surveyed Charles's legislation for Spain.

87. Konetzke, *Colección*, I, 175–6, royal warrant to the governor of Nicaragua, 9 Sep. 1536.

88. AGI *Patronato* 193/18/213–33, dossier about 'lo del río de Chagres', including a royal warrant to Francisco de Barrionuevo, gobernador de Tierra Firme (undated but Jan. 1534). I thank Bethany Aram for drawing this reference to my attention.

89. AGI *IG* 737/63, 'Lo que resulta para consultar a Vuestra Magestad lo que scriven los del consejo de Indias', mid-Nov. 1550 (undated, but the *consulta* mentioned the recent death of Licenciado Villalobos, fiscal of the council, on 8 Nov. 1550, and so was written very soon afterwards); AGI *México* 1089/4/419v–423v, three royal warrants dated Toro, 21 Sep. 1551, concerning the new 'estudio y universidad' in Mexico. Proof that the measure took effect appears in Gerhard, *Síntesis*, 63,

mandamiento 253, in which the viceroy ordered on 20 Nov. 1553 that the prior of the local Dominican convent be paid 100 pesos for his salary as professor of theology, since he had 'taught on every one of the days that he was required to do so' for the previous six months.

90. Lee, *Libros de Cabildos*, IV, 258, instructions to procuradores, 23 Jan. 1550; AGI *Lima* 566/6/368–368v and 382v–383, warrant to the Audiencia of Lima, 1 May 1551 and charter creating a new university in Mexico, 12 May 1551, both signed in Valladolid.

91. The websites maintained by the Universidad Nacional Mayor de San Marcos claim that its foundation charter was signed in Valladolid on 12 May 1551 either by Charles (who was in Augsburg) or by Joanna (who was in Tordesillas). In fact it was signed 'La reyna': the style used at the time by Charles's daughter, María, queen of Bohemia and regent in Spain.

92. *CDCV*, III, 403–4, Charles to Philip, Mar. 1552. (The emperor devoted special attention to the potential Portuguese threat to his own transatlantic possessions, a problem to which Mendoza's 'Relación' – see next note – devoted much attention: a coincidence that identifies both documents.)

93. *CDCV*, III, 255–7, 'Relaçión de don Antonio de Mendoça' (also printed in Hanke, *Los virreyes*, I, 57–8, with an important correction: 'mudar' instead of 'mandar').

94. AGNM *Mercedes* II/257, 'Provisión del rey para la libertad de los de Tascala', 29 Mar. 1541, reissued 4 Apr. 1542. Gibson, *Tlaxcala*, 80–2, discusses the conflicting legislation.

95. Hanke, *Los virreyes*, I, 131, instructions for Velasco, 16 Apr. 1550; AGNM *Mercedes* III/102 (*expediente* 253), *mandamiento* in favour of the son of the late Sebastián Rodríguez, 18 July 1550, one of many such orders.

96. *CDCV*, III, 577–92, Charles to Philip, 2 Apr., with a postscript dated 27 Apr. 1553; Kamen, *Felipe*, 60–1, quoting an exchange about indigenous inhabitants from Sep. 1554.

97. Bataillon, 'Pour l'epistolario', 384–7, Las Casas to Soto, May 1549, referring to previous epistolary exchanges.

98. Las Casas, *Brevíssima relación*, ff. 3–3v (Dedication) and ff. 63v–64 ('Sumario' of the charge by Fray Domingo de Soto); Beltrán de Heredía, *Domingo de Soto*, 645, Maximilian and María, regents, to Soto, 7 July and 4 Aug. 1550; Castilla Urbano, 'La superación', 41, council of the Indies to Charles, 15 Dec. 1554. Castilla Urbano provides the best concise account of the work of the committee, which met in Valladolid Aug.–Sep. 1550 and Apr.–May 1551. La Gasca only participated in the second session.

99. Lippens, 'Jean Glapion', XLV, 39–41 (Glapion died before he left Spain); Castet, *Annales*, VIII, 225 (noting Glapion's efforts to create and lead a group of Franciscan missionaries from the Netherlands to America); Beltrán de Heredía, *Domingo de Soto*, Part II, includes several letters to and from Soto on American affairs.

100. Konetzke, *Colección*, 113–20, 'Ordenanzas' issued 4 Dec. 1528, and 131–2, 'Consulta del consejo', 10 Dec. 1529. See other examples from 1525 and 1535 on pp. 350 and 354 above, and in Konetzke, *Colección*, 103–6 (1528: charter of Charles and Joanna 'queriendo en esto descargar nuestras conciencias reales'), 130–1 (1529: charter issued 'para descargo de nuestras conciencias'); and so on.

101. Martínez, *Documentos*, III, 136 (Petition of Francisco Núñez to Charles, May 1530) and 266–77 (Relación of the Audiencia to Charles, 1531), and IV, 62–77 (*Relación* of Cortés to Charles, 1533). Other examples (among many) from Cortés at ibid., 132–5 (1535), 190 (1539), 210–15 (1540), 243–5 (1543), 257–70 (1544) and 328 (will of Cortés, clause XXXVII, 12 Oct. 1547).

102. Pérez de Tudela Bueso, *Documentos*, II, 544–7, La Gasca to the magistrates of Arica, 28 Sep. 1549, minute. Although La Gasca did not identify the recipient of this remarkable letter, full of references to Charles's 'delicada conciencia', I deduce Arica because it is precisely 170 leagues from Potosí.

103. Espinosa to Charles, Panama, 21 July 1533 (p. 368 above); *Este es vn traslado*, f. 4 (I thank Danielle Anthony for bringing this rare pamphlet to my attention).

PORTRAIT OF THE EMPEROR IN HIS PRIME

1. Firpo, *Relazioni*, I, 336, Relation of Giovanni Micheli, 13 May 1557 (partial English translation in *CSPV*, VI/2, 1,043–85); BMECB *Ms. Granvelle*, 8/189, Gonzalo Pérez to Antoine Perrenot de Granvelle, 19 Feb. 1564 (minute in AGS *E* 525/81), trying to excuse the slow development of Charles's grandson, don Carlos.

2. Ball and Parker, *Cómo ser rey*, instruction of 6 May 1543. For more on this document see ch. 11 and Pl. 9; for his linguistic limitations in 1517–18, see ch. 4.

3. Sanuto, *I diarii*, LII, cols 302–7, letter of Hironimo Bontempo, Bologna, 25 Nov. 1529; ASF *MdP* 4296/57v, Alessandro Serristori to Duke Cosimo, 16 Oct. 1537 ('Sua Maestà nelle riposte che mi faceva sempre parlò in lingua Toscana'); TNA *SP* 68/11 no. 611, Dudley and Morison to Privy Council, 25 Jan. 1553. MacCulloch, *Thomas Cromwell*, 27–8 and 587–8, noted that many of Henry VIII's ministers, including Richard Morison, were fluent in Italian.

4. Sanuto, *I diarii*, XXIX, cols 371–2, Corner's report on the coronation at Aachen ('perchè lei non parla anchora molto promptamente lo idioma aleman'); *L&P Henry VIII*, III/1, 428–30, Spinelly to Wolsey, 2 Feb. 1521; Górski, *Acta Tomiciana*, VII, 197, Dantiszek to King Sigismund, Madrid, 16 Mar. 1525, Latin, but with Charles's German words transcribed in the Gothic script used in German texts (Spanish translation in Fontán and Axer, *Españoles y polacos*, 172).

5. Lenz, *Briefwechsel*, II, 225–32, Martin Bucer to Heinrich Bullinger, 23 Dec. 1543 (Charles 'germanica respondebat'). On the emperor's idiosyncratic German at the Diet of Augsburg in 1530 see p. 196.

6. Sastrow, an eyewitness, recorded Charles's remarks in Low German or Dutch in 1547–8: 'Wel, Carlevitz, how zal het nu wel worden?' (to Christoph von Carlowitz, chief adviser to Maurice of Saxony); 'Wel, ik zal u leeren lachgen' (to the landgrave of Hesse); and 'Vesali, gy zult naar Carlevitz gaan, die zal ieswat schik zyn; ziet, dat gy hem helpt' (Andreas Vesalius was Charles's personal physician as well as one of the greatest anatomists of his day): see Sastrow, *Herkommen*, II, 16, 29–30 and 84. Weinrich, 'Sprachanekdoten', 185, suggested that Charles's Low German and Dutch may have been interchangeable (although he cited no source); de Grauw, 'Quelle langue', 158, noted that Charles would have heard 'Brabançon' spoken around his palace in Mechelen (and Maximilian encouraged him to learn it: p. 30 above).

7. BL *Cott. Ms.* Vespasian C.III/227–31, Lee to Wolsey, 21 Mar 1526; Illescas, *Segunda parte*, 197–8 (perhaps quoting an anecdote first found in Giovio, *Delle Historie*, book XXVII, who alleged that it happened when Charles arrived in Genoa in 1529); *NBD*, V, 193, Nuncio Poggio to Paul III, 20 Apr. 1540 (quoting Charles at an audience); Ball and Parker, *Cómo ser rey*, 151, Instructions of 4 May 1543; Reiffenberg, *Lettres*, 76–8, van Male to Praet, 23 Nov. 1552 (van Male used the Greek word for 'brag').

8. Sanuto, *I diarii*, LIII, col. 384, Marco Antonio Magno to Marco Contarini, 20 July 1530; idem, LVII, cols 212–14, Relation of Marco Minio and other ambassadors, Nov. 1532, after eighteen days 'sempre cavalcando con la Cesarea Magestad'. The evidence contradicts the categorical assertion of Alfred Morel-Fatio that Charles 'was never capable of speaking for ninety minutes in Italian' and 'did not understand German': Morel-Fatio, 'L'espagnol', 218.

9. Fabrizi d'Acquapendente, *De Locutione*, 23, offered two versions of this anecdote, claiming that one came from 'a German'. This seems to be the first iteration of the story in print, but since Fabrizi was born in 1533 and first published his short treatise on speech in 1601 he clearly related hearsay. Subsequent versions of this 'itinerant anecdote' later appeared in English, French, German and Russian: see details in Buceta, 'El juicio', 11–14, and Weinrich, 'Sprachanekdoten', 182–3.

10. Admittedly, Erasmus stressed that rulers must learn languages – see Pollnitz, 'Old words', 146–7 – but there is no evidence that Charles paid heed.

11. *NBD*, 1. Ergänzungsband 1530–1531, 414, Aleandro to Cardinal Salviati, 19 Nov. 1531. Initially, Aleandro felt nervous because several of his contemporaries claimed that he was a Jew; and so 'I replied with a smile that I did not want His Majesty to be outraged, like the Lutherans, if I told him that the script was Hebrew'. On Maximilian's insistence on linguistic proficiency, see ch. 2 above.

12. Cienfuegos, *La heroyca vida*, 47–9 (based in part on Ribadeneyra, *Vida*, f. 11v–12). See also p. 235 above on Charles's visit to the university of Salamanca at the same time.

13. Bataillon, 'Charles-Quint', 257–8, Nicholas Curtz to Charles, Nuremberg, 21 Mar. 1543. Gonzalo Sánchez-Molero, *Regia biblioteca*, I, 331–2, speculated on the fate of the instrument by Apian and the book by Copernicus.

14. Neefe, *Tafel-Reden*, 2–3, relating his conversations with Ferdinand in 1563–4 (my thanks to Annemarie Jordan Gschwend for this reference).

15. ASF *MdP* 652/355, Agnolo Niccolini to Lorenzo Pagni, 25 July 1541; AGS *E* 73/239, Charles to Los Cobos, 11 Aug. 1546, decrypt. See also Charles's impressive writing desk from 1532, currently in the Victoria and Albert Museum, London (# 11–1891), described by Jordano, 'The *plus oultra* writing cabinet', and Rosenthal, 'Plus Ultra', 226–7. Sometimes, Charles's insistence on writing holograph letters could cause delays, see (for example) *CMH*, I, 551–3, Granvelle to Marie, 16 Nov. 1532, explaining that Charles had ordered a secretary to prepare some letters to her and the empress, 'but he has put off signing them, hoping from one day to the next that he could write to you both with his own hand'. Since he had not found time, Granvelle decided to explain why others would hear news before she did.

16. Firpo, *Relazioni*, II, 829, Relation of Marino Cavalli, 1551, after three years spent at the imperial court.

17. *NBD*, IX, 71–3, Cardinal Otto Truchsess von Waldburg to Cardinal Farnese, 9 June 1546; Turba, *Venetianische Depeschen*, I, 673–7, Mocenigo to the Doge, 7/8 Sep. 1546 (the ambassador wrote that the council met 'fino alle 5 hore di notte', which according to the Venetian measurement of time meant five and a half hours after sunset. In Ingolstadt in mid-September – because 8 Sep. was 18 Sep. according to the Gregorian Calendar – the sun sets around 7.20 p.m., so '5 hore di notte' meant just after midnight.

18. ASP *GG* busta 43, unfol., Gonzaga's instructions to Gonzalo Girón, 20 Dec. 1553, copy; and ibid., Musi to Gonzaga, 13 Dec. 1553, copy, reporting a conversation with Juan de Figueroa.

19. Tellechea Idígoras, *Así murió*, 96, testimony of Francisco de Toledo to the Inquisition, relating an indiscretion by his brother, the count of Oropesa; *NBD*, XI, 72–3, Bertano to Farnese, 13 Aug. 1548. For more on this exchange see ch. 15 below; and on Soto's advice to execute John Frederick of Saxony, see ch. 12 above. Maurenbrecher, *Karl V*, pp. 29*–32*, published Soto's only surviving paper of advice to Charles, a fire-eating analysis in Feb. 1546 'on the enterprise of Germany'. See also the short article on Soto by Carro, 'Influencia'.

20. *CDCV*, III, 177–8, Charles to María and Maximilian, 25 Jan. 1550. Although the emperor never defaulted on his loans, less than six months after his accession as king of Castile Philip II decreed a suspension of all interest payments and the forcible conversion of outstanding loans to low-interest bonds.

21. BNE *Ms.* 9937/23–23v, notes for his chronicle by Florián de Ocampo, Jan. 1550; Beltrán de Heredía, *Domingo de Soto*, 642–4, Soto to Charles and to Francisco de Eraso, Salamanca, 1 July 1550, both holograph. All the criticisms attributed to Soto about selling assets promiscuously were well founded: see p. 447 above.

22. Beltrán de Heredía, *Domingo de Soto*, 636–7, Valdés to Soto, 16 Apr. 1549 (one of several similar letters); Bataillon, 'Pour l'epistolario', 384–7, Las Casas to Soto, May 1549, referring to previous epistolary exchanges. See also Lehnhoff, *Die Beichtväter*, 71–5.

23. Lefèvre-Pontalis, *Correspondance*, 10, Selve to Francis I, 10 July 1546, quoting Chancellor Wriothesley; *NBD*, XII, 235–8, Nuncio Camaiani to Cardinal del Monte, 12 Mar. 1552. See pp. 137 and 206–7 for earlier examples of Charles bypassing his ministers and allies.

24. Reiffenberg, *Histoire*, 415–17, account of the chapter of the Order held in Jan. 1546 at Utrecht (like Tournai, a territory acquired by Charles). The account is terser than usual, and may reflect an incomplete record: ibid., p. VIII.

25. Braudel, *La Méditerranée*, 320–1 and 326. Braudel once told me that he preferred 'Distance: public enemy number one' as the translation of 'L'espace: ennemi numéro 1' to that of the English edition: 'Distance, the first enemy': F. Braudel, *The Mediterranean and the Mediterranean world in the age of Philip II*, vol. I (London, 1972), 355.

26. *CWE*, XI, 54–6 (# 1554), Erasmus to Lallemand, 24 Feb. 1525; *CWE*, XV, 265–7 (# 2198), Valdés to Erasmus, July 1529; *CCG*, IV, 558, Granvelle to Morillon, 11 May 1573.

27. ADN *B* 2177, register of Simon Longin for 1502, unfol., included payments to Francisco de Taxis among the 'menus voyaiges et messageries'; Alcázar Molina, 'La política postal española', 227–9 (on the contract of 1516); Behringer, *Im Zeichen des Merkur*, 65–98; Pettegree, *The invention*, 17–18 and 169.

28. *LCK*, II, 361, Charles to Ferdinand, 11 Jan. 1530; Mártir de Angléria, *Epistolario*, III, 364–5 (# 643), to the marquesses of Los Vélez and Mondéjar, 15 July 1519; BNMV, *Ms. Italiani, Classe* VII, Cod. 1009/164v, Contarini to the Signory, Brussels, 22 Jan. 1522; Behringer, *Im Zeichen des Merkur*, 81 (a courier left Rome at 'ore 20' on 17 June 1545 and arrived in Worms at 'ore 11' on 23 June).

29. *KFF*, I, xxviii–xxx, and II/1, ix–xii. Strohmeyer, *Die Korrespondenz*, 61–6, showed that letters exchanged between the Austrian and Spanish Habsburgs in the 1560s took between nineteen and eighty-five days to reach their destination.

30. RAH *Salazar* A-60/125, bishop of Osma to Perrenot, 1 Feb. 1557; Fagel, *De Hispano-Vlaamse Wereld*, 317.

31. *SP*, VI, 451–76, Tunstal and Sampson to Henry VIII, 11 Aug. 1525 (Henry had signed the letters on 3 July); *LCK*, I, 270, prince of Orange to Charles, 14 June 1528; AGS *E* 874/8, Vega to Charles, 8 Feb. 1547.

32. *SP*, IX, 355–60, Bonner to Henry, 15 Apr. 1543.

33. Tracy, *Emperor*, 109.

34. Lanz, *Aktenstücke*, 496–500, Charles's instructions for his ambassadors in England, 13 Dec. 1521; HHStA *Belgien PA* 2/4/68, Charles to Margaret, 25 Aug. 1522, copy; RAH *Ms.* 9/4817/247, Charles to his ambassadors in Rome, 10 Jan. 1525, minute; AGS *PR* 17 no. 35, Charles's instructions to Figueroa, Feb. 1529; AGS *PR* 16 no. 75, Charles's instructions to Juan de Vega, 4 July 1543.

35. AA 4/95, Charles to Alba, 27 Oct. 1543, holograph.

36. AGS *PR* 17 no. 35, Charles's instructions to Figueroa, Feb. 1529; *PR* 45 no. 21, Charles's instructions to Soria, 19 Apr. 1529. Much of Soria's personal archive has survived, revealing the extent of his correspondence with other imperial servants and subjects in Italy: see Ibarra y Rodríguez and Arsenio de Izaga, 'Catálogo', and Pizarro Llorente, 'Un embajador'. See also BNE *Ms.* 20214/62, a collection of seventeen Latin letters from Soria to the young Antoine Perrenot while he was a student at Padua, 1538–9

37. Firpo, *Relazioni*, II, 465–6, Relation of Navagero, July 1546. Some ambassadors noted that Charles likewise lost his 'solemnity' when engaged in jousts and other sports. Sepúlveda, *Historia de Carlos V*, Book XXX ch. 24, asserted that the emperor 'placed himself at risk in battle beyond what a sovereign or general should do'.

38. *LCK*, I, 300–8, Margaret to Charles, 26 May 1529 (Charles the Bold died in battle in 1477; Charles of France, to whom Margaret had once been engaged, was routed at the battle of Fornovo in 1495); *KFF*, V, 211–12, Marie to Ferdinand, 12 Apr. 1535. For Marie's opposition to Charles's exposure in battle in 1538, see ch. 9 above.

39. HSA *B* 2032, Charles to Lope Hurtado de Mendoza, his ambassador in Portugal, 30 Aug. 1549 (conveniently forgetting that he had appointed Luis his second-in-command during the Tunis campaign); *SP*, IX, 683–93, Paget and Wotton to Henry VIII, 2 June 1544 (Charles had made the same argument during the Tunis campaign).

40. HHStA *Hs. Blau* 596/1/139v–140v, Charles to Ferdinand, 21 and 26 Mar. 1547, holograph postscripts. Movements from Foronda, *Viajes*, 589.

41. García Fuentes, 'Testigo', 93, from the chronicle of Bernabé de Busto; ASF *MdP* 4308, unfol., Bernardo de' Medici to Cosimo, 8 June 1551; De Witte, 'Cornelis', 184–8, letters to Marie of Hungary, Apr.–Aug. 1548 (bizarrely, De Witte insisted that Baersdorp addressed his letters to Empress Isabella, who died in 1539: in fact he wrote to Marie).

42. Von Ranke, *Deutsche Geschichte*, V, 370–1, 'Sommaire de l'Ambassade de feu monsieur de Vienne vers l'empereur Charles V, en l'année 1550'. Charles took a German sauna with him to Yuste: see ch. 16 below.

43. Morel-Fatio, *Historiographie*, 171, listed the seventeen attacks of gout between 1528 and 1550 recorded in the emperor's *Memoirs*.

44. Gachard, *Trois années*, 69, Navagero to the Signory, 18 Jan. 1545; ASF *MdP* 3101A/1085, Francesco di Paolo Vinta to Duke Cosimo, 2 Apr. 1548 (from Milan, hence the attention paid to the appearance of a portrait rather than to its subject).

45. De Witte, 'Cornelis', 187–8, letters to Marie of Hungary, 10 July and 7 Aug. 1548; Giles, *The whole works*, I, ii, 267–8, Roger Ascham to Edward Raven, Augsburg, 29 Jan. 1551; Von Ranke, *Deutsche Geschichte*, V, 370–1, 'Sommaire' of Marillac, 1550–1.

46. Sastrow, *Herkommen*, II, 86–8, based on his observation of the emperor's mealtimes in Brussels, and during the Diets at Augsburg, Speyer (twice) and Worms (for an alternative translation see *Social Germany*, 230–1). See earlier observations on Charles's table manners at p. 210 above. Rijksmuseum, Amsterdam, BK-NM-562–566, is a portable cutlery set (a fork and four knives) made for Charles in Italy in 1532, and perhaps the ones observed by Sastrow.

47. ASF *MdP* 4308, unfol., Bernardo de' Medici to Cosimo, 22 July 1550 ('certo è eccellentissimo imberciatore'); Reiffenberg, *Lettres*, 19–21, van Male to Praet, 9 June 1551.

48. *SP*, X, 319–21, and TNA *SP* 1/212/42, Paget to Petrie, 1 Mar. and 16 Dec. 1545; *NBD*, VIII, 68–70, Verallo to Cardinal Farnese, 9 Feb. 1545 (italics added).

49. Alarcón, *Viajes*, 66–9 (description from Sep. 1872); Ordi, 'The severe gout', 519. See also Appendix II.

50. Sastrow, *Herkommen*, II, 88 (for an alternative translation see *Social Germany*, 231). At the Hotel Adelshof in Halle, Germany, dedicated Carlophiles can eat the exact menu served to Charles when in 1541 and again in 1546 he stayed in the large house that stood on the site: Ozment, *The bürgermeister's daughter*, 145. Although the hotel supplies the food, to enjoy dining like the emperor to the full, please bring your own jesters.

51. Rassow, *Die Kaiser-Idee*, 433–6, 'Las pláticas que el emperador passó con [el embajador francés] por la misma forma y palabras', by Idiáquez, 1538 (italics added); ASF *MdP* 4306/71, Bernardo de' Medici to Duke Cosimo, 28 June 1548.

52. BL *Cott. Ms.* Vespasian C.XIII/258, John Brereton to Wriothesley, Valladolid, 23 June 1537; Nott, *The works*, II, 518–23, 'Sir Thomas Wyatt's memorial', Nov. 1537.

53. Enzinas, *Mémoires*, I, 205–7, describing the audience on 25 Nov. 1543 at which he presented the emperor with a copy of *El nvevo testamento . . . dedicado a la Cesarea Magestad. Habla Dios*. Enzinas was lucky: two weeks before, Charles had banned his book as heretical, but did not realize that its author now stood before him (Enzinas, *Mémoires*, I, 642–4). Sastrow likewise reported that every day after dinner Charles 'took his seat in one of the window recesses, where everybody could approach him or hand him a petition and explain his reasons. The emperor gave his decision on the spot' (Sastrow, *Herkommen*, II, 88).

54. ASF *MdP* 4308, unfol., Bernardo de' Medici to Cosimo, 29 June 1551; *CSPF Edward VI*, 137–8, Dr Wotton to the Privy Council, 30 June 1551. For other 'pungent words' uttered at an audience in 1548, see p. 333 above.

55. Von Ranke, *Deutsche Geschichte*, V, 366–70, Marillac's report on his embassy, 1550. See the identical conclusion of Ambassador Thomas Wyatt in 1538: 'The emperor pays no attention to people except when he needs them' (Brigden, *Thomas Wyatt*, 374, translated from Wyatt's complaint to an Italian ambassador).

56. *NBD*, XII, 198–200, Camaiani to Pope Julius, 22 Feb. 1552.

57. Lenz, *Briefwechsel*, II, 225–32, Bucer to Bullinger, 23 Dec. 1543, Latin.

CHAPTER 14: PATERFAMILIAS, 1548–51

1. Bodart, *Tiziano*, 209, Ambassador Leonardi to the duke of Urbino, 18 Mar. 1530; Firpo, *Relazioni*, II, 541 (Mocenigo) and III, 55 (Badoer). On the erroneous suggestion that Charles sired a fourth illegitimate daughter, see Appendix IV.

2. Crutzen, 'L'origine', 159–62, cited Charles's warrant granting Jeanne an annual pension of £24 on 1 Aug. 1522, no doubt shortly after she had given birth; his warrant of 31 Oct. 1542, just after Jeanne's death, ordering the pension to be transferred to her daughters; and a petition for money submitted in 1559 by two of Jeanne's siblings to Margarita of Parma, their niece and now regent of the Netherlands, reminding her that they were 'poor people of good family' who 'gained their living from weaving tapestries'.

3. *KFF*, I, 474–8, Charles to Ferdinand, 4 Oct. 1526 (on a plan to marry 'ma bastarde qu'est en Flandres' to the prince of Ferrara); AGS *PR* 45/18, Instructions to Leyva and Caracciolo, 27 June 1529 (offering her to Mantua); AGS *PR* 45/84, marriage treaty signed in Barcelona, 23 June 1529; RAH *Ms. Salazar* A-44/135, Charles's act legitimizing Margarita, 9 July 1529.

4. AGS *E* 867/3 and 6, Charles to Lope Hurtado de Mendoza, 2 Jan. 1538, and to the marquis of Aguilar, 3 Feb. 1538.

5. Gachard, *Correspondance de Marguerite*, II, v–vii, Charles to Margarita, 11 Apr. and 15 Aug. 1540, both holograph. Margarita's letters to Charles have evidently disappeared, but the English ambassador overheard imperial courtiers 'speaking of a divorce' between Margarita and Octavio: Powell, *The complete works*, I, 242, Thomas Wyatt to Thomas Cromwell, Ghent, 2 Apr. 1540.

6. Giovio, *Pauli Iovii opera*, I, 312–13, Giovio (travelling with the emperor) to Nicolas Raynce and Girolamo Angleria, 7 June 1543 ('Il bel duca Ottavio chiavò in Pavia quattro volte la prima notte la sua Madama'); *NBD*, VIII, 520–6, Nuncio Dandini to Cardinal Farnese, 5–6 Jan. 1546 (on Charles's interest in the twins).

7. AGS *E* 644/101, Charles to Diego Hurtado de Mendoza, 19 Sep./7 Oct. 1547 (about 'the illness of the duke of Camarino'). On Margarita's later career, see d'Onofrio, *Il carteggio intimo*; de Iongh, *Madama*; and Steen, *Margaret*. When he grew up, Alessandro Farnese became one of Spain's most successful generals.

8. The original reads 'le yzo hazer *una señal* nela pierna derecha'. What did the word 'señal' signify? Two years earlier, Charles complained that Spanish settlers 'hierran de *una señal* en el rostro' free native Americans to suggest that they were slaves (and tried to regulate the practice): Konetzke, *Colección*, I, 109–11, royal order of 20 Nov. 1528, issued 'after consultation with me, the king'. The sense here is clearly branding, and so Charles may have ordered that his daughter be branded (rather than merely tattooed).

9. AGS *E* 142/135, 'Breve Relación del caso de la Señora Orsolina de la Peña' submitted to Philip II by Camillo Enobarbo in 1562, together with supporting documents that included f. 134, two autograph letters of Charles to Ursolina della Penna, 13 and 19 Apr. 1536, in French and Italian, and f. 142, Tadea to Philip II, 12 Oct. 1562. Imperfect transcripts of these documents appeared in *CODOIN*, LXXXVIII, 512–21. Gossart, 'Deux filles', discussed them.

10. BNMV *Ms. Italiani*, Classe VII, cod. 1009/408v, Gasparo Contarini to the Council of Ten, 28 Jan. 1525 (mentioning 'la fiola de la Maestà Cesarea, la qual hebbe in Vagliadolid ja 18 mesi'). On Girolamo da Nogarola and the mysterious imperial gift of 'due milia [scudi] per maritare una sua figliuola' in May 1524, see Cicogna, *Delle Inscrizioni*, VI, 240–1.

11. AGS *E* 5/231, Prioress María de Aragón to Henry of Nassau, 28 Mar. 1524, holograph (partially printed in *CODOIN*, LXXXVIII, 510–11). Díaz del Valle y de la Puerta, *Historia del reyno de León*, II, parte 1ª, f. 86, stated (without providing a source) that 'otra hija del César fue doña Juana de Austria que murió de edad de 7 años el de 1530, siendo novicia en el convento de Augustinos en la villa de Madrigal donde yaze'. Zurdo Manso and Cerro Calvo, *Madrigal*, 40, claimed (also without providing a source) that in 1530 Juana 'murió ahogada en el pozo del convento'. I thank Ruth MacKay and Felipe Vidales del Castillo for discussing the fate of Juana with me.

12. *KFF*, III/2, 223–33, Charles to Ferdinand, 29 July 1531, holograph. Despite his profession that he was 'about to leave', Charles remained in the Netherlands for more than five months.

13. *CODOIN*, XIV, 16–17, Loaysa to Charles, 8 June 1530; Sanuto, *I diarii*, LIII, cols 208–10, letter of Zuan Francesco Masardo, Innsbruck, 5 May 1530; Ribier, *Lettres*, II, 633–7 (also printed in Cimber and Danjou, *Archives curieuses*, 1ᵉ série, III, 296–306), Charles's recollections at an audience in 1556, recorded by an anonymous French eyewitness.

14. Rosso, *Istoria*, 70; Poumarède, 'Le voyage', 283, Ambassador Alfonso Rossetti to Ercole of Este, 1 Mar. 1536; Cosentini, *Una dama*, 66–80 (his regret recorded on p. 76).

15. Gayangos, *Relaciones de Pedro de Gante*, 17–19; Keniston, *Francisco de Los Cobos*, 204, Vázquez to Los Cobos, 13 Feb. 1538; March, *Niñez*, II, 345, Doña Estefanía de Requesens to her mother, 23 Mar. 1538. The emperor had rejoined his wife in Valladolid on 27 Nov. 1537 and left her again on 21 Dec.

16. Panzer, *Barbara*, ch. 2, suggests that Barbara may have caught Charles's eye when he went hunting in Geisling, near Regensburg, where her parents owned property, and later visited him in the Gasthof 'Zum goldenen Kreuz' in Regensburg (see Pl. 5 in her book). Ozment, *The bürgermeister's daughter*, ch. 2, revealed how easily clandestine affairs could develop in Charles's Germany.

17. BMECB *Ms. Granvelle* V/423–4, codicil signed by Charles, 6 June 1554, enclosing the affidavit signed by Massi on 13 June 1550 (copies made from the originals in 1624). *PEG*, IV, 495–500, printed both texts, but omitted the descriptions and annotations made by the copyist. The emperor's precise description regarding Gerónimo's conception and birth suggests that he was the only illegitimate child conceived after the empress's death – or at least the only one still alive in 1554. For more on the codicil, see ch. 15.

18. Gachard, *Études*, 9–10 and 21 (warrants issued by the treasury of the Netherlands in 1551 in favour of Hieronymus Kegel Piramus), and 14 (details of Barbara's household in 1571). No surviving documents reveal when Barbara married Hieronymus, but the coincidence that her son received the same name as his stepfather suggests that Barbara knew her future husband before Charles sequestered the boy.

19. GRM, II, 506–7, Quijada to Philip, 12 Oct. 1558 (the secret messenger who conveyed the money was Ogier Bogart, who had witnessed the document empowering François Massi to take charge of Gerónimo in 1550). For more on Barbara's sad existence until she died in 1597, see Lafuente, 'La madre', Lozano Mateos, 'Noticias', and Panzer, *Barbara*.

20. Gonzalo Sánchez-Molero, *Felipe II: la educación*, 198–241, describes the selection of a preceptor. Charles signed Silíceo's title as *maestro* on 1 July 1534, a few days after hearing him lecture: March, *Niñez*, I, 104. Gonzalo, op. cit., 237, stated that the empress accompanied her husband to Salamanca, and so probably played a part in selecting Silíceo, but in fact she travelled directly from Segovia to Valladolid (Girón, *Crónica*, 43).

21. Gonzalo Sánchez-Molero, *Felipe II: la educación*, 242–56 (on the selection of Zúñiga); Fernández de Oviedo, *Libro de la Cámara Real*, 1–3.

22. March, *Niñez*, I, 230, Zúñiga to Charles, 11 Feb. 1536 – explaining why he had been absent when Philip became injured in a fight between two of his pages. Martínez Millán, *La Corte*, II, 100, gave the household size.

23. Gonzalo Sánchez-Molero, *Felipe II: la educación*, 243, quoting Francisco de Monzón, *Libro primero del espejo del prínçipe christiano* (Lisbon, 1544).

24. March, *Niñez*, I, 68–70, 72, Silíceo to Charles, 25 Feb. 1536 and 19 Mar. 1540. See also the complaints of López de la Cuadra early in 1543 that 'in the past two years, His Highness has spent no more than fifteen to twenty days in learning to write' and 'in the past four months has spent only five hours studying Latin': Martínez Millán, *La Corte*, II, 143 n. 724.

25. Gonzalo Sánchez-Molero, *Felipe II: la educación*, 258–9.

26. March, *Niñez*, I, 230, Zúñiga to Charles, 9 Feb. 1536. Gonzalo Sánchez-Molero, *Felipe II: la educación*, 260–73, described Philip's religious formation, and identified the Rosarium as the one illuminated by Simon Bening now in the Chester Beatty Library in Dublin (ibid., 266–7).

27. March, *Niñez*, I, 227, Zúñiga to Charles, 25 Aug. 1535 (Zúñiga had served Charles since 1506, when the future emperor was only six, which gave force to his parallel).

28. Martínez Millán, *La Corte*, II, 129–46, is enlightening on the emperor's efforts to keep Philip and his sisters apart. For one example, see *CDCV*, II, 229, Charles to Philip, Metz, 6 July 1544 – that is, the emperor found time to micro-manage his children's lives just as he began his invasion of France.

29. Charles's treatment of his daughters contrasted sharply with the loving and caring letters that Philip II wrote to his daughters in the 1580s: see Parker, *Imprudent king*, 167–70.

30. AGS *CSR* 106/470–1, Albalá to 'el bachiller Christobal de Estrella', 4 Feb. 1541. Gonzalo Sánchez-Molero, *Felipe II: la educación*, 499–572, provided an admirable biography of each preceptor.

31. HHStA *Ms. Blau* 596/1/45v–46, Charles to Ferdinand, 4 Nov. 1542; BL *Addl. Ms.* 28,706/1–16 contain the major documents concerning Philip's Portuguese marriage sent to Charles's ambassador in Lisbon on 23 Sep. 1542. Even then, the papal Bull failed to cover all instances of consanguinity, and

Charles had to secure another one 'suppliendo el deffecto de la dispensación que se concedió quando os casastes con la princesa': *CDCV*, II, 636–9, Charles to Philip, 8 July 1548.

32. Ball and Parker, *Cómo ser rey*, 70–7, Charles to Philip, 4 May 1543 (whence all subsequent quotations from this document come). Charles did not care about exposing his daughter Margarita or his niece Christina to teenage sex: see above.

33. The normally compliant Borja refused to obey the emperor's outrageous order, fearing that 'de mi yda se podría rescrescer algo de que Vuestra Magestad fuesse deservido'. He and the duchess therefore stayed at home until long after Philip and his wife had consummated their union: see *Sanctus Franciscus Borgia*, II, 460–4 and VI, 609–11, Francisco de Borja, duke of Gandía, to Charles, Philip and Los Cobos, all on 2 Oct. 1543.

34. BZ 144/39 and Riba García, *Correspondencia*, 25–6, Mateo Vázquez to Philip II with rescripts, 28 Dec. 1574 and 21 Mar. 1576.

35. *CDCV*, II, 172–3 and 183, Charles to Philip, 27 Oct. and 15 Nov. 1543, and 189–93, Philip to Charles, 4 Feb. 1544, minute.

36. Gonzalo Sánchez-Molero, *Felipe II. La mirada*, 124.

37. March, *Niñez*, I, 323–6, Charles to Zúñiga, 17 Feb. 1545.

38. *CDCV*, II, 332 and 343, Charles to Philip, 13 Jan. and 17 Feb. 1545; March, *Niñez*, I, 324, Charles to Zúñiga, Brussels, 17 Feb. 1545, all with holograph postscripts.

39. Gonzalo Sánchez-Molero, *El aprendizaje*, 166, prints part of the document, presented to Philip in a private ceremony of investiture on 16 Sep. 1546.

40. *CDCV*, II, 407, Charles to Philip, 2 Aug. 1545, postscript; AGS *E* 641/11–12, Charles to Los Cobos, 3 Aug. 1545, holograph postscript.

41. AGS *E* 644/20, Charles to Philip, 25 Dec. 1547; *CDCV*, II, 564–9, Charles's instructions to Alba, [18 Jan. 1548].

42. *CDCV*, II, 569–92, Instructions, 18 Jan. 1548, from which all quotations come. Granvelle's copy, which seems to be an earlier draft, was printed in *PEG*, III, 267–318. Charles may have worked from a draft prepared by Granvelle, as he seems to have done when drafting his instructions of 1539 (ch. 10); or he may have worked alone, as he did with his instructions in 1543 (ch. 11). Since no original appears to have survived, certainty is impossible.

43. The text in Granvelle's archive omitted the paragraph about Pier Luigi Farnese and Piacenza, so perhaps Charles added it himself (*CDCV*, II, 576 n. 691). Paul III was Octavio's grandfather and so had strong views on this subject.

44. Gachard, 'Mémoire', 29, Manrique to Cisneros, 8 Mar. 1516. See also the abortive partition plan proposed to Charles by Margaret of Austria and her council in 1519: ch. 4 above.

45. Pietschmann, 'Carlos V y la formación', 440–4, and idem, 'Carlos V y América', 267–75, provided an excellent analysis of the three paragraphs of Charles's Political Testament devoted to America, the emperor's only substantial consideration of their affairs. Remarkably, he omitted two other important issues: Spain's 'just title' to govern, and Church affairs.

46. Pietschmann, 'Carlos V y la formación', 444–5.

47. *CDCV*, II, 612–15, Charles to Philip, 9 Apr. 1548. The emperor justified his choice in part because of the 'good sense and prudence' with which Maximilian 'is handling the affairs of the Empire in my place' at the Diet of Augsburg.

48. ASF *MdP* 4307, unfol., Bernardo de' Medici to Duke Cosimo, 28 Sep. 1548.

49. ASF *MdP* 4307, unfol., Bernardo de' Medici to Duke Cosimo, 9 Nov. 1548 and 6 Apr. 1549.

50. BL *Eg. Ms.* 2148/16v, account of the 'prince of Spayne's' entry to Mantua by Thomas Hoby, an eyewitness.

51. *RTA*, XVIII, 2082–2176, prints the debates at the Diet concerning the 'Burgundischer Vertrag' in Mar.–June 1548.

52. Frieder, *Chivalry*, 133–58 described and dissected 'les fêtes de Binche'. In 2003 UNESCO declared the annual carnival at Binche a 'Masterpiece of the Oral and Intangible Heritage of Humanity'.

53. ASF *MdP* 4307, unfol., Bernardo de' Medici to Duke Cosimo, 28 June 1549; and *MdP* 4308, unfol., same to same, 7 Dec. 1549.

54. Firpo, *Relazioni*, II, 831, Relation of Marino Cavalli, 1551.

55. Giles, *The whole works*, I/2, 255, Roger Ascham to Edward Raven, 29 Jan. 1551 (describing the passenger barges that plied the Rhine).

56. Reiffenberg, *Lettres*, 12–13, van Male to Louis de Praet (his patron), 17 July 1550. Some have claimed that the emperor dictated his memoirs to van Male, but his letter clearly stated that Charles 'scriberet in navi'. Morel-Fatio, *Historiographie*, 160, argued that Charles stopped writing his memoirs when he reached Mainz on 18 June, but this seems unfounded: he embarked on the Rhine at Cologne on 14 June and travelled upstream on his barge until he reached Speyer on 23 June (Foronda, *Viajes*, 617–18). For more on the *Memoirs*, see Appendix I.

57. Reiffenberg, *Lettres*, 12–13, van Male to Louis de Praet, 17 July 1550; Zimmerman, 'The publication', 89, Bernardo de' Medici, bishop of Forlì, to Duke Cosimo, Augsburg, 19 Dec. 1550.
58. Ribadeneyra, *Vida*, 109v–10. Unfortunately, Ribadeneyra gave no date, stating unhelpfully that this exchange took place on 'no sé qual de las vezes que estuuo el padre Francisco en Iuste con el emperador'; but the most likely occasion was Dec. 1557, when the future saint spent two whole days visiting the emperor: GRM, I, 235.
59. *CDCV*, IV, 486: I cite throughout from this version.
60. Morel-Fatio, *Historiographie*, 170–1, listed the various 'numérotages' in the *Memoirs*.
61. *CDCV*, IV, 532, described 'la primera falta o yerro' of 'los de la Liga de Schmalkalden', and ibid., 560, highlighted the 'sexta falta y error'.
62. Pacheco, *Libro de descripción*, no. 84. Mexía ended his *Historia Ymperial*, published in Apr. 1547, with a call for someone to write a worthy history of Charles. He started his new commission at once, using documents from the Biblioteca Colombina in his native Seville, but had only reached the year 1530 when he died.
63. Giovio, *Pauli Iovii opera*, II, 170–1, Giovio to Charles, 14 Aug. 1550; ASF *MdP* 4308, unfol., Bernardo de' Medici, bishop of Forlì, to Cosimo, 8 Nov., 1, 9 and 19 Dec. 1550, and 9 Jan. 1551 (some partly published in Zimmerman, 'The publication', 87–90). For more on Charles and his historians, see Kagan, *Clio*, ch. 2; on Ávila's work as *protocronista*, see Gonzalo Sánchez-Molero, 'Acerca', 177–8, and idem, *El César*, 275–83.
64. Pérez de Tudela Bueso, *Documentos*, I, 207–9, La Gasca to van Male, Palencia, 23 Aug. 1553, responding to the request for details; Gómara, *Hispania Victrix* (printing 'acabóse a veinte días del mes de agosto', 1553; the previous year, an earlier version was printed in Zaragoza); Pérez Pastor, *La imprenta*, 94–7, *real cédula* of 17 Nov. 1553, followed by statements from the booksellers of Seville in Feb. 1554.
65. *LCK*, II, 562, Charles to Marie, 25 Apr. 1547; *CDCV*, IV, 559, noted the contrasting accounts of the ford incident in both Ávila and the *Memoirs*.
66. Kagan, 'La propaganda', 213–14, listed the productions of the emperor's publicity agency in 1548–9.
67. Plon, *Leone Leoni*, 370–2, Leoni to Perrenot, 14 Aug. 1555, described progress on his various commissions; Sepponen, 'Imperial materials', n. 5, gave their locations in 2014.
68. Ozment, *The bürgermeister's daughter*, 52, Anna Büschler to Erasmus Schenkin of Limpurg, then at Worms, 9 May 1521. The Kunsthistorisches Museum, Vienna, Kunstkammer, contains another piece from a set of draughts bearing Charles's likeness made in Augsburg in the 1540s (Inv.-Nr KK_3853). Gunn, *War*, 250, surveyed the media used to propagate Charles's image in the Netherlands.
69. Plon, *Leone Leoni*, 362–3, Leoni to Perrenot, 1550. Ando, *Imperial ideology*, especially chs 7 and 8, provided a brilliant account of how the Roman emperors (whom Charles took as his role models) projected themselves through a wide range of media.
70. Reiffenberg, *Lettres*, 12–13, van Male to Praet, 17 July 1550, postscript (on the project for a Latin text). Morel-Fatio, *Historiographie*, 172–3, argued convincingly that Ferdinand was the target audience for the *Memoirs*.
71. Bernays, *Urkunden*, 2e Abteilung, IV/2, 822 and 826, Jacob Sturm and others to the magistrates of Strasbourg, 15 and 31 Dec. 1547; Turba, *Venetianische Depeschen*, II, 412–14, Mocenigo and Badoer to the Signory, 19 Apr. 1548; NBD, X, 377–80, Cardinal Santa Croce to Cardinal Farnese, 15 June 1548. AGS E 1199/26, Granvelle to Alba, 19 Oct. 1548, reported that the emperor's enemies were spreading the rumour that 'the prince is coming to be made king of Italy and king of the Romans'.
72. Von Bucholtz, *Geschichte*, IX, 726–8, Ferdinand to Marie, 29 Mar. 1549, and 729–30, Marie's reply, 13 Apr. 1549. I have followed the brilliant discussion of when and why Charles changed his mind on the imperial succession in Rodríguez-Salgado, 'El ocaso', 53–7
73. Von Bucholtz, *Geschichte*, IX, 495–7, Marie to Ferdinand, 1 May 1550 (I have translated 'nostre maison' as 'our dynasty'). Philip's 'wide-ranging rationale' is probably the one printed by Lanz, *Staatspapiere*, 450–61, 'Denkschrift über die Succession in der Kaiserwürde'.
74. Von Druffel, *Beiträge*, III, 161–5, and Gachard, 'Charles-Quint', col. 793 note, two letters from Ferdinand to Marie, the first undated and the second sent on 19 July 1550.
75. *CSPSp*, X, 156–7, Perrenot to Marie, 16 Aug. 1550; *PEG*, III, 448, Perrenot to Renard, 2 Sep. 1550.
76. *LCK*, III, 12, Ferdinand to Charles, 14 Dec. 1550, and 15–21, Charles to Marie, 16 Dec. 1550 (transposing Charles's report of the acrimonious exchange into direct speech). Rodríguez-Salgado, 'El ocaso', 57–8, provides a concise account of the argument.
77. *LCK*, III, 15–21, Charles to Marie, 16 Dec. 1550; Turba, *Venetianische Depeschen*, II, 508–10, Mocenigo and Badoer to the Signory, 15 Feb. 1551.

78. Von Dollinger, *Dokumente*, 168–77, and von Druffel, *Beiträge*, III, 196–201, printed the numerous documents signed by Philip and Ferdinand in Augsburg on 9 Mar. 1551, many of them drafted by Marie. *CSPSp*, X, 245–6, printed the final agreement in English translation.

79. Friedensburg, 'Karl V.', 76–81, Giovanni Michele to the council of Ten, Dec. 1551, reporting Maximilian's indiscretions; *CODOIN*, XCVIII, 24–8, Ferdinand to the bishop of Aquila, Philip II's ambassador, 22 July 1558, in a letter reneging on the promise to invest his nephew as Imperial Vicar in Italy. Edelmayer, 'Carlos V', and Laubach, 'Karl V.', expertly analysed the complex succession debates at Augsburg.

80. Giles, *The whole works*, III, 9, Ascham, *A report*; TNA *SP* 68/7 no. 358, Morison to the English Privy Council, 26 May 1551. Vandenesse also reported that 'the separation of father and son was hard': Gachard, *Voyages*, II, 463.

CHAPTER 15: THE EMPEROR'S LAST CAMPAIGNS, 1551–4

1. Gutiérrez, *Trento*, I, 74–80, 107–10 and 290–5, Charles to Diego Hurtado de Mendoza, 18 Mar. and 30 Oct. 1551 and 19 Apr. 1551 (draft). Charles had urged the popes to convene the general council at Trent since 1524: RAH *Ms.* 9/4817 f. 216–25v, Charles to Sessa, 18 July 1524.

2. Gutiérrez, *Trento*, I, 132–5, Protest, 3 Jan. 1551; ibid., III, 22–9, on the letters of summons; Buschbell, *Concilium Tridentinum*, XI/2, 771–7, Julius to his legate at Trent, 16 Jan. 1552, on the joke.

3. Gutiérrez, *Trento*, I, 425–8, and II, 63–77, Charles to Toledo, 8 Oct. 1551 and 5 Jan. 1552 (*CSPSp*, X, 431–5, provided a full English translation of the latter).

4. Gutiérrez, *Trento*, II, 240–6, 'Resultan los puntos que se han consultado a Su Magestad', undated but Feb. 1552; Buschbell, *Concilium Tridentinum*, XI/2, 771–7, Julius to his legate at Trent, 16 Jan. 1552. Gutiérrez, op. cit., III, 397–8, saluted Charles's achievement in persuading at least some Lutheran states – including Brandenburg, Württemberg and Strasbourg – to send formal delegations to Trent.

5. Gutiérrez, *Trento*, II, 281–91, Charles to Diego Hurtado de Mendoza, 27 Feb. 1552, minute (*CSPSp*, X, 457–64, provided a full English translation of the latter). Philip II would draw a similar parallel between his interests and those of God: *FBD*, 225.

6. Giles, *The whole works*, III, 10, Ascham's *Report*; Vos and Hatch, *Letters*, 236, Ascham to Cheke, 7 July 1553. See the similar assessment of the French ambassador Marillac slightly earlier, quoted on pp. 503–4 below.

7. Tytler, *England*, I, 301–7, Sir John Mason to the Privy Council, 29 June 1550; Rymer, *Foedera*, XV, 211–17, treaty of Boulogne, 24 Mar. 1550; Alberì, *Relazioni*, serie I, vol. 2, Final Relation of Giovanni Capello, 1554.

8. ASF *MdP* 4308, unfol., Bernardo de' Medici to Cosimo, 29 Sep. and 3 Oct. 1550 (on the 'festa maxime' at Charles's court to celebrate the capture of Mahdia); *LCK*, III, 9–11 and 55–7, Charles to Suleiman, 31 Oct. 1550 and 8 Mar. 1551. Apart from Mahdia (then known as Africa), Doria also captured Monastir and Susa in modern Tunisia: see operational details in Alonso Acero, 'Cristiandad', and idem, 'El norte de África'.

9. Giles, *The whole works*, III, 14, Ascham's *Report*.

10. *PEG*, III, 504–10, instructions of Julius to the bishop of Imola, 31 Mar. 1551; Dumont, *Corps*, IV, part iii, 26–7, secret treaty between Henry II and Farnese, 27 May 1551. Philip's visit is mentioned in AGS *E* 646/53, Charles to Philip, 9 July 1551.

11. *LCK*, III, 68–71, Charles to Ferdinand, 15 Aug. 1551; AGS *CMC* 1a/1231, Accounts of García Portillo, payments in Oct. 1551 to the 'ynfantería y caballería spañola que quedó en guardia y presidio de las tres fuertes del ducado de Wirtemberg . . . al tiempo que salieron de las dichas fuertes de Wirtemberg . . . para baxar en Italia al cerco de Parma' and to three companies of German guards under the count of Nassau. The emperor's appreciation of the strategic value of Parma appears in *CDCV*, II, 128, Charles to Philip, 19 June 1543, and 576, his Political Testament of 1548.

12. Vos and Hatch, *Letters*, 132–8, Ascham to Cheke, 11 Nov. 1550, described Charles's Lutheran opponents; Rein, *The Chancery of God*, and Moritz, *Interim und Apokalypse*, detailed the resistance of Magdeburg.

13. Von Druffel, *Briefe*, I, 474–6, Henry to Marillac, his ambassador at the imperial court, 10 Aug. 1550.

14. Ibid., I, 234–7, Ferdinand to Charles, 21 June 1549; *LCK*, II, 622–6 and 637–8, Maurice to Philip, 27 Jan. 1549 and reply 31 Aug. 1549; Giles, *The whole works*, III, 57, Ascham's *Report*. Issleib, *Aufsätze*, 494–7, documented the efforts of Maurice and others to pressure the prince to plead for the landgrave's release, culminating in Charles's rejection, 10 Apr. 1549. Imprisoning the landgrave was not cheap: the 300 Spanish soldiers guarding the landgrave cost Charles 67,000 ducats between 1547 and 1552 (AGS *CMC* 1a/1519/V, payment to Diego de Torralva).

15. Turba, 'Verhaftung', 228–31, printed the declarations against Hesse and against John Frederick (condemned 'to prison for the rest of his life') from ÖNB *Codex Vindobonensis Palatinus* 9363, a volume full of documents concerning the imprisonment of the two Lutheran leaders.

16. *LCK*, III, 60–7, Charles to Viglius, 17 Mar. 1551, and Viglius's reply, 25 Mar. 1551. Benavent Benavent and Bertomeu Masiá, *El secuestro*, 82–99, printed documents concerning the landgrave's unsuccessful attempt to escape. See also Mariotte, *Philippe*, 273–5.

17. Dumont, *Corps*, IV, part iii, 31–3, treaty of Lochau, 5 Oct. 1551, ratified by Henry at Chambord, 15 Jan. 1552 (German text in von Druffel, *Briefe*, III, 340–50). Weber, 'Le traité', offers an excellent account of the tortuous negotiations that led to the treaty of Chambord.

18. Gachard, *Rapport*, 171, Marnix to Margaret, 12 Mar. 1519; AGS *E* 64/197, Loaysa to Charles, 5 Jan. 1544, with 'puntos' on the dorse, each one with a note of Charles's replies.

19. Giles, *The whole works*, I/2, 313, Ascham to the Master and Fellows of St John's College, Cambridge, Augsburg, 12 Oct. 1551; and III, 19–20, Ascham's *Report*, written in June–July 1553 (see also letters from Charles's other ministers at this time refusing to believe the rumours of an impending disaster, cited in von Druffel, *Briefe*, I, 854 n. 1). Lutz, *Christianitas afflicta*, 72–84, discussed the flawed decision-making at the imperial court at this time; Janis, *Groupthink*, analysed the broader phenomenon.

20. *NBD*, VIII, 717, report of the nuncio's conversation with the cardinal of Augsburg, 8 June 1545; *NBD*, XI, 48–54, Pietro Bertano, bishop of Fano, to Cardinal Farnese, Augsburg, 29 July 1548; ibid., 563–4, Marino Cavalli to the council of Ten, Augsburg, 21 Aug. 1548 (thus less than a month after Bertano's revelations).

21. References located through the Medici Archive Project: Doc IDs # 3820 (1543), # 2367 (1545), and # 4480 (1547). My thanks to Maurizio Arfaioli for sharing them with me.

22. ASP *GG* b 43, unfol., Natale Musi to Gonzaga, 13 Dec. 1553, and Gonzaga's instructions to Gonzalo Girón, his envoy to Charles, 20 Dec. 1553, both dealing with criticism of Gonzaga over the previous two years.

23. *NBD*, XI, 73 n. 1, Granvelle to Marie, 15 Aug. 1548. Soto eventually prevailed in this matter: Charles did later insist that urban Lutheran preachers must either renounce their creed or depart (see ch. 12 above). Beltrán de Heredía, *Domingo de Soto*, 231, asserted that Granvelle forced out Pedro de Soto, and eighteen months later also his successor as imperial confessor, Domingo de Soto. Juan Ginés de Sepúlveda, *Historia de Carlos V*, Book XXX, ch. 36, noted that after the death of Los Cobos and Granvelle, Charles discussed his decisions with 'very few'.

24. *NBD*, XVI, 121–4, Martinengo to Cardinal del Monte, 29 Mar. 1552; Gachard, 'Charles-Quint', col. 831 n. 1, Perrenot to Marie, 17 Nov. 1551. See also *NBD*, XII, 28–30, Bertano to Julius III, 8 June 1551, complaining about the difficulty of getting an audience, and still more a decision, from Charles because he spent so much time hunting.

25. Gachard, 'Charles-Quint', col. 830 n. 3, Perrenot to Marie, 14 June 1551.

26. *LCK*, III, 78–83, Marie to Perrenot, 5 Oct. 1551. Charles left Augsburg for Innsbruck on 2 Nov.

27. Giles, *The whole works*, III, 9 and 28–30, Ascham's *Report* (which, alas, ends when Maurice began his march towards Innsbruck). Von Druffel, *Beiträge*, I, 674, Gerhard Veltwyk to Charles V, July 1551, recorded Frederick's anger against Ávila.

28. *NBD*, XII, 155–60, Nuncio Camaiani to del Monte, 27 Jan. 1552. Charles had not seen his daughter since 1543; the grandchildren he met were Anna, two years old, who would later marry his son Philip, and Ferdinand, aged nine months, who died the following year. María was also pregnant (her son Rudolf, the future Emperor Rudolf II, was born in July) and she remained in Innsbruck with her father until 11 Feb. 1552.

29. ASF *MdP* 4313 # 44, Pandolfini to Duke Cosimo, 28 Dec. 1551; *NBD*, XII, 143–6, Camaiani to del Monte, 12 Jan. 1552.

30. Grata, *Des lettres*, 258–60, Perrenot to Niccolò Belloni, 1 Jan. 1552; von Druffel, *Beiträge*, II, 54–9, Perrenot to Viglius, 24 Jan. 1552; Gachard, 'Charles-Quint', col. 834 n. 1, Perrenot to Marie, 27 Jan. 1552, and Charles to Marie, 26 Feb. 1552.

31. *LCK*, III, 98–106, Instructions to M. de Rye, 3 Mar. 1552, listing the concessions that Charles was now prepared to make; von Druffel, *Briefe*, II, 70–1, Charles to Marie, 28 Jan. 1552, holograph postscript.

32. Dumont, *Corps*, IV, part iii, 33–4, Oath of the city of Metz, 21 Apr. 1552.

33. Gachard, 'Charles-Quint', col. 838 n. 2, Charles to Marie, 21 Mar. 1552; *LCK*, III, 107–8, Secret instructions to M. de Rye, 3 Mar. 1552.

34. Fernández Álvarez, *Política mundial*, 306–17, Instructions to Juan Manrique de Lara, 28 Mar. 1552, and AGS *E* 90/7–9, further instructions on 29 Mar. 1552; *CDCV*, IV, 485, Charles to Philip, [29] Mar. 1552 (Fernández Álvarez deduces the date and manner of transfer at ibid., p. 471).

35. *LCK*, III, 159–62, Charles to Ferdinand, 4 Apr. 1552, holograph. Charles's order that his secretary must not send this letter until after he had left Innsbruck demonstrated how much he now distrusted his brother.
36. *CDCV*, III, 420, Charles to Philip, 9 Apr. 1552; Fernández Álvarez, *Política mundial*, 306–17, Instructions to Juan Manrique, 28 Mar. 1552. Both messengers reached Philip at the same time.
37. Gachard, 'Charles V', col. 838 n. 6, Charles to Marie, 15 Apr. 1552.
38. Sandoval, *Historia*, II, 534.
39. *NBD*, XIII, 1 n. 1, Ambassador Savoie to the duke of Ferrara, 22 May 1552; AST *LM Vienna*, 2/348, Stroppiana to Emanuel Philibert of Savoy, 20 May 1552. The Florentine ambassador reported that 'the emperor left Innsbruck in such a hurry that I scarcely had time to pack', and then 'rode the whole night, arriving four hours after sunrise' at Sterzing: ASF *MdP* 4314/134, Pandolfini to Duke Cosimo, 20 May 1552. According to tradition, the emperor fled from Innsbruck in the closed campaign litter now in the Real Armería in Madrid.
40. Greppi, 'Extraits', 219–20, Stroppiana to Emanuel Philibert, Villach, 30 May 1552.
41. *LCK*, III, 300–3 and 305–8, Ferdinand to Charles, Passau, 27 and 28 June 1552.
42. Ibid., 318–29, Charles to Ferdinand, 30 June 1552 (von Druffel, *Briefe*, II, 645–50, printed a different version of the same letter, followed by a list of the concessions Charles was prepared to make: ibid., 650–5).This letter is also the source of all quotations in the next paragraph. See further details of the debate over the treaty in Greppi, 'Extraits', 227–8, Stroppiana to Emanuel Philibert, 10 July 1552.
43. *LCK*, III, 329, Charles to Ferdinand, 30 June 1552, holograph postscript; von Druffel, *Briefe*, II, 658, Charles to Maximilian, Villach, 1 July 1552, holograph.
44. BNE *Ms.* 7915, unfol., Raimundo de Tassis to Perrenot, Madrid, 9 June 1552; von Druffel, *Briefe*, II, 681–7, Charles to Marie, Lienz, 16 July 1552; *NBD*, XIII, 20–2, Camaiani to del Monte, 5 July 1552 (italics added).
45. AGS *E* 647/30, Luis de Orejuela to Gonzalo Pérez, Brixen, 28 July 1552; Turba, *Venetianische Depeschen*, II, 536–9, Marc'Antonio Damula to the Signory, Innsbruck, 4 Aug. 1552. Von Druffel, *Briefe*, III, 532–5, printed Charles's Ratification of the treaty of Passau, Munich, 15 Aug. 1552.
46. *CDCV*, III, 478, Charles's instruction to Figueroa, [6] Sep. 1552 (on this date, see n. 48 below).
47. *NBD*, XIII, 107–11, Camaiani to del Monte, Esslingen, 9 and 11 Sep. 1552. The Florentine ambassador noted that Charles 'rode in full armour': ASF *MdP*, 4314, unfol., Pandolfini to Cosimo, 13 Sep. 1552.
48. AGS *E* 90/97–8, Eraso to Philip, 27 Sep. 1552; *CDCV*, III, 478, Charles's instruction to Figueroa, his envoy to Philip, [6] Sep. 1552. Fernández Álvarez (loc. cit.) dated the document 18 Sep., but Lutz, *Christianitas afflicta*, 106, plausibly proposed a date of 4, 5 or 6 Sep.
49. AGS *E* 648/85, Charles to Ferrante Gonzaga, 28 June 1552; Brandi, 'Karl V. vor Metz', 26–30, Charles to Marie, 23 Sep. 1552.
50. *LCK*, III, 512–13, Charles to Marie, 13 Nov. 1552, holograph; AGS *E* 90/97–8, Eraso to Philip, 27 Sep. 1552.
51. *NBD*, XIII, 92–6 and 116–20, Camaiani to del Monte, 22–23 Aug. and 16 Sep. 1552, both cyphered.
52. *CDCV*, III, 542, Charles to Philip, 25 Dec. 1552, explaining why and how he had besieged Metz; AGS *E* 90/97–8, Eraso to Philip, 27 Sep. 1552. The Florentine ambassador noted that Charles 'did not want Albert Alcibiades to kiss his hand', but Alba convinced him that it was necessary: ASF *MdP*, 4314, unfol., Pandolfini to Cosimo, 23 Nov. 1552.
53. AGS *E* 90/97–8, Eraso to Philip, 27 Sep. 1552; Zeller, *Le siège*, 105–6, Charles to Marie, 21 Oct. 1552.
54. GRM *Introduction*, 28 n. 1, Bossu to Marie, 23 Oct. and 21 Nov. 1552; Le Petit, *La grande chronique*, II, 208.
55. *CDCV*, III, 543, Charles to Philip, 25 Dec. 1552; ASF *MdP*, 4314, unfol., Pandolfini to Cosimo, 29 Nov. 1552. See also Zeller, *Le siège*, 126–7, Charles to Marie, 14 Nov. 1552, criticizing 'those who say that I am hazarding my entire reputation if I do not prevail'.
56. Zeller, *Le siège*, 145–6, Charles to Marie, 11 Dec. 1552 (about the mines); *NBD*, XIII, 395–402, report of Camaiani's secretary on his clandestine visit to the siege-works around Metz, 20 Nov.–12 Dec. 1552; Turba, *Venetianische Depeschen*, II, 578–80, Damula to the Signory, 20 Dec. 1552.
57. Brantôme, *Oeuvres complètes*, IV, 89 ('Ç'a été le plus beau siège qui fût jamais'); Greppi, 'Extraits', 233–4, Stroppiana to Savoy, 31 Dec. 1552; TNA *SP* 68/11 no. 604, Richard Morison to the Privy Council, Jan. 1553; *CCG*, IV, 554, Perrenot to Morillon, 18 Mar. 1573.
58. Zeller, *Le siège*, 153–4, Charles to Marie, 20 Dec. 1552; Reiffenberg, *Lettres*, 76–8, van Male to Praet, 23 Nov. 1552 (ibid., 44–5, same to same, 5 May 1551, also mentioned the emperor 'repeatedly reading the Psalms of David, which inspire him'); Pérez de Tudela Bueso, *Documentos*, I, 207–9, La Gasca to van Male, 23 Aug. 1553, commenting on the emperor's book recently sent from the Netherlands.

59. Zeller, *Le siège*, 154–5, Charles to Marie, 22 Dec. 1552 (he did not yet know that Hesdin had surrendered on the 18th). He gave the same rationale to his son: *CDCV*, III, 553, Charles to Philip, 25 Dec. 1552.

60. Zeller, *Le siège*, 258–63, and Rosenthal, 'Plus Ultra', 216, discussed the celebratory medals.

61. Greppi, 'Extraits', 238, Stroppiana to Savoy, 10 Feb. 1553; Turba, *Venetianische Depeschen*, II, 590–2, Damula to the Signory, 11 Feb. 1553; Rigault, 'Une relation inédite', 302.

62. Linas, *Translation*, and Finot, 'Compte', documented the transfer of the duke's bones from Nancy to Luxemburg in 1550 (and on to Bruges in 1562).

63. Turba, *Venetianische Depeschen*, II, 587–9, Damula to the Signory, 23 Jan. 1553 (with details on the composition of the opposing factions at Charles's court).

64. Spanish calculations by Tracy, *Emperor*, 240–5; Netherlands totals from ADN *B* 2482, 2493, and Henne, *Histoire*, X, 87, Accounts of Receiver-General Robert de Bouloingne for 1550, 1552 and 1553. See also Braudel, 'Les emprunts'.

65. Reiffenberg, *Lettres*, 89–92, van Male to de Praet, 24 Dec. 1552; GRM *Introduction*, 30 n. 1, Cornelis van Baersdorp to Marie, 30 Dec. 1552; TNA *SP* 68/11 no. 604, Morison to the Privy Council, Jan. 1553, holograph.

66. Turba, *Venetianische Depeschen*, II, 590–2, Damula to the Signory, 11 Feb. 1553; Greppi. 'Extraits', 237, Stroppiana to Savoy, 4 Feb. 1553. A Florentine envoy also feared that Charles would soon die: ASF *MdP*, 4314, unfol., Bartolomeo Concini to Duke Cosimo, 5 and 10 Jan. 1553.

67. Henne, *Histoire*, X, 13–17, printed Charles's speech on 13 Feb. 1553; Turba, *Venetianische Depeschen*, II, 603–7, Damula to the Signory, 19 May 1553.

68. AGS *E* 98/274–5, Memorial of Francisco Duarte, sent to Philip in Sep. 1553 but composed over a long period and incorporating an oral report from 'NN' – Nicholas Nicolay – also undated, but certainly completed before June, when Duarte left the Netherlands; Turba, *Venetianische Depeschen*, II, 603–7, Damula to the Signory, 19 May 1553 (on Praet); *PEG*, III, 639–41, Charles to Perrenot, 20 Apr. 1553.

69. *CDCV*, III, 577–92, Charles to Philip, 2 Apr. 1553, with a postscript dated 27 Apr. – evidently the date on which Charles entrusted the letter to the duke of Alba, because the prince replied to this one; ibid., 592–5, Philip to Charles, 18 May 1553. All quotations in this and the subsequent paragraph come from this letter.

70. *CDCV*, III, 583–4, Charles to Philip, Brussels, 2 Apr. 1553.

71. Martens, *Militaire architectuur*, 225, Roeulx to Marie of Hungary, 5 Apr. 1553; ibid., 283–4, Order of Charles V, 19 June 1553; Rabutin, *Commentaires*, I, 199 (on Thérouanne), and 203 (on Hesdin).

72. *NBD*, XIII, 259–61 and 269–78, bishop of Imola to the pope, 28 May, 8 and 10 June 1553 (Perrenot quoted in the second letter). Charles was no doubt aware of an assassination attempt planned in 1546: Henne, *Histoire*, VIII, 298, letter from Roeulx to Marie.

73. *NBD*, XIII, 298–9, Imola to the pope, 29 Aug. 1553, cyphered insert; TNA *SP* 69/1/69, Bishop Thirlby to the Privy Council, 10 Sep. 1553, and *SP* 69/1/1, Thirlby and Mason to Queen Mary, 10 Oct. 1553. On the 1553 campaign, see Martens, *Militaire architectuur*, ch. 5.

74. AGS *E* 1498/6, untitled paper of late 1554 that begins 'Al tiempo que falesció el Rey Eduardo'; *PEG*, IV, 108–16, Charles to Renard, 20 Sep. 1553, setting forth the arguments to be made to Mary and her council in favour of the 'Spanish match'.

75. *PEG*, IV, 78–7 and 97, Renard to Perrenot, 15 Aug. and 8 Sep. 1553; Gachard, *Voyages*, IV, 99, ambassadors in England to Charles, 16 Aug. 1553, narrating their audience with Mary; ibid., 105, Charles to his ambassadors in England, 22 Aug. 1553; and *PEG*, IV, 113–15, Charles to Renard, 20 Sep. 1553.

76. Gachard, *Voyages*, IV, 12, 11/15 Sep. 1553 (the envoy was Diego de Azevedo, 'coming from the emperor and having visited and seen Queen Mary of England'); *CSPSp*, XI, 177–8, Philip to Charles, 22 Aug. 1553, holograph minute, replying to the emperor's letters dated 30 July 1553. Only after this letter arrived in Brussels on 11 Sep. did serious marriage negotiations begin: *PEG*, IV, 102–4, Perrenot to Renard, 13 Sep. 1553. Rodríguez-Salgado, *Changing face*, 77–9, recorded the strange history of the undelivered letter of 8 Aug. 1553, in which Philip promised to marry his cousin María of Portugal.

77. *PEG*, IV, 108–16, Charles to Renard, 20 Sep. 1553, instructed him to make the crucial concession that Don Carlos would not inherit the Netherlands; *CSPSp*, XI, 326, Renard to Philip, 29 Oct. 1553, urged linguistic study (ironically the prince could not read this critical letter in French and so his clerks had to prepare a Spanish translation).

78. *CDCV*, III, 636–9, Charles to Philip, 16 and 26 Dec. 1553; *CODOIN*, III, 451–3, same to same, 21 Jan. 1554; AGS *E* 807/36–2, 'Escriptura ad cautelam', 4 Jan. 1554.

79. *CDCV*, III, 667, Charles to Philip, 13 Mar. 1554.

80. ASF *MdP* 4316, unfol., Pandolfini to Duke Cosimo, 31 Dec. 1554; AGS *E* 90/147–8, Eraso to Philip, 12 Dec. 1553, minute; *CDCV*, III, 641–4, Charles to Philip, 30 Dec. 1553; *CDCV*, III, 645–6, Charles

to Philip, 19 Jan. 1554. That same day, Secretary Diego de Vargas complained that Charles's ministers 'were all confused because for four or five months he has replied to none of them: AGS E 508/13, Vargas to Philip, 19 Jan. 1554.

81. *NBD*, XIII, 298–9, Nuncio Imola to Cardinal del Monte, 24 June 1553. For other descriptions of Charles's cottage (often referred to as his 'casita' or 'casino'), see Ribier, *Lettres*, II, 633–7; GRM *Introduction*, 77–9; and Heymans, *Le palais du Coudenberg*, 196.

82. *NBD*, XIV, 62–4, Nuncio Muzzarelli to Monte, Brussels 5 May 1554; Zanetti, *Janello*, 53, Charles charter in favour of Janello, 7 Mar. 1552. Zanetti's book, the catalogue of an exhibition mounted in Cremona (Janello's home town), presented fascinating material on the 'prince of clockmakers' and his work.

83. Morales, *Las antigüedades*, ff. 91v–94v (the entry on the 'Microcosm' was the longest concerning a contemporary monument in the entire book); Thieulaine, 'Un livre', 179; Firpo, *Relazioni*, III, 54–5, Relation of Badoer, spring 1557 ('*pottaggio di relogi*').

84. Fernández Álvarez, *Felipe II y su tiempo*, 761, count of Buendía to Philip, 2 Sep. 1552.

85. *CDCV*, IV, 40, Charles to Philip, 30 Apr. 1554; 46, Philip to Charles, 11 May 1554; and 109–10, Philip's instructions to Joanna, 12 July 1554. For more on the process by which Joanna became regent, see Rodríguez-Salgado, *Changing face*, 86–8.

86. TNA *SP* 69/4/147, Mason to Queen Mary, Brussels, 20 June 1554.

87. AGS *PR* 29/10, fifth and last testament of Charles V, Brussels, 6 June 1554 (published with some variations in *CDCV*, IV, 66–98, which noted several errors and omissions in the text published by Sandoval, *Historia*, II, 639–56). Fernández Álvarez, *Carlos V*, 761–79, provided an excellent analysis of this document, noting (among other things) that it cited the will of Isabella the Catholic (and only hers).

88. BMECB *Ms. Granvelle*, V/265–8, codicil to Charles's will, 6 June 1554 written 'in the same imperial hand', copy made in 1624 from a lost original (partially printed in *PEG*, IV, 495–6). Although the emperor signed his testament that day in the presence of three notaries and seven witnesses, he wrote and signed the codicil alone, using his 'small secret seal'. See ch. 14 above for more on Charles's treatment of his four illegitimate children and their mothers.

89. AGS *PR* 55 no. 30, Instructions of Charles to Eraso, Béthune, 1 Sep. 1554, minute, mentioning the 'general document in Latin' (which has apparently not survived) that 'I drew up in Namur' (according to Foronda, *Viajes*, the emperor was in Namur between 27 July and 2 Aug. 1554). Charles gave his son a box containing all his extant testaments in the abdication ceremony on 16 Jan. 1556: Mayr, 'Die letzte Abdankung', 156–8, 'Ragionamento'.

90. TNA *SP* 69/4/119, 127 and 153, Mason to Mary, 4, 11 and 26 June 1554; ASF *MdP* 4317, unfol., Pandolfini to Cosimo, 10 June 1554 (it must have been a long audience, but mercifully the ambassador omitted the secret of the emperor's preferred haemorrhoid treatment from his report 'because it really isn't important'); *CSPV*, V, 516–17, Damula to the Signory, 30 June 1554. The nuncio also noted that Charles now rode in the park every day: *NBD*, XIV, 58–62 and 79–82, Girolamo Muzzarelli, archbishop of Consa, to del Monte, 5 May and 15 June 1554.

91. *CDCV*, IV, 98–102, Charles to Philip, 29 June 1554, minute.

92. *NBD*, XIV, 93–4, Muzzarelli to del Monte, 8 July 1554; TNA *SP* 69/4/165, Mason to Secretary Petrie, 10 July 1554. The nuncio also reported that Charles's council of war opposed his strategy (*NBD*, XIV, 90 n. 1, Muzzarelli to del Monte, 6 July 1554); so did the Florentine ambassador (ASF *MdP* 4317, unfol., Pandolfini to Cosimo, 4 July 1554).

93. TNA SP 69/5/18, Mason to the Privy Council, 13 Aug. 1554, noting that the campaign would have been very different if 'they had been 2 castells of Millan'.

94. ASF *MdP*, 4317, unfol., Pandolfini to Cosimo, 22 July 1554 (adding 'this shows how much he enjoys being with the army'); *NBD*, XIV, 97 n. 8 and 100–2, Muzzarelli to del Monte, 15 and 22 July 1554; Thieulaine, 'Un livre', 185, 191; Anon., 'Dagverhaal', 282–3, 286.

95. TNA *SP* 69/5/2, Mason to Mary, 2 Aug. 1554; AGS *E* 508/187, 'Lo que vos, Mos de Obremon, gentil-hombre de nuestra cámara, hauéys de hazer en Inglaterra', 'del campo', 4 Aug. 1554, minute.

96. Salignac, *Le voyage*, sig. Gi', part of an account of the campaign by a French eyewitness; Gachard, 'L'abdication', 882 n. 2, Marie to the bailli of Brabant, 17 Aug. 1554.

97. TNA *SP* 69/5/18, Mason to the Privy Council, 13 Aug. 1554. The ambassador knew whereof he spoke, since he had served at Charles's court intermittently for twenty years: see *ODNB* s.v. 'Sir John Mason'.

98. AGS *E* 508/194, Charles to Philip and to Alba, 'de nuestro exército cerca de Renti', 15 Aug. 1554, Assumption Day, the same letter with different holograph postscripts, both minutes. (*CDCV*, IV, 121–2, incorrectly dates these letters 25 Aug.); Gachard, 'L'abdication', 883 n. 1, Charles to Marie, 16 Aug. 1554.

99. AGS *PR* 55 no. 30, Instructions of Charles to Eraso, Béthune, 1 Sep. 1554, minute.

CHAPTER 16: RESTLESS RETIREMENT, 1555–8

1. TNA *SP* 69/5/58, Mason to Queen Mary, Brussels, 10 Oct. 1554; *NBD*, XIV, 140 n. 6, Nuncio Muzzarelli to Cardinal del Monte, 14 Oct. 1554 (Charles 'went hunting yesterday'); Tytler, *England*, II, 456, Mason to Philip and Mary, 9 Nov. 1554; AGS *E* 508/235–6, Secretary Diego de Vargas to Philip, 30 Nov. 1554; Tytler, *England*, II, 462–6, Mason to the Privy Council, 25 Dec. 1554 (Mason wrote the passage in italics in French, adding – unfortunately for historians – 'which, for that it were too long to write, I do omit').

2. *CODOIN*, III, 531–6, Ruy Gómez to Eraso, 12 Aug. 1554, and reply, 29 Nov. 1554 (annotations by Philip on Eraso's reply show that the prince himself read his father's spiteful words).

3. AGS *PR* 55 no. 30 and no. 27 ff. 124–7, Instructions of Charles to Eraso, 1 Sep. 1554 (only no. 30 is dated, but Eraso evidently also took with him the undated instructions in no. 27).

4. Tytler, *England*, II, 451–7, Mason to Philip and Mary, 9 Nov. 1554.

5. *CSPV*, VI/1, Badoer to the Signory, 3 Jan. 1556. *CDCV*, IV, 118–232, printed a selection of the competing correspondence of Charles and Philip with Joanna.

6. *CDCV*, IV, 127–30, Philip to Charles, London, 16 Nov. 1554; Morel-Fatio, 'Une histoire', 30–1.

7. TNA *SP* 69/6/67–9, Mason to Queen Mary, 11 Apr. 1555.

8. Pastor, *History of the popes*, XIV, 130, report of the Venetian envoy after an audience with Paul IV, July 1555. Lutz, *Christianitas afflicta*, 374–98, provided an excellent account of these developments.

9. ASF *MdP* 4318 unfol., Pandolfini to Duke Cosimo, 31 May 1555; Ribier, *Lettres*, II, 633–7 (Mar. 1556).

10. TNA *SP* 69/6/67–9, Mason to Queen Mary, 11 Apr. 1555; *CSPV*, VI/1, 39–41, Badoer to the Signory, 6 Apr. 1555; TNA *SP* 69/6/75, Mason to the Privy Council, 26 Apr. 1555 (printed with some errors in Tytler, *England*, II, 466–8). In fact Charles had received the insignia in Feb. 1509, forty-six years before: see ch. 1.

11. Jordan Gschwend, 'Verdadero padre', 3,030–1, Anna de Andrade to Catalina, Charles's youngest sister and queen of Portugal, Brussels, 15 Aug. 1554; Bataillon, 'Charles-Quint', 402, quoting Fray Cipriano de Huerga's sermon in Alcalá on 19 Apr. 1556. Sepúlveda, *Historia de Carlos V*, Book XXX, ch. 25, claimed that 'around the age of fifty, his teeth began to fall out'.

12. Aram, *Juana*, 277–8, noted the sigh of relief among Philip's courtiers on hearing of his grandmother's death. Stirling-Maxwell, *Notices*, 27, recorded the emperor's decree in Jan. 1556 permitting others to recommence wearing silk, but stating that he would continue to wear mourning for his mother until he died.

13. *LCK*, III, 622–8 and 681–3, Charles to Ferdinand, 8 [*recte* 10] June 1554 and 19 Sep. 1555 (Charles wrote that he had decided 'de non me plus *enveloper* en ce point de religion' – a very strong statement). *RTA*, XX/4, 3,012–3,158, printed all 144 articles of the *Reichsabschied*, issued on 25 Sep. 1555, with the religious peace at its heart. Tüchle, 'The peace', provided an excellent overview of the framing and implementation of the peace.

14. *CSPV*, VI/1, 186–8, Badoer to the Signory, Brussels, 14 Sep. 1555; *NBD*, XIV, 302–4, Muzzarelli to Paul IV, 15 Sep. 1555; Gachard, *Analectes Belgiques*, 70–2, Charles to the governor of Hainaut, 26 Sep. 1555.

15. Gachard, 'L'abdication', 891–4, on the delinquent provinces (Hainaut and Guelders; Overijssel and Drenthe), and 901 and 923–48 on the rest. See also the account of these events in *CSPV*, VI/1, 214–16 and 218–20, Badoer to the Signory, Brussels 16 and 23 Oct. 1555; and GRM *Introduction*, 82 n. 3 on the total ('There were more than 1,000 people in the great hall'). Le Petit, *La grande chronique*, II, 235, printed Charles's speech on this occasion.

16. Gachard, *Analectes Belgiques*, 77–9, quoting an eyewitness; ASF *MdP* 4319/240v, Ricasoli to Duke Cosimo, 22/26 Oct. 1555; *SLID*, III, 142 n. 111, 'Escrito de Corte'. Other eyewitnesses noted that the emperor '*mist ses lunettes*' and held '*zekere rolleken*' as he spoke: see GRM *Introduction*, 87 n. 1, and *CSPV*, VI/1, 221–4, Badoer to the Signory, 26 Oct. 1555.

17. Speech and events reconstructed from Gachard, *Analectes Belgiques*, 87–91, 'Receuil de ce que l'empereur dit de bouche aux estatz generaulx', almost certainly compiled by Perrenot from the 'notes' used by Charles (I have used the first person); Le Petit, *La grande chronique*, II, 236; Stirling-Maxwell, *Notices*, 14–19, Badoer to the Signory, 26 Oct. 1555; and Kervyn de Lettenhove, *Relations politiques*, I, 4–7, Mason to Petrie, 27 Oct. 1555, with a 'Note' of the proceedings. Other details from ASF *MdP* 4319/240v, Ricasoli to Duke Cosimo, 22/26 Oct. 1555; *SLID*, III, 142 n. 111, 'Escrito de Corte'; and the Spanish *Cancionero* and Ieper Manuscript cited in GRM. For the difficulties in reconciling these and other accounts of the ceremony, see p. 572 below.

18. GRM *Introduction*, 98, printed an account by Joachim Viglius of 'every word the king spoke'. Sir John Mason noted with disapproval that 'the king could not himself well speake unto the people in such language as apperteyned': Kervyn de Lettenhove, *Relations politiques*, I, 6. *PEG*, IV, 486–9, printed Charles's act of abdication as ruler of the Netherlands, Brussels, 25 Oct. 1555.

19. Gachard, *Analectes Belgiques*, 102–6, letters patent, 25 Oct. 1555. Since the ceremony left everyone exhausted, Philip and the States-General did not exchange oaths until the following day: ibid., 79–80.
20. *CSPV*, VI/1, 242–3 and 288–9, Badoer to the Signory, 11 Nov. and 22 Dec. 1555.
21. Stirling-Maxwell, *Notices*, 28–33, Badoer to the Signory, 16 Jan. 1556 (summarized in *CSPV*, VI/1, 317–18). See also the contemporary account of the ceremony printed by Mayr, 'Die letzte Abdankung', 156–8. Did Charles use the same notes for this speech? The sources are silent.
22. GRM *Introduction*, 110–42, provides details on each renunciation; AGS *PR* 45/9, Charles's nomination of Philip as his vicar-general in Italy, 16 Jan. 1556. Obstruction by Aragonese officials forced Charles to make a second renunciation of that crown in July 1556, and even then Philip was formally recognized as king only when he went there in person in 1564: Buyreu Juan, *La corona de Aragón*, 85–90.
23. *CSPV*, VI/1, 321–2, Badoer to the Signory, 19 Jan. 1556; Rodríguez-Salgado, 'Los últimos combates', 97, Charles to Maximilian, Jan. 1556.
24. Stirling-Maxwell, *Notices*, 14–19, Badoer to the Signory, 31 Mar. 1556 (summarized in *CSPV*, VI/1, 394–5).
25. Ribier, *Lettres*, II, 633–7 (also printed in Cimber and Danjou, *Archives curieuses*, 1ᵉ série, III, 296–306), eyewitness account of the French embassy in Mar. 1556; *CSPV*, VI/1, 389–90, Badoer to the Signory, 28 Mar. 1556 (Fregoso's children); Paredes, 'The confusion' (the tapestries). No doubt Charles remembered the poignant stanzas 330–3 towards the end of *The resolute knight*, about the inexorable loss of functions that came with age: La Marche, *Le chevalier délibéré*, 283–5.
26. ASF *MdP* 4319/528, Ricasoli to Duke Cosimo, 31 Mar. 1556; Kervyn de Lettenhove, *Relations politiques*, I, 43, Mason to Peter Vannes, 29 June 1556.
27. *CSPV*, VI/1, 468–71, Badoer to the Signory, 31 May 1556.
28. *LCK*, III, 693, Charles to Ferdinand, 3 Nov. 1556. Ibid., III, 698–9 and 702–3, same to same, 5, 16 and 28 May 1556, filled with complaints about the delays.
29. Badoer noted the tears as Charles left Brussels: Stirling-Maxwell, *Notices*, 51–2. On the 600-day imperial interregnum, see Neuhaus, 'Von Karl V. zu Ferdinand I.'. Kohler, *Quellen*, 480–2, printed Charles's concession of full powers to his brother, dated 3 Aug. 1556.
30. *PEG*, IV, 469–80, Marie to Charles, undated but late Aug. 1555 (a fascinating letter). Rumours that Marie intended to retire to Spain with her brother had long circulated at court: *NBD*, XIV, 176–7, Muzzarelli to Monte, 18 Nov. 1554, relating 'li discorsi de speculativi'.
31. ASF *MdP* 4320/152–3, Ricasoli to Duke Cosimo, 29 Aug. 1556. The ambassador added 'I was astonished that he confided in me for so long'. Paul IV had just turned eighty; he would outlive Charles by almost a year.
32. *CSPV*, VI/1, 622–4, Badoer to the Signory, 16 Sep. 1556; BNF *F.f.* 16,121/295–316, 'Discours de l'embarquement de l'empereur', compiled by an agent of the French ambassador on 30 Oct. 1556. See also *SLID*, III, 169 n. 137, entries from the log kept by the commander of Charles's fleet, Luis de Carvajal.
33. AGS *E* 883/15, Juan Manrique de Lara to Princess Joanna, Rome, 1 Apr. 1556 (the pope said that 'hera la más rrara cosa que se havía visto'); Ribadeneyra, *Vida*, f. 98v (based on what Borja 'himself told me some years later', adding that although initially kept a secret, Charles told Borja at their meeting: 'Now that I have followed through, you can talk about it'); Sigüenza, *Historia*, II, 148 (claiming that Charles ordered this inspection of Yuste 'more than twelve years before' the visit of Prince Philip in 1554 – in other words, in or before 1542). The 'so-and-so' was surely Luis de Ávila y Zúñiga, who lived close to the convent at Yuste, with which he would have been familiar (as Charles was not). Ávila was also probably one of the 'learned and prudent men' mentioned by Sigüenza.
34. AGS *PR* 55/30, Instructions to Francisco de Eraso on what he must say to Philip, 1 Sep. 1554; Stirling-Maxwell, *Notices*, 28–33, Badoer to the Signory, 16 Jan. 1556 (summarized in *CSPV*, VI/1, 317–18), substituting the first for the third person in both.
35. Mignet, *Charles-Quint*, 188 n. 1, Lorenzo Pirez de Tavora to John III, Yuste, 15 Feb. 1558.
36. Anon., *La renunciación*, first item (a two-page broadsheet published in 1556, which included the words 'desde su niñez tuuo propósito de lo hacer así'). In 1550–1 Charles had translated *The resolute knight* from French into Spanish: Gonzalo Sánchez-Molero, *Regia biblioteca*, I, 314–15, and Checa Cremades, 'El caballero'.
37. GRM *Introduction*, 40–1, Charles's warrant to García de Castro, 30 June 1553, and to Philip, 17 Dec. 1553 (Gachard argued that both documents were written in 1554, not 1553, but this makes no sense because the monks at Yuste actually *received* the 3,000 ducats on 25 June 1554). Pizarro Gómez, 'El monasterio', 97–9 and 103, described the phase of construction work that began in 1539, the year of the empress's death: a tantalizing clue that Charles may have already considered retiring to Yuste.
38. GRM, II, 4 (Corral); GRM *Introduction*, 163–4, Fray Juan de Ortega to Charles, 9 Aug. 1554. The same configuration would later characterize Philip's apartments at El Escorial.

39. Checa Cremades, 'Venezia', 140, Titian to Cardinal Farnese, 16 Jan. 1567; Checa Cremades, *Inventarios*, I, 265, Inventory dated 18 Aug. 1556 ('Premièrement de la Trinité, faicte par Tisiane, en grande forme, sur toile').

40. ADN *B* 2510/636, Account of Receiver-General Robert de Bouloingne for 1555 (Vermeyen); Checa Cremades, *Inventarios*, I, 266 and 299, the 1556 and 1558 inventories: portrait of 'la rreyna de Ynglaterra' by '*Tomás Moro*'. Both Mancini, 'Los últimos cuadros', and Baker-Bates, 'The "cloister life"', reproduced and discussed the religious paintings that Charles took with him to Yuste.

41. Checa Cremades, *Inventarios*, I, 261–5 ('Inventario de vajillas, pinturas y objetos litúrgicos', Brussels, 18 Aug. 1556), and 597–8 (Inventory post-mortem of Charles's goods). Zanetti, *Janello*, included reproductions of 'small round portable clocks' similar to the ones that accompanied Charles.

42. Gonzalo Sánchez-Molero, *Regia biblioteca*, I, 311–37, discussed the books Charles took with him to Yuste and their focus on 'ars moriendi' (*The resolute knight* fell into this category), and noted that at Yuste the emperor could and did read other books brought by visitors. Ibid., I, 263–94 discussed the books deposited in 1543 in the archive-fortress of Simancas. The 'Estatutas' volume is now IVdeDJ signatura 26-I-27 (a facsimile was published in 1998).

43. Rodríguez-Salgado, 'Los últimos combates', 97, Charles to Maximilian, Jan. 1556; GRM, II, 8 and 19 (from Corral's 'Historia breve'). Reglá had come to Charles's notice by 1551, when the emperor sent him to the council of Trent so that 'aya allí letrados de la corona de Aragón': AGS *E* 646/49, Charles to María, 9 July 1551.

44. GRM, I, 4, Fray Juan de Ortega to Juan Vázquez de Molina, Yuste, 5 Oct. 1556, and 5–6, Gaztelú to Vázquez de Molina, Laredo, 6 Oct. 1556. *SLID*, III, 166–7 and nn. 130–1, printed Philip's letters about preparations.

45. GRM, I, 7–11, Quijada to Vázquez de Molina, 6 and 8 Oct. 1556.

46. *CSPV*, VI/1, 638–40, Giovanni Michiel to the Signory, 22 Sep. 1556, and 631–3, Bernardo Navagero to the Signory, 19 Sep. 1556; *CSPV*, VI/2, 719–23, Navagero and Pebo Capella to the Signory, 20 Oct. 1556. On Paul's legal moves against the emperor in 1556–7, see Tellechea Idígoras, 'Lo que el emperador no supo'. Paul had served as a papal diplomat at Charles's court in the Netherlands in 1516–17 and in Spain in 1518–19, later claiming that he had resigned 'because he could not bear the tyranny of Charles': *CSPV*, VI/1, 700–4, Navagero and Capella to the Doge, Rome, 12 Oct. 1556, after an audience.

47. GRM, I, 6–7, Quijada to Vázquez de Molina, Laredo, 6 Oct. 1556; *SLID*, III, 232 ('Retiro, estancia y muerte'); GRM, II, lxvii n. 1, Charles to the count of Alcaudete, 6 Sep. 1557 (together with more examples of Charles refusing to become involved in public affairs). For the emperor's use of 'en mi tiempo', see GRM, I, 300, and II, 485–6.

48. *SLID*, III, 234–6 ('Retiro, estancia y muerte'). See also p. 343 above for Charles's praise of bed linen made of American feathers sent to keep him warm.

49. GRM, I, 39–43, Quijada to Vázquez de Molina, and Gaztelú to the same, Jarandilla, 14 and 15 Nov. 1556; *SLID*, III, 236. See also *SLID*, I, map facing p. 144, 'Itinerario de Carlos V, desde Bruselas a Yuste'.

50. GRM, I, 41–51, Gaztelú to Vázquez de Molina, 15, 18 and 20 Nov. 1556, and Quijada to the same, 18 and 20 Nov. 1556 – letters filled with complaints. Gaztelú referred to the twenty-seven days of rain in a later letter: GRM, II, 145 n. 1, to Vázquez de Molina, 28 Dec. 1557.

51. Stirling-Maxwell, *The cloister life*, 50.

52. GRM, I, 84–6, Quijada to Vázquez de Molina, 6 Jan. 1557.

53. Clifford, *Photographic scramble*, 19 (I thank Patrick Lenaghan for this reference); Perla, 'Anton van den Wyngaerde', 35 (the same article convincingly dated the drawing to 1567).

54. GRM, II, 13 (Hernando del Corral); GRM, II, 264–5, Quijada to Joanna, 31 Oct. 1557 (Charles the gardener). Other information from Perla, 'Una visita', and idem, 'Anton van den Wyngaerde'.

55. GRM, I, 234–5, Quijada to Vázquez de Molina, 27 Dec. 1557 (the sauna); Martín González, 'El palacio', XXIII, 39–40 (building accounts).

56. Details from Checa Cremades, *Inventarios*, I, 281–834, Inventory post-mortem of Charles's goods; and Martín González, 'El palacio', XXIII, 51 (17,500 ducats, plus the items appropriated without compensation by Philip).

57. Gonzalo Sánchez-Molero, *Regia biblioteca*, I, 324–5, quoted Sigüenza and tentatively identified the Book of Hours as BNE *Ms.* Vit/24/3, available online at http://bdh-rd.bne.es/viewer. vm?id=0000051953&page=1.

58. GRM, II, 22–6. Sigüenza later included Corral's account virtually verbatim (without acknowledgement) in his *Historia*: GRM, II, pp. vi–x, and *SLID*, II, 233–7, notes, pointed out the discrepancies.

59. *SLID*, II, 35, from the 'Vida y fin' written by Prior Martín de Angulo ('¡Oh, hideputa bermejo! Aquél erró').

60. Sandoval, *Historia*, 'Historia de la vida que el emperador Carlos V rey de España hizo retirado en el monasterio de Iuste', Book VII, italics added. Francisco Guerrero (1528–99) presumably presented his *Sacrarum cantionum quae vulgo moteta nuncupata, 4 et 5 vocum* (Seville, 1555). Charles's daughter Joanna owned a copy at her death, perhaps inherited from the emperor.
61. Sepúlveda, *Historia de Carlos V*, VI, p. CIV (Sepúlveda to van Male, 1 June 1557, about Sleidan) and 155–6 (Book XXX: 31, on the interview); GRM, I, 308–10, Charles to Vázquez de Molina, 9 July 1558. See Appendix I below on the *Memoirs*.
62. GRM, II, 25 (Corral); GRM, I, 89–90, Gaztelú to Vázquez de Molina, 16 Jan. 1557. Cadenas y Vicent, *Carlos*, 97, noted 237 surviving letters.
63. Rodríguez-Salgado, *Changing face*, 132.
64. Kervyn de Lettenhove, *Relations politiques*, I, 54–9, Philip's instructions to Ruy Gómez, 2 Feb. 1557 (changing third person to first).
65. AGS *E* 128/326, Charles to Philip, Yuste, 15 Nov. 1557, with a holograph postscript; and *E* 128/317, 'Relación de cartas del emperador a Su Magestad.' Eraso endorsed both documents.
66. GRM, II, 186–7 and 195–6, Charles to Valdés, 18 May and 2 June 1557 (see the rest of the acrimonious correspondence at pp. 188–203). Charles had nominated Valdés to Seville after Loaysa died in 1546; Valdés eventually loaned 50,000 ducats instead of the 150,000 requested.
67. BNE *Ms.* Caja 18,667/90, Secretary Vargas to Juan de Vega, 4 Nov. 1557, copy (the visitor was Ruy Gómez da Silva); *CODOIN*, XCVII, 335–9, an anonymous minister, almost certainly Gutierre López de Padilla, to Ruy Gómez, Valladolid, 4 Jan. 1558.
68. GRM, I, 170, Quijada to Vázquez de Molina, 4 Sep. 1557; ibid., I, 218, Gaztelú to the same, 23 Nov. 1557.
69. *CDCV*, IV, 296–7, Charles to Joanna, 31 Jan. 1557; and 415, Charles to Philip, 31 Mar. 1558, holograph postscript. Although Oran was saved, in July 1558 a Franco-Turkish fleet captured and sacked Ciutadella on Menorca – 'the greatest disaster suffered by the Spanish Monarchy in the Mediterranean in the 16th century' – but Charles probably died before hearing about it: Vidal, 'La defensa', 586–7.
70. *CDCV*, IV, 309–11, Charles to Joanna, 1 Apr. 1557, copy of holograph; GRM, I, 148–9, Gaztelú to Vázquez de Molina, 12 May 1557 (reporting a rant by the emperor).
71. *CODOIN*, XCVII, 335–9, an anonymous minister, almost certainly Gutierre López de Padilla, to Ruy Gómez, Valladolid, 4 Jan. 1558.
72. Tellechea Idígoras, *Tiempos Recios*, IV, 329–32, Charles to Joanna, and AGS *E* 128/1, Charles to Philip, both from Yuste on 25 May 1558. Ironically, despite this zeal, Charles's library at Yuste included several works condemned by the inquisition: see details in Gonzalo Sánchez-Molero, *Regia biblioteca*, I, 322–4, who concluded unkindly (but accurately): 'Heresy arrived at Yuste in the emperor's baggage.'
73. Rodríguez-Salgado, *Changing face*, 211; and 'Los últimos combates', 104.
74. Quotations from the letters cited above, with italics added.
75. GRM, II, 120–3, Quijada to Vázquez de Molina, 6 Dec. 1557; *SLID*, III, 544, Mathys to Philip, 1 Apr. 1558.
76. GRM, II, 22 (Fray Hernando del Corral, noting the visit of the future Don John in a chapter that stressed how few visitors Charles allowed). The only other eyewitness to record the visit of Doña Magdalena ('whom His Majesty had asked to visit him') did not mention Gerónimo, no doubt because he did not know the boy's true identity: GRM, II, 454–5, Gaztelú to Vázquez de Molina, 19 July 1558.
77. GRM, I, 449–50, Quijada to Philip, 13 Dec. 1558, explaining to his new master how he intended to raise Gerónimo until Philip returned and stating that Charles wanted 'this to remain secret until Your Majesty's arrival and that thereafter we should do whatever Your Majesty might order'. (Naturally, Charles had assumed he would still be alive when Philip returned.) Corral stated that the future Don John of Austria stood close to Quijada throughout the exequies (GRM, II, 54–5). The historical novel by Uslar Pietri, *La visita en el tiempo*, begins as the eleven-year-old Don John watches Quijada and others compile an inventory of the goods of the late emperor, whom he does not yet know was his father. (I thank José Luis Gonzalo Sánchez-Molero for this reference.) In 1563 some of those goods were purchased for 'the use of Don John of Austria': Checa Cremades, *Inventarios*, I, 558–62.
78. Checa Cremades, *Inventarios*, I, 288, 'Inventario Postmórtem', commenced 28 Sep. 1558.
79. On the herbal cure for the imperial haemorrhoids see the letters printed in GRM, I, 121–5 and 144–6, and II, 109–10. García Simón, *El ocaso*, ch. 6, described the emperor's litany of health problems while at Yuste.
80. GRM, II, 314–15, Ávila to Vázquez de Molina, 28 Feb. 1558; *SLID*, III, 544, Mathys to Philip, 1 Apr. 1558 (translated from Latin).

81. GRM, II, 470–2, Quijada to Vázquez de Molina, 9 Aug. 1558 ('por el gran calor que haze y él [Charles] siente, duerme ventanas y puertas abiertas').
82. GRM, I, lxxxix–xc, 'Historia breve' by Corral, reprinted *SLID*, II, 125. Although Sigüenza embellished the story in his *Historia* (*SLID*, II, 249–50), he clearly relied on Fray Hernando's account. An inscription at Yuste records that 'the emperor was sitting down here when he fell ill on 31 August 1558 at 4 p.m.' (Fernández Álvarez, *Carlos V: el César*, 846 n. 20).
83. GRM, I, 331–6, Dr Mathys to Vázquez de Molina, 3 and 4 Sep. 1558, and Quijada to Vázquez de Molina and Joanna, 4 Sep. 1558 (two letters); ibid., I, 353–4, Mathys to Vázquez de Molina, 8 Sep. 1558; ibid., I, 370–3, Quijada to Philip, 17 Sep. 1558.
84. AGS *PR* 29/11, 'Codicillo original que otorgó el emperador Don Carlos', 9 Sep. 1558 (printed in Sandoval, *Historia*, II, 657–61, but without indicating the numerous attached affidavits, additions and signatures).
85. GRM, I, 365–6 and 377, Quijada to Vázquez de Molina, 14 and 18 Sep. 1558, both holograph; and ibid., 374–5, Mathys to Vázquez de Molina, 18 Sep. 1558. *SLID*, III, 633–75, published a day-by-day account of the emperor's last three weeks compiled from the surviving sources in Simancas by the archivist Tomás González (see pp. 570–1 above).
86. GRM, II, 506–7, Quijada to Philip, 12 Oct. 1558.
87. GRM, II, 413–14, Mathys to Vázquez de Molina, 30 May and 19 June 1558; Gonzalo Sánchez-Molero, *Regia biblioteca*, I, 323–4. Gonzalo Sánchez-Molero, *El César*, 346, suggested that Charles possessed a French Bible, burnt before his death; and on p. 344 he demonstrated that the imperial library at Yuste included a work by Erasmus (his *Precatio Dominica*) even though all previous scholars have denied it. On Dr Egidio, favoured by Charles and defended by Domingo de Soto, see Luttikhuizen, *Underground Protestantism*, 188–99; on Constantino, who accompanied Philip II on his grand tour in 1548 and again to England, see ibid., 200–11.
88. Tellechea Idígoras, 'Carlos V', 51–2, and idem, *Así murió*, 79–80, testimony of Fray Luis de San Gregorio, an eyewitness of the exchange. Joanna had warned her father 'to be cautious' when he met Carranza because, according to Valdés, some of the Lutherans imprisoned in Valladolid had incriminated the archbishop (AGS *E* 128/393–5, Joanna to Charles, 8 Aug. 1558, a holograph insert – a highly unusual practice). Don Francisco de Toledo later testified that 'he had heard that His Majesty did not really want [Carranza] there': Tellechea Idígoras, *Así murió*, 93–4.
89. Tellechea Idígoras, *Así murió*, 14–15, citing a passage, later deleted, from Carranza's unpublished manuscript *De recta spe filiorurm Adae*, in which the archbishop described Charles's final agony. The painting was presumably Vermeyen's *Man of sorrows*.
90. Tellechea Idígoras, *Así murió*, 67 and 69, testimony of Fray Francisco de Ángulo, an eyewitness of the exchange.
91. GRM, I, 385–6 and 405–7, Quijada to Vázquez de Molina, 21 and 26 Sep. 1558, and 408–11, Quijada to Philip, 30 Sep. 1558; Tellechea Idígoras, *Así murió*, 70, 61–2 and 94–6, testimony of Fray Francisco de Ángulo, Fray Marcos de Cardona, and Francisco de Toledo (reporting, inter alia, something he heard from his brother, the count of Oropesa). Tellechea Idígoras, *Así murió*, 51–101, printed all the eyewitness depositions. Inquisitor-General Valdés had Carranza arrested in 1559, and he would spend the next seventeen years in prison while first Spanish and then Roman Inquisitors searched for evidence of heresy. *FBD*, 330–48, offers an overview of 'the trial of the century'.
92. Ordi, 'The severe gout', quotation from p. 519; Zulueta, 'The cause', 109; and Zulueta, *Tuan nyamok*, 336–43. For the authenticity of the detached digit, see Appendix II below.
93. Zulueta, 'The cause', 107; idem, *Tuan nyamok*, 342–3.

CHAPTER 17: THE EMPEROR IN LEGEND AND HISTORY

1. Young Marcel probably fell asleep over Jules Michelet's book for children, *François Ier et Charles-Quint 1515-1547* (Paris, 1887).
2. GRM, I, 405–7, Quijada to Vázquez de Molina, 26 Sep. 1558; *SLID*, II, 136 (Corral); Snouckaert van Schouwenburg, *De republica*, first licensed for publication in Ghent in May 1559 and frequently reprinted.
3. Marín Cruzado, 'El retrato', 123, noted three distinct representations of Charles V as one of the Three Kings; Archivo Municipal de Zaragoza, caja 7775, Pope Leo X to Ferdinand of Aragon, 1 Nov. 1515 (my thanks to Bethany Aram for sharing with me this amazing document). Checa Cremades, *Carlos V*, 163–71, provided an excellent survey of 'The image of the emperor as the new messiah'.
4. *NBD*, 2. *Ergänzungsband 1532*, 424–8, Aleandro to Sanga, 21 Aug. 1532, and 441–4, Aleandro to Pope Clement, 1 Sep. 1532. For more on Charles and Molcho (or Molkho), see Lenowitz, *The Jewish Messiahs*, 103–23 (Fig. 5.2, on p. 106, shows Molcho's banner and robe), and Fraenkel-Goldschmidt,

The historical writings, 187–99 and 323–4 (Joseph of Rosheim's account). For more on Charles's messianic contemporaries, see Parker, 'The place', 167–73.

5. Menegus Bornemann, 'Los títulos', 225–30, printed the original titles of Ocoyoacac, a town on the road from Mexico City to Toluca, in which 'our great king Charles V' featured prominently. See also Ruiz Medrano, *Mexico's indigenous communities*, 112–24 and 175–8.

6. Los Santos, *Descripción*, 167–8 and 176; [Caimo], *Lettere*, II, 32–53, letter from El Escorial on 22 Aug. 1755. For more on the imperial cadaver, see Appendix II below.

7. Leti, *Vita*, IV, 412–13 (totals) and 463 (quotation). Auernhammer and Däuble, 'Die exequien', 154–7, and Schraven, *Festive funerals*, table 2.1, provided incomplete lists of funeral services for Charles. Thomas, *Gesammelte Schriften*, I, 435–6, listed the publications down to 1743 that mentioned the 'grosser Totenfeier' in Augsburg, starting with a contemporaneous illustrated manuscript account: ÖNB *Ms. Codex* 7566.

8. Calvete de Estrella, *El tvmvlo* (Valladolid); *La magnifiqve et svmptvevse pompe fvnèbre* (Brussels); Anon., *Aigentliche unnd wahrhaffte Beschreibung* and Thomas, *Gesammelte Schriften*, I, 433–52 (Augsburg).

9. Calvete de Estrella, *El tvmvlo*, f. 6v. Abella Rubio, 'El túmulo', included three reconstructions of the images described by Calvete; Redondo Cantera and Serrão, 'El pintor portugués', documented the duration of Calvete's work on the catafalque. For the ceremonies in other Spanish cities, see Bouza Brey, 'Las exequias' (Santiago de Compostela); Checa Cremades, 'Un programa' (Alcalá de Henares); and Noguiera, 'Les répercussions', 211–13. Sandoval, *Historia*, II, 620–37, published a detailed description of the exequies in Brussels and in Rome (4 Mar. 1559).

10. Burgon, *Life and times*, I, 254–5, Richard Clough to Thomas Gresham, 2 Jan. 1559. On the 1516 ceremony, see ch. 3 above.

11. Rose, 'La hija pródiga', described the commemoration in Lima and suggested (p. 129 n. 1) that Potosí and perhaps Cuzco and Quito also staged exequies.

12. Cervantes de Salazar, *Túmulo Imperial*, 191, 195 (summary in Peset Reig, 'Fundación', 552–3, with an analysis of the texts in Sanchis Amat, 'Los poemas'). The copy of this work in the Biblioteca de la Universidad Complutense de Madrid includes a complete print of the catafalque (other copies reproduced only part): see http://alfama.sim.ucm.es/dioscorides/consulta_libro. asp?ref=B22329791&idioma=0. Olton, 'To shepherd', reproduced and discussed the image of the catafalque from the Tlatelolco Codex, completed in 1562. Bossuyt, 'Charles', 160, noted the Morales connection.

13. Aguirre Landa, 'Viejos y nuevos', 41–4, described the contents of AGS *CSR* 180, 134 and 142 respectively. Varela, *La muerte*, 85 and 145, noted that the will of the Catholic Monarchs called for a more modest 10,000 Masses, whereas that of Philip IV required 100,000 Masses and that of Philip V demanded 200,000.

14. AGS *CSR* 133 legajo 11, f. 108 (total debts exceeded 200,000 ducats); f. 129, *real cédula* of July 1559; and f. 113, *Consulta de descargos*, and Philip's rescript, 11 Feb. 1579.

15. Mulcahy, *Philip II*, 50. Pérez de Tudela, 'El cenotafio', provides a brilliant description of the statues of Charles and his family in the Escorial, and how they arrived there. Perhaps in hope that the commission might be completed in his lifetime, Philip reduced the funeral group from seven to five by eliminating his two infant brothers.

16. *CCG*, XI, 277–8, Juan de Idiáquez to Cardinal Granvelle, El Escorial, 22 Sep. 1584. See *CODOIN*, VII, 90–118 ('Memorias' of Fray Juan de San Jerónimo') and Varela, *La muerte*, 27–8, on the migration of Charles's body to the Escorial. The azulejos of 1577–8 in the Sala Cantarera of the Alcázar were open to visitors in 2015–17.

17. BZ 144/39, Mateo Vázquez to Philip and rescript, 28 Dec. 1574 (for the context, see ch. 11 above). For more examples of the emperor's influence on his son, see Tellechea Idígoras, *Fray Bartolomé*, I, 319–21, Interrogation of Philip by the Inquisition, 11 Jan. 1560, and Ball and Parker, *Cómo ser rey*, 26–7.

18. Fernández Terricabras, 'La reforma de las Órdenes', 193, Philip to Luis de Requesens, May 1569, italics added. For more examples, see *FBD*, chs 5 and 8.

19. Parker, 'The place of Tudor England', 205, Philip to the duke of Alba, 14 Sep. 1571 (part of a discussion of Philip's attempts to overthrow Elizabeth in 1569–71); AGS *E* 165/2–3, Philip to Archduke Albert, 14 Sep. 1587.

20. *LCK*, III, 512–13, Charles to Marie, 13 Nov. 1552, holograph; BZ 144/61, Vázquez to Philip, and rescript, 31 May 1575. For more on such strategic continuities, see Parker, 'Incest'.

21. Plaisant, *Aspetti e problemi*, 111, Mendo Rodríguez de Ledesma to Philip III, 14 Sep. 1600.

22. AGI *Patronato* 29/13, challenge of Aguirre, 1561; AGS *E* 531/91, Fray Lorenzo de Villavicencio to Philip II, 6 Oct. 1566. The inscription beneath the bust (by Leone and Pompeo Leoni) reads:

'CAROLO QUINTO/ ET E ASSAY QUESTO PERCHE SE/ SA PER TUTO IL MONDO IL RESTO'.
http://plasenciahistorica.blogspot.com/2009/07/busto-de-carlos-v.html

23. ASP *CF* 127 [*Spagna* 4], unfol., count of Olivares to Octavio, duke of Parma, 2 Nov. 1568; BNE *Ms.* 20210/69/20, Philip to Don John, 3 Mar. 1570, holograph; AGS *CS* 2a/280/1485-6, 1519-20, 1532-3, 1540-1, 1646-7 and 1655-6 describe guns cast by 'Gregorio Lefer' or 'de la fundición de Alemaña' embarked on Armada ships in 1587-8. I thank Colin and Paula Martin for helping me identify the lost Löffler guns.

24. Mendieta, *Historia*, 470 (Book IV, ch. 29); Covarrubias, *Tesoro de la lengva castellana*, f. 202v; Sandoval, *Historia*, II, 618 (Book XXXII, ch. 17); Cervantes, *Don Quijote*, I, ch. 39 and II, ch. 8; Elliott 'Monarquía', 699, petition of Olivares, June 1638; Ponce de León, 'La arquitectura', on the emulation of Yuste at Loeches.

25. De Grieck, *De heerlycke ende vrolycke daeden*, introduction; Lox, *Van stropdragers*, passim.

26. Campanella, *De monarchia*, 98-9.

27. Brandi, 'Die politische Testamente', 277-86 (the 'last instructions'). For a detailed consideration of this forgery, see Appendix III below. Richard Kagan reminds me that Charles also featured in the 1941 Hollywood movie *The Maltese Falcon*.

28. Details from Peiró Martín, *En los altares*, 167-86, quoting Fernández Álvarez, *Evolución del pensamiento histórico en los tiempos modernos* (Madrid: Editora Nacional, 1974), 127. His view remained the same in 1999: Fernández Álvarez concluded his biography 'Carlos V, el único emperador del Viejo y Nuevo Mundo: un hombre para la Europa del año 2000' (*Carlos V: el César*, 853).

29. De Gaulle, *Discours*, 428 (from a speech delivered on 3 July 1962); Terlinden, *Carolus Quintus* (1975), beautifully illustrated thanks to a subsidy from the Banque de Paris et des Pays-Bas; Barón Crespo, 'La Europa' (delivered to a conference on Charles and Europe, italics added). In 2018, Barón Crespo received a 'Charles V European Award' from the European Academy of Yuste Foundation for furthering European unification.

30. Rassow, 'Das Bild', 15 (italics added); Torraca, *Studi*, 104-16 and 543-70. The text of '*La ricevuta dell'imperatore alla Cava*' first appeared in an early seventeenth-century manuscript of 'Farse cavaiole', but must have been composed several years earlier. For details on Charles's passage through Cava on 22 Nov. 1535, and its cost, see Saletta, 'Il viaggio', part II, 86-8.

31. Haton's *Mémoires* translated by Potter, 'Emperor Charles', 138 n. 18; Knox, *The history*, 79, quoting 'A faithful admonition of Johne Knox to the professours of God's truthe in England' (1554). The same work equated 'mischievous Mary' Tudor with Jezebel.

32. Sepúlveda, *Historia de Carlos V*, Book XXVI:88, Book XXVII:34, and most of Book XXX criticized the emperor. Although Florián de Ocampo (like Sepúlveda) never published his history of Charles, the notebooks he kept on events during the 1550s included many complaints about how the central government pursued policies deleterious to Castile: BNE *Ms.* 9937, 'Noticias de varios sucesos'.

33. Daza, *Quarta parte*, Book II ch. 36 (pp. 137-8, also in Sandoval, *Historia*, II, 637-9 and *SLID*, II, 63-6: Méndez only revealed his vision on his deathbed in 1582); Ganz, 'Charlemagne in Hell' (my thanks to Fritz Graf for this succulent reference).

34. Burton, *Life*, II, 84-5, Hume to Robertson, c. 1760; Robertson, *The history*, III, 276-80 (assessment) and 518-26 (index entry for 'Charles V'). On the positive side, Robertson was the first to argue that Charles's reign saw the emergence of a new political system in Europe characterized by the concept of a balance of power. Details on how Charles made his first Scottish biographer rich from *ODNB*, s.v. William Robertson.

35. Von Ranke, *Deutsche Geschichte*; Baumgarten, *Geschichte Karls V.*; Stirling-Maxwell, *The cloister life*, 260. See also the negative verdict of Gustave Bergenroth quoted in the Preface above.

36. Michelet, *Histoire*, 263 (the epithet 'bookworm' seems odd, given how little time Charles devoted to reading); Galasso, 'La storiografia', 155-6.

37. Peiró Martín, *En los altares*, 111-13; Clifford, *Photographic scramble*, 18-19 (published c. 1860, accompanied by the earliest known photographs of the site). After Miguel de Unamuno visited Yuste in 1908, he complained in similar terms about the difficult trail from Cuacos, and the desolation when he reached the monastery: Unamuno, *Obras completas*, VI, 277-82, 'Yuste'.

38. Fernández Álvarez, *Carlos V: el César*, 849 (describing his first visit to Yuste 'in 1955 or 1956'); Brandi, *The emperor*, 12, 15 ('Introduction: Charles's character and place in history'), italics added.

39. Erasmus, *Adages* (Paris 1500, often reprinted), 87-91 (Adage 1-V-18: 'Multa novit vulpes, verum echinus unum magnum').

EPILOGUE: THE BALANCE OF THE REIGN

1. Braudel, 'Les emprunts', 200.

2. Von Ranke, *Deutsche Geschichte*, V, 366–70, 'Sommaire de l'Ambassade de feu monsieur de Vienne vers l'empereur Charles V, en l'année 1550', a section entitled 'Des pars bonnes ou mauvaises qui sont en l'empereur'. Marillac had served as French ambassador in England 1539–43 and at Charles's court 1547–51. ASF *MdP* 3464/29–70, Serristori to Duke Cosimo, 17 Sep. 1547, offered a striking example of Marillac's assertion about the beneficial effects of the emperor's reputation for piety: Serristori claimed that Charles could not have been involved in the recent murder of Pier Luigi Farnese (ch. 12) 'because he is such a Christian and Catholic prince'.

3. ASF *MdP* 4308, unfol., Bernardo de' Medici to Duke Cosimo, Augsburg, 19 Jan. 1551.

4. Gayangos, *Relaciones de Pedro de Gante*, 34 (almost drowned); Gachard, *Voyages*, II, 156 (two sources on the incident at Amboise, 14 Dec. 1539). Buttay-Jutier, *Fortuna*, 391 and 419–20, discussed an unpublished treatise of 1544 by Girolamo Borgia that dissected Charles's 'very favourable Fortune'.

5. *RVEC*, 794–9, Salinas to Ferdinand, 18 Mar. 1537; Vilar Sánchez, *Carlos V*, 397–9 (on the damage inflicted by his fall in 1532).

6. Gayangos, *Relaciones de Pedro de Gante*, 195 (Orange killed during the siege of St Dizier in 1544).

7. Henne, *Histoire*, VIII, 298 (letter from Roeulx to Marie, 1546 about the assassination attempt); Sastrow, *Herkommen*, II, 50–5 (about the mutineers: alternative English text see *Social Germany*, 219–20); Greppi, 'Extraits', 145, Stroppiana to duke of Savoy, 24 Aug. 1547 (about the drunken soldier). Assassins removed several of Charles's enemies, including Pier Luigi Farnese and Lorenzino de' Medici as well as Rincón and Fregoso.

8. Michaud and Poujoulat, *Nouvelle collection . . . Vieilleville*, 113–15, 'Entretien de M de Vieilleville avec le comte de Nassau' in 1551. Nassau was particularly concerned that his son, Prince William of Orange, 'will never gain favour with the emperor' because he was not Spanish. He was wrong.

9. Specifically, he entrusted Margarita to André de Douvrin, a courtier; Tadea to 'Joanna Borgognona' (who accompanied Tadea's pregnant mother from Charles's court to Italy); Joanna to Henry of Nassau; and Gerónimo to Luis Quijada: see ch. 14 for more details. On Charles's concern that his son should become a 'verdadero príncipe de Castilla', see *FBD*, ch. 1.

10. BL *Cott. Ms.* Vespasian C.II/105–6, Thomas Boleyn and Richard Sampson to Wolsey, 8 Mar. 1523; *NBD*, VI, 338–41, Charles to Ferdinand, Bruges, 2 July 1540 ('je ne puis estre soubstenu sinon de mes royaulmes d'Espaigne'); Braudel, 'Les emprunts', 195 ('un pour les Pays-Bas, quatre pour la Castille'). In the summer of 1556, Philip II confirmed that since 1551 Spain had transferred to the Netherlands, either in cash or credit, eleven million ducats to pay for his father's wars: AGS *E* 513/114, untitled document that began 'La magestad del rei nuestro señor hoyó'.

11. HHStA *Belgien PA* 35/1/256–66, Charles to Granvelle, [28] Dec. 1541; HHStA *Hs. Blau* 596/1/7 and 11, Charles to Ferdinand, 8 Mar. and 10 May 1542. Kohler, *Carlos V*, 130–5, listed and evaluated the German ministers who served Charles.

12. Lanz, *Aktenstücke*, II/1, 128–9, Elna and Le Sauch to Margaret, London, 19 Mar. 1520; AGS *E* 1555/103, Charles to Miguel Mai, 16 May 1529 (apologizing that he could not reply properly to seven of his letters, because he lacked the correct cypher key); AGS *E* 1555/130, Charles to 'Fulano y fulano, mis embaxadores', 16 Sep. 1529. See also AGS *E K* 1485/6, Granvelle to Los Cobos, 6 Jan. 1540, apologizing to his closest colleague that he could not write 'in my own hand because I do not know how to write [Spanish]'; and AGS *E* 638/88, a joint *consulta* by Los Cobos and Granvelle in Feb. 1532, with the former writing in Spanish and the latter in French. Charles replied to each minister in their own language.

13. Glapion quoted on p. 138 above; Piot, 'Correspondance politique', 80–3, Gattinara to Barroso, imperial ambassador in Portugal, 13 Jan. 1522; *NBD*, XIII, 20–2, Camaiani to del Monte, 5 July 1552 (italics added).

14. Pietschmann, 'Los problemas', 54, 59; HHStA *Belgien PA* 2/4/68, Charles to Margaret, 25 Aug. 1522; *CMH*, I, 410–17 and 461–3, Charles to Marie, 21 Aug. and 20 Sep. 1531, both holograph. Henne, *Histoire*, VI, 23–34, provided details on the prolonged persecution of the rioters and looters. On measures against the descendants of Comuneros in 1552, see p. 140 above.

15. AGS *GA* 2/29–30, Charles to the empress, 30 Aug. 1529; *CDCV*, I, 186, Margaret to the empress, 15 Dec. 1529 (Margaret was right: the younger prince became King Henry II, Charles's implacable enemy: see ch. 15 above); Serristori, *Legazioni*, 18, Serristori, Florentine ambassador, to Duke Cosimo, 2 Oct. 1537, quoting Granvelle on how the emperor viewed Filippo Strozzi: 'Uomo morto non fa guerra'. Soon afterwards, Strozzi was found dead in his prison cell.

16. *CSPSp*, VI/1, 540–2, Badoer to the Signory, 25 July 1556; *L&P Henry VIII*, XIV/2, 285–8, Edmund Bonner to Thomas Cromwell, 30 Dec. 1539; TNA *SP* 1/170/23–33, Paget to Henry VIII, 19 Apr. 1542,

with a postscript on the 22nd, quoting the Admiral of France; AGS *E* 874/17–18, Juan de Vega to Charles, 19 Feb. 1547 (reporting on an audience with the pope).

17. HHStA *Hs. Blau* 596/1/148v–51 Charles to Ferdinand, 28 June 1547, register copy. Fernández Álvarez believed the emperor and held up 'su respeto a la palabra dada' as one of Charles's greatest virtues (*Carlos V: el César*, 853); but this volume is full of examples of Charles consciously telling lies or getting his minsters to tell lies on his behalf. See, for example, the numerous instructions to his officials in Seville to sequester cargoes belonging to individuals and to lie about it: pp. 368–9 above.

18. Poumarède, 'Le "vilain et sale assassinat"', 7–8 (quoting Blaise de Monluc's *Commentaries*, published 1590, and a manifesto by the French Directorate on 7 May 1799), and 38–43 (citing discussion of the murders by Bodin, Gentili, Grotius, Wiquefort, Vattel and other experts in international law). Williams, 'Re-orienting', 24–6, noted how Giovio included a discussion of the murder in his *History of his own times* (1552-3), leading imperial apologists to rally to Charles's support.

19. Gunn, *War*, 27. See also the quotations from military experts concerning the difference between besieging a town fortified 'à l'antiqua' and an artillery fortress in ch. 15 above. See also Parker, *The military revolution*, ch. 1.

20. Machiavelli (with Pedro Navarro), 'Relazione di una visita fatta per fortificare Firenze' (Apr. 1526); Robert, 'Philibert', XL, 19–20 and 277–9, Châlons to Charles, 25 Sep. and 25 Oct. 1529, holograph. The prince was killed in action a week before the surrender. Blockmans discussed these letters in 'Logistics', 38–43, and again in *Emperor*, 140–6.

21. Robert, 'Philibert', XL, 282–4, Châlons to Charles, Oct. 1529, holograph; Rodríguez Villa, *Memorias*, 258–9, Ferrara to his ambassador at the imperial court, 2 Aug. 1527; Sherer, '"All of us"', 903 (map of the 1537-8 mutinies) and 912 (etiquette); Sastrow, *Herkommen*, II, 50–5 (Sastrow's eyewitness account of how mutineers at Augsburg in 1547 confronted Charles in person); Thieulaine, 'Un livre', 147–8 (the mutiny of the garrisons of Cambrai, Douai and St Omer in 1553).

22. *PEG*, V, 165, Juan de Vega to Philip II, Nov./Dec. 1557, with 'puntos' that his successor as viceroy of Sicily should know.

23. Tracy, *Emperor*, 182 (Table 8.1) and 247 (Table 11.2); AGS *E* 513/114, untitled document that began 'La magestad del rei nuestro señor hoyó', detailed the king's debts in each state in summer 1556; AGS *E* 8340/85, the 'Decreto de suspensión' of May 1557.

24. *NBD*, XIV, 82–3, Nuncio Muzzarrelli to Cardinal del Monte, 18 June 1554.

25. *RTA*, II (212 pp.), X (250 pp.) and XVIII (314 pp.) Calculations are facilitated by the editors' decision to arrange the Acta by theme, not date. *RTA* for the Diets of Augsburg (1530) and Regensburg (1541) are not yet published, but the discussion of religion figured prominently in the agenda for both assemblies.

26. *LWB*, V, 197–9, Hesse to Luther, 9 Dec. 1529.

27. Suri, *The impossible presidency*, 192, 289.

28. *CWE*, II, 193–6 (# 413), Erasmus to John Fisher, 5 June 1516. See also ch. 3 above.

29. TNA *SP* 1/87/81–3, Vaughan to Cromwell, Brussels, 7 Dec. 1534, holograph. Vaughan loyally assured Cromwell that neither Carondolet 'nor yet the chef counsyllor of no one prynce in Christendome' transacted 'half the busyness, no not the tenth part, that you have'. On Vaughan's career see his entry in *ODNB*. Gunn, Grummit and Cools, *War*, provided an excellent survey of how the Military Revolution increased the workload of government at all levels. For instance, at St Omer (which left immaculate records) by the 1540s 'two-thirds of the magistracy's correspondence … concerned military affairs'.

30. Claretta, *Notice*, 69–84, 'Première représentation de Mercurin de Gattinara à l'empereur' (although Claretta dated the document to 1526, Gattinara twice mentioned that he had served as chancellor for four and a half years: since he took the oath of office in Oct. 1518, he must have composed the Remonstrance in Apr. 1523); ibid., 84–92, 'Deuxième représentation de Mercurin de Gattinara à l'empereur', in Italian, with passages from the French original in Bornate, 'Historia', 311 n. 4 (although the document is undated, *BKK*, II, 152–3, convincingly argued that Gattinara prepared it in Apr.–May 1523).

31. Claretta, *Notice*, 69–92; *CDCV*, IV, 511 (Charles's *Memoirs*); *CDCV*, III, 478, Charles's instruction to Figueroa, [6] Sep. 1552; Heine, *Briefe*, 494–5, Loaysa to Charles, 8 May 1532, and 445–7, same to same, 12 Sep. 1531.

32. Von Druffel, *Briefe*, II, 835–8, Perrenot to Marie, from 'the camp before Metz', 16 Dec. 1552 (a false hope in this case). On Philip II's Messianic vision, which rivalled that of his father, see Parker, *Grand Strategy*, 99–102; and Parker, 'The place'.

33. *CWE*, V, 108–13 (# 657), Erasmus to Henry VIII, 9 Sep. 1517; Michaud and Poujoulat, *Nouvelle collection… Vieilleville*, 113–15, 'Entretien de M de Vieilleville avec le comte de Nassau' in 1551. See Martínez Millán, *La Corte*, III, for biographies of most of Charles's councillors.

34. Cedillo, *El Cardenal*, II, 334-6, Charles to Cisneros, 30 Aug. 1516; *KFF*, III, 25-41, Charles's instructions to Ferdinand, 16 Jan. 1531. The preceding chapters contain numerous examples of Charles delegating decisions.
35. *PEG*, I, 603, Charles's instructions to Baron Balançon, Regensburg, 3 Apr. 1532; *CMH*, II, 257-8, Charles to Marie, 31 July 1533 (he made the same point one more time in the same document).
36. Gayangos, *Relaciones de Pedro de Gante*, 48 (Aigues Mortes); Brigden, *Thomas Wyatt*, 439, quoting Charles's statement at an audience on 11 Mar. 1539; HHStA *Hs. Blau* 596/1/27-35v, Charles to Ferdinand, 11 Aug. 1542.
37. *LCK*, II, 177-9, Charles to Nassau, 10 May 1535 (see ch. 9 above for the context); Alonso Acero, 'El norte de África', 397-8 (see ch. 15 above for the context); ASF *MdP* 4320/152, Ricasoli to Duke Cosimo, 29 Aug. 1555.
38. *CMH*, II, 129, Charles to Marie, 8 Apr. 1533 (a challenging document reproduced in facsimile as well as transcription); Powell, *The complete works*, I, 197-8, Sir Thomas Wyatt to Henry VIII, 7 Jan. 1540 (also printed in *SP*, VIII, 219-32).
39. Baronius, *Annales*, XXXII, 125 (Giovio at Charles's coronation as king of the Lombards); Flaminio, *Oratio*, f. III (after the imperial coronation); *LCK*, II, 200, Charles to Jean Hannart, 16 Aug. 1535. See also an identical message in *CDCV*, I, 441-4, Charles to Soria, 16 Aug. 1535. In the euphoria that followed his capture of Tunis, several contemporaries genuinely believed that Charles could take Constantinople: see Giovio, *Pauli Iovii opera*, I, 165, Giovio to Duke Francesco Sforza, 14 Sep. 1535 ('God grant that the pope may be able to celebrate Mass in Santa Sophia in Constantinople in the summer of 1536'); and Gilliard, 'La política', 229, Secretary of State Antoine Perrenin to Leonard de Gruyères, 31 Dec. 1535 ('the emperor has the power to take Constantinople, and I pray that God will give him the grace to triumph there').
40. Kissinger, *White House Years*, 167; Burbank and Cooper, *Empires*, 2-3, 12-15.
41. Koenigsberger, 'The empire', 350-1.
42. *PEG*, II, 123-4, Charles's instructions to Noircarmes, June 1534; Powell, *The complete works*, I, 168, Wyatt to Henry VIII, 12 Dec. 1539; *PEG*, II, 566, Charles to M. de Bonvalot, his ambassador in France, 24 Mar. 1540.
43. Loaysa in 1532 quoted p. 211 above; BL *Harl. Ms.* 282/297v, Sir Thomas Wyatt to Henry VIII, 7 Jan. 1540 (about Henry's demand that Charles hand over Robert Brancetour: Powell, *The complete works*, 193-4, reads '*change* myn honour', but the original clearly reads '*charge*'); Beltrán de Heredía, *Domingo de Soto*, 654-5, Soto to Charles, 25 Aug. 1552, reminding him 'of something that I heard Your Majesty say', presumably while he served as imperial confessor in 1548-50. For more on these continuities, see Chabod, *Carlos V*, 26-38.
44. Gonzalo Sánchez-Molero, *Regia biblioteca*, I, 259-62, discussed this volume, for which in 1537 Charles paid Simon Bening £452 for the illuminations.
45. Jover Zamora, *Carlos V*, 411-12, Charles to the empress, 18 May 1536. Rodríguez-Salgado, 'The art of persuasion', 71-8, cited other examples of this high-level blackmail towards both the empress and Marie.
46. AGS *E* 640/80, Charles to Vázquez de Molina, Metz, 6 July 1544; *CSPSp*, X, 327, Charles to Marie, 9 July 1551; Gutiérrez, *Trento*, II, 240-6, 'Resultan los puntos que se han consultado a Su Magestad', undated but Feb. 1552; *CDCV*, III, 543, Charles to Philip, 25 Dec. 1552. For other examples of the significance of 'reputation' to Charles, and how it changed somewhat over time, see Hatzfeld, 'Staatsräson'.
47. *RTA*, II, 594-6, copy of Charles's paper 'fait de ma main' on the night of 18-19 Apr. 1521; *SP*, VIII, 219-32, Wyatt to Henry VIII, Paris, 7 Jan. 1540, holograph draft. Despite this claim, Charles could and did occasionally 'altre my inquisition'. Brigden, *Thomas Wyatt*, 423-5, noted his intervention in two cases; and a paper of advice given to Philip in 1556 urged him to 'Take care that Inquisition is properly run, and that it is not used as an excuse to harm anyone' – hardly a ringing endorsement (Merriman, 'Charles V's last paper', 491).
48. La Gasca on Charles's fear of Hell quoted on p. 375 above; Rodríguez-Salgado, 'El ocaso', 71-3, cited these and other late examples of Charles's conscience dictating policy. Lutz, 'Karl V', 153, considered 'conscience' and 'scruples' to be 'zwei Leitmotive' of Charles's statecraft, but of course there were exceptions: Charles fought in alliance with Henry VIII, condemned as a heretic, in 1543-4; with Maurice of Saxony and other Lutheran rulers both then and in 1546-7; and with Albert Alcibiades in 1552.
49. *CDCV*, IV, 485, Charles to Philip, 1552. See ch. 6 above for his self-doubts in 1525 and ch. 11 for those in 1543.
50. AGS *E* 60/193-4, Loaysa to Charles, 9 Sep. [1543] holograph, to be placed directly 'in His Majesty's hands'; Rassow, *Die Kaiser-Idee*, 433-7, 'Las pláticas que el emperador passó con [el embajador

francés]', sent by Idiáquez to Los Cobos and Granvelle, Feb. 1538. In the 1520s, Charles also pursued personal diplomacy by inserting a special sign in his holograph letters to indicate matters 'that I have set my heart on': see ch. 6 above.

51. Rodríguez-Salgado, 'Charles V and the dynasty', 80–1; Rabe and Marzahl, '"Comme représentant"', 79 (citing on p. 80 the notable failure of Charles's first attempts at delegation: in the Netherlands in 1517–20, in Germany in 1519–20, and in Spain in 1520–1).

52. Villar García, 'Cartas', 81–5, Charles to Rodrigo Mexía, 20 Feb. and 28 July 1529 (no doubt similar letters went out to all Charles's vassals); *CDCV*, I, 292–4, Charles to the empress, 13 June 1531.

53. AGS *E* 644/102, Charles to Diego Hurtado de Mendoza, 7 Oct. 1547. For another example of Charles taking advantage of enforced leisure while sailing to make plans, this time in Mallorca in 1541, see p. 273 above.

54. Ando, *Imperial ideology*, xiii, 27, and most of Part 2, where 'charisma' is one of the most common words.

55. Preciado, *Juan de Anchieta*, Introduction (royal warrant dated 5 Aug. 1519); González de Ávila, *Historia*, 474–80 (Cabeza de Vaca). See details in ch. 1 above about Servels; and in ch. 14 about Jeanne.

56. Garibay, 'Memorias', 420–1; ASF *MdP* 4307, unfol., Bernardo de' Medici to Duke Cosimo, 30 Dec. 1548, and Brantôme, *Oeuvres*, I, 313–18, both narrated the death of Buren on 23 Dec. 1548; Beltrán de Heredía, *Domingo de Soto*, 643–4 and 655, Soto to Eraso, 1 July 1550 (six months after returning to Spain) and 25 Aug. 1552. For examples of Charles's ability to 'work a crowd', see pp. 219–20 above.

57. Gutiérrez, *Trento*, II, 117–18, Perrenot to the bishop of Segorbe, 19 Jan. 1552, minute; Gachard, *Correspondance de Guillaume le Taciturne*, I, 40–1, Marie to Orange, 27 Oct. 1552.

58. Grunberg, 'Le vocabulaire', 18–21; Headley, 'The Habsburg world empire', 47 (Duke Philip the Good and his son Charles had founded the convent at Scheut in 1456); Lapèyre, *Une famille*, 127–37, 'Le marchand devant Dieu'; Guyon, *Mémoires*, 78 (admittedly the tournament involved 1,500 warriors on each side, with the victors 'pillaging and sacking' a mock castle), 84, 94. By contrast Guyon omitted Charles's treatment of Ghent in 1540, of which he was an eyewitness, because 'to narrate it all would make me too verbose'.

59. *CLC*, IV, 354–6, petition of the Cortes, 15 July 1523; Espinosa, *The empire*, 257, quoting letters from the magistrates of Calahorra and Valladolid to Charles, 7 and 8 Dec. 1526; Villar García, 'Cartas', 77, Rodrigo Mexía to Charles, June 1528; RAH *Salazar* A-43/176–7v, Juan Pérez to Charles, 19 Sep. 1528. See also the similar wishes expressed by Charles's ministers: ch. 9 above.

60. Ariosto, *Orlando furioso* (Ferrara, 1532), canto XV, stanzas 23–25 (Ariosto met Charles during his visit to Mantua in 1532, and presented a copy of his work; in return Charles apparently made him Poet Laureate); Meertens, 'Een esbatement'.

61. *CLC*, V, 355–7, petition of the Cortes, 25 Apr. 1548, on hearing that Charles had ordered his children Philip and María to join him in Germany; Thieulaine, 'Un livre', 185 and 191, entries for Aug. 1554. Charles's regents also regularly argued that only his presence could avert catastrophe, but they were biased: if he were present, they could not be blamed should a catastrophe nevertheless occur.

62. Thieulaine, 'Un livre', 179 (the lawyer was correct: for the role of Robert de la Marck, lord of Sedan, in 1521 see p. 131).

63. RAH *Muñoz* 80/101v, Bishop Bastidas of Venezuela to Charles, 20 Jan. 1535. Charles had granted the Welser Company of Augsburg the rights to explore and develop Venezuela and they sent out several hundred German colonists, including Philipp von Hutten, cousin of a prominent rebel against Charles, Ulrich von Hutten. More is known about him than about almost any other conquistador: see Schmitt and von Hutten, *Das Gold*. See also the suggestion of a Spanish pamphlet suggesting that Gonzalo Pizarro had been a Lutheran in ch. 13 above.

64. Chabod, *Storia*, 261 and 302–3, quoting Caracciolo to Charles, June 1537, and the will of the marquis del Vasto, 28 Mar. 1546.

65. Braudel, 'Charles-Quint', 202–4. Braudel perhaps forgot that Penelope's cunning strategy of unravelling by night the weaving she had done by day eventually came to an end: four years after she heard that Odysseus was dead, 'my maidens, disrespectful bitches', told her suitors who 'came upon me and caught me and upbraided me loudly. So I finished my web against my will' (Homer, *Odyssey*, 19.150–158).

66. Escamilla, 'Le règne', 6–7. Wiesflecker, *Kaiser Maximilian*, V, 179–91, and Cauchies, *Philippe*, 54, both concluded that without Habsburg resources the Burgundian Netherlands would not have remained independent.

67. Edelmayer, 'El Sacro Imperio', 169–76. For a time Ferdinand regarded the Religious Peace of Augsburg as another interim agreement and expected further colloquies to find a formula of concord for all Christian confessions; but the first one, at Worms in 1557, broke down because the Lutherans could not even agree among themselves: see Liebing, 'Frontière infranchissable'.

68. Bofarull y Sans, *Predilección*, 64–6, Charles to the viceroy of Catalonia, 2 Jan. 1533; Carretero Zamora, *Gobernar*, 162–3 and 402.

69. Tellechea Idígoras, *Tiempos Recios*, IV, 374–7, 'Lo que el consejo de la Inquisición demanda al Rey', June 1558; and 436–42, Joanna's pragmática of Valladolid, 7 Sep. 1558, incorporating much of the 'demanda'. Fernández Terricabras, 'De la *crisis*', 56–9, described the measures to control heresy taken in Castile in 1558–9; Bujanda, *Index*, itemized and identified the books prohibited in the Index of 1559.

70. Aram, *Juana*, ch. 6, recorded Borja's three extended visits to Queen Joanna at Tordesillas in 1554–5; on his visits to Yuste in 1557–8, see ch. 16 above.

71. Tellechea Idígoras, *Tiempos Recios*, IV, 953–4, 995–6, Feria to Bishop Quadra (his successor as Spanish ambassador in England), Mechelen, 4 Dec. 1559 and 21 Jan. 1560. Fernández Terricabras, 'De la *crisis*', provided a brilliant discussion of the cordon sanitaire created in Spain in 1558–9, noting that although the rhythm of persecution was slower and initially less palpable in the crown of Aragon eventually the process affected all Spain.

72. Powell, *The complete works*, I, 128, 'Note of remembraunce by Sir Thomas Wiat', Toledo, Dec. 1538.

73. Ando, *Imperial ideology*, 27. See also chs 14, 15 and 16 above for the tense relations between Charles and Philip. See Parker, *Imprudent king*, 370–1, for the prince's 'anal' personality.

74. Álvarez, 'The role', detailed each inbreeding coefficient and explains how they were calculated. Weber, 'Zur Heiratspolitik Karls V', provided the best analysis of how the emperor pursued matrimonial imperialism, with special reference to France, accompanied by striking explanatory diagrams.

75. Deswarte-Rosa, 'Espoirs', 270 and 293–4, quoting letters from Luis de Sarmiento, Spanish ambassador in Lisbon, to Charles, 23 Oct. 1539, and to Los Cobos, 21 Jan. and 21 Mar. 1540 (italics added).

76. Tellechea Idígoras, *El Papado y Felipe II*, I, 199–202, Pius V to Philip II, undated holograph (but Philip's reply rejecting this argument stated that Pius had sent it with a letter dated 20 Dec. 1568).

77. *Acta Pacis Westphalicae*, Series II B 5/1, 390–1, Servien to Lionne, 21 Jan. 1647. Louis married Maria Theresa in 1660.

78. Pociecha, *Polska*, 5.

79. TNA *SP* 1/37/212 Wolsey to Louise of Savoy, [undated but 20 Mar. 1526] French, copy.

80. *CDCV*, II, 579–80, Charles's 'Political Testament', Jan. 1548. Admittedly, in 1529 Charles ceded to Portugal his rights to the Moluccas in return for a large cash sum, but he retained the option to repurchase them at a future date; and in 1543 he seriously considered the pope's offer to buy Milan from him, but eventually declined.

81. Tyler, *The emperor*, 279, 285.

82. *CSPV*, V, 519, Damula to the Signory, 8 July 1554, quoting Perrenot.

83. Sastrow, *Herkommen*, II, 647–8 (fonts as in the original), written in the 1590s (for an alternative translation see *Social Germany*, 278–9); Mignet, *Charles-Quint*, 188 n. 1, Charles's comment to a Portuguese envoy in Feb. 1558.

84. Heine, *Briefe*, 494–5, Loaysa to Charles, 8 May 1532.

85. TNA *SP* 1/170/23–33, Paget to Henry VIII, Chablis in Burgundy, 19 Apr. 1542 with a postscript on the 22nd, quoting the Admiral of France.

86. Gutiérrez, *Trento*, I, 411–14, Mendoza to Charles, Rome, 27 Sep. 1551. For the parallel views of Perrenot, and for the catastrophic consequences, see ch. 15.

87. Huizinga, *Geschonden wereld*, 62 (evidently Charles did not interest Huizinga: even *The waning of the Middle Ages* mentioned him only three times); Robertson, 'Empire and union' (an essay first published in 1995), 14.

88. Braudel, *Les écrits*, II, 395, from Braudel's paper at a conference in 1972. He referred to Marcel Bataillon (1895–1977), author of *Érasme et l'Espagne, recherches sur l'histoire spirituelle du XVIe siècle*, first published in 1937, and of many other works on the Dutch humanist and his circle.

APPENDICES

1. Snouckaert van Schouwenburg, *De republica*, 137; Cadenas y Vicent, *Las supuestas 'Memorias'*, 361–2.

2. I thank M. Olivier Wagner, archiviste-paléographe of the BNF, for confirming that the watermark of *Ms. Port.* 61 resembles Briquet no. 5704, and that the manuscript once belonged to Mazarin.

3. Sánchez Alonso, *Fuentes*, II, 44, no. 4806. BNF *Ms. Port.* 15, 16 and 23, and *Ms. Esp.* 166, are all Moura manuscripts. I thank Fernando Bouza for drawing this to my attention.

4. Reiffenberg, *Lettres*, 12–13, van Male to Louis de Praet, 17 July 1550. In *CDCV*, IV, 361–81, Fernández Álvarez disposed of several misconceptions concerning the manuscript, including the claim by von Ranke (*Deutsche Geschichte*, VI, 73–9, 'Über die autobiographischen Aufzeichnungen Carls V') that a Spanish version 'must have' once existed. On whether Charles wrote or dictated his *Memoirs*, see p. 657 n. 56 below.

5. Gonzalo Sánchez-Molero, *El César*, 294–392, and *Regia biblioteca*, I, 303–4 and 328–31.

6. Fernández Álvarez, *CDCV*, IV, 471 n. 36, plausibly suggests that Charles entrusted his *Memoirs* to a confidential messenger, Juan Manrique, in Mar. 1552.

7. *PEG*, VI, 290, Perrenot to Philip, 7 Mar. 1561; Checa Cremades, *Inventarios*, I, 291, entry in the Inventory of Charles's property at Yuste (stating that the papers belonged to 'Guillermo Miguel Lineo', meaning 'Malineo', the form of 'van Male' used by most of his Spanish contemporaries). Gonzalo Sánchez-Molero, *El César*, 363, noted the presence of historical works at Yuste and took it as evidence that the emperor planned to work further on his *Memoirs*.

8. Gonzalo Sánchez-Molero, *Regia biblioteca*, I, 328, Morales to Jerónimo Zurita, 20 Nov. 1564; Domingo Malvadi, *Bibliofilia Humanista*, 449–51, Páez de Castro to Zurita, 30 Jan. 1569. It appears that Páez died before he managed to see the manuscript. For the links between Páez and 'Malineo', see ibid., 542, a note of Páez's papers delivered posthumously to the king: 'Otro cuaderno en que hay diversos dichos y particularidades de las condiciones y costumbres del emperador referidas al doctor Páez por Guillermo Malineo.'

9. Gonzalo Sánchez-Molero, *El César*, 295.

10. Kervyn de Lettenhove, *Commentaires*. The manuscript was then catalogued as BNF *F. f.* 10,230. *CDCV*, IV, 461–81, provides further details on the manuscript and its various editions.

11. Morel-Fatio, *Historiographie*, 168 n.1. Erudite discussions of the *Memoirs* can also be found in Brandi, 'Die politischen Testamente', 286–93; Fernández Álvarez, 'Las "Memorias" de Carlos V'; Kagan, 'La propaganda'; and Gonzalo Sánchez-Molero, *El César*, 283–302 and 360–4. For their content, see ch. 14 above.

12. I thank Almudena Pérez de Tudela, Felipe Vidales del Castillo and Patrick Lenaghan for bringing to my attention several crucial works on this topic, and for sharing their erudition.

13. Los Santos, *Descripción breue*, 167–8 and 176; [Caimo], *Lettere*, II, 32–53, letter from El Escorial, 22 Aug. 1755. Varela, *La muerte*, 18–19, notes that Charles's father was embalmed in 1506, as was his mother in 1555, so the technology was available to do the same with the imperial cadaver had those around his deathbed decided it was necessary.

14. Zulueta, *Tuan nyamok*, 338–9; Salomone, 'Se busca malaria'.

15. Stirling-Maxwell, *The cloister life* [1891 edition], 408 n. 2, Layard to Stirling-Maxwell, 17 May 1871; Thausing, 'Die Leiche'; Vilar Sánchez, *Carlos V*, 397–9 (the injured leg).

16. Alarcón y Ariza, *Viajes*, 66–9.

17. 'El emperador Carlos V, copiado del natural en 1871', *La ilustración de Madrid. Revista de política, ciencias, artes y literatura*, III, no. 49 (13 Jan. 1872), 11, Rico to Mariano Fortuny, El Escorial, 18 Dec. 1871. The same issue printed the engraving on p. 9.

18. Bodart, 'Il mento "posticcio"'.

19. Zulueta, *Tuan nyamok*, 336. It seems likely that the photograph that inspired Zulueta was not of the mummy of Charles V. Although he saw it in the international press in Paris, presumably it originated in Spain, but a search of the main Spanish newspapers (*El Liberal*, *La Libertad*, *La Voz*, *El Sol*, *El Heraldo de Madrid*, *Estampa*, *Crónica*, *El Socialista*, *Mundo Obrero* and *CNT*) between July and Dec. 1936, the period of Zulueta's residence in Paris, revealed nothing about an assault on the Pantheon of the Kings and no photograph of the desecration of the imperial mummy. A search of the archive of a French photographer living in Madrid in 1936, who sent images and information back to France, also revealed nothing (Archivo Deschamps, conserved in the Archivo de la Memoria Histórica, Salamanca). In 2016 an interview with two Augustinian priests who had been students at El Escorial in 1936 confirmed that although Republican militia units certainly assaulted El Escorial, taking away many priests and shooting them at Paracuellos de Járama, they did not desecrate the Pantheon. Consequently, the photo seen by Zulueta cannot have been the mummy of Charles V. Perhaps the international press published a photo of a militiaman with a mummy, taken in some location where tombs were desecrated, and either printed the wrong caption or else Zulueta misremembered the caption. Either way, the error proved fruitful, because it convinced Zulueta that he could prove malaria had killed the emperor.

20. Salomone, 'Se busca malaria', citing a note from Pedro Larrea to the Dirección General del Patrimonio Nacional in Dec. 2004; Zulueta, *Tuan nyamok*, 341, wrote that a senior official of Patrimonio Nacional told him about the detached digit while he was looking at a portrait of the family of Carlos IV in 'una exposición de retratos' in the Prado, and the Prado mounted such an exhibition between Oct. 2004 and Feb. 2005; Beruete, 'Martín Rico', 540–1.

21. Patrimonio Nacional, no. 10044506, includes a letter to Alfonso XIII signed by the marquis of Miraflores and the dowager marchioness of Martorell on 31 May 1912; and a statement that they acquired the digit on 14 Sep. 1870. I thank Pilar Benito García for permission to consult these items.

22. Zulueta, *Tuan nyamok*, 339–43. The results appeared in Ordi, Zulueta et al., 'The severe gout', and Zulueta, 'The cause of death'.

23. Rico y Ortega, article in *La ilustración de Madrid*, 10–11, letter to Fortuny, 18 Dec. 1871, italics added.

24. Salomone, 'Se busca malaria', reported that the *New England Journal of Medicine*, which published the results of the tests, asked for a DNA match, 'pero los investigadores no obtuvieron permiso para ello'. This is regrettable because in 2014 a perfect mitochondrial DNA match was made between the recently excavated skeletal remains uncovered on the site of a friary in Leicester and a living descendant of the Plantagenet dynasty, proving beyond all doubt that the skeleton was that of King Richard III of England.

25. I thank Daniel C. Anderson, Paul Hammer, David Lagomarsino, Linda Levy Peck, Mary Robertson, Mía Rodríguez-Salgado, Andrew Thrush and Vanessa Wilkie for sharing with me their erudition and their suggestions to help me compile this Appendix.

26. The printed texts are Anon., *The advice*, and Teissier, *Instructions* (with two subsequent editions, published in The Hague in 1700 and 1788). Mayer, 'Das politische Testament', discussed thirteen Italian manuscript texts he found in the archives and libraries of Rome, and quoted extensively from one of them, but he ignored at least twelve more in Scottish, English, French, German, American and other Italian libraries.

27. Mayr, 'Die letzte Abdankung', 156–8, published the document, from HHStA *Hs.* 630/89–90. The document is dated 16 Jan. 1555, old style. For more on these documents, see ch. 15 above.

28. The Venetian ambassador provided a detailed account of the emperor's speech that day: see pp. 466–7 above.

29. RAH *Ms.* 9/5949/12 (formerly *Varios de Historia* Sign. Est 27, gr. 5a, E., no. 134, tomo I, f. 12), 'Puntos que enbió el emperador Don Carlos de gloriosa memoria al rey Don Phelipe su hijo quando dio su vuelta a Spaña. De la manera que mejor se havía de gobernar', printed by Merriman, 'Charles V's last paper', 491.

30. Brandi, 'Aus den Kabinettsakten', 183–4, Paper of advice from Gattinara, Nov.–Dec. 1523. Among other things, Gattinara recommended 'that the Muslims and infidels . . . in your kingdoms should be expelled': to which Charles replied, 'This is not the right time' but 'the chancellor may propose the preparations that would be required to achieve this, and tell me about them later'.

31. If Charles did provide a paper of advice to his son in 1555–6, he was not alone: see those mentioned by Houssiau, 'Comment gouverner'.

32. Mayer, 'Das politische Testament', 476–87, detailed the errors.

33. National Library of Scotland *Ms. Adv.* 23.I.6, 'Ragionamento di Carlo V Imperatore tenuto al re Philippo suo figiuolo . . . riscritto l'anno MDXCII'; Craigie, *The Basilicon Doron*, II, 64–6 ('The literary antecedents of *Basilicon Doron*') and 171–3 (on Pemberton).

34. The titles of Hunt *HA Papers* Box 15 (8A), and BL *Lansdowne* Ms. 792, no. 1, respectively, italics added. All known copies, partial and complete, are described in http://www.celm-ms.org.uk/authors/howardhenryearlofnorthampton.html, entries HoH 28–HoH 51.

35. Hunt, *HA Correspondence* 6909, Howard's Dedicatory Epistle to Elizabeth, f. 1v.

36. I thank Paul Hammer for pointing out to me that Howard and Castelvetro both belonged to the political and cultural circle of Penelope, Lady Rich, and for suggesting that Howard presented his translation to Elizabeth in Dec. 1592, because he told her that he had suffered 'twelve yeares sequestratacon from the comfort of your cheerfull looks', and she imprisoned him in Dec. 1580: emails from Hammer to Parker, 20 Aug. and 2 Sep. 2014.

37. Hunt, *HA Correspondence* 6909, Howard's Dedicatory Epistle to Elizabeth, f. 2v.

38. Teissier, *Instructions*, 'Avertissement' (unfoliated). The prince was the future King Frederick William I of Prussia (1688–1740).

39. Stübel, 'Die Instruktion Karls V', prints the German text and notes how it diverges from Teissier.

40. Mayer, 'Das politische Testament', 491–4; Brandi, 'Die politischen Testamente', 277–86.

41. I thank Bethany Aram, José Luis Gonzalo Sánchez-Molero, Annemarie Jordan Gschwend, Ruth MacKay and Felipe Vidales del Castillo for help with this Appendix.

42. AGS *PR* 29/59, notarized copy of the will of Germaine de Foix, 28 Sep. 1536, sent by Calabria to the empress with a letter dated 18 Oct. 1536. The original is at Archivo del Reino de Valencia, *Clergat*, Caixa 1824, no. 25.

43. Ríos Lloret, *Germana*, 114.

44. BNE *Ms.* 1758, Anon., 'Voyages de l'empereur', f. 15, the last entry in a genealogy starting with Pharamond; *Llibre de memòries de la Ciutat i Regne de València*, a manuscript history (Francesc Joan compiled entries for the 1530s: I thank José Luis Gonzalo Sánchez-Molero for this reference).

45. AGS *PR* 30, no. 19, 'Inventario de las joyas, plata y recámara de la emperatriz', ff. 1v–2, Charles to María, Augsburg, 24 Apr. 1551. Checa Cremades, *Inventarios*, II, 2258, published the text from another copy of Charles's letter in the 'Libro de partiçyon que se hizo de la rrecámara que fue de la emperatriz', compiled in 1555. I thank Annemarie Jordan Gschwend for identifying the 'hilo de perlas' worn by María in a painting done by a Netherlands artist circa 1557: Kunsthistorisches Museum, Vienna, Gemäldegalerie, Inv.-Nr. GG_1042.

ACKNOWLEDGEMENTS

1. Gardiner, *The literary Memoranda*, II, 69–70, Prescott's journal entry from 1 Apr. 1841; Temple, *A sort of conscience*, 2 (italics added). Temple planned to complete his biography of Edward Wakefield and his brothers 'in three to five years, but ended only after eleven. I underestimated the time it would take to research and write about an entire family'. In 1999, Manuel Fernández Álvarez provided a similar account of his engagement with Charles V. He started in 1942, working on a doctoral thesis to explain why the alliance between Spain and England forged in 1553 should have foundered; expanded his scope in 1956 when asked to organize something suitable for the quatercentenary of the emperor's death; and published an ambitious biography in 1999, just in time to commemorate the quincentenary of the emperor's birth (*Carlos V: el César*, 21–2).

2. Giles, *The whole works*, I.ii, 267–8, Ascham to Edward Raven, 29 Jan. 1551. The vicar of Epperstone at this time was Christopher Wansforth. He, Ascham and Raven were all educated at St John's College, Cambridge, which may explain the parallel. I thank John Morrill and Tracey Akehurst for illuminating this point for me.

3. Koenigsberger and Parker, 'Charles V'. Koenigsberger's exam question was probably inspired by Tyler, *The emperor*, 285: 'The means at his disposal to face the demands upon him always fell short of what he needed to exploit a victory or a diplomatic success.'

4. Ball and Parker, *Cómo ser rey*.

5. See, for example, Brandi's account of Charles's siege of Metz, in whose garrison he had served as 'erster Adjutant der Festung' in 1917–18 (Brandi, 'Karl V. vor Metz', 1), and his appreciation of the terror of digging mines and counter-mines (Brandi, *The emperor*, 641). In his last lecture, in 1945, published in Plassmann, *Karl Brandi*, 39–43, Brandi drew on his experience as a 'Frontkämpfer des ersten Weltkrieges'. Ericksen, *Complicity*, 62–74, discusses the impact of Brandi's war service on his patriotism and his politics before and after the rise of Hitler.

6. Ericksen, *Complicity*, 91, from a letter by Brandi in Jan. 1934. The colleague was the ancient historian Ulrich Kahrstedt, also a professor at Göttingen. Brandi issued his challenge immediately, 'while still in my robes'.

7. Not all the foreign editions were satisfactory: see the shortcomings of the 1939 French translation excoriated by Bataillon, 'Le Charles-Quint de Karl Brandi', 300–2. C. V. Wedgwood provided a more reliable English translation.

8. Gardiner, *The literary Memoranda*, II, 145, Prescott's journal entry from 23 Apr. 1845, emphasis in the original. In 1856, Prescott supplied 'An account of the emperor's life after his abdication' to Robertson's *History*: see I, iii–vi, and III, 331–510. For Robertson's negative view of Charles, see p. 500 above.

9. Cartwright, *Gustave Bergenroth*, 153, Bergenroth to David Douglas, 1 Aug. 1866.

10. For more on the Bergenroth transcripts, and their colourful collector, see p. 570 above.

11. Cartwright, *Gustave Bergenroth*, 89, n. 1, J. S. Brewer to Lord Romilly, Valladolid, 21 Aug. 1861.

12. Atlas, *The shadow*, 31.

NOTE ON DATES AND QUOTES

1. Compare Le Glay, *Correspondance*, II, 155–6, with Walther, 'Review of Kreiten', 282. Schlegelmilch, *Die Jugendjahren*, 96 n. 256, confirmed Walther's date. Cheney, *Handbook of dates*, 83–161, gives a French Style calendar for each year, arranged by the date of Easter.

2. Talbot, 'Ore italiane'; Sanuto, *I diarii*, XXXI, cols 80–2, Gasparo Contarini to the Doge, 6 July 1521, 'at two o'clock at night'. Since Charles and all his European contemporaries used the Julian Calendar, to calculate sunset accurately it is necessary to add ten days: so sunset on 4 July 1521 would be the same as sunset on 14 July today.

3. Powell, *The complete works*, I, xxi.

NOTE ON SOURCES

1. Sánchez Alonso, *Fuentes*, II, 1 (see pp. 36–165 for works on 'España en el período 1516–1556'); Dixon and Fuchs, *The histories*. In 2001, Kohler, 'Una mirada', provided a useful overview of sources for the study of the emperor.

2. Foronda y Aguilera, *Estancias y viajes*, online at http://www.cervantesvirtual.com/bib/historia/CarlosV/5_3_foronda_1.shtml. Gould, 'The adventure', presents a delightful appreciation of Foronda and his work. Vilar Sánchez, *Carlos V*, 400–1, provided a somewhat different account of where Charles spent his time.

3. See the overview at http://karl-v.bsz-bw.de/einl.htm which links to the POLKAweb site. To use POLKAweb click the button 'Gesamtsuche'; to find letters sent by Charles in (say) 1543, set 'Suchart' at 'Standard', type in 'Karl' as 'Absender', and type in the 'Datum' boxes: '01.01.1543 bis 31.12.1543': this brings up 362 letters, in chronological order. Click on each item for details.

4. BL *Department of Manuscripts Departmental Archive*, 'Papers regarding purchase and acquisition of manuscripts, 1871–1873', ff. 1–4, John Dahlberg Acton to J. Winter Jones, 12 Aug. 1869, and Paul Friedmann to Edward Bond, 14 June 1869. Ibid., ff. 1–95 contain the correspondence between the Museum librarians and Bergenroth's heirs and assigns about the collection, 1869–71. Cartwright, *Gustave Bergenroth*, narrates Bergenroth's life and prints some correspondence about his projected biography of Charles V.

5. BL *Department of Manuscripts Departmental Archive*, 'Papers regarding purchase and acquisition of manuscripts, 1871–1873', ff. 446–57 contains the angry correspondence between the Museum and Friedmann about the eleven withheld volumes; Rzepka, *Historia kolekcji*, 121–2, provided a brief description of the Kraków collection. Further volumes of Bergenroth's transcripts, though not all related to Charles, may be found at TNA *PRO* 31/11 (fourteen volumes of transcripts from Spanish archives, most of them published in *CSPSp*; TNA *PRO* 31/11/11 contains keys to cyphers); and BNE *Ms.* 18550/2 (a volume of 376 ff. containing Bergenroth transcripts, most of them published in *CSPSp*).

6. Martínez Millán, *La Corte*.

7. Checa Cremades, *Inventarios*. Vol. I included nine inventories for Charles and one for his mother; vol. II included nine inventories for the empress; vol. III included inventories for Charles's aunt Margaret (twenty-two) and for his siblings Eleanor (two), Isabeau (seven), Ferdinand (four), Marie (four) and Catalina (five), together with indexes that cover all three volumes.

8. *SLID*, II, 21–69.

9. *SLID*, II, 71–154 (GRM, II, 1–69, published the same text, albeit Gachard could not identify its author). In the 1620s, Fray Luis de Santa María wrote *A la cassa y monasterio Ymperial de St Hr.mo. de Yuste*. In 1999 the monastery of Yuste acquired a nineteenth-century copy of this manuscript, and produced a facsimile edition, Madrid, 2000; but the passages on Charles V seem to replicate those of Corral.

10. Stirling-Maxwell, *The cloister life* (1852), Pichot, *Charles-Quint* (1854), and Mignet, *Charles-Quint* (1854), all worked from the transcripts of Simancas documents made by González and acquired in 1844 for CADMA by Mignet, its director. Gachard, *Retraite et mort* (3 vols, 1854–6), used transcripts of the same documents, most of them concerning Belgium, made for him in Simancas by García González and his staff.

11. Sánchez Loro, *La inquietud postrimera de Carlos V* (1957–8), part of the 'Publicaciones de la Jefatura Provincial del Movimiento'. Although his enthusiasm for the Fascist regime led Sánchez Loro into both errors and odious value judgements, his trilogy constituted a solid scholarly achievement that deserves to be better known.

12. AGS *CSR* legajos 128–80. Aguirre, 'Viejos y nuevos', 40–4, provided the best available description of this important but neglected series.

13. ADN *B* 2268 (79,071), contains the last two membranes of a parchment roll listing all items removed from 'la chambre de nos joyaulx à Bruxelles selon qu'elles sont comprinses en vostre inventaire pour nous en servir en nostre prochain voyaige d'espaigne', signed by Charles on 30 June 1517.

14. Dekker, *Egodocuments*, 7. See also the excellent articles on the subject in a special issue of *German History*, XXVIII/3 (2010).

15. Neefe, *Tafel-Reden* of Ferdinand and his doctor; *LWT*, six volumes of Luther's so-called 'table talk'. Chabod and the similar opinions of other historians quoted on p. ix above.

16. See the overview of the emperor's self-promoting projects, and those involved, in Silver, *Marketing Maximilian*, 37–40.

17. Bornate 'Mémoire', 394; Rivera Rodríguez, *Carlos V*, 25. Brandi, *Kaiser Karl* II, 42–5, listed and discussed the sources on Gattinara available when he wrote in 1941. In 1981, the chancellor's own

archive, now in AS Vercelli, became available to historians and it formed the basis of the studies by Headley, *The emperor*, Boone, *Mercurino*, and Rivera Rodríguez, *Carlos V.*

18. Laiglesia, *Estudios*, I, 41–92, published a dozen instructions signed by Charles in May 1543. For the two papers of advice, see ch. 11 above, and Ball and Parker, *Cómo ser rey*. On the mysterious 'last instructions' for Philip allegedly delivered by Charles in 1555 or 1556, see Appendix III above.

19. Firpo, *Relazioni*, II, 829, Relation of Marino Cavalli, 1551; Brandi, 'Eigenhändige Aufzeichnungen', 256–60.

20. *KFF*, II/2, 549–63, (also printed in *LCK*, I, 360–73), Charles to Ferdinand, 11 Jan. 1530, minute. Contarini suggested that Charles saw such letters as a means of planning: Alberì, *Relazioni*, 2nd series III, 269–70, Relation of Gasparo Contarini, 4 Mar. 1530.

21. *LWT*, II, 182 (# 1687) and III, 233 (# 3245), a comment by Luther in June–July 1532. Carretero Zamora, *Gobernar*, 59–76, analysed the various 'razonamientos' delivered to the Cortes of Castile by Charles or in his name; Reiffenberg, *Histoire*, printed the records of the Greffier. Santa Cruz, *Crónica*, II, 454–8, printed a 'razonamiento' that he claimed Charles had provided to his council on 16 Sep. 1528, to justify his plan to go to Italy. Rassow, *Die Kaiser-Idee*, 11ff, accepted it as genuine and made it the foundation of what he discerned as the imperial 'Programme for 1528'; but Brandi deemed it a fake on stylistic grounds: *BKK*, II, 195–6, and 'Eigenhändige Aufzeichnungen', 229–35. Later Beinert, 'Kaiser Karls V. Rede', argued that Santa Cruz's text was genuine, but I find Brandi's rationale convincing and therefore omit the document.

22. See the various accounts of the harangue published by Morel-Fatio, 'L'espagnol', and Cadenas, *Discurso*; for the abdication speech, see the accounts of Federico Badoer to the Signory of Venice, 26 Oct. 1555 (printed by Stirling-Maxwell, *Notices*, 14–19, and in part in *CSPV*, VI/1, 221–4, including the deciphered text of a coded passage); Giovanni Battista Ricasoli to Duke Cosimo of Florence, 26 Oct. 1555 (ASF *MdP* 4319/237–41, printed in part by von Ranke, *Deutsche Geschichte*, V, 380); and Sir John Mason to Secretary of State Petrie, 27 Oct. 1555, with a 'Note' of the proceedings (printed by Kervyn de Lettenhove, *Relations politiques*, I, 4–7).

23. *SLID*, III, 142 n. 111, 'Escrito de Corte de la cesión que Su Majestad ha hecho' (ibid., II, 635–8, printed yet another account by a Spanish eyewitness).

24. Heuterus, *Rerum Belgicarum*, book XIV; 'Receuil' printed by Gachard, *Analectes Belgiques*, 87–91. Several copies exist: see GRM *Introduction*, 88 n. 1, and Gachard, 'L'abdication', 908 n. 1.

25. Baumgarten, *Geschichte*, III, vi; Roper, '"To his most learned and dearest friend"', 285 (Roper noted that 'because Luther wrote so much, his letters have shaped the way in which Reformation history has itself been written': ibid., 283). Charles published his exchanges with Francis in *Apologie de Charles-Quint* (1535: discussed in Gachard, 'Lettre', 306–9). For an example of Charles writing to a trusted minister in his own hand, addressing and sealing the letter himself explicitly so that his other ministers would not know its contents, see BMECB *Ms. Granvelle*, I, 153–5, Charles to Baron Montfort, 23 Dec. 1528 (p. 206 above); and the secret instructions to Philip dated 6 May 1543.

26. Laferl, 'Las relaciones', 115; *CMH* (2 vols) and *KFF* (initially arranged according to the date when Ferdinand received each letter, so a letter from Charles written earlier may come later, because Ferdinand did not know its contents when he wrote). Spielman and Thomas, 'Quellen', published a cache of twelve letters from Charles to Ferdinand 1514–17; von Bucholtz, *Geschichte*, IX, published extracts from many letters exchanged between Ferdinand and his siblings; *LCK* also published many of the more important letters exchanged between Charles, Ferdinand and Marie; Árpad, 'Kiadatlan', published letters about Hungary exchanged between Charles and Ferdinand Oct. 1541–Nov. 1542.

27. Mazarío Coleto, *Isabel*. The imperial spouses also exchanged special messengers expressly to bring news of their health. In 1956, Royall Tyler regretted 'the disappearance during or after World War II, of the material collected by Fritz Walser for a publication of Charles's correspondence with his Empress' (*The emperor*, 356). It has not reappeared.

28. AGS *E* 142/134 and 134bis, Charles to Ursolina de la Penna, Rome, 13 and 19 Apr. 1536. For more on Ursolina and Tadea, see ch. 14 above.

29. Moeller, *Éléonore*, 327, prints the text, now in AGS *E K* 1483, B2 # 3, noting the double irony that although the letter can now be read by anyone, and although it travelled halfway around Europe (from Zealand, where it was written, to Spain in 1517; from there to Paris in 1812 and back again in 1942), it was never read by the sole person meant to see it because Charles plucked it from between his sister's breasts before she could open it.

30. Gachard, *Correspondance de Marguerite*, II, ii–xiii and lvii–lix, published the full texts of Charles's letters (two of them holograph) from 1539, 1540 and 1556, and summaries of most of the rest. No letters from Charles to his children convey the playful yet passionate affection found in those of Philip II when separated from his teenage daughters in 1580–3: Bouza, *Cartas*.

31. Gachard, *Correspondance de Charles*; von Höfler, 'Monumenta Hispanica I: Correspondenz des Gobernadors von Castilien . . . mit Kaiser Karls V. im Jahre 1520'; Viaud, *Lettres*.

32. Heine, *Briefe* (letters to Charles from 1530, 1531 and 1532, published in Spanish with a German translation and apparatus criticus), and *CODOIN*, XIV, 1–234, and XCVII, 213–84 (letters to Charles and Los Cobos from 1530 and 1531, including some to Charles omitted by Heine). On Loaysa's career see Nieva Ocampo, 'El confesor'; Martínez Pérez, *El confesor*, ch. 4; and Lehnhoff, *Die Beichtväter*, 34–59.

33. Maurenbrecher, *Karl V*, 29*–32*, published Soto's 'parescer' to Charles 'sobre la empresa de Alemania'. See also Carro, 'Influencia'; Martínez Pérez, *El confesor*, ch. 9; and Lehnhoff, *Die Beichtväter*, 65–71.

34. Beltrán de Heredía, *Domingo de Soto*, 207–36, and 615–55 (Soto to Charles, 25 Aug. 1552, a letter of consolation after hearing of the emperor's flight from Villach, at pp. 654–5). See also Lehnhoff, *Die Beichtväter*, 71–5.

35. Escoriaza's letters quoted in chs 8 and 9; De Witte, 'Cornelis', published thirteen letters from Baersdorp, eleven of them from Augsburg in 1548 (although he did not write to the empress, who died in 1539, as de Witte repeatedly claimed, but to Marie); Mathys's letters appeared in GRM; Reiffenberg, *Lettres*, published van Male's thirty-four letters to Louis de Praet.

36. Ribadeneyra, *Vida del P. Francisco de Borja* (1592; the seven published volumes of papers by or about Borja also contain much on Charles: *Sanctus Franciscus Borgia*); Sandoval, *Historia*, 'Historia de la vida . . . Iuste', Books XII–XV.

37. Confirmed in an email from Archivist David Fliri of the HHStA dated 23 July 2018.

38. The first two volumes of *CSPSp*, covering 1520–5, omitted documents from HHStA, but the *Further Supplement* edited by Garrett Mattingly, published in 1947, printed an English précis of these (except for those printed by Lanz, *Aktenstücke und Briefe*, because a précis already existed in *L&P Henry VIII*). The same volume contains a précis of many documents once in HHStA but later returned to AGRB: see details in *CSPSp Further Supplement*, vii.

39. Akademische Druck- und Verlagsanstalt of Graz published a facsimile in 1976 (*Codices selecti*, LVII). The Morgan Library and Museum, Ms. M.491, is a very similar Book of Hours made for Charles in 1533, perhaps copied from the Vienna item: all miniatures can be viewed online at http://corsair. themorgan.org/cgi-bin/Pwebrecon.cgi?DB=Local&Search_Arg=%22ms+m.491%22+ica&Search_Code=GKEY^&CNT=50&HIST=1.

40. Aerts, 'L'âge', 579–80 (a list of Gachard's archive-seeking forays and their fruit), and 590 (quoting Reiffenberg).

41. Aerts, 'L'âge', 595 (list of the volumes of documents – almost entirely about politics and diplomacy – published by Gachard between 1830 and 1885). Gachard, *Carlos V* (2015), is a Spanish translation of his long essay on the emperor in the *Biographie Nationale de Belgique* (1872), with an appreciation of Gachard and his work by Gustaaf Janssens.

42. On Gachard's remarkable sixty-year career as archivist and historian see https://dutchrevolt.leiden. edu/dutch/geschiedschrijvers/Pages/Gachard.aspx; Wellens, 'Études'; Aerts, 'L'âge' (with some criticisms of Gachard's zeal for rearranging series by date, without regard to provenance); and, most recently, s.v. in *Nationaal Biografisch Woordenboek*, XXII, 311–45.

43. Janssens, 'Fuentes flamencas', 201 n. 41, notes the difficulty of identifying the current location of the documents printed by Lanz, and offers some guidelines.

44. BRB *Ms.* II-2270, printed with some errors by Gossart, *Charles-Quint*, 217–20. On its provenance, see *De Nederlandsche Spectator*, Jaargang 1894, p. 175 (no. 22, 2 June 1894, p. 1), which mentioned the document in its announcement of the auction. On its content, see p. 68 above.

45. Gachet, 'Extrait', 269, and Gachard, 'Notice', 243–4.

46. It is probably not in the part of the collection that remained at Chimay, because it did not appear in E. Dony, 'Les archives du château de Chimay. Recueil d'analyses, textes et extraits', BCRH, LXXXVI (1922), 11–162. I thank Wim Blockmans, Claude de Moreau de Gerbehaye, Pierre-Jean Niebes, John O'Neill and Steven Thiry for assistance in trying to locate the Registre.

47. For an excellent example of how to exploit the documents in AS Milan from Charles's reign that survived World War II, see Rabà, *Potere e poteri*. *CSP Milan* is available in digital form via BHO.

48. Gerhard, *Síntesis*, 12. Gerhard provided an analysis of the 2,911 warrants in the four volumes that cover 1548–53 – AGNM *Civil* 1271, AGNM *Mercedes* III, Kraus Ms. and Ayer Ms. – organized into twenty-nine geographical areas and six topics. This arrangement may be helpful for historians of early colonial Mexico but it precludes any measurement of the daily flow of business.

49. O'Gorman, 'Mandamientos', published a transcript of all ninety-two orders registered in this volume. Five warrants cited a royal decree. By 1550, Mendoza issued up to eleven warrants a day.

50. To sample this wonderful resource, type PARES [Portal de Archivos Españoles] into your browser and choose the option 'Búsqueda Sencilla'. Under 'Buscar' type 'Testamento Carlos V' and the dates '1554' to '1558'; of the thirteen series in four archives displayed, choose 'Archivo General de Simancas, Patronato Real', and of the five documents listed click on the last one: 'Testamento del emperador Carlos V, 6 June 1554'. Wherever you live, and whatever the hour, you can now read all 100 folios of that document online, and print out whatever interests you.

51. Danvila, *Historia*, I, 10–16, trumpeted his efforts to relocate to Madrid the AGS transcripts that he published, and thus avoid not only palaeographic challenges but also the need to live in 'a village where a visitor is unlikely to find decent accommodation'.

52. AGS *Estado K*, the papers of the council of State concerning France have been heavily used. By contrast, documents stolen from other series because of their importance, now in AGS *E* 8334–8343, have been largely neglected.

53. Núñez Contreras, *Un registro*, published a helpful summary of the contents of each document.

54. BNE *Ms.* 18,634 no. 58 (formerly ff. 260–2), 'Lo que el Comendador Mayor scrivió a Su Magestad desde Gante', undated but from the second week of Apr. 1531. *CDCV*, I, 260–3, published this fascinating *consulta*, but with numerous errors of transcription and no firm date.

55. Moreno Gallego, 'Letras misivas', 45–9, plausibly argues that the BR collection was acquired in Besançon by the count of Gondomar in the 1630s, and entered the BR with the rest of the Gondomar collection in 1806. Most of the documents have been digitized, but currently (2018) they can only be consulted in the library itself.

56. In 1921 the last descendant of the Requesens family entrusted the archive to the Jesuit Order in Catalonia. It entered the ANC in 2011.

57. There are three guides to ADN *Lettres missives*: a printed catalogue by Bruchet, available online, and two guard book catalogues, one arranged by correspondent and the other by date, available only in the ADN catalogue room.

58. See the 'Note on dates and quotes' above for more about the problems of dating these letters. Walther stressed the need for a new critical edition of the whole correspondence between father and daughter, with correct dates and transcripts: unfortunately, no one has yet answered his call.

59. The two registers of Ambassador Marillac's correspondence in 1548–9, analysed in *BNP*, II, 88–105, are now available online: BNF *F. f.* 3098–3099 (formerly *Mss.* 8625–8626), with copies (also online) at BNF *Cinq Cents de Colbert* 397–398 and *Clairambault* 343. Marillac's diplomatic correspondence for 1550, analysed in *BNP*, II, 106–14, is now at BNF *NAF* 7060 (formerly *Ms.* Brienne 89). It is not yet available online.

60. Two detailed catalogues of these documents were made when they were still in Paris: Daumet, 'Inventaire'; and Paz, *Catálogo*. For some details on Tirán, and on the documents he stole from Spanish archives that migrated to ANF, see https://francearchives.fr/en/facomponent/56390733ecad e52ac4b13529b82e7009b51887b9. The boxes of documents returned to Simancas by CADMA (now AGS *E* 8334–8343) bore the stamp of the German *Militärbefehlshaber in Frankreich*, ordering all customs officials to allow them free passage, dated 16 Oct. 1941.

61. Gutiérrez, *Trento*, III, 6–10, described these volumes.

62. Moreno Gallego, 'Letras misivas', offers the best explanation to date on the dispersion of the cardinal's papers. Van Durme, 'Les Granvelle', provides a helpful overview of the Granvelle family and their work for Charles.

63. The New York Public Library, Obadiah Rich Collection, Mss. 79–82, contains transcripts of some but not all the RAH documents, and some other Pizarro-La Gasca material apparently not in the RAH: see Brownrigg, *Colonial*, 70–85. *CODOIN*, XLIX and L, also printed many documents connected with La Gasca's pacification of Peru; and Saville, 'Some unpublished letters', published five important letters from La Gasca to the Spanish authorities in Guatemala, revealing how he adroitly mobilized the resources of the entire hemisphere to crush Pizarro's rebellion. See also La Gasca noted on p. 579 above.

64. I thank Clay Stalls and the late Bill Frank, curators of California and Hispanic Collections at the Huntington, for their help in compiling this description of the Pizarro-La Gasca papers.

65. Saletta, 'Il viaggio'. I thank Claudia Möller Recondo for help in calculating the emperor's movements. See also map 1, p. xiv, above.

66. Baumgarten, *Geschichte*, III, v–vi. He continued: 'what we really need is the publication of the entire correspondence of Charles V'. Amen.

67. BL *Cott. Ms.* Galba B.III f. 57, Young and Boleyn to Henry VIII, Brussels, 3 Nov. 1512, register copy.

68. Senatore, *'Uno mundo de carta'*, 274, Galeazzo Maria Sforza to Giovan Pietro Panigarola, 21 Mar. 1476. Senatore's title comes from the complaint of a Milanese ambassador in 1448 that his master's

multilateral diplomacy would create 'uno mundo de carta': a century later, his prediction had come true.

69. Muller, *Letters*, 81–91, Stephen Gardiner's instructions to Edmund Bonner, going to Charles's court, 20 Aug. 1538; Merriman, *Life and letters*, II, 92–4, Thomas Cromwell to Thomas Wyatt, 10 Oct. 1537; Gleason, *Gasparo Contarini*, 34–7. Contarini served as Venetian ambassador to Charles in 1521–5, as ambassador to the pope at the Bologna summit in 1529–30, and as papal legate at the Diet of Regensburg in 1541: this allowed him to compare the young with the mature emperor.

70. Merriman, *Life and letters*, II, 116, Thomas Cromwell to Thomas Wyatt, 22 Feb. 1538; Turba, *Venetianische Depeschen*, I, 240, Mocenigo to the Doge, Toledo, 22 Nov. 1538. See also ibid., 67–76, a combined report from the diplomatic summit at Nice, 24 May 1538, sent 'per oratores quinque' (those accredited to the French, Imperial and papal courts) after their long audience with Charles, providing 'tutto il ragionamento di Sua Maestà con l'ordine et parole istesse quanto più fedelmente havemo potuto' because they realized they were 'di somma importantia'. De Vivo, 'Archives of speech', stressed the value of such records.

71. Nott, *The works*, II, xii; Powell, *The complete works*, I, 76–7 (diplomats concealing their failures with a bodyguard of detail) and 204–12, Wyatt to Henry VIII, 3 Feb. 1540 (Charles interrupting, laughing and wagging his head). Brigden, *Thomas Wyatt*, chs 11–14, provided a wonderful account of the world of an ambassador at Charles's court. On his resort to composing poems (with titles like 'Tagus, fare well') to alleviate the misery of life in Spain, see Powell, 'Thomas Wyatt's poetry'.

72. *SP*, IX, 638–47, Wotton to Henry, Speyer, 9 Apr. 1544 (italics added); TNA *SP* 1/182/157–64, 'Articles concluded between the viceroy and the king's highness commissioners for ye invasion of France', undated but 31 Dec. 1543.

73. *NBD*, XIV, 82–3, Nuncio Muzzarrelli to Cardinal del Monte, 18 June 1554 (emperor absorbed by 'questi tumulti di guerra'); *NBR* XIII, 259–61, Nuncio Imola to Julius III, 28 May 1553 (for four months Charles had been too ill to grant audiences); ibid., 116–20, Nuncio Camiani to Monte, 16 Sep. 1552, and Giles, *The whole works*, I/2, 334–6, Ascham to Morison, 1 Oct. 1552 (banishment to Speyer). Nevertheless, maintaining a news blackout was easier said than done: *NBD*, XIII, 395–402, printed a detailed report by the nuncio's secretary after a secret twelve-day visit to the Imperial camp before Metz.

74. TNA *SP* 1/225/145, Stephen Vaughan to Secretary of State Paget, Antwerp, 6 Oct. 1546; Górski, *Acta Tomiciana*, V, 80–1, Dantiszek to Piotr Tomicki, Barcelona, 17 Aug. 1519, Latin (Spanish translation in Fontán and Axer, *Españoles y polacos*, 143–4). The ambassador claimed proficiency in the first 'faculty' and said he received daily instruction in the second; but 'no one succeeds in the other two without a prior disposition'.

75. BL *Cott. Ms.* Vespasian C.III/257–66, Lee to Henry VIII, 7 Sep. 1526; BAV *Vat. Lat.* 6753/203v–215, Navagero to the Signory, 6 Sep. 1526 (English summary in *CSPV*, III, 601–6); Serassi, *Delle lettere*, II, 57–71, Castiglione to Capua, 8 Sep. 1526. No dispatch from the French ambassador has survived.

76. TNA *SP* 1/22/9, endorsed 'copie of the emperours letter'. On Spinelly's career and intelligence network, see Behrens, 'The office'.

77. Rassow, *Die Kaiser-Idee*, 433–7, 'Las pláticas que el emperador passó con el señor de Pressiu', sent by Idiáquez to Los Cobos and Granvelle, Feb. 1538. For further details see ch. 10 above.

78. HSA *B* 2954 is a fine collection of holograph letters exchanged between Charles, Henry, Francis and his mother (and regent) Louise of Savoy in the 1520s; Gachard, *Correspondance de Charles*, published their letters; Vañes, 'Cartas' published sixty-three letters from Charles to Clement.

79. MacCulloch, *Thomas Cromwell*, xxiii. I have chosen the printed numbering when citing documents from TNA *SP* and the most recent numbering when citing documents from the BL *Cotton Ms.* because that is what *SPO* used.

80. *L&P Henry VIII*, V, pp. i–viii, James Gairdner's account of Brewer's achievement.

81. *RVEC*, 6. The volume, purchased by the RAH in 1801, is currently *Ms.* 9–5492.

82. *Archivio Mediceo del Principato. Inventario Sommario*, ed. by M. del Piazzo (Rome, 1951), 145–155: 'Germania: Corte Imperiale'.

83. ASF *MdP* 652/355, Ambassador Niccolini to Pagni, Regensburg, 25 July 1541 [Bia, Doc ID# 22385].

84. *NBD*, VIII, 717, report of a papal diplomat in Worms, 8 June 1545: Stroppiana 'dorme in camera della Maestà Cesarea'.

85. Sanuto, *I diarii*, XL, cols 285–6, reported how on 14 Nov. 1525, Contarini, 'dressed in black velvet', spent 'three and a half hours' reading his *Relazione* to the Senate 'in a very low voice that could scarcely be heard'. Only Venice required its ambassadors to present a 'Final Relation' after each embassy. A few Tuscan diplomats did so, but it never became standard practice.

86. Apparently, Andrea Navagero did not deliver a *Relazione*, no doubt because Charles arrested and imprisoned him: see ch. 8 above.

87. Alberì, *Relazioni*; Firpo, *Relazioni*. Gleason, *Gasparo Contarini*, 34–8, provides a succinct description of the genre.

88. Leva, 'Marino Sanuto', 117.

89. One tiny example: *CSPV*, III, 160–1, Contarini to the Signory, 16 July 1521, says the ambassador and Charles were 'in consultation well nigh two hours'; yet both Sanuto's text and Contarini's register copy say 'quasi hore 3' (Sanuto, *I diarii*, XXI, cols. 318–20; BNMV *Ms. Italiani Clase VII*, cod. 1009/75–7). Nevertheless, some of Brown's transcripts in *CSPV* include decrypts of passages coded in the original for which the key is now lost, and thus provide more information than the originals.

90. Fontán and Axer, *Españoles y polacos*, 324, Krysztof Szydlowiecki to Dantiszek, 27 Apr. 1530, thanking him for sending a portrait of Cortés, and noting that King Ferdinand had given him a 'book of the *Cartas de Relación*', no doubt a copy of ÖNB *Codex Vindobonensis* S. N. 1600 (see p. 575 above).

91. Printing details on Snouckaert from Pettegree and Walsby, *Netherlandish books*, II, 1231, # 28103–# 28110. Snouckaert left an archive: see http://www.gahetna.nl/collectie/archief/pdf/NL-HaNA_1.10.76. ead.pdf, p. 36. See also the entries for each chronicler in the bibliography.

92. Redondo, *Antonio*, 304, and Druez, 'Perspectives', 86, both charted the overlapping appointments of Charles's chroniclers.

93. For full publication details see the entry for each chronicle in the Bibliography to this volume. Morel-Fatio never published further instalments of his *Historiographie*, but for updates see Chabod, *Carlos V*, 142–8; Kagan, *Clio*, ch. 2; Chaunu and Escamilla, *Charles*, 1,134–9; and the detailed studies of García Fuentes, 'Bernabé de Busto', and Cuart Moner, 'Juan Ginés'.

94. Morel-Fatio, *Historiographie*, 61–6, and Cuart Moner, 'Juan Ginés', 359–63, noted that Sepúlveda included material provided to him directly by Charles (for example, on the Cortes of Castile and the meeting with Francis at Aigues Mortes in 1538), as well as what he had seen for himself while accompanying the emperor in 1542–3 and what he learned from other eyewitnesses (for example, from Antonio de Fonseca concerning the burning of Medina del Campo in 1520 and from a servant whom he ordered to accompany Charles to Algiers in 1541).

95. Beinert, 'Kaiser Karls V. Rede', Redondo, *Antonio*, 303–49, and Civil, 'Enjeux', examined in detail the passages in Santa Cruz plagiarized from Guevara. Morel-Fatio, *Historiographie*, 102–3, cited a letter from Santa Cruz that recorded a conversation with Charles in 1556, on his way to Yuste.

96. Mariscal, 'A clown', 67. Two editions of this idiosyncratic work appeared in the 1980s: see the Bibliography under 'Zúñiga' for details.

97. See Delsalle, 'Un homme', for some details on Guyon and his *Mémoires*.

98. See details in Gonzalo Sánchez-Molero, 'Acerca de los *Hechos del Emperador*'.

99. Zimmerman, 'The publication', 59–61; Giovio, *Pauli Iovii opera: II, Epistularum pars altera*, 105, Giovio to Saxony and Hesse, 29 Aug. 1547.

100. In 1562 his *Historiae* appeared in two distinct Spanish translations, provoking a hostile counterblast, *El antijovio*, five years later: Cuart Moner, 'Jovio en España'.

101. Mignet, *Charles-Quint*, 282–3 (Charles called both Sleidan and Giovio liars); Sleidan, *De statu*, sig. Aiii. Sepúlveda, *Historia de Carlos V*, VI, pp. CIV–CVII, Sepúlveda to van Male, 1 June 1557, reported receiving a copy of Sleidan's book from Luis de Ávila, 'with assurances that it would come in useful for revising what I had written on events in Germany', demonstrating that the work became known at the imperial court almost at once. Sleidan's work went on the Index of Prohibited Books in 1558. For more on the author and his *Commentaries*, see Kess, *Johann Sleidan*, especially ch. 5.

102. Gomara, *Annals*, a bilingual edition in Spanish and English. The editor, R. B. Merriman, suggested that Gómara composed this work, which extols Charles at every turn, explicitly to secure a reversal of the decision to ban his earlier *Historia de las Indias*.

103. Redondo, *Antonio*, 303–49, expertly examined the overlaps between Guevara, Santa Cruz and Sandoval.

104. Thomas, *Annalium*, published posthumously in 1624 with a German translation four years later. On the frustrated love-match, see ch. 3 above.

105. Fagel, 'Carlos de Luxemburgo', 30 and 63 n. 2, listed these sites and included reproductions of them. For the excavations at the Coudenberg palace, and on the park that surrounded it, see Heymans, *Le palais du Coudenberg*, 195–6 and 209. By chance, the 'chapelle de Charles-Quint' survived the fire, but was demolished in 1775.

106. Rosenthal, *The palace*, and Tafuri, *Interpreting*, ch. 6.

107. Details in Checa Cremades, *Monumentos restaurados*; Baker-Bates, 'The "cloister life "'; and Martín González, 'El palacio'.

108. See, for example, the splendid set of nineteen wooden game pieces, with a portrait on one side and an identification on the other, reproduced in Haag, *Frauen*, 82.

109. Luis Zapata de Chaves, writing about Charles in the 1580s, suggested that 'Cobos was his Favourite in matters of state, and Don Luis de Ávila in his private affairs': Gayangos, *Miscelánea*, 185. On the Museo Carolino, see Gonzalo Sánchez-Molero, 'Acerca de los *Hechos del Emperador*', 436–8; and Marcks, 'Die Antikensammlung'. For the aborted sale, see http://www.hoy.es/plasencia/busto-carlos-palacio-20171212220145-nt.html.

110. Ferer, *Music*, 240. See also pp. 24, 161–6 and 182–201, where she linked some compositions with certain events.

111. Gachard, 'Particularités', 128–9 (reprinted in Gachard, *Études*, II, 352–3); Schlegelmilch, *Die Jugendjahre*.

112. *CDCV*, IV, 11, part of a revealing account of how the historian who commissioned the project, Cayetano Alcázar, 'gave me a hand when so many turned their backs on me'. He repeated the story in Fernández Álvarez, *Carlos V. Un hombre*, 11.

113. *CDCV* purposely omitted documents already published in major collections: not only *CODOIN* but also *LCK* (with 1,009 documents from Brussels) and *PEG* (739 documents from Charles's reign, almost all from Besançon). Peiró Martín, *En los altares*, 174–5 and 184–5, provided interesting details on the making of *CDCV* by the 'falangista de juventud y ocasión Manuel Fernández Álvarez'.

114. Cohn, 'Did bribery', 2.

115. From B. Greiff, 'Was Kayser Carolus dem V^{ten} die Römisch Künglich Wal cost im 1520', *Jahresbericht des historischen Kreis-Vereins in Schwaben und Neuburg*, XXXIV (Augsburg, 1868), 9–50 (also published as an offprint).

116. Tyler, *The emperor*, 357–8; *BKK*, II, 28–9; Dixon, 'Charles V', 106–8. Chabod, *Carlos V*, 152, also ranked Brandi's biography the best. See also his long essay on 'Carlos V en la obra de Brandi' (op. cit., 577–606) and his introduction to the Italian edition of Brandi's biography (idem, pp. 607–29). Royall Tyler (1884–1953), fluent in four languages and proficient in three more, served in both world wars (the first in the US infantry, the second in US intelligence) and worked for both the League of Nations and the United Nations, as well as editing the last five volumes of *CSPSp* between 1913 and 1954 – all activities that provided insights into Charles and the problems he faced. For a thoughtful consideration of the biographies by Brandi, Tyler and others, see Galasso, 'L'opera'.

117. *BKK*, II, 196, admitted that a document in the RAH, Madrid, cited by an earlier historian, 'ist mir unbekannt geblieben'. It is significant that the various archival guides published in *B&S* omit ADN. For more on Brandi and his works on Charles, see Plassmann, *Karl Brandi*, and p. 581 above.

118. Simons, *Keizer Karel*; Fagel, 'A broken portrait', 77–8.

119. Möller Recondo, 'Carlos V', 375–80, listed the categories and contents of the Biblioteca Virtual Cervantes site.

120. Atlas, *The shadow*, 327

121. *CSPSp*, VI/2, 105, Charles to Eustache Chapuys, 12 Aug. 1542; Brandi, 'Die politischen Testamente', *B&S*, II, 259 n. 1, Perrenot to Ferdinand, 9 May 1557 (documents from the imperial chancery that 'etliche fur Algers verloren wordten').

122. Vargas-Hidalgo, *Guerra y diplomacia*, xi, 'Informe' by Gabriel de Zayas, 4 Oct. 1592. See also Gachard, *Correspondance de Marguerite*, I, ii n. 3, Courtewille to Viglius, 23 Dec. 1559.

123. HHStA *Hs. Blau* 595/188, and 596/1/277, both record that the register 'a esté collationé en l'an 1558 et trouvé concorder avec les lettres originalles'. Head, 'Configuring', 504–6, notes that compiling such registers became standard practice among Habsburg archivists in the 1520s.

124. TNA *SP* 1/88/162, Richard Pate to Cromwell, 11 Dec. 1534; *KFF*, V, 11, quoting Herwig Wolfram; *CMH*, I, 384–9 and 447–8, Mary to Charles, 3 Aug. and 4 Sep. 1532.

125. Walther, *Die Anfänge*, 246, Maximilian to Margaret, 7 Dec. 1516, copy; *KFF*, II/1, 96–7, Charles to Ferdinand, 1 July 1527 (Ferdinand's letter of 9 May has been lost, which may mean that Charles destroyed it).

126. *CSPSp*, I, xiii–xv. In 2018 the Spanish CNI began to use modern techniques of cryptanalysis on sixteenth-century documents, starting with the coded letters sent by the Gran Capitán in Naples to King Ferdinand in Spain.

127. Kreiten, *Der Briefwechsel*, 248–9, Maximilian to Margaret, 29 Apr. 1508, holograph; BL *Cott. Ms. Galba* B.V/241, Margaret to Wolsey, Ghent, 12 May 1517 ('car ce sont choses que pourroit mieulx a dire de bouche que par lettre'); Danvila, *Historia*, II, 489, Adrian to Charles, 31 Aug. 1520.

128. AHN Nobleza *Frías* C.23 D.5, Charles to the count of Haro, 19 Aug. 1528; HHStA *Hs. Blau* 596/1/103–4, Charles to Ferdinand, 18 Apr. 1546, register copy.

129. ADN *B* 2249 (77,795), receipt signed by 'maistre Adriaen Florencii', 1 Oct. 1515; ADN *B* 2510/608 and 621, account of Receiver-General Bouloingne for 1555 (italics added).

130. *PEG*, II, 460–1, Charles to Ambassador Hannart, 25 May 1536, minute; Ball and Parker, *Cómo ser rey*, 86 and 133, Charles's instruction of 6 May 1543.

131. Caro, *The years of Lyndon Johnson: The path to power*, 776–7; Caro, *The years of Lyndon Johnson: Master of the Senate*, 1,052–3; and an interview with Caro on the NPR programme 'Fresh Air' on 13 May 2013, http://www.npr.org/books/authors/151439873/robert-a-caro. For an early modern example of 'unknown unknowns', see MacCulloch, *Thomas Cromwell*, 1–3, noting the dearth of outgoing letters in Cromwell's own archive and postulating that 'Such a vast loss of the out-tray can only be the result of deliberate destruction'. For a twentieth-century parallel, see Clark, *The sleepwalkers*, 19, noting that the leading Serbian politician Nikola Pašić (1845–1926) 'tended not to commit ideas and decisions to paper, or even, indeed, to the spoken word. He was in the habit of regularly burning his papers.'

132. Cadenas y Vicent, *Entrevistas*; Daza, *Quarta parte*, 137–8 (the vision of Fray Gonzalo Méndez: see ch. 17).

BIBLIOGRAPHY

So much has been written about Charles V that a comprehensive bibliography of works about him would require a separate volume. The list below provides details only for printed works cited in this biography.

PRINTED PRIMARY SOURCES

Acta Pacis Westphalicae, ed. K. Repgen, Series II, Part B, *Die franzözischen Korrespondenzen*, 8 vols to date (Münster, 1979–2011)

Álamos de Barrientos, Balthasar, *Discurso político al rey Felipe III* (1598; ed. M. Sánchez, Madrid, 1990)

Alba, duke of, *see* Berwick y Alba, duchess of and duke of

Alberì, E., *Relazioni degli ambasciatori veneti al Senato*, 15 vols in three series (Florence, 1839–63); *see also* Firpo, L.

Albicante, Giovanni Alberto, *Trattato del'intrar in Milano di Carlo V, C[esare] sempre Aug[usto], con le proprie figure de li archi* (Milan, 1541)

Álvarez, Vicente, *Relación del camino y buen viaje que hizo el príncipe de España don Phelipe* (1552); reprinted in Calvete de Estrella, *El felicíssimo viaje* (2001 edition), 595–681

Anon., *Warhafftige und gewise newe Zeytung, Wie die Roem. Key. Mey. auff den xx. Octobris, deß xlj. Jars, mit einer treffenlichen Armada, die Statt Algiero zu Erobern, daselbst ankommen* (Augsburg, 1541)

Anon., *La renunciación que [e]l emperador Nuestro Señor ha hecho de todos los reynos de Castilla y Aragón y de todo quanto tenía. Las mercedes que ha en la última consulta. Las treguas que se han hecho entre su magestad y el rey de Francia* (Valencia, 1556)

Anon., *The advice of Charles the Fifth, Emperor of Germany, and King of Spain, to his son Philip the Second upon his resignation of the crown of Spain to his said son* (London, 1670)

Anon., 'Dagverhaal van den veldtogt van Keizer Karel V in 1554', ed. R. Macaré, in *Kronijk van het Historisch Genootschap gevestigd te Utrecht*, VII (1851), 280–308

Anon., *Cartas de Indias* (Madrid, 1877)

Árpád, K., 'Kiadatlan levelek a német birod. Magyarországi nagy hadi vállallatának történetéhez 1542', in *Történelmi Tár. Évnegyedes folyóirat Kiadja a Magyar Történelmi társulat* (Budapest, 1880), 490–540

Arteaga Garza, B. and G. Pérez San Vicente, *Cedulario cortesiano* (Mexico City, 1949)

Ascham, Roger, *A report and discourse, see* Giles, J. A.

Ávila y Zúñiga, Luis de, *Comentario del illustre señor don Luis de Ávila y Zúñiga, comendador mayor de Alcántara: de la Guerra de Alemaña hecha de Carlo V Máximo, emperador romano, rey de España, en el año de M.D.XLVI y M.D.XLVII* (1548; Antwerp 1550)

Avonto, L., *Mercurino Arborio di Gattinara e l'America: documenti inediti per la storia delle Indie Nuove nell'archivio del Gran Cancelliere di Carlo V* (Vercelli, 1981)

Balan, P., *Monumenta reformationis lutheranae ex tabulariis secretioribus Santissimi sedis, 1521–1525* (Regensburg, 1884)

Ball, R. and G. Parker, *Cómo ser rey. Las Instrucciones secretas de Carlos V en mayo de 1543. Edición crítica* (Madrid, 2014)

Barillon, Jean, *Journal de Jean Barrillon, secrétaire du Chancelier Duprat 1515–1521*, ed. P. de Vaissière, 2 vols (Paris, 1897–9)

Baronius, Cesare, et al., *Annales ecclesiastici denuo et accurate excuse*, 37 vols (Paris and Bar-le-Duc, 1864–83)

Bauer, W., R. Lacroix, C. Laferl, C. Thomas and H. Wolfram, *Die Korrespondenz Ferdinands I. I. Familienkorrespondenz*, 5 vols to date (Vienna, 1912–2015: Veröffentlichungen der Kommission für Neuere Geschichte Österreichs, XI, XXX, XXXI, LVIII, XC and CIX)

BIBLIOGRAPHY

Beatis, Antonio de, *The travel journal of Antonio de Beatis: Germany, Switzerland, the Low Countries, France and Italy, 1517–1518* (London, 1979: Hakluyt Society 2nd series CL)

Beinert, B., 'El Testamento Político de Carlos V de 1548. Estudio crítico', in *Carlos V. Homenaje de la Universidad de Granada* (Granada, 1958), 401–38

Beinert, B., 'Kaiser Karls V. Rede im Staatsrat vom September 1528. Zum Quellenwert der Reden bei Santa Cruz', *Jahrbuch für Geschichte von Staat, Wirtschaft und Gesellschaft Lateinamerikas*, IV (1967), 127–61

Beltrán de Heredía, V., *Cartulario de la Universidad de Salamanca (1218–1600)*, II (Salamanca, 1970)

Benavent Benavent, J. and M. J. Bertomeu Masiá, *El secuestro que ordenó Carlos V: introducción, documentos inéditos y notas* (Valencia, 2012)

Berichte und Studien zur Geschichte Karls V., 20 articles (Göttingen, 1930–42); *see individual entries under* Brandi, Hasenclever, Looz-Corswarem, Stix and Walser

Bernays, J., H. Gerber et al., eds, *Urkunden und Akten der Stadt Strassburg. Zweite Abteilung: Politische Correspondenz der Stadt Strassburg im Zeitalter der Reformation*, 5 vols (Strasbourg, 1882–1935)

Bertomeu Masiá, M. J., *La guerra secreta de Carlos V contra el papa. La cuestión de Parma y Piacenza en la correspondencia del cardenal Granvela. Edición, estudio y notas* (Valencia, 2009)

Berwick y Alba, duchess of, *Documentos escogidos del Archivo de la Casa de Alba* (Madrid, 1891)

Berwick y Alba, duke of, *Correspondencia de Gutierre Gómez de Fuensalida, embajador en Alemania, Flandes e Inglaterra 1496–1509* (Madrid, 1907)

Berwick y Alba, duke of, 'Correspondencia de Carlos V con el marqués del Vasto, gobernador del Milanesado (años 1540–1542)', *BRAH*, LXXXVIII (1926), 71–145

Berwick y Alba, duke of, *Epistolario del III duque de Alba*, 3 vols (Madrid, 1952)

Bofarull y Sans, F. de, *Predilección del emperador Carlos V por los catalanes: memoria documentada* (Barcelona, 1895)

Boom, G. de, 'Voyage et couronnement de Charles-Quint à Bologne', *BCRH*, CI (1936), 55–106

Borgia, Francisco, *see Sanctus Franciscus Borgia*, Cienfuegos, *and* Ribadeneyra

Bornate, C., 'Mémoire du chancelier de Gattinara sur les droits de Charles-Quint au duché de Bourgogne', *BCRH*, LXXVI (1907), 391–533

Bornate, C., 'Historia vite et gestorum per dominum magnum cancellarium (Mercurino Arborio di Gattinara), con note, aggiunte e documenti', in Bornate, *Miscellanea di storia italiana*, 3rd series XVII (XLVIII) (1915), 231–585

Borrás Gualis, G. M., J. F. Criado Mainar and M. Serrano Marqués, eds, *La imagen triunfal del Emperador. La jornada de la coronación imperial de Carlos V en Bolonia y el friso del Ayuntamiento de Tarazona* (Madrid, 2000)

Bourrilly, V.-L., ed., *Histoire journalière d'Honorat de Valbelle (1498–1539): journal d'un bourgeois de Marseille au temps de Louis XII et de François Ier*, 2 vols (Aix-en-Provence, 1985)

Bouza Álvarez, F. J., ed., *Cartas de Felipe II a sus hijas* (2nd edition, Madrid, 1998)

Braamcamp Freire, A., 'Ida da Imperatriz D. Isabel para Castela', *Academia das Sciências de Lisboa: Boletim da Classe de Letras (antigo Boletim da Segunda Classe)*, XIII/2 (1919), 561–657

Bradford, W., ed., *Correspondence of the Emperor Charles V and his ambassadors at the courts of England and France* (New York, 1850)

Brandenburg, E., et al., eds, *Politische Korrespondenz des Herzogs und Kurfürsten Moritz von Sachsen*, 6 vols (Leipzig and Berlin, 1900–2006)

Brandi, K., 'Die politischen Testamente Karls V', *B&S*, II (1930), 258–93

Brandi, K., 'Die Überlieferung der Akten Karls V im Haus-, Hof-, und Staatsarchiv, Wien', in four parts, *B&S*, IV (1931), 241–77, V (1932), 18–51, VII (1933), 229–59 and XI (1933), 513–78

Brandi, K., 'Eigenhändige Aufzeichnungen Karls V. aus dem Anfang des Jahres 1525. Der Kaiser und sein Kanzler', *B&S*, IX (1933), 219–33

Brandi, K., 'Die Testamente und politische Instruktionen Karls V., inbesondere diejenigen der Jahre 1543/44', *B&S*, XII (1935), 31–107

Brandi, K., 'Nach Pavia. Pescara und die italienischen Staaten, Sommer und Herbst 1525', *B&S*, XVII (1939), 139–231

Brandi, K., 'Aus den Kabinettsakten des Kaisers', *B&S*, XIX (1941), 161–257

Brantôme, Pierre de Bourdeille, lord of, *Oeuvres complètes de Pierre de Bourdeille, seigneur de Brantôme*, ed. L. Lalanne, 11 vols (Paris, 1864–82)

Bretschneider, K. G. et al., eds, *Corpus Reformatorum*, 101 vols to date (Halle, 1834–)

Brieger, T., ed., *Quellen und Forschungen zur Geschichte der Reformation. I. Aleander und Luther 1521: die vervollständigen Aleander-Depeschen nebst Untersuchungen über den Wormser Reichstag* (Gotha, 1884)

Brizio, E., ' "The country is large, and beautiful and happy." Lelio Pecci's travel journal of his 1549 mission to Flanders', *Quaderni d'italianistica*, XXXI/2 (2010), 51–89

Brown, R., *Four years at the Court of Henry VIII. Selections of despatches written by the Venetian ambassador Sebastian Giustinian [1515–1519]*, 2 vols (London, 1854)

Brownrigg, E. B., *Colonial Latin American manuscripts and transcripts in the Obadiah Rich Collection: an inventory and index* (New York, 1978)

Bruchet, M. and E. Lancien, *L'itinéraire de Marguerite d'Autriche, gouvernante des Pays-Bas* (Lille, 1934)

Bujanda, J. M. de, *Index de l'Université de Louvain, 1546, 1550, 1558* (Geneva, 1986)

Burgon, J. W., *The life and times of Sir Thomas Gresham*, 2 vols (London, 1839)

Burnet, Gilbert, *History of the Reformation of the Church of England* (new edition, London, 1820), part III, ii, 'A collection of records, letters and original papers'

Burton, J. H., ed., *Life and correspondence of David Hume*, 2 vols (Edinburgh, 1846)

Buschbell, G. et al., eds, *Concilium Tridentinum. Diariorum, actorum, epistularum, tractatuum nova collectio*, 13 vols in 18 (Freiburg-im-Breisgau, 1901–2001)

Busto, Bernabé de, *Geschichte des Schmalkaldischen Krieges*, ed. Otto Adalbert, count of Looz-Corswarem (Burg, 1938: *Texte und Forschungen im Auftrage der Preussichen Akademie der Wissenschaften*, I). *See also* García Fuentes

Cadenas y Vicent, V. de, *El Protectorado de Carlos V en Génova: la 'condotta' de Andrea Doria* (Madrid, 1977)

Cadenas y Vicent, V. de, *Discurso de Carlos V en Roma en 1536* (Madrid, 1982)

Cadenas y Vicent, V. de, *Entrevistas con el Emperador Carlos V* (2nd edition, Madrid, 1983)

Cadenas y Vicent, V. de, *Doble coronación de Carlos V en Bolonia, 22–24/II/1530* (Madrid, 1983)

Cadenas y Vicent, V. de, *Carlos I de Castilla, señor de las Indias* (Madrid, 1988)

Cadenas y Vicent, V. de, *Las supuestas 'Memorias' del Emperador Carlos V* (Madrid, 1989)

Cadenas y Vicent, V. de, *Diario del emperador Carlos V. Itinerarios, permanencias, despachos, sucesos y efemérides relevantes de su vida* (Madrid, 1992)

Cadenas y Vicent, V. de, *Caminos y derroteros que recorrió el emperador Carlos V: noticias fundamentales para su historia* (Madrid, 1999)

Cadenas y Vicent, V. de, *Carlos de Habsburgo en Yuste, 3-II-1557–21-IX-1558* (3rd edition, Madrid, 2000)

Cadenas y Vicent, V. de, 'Un documento "A barras derechas" de Carlos V', *Hidalguía*, CCXCIV (2002), 685–712

[Caimo, N.], *Lettere d'un vago italiano ad un suo amico*, 2 vols (Milan, 1761–8)

Calderón Ortega, J. M., *Testamento del Rey Fernando el Católico, 22 de enero de 1516. Original conservado en la Fundación Casa de Alba* (Madrid, 2016)

Calendar of Letters, Despatches, and State Papers, relating to the negotiations between England and Spain, preserved in the archives at Vienna, Simancas, Besançon, Brussels, Madrid and Lille, 13 vols, ed. G. A. Bergenroth, P. de Gayangos et al. (London, 1862–1954)

Calendar of State Papers, Foreign Series, of the reign of Edward VI, 1547–1553, ed. W. B. Turnbull (London, 1861)

Calendar of State Papers, Foreign Series, of the reign of Mary, 1553–1558, ed. W. B. Turnbull (London, 1861)

Calendar of State Papers, Foreign Series, of the reign of Elizabeth, 23 vols, ed. J. Stevenson et al. (London, 1863–1950)

Calendar of State Papers and Manuscripts in the Archives and Collections of Milan, 1385–1618, ed. A. B. Hinds (London, 1912)

Calendar of State Papers and Manuscripts relating to English Affairs existing in the archives and collections of Venice, 38 vols, ed. H. F. Brown et al. (London, 1864–1947)

Calvete de Estrella, Juan Cristóbal, *El felicíssimo viaje del muy alto y muy poderoso Príncipe don Phelippe* (Antwerp, 1552; ed. P. Cuenca, Madrid, 2001)

Calvete de Estrella, Juan Cristóbal, *El tvmvlo imperial, adornado de Historias y Letreros y Epitaphios en prosa y verso latín* (Valladolid, 1559)

Calvete de Estrella, Juan Cristóbal, *Rebelión de Pizarro en el Perú y vida de don Pedro Lagasca*, ed. A. Paz y Melía, 2 vols (composed 1565–7; Madrid, 1889)

Campanella, Tommaso, *De monarchia hispanica discursus* (Amsterdam, 1640)

Canestrini, G. and A. Desjardins, *Négociations diplomatiques de la France avec la Toscane*, 6 vols (Paris, 1859–86)

Caroli Romanorum regis recessuri adlocutio in conventu Hispaniarum (Rome, 1520)

Castet, Silvestre, *Annales des Frères Mineurs composées en Latin abbregées & traduites en François*, VIII (Toulouse, 1682)

BIBLIOGRAPHY

Castiglione, Baldassare, *Il libro del Cortegiano* (1528; ed. G. Preti, Turin, 1965)

Castiglione, Baldassare, *see also* Serassi *and* Volpi

Catalogue: Charles-Quint et son temps (2nd edition, Ghent, 1955)

Catalogue des Actes de François Ier, 10 vols (Paris, 1887–1908)

Cauchies, J.-M., ed., *Jean Lemaire des Belges. Le carnet de notes d'un chroniqueur: août 1507–février 1509* (Brussels, 2008)

Causa formada en 1526 a D. Antonio de Acuña, obispo de Zamora, por la muerte que dió a Mendo de Noguerol, alcalde de la fortaleza de Simancas (Valladolid, 1849)

Cavalcanti, Bartolommeo, *Trattati sopra gli ottimi reggimenti delle repubbliche antiche e moderne* (1552; Venice 1571; reprinted Milan, 1805)

Cedillo, Jerónimo López de Ayala, count of, *El cardenal Cisneros: gobernador del reino. Estudio histórico*, 3 vols (Madrid, 1921–8)

Cervantes Saavedra, Miguel de, *El ingenioso hidalgo Don Quijote de la Mancha*, 2 parts (Madrid, 1605–15)

Cervantes de Salazar, Francisco, *Túmulo Imperial de la Gran Ciudad de México* (Mexico City, 1560; reprinted in E. O'Gorman, ed., *México en 1554 y Túmulo Imperial*, Mexico City, 1963)

Champollion-Figeac, A., *Captivité du roi François Ier* (Paris, 1847)

Charles V, *Mémoirs, see* Cadenas y Vicent *and* Kervyn de Lettenhove

Charrière, E., ed., *Négociations de la France dans le Levant*, 4 vols (Paris, 1848–60)

Charvet, E.-L.-G, ed., *Lettres et documents pour servir à l'histoire du XVIe siècle et à celle de Eustache Chapuys, ambassadeur de Charles-Quint. Première partie: correspondance avec Henri-Cornelius Agrippa de Nettesheim* (Lyons, 1875)

Chastellain, Georges, 'Chronique', in Baron Kervyn de Lettenhove, *Oeuvres de Georges Chastellain*, 8 vols (Brussels, 1864–6)

Checa Cremades, F., ed., *Los inventarios de Carlos V y la familia imperial*, 3 vols (Madrid, 2010)

Checa Cremades, F., 'Emperor Charles V: Inventories, possessions and collections', in Checa Cremades, *Los inventarios de Carlos V*, I, 39–834

Chmel, Joseph, ed., *Urkunden, Briefe und Ackenstücke zur Geschichte Maximilians I. und seiner Zeit* (Stuttgart, 1845: Bibliothek des literarischen Vereins in Stuttgart, X)

Chmel, J., 'Review of Lanz', *Correspondenz Karls V.*, vol. I, in *Jahrbücher der Literatur*, CXI (July–Sep. 1845), 174–198

Chytraeus, David, *Chronicon Saxoniae et vicinarum aliquot gentium, ab anno Christi 1500 usque ad M.D.XCIII* (Leipzig, 1593); German version, *Chronicon, was in Sachsenn und benachbartenn ordischen und andern Lendern die nechsten hundert Jahr hero füre in Zustand gewesen* (Leipzig, 1598)

Cicogna, Emmanuele Antonio, *Delle Inscrizioni Veneziane*, VI (Venice, 1853)

Cienfuegos, Álvaro de, *La heroyca vida, virtudes y milagros del grande S. Francisco de Borja* (Madrid, 1702)

Cieza de León, Pedro, *Primera parte de la Chrónica del Perú* (Antwerp, 1554)

Cimber, L., and F. Danjou, eds, *Archives curieuses de l'histoire de France depuis Louis XI jusqu'à Louis XVIII, ou collection de pièces rares et intéressantes. Publiées d'après les textes conservés à la Bibliothèque Royale, et accompagnées de notices et d'éclaircissemens*, 1e série, 15 vols (Paris, 1834–7)

Claretta, M., *Notice pour server à la vie de Mercurin de Gattinara, Grand Chancelier de Charles-Quint d'après des documents originaux* (Chambéry, 1898; also published as *Mémoires et documents publiés par la Société savoisienne d'Histoire et d'Archéologie*, 2nd series XII (1898)), 245–344

Colección de Documentos Inéditos para la historia de España, 112 vols (Madrid, 1842–95)

Colección de Documentos Inéditos relativos al descubrimiento, conquista y organización de las antiguas posesiones de América y Oceania, 42 vols (Madrid, 1864–84)

Colección de Documentos Inéditos relativos al descubrimiento, conquista y organización de las antiguas posesiones españoles de Ultramar, 25 vols (Madrid, 1885–1932)

Correspondance du Cardinal de Granvelle, ed. E. Poullet and C. Piot, 12 vols (Brussels, 1877–96)

Cortes de los antiguos reinos de León y de Castilla, ed. M. Colmeiro, 7 vols (Madrid, 1861–1903)

Cortés, Hernán, *Cartas de relación* (ed. M. Hernández, Madrid, 1985)

Cortijo Ocaña, A. and A., *Cartas desde México y Guatemala (1540–1635). El proceso Díaz de Reguera (Bancroft Library Ms. 92/83z)* (Cáceres, 2003)

Cosenza, John, archbishop of, 'Copia litterarvm reverendissimo domini Ioannis Archiepiscopi Consentini apvd Cesaream Maiestatem nuntij apostoloici', in *Provinciae sive regiones in India occidentali noviter repertae in vltima navigatione* (n.p., 1520)

Covarrubias Orozco, Sebastián de, *Tesoro de la lengua castellana, o española* (Madrid, 1611)

Craigie, J., ed., *The Basilicon Doron of King James VI*, 2 vols (Edinburgh, 1944, 1950: Scottish Texts Society, 3rd series XVI, XVIII)

Danvila y Collado, M., *El poder civil en España. V: Documentos e ilustraciones* (Madrid, 1885)

690

BIBLIOGRAPHY

Danvila y Collado, M., *Historia crítica y documentada de las Comunidades de Castilla*, 6 vols (Madrid 1897–1900: Memorial histórico español, XXXV–XL)

Daumet, G., 'Inventaire de la Collection Tirán', *BH*, XIX (1917), 189–99, XX (1918), 36–42 and 233–48, and XXI (1919), 218–30 and 282–95

Daza, Antonio, *Quarta parte de la chrónica general de nuestro padre San Francisco y su apostólica orden* (Valladolid, 1611)

De Gaulle, C., *Discours et messages, III: Avec le renouveau, mai 1958 – juillet 1962* (Paris, 1970)

De Grieck, Jan, *De heerlycke ende vrolycke daeden van keyser Carel den V; Les actions heroiques et plaisantes de l'empereur Charles V* (Antwerp, 1675)

De Witte, A., 'Cornelis van Baersdorp, lijfarts van Keizer Karel. Korrespondentie 1548–1561', *Scientiarum Historia: Tijdschrift voor de Geschiedenis van de Wetenschappen en de Geneeskunde*, I (1959), 177–90

Deutsche Reichstagsakten, jüngere Reihe. Deutsche Reichstagsakten unter Kaiser Karl V., ed. A. Kluckhohn et al., 20 vols, some in multiple parts (Gotha and Munich, 1893–2009)

Díaz del Valle y de la Puerta, Lázaro, *Historia del reyno de León y principado de Asturias*, II part 1 (1665: manuscript copy in BL *Egerton* 1878)

Dittich, F., 'Nuntiaturberichte Giovanni Morones vom Reichstage zu Regensburg, 1541', *Historisches Jahrbuch der Görresgesellschaft*, IV (1883), 395–472, 618–73

Dolce, Lodovico, *Le vite di tutti gl'imperadori romani da Giulio Cesare fino a Massimiliano, tratte per M. Lodovico Dolce dal libro spagnolo del Signor Pietro Messia* (Venice, 1561, reprinted 1664)

Dolce, Lodovico, *Vita dell'inuittiss. e gloriosiss. Imperador Carlo Quinto* (Venice, 1561)

D'Onofrio, G. I., *Il carteggio intimo di Margherita d'Austria, duchessa di Parma e Piacenza. Studio critico di documenti farnesiani* (Naples, 1919)

Du Bellay, Martin and Guillaume, *Mémoires de Martin et Guillaume du Bellay*, ed. V.-L. Bourrilly and F. Vindry, 4 vols (Paris, 1908–19)

Duller, E., *Neue Beiträge zur Geschichte Philipps des Grossmüthigen, Landgrafen von Hessen, bisher ungedruckte Briefe dieses Fürsten und seiner Zeitgenossen, Karls V., Ferdinands I., der Königin Maria von Ungarn usw.* (Darmstadt, 1842)

Dumont, Jean, *Corps universel diplomatique du droit des gens; contenant vn recueil des traitez d'alliance, de paix, de treve, de neutralité, de commerce, d'échange . . . & autres contrats, qui ont été faits en Europe, depuis le regne de l'empereur Charlemagne jusques à présent*, 8 vols (Amsterdam, 1726–31)

Du Puys, Remy, *La tryumphante entrée de Charles, prince des Espagnes, en Bruges* (Paris 1515; ed. S. Anglo, New York, 1970)

Dürer, Albrecht, *Diary of his journey to the Netherlands, 1520–1521, accompanied by The Silverpoint Sketchbook, and paintings and drawings made during his journey*, ed. J.-A. Goris and G. Marlier (Greenwich, CT, 1971)

Dürer, Albrecht, *Schriftlicher Nachlass*, ed. H. Rupprich, I (Berlin, 1956)

Eichberger, D., 'Margaret of Austria and the documentation of her collection in Mechelen', in Checa Cremades, *Los inventarios de Carlos V*, III, 2,337–2,563

Ellis, H., *Original letters illustrative of English history including numerous royal letters from autographs in the British Museum, and one or two other collections*, 3 series, 11 vols, 2nd edition (London, 1824–46)

Enzinas, Francisco de, *Mémoires de Francisco de Enzinas. Texte latin inédit avec la traduction française du XVIe siècle en regard, 1543–1545*, ed. C. A. Campan, 2 vols (Brussels, 1862–3)

Erasmus, Desiderius, *Erasmi opuscula, a supplement to the Opera omnia*, ed. W. K. Ferguson (The Hague, 1933)

Erasmus, Desiderius, *The Collected Works of Erasmus: The Correspondence*, ed. W. K. Ferguson, J. Estes et al., 18 vols to date (Toronto, 1974–2018)

Erasmus, Desiderius, *Opus epistolarum Des. Erasmi Roterodami*, ed. P. S. Allen et al., 2nd edition, 12 vols (Oxford, 1992)

Erasmus, Desiderius, *The adages of Erasmus, selected by William Barker* (Toronto, 2001, selected from *CWE*, vols XXXI–XXXVI)

Erasmus, Desiderius, *The education of a Christian Prince*, ed. L. Jardine (1516; Cambridge, 1997)

Este es vn traslado de vna carta que fue embiada dela ciudad del Cuzco prouincia del Peru a esta muy noble y muy leal ciudad de Sevilla, en que cuenta muy por estenso la victoria que vuo el muy magnifico y reverendo señor el señor licenciado de La Gasca, Presidente y gouernador de las prouincias del Peru contra Gonçalo Piçarro: assi mismo cuenta del número y personas señaladas de que se hizo justicia (n.d., but Seville, 1549)

Esteban, E., 'De las cosas necesarias para escribir historia (Memorial inédito del Dr Páez de Castro al Emperador Carlos V)', *La Ciudad de Dios. Revista religiosa, científica y literaria*, XXVIII (1892), 601–10, and XXIX (1892), 27–38

Fabrizi d'Acquapendente, Girolamo, *De Locutione et ejus instrumentis liber* (Padua, 1603)

BIBLIOGRAPHY

Fagel, R., 'Het Bourgondische hof van Karel V als koning van Spanje. De hofstaat van 21 juni 1517', *BCRH*, CLXXX (2014), 69–137

Faminio, Giovanni Antonio, *Oratio ad Carolum quintum Romanorum imperatorum* (Bologna, 1531)

Fernández Álvarez, M., *Corpus Documental de Carlos V*, 5 vols (Salamanca, 1973–81)

Fernández Álvarez, M. and J. L. de la Peña, eds, *Testamento de Carlos V* (Madrid, 1983)

Fernández de Navarrete, M., *Colección de los viages y descubrimientos que hicieron por mar los españoles desde fines del siglo XV, con varios documentos inéditos concernientes a la historia de la marina castellana y de los establecimientos españoles en Indias*, 5 vols (Madrid, 1829–59)

Fernández de Oviedo, Gonzalo, 'Relación de lo sucedido en la prisión del rey de Francia, desde que fue traído en España', *CODOIN*, XXXVIII, 404–530

Fernández de Oviedo, Gonzalo, *Libro de la Cámara Real del Prínçipe Don Juan e offiçios de su casa y serviçio ordinario* (1548; ed. S. Fabregat Barrios, Valencia, 2006)

Finot, J., 'Compte des sommes dépensées pour le transport des restes mortels de Charles-le-Téméraire de Nancy à Luxembourg, en 1550', *Bulletin du comité travaux historiques et scientifiques: section d'archéologie*, 1884/3, 293–303

Firpo, L., ed., *Relazioni di ambasciatori veneti al Senato. I. Inghilterra* (Turin, 1965)

Firpo, L., ed., *Relazioni di ambasciatori veneti al Senato. II. Germania 1506–1554* (Turin, 1970)

Firpo, L., ed., *Relazioni di ambasciatori veneti al Senato. III. Germania 1557–1654* (Turin, 1970)

Firpo, L., ed., *Relazioni di ambasciatori veneti al Senato. VIII. Spagna 1497–1598* (Turin, 1981)

Fisher, H. A. L., *see* Sastrow, Bartolomaus

Florange, Robert de la Marck, lord of, *Mémoires du Maréchal de Florange, dit le jeune adventureux*, ed. R. Goubaux and P.-A. Lemoisne, 2 vols (Paris, 1913–24)

Fontán, A. and J. Axer, *Españoles y polacos en la Corte de Carlos V. Cartas del embajador Juan Dantisco* (Madrid, 1994); *see also* Górski

Foronda y Aguilera, M., *Estancias y viajes del emperador Carlos V desde el día de su nacimiento hasta él de su muerte* (2nd edition, Madrid, 1914; available online, with some omissions, at http://www.cervantesvirtual.com/bib/historia/CarlosV/1542.shtml)

Förstemann, K. E., ed., *Urkundenbuch zur Geschichte des Reichstages zu Augsburg im Jahre 1530*, 2 vols (Halle, 1833–5)

Foucard, C., *Relazioni dei duchi di Ferrara e di Modena coi re di Tunisi: cenni e documenti raccolti nell'Archivio di Stato in Modena* (Modena, 1881)

Freher, Marquand, *Rerum Germanicarum Scriptores Varii, qui, praemissis quibusdam superioris saeculi, sub Carolo V. Imp. memorabiliter acta potissimum complectuntur*, III (Strasbourg, 1717)

Friedensburg, W., 'Am Vorabend des Schmalkaldischen Krieges. Denkschrift aus der Umgebung Kaiser Karls V', *Quellen und Forschungen aus italienischen Archiven und Bibliotheken*, II (1897), 140–51

Friedensburg, W., 'Karl V. und Maximilian II. (1551). Ein venetianischer Bericht über vertrauliche Äusserungen des Letzteren', *Quellen und Forschungen aus italienischen Archiven und Bibliotheken*, IV (1902), 72–81

Friedensburg, W., 'Aktenstücke zur Politik Kaiser Karls V. im Herbst 1541', *Archiv für Reformationsgeschichte*, XXIX (1932), 35–66

From Panama to Peru. The conquest of Peru by the Pizarros, the rebellion of Gonzalo Pizarro, and the pacification by La Gasca. Epitome of the original signed documents (London, 1925)

Gachard, L. P., *Analectes Belgiques: ou recueil de pièces inédites, mémoires, notices, faits et anecdotes concernant l'histoire de Pays-Bas*, I (Brussels, 1830)

Gachard, L. P., *Collection de documents inédits concernant l'histoire de la Belgique*, I (Brussels, 1832)

Gachard, L. P., 'Lettre à M. Gerlache', *BCRH*, II (1838), 305–24

Gachard, L. P., *Rapport à Monsieur le Ministre de l'Intérieur sur les différentes séries de documents concernant l'histoire de la Belgique qui sont conservés dans les archives de l'ancienne chambre des comptes de Flandres à Lille* (Brussels, 1841)

Gachard, L. P., 'Particularités et documents inédits sur Philippe de Commines, Charles le Téméraire et Charles-Quint', *Trésor national: recueil historique, littéraire, scientifique, artistique, commercial et industriel*, II (1842), 121–31 (reprinted in Gachard, *Études et notices historiques concernant l'histoire des Pays-Bas*, II, 343–56)

Gachard, L. P., 'Mémoire adressé au cardinal d'Espagne, le 8 mars 1516, par l'évêque de Badajoz', *BCRH*, X (1845), 6–35

Gachard, L. P., 'Notice des archives de M. le duc de Caraman, précédée de recherches historiques sur les princes de Chimay et les comtes de Beaumont', *BCRH*, XI (1845), 109–256

Gachard, L. P., *Relation des troubles de Gand sous Charles-Quint, par un anonyme; suivie de trois cent trente documents inédits sur cet événement* (Brussels, 1846)

Gachard, L. P., *Correspondance de Guillaume le Taciturne, prince d'Orange*, 6 vols (Brussels, 1847–57)

Gachard, L. P., *Lettres inédites de Maximilien, duc d'Autriche, roi des Romains et empereur, sur les affaires des Pays-Bas*, 2 vols (Brussels, 1851–2)

Gachard, L. P., 'Notice historique et descriptive des archives de la ville de Gand', *Mémoires de l'Académie Royale des Sciences, des Lettres et des Beaux-Arts de Belgique*, XXVII (1853), 1–162

Gachard, L. P., 'Sur les Commentaires de Charles-Quint', *Bulletin de l'Académie Royale des sciences, des lettres et des beaux-arts de Belgique*, XXI/1 (1854), 502–7

Gachard, L. P., 'L'abdication de Charles-Quint', *Bulletin de l'Académie Royale des sciences, des lettres et des beaux-arts de Belgique*, XXI/2 (1854), 880–942

Gachard, L. P., *Retraite et mort de Charles-Quint au monastère de Yuste. Lettres inédites publiées d'après les originaux conservés dans les archives royales de Simancas*, Introduction and 2 vols (Brussels, 1854–6)

Gachard, L. P., *Analectes historiques*, 5 vols (Brussels, 1856–71: vol. I contains *Analectes* series 1–4; vol. II contains series 5–7; vol. III contains series 8–10; vol. IV contains series 11–13; vol. V contains series 14–17)

Gachard, L. P., *Correspondance de Charles-Quint et d'Adrien VI* (Brussels, 1859)

Gachard, L. P., *La captivité de François Ier et le traité de Madrid: étude historique* (Brussels, 1860; also published in *Bulletin de l'Académie royale de Belgique*, 2ᵉ série, IX)

Gachard, L. P., *Trois années de l'histoire de Charles-Quint, 1543–1546 d'après les dépêches de l'ambassadeur vénetien Navagero* (Brussels, 1865)

Gachard, L. P., *Correspondance de Marguerite d'Autriche, duchesse de Parme, avec Philippe II*, 2 vols (Brussels, 1870)

Gachard, L. P., *La Bibliothèque Nationale à Paris. Notice et extraits des manuscrits qui concernent l'histoire de la Belgique*, 2 vols (Brussels, 1875–7)

Gachard, L. P., *Études et notices historiques concernant l'histoire des Pays-Bas*, 3 vols (Brussels, 1890)

Gachard, L. P. and C. Piot, *Collection des voyages des souverains des Pays-Bas*, 4 vols (Brussels, 1876–82)

Gachet, E., 'Extrait de l'inventaire des titres et papiers autrefois déposés aux archives du château à Boussu et actuellement au château de Beaumont', *BCRH*, II (1838), 258–85

Gachet, E., 'Expédition de Charles-Quint contre Tunis en 1535', *BCRH*, VIII (1844), 7–54

Gairdner, J., ed., *Letters and papers illustrative of the reigns of Richard III and Henry VII*, 2 vols (London, 1861–3)

Gairdner, J., ed., ' "The Spouselles" of the princess Mary, daughter of Henry VII, to Charles prince of Castile, A D 1508', *Camden Miscellany*, IX (London, 1893: Camden Society, New Series, LIII)

Galíndez de Carvajal, Lorenzo, *Anales breves del reinado de los Reyes Católiocos*, in *CODOIN*, XVII, 227–422

García Cerezada, Martín, *Tratado de las campañas y otros acontecimientos de los ejércitos del Emperador Carlos V en Italia, Francia, Austria, Berbería y Grecia desde 1521 hasta 1545 por Martín García Cerezada, cordovés, soldado en aquellos ejércitos*, ed. G. Cruzada Villaamil, marqués de la Fuensanta del Valle, 3 vols (Madrid, 1873–6)

García Fuentes, J. M., 'Testigo de Mühlberg', *Chronica nova*, VI (1971), 79–94

García Fuentes, J. M., 'Bernabé de Busto, cronista de Carlos V', in Castellano Castellano and Sánchez-Montes González, *Carlos V*, I, 177–93

García Martínez, S., 'Estudio preliminar', in Martí de Viciana, *Crónica de la ínclita y coronada ciudad de Valencia* (Valencia, 1983), 24–222

Gardiner, C. H., ed., *The literary memoranda of William Hickling Prescott*, 2 vols (Norman, OK, 1961)

Garibay y Zamalloa, Esteban de, 'Memorias de Garibay', in P. de Gayangos, ed., *Memorial histórico español*, VII (Madrid, 1854)

Gattinara, Mercurino Arborio di, *see* Boone *and* Bornate

Gayangos, P. de, see *Calendar of State Papers*

Gayangos, P. de and V. de la Fuente, eds, *Cartas del Cardenal Fray Francisco Jiménez de Cisneros dirigidas á Don Diego López de Ayala* (Madrid, 1867)

Gerhard, P., *Síntesis e índice de los mandamientos virreinales, 1548–1553* (Mexico City, 1992)

Giles, J. A., ed., *The whole works of Roger Ascham, now first collected and revised, with a life of the author*, 3 vols (London, 1864–5)

Giordano, Gaetano, *Della venuta e dimora in Bologna del sommo pontefice Clemente VII per la coronazione di Carlo V. Imperatore, celebrate l'anno MDXXX. Cronaca con note ed incisioni* (2nd edition, Bologna, 1842)

Giovio, Paolo, *Delle Istorie del suo tempo, di Mons. Paolo Giovio da Como, vescovo di Nocera tradotte da M. Lodovico Domenichi*, 2 vols (Venice, 1572; Latin edition, Florence, 1550–2)

Giovio, Paolo, *Pauli Iovii opera*, ed. G. G. Ferrero et al., 9 vols (Rome 1956–87)

Girón, Pedro, *Crónica del emperador Carlos V*, ed. J. Sánchez Montes, prologue by P. Rassow (Madrid, 1964)

Godefroy, Jean, *Lettres du roi Louis XII, et du cardinal George d'Amboise. Avec plusieurs autres lettres, mémoires & instructions écrites depuis 1504 jusques et compris 1514*, 4 vols (Brussels and The Hague, 1712–13)

González de Ávila, Gil, *Historia de las antigüedades de la ciudad de Salamanca: vidas de sus obispos y cosas sucedidas en su tiempo* (Salamanca, 1606)

Górski, Stanisłav, *Acta Tomiciana: Epistole. Legationes. Responsa. Actiones. Res Geste; Serenissimi Principis Sigismundi, Ejus Nominis Primi, Regis Polonie, Magni Ducis Lithuanie, Russie, Prussie, Masovie Domini*, ed. W. Pociecha et al., 18 vols (Poznań and Warsaw, 1852–1999); *see also* Fontán, A.

Gorter-van Royen, L. and J.-P. Hoyois, eds, *Correspondance de Marie de Hongrie avec Charles-Quint et Nicolas de Granvelle. I: 1532 et années antérieures* (Leuven, 2009)

Gorter-van Royen, L. and J.-P. Hoyois, eds, *Correspondance de Marie de Hongrie avec Charles-Quint et Nicolas de Granvelle. II: 1533* (Leuven, 2018)

Grata, G., *Des lettres pour gouverner: Antoine Perrenot de Granvelle et l'Italie de Charles-Quint dans les manuscrits Trumbull* (Besançon, 2014)

Greppi, G., 'Extraits de la correspondance diplomatique de Jean-Thomas de Langosco, comte de Stroppiana, et de Claude Malopera, ambassadeurs du duc de Savoie à la cour de Charles-Quint: 1546–1559', *BCRH*, 2nd series XII (1859), 117–270

Guicciardini, Francesco, *Opere inedite di Francesco Guicciardini*, ed. G. Canestrini, 10 vols (Florence, 1857–67)

Guicciardini, Francesco, *Istoria d'Italia*, 4 vols (Milan, 1882)

Gutiérrez, C., *Trento: un concilio para la union (1550–1552)*, 3 vols (Madrid, 1981)

Guyon, Fery de, *Mémoires de Fery de Guyon, écuyer, bailly général d'Anchin et de Pesquencourt*, ed. A. L. P. de Robaulx de Soumoy (Brussels, 1858)

ha-Kohen, Joseph, *Sefer divre ha-yamin le-malkhe sarfat u-malkhe vet Otoman ha-Togar* (Venice, 1554), translated by C. H. F. Bailloblotzky as *The chronicles of Rabbi Joseph ben Joshua ben Meir, the Sphardi*, 2 vols (London, 1835–6)

Halkin, L.-E. and G. Dansaert, *Charles de Lannoy, vice-roi de Naples* (Brussels, 1934)

Hamy, A., *Entrevue de François Premier avec Henry VIII à Boulogne-sur-Mer, en 1532. Intervention de la France dans l'affaire du divorce, d'après un grand nombre de documents inédits* (Paris, 1898)

Hanke, L., ed., *Los virreyes españoles en América durante el gobierno de la casa de Austria. México I* (Madrid, 1976: BAE, CCLXXIII)

Hasenclever, A., 'Die Geheimartikel zum Frieden von Crépy von 19. September 1544', *Zeitschrift für Kirchengeschichte*, XLV (1926), 418–26

Hasenclever, A., 'Die Überlieferung der Akten Karls V. in Pariser Archiven und Bibliotheken', *B&S*, X (1933), 437–69

Heine, G., *Briefe an Kaiser Karl V., geschrieben von seinem Beichtvater in den Jahren 1530–1532* (Berlin, 1848)

Heuterus, Pontus, *Rerum Belgicarum et Austriacarum libri XV* [1598], in Heuterus, *Opera historica omnia; Burgundica, Austriaca, Belgica* (3rd edition, Leuven, 1651)

Historical Manuscript Commission: Fifteenth Report, Appendix, Part II: The Manuscripts of J. Eliot Hodgkin (London, 1897)

Holanda, Francisco de, *De la pintvra antigva* (1548; Spanish edition 1563, ed. E. Tormó, Madrid, 1921)

Hortleder, Friedrich, *Der Römischen Keyser- vnd Königlichen Maiesteten, auch deß Heiligen Rö[mischen] Reichs geistlicher und weltlicher Stände ... Handlungen und Auszschreiben, Send-Brieffe/Bericht/ Unterricht/Klag- vnd Supplication-Schrifften ... Von den Vrsachen deß Teutschen Kriegs Kaiser Carls deß V. wider die Schmalkaldische Bunds-Oberste/Chur- und Fürsten/Sachsen und Hessen* (Weimar, 1618)

Howard, K. D., ed., *Discursos de Nicolao Machiaueli. Juan Lorenzo Ottevanti's Spanish translation of Machiavelli's Discourses on Livy (1552)* (Tempe, 2016)

Ibarra y Rodríguez, E. and G. Arsenio de Izaga, 'Catálogo de los documentos del archivo de Lope de Soria, embajador del emperador Carlos V', *BRAH*, XCVIII (1931), 363–416

Illescas, Gonzalo de, *Segunda parte de la historia pontifical y cathólica, en la qual se prosigven las vidas y hechos de Clemente Quinto y de los demás pontífices sus predecessores hasta Pio Quinto* (1564; 5th edition, Barcelona, 1606)

Inventaire sommaire des Archives Départementales antérieures à 1790. Nord: Archives civiles, Série B: Chambre des Comptes de Lille, ed. C. Dehaisnes, J. Finot and M. Bruchet, 9 vols (Lille, 1863–1908)

Janssens, G., 'Fuentes flamencas para el reinado de Carlos V en los Países Bajos', in Castellano Castellano and Sánchez-Montes González, *Carlos V*, I, 195–207

Kannengiesser, P., *Karl V und Maximilien Egmont, Graf von Büren: ein Beitrag zur Geschichte des schmalkaldischen Krieges* (Freiburg, 1895)

Kaulek, J., ed., *Correspondance politique de MM. de Castillon et de Marillac, ambassadeurs de France en Angleterre (1537–1542)* (Paris, 1885)

Keniston, H., ed., *Memorias de Sancho Cota* (Cambridge, MA, 1964: Harvard Studies in Romance Languages, XXVIII)

Kervyn de Lettenhove, J., *Commentaires de Charles-Quint* (Paris, 1862; translated as *The autobiography of the Emperor Charles V. Recently discovered in the Portuguese language by Baron Kervyn de Lettenhove*, London, 1862; *Aufzeichnungen des Kaiser Karl's des Fünften. Zum ersten mal herausgegeben von Baron Kervyn van Lettenhove*, Leipzig, 1862; and *Comentarios del emperador Carlos V*, Madrid, 1862)

Kervyn de Lettenhove, J., *Relations politiques des Pays-Bas et de l'Angleterre sous le règne de Philippe II*, 11 vols (Brussels, 1882–1900)

Knox, John, *The history of the Reformation of religion in Scotland*, ed. W. McGavin (Glasgow, 1881)

Kohler, A., *Quellen zur Geschichte Karls V.* (Darmstadt, 1990: Ausgewählte Quellen zur deutschen Geschichte der Neuzeit, XV)

Konetzke, R., ed., *Colección de documentos para la formación social de Hispanoamérica 1493–1810*, I (Madrid, 1953)

Kreiten, H., *Der Briefwechsel Kaiser Maximilians I. mit seiner Tochter Margareta von Österreich. Untersuchungen über die Zeitfolge des durch neue Briefe ergänzten Briefwechsels* (Vienna, 1907); *see also* Walther, 'Review'

La Fuente, V. de, ed., *Cartas de los Secretarios del Cardenal D. Fr. Francisco Jiménez de Cisneros durante su regencia en los años de 1516 y 1517* (Madrid, 1876)

La magnifiqve et svmptvevse pompe fvnèbre faite avs obsèqves et fvnérailles dv trèsgrand et trèsvictorieus empereur Charles cinqvième celebrées en la vile de Brvxelles le XXIX iovr de décembre MDLVIII (Antwerp, 1559)

La Marche, Olivier de, *Mémoires d'Olivier de La Marche, Maître d'Hôtel et Capitaine des Gardes de Charles Le Téméraire*, ed. H. Beaune and J. d'Arbaumont, 4 vols (Paris, 1883–8)

La Marche, Olivier de, *Le chevalier délibéré (The resolute knight)*, ed. C. W. Carroll (Tempe, 1999)

Laiglesia, F. de, *Estudios históricos 1515–1555*, 3 vols (Madrid, 1918–19)

Lanz, K., *Correspondenz des Kaisers Karl V., aus dem königlichen Archiv und der Bibliothèque de Bourgogne zu Brüssel*, 3 vols (Leipzig, 1844–6)

Lanz, K., *Staatspapiere zur Geschichte des Kaisers Karl V. aus dem königlichen Archiv und der Bibliothèque de Bourgogne zu Brüssel* (Stuttgart, 1845)

Lanz, K., *Aktenstücke und Briefe zur Geschichte Kaiser Karl V.*, 2 vols (Vienna, 1853–7: Monumenta Habsburgica. Sammlung von Aktenstücken und Briefen zur Geschichte des Hauses Habsburg dem Zeitraume von 1473 bis 1576. Zweite Abtheilung. Kaiser Karl V. und König Philipp II)

Las Casas, Bartolomé de, *Brevíssima relación de la destruyción de las Indias* (Seville, 1552)

Las Casas, Bartolomé de, *Historia de las Indias*, ed. Marqués de la Fuensanta del Valle and J. Sancho Rayón, 5 vols (Madrid, 1875)

Laurent, *Recueil, see Recueil des Ordonnances*

Le Glay, A. J. G., ed., *Correspondance de l'empereur Maximilien Ier et de Marguerite d'Autriche, sa fille, gouvernante des Pays-Bas, de 1507 à 1519*, 2 vols (Paris, 1839)

Le Glay, A. J. G., ed., *Négociations diplomatiques entre la France et l'Autriche durant les trente premières années du 16e siècle*, 2 vols (Paris, 1845)

Le Petit, Jean François, *La grande chronique ancienne et moderne de Hollande, Zélande, Westfrise, Vtrecht, Frise, Overyssel & Groeningen, jusques à la fin de 1600*, 2 vols (Dordrecht, 1601)

Lee, B. T., ed., *Libros de Cabildos de Lima, IV (1548–1553)* (Lima, 1935)

Lefèvre-Pontalis, G., ed., *Correspondance politique de Odet de Selve: ambassadeur de France en Angleterre (1546–1549)* (Paris, 1888)

Lemaire des Belges, Jean, *Chronique de 1507*, ed. A. Schoysman (Brussels, 2001)

Lemaire des Belges, Jean, *Le carnet de notes d'un chroniqueur: août 1507–février 1509*, ed. J.-M. Cauchies (Brussels, 2008)

Lenz, M., ed., *Briefwechsel Landgraf Philipp's des Grossmüthigen von Hessen mit Bucer*, 3 vols (Stuttgart and Leipzig, 1880–91)

Leonardo de Argensola, Bartolomé, *Primera parte de los Anales de Aragón que prosigue los del Secretario Gerónimo Zurita desde el año MDXVI* (Zaragoza, 1630)

Lestocquoy, J., ed., *Correspondance des nonces en France Capodiferro, Dandino et Guidiccione, 1541–1546. Légations des cardinaux Farnèse et Sadolet et missions d'Ardinghello, de Grimani et de Hieronimo da Correggio* (Paris and Rome, 1963)

Leti, Gregorio, *Vita del invitissimo imperadore Caroli V, Austriaco*, 4 vols (Amsterdam, 1700)

Letters and papers, foreign and domestic, of the reign of Henry VIII, ed. J. S. Brewer, J. Gairdner and R. H. Brodie, 21 vols, some in multiple parts (London, 1872–1920)

BIBLIOGRAPHY

Leva, G. de, *Storia documentata di Carlo V in correlazione all'Italia*, 5 vols (Venice, 1863–94)

Libro primero de Cabildos de Lima, descifrado y anotado por Enrique Torres Saldamando, con la colaboración de Pablo Patrón y Nicanor Boloña, 3 vols (Lima, 1888)

Libros de Antaño, VIII. Viajes por España de Jorge de Einghen, del Barón León de Rosmithal de Blatna, de Francesco Guicciardini, y de Andrés Navajero, ed. A. M. Fabié (Madrid, 1879)

Lima Cruz, M. A., ed., *Diogo do Couto e a Decada Oitava da Asia* (c. 1600; Lisbon, 1993)

Linas, Ch. de, *Translation des restes de Charles le Téméraire de Nancy à Luxembourg, Manuscrit d'Antoine de Baulaincourt, Roi d'Armes de la Toison d'Or* (Nancy, 1855)

Looz-Corswarem, Graf O. A., 'Die römische Korrespondenz Karls V. in Madrid und Simancas', *B&S*, XIII (1935), 109–90

Looz-Corswarem, Graf O. A., 'Die Korrespondenz Karls V. mit Philipp und mit der Regentschaft in Spanien (1539–1556) im Archiv zu Simancas', *B&S*, XV (1935), 227–68

López de Gómara, Francisco, *Hispania Victrix. Primera y segunda parte de la Historia General de las Indias con todo el descubrimiento y cosas notables que han acaecido dende que se ganaron hasta el año de 1551. Con la conquista de México y de la Nueva España* (2nd edition, Medina del Campo, 1553)

López de Gómara, Francisco, *Annals of the Emperor Charles V*, ed. R. B. Merriman (Oxford, 1912)

López de Gómara, Francisco, *Guerras de mar del Emperador Carlos V*, ed. M. A. de Bunes Ibarra and N. E. Jiménez (Madrid, 2000)

López Medel, Tomás, *Colonización de América. Informes y Testimonios 1549–1572*, ed. L. Pereña et al. (Madrid, 1990: *Corpus Hispanorum de Pace*, XXVIII)

Los Santos, Francisco de, *Descripción breue del monasterio de S. Lorenzo el Real del Escorial, vnica marauilla del mundo* (Madrid, 1657; 2nd edition, 1667)

Lozano Mateos, E., 'Noticias documentales sobre Bárbara Blomberg', *Altamira: revista de estudios montañeses*, I (1968–71), 15–138

Lüdecke, H., *Lucas Cranach der Ältere im Spiegel seiner Zeit: aus Urkunden, Chroniken, Briefen, Reden und Gedichten* (Berlin, 1953)

Luther, Martin, *Dr Martin Luthers Werke, Kritische Gesamtausgabe. Abteilung 1: Schriften*, 56 vols (Weimar, 1883–1929)

Luther, Martin, *Dr Martin Luthers Werke, Kritische Gesamtausgabe. Abteilung 2: Tischreden*, 6 vols (Weimar, 1912–21)

Luther, Martin, *Dr Martin Luthers Werke, Kritische Gesamtausgabe. Abteilung 4: Briefwechsel*, 18 vols (Weimar, 1930–85)

Machiavelli, Niccolò, 'Relazione di una visita fatta per fortificare Firenze' [1526], in S. Bertelli, ed., *Niccolò Macchiavelli: Arte della guerra e scritti politici minori* (Milan, 1961), 289–302

Machiavelli, Niccolò, *Discursos de Nicolao Machiaueli, dirigidos al muy alto y poderoso señor don PHILIPPI principe de España nuestro señor* (Medina del Campo, 1552); *see also* Howard, K. D.

Maldonado, Juan, *La revolución comunera. El movimiento de España, o sea historia de la revolución conocida con el nombre de Comunidades de Castilla* (original edition, Latin, 1545; Spanish translation ed. V. Fernández Vargas, Madrid, 1975)

Mancini, M., ed., *Tiziano e le Corti d'Asburgo nei documenti degli archivi Spagnoli* (Venice, 1997)

March, J. M., *Niñez y juventud de Felipe II: documentos inéditos sobre su educación civil, literaria y religiosa y su iniciación al gobierno (1527–1547)*, 2 vols (Madrid, 1941–2); *see also* Requesens, Estefanía de

Martínez, J. L., ed., *Documentos cortesianos*, 4 vols (Mexico City, 1990–3)

Mártir de Anglería, Pedro, *Epistolario de Pedro Mártir de Anglería* (Spanish translation ed. José López de Toro, 4 vols, Madrid, 1953–7: Documentos inéditos para la historia de España, IX–XII)

Martyr de Angleria, Peter, *Opus epistolarum Petri Martyris Anglerii Mediolanensis* (1530; Amsterdam, 1670)

Maurenbrecher, W., *Karl V. und die deutschen Protestanten 1545–1555, nebst einem Anhang von Aktenstücken aus dem spanischen Staatsarchiv von Simancas* (Düsseldorf, 1865)

Maximilian I, Emperor, *Kaiser Maximilians I. Weisskunig*, ed. H. T. Musper, 2 vols (Stuttgart, 1956)

Mayer, E. W., 'Das politische Testament Karls V. von 1555', *Historische Zeitschrift*, CXX (3rd series, XXIV, 1919), 452–94

Mayr, J. K. 'Das politische Testament Karls V', *Historische Blätter, herausgegeben vom Haus Hof- und Staatsarchiv in Wien*, I (1921), 218–51

Mayr, J. K., 'Die letzte Abdankung Karls V. (16 Jänner 1556)', *B&S*, III (1931), 143–58

Medina, J. T., *La imprenta en Lima (1584–1824)*, I (Santiago de Chile, 1904)

Mencke, Johann Burkhard, *Scriptores rerum Germanicarum, praecipue Saxonicarum: in quibus scripta et monumenta illustria, pleraque hactenus inedita, tum ad historiam Germaniae generatim, tum speciatim Saxoniae Sup. Misniae, Thuringiae et varisciae spectantia*, 3 vols (Leipzig, 1728–30)

Mendieta, Gerónimo de, *Historia ecclesiástica indiana*, ed. J. García Icazbalceta (Mexico City, 1880)

Merriman, R. B., 'Charles V's last paper of advice to his son', *AHR*, XXVIII/3 (1923), 489–91

Merriman, R. B., ed., *Life and letters of Thomas Cromwell*, 2 vols (Oxford, 1902)

Mexía, Pedro de, *Historia del Emperador Carlos V, por el magnífico caballero Pedro Mexía, veintecuatro de Sevilla*, ed. J. de Mata Carriazo (Madrid, 1945)

Michaud, J. and J. J. F. Poujoulat, eds, *Nouvelle collection des mémoires pour servir à l'histoire de France, 1ère série IX: Vieilleville, Castelnau, Mergey, La Noue* (Paris, 1838)

Mogen, Ludwig G., *Historia captivitatis Philippi Magnanimi, Hassiae Landgravii* (Frankfurt and Leipzig, 1766)

Molinet, Jehan, *Chroniques*, ed. J.-A. Buchon, 5 vols (Paris 1827–8)

Möllenberg, W., 'Die Verhandlung im schmalkaldischen Lager vor Giengen und Landgraf Philipps Rechenschaftsbericht', *Zeitschrift des Vereins für hessische Geschichte und Landeskunde*, XXXVIII (1904), 31–62

Mone, F. J., 'Briefwechsel über die Kaiserwahl Karls V', *Anzeiger für Kunde der teutschen Vorzeit*, V (Karlsruhe, 1836), cols 13–37, 118–36, 283–98 and 396–411

Monluc, Blaise de, *Commentaires*, ed. J. Courteault (Paris, 1911)

Morales, Ambrosio de, *Las antigüedades de las ciudades de España* (Alcalá de Henares, 1575)

Morel-Fatio, A., *Historiographie de Charles-Quint* (Paris, 1913)

Morel-Fatio, A., 'Une histoire inédite de Charles-Quint par un fourier de sa cour (Hugues Cousin)', *Mémoires de l'Institut National de France. Académie des Insciptions et Belles Lettres*, XXXIX (1914), 1–40

Morgan, H., *Ireland 1518: Archduke Ferdinand's visit to Kinsale and the Dürer connection* (Cork, 2015)

Morsolin. B., 'Francesco Chiericati, vescovo e diplomatico del secolo decimosesto', *Atti dell'Academia Olimpica di Vicenza*, III (1873), 121–237

Mugnier, F., 'Les faictz et guerre de l'Empereur Charles-Quint contre la Ligue de Smalkade (1546–1547)', *Mémoires et documents publiés par la Société savoisienne d'histoire et d'archéologie*, XL (1901), 238–368

Muller, J. A., ed., *The letters of Stephen Gardiner* (London, 1933)

Muratori, Lodovico Antonio, *Delle antichità Estensi ed Italiane*, 2 vols (Modena, 1727–40)

Nader, H., ed., *The Book of Privileges issued to Christopher Columbus by King Fernando and Queen Isabel, 1492–1502* (Los Angeles, 1996: Reportium Columbianum, II)

Naujoks, E., ed., *Kaiser Karl V. und die Zunftverfassung. Ausgewählte Aktenstücke zu den Verfassungsänderungen in den oberdeutschen Reichsstädten (1547–1556)* (Stuttgart, 1985: Veröffentlichungen der Kommission für geschichtliche Landeskunde in Baden-Württemberg, A 36)

Navagero, Andrea, *see* Cicogna

Neefe, Johannes, *Des allerdurchleuchtigsten römischen keysers Ferdinand des Ersten denkwürdiger Tafel-Reden* (Dresden, 1674)

Nichols, J. G., ed., *Literary remains of King Edward the Sixth. Edited from his autograph manuscripts, with historical notes and a biographical memoir* (London, 1857)

Nicolson, N. and J. Trautmann, eds, *The letters of Virginia Woolf. Volume VI: 1936–1941* (New York, 1975)

Nordman, D., *Tempête sur Alger: l'expédition de Charles Quint en 1541* (Paris, 2011)

Nott, G. F., ed., *The works of Henry Howard, earl of Surrey, and of Sir Thomas Wyatt, the elder*, 2 vols (London, 1815–16); *see also* Powell, J.

Núñez Alba, Diego, *Diálogos de la vida del soldado* (Salamanca, 1552; reprint, ed. A. M. Fabié, Madrid, 1890)

Núñez Contreras, L., *Un registro de Cancilleria de Carlos V: el manuscrito 917 de la Biblioteca Nacional de Madrid. Estudio, edición, traducción y notas* (Madrid, 1965)

Nuntiaturberichte aus Deutschland. Nebst ergänzenden Aktenstücken, Erste Abteilung 1533–1559, ed. W. Friedensburg, L. Cardauns et al., 17 vols, with two *Ergänzungsbände* covering 1530–2 (Gotha, 1892–1981)

O'Gorman, E., 'Mandamientos del virrey don Antonio de Mendoza', *Boletín del Archivo General de la Nación*, VI (1935), 2–22, and X (1939), 213–311

Ordonnances des rois de France. Règne de François Ier, 9 vols (Paris, 1902–92)

'P. P.', 'L'expédition espagnole de 1541 contre Alger', *Revue Africaine*, CCII (1891), 177–206

Pacheco, Francisco, *Libro de descripción de verdaderos retratos de ilustres y memorables varones* (1599; Seville, 1999)

Pacheco de Leiva, E., *La política española en Italia. Correspondencia de don Fernando Marín, abad de Nájera, con Carlos V. I. 1521–24* (Madrid, 1919)

Páez de Castro, Juan, *see* Esteban, E.

Papiers d'État du Cardinal de Granvelle, ed. C. Weiss, 9 vols (Paris, 1841–52)

BIBLIOGRAPHY

BIBLIOGRAPHY

Paso y Troncoso, F. del, et al., eds, *Epistolario de Nueva España, 1505–1818*, 16 vols (Mexico City, 1939–42)

Pastor, L., 'Die Correspondenz des Cardinals Contarini während seiner deutschen Legation (1541), aus dem päpstlichen Geheim-Archiv', *Historisches Jahrbuch der Görresgesellschaft*, I (1880), 321–92 and 473–501

Paz, J., *Catálogo de documentos españoles existentes en el Archivo del Ministerio de Asuntos Extranjeros de París* (Madrid, 1932)

Pérez de Tudela Bueso, J., *Documentos relativos a don Pedro de La Gasca y a Gonzalo Pizarro*, 2 vols (Madrid, 1964: Archivo Documental Español, XXI–XXII)

Pérez Pastor, C., *La imprenta en Medina del Campo* (Madrid, 1895)

Pettegree, A. and M. Walsby, eds, *Netherlandish books: Books published in the Low Countries and Dutch books printed abroad before 1601*, 2 vols (Leiden, 2011)

Pinchart, A., *Archives des arts, sciences et lettres. Documents inédits*, 3 vols (Ghent, 1860–81)

Piot, C., 'Correspondance politique entre Charles-Quint et le Portugal de 1521 à 1522', *BCRH*, 4ᵉ série VII (1879), 11–110

Plon, E., *Leone Leoni, sculpteur de Charles-Quint, et Pompeo Leoni, sculpteur de Philippe II* (Paris, 1887)

Plutarch's Lives: The Dryden translation, ed. A. H. Clough, 2 vols (New York, 2001)

Pocock, N., *Records of the Reformation: The divorce 1527–1533*, 2 vols (Oxford, 1870)

Pogo, A., 'The Anonymous *La Conquista Del Perú* (Seville, April 1534) and the *Libro Vltimo Del Svmmario Delle Indie Occidentali* (Venice, October 1534)', *Proceedings of the American Academy of Arts and Sciences*, LXIV/8 (1930), 177–286

Porras Barrenechea, R., *Cedulario del Perú, siglos XVI, XVII y XVIII*, 2 vols (Lima, 1944–8: Colección de documentos inéditos para la historia del Perú, I–II)

Porras Barrenechea, R., *Cartas del Perú, 1524–1543* (Lima, 1959: Colección de documentos inéditos para la historia del Perú, III)

Porras Barrenechea, R., *Las relaciones primitivas de la conquista del Perú* (Lima, 1967)

Powell, J., ed., *The complete works of Sir Thomas Wyatt the Elder*, I (Oxford, 2016); *see also* Nott, G. F.

Preuschen, E., 'Ein gleichzeitiger Bericht über Landgraf Philipps Fussfall und Verhaftung', in J. R. Dieterich, ed., *Philipp der Grossmütige. Beiträge zur Geschichte seines Lebens und seiner Zeit* (Marburg, 1904), 144–54

Rabe, H., *Karl V., politische Korrespondenz: Brieflisten und Register*, 20 vols (Konstanz, 1999)

Rabe, H., P. Marzahl, G. Rill, H. Stratenwerth and C. Thomas, 'Stückverzeichnis zum Bestand Belgien PA des Haus- Hof- und Staatsarchivs Wien', *MÖStA*, XXIX (1976), 436–93, XXX (1977), 346–97, XXXII (1979), 267–305, XXXIII (1980), 284–345, XXXIV (1981), 345–400, XXXV (1982), 365–403, XXXVI (1983), 283–328, XXXVII (1984), 377–447, XXXIX (1986), 307–71

Rabelais, François, *Lettres écrites d'Italie par François Rabelais (Décembre 1535–Février 1536)*, ed. V. L. Bourrilly (Paris, 1910)

Rabutin, François de, *Commentaires des dernières guerres en la Gaule Belgique* (Paris, 1823: Collection complète des mémoires relatifs à l'histoire de France, XXXI)

Rassow, P., 'La primera firma del Emperador Carlos V', *Investigación y progreso*, I, no. 8 (1927), 57–8

Recueil d'aucunes lectres escriptures par lesquelles se comprend la vérité des choses passées entre la majesté de l'empereur Charles cinquième et François roi de France (Antwerp, 1536)

Recueil des ordonnances des Pays-Bas, Deuxième série, 1506–1700: Règne de Charles Quint, 1506–1555, ed. C. Laurent, J. Lameere and H. Simont, 6 vols (Brussels, 1893–1922)

Reiffenberg, Frédéric, baron de, *Histoire de l'Ordre de la Toison d'Or, depuis son institution jusqu'à la cessation des chapitres généraux, tirée des archives même de cet Ordre* (Brussels, 1830)

Reiffenberg, Frédéric, baron de, *Lettres sur la vie intime de l'Empereur Charles-Quint, écrites par Guillaume van Male, gentilhomme de sa chambre* (Brussels, 1843)

Requesens, Estefania de, *Cartes íntimes d'una dama catalana del s XVI. Epistolari a la seva mare la comtessa de Palamós*, ed. Maite Guisando (Barcelona, 1987)

Retz, Jean-François-Paul de Gondi, cardinal de, *La congiura del conte Gian Luigi Fieschi*, ed. C. de Marchi (Palermo, 1990)

Riba García, C., ed., *Correspondencia privada de Felipe II con su secretario Mateo Vázquez 1567–91* (Madrid, 1959)

Ribadeneyra, Pedro de, *Vida del P. Francisco de Borja, que fue duque de Gandía, y después religioso y III. General de la compañía de Iesús* (Madrid, 1592)

Ribier, Guillaume, *Lettres et mémoires d'estat des roys, princes, ambassadeurs et autres ministres, sous les règnes de François I, Henry II et François II*, 2 vols (Paris, 1666)

Rico y Ortega, Martín, untitled article and engraving in *La ilustración de Madrid. Revista de política, ciencias, artes y literatura*, III, no. 49 (13 Jan. 1872), 9–11

Rigault, J., 'Une relation inédite du siège de Metz en 1552', *Annales de l'Est*, 5th series III (1952), 293–306

Robert, U., 'Philibert de Châlon, prince d'Orange (1502–30). Lettres et documents', *BRAH*, XXXIX (1901), 5–288, 337–81, 433–46, and XL (1902), 15–40, 273–321, 369–418 and 465–97

Roca, P., *Catálogo de los manuscritos que pertenecieron a D. Pascual de Gayangos existentes hoy en la Biblioteca Nacional* (Madrid, 1904)

Rodríguez Raso, R., *Maximiliano de Austria, gobernador de Carlos V en España. Cartas al emperador* (Madrid 1963)

Rodríguez Villa, A., *Memorias para la historia del asalto y saqueo de Roma en 1527 por el Ejército Imperial, formadas con documentos originales, cifrados é inéditos en su mayor parte* (Madrid, 1875)

Rodríguez Villa, A., *Italia desde la batalla de Pavía hasta el Saco de Roma. Reseña histórica escrita en su mayor parte con documentos originales, inéditos y cifrados* (Madrid, 1885)

Rodríguez Villa, A., *El Emperador Carlos V y su corte según las cartas de don Martín de Salinas, embajador del Infante don Fernando, 1522–1539* (Madrid, 1903)

Rosso, Gregorio, *Istoria delle cose di Napoli sotto l'Impero di Carlo V, scritta per modo di Giornali da Gregorio Rosso* (Naples, 1770: *Raccolta di tutti i più rinomati scrittori dell' istoria generale del regno di Napoli*, VIII)

Ruscelli, Girolamo, *Delle lettere di Principi, le quali o si scrivono da principi o a principi o ragionano di principi*, 3 vols (Venice, 1562–81)

Rymer, Thomas, *Foedera, conventiones, literae, et cujuscunque generis acta publica, inter reges Angliae et alios quosvis imperatores, reges, pontifices, principes, vel communitates, ab ineunte sæculo duodecimo, viz. ab anno 1101, ad nostra usque tempora*, 20 vols (London, 1727–9)

Rzepka, A., R. Sosnowski and P. Tylus, *Historia kolekcji rękopisów romańskich z byłej Pruskiej Biblioteki Państwowej w Berlinie, przechowywanych w Bibliotece Jagiellońskiej w Krakowie – studium ogólne/The history of the collection of Romance manuscripts from the former Preussische Staatsbibliothek zu Berlin, kept at the Jagiellonian Library in Kraków – the overall study* (Kraków, 2011)

Salignac, Bertrand de, *Le voyage du Roy au Pays-Bas de l'Empereur en l'an MDLIIII* (Paris, 1554)

Sánchez Alonso, B., *Fuentes de la historia española e hispanoamericana: ensayo de bibliografía sistemática de impresos y manuscritos que ilustran la historia política de España y sus antiguas provincias de ultramar*, 3 vols (3rd edition, Madrid, 1952)

Sánchez Loro, D., *La inquietud postrimera de Carlos V*, 3 vols (Cáceres, 1957–8)

Sancho de la Hoz, Pedro, 'Relación de lo sucedido en la conquista y pacificación de estas provincias de la Nueva Castilla', in E. de Vedia, ed., *Historiadores primitivos de Indias*, II (Madrid, 1853), 125–258

Sanctus Franciscus Borgia, Quartus Gandiae Dux et Societatis Iesu Praepositus Generalis Tertius 1510–1572. Monumenta Borgia, 7 vols (Rome and Valencia, 1894–2007)

Sandoval, Prudencio de, *Historia de la vida y hechos del Emperador Carlos V* (1604–6), ed. Carlos Seco Serrano, 3 vols (Madrid, 1955) (BAE, LXXX–LXXXII)

Sansovino, Francesco, *Il simolacro di Carlo Quinto imperadore* (Venice, 1567)

Santa Cruz, Alonso de, *Crónica del emperador Carlos Quinto, compuesta por Alonso de Santa Cruz*, ed. R. Beltrán y Rózpide and A. Blázquez y Delgado-Aguilera, 5 vols (Madrid, 1920–5)

Sanuto, Marino, *I diarii di Marino Sanuto*, ed. F. Stefani, G. Berchet and N. Barozzi, 58 vols (Venice, 1879–1903)

Sastrow, Bartolomaus, *Bartholomäi Sastrowen Herkommen, Geburt und Lauff seines gantzen Lebens: auch was sich in dem Denckwerdiges zugetragen, so er mehrentheils selbst gesehen und gegenwärtig mit angehöret hat / von ihm selbst beschrieben aus der Handschrift herausgegeben und erläutert*, ed. G. C. F. Mohnike, 3 vols (Greifswald, 1823–4); abridged English text, *Social Germany in Luther's time, being the memoirs of Bartholomew Sastrow*, ed. H. A. L. Fisher (Westminster, 1902), republished as *Bartholomew Sastrow, being the memoirs of a German Burgomaster* (London, 1905)

Saville, M. H., 'Some unpublished letters of Pedro de La Gasca relating to the conquest of Peru', *Proceedings of the American Antiquarian Society*, XXVII (1917), 336–57

Schertlin von Burtenbach, Sebastian, *Leben und Thaten des weiland wohledlen und gestrengen Herrn Sebastian Schertlin von Burtenbach durch ihn selbst deutsch beschreiben*, ed. O. Schönhuth (Münster, 1858)

Scheurer, Rémy, ed., *Correspondance du cardinal Jean du Bellay*, 7 vols (Paris, 1969–2016)

Scheurl, Christoph, *Einritt Keyser Carlen in die alten keyserlichen haubtstatt Rom, den 5 Aprilis 1536* (Nuremberg, 1536)

Schmitt, E. and F. K. von Hutten, eds, *Das Gold der Neuen Welt. Die Papieren des Welser Konquistadors und Generalkapitans von Venezuela Philipp von Hutten 1534–1541* (Hildburghausen, 1996)

Schultze, V., 'Dreizehn Despeschen Contarini's aus Regensburg an den Cardinal Farnese (1541)', *Zeitschrift für Kirchengechichte*, III (1878–9), 150–84

Sepúlveda, Juan Ginés de, *Historia de Carlos V*, ed. E. Rodríguez Peregrina and B. Cuart Moner, 6 vols (*Obras completas de Juan Ginés de Sepúlveda*, vols I, II, X, XII, XIII and XIV: Pozoblanco, 1995–2010)

BIBLIOGRAPHY

Serassi, Pierantonio, *Delle lettere del conte Baldessar Castiglione, ora per la prima volta date in luce*, 2 vols (Padua, 1769–71)

Serristori, L., *Legazioni di Averardo Serristori, Ambasciatore di Cosimo I a Carlo Quinto e in corte di Roma (1537–1568)* (Florence, 1853)

Sigüenza, José de, *Historia de la Orden de San Jerónimo*, ed. J. Catalina García, 2 vols (Madrid, 1600, reprinted Madrid, 1907–9)

Sigüenza, José de, *La fundación del Monasterio de El Escorial* (vol. III of his *Historia de la Orden de San Jerónimo*, Madrid, 1605, reprinted Madrid, 1988)

Sleidan, Johannes, *De statu religionis et reipublicae Carolo V Caesare commentarii* (1555; Strasbourg, 1612)

Snouckaert van Schouwenburg, Willem (*alias* Gulielmus Zenocarus a Scauwenburgo), *De republica, vita, moribus, gestis, fama, religione, sanctitate imperatoris caesaris augusti quinti Caroli, maximi monarchae, libri septem* (Ghent, 1559)

Social Germany, see Sastrow, Bartolomaus

Spielman, D. C. and C. Thomas, 'Quellen zur Jugend Erzherzog Ferdinands in Spanien. Bisher unbekannte Briefe Karls V. an seinen Bruder (1514–1517)', *MÖStA*, XXXVII (1984), 1–34

Spinola, M., L. T. Belgrano and F. Podestà, 'Documenti ispano-genovesi dell'archivio di Simancas', *Atti della Società ligure di storia patria*, VIII (1868), 1–291

State Papers, published under the authority of His Majesty's Commission. King Henry the Eighth, 5 parts in 11 vols (London, 1830–52)

Stirling-Maxwell, W., *Notices of the emperor Charles V in 1555 and 1556: selected from the despatches of Federigo Badoer, ambassador from the republic of Venice to the court of Bruxelles* (London, 1856)

Stirling-Maxwell, W., ed., *The chief victories of the emperor Charles V, designed by Martin Heemskerck in M.D.L.V* (London and Edinburgh, 1870)

Stirling-Maxwell, W., ed., *Entry of the Emperor Charles V into Bologna on the 5th of November MDXXIX* (Florence, London and Edinburgh, 1875)

Stirling-Maxwell, W., ed., *The procession of Pope Clement VII and the emperor Charles V after the coronation at Bologna on the 24th February MDXXX, designed and engraved by Nicolas Hogenberg* (Edinburgh, 1875)

Stix, F., 'Die Geheimschriftenschlüssel der Kabinettskanzlei des Kaisers', *B&S*, XIV (1935), 207–26, and XVI (1937), 61–70

Strohmeyer, A., *Die Korrespondenz der Kaiser mit ihren Gesandten in Spanien. I. Briefwechsel 1563–1565* (Vienna and Munich, 1997)

Stübel, B., 'Die Instruktion Karls V. für Philip II. vom 25. Oktober 1555, deutscher Text', *Archiv für österreichische Geschichte*, XCIII (1905), 181–248

Stumpf, A. S., *Baierns politische Geschichte*, I (Munich, 1816–17)

Tamalio, R., *Ferrante Gonzaga alla corte spagnola di Carlo V, nel carteggio privato con Mantova (1523–1526). La formazione da 'cortegiano' di un generale dell'Impero* (Mantua, 1991)

Tausserat-Radel, A., ed., *Correspondance politique de Guillaume Pellicier, ambassadeur de France à Venise (1540–1542)*, 2 vols (Paris, 1899)

Teissier, Antoine, *Instructions de l'Empereur Charles V à Philippe II, roi d'Espagne, et de Philippe II au prince Philippe son fils. Mises en françois, pour l'usage de monseigneur le Prince Electoral, par Antoine Teissier conseiller & hist. de S. S. E. de Brandebourg* (Berlin, 1699)

Tellechea Idígoras, J. I., *Fray Bartolomé Carranza. Documentos históricos*, 7 vols (Madrid, 1962–94)

Tellechea Idígoras, J. I., *Así murió el emperador. La última jornada de Carlos V (Yuste, 21 Septiembre 1558)* (1958; 2nd edition, Salamanca, 1995)

Tellechea Idígoras, J. I., *El Papado y Felipe II. Colección de Breves Pontificios*, 3 vols (Madrid, 1999–2002)

Thausing, M., 'Die Leiche Kaiser Karls V', *Mittheilungen des Instituts für Oesterreichische Geschichtsforschung*, II (Innsbruck, 1881), 459–60

Thieulaine, Jean, 'Un livre de raison en Artois (XVIᵉ siècle). Extraits historiques', ed. X. de Gorguette d'Argoeuves, *Mémoires de la Société des Antiquaires de la Morinie*, XXI (1889), 141–99

Thomas, Hubert (also known as 'Leodius'), *Annalium de vita et rebus gestis illustrissimi principis, Friderici II. electoris palatini, libri XIV* (Frankfurt, 1624; German translation, *Spiegel des Humors grosser Potentaten: anzuschawen vorgestellet in der Beschreibung des Lebens von der Regierung weiland Pfaltzgraffen Friedrichen des Andern, Churfürstens, etc.* (Schleusingen, 1628)

Turba, G., ed., *Venetianische Depeschen vom Kaiserhofe (Dispacci di Germania)*, 3 vols (Vienna 1889–95)

Tytler, P. F., *England under the reigns of Edward VI and Mary, with the contemporary history of Europe, illustrated in a series of original letters never before printed*, 2 vols (London, 1839)

Valdés, Alfonso de, *Relación de las nuevas de Italia: sacadas de las cartas que los capitanes y comisario del Emperador y Rey nuestro señor han escripto a su magestad: assi de la victoria contra el rey de Francia como de otras cosas alla acaecidas: vista y corregida por el señor gran Chanciller e consejo de su magestad* (Madrid, 1525)

Valdés, Alfonso de, *Diálogo de las cosas acaecidas en Roma. Diálogo en que particularmente se tratan las cosas acaecidas en Roma el año de 1527, a gloria de Dios y bien universal de la República Cristiana* (c. 1528: ed. J. F. Montesinos, Madrid, 1928)

Valdés, Alfonso de, *Diálogo de Mercurio y Carón: en que allende de muchas cosas graciosas y de buena doctrina se cuenta lo que ha acaescido en la guerra desdel año de mill y Qujnjentos y veynte y vno hasta los desafíos de los Reyes de Francia & Ynglaterra hechos al Emperador en el año de MDXXVIII* (c. 1529; ed. J. F. Montesinos, Madrid, 1929)

van den Bergh, L. P. C., *Correspondance de Marguerite d'Autriche, gouvernante des Pays-Bas, avec ses amis, sur les affaires des Pays-Bas de 1506–1528*, 2 vols (Leiden 1845–7)

Vandenesse, Jean de, 'Journal des voyages de Charles-Quint', in Gachard, *Collection des voyages*, II (Brussels, 1874), 53–463

van den Gheyn, J., *Catalogue des Manuscrits de la Bibliothèque Royale de Belgique*, VII (Brussels, 1907)

van der Elst, Laurentius, *Basilicae Bruxellensis sive monumenta antiqua inscriptiones et coenotaphia ecclesiae Collegiatae S. S. Michaeli*, 2 vols (Mechelen, 1743)

vander Linden, H., 'Articles soumis à Charles-Quint par son chancelier Gattinara concernant l'office de la chancellerie en 1528 [*recte* 1526]', *BCRH*, C (1937), 265–80

van Salenson, Gerardt, *Die warachtige geschiedenisse van allen gheleefweerdighe saken vanden alder onuerwinnelijsten ende alder moghensten Keyser van Roomen Carolus de vijfste van dien name, coninck van Spaengnien* (Ghent, 1564)

Vañes, C. A., 'Cartas originales de Carlos V al Papa Clemente VII', *Ciudad de Dios: Revista agustiniana*, CCXXIII (2010), 725–62, and CCXXIV (2011), 155–89

Vargas-Hidalgo, R., *Guerra y diplomacia en el Mediterráneo: correspondencia inédita de Felipe II con Andrea Doria y Juan Andrea Doria* (Madrid, 2002)

Varillas, Antoine, *La Pratique de l'éducation des princes, contenant l'histoire de Guillaume de Croÿ, surnommé Le Sage, seigneur de Chièvres, gouverneur de Charles d'Autriche qui fut Empereur, Cinquième du Nom* (Amsterdam, 1686)

Vera y Figueroa, Juan Antonio, *Epítome de la vida y hechos del invicto emperador Carlos V* (Milan, 1646)

Viaud, A., ed., *Lettres des souverains portugais à Charles-Quint et à l'impératrice (1528–1532), suivies en annexe de lettres de D. María de Velasco et du duc de Bragance, conservées aux archives de Simancas* (Lisbon and Paris, 1994)

Viciana, Martí de, *Libro tercero de la crónica de la ínclita y coronada ciudad de Valencia y de su reino*, ed. J. Iborra (1564; Valencia, 2002)

Viciana, Martí de, *Libro quarto de la crónica de la ínclita y coronada ciudad de Valencia y de su reino*, ed. J. Iborra (1566; Valencia, 2005)

Viglius (Wigle van Aytta van Zwichem), *see* von Druffel

Vilanova, R. de Vilanova de Rossello, count of, *Capítulo del Toisón de Oro celebrado en Barcelona el año 1519* (Barcelona, 1930)

Villar García, M. B., 'Cartas de Carlos V a Rodrigo Mexía (1520–1531)', *Studia histórica: historia moderna*, II (1984), 47–94

Vital, Laurent, 'Premier voyage de Charles-Quint en Espagne, de 1517 à 1518', in Gachard, *Collection des voyages*, III (Brussels, 1876), 1–314; *see also* Morgan, H.

Vitoria, Francisco de, *Relectio de Indis o libertad de los indios*, ed. L. Pereña and J. M. Pérez Prendes (Madrid, 1967: *Corpus Hispanorum de Pace*, V)

Voigt, G., 'Die Geschichtschreibung über den Zug Karls V gegen Tunis', *Abhandlung der philologisch-historischen Classe der königlich sächsischen Gesellschaft der Wissenschaften*, VI (Leipzig, 1874), 161–243

Voigt, G., 'Die Geschichtschreibung über den Schmalkaldischen Krieg', *Abhandlung der philologisch-historischen Classe der königlich sächsischen Gesellschaft der Wissenschaften*, VI (Leipzig, 1874), 567–758

Volpi, Giovanni Antonio and Gaetano, *Opere volgari e latine del Conte Baldessar Castiglione. Novellamente raccolte, ordinate, ricorrette, ed illustrate, come nella seguente letters può vedersi* (Padua, 1733)

Voltes Bou, P., *Documentos de tema español existentes en el Archivo de Estado de Viena* (Barcelona, 1964)

von Bucholtz, F. B., *Geschichte der Regierung Ferdinand des Ersten: aus gedruckten und ungedruckten Quellen*, 9 vols (Vienna, 1831–8)

von Dollinger, J. J. I., *Dokumente zur Geschichte Karl's V., Philipp's II. und ihrer Zeit aus spanischen Archiven* (Regensburg, 1862)

von Druffel, A., *Briefe und Akten zur Geschichte des 16. Jahrhunderts, mit besonderer Rücksicht auf Bayerns Fürstenhaus. Beiträge zur Reichsgeschichte 1546–1555*, 4 vols (Munich, 1873–96; vol. IV co-edited by Karl Brandi)

BIBLIOGRAPHY

von Druffel, A., ed., *Des Viglius van Zwichem Tagebuch des Schmalkaldischen Donaukriegs* (Munich, 1877)

von Gévay, A., *Urkunden und Actenstücke zur Geschichte der Verhältnisse zwischen Österreich, Ungern und der Pforte im XVI. und XVII. Jahrhunderte, aus Archiven und Bibliotheken. I, part V: Gesandtschaft König Ferdinands I. an Sultan Suleiman I. 1531–1532* (Vienna, 1838)

von Höfler, C. R., 'Monumenta Hispanica I: Correspondenz des Gobernadors von Castilien, Grossinquisitors von Spanien, Cardinals von Tortosa, Adrian von Utrecht mit Kaiser Karl V. im Jahre 1520', *Abhandlungen der königlichen böhmischen Gesellschaft der Wissenschaften, VI. Folge, 10. Band: Classe für Philosophie, Geschichte und Philologie Nr. 4* (Prague 1881), 3–90,

von Höfler, C. R., 'Monumenta Hispanica II. Spanische regesten von 1515 bis Ende 1520', *Abhandlungen der königlichen böhmischen Gesellschaft der Wissenschaften, VI. Folge, 11. Band: Classe für Philosophie, Geschichte und Philologie Nr. 5* (Prague 1882), 1–98

von Höfler, C. R., 'Zur Kritik und Quellenkunde der ersten Regierungsjahre Kaiser Karls V. III Abteilung. Das Jahr 1521, nach den authentischen Correspondenzen im Archive zu Simancas zusammengestellt', *Denkschriften der kaiserlichen Akademie der Wissenschaften, Philosophisch-Historische Classe*, XXXIII (Vienna, 1883), 1–206

von Höfler, C. R., 'Kritische Untersuchungen über die Quellen der Geschichte Phillipps des Schönen, Erzherzogs von Oesterreich, Herzogs von Burgund, Königs von Castilien', *Sitzungsberichte der kaiserlichen Akademie der Wissenschaften*, CIV (1883), 169–256

von Höfler, C. R., 'Antoine de Lalaing, seigneur de Montigny, Vincenzo Quirino und Don Diego de Guevara als Berichtserstatter über König Phillipp I. in den Jahren 1505, 1506', *Sitzungsberichte der kaiserlichen Akademie der Wissenschaften*, CIV (1883), 433–510

von Höfler, C. R., 'Depeschen des Venetianischen Botschafters bei Erzherzog Philipp, Herzog von Burgund, König von Leon, Castilien, Granada, Dr Vincenzo Quirino 1505–1506', *Archiv für österreichische Geschichte*, LXVI (1885), 45–256

von Kraus, V., 'Itinerarium Maximilian I. 1508–1518: mit eingeleitenden Bemerkungen über das Kanzleiwesen Maximilians I.', *Archiv für österreichische Geschichte*, LXXXVII (1899), 229–318

Vos, A. and M. Hatch, *Letters of Roger Ascham* (New York, 1989)

Walser, F., 'Spanien und Karl V. Fünf spanische Denkschriften an den Kaiser', in *B&S*, VI (1932), 120–81

Weert, Josse de, 'Cronycke van Nederlant, besonderlyck der stadt Antwerpen', in C. Piot, ed., *Chroniques de Brabant et de Flandre* (Brussels, 1879), 71–179

Wiesflecker-Friedhuber, I., ed., *Quellen zur Geschichte Maximilians I. und seiner Zeit* (Darmstadt, 1996)

Winckelmann, O., ed., *Politische Correspondenz der Stadt Strassburg im Zeitalter der Reformation, III. 1540–1545* (Strasbourg, 1898)

Xérez, Francisco de, *Verdadera relación de la conquista del Perú y provincia del Cuzco llamada la nueva Castilla* (Seville, 1534; Madrid 1891)

Zapata de Chaves, Luis, *Miscelánea*, in P. de Gayangos, ed., *Memorial Histórico Español*, XI (Madrid, 1859)

Zúñiga, Francés de, *Francesillo de Zúñiga: Crónica burlesca del emperador Carlos V*, ed. D. Pamp de Avalle-Arce (Barcelona, 1981)

Zúñiga, Francés de, *Don Francés de Zúñiga: Crónica burlesca del emperador Carlos V*, ed. J. A. Sánchez Paso (Salamanca, 1989)

Zurita, Jerónimo, *Historia del Rey don Hernando el Católico: de las empresas y ligas de Italia* (Zaragoza, 1580)

Zurita, Jerónimo, *Los cinco libros postreros de la historia de don Hernando el Católico: de las empresas y ligas de Italia* (Zaragoza, 1610)

SECONDARY SOURCES

Abella Rubio, J. J., 'El túmulo de Carlos V en Valladolid', *Boletín del Seminario de Estudios de Arte y Arquaeología*, XLIV (1978), 177–200

Aerts, E., L. de Mecheleer and R. Wellens, 'L'âge de Gachard. L'archivistique et l'historiographie en Belgique (1830–85)', in I. Cotta et al., eds, *Archivi e storia nell'Europa del XIX secolo: alle radici dell'identità culturale europea. Atti del convegno internazionale di studi nei 150 anni dall'istituzione dell'Archivio Centrale, poi Archivio di Stato, di Firenze; Firenze, 4–7 dicembre 2002* (Florence, 2006), 571–99

Aguirre Landa, I., 'Viejos y nuevos documentos en torno a Carlos V', in Castellano Castellano and Sánchez-Montes González, *Carlos V*, I, 35–46

Alarcón y Ariza, Pedro Antonio de, *Viajes por España* (2nd edition, Madrid 1892)

Alcázar Molina, C., 'La política postal española en el siglo XVI en tiempo de Carlos V', in *Carlos V (1500–1558). Homenaje*, 219–32

BIBLIOGRAPHY

Allo Manero, A., 'Exequias del emperador Carlos V en la monarquía hispana', in M. J. Redondo Cantera and M. A. Zalama, eds, *Carlos V y las artes. Promoción artística y familia imperial* (Valladolid, 2000), 261–81

Alonso Acero, B., 'Cristiandad versus Islam en el gobierno de Maximiliano y María (1548–1551)', in Castellano Castellano and Sánchez-Montes González, *Carlos V*, III, 15–29

Alonso Acero, B., 'El norte de África en el ocaso del emperador (1549–1558)', in Martínez Millán, *Carlos V y la quiebra*, I, 387–414

Alonso Acero, B. and J. L. Gonzalo Sánchez-Molero, 'Alá en la corte de un príncipe cristiano: el horizonte musulmán en la formación de Felipe II (1532–1557)', *Torre de los Lujanes*, XXXV (1998), 109–140

Altmeyer, J. J., *Isabelle d'Autriche et Christiern II* (Brussels, 1842)

Alvar Ezquerra, A., 'El gobierno de la emperatriz y la consolidación de la dinastía', in A. Alvar Ezquerra, J. Contreras Contreras and J. I. Ruiz Rodríguez, eds, *Política y cultura en la época moderna (Cambios dinásticos. Milenarismos, mesianismos y utopías)* (Alcalá de Henares, 2004), 51–63

Alvar Ezquerra, A., *La emperatriz. Isabel y Carlos V, amor y gobierno en la corte española del Renacimiento* (Madrid, 2012)

Álvarez, G., F. C. Ceballos and C. Quinteiro, 'The role of inbreeding in the extinction of a European royal dynasty', *PLoS ONE* 4(4): e5174. doi:10.1371/journal.pone.0005174

Anatra, B, 'Los itinerarios de Carlos V', in Castellano Castellano and Sánchez-Montes González, *Carlos V*, III, 37–45

Ando, C., *Imperial ideology and provincial loyalty in the Roman Empire* (Berkeley, 2000)

Angermeier, H., 'Der Wormser Reichstag 1495 in der politischen Konzeption König Maximilians I', in Lutz and Müller-Luckner, *Das römisch-deutsche Reich*, 1–13

Anthony, D., 'Intimate invasion: Andeans and Europeans in 16th-century Peru' (Ohio State University Ph.D. thesis, 2018)

Aram, B., *La reina Juana. Gobierno, piedad y dinastía* (Madrid, 2001)

Aram, B., *Juana the Mad: Sovereignty and dynasty in Renaissance Europe* (Baltimore, 2005)

Arfaioli, M., *The black bands of Giovanni: Infantry and diplomacy during the Italian wars (1526–1528)* (Pisa, 2005)

Arfaioli, M., 'A clash of dukes: Cosimo I de' Medici, William of Cleves and the "Guerra di Dura" of 1543' (forthcoming)

Arias de Saavedra Alias, I., 'La Universidad de Granada en la época de Carlos V', in Castellano Castellano and Sánchez-Montes González, *Carlos V*, V, 53–76

Armitage, D., ed., *Theories of empire 1450–1800* (Aldershot, 1998)

Arnade, P., 'Privileges and the political imagination in the Ghent Revolt of 1539', in Boone and Demoor, *Charles V*, 103–24

Arregui Zamorano, P., 'Carlos V: el despliegue de las Audiencias en el Nuevo Mundo', in Castellano Castellano and Sánchez-Montes González, *Carlos V*, II, 63–84

Auernhammer, A. and F. Däuble, 'Die exequien für Karl V. in Augsburg, Brüssel und Bologna', *Archiv für Kulturgeschichte*, LXII–LXIII (1980–1), 101–57

Baker-Bates, Piers, 'The "cloister life" of the Emperor Charles V: Art and ideology at Yuste', *Hispanic Research Journal*, XIV (2013), 427–45

Barón Crespo, E., 'La Europa de Carlos V y la Europa de Maastricht', *Correspondance: Revista hispano-belga*, no. Extra I (1994), 13–20

Bataillon, M., 'Charles-Quint et Copernic', *BH*, XXV (1923), 256–8

Bataillon, M., 'Le Charles-Quint de Karl Brandi', *BH*, XLII/4 (1940), 296–302

Bataillon, M., 'Charles-Quint bon pasteur, selon Fray Cipriano de Huerga', *BH*, L (1948), 398–406

Bataillon, M., 'Pour l'epistolario de Las Casas. Une lettre et un brouillon', *BH*, LVI (1954), 366–87

Bataillon, M., *Erasmo y España. Estudios sobre la historia espiritual del siglo XVI* (1937; 2nd edition, 1966)

Bataillon, M., 'Charles-Quint, Las Casas et Vitoria', in *Charles-Quint*, 77–92

Bataillon, M., 'Plus oultre: la cour découvre le nouveau monde', in Jacquot, *Les fêtes de la Renaissance*, II, 13–27

Bauer, W., *Die Anfänge Ferdinands I.* (Vienna and Leipzig, 1907)

Baumgarten, H., *Geschichte Karls V.*, 3 vols (Stuttgart, 1885–92)

Behrens, B., 'The office of English resident ambassador: Its evolution as illustrated by the career of Sir Thomas Spinelly', *TRHistS*, XVI (1933), 161–95

Behringer, W., *Im Zeichen des Merkur: Reichspost und Kommunikationsrevolution in der Frühen Neuzeit* (Göttingen, 2003)

Belenguer Cebrià, E., ed., *De la unión de coronas al imperio de Carlos V*, 3 vols (Madrid, 2000)

Beltrán de Heredía, V., *Domingo de Soto. Estudio biográfico documentado* (Salamanca, 1960)

BIBLIOGRAPHY

Bietenholz, P. G. and T. B. Deutscher, *Contemporaries of Erasmus: A biographical register of the Renaissance and Reformation*, 3 vols (Toronto, 1985–7)

Blockmans, W. P., 'Autocratie ou polyarchie? La lutte pour le pouvoir politique en Flandre de 1482 à 1492, d'après des documents inédits', *BCRH*, CXL (1974), 257–368

Blockmans, W. P., 'Unidad dinástica, diversidad de cuestiones', in García García, *El imperio de Carlos V*, 29–44

Blockmans, W. P., 'The emperor's subjects', in Soly, *Charles V*, 227–83

Blockmans, W. P., *Emperor Charles V, 1500–1558* (London, 2002)

Blockmans, W. P., 'Logistics of warfare in central Italy 1527–30', in Boone and Demoor, *Charles V*, 35–46

Blockmans, W. P. and N. Mout, eds, *The world of the Emperor Charles V* (Amsterdam, 2004)

Bodart, D. H., *Tiziano e Federico II Gonzaga. Storia di un rapporto di committenza* (Rome, 1998)

Bodart, D. H., 'Algunos casos de anacronismo en los retratos de Carlos V', *Boletín del Museo del Prado*, XVIII (2000), 7–24

Bodart, D. H., 'Frédéric Gonzague et Charles Quint. Enjeux artistiques et politiques des premiers portraits impériaux par Titien', in S. Ferino-Pagden and A. Beyer, eds, *Tizian versus Seisenegger. Die Portraits Karls V. mit Hund. Ein Holbeinstreit* (Turnhout, 2006), 19–31

Bodart, D. H., 'Il mento "posticcio" dell'imperatore Carlo V', *Micrologus: Natura, scienze e società medievali*, XX (2012), 465–83

Bonal Zazo, J. L., 'Disposiciones Carolinas en la base de datos *Legislación Histórica de España*', in Gonzalo Sánchez-Molero and Miranda Díaz, *La bibliografía*, 391–443

Bond, K. L., 'Costume albums in Charles V's Habsburg empire' (Cambridge University Ph.D. thesis, 2017)

Boom, G. de, *Marguerite d'Autriche-Savoie et la pré-Renaissance* (Paris, 1935)

Boom, G. de, *Les voyages de Charles-Quint* (Brussels, 1957)

Boone, M., 'From cuckoo's egg to "Sedem Tyranni". The princely citadels in the cities of the Low Countries, or the city's spatial integrity hijacked (15th–early 16th centuries)', in M. C. Howell and M. Boone, eds, *The power of space in late medieval and early modern Europe: The cities of Italy, Northern France and the Low Countries* (Turnhout, 2013), 77–95

Boone, M. and M. Demoor, eds, *Charles V in context: The making of a European entity* (Ghent, 2003)

Boone, R. A., *Mercurino di Gattinara and the creation of the Spanish Empire* (London, 2014)

Bossuyt, I., 'Charles V: a life story in music. Chronological outline of Charles's political career through music', in F. Maes, ed., *The empire resounds: Music in the days of Charles V* (Leuven, 1999)

Bourrilly, V.-L., 'Les diplomates de François 1er Antonio Rincon et la politique orientale de François 1er (1522–41)', *Revue hististorique*, CXIII (1913), 64–83 and 268–308

Bourrilly, V.-L., 'Charles-Quint en Provence (1536)', *Revue historique*, CXXVII (1936), 209–80

Bouza Brey, P., 'Las exequias del emperador Carlos I en la catedral de Santiago', *Cuadernos de estudios gallegos*, XIV (1959), 267–76

Boyd-Bowman, P., 'Patterns of Spanish emigration to the Indies until 1600', *Hispanic American Historical Review*, LVI (1976), 580–604

Brading, D., *The first America: The Spanish Monarchy, Creole patriots, and the liberal state, 1492–1867* (Cambridge, 1991)

Brady, T. A., 'Imperial destinies: A new biography of the Emperor Maximilian I', *Journal of Modern History*, LXII (1990), 298–314

Brady, T. A., *Protestant politics: Jacob Sturm (1489–1553) and the German Reformation* (Boston, 1995)

Brandi, K., 'Karl V. vor Metz', *Elsass-Lothringisches Jahrbuch*, XVI (1937), 1–30

Brandi, K., *The Emperor Charles V: The growth and destiny of a man and of a world-empire* (London, 1939; translation of *Kaiser Karl V. Werden und Schicksal einer Persönlichkeit und eines Weltreiches*: Munich, 1937)

Brandi, K., *Kaiser Karl V, II: Quellen und Erörterungen* (Munich, 1941)

Braudel, F., *La Méditerranée et le monde méditerranéen à l'époque de Philippe II* (Paris, 1949)

Braudel, F., 'Les emprunts de Charles-Quint sur la place d'Anvers', in *Charles-Quint*, 191–201

Braudel, F., 'Charles-Quint: témoin de son temps, 1500–1558', in Braudel, *Écrits sur l'histoire*, II (Paris, 1994), 167–207 (originally published in Italian in 1966)

Bregnsbo, M., 'Carlos V y Dinamarca', in Kohler, *Carlos V/Karl V*, 487–97

Brendecke, A., *Imperio e información. Funciones del saber en el dominio colonial español* (Madrid, 2013; translation of *Imperium und Empirie. Funktionen des Wissens in der spanischen Kolonialherrschaft*, Cologne, 2009); revised and shortened English translation: *The empirical empire: Spanish colonial rule and the politics of knowledge* (Berlin, 2016)

Bridgman, N., 'La participation musicale à l'entrée de Charles Quint à Cambrai, le 20 janvier 1540', in Jacquot, *Les fêtes de la Renaissance*, II, 235–53

BIBLIOGRAPHY

Brigden, S., *Thomas Wyatt: The heart's forest* (London, 2012)

Brothers, C., 'The Renaissance reception of the Alhambra: The letters of Andrea Navagero and the palace of Charles V', *Muqarnas: An Annual on Islamic Art and Architecture*, XI (1994), 79–102

Buceta, E., 'El juicio de Carlos V acerca del español y otros pareceres sobre las lenguas romances', *Revista de filología española*, XXIV (1937), 11–23

Burbank, J. and F. Cooper, *Empires in world history: Power and the politics of difference* (Princeton, 2010)

Burbure, L. de, 'Bredeniers, Henri', *Bibliographie nationale de Belgique*, II (Brussels, 1873), cols 921–4

Burke, P., 'Presenting and re-presenting Charles V', in Soly, *Charles V*, 393–475

Bustamante García, A., 'Las tumbas reales de El Escorial', in *Felipe II y el arte de su tiempo* (Madrid, 1998), 55–78

Buttay-Jutier, F., *Fortuna. Usages politiques d'une allégorie morale à la Renaissance* (Paris, 2008)

Cabrero Fernández, L., 'El empeño de las Molucas y los tratados de Zaragoza: cambios, modificaciones y coincidencias entre el no ratificado y el ratificado', in L. A. Ribot García et al., eds, *El Tratado de Tordesillas y su época*, II (Valladolid, 1995), 1,091–1,132

Cadenas y Vicent, V. de, 'Una calumnia gratuita levantada al emperador Carlos V por uno de sus mejores historiadores: Manuel Fernández Álvarez', *Hidalguía*, CCLXX (1998), 625–46

Cadenas y Vicent, V. de, 'Aclarada la calumnia del académico y catedrático Manuel Fernández Álvarez: la "Infanta de Castilla Isabel" tiene padres conocidos: los últimos reyes de Napoles', *Hidalguía*, CCLXXI (1998), 859–61

Carande, R., *Carlos V y sus banqueros*, 3 vols (Madrid, 1943–67)

Carande, R., 'Carlos V: viajes, cartas y deudas', in *Charles-Quint*, 203–36

Carande, R., 'Solimán no llega a Viena (1532) y de España sale un tesoro recibido de Francisco I', in *Studi in onore di Amintore Fanfani*, IV (Milan, 1962), 185–218

Carlos V (1500–1558). Homenaje de la Universidad de Granada (Granada, 1958)

Carlos Morales, C. J. de, *El consejo de Hacienda de Castilla, 1523–1602. Patronazgo y clientelismo en el gobierno de las finanzas reales durante el siglo XVI* (Valladolid, 1996)

Caro, R. A., *The years of Lyndon Johnson. I: The path to power* (1982; 2nd edition, New York, 1990)

Caro, R. A., *The years of Lyndon Johnson. III: Master of the Senate* (New York, 2003)

Carretero Zamora, J. M., *Gobernar es gastar. Carlos V, el servicio de las Cortes de Castilla y la deuda de la Monarquía Hispánica, 1516–1556* (Madrid, 2015)

Carro, V. D., 'Influencia de fray Pedro de Soto sobre Carlos V y el Papa en la guerra contra los protestantes', *Ciencia Tomista*, XXXII (1925), 55–71

Cartwright, J., *Christina of Denmark: Duchess of Milan and Lorraine, 1522–1590* (New York, 1913)

Cartwright, W. C., *Gustave Bergenroth: A memorial sketch* (Edinburgh, 1870)

Castellano Castellano, J. L. and F. Sánchez-Montes González, eds, *Carlos V. Europeísmo y universalidad*, 5 vols (Madrid, 2001)

Castilla Urbano, F., 'La superación de la polémica de la conquista: del enfrentamiento Sepúlveda-Las Casas a las propuestas de Acosta', *Revista inclusiones. Revista de humanidades y ciencias sociales*, II (2015), 29–51

Cauchies, J.-M., 'L'Archiduc Philippe d'Autriche, dit le Beau', *Handelingen van het Koninklijke Kring voor oudheidkunde, letteren en geschiedenis van Mechelen*, XCV (1992), 45–53

Cauchies, J.-M., *Philippe le Beau. Le dernier duc de Bourgogne* (Leuven, 2003: Burgundica VI)

Cauchies, J.-M., ' "Croit conseil" et ses "ministres": l'entourage politique de Philippe le Beau (1494–1506)', in A. Marchandisse and J.-L. Kupper, eds, *A l'ombre du pouvoir: les entourages princiers au Moyen Age* (Liège, 2003), 385–405

Cauchies, J.-M., ' "No tyenen más voluntad de yr a España que de yr al infierno!". Los consejeros "flamencos" de Felipe el Hermoso y del joven Carlos V frente a la herencia española', in A. Álvarez-Ossorio Alvariño and B. J. García García, eds, *La Monarquía de las naciones. Patria, nación y naturaleza en la Monarquía de España* (Madrid 2004), 121–30

Cauchies, J.-M. and M. van Eeckenrode, ' "Recevoir madame l'archiduchesse pour faire incontinent ses nopces . . .". Gouvernants et gouvernés autour du mariage de Philippe le Beau et de Jeanne de Castille dans les Pays-Bas (1496–1501)', in Cauchies and van Eeckenrode, eds, *Die Erbtochter, der fremde Fürst und das Land* (Luxemburg, 2013: Publications du Centre luxembourgeois de Documentation et d'Etudes médiévales, XXXVIII), 263–77

Chabod, F., *Lo stato di Milano nell'impero di Carlo V* (Rome, 1934)

Chabod, F., 'Contrasti interni e dibattiti sulla politica generale di Carlo V', in Rassow and Schalk, *Karl V*, 51–66, reprinted in Chabod, *Carlos V*, 253–70 (citations from the latter)

Chabod, F., 'Milán o los Países Bajos? Las discusiones en España sobre la "Alternativa" de 1544', in *Carlos V (1500–1558)*, 331–372, reprinted in Chabod, *Carlos V*, 211–51 (citations from the latter)

BIBLIOGRAPHY

Chabod, F., *Storia di Milano nell'epoca di Carlo V* (Turin, 1971: *Opere di Federico Chabod*, III/2, first published in 1961 as vol. IX of the Treccani *Storia di Milano*)

Chabod, F., *Carlos V y su imperio* (Mexico City, 1992; Italian original 1985)

Charles-Quint et son temps (Paris, 1959)

Chaunu, P. and M. Escamilla, *Charles Quint* (2nd edition, Paris, 2013)

Checa Cremades, F., 'Un programa imperialista: el túmulo erigido en Alcalá de Henares en memoria de Carlos V', *Revista de Archivos, Bibliotecas y Museos*, LXXXII (1979), 369–79

Checa Cremades, F., 'El caballero y la muerte (sobre el sentido de la muerte en el Renacimiento)', *Revista de la Universidad Complutense*, Año 1982, 242–57

Checa Cremades, F., *Carlos V y la imagen del héroe en el Renacimiento* (Madrid, 1987)

Checa Cremades, F., ed., *Monumentos restaurados: El monasterio de Yuste* (Madrid: Monumentos restaurados VII, 2007)

Checa Cremades, F., ed., *Museo Imperial. El coleccionismo artístico de los Austrias en el siglo XVI* (Madrid: Villaverde, 2013)

Checa Cremades, F., M. Falomir and J. Portús, eds, *Carlos V: retratos de familia* (Madrid, 2000)

Cheney, C. R., *Handbook of dates for students of English history* (corrected edition, Cambridge, 1996)

Civil, P., 'Enjeux et stratégies de la politique imperiale à travers les portraits de Charles-Quint', in F. Crémoux and J.-L. Fournel, eds, *Idées d'empire en Italie et en Espagne, XIVe–XVIIe siècle* (Rouen, 2010), 103–20

Clark, C., *The sleepwalkers: How Europe went to war in 1914* (New York, 2012)

Clifford, C., *Photographic scramble through Spain* (London, n.d. but c. 1860)

Cline, H. F., 'Hernando Cortés and the Aztec Indians in Spain', *The Quarterly Journal of the Library of Congress*, XXVI/2 (1969), 70–90

Close, C. W., 'City-states, princely states, and warfare: Corporate alliance and state formation in the Holy Roman Empire (1540–1610), *European History Quarterly*, XLVII (2017), 205–28

Cohn, H. J., 'Did bribery induce the Imperial Electors to choose Charles V as emperor in 1519?', *German History*, XIX (2001), 1–27

Colón de Carvajal, A., 'Don Fernando de Valdés Salas, Letrado del II Almirante de las Indias', *e-SLegal History Review*, XVI (2013), 1–8

Coniglio, G., *Il regno di Napoli al tempo di Carlo V* (Naples, 1951)

Cosentini, L., *Una dama Napoletana del XVI secolo: Isabella Villamarina, principessa di Salerno* (Trani, 1896)

Couper, R. T. L., P. L. Fernandez and P. L. Alonso, 'The severe gout of Emperor Charles V', *New England Journal of Medicine*, CCCLV (2006), 1,935–6

Crouzet, D., *Charles de Bourbon, connétable de France* (Paris, 2003)

Crouzet, D., *Charles Quint: empereur d'une fin des temps* (Paris, 2016)

Crutzen, G., 'L'origine maternelle et la naissance de Marguerite de Parme, régente des Pais-Bas', *Revue de l'instruction publique (supérieure et moyenne) en Belgique*, XXV (1882), 153–69

Cuart Moner, B., 'Jovio en España. Las traducciones castellanas de un cronista del emperador', in Castellano Castellano and Sánchez-Montes González, *Carlos V*, V, 197–224

Cuart Moner, B., 'Juan Ginés de Sepúlveda, cronista del Emperador', in Martínez Millán, *Carlos V y la quiebra*, III, 342–67

Dall'Aglio, S., *The duke's assassin: Exile and death of Lorenzino de' Medici* (New Haven and London, 2015 (translated from the Italian original, Florence, 2011)

Dandelet, T. J., *The Renaissance of empire in early modern Europe* (Cambridge, 2014)

Dandelet, T. J., 'Imagining Marcus Aurelius in the Renaissance: Forgery, fiction, and history in the creation of the imperial ideal', in A. Blair and A.-S. Goeing, *For the sake of learning: Essays in honor of Anthony Grafton*, 2 vols (Leiden, 2016), II, 729–42

De Courcelles, D., *Escribir la historia, escribir historias en el mundo hispánico* (Mexico City, 2009)

Decrue, F., *Anne de Montmorency: Grand Maître et Connétable de France: à la cour, aux armées et au conseil du roi Francois Ier* (Paris, 1885)

De Grauw, L., 'Quelle langue Charles-Quint parlait-il?', in Boone and Demoor, *Charles V*, 147–62

De Iongh, J., *Madama. Margaretha van Oostenrijk. Hertogin van Parma en Piacenza, 1522–1586* (3rd edition, Amsterdam, 1981)

Dekker, R., ed., *Egodocuments and history: Autobiographical writing in its context since the Middle Ages* (Hilversum, 2002)

Delsalle, P., 'Un homme de guerre au service de Charles Quint et de Philippe II: Fery de Guyon', in *Actes du cinquantième congrès de la fédération des sociétés savantes du Nord de la France* (2010), 6–10

Deswarte-Rosa, S., 'Espoirs et désespoir de l'Infant D. Luís', *Mare Liberum*, III (1991), 241–98

706

De Vivo, F., 'Archives of speech: Recording diplomatic negotiation in late medieval and early modern Italy', *European History Quarterly*, XLVI (2016), 519–44

Di Blasi, G. E., *Storia cronologica dei vicerè, luogotenenti e presidenti del Regno di Sicilia* (Palermo, 1842)

Dixon, C. S., 'Charles V and the historians: Some recent German works on the emperor and his reign', *German History*, XXI (2003) 104–24

Dixon, C. S. and M. Fuchs, *Nationale Perspektiven von Persönlichkeit und Herrschaft / The histories of the Emperor Charles V* (Münster, 2005)

Dobras, W., 'Karl V., Ferdinand I. und die Reichsstadt Konstanz', in Rabe, *Karl V. Politik und politisches System*, 191–221

Domingo Malvadi, A., *Bibliofilia Humanista en tiempos de Felipe II: la biblioteca de Juan Páez de Castro* (Salamanca, 2011)

Domínguez Casas, R., 'Estilo y rituales de corte', in Zalama and Vandenbroeck, *Felipe I el Hermoso*, 89–103

Doussinague, J. M., *La política internacional de Fernando el Católico* (Madrid, 1944)

Doussinague, J. M., *El testamento político de Fernando el Católico* (Madrid, 1950)

Druez, L., 'Perspectives comparées du règne de Charles-Quint: histoire officielle, histoire luthérienne, histoire italienne', in C. Grell, ed., *Les historiographes en Europe de la fin du Moyen Age à la Révolution* (Paris, 2006), 77–107

Dunham, W. H., 'Henry VIII's whole council and its parts', *Huntington Library Quarterly*, VII (1943), 7–46

Edelmayer, F., 'Carlos V y Fernando I. La quiebra de la monarquía universal', in Martínez Millán, *Carlos V y la quiebra*, I, 151–61

Edelmayer, F., 'El Sacro Imperio en la época de Carlos V. El problema de la Reforma protestante', in Castellano Castellano and Sánchez-Montes González, *Carlos V*, III, 169–76

Edelmayer, F., 'Ferdinand I and his inventories', in Checa Cremades, *Los inventarios de Carlos V*, III, 2,653–63

Egido, T., 'Carlos V y Lutero', in Castellano Castellano and Sánchez-Montes González, *Carlos V*, V, 225–42

Eichberger, D., 'A noble residence for a female regent: Margaret of Austria and the "Court of Savoy" in Mechelen', in H. Hills, ed., *Architecture and the politics of gender in early modern Europe* (Aldershot, 2003), 25–46

Elliott, J. H., 'Monarquía compuesta y Monarquía universal en la época de Carlos V', in Castellano Castellano and Sánchez-Montes González, *Carlos V*, V, 699–710

Ericksen, R. P., *Complicity in the Holocaust: Churches and universities in Nazi Germany* (Cambridge, 2012)

Escallier, E. A., *L'abbaye d'Anchin, 1079–1792* (Lille, 1852)

Escamilla, M., 'Le règne de Charles Quint: un bilan impossible?', in Molinié-Bertrand and Duviols, *Charles Quint*, 5–22

Espinosa, A., *The empire of the cities: Emperor Charles V, the Comunero revolt and the transformation of the Spanish system* (Leiden, 2009)

Fagel, R., *De Hispano-Vlaamse Wereld. De contacten tussen Spanjaarden en Nederlanders 1496–1555* (Brussels, 1996)

Fagel, R., 'Carlos de Luxemburgo: el futuro emperador como joven príncipe de Borgoña (1500–1515)', in Navascués Palacio, *Carolus V*, 29–63

Fagel, R., 'A broken portrait of the emperor: Charles V in Holland and Belgium, 1558–2000', in Dixon and Fuchs, *Nationale Perspektiven*, 63–89

Fagel, R., 'Don Fernando en Flandes (1518–1521): un príncipe sin tierra', in A. Alvar and F. Edelmayer, eds, *Fernando I, 1503–1564: socialización, vida privada y actividad pública de un Emperador del renacimiento* (Madrid, 2004), 253–71

Fagel, R., 'Un heredero entre tutores y regentes: casa y corte de Margarita de Austria y Carlos de Luxemburgo (1506–1516)', in Martínez Millán, *La Corte*, I, 115–38

Fagel, R., 'Adrian of Utrecht in Spain (1515–1522): A career in the service of a Habsburg prince', *Fragmenta*, IV (2010), 23–45

Fagel, R., 'Poner la corte en orden, poner orden en la corte. Los cambios en la casa de Borgoña alrededor del primer viaje hispánico de Carlos V (1515–1517)', in J. E. Hortal Muñoz and F. Labrador Arroyo, eds, *La casa de Borgoña. La casa del rey de España* (Leuven, 2014), 51–72

Ferer, M. T., *Music and ceremony at the court of Charles V: The Capilla Flamenca and the art of political promotion* (Woodbridge, 2012)

Fernández Álvarez, M., 'Las "Memorias" de Carlos V', *Hispania*, LXXIII (1958), 690–718

Fernández Álvarez, M., *Política mundial de Carlos V y Felipe II* (Madrid, 1966)

BIBLIOGRAPHY

Fernández Álvarez, M., *La España del Emperador Carlos V (1500–58; 1517–56)* (Madrid, 1966: Historia de España Menéndez Pidal, XVIII)

Fernández Álvarez, M., 'Las instrucciones políticas de los Austrias mayores. Problemas e interpretaciones', *Gesammelte Aufsätze zur Kulturgeschichte Spaniens*, XXIII (1967), 171–88

Fernández Álvarez, M., *Charles V* (London, 1975)

Fernández Álvarez, M., *Felipe II y su tiempo* (Madrid, 1998)

Fernández Álvarez, M., *Carlos V: el César y el Hombre* (Madrid, 1999)

Fernández Álvarez, M., *Carlos V. Un hombre para Europa* (Madrid, 1999)

Fernández Terricabras, I., 'La reforma de las Órdenes religiosas en tiempos de Felipe II. Aproximación cronológica', in E. Belenguer Cebrià, *Felipe II y el Mediterráneo*, 4 vols (Madrid, 1999), II, 181–204

Fernández Terricabras, I., 'De la *crisis* al *viraje*. Los inicios de la política confesional de Felipe II', in M. Boeglin, I. Fernández Terricabras and D. Kahn, eds, *Reforma y disidencia religiosa. La recepción de las doctrinas reformadas en la Península Ibérica en el siglo XVI* (Madrid, 2018), 53–73

Fortea Pérez, J. I., 'Las Cortes de Castilla en los primeros años de Carlos V, 1518–1536', in Belenguer Cebrià, *De la unión*, I, 411–43

Fortea Pérez, J. I., 'Las últimas Cortes del reinado de Carlos V (1537–1555)', in Castellano Castellano and Sánchez-Montes González, *Carlos V*, II, 243–73

Fraenkel-Goldschmidt, C., ed., *The historical writings of Joseph of Rosheim: Leader of Jewry in early modern Germany* (Leiden, 2006)

Frieder, B., *Chivalry and the perfect prince: Tournaments, art and armor at the Spanish Habsburg court* (Kirksville, MO, 2007)

Fuchs, B., *Exotic nation: Maurophilia and the construction of early modern Spain* (Philadephia, 2009)

Fuchs, M., *Karl V. – Eine populäre Figur? Zur Rezeption des Kaisers in deutschsprachiger Belletristik* (Münster, 2002)

Fürstenwerth, L., *Die Verfassungsänderungen in den oberdeutschen Reichsstädten zur Zeit Karls V.* (Göttingen, 1893)

Gachard, L. P., 'Charles-Quint', in *Biographie nationale de Belgique*, III (Brussels, 1872), cols 523–960. Spanish translation: L. P. Gachard, *Carlos V* (Pamplona, 2015)

Gachard, L. P., *Don Juan d'Autriche: Études historiques* (Brussels, 1869)

Galasso, G., 'L'opera del Brandi e alcuni studi recenti su Carlo V', *Rivista storica italiana*, LXXIV (1962), 93–119

Galasso, G., 'La storiografia italiana e Carlo V da G. De Leva a F. Chabod (1860–1960)', in Castellano Castellano and Sánchez-Montes González, *Carlos V*, I, 145–57

Ganz, D. M., 'Charlemagne in Hell', *Florilegium*, XVII (2000), 176–94

García-Baquero González, A., 'Agobios carolinos y tesoros americanos: los secuestros de las remesas de particulares en la época del emperador', in Castellano Castellano and Sánchez-Montes González, *Carlos V*, I, 309–36

García Cárcel, R., *Las Germanías de Valencia* (Barcelona, 1975)

García-Frías Checa, C., ed., *Carlos V en Yuste. Muerte y gloria eterna* (Madrid, 2008)

García Fuentes, J. M., 'Bernabé de Busto, cronista de Carlos V', in Castellano Castellano and Sánchez-Montes González, *Carlos V*, IV, 177–93

García García, B., ed., *El imperio de Carlos V. Procesos de agregación y conflictos* (Madrid, 2000)

García Simón, A., *El ocaso del emperador: Carlos V en Yuste* (Madrid, 1995)

Gibson, C., *Tlaxcala in the sixteenth century* (1952; 2nd edition, Stanford, 1967)

Giménez Fernández, M., *Bartolomé de Las Casas*, 2 vols (Madrid, 1953–60)

Glagau, H., 'Landgraf Philipp von Hessen im Ausgang des Schmalkaldischen Krieges', *Historische Vierteljahrschrift*, N. F. VIII (1905), 17–56

Gleason, E., *Gasparo Contarini: Venice, Rome and reform* (Berkeley, 1993)

Godin, A., 'La société au XVIe siècle vue par J. Glapion (1460?–1522), frère mineur, confesseur de Charles-Quint', *Revue du Nord*, XLVI (1964), 341–70

Gómez-Salvago Sánchez, M., *Fastos de una boda real en la Sevilla del quinientos (estudio y documentos)* (Seville, 1998)

González García, J. L., 'La memoria del emperador: libros, imágenes y devociones de Carlos V en Yuste', in Checa Cremades, *Monumentos restaurados*, 109–34

González García, J. L., 'Prácticas de reciclaje y auto-consciencia familiar en el coleccionismo artístico de los Habsburgo', in Checa Cremades, *Museo Imperial*, 43–52

Gonzalo Sánchez-Molero, J. L., *El aprendizaje cortesano de Felipe II (1527–1546). La formación de un príncipe del Renacimiento* (Madrid, 1999)

Gonzalo Sánchez-Molero, J. L., *Regia Bibliotheca. El libro en la corte española de Carlos V*, 2 vols (Mérida, 2005)

708

Gonzalo Sánchez-Molero, J. L., 'El caballero, la muerte, y el libro: las lecturas del emperador en Yuste', in García-Frías Checa, *Carlos V en Yuste*, 145–77

Gonzalo Sánchez-Molero, J. L., *El César y los libros. Un viaje a través de las lecturas del emperador desde Gante a Yuste* (Yuste, 2008)

Gonzalo Sánchez-Molero, J. L., 'Acerca de los *Hechos del Emperador*, una ficción bibliográfica cervantina', in Gonzalo Sánchez-Molero and Miranda Díaz, *La bibliografía*, 375–462

Gonzalo Sánchez-Molero, J. L., *Felipe II. La educación de un 'felicísimo príncipe' (1527–1545)* (Madrid, 2013)

Gonzalo Sánchez-Molero, J. L., *Felipe II. La mirada de un rey* (Madrid, 2014)

Gonzalo Sánchez-Molero, J. L. and B. Miranda Díaz, eds, *La bibliografía sobre el emperador Carlos V. Perspectivas históricas y temáticas* (Yuste, 2010)

Gorter-van Royen, L., 'María de Hungría, regente de los Países Bajos, a la luz de su correspondencia', in Kohler, *Carlos V/ Karl V*, 193–202

Gossart, E., 'Deux filles naturelles de Charles-Quint: Thadée et Jeanne', *Revue de Belgique*, 2ᵉ série VI (1892), 247–52

Gossart, E., *Charles-Quint et Philippe II. Étude sur les origines de la prépondérance politique de l'Espagne en Europe* (Brussels, 1896: Mémoires couronnés et autres mémoires publiés par l'Académie royale des sciences, des lettres et des beaux-arts de Belgique, LIV)

Gossart, E., *Notes pour servir à l'histoire du règne de Charles-Quint* (Brussels, 1897: Mémoires couronnés et autres mémoires publiés par l'Académie royale des sciences, des lettres et des beaux-arts de Belgique, LV)

Gossart, E., *Charles-Quint: roi d'Espagne, suivi d'une étude sur l'apprentissage politique de l'empereur* (Brussels, 1910)

Gould, A. B., 'The adventure of the missing fortnight', *The Atlantic Monthly*, CXXIV (1919), 34–44

Grunberg, B., 'Le vocabulaire de la "conquista". Essai de linguistique historique appliquée à la conquête du Mexique d'après les chroniques des conquistadores', *Histoire économique et sociale*, IV (1985), 3–27

Guilmartin, J. F., *Gunpowder and galleys: Changing technology and Mediterranean warfare at sea in the sixteenth century* (Cambridge, 1974)

Gunn, S. J., 'The duke of Suffolk's march on Paris in 1523', *EHR*, CI (1986), 596–634

Gunn, S. J., D. Grummit and H. Cools, *War, state, and society in England and the Netherlands, 1477–1559* (Oxford, 2007)

Gwyn, P., 'Wolsey's foreign policy: The conferences at Calais and Bruges reconsidered', *Historical Journal*, XXIII (1980), 755–72

Haag, S., D. Eichberger and A. Jordan Gschwend, *Frauen, Kunst und Macht: Drei Frauen aus dem Haus Habsburg* (exhibition catalogue from the Kunstmuseum, Vienna, 2018)

Häberlein, M., 'Jakob Fugger und die Kaiserwahl Karls V. 1519', in J. Burkhardt, ed., *Die Fugger und das Reich. Eine neue Forschungsperspektive zum 500jährigen Jubiläum der ersten Fuggerherrschaft Kirchberg-Weissenhorn* (Augsburg, 2008: Studien zur Fuggergeschichte, XLI), 65–81

Häberlein, M., *The Fuggers of Augsburg: Pursuing wealth and honor in Renaissance Germany* (Charlottesville, 2012)

Hampe Martínez, T., 'Don Pedro de La Gasca y la proyección del mundo universitario salmantino en el siglo XVI', *Mélanges de La Casa de Velázquez*, XXII (1986), 171–95

Hampe Martínez, T., *Don Pedro de La Gasca (1493–1567): su obra política en España y América* (Palencia, 1990)

Hanke, L., *The Spanish struggle for justice in the conquest of America* (Boston, 1949)

Haring, C. H., 'Ledgers of the royal treasurers in Spanish America in the sixteenth century', *Hispanic-American Historical Review*, II (1919), 173–87

Hatzfeld, L., 'Staatsräson und Reputation bei Kaiser Karl V', *Zeitschrift für Religions- und Geistesgeschichte*, XI (1959), 32–58

Hauser, H., *Le traité de Madrid et la cession de la Bourgogne à Charles-Quint; étude sur le sentiment national bourguignon en 1525–1526* (Dijon, 1912; also published in *Revue bourguignonne*, XXII)

Head, R. C., 'Configuring European archives: Spaces, materials and practices in the differentiation of repositories from the late Middle Ages to 1700', *European History Quarterly*, XLVI (2016), 498–518

Headley, J. M., 'The Habsburg world empire and the revival of Ghibellinism', in Armitage, *Theories of empire*, 45–79

Headley, J. M., *The emperor and his chancellor: A study of the imperial chancellery under Gattinara* (Cambridge, 1983)

Headley, J. M., 'The emperor and his chancellor: Disputes over empire, administration and pope (1519–1529)', in Martínez Millán, *Carlos V y la quiebra*, I, 21–35

Heikamp, D., *Mexico and the Medici* (Florence, 1972: Quaderni d'arte, VI)

BIBLIOGRAPHY

Hein, J., 'Isabella of Austria, queen of Denmark', in Checa Cremades, *Los inventarios de Carlos V*, III, 2,613–23

Henne, A., *Histoire du règne de Charles-Quint en Belgique*, 10 vols (Brussels, Paris, Madrid and Leipzig, 1858–9)

Hernando Sánchez, C. J., *Castilla y Nápoles en el siglo XVI. El Virrey Pedro de Toledo* (Salamanca, 1994)

Hess, A. C., 'The Ottoman conquest of Egypt (1517) and the beginning of the sixteenth-century world war', *International Journal of Middle Eastern Studies*, IV (1973), 55–7

Hewlett, M., 'Fortune's fool: The influence of humanism on Francesco Burlamacchi, "hero" of Lucca', in K. Eisenbichler and N. Terpstra, eds, *The Renaissance in the streets, schools, and studies: Essays in honour of Paul F. Grendler* (Toronto, 2008), 125–56

Heymans, V., *Le palais du Coudenberg à Bruxelles: Du château médiéval au site archéologique* (Brussels, 2014)

Hillerbrand, H. J., 'Martin Luther and the bull *Exsurge Domine*', *Theological Studies*, XXX (1969), 108–12

Huizinga, J., *Herfsttij der Middeleeuwen*, in Huizinga, *Verzamelde werken*, III (ed. L. Brummel) (Haarlem, 1949; 1st edition, 1919)

Huizinga, J., *Geschonden wereld. Een beschouwing over de kansen op herstel van onze beschaving* (2nd edition, Haarlem, 1945)

Ilardi, V., 'Crosses and carets: Renaissance patronage and coded letters of recommendation', *AHR*, XCII (1987), 1,127–49

Isom-Verhaaren, C., ' "Barbarossa and his army, who came to succor all of us": Ottoman and French views of their joint campaign of 1543–1544', *French Historical Studies*, XXX (2007), 395–425

Issleib, S., *Aufsätze und Beiträge zu Kurfürst Moritz von Sachsen (1877–1907)*, 2 vols (Cologne, 1989)

Jacqueton, G., *La politique extérieure de Louise de Savoie. Relations diplomatiques de la France et de l'Angleterre pendant la captivité de Francois Ier (1525–1526)* (Paris, 1892)

Jacquot, J., ed., *Fêtes et cérémonies au temps de Charles Quint* (Paris, 1960; reprinted 1975)

Janis, I. L., *Groupthink: Psychological studies of policy decisions and fiascos* (New York, 1983)

Johnson, C. L., *Cultural hierarchy in sixteenth-century Europe: The Ottomans and the Mexicans* (Cambridge, 2011)

Jordan Gschwend, A., '*Ma meilleure sœur*: Leonor of Austria, queen of Portugal and France', in Checa Cremades, *Los inventarios de Carlos V*, III, 2,569–92

Jordan Gschwend, A., '*Verdadero padre y señor*: Catherine of Austria, queen of Portugal', in Checa Cremades, *Los inventarios de Carlos V*, III, 3,015–44

Jordano, A., 'The *plus oultra* writing cabinet of Charles V: Expression of the sacred imperialism of the Austrias', *Journal of Conservation and Museum Studies*, IX (2012), 14–26

Jover Zamora, J. M., *Carlos V y los españoles* (Madrid, 1963; 2nd edition, 1987)

Junghans, H., 'Kaiser Karl V. am Grabe Martin Luthers in der Schlosskirche zu Wittenberg', *Lutherjahrbuch*, LIV (1987), 100–13

Juste, T., *Charles-Quint et Marguerite d'Autriche. Etude sur la minorité, l'émancipation et l'avènement de Charles-Quint à l'Empire (1477–1521)* (Brussels and Leipzig, 1858)

Kagan, R. L., 'Las cronistas del emperador', in Navascués Palacio, *Carolus V*, 183–212

Kagan, R. L., 'La propaganda y la política: las memorias del Emperador', in Castellano Castellano and Sánchez-Montes González, *Carlos V*, I, 209–16

Kagan, R. L., *Clio and the crown: The politics of history in medieval and early modern Spain* (Baltimore, 2009)

Kalkar, C. H., 'Isabella von Österreich, Gemahlin Christierns des Zweiten, Königin von Dänemark', *Archiv für Staats- und Kirchengeschichte der Herzogthümer Schleswig-Holstein und Lauenburg und der angrenzenden Länder und Städte*, V (1843), 443–519

Kamen, H., *Felipe de España* (Madrid, 1997)

Keniston, H., *Francisco de Los Cobos, secretary of the Emperor Charles V* (Pittsburgh, 1958)

Kess, A., *Johann Sleidan and the Protestant vision of History* (Aldershot, 2008)

Kissinger, H., *White House years* (Boston, 1979)

Kleinschmidt, H., *Charles V: The world emperor* (Stroud, 2004)

Knecht, R., 'Charles V's journey through France, 1539–40', in J. R. Mulryne and E. Goldring, eds, *Court festivals of the European Renaissance. Art, politics and performance* (Aldershot, 2002), 153–70

Knecht, R. J., *Francis I* (Cambridge, 1982)

Koenigsberger, H. G., 'The empire of Charles V in Europe', in G. R. Elton, ed., *The New Cambridge Modern History. II: The Reformation* (1958; 2nd edition, Cambridge, 1990), 339–76

Koenigsberger, H. G. and G. Parker, 'Charles V', *Sussex Tapes Pre-recorded educational discussions* (Devizes, 1982)

BIBLIOGRAPHY

Kohler, A., *Antihabsburgische Politik in der Epoche Karls V.: die reichsständische Opposition gegen die Wahl Ferdinands I. zum römischen König und gegen die Anerkennung seines Königstums (1524–1534)* (Göttingen, 1982)

Kohler, A., *Carlos V, 1500–1558. Una biografía* (Madrid, 2000; original German edition, Munich, 1999)

Kohler, A., ed., *Carlos V/Karl V. 1500–2000* (Madrid, 2001)

Kohler, A., 'Una mirada retrospectiva a los últimos 500 años. Balance y déficit de una "interminable" historia de la investigación', in Kohler, *Carlos V/Karl V*, 3–11

Konetzke, R., 'La legislación sobre inmigración de extranjeros en América durante el reinado de Carlos V', in *Charles-Quint*, 93–111

Kouri, E. and T. Scott, eds, *Politics and society in early modern Europe: Festschrift for Geoffrey Elton* (Basingstoke, 1987)

Laferl, C. F., 'Las relaciones entre Carlos V y Fernando I a través de la correspondencia familiar de Fernando I (1533–1534). Idiomas, contenidos y jerarquía entre hermanos', in Kohler, *Carlos V/Karl V*, 105–17

Lafuente, M., 'La madre de Don Juan de Austria', in C. de Ochoa, ed., *Antología española. Colección de trozos escogidos de los mejores hablistas, en prosa y verso, desde el siglo XV hasta nuestros días* (Paris, 1860), 298–309

Lapèyre, H., *Une famille des marchands: les Ruiz. Contribution à l'étude du commerce entre la France et l'Espagne au temps de Philippe II* (Paris, 1955)

Laubach, E., 'Wahlpropaganda und Wahlkampf um die deutsche Königswürde 1519', *Archiv für Kulturgeschichte*, LIII (1971), 207–48

Laubach, E., 'Karl V., Ferdinand und die Nachfolge im Reich', *MÖStA*, XXIX (1976), 1–51

Le Person, X., 'A moment of "resverie": Charles V and Francis I's encounter at Aigues-Mortes (July 1538)', *French History*, XIX (2005), 1–27

Lehnhoff, O., *Die Beichtväter Karls V. Ihre politische Tätigkeit und ihr Verhältnis zum Kaiser* (Alfeld, 1932)

Lenowitz, H., *The Jewish Messiahs, from the Galilee to Crown Heights* (Oxford, 1998)

Leva, G. de, 'Marino Sanuto', *Archivio Veneto*, XXXVI (1888), 109–26

Levin, M., 'A failure of intelligence: Gómez Suárez de Figueroa and the Fieschi conspiracy, 1547', *Bulletin for Spanish and Portuguese Historical Studies*, XXXVIII (2013), 20–37

Lhotsky, A., *Festschrift des Kunsthistorischen Museums zur Feier des fünfzigjährigen Bestandes. II. Die Geschichte der Sammlungen*, 2 vols (Vienna, 1941–5)

Liebing, H., 'Frontière infranchissable?' L'accès des Réformés à la paix d'Augsbourg, 1555–1577', in R. Sauzet, *Les frontières religieuses en Europe du XVe au XVIIe siècle* (Paris, 1992), 215–23

Lippens, H., 'Jean Glapion, défenseur de la Réforme de l'Observance, conseiller de l'empereur Charles-Quint', *Archivum franciscanum historicum*, XLIV (1951), 3–70, and XLV (1952), 3–71

Lox, H., *Van stropdragers en de pot van Olen. Verhalen over Keizer Karel* (Leuven, 1999)

Luttenberger, A. P., 'Reichspolitik und Reichstag unter Karl V.: Formen zentralen politischen Handelns', in H. Lutz and A. Kohler, eds, *Aus der Arbeit an den Reichstagen unter Kaiser Karl V.: 7 Beiträge zu Fragen der Forschung und Edition* (Göttingen, 1986), 18–68

Luttenberger, A. P., 'La política religiosa de Carlos V en el Sacro Imperio Romano', in Kohler, *Carlos V/Karl V*, 43–90

Luttikhuizen, F., *Underground Protestantism in sixteenth-century Spain: A much-ignored side of Spanish history* (Göttingen, 2017)

Lutz, H., *Christianitas afflicta. Europa, das Reich, und die päpstliche Politik im Niedergang der Hegemonie Kaiser Karls V 1552–1556* (Göttingen, 1964)

Lutz, H., 'Karl V. Biographische Probleme', in G. Klingenstein, H. Lutz and G. Stourzh, eds, *Biographie und Geschichtswissenschaft. Aufsätze zur Theorie und Praxis biographischer Arbeit* (Vienna, 1979: Wiener Beiträge zur Geschichte der Neuzeit, VI), 151–82

Lutz, H. and E. Müller-Luckner, eds, *Das römisch-deutsche Reich im politischen System Karls V.* (Munich and Vienna, 1982: Schriften des historischen Kollegs, I)

MacCulloch, D., *Thomas Cromwell: A revolutionary life* (New York, 2018)

Mancini, M., 'Los últimos cuadros del emperador en Yuste', in Checa Cremades, *Monumentos restaurados*, 163–82

Maples, W. R., 'The death and mortal remains of Francisco Pizarro', *Journal of Forensic Sciences*, XXXIV (1989), 1,021–36

Marcks, C., 'Die Antikensammlung des D. Luis de Ávila y Zúñiga, Marqués de Mirabel', in Plasencia', *Madrider Mitteilungen*, XLII (2001), 155–208

Marín Cruzado, O., 'El retrato real en composiciones religiosas de la pintura del siglo XVI: Carlos V y Felipe II', in W. Rincón García, ed., *El arte en las cortes de Carlos V y Felipe II* (Madrid, 1999), 113–26

BIBLIOGRAPHY

Mariotte, J.-Y., 'François Ier et la Ligue de Schmalkalde', *Revue Suisse d'Histoire*, XVI (1966), 206–42

Mariotte, J.-Y., 'Charles Quint "faussaire"?: l'arrestation de Philippe de Hesse, 9 juin 1547', in D. Dinet and F. Igersheim, eds, *Terres d'Alsace, chemin de l'Europe: mélanges offerts à Bernard Vogler* (Strasbourg, 2003), 377–404

Mariotte, J.-Y., *Philippe de Hesse (1504-1567). Le premier prince protestant* (Paris, 2009)

Mariscal, G., 'A clown at court: Francesillo de Zúñiga's *Crónica burlesca*', in N. Spadaccini and J. Talens, eds, *Autobiography in early modern Spain* (Minneapolis, 1988), 59–75

Martens, P., *Militaire architectuur en vestingoorlog in de Nederlanden tijdens het regentschap van Maria van Hongarije (1531-1555). De ontwikkeling van de gebastioneerde vestingbouw*, 2 vols (Leuven, 2009)

Martín González, J. J., 'El palacio de Carlos V en Yuste', *Archivo español de arte*, XXIII (1950), 27–51 and 235–51, and XXIV (1951), 125–40

Martínez, J. L., *Hernán Cortés* (Mexico City, 1990)

Martínez Millán, J., 'La historiografía sobre Carlos V', in idem, *La Corte*, I, 17–41

Martínez Millán, J., ed., *La Corte de Carlos V*, 5 vols (Madrid, 2000)

Martínez Millán. J., ed., *Carlos V y la quiebra del humanismo político en Europa, 1530-1558*, 4 vols (Madrid, 2000)

Martínez-Peñas, L., *Las Cartas de Adriano. La guerra de las Comunidades a través de la correspondencia del Cardenal-Gobernador* (Madrid, 2010)

Martínez Pérez, L., *El confesor del rey en el antiguo régimen* (Madrid, 2007)

Mazarío Coleto, M. del C., *Isabel de Portugal, emperatriz y reina de España* (Madrid, 1951)

Meertens, P. J., 'Een esbatement ter ere van keizer Karel V (Een Leids rederrijkersspel uit 1552)', *Jaarboek de Fonteine. Jaargang 1967*, 75–81

Menegus Bornemann, M., 'Los títulos primordiales de los pueblos indios', *Estudis*, XX (1994), 207–31

Merluzzi, M., 'Mediación política, redes clientelares y pacificación del reino en el Perú del siglo XVI. Observaciones a partir de los papeles "Pizarro-La Gasca"', *Revista de Indias*, LXVI (2006), 87–106

Merluzzi, M., '"Con el cuidado que de vos confío": Las instrucciones a los virreyes de Indias como espejo de gobierno y enlace con el soberano', *Libros de la Corte.es*, IV/4 (2012), 154–65

Merriman, R. B., *The rise of the Spanish empire in the Old World and the New. III: The emperor* (London, 1918)

Mesnard, P., 'L'expérience politique de Charles Quint et les enseignements d'Erasme', in Jacquot, *Les fêtes de la Renaissance*, II, 45–66

Michelet, J., *Histoire de France au seizième siècle: Renaissance* (Paris, 1855: *Histoire de France*, VII)

Mignet, F. A., *Charles-Quint: son abdication, son séjour et sa mort au monastère de Yuste* (Paris, 1854)

Mignet, F. A., *Rivalité de François 1er et de Charles-Quint*, 2 vols (3rd edition, Paris, 1886)

Millar, A., 'Olivier de la Marche and the Court of Burgundy, c. 1425–1502' (Edinburgh University Ph.D. thesis, 1996)

Mitchell, B., *The majesty of the state: Triumphal progresses of foreign sovereigns in Renaissance Italy (1494-1600)* (Florence, 1986)

Moeller, B., 'Luther in Europe: His works in translation, 1517–46', in Kouri and Scott, *Politics*, 235–51

Moeller, C., *Éléonore d'Autriche et de Bourgogne, reine de France. Un épisode de l'histoire des cours au XVIe siècle* (Paris, 1895)

Molinié-Bertrand, A. and J.-P. Duviols, eds, *Charles Quint et la monarchie universelle* (Paris, 2001)

Möller Recondo, C., 'Carlos V como categoría bibliográfica - en español - en la red', in Gonzalo Sánchez-Molero and Miranda Díaz, *La bibliografía*, 355–90

Morales Foguera, J. M., 'El viaje triunfal de Carlos V por Sicilia tras la victoria de Túnez', *Imago: revista de emblemática y cultura visual*, VII (2015), 97–111

Morales Ortiz, A., *Plutarco en España: traducciones de Moralia en el siglo XVI* (Murcia, 2000)

Morel-Fatio, A., 'L'espagnol langue universelle', *BH*, XV (1913), 207–25

Moreno Gallego, V., 'Letras misivas, letras humanas, letras divinas. La correspondencia del Cardenal Granvela en la Real Biblioteca y sus cartas de autores', *Cuadernos de historia moderna. Anejos*, IV (2005), 31–55

Moritz, A., *Interim und Apokalypse. Die religiösen Vereinheitlichungsversuche Karls V. im Spiegel der magdeburgischen Publizistik 1548-1551/2* (Tübingen, 2009)

Mulcahy, R., *Philip II of Spain: Patron of the Arts* (Dublin, 2004)

Navascués Palacio, P., ed., *Carolus V Imperator* (Madrid, 1999)

Necipoglu, G., 'Suleiman the Magnificent and the representation of power in the context of Ottoman-Habsburg-Papal rivalry', in H. Inalcik and C. Kafadar, eds, *Süleymân the Second and his time* (Istanbul, 1993), 163–94

Neuhaus, H., 'Von Karl V. zu Ferdinand I. – Herrschaftsübergang im Heiligen Römischen Reich 1555–1558', in C. Roll, B. Braun and H. Stratenwerth, eds, *Recht und Reich im Zeitalter der Reformation: Festschrift für Horst Rabe* (Fankfurt, 1996), 417–40

Newson, L. A., 'The demographic impact of colonization' in V. Bulmer-Thomas, J. Coatsworth and R. Cortes Conde, eds, *The Cambridge Economic History of Latin America*, 2 vols (Cambridge, 2006), I, 143–84

Nieva Ocampo, G., 'El confesor del emperador: la actividad política de fray García de Loaysa y Mendoza al servicio de Carlos V (1522–1530)', *Hispania. Revista española de historia*, LXXV (2015), 641–68

Noguiera, P., 'Les répercussions de la politique de Charles Quint en Galice: l'exemple de la ville de La Corogne', in Molinié-Bertrand and Duviols, *Charles Quint*, 205–13

Oberman, H. A., 'The impact of the Reformation: Problems and perspectives', in Kouri and Scott, *Politics*, 3–31

Olton, E. D., 'To shepherd the empire: The catafalque of Charles V in Mexico City', in J. Beusterien and C. Cortez, eds, *Death and afterlife in the early modern Hispanic world: Hispanic Issues Online*, VII (Fall 2010), 10–26 http://hispanicissues.umn.edu/DeathandAfterlife.html

Ordi, J., J. de Zulueta et al., 'The severe gout of Holy Roman Emperor Charles V', *New England Journal of Medicine*, CCCV/5 (3 Aug. 2006), 516–20

Orts i Bosch, P. M., 'Margarida o Isabel. Dos noms per a una mateixa filla illegítima de l'emperador Carles d'Austria', *Afers: fulls de recerca i pensament*, XXVII (2012), 401–5

Owens, J. B., *'By my absolute royal authority': Justice and the Castilian commonwealth at the beginning of the first global age* (Rochester, 2005)

Ozment, S., *The bürgermeister's daughter: Scandal in a sixteenth-century German town* (New York, 1996)

Pacini, A., *La Genova di Andrea Doria nell'impero di Carlo V* (Florence, 1999)

Paget, H., 'The youth of Anne Boleyn', *HR*, LIV (1981), 162–70

Paillard, C., 'Le voyage de Charles-Quint en France en 1539–1540', *Revue des questions historiques*, XXV (1879), 506–50

Paillard, C. and G. Hérelle, *L'invasion allemande en 1544: fragments d'une histoire militaire et diplomatique de l'expédition de Charles V* (Paris, 1884)

Pánek, J., 'Emperador, rey y revuelta estamental. Los estamentos de Bohemia y su postura ante la política imperial de Carlos V y Fernando I durante la época de la guerra de Esmalcalda', in Kohler, *Carlos V/ Karl V*, 137–49

Panzer, M. A., *Barbara Blomberg: Bürgerstochter, Kaisergeliebte und Heldenmutter* (Regensburg, 1995; revised edition, 2017)

Pardanaud, C., 'Plaider, convaincre, entrer en scène: Éléonore d'Autriche et la libération des enfants de France, d'après sa correspondance inédite', *Seizième siècle*, IV (2008), 195–216

Paredes, C., 'The confusion of the battlefield: A new perspective on the tapestries of the battle of Pavia (c. 1525–1531)', *Journal of the International Association of Research Institutes in the History of Art*, 0102 (Oct.–Dec. 2014) http://www.riha-journal.org/articles/2014/2014-oct-dec/paredes-battle-of-pavia

Parker, G., *The Army of Flanders and the Spanish Road, 1567–1659: The logistics of Spanish victory and defeat in the Low Countries' Wars* (1972; 3rd edition, Cambridge, 2004)

Parker, G., 'The place of Tudor England in the Messianic vision of Philip II of Spain', *TRHistS*, 6th series XII (2002), 167–221

Parker, G., *Felipe II. La biografía definitiva* (Barcelona, 2010)

Parker, G., *Imprudent king: A new life of Philip II* (New Haven and London, 2014)

Parker, G., 'Incest, blind faith, and conquest: The Spanish Hapsburgs and their enemies', in J. Lacey, ed., *Great strategic rivalries: From the Classical World to the Cold War* (Oxford, 2016), 209–33 and 580–5

Pascual Barroso, A., *Dos niños príncipes franceses cautivos en Castilla (1526–1530)* (Pedraza, 2013)

Pastor, L., *The history of the popes from the close of the Middle Ages, drawn from the secret archives of the Vatican and other original sources*, 40 vols (London, 1899–1953; original German edition 1886–1933)

Peiró Martín, I., *En los altares de la patria. La construcción de la cultura nacional española* (Madrid, 2017)

Pereña Vicente, L., 'El emperador Carlos V en la encrucijada de América: Proyecto de reconversión colonial', in Castellano Castellano and Sánchez-Montes González, *Carlos V*, II, 379–410

Pérez, J., 'Moines frondeurs et sermons subversifs en Castille pendant le premier séjour de Charles-Quint en Espagne', *BH*, LXVII (1965), 5–24

Pérez, J., *La revolución de las Comunidades de Castilla (1520–1521)* (6th edition, Madrid, 1998)

Pérez Bustamente, C., 'Actividad legislativa de Carlos V en orden a las Indias', in *Charles-Quint*, 113–21

Pérez de Tudela, A., 'El cenotafio de Carlos V en la Basílica de El Escorial', in S. F. Schröder, ed., *Leone y Pompeo Leoni. Actas del congreso internacional* (Turnhout, 2012), 132–48

Perla, A., 'Anton van den Wyngaerde y el palacio de Carlos V en Yuste', *Espacio, tiempo y forma, serie VII: historia del Arte*, XX–XXI (2007–8), 23–36

BIBLIOGRAPHY

Perla, A., 'Una visita al monasterio de San Jerónimo de Yuste', in Checa Cremades, *Monumentos restaurados*, 15–82

Perrone, S. T., *Charles V and the Castilian assembly of clergy: Negotiations for the ecclesiastical subsidy* (Leiden, 2008)

Peset Reig, M., 'Fundación y primeros años de la Universidad de México', in Castellano Castellano and Sánchez-Montes González, *Carlos V*, V, 541–63

Petritsch, E. D., 'Der habsburgisch-osmanische Friedensvertrag des Jahres 1547', *MÖStA*, XXXVIII (1985), 49–80

Philipp, M., *Ehrenpforten für Kaiser Karl V.: Festdekorationen als Medien politischer Kommunikation* (Berlin, 2011)

Pichot, A., *Charles-Quint. Chronique de sa vie intérieure et de sa vie politique, de son abdication, et de sa retraite dans le cloître de Yuste* (Paris, 1854)

Pietschmann, H., 'Carlos V y la formación del estado en las Indias', in Castellano Castellano and Sánchez-Montes González, *Carlos V*, II, 437–69

Pietschmann, H., 'Carlos V y América: el soberano, la corte y la política', in Kohler, *Carlos V/Karl V*, 265–78

Pietschmann, H., ed., *Alemania y México: percepciones mutuas en impresos, siglos XVI–XVIII* (Mexico City, 2005)

Pirenne, H., *Histoire de la Belgique. III. De la mort de Charles le Téméraire à l'arrivée du duc d'Albe dans les Pays-Bas (1567)* (Brussels, 1907)

Pizarro Gómez, F. J., 'El monasterio de Yuste y Carlos V', in García-Frías Checa, *Carlos V en Yuste*, 95–111

Pizarro Llorente, H., 'Un embajador de Carlos V en Italia: Don Lope de Soria (1528–1532)', in Martínez Millán, *Carlos V y la quiebra*, IV, 119–55

Plaisant, M. L., *Aspetti e problemi di politica spagnola (1556–1619)* (Padua, 1973)

Plassmann, E., *Karl Brandi (1868–1946) zur fünfundzwanzigsten Wiederkehr seines Todestag* (Bochum, 1972)

Pleij, H., *De sneeuwpoppen van 1511. Stadscultuur in de late Middeleeuwen* (Amsterdam/Leuven, 1988)

Pociecha, W., *Polska wobec elekcji Cesarza Karola V. w roku 1519* [*Poland against the election of Emperor Charles V in 1519*] (Wrocław, 1947)

Podestà, G. L., *Dal delitto político alla política del delitto. Finanza pubblica e congiure contro i Farnese nel ducato di Parma e Piacenza dal 1545 al 1622* (Milan, 1995)

Pollnitz, A., 'Old words and the New World: Liberal education and the Franciscans in New Spain, 1536–1601', *TRHistS*, 6th series XXVII (2017), 123–52

Ponce de León, P., 'La arquitectura del palacio-monasterio de Loeches. El sueño olvidado de un Valido; la emulación de un real retiro' (Ph.D. thesis, 2013, online at http://oa.upm.es/22388/1/PEDRO_PONCE_DE_LEON.pdf)

Potter, D., *Henry VIII and Francis I: The Final Conflict, 1540–47* (Leiden, 2011)

Potter, D., *Renaissance France at war: Armies, culture and society, c. 1480–1560* (Woodbridge, 2008)

Poumarède, G., 'Le voyage de Tunis et d'Italie de Charles Quint ou l'exploitation politique du mythe de la Croisade (1535–1536)', *Bibliothèque d'Humanisme et Renaissance*, LXVII (2005), 247–85

Poumarède, G., 'Le "vilain et sale assassinat" d'Antonio Rincon et Cesare Fregoso (1541). Un incident diplomatique exemplaire?', in L. Bély and G. Poumarède, eds, *L'incident diplomatique (XVIe–XVIIIe siècle)* (Paris, 2009), 7–44

Powell, J., 'Thomas Wyatt's poetry in Embassy: Egerton 2711 and the production of literary manuscripts abroad', *Huntington Library Quarterly*, LXVII (2004), 261–82

Powell, J. E., *Joseph Chamberlain* (London, 1977)

Preciado, D., ed., *Juan de Anchieta (c 1462–1523): Cuatro Pasiones Polifónicas* (Madrid, 1995)

Press, V., 'Die Bundespläne Karls V. und die Reichsverfassung', in Lutz and Müller-Luckner, *Das römisch-deutsche Reich*, 55–106

Rabà, M. M., *Potere e poteri. 'Stati', 'privati' e communità nel conflitto per l'egemonia in Italia settentrionale (1536–1558)* (Milan, 2016)

Rabe, H., *Reichsbund und Interim. Die Verfassungs- und Religionspolitik Karls V. und der Reichstag von Augsburg 1547/1548* (Cologne, 1971)

Rabe, H., 'Die politische Korrespondenz Kaiser Karls V. Beiträge zu ihrer wissenschaftlichen Erschließung', in Rabe, *Karl V. Politik und politisches System*, 11–39

Rabe, H., ed., *Karl V. Politik und politisches System. Berichte und Studien aus der Arbeit an der politischen Korrespondenz des Kaisers* (Konstanz, 1996)

Rabe, H. and P. Marzahl, '"Comme représentant nostre propre personne" – the regency ordinances of Charles V as a historical source', in Kouri and Scott, *Politics*, 78–102

Ramos, D., *Hernán Cortés. Mentalidad y propósitos* (Madrid, 1992)

BIBLIOGRAPHY

Rassow, P. E., *Die Kaiser-Idee Karls V dargestellt an der Politik der Jahre 1528–1540* (Berlin, 1932)

Rassow, P. E., 'Das Bild Karls V. im Wandel der Jahrhunderte', in Rassow and Schalk, *Karl V*, 1–17

Rassow, P. E., 'Karls V. Tochter Maria als Eventual-Erbin der spanischen Reiche', *Archiv für Reformationsgeschichte*, XLIX (1959), 161–8

Rassow, P. E. and F. Schalk, eds, *Karl V: der Kaiser und seine Zeit* (Cologne and Graz, 1960)

Redondo, A., 'Luther et l'Espagne de 1520 à 1536', *Mélanges de la Casa de Velázquez*, I (1965), 109–65

Redondo, A., *Antonio de Guevara (1480?–1545) et l'Espagne de son temps. De la carrière officielle aux oeuvres politico-morales* (Geneva, 1976)

Redondo, A., 'La comunicación sobre la victoria de Pavía de 1525: los canales de la propaganda imperial (cartas manuscritas, pliegos impresos, oralidad) y los restos correspondientes', in G. Ciappelli and V. Nider, eds, *La invención de las noticias: las relaciones de sucesos entre la literatura y la información (siglos XVI–XVIII)* (Trent, 2017), 255–71

Redondo Cantera, M. J. and J. Serrão, 'El pintor portugués Manuel Denis, al servicio de la Casa Real', in M. Cabañas Bravo, ed., *El arte foráneo en España. Presencia e influencia* (Madrid, 2005), 61–78

Rein, N. B., 'Faith and empire: Conflicting visions of religion in a late Reformation controversy – the Augsburg Interim and Its Opponents, 1548–50', *Journal of the American Academy of Religion*, LXXI (2003), 45–74

Rein, N., *The Chancery of God: Protestant Propaganda against the Empire, Magdeburg 1546–1551* (Aldershot, 2008)

Reinhard, W., '"Governi stretti e tirannici". Las ciudades y la política del emperador Carlos V, 1515–1556', in Kohler, *Carlos V/Karl V*, 151–77

Restall, M., *When Montezuma met Cortés: The true story of the meeting that changed history* (New York, 2018)

Richardson, G., *The Field of Cloth of Gold* (New Haven and London, 2013)

Ríos Lloret, R. E., *Germana de Foix: Una mujer, una reina, una corte* (Valencia, 2003)

Ríos Lloret, R. E. and S. Vilaplana Sánchis, eds, *Germana de Foix i la societat cortesana del seu temps* (Valencia, 2006)

Rivera Rodríguez. M., *Carlos V y el sueño del Imperio* (Madrid, 2005)

Robertson, J., 'L'entrée de Charles-Quint à Londres en 1522', in Jacquot, *Les fêtes de la Renaissance*, II, 169–81

Robertson, J., 'Empire and union: Two concepts of the early modern European political order', in Armitage, *Theories of empire*, 11–44

Robertson, W., *The history of the reign of the Emperor Charles V*, 3 vols (London, 1769; revised edition, 1787; reprinted with an addition by W. H. Prescott, Philadelphia, 1860)

Rodocanachi, E., 'Jeunesse d'Adrien VI', *Revue historique*, CLXVIII (1931), 300–7

Rodríguez-Salgado, M. J., *The changing face of Empire: Charles V, Philip II, and Habsburg authority, 1551–1559* (Cambridge, 1988)

Rodríguez-Salgado, M. J., 'Charles V and the dynasty', in Soly, *Charles V*, 27–111

Rodríguez-Salgado, M. J., 'Carolus Africanus? El emperador y el Turco', in Martínez Millán, *Carlos V y la quiebra*, I, 487–531

Rodríguez-Salgado, M. J., 'El ocaso del imperio carolino', in García García, *El imperio de Carlos V*, 47–79

Rodríguez-Salgado, M. J., 'Buenos hermanos y aliados perpetuos: Carlos V y Enrique VIII', in Kohler, *Carlos V/Karl V*, 443–85

Rodríguez-Salgado, M. J., 'La granada, el león, el águila y la rosa (las relaciones con Inglaterra 1496–1525', in Belenguer Cebrià, *De la unión*, III, 315–55

Rodríguez-Salgado, M. J., 'Obeying the Ten Commandments: Charles V and France', in Blockmans and Mout, *The world of the Emperor Charles V*, 15–67

Rodríguez-Salgado, M. J., 'Los últimos combates de un caballero determinado', in Checa Cremades, *Monumentos restaurados*, 83–146

Rodríguez-Salgado, M. J., 'Ferrante Gonzaga: The champion of innocence', in G. Signorotto, ed., *Ferrante Gonzaga. Il Mediterraneo, L'Impero (1507–1557)* (Rome, 2009), 139–96

Rodríguez-Salgado, M. J., 'The art of persuasion: Charles V and his governors', in P. Hoppenbrouwers, A. Janse and R. Stein, eds, *Power and persuasion: Essays on the art of state building in honour of W. P. Blockmans* (Turnhouse, 2010), 59–82

Rodríguez Villa, A., *La Reina Doña Juana la Loca. Estudio histórico* (Madrid, 1892)

Roper, L., '"To his most learned and dearest friend": reading Luther's letters', *German History*, XXVIII (2010), 283–95

Roper, L., *Martin Luther: Renegade and prophet* (London, 2016)

Rose, S. V., 'La hija pródiga del imperio: honras fúnebres a Carlos V en la Ciudad de los Reyes', *Revista destiempos* (Mexico City), III, no. 14 (Mar.–Apr. 2008), 129–41

Rosenthal, E. E., 'The house of Andrea Mantegna in Mantua', *Gazette des Beaux-Arts*, LX (1962), 327–48

Rosenthal, E. E., 'Plus Ultra, Non plus Ultra, and the columnar device of Emperor Charles V', *Journal of the Warburg and Courtauld Institutes*, XXXIV (1971), 204–28

Rosenthal, E. E., 'The invention of the columnar device of the Emperor Charles V at the Court of Burgundy in Flanders in 1516', *Journal of the Warburg and Courtauld Institutes*, XXXVI (1973), 198–230

Rosenthal, E. E., *The palace of Charles V in Granada* (Princeton, 1985)

Ruble, A. de, *Le mariage de Jeanne d'Albret* (Paris, 1877)

Ruiz Medrano, E., *Mexico's indigenous communities, their lands and histories, 1500–2010* (Boulder, CO, 2010)

Russell, J. G., 'The search for universal peace: The conferences of Calais and Bruges in 1521', *BIHR*, XLIV (1971), 162–93

Russo, A., 'Cortés's objects and the idea of New Spain', *Journal of the History of Collections*, XXIII/2 (2011), 229–52

Sadlack, E. A., *The French queen's letters: Mary Tudor Brandon and the politics of marriage in sixteenth-century Europe* (New York, 2011)

Saint-Saëns, A., ed., *Young Charles V, 1500–1531* (New Orleans, 2000)

Salazar, J. de, 'Sobre una posible hija de Carlos V y de Germana de Foix', *Boletín de la Real Academia Matritense de Heráldica y Genealogía*, XXVIII (1998), 14–16

Saletta, V., 'Il viaggio di Carlo V in Italia 1535–1536', *Studi Meridionali*, IX (1976), 286–327, 452–79; X (1977), 78–114, 268–92, 420–42; XI (1978), 329–39

Salomone, M. 'Se busca malaria en la momia del emperador Carlos V', *El País*, 3 Aug. 2006, archived at http://elpais.com/diario/2006/08/03/revistaverano/1154556001_850215.html, accessed 16 Jan. 2018

Salonia, M., *Genoa's freedom: Entrepreneurship, republicanism and the Spanish Atlantic* (Lanham, MD, 2017)

Salvador, G., 'El hablar de Cúllar-Baza', *Revista de filología española*, XLII (1958–9), 37–89

Sánchez Agesta, L., 'El "poderío real absoluto" en el testamento de 1554 – sobre los orígenes de la concepción de Estado', in *Carlos V (1500–1558)*, 439–60

Sanchis Amat, V. M., 'Los poemas castellanos del Túmulo Imperial de la gran ciudad de México (1560). Edición y comentario', *Revista de cancioneros impresos y manuscritos*, VI (2017), 244–73

Sardella, P., *Nouvelles et speculations à Venise au début du XVIe siècle* (Paris, 1948)

Schilling, D., 'L'education de Charles-Quint', in Saint-Saëns, *Young Charles V*, 1–11

Schilling, H., 'Veni, vidi, Deus vixit – Karl V. zwischen Religionskrieg und Religionsfrieden', *Archiv für Religionsgeschichte*, LXXXIX (1998), 144–66

Schlegelmilch, A. M., *Die Jugendjahre Karls V. Lebenswelt und Erziehung des burgundischen Prinzen* (Cologne, 2011)

Schraven, M., *Festive funerals in early modern Italy: The art and culture of conspicuous commemoration* (London, 2017)

Schüz, A., *Der Donaufeldzug Karls V. im Jahre 1546* (Tübingen, 1930)

Schwaller, J. F., with Helen Nader, *The first letter from New Spain: The lost petition of Cortés and his company, June 20, 1519* (Austin, TX, 2014)

Scribner, B., *The German Reformation* (Houndmills, 1986)

Semboloni Capitani, L., *La construcción de la autoridad virreinal en Nueva España (1535–1595)* (Mexico City, 2014)

Senatore, F., *'Uno mundo de carta': forme e strutture della diplomazia sforzesca* (Naples, 1998)

Sepponen, W., 'Imperial materials: Site and citation in Leone and Pompeo Leoni's Charles V and Furor', in D. Odell and J. Buskirk, eds, *Midwestern Arcadia: Essays in Honor of Alison Kettering* (Carleton, 2014), 122–31

Sepúlveda, R., *El monasterio de San Jerónimo el Real de Madrid. Estudio histórico-literario* (2nd edition, Madrid, 1888)

Setton, K. M., *The papacy and the Levant, 1204–1571*, 4 vols (Philadelphia, 1984)

Sherer, I., ' "All of us, in one voice, demand what's owed us": Mutiny in the Spanish infantry during the Italian Wars, 1524–1538', *Journal of Military History*, LXXVIII (2014), 893–926

Sherer, I., *Warriors for a living: The experience of the Spanish infantry during the Italian Wars, 1494–1559* (Leiden, 2017)

Silver, L., 'Shining armor: Maximilian I as Holy Roman Emperor', *Art Institute of Chicago Museum Studies*, XII/1 (1985), 8–29

Silver, L., 'Shining armor: Emperor Maximilian, chivalry and war', in P. F. Cuneo, ed., *Artful armies, beautiful battles: Art and warfare in the Early Modern Europe* (Leiden, 2001), 61–86

Silver, L., *Marketing Maximilian: The visual ideology of a Holy Roman Emperor* (Princeton, 2008)

Simons, B., ed., *Keizer Karel 1500–2000. Het Keizer Karel Jaar in Vlaanderen: Nabeschouwingen* (Brussels, 2000)

Smith, P., *Erasmus: A study of his life, ideals and place in history* (2nd edition, New York, 1962)

Soly, H., ed., *Charles V 1500–1558 and his time* (Antwerp, 1999)

Speakman Sutch, S. and A. L. Prescott, 'Translation as transformation: Oliver de La Marche's "Le Chevalier Délibéré" and its Hapsburg and Elizabethan permutations', *Comparative Literature Studies*, XXV/4 (1988), 281–317

Steen, C. R., *Margaret of Parma: A life* (Leiden, 2013)

Stirling-Maxwell, W., *The cloister life of the emperor Charles V* (2nd edition, Boston, 1853)

Stone, M. W. F., 'Adrian of Utrecht and the university of Louvain: theology and the discussion of moral problems in the late fifteenth century', *Traditio*, LXI (2006), 247–87

Stone, M. W. F., 'Adrian of Utrecht as a moral theologian', in Verweij, *De paus uit de Lage Landen*, 19–44

Strøm-Olsen, R., 'Dynastic ritual and politics in early modern Burgundy: The baptism of Charles V', *Past & Present*, CLXXV (2002), 34–64

Struick, J. E. A. L., *Gelre en Habsburg, 1492–1538* (Arnhem, 1960)

Suri, J., *The impossible presidency: The rise and fall of America's highest office* (New York, 2017)

Tafuri, M., *Interpreting the Renaissance: Princes, cities, architects* (New Haven and London, 2006; original Italian edition, 1992)

Talbot, M., 'Ore italiane: The reckoning of the time of day in pre-Napoleonic Italy', *Italian Studies*, XL (1985), 51–62

Tamussino, U., *Margarete von Österreich, Diplomatin der Renaissance* (Graz, 1995)

Tellechea Idígoras, J. I., 'Carlos V y Bartolomé Carranza: un navarro junto al lecho de muerte del emperador', *Príncipe de Viana*, XIX (1958), 33–82

Tellechea Idígoras, J. I., 'El último mensaje de Felipe II a Carlos V', in Castellano Castellano and Sánchez-Montes González, *Carlos V*, V, 643–62

Tellechea Idígoras, J. I., 'Lo que el emperador no supo. Proceso de Paulo IV a Carlos V y Felipe II', in Martínez Millán, *Carlos V y la quiebra*, IV, 181–95

Tellechea Idígoras, J. I., *Paulo IV y Carlos V. La renuncia del Imperio a debate* (Madrid, 2001)

Tellechea Idígoras, J. I., *El Arzobispo Carranza. 'Tiempos Recios'*, 4 vols (Salamanca, 2003–7)

Temple, P., *A sort of conscience: The Wakefields* (Auckland, 2002)

Terlinden, C., *Carolus Quintus, Charles Quint, empereur des deux mondes* (Brussels, 1965)

Thomas, B., *Gesammelte Schriften zur historischen Waffenkunde*, 2 vols (Graz, 1977)

Thomas, H., *The Golden Empire: Spain, Charles V and the creation of America* (New York, 2011)

Tondat, R., 'De Geboorteplaats van Keizer Karel', *Handelingen der Maatschappij voor geschiedenis en Oudheidkunde te Gent*, new series LV (2001), 457–61

Torre Revello, J., 'La crónica de las exequias de Carlos V en la Ciudad de los Reyes. Año 1559', *Boletín del Instituto de Investigaciones Históricas*, XIV nos 51–2 (1932), 60–78

Tracy, J. D., *Emperor Charles V, impresario of war: campaign strategy, international finance, and domestic politics* (Cambridge, 2002)

Tubau, X., 'Alfonso de Valdés y la política imperial del canciller Gattinara', in E. Fosalba et al., eds, *Literatura, sociedad y política en el Siglo de Oro* (Barcelona, 2010), 17–43

Tüchle, H., 'The peace of Augsburg: New order or lull in the fighting', in H. Cohn, ed., *Government in Reformation Europe, 1520–1560* (Basingstoke, 1971), 144–65 (first published in German in 1955)

Turba, G., 'Verhaftung und Gefangenschaft des Landgrafen Philipp von Hessen 1547–1550', *Archiv für österreichische Geschichte*, LXXXIII (1897), 107–232

Turetschek, C., *Die Türkenpolitik Ferdinands I. von 1529 bis 1532* (Vienna, 1968: Dissertationen der Universität Wien, X)

Tyler, R., *The Emperor Charles the Fifth* (London, 1956)

Unamuno, M. de, *Obras completas*, VI (Madrid, 2001)

Uslar Pietri, A., *La visita en el tiempo* (Barcelona, 1990)

van den Boogert, B., 'Mary of Hungary as a patron of the arts', in Checa Cremades, *Los inventarios de Carlos V*, III, 2,807–22

van Deusen, N. E., 'Coming to Castile with Cortés: Indigenous "servitude" in the 16th century', *Ethnohistory*, LXII (2015), 285–308

van Durme, M., 'Les Granvelle au service des Habsbourg', in K. de Jonge and G. Janssens, eds, *Les Granvelle et les anciens Pays-Bas. Liber doctori Mauricio van Durme dedicatus* (Leuven, 2000), 11–81

Varela, J., *La muerte del rey. El ceremonial funerario de la monarquía española, 1500–1885* (Madrid, 1990)

Venturelli, P., 'L'ingresso trionfale a Milano dell'imperatore Carlo V (1541) e del Príncipe Filippo (1548). Considerazioni sull'apparire e l'accoglienza', in Martínez Millán, *Carlos V y la quiebra*, III, 51–83

BIBLIOGRAPHY

Verweij, M., ed., *De paus uit de Lage Landen: Adrianus VI 1459–1523. Catalogus bij de tentoonstelling ter gelegenheid van het 550ste geboortejaar van Adriaan van Utrecht* (Leuven, 2009)

Vidal, J. J., 'La defensa del reino de Mallorca en la época de Carlos V (1535–1558)', in Martínez Millán, *Carlos V y la quiebra*, I, 541–89

Vigo, G., *Uno stato nell' impero. La difficile transizione al moderno nella Milano di età spagnola* (Milan, 1994)

Vilar Sánchez, J. A., *1526. Boda y luna de miel del emperador Carlos V* (Granada, 2000)

Vilar Sánchez, J. A., *Carlos V: emperador y hombre* (Madrid, 2015)

Viseglia, M. A., 'Il viaggio cerimoniale di Carlo V dopo Tunisi', *Dimensioni e problemi della ricerca storica, Rivista del Dipartimento di Storia Moderna e Contemporanea dell'Università di Roma La Sapienza*, II (2001), 5–50 (a corrected version of the essay published in Martínez Millán, *Carlos V y la quiebra*, II, 133–72)

von Druffel, A., 'Kaiser Karl V. und die Römische Kurie 1544–1546, erste Abtheilung', *Abhandlungen der historischen Klasse der königlich bayerischen Akademie der Wissenschaften*, XIII/2 (1877), 147–277

von Ostenfeld-Suske, K., 'Juan Páez de Castro, Charles V, and a method for royal historiography', in P. Baker et al., eds, *Portraying the prince in the Renaissance: The humanist depiction of rulers in histo-riographical and biographical texts* (Berlin and Boston, 2016), 363–89

von Pölnitz, G., *Jakob Fugger*, 2 vols (Tübingen, 1949–51)

von Ranke, L., *Deutsche Geschichte im Zeitalter der Reformation*, 6 vols (4th edition, Leipzig, 1867–8)

von Rommel, C., *Philipp der Grossmüthige, Landgraf von Hessen*, 3 vols (Giessen, 1830)

Walser, F., *Die spanischen Zentralbehörden und der Staatsrat Karls V.: Grundlagen und Aufbau bis zum Tode Gattinaras* (ed. R. T. Wohlfeil, Göttingen, 1959)

Walther, A., 'Review of Kreiten, *Der Briefwechsel Kaiser Maximilians I*', *Göttingische gelehrte Anzeigen*, CLXX (1908), 253–86

Walther, A., *Die burgundischen Zentralbehörden unter Maximilian I. und Karl V.* (Leipzig, 1909)

Walther, A., *Die Anfänge Karls V.* (Leipzig, 1911)

Weber, H., 'Le traité de Chambord (1552)', *Charles-Quint, le Rhin et la France. Droit savant et droit pénal à l'époque de Charles-Quint* (Strasbourg, 1973: Publications de la Société savante d'Alsace et des régions de l'Est, collection Recherches et Documents, XVII), 81–94

Weber, H., 'Zur Heiratspolitik Karls V', in Lutz and Müller-Luckner, *Das römisch-deutsche Reich*, 129–60

Weinrich, H., 'Sprachanekdoten um Karl V', in idem, *Wege der Sprachkultur* (Stuttgart, 1985), 181–92

Wellens, R., *Inventaire des papiers, notes et manuscrits de Louis-Prosper Gachard, archiviste général du royaume (1800–1885)* (Brussels, 1983)

Wellens, R., 'Études et travaux relatifs à la vie et à l'œuvre de Louis-Prosper Gachard. Une approche bibliographique', in J. Paviot, ed., *Liber Amicorum Raphael de Smedt, III. Historia* (Leuven, 2001: Miscellanea Neerlandica, XXV), 415–22

Wetter, O., et al., 'The year-long unprecedented European heat and drought of 1540 – a worst case', *Climatic change*, CXXV (2014), 349–63, and 'Supplementary Information' online

Wiesflecker, H., *Kaiser Maximilian I. Das Reich, Österreich und Europa an der Wende zur Neuzeit. I. Jugend, burgundisches Erbe und Römisches Königtum bis zur Alleinherrschaft, 1459–1493* (Munich, 1971); *II. Reichsreform und Kaiserpolitik, 1493–1500. Entmachtung des Königs im Reich und in Europa* (Munich, 1975); *III. Auf der Höhe des Lebens, 1500–1508. Der grosse Systemwechsel. Politischer Wiederaufstieg* (Munich, 1977); *IV. Gründung des habsburgischen Weltreiches, Lebensabend und Tod, 1508–1519* (Munich, 1981); *V. Der Kaiser und seine Umwelt: Hof, Staat, Wirtschaft, Gesellschaft und Kultur* (Munich, 1986)

Wijsman, H., 'Philippe le Beau et les livres: rencontre entre une époque et une personnalité', in Wijsman, ed., *Books in transition at the time of Philip the Fair: Manuscripts and books in the late fifteenth and early sixteenth century Low Countries* (Turnhout, 2010), 17–92

Williams, M. K., 'Re-orienting a Renaissance diplomatic *cause celèbre*: The 1541 Rincón-Fregoso affair', in S. Brzeziński and A. Zarnóczki, eds, *A divided Hungary in Europe: Exchanges, networks and representations, 1541–1699. II: Diplomacy, information flow and cultural exchange* (Newcastle, 2014), 11–29

Wohlfeil, R., 'Retratos gráficos de Carlos V al servicio de la representación y la propaganda', in Kohler, *Carlos V/Karl V*, 307–31

Zalama, M. A., 'Felipe I el Hermoso y las artes', in Zalama and Vandenbroeck, *Felipe I el Hermoso*, 17–48

Zalama, M. A., *Juana I. Arte, poder y cultura en torno a una reina que no gobernó* (Madrid, 2010)

Zalama, M. A., 'Origen y destino de la colección de tapices de la reina Juana I', in Checa Cremades, *Museo Imperial*, 53–69

Zalama, M. A. and P. Vandenbroeck, eds, *Felipe I el Hermoso. La Belleza y la locura* (Madrid, 2006)

Zanetti, C., ed., *Janello Torriani, a Renaissance genius* (Cremona, 2016)

BIBLIOGRAPHY

Zeller, G., *Le siège de Metz par Charles-Quint* (Nancy, 1943)

Zimmerman, T. C. Price, 'The publication of Paolo Giovio's Histories: Charles V and the revision of Book XXXIV', *La Bibliofilia*, VII (1972), 49–90

Zimmerman, T. C. Price, *Paolo Giovio: The historian and the crisis of sixteenth-century Italy* (Princeton, 1995)

Zulueta, J. de, 'The cause of death of Emperor Charles V', *Parassitologia*, XLIX (June 2007), 107–9

Zulueta, J. de, *Tuan nyamok [El señor de los mosquitos]. Relatos de la vida de Julián de Zulueta contados a María García Alonso* (Madrid, 2011)

Zurdo Manso, F. and E. del Cerro Calvo, *Madrigal de las Altas Torres: recuerdos para una historia* (Ávila, 1996)

MAPS, FIGURES AND PLATES

PLATES

1. Young Habsburgs study at school c. 1510. Hans Burgkmair, *Der Weiss Kunig*, Museum of Fine Arts, Boston, A57.40.

2. Charles's first signature, 1504. Real Academia de la Historia, Madrid, *Salazar y Castro Ms.* A-10 f. 35 (formerly f. 42). Courtesy of the publications department of the Royal Academy of History in Spain/Real Academia de la Historia.

3. Charles's first letter in French, 1508. British Library, London, *Cotton Ms.* Galba B/III f. 109, Charles to Mary Tudor, 18 Dec. 1508. © The British Library Board/Scala, Florence.

4. Martial sports for boys, c. 1514. (A) Hans Burgkmair, *Der Weiss Kunig*, f. 101. Akg-images/Erich Lessing. (B) Kunsthistorisches Museum, Vienna, Hofjagt- und Rüstkammer/Sammlung für Plastik und Kunstgewerke, Inv. 81, 82. Akg-images/Album.

5. Happy family, 1511. Stadarchief, Mechelen, B-MEa-ms-ss., 'Mechels Koorboek', f. 1v. Akg-images/Album.

6. The resolute knight meets Death. Biblioteca Nacional de España, *Ms.* 1475, *El caballero determinado*, f. 126, engraving by Arnold Nicolai. © Biblioteca Nacional de España.

7. Charles makes his ceremonial 'entry' to Bruges as count of Flanders in 1515. Österreichische Nationalbibliothek, Vienna, Codex 2591: 'Le tryumphante et solomnelle entrée faicte sur le joyeulx advenement de . . . Charles prince des Espagnes . . . en la ville de Bruges', f. 41r.

8. Charles unbuttons himself in a holograph note to his friend, Count Henry of Nassau, 22 January 1518. Bibliothèque Royale, Brussels, Ms. II-2270, Charles to Henry of Nassau, 22 Jan. 1518, holograph, first and last sheets. © Bibliothèque royale de Belgique/Koninklijke Bibliotheek van België.

9. Charles's secret instruction to Prince Philip, Palamos, 6 May 1543. Hispanic Society of America, New York, *Ms.* B 2955 ff. 13 and 17v. Courtesy of the Department of Manuscripts and Rare Books, The Hispanic Society of America, New York.

10. Charles almost writes in German, 1519. Bayerische Hauptstaatsarchiv, Munich, Kasten Blau (Pfalz), 103/2, Charles to Elector Palatine, Barcelona, 2 May 1519. Akg-images/Album.

11. Mary Tudor wearing a brooch with jewels that reads 'the emp[er]our', 1522. National Portrait Gallery, London, 6453, Miniature by Lucas Horenbout. Heritage Images/Fine Art Images/Akg-images.

12. A suit of combat armour for Charles, 1525. Armería Real, Madrid, No. de Inventario 19000265. A19. Akg-images/Album/Oronoz.
13. Discussion points drawn up for Charles before one of his meetings with Pope Clement VII in Bologna, 1529. Archivo General de Simancas *Patronato Real* 16/96, 'Las cosas que Su Magestad ha de tener memoria para hablar y suplicar a Su Santidad son las siguientes'. © Archivo General de Simancas.
14. Francis I captured at the battle of Pavia. Capodimonte Museum, Naples, tapestry designed by Bernard van Orley, woven in the workshop of Willem and Jan Dermoyen between 1528 and 1531. Photo: Scala.
15. Charles V and his grandparents in Bruges, 1531. Renaissancezaal, Paleis van het Brugse Vrije, Bruges. Aurora Photos/Alamy Stock Photo.
16. Joanna and Charles, monarchs of Aragon, 1528. Bibliothèque Nationale de France, Paris, Département des monnaies, médailles et antiques, Espagne 33/44. © Sarah Bauwens.
17. Emperor Charles eclipses Sultan Suleiman, 1532. Metropolitan Museum of Art, New York: Accession # 1986.319.70, bronze. Diameter: 108 mm. Akg-images.
18. Charles with a book and gloves by Christoph Amberger, 1532. Gemäldegalerie, Staatliche Museen zu Berlin, Preussischer Kulturbesitz, Inv. 556. Akg-images.
19. Portraits of Charles by Jakob Seisenegger and Titian, 1532–3. (A) Museo del Prado, Madrid, P00409; (B) Kunsthistorisches Museum, Vienna, Inv. A 114. Akg-images/Album/Oronoz.
20. Charles reviews his army at Barcelona before embarking for Tunis, 1535. Cartoon by Jan Cornelisz Vermeyen, Kunsthistorisches Museum, Vienna, Gemäldegalerie 2038. Akg-images.
21. Statue of Charles in the Piazza Bologni, Palermo, 1535/1630. By Scipio Li Volsi.
22. Charles enters Rome in triumph, 1536. Christoph Scheurl, *Einritt Keyser Carlen in die alten keyserlichen haubtstatt Rom* (Nuremberg, 1536), frontispiece.
23. Map of eastern France, 1544. Biblioteca Nacional de España, *Ms.* MR/43/283, 'Descripció de parte de Francia por donde entró el emperador'. Akg-images/Album.
24. Charles besieged in his camp outside Ingolstadt, September 1546. Luis de Ávila y Zúñiga, *Comentario del illustre Señor don Luis de Ávila y Zúñiga, comendador mayor de Alcántara, de la guerra en Alemaña* (Antwerp, 1550), pull-out facing f. 21v. © The Princeton Theological Seminary Library.
25. *Charles at the battle of Mühlberg* by Titian, 1547. Museo Nacional del Prado, Inv. P00410. Akg-images/Album.
26. Charles and his war council, 1545. Staatsbibliothek München, Cod. Germ. 3663, Hans Döring, 'Ratthschlag auff des Kriegsherrn Ubergeben Artickell an die Kriegs Rath', f. 120v, woodcut.
27. Charles in Augsburg by Titian, 1548. Alte Pinakothek, Munich, accession number 632. Akg-images/Album.
28. Procuring all the necessary dispensations for Prince Philip's incestuous first marriage, 1543. British Library, London, *Additional Ms.* 28,706/52 'Los parentescos que hay entre el príncipe de Castilla don Phelipe . . . y la señora Infanta de Portugal'. © The British Library Board/Scala, Florence.
29. Charles vanquishes Fury by Leone and Pompeo Leoni, 1549–64. Museo Nacional del Prado © Photo MNP / Scala, Florence.
30. Charles played at draughts. Victoria and Albert Museum, London, A.513-1910. © Victoria and Albert Museum, London.
31. Charles and Philip by Leone Leoni. Metropolitan Museum of Art, New York, The Milton Weil Collection, 1938 [38.150.9].
32. Charles abdicates, 1555. Frans Hogenberg, *Events in the history of the Netherlands*, Metropolitan Museum of Art, New York, the Elisha Wittelsey Collection, 59.570.200 (1-368). Akg-images.
33. Charles after his abdication, attributed to Simon Bening, 1556. Oil on vellum on card, private collection.
34. *The Last Judgement* by Titian, 1551–4. Museo Nacional del Prado, # 432. Akg-images/Album.
35. The imperial apartments at the monastery of Yuste by Antoon van den Wyngaerde. Albertina, Vienna, Inv. 26.336. Patrimonio Nacional.
36. Funeral obsequies for Charles in Brussels, 1558. Biblioteca Nacional de España, *E. R. 2901 no 15*: Frans Hogenberg, *Sucesos de Europa* (Amberes, 1559), # 15 'Cortejo fúnebre de Bruselas'. © Biblioteca Nacional de España.
37. Funeral obsequies for Charles in Valladolid, 1558. Juan Cristóbal Calvete de Estrella, *El túmulo imperial* (Valladolid, 1559), fold-out print after f. 37.
38. A cannon confiscated from German Lutherans and embarked on the Spanish Armada. AGS *Mapas, Planos y Dibujos* V-18, drawing of a full cannon done for Philip II in 1587, redrawn by Colin Martin four centuries later. (Courtesy of Colin Martin.)
39. Charles in his sarcophagus, 1870. Postcard, private collection. Photo © Ken Welsh/Bridgeman.

INDEX

Acton, Lord, historian, 558

Acuña, Antonio de, bishop of Zamora and Comunero leader, 113–15, 139–40, 160, 209

Admiral of Castile, Fadrique Enríquez de Velasco, co-regent of Castile, 138

Admiral of France, *see* Coligny, Gaspar de

Adrian of Utrecht (Adrian Florensz Boeyers), Charles's preceptor, governor of Castile, inquisitor-general, and later Pope Adrian VI, 30–2, 34–5, 54–6, 70, 81, 91, 105, 107, 110–13, 115, 116, 125, 128, 135, 138, 140, 144, 377, 378, 383, 515, 594, 602 n. 27, 611 n. 26

Aeneid, poem by Virgil, xi

Africa
> north, x, 51, 52, 55, 75, 77, 109, 114, 209, 236–43, 244, 248, 257–8, 268, 269, 271, 273–7, 280, 282, 309, 314, 315, 382, 387, 427, 465, 492, 493–4, 516, map 4 (241)
> slaves from, 342–4, 358, 370

Agincourt, battle of (1415), 147

Aguirre, Lope de, rebellious colonist in Peru, 496

Alarcón y Ariza, Pedro Antonio de, travel writer, 538, 540

Alba, Fernando Álvarez de Toledo, third duke of, 230, 238–9, 246, 286, 289, 291, 309–10, 321, 322–3, 327–8, 328, 363, 386, 419, 425, 439–40, 443, 445, 458, Pl. 9

Albert Alcibiades of Brandenburg-Külmbach, 300, 433, 435, 440–3

Albret, Henry d', king of Navarre, 59, 125, 131, 133, 148, 286, 455, 617 n. 56

Albret, Jeanne d', queen of Navarre, 267, 283

Alcalá, Universidad Complutense at, 364, 371, 463, 669 n. 9

Aleandro, Girolamo, humanist and papal diplomat, 111–21, 125, 126, 127, 183, 194, 196, 198, 202, 228, 378, 491, 586–7, 652 n. 11

Alexander the Great, xi, 99, 190, 226–31, 491, 517, 534

Alfonso de Aragón, archbishop of Zaragoza, 54–5, 82, 85

Alfonso XIII, king of Spain, 540

Algiers, xiii, 75, 77, 237, 248, 250, 251, 260, 270–7, 280–1, 301, 306, 354, 359, 367, 397, 442, 457, 483, 495, 505, 514, 531, 590, 593, 636 n. 82, 649 n. 56, 684 n. 94

Alhambra (Granada), 161, 162, 231, 273, 590

Almagro, Diego de, Spanish colonist in Peru, 355, 357, 361

'Alternative', the (1544–5), 308–11, 408, 413, 517, 529

Amberger, Christoph, painter, Pl. 18

America, 19, 58, 86, 106, 145, 182, 196, 209, 239, 292, 342–75, 381, 385, 418–19, 435, 447, 454, 482, 492–3, 507, 511, 513, 517, 519, 523, 526–7, 531, 577

Ana of Austria, archduchess, queen of Spain (niece and spouse of Philip II), 434, 528, 660 n. 28

Anchieta, Juan de, preceptor and composer, 12, 21, 522, 599 n. 27

Anchin, monastery at, 4

Ando, Clifford, historian, 521–2

Angoulême, Charles, duke of (after 1536, duke of Orléans), 250, 258–9, 263–7, 282, 283, 286–7, 306, 308–11, 314, 403, 504, 641 n. 18

Anna Jagiellon, queen of Hungary and Bohemia, spouse of Ferdinand, 40, 48, 132, 168

Anne of Austria, infanta of Spain, queen of France, 535

Anne of Brittany, duchess, queen of France, 39

Antwerp, 4, 20, 26, 31, 76, 286, 299, 416

Apian, Peter, geographer, 379, 473

Arabian peninsula, 77–8

Aragon, 51, 85; *see also* Ferdinand the Catholic; Katherine of Aragon

Aram, Bethany, historian, 53, 79

archives, 155, 245, 249, 268, 277, 498, 500–1, 549–50, 568–95, 682 n. 50, 686 n. 131; *see also* Simancas

Arévalo, 403

Arfaioli, Maurizio, historian, 177, 181

Arica (viceroyalty of Peru), 374–5, 651 n. 102

Ariosto, Lodovico, poet, 523–4, 597 n. 1

Aristotle, philosopher, 31, 32

Armed Diet, *see* Augsburg, Diet of (1547–8)

722

INDEX

council of the Indies, 184, 210, 350, 352, 355, 360, 361, 362, 370–1, 374, 419, 579
council of Trent, 293, 306, 314, 333–6, 425–6, 429, 505, 509, 519, 522, 532, 570, 666 n. 43
Couto, Diogo do, chronicler, 624 n. 26
Covarrubias, Sebastián de, lexicographer, 497
Cranach, Lucas, artist, 34–5
Crépy, treaty of (1544), 305–6, 308, 310–12, 314, 411, 427, 504
Cromwell, Thomas, English minister, 513, 593, 672 n. 29, 686 n. 131
Croÿ, Adrien de, count of Roeulx, 449
Croÿ, Charles de, prince of Chimay, see Chimay, Charles de Croÿ
Croÿ, Guillaume de, baron of Chièvres, see Chièvres, Guillaume de Croÿ
Croÿ, Guillaume de, cardinal archbishop of Toledo (Chièvres's nephew), 19, 81–2, 113, 128, 607 n. 20
Croÿ, Robert de, archbishop of Cambrai, 113–14, 612 n. 38
Crusades, 33, 230
Cuba, 345, 347, 351, 370, 374–5
Cuzco, 356, 365–6, 669 n. 11
cyphers, 251, 379, 385, 386, 507, 549, 573, 594, 639 n. 29, 685 n. 126

Dantiszek (Dantiscus), Jan, Polish diplomat, 145, 162, 176, 377–8, 584, 588
Daza, Fray Antonio, 499–500
Denia, Bernardo de Sandoval y Rojas, marquis of, 79–80, 86
Denmark, 40, 254, 261, 268, 283, 286, 299, 412
Diet (Reichstag) of Holy Roman Empire, see Augsburg; Regensburg; Speyer; Worms
Dijon, 14, 135–6, 163, 300, 454, 579, Pl. 23
diplomatic correspondence, 582–8
disease, 126–7, 181, 255; see also malaria; plague; smallpox; venereal disease
Dolce, Lodovico, biographer, 208
Don Carlos, prince of Asturias, 404, 455, 474, 492, 528
Don John of Austria, Charles's illegitimate son, 400–1, 455, 484, 486, 497, 506, 655 n. 17, 667 nn. 76–7, 670 n. 9
Donauwörth, 319, 321
Doria, Andrea, Genoese admiral and patrician, 169–70, 178, 180, 181–2, 186, 229, 233, 239, 240, 253, 255, 256, 260, 262, 272, 276, 280, 288, 337–9, 410, 427, 503, 511
Doria, Giannettino, Genoese patrician, 337
Dorothea of Denmark, princess, Charles's niece, 215–16, 317
Dragut, Barbary corsair, 427–8
dreams, 33, 86, 182, 499–500
Dubois, Adrian, imperial servant, 401
duels, 29, 34, 169, 175–80, 186, 219, 237, 252, 255, 322–3, 433, 518, 548–9, 573
Düren, 295, 301, 505
Dürer, Albrecht, artist, 19, 37, 90, 116, 347, 598 n. 25

Eck, Dr Johann, Catholic theologian, 120–3
Edelmayer, Friedrich, historian, 525
Edward VI, king of England and Ireland, 391, 412, 427, 450
Eeklo, Charles not born in, 597 n. 6
Egidio, see Gil, Juan
Egypt, 77
El Escorial, monastery of San Lorenzo de, 491, 494, 498, 536, 537–41, 570, 579, 627 n. 15, 665 n. 38, 669 n. 15, 676 n. 19, Pl. 39
Eleanor of Austria, queen of Portugal and France, Charles's sister, xvi, 8, 9, 12, 16, 20, 21–2, 26, 39, 63–5, 66, 76, 78, 82–3, 87, 91, 93, 114, 138, 143, 144, 154–8, 164, 187, 188, 212, 214, 214, 216, 219, 236, 250–1, 262, 263, 308, 448, 463, 469, 480, 484, 487, 494, 504, 518, 573, 588, 590, 628 n. 38, Pl. 1
Electors (Kurfürsten) of the Holy Roman Empire, 79–80, 87–8, 90–4, 99, 103, 116, 118, 120, 122–4, 177, 194–5, 199, 227, 317, 328–33, 421–2, 429, 430, 469
Elton, Geoffrey, historian, 513
encomienda system, 348–9, 352, 357, 359, 361, 363–4, 367, 373–4, 381, 413, 447, 519
England, x, 16, 22–4, 38–40, 53, 59–60, 101–4, 107–8, 133–8, 144, 164, 165, 166, 168, 171, 174, 176–7, 186–7, 233, 236, 239, 254, 262–4, 284, 313, 319, 323, 328, 346, 347, 386, 412–13, 417, 427, 450–5, 458, 460–1, 464, 465, 495, 505, 507, 513, 525, 530, 531, 543–4
Enzinas, Francisco de, Protestant, 391, 654 n. 53
Erasmus, Desiderius, humanist, xv, 22, 31, 61, 67, 70, 82, 99–100, 117–18, 126, 136, 161, 189, 205–6, 209, 383, 402, 487, 502, 513, 515, 532, 596 n. 5, 608 n. 33, 652 n. 10, 668 n. 87
Eraso (Erasso), Francisco de, imperial secretary, 379, 442, 443, 452, 460–1, 481, 522, 536
Ercilla, Alonso de, colonist and poet, 497
Escamilla, Michèle, historian, 525
Escoriaza, Fernan López de, Charles's physician, 200, 225–6, 573
executive diplomacy by Charles, 251–2, 315–16, 511–12, 520–1
exequies for Charles (1558–9), 491–2
Exsurge, domine, papal bull (1520), 117–18, 120
Eyck, Jan van, painter, 19

Farnese, Alessandro, cardinal, 313
Farnese, Alessandro, duke of Parma, Charles's grandson, 398
Farnese, Alessandro, see Paul III, pope
Farnese, Octavio, duke of Camerino and later of Parma, Charles's son-in-law, 397–8, 410–11, 419, 428, 496, 508, 576
Farnese, Pier Luigi, duke of Parma, 294, 314, 333–4, 338–40, 425, 508, 576